BRADFORD'S
POCKET
CROSSWORD
SOLVER'S
DICTIONARY

ANNE R. BRADFORD

Collins

Published by Collins
An imprint of HarperCollins Publishers
Westerhill Road
Bishopbriggs
Glasgow G64 2QT

Third Edition 2017

10 9 8 7 6 5 4 3 2 1

© Anne R. Bradford 2008, 2014, 2017

This edition: © Anne R. Bradford 2017

The Author hereby asserts her moral rights
to be identified as the author of this work.

ISBN 978-0-00-824882-6

Collins® is a registered trademark of
HarperCollins Publishers Limited

www.collinsdictionary.com

Typeset by Davidson Publishing
Solutions, Glasgow

Printed and bound by CPI Group (UK) Ltd,
Croydon CR0 4YY

The contents of this publication are
believed correct at the time of printing.
Nevertheless the Publisher can accept no
responsibility for errors or omissions,
changes in the detail given or for any
expense or loss thereby caused.

HarperCollins does not warrant that any
website mentioned in this title will be
provided uninterrupted, that any website
will be error free, that defects will be
corrected, or that the website or the server
that makes it available are free of viruses
or bugs. For full terms and conditions
please refer to the site terms provided on
the website.

A catalogue record for this book is
available from the British Library.

If you would like to comment on any
aspect of this book, please contact us at
the given address or online.
E-mail: dictionaries@harpercollins.co.uk
facebook.com/collinsdictionary
@collinsdict

MIX
Paper from
responsible sources
FSC™ C007454

This book is produced from independently certified
FSC™ paper to ensure responsible forest management.

For more information visit:
www.harpercollins.co.uk/green

HarperCollins
P U B L I S H E R S
200

Contents

Author's Preface

Word puzzles have existed nearly as long as words themselves with examples being found during archaeological excavations. In his book, *The Anatomy of the Crossword*, D.St.P. Barnard describes letter patterns in triangular or diamantine form and an ingenious word square discovered at a Roman site at Cirencester.

Word puzzles are a source of pleasure even to quite young children. I myself remember playing a game where we each had a square grid – 5×5 or 6×6 – and we took turns choosing a letter to insert in it until all the squares were occupied, scoring points for any proper words that appeared either across the grid or down.

The Victorians were fond of acrostics, usually in verse form with the initial letters of each line giving the solution. Double acrostics went a step further with both the initial and last letters of each line being employed. At first these tended to be tributes of a sort. They became quite difficult puzzles when the initial verse was turned into a definition of the answer, and the subsequent lines became clues to the acrostic part.

> We shun the light and fly by night (BAT (initial letter) OWL (final))
> 1. An interjection that may make you start   BoO
> 2. A feathered foe may pierce you to the heart   ArroW
> 3. A tax oft levied on a horse and cart   ToLL

Many years later we were playing a simpler version (BAT is the only answer).

> My first is in cable, but not in wire
> My second in arson, but not in fire
> My last is in lettuce, though not in bean
> My whole in daylight is rarely seen.

Spoken word games were equally popular before the age of electronics. 'I-spy' is still with us and repetitive round games are very good for the memory. For example, 'I love my love with an A because she is – adorable', to be repeated by the next player who adds 'I love my love with a B because she is – beautiful' and on through the alphabet, but ignoring X and Z for the most part.

Acrostics were followed by the earliest form of the crossword as we know it, consisting of simple grids which allowed for both across and down answers, hence 'cross' words. The USA was the first country to provide this exercise in regular print when the *New York World* introduced it in 1913. More than a decade passed before such puzzles appeared in Britain, with *The Sunday Times* being the first to publish one, in 1925. People soon became addicted and the popular postcard manufacturers were quick to bring out postcards with a crossword theme, as in this illustration:

One of the thirty-seven comic crossword designs by Donald McGill.
Reproduced with consent from the Donald McGill Archive & Museum, Ryde.

My mother and at least one of her sisters loved crosswords, so I was introduced to them at an early age. She had taught me to read and write long before I started school – entry in those days being after the 5th birthday – but although I had a passion for words I did no regular crossword puzzles until my late teens, and it was a few years more before I really took them seriously. I struggled with the weekly Ximenes puzzle in the weekend paper, learning many new words. He was particularly fond of 'lat', a form of pillar, so I started to write down a sort of memorandum. It was then that the idea came to me of a 'reverse dictionary' where headword and definition would change place. Full of enthusiasm, and by this time staying at home raising a family, I wrote to several leading dictionary publishers, none of whom were interested – possibly rightly so because when I pressed ahead with the project regardless, it was over 20 years before I had anything like enough material for a book. I analysed each crossword I completed (as I do still), selecting synonyms, cross-references, familiar adjectives and also anagram indicators. These were entered into alphabetical files and each week I worked out the percentage already included, having a target of 70% in mind in order to make a book worthy of publication. It was quite a few years before I converted to an alphabetical main file, my back-up ones being indexed by page numbers. Besides analysing puzzles I was also working my way through English dictionaries and other word books in search of further material, and barely arriving at the end of one before a new edition of another reached the market.

It was about 25 years before my labours bore fruit with the eventual appearance of *Longman's Crossword Solver's Dictionary* in 1986, but the firm was taken over by Penguin around 1990 and the reference section closed down, so I was once again seeking a publisher. A year or so later I was lucky to find Peter Collin, who published only reference works. The name *Collin's Crossword Solver's Dictionary* was unsuitable for obvious reasons, and so it became Bradford's, but might well have been Collins when this company took it on in 2002. Happily they decided my surname was sufficiently established and should remain.

Who knows how long crosswords will survive, given our present electronic age and the advance of numerical puzzles. I am delighted to have been involved with them for most of my life, and to have made so many friends along the way. My sincere thanks to you all for your encouragement and for keeping me on my toes, and to the team at Collins who are so supportive.

Anne R. Bradford

Solving Crossword Clues

Crossword puzzles tend to be basically 'quick' or 'cryptic'. A 'quick' crossword usually relies on a one- or two-word clue which is a simple definition of the answer required. Many words have different meanings, so that the clue 'ball' could equally well lead to the answer 'sphere', 'orb', or 'dance'. The way to solve 'quick' crosswords is to press on until probable answers begin to interlink, which is a good sign that you are on the right track.

'Cryptic' crosswords are another matter. Here the clue usually consists of a basic definition, given at either the beginning or end of the clue, together with one or more definitions of parts of the answer. Here are some examples taken from all-time favourites recorded over the years:

1. *'Tradesman who bursts into tears'* (**Stationer**)

   Tradesman is a definition of stationer. *Bursts* is cleverly used as an indication of an anagram, which *into tears* is of stationer.

2. *'Sunday school tune'* (**Strain**)

   Here *Sunday* is used to define its abbreviation S, *school* is a synonym for train, and put together they give strain, which is a synonym of *tune*.

3. *'Result for everyone when head gets at bottom'* (**Ache**)
   (used as a 'down' clue)

   This is what is known as an '& lit' clue, meaning that the setter has hit on a happy composition which could literally be true. *Everyone* here is a synonym for each, move the *head* (first letter) of the word to the *bottom*, and the answer is revealed, the whole clue being the definition of the answer in this case.

4. *'Tin out East'* (**Sen**)

   In this example, *tin*, implying 'money', requires its chemical symbol Sn to go *out*(side) *East*, or its abbreviation, E, the whole clue being a definition of a currency (sen) used in the East.

5. *'Information given to communist in return for sex'* (**Gender**)

   Information can be defined as gen, *communist* is almost always red, *in return* indicates 'reversed', leading to gen-der, a synonym for *sex*.

6. *'Row about no enclosure of this with sardines'* (**Tin-opener**)

   Row is a synonym for tier, *about* indicates 'surrounding', *no enclosure* can be no pen, leading to ti-no pen-er, and another '& lit' clue.

7. *'Cake-sandwiches-meat, at Uncle Sam's party'* (**Clambake**)

   Meat here is lamb, *sandwiches* is used as a verb, so we have C-lamb-ake, which is a kind of party in America. *Uncle Sam* or US is often used to indicate America.

8. *'Initially passionate meeting of boy and girl could result in it'* (**Pregnancy**)

   Initially is usually a sign of a first letter, in this case 'p' for *passionate* + Reg (a *boy*) and Nancy (a *girl*), and another clever '& lit'.

With 'cryptic' clues the solver needs to try to analyse the parts to see what he or she is looking for – which word or words can be the straight definition, and which refer to the parts or hint at anagrams or other subterfuges. Whilst it would be unrealistic to claim total infallibility, practice has shown that in most crosswords some 90% of the answers are to be found in this work.

Anne R. Bradford

How to Use the Dictionary

This dictionary is the result of nearly sixty years' analysis of some 475,000 crossword clues, ranging from plain 'quick' crosswords requiring only synonyms to the different level of cryptic puzzles. Therefore the words listed at each entry may be connected to the keyword in various ways, such as:

- a straightforward synonym

- a commonly-associated adjective

- an associated or proper noun

- a pun or other devious play on words

Keywords are listed alphabetically; in cases where the heading consists of more than one word, the first of these words is taken to be the keyword, and in cases where the end of a word is bracketed, the material up to the opening bracket is taken to be the keyword. Keywords marked with the symbol ▶ refer the user to other entries where additional information may be found. Keywords marked with the symbol ▷ give leads to anagrams and other ploys used by crossword setters. If the keywords found in the clue do not lead directly to the required answer, the solver should look under words given as cross-references to other entries. These are indicated by the symbol →, with the cross-referenced word shown in capitals.

Publisher's Note
All words included in this publication have been sourced from crossword puzzles published in the last sixty years, and no word is excluded on the grounds of religion, gender, or race. The presence of any word does not in any way represent the views of the author or the Publisher, HarperCollins.

The Crossword Club

If you are interested in crosswords, you might like to consider joining the Crossword Club. Membership is open to all who enjoy tackling challenging crosswords and who appreciate the finer points of clue-writing and grid-construction. The Club's magazine, *Crossword*, contains two prize puzzles each month. A sample issue and full details are available on request.

The Crossword Club
Coombe Farm
Awbridge
Romsey, Hants.
SO51 0HN
UK

email: bh@thecrosswordclub.co.uk
website address: www.thecrosswordclub.co.uk

About the Author

Anne Bradford's love of words began to make itself evident even in her schooldays, when, as Head Girl of her school, she instituted a novel punishment – instead of making rulebreakers write lines, she had them write out pages from a dictionary, on the grounds that this was a more useful exercise. Little did she know this was soon to be her own daily routine!

As Anne tells in her preface, she conceived the idea for the dictionary pretty well along with her first child. Over the space of 25 years, Anne continued to build on her collection of solutions, analysing every crossword clue as she solved it and adding it to her steadily growing bank of entries. This unique body of material eventually reached such proportions that she had the idea of offering it to her fellow crossword solvers as a reference book, and since then, the book has gone from strength to strength, providing valuable help to countless cruciverbalists over a number of editions.

Anne Bradford continues to devote time each day to solving crosswords, averaging some 20 a week – both quick and cryptic – and still avidly collects new solutions for her *Crossword Solver's Dictionary* at a rate of around 150 a week, compiling each solution by hand (without the use of a computer!). This latest edition therefore includes much new material, gleaned by a true crossword lover who not only solves crosswords but, as an active member of the Crossword Club, can offer the user an insight into the mind of a cunning crossword compiler.

Aa

A, An Ack, Adult, Ae, Alpha, Angstrom, Argon, D, Ein, Her, If, L, One, Per, They

Abandon(ed), Abandonment Abdicate, Abnegate, Abort, Adrift, Aguna(h), Amoral, Apostasy, Back down, Cade, Cancel, Castaway, Cast off, Chuck, Corrupt, Decommission, Defect, Derelict, **→ DESERT**, Desolate, Desuetude, Dice, Discard, Disown, Dissolute, Disuse, Ditch, Drop, Dump, Elan, Evacuate, Expose, Flagrant, Forhoo(ie), Forhow, Forlend, Forsake, Gomorra, Gretel, Hansel, Homeless, Immoral, Jack(-in), Jettison, Jilt, Leave, Licentious, Lonely, Loose, Louche, Mad, Maroon, Old, Orgiastic, Profligate, Quit, Rakish, Rat, Relinquish, Renounce, Reprobate, Resign, Scrap, Scrub, Shed, Shelve, Sink, Strand, Vacate, Waive, Wanton, Wild, Yield

Abase Degrade, Demean, Disgrace, Eat crow, Embrute, Grovel, **→ HUMBLE**, Kowtow, Lessen

Abate(ment) Allay, Appal, Decrescent, Deduction, Diminish, Ending, Lyse, Lysis, Moderate, Reduce, Remit, **→ SUBSIDE**

▷**Abate** *may indicate* a contention

Abbey Abbacy, Ampleforth, Bath, Buckfast, Cloister, Downside, Fonthill, Fountains, Glastonbury, Györ, Je(r)vaulx, Medmenham, Melrose, Minster, Nightmare, Northanger, Priory, Rievaulx, Tintern, Westminster, Whitby, Woburn

Abbot Aelfric, Archimandrite, Brother, Eutyches, Friar

Abbreviate, Abbreviation Abridge, Ampersand, Compendium, Condense, Curtail, **→ SHORTEN**, Sigla

Abdicate, Abdication Cede, Disclaim, Disown, Resign

Abdomen Belly, C(o)eliac, Epigastrium, Gaster, Hypochondrium, Opisthosoma, Paunch, Pleon, **→ STOMACH**, Tummy, Venter, Ventral

Abduct(ed), Abduction Asport, Enlèvement, Kidnap, Rapt, Ravish, Shanghai, Steal

Abet(tor) Aid, Back, Candle-holder, Second

Abeyance, Abeyant Dormant, Shelved, Sleeping, Store

Abhor(rent) **→ DETEST**, Dissent, **→ HATE**, Loathe, Shun

Abide (by) Accept, Adhere, Dwell, Inhere, **→ LAST**, Lie, Live, Observe, Remain, Stand, Tarry

Ability Acumen, Aptitude, Calibre, Capacity, Cocum, **→ COMPETENCE**, Efficacy, ESP, Facility, Faculty, Ingine, Initiative, Instinct, Lights, Potential, Power, Prowess, Savey, Savoir-faire, Savv(e)y, Skill, Talent, Tenacity

Abject Base, Craven, Grovel, Humble, Servile, Slave

Able Ablins, Accomplished, **→ ADEPT**, Aiblins, Apt, Can, Capable, **→ COMPETENT**, Fere, Fit, Idiot savant, Literate, Proficient, Seaman, Streetwise, Yibbles

Abnormal(ity) Anomalous, Aplasia, Atypical, Autism, → DEVIANT,
Dysfunction, Ectopic, Erratic, Etypical, Exceptional, Freakish, Hare-lip,
Malocclusion, Odd, Peloria, Phenocopy, Preternatural, → QUEER, Sport, Teras,
Trisome, Unconventional, Unnatural, Varus

Abode Domicile, Dwelling, Habitat, → HOME, In(n), Lain, Libken, Lien, Limbo,
Midgard, Remain, Seat

Abolish, Abolition(ist) Abrogate, Annihilate, Annul, Axe, → BAN, D, Delete,
Destroy, Eradicate, Erase, Extirpate, John Brown, Nullify, Remove, Repeal,
Rescind, Scrap, Tubman, Wilberforce

Abominable, Abominate, Abomination Anathema, Bane, Cursed, → HATE,
Nefandous, Nefast, Revolting, Snowman, Vile, Yeti

Aboriginal, Aborigine Awakabai, Black-fellow, Boong, Bushman, Devil's
Marbles, Dharuk, Dhurga, Dieri, Diyari, Gin, Indigenous, Inuit, Kipper, Lubra,
Maori, Mary, Myall, Negro, Nisga'a, Nyunga(r), Siwash, Vedda(h), Warlpiri,
Wemba, Weniba, Wergaia, Wiradhui, Wiradjai, Yagara, Yupik

Abound(ing) Bristle, Copious, Enorm, Flush, Overflow, Rich, Rife, Swarm, Teem

About A, Almost, Anent, Around, C, Ca, Cir(c), Circa, Circiter, Concerning,
Encompass, Environs, Going, Near, Of, On, Over, Re, Regarding, Round, Soon
at, Upon

▷**About** *may indicate* one word around another

Above Abune, Over, Overhead, Overtop, Owre, Sopra, Superior, Supra-, Ubi
supra, Upon, Us

Abrade, Abrasive Alumina, Carborundum®, Chafe, Emery, Erode, File, Garnet
paper, → GRATE, Ground glass, Rub, Sand(paper), Scrape

Abreast Afront, Alongside, Au courant, Au fait, Beside, Level, Up

Abridge(ment) Audley, Compress, Condense, Contract, Cut, Digest, Dock, Edit,
Epitome, Pot, Shorten, Trim

Abroad Afield, Away, Distant, Elsewhere, Forth, Out, Overseas

▷**Abroad** *may indicate* an anagram

Abrupt(ly) Bold, Brusque, Curt, Gruff, Jerky, Offhand, Premorse, Prerupt,
Sharp, Short, Staccato, Terse

▷**Abrupt** *may indicate* a shortened word

Abscond Bolt, Decamp, Desert, Elope, Escape, Flee, Jump ship, Levant, Run
away, Truant, Welch, Welsh

Absence, Absent(ee), Absent-minded(ness) A, Abs, Abstracted, Away,
AWOL, Distant, Distracted, Distrait, Dreamy, Drought, Exeat, Exile, Gone,
Hookey, Lack, Malingerer, Missing, Mitch, No show, Oblivious, Sabbatical,
Scatty, Skip, Truant, Vacuity, Vague, Void, Wool-gathering

Absolute(ly) Arrant, Bang, Complete, Dead, Deep-dyed, Downright, Fairly,
Flat, Heartily, Implicit, Indeed, Ipso facto, Just, Literally, Meer, Mere, Mondo,
Nominative, Not half, Okey-doke(y), Outright, Plenary, Plumb, Quite,
Real, Sheer, Simply, Thorough, Total, Truly, Unadulterated, Unbounded,
Unconditional, Unmitigated, Unqualified, Utter, Veritable, Very, Yeah

Absolve, Absolution Assoil, Clear, Exculpate, Excuse, Exonerate, Pardon,
Redeem, Shrift, Shrive

Absorb(ed), Absorbent, Absorbing, Absorption Assimilate, Autism,
Blot, Consume, Desiccant, Devour, Digest, Dope, Drink, Eat, → ENGROSS,
Enrapt, Imbibe, Immerse, Ingest, Inhaust, Intent, Merge(r), Occlude, Occupy,
Permeable, Porous, Preoccupation, Preoccupied, Rapt, Sorbefacient, Spongy,
Subsume, Unputdownable, Yrapt

Abstain(er), Abstemious, Abstention, Abstinence, Abstinent Band of Hope, Celibacy, Chastity, Continent, Desist, Eschew, Fast, Forbear, Forgo, Maigre, Nazarite, Nephalism, Rechab(ite), Refrain, Resist, Sober, Teetotaller, Temperate, TT, Virtue

Abstract(ed), Abstraction Abrege, Abridge, Academic, Appropriate, Brief, Compendium, Deduct, Digest, Discrete, Dreamy, Epitome, Essence, Inconscient, Metaphysical, Musing, Notional, Précis, Preoccupied, Prepossessed, Prescind, Résumé, Reverie, Scatty, Stable, Steal, Subduct, Summary, Tachism

Absurd(ity) Apagoge, Charade, Cockeyed, Fantastic, Farcical, Folly, Gonzo, Inept, Irrational, Laputan, Ludicrous, Nonsense, Paradox, Preposterous, Priceless, Ridiculous, Risible, Silly, Solecism, Stupid, Toshy

Abundance, Abundant Abounding, A-gogo, Ample, Aplenty, Bounty, Copious, Corn in Egypt, Cornucopia, Cosmic, Excess, Flood, Flush, Fouth, Fowth, Fruitful, Galore, Lashings, Lavish, Liberal, Luxuriance, Manifold, Mickle, Mine, Mint, Muckle, Natural, Oodles, Oodlins, Opulent, Over, Plenitude, Plenteous, → **PLENTIFUL**, Plenty, Pleroma, Plethora, Plurisie, Profusion, Prolific, Relative, Replete, Rich, Rife, Rock and manger, Routh, Rowth, Sonce, Sonse, Store, Stouth and routh, Superabound, Surfeit, Tallents, Teeming, Tons, Uberous

Abuse(r), Abusive Assail, Becall, Billingsgate, Blackguard, Chemical, Clapperclaver, Contumely, Cruelty, Diatribe, Ear-bashing, Flak, Fustilarian, Fustil(l)irian, Hail, Hate mail, Ill-treat, Ill-use, Injury, Insolent, Insult, Invective, Jobbery, Limehouse, Malpractice, Maltreat, Miscall, Misuse, Mofo, Molest, Mud, Obloquy, Oppress, Opprobrium, Philippic, Rail, Rampallian, Rate, Rayle, Revile, Satire, Scarab(ee), Scurrilous, Slang, Slate, Sledging, Snash, Solvent, Stick, Strap, Tirade, Torture, Traduce, Verbal, Vilify, Violate, Vituperation, Wosbird

Abut Adjoin, Border, Touch

Academic(ian) A, Chair, Della-Cruscan, Don, Erudite, Fellow, Hypothetic(al), Immortals, Literati, Master, Pedantic, PRA, RA, Reader, Rector, Scholar

Academy, Academic A, Athenaeum, Bookish, Dollar, Donnish, Forty, Learned, Loretto, Lyceum, Military, Oxbridge, Plantilla, RA, St Cyr, Sandhurst, Seminary, Studious, The Shop, West Point

Accelerate, Acceleration, Accelerator Bevatron, Collider, Cyclotron, G, Gal, Grav, Gun, Hasten, Increase, Linac, Linear, Rev, Speed, Stringendo, Supercollider, Synchrotron, Throttle

Accent(ed), Accentuate Acute, Beat, Breve, Brogue, Bur(r), Circumflex, Cut-glass, Doric, Drawl, Enclitic, Enhance, Gammat, Grave, Hacek, Intonation, Kelvinside, Lilt, Long, Macron, Marcato, Martelé, Mockney, Morningside, Mummerset, Nasal, Orthotone, Oxford, Oxytone, Pitch, Rhotic, Rhythm, Rinforzando, Sforzando, Stress, Tittle, Tone, Twang

Accept(able), Acceptance, Accepted, Accepting A, Accede, Adequate, Admit, Adopt, Agree, Allow, Alright, Approbate, Bar, Believe, Buy, Can-do, Common, Compliant, Consent, Cool, Cosher, Decent, Done, Eligible, Embrace, Epenthesis, Freeload, Going, Grant, Idee recue, Include, Kosher, Meet, Nod, Obey, On, Orthodox, Pocket, Putative, Realise, Receive, Resipiscence, Satisfactory, Settle, Stand, Street cred, Suppose, Swallow, Take (on board), Tolerate, U, Valid, Wear, Widespread

Access(ible), Accessibility, Accession Arrival, Avenue, Blue-jacking, Card, Come-at-able, Conditional, Credit, Door, Entrée, → **ENTRY**, Fit, Gateway, Get-at-able, Ingo, Key, Manhole, Near, Open, Passe-partout, Passkey, Password,

Ping, Random, Recourse, Remote, Sequential, Sociable, Spasm, Telnet, Wayleave

Accessory, Accessories Abettor, Addition, Aide, Ally, Ancillary, Appendage, Appurtenance, Attachment, Attribute, Bandanna, Bells and whistles, Cribellum, Cuff-links, Extra, Findings, Staffage, Trappings, Trimming, Umbrella

Accident(al) Adventitious, Arbitrary, Bechance, Blowdown, Blunder, Calamity, →CHANCE, Circumstance, Contingency, Contretemps, Crash, Criticality, Disaster, Double flat, Fall, Fluke, Hap, Hit and run, Inadvertent, Meltdown, Mischance, Mishap, Note, Pile up, Prang, Promiscuous, Random, Rear-ender, Shunt, Smash, Smash-up, Spill, Stramash, Unintentional, Unmeant, Wreck

Acclaim Accolade, Applaud, Brava, Bravo, Cheer, Clap, Credit, Eclat, Encomium, Fame, Fanfare, Hail, Kudos, Ovation, Praise, Salute, Toast, Zindabad

Accolade Award, Brace, Dubbing, Honour, Palm, Token

Accommodate, Accommodating, Accommodation Accustom, Adapt, Almshouse, Amenable, B and B, Bedsit, Berth, Board, Botel, Bunkhouse, Camp, Chalet, Chambers, Compromise, Crashpad, Flotel, Gaff, Gite, Grace and favour, Hall, Homestay, Hostel, Hotel, House, Humour, Lend, Loan, Lodge, Lodgement, Minshuku, Motel, →OBLIGE, Parador, Pension, Penthouse, Pew, Pliant, Prefab, Quarters, Rapprochement, Recurve, Room, Single-end, Sorehon, Stabling, Stateroom, Steerage, Storage, Tent, Timeshare, Wharepuni, Youth hostel

▷**Accommodating** *may indicate* one word inside another

Accompany(ing), Accompanied (by), Accompaniment, Accompanist Accessory, Alberti, And, Attach, Attend, Chaperone, Chum, Concomitant, Consort, Continuo, Descant, Duenna, Enclose, →ESCORT, Fixings, Harmonise, Herewith, Obbligato, Obligate, Obligato, Trimmings, Vamp, Wag

Accomplice Abettor, Aide, →ALLY, Bagman, Bonnet, Collaborator, Confederate, Federarie, Federary, Partner, Shill, Stale, Swagsman

Accomplish(ed), Accomplishment Able, →ACHIEVE, Arch, Attain, Clever, Complete, Done, Doss, Effect, Expedite, Exploit, Galant, Master, Over, Perform, Polished, Prowess, Put through, Realise, Ripe, Savant

Accord, According(ly), According to After, Agree, Ala, Allow, As per, Attune, Chime, Congree, Consensus, Give, Grant, Harmony, Jibe, Meet, One, Per, So, Sort, Thus

Accost Abord, Approach, Greet, Hail, Importune, Molest, Solicit, Tackle

Account(s) AC, Appropriation, Audit, Battels, Behalf, Bill, Books, Budget, Cause, Charge, Chequing, Chronicle, Control, Current, Deposit, Description, Detailed, Discretionary, Due, Enarration, Expense, Explain, Explanation, Exposition, ISA, Ledger, Log, Long, Memoir, Narration, Nominal, Overdue, Procès-verbal, Reason, Recital, Record, Regest, Register, Relation, →REPORT, Repute, Résumé, Sake, Statement, Suspense, Swindlesheet, Tab, Tale, TESSA, Thesis, Version, Viable

Accountancy, Accountant Auditor, Bean counter, Bookkeeper, CA, Cost, Double entry, Liquidator, Purser, Reckoner, Single entry

Accumulate, Accumulation Adsorb, Aggregate, →AMASS, Augment, Backlog, Collect, Drift, Gather, Hoard, Lodg(e)ment, Multiply, Oedema, Pile, Pool, Run up, Save, Uplay

Accuracy, Accurate(ly) Bang-on, Cocker, →CORRECT, Dead-on, Exact, Fair, Faultless, Fidelity, Griff, Minute, Precise, Realistic, Right, Spot-on, To scale, True, Unerring, Veracious, Word-perfect

Accusation, Accuse(d) Allege, Arraign, Asperse, Attaint, Bill, Blame, Calumny, Censure, Challenge, Charge, Criminate, Denounce, Dite, Gravamen, Impeach,

Impute, Incriminate, Indictment, Information, Name, Panel, Plaint, Prosecute, Recrimination, Suspect, Tax, Threap, Threep, Traduce, Wight, Wite, Wyte

Accustom(ed) Acquaint, Attune, Enure, General, Habituate, Harden, Inure, Wont, Woon

Ace(s) Basto, Blackjack, Crack, Demon, Dinger, →**EXPERT**, Jot, Master, Mega, Mournival, One, Quatorze, Smashing, Spadille, Spadill(i)o, Spot, Tib, Virtuoso, Whizz, Wonderful

Ache, Aching Aitch, Die, Hunger, Long, Mulligrubs, Nag, Otalgia, Pain, Sore, Stitch, Stound, Stownd, Work, Yearn, Yen

Achieve(ment) Accomplish, Acquisition, Attain, Big League, Come, Compass, Coup, Cum laude, →**EFFECT**, Enacture, Exploit, Feat, Fulfil, Gain, Hatchment, Masterpiece, Realise, Res gestae, Satisfice, Satisfy, Stroke, Succeed, Threepeat, Triumph, Trock, Troke, Truck

Acid(ity) Acrimony, Corrosive, Drop, Etchant, Hydroxy, Reaction, Ribosomal, Ribozyme, Sharp, Solvent, Sour, Tart, Vinegar, Vitriol

Acknowledge(ment) Accept, Admit, Agnise, Allow, Answer, Avow, Con, Confess, Grant, Greet, Mea culpa, Nod, Own, Profess, React, Receipt, Recognise, Respect, Righto, Roger, Salute, Ta, Thank you, Touché, Wilco

Acoustic(s) Harmonics, Phenocamptics, Sonics

Acquaint(ance), Acquainted Advise, Cognisant, Contact, Enlighten, Familiar, →**INFORM**, Knowledge, Nodding, Notify, Tell, Versed

Acquire, Acquisition, Acquisitive Acquest, Adsorb, Cop, Earn, Ern, Gain, →**GET**, Glom, Grasping, Irredentist, Land, Learn, Obtain, Procure, Purchase, Rapacity, Secure, Steal, Take-over, Target, Usucap(t)ion

Acquit(tal) Absolve, Assoil, Cleanse, Clear, Exonerate, Free, Loose, Loste, Pardon, Vindicate

Acrid, Acrimonious, Acrimony Acid, Bitter(ness), Empyreuma, Mordant, Resentment, Rough, Sour, Spleen, Surly, Virulent, Vitriolic

Acrobat(s), Acrobatics Equilibrist, Gymnast, Hot dog, Ropedancer, Rope-walker, Splits, Trampoline, Trick cyclist, Tumbler

Across A, Ac, Athwart, Betwixt, O'ed, Opposite, Over, Through, Transit

Act(ing), Action, Active, Acts A, Actus reus, Affirmative, Afoot, Antic, Assist, Atonement, Auto, Barnstorm, Barrier, Behave, Blitz, Business, Camp, Capillary, Caretaker, Case, Caster, Catastasis, Cause, Charade, Class, Conduct, Consolation, COPPA, Deal, Declaratory, →**DEED**, Detinue, Dido, Do, Enabling, Evasive, Excitement, Exert, Exploit, Factory, Feat, Feign, Forthcoming, Function, Habeas corpus, Homestead, Identic, Impersonate, Impro(visation), Industrial, Juristic, Law, Litigate, Lock-out, Locutionary, Masterstroke, Measure, Method, Mime, Movement, Mutiny, Navigation, Onstage, Overt, Perform(ance), Perlocutionary, Play, Positive, Practice, Pretence, Private, Procedure, Process, Public, Quia timet, Qui tam, Quiver, Rearguard, Reflex, Reform bill, Represent, Rising, Roleplay, Secondary, Septennial, Serve, Settlement, Sham, Showdown, Shtick, Sick-out, Simulate, Speech, Sprightly, Strike, Stunt, Suit, Tactic, Terminer, Test, Theatricise, Transitory, Treat, Truck, Turn, Union, War

Activate Arm, Energise, Goad, Spark, Spur, Stur, Styre, Trigger

Active, Activist, Activity A, Agile, Alert, Alive (and kicking), Animated, Astir, At, Athletic, Brisk, Business, Busy, Cadre, Campaigner, Deedy, DIY, Do(ing), Dynamited, Dynamo, Ecowarrior, Effectual, Energetic, Energic, Erupting, Exercise, Extra-curricular, Floruit, Fluster, Game, Go-go, Goings-on, Hum, Hyper, In play, Leish, Licht, Live, Mobile, Motile, Nimble, Nippy, Ongo, On the go, Op,

Operant, Optical, Overdrive, Play, Rambunctious, Residual, Shenanigan, Sideline, Spree, Sprightly, Springe, Spry, Sthenic, Stir, Surge, Third house, Vacuum, Voice, Wick, Wimble, Working, Ya(u)ld, Zionist

Actor(s), Actor-like Agent, Alleyn, Artist, Ashe, Barnstormer, Benson, Betterton, Bit player, Borgnine, Brando, Burbage, Cast, Character, Company, Co-star, Diseur, Donat, Gable, Garrick, Gielgud, Guiser, Ham, Hamfatter, Heavy, Histrio(n), Impersonator, Jay, Juve(nile), Kean, Keaton, Luvvie, MacReady, Mime(ster), Mummer, Olivier, O'Toole, Pantomimist, Performer, Player, Playfair, Protagonist, RADA, Roscian, Roscius, Savoyard, Scofield, Sim, Spear-carrier, Stager, Strolling, Super, Theatrical, Thespian, Tragedian, Tree, Tritagonist, Trouper, Understudy, Utility man, Wolfit

Actress Bankhead, Bow, Buffa, Dietrich, Duse, Figurant, Garbo, Harlow, Ingenue, Loren, Pierrette, Siddons, Soubrette, Starlet, Swanson, Terry, West

Actual(ity), Actually De facto, Entelechy, Literal, Live, Material, Real, Real-life, True, Very

Acute Astute, Dire, Fitché, Incisive, →**INTENSE**, Keen, Quick-witted

▶**Ad** *see* **ADVERT(ISE)**

Adage Aphorism, Gnome, Maxim, Motto, Paroemia, Proverb, Saw, Saying, Truism

Adamant Firm, Inexorable, Obdurate, Rigid, Unbending

Add(ed), Addendum, Adder, Adding Accrue, Adscititious, Annex, →**APPENDIX**, Attach, Cast, Contribute, Coopt, Death, Dub, Ech(e), Eik, Eke, Elaborate, Embroider, Enhance, Enlarge, Forthgoing, Fortify, Insert, Lace, Reckon, Reinforce, Retrofit, Score, Spike, Sum, Summate, Top up, Tot(e), Total

Addict(ion), Addicted, Addictive Abuser, Acid freak, Acidhead, A colt's tooth, Alcoholic, Blunthead, Buff, Chocoholic, Devotee, Dopehead, Etheromaniac, Fan, Fiend, Freak, Given, Glue-sniffing, Habit-forming, Hophead, Hound, Hype, Jones, Joypopper, Junkie, Mainliner, Mania, Narcotist, Need, Opiate, Opioid, Opium, Pillhead, Pillpopper, Pothead, Shithead, Shooter, Shopaholic, Slave, Snowbird, Space-cadet, Speedfreak, Stoner, Sybaritism, Theism, User, Wino, Workaholic

Addition(al), Additive Adipate, Advene, Also, And, Antiknock, Appendage, Carrag(h)anin, Carrageenan, Codicil, Cyclamate, Dextran, Encore, Epexegesis, Etc, Excess, Extension, →**EXTRA**, Footnote, Increment, Mae, Mo, New, Odd, On, Other, Padding, Plus, Preservative, PS, Rider, Spare, Suffix, Supplementary, Top-up

Address, Address system Accommodation, →**ATLAS**, Bach, Call, Cariad, Chuck, Cousin, Dedication, Delivery, Diatribe, Discourse, Effendi, Inaugural, IP, Jimmy, Kiddo, Lala, Lecture, Letterhead, Mac, Milord, Orate, Past master, Pastoral, Poste-restante, Salute, Sermon, Speech, Squire, Tannoy®, URL, Web(site), You-all

Adept Able, Adroit, Buff, Dab, Deacon, Don, →**EXPERT**, Fit, Handy, Mahatma, Master, Past master

Adequate Condign, Does, Due, Egal, Equal, Ere-now, Passable, Proper, →**SUFFICIENT**, Tolerable, Valid

Adhere(nt), Adherence, Adhesive Allegiance, Ally, Blutack®, Bond, Burr, Cement, Child, Cling, Conform, Dextrin, Disciple, Emplastic, Epoxy, Follower, Glair, Glue, Gum, Jain(a), Leech, Loyalist, Mixtion, Moonie, Mucilage, Nomism, Partisan, Paste, Resin, Sectator, Servitor, Stand pat, Sticker, Supporter, Synechia, Votary, Waterglass

Adjacent, Adjoining Bordering, Conterminous, Contiguous, Handy, Neighbouring, Nigh

Adjourn(ment) Abeyance, Delay, Moratoria, →**POSTPONE**, Prorogate, Recess, Rise, Suspend

Adjunct Addition, Aid, Ancillary, Rider

Adjust(able), Adjustment, Adjuster Accommodate, Adapt, Attune, Coapt, Dress, Ease, Fit, Gang, Gauge, Handicap, J'adoube, Modify, Modulate, Orientate, Prepare, Preset, Primp, Redo, Reduce, Regulate, Resize, Retrofit, Scantle, Scotopia, Sliding, Suit, Tailor, Temper, Toe-in, Tram, Trim, True, Tune, Tweak
▷**Adjust** *may indicate* an anagram

Ad-lib Ex tempore, Improvise, Wing it

Administer, Administration, Administrator Adhibit, Anele, Apply, Arrondissement, Bairiki, Control, Curia, →**DIRECT**, Dispence, Dispense, Executive, Front office, Intendant, Intinction, Leadership, →**MANAGE**, MBA, Penpusher, Pepys, Provost, Regime, Registrar, Run, Secretariat, Steward, Sysop, Trustee, Whitehall

Admirable, Admiration, Admire(d), Admirer Beau, Clinker, Clipper, Conquest, Crichton, Envy, Esteem, Estimable, →**EXCELLENT**, Fine, Flame, Fureur, Gaze, Gem, Ho, Iconise, Idolater, Laudable, Lionise, Partisan, Popularity, Rate, Regard, Respect, Ripping, Rocking, Stotter, Suitor, Swain, Toast, Tribute, Venerate, Wonder, Worthy

Admission, Admit(ter), Admit(ting), Admitted, Admittance Accept, Access, Acknowledge, Agree, Allow, Avow, Cognovit, Concede, →**CONFESS**, Enter, Entrée, Entry, Estoppel, Gateman, Give, Grant, Induct, Ingress, Initiate, Intromit, Ordain, Ordination, Owe, Own (up), Privy, Recognise, Shrift, Take, Tho(ugh), Turnstile, Yield

Admonish, Admonition Advice, Caution, Chide, Lecture, Moralise, Rebuke, →**SCOLD**, Tip, Warn

Ado Bother, Bustle, Fuss, Lather

Adolescent Bodgie, Developer, Grower, Halflin, Immature, Juvenile, Neanic, Teenager, Tweenager, Veal, Widgie, Youth

Adopt(ed) Accept, Affiliate, Allonym, Assume, Catch on, Embrace, Espouse, Father, Foster, Latch on, Mother

Adoration, Adore(r), Adoring Doat, Dote, Goo-goo, Homage, Love, Pooja(h), Puja, Revere, Venerate, Worship, Zoolater

Adorn(ed), Adornment Antefix, Aplustre, Attrap, Banderol, Bedeck, Bedight, Begem, Bejewel, Caparison, Clinquant, Deck, Dight, Drape, Embellish, Emblaze, Emblazon, Embroider, Enchase, Equip, Festoon, Flourish, Furnish, Garland, Garnish, Grace, Graste, Jewellery, Ornament, Riband, Story, Tassel, Tattoo, Tatu, Tinsel

Adroit(ness) Address, Adept, Clever, Dextrous, Expert, Neat, Skilful, Slick

Adulate, Adulation Flatter(y), Praise, →**WORSHIP**

Adult Amadoda, Grown-up, Imago, Man, Mature, Upgrown, X

Advance(d), Advancement A, Abord, Accelerate, Ante, Approach, Ascend, Assert, Better(ment), Breakthrough, Bring on, Charge, Develop, Early, Elevation, Evolué, Extreme, Far, Fast-forward, Fore, Forge, Forward, Further, Get on, Haut(e), Hi-tec(h), Impress, Imprest, Incede, Late, Lend, →**LOAN**, March, Mortgage, Onrush, Outcome, Overture, Pass, Piaffe, Posit, Postulate, Precocious, Prefer, Prepone, Prest, Process, Progress, →**PROMOTE**, Propose, Propound, Push, Retainer, Ripe, Rise, Sub, Submit, Tiptoe, Top end, Ultramodern, Upfront, Upgang

Advantage(ous) Accrual, Ad, Aid, →ASSET, Avail, Batten, Benefit, Bisque, Boot, Bright, Edge, Emolument, Expedient, Exploit, Favour, Fruit, Gain, Grouter, Handicap, Handle, Head-start, Help, Inside (track), Interess, Interest, Lever(age), Mess of pottage, Nonmonetary, Obvention, Odds, One-up, Oneupmanship, Oyster, Percentage, Plus, Privilege, Prize, Pull, Purchase, Sake, Salutary, Serviceable, Start, Stead, Strength, Toe-hold, Trade, Trump card, Upstage, Use, Van, Whiphand

Adventure(r), Adventuress, Adventurous Argonaut, Assay, Bandeirante, Buccaneer, Casanova, Condottiere, Conquistador, Dareful, Daring, Emprise, Enterprise, Escapade, Filibuster, Gallant, Gest, Lark, Mata Hari, Mercenary, Merchant, Picaresque, Picaro, Risk, Routier, Rutter, Swashbuckler, Vamp, Viking, Voyage

Adversary Anti, Arch-enemy, Cope(s)mate, Enemy, Foe, Nemesis, Opponent

Adverse, Adversity Calamity, Cross, Down, Downside, Harrow, Misery, Reversal, Setback, Unfavourable, Untoward, Woe

Advert(ise), Advertisement, Advertiser, Advertising Above the line, Ad, Allude, Attack, Banner, Bark, Bill, Circular, Classified, Coign(e), Coin, Commercial, Copy, Display, Dodger, Earpiece, Flysheet, Hard sell, Hype, Jingle, Knocking copy, Madison Avenue, Mailshot, Market, Noise, →NOTICE, Out, Parade, Personnel, Placard, Playbill, Plug, Proclaim, Promo, Promote, Promulgate, Prospectus, Puff, Quoin, Refer, Sandwich board, Shoutline, Showbill, Skyscraper, Sky-write, Splash, Sponsor, Stunt, Subliminal, Teaser, Throwaway, Tout, Trailer, Trawl, Wrap around

Advice Conseil, Counsel, →GUIDANCE, Guideline, Information, Invoice, Opinion, Read, Recommendation, Re(e)de, Reed, Tip (off)

Advise(d), Adviser, Advisable Acquaint, Apprise, Assessor, Avise(ment), Back-seat driver, Brains trust, CAB, Consultant, Cornerman, Counsel, Enjoin, Enlighten, Exhort, Expedient, Inform, Instruct, Mentor, Monitor, Oracle, Peritus, Prudent, Ralph, →RECOMMEND, Starets, Staretz, Tutor, Urge, Warn, Weld, Wise

Advocate(d) Agent, Argue, Attorney, Back, Devil's, Endorse, Exponent, Gospel, Intercede, Lawyer, Move, Paraclete, Peat, Peddle, Pleader, Pragmatist, Preach, Proponent, Silk, Statist, Syndic, Urge

Aerial Antenna, Clover leaf, Communal, Dipole, Directional, Dish, Ethereal, Lead-in, Loop, Minidish, Parabolic, Squarial

Aerodrome →AIRPORT, Landing field, Rotor-station

▶**Aeroplane** *see* AIRCRAFT

Affable, Affability Amiable, Avuncular, Benign, Bonhomie, Cordial, Gracious, Hearty, Pleasant, Suave, Urbane

Affair(s) Amour, Business, Carry on, Cerne, Concern, Current, Dreyfus, Event, Extra-marital, Fight, Fling, Go, Intrigue, Liaison, Matter, Pash, Pidgin, Pi(d)geon, Ploy, Relationship, Res, Romance, Shebang, Subject, Thing

Affect(ed), Affectation, Affection(ate), Affecting Air, Alter, Arty, Breast, Camp, Chi-chi, Concern, Cordial, Crachach, Crazy, Distress, Effete, Emotive, Endearment, Euphuism, Foppery, Frappant, Grip, Heartstrings, High-sounding, Hit, Ladida, Lovey-dovey, Mannered, Mimmick, Minnick, Minnock, Mouth-made, Mwah, Phoney, Play at, →POSE, Poseur, Precieuse, Preciosity, Pretence, Spoilt, Stag(e)y, Storge, Stricken, Strike, Supervene, Susceptible, Sway, Tender, Topophilia, Touched, Touchy-feely, Tushery, Twee, Unction, Unnatural, Vain, Warm, Yah

Affiliate, Affiliation Adopt, Associate, Merge, Unite

Affinity Bro, Kin(ship), Penchant, Rapport, Tie

Affirm(ative), Affirmation Assert, Attest, Avow, Maintain, Positive, Predicate, Profess, Protestation, State, Uh-huh, → VERIFY

Afflict(ed), Affliction Aggrieve, Asthma, Cross, Cup, Curse, Dead leg, Disease, Furnace, Harass, Hay fever, Hurt, Lacerate, Lumbago, Molest, Nosology, Oppress, Palsy, Persecute, Pester, Plague, Scourge, Smit, Sore, → SORROW, Stricken, Teen, Tene, Tic, Tine, Tribulation, → TROUBLE, Try, Unweal, Visitation, Woe

Affluence, Affluent Abundance, Ease, Fortune, Grey panther, Inflow, Moneyed, Opulence, Upmarket, Wealth

Afford Bear, Manage, Offer, Provide, Run to, Spare

Affront Assault, Defy, Facer, → INSULT, → OFFEND, Outrage, Scandal, Slight, Slur

Afraid Adrad, Alarmed, Chicken, Fearful, Funk, Nesh, Rad, Regretful, Scared, Timorous, Windy, Yellow

Africa(n) Abyssinian, Adamawa, Akan, Algerian, Amakwerekwere, Angolan, Ashanti, Baganda, Bambara, Bantu, Barbary, Barotse, Basotho, Basuto, Bechuana, Beento, Bemba, Beninese, Berber, Biafran, Bintu, Black, Boer, Botswana(n), Bushman, Caffre, Cairene, Carthaginian, Chewa, Chichewa, Ciskei, Congo(l)ese, Cushitic, Dagomba, Damara, Dark continent, Dinka, Duala, Dyula, Efik, Eritrean, Ethiopian, Fang, Fantee, Fanti, Fingo, Flytaal, Fula(h), Gabonese, Galla, Gambian, Ganda, Gazankulu, Grikwa, Griqua, Guinean, Gullah, Hamite, Hausa, Herero, Hutu, Ibibio, Ibo, Igbo, Impi, Ivorian, Kabyle, Kenyan, Khoikhoi, Khoisan, Kikuyu, Kongo, Lango, Lesotho, Liberian, Libyan, Lowveld, Lozi, Luba, Luo, Maghreb, Maghrib, Malagasy, Malawi, Malian, Malinke, Mande, Mandingo, Mandinka, Masai, Mashona, Matabele, Mende, Moor, Moroccan, Mossi, Mozambican, Mswahili, Munt(u), Mzee, Nama(qua), Namibian, Ndebele, Negrillo, Ngoni, Nguni, Nilot(e), Nubian, Nuer, Numidian, Nyanja, Oromo, Ovambo, Pedi, Pied noir, Pondo, Qwaqwa, Rastafarian, Rhodesian, Rwandan, Sahelian, San, Senegalese, Shilluk, Shluh, Shona, Somali, Songhai, Songhay, Sotho, Soweto, Sudanese, Susu, Swahili, Swazi, Tanzanian, Temne, Tiv, Togolese, Tonga, Transkei, Transvaal, Tshi, Tsonga, Tswana, Tuareg, Tunisian, Tutsi, Twi, Ugandan, Uhuru, Venda, Voltaic, Waswahili, Watu(t)si, Wolof, X(h)osa, Yoruban, Zairean, Zulu

After(wards) About, At, Behind, Belated, Beyond, Eft, Epi-, → LATER, On, Past, Post hoc, Rear, Since, Sine, Subsequent, Syne

▷**After injury** *may indicate* an anagram

Afternoon A, Arvo, Ex-am, PM, Postmeridian, Undern

Afterpiece, Afterthought Addendum, Codicil, Epimetheus, Exode, Footnote, Note, PS, Supplement

Again Afresh, Agen, Ancora, Anew, Back, Bis, De novo, Ditto, Do, Eft, Eftsoons, Encore, Iterum, Mair, More, Moreover, O(v)er, Re-, Recurrence, Reprise, Than, Then

Against A, Anent, Anti, Beside, Con, Counter, For, Gainsayer, Into, Nigh, On, One-to-one, Opposing, To, V, Versus

Age(d), Ages, Aging Absolute, Ae, Aeon, Antique, Bronze, Chair-days, Chellean, Cycle, Dark, Date, Discretion, Distress, Eon, Epact, Epoch(a), Era, Eternity, Generation, Golden, Heroic, Ice, Iron, Jurassic, Kalpa, Mature, Mesolithic, Middle, Millennium, Neolithic, New, Paleolithic, Period,

Pre-Cambrian, Radiometric, Reason, Season, Senescence, Senility, Space, Steam, Stone, Wrinkly

Agency, Agent Advertising, Alkylating, Ambassador, Antistatic, Autolysin, Bailiff, Baking soda, Bargaining, Bicarb(onate), Broker, Bureau, Buyer, Catalyst, Cat's paw, Chelating, Chemical, Child support, Commission, Complexone, Confidential, Consul, Consular, Counter, Countryside, Crown, Dating, Defoaming, Developing, Dicumaral, Disclosing, Distributor, Doer, Double, Emissary, Envoy, -er, Escort, Estate, Exciseman, Executant, Executor, Factor, Forwarding, Free, Galactagogue, G-man, Go-between, Good offices, Hand, House, Implement, Indian, Influence, Instrument, Intermediary, Isinglass, Itar Tass, Law, Leavening, Legate, Literary, Magic bullet, Masking, Mata Hari, Means, Medium, Melanin, Mercantile, Mitogen, Mole, Moral, Mouthwash, Narco, Nerve, Nucleating, OO, Operation, Orange, Oxidizing, Parliamentaire, Parliamentary, Patent, Pathogen, Pawn, Peace corps, Penetration, Pinkerton, Press, Provocateur, Proxy, Realtor, Reducing, Rep(resentative), Reuters, Riot, Road, Runner, Salesman, Secret (service), Shipping, Ship's husband, SIS, Solvent, Soman, Spook, Spy, Stock, Surfactant, Tass, Third party, Ticket, Tiger team, Tool, Training, Travel, UNESCO, Virino, Voice, Welfare, Wetting, Wire service

Agenda Business, Order paper, Programme, Remit, Schedule

Aggravate Annoy, Exacerbate, Exasperate, Harass, Inflame, Irk, Needle, Nettle, Provoke, Rankle, Try, Vex

Aggression, Aggressive(ly), Aggressor, Aggro Anti-Imperialism, Attack, Ballbreaker, Bare-knuckle, Battleaxe, Bellicose, Belligerent, Biffo, Bovver, Bullish, Butch, Defiant, Enemy, Feisty, Foe, Go-getter, Gungho, Hard-hitting, Hawk, Invader, Laddish, Lairy, Macho, Militant, Nasty, On-setter, Pushing, Rambo, Rampant, Sabre-rattling, Shirty, Tooth and nail, Truculent, Violent, Wild

Agile Acrobatic, Deft, Lissom(e), Nifty, Nimble, Quick, Spry, Supple, Swank, Twinkletoes, Wiry

Agitate(d), Agitation, Agitator Acathisia, Activist, Ado, Agitprop, Akathisia, Alarm, Arouse, Boil, Bolshie, Bother, Bristling, Churn, Commotion, Convulse, Dismay, Distraught, →**DISTURB**, Ebullient, Emotion, Euoi, Euouae, Evovae, Excite, Extremist, Fan, Ferment, Firebrand, Flap, Fluster, Frenzy, Fuss, Fusspot, Goad, Heat, Hectic, Het (up), Impatience, Jumpy, Khilafat, Lather, Militant, Overwrought, Perturb, Pother, Protest, Rabble-rouser, Rattle, Restless, Rouse, Ruffle, Seethed, Shake, Stew, Stir(-up), Tailspin, Tempest(uous), Tizzy, Toss, Tremor, Trouble, Turbulent, Turmoil, Twitchy, Twittery, Unrest, Welter, Whisk

▷**Agitate** *may indicate an anagram*

Agonise, Agony Ache, Anguish, Ecstasy, Heartache, →**PAIN**, Torment, Torture

Agree(ing), Agreed, Agreement Accede, Accept, Accord, Acquiescence, Adhere, Agt, Align, Aline, Allow, Amen, Analogy, Assent, Ausgleich, Aye, Camp David, Cartel, Charterparty, Chime, Coincide, Collective, Compact, Comply, Concert, Concord(at), Concordance, Concur, Condone, Conform, →**CONSENT**, Consist, Contract, Convention, Correspond, Covenant, Covin, Covyne, Cushty, Deal, Deffo, Determine, Embrace, Entente, Equate, Finalise, Gentleman's, Harmony, Homologous, Identity, Knock-for-knock, League, Like-minded, Munich, National, Nod, Non-con, Nudum pactum, Okay, On, Pact(um), Pair, Plant, Plea bargaining, Predetermine, Prenuptial, Procedural, Productivity, Protocol, Recognise, Reconcile, Repo, Repurchase, Right(o), Roger, Sanction, Service, Settlement, Side, Square, Standstill, Substantive, Suit, Sympathy,

Synastry, Sync(hronise), Tally, Technology, Trade, Treaty, Trucial, Unanimous, Union, Unison, Unity, Wilco, Wukkas, Yalta, Yea, Yea-say, Yes

Agreeable Amene, Comfy, Harmonious, Obliging, Pleasant, Sapid, Sweet, Well-disposed, Willing, Winsome

▷**Ague(ish)** *may indicate* an anagram

Ahead Anterior, Before, Fast, Foreship, Forward, Frontwards, Onward, Precocious, Up

Aid(s), Aide Accessory, ADC, Adjutant, Artificial, Assist, Audiovisual, Audiophone, Caliper, Decca, →**DEPUTY**, Fresh-card, Galloper, Gift, Grant, Help(line), Key, Legal, Lend-lease, Life-saver, Monitor, Optophone, PA, Relief, Satnav, Seamark, Serve, Sex, Sherpa, Stepping-stone, Succour, Support, Visual, Zimmer®

Ail(ment), Ail(ing) Affect, Afflict(ion), Complaint, Croup, Disease, Disorder, Enteritis, Malady, Misorder, Narks, Occupational, Pink-eye, Pip, Queasy, Sickness, Suffer, TB, Unwell

Aim Approach, Aspire, Bead, Bend, End, Ettle, Eye, Goal, Hub, Intent, Level, Mark, Mint, Mission, Object, Peg, Plan, Plank, Point, Point blank, Purpose, Quest, Reason, Sake, Seek, Sight(s), Target, Tee, Telos, Train, Try, View, Visie, Vizy, Vizzie

Aimless Drifting, Erratic, Haphazard, Random, Unmotivated

Air(s), Airer, Air-space, Airy Affectation, Ambience, Anthem, Appearance, Arioso, Atmosphere, Attitude, Aura, Bearing, Breath, Clothes horse, Ether(eal), Expose, Greensleeves, Heat-island, Inflate, Lift, Lullaby, Madrigal, Maiden, Manner, Melody, Microburst, Mien, Night, Ozone, Parade, Poseur, Screen, Serenade, Shanty, Sinus, Tidal, →**TUNE**, Ventilate, Wind

Aircraft, Airship Aerodyne, Aerostat, Angels, AST, Auster, Autoflare, Autogiro, Autogyro, Aviette, Avion, Biplane, Blimp, Boeing, Brabazon, Bronco, Broomstick, Camel, Canard, Canberra, Chaser, Chopper, Coleopter, Comet, Concorde, Convertiplane, Corsair, Crate, Cropduster, Cyclogiro, Delta-wing, Dirigible, Dive-bomber, Doodlebug, Drone, Eagle, Enola Gay, Eurofighter, F, Ferret, Fixed-wing, Flivver, Flying fortress, Flying wing, Fokker, Freedom-fighter, Freighter, Galaxy, Glider, Gotha, Gyrodyne, Gyroplane, Hang-glider, Harrier, Hawkeeze, Heinkel, Helicopter, Helo, Hercules, Hunter, Hurricane, Interceptor, Intruder, Jet star, Jumbo, Jump-jet, Kite, Lancaster, Liberator, Lifting-body, Link trainer, Lysander, Messerschmitt, Microjet, Microlight, Microlite, MIG, Mirage, Monoplane, Mosquito, Moth, Multiplane, Nacelle, Nightfighter, Nightfinder, Nimrod, Oerlikon, Orion, Ornithopter, Orthopter, Parasol, Penguin, Phantom, →**PLANE**, Provider, Prowler, Pusher, Ramjet, Rigid, Rotaplane, Runabout, Scout, Scramjet, Semi-rigid, Shackleton, Skiplane, Skyhawk, Sopwith, Sopwith Camel, Spitfire, SST, Stack, Starfighter, Starlifter, Stealth bomber, STOL, Stratocruiser, Stratotanker, Stuka, Super Sabre, Sweptwing, Swing-wing, Tankbuster, Taube, Taxiplane, Thunderbolt, Thunderchief, Tomcat, Tornado, Torpedo bomber, Towplane, Tracker, Trident, Tri-jet, Triplane, Turbofan, Turbo-jet, Turbo-prop, Turboramjet, Variable geometry, Vessel, Vigilante, Viking, Viscount, Vomit comet, Voodoo, VTOL, War bird, Widebody, Wild weasel, Zeppelin

Aircraftsman, Airman AC, Aeronaut, AR, Bleriot, Co-pilot, Kiwi, LAC, Observer, RAF

Airline, Airway Aeroflot, Anthem, BAC, BEA, Bronchus, Carrier, Duct, El Al, Iberia, JAL, Larynx, Lot, Purple, SAS, S(ch)norkel, Trochea, TWA, Upcast, Vent, Weasand(-pipe), Windpipe

▶**Airman** *see* **AIRCRAFTSMAN, FLIER**

Airport Chiang Kai Shek, Drome, Dyce, Entebbe, Faro, Gander, Gatwick, Greenham Common, Heliport, Idlewild, John Lennon, Kennedy, La Guardia, Landing strip, Le Bourget, Lod, Luton, Lympne, O'Hare, Orly, Runway, Shannon, Stansted, Stolport, Tegal, Terminal, Vertiport, Wick

Air-tight Hermetic, Indisputable, Sealed

Akin Alike, Cognate, Congener, Kindred, Sib

Alarm(ed), Alarming, Alarmist Affear, Affright, Agitation, Alert, Arouse, Bell, Bleep, Bugaboo, Caution, Dismay, False, Flap, Fricht, Fright, Frit, Ghast, Hairy, Larum, Panic, Perturb, Radio, Rouse, Scaremonger, Siren, Smoke, Startle, Tirrit, Tocsin, Trepidation, Unease, Unnerve, Warn, Yike(s)

Alas Ah, Alack, Ay, Eheu, Ha, Haro, Harrow, Io, Lackadaisy, Lackaday, O, Oh, Ohone, O me, Waesucks, Waly, Wel(l)away, Well-a-day, Wellanear, Woe

Albatross Alcatras, Black-footed, Golf, Gooney(-bird), Millstone, Omen, Onus, Quaker-bird

Alchemic, Alchemist, Alchemy Adept, Arch-chimic, Brimstone, Cagliostro, Faust(us), Hermetic(s), Multiplier, Quicksilver, Sal ammoniac, Sorcery, Spagyric, Spagyrist, Witchcraft

Alcohol(ic) Acrolein, Aldehyde, Bibulous, Blue ruin, Booze, Borneol, Catechol, Cetyl, Chaptalise, Cholesterol, Choline, Citronellol, Cresol, Diethyl, Diol, Dipsomaniac, Drinker, Ethal, Ethanol, Ethyl, Farnesol, Firewater, Fusel-oil, Geraniol, Glycerin(e), Grain, Grog, Gut-rot, Hard, Inebriate, Inositol, Isopropyl, Jakey, Lauryl, Linalool, Malt, Manniferous, Mannite, Mannitol, Mercaptan, Mescal, Mescalin(e), Methanol, Meths, Moonshine, Nerol, Phytol, Pisco, Polyol, Potato spirit, Propyl, Pyroligneous, Rotgut, Rubbing, Scrumpy, Sorbitol, Sphingosine, Spirits, Sterol, Taplash, Thiol, Wash, White lightning, Wino, Witblits, Xylitol

Alcove Apse, Bay, Bole, Dinette, Niche, Nook, Recess, Reveal

Ale, Alehouse Audit, Barleybree, Barley-broo, Barley-broth, Beer, Brown, Bummock, CAMRA, Draught, Feast, Humming, Humpty-dumpty, Keg, Lager, Lamb's wool, Light, Mild, Morocco, Nappy, Nog, Nogg, October, Porter, Purl, Real, Stout, Swats, Tiddleywink, Tipper, Whitsun, Wort, Yard, Yill

Alert Agog, Amber, Arrect, Astir, Astute, Attentive, Aware, Bleep, Conscious, Gleg, Gogo, Intelligent, Presential, Qui vive, Red, Scramble, Sharp, Sprack, Sprag, Stand-to, Tentie, Up and coming, Vigilant, Volable, Warm, Wary, Watchful, Yellow

Alga(e) Anabaena, Blanketweed, Chlorella, Chlorophyte, Conferva, Desmid, Diatom, Dulse, Heterocontae, Isokont, Jelly, Nostoc, Pleuston, Pond scum, Prokaryon, Protococcus, Rhodophyte, Scum, Sea-lace, Seaweed, Spirogyra, Star-jelly, Stonewort, Ulothrix, Ulotrichales, Valonia, Volvox, Yellow-green, Zooxanthella

Algebra Boolean, Linear, Quadratics

Alias Aka, Byname, Epithet, Moni(c)ker, Nick(name), Pen-name, Pseudonym

Alien(ate), Alienation A-effect, Amortise, Devest, Disaffect, Drop-out, Ecstasy, Erotic, Estrange, ET, Exotic, External, Foreign, Hostile, Little green man, Martian, Metic, Outlandish, Philistine, Repugnant, Strange(r), Vulcan

Alight Alowe, Avail(e), Avale, Detrain, Disembark, Dismount, Flambe, In, Lambent, Land, Lit, Perch, Pitch, Rest, Settle

Align Arrange, Associate, Collimate, Dress, Juxtapose, Marshal, Orient, Synchronize

▶**Alike** *see* **LIKE(NESS)**

Alive Alert, Animated, Breathing, Extant, Quick, Teeming

Alkali(ne), Alkaloid Antacid, Apomorphine, Base, Bebeerine, Berberine, Betaine, Borax, Brak, Brucine, Caffein(e), Capsaicin, Chaconine, Codeine, Colchicine, Curarine, Emetin(e), Ephedrine, Ergotamine, Gelsemin(in)e, Guanidine, Harmalin(e), Harmin(e), Hydrastine, Hyoscine, Hyoscyamine, Ibogaine, Kali, Limewater, Lobeline, Lye, Narceen, Narceine, Nicotine, Papaverine, Physostigmine, Piperine, Potash, Quinine, Reserpine, Rhoeadine, Scopaline, Scopolamine, Soda, Sparteine, Stramonium, Thebaine, Theine, Theobromine, Theophylline, Totaquine, Tropine, Tubocurarine, Veratrin(e), Vinblastine, Vincristine, White, Yohimbine

All A, En bloc, → ENTIRE, Entity, Every man Jack, Finis, Omni, Pan, Quite, Sum, → TOTAL, Toto, Tutti, Whole

All at once Holus-bolus, Per saltum, Suddenly

Allay Calm, Lessen, Quieten, Solace, Soothe

Allegation, Allege(d) Assert, Aver, Claim, Declare, Mud, Obtend, Plead, Purport, Represent, Smear, So-called

Allegiance Faith, Foy, Loyalty, Tribalism

Allegory, Allegorical Apologue, Fable, Mystic, Myth, Parable

Alleviate Alleg(g)e, Calm, Mitigate, Mollify, Palliate, → RELIEVE, Temper

Alley Aisle, Blind, Bonce, Bowling, Corridor, Ginnel, Lane, Laura, Marble, Passage, Rope-walk, Tin Pan, Vennel, Walk, Wynd

Alliance Agnation, Axis, Bloc, Cartel, Coalition, Combine, Compact, Entente, Federacy, → LEAGUE, Marriage, NATO, Syndicate, Union

Alligator Al(l)igarta, Avocado, Caiman, Cayman

Allocate, Allocation Allot, Apportion(ment), Distribute, Earmark, Placement, Ration, Share, Soum, Zone

Allot(ment), Allow(ance), Allowed, Allowing Abear, Alimony, Allocation, Although, Attendance, Award, Brook, Budget, Bug, Cap, Cater, Confess, Countenance, Discount, Down, Draft, Empower, Excuse, Field, Fya, Grant, Indulge, Latitude, Let, License, Licit, Mete, Pension, → PERMIT, Pin-money, Portion, Prebend, Privy purse, Quota, Ration, Rebate, Sanction, Share(-out), Stipend, Suffer, Table money, Though, Tolerance, Viaticum, Vouchsafe, Whack, Yield

▶**Allow(ance)** *see* ALLOT(MENT)

Alloy Albata, Alnico®, Amalgam, Babbitt, Bell-metal, Billon, Blend, Brass, Britannia metal, Bronze, Cermet, Chrome(l), Compound, Constantan, Cupronickel, Duralumin®, Dutch leaf, Electron, Electrum, Ferrosilicon, Gunmetal, Invar®, Kamacite, Latten, Magnalium, Magnox, Marmem, Mischmetal, Mix, Monel®, Nicrosilal, Nimonic, Nitinol, Occamy, Oreide, Orichalc, Ormolu, Oroide, Osmiridium, Paktong, Pewter, Pinchbeck, Platinoid, Potin, Shakudo, Shibuichi, Similor, Solder, Speculum, Spelter, Steel, Stellite®, Tambac, Terne, Tombac, Tombak, Tutenag, White metal, Y, Zircal(l)oy, Zircoloy

▷**Alloy** *may indicate* an anagram

All right A1, Assuredly, Fit, Hale, Hunky(-dory), OK, Safe, Tickety-boo, Well

All the same Even so, Nath(e)less, Nevertheless

Allude, Allusion Cite, Hint, Imply, Innuendo, Mention, Refer, Reference, Suggest

Allure, Alluring Agaçant(e), Charm, Circe, Decoy, Delilah, Glam, Glamour, Houri, It, Magnet(ic), SA, Seduce, Seductive, Siren, Tempt, Trap, Trepan, Vamp

Ally, Allied Accomplice, Agnate, Aide, Alley, Alliance, Ami, Backer, Belamy, Co-belligerent, Cognate, Colleague, Compadre, Dual, Foederatus, German(e), Holy, Marble, Marmoreal, Pal, Partner, Plonker, Related, Taw, Unholy, Unite

Almanac Calendar, Clog, Ephemeris, Morrison, Nostradamus, Whitaker's, Wisden, Zadkiel

Almost Anear, Anigh, Close on, Most, Near(ly), Nigh(ly), Ripe, Une(a)th, Virtually, Well-nigh, Welly

Alms, Alms-giving Awmous, Charity, Dole, Eleemosynary, Handout

Alone Dernful, Eremite, Hat, Hermit, Jack, Lee-lane, Onely, Secco, Separate, Single, Singly, Sola, Solo, Solus, Unaccompanied, Unaided, Unholpen

Along, Alongside Abeam, Aboard, Abreast, Apposed, Beside, By, Parallel, Synchronous

Alphabet ABC, Absey, Augmented Roman, Black-out, Brahmi, Braille, Chalcidian, Christcross, Cyrillic, Deaf, Devanagari, Estrang(h)elo, Finger, Futhark, Futhorc, Futhork, Glagol, Glagolitic, Glossic, Grantha, Hangul, Horn-book, International, IPA, ITA, Kana, Kanji, Katakana, Kufic, Latin, Manual, Nagari, Og(h)am, Pangram, Phonetic, Pinyin, Romaji, Roman, Runic, Signary, Slavonic, Syllabary

Alpine, Alps Australian, Bernese, Cottian, Dinaric, Eiger, Gentian, Graian, Julian, Laburnum, Lepontine, Maritime, Matterhorn, Ortles, Pennine, Rhaetian, Rock plant, Savoy, Southern, Transylvanian, Tyrol, Western

Also Add, And, Eke, Item, Likewise, Moreover, Plus, Too, Und, Withal

Altar, Altar-cloth, Altarpiece Diptych, Dossal, Dossel, Family, Polyptych, Retable, Shrine, Tabula, Triptych

Alter, Alteration Adapt, Adjust, Airbrush, Bushel, Change, Changeover, Chop and change, Convert, Correct, Customise, Evolve, Falsify, Lib, Material, Modify, Modulate, Munge, Mutate, Recast, Refashion, Revise, Transient, Transmogrify, Transpose, Up-end, Variance, →**VARY**

▷**Alter(native)** *may indicate* an anagram

Alternate, Alternating, Alternation, Alternative Aka, Boustrophedon, Bypass, Exchange, Instead, Intercut, Metagenesis, →**OPTION**, Or else, Ossia, Other, Rotate, Second best, Solidus, Staggered, Stop-go, Systaltic, Tertian, Variant, Vicissitude

▷**Alternately** *may indicate* every other letter

Although Admitting, Albe(e), All-be, But, Even, Howsomever, Whereas, While, Whilst

Altitude Elevation, Height, Meridian, Pressure, Rated, Snowline

▷**Altogether** *may indicate* words to be joined

Altruistic, Altruism Heroic, Humane, Philanthropic, Selfless(ness), Unselfish

Always Algate(s), Ay(e), Constant, E'er, Eternal, Ever(more), Forever, For keeps, I, Immer, Sempre, Still

Amass Accumulate, Assemble, Collect, Gather, Heap, Hoard, Pile (up), Upheap

Amateur(s) A, AA, Armchair, Beginner, Corinthian, Dabbler, Dilettante, DIY, Hacker, Ham, Inexpert, L, Lay(man), Newbie, Novice, Prosumer, Tiro, Tyro

Amaze(d), Amazement, Amazing Agape, Agog, Astonish, Astound, Awhape, Bewilder, Cor, Criv(v)ens, Dum(b)found, Flabbergast, Gasser, Gobsmack, Goodnow, Grace, Incredible, Magical, Monumental, O, Open-eyed, Open-mouthed, Perplex, Poleaxe, Pop-eyed, Prodigious, Stagger, Strewth, Stupefaction, Stupendous, Thunderstruck, Unreal, Wow

Ambassador At-large, Diplomat, Elchee, Elchi, Eltchi, Envoy, Extraordinary, Fetial, HE, Internuncio, Ledger, Legate, Leidger, Leiger, Lieger, Minister, Nuncio, Plenipo, Plenipotentiary, Pronuncio

Ambience Atmosphere, Aura, Milieu, Setting

Ambiguous, Ambiguity Amphibology, Cryptic, Delphic, Double, Elusive, Enigmatic, Epicene, Equivocal, Gnomic, Inexactness, Loophole, Oracular, Weasel words

Ambition, Ambitious Adventurer, Aim, Aspiring, Careerism, Dream, Drive, Emulate, Go-ahead, Goal, Go-getter, Grail, High-flier, Holy Grail, Keen, Office-hunter, Purpose, Pushy, Rome-runner, Thrusting, Type A

Amble Meander, Mosey, Pace, Pootle, Saunter, Single-foot, Stroll, Traipse

Ambulance, Ambulanceman Badger, Blood-wagon, Meat wagon, Pannier, Van, Yellow-flag, Zambu(c)k

Ambush(ed) Ambuscade, Belay, Bushwhack, Emboscata, Embusque, Forelay, Forestall, Latitant, Lie in wait, Lurch, Perdu(e), Trap, Watch, Waylay

Amen Ammon, Approval, Inshallah, Verify

Amend(ment) Alter, Change, Correct, Edit, Expiate, Fifth, Insertion, Protocol, Redress, Reform, Repair, Restore, **→ REVISE**, Satisfy

▷**Amend** *may indicate* an anagram

America(n) A, Algonki(a)n, Algonqu(i)an, Am, Angeleno, Basket Maker, Caddo, Cajun, Canadian, Carib, Chicano, Chickasaw, Chinook, Copperskin, Digger, Doughface, Down-easter, Federalist, Flathead, Fox, Gringo, Gullah, Guyanese, Huron, Interior, Joe, Jonathan, Latino, Miskito, Mission Indian, Mistec, Mixtec, Mound builder, Native, New World, Norteno, Olmec, Paisano, Redneck, Salish, Stateside, Statesman, Statist, Tar-heel, Tico, Tupi, Uncle Sam, US(A), WASP, Yankee (Doodle), Yanqui

Amiable, Amicable Friendly, Genial, Gentle, Inquiline, Mungo, Peaceful, Sweet, Warm

Amid(st) Among, Atween, Between, Inter, Twixt

Amiss Awry, Ill, Up, Wrong

Ammunition Ammo, Birdshot, Buckshot, Bullets, Chain-shot, Grenade, Round, Shot, Slug, Tracer

Among Amid(st), In, Inter al, Within

Amorous(ly) Erotic, Fervent, Lustful, Nutty, Romantic, Sheep's eyes, Warm

Amount Come, Degree, Dose, Element, Figure, Glob, Gobbet, Handful, Lashings, Levy, Lot, Measure, Nip, Number, Ocean, Offset, Outage, Plethora, Pot(s), Premium, Price, Quantity, Quantum, Shedload, Span, Stack, Stint, Sum, Throughput, Trace, Volume, Whale, Wheel

Amphibian(s), Amphibious Amb(l)ystoma, Amtrack, Anura, Axolotl, Batrachian, Caecilia, Caecilian, Desman, Eft, Frog, Guana, Hassar, Herpetology, Horned toad, Mermaid, Mudpuppy, Newt, Olm, Ophiomorph, Proteus, Rana, Salamander, Salientia, Seal, Siren, Tadpole, Tree frog, Urodela(n), Urodele, Weasel

Amphitheatre Arena, Bowl, Coliseum, Colosseum, Ring, Stage

Ample, Amplitude Bellyful, Copious, Enough, Generous, Good, Large, Much, Opulent, Profuse, Rich, Roomy, Round, Sawtooth, Spacious, Uberous, Voluminous

Amplifier, Amplify Booster, Double, Eke, Enlarge, Hailer, Laser, Loud hailer, Maser, Megaphone, Push-pull, Solion, Soundboard, Transistor, Treble

Amulet Charm, Fetish, Pentacle, Talisman, Telesm, Tiki, Token

Amuse(ment), Amusing(ly) Account, Caution, Disport, Diversion, Divert, Drole, Droll, Entertain, Game, Gas, Glee, Hoke, Hoot, Jocular, Killing, Laughter, Levity, Light, Occupy, Pantheon, Pleasure, Popjoy, Priceless, Rich, Riot, Scream, Slay, Solace, → **SPORT**, Tickle, Titillate

▶**An** see **A**

Anaesthetic, Anaesthetise(d), Anaesthetist Analgesic, Apgar, Avertin®, Basal, Benzocaine, Bupivacaine, Chloralose, Chloroform, Cocaine, Epidural, Ether, Eucain(e), Fluothane, Freeze, Gas, General, Halothane, Hibernation, Jabber, Ketamine, Lignocaine, Local, Metopryl, Morphia, Novocaine, Number, Opium, Orthocaine, Phenacaine, Phencyclidine, Procaine, Stovaine, Trike, Twilight sleep, Under, Urethan(e)

Analogous, Analogy Akin, Corresponding, Like, Parallel, Similar

Analyse(r), Analysis Alligate, Anagoge, Anatomy, Assay, Assess, Blot, Breakdown, Combinatorial, Conformational, Construe, Critique, Dimensional, Discourse, Dissect, Emic, E-nose, Esda, Eudiometer, Examine, Fourier, Gap, Harmonic, Lexical, Linguistic, Logical, Numerical, Parse, Post-mortem, Process, Qualitative, Quant, Quantitative, Reductionism, Resolution, Rundown, Sabermetrics, Scan(sion), Semantics, Sift, Spectral, Statistician, Swot, Systems, Test, Unpick

▷**Analysis** may indicate an anagram

Analyst Alienist, Jung, Lay, Psychiatrist, Quant(ative), Researcher, Shrink, Systems, Trick cyclist

Anarchist, Anarchy Bakunin, Black Bloc(k), Black Hand, Bolshevist, Chaos, Kropotkin, Lawless, Provo, Punk, Rebel, Revolutionary, Riotous, Trotskyite, Unrule

Anatomy, Anatomist Bones, Cuvier, De Graaf, Dubois, Framework, Henle, Histology, Hunter, Malpighi, Meibom, Osteology, Pacini, Prosector, Puccini, Schneider, Spiegel, Topology

Ancestor, Ancestral, Ancestry Adam, Avital, Dawn man, Descent, Elder, Extraction, For(e)bear, Gastraea, Hereditary, Humanoid, Kachina, Lin(e)age, Parent, Parentage, Pedigree, Primogenitor, Proband, Profectitious, Progenitor, Propositus, Roots, Sire, Tree

Anchor(age) Atrip, Berth, Bower, Cell, Deadman, Drag, Eremite, Grapnel, Hawse, Hermit, Host, Kedge, Killick, Killock, Laura, Mud-hook, Nail, Presenter, Ride, Roads(tead), Root, Scapa Flow, Sheet, Spithead, Stock

Ancient Antediluvian, Archaic, Auld-warld, Early, Gonfanoner, Historic, Hoary, Iago, Immemorial, Lights, Neanderthal, Neolithic, Ogygian, Old-world, Primeval, Primitive, Pristine, Ur, Veteran

And Als(o), Ampassy, Ampersand, Amperzand, Ampussyand, Besides, Et, Furthermore, 'n', Plus, Und

Anecdote(s) Ana, Exemplum, Personalia, Story, Tale, Yarn

Angel(s) Abdiel, Adramelech, Apollyon, Archangel, Ariel, Arioch, Asmadai, Azrael, Backer, Banker, Beelzebub, Belial, Benefactor, Cake, Cherub, Clare, Deva, Dominion, Dust, Eblis, Fallen, Falls, Gabriel, Guardian, Heavenly host, Hierarchy, Host, Investor, Israfel, Ithuriel, Lucifer, Nurse, Power, Principality, Raphael, Recording, Rimmon, Saint, St, Seraph, Spirit, Throne, Uriel, Uzziel, Virtue, Watcher, Zadkiel, Zephiel

Anger, Angry → **ANNOY**, Apeshit, Bate, Berserk, Bile, Black, Boiling, Bristle, Choler(ic), Conniption, Cross, Dander, Disgruntled, Displeased, Dudgeon, Enrage, Exasperation, Face, Fiery, Fired up, Fuff, Fury, Gnar, Gram, Hacked off,

Heat, Het up, Horn-mad, Huff, Incense, Inflame, Infuriate, Iracund, Irascible, Ire, Kippage, Livid, Mad, Monkey, Moody, Nettle, Pique, Provoke, Radge, Rage, Rampant, Ratty, Renfierst, Rile, Roil, Rouse, Sore, Spleen, Steam, Stroppy, Tamping, Tantrum, Tarnation, Teed off, Teen(e), Temper, Tene, Tooshie, Vex, Vies, Warm, Waspish, Waxy, Worked-up, Wound up, Wrath, Wroth, Yond

Angle(d), Angler, Angular, Angles, Angling Acute, Aglee, Argument, Aspect, Attitude, Axil, Azimuthal, Baiter, Canthus, Cast, Catch, Chiliagon, Coign, Complementary, Conjugate, Contrapposto, Corner, Cos, Critical, Diedral, Diedre, Dihedral, Elbow, Elevation, Ell, Exterior, Facial, Fish, Fish-hook, Fork, Geometry, Gonion, Hade, Hip, Hour, Hyzer, In, Incidence, Interior, L, Laggen, Laggin, Latitude, Loft, Longitude, Mitre, Mung, Negative, Nook, Oblique, Obtuse, Parallax, Pediculate, Perigon, Peterman, Phase, Piend, Piscator, Pitch, Pitch-cone, Plan, Plane, Polyhedral, Position, Positive, Quoin, Radian, Rake, Re-entrant, Reflex, Right, Rod(ster), Rod(s)man, Round, Salient, Sally, Saltchucker, Sine, Sinical, Slip, Solid, Spherical, Stalling, Steeve, Steradian, Straight, Supplementary, Sweepback, The gentle craft, Trotline, Vertical, Viewpoint, Visual, Walton, Waltonian, Washin, Weather, Wide-gab

Anglican(s) CE-men, Conformist, Episcopal

Angora Goat, Mohair, Rabbit

Anguish(ed) Agony, Distress, Gip, Gyp, Hag-ridden, Heartache, Misery, → **PAIN**, Pang, Sorrow, Throes, → **TORMENT**, Torture, Woe

Animal(s) Acrita, Anoa, Armadillo, Atoc, Bag, Bandog, Barbastel, Beast, Bestial, Brute, Cariacou, Carnal, Chalicothere, Cleanskin, Coati, Creature, Criollo, Critter, Fauna, Felis, Feral, Gerbil, Guanaco, Herd, Huanaco, Ichneumon, Jacchus, Jerboa, Kinkajou, Klipdas, Mammal, Marmoset, Marmot, Meiofauna, Menagerie, Moose, Morken, Noctule, Oribi, Parazoon, Party, Pet, Political, Protozoa, Pudu, Pygarg, Quadruped, Quagga, Rac(c)oon, Rhesus, Rotifer, Sensual, Sloth, Stud, Tarsier, Teledu, Urson, Waler, Xenurus, Yale, Yapock, Zerda, Zoo

Animate(d), Animation Activate, Actuate, Alive, Arouse, Biophor, Cartoon, Ensoul, Excite, Fire, Frankenstein, Frisky, Heat, Hot, Inspire, Lit, Live, Morph, Mosso, Perky, Rouse, Spark, Spiritoso, Spritely, Stop-motion, Toon, Verve, Vivacity

Animosity Enmity, Friction, Hostility, Malevolence, Malice, Pique, Rancour, Strife

Ankle Coot, Cuit, Cute, Hock, Hucklebone, Knee, Malleolus

Annal(s) Acta, Archives, Chronicles, Register

Annex(e) Acquire, Add, Affiliate, Attach, Codicil, Extension, Lean-to, Subjoin

Annihilate Abolish, Destroy, Erase, Exterminate, Slay, Unbe

Anniversary Birthday, Feast, Jubilee, Obit, Yahrzeit

Announce(r), Announcement Banns, Bellman, Bill(ing), Blazon, Bulletin, Communiqué, Crier, Decree, Disclose, Divulgate, Flash, Gazette, Herald, Hermes, Impart, Inform, Intimate, Meld, Name and shame, Newsflash, Notice, Oracle, Post, Preconise, Press release, Proclaim, Profess, Promulgate, Pronunciamento, Publish, Release, → **REPORT**, Speaker(ine), State, Statement, Tannoy, Trumpet

Annoy(ance), Annoyed, Annoying Aggravate, Aggrieve, Anger, Antagonise, Badger, Bane, Bother, Bug(ger), Bugbear, Chafe, Chagrin, Choleric, Contrary, Cross, Displeasance, Displeasure, Disturb, Drag, Drat, Fash, Fleabite, Frab, Fumed, Gall, Gatvol, Get, Gordon Bennett, Hack off, Hang, Harass, Hatter,

Hector, Hip, Hoots, Huff, Hump, Incense, Irk, → **IRRITATE**, Miff, Mischief, Molest, Nag, Nark, Needle, Nettle, Niggle, Noisome, Noy(ance), Peeve, Perisher, Pesky, Pester, Pipsqueak, Pique, Plague, Provoke, Rankle, Rats, Resentful, Ride, Rile, Roil, Rub, Shirty, Sting, Testy, Tiresome, Tracasserie, Troublesome, Try, Vex

Annual, Annuity Almanac, Bedder, Book, Consolidated, Contingent, Deferred, Etesian, → **FLOWER**, Half-hardy, Hardy, Immediate, Pension, Perpetuity, → **PLANT**, Rente, Tontine, Yearbook, Yearly

Annul(ment) Abolish, Abrogate, Cashier, Cassation, Dissolution, Invalidate, Irritate, Negate, Repeal, Rescind, Reversal, Revoke, Vacate, Vacatur, Vacuate, → **VOID**

▶**Annunciation** see **ANNOUNCE(R)**

▷**Anomaly** may indicate an anagram

Anon Again, Anew, Erelong, Later, Soon

Anonymous Adespota, Anon, A.N.Other, Faceless, Grey, Impersonal, Nameless, Somebody, Unknown, Unnamed, Valentine

Answer(ing), Answer(s) A, Acknowledge, Amoebaean, Ans, Antiphon, Because, Comeback, Crib (sheet), Defence, Dusty, Echo, Key, Lemon, Light, No, Oracle, Rebuttal, Rebutter, Rein, Rejoin(der), Repartee, Reply, Rescript, Respond, Response, Retort, Return, Riposte, Serve, Sol, Solution, Solve, Verdict, Yes

Ant(s), Anthill Amazon, Army, Bull(dog), Carpenter, Colony, Driver, Dulosis, Emmet, Ergataner, Ergates, Ergatogyne, Fire, Formic, Formicary, Myrmecoid, Myrmidon, Nasute, Neuter, Pharaoh, Pismire, Red, Sauba, Slave-maker, Soldier, Termite, Thief, Velvet, White, Wood

Ante Bet, Punt, Stake

Ant-eater Aardvark, Banded, Echidna, Edental, Giant, Manis, Numbat, Pangolin, Scaly, S(e)ladang, Spiny, Tamandu, Tamandua, Tapir

Antelope Addax, Blackbuck, Blaubok, Blesbok, Bloubok, Bluebuck, Bongo, Bontebok, Bubal(is), Bushbuck, Chamois, Chikara, Dikdik, Duiker, Duyker, Dzeren, Eland, Elk, Gazelle, Gemsbok, Gerenuk, Gnu, Goa, Goral, Grysbok, Hartebees, Hartebeest, Impala, Inyala, Kaama, Kid, Klipspringer, Kob, Kongoni, Koodoo, Kudu, Lechwe, Madoqua, Nagor, Nilgai, Nilgau, Nyala, Nylghau, Oribi, Oryx, Ourebi, Pale-buck, Pallah, Prongbuck, Pronghorn, Puku, Pygarg, Reebok, Reedbuck, Rhebok, Sable, Saiga, Sasin, Sassaby, Serow, Sitatunga, Situtunga, Steenbok, Steinbock, Stemback, Stembok, Suni, Takin, Thar, Topi, Tragelaph, Tsessebe, Waterbuck, Wildebeest

Antenna Aerial, Dipole, Dish, Feeler, Horn, Rabbit's ears, Sensillum, Squarial, TVRO

Anterior Anticous, Earlier, Front, Prior

Anthem Die Stem, Hymn, Introit, Isodica, Marseillaise, Motet(t), National, Offertory, Psalm, Red Flag, Responsory, Song, Theme, Tract

Anthology Album, Ana, Chrestomathy, Digest, Divan, Florilegium, Garland, Pick, Spicilege

Anti Against, Agin, Averse, Con, Gainst, Hostile

Anti-bacterial, Antibiotic Aclarubicin, Actinomycin, Allicin, Avoparcin, Bacitracin, Carbenicillin, Cecropin, Cephalosporin, Cipro®, Cloxacillin, Colistin, Cycloserine, Doxorubicin, Doxycycline, Drug, Erythromycin, Gentamicin, Gramicidin, Griseofulvin, Interferon, Interleukin, Kanamycin, Lincomycin, Macrolide, Magainin, Methicillin, Mitomycin, Neomycin, Nystatin, Opsonin,

Oxacillin, Oxytetracycline, Penicillin, Polymyxin, Puromycin, Rifampicin, Rifamycin, Spectinomycin, Streptokinase, Streptomycin, Streptothricin, Terramycin®, Tetracycline, Tyrocidine, Tyrothricin, Virginiamycin

Antibody Agglutinin, Alemtuzumab, Amboceptor, Antitoxin, Blocker, Catuximab, H(a)emolysin, IgA/E/G/M/O, Isoagglutinin, Lysin, Monoclonal, Precipitin, Reagin, Rituximab, Trastuzumab

Antic(s) Caper, Dido, Frolic, Gambado, Hay, Prank, Shenanigan, Stunt

Anticipate, Anticipation Against, Antedate, Augur, Await, Dread, Drool, Envisage, → **EXPECT**, Forecast, Foresee, Forestall, Foretaste, Forethought, Hope, Intuition, Pre-empt, Preparation, Prevenancy, Prolepsis, Prospect, Type

Anticlimax Bathos, Comedown, Deflation, Disappointment, Letdown

Antidote Adder's wort, Alexipharmic, Angelica, Antivenin, Bezoar, Contrayerva, Cure, Emetic, Guaco, Mithridate, Nostrum, Orvietan, Picrotoxin, Remedy, Ribavirin, Senega, Theriac(a), (Venice-)Treacle

Antipathy Allergy, Animosity, Aversion, Detest, → **DISLIKE**, Enmity, Intolerance, Repugnance

Antiquated, Antique, Antiquarian Ancient, Archaic, A(u)stringer, Bibelot, Curio, Dryasdust, Egyptian, Egyptologist, FAS, Fogram(ite), Fog(e)y, Fossil, Moth-eaten, Old-fangled, Ostreger, Relic

Antiseptic Acriflavine, Borax, Carbolic, Cassareep, Creosote, Cresol, Dettol®, Disinfectant, Eupad, Eusol, Formaldehyde, Formalin, Formol, Germicide, Guaiacol, Iodine, Lister, Merbromin, Phenol, Sterile, Thymol, Tutty

Antisocial Aggro, Hoodie, Hostile, Ishmaelitish, Litterbug, Litter-lout, Loner, Misanthropic, Oik, Psychopath, Standoffish

Antithesis Contrary, Converse, Opposite

Anvil Bick-iron, Block, Incus, Stiddie, Stithy

Anxiety, Anxious Abdabs, Angst, Brood, Care(ful), Cark, Concern, Disquiet, Dreading, Dysthymia, Eager, Edgy, Fanteeg, Fantigue, Fantod, Fear, Fraught, Fretting, Grave, Habdabs, Heebie-jeebies, Hung-up, Hypochondria, Impatient, Inquietude, Itching, Jimjams, Jumpy, Keen, Nerviness, Panic, Reck, Restless, Scruple, Separation, Shpilkes, Solicitous, Stewing, Stress, Suspense, Sweat, Tension, Toey, Trepidation, Twitchy, Unease, Unquiet, Upset, Uptight, White-knuckle, Willies, Worriment, Worryguts, Worrywort

Any Arrow, Ary, Some

Anybody, Anyone One, Whoso, You

Anyhow, Anyway Anyroad(s), However, Leastways, Leastwise, Regardless

Anything Aught, Oucht, Ought, Owt, Whatnot

▷**Anyway** *may indicate* an anagram

Apart Aloof, Aside, Asunder, Atwain, Beside, Separate

Apartment Atrium, Ben, Condo(minium), Cubicle, Digs, Duplex, Flat, Insula, Mansion, Paradise, Penthouse, Pied-a-terre, Quarters, Room, Simplex, Solitude, State, Suite, Unit

Apathetic, Apathy Accidie, Acedia, Incurious, Indifferent, Inertia, Languid, Lethargic, Listless, Lobotomized, Lukewarm, Mopish, Pococurante, Stoical, Torpid, Unenthusiastic

Ape(-like), Apeman Anthropoid, Barbary, Big-foot, Catarrhine, Copy, Dryopithecine, Gelada, Gibbon, Gorilla, → **IMITATE**, Magot, Mimic, → **MONKEY**, Naked, Orang, Paranthropus, Parrot, Pongid, Pongo, → **PRIMATE**, Proconsul, Replicate, Simian, Simulate, Troglodyte, Yowie

Apex Acme, Culmen, Gonion, Keystone, Knoll, Knowe, Summit, Vertex

Aphorism Adage, Epigram, Gnome, Maxim, Pensée, Proverb, Sutra

Aphrodisiac, Aphrodite Cytherean, Erotic, Idalian, Paphian, Philter, Philtre, Spanish fly, Urania, Yohimbine

Apologetic, Apologist, Apology Advocate, Ashamed, Cut up, Excuse, Justifier, Mockery, My bad, Oops, Pardon, Scuse, Sir-reverence

Apostle, Apostolic Cuthbert, → DISCIPLE, Evangelist, Johannine, Jude, Matthew, Pauline, Spoon, Thad(d)eus, Thomas, Twelve

Apothecary Chemist, Dispenser, Druggist, LSA, Pharmacist, Pottingar

Appal(ling) Abhorrent, Abysmal, Affear(e), Aghast, Dismay, Egregious, Execrable, Frighten, Horrify, Piacular, Tragic

▷**Appallingly** *may indicate* an anagram

Apparatus Absorptiometer, Aerator, Alkalimeter, Appliance, Aqualung, Aspirator, Block and tackle, Breeches buoy, Bridgerama, Caisson, Calorimeter, Churn, Clinostat, Codec, Commutator, Condenser, Converter, Convertor, Critical, Cryostat, Cyclotron, Decoy, Defibrillator, Desiccator, → DEVICE, Digester, Ebullioscope, Effusiometer, Egg, Electrograph, Electrophorus, Electroscope, Elutriator, Enlarger, Equipment, Gadget, Gasogene, Gazogene, Generator, Giant('s) stride, Gyroscope, Heater, Heliograph, Helioscope, Hemocytometer, Hodoscope, Holophote, Horse, Hydrophone, Hygrostat, Incubator, Inhalator, Injector, Inspirator, Installation, Instrument, Iron lung, Isotron, Langmuir-trough, Lease-rod, Life-preserver, Loom, Microreader, Mimeograph, Mine-detector, Nephoscope, Nitrometer, Oscillator, Oscillograph, Oxygenator, Pasteuriser, Peat-seeker, Percolator, Phon(o)meter, Photophone, Photostat®, Phytotron, Plate-warmer, Plethysmograph, Plumber's snake, Pommel horse, Potometer, Projector, Proto®, Pulmotor®, Push-pull, Radiator, Radiosonde, Rattlebag, Rattletrap, Rectifier, Replenisher, Resistor, Respirator, Respirometer, Resuscitator, Retort, Rotisserie, Scrubber, Searchlight, Seeder, Semaphore, Set, Skimmer, Slide rest, Smoker, Snake, Sniffer, Snorkel, Snowbox, Soundboard, Spectrometer, Spirophore, Starter, Steamer, Stellarator, Steriliser, Still, Substage, Switchgear, Tackle, Tackling, Talk-you-down, Telecine, Teleprinter, Teleseme, Tellurian, Transformer, Transmitter, Tribometer, Tuner, Ventouse, Wheatstone's bridge, ZETA

Apparel Attire, Besee, → COSTUME, Garb, Raiment, Wardrobe, Wardrop

Apparent(ly) Ap, Clear, Detectable, Evident, Manifest, Open, Ostensible, Outward, Overt, Palpable, Plain, Prima facie, Seeming, Semblance, Visible

▷**Apparent** *may indicate* a hidden word

Apparition Avatar, Dream, Eidolon, Fetch, Ghost, Hallucination, → ILLUSION, Phantom, Shade, Spectre, Vision, Visitant, Wraith

Appeal(ing) Ad, Attract, Beg, Cachet, Call, Catchpenny, Charisma, Charm, Cri de coeur, Cry, Dreamy, Entreat, Entreaty, Epirrhema, Exhort, Eye-catching, Fetching, Glamorous, Howzat, Intil, Invocation, It, Mediagenic, Miserere, O, Oath, Oomph, Plead, Popular, SA, Screeve, Sex(iness), Solicit, SOS, Suit, Yummy

Appear(ance) Advent, Air, Arise, Arrival, Aspect, Brow, Cameo, Colour, Debut, Effeir, Effere, Emerge, Enter, Entrance, Facade, Feature, Figure, Garb, Guise, Hue, Image, Looks, Loom, Manifestation, → MANNER, Materialise, Mien, Occur, Ostent, Outward, Phenomenon, Physiognomy, Pop-up, Presence, Represent, Rise, Seem, Semblance, Show, Species, Spectre, Spring, Veneer, View, Visitation, Vraisemblance, Whistle-stop

Appease(ment) Allay, Atone, Calm, Conciliation, Danegeld, Mitigate, Munichism, Pacify, Placate, Propitiate, Relieve, Satisfy, Soothe, Sop, Sweeten

Append(age) Addition, Adjunct, Annex, Antennule, Codpiece, Hanger-on, Lobe, Lug, Nose-leaf, Pendicle, Postfix, Proboscis, Stipule, Tail, Tentacle, Uvula

Appendix Addendum, Apocrypha, Codicil, Grumbling, Label, Pendant, Pendent, Rider, Schedule, Vermiform

Appetite, Appetitive, Appetise(r), Appetize(r) Amuse-bouche, Amuse-gueule, Angels on horseback, Antepast, Antipasto, Aperitif, Appestat, Bhagee, Bhajee, Bulimia, Bulimy, Canapé, Concupiscence, Concupy, Crudités, Dim-sum, Entremes(se), Entremets, Flesh, Hunger, Inner man, Limosis, Malacia, Meze, Nacho, Orectic, Orexis, Passion, Pica, Polyphagia, Relish, Tapa(s), Titillate, Twist, Ventripotent, Whet, Yerd-hunger, Yird-hunger

Applaud, Applause Bravo, →**CHEER**, Clap, Claque, Eclat, Encore, Extol, Olé, Ovation, Praise, Root, Tribute

Apple Alligator, Bad, Baldwin, Balsam, Biffin, Blenheim orange, Bramley, Cashew, Charlotte, Codlin(g), Cooker, Costard, Crab, Custard, Eater, Granny Smith, Greening, Jenneting, John, Jonathan, Kangaroo, Leather-coat, Love, Mammee, Medlar, Nonpareil, Pearmain, Pippin, Pomace, Pome(roy), Pomroy, Pupil, Pyrus, Quarantine, Quarenden, Quar(r)ender, Quarrington, Queening, Redstreak, Reinette, Rennet, Ribston(e), Ripstone, Rotten, Royal gala, Ruddock, Russet, Seek-no-further, Snow, Sops-in-wine, Sturmer (Pippin), Sugar, Sweeting, Thorn, Toffee, Winesap

Application, Applicable, Apply, Appliance(s) Address, Adhibit, Appeal, Appose, Assiduity, Astringent, Barrage, Blender, Concentration, Devote, Diligence, Dispose, Dressing, Exercise, Exert, Foment, Fridge, Gadget, Germane, Implement, Impress, Inlay, Juicer, Kettle, Lay, Liquidiser, Lotion, Machine, Ointment, Pertinent, Petition, Plaster, Poultice, Put, Resort, Rub, Sinapism, Stupe, Talon, Toggle, Truss, →**USE**, White goods

Appoint(ee), Appointment Advowson, Assign, Berth, Co-opt, Date, Delegate, Depute, Designate, Dew, Due, Executor, Induction, Installation, Make, Name, →**NOMINATE**, Nominee, Office, Ordain, Place, Position, Post, Posting, Rendezvous, Room, Set, Tryst

▷**Appointed** *may indicate* an anagram

Appraise, Appraisal Analyse, →**EVALUATE**, Eye-up, Gauge, Judge, Once-over, Review, Tape, Valuate, →**VALUE**, Vet

Appreciate, Appreciation Accrue, Acknowledgement, Admire, Cherish, Clap, Comprehensible, Dig, Empathy, Endear, Esteem, Feel, Grasp, Gratefulness, Gratitude, Increase, Phwoar, Prize, Realise, Recognise, Regard, Relish, Rise, Sense, Stock, Taste, Thank you, Treasure, →**VALUE**, Welcome

Apprehend(ing), Apprehension Afears, Alarm, Anticipate, Arrest, Attuent, Awestruck, →**CATCH**, Collar, Fear, Foreboding, Grasp, Insecure, Insight, Intuit, Noesis, Perceive, Presentiment, Quailing, See, Suspense, Take, Toey, Trepidation, Uh-oh, Unease, Uptake

Apprehensive Jumpy, Nervous, Uneasy

Apprentice(ship) Article, Cub, Devil, Garzone, Improver, Indent(ure), Jockey, L, Learner, Lehrjahre, Novice, Noviciate, Novitiate, Printer's devil, Pupillage, Trainee, Turnover

Approach(ing), Approachable Abord, Access, Accost, Advance, Anear, Angle, Anigh, Appropinquate, Appulse, Asymptotic, Avenue, Close, Coast, Come, Converge, Cost(e), Draw nigh, Drive, Driveway, Fairway, Feeler, Gate, Imminent, Ingoing, Line, Near, Nie, Open, Overture, Pitch, Procedure, Road, Run-in, Run-up, Stealth, Strategy, Verge, Warm

Appropriate(ly), Appropriateness Abduct, Abstract, Annex, Applicable, Apposite, Apt, Aright, Arrogate, Asport, Assign, Bag, Befitting, Borrow, Collar, Commandeer, Commensurate, Condign, Confiscate, Congruous, Convenient, Decent, Due, Element, Eligible, Embezzle, Expedient, Fit, Germane, Good, Happy, Hijack, Hog, Impound, In keeping, Jump, Just, Meet, Nick, Pertinent, Pilfer, Pocket, Pre-empt, Proper, Propriety, Relevant, Right, Seise, Seize, Sequester, Sink, Snaffle, Steal, Suit(ed), Swipe, Take, Timely, Trouser, Usurp

Approval, Approve(d), Approbation Accolade, Accredit, Admire, Adopt, Allow, Amen, Applaud, Assent, Attaboy, Aye, Blessing, Bravo, Brownie points, Change, Cheer, Clap, Credit, Cushty, Dig, Endorse, Favour, For, Green light, Hear hear, Hubba-hubba, Hurra(h), Imprimatur, Initial, Kitemark, Know, Laud, Nod, Official, Okay, Olé, Orthodox, Pass, Plaudit, Praise, Rah, Ratify, Recognise, Recommend, Right-on, Rubber-stamp, Sanction, Stotter, Thumbs-up, Tick, Tribute, Vivat, Voice, Warm to, Yay, Yes

Approximate(ly), Approximation Almost, Around, Ballpark, Circa, Close, Coarse, Estimate, Guess, Imprecise, Near, Rough and ready, Roughly

Apron Airside, Barm-cloth, Bib, Blacktop, Brat, Bunt, Canvas, Fig-leaf, Napron, Pinafore, Pinny, Placket, Rim, Stage, Tablier, Tier

Apt(ly) Apposite, Appropriate, Apropos, Ben trovato, Capable, Evincive, Fit, Gleg, Happy, Inclined, Liable, Prone, Suitable, Tends

Aptitude Ability, Bent, Ear, Eye, Faculty, Feel, Flair, Gift, Knack, Know-how, Nose, Skill, Talent, Taste, Tendency, Touch, Viability

Aqueduct Canal, Channel, Conduit, Hadrome, Xylem

Arab(ian), Arabia, Arabic Abdul, Adnan, Algorism, Ali (Baba), Baathist, Bahraini, Bahrein, Bedouin, Bedu, Druse, Druz(e), Effendi, Fedayee(n), Gamin, Geber, Hani, Hashemite, Hassaniya, Himyarite, Horse, Iraqi, Jawi, Kuwaiti, Lawrence, Moor, Mudlark, Nabat(a)ean, Nas(s)eem, Omani, Omar, PLO, Saba, Sab(a)ean, Saracen, Seleucid, Semitic, Sheikh, Syrian, UAR, Urchin, Yemen(i)

Arbitrary Despotic, Haphazard, Peculiar, Random, Wanton, Whim

Arbitrate, Arbitration, Arbitrator, Arbiter ACAS, Censor, Daysman, Judge, Negotiator, Ombudsman, Pendulum, Prud'homme, Ref(eree), Umpire

Arboreal, Arbour Bower, Dendroid, Pergola, Trellis

Arc Azimuth, Bow, Carbon, →**CURVE**, Dink, Flashover, Fogbow, Foil, Halo, Hance, Haunch, Limb, Octant, Quadrant, Rainbow, Reflex, Semicircle, Trajectory

Arcade Amusement, Burlington, Cloister, Gallery, Loggia, Triforium, Video

Arcane Esoteric, Mystic, Obscure, Occult, Orphism, Recherché, Rune, Secret

Arch(ed), Arching Acute, Admiralty, Alveolar, Arblaster, Arcade, Arcature, Archivolt, Camber, Chief, Counterfort, Crafty, Cross-rib, Ctesiphon, →**CUNNING**, Curve, Discharging, Eyebrow, Fallen, Flying buttress, Fog-bow, Gothic, Hance, Haunch, Instep, Intrados, Inverted, Keystone, Knowing, Lancet, Lierne, Limb-girdle, Marble, Neural, Norman, Ogee, Ogive, Opistholomos, Pelvic, Plantar, Pointed, Portal, Proscenium, Recessed, Relieving, Roguish, Roman, Saddlebow, Safety, Saucy, Segmental, Shouldered, Skew, Sly, Soffit, Span, Squinch, Stilted, Trajan, Triumphal, Vault

Archaeological, Archaeologist, Archaeology Bell, Carter, Childe, Dater, Dig, Evans, Industrial, Layard, Leakey, Mallowan, Mycenae, Petrie, Pothunter, Qumran, Schliemann, Sutton Hoo, Type-site, Wheeler, Winckelmann, Woolley

Archangel Azrael, Gabriel, Israfeel, Israfel, Israfil, Jerahmeel, Michael, Raguel, Raphael, Sariel, Satan, Uriel, Yellow

Archbishop Anselm, Augustine, Cosmo, Cranmer, Davidson, Dunstan, Ebor, Elector, Hatto, Lambeth, Lanfranc, Lang, Langton, Laud, Metropolitan, Morton, Primate, Scroop, Temple, Trench, Tutu, Whitgift

Archer(y) Acestes, Bow-boy, → **BOWMAN**, Cupid, Eros, Hood, Petticoat, Philoctetes, Sagittary, Tell, Toxophilite

Archetype Avatar, Model, Pattern

Architect(ure), Architectural Baroque, Bauhaus, Bricolage, Byzantine, Cartouche, Community, Composite, Computer, Corinthian, Data-flow, Decorated style, Domestic, Doric, Early English, Elizabethan, Flamboyant, Georgian, Gothic, Greek Revival, Ionic, Italian, Landscape, Listed, Lombard, Maker, Moorish, Moresque, Mudejar, Naval, Neoclassical, Neo-gothic, Norman, Palladian, Pelasgian, Perpendicular, Picnostyle, Planner, Queen Anne, Romanesque, Saracenic, Saxon, Spandrel, Spandril, Tudor, Tudorbethan, Tuscan, Vitruvian

Archive(s) Morgue, Muniment, PRO, Records, Register

Arctic Estotiland, Frigid, Hyperborean, In(n)uit, Inupiat, Polar, Tundra

Ardent, Ardour Aflame, Aglow, Boil, Broiling, Burning, Enthusiasm, Fervent, Fervid, Fiery, Flagrant, Flaming, Gusto, Heat, Het, → **HOT**, In, Mettled, Mettlesome, Passion(ate), Perfervid, Rage, Spiritous, Vehement, Warm-blooded, Zealous, Zeloso

Area Acre, Aleolar, Apron, Arctogaea, Are, Assisted, Bailiwick, Beat, Belt, Built-up, Catchment, Centare, Centre, Chill-out, Clearing, Conurbation, Courtyard, Craton, Depressed, Dessiatine, Development, Disaster, District, Docklands, Domain, Downtown, Eruv, Extent, Forecourt, Goal, Grey, Growth, Hectare, Henge, Hide, Hinterland, Hotspot, Input, Landmass, Latitude, Locale, Locality, Lodg(e)ment, Metroplex, Milieu, Mofussil, Neogaea, Nidderdale, No-go, No-man's-land, Notogaea, Pale, Parish, Penalty, Place, Plot, Precinct, Province, Purlieu, Quad, Quarter (section), Range, Redevelopment, → **REGION**, Renosterveld, Res(ervation), Reserve, Rest, Restricted, Riding, Rule, Sector, Service, Shire, Site, Slurb, Special, Staging, Sterling, Subtopia, Sun belt, Support, Surface, Target, Tartary, Technical, Terra, Terrain, Territory, Theatre, Tract, Tundra, Uptown, Urban, Ure, Weald, White, Wilderness, Work station, Yard, Zone

Arena Battleground, Centre court, Circus, Cockpit, Dohyo, Field, Maidan, Olympia, → **RING**, Snowdome, Stadium, Tiltyard, Venue

Argue, Argument(ative) Altercation, Argy-bargy, Bandy, Barney, Beef, Bicker, Blue, Cangle, Conflict, Contend, Contest, Contra, Cosmological, Debate, Difference, Dilemma, Ding-dong, Dispute, Dissent, Enthusiasm, Exchange, Expostulate, Fray, Free-for-all, Hysteron proteron, Logic, Mexican standoff, Moot, Object, Odds, Patter, Plead, Polylemma, Propound, Pros and cons, Quarrel, Quibble, → **REASON**, Rebut, Remonstrate, Row, Run-in, Scene, Sequacious, Socratise, Sophistry, Spar, Spat, Straw man, Stroppy, Stushie, Summation, Teleological, Third man, Tiff, Transcendental, Verbal, Vociferate, Words, Wrangle, Wrestle

Aria Ballad, Cabaletta, Cantata, Cavatina, Melody, Nessun dorma, Song

Aris Arse, → **BOTTOM**, Can

Arise Appear, Develop, Emanate, Emerge, Stem, Upgo, Wax

Aristocracy, Aristocrat(ic) Blood, Blue blood, Classy, Debrett, Duc, Elite, Gentle, Gentry, Grandee, High-hat, Milord, Nob, Noble, Optimate, Passage, Patrician, Thegn, Toff, Tony, U-men, Upper-crust, Viscount, Well-born

Arm(ed), Arms Akimbo, Arsenal, Bearing, Brachial, Branch, Bundooks, Canting, Cove, Crest, Cross bow, Embattle, Equip, Escutcheon, Estoc, Fin, Firth, Frith, Gnomon, Halbert, Hatchment, Heel, Heraldic, Inlet, Jib, Krupp, Limb, Loch, Long, Member, Munitions, Musket, Olecranon, Pick-up, Quillon, Radius, Rail, Ramous, Rocker, Rotor, SAA, Secular, Shield, Shotgun, Side, Small(-bore), Smooth-bore, Spiral, Tappet, Tentacle, Timer, Tone, Tooled-up, Transept, Tremolo, Ulnar, Water pistol, → **WEAPON**, Whip

▷ **Arm** *may indicate* an army regiment, etc.

Armadillo Dasypod, Dasypus, Fairy, Giant, Pangolin, Peba, Pichiciego, Tatou(ay), Xenurus

Armour(ed), Armoury Ailette, Armet, Barbette, Beaver, Besagew, Bevor, Brasset, Brigandine, Buckler, Byrnie, Camail, Cannon, Casemate, Casspir, Cataphract, Chaffron, Chain, Chamfrain, Chamfron, Chausses, Corium, Cors(e)let, Couter, Cuirass, Cuish, Cuisse, Culet, Curat, Curiet, Cush, Defence, Fauld, Garderobe, Garniture, Gear, Genouillère, Gorget, Greave, Habergeon, Hauberk, Jack, Jambe, Jambeau, Jazerant, Jesserant, Lamboys, Mail, Mentonnière, Mesail, Mezail, Nasal, Palette, Panoply, Panzer, Pauldron, Petta, Placcat, Placket, Plastron, Poitrel, Poleyn, Pouldron, Rerebrace, Rest, Roundel, Sabaton, Secret, → **SHIELD**, Solleret, Spaudler, Splint, Stand, Tace, Tank, Taslet, Tasse(t), Thorax, Tonlet, Tuille, Vambrace, Vantbrass, Visor, Voider

Army Arrière-ban, Arrière-garde, BEF, Blue Ribbon, Church, Colours, Confederate, Crowd, Federal, Fyrd, Golden (Horde), Horde, Host, IRA, Junior Service, Land, Landwehr, Legion, Line, Military, Militia, Mobile Command, Multitude, Para-military, Red, SA, Sabaoth, Sally, Salvation, SAS, Sena, Service, Soldiers, Squad, Standing, Stratonic, Swarm, TA, Tartan, Terracotta, Territorial, Thin red line, Volunteer, War, Wehrmacht

▷ **Army** *may indicate* having arms

Aroma(tic) Allspice, Aniseed, Aryl, Balmy, Camphor, Coriander, Fenugreek, Fragrant, Nose, Odorous, Pomander, Spicy, Vanillin, Wintergreen

Around About, Ambient, Circa, Near, Peri-, Skirt, Tour

▷ **Around** *may indicate* one word around another

Arouse(d), Arousal Alarm, Displease, → **EXCITE**, Fan, Fire, Goad, Incite, Indignant, Inflame, Inspire, Must(h), Needle, Provoke, Stimulate, Stole, Suscitate, Urolagnia, Waken, Whet

Arrange(r), Arrangement Adjust, Array, Attune, Ausgleich, Bandobast, Bank, Bundobust, Cohabitation, Collate, Concert, Concinnity, Configuration, Coordinate, Design, Display, Dispose, Do, Drape, Dress, Echelon, Edit, Engineer, Finger, Fix, Foreordain, Format, Formation, Formwork, Grade, Ikebana, Layout, Lineation, Marshal, Modus vivendi, Neaten, Orchestrate, Orchestration, Ordain, → **ORDER**, Ordonnance, Organise, Pack, Pattern, Perm, Permutation, Plan, Position, Prepare, Prepense, Quincunx, Redactor, Regulate, Run, Rustle up, Schedule, Schema, Scheme, Score, Set(ting) (up), Settle, Sort, Spacing, Stack, Stage-manage, Stereoisomerism, Stow, Straighten, Structure, Style, Syntax, System, Tabulate, Tactic, Taxis, Tidy, Timeshare, Transcribe, Vertical

▷ **Arrange** *may indicate* an anagram

Array(ed) Attire, Caparison, Deck, Herse, Logic, Marshal, Matrice, Muster, Ula

Arrear(s) Aft, Ahint, Backlog, Behind, Debt, Owing

Arrest(ed), Arresting Abort, Alguacil, Alguazil, Ament, Apprehend, Attach, Attract, Blin, Book, Bust, Caption, Capture, Cardiac, Catch, Cessation, Check, Citizen's, Collar, Detain, False, Furthcoming, Hold, House, Infangthief, Knock,

Lag, Lift, Lightning, Nab, Nail, Nick, Nip, Nobble, Pinch, Pull in, Restrain, Retard, Riveting, Round-up, Run-in, Salient, Sease, Seize, Snaffle, Snatch, Spellbind, Stasis, Stop, Sus(s), Turn in

Arrival, Arrive, Arriving, Arriviste Accede, Advent, Attain, Come, Entrance, Get, Happen, Hit, Inbound, Influx, Johnny-come-lately, Land, Natal, Nativity, Newcomer, Parvenu, Pitch up, Reach, Roll up, Strike

Arrogance, Arrogant Assumption, Boastful, Bold, Bravado, Bumptious, Cavalier, Cocksure, Cocky, Contemptuous, Disdain, Dogmatic, Effrontery, Haughty, Haut(eur), High, High and mighty, High-handed, High-hat, Hogen-mogen, Hoity-toity, Hubris, Imperious, Jumped up, Lordly, Morgue, Overweening, Presumption, Pretentious, Proud, Proud-stomached, Prussianism, Side, Snobbish, Surquedry, Surquedy, Toploftical, Topping, Uppity, Upstart, Yuppy

Arrow, Arrow-head Acestes, Any, Ary, Bolt, Cloth-yard shaft, Dart, Filter, Flechette, Missile, Pheon, Pointer, Quarrel, Reed, Sagittate, Shaft, Sheaf, Straight

Arsenal Ammo, Armo(u)ry, Depot, Fire-arms, Magazine, Side, Toulon

Arson(ist) Firebug, Pyromania, Torching

Art(s), Arty, Art movement, Art school, Art style Abstract, Alla prima, Applied, Arte Povera, Bauhaus, Bloomsbury, Bonsai, Britart, Brut, Chiaroscuro, Clair-obscure, Clare-obscure, Click, Clip, Cobra, Collage, Commercial, Conceptual, Constructivism, Contrapposto, Craft, Cubism, Culture vulture, Cunning, Curious, Dada, Daedal(e), Deco, Decorative, Dedal, De Stijl, Die Brucke, Diptych, Divisionism, Enamel(ling), Expressionism, Fauvism, Feat, Fine, Finesse, Flemish, Folk, Futurism, Genre, Graphic, Grisaille, High Renaissance, Humanities, Ikebana, Impressionist, Jugendstil, Kakemono, Kano, Ka pai, Kinetic, Kirigami, Kitsch, Knack, Lacquerware, Land, Liberal, Mandorla, Mannerism, Martial, Masterwork, Mehndi, Minimal, Modern(e), Montage, Motivated, Music, Nabis, Nazarene, Neoclassical, Neo-impressionism, New Wave, Nihonga, Noli-me-tangere, Nouveau, Objets trouves, Optical, Origami, Orphic Cubism, Orphism, Outsider, Pastiche, Performance, Perigordian, Plastic, Pointillism, Pop, Postimpressionism, Postmodern, Practical, Pre-Raphaelite, Primitive, Psychedelic, Public, Purism, Quadratura, Quadrivium, Relievo, Repousse, Sienese, → **SKILL**, Social realism, Stained glass, Still-life, Suprematism, Surrealism, Synchronism, Tachism(e), Tactics, Tatum, Tenebrism, Tessera, Toreutics, Trecento, Triptych, Trivium, Trompe l'oeil, Trouvé, Tsutsumu, Ukiyo-e, Useful, Verism, Virtu, Visual, Vorticism

▷**Art** *may indicate* an -est ending

▷**Artefact** *may indicate* an anagram

Artery Aorta, Brachial, Carotid, Coronary, Duct, Femoral, Iliac, Innominate, M1, Pulmonary, Route

Artful Cute, Dodger, Foxy, Ingenious, Quirky, Shifty, Sly, Subtle, Tactician, Wily

Article(s) A, An, Apprentice, Artefact, Clause, Column, Commodity, Cutting, Definite, Doctrine, Feature, Feuilleton, Gadget, Indefinite, Indenture, Item, Leader, Leading, Object, Op-ed, Paper, Part, Piece, Pot-boiler, Report, Shipping, Sidebar, Specify, The, Thing, Thirty-nine, Treatise, Turnover, Utensil, Ware

Articulation, Articulate(d) Clear, Diarthrosis, Distinct, Eloquent, Enounce, Express, Fluent, Gimmal, Hinged, Intonate, Jointed, Lenis, Limbed, Lisp, Pretty-spoken, Pronounce, Single-tongue, Tipping, Tonguing, Utter, Verbalise, Vertebrae, Vocal, Voice, Wrist

Artifice(r), Artificial Bogus, Chouse, Contrived, Davenport-trick, Dodge, Ersatz, Factitious, False, Feint, Finesse, Guile, Hoax, Inauthentic, In vitro, Logodaedaly, Made, Man-made, Mannered, Opificer, Phoney, Postiche, Pretence, Prosthetic, Pseudo, Reach, Ruse, Sell, Set, Sham, Spurious, Stratagem, → **STRATEGY**, Synroc, Synthetic, Theatric, → **TRICK**, Unnatural, Wile, Wright

Artillery(man) Battery, Cannon(ier), Cohorn(e), Fougade, Fougasse, Guns, Mortar, Ordnance, Pyroballogy, RA, Rafale, Ramose, Ramus, Train

Artisan Craftsman, Decorator, Joiner, Journeyman, Mechanic, Pioneer, Pioner, Pyoner, Weaver, Workman

Artist(e), Artistic Aesthetic, Animator, Bohemian, Cartoonist, Colourist, Cubist, Dadaist, Daedal(e), Deccie, Decorator, Enameller, Escape, Etcher, Fine, Foley, Gentle, Gilder, Graffiti, ICA, Illustrator, Impressionist, Landscapist, Limner, Linear, Maestro, Make-up, Master, Mime, Miniaturist, → **MUSICIAN**, Nabis, Nazarene, Oeuvre, Orphism, → **PAINTER**, Pavement, Paysagist, Perspectivist, Piss, Plein-airist, Pre-Raphaelite, Primitive, Quick-change, RA, Rap, Screever, Sideman, Sien(n)ese, Stripper, Surrealist, Tachisme, Tagger, Tap dancer, Touch, Trapeze, Trecentist, Virtuose, Virtuoso, Water-colourist

Artless Candid, Homespun, Ingenuous, Innocent, Naive, Open, Seely

As Aesir, Als, Arsenic, Coin, Eg, Forasmuch, Kame, Qua, Ridge, 's, Since, So, Thus, Ut, While

As before Anew, Ditto, Do, Stet

Ascend(ant), Ascent, Ascension Anabasis, Climb, Dominant, Escalate, Gradient, Pull, Ramp, Right, Rise, Sclim, Sklim, Slope, Up, Upgang, Uphill, Uprise, Zoom

Ascertain Determine, Discover, → **ESTABLISH**, Prove

Ascribe Assign, → **ATTRIBUTE**, Blame, Credit, Imply, Impute

Ash(es), Ashen, Ashy Aesc, Aizle, Bone, Breeze, Cinders, Cinereal, Clinker(s), Easle, Embers, Fraxinas, Griseous, Kali, Pallor, Pearl, Pozz(u)olana, Prickly, Rowan, Ruins, Sorb, Stinking, Tephra, Urn, Varec, Volcanic, Wednesday, White, Witchen, Yg(g)drasil(l)

Ashamed Abashed, Embarrassed, Hangdog, Mortified, Repentant, Sheepish, Shent

Ashore Aland, Beached, Coast, Grounded, Stranded

Asia(n), Asiatic Afghan, Angaraland, Armenian, Azerbaijani, Balinese, Bengali, Bithynia, Cambodian, Cantonese, Desi, E, Evenki, Ewenki, Harijan, Harsha, Hun, Hyksos, Indian, Indonesian, Jordanian, Karen(ni), Kazakh, Kirghiz, Korean, Kurd, Kyrgyz, Lao(tian), Lydian, Malay, Medea, Media, Mongol, Naga, Negrito, Nepalese, Pasht(o)um, Pathan, Punjabi, Pushtu, Samo(y)ed, Saudi, Shan, Siamese, Sindi, Sogdian, Sri Lankan, Tamil, Tatar, Tibetan, Turanian, Turk(o)man, Uzbeg, Uzbek, Vietnamese

Aside Apart, By(-speech), Despite, Private, Separate, Shelved, Sotto voce, Stage whisper

Ask Bed, Beg, Beseech, Bid, Cadge, Charge, Demand, Desire, Eft, Enquire, Entreat, Evet, Implore, Intreat, Invite, Lobby, Newt, Petition, Pray, Prithee, Pump, Query, Quiz, Request, Require, Rogation, Seek, Solicit, Speer, Speir, Touch

Askance Asconce, Askew, Oblique, Sideways

Asleep Dormant, Dove, Inactive, Napping

Aspect Angle, Bearing, Brow, Face, Facet, Facies, Feature, Hue, Look, Mien, Nature, Outlook, Perfective, Perspective, Phase, Sextile, Side, → **VIEW**, Visage, Vista

Aspersion, Asperse Calumny, Defame, Innuendo, Libel, Slander, Slur, Smear, Traduce

Asphalt Bitumen, Blacktop, Gilsonite®, Jew's pitch, Pitch, Uinta(h)ite

Aspirant, Aspirate, Aspiration, Aspire Ambition, Breath, Buckeen, Challenger, Desire, Dream, Endeavour, Ettle, Goal, H, Hope(ful), Pretend, Pursue, Rough, Spiritus, Wannabe(e), Would be, Yearn, Yuppie

Assail(ant) Afflict, Assault, Batter, Bego, Belabour, Bepelt, Beset, Bombard, Foe, Harry, Impugn, Oppugn, Pillory, Ply, Revile

Assassin(ate), Assassination Attentat, Booth, Brave, Bravo, Brutus, Casca, Cassius, Corday, Cut-throat, Dallas, Frag, Gar(r)otte, Gunman, Highbinder, Hitman, Hit squad, Killer, Ninja, Oswald, Sword, Sworder, Thuggee, Triggerman, Tyrannicide

Assault ABH, Assail, Assay, Attack, Battery, Bombard, GBH, Hamesucken, Head-butt, Indecent, Invasion, Knee, Maul, Molest, Mug, Push, → **RAID**, Stoor, Storm, Stour, Stowre, Work over

Assemble(d), Assembly Aggregate, Amass, Audience, Ball, Band, Bevy, Bottom-hole, Brood, Chapter, Church, Clutch, → **COLLECTION**, Company, Conclave, Congregate, Convention, Convocation, Convoke, Corroboree, Council, Court (baron), Covey, Diet (of Worms), D(o)uma, Fit, Flotilla, Folkmote, Forgather, Fuel, Gather(ing), General, Group, House, Jirga, Lekgotla, Levee, Loya jirga, Mass, Meet, → **MEETING**, Moot, Murder, Muster, National, Nide, Oireachtas, Panegyry, Parishad, Parliament, Prefabrication, Primary, Quorum, Rally, Rallying-point, Reichstag, Relie, Resort, Riksdag, Rodeo, Roll up, Sanghat, School, Scratch, Sedge, Sejm, Senate, Senedd, Sheaf, Society, Squadron, String, Student, Synagogue, Synod, Tribunal, Troop, Troupe, Turn out, Unlawful, Vidhan Sabha

Assent Accede, Acquiesce, Agree, Amen, Aye, Comply, Concur, Jokol, Nod, Placet, Sanction, Viceregal, Yea, Yield

Assert(ing), Assertion, Assertive Affirm, Allege, Bumptious, Claim, Constate, Contend, → **DECLARE**, Dogmatic, Forceful, Ipse-dixit, → **MAINTAIN**, Pose, Predicate, Proclaim, Protest, Pushing, Pushy, Swear (blind), Thetical

Assess(ment), Assessor Affeer, Appraise, Consider, Critique, Eleven-plus, Estimate, Evaluate, Formative, Gauge, Guesstimate, Inspect, → **JUDGE**, Levy, Measure, Perspective, Rating, Referee, Report, Risk, Scot and lot, Size up, Stocktake, Summative, Tax, Value, Weigh

Asset(s) Advantage, Capital, Chargeable, Chattel, Current, Fixed, Intangible, Inventory, Liquid, Plant, Property, Resource, Seed corn, Talent, Tangible, Virtue

Assign(ation), Assignment Allocate, → **ALLOT**, Apply, Aret, Ascribe, Attentat, Attribute, Award, Date, Dedicate, Depute, Detach, Detail, Duty, Entrust, Errand, Fix, Give, Grant, Impute, Mission, Ordain, Point, Quota, Refer, Sort, Tak(e), Tryst

Assimilate(d) Absorb, Blend, Digest, Esculent, Fuse, Imbibe, Incorporate, Merge, Osmose

Assist(ance), Assistant Acolyte, Adjunct, Adviser, Aid(e), Ally, Alms, Attaché, Attend, Au pair, Batman, Befriend, Busboy, Cad, Collaborate, Counterhand, Deputy, Dresser, Facilitate, Factotum, Famulus, Girl Friday, Gofer, → **HAND**, Help, Henchman, Legal aid, Matross, Nipper, Number two, Offsider, Omnibus, Orderly, Proproctor, Reinforce, Relief, Second, Secretary, Server, Service, Servitor, Sidekick, Sidesman, Stead, Subeditor, Subsidiary, Suffragan, → **SUPPORT**, Tawny Owl, Underling, Usher, Whipper-in

Associate(d), Association Accomplice, Affiliate, Alliance, Attach, Bedfellow, Brotherhood, Cartel, Chapel, Club, Colleague, Combine, Community, Company, Comrade, →CONNECT, Consort(ium), Contact, Correlate, Crony, Familiar, Fellow, Fraternise, Fraternity, Goose club, Guild, Hobnob, Identify, Inquiline, Join, Kindred, League, Liaison, Link, Member, MENSA, Mix, Partner(ship), Probus, Relate, Ring, Stablemate, Staff, Syndicate, Synonymous, Tenants', Trade, UN(A), Union, Wiener Werkstatte, Word, Yoke-fellow

▷**Assorted** *may indicate* an anagram

Assuage Allay, Appease, Beet, Calm, Ease, Mease, Mitigate, Mollify, Relieve, Slake, Soften, Soothe

Assume(d), Assuming, Assumption Adopt, Affect, Arrogate, Artificial, Attire, Axiom, Believe, Don, Donné(e), Feign, Gather, Hypothesis, Lemma, Occam's Razor, Posit, Postulate, Preconception, Premise, Premiss, Presuppose, Pretend, Pretentious, Principle, Putative, Saltus, Say, Side, Simulate, Suppose, Surmise, Take

▷**Assumption** *may indicate* 'attire'

Assure(d), Assurance Aplomb, Aver, Avouch, Belief, Calm, →CERTAIN, Comfort, Confidence, Confirm, Earnest, Gall, Guarantee, Knowing, Life, Pledge, Poise, Promise, Secure, Self-confidence, Term, Thoughten, Warranty

Asteroid Ceres, Eros, Hermes, Hygiea, Icarus, Juno, Minor planet, Pallas, Planetoid, Sea-star, Star, Starfish

Astonish(ed), Astonishing, Astonishment, Astound Abash, Admiraunce, Amaze, Banjax, Bewilder, Bowl over, Confound, Corker, Crikey, Daze, Donnert, Dumbstruck, Dum(b)found, Flabbergast, Gobsmack, Open-eyed, Open-mouthed, Phew, Rouse, Shake, Singular, Stagger, Startle, Stupefaction, Stupefy, Stupendous, Surprise, Thunderstruck, Wide-eyed, Wow

Astray Abord, Amiss, Errant, Lost, Will, Wull

Astride Athwart, En cavalier, Spanning, Straddle-back

Astringent Acerbic, Alum, Catechu, Gambi(e)r, Harsh, Kino, Myrobalan, Obstruent, Puckery, Rhatany, Sept-foil, Severe, Sour, Stypsis, Styptic, Tormentil, Witch-hazel

Astrologer, Astrology, Astrological Archgenethliac, Chaldean, Culpeper, Faust, Figure-caster, Genethliac, Lilly, Magus, Midheaven, Moore, Nostradamus, Soothsayer, Starmonger, Zadkiel

Astronaut Aldrin, Cosmonaut, Gagarin, Glenn, Lunarnaut, Spaceman, Spacer

Astronomer, Astronomy, Astronomical Airy, Almagest, Aristarchus, Azimuth, Barnard, Bessel, Bliss, Bradley, Brahe, Callipic, Cassegrain, Cassini, Celsius, Christie, Coal sack, Copernicus, Dyson, Eddington, Encke, Eratosthenes, Eudoxus, Flamsteed, Galileo, Gamma-ray, Graham-Smith, Hale, Halley, Herschel, Hertzsprung, Hewish, Hipparchus, Hoyle, Hubble, Huggins, Jeans, Kepler, Lagrange, Laplace, Leverrier, Lockyer, Lovell, Maskelyne, Meton, Moore, Olbers, Omar Khayyam, Oort, Planetesimal, Planetology, Pond, Ptolemy, Quadrivium, Radio, Reber, Rees, Roche, Roemer, Russell, Ryle, Schwarzschild, Seyfert, Sosigenes, Spencer-Jones, Tycho Brahe, Urania, Uranography, Wolfendale, Woolley

Astute Acute, Canny, Crafty, Cunning, Downy, Perspicacious, Shrewd, Subtle, Wide, Wily

As well Additionally, Also, Both, Eke, Even, Forby, To boot, Too

Asylum Bedlam, Bin, Bughouse, Frithsoken, Funny-farm, Girth, Grith, Haven, Institution, Loony bin, Lunatic, Madhouse, Magdalene, Nuthouse, Political, Rathouse, Refuge, Retreat, Sanctuary, Shelter, Snake-pit

Asymmetric(al) Contrapposto, Lopsided, Skew

Atheist Doubter, Godless, Infidel, Irreligious, Sceptic

Athlete, Athletic(s) Agile, Agonist, Blue, Coe, Discobolus, Field, Gymnast, Hurdler, Jock, Leish, Miler, Milo, Nurmi, Olympian, Owens, Pacemaker, Runner, Sexual, Shamateur, Shot-putter, Sportsman, Sprinter, Track, Track and field, Triple jump

Atlas Linguistic, Maps, Range, Silk, Telamon

▷**At last** *may indicate* a cobbler

Atmosphere Aeropause, Afterdamp, Air, Ambience, Aura, Chemosphere, Climate, E-layer, Elements, Epedaphic, E-region, Ether, Exosphere, F-layer, Fug, Geocorona, Ionosphere, Lid, Magnetosphere, Mesophere, Meteorology, Miasma, Mood, Ozone, Stratosphere, Thermosphere, Tropopause, Troposphere, Upper, Vibe(s), Vibrations

Atom(ic), Atoms, Atomism Boson, Chromophore, Dimer, Electron, Excimer, Fusion, Gram, Ion, Iota, Isobare, Isotone, Isotope, Ligand, Logical, Molecule, Monad, Monovalent, Muonic, Nematic, Nuclide, Particle, Pile, Radionuclide, Side-chain, Species, Steric, Substituent

Atone(ment) Aby(e), Acceptilation, Appease, Assoil, Expiate, Purge, Redeem, Redemption, Yom Kippur

▷**At random** *may indicate* an anagram

Atrocious, Atrocity Abominable, Brutal, Diabolical, Enorm, Flagitious, Heinous, Horrible, Massacre, Monstrous, Outrage, Piacular, Terrible, Vile

▷**At sea** *may indicate* an anagram

Attach(ed), Attachment Accessory, Adhesion, Adhibition, Adnate, Adnation, Adscript, Affix, Allonge, Bolt, Bro, Byssus, Covermount, Curtilage, Devotement, Devotion, Distrain, Dobby, Extra, Eyehook, Feller, Fixation, Glue, →**JOIN**, Menge, Moor, Obconic, Piggyback, Pin, Reticle, Sew, Sidecar, Snell, Stick, Tack on, Tendon, Tendril, Tie, Weld

Attack(ing), Attacker Affect, Aggression, Airstrike, Alert, Ambuscade, Ambush, Apoplexy, Assail, Assault, Assiege, Banzai, Batter, Belabour, Beset, Blitz(krieg), Bombard, Bout, Broadside, Brutalise, Calumny, Campaign, Carte, Charge, Clobber, Club, Counteroffensive, Coup de main, Denounce, Depredation, Discomfit, Excoriate, Feint, Fit, Foray, Fork, Forward, Gas, Glass, Happy-slapping, Harry, Hatchet job, Headbutt, Heart, Heckle, Iconoclast, Impingement, Incursion, Infestation, Inroad, Invade, Inveigh, Jump, Knee, Lampoon, Lash out, Let fly, Maraud, Molest, Mug, Offence, Offensive, Onfall, Onrush, Onset, Onslaught, Oppugn, Outflank, Panic, Philippic, Pillage, Pin, Poke, Polemic, Pounce, Pre-emptive, Push, Raid, Rally, Sail, Sandbag, Savage, Second strike, Seizure, Siege, Skitch, Slam, Snipe, Sortie, Spasm, Storm, Strafe, Straff, Strike, Thrust, Tilt, Vituperate, Wage, Warray, Zap

Attain(ment) Accomplish, Achieve, Arrive, Earn, Fruition, Get, Land, Reach

Attempt Attentat, Bash, Bid, Burl, Crack, Debut, Effort, Egma, Endeavour, Essay, Go, Mint, Nisus, Offer, Potshot, Seek, Shot, Shy, Spell baker, Stab, Strive, Tackle, Trial, →**TRY**, Venture, Whack, Whirl

Attend(ance), Attendant Accompany, Acolyte, Aide, Appearance, Batman, Bearer, Bell-hop, Bower woman, Chaperone, Commissionaire, Courtier, Doula, Dresser, Entourage, Equerry, Escort, Esquire, Footman, Gate(-keeper), G(h)illie, Gilly, Hear, →**HEED**, Jack, Janitor, Keeper, →**LISTEN**, Loblolly-boy, Marshal, Note, Orderly, Outrider, Page, Pew-opener, Presence, Respect, Satellite, Second, S(a)ice, Sort, Steward, Syce, Therapeutic, Trainbearer, Trolleydolly, Up at, Usher, Valet, Visit, Wait, Watch, Zambuck

Attention, Attentive Achtung, Alert, Assiduity, Care(ful), Concentration, Court, Coverage, Dutiful, Ear, Eye, Focus, Gallant, Gaum, Gorm, Hark, Heed, Mind, Note, Notice, Observant, Present, Punctilious, Qui vive, **→ REGARD**, Respect, Spotlight, Tentie, Tenty, Thorough, Thought, Uxorious, Voila

Attest Affirm, Certify, Depose, Guarantee, Notarise, Swear, **→ WITNESS**

Attic Bee-bird, Garret, Greek, Koine, Loft, Mansard, Muse, Salt, Sky parlour, Solar, Soler, Sollar, Soller, Tallat, Tallet, Tallot

Attire Accoutre, Adorn, Apparel, Clobber, Clothe, Clothing, **→ DRESS**, Garb, Habit, Slacks

Attitude Air, Aspect, Behaviour, Demeanour, Light, **→ MANNER**, Mindset, Nimby, Outlook, Pose, Position, Possie, Posture, Propositional, Scalogram, Sense, Song, Spirit, Stance, Tone, Uppity, Viewpoint

Attorney Advocate, Counsellor, DA, Lawyer, Private, Proctor, Prosecutor, Public

Attract(ion), Attractive(ness), Attractor Bait, Beauté du diable, Becoming, Bedworthy, Bewitch, Bonnie, Bonny, Catchy, Charisma, **→ CHARM**, Comely, Cute, Dinky, Dish(y), **→ DRAW**, Engaging, Entice, Eye-catching, Fascinate, Fetching, Goodly, Great, Heartthrob, Hot, Hot stuff, Hotty, Hunky, Inviting, Jolie laide, Loadstone, Looker, Luscious, Magnet(ism), Ornamental, Pack in, Personable, Pheromone, Photogenic, Picture postcard, Picturesque, Plum, Popsy, Prepossessing, Pretty, Seduce, Sexpot, Sideshow, Smasher, Snazzy, Striking, Stunner, Taking, Tasteful, Tasty, Tempt, Toothsome, Tottie, Totty, Triff(ic), Va-va-voom, Winning, Winsome, Zoophilia

Attribute, Attribution Accredit, Allot, Ap(p)anage, Ascribe, Asset, By, Credit, Gift, Impute, Lay, Metonym, Owe, Proprium, Quality, Refer, Resource, Shtick, Strength

Aubergine Brinjal, Brown jolly, Egg-apple, Egg-plant, Mad-apple

Auburn Abram, Chestnut, Copper, Vill(age)

Auction(eer) Barter, Bridge, Cant, Dutch, Hammer, Outcry, Outro(o)per, Roup, Sale, Subhastation, Tattersall, Trade sale, Vendue, Warrant sale

Audacious, Audacity Bald-headed, Bold, Brash, Cheek, Chutspah, Chutzpah, Cool, Der-doing, Devil-may-care, Effrontery, Face, Hardihood, Indiscreet, Insolence, Intrepid, Neck, Nerve, Rash, Sauce

Audience, Auditorium Assembly, Court, Durbar, Gate, House, Interview, Pit, Sphendone, Theatre, Tribunal

Audit(or) Accountant, Check, Ear, Examine, Inspect, Listener, Medical, Vet

Augment(ed) Boost, Eche, Eke, Grow, Ich, Increase, Pad, Supplement, Swell, Tritone

Augur(y) Bode, Divination, Ornithoscopy, Portend

Aunt(ie) Agony, Augusta, BBC, Beeb, Giddy, Naunt, Sainted, Tia, Welsh

Aura Aroma, Halo, Mystique, Nimbus, Odour, Vibe(s), Vibrations

Austere, Austerity Astringent, Bleak, Dantean, Dervish, Dour, Hard, **→ HARSH**, Moral, Plain, Rigour, Self-disciplined, Stern, Stoic, Stoor, Strict, Vaudois, Waldensian

Australia(n) A, Alf, Antichthone, Antipodean, .au, Aussie, Balt, Banana-bender, Bananalander, Billjim, Bodgie, Canecutter, Cobber, Currency, Darwinian, Digger, Gin, Godzone, Gumsucker, Gurindji, Koori, Larrikin, Myall, Norm, Ocker, Ossie, Outbacker, Oz(zie), Pintupi, Roy, Sandgroper, Strine, Sydneysider, Wallaby, Yarra-yabbies

Authentic(ate), Authentication Certify, Des(h)i, Echt, Genuine, Honest, Notarise, Official, Probate, Ratify, Real, Sign, Simon-pure, Test, True, Validate

Author(ess) Anarch, Architect, Auctorial, Biographer, Chronicler, Hand, Inventor, Me, Parent, Penman, Playwright, Rhymer, Scenarist, Volumist, Wordsmith, →WRITER

▷**Author** *may refer to* author of puzzle

Authorise(d), Authorisation Accredit, Chit, Clearance, Command, Consent, Depute, Empower, Enable, Entitle, Exequatur, ID card, Imprimatur, Initial, Legal(ise), Legit, →LICENCE, Licit, Mandate, Official, OK, Passport, →PERMIT, Plenipotentiary, Proxy, Ratify, Rubber-stamp, Sanction, Sign, Signature, Stamp, Undersign, Warrant

Authority, Authoritarian, Authoritative Ascetic, Canon, Chair, Charter, Circar, Cocker, Commission, Commune, Crisp, Curule, Definitive, Domination, Domineering, Dominion, Establishment, Ex cathedra, Expert, Fascist, Free hand, Gravitas, Hegemony, Inquirendo, Jackboot, Leadership, Licence, License, Light, Local, Magisterial, Mana, Mandate, Mantle, Mastery, Name, Omnipotence, Oracle, Permit, PLA, Potency, →POWER, Prefect, Prestige, Pundit, Regime, Remit, Right, Rod, Savant, Say-so, Sceptre, Sircar, Sirkar, Source, Supremacy, Supremo, Sway, Top-brass, Tyrannous, Unitary, Warrant

Autocrat(ic) Absolute, Caesar, Cham, Despot, Neronian, Tenno, Tsar, Tyrant

Automatic, Automaton Android, Aut, Browning, Deskill, Instinctive, Knee-jerk, Machine, Mechanical, Pistol, Reflex, Robot, RUR, Zombi(e)

Auxiliary Adjunct, Adjuvant, Adminicle, Aide, Ancillary, Be, Feldsher, Foederatus, Have, Helper, Ido, Modal

Avail(able) Abounded, Benefit, Dow, Eligible, Going, Handy, In season, On, On call, On hand, On tap, Open, Out, Pickings, Potluck, →READY, Serve, To hand, Up for grabs, Use, Utilise, Worth

Avalanche Deluge, Icefall, Landfall, Landslide, Landslip, Lauwine, Rockfall, Slide, Slip, Snowdrop

Avarice, Avaricious Cupidity, Gimmes, Golddigger, Greed, Money-grubbing, Pleonexia, Predatory, Shylock, Sordid

Avenge(r) Alecta, Eriny(e)s, Eumenides, Goel, Kurdaitcha, Megaera, Nemesis, Punish, Redress, Requite, →REVENGE, Tisiphone, Wreak

Avenue Allee, Alley, Approach, Arcade, Channel, Corso, Cradle-walk, Hall, Mall, Passage, Vista, Way, Xyst(us)

Average Adjustment, Av, Batting, Dow Jones, Everyman, Fair, Mean, Mediocre, Middle-brow, Middling, Moderate, Norm, Par, Run, Soso, Standard, Usual

Averse, Aversion, Avert Against, Antipathy, Apositia, Disgust, Distaste, Hatred, Horror, Opposed, Pet, Phengephobia, Phobic, Photophobia, Risk, Scunner, Sit(i)ophobia

Avert Avoid, →DEFLECT, Forfend, Parry, Ward

Aviator Airman, Alcock, Bleriot, Brown, Co-pilot, De Havilland, Earhart, Flier, Hinkler, Icarus, Johnson, Lindbergh, Pilot, Yeager

Avid Athirst, →EAGER, Greedy, Keen

Avoid(er), Avoidance Abstain, Ba(u)lk, Boycott, Buck, Bypass, Cop-out, Cut, Dodge, Duck, Elude, Escape, Eschew, Evade, Evitate, Evite, Fly, Forbear, Gallio, Hedge, Miss, Needless, Obviate, Parry, Prevaricate, Save, Scape, Scutage, Secede, Shelve, Shirk, Shun, Sidestep, Skirt, Skive, Spare, Spurn, Tergiversate, Waive

Avow(ed) Acknowledged, Affirm, Declare, Own, Swear

Await(ed) Abide, Bide, Expect, Godot, Tarry

Awake(ning) Aware, Conscious, Conversion, Fly, Rouse, Vigilant

Award Academy, Accolade, Acquisitive, Addeem, Addoom, Allot, Alpha, Apple, Arbitrament, Aret(t), Bafta, Bar, Bestow, Bursary, Cap, Charter Mark, Clasp, Clio, Compensation, Crown, Degree, Emmy, Exhibition, Genie, Gold disc, Golden handshake, Grammy, Grant, Juno, Lourie, Medal, Meed, Mete, MOBO, Oscar, Palatinate, Palme d'Or, Premium, Present(ation), → **PRIZE**, Purse, Rosette, Scholarship, Tony, Trophy, Yuko

Aware(ness) Alert, Aware, Coconscious, Cognisant, Conscious, Conversant, Enlightenment, ESP, Est, Hep, Hip, Informed, Knowing, Liminal, Mindshare, Onto, Open-eyed, Panaesthesia, Prajna, Presentiment, Samadhi, Scienter, Sensible, Sensile, Sensitive, Sentience, Streetwise, Vigilant, Weet, Wit, Wot

Away Abaxial, Absent, Afield, Apage, Aroint, Avaunt, Beyond, By, For-, Forth, Fro(m), Go, Hence, Off, Out, Past

▷**Away** *may indicate* a word to be omitted

Awe(d) Dread, D(o)ulia, Fear, Intimidate, Loch, Overcome, Popeyed, Regard, Respect, Reverent, Scare, Solemn, Wonderment

Awful(ly) Alas, Appalling, Deare, Dere, Dire, Fearful, Horrendous, Lamentable, Nasty, O so, Piacular, Rotten, Terrible, Third rate, Unspeakable

▷**Awfully** *may indicate* an anagram

Awkward(ness) All thumbs, Angular, Blate, Bolshy, Bumpkin, Cack-handed, Clumble-fisted, Clumsy, Complicated, Contrary, Corner, Crabby, Cubbish, Cumbersome, Cussed, Disconcerting, Dub, Embarrassing, Farouche, Fiddly, Fix, Gangly, Gauche, Gawky, Graceless, Handless, Hobbledehoy, Howdy-do, Inconvenient, Inelegant, Inept, Jam(pot), Kittle-cattle, Knotty, Lanky, Loutish, Lurdan(e), Lurden, Maladdress, Mauther, Mawr, Naff, Nasty, Nonconformist, Ornery, Perverse, Refractory, Slouch, Slummock, So-and-so, Spot, Sticky, Stiff, Stroppy, Stumblebum, Swainish, Ticklish, Twiddley, Uncoordinated, Uncouth, Uneasy, Ungainly, Ungraceful, Unhandy, Unwieldy, Wooden, Wry

Awry Agley, Amiss, Askent, Askew, Athwart, Cam, Haywire, Kam(me), Pear-shaped, Wonky

Axe(s) Abolish, Adz(e), Bill, Celt, Chop(per), Cleaver, Ditch, Gisarme, Gurlet, Halberd, Halbert, Hatchet, Hew, Holing, Ice, Palstaff, Palstave, Partisan, Piolet, Retrench, Sax, Scrub, Sparth(e), Sperthe, Spontoon, Thunderbolt, Tomahawk, Twibill, X, Y, Z

Axeman Bassist, Guitarist, Hendrix

Axiom Adage, Motto, Peano's, Proverb, Saw, Saying

Aye Eer, Ever, Yea, Yes

Bb

B Bachelor, Black, Book, Born, Boron, Bowled, Bravo, Flipside

Babble(r) Blather, Chatter, Gibber, Haver, Jabber, Lallation, Lurry, Prate, Prattle, Psycho, Runnel, Tonguester, Tonguework, Twattle, Waffle, Witer

Baboon Ape, Bobbejaan, Chacma, Cynocephalus, Dog-ape, Drill, Gelada, Hamadryas, Mandrill, Sphinx

Baby Bairn, Band-Aid®, Blue, Bub, Bunting, Coddle, Duck, Grand, Infant, Jelly, Litter, Neonate, Nursling, Pamper, Papoose, Preverbal, Rugrat, Sis, Small, Sook, Spoil, Suckling, Tar, Test tube, Tot, Wean

Bachelor Alumnus, BA, Bach, Benedict, Budge, Celibate, En garçon, Knight, Pantagamy, Parti, Single, Stag, Wifeless

Bacillus Comma, Germ, Micrococcus, Tubercle, Virus

Back(er), Backing, Back out, Back up, Backward Abet, Accompany, Addorse, Aft, Again, Ago, Aid, Anticlockwise, Arear, Arrear, Assist, Backare, Bankroll, Behind, Buckram, Champion, Chorus, Consent, Countenance, Croup, Cry off, Culet, Defender, Donor, Dorsal, Dorse, Dorsum, Dos, Ebb, Empatron, Encourage, Endorse, Fakie, Finance, Frae, Fro, Full, Fund(er), Gaff, Grubstake, Half, Help, Hind, Historic, Incremental, La-la, Late, Notaeum, Notal, Notum, On, Patronise, Pendu, Poop, Pronotum, Punt, Rear(most), Rearwards, Reinforce, Reinforcement, Reticent, Retral, Retro(grade), Retrogress, Retrorse, Retrospective, Return, Rev, Reverse, Ridge, Root, Running, Scenery, Shy, Spinal, Sponsor, Standby, Stern, Sternboard, Sternway, **→ SUPPORT**, Sweeper, Syndicate, Tail, Telson, Tergum, Third, Thrae, Three-quarter, Tonneau, Ulu, Uphold, Verso, Vie, Vo, Wager, Watteau

▷ **Back(ing)** *may indicate* a word spelt backwards

Backbone Atlas, Chine, Grit, Guts, Mettle, Spina, Spine

Backchat Lip, Mouth, Sass

Backer Angel, Benefactor, Funder, Patron, Punter, Seconder, Sponsor

Backgammon Acey-deucy, Blot, Lurch, Tick-tack, Trick-track, Tric-trac, Verquere

Background Antecedence, Chromakey, Cyclorama, Fond, History, Horizon, Natural, Retrally, Setting, Ulterior

Back problem Kyphosis, Lumbago, Osteoporosis, Scolioma, Scoliosis

Backslide(r), Backsliding Apostate, Lapse, Regress, Relapse, Revert

Bacon Danish, Essayist, Flitch, Francis, Gammon, Green, Lardo(o)n, Pancetta, Pig(meat), Pork, Rasher, Roger, Smoked, Spec(k), Streaky, Verulam

Bacteria, Bacteriologist, Bacterium Acidophilus, Actinomycete, Aerobe, Bacilli, Bacteriological, Baregin, **→ BUG**, Cocci, Culture, E-coli, Enterococcus, Foul-brood, **→ GERM**, Hib, Intestinal flora, Koch, Legionella, Listeria, Lysogen, Microbe, Micrococcus, Microphyte, Mother, MRSA, Nitrifying, Nitrite,

Nostoc, Operon, Packet, Pasteur, Pasteurella, Pathogen, Peritrich(a), Petri, Pneumococcus, Proteus, Pus, Salmonella, Septic, Serogroup, Serotype, Serum, Spirilla, Spirulina, Spore, Staph, Strep(tococcus), Superbug, Vibrio, Vincent's angina

Bad(die), Badness Abysmal, Addled, Chronic, Crook, Defective, Degenerate, Diabolic, Drastic, Dud, Duff, Dystopia, Egregious, Evildoer, Execrable, Faulty, Fearful, Fourth-rate, Half-pie, Heinous, Ill (timed), Immoral, Inferior, Injurious, Lither, Lulu, Mal(vu), Naughty, Nefandrous, Nefarious, Nice, Off, Ominous, Oncus, Onkus, Parlous, Piacular, Poor, Rank, Reprobate, Ropy, Scampish, Scoundrel, Shocking, Sinful, Spoiled, The pits, Turpitude, Undesirable, Unspeakable, Useless, Wack, Wick, **→ WICKED**

▷**Bad(ly)** *may indicate* an anagram

Badge Brassard, Brooch, Button, Chevron, Cockade, Cockleshell, Comm, Cordon, Crest, Eagle, Emblem, Ensign, Epaulet, Episemon, Fáinne, Film, Flash, Garter, Gorget, ID, Insigne, Insignia, Kikumon, Mark, Mon, Numerals, Orange, Pilgrim's sign, Pin, Rondel, Rosette, Scallop(-shell), Shield, Shouldermark, **→ SIGN**, Symbol, Tiger, Token, Totem, Vernicle, Vine branch, Vine-rod, Wings

Badger →ANNOY, Bait, Bedevil, Beset, Brock, Browbeat, Bug, Bullyrag, Cete, Dassi(e), Ferret, Gray, Grey, **→HARASS**, Harry, Hassle, Hog, Honey, Hound, Nag, Pester, Plague, Provoke, Ratel, Ride, Roil, Sand, Sow, Teledu, Wisconsin

Bad luck Ambs-ace, Ames-ace, Deuce-ace, Hoodoo, Jinx, Jonah, Shame, Voodoo

Bad-tempered Carnaptious, Crabby, Curmudgeon, Curnaptious, Curst, Grouchy, Grum(py), Irritable, Marabunta, Moody, Patch, Scratchy, Shirty, Sour, Splenetic, Stroppy

Baffle(d), Baffling Anan, Balk, Bemuse, Bewilder, Confound, Confuse, Elude, Evade, Floor, Flummox, Foil, Fox, Get, Hush-kit, Mate, Muse, Mystify, Nark, Nonplus, Perplex, Pose, Puzzle, Stump, Throw, Thwart

Bag(gage), Bags Acquire, Air, Albatross, Alforja, Amaut, Amowt, Bedroll, Besom, Bin-liner, Bladder, Blue, Body, Bounty, Briefcase, Bulse, Bum, Buoyancy, Caba(s), Cachet, Caecum, Capture, Carpet, Carrier, Carryall, Case, Cecum, Claim, Clutch, Cly, Cod, Colostomy, Cool(er), Corduroy, Crone, Crumenal, Cyst, Daypack, Dilli, Dilly, Dime, Diplomatic, Ditty, Doggy, Dorothy, Douche, Duffel, Dunnage, **→EFFECTS**, Emery, Excess, Fanny pack, Fishwife, Flannels, Flotation, Follicle, Game, **→GEAR**, Gladstone, Goody, Grab, Green, Grip, Gripsack, Grow, Haversack, Holdall, Ice, Impedimenta, Jelly, Jiffy®, Kill, Knapsack, Ladies' companion, Lavender, Loose, Materiel, Meal-poke, Messenger, Minx, Mixed, Money, Monkey, Moon, Mummy, Musette, Musk, Muzzle, Mystery, Nap, Necessaire, Net, Nunny, Organiser, Overnight, Overnighter, Oxford, Packsack, Pantaloons, Plastic, Plus fours, Pochette, Pock(et), Pocketbook, Poke, Politzer's, Poly(thene), Port(manteau), Portmantle, Portmantua, Post, Pot, Pouch, Pounce, Pudding, Punch, Purse, Rake, Red, Reticule, Ridicule, Rucksack, Sabretache, Sac(cule), Sachet, Sack, Saddle, Sag, Satchel, Scent, School, Scrip, Scrotum, Sea, Shapeless, Shopper, Sick, Slattern, Sleeping, Specialty, Sponge, Sporran, Stacks, Steal, Sugar, Survival, Tea, Toilet, Tool, Tote, **→TRAP**, Trews, Trollop, Trouse(r), Tucker (box), Udder, Unmentionables, Valise, Vanity, Viaticals, Waist, Wallet, Water, Weekend, Win, Woolpack, Work, Wrap, Wrapping, Ziplock

Bagpipe Chanter, Chorus, Cornemuse, Drone, Gaita, Musette, Pibroch, Piffero, Skirl, Sourdeline, Uillean, Zampogna

Bail(er), Bailment Bond, Ladle, Mainpernor, Mainprise, Mutuum, Remand, Replevin, Replevy, Scoop

Bailiff Adam, Beagle, Bum, Factor, Grieve, Land-agent, Philistine, Reeve, Steward, Tipstaff, Water

Bait Angleworm, Badger, Bait, Berley, Brandling, Burley, Chum, Dap, Decoy, Entice, Gentle, Harass, Incentive, Lobworm, Lug(worm), Lure, Mawk, → **RAG**, Ragworm, Sandworm, Teagle, Tease, Tempt, Tole, Toll

Bake(r), Baked, Baking Alaska, Batch, Baxter, Coctile, → **COOK**, Fire, Icer, Kiln-dry, Mr Bun, Oven, Pieman, Roast, Scorch, Shir(r)

Balance(d) Account, Beam, Counterpoise, Countervail, Counterweight, Equate, Equilibrium, Equipoise, Equiponderate, Even, Fixed, Gyroscope, Gyrostat, Horn, Hydrostatic, Isostasy, Launce, Level-headed, Libra, Librate, Meet, Otocyst, Otolith, Pease, Peise, Perch, Peyse, Poise, → **REMAINDER**, Remnant, Residual, Rest, Scale, Spring, Stability, Stand, Steelyard, Symmetry, Together, → **TOTAL**, Trade, Trial, Trim, Tron(e), Unicycle

Balcony Circle, Gallery, Loggia, Mirador, Moucharaby, Pew, Porch, Sundeck, Tarras, Terrace, Veranda(h)

Bald, Baldness Alopecia, Apterium, Awnless, Barren, Calvities, Coot, Crude, Egghead, Fox-evil, Glabrous, Hairless, Madarosis, Open, Peelgarlic, Pilgarlic(k), Pollard, Psilosis, Slaphead, Smoothpate, Tonsured

Bale Bl, Bundle, Evil, Pack, Truss

Ball(s) Agglomerate, Alley, Ally, Ammo, Aniseed, Beach, Bead, Beamer, Bearings, Bobble, Bolus, Bosey, Bosie, Bouncer, Bowl, Break, Buckshot, Cap, Cherry, Chinaman, Clew, Clue, Condylar, Cotill(i)on, Cramp, Croquette, Crystal, Cue, Curve, Daisy-cutter, → **DANCE**, Delivery, Dink, Dollydrop, Doosra, Full-pitch, Full-toss, Fungo, Gazunder, → **GLOBE**, Glomerate, Gobstopper, Googly, Goolies, Gool(e)ys, Grounder, Grub(ber), Grubhunter, Gutta, Gutter, Gutty, Hank, Hop, Hunt, Inswinger, Ivory, Jinglet, Knob, Knur(r), Leather, Leg-break, Leg-cutter, Lob, Long-hop, Marble, Masque(rade), Medicine, Minié, Moth, Nur(r), O, Off-break, Off-spin, Outswinger, Over, Overarm, Parrel truck, Pea, Pellet, Pill, Pompom, Pompon, Prom, Puck, Quenelle, Rissole, Root, Rover, Rundle, Seamer, Sneak, Sphere, Spinner, Strike, Swiss, Tea, Testes, Tice, Time, Witches, Wood, Wrecker's, Wrecking, Yorker, Zorb®

Ballast Kentledge, Makeweight, Stabiliser, Trim, Weight

Ballerina Coryphee, Dancer, Pavlova

Ballet, Ballet movement, Ballet-system Arabesque, Assemblé, Balancé, Ballon, Battement, Bolshoi, Brisé, Cabriole, Cambré, Chainé, Changement, Checkmate, Cinderella, Daphnis and Chloe, Développé, Écarté, Echappé, Enchainement, Entrechat, Firebird, Fouetté, Giselle, Jeté, Kirov, Laban, Mayerling, Nutcracker, Pas de basque, Pas de bourrée, Pas de chat, Petit battement, Petrushka, Pirouette, Plastique, Pointe, Port de bras, Relevé, Saut

Balloon(ist) Aeronaut, Aerostat, Airship, Bag, Barrage, Billow, Blimp, Bloat, Dirigible, Distend, Dumont, Enlarge, Fumetto, Glass, Hot air, Lead, Montgolfier, Pilot, Rawinsonde, Swell, Weather, Zeppelin

Ballot Election, Mulligan, → **POLL**, Referendum, Second, Secret, Suffrage, Ticket, Vote

Balm(y) Anetic, Arnica, Balsam, Calamint, Emollient, Fragrant, Garjan, Gilead, Gurjun, Lemon, Lenitive, → **MILD**, Mirbane, Myrbane, Nard, Oil, Opobalsam, Ottar, Redolent, Remedy, Soothe, Spikenard, Tolu, Unguent

Balsam Canada, Copaiba, Copaiva, Nard, Noli-me-tangere, Peruvian, Resin, Spikenard, Tamanu, Tolu(ic), Touch-me-not, Tous-les-mois, Turpentine

Ban(ned) Abolish, Accurse, Anathema, Black(ing), Censor, Curfew, Debar, D-notice, Embargo, Estop, Exclude, Excommunicate, Forbid, For(e)say,

For(e)speak, Gag, Gate, Green, Moratorium, No, Outlaw, Prohibit, Proscribe, Suppress, Taboo, Tabu, Test, Verboten, Veto

Banal Anorak, Corny, Flat, Hackneyed, Jejune, Mundane, Ordinary, Platitudinous, →**TRITE**, Trivial

Banana(s) Abaca, Hand, Loco, →**MAD**, Musa, Plantain, Raving, Split, Top, Zany

Band(ed), Bands Absorption, Alice, Anadem, Anklet, Armlet, Belt, Border, Braid, Brake, Brass, Brassard, Brassart, Caravan, CB, Channel, Chevron, Chinstrap, Chromosome, Circlet, Citizens', Closet, Cohort, Collar, Collet, Combo, Company, Conduction, Corslet, Coterie, Crape, Crepe, Crew, Deely boppers, Dog collar, Elastic, ELO, Endorse, Energy, Facia, Falling, Fascia, Ferret, Ferrule, Fess, Filament, Fillet, Fourchette, Fraternity, Frequency, Frieze, Frog, Frontlet, Galloon, Gamelan, →**GANG**, Garage, Garland, Garter, Gasket, Gaskin, Geneva, German, Gird, Girr, Girth, Group, Guard, →**HOOP**, Hope, Iron, Jazz, Jug, Kara, Kitchen, Label, Lytta, Macnamara's, Maniple, Massed, Military, Mourning, Noise, Obi, One-man, Orchestra, Pack, Pass, Patte, Pipe, Plinth, Property, Puttee, Rib, Ribbon, Ridge, Rim, Ring, Robbers, Round, Rubber, Sash, Scarf, Screed, Sect, Shadow, Sheet, Shoe, Snood, Speckled, Steel, Strake, Strand, Strap, Stratum, String, Stripe, Succinctory, Swath(e), Sweat, Tape, Tendon, Thecla, Thoroughbrace, Tie, Tippet, Tourniquet, Train, Trangle, Tribute, Troop, Troupe, Tumpline, Turm, Tyre, Unite, Valence, Vitrain, Vitta, Wanty, Wedding, Weed, Weeper, Welt, Wings, With(e), Wristlet, Zona, Zone, Zonule

Bandage Bind, Dressing, Fillet, Gauze, Lint, Living, Pledget, Roller, Sling, Spica, Swaddle, Swathe, T, Tape, Truss, Wadding

Bandit Apache, Bravo, Brigand, Desperado, Ishmael, Outlaw, Pirate, Rapparee, →**ROBBER**, Slot machine, Turpin

Bane Curse, Dioxin, Evil, Harm, Nemesis, Poison

Bang(er) Amorce, Andouillette, Beat, Big, Cap, Chipolata, Clap, Cracker, Crock, Explode, Firecracker, Flivver, Fringe, Haircut, Heap, Implode, Jalopy, Jammy, Maroon, Pep(p)eroni, Rattletrap, Report, Sausage, Sizzler, Slam, Thrill, TNT, Wham, Wurst

Bangle Anklet, Armlet, Bracelet, Kara

Banish(ment) Ban, Debar, Deport, Depose, Dispel, Excommunicate, Exile, Expatriate, Expel, Extradition, Forsay, Maroon, Ostracise, →**OUTLAW**, Relegate, Rusticate

Bank(ing), Bank on An(n)icut, Asar, Backs, Bar, Bay, Beneficiary, Bet, Bk, Blood, Bluff, Bottle, Brae, Brim, Bund, Camber, Cay, Central, Chesil, Clearing (house), Cloud, Commercial, Cooperative, Data, Depend, Deposit, Dogger, Down, Drawee, Drift, Dune, Dyke, Earthwork, Escarp, Fog, Gene, Giro, Glacis, Gradient, Gradin(e), Hack, Hele, Hill(side), Home, Incline, Jodrell, Kaim, Kame, Land, Left, Lender, Levee, Link, Lombard Street, Memory, Merchant, Mound, Nap, National, Needle, Nore, Overslaugh, Oyster, Parapet, Penny, Piggy, Pot, Private, Rake, Ramp, Rampart, RBS, Reef, →**RELY**, Reserve, Retail, Ridge, Rivage, Riverside, Rodham, Row, Sandbar, Savings, Seed, Shallow, Shelf, Side, Slope, Soil, Sperm, Spit, Staithe, State, Sunk, Telephone, Terrace, Terreplein, Tier, Treasury, Trust, Vault, Wells Fargo, West, World

Banker Agent, Aileron, Cert(ainty), Financial, Fugger, Gnome, Lender, Lombard, Medici, →**RIVER**, Rothschild, Shroff, Teller

▷**Banker** *may indicate* a river

Bankrupt(cy) Break, Broke, Bung, Bust, Cadaver, Carey Street, Chapter-eleven, Crash, Debtor, Deplete, Duck, Dyvour, Fail, Fold, Insolvent, Penniless,

Receivership, Ruin, Rump, Scat, Sequestration, Skatt, Smash

▷**Bankrupt** *may indicate* 'red' around another word

Banner Banderol(e), Bandrol, Bannerol, Blue blanket, →**FLAG**, Gumphion, Labarum, Oriflamme, Sign, Standard, Streamer

Banquet Beanfeast, Dine, Feast, Junket, Nosh-up, Spread

Banter Backchat, Badinage, Borak, Borax, Chaff, Dicacity, Dieter, Jest, →**JOKE**, Josh, Persiflage, Picong, Rag, Rally, Repartee, Ribaldry, Roast, Rot, Tease

Baptise(d), Baptism, Baptist Affusion, Amrit, Christen, Clinical, Conditional, Dip, Dipper, Dopper, Dunker, Hypothetical, Illuminati, Immersion, John, Mandaean, Mersion, Palingenesis, Private, Sprinkle, Tinker

Bar(s) Address, Angle-iron, Apartheid, Asymmetric, Axletree, Bail, Ban, Baulk, Beam, Bilboes, Billet, Bistro, Blackball, Blacklist, Block(ade), Bloom, Bolt, Boom, Bottega, Brasserie, Buffet, Bull, Bullion, Bumper, But, Buvette, →**CAGE**, Cake, Came, Candy, Cantina, Capo, Capstan, Channel, Clasp, Clip joint, Cocktail, Coffee, Colour, Counter, Cramp(on), Cross(head), Crow, Crush, Currency, Dive, Doggery, Double, Draw, Drift, Dumbbell, Efficiency, Espresso, Estaminet, Estop(pel), Except, Exchange, Exclude, Fern, Fid, Flinders, Fonda, Forbid, Foreclose, Forestall, Fret, Gad, Gastropub, Gin palace, Glazing, Grate, Grid, Grog-shop, Gunshop, Hame, Handrail, Handspike, Heck, Hershey, →**HINDRANCE**, Horizontal, Hound, Hyphen, Impediment, Ingot, Inn, Inner, Judder, Juice, Karaoke, Keeper, Kickstand, Knuckleduster, Latch, Let, Lever, Limbo, Line, Lingot, Local, Lock out, Lounge, Macron, Mandrel, Mandril, Measure, Menu, Merchant, Milk, Muesli, Mullion, Nail, Nanaimo, Navigation, Nineteenth hole, No-go, Norman, Obstacle, Obstruct, Omerta, Onely, Outer, Oxygen, Parallel, Perch, Pile, Pinch, Pole, Posada, Prescription, Prevent, Private, Prohibit, Pub, Public, Rack, Raddle, Rail, Ramrod, Rance, Raw, Reach, Restrict, Rib, Risp, Rod, Roll, Roo, Rung, Saddle, Salad, Saloon, Sand, Sans, Save, Saving, Scroll, Shaft, Shanty, Shet, Shut, Singles, Skewer, Slice, Slot, Snack, Snug, Soap, Spacer, Spar, Speakeasy, Spit, Splinter, Spoke, Sprag, Status, Stave, Stemmer, Stick, Stretcher, Stripe, Strut, Suspend, Sway, Swee, T, Tap(-room), Tapas, Taphouse, Task, Tavern(a), Temple, Tiki, Title, Toll, Tombolo, Tommy, Tool, Torsion, Tow, Trace, Trangle, Transom, Trapeze, Trundle, Type, U-bolt, Vinculum, Wall, Ward, Wet, Whisker, Window, Wine, Wire, Wrecking, Z, Zed

Barb(ed) Bur(r), Cutter, Fluke, Harl, Herl, →**HOOK**, Jag(g), Jibe, Pheon, Prickle, Ramus, Tang, Thorn, Vexillum

Barbarian, Barbaric Boor, Fifteen, Foreigner, Goth, Heathen, Hun, Inhuman, Lowbrow, Outlandish, Philistine, Rude, Savage, Tartar, Tatar(ic), Vandal

Barbecue Braai(vleis), Chargrill, Cook-out, Flame-grill, Grill, Hangi, Hibachi, Roast, Spit

Barber Epilate, Figaro, Hair, Scrape(r), Shaver, Strap, Sweeney Todd, Tonsor, Trimmer

Bare, Bare-headed Adamic, Aphyllous, Bald, Barren, Blank, Bodkin, Cere, Décolleté, Denude, Hush, Lewd, Marginal, Mere, Moon, →**NAKED**, Nude, Open, Plain, Scablands, Scant, Sear, Stark(ers), Timber line, Topless, Uncase, Uncover, Unfurnished, Unpainted, Unveil

Barely Hardly, Just, Merely, Scarcely, Scrimp

Bargain(ing) Agreement, Bargoon, Barter, Bon marche, Braata, Chaffer, Champerty, →**CHEAP**, Cheapo, Collective, Compact, Compromise, Contract, Coup, Deal, Dicker, Distributive, Effort, Find, Go, Haggle, Higgle, Horse-trade, Huckster, Indent, Integrative, Negotiate, Option, →**PACT**, Plea, Productivity,

Scoop, Snip, Steal, Supersaver, Time, Trade, Trock, Troke, Truck, Wanworth, Wheeler-dealing

Barge Birlinn, Bucentaur, Budgero(w), Butty, Casco, Elbow, Gabbard, Gabbart, Galley-foist, Gloriana, Hopper, Intrude, Jostle, Keel, Lighter, Nudge, Obtrude, Pra(a)m, Ram, Scow, → **SHIP**, Thrust, Trow, Wherry

▷**Barge** *may indicate* an anagram

Bark Angostura, Ayelp, Bass, Bast, Bay, Bowwow, Canella, Cascara, Cascara sagrada, Cassia, China, Cinchona, Cinnamon, Cork, Cortex, Hack, Honduras, Jamaica, Kina, Kinakina, Liber, Mezereon, Mezereum, Myrica, Parchment, Peel, Pereira, Peruvian, Quebracho, Quest, Quill, Quillai, Quina, Quinquina, Rind, Salian, Sassafras, Scrape, Shag, → **SHIP**, Skin, Tan, Tap(p)a, Waff, Waugh, Winter's, Woof, Wow, Yaff, Yelp, Yip

Bar-keep(er), Barmaid, Barman, Bartender Advocate, Ale-wife, Barista, Bencher, Curate, Hebe, Luckie, Lucky, Portia, Tapster, Underskinker

Barley (water) Awn, Bear, Bere, Bigg, Malt, Pearl, Scotch, Truce

Barn Bank, Byre, Cowshed, Dutch, Grange, Skipper, Tithe

Barnacle Acorn, Cirriped(e), Cypris, Goose(neck), Limpet, Sticker

Baroque Gothic, Ornate, Rococo

▷**Barrack(s), Barracking** Asteism, Boo, Cantonment, Casern(e), Cat-call, Garrison, Glasshouse, Heckle, Irony, Jeer, Quarters

Barrage Balloon, Boom, Broadside, Fusillade, Heat, Salvo, Shellfire

Barrel Bbl, Bl, Butt, Cade, Capstan, Cascabel, Cask, Chase, Clavie, Croze, Cylinder, Drum, Hogshead, Keg, Kibble, Morris-tube, Oak, Organ, Pièce, Run(d)let, Tan-vat, Thrall, Tierce, Tun, Vat, Wood

Barren Addle, Arid, Badlands, Bleak, Blind, Blunt, Clear, Dry, Eild, → **EMPTY**, Farrow, Fruitless, Hardscrabble, Hi(r)stie, Jejune, Sterile, Unbearing, Unfruitful, Waste, Wasteland, Wilderness, Yeld, Yell

Barrier Baffle, Bail, Barrage, Barricade, Bayle, Block, Boom, Breakwater, Cauld, Checkrail, Cheval de frise, Chicane, Cordon (sanitaire), Crash, Crush, → **DAM**, Defence, Deterrent, Drawgate, Dyke, Fence, Floodgate, Fraise, Gate, Guard rail, Ha-ha, Handicap, Heat, Hedge, Hindrance, Hurdle, Mach, Obstruct, Pain, Paling, Potential, Rail(-fence), Rampart, Restraint, Revetment, Ring fence, Roadblock, Rope, Sandbag, Screen, Skreen, Sonic, Sound, Spina, Stockade, Thames, Thermal, Tollgate, Trade, Transonic, Traverse, Turnpike, Turnstile, Vapour, → **WALL**

Barrister Advocate, Attorney, Brief, Counsel, Devil, Lawyer, Recorder, Revising, Rumpole, Serjeant(-at-law), Silk, SL, Templar, Utter

Barrow Applecart, Clyde, Dolly, Handcart, Henge, How, Hurley, Kurgan, Molehill, Mound, Pushcart, Tram, Trolley, Truck, Tumulus

Barter Chaffer, Chop, Dicker, → **EXCHANGE**, Haggle, Hawk, Niffer, Permutate, Sco(u)rse, Swap, → **TRADE**, Traffic, Truck

Base Aggregate, Air, Airhead, Alkali, Bag, Bed, Beggarly, Billon, Board, Bottom, Brest, Camp, Choline, Degenerate, Degraded, Diethyl, Dog, Down, E, → **ESTABLISH**, Floor, Fond, Foot, Foothold, Footstall, Fort Knox, Found, Foundation, Fundus, Harlot, Hydroxide, Ignoble, Ignominious, Imidazole, Infamous, Iniquitous, Install, Knowledge, La Spezia, Leuco, Lewis, Litmus, → **LOW**, → **MEAN**, Nefarious, Nook, Oasis®, Octal, Partite, Patten, Platform, Plinth, Podium, Predella, Premise, Ptomaine, Purin(e), Raca, Rascally, Ratty, Rests, Ribald, Root, Roux, Rude, Scapa Flow, Servile, Shameful, Shand, Sheeny,

Snide, Socle, Soda, Sordid, Springing, Staddle, → **STAND**, Station, Substrate, Ten, Tetracid, Torus, Turpitude, Unworthy, Vile

Bash Attempt, Belt, Bonk, Clout, Dint, Go, Hit, Rave, Shot, Slog, Strike, Swat, Swipe

Bashful Awed, Blate, Coy, Diffident, Modest, Prudish, Retiring, Shamefast, Sheep-faced, Sheepish, → **SHY**

Basic(s), Basically, Basis ABC, Abcee, Abecedarian, Alkaline, Aquamanale, Aquamanile, At bottom, At heart, Bare, Bedrock, Brass tacks, Cardinal, Crude, Elemental, → **ESSENTIAL**, Fiducial, Fond, Foundation, Fundamental, Ground(work), Gut, In essence, Integral, Intrinsic, Logic, Meat and potatoes, Need-to-know, Nitty-gritty, No-nonsense, Nuts and bolts, One-horse, Ontology, Presumption, Primordial, Principle, Protoplasm, Radical, Rudimentary, Spit-and-sawdust, Staple, Substance, Substratum, Underlying, Unsophisticated, Uracil

Basin Artesian, Aspergillum, Aspersorium, Bidet, Bowl, Brazil, Canning, Catch, Chott, Cirque, Corrie, Cwm, Dish, Dock, Great, Lavabo, Laver, Minas, Monteith, Ocean, Okavango, Pan, Park, Piscina, Playa, Porringer, Pudding, Reservoir, Scapa Flow, Sink, Slop(-bowl), Stoop, Stoup, Tank, Tidal, Washhand

Bask Apricate, Revel, Sun, → **WALLOW**

Basket, Basket-work Bass, Bassinet, Bread, Buck, Cabas, Canasta, Car, Chip, Cob, Coop, Corbeil(le), Corf, Creel, Cresset, Fan, Flasket, Frail, Gabion, Goal, Hamper, Hask, Junket, Kipe, Kit, Kite, Leap, Litter, Maund, Mocuck, Moses, Murlain, Murlan, Murlin, Osiery, Pannier, Ped, Petara, Plate, Pottle, Punnet, Rip, Round file, Scull, Scuttle, Seed-lip, Skep, Skull, Trout, Trug, Van, Wagger-pagger(-bagger), Waste(-paper), Wicker(-work), Will(e), Wisket

Bass Alberti, Ale, Alfie, B, Black, Continuo, Deep, Double, El-a-mi, Fish, Ground, Low, Ostinato, Serran, String

▷**Bastard** *may indicate* an anagram

Bat(sman), Bat's wing, Batter, Batting, Batty Ames, Assail, Barbastelle, Baton, Blink, Close, Club, Cosh, Crackers, Crease, Cudgel, Dad, Die Fledermaus, Eyelid, Flittermouse, Flutter, Fungo, Grace, Hatter, Haywire, Hit, Hobbs, Hook, Horseshoe, In, Ink mouse, Kalong, Knock, Language, Lara, Man, Mastiff, Maul, May, Mormops, Myopic, Nictate, Nictitate, Night, Nightwatchman, Noctilio, Nora, Opener, Paddle, Patagium, Pinch-hit, Pipistrel(le), Poke, Pummel, Rabbit, Racket, Racquet, Ram, Rearmouse, Ruin, Sauch, Scorer, Serotine, Sledge, Spectre, Stick, Stonewall, Striker, Swat, Switch hitter, Tail(ender), Trunnion, Vampire, Viv, Whacky, Willow, Wood

Batch Bake, Bunch, Clutch, Crop, Tranche

Bath(room), Bath-house Aerotone, Aeson's, Aquae sulis, Bagnio, Bain-marie, Balneotherapy, Banya, Bed, Bidet, Blanket, Blood, Bubble, Caldarium, Cor, Dip, En suite, Epha, Foam, Hammam, Hip, Hummaum, Hummum, Jacuzzi®, Lav, Laver, Mik vah, Mud, Mustard, Oil, Oliver, Piscina, Plunge, Salt, Sauna, Shower, Sitz, Slipper, Soak, Spa, Sponge, Steam, Stew, Stop, Sudarium, Tepidarium, Therm, Tub, Turkish, Tye, Vapour, Whirlpool, Wife

Bathe(r), Bathing Archimedes, Balneotherapy, Bay(e), Beath, Bogey, Bogie, Dip, Dook, Embay, Foment, Immerse, Lave, Lip, Skinny-dip, Souse, Splash, Stupe, → **SWIM**, Tub, → **WASH**

Baton Mace, Rod, Sceptre, Staff, Truncheon, Wand

▷**Bats, Batting** *may indicate* an anagram

Battalion Bn, Corps, Troop

Batter(ed) Bombard, Bruise, Buffet, Decrepit, Pound, Thump

Battery Artillery, Button-cell, Cannonade, Drycell, Field, Heliac, Henhouse, Li(thium)-ion, Masked, Nicad, Nickel cadmium, NIMH, Pra(a)m, Solar, Transducer, Troop, Voltaic, Waffle

Battle(s), Battleground Action, Affair, Ben, Campaign, Clash, Cockpit, Combat, → **CONFLICT**, Darraign, Deraign, Encounter, Engagement, Field, → **FIGHT**, Fray, Front, Joust, Maiden, Martian, Royal, Running, Sarah, Sciamachy, Skiamachy, Spurs, Stoor, Stour, Stowre, Theatre, Theomachy, Wage, → **WAR**, Wargame

Battle-axe Amazon, Bill, Gorgon, Halberd, Ogress, Sparth(e), Termagant, Termagent, Turmagant, Turmagent

Battlement Barmkin, Crenellate, Merlon, Rampart

Battleship Carrier, Destroyer, Dreadnought, Gunboat, Man-o'-war, Potemkin, Repulse

Bauble Bagatelle, Gaud, Gewgaw, Trifle

Bawl Bellow, Gollar, Howl, Weep

Bay Ab(o)ukir, Arm, Baffin, Bantry, Bark, Bell, Bengal, Bez, Bight, Biscay, Bonny, Botany, Broken, Brown, Byron, Cape Cod, Cardigan, Chesapeake, Classis, Cove, Covelet, Creek, Cubicle, Daphne, Delagoa, Discovery, Dundalk, Dvina, False, Famagusta, Fleet, Freshwater, Frobisher, Fundy, Galway, Gdansk, Georgian, Gibraltar, Glace, Golden, Green, Guanabara, Harbour, Hawke's, Herne, Hervey, Horse, → **HOWL**, Hudson, Inhambane, Inlet, Ise, Islands, James, Jervis, Laura, Laurel, Lobito, Loblolly, Lutzow-Holm, MA, Magdalena, Manila, Massachusetts, Narragansett, Niche, Oleander, Oriel, Pegasus, Pigs, Plymouth, Poverty, Recess, Red, Roan, St Austell, San Pedro, Scene, Shark, Sick, Sligo, Stall, Suvla, Swansea, Tampa, Tasman, The Wash, Thunder, Tralee, Trincomalee, Ungava, Vae, Vigo, Voe, Vyborg, Waff, Wash, Wick, Yowl

Bazaar Alcaiceria, Emporium, Fair, Fete, Market, Pantechnicon, Sale, Sook, Souk

Beach(head) Anzio, Bikini, Bondi, Chesil, Coast, Ground, Hard, Lido, Littoral, Machair, Miami, Myrtle, Plage, Sand, Sea-coast, Seashore, Seaside, Shingle, Shore(line), Strand, Waikiki

Beacon Belisha, Brecon, Fanal, Lantern, Lighthouse, Lightship, Need-fire, Pharos, Racon, Radar, Radio, Signal

Bead(s), Beaded Adderstone, Aggri, Aggry, Astragal, Baily's, Bauble, Blob, Bugle, Chaplet, Crab's-eyes, Crab-stones, Dewdrop, Drop, Droplet, Gaud, Job's tears, Love, Nurl, Paternoster, Poppet, Poppit, Prayer, Rosary, Sabha, St Cuthbert's, Spacer, Spacer plate, Taktite, Tasbih, Tear, Wampum(peag), Worry

Beak AMA, Bailie, Bill, Cad, Cere, Coronoid, Gar, JP, Kip(p), Magistrate, Master, Metagnathous, Mittimus, Nasute, Neb, Nose, Pecker, Prow, Ram, Rectal, Rostellum, Rostrum

Beam(ing) Arbor, Balance, Ba(u)lk, Bar, Binder, Boom, Bowstring, Box, Breastsummer, Broadcast, Bum(p)kin, Cantilever, Carline, Carling, Cathead, Collar, Crossbar, Crosshead, Crosspiece, Deck, Effulge, Electron, Girder, Grin, Hammer, Hatch, I, Irradiate, Joist, Ke(e)lson, Landing, Laser, Lentel, Lintel, Manteltree, Maser, Molecular, Moonlight, Needle, Outrigger, Particle, Pencil, Principal, Proton, Purlin, Putlock, Putlog, Radiant, Radio, → **RAFTER**, → **RAY**, Rayon, Refulgent, Rident, Ridgepole, Rood, Roof-tree, Sandwich, Scale, Sealed, Searchlight, Shaft, Shine, Shore, Sleeper, Smile, Soffit, Spar, Stanchion, Stemson, Sternpost, Sternson, Straining, Streamer, Stringer, Stringpiece,

Summer, Sunlight, Support, Tailing, Tie, Timber, Transom, Trave, Trimmer, Truss, Universal, Walking, Weigh-bauk, Yard, Yardarm

Bean Abrus, Adsuki, Aduki, Adzuki, Arabica, Berry, Black, Black-eye, Borlotti, Broad, Bush, Butter, Cacao, Calabar, Castor, Cluster, Cocoa, Coffee, Cow-pea, Edamame, Fabaceous, Fava, Flageolet, French, Frijol(e), Garbanzo, Gram, Haricot, Harmala, Head, Horse, Hyacinth, Jack, Jelly, Jequirity, Jumping, Kidney, Lablab, Legume, Lentil, Lima, Locust, Molucca, Moth, Mung, Nelumbo, Nib, Noddle, Ordeal, Pichurim, Pinto, Pulse, Runner, St Ignatius's, Scarlet, Silverskin, Snap, Snuffbox, Soy(a), String, Sugar, Tepary, Tonga, Tonka, Tonquin, Urd, Wax, Winged

Bear(er), Bear lover Abide, Abrooke, Andean, Arctic, Arctophile, Aurora, Baloo, Balu, Barley, Beer, Bigg, Breed, Brook, Brown, Bruin, Brunt, →CARRY, Cave, Churl, Cinnamon, Coati-mondi, Coati-mundi, Cub, Demean, Dree, Ean, →ENDURE, Engender, Exert, Fur-seal, Gest(e), Gonfalonier, Great, Grizzly, Hack, Ham(m)al, Harbinger, Have, Hod, Hold, Honey, Humf, Hump(h), Jampanee, Jampani, Keb, Kinkajou, Koala, Kodiak, Koolah, Lioncel(le), Lionel, Lug, Mother, Nandi, Nanook, Owe, Paddington, Panda, Pertain, Polar, Pooh, Produce, Rac(c)oon, Roller, Rupert, Russia, Sackerson, Seller, Shoulder, Sit, Sloth, Spectacled, Stand, Stay, Stomach, →SUFFER, Sun, Sunbear, Sustain, Targeteer, Teddy, Teem, Thole, Throw, Tolerate, Tote, Transport, Undergo, Upstay, Ursine, Water, Whelp, White, Wield, Withstand, Wombat, Woolly, Yean, Yield, Yogi

Beard(ed) Arista, Awn, Balaclava, Barb, Beaver, Charley, Charlie, Confront, Defy, Escort, Face, Five o'clock shadow, Fungus, Goatee, Hair(ie), Hairy, Hear(ie), Imperial, Kesh, Mephistopheles, Newgate frill, Newgate fringe, Outface, Peak, Rivet, Stubble, Tackle, Vandyke, Whiskerando, Whiskery, Ziff

▷**Bearhug** *may indicate* Teddy or similar around a word

Bearing(s) Air, Allure, Aspect, Babbitt, Ball, Behaviour, Billet, Bush, Carriage, Deportment, Direction, E, Endurance, Gait, Germane, Gest, Gudgeon, Hatchment, Haviour, Heading, →HERALDIC, Hugger-mugger, Manner, Martlet, Mascle, Middy, Mien, N, Needle, Nor, Pall, Pheon, Port, Presence, Reference, Relevant, S, Seme(e), Subordinary, Teeming, Tenue, Thrust, W, Yielding

▷**Bearing** *may indicate* compass points

Beast(ly) →ANIMAL, Behemoth, Brute, Caliban, Caribou, →CREATURE, Dieb, Dragon, Dzeren, Fatstock, Gargoyle, Gayal, Genet, Godzilla, Grampus, Hog, Hy(a)ena, Jumart, Kinkajou, Lion, Mammoth, Marmot, Mastodon, Mhorr, Narwhal, Ogre, Oliphant, Oryx, Panda, Potto, Quagga, Queen's, Rac(c)oon, Rhytina, Rother, Sassaby, Steer, Sumpter, Swinish, Teg, Wart-hog, Yahoo, Yak, Yale, Zizel

Beat(ing), Beaten, Beater Anoint, Arsis, Athrob, Bandy, Bang, Baste, Bastinado, Batter, Battue, Battuta, Beetle, Belabour, Belt, Bepat, Best, Blatter, Bless, Cadence, Cane, Chastise, Clobber, Club, Clump, Cob, Conquer, Cream, Cuff, Curry, Debel, →DEFEAT, Ding, Donder, Dress, Drub, Drum, Dunt, Elude, Excel, Fatigue, Faze, Feague, Feeze, Fibbed, Flagellate, Flail, Flam, Flap, Float, Flog, Floor, Flush, Fly, Fustigate, Hammer, Hiding, Hollow, Horsewhip, Ictus, Jole, Joll, Joule, Jowl, Knock, Knubble, Lace, Laidy, Lambast(e), Larrup, Lash, Lather, Latin, Laveer, Lay, Lick, Lilt, Lounder, Mall, Malleate, Manor, Mell, Mersey, Mullah, Muller, Nubble, Onceover, Outclass, Outdo, Outflank, Outshine, Outstrip, Outstroke, Overwhelm, Palpitate, Pandy, Paradiddle, Pash,

Paste, Pelt, Pip, Ploat, Pommel, Pound, Prat, Pug, Pulsate, Pulsatile, Pulse, Pummel, Pun, Quop, Raddle, Ram, Ratten, Resolve, Retreat, Rhythm, Ribroast, Rope's end, Round, Rout, Ruff(le), Scourge, Slat, Slipper, Smite, Soak, Sock, Sort, Strike, Surpass, Swinge, Swingle, Syncopation, Systole, Taber, Tabor, Tact, Tala, Tan, Tattoo, Thesis, Thrash, Thresh, Throb, Thud, Thump, Thwack, Tick, Time, Tired, Top, Torture, Trounce, Tuck, Verberate, Vibrate, Wallop, Wappend, Weary, Welt, Wham, Whip, Whisk, Whitewash, Whup, Wraught, Ybet, Yerk, Yirk

▷**Beaten-up** *may indicate* an anagram

Beaut(y), Beautiful, Beautify Advantage, Angelic, Astrid, Belle, Bellibone, Bonny, Bright, Camberwell, Charmer, Colleen, Comely, Corker, Cracker, Dish, Embellish, Enhance, Exquisite, Eye candy, Eyeful, Fair, Fairness, Fine, Glamour (puss), Glorious, Glory, Grace, Helen, Houri, Hyperion, Junoesque, Kanta, Lana, Looks, Monism, Ornament, Peri, Picture, Pink, Pride, Pulchritude, Purler, Scenic, Sheen, Smasher(oo), Smicker, Specious, Stunner, Sublime, To kalon

Beaver Beard, Castor, Eager, Grind, Oregon, Rodent, Sewellel

Because (of) As, Forasmuch, Forwhy, Hence, In (that), Inasmuch, Ipso facto, Sens, Since

Beckon Gesture, Nod, Summons, Waft, Wave, Wheft

Become, Becoming Apt, Besort, Decent, Decorous, Dignified, Enter, Fall, Fit, Flatter, Get, Go, Grow, Happen, Occur, Seemly, Suit, Wax, Worth

Bed(s), Bedding, Bedstead Air, Allotment, Amenity, Apple-pie, Arroyo, Bacteria, Base, Bassinet, Berth, Border, Bottom, Bottomset, Box, Bundle, Bunk, Caliche, Camp, Capillary, Carrycot, Channel, Charpoy, Cill, Cot(t), Couch(ette), Counterpane, Couvade, Coverlet, Cradle, Crib, Cross, Cul(t)ch, Day, Divan, Doona, Doss, Duvet, Erf, False, Feather, Filter, Flock, Fluidized, Flying, Form, Four-poster, Futon, Gault, Greensand, Hammock, Inlay, Kago, Kang, Kingsize, Kip, Knot, Knot garden, Lay(er), Lazy, Lilo®, Linen, Litter, Marriage, Mat, Matrix, Mattress, Mosquito net, Murphy, Naked, Nap, Nest, Nookie, Oyster, Pad, Paillasse, Pallet, Palliasse, Pan, Parterre, Passage, Patch, Pavement, Pay, Pig, Pit, Plank, Plant, Plot, Procrustean, Puff, Queensize, Quilt, Retire, River, Rollaway, Roost, Rota, Sack, Scalp, Settle, Shakedown, Sill, Sitter, Sleep, Sofa, Spawning, Standing, Stratum, Stretcher, Sun, T(h)alweg, Tanning, Test, The downy, Thill, Trough, Truckle, Trundle, Twin, Wadi, Wady, Ware, Water, Wealden, Wedding

Bed-bug B, B flat, Chinch, Flea, Louse, Vermin

Bedchamber, Bedroom Boudoir, Bower, Br, Chamber, Cubicle, Dorm(itory), Dormer, Dorter, Ruelle, Ward

▷**Bedevilled** *may indicate* an anagram

Bee Afrikanised, Athenia, Bike, Bumble, Carpenter, Cuckoo, Deborah, Debra, Deseret, Dog, Drone, Drumbledor, Dumbledore, Group, Hiver, Honey, Humble, Husking, Killer, King, Lapidary, Leaf-cutter, Mason, Melissa, Pollinator, Queen, Solitary, Spell, Spell-down, Swarm, Trixie, Worker

Beech Hornbeam, Mast, Tree

Beef(y) Aitchbone, Baron, Bleat, Brawny, Bresaola, Bull(y), Bullock, Carp, Carpaccio, Charqui, Chateaubriand, Chuck, Clod, Complain, Corned, Filet mignon, Flank, Gripe, Groan, Grouch, Grouse, Hough, Jerk, Keema, Liebig, Mart, Mice, Moan, Mousepiece, Muscle(-bound), Neat, Ox, Pastrami, Peeve, Plate, Porterhouse, Rother, Salt-horse, Sauerbraten, Sey, Shin, Silverside, Sirloin, Stolid, Stroganoff, Topside, Tournedos, Tranche, Undercut, Vaccine, Wagyu, Whine

Beer Ale, Alegar, Amber fluid, Amber liquid, Bantu, Barley sandwich, Bitter, Black, Bock, Chaser, Coldie, Draught, Drink, Dry, Entire, Export, Gill, Ginger, Granny, Grog, Guest, Heavy, Herb, Home-brew, Kaffir, Keg, Kvass, Lager, Lambic, Lite, Lush, Malt, March, Middy, Mild, Milk stout, Mum, Near, Nog, October, Pils(e)ner, Pint, Pony, Porter, Real, Real ale, Rice, Root, Round, Saki, Scoobs, Sherbet, Six-pack, Skeechan, Slip, Small, Spruce, Stingo, Stout, Stubby, Suds, Swankie, Swanky, Swats, Swipes, Switchel, Table, Taplash, Tinnie, Tipper, Tshwala, Tube, Turps, Wallop, Wheat, Zythum

Beet Blite, Chard, Fat-hen, Goosefoot, Mangel(wurzel), Seakale, Silver, Spinach

Beetle Ambrosia, Argus tortoise, Asiatic, Bacon, Bark, Batler, Bee, Blister, Bloody-nosed, Boll weevil, Bug, Bum-clock, Buprestus, Burying, Bustle, Buzzard-clock, Cabinet, Cadelle, Cane, Cantharis, Cardinal, Carpet, Carrion, Chafer, Christmas, Churchyard, Click, Clock, Cockchafer, Cockroach, Coleopterous, Colorado, Darkling, Deathwatch, Devil's coach-horse, Diamond, Diving, Dor(r), Dor-fly, Dumbledore, Dung, Elater, Elmbark, Elytron, Elytrum, Firefly, Flea, Furniture, Glow-worm, Goliath, Gregor, Ground, Hammer, Hangover, Hercules, Hop-flea, Hornbug, Impend, Japanese, Jewel, June bug, Ladybird, Ladybug, Larder, Leaf, Leather, Longhorned, Mall(et), Maul, May-bug, Minotaur, Oil, Overhang, Pinchbuck, Pine-chafer, Potato, Project, Protrude, Rhinoceros, Roach, Rosechafer, Rove, Saw palmetto, Scarab(ee), Scavenger, Scurry, Sexton, Skelter, Sledge(-hammer), Snapping, Snout, Spanish fly, Spider, Squirr, Stag, Tiger, Tumble-bug, Turnip-flea, Typographer, VW, Water, Weevil, Whew, Whirligig, Wireworm, Woodborer

Before(hand) A, Advance, Already, An, Ante, Avant, By, Coram, Earlier, Early, Ere, Erst(while), First, → **FORMER**, Or (e'er), Parava(u)nt, Pre, Previously, Prior, Pro, Sooner, Till, To, Until, Van, Zeroth

Befriend Assist, Cotton, Fraternise, Support

Beg(gar), Beggarly, Begging Ask, Badgeman, Beseech, Bey, Blighter, Blue-gown, Cadge, Calendar, Crave, Down and outer, → **ENTREAT**, Exoration, Flagitate, Fleech, Gaberlunzie, Gangrel, Hallan-shaker, Implore, Impoverish, Lackall, Lazar(us), Lazzarone, Limitary, Maund, Mendicant, Montem, Mooch, Mouch, Mump, Niggardly, Panhandle, Pauper, Penniless, → **PLEAD**, Pled, Pray, Prig, Procreate, Prog, Rag, Randy, Ruffler, Schnorr(er), Screeve, Scrounge, Shool(e), Skelder, Skell, Solicit, Standpad, Sue, Suppliant, Supplicate, Thig(ger), Toe-rag, Touch, Undo, Uprightman, Whipjack

Begin(ner), Beginning Ab initio, Ab ovo, Alpha, Alphabetarian, Author, B, Black, Cause, Che(e)chako, Clapdash, Commence, Daw, Dawn, Deb, Debut, Embryo, Enter, Exordium, Fall-to, Found, Fountainhead, Genesis, Germ, Get at, Go, Greenhorn, Inaugural, Inception, Inchoate, Incipient, Incipit, Initial, Initiate, Intro, Johnny-raw, L, Launch, Lead, Learn, Learner, Logos, Nascent, Neophyte, Noob, → **NOVICE**, Onset, Ope(n), Ord, → **ORIGIN**, Outbreak, Outset, Pose, Prelim(inary), Primer, Rookie, Seed, Set, Set forth, Shoot, → **START**, Startup, Strike up, Takeoff, Tenderfoot, Threshold, Tiro, To-fall, Yearn

Behave(d), Behaviour, Behaving Abear, Accepted, Act, Appeasement, Attitude, Carriage, Conduct, Consummatory, Convenance, Decorum, Demean, Do, Effrontery, Etepimeletic, Ethics, Ethology, Form, Freak out, Guise, Horme, Life style, → **MANNER**, Meme, Nature, Netiquette, Noblesse oblige, Obey, Orientation, Practice, Praxeology, Quit, React, Response, Ruly, Strong meat, Tribalism

Behind(hand) Abaft, Aft(er), Ahent, Ahind, Ahint, Apoop, Arear, Arere, Arrear, Astern, Backside, Beneath, Bottom, Bum, Buttocks, Can, Croup, Derrière, Fud, Fundus, Late, Overdue, Prat, → **REAR**, Rump, Slow, Tardy, Tushie

Being Cratur, Creature, Critter, Ens, Entia, Entity, Esse, Essence, Existence, Human, Man, Metaphysics, Mode, Nature, Omneity, Ontology, Organism, → **PERSON**, Saul, Soul, Subsistent, Substance, Wight

Belch Boak, Boke, Brash, Burp, Emit, Eruct, Erupt, Rift, Spew, Toby, Yex

Belief, Believe, Believed, Believer, Believing Accept, Accredit, Adam and Eve, Bigot, Buy, Capernaite, Catechism, Chiliasm, Conviction, Creationism, Credence, Credit, Creed, Cult, Culture, Deem, Deist, Di(o)physite, Doctrine, Doxy, Dyophysite, Evangelical, Faith, Gnostic, Guess, Heresy, Heterodoxy, Hold, Holist, Idea, Ideology, Idolater, Imagine, Islam, Ism, Latitudinarian, Lore, Ludism, Mechanist, Messianist, Methink, Monotheist, Mysticism, Notion, Opine, → **OPINION**, Ovist, Pantheism, Pelagianism, Persuasion, Physicism, Pluralism, Postmillenarian, Presumption, Rasta, Religion, Reputed, Revelationist, S(h)aivism, Second Coming, Secularism, Seeing, Solipsism, Superstition, Supremacist, Swallow, Tenet, Test, Tetratheism, Thanatism, Theist, Theosophy, Think, Threap, Threep, Traducianism, Trinitarian, Triphysite, Trow, Trust, Umma(h), Unitarian, Wear, Ween, Wis(t)

Belittle Cheapen, Decry, Demean, Depreciate, Derogate, Detract, Diminish, Discredit, Disparage, Humble, Slight

Bell(s) Acton, Agogo, Angelus, Ben, Bob, Bow, Bronte, Cachecope, Canterbury, Carillon, Chime, Clanger, Crotal, Curfew, Currer, Daisy, Diving, Division, Ellis, Gong, Grandsire, Inventor, Jar, Knell, Liberty, Low, Lutine, Market, Mass, Muffin, Passing, Pavilion, Peal, Peter, Pinger, Ring, Roar, Sacring, Sanctus, Tailor, Tantony, Tenor, Tent, Tintinnabulum, Toll, Tom, Triple, Tubular, Vair, Vesper, Wind

Bellow(s) Buller, Holla, Holler, Moo, Rant, Rave, Roar, Saul, Thunder, Troat, Tromp(e), Trumpet, Windbag

Belly Abdomen, Alvine, Bag, Beer, Beer-gut, Boep, Bunt, Calipee, Celiac, Coeliac, Gut, Kite, Kyte, Paunch, Pod, → **STOMACH**, Swell, Tum(my), Venter, Wame, Weamb, Wem(b), Womb

Belong, Belonging(s) Appertain, Apply, Appurtenant, Chattels, Effects, Inhere, Intrinsic, Our, Paraphernalia, Pertain, → **PROPERTY**, Relate, Roots, Things, Traps

Beloved Alder-lief(est), Amy, David, Dear, Esme, Inamorata, Joy, Leve, Lief, Loor, Morna, Pet, Popular, Precious

Below Beneath, Inf(erior), Infra, Nether, Sub, Subjacent, Under, Unneath

Belt(ed) Baldric(k), Band, Bandoleer, Bandolier, Baudric(k), Bible, Black, Cartridge, Chastity, Cholera, Clitellum, Clobber, Clock, Clout, Commuter, Conveyor, Copper, Cotton, Crios, Equator, Fan, Flog, Galvanic, Garter, Gird(le), Girt, Hydraulic, Inertial, Judoka, Kuiper, Lap, Larrup, Life, Lonsdale, Mitre, Orion's, Orogenic, Polt, Pound, Roller, Roll-on, Safety, Sahel, Sam Browne, Sash, Seat, Slug, Speed, Stockbroker, Storm, Strap, Stratosphere, Surcingle, Suspender, Swipe, Taiga, Tawse, Tear, Thump, Tore, Tract, Van Allen, Wampum, Wanty, Webbing, Wing, Zodiac, Zone, Zonulet, Zoster

Bemoan → **LAMENT**, Mourn, Rue, Sigh, Wail

Bemuse Infatuate, Stonn(e), Stun, Stupefy, Throw

Bench Banc, Bink, Counter, Court, Cross, Exedra, Form, Knifeboard, Magistrates, Opposition, Pew, Rout seat, Rusbank, Settle, Siege, Stillage, Thoft, Thwart, Treasury, Trestle

Bend(er), Bending, Bends Angle, Arc, Arch, Articular, Bight, Binge, Bow, Buck(le), Bust, Camber, Carrick, Chicane, Circumflect, Contort, Corner,

Crank(le), Crimp, Cringe, →**CROOK**, Crouch, Curl, Curve, Diffraction, Dog-leg, Elbow, Engouled, Epinasty, Es(s), Falcate, Fawn, Flex(ural), Flexion, Flexure, Fold, Geller, Geniculate, Genu, Genuflect, Grecian, Hairpin, Hinge, Hook, Horseshoe, Hunch, Inflect, Jag, Knee(cap), Kneel, Knot, Kowtow, Mould, Nutant, Orgy, Ox-bow, Pitch, Plash, Pliant, Plié, Ply, Recline, Reflex, Retorsion, Retortion, Retroflex, Riband, S, Sag, Scarp, Souse, Spree, Spring, Stave, Stoop, Swan-neck, Trend, Twist, U, Ups(e)y, Uri, Wale, Warp, →**YIELD**, Z

▷**Bendy** *may indicate* an anagram

Beneath Below, Sub, Under, Unworthy

Benefactor, Benefactress Angel, Backer, Barmecide, Carnegie, Donor, Fairy Godmother, Maecenas, →**PATRON**, Philanthropist, Promoter

Beneficial, Beneficiary, Benefit, Benefice, Beneficent Advantage, →**AID**, Alms, Ameliorate, Asset, Avail, Behalf, Behoof, Behove, Bespeak, Bonus, Boon, Boot, Charity, Collature, Commendam, Commensal, Conferee, Devisee, Disablement, Dole, Donee, Endorsee, Enjoy, Enure, FIS, For, Fringe, Fund-raiser, Gain, Grandisonian, Grantee, Healthful, Housing, Incapacity, Incumbent, Inheritor, Injury, Interest, Inure, Invalidity, Legal aid, Living, Manna, Maternity, Ménage, Mileage, Neckverse, Pay, Perk, Perquisite, Plenarty, Plus, Portioner, Postulate, Prebend, Profit, Sake, Salutary, Sanative, Serve, Service, Sickness, Sinecure, Spin-off, Stipend, Supplementary, Symbiotic, Trickle down, UB40, Unalist, Unemployment, Use, Usufruct, Va(u)ntage, Well-being, Wholesome, Wonderful, Workfare

Benevolence, Benevolent Charitable, Clement, Dobbie, Dobby, Goodwill, Humanitarian, Kind, Liberal, Nis(se), Philanthropy, Pickwickian, Sprite

Benign Affable, Altruistic, Gracious, Innocuous, Kindly, Trinal

Bent Akimbo, Bowed, Brae, Concave, Coudé, Counterfeit, Courb, Criminal, Crooked, Curb, Determined, Dorsiflex, Falcate, Fiorin, Flair, Habit, Heath, Inclination, Ingenium, Intent, Inverted, Leant, Out, Peccant, Penchant, Ply, Predisposition, Reclinate, Redtop, Scoliotic, Stooped, Swayed, Talent, Taste, Twisted

▷**Bent** *may indicate* an anagram

Bequeath, Bequest Bestow, Chantr(e)y, Demise, Endow, Heirloom, →**LEAVE**, Legacy, Mortification, Pass down, Pittance, Testament, Transmit, Will

Berate(d) Censure, Chastise, Chide, Jaw, Reproach, Scold, Slate, Vilify

Bereave(d), Bereavement Deprive, Loss, Mourning, Orb, Sorrow, Strip, Widow

Berry Acai, Allspice, Bacca, Blackcurrant, Cow, Cubeb, Fruit, Goji, Goosegog, Haw, Hound's, Konini, Miracle, Mistletoe, Pea, Pepo, Persian, Pimento, Poke, Pottage, Quinsy, Raccoon, Rhein, Rhine, Rowan, Sal(l)al, Salmonberry, Slae, Sloe, Snow, Sop, Sun, Tay, Tomatillo, Winter, Wolf

Berserk Amok, Baresark, Frantic, Frenzy, Gungho, Rage

Berth Anchorage, Bunk, Cabin, Couchette, Dock, Marina, Moor, Seat, Space

Beseech Beg, Crave, Entreat, Implore, Invoke, Obsecrate

Beset Amidst, Assail, Assiege, Badger, Bego, Embattled, Environ, Harry, Obsess, Perplex, Scabrid, Siege

Beside(s) Adjacent, Along, And, At, Au reste, By, Else, Forby(e), Moreover, Next, On, To, Withal

Besiege(d) Beset, Best(ed), Blockade, Gherao, Girt, Invest, Obsess, Plague, Poliorcetic, Surround

▷**Besiege** *may indicate* one word around another

Besot(ted) Dotard, Infatuate, Intoxicate, Lovesick, Smitten, Stupefy

Best A1, Ace, All-time, Aristocrat, Beat, Bonzer, Cap, Cat's whiskers, Champ(ion), Choice, Conquer, Cream, Creme, Damnedest, Defeat, Deluxe, Elite, Every, Eximious, Finest, First, Flower, Foremost, Greatest, Highlight, Ideal, Nicest, Optima, Outdo, Outwit, Overcome, Peak, Peerless, Pick, Pink, Plum, Purler, Ream, Sunday, Super, Supreme, The, Tiptop, Top (flight), Topper, Transcend, Ultimate, Utopian, Vanquish, Wale, World-class

Bet(ting), Betting System Accumulator, A cheval, Ante, Antepost, Back, Banco, Banker, Daily double, Dice, Double, Fixed odds, Flutter, Gaff, Gamble, Go, Hedge, Impone, Lay (odds), Long shot, Martingale, Mise, Note, Pari-mutuel, Parlay, Perfecta, Pip, Place, Pot, Punt, Quadrella, Quinella, Ring, Risk, Roulette, Saver, Set, SP, Spec, Sport, Stake, Take, Tattersalls, Tatts, Totalisator, Totalise, Tote, Treble, Triella, Trifecta, → **WAGER**, Win, Yankee

Betray(al), Betrayed, Betrayer Abandon, Abuse, Belewe, Bewray, Breach, Cornuto, Cuckold, Desert, Disclose, Divulge, Dob, Dobbin, Double-cross, Giveaway, Grass, Judas, Proditor, Renegade, Renege, Rumble, Sell, Sellout, Shop, Sing, Sinon, Split on, Stab, Telltale, Traditor, Trahison, Traitor, Treachery, Treason, Turncoat

Betroth(ed), Betrothal Affiance, Affy, Assure, Engage, Ensure, Espouse, Fiancé(e), Handfasting, Pledge, Promise, Sponsalia, Subarr(h)ation

Better Abler, Ameliorate, Amend, Apter, Bigger, Buck, Cap, Comparative, Cured, Edify, Fairer, Gambler, Gamester, Imponent, Improve, Layer, Master, Meliorate, Mend, Mitigate, Outdo, Outpeer, Outpoint, Piker, Preponderate, Punter, Race-goer, Reform, Score off, Superior, Surpass, Throw, Top, Turfite, Work, Worst

Between Amid, Bet, Betwixt, Inter, Interjacent, Linking, Mesne, Twixt

Beverage Ale, Cocoa, Coffee, Cordial, Cup, → **DRINK**, Mobbie, Mobby, Nectar, Tea

Bevy Flock, Group, Herd, Host

Beware Cave, Fore, Heed, Look out, Mind, Mistrust, Tut

Bewilder(ed), Bewildering, Bewilderment Amaze, Astound, Baffle, Buffalo, Confound, Confuse, Consternation, Daze, Distract, Flummox, Mate, Maze, Mind-boggling, Mystify, Obfuscate, Perplex, Stun, Taivert, Tutulbay, Wander, Will, Wull

Beyond Above, Ayont, Besides, Farther, Outwith, Over, Past, Thule, Trans, Ulterior, Ultra

Bias(ed) Angle, Bent, Colour, Discriminatory, Forward, Imbalance, One-sided, Partial, Parti pris, Partisan, Penchant, Preconception, Predilection, → **PREJUDICE**, Prepossess, Set, Skew, Slant, Slope, Spin, Tendency, Warp

Bible, Biblical Alcoran, Alkoran, Antilegomena, Apocrypha, ASV, Authority, AV, Avesta, Bamberg, Book, Breeches, Coverdale, Cranmer, Cromwell, Douai, Douay, Family, Gemara, Geneva, Gideon, Good book, Goose, Gospel, Haggada, Helachah, Heptateuch, Hermeneutic, Hexapla, Hexateuch, Itala, Italic, King James (version), Leda, Mazarin(e), Midrash, Missal, Murderer, NT, Omasum, OT, Pentateuch, Peshito, Peshitta, Peshitto, Polyglot, Psalter, Revised Version, RSV, RV, Scriptures, Septuagint, Stomach, Talmud, Tanach, Tantra, Targum, Taverners, Text, Tyndale, Vinegar, Vulgate, Whig, Wyclif(fe), Zurich

Bicker(ing) Argue, Bowl, Brawl, Coggie, Dispute, Spat, Tiff, Wrangle

Bicycle, Bike(r) All-terrain, Bee, Bone-shaker, Chopper, Coaster, Crog(gy), Dandy-horse, Draisene, Draisine, Hell's Angels, Hobby, Kangaroo, Mixte,

Moped, Mount, Mountain, Ordinary, Pedal, Penny-farthing, Racer, Raleigh®, Roadster, Rocker, Safety, Scooter, Ski-bob, Solo, Spin, Stationary, Swarm, Tandem, UCI, Velocipede

Bid(der), Bidding (system) Abundance, Acol, Apply, Blackwood, Call, Canape, Command, Contract, Cue, Declare, Double, Gone, INT, Invite, Misère, Nod, NT, →**OFFER**, Order, Pass, Pre-empt(ive), Proposal, Puffer, Redouble, Rescue, Summon, Take-out, Take-over, Tell, Tender, Vied

Big Altruistic, Beamy, Bulky, Bumper, Burly, Capacious, Cob, Corpulent, Enormous, Fat, Ginormous, Gross, →**LARGE**, Loud, Massive, Mighty, Obese, Roomy, Stonker, Strapping, Substantial, Swopper, Thumping, Tidy, Vast, Whacker, Whopper

Bighead(ed) Besserwisser, Ego, Uppity

Bigot(ed) Chauvinist, Dogmatist, Fanatic, Hide-bound, Intolerant, Racialist, Racist, Redneck, Wowser, Zealot

Bigshot, Bigwig Cheese, Nob, Swell, Titan, Toff, →**VIP**

Bile, Bilious(ness) Cholaemia, Choler, Gall, Icteric, Melancholy, Scholaemia, Venom

Bilge Leak, Pump, Rhubarb, Rot, Waste

Bill(ed), Billy Ac(c), Accommodation, Accompt, Account, Act, Ad, Addition, Allonge, Appropriation, Barnacle, Beak, Becke, Budd, Buffalo, Bunter, Can, Caress, Carte, Charge, Cheque, Chit(ty), Cody, Coo, Coronoid, Cross(-bencher), Debt, Demand, Dixy, Docket, Double, Due, Egg-tooth, Enabling, Exactment, Fee, Fin, Finance, Foreign, Gates, Goat, Hybrid, Inland, Invoice, Kaiser, →**LAW**, Lawin(g), Legislation, Liam, Liar, Line-up, List, Measure, Menu, Nail, Neb, Ness, Nib, →**NOTE**, Notice, Paper, Petition, Platypus, Police, Pork barrel, Portland, Poster, Private, Programme, Pruning, Public, Puffing, Reckoning, Reform, Rostral, Rostrum, Score, Selsey, Short, Shot, Show, Sickle, Silly, Sparth(e), Sperthe, Spoon, Sticker, Tab, Tariff, Tenner, Tenuirostral, Tomium, Trade, Treasury, True, Twin, Victualling, Watch, Willy

Billiards, Billiards player, Billiards stroke Bar, Cueist, Jenny, Lagging, Massé, Nursery cannon, Pills, Pool, Potter, Pyramids, Short jenny, Snooker, String, Whitechapel

Billow Roil, Roller, Rule, Surge, Swell, Wave

▶**Billy** see **BILL(ED)**

Bin Bing, Box, Chilly, Container, Crib, Crock, Discard, Hell, Litter, Loony, Receptacle, Snake-pit, Stall, Throw away, Wagger-pagger, Wheelie, Wheely

Bind(er), Binding Adherent, Adhesive, Alligate, Apprentice, Astrict, Astringent, Bale, Bandage, Bandeau, Bandster, Bias, Boyer, Brail, Burst, Calf, Cement, Cerlox®, Chain, Cinch, Circuit, Clamp, Colligate, Complain, Cord, Cramp-iron, Cummerbund, Dam, De Vigneaud, Drag, Edge, Embale, Enchain, Engage, Enslave, Enwind, →**FASTEN**, Fetter, Final, Gird, Girdle, Half-calf, Half-leather, Haworth, Hay-wire, Hold, Hole, Hopkins, Incumbent, Indenture, Iron, Keckle, Krebs, Lash(er), Law-calf, Leash, Ligament, Ligature, Mail, Marl, Marry, Martin, Meyerhof, Morocco, Muslin, Obi, Obligate, Oblige, Oop, Organdie, Oup, Parpen, Paste grain, Perfect, Pinion, Porter, Quarter, Raffia, Red Tape, Restrict, Ring, →**ROPE**, Seize, Sheaf, Spiral, Strap, Stringent, Swathe, Tape, Tether, Thirl, Thong, Three-quarter, Tie, Tree-calf, Truss, Twine, Unsewn, Valid, Whip, Withe, Yapp, Yerk, Yoke

Binge, Binging Bat, Beano, Bend(er), Blind, Carouse, Dipsomania, →**DRINK**, Drinking-bout, Engorge, Gorge, Party, Pig out, Riot, Soak, Souse, Spree, Toot, Tout

Bingo Beano, Housey-housey, Lotto, Tombola

Binocular(s) Glasses, Jumelle, OO, Stereoscope

Biographer, Biography Boswell, CV, Hagiography, History, Life story, Memoir, Plutarch, Potted, Profile, Prosopography, Strachey, Suetonius, Vita

Biology, Biologist Algology, Berg, Bordet, Carrel, Cladistics, Cohen, Dawkins, Delbruck, Genetics, Haller, Kendrew, Kinsey, Mendel, Molecular, Morphology, Phenetics, Shatten, Stoechiology, Stoich(e)iology, Taxonomy, Transgenics, Weismann

Birch Betula, Birk, Cane, Cow, Flog, Hazel, Kow, Larch, Larrup, Reis, Rice, Rod, Silver, Swish, Thrash, Twig, Whip, Withe

Bird(s) Al(l)erion, Altricial, Bertram, Brood, Damsel, Dawn chorus, Doll, Early, Flier, Fowl, Gal, → **GIRL**, Grip, Hen, Layer, Left, Limicoline, Nestling, Ornithology, Pecker, Pen, Perching, Poultry, Praecoces, Prison, Quod, Raptor, Rare, Roaster, Sentence, Sis, Skirt, Stretch, Visitant, Warbler

▷**Bird** *may indicate* a prison sentence

Birth Burden, Congenital, Delivery, Drop, Extraction, Genesis, Geniture, Jataka, Lineage, Multiple, Nativity, Origin, Parage, Parthenogenesis, Parturition, Water, Whelp(ing)

Birthday Anniversary, Genethliac, Prophet's

Birthmark Blemish, Mole, Mother-spot, Naevus, Port wine stain, Stigmata

Birthright Heritage, Mess, Patrimony

Biscuit Abernethy, Amaretto, Bake, Bath-oliver, Biscotto, Bourbon, Brown George, Butterbake, Charcoal, Cookie, Cracker, Cracknel, Crispbread, Custard cream, Dandyfunk, Digestive, Dunderfunk, Fairing, Flapjack, Florentine, Fly cemetery, Garibaldi, Gingersnap, Hardtack, Jammy dodger, Jumbal, Kiss, Lavash, Lebkuchen, Macaroon, Marie, Mattress, Nut, Oliver, Osborne, Parkin, Perkin, Petit four, Pig's ear, Poppadom, Poppadum, Pretzel, Puff, Ratafia, Rice, Rusk, Sea, Ship's, Shortbread, Snap, Sponge finger, Sweetmeal, Tack, Tan, Teiglach, Tollhouse cookie, Wafer, Zwieback

Bishop(ric) Aaronic, Abba, Aberdeen, Aidan, Ambrose, Apollinaris, Bench, Berkeley, Bp, Cambrensis, Cantuar, Chad, Chorepiscopal, Coadjutor, Coverdale, Cranmer, Diocesan, Dunelm, Ebor, Ely, Eparch, Episcopate, Eusebian, Exarch, Exon, Golias, Hatto, Henson, Jansen, Latimer, Lord, Magpie, Man, Metropolitan, Missionary, Norvic, Odo, Ordainer, Patriarch, Peter, Petriburg, Piece, Polycarp, Pontiff, Prelate, Priest, Primate, Primus, Proudie, Ridley, Roffen, RR, St Swithin, Sarum, Sleeve, Sodor and Man, Suffragan, The purple, Titular, Tulchan, Weed, Winton, Wrexham

Bison Bonas(s)us, Buffalo, Ox, Wisent

Bit Ate, Baud, Byte, Cantle(t), Chad, Cheesecake, Chip, Chunk, Coin, Crumb, Curb, Curn, Dash, Degree, Drib, Excerpt, Fleck, Fraction, Fraise, Haet, Hait, Hate, Ion, Iota, Jaw, Jot, Leptum, Mite, Modicum, Morsel, Mote, Mu, Nit, Ort, Ounce, Pelham, Peni, Penny, → **PIECE**, Pinch, Port, Rap, Rare, Ratherish, Rowel, Scintilla, Scrap, Section, Shaving, Shiver, Shrapnel, Shred, Smattering, Smidge(n), Smidgeon, Smidgin, Snaffle, Snatch, Snippet, Soupcon, Spale, Speck(le), Splinter, Spot, Stop, Suspicion, Tad, Tait, Tate, Threepenny, Trace, Unce, Vestige, What, Whit

Bite(r), Biting, Bitten Astringent, Begnaw, Canapé, Caustic, Champ, Chelicera, Chew, Cold, Eat, Engouled, Erose, Etch, Gnash, Gnat, Gnaw, Hickey, Hickie, Incisor, Knap, Masticate, Midge, Molar, Mordacious, Mordant, Morsel, Morsure, Nacho, Nibble, Nip(py), Occlude, Pium, Pointed, Premorse, Rabid, Raw, Sarcastic, Sharp, Shrewd, Snack, Snap, Tart, Teeth

Bitter(ness), Bitters Absinth, Acerb, Acid, Acrimonious, Ale, Aloe, Angostura, Astringent, Bile, Caustic, Eager, Edge, Envenomed, Ers, Fell, Gall, Heated, Jaundiced, Keen, Keg, Marah, Maror, Myrrh, Picamar, Pique, Radicchio, Rancorous, Rankle, Resentful, Sarcastic, Sardonic, Snell, Sore, Spleen, Tannin, Tart(aric), Venom, Verjuice, Virulent, Vitriolic, Wersh, Wormwood, Wry

Bizarre Antic, Curious, Eccentric, Exotic, Fantastic, Gonzo, Grotesque, Kafkaesque, Odd, Offbeat, Off-the-wall, Outlandish, Outré, Pythonesque, Queer, Strange, Surreal, Weird

▷**Bizarre** *may indicate* an anagram

Black(en), Blackness, Black-out Afro-American, Asperse, Atramental, B, Ban, BB, Bess, Blae, Boycott, Carbon, Charcoal, Cilla, Coal, Coloured, Cypress, Death, Debar, Demonise, Denigrate, Dwale, Ebon(y), Eclipse, Ethiop, Evil, Graphite, Grime, Heben, Hole, Ink(y), Ivory, Japan, Jeat, Jet, Jim Crow, Kohl, Malign, Market, Melanic, Melano, Moke, Moor, Muntu, Myall, Negritude, Negro, Niello, Niger, Nigrescent, Nigritude, Obliterate, Obscure, Outage, Oxford, Piceous, Pitch, Platinum, Pongo, Prince, Pudding, Raven, Sable, Scab, School, Scorch, Sheep, Sloe, Solvent, Sombre, Soot, Sooterkin, Soul brother, Soul sister, Starless, Stygian, Swart(y), Swarth(y), Tar, Uncle Tom, Weeds

Blackberry Acini, Bramble, Mooch, Mouch

Blackbird Collybird, Crow, Jackdaw, Merl(e), Ousel, Raven

Blackjack Billie, Billy, Cosh, Flag, Sphalerite, Tankard, Truncheon, Vingt(-et)-un

Blackmail(er) Bleed, Chantage, Chout, Exact, Extort, Greenmail, Honey-trap, Ransom, Strike, Vampire

Blackout ARP, Eclipse, Faint, Power cut, Shallow water, Swoon, Syncope

Blacksmith Brontes, Burn-the-wind, Farrier, Forger, Harmonious, Plater, Shoer, Vulcan

Blade(s) Acrospire, Andrew Ferrara, Bilbo, Brand, Brown Bill, Catling, Cleaver, Co(u)lter, Cutlass, Dandy, Espada, Faible, Foible, Forte, Froe, Gleave, Gouge, Guillotine, Hydrofoil, Kris, Lance, Lawnmower, Leaf, Man, Mouldboard, Oar, Paddle, Palmetto, Peel, Propeller, Rachilla, Rapier, Razor, Rip, Rotor, Scalpel, Scapula, Scimitar, Scull, Skate, Spade-, Spatula, Spatule, Spear, Spoon, Stiletto, Stock, Sweep, Switch, →**SWORD**, Symitar, Toledo, Vane, Vorpal, Wash, Web

Blame(worthy) Accuse, Censure, Condemn, Confound, Culpable, Decry, Dirdam, Dirdum, Fault, Guilt, Incriminate, Inculpate, Odium, Rap, Reproach, Reprove, Stick, Thank, Twit, Wight, Wite, Wyte

Blameless Innocent, Irreproachable, Lily-white

Blanch Bleach, Etiolate, Scaud, Whiten

Bland Anodyne, Flavourless, Insipid, Mild, Neutral, Pigling, Sleek, Smooth, Suave, Tasteless, Unctuous

Blank Burr, Cartridge, Deadpan, Empty, Erase, Flan, Flyleaf, Ignore, Lacuna, Mistigris, Planchet, Shot, Space, Tabula rasa, →**VACANT**, Vacuous

Blanket Across the board, Afghan, All-over, Bluey, Chilkat, Comprehensive, Counterpane, Cover, Envelop, General (purpose), Kaross, Mackinaw, Manta, Obscure, Overall, Overlay, Poncho, Quilt, Rug, Saddle, Sarape, Security, Serape, Shabrack, Smog, Space, Stroud, Umbrella, Wagga, Wet, Whittle

Blast(ed), Blasting Blight, Blore, Blow, Bombard, Dang, Darn, Dee, Drat, Dynamite, Expletive, Explode, Fanfare, Flaming, Flurry, Fo(e)hn, Gale, Grit, Gust, Hell, Pan, Parp, Planet-struck, Pryse, Rats, Ruddy, Scarth, Scath(e), Sere, Shot, Sideration, Skarth, Sneeze, Stormer, Tantara, Toot, Tout, Tromp(e), Trump(et), Volley

Blatant Conspicuous, Flagrant, Hard-core, Noticeable, Strident, Unashamed, Vulgar

Blaze(r), Blazing Afire, Beacon, Bonfire, Burn, Cannel, Conflagration, Firestorm, → **FLAME**, Flare, Glare, Inferno, Jacket, Low(e), Lunt, Palatinate, Race, Ratch, Sati, Star, Sun, Tead(e)

Bleach(er) Agene, Blanch, Chemic, Chloride, Decolorate, Etiolate, Fade, Frost, Keir, Kier, Peroxide, Whiten, Whitster

Bleak Ablet, Bare, Barren, Blay, Bley, Dour, Dreary, Dreich, Gaunt, Midwinter, Raw, Soulless, Wintry

Bleed(er), Bleeding Breakthrough, Cup, Diapedesis, Ecchymosis, Emulge, Epistaxis, Extort, Extravasate, Fleam, Haemorrhage, Leech, Menorrhagia, Menorrh(o)ea, Metrorrhagia, Milk, Purpura, Rhinorrhagia, Root-pressure

Blemish Birthmark, Blot, Blotch, Blur, Botch, Defect, Eyesore, Flaw, Imperfection, Lepra, Mackle, Mark, Milium, Mote, Naevus, Scar, Smirch, Smudge, Spot, Stain, Sully, Taint, Tash, Verruca, Vice, Wart, Wen

Blend(ing) Amalgam, Coalesce, Commix, Contemper, Contrapuntal, Counterpoint, Electrum, Fit, Fuse, Go, Harmonize, Hydrate, Interfuse, Interlace, Intermix, Liquidise, Meld, Melt, → **MERGE**, Mingle, Mix, Osmose, Portmanteau, Scumble, Sfumato, Stir, Synalepha

▷**Blend** *may indicate an anagram*

Bless(ing), Blessed(ness) Amen, Anoint, Approval, Asset, Beatitude, Benedicite, Benediction, Benison, Benitier, Bensh, Bismillah, Bonus, Boon, Brachah, Brocho, Charmed, Consecrate, Cup, Damosel, Darshan, Elysium, Ethereal, Felicity, Gesundheit, Giver, Gwyneth, Hallow, Holy (dam), Kiddush, Luck, Macarise, Mercy, Mixed, Sain, Saint, Sanctify, Sanctity, Sneeze, Urbi et orbi, Xenium

Blight Afflict, Ague, American, Apple, Bespot, Blast, Destroy, Early, Eyesore, Late, Rot, → **RUIN**, Rust, Sandy, Shadow, Viticide, Waldersterben, Wither

Blimey Coo, Cor, Crimini, Crumbs, O'Riley, Strewth

Blind(ness), Blind spot Amaurosis, Amblyopia, Artifice, Austrian, Bedazzle, Beesome, Binge, Bisson, Blend, Blotto, Camouflage, Carousal, Cecity, Chi(c)k, Cog, Colour, Concealed, Dazzle, Drop serene, Drunk, Eyeless, Feint, Festoon, Flash, Gravel, Hemeralopia, Homer, Hood, Invisible, Jalousie, Legless, Meropia, Mole, Nyctalopia, Onchocerciasis, Persian, Persiennes, Pew, Pickled, Prestriction, Rash, River, Roller, Sand, Scotoma, Seel, Shade, Shutter, Sightless, Slat, Snow, Stimie, Stimy, Stymie, Sun, Swear, Teichopsia, Typhlology, Venetian, Visually challenged, Word, Yblent

Blindfold Bandage, Hood, Hoodwink, Muffle, Seal, Wimple

Blink, Blinker(s), Blinkered, Blinking Bat, Blinders, Bluff, Broken, Flash, Haw, Idiot, Insular, Nictate, Owl-cyed, Owly, Twink, Wapper, Water, Wink

Bliss(ful) Beatitude, Bouyan, Cheer, Composer, Delight, → **ECSTASY**, Eden, Elysium, Glee, Happy, Heaven, Ignorance, Joy, Married, Millenium, Nirvana, Paradise, Rapture, Seventh heaven, Sion, Tir-na-nog, Utopia, Valhalla, Walhalla, Wedded

Blister(ed), Blistering Blab, Blain, Bleb, Bubble, Bullate, Cantharidine, Epispastic, Fever, Herpes, Measle, Overgall, Pemphigus, Phlyct(a)ena, Scorching, Tetter, Vesicant, Vesicle

Blitz Attack, Bombard, Onslaught, Raid

Blizzard Buran, Gale, Snowstorm, Whiteout

Bloat(ed), Bloater Buckling, Gross, Puff, Strout, Swell, Swollen, Tumefy, Tumid, Turgid, Two-eyed steak, Yarmouth

Blob Bead, Bioblast, Dollop, Drop, Globule, O, Pick, Spot, Tear

Bloc Alliance, Cabal, Cartel, Party

Block(er), Blockage, Blocked, Blocking Altar, Anvil, Ashlar, →**BAR**, Barber's, Barracks, Barricade, Barrier, Battle-axe, Brake, Breeze, Brick, Briquet(te), Building, Bung, Bunt, Capital, Choke, Chunk, Cinder, Cleat, Clint, Clog, Clot, Cloy, Compass, Condo(minium), Congest, Constipated, Cylinder, Dado, →**DAM**, Dead-eye, Debar, Defect, Delete, Dentel, Dentil, Die, Dit, Eclipse, Embolism, Encompass, Erratic, Fiddle, Filibuster, Fipple, Frog, Gypsum, Hack-log, Head off, Heart, High-rise, Hunk, Ileus, Impasse, Impede, Impost, Ingot, Input, Insula, Interclude, Interrupt, Investment, Ischaemia, Jam, Licence, Lifestyle, Lingot, Lodgment, Log-jam, Lump, Ministroke, Monkey, Mounting, Nog, Oasis®, Obstacle, →**OBSTRUCT**, Occlude, Pad, Page, Parry, Pile-up, Planer, Plinth, Pre-empt, Prevent, Ram, Scotch, Seal, Sett, Siege, Snooker, Stalemate, Stap, Starting, Stenosis, Stimie, Stimy, Stone, Stonewall, Stop, Stumbling, Stymie, Sun(screen), Tamp, Tetrapod, Thwart, Tint, Tower, Tranche, Trig, Triglyph, Truck, Veto, Vibropac®, Wedge, Wig, Writer's

Bloke Beggar, Chap, Codger, Cove, Fellow, Geezer, Gent, Man, Oik

Blond(e) Ash, Bombshell, Cendré, Fair, Goldilocks, Nordic, Platinised, Platinum, Strawberry, Tallent, Towhead

Blood(y), Blood-letter, Blood-letting A, Ancestry, B, Bally, Blue, Bluggy, Blut, Buck, Butchery, Claret, Clot, Cold, Cruor, Cup, Dutch pink, Ecchymosis, Ensanguine, Epigons, Factor, Family, H(a)emal, Haematoma, Ichor, Introduce, Kin, Knut, Menses, Microcyte, Nut, O, Opsonin, Parentage, Penny dreadful, Persue, Pigeon's, Plasma, Platelet, Properdin, Pup, Purple, Race, Rare, Red, Rh negative, Rh positive, Ruby, Sang, Schistosoma, Serum, Show, Stroma, Thrombin, Toff, Type, Venisection, Welter

Bloodless Anaemic, Isch(a)emic, Wan, White

Blood-sucker Anoplura, Asp, Bed bug, Dracula, Flea, Gnat, Ked, Leech, Louse, Mosquito, Parasite, Reduviid, Soucouyant, Sponger, Tick, Vampire(-bat)

Blood vessel Artery, Vein, Venule

Bloom(er), Blooming Anthesis, Bally, Blossom, Blow, Blush, Boner, Bread, Clanger, Cobalt, Dew, Dratted, Error, Film, Flipping, Florence, Florescent, Flourish, Flowery, Flush, Full-blown, Gaffe, Glaucous, Heyday, Howler, Knickers, Loaf, Miscalculation, Nickel, Out, Peach, →**PLANT**, Pruina, Rationals, Reh, Remontant, Rosy, Ruddy, Thrive, Underwear

▷**Bloomer** *may indicate* a flower

Blossom Blow, Burgeon, Catkin, Develop, Festoon, Flourish, Flower, Marybud, May, Orange, Pip, Springtime

Blot (out) Atomy, Blob, Cartel, Delete, Disgrace, Eclipse, Eyesore, Obliterate, Obscure, Pad, Smear, Smudge, Southern, Splodge, Splotch

Blotch(y) Blemish, Giraffe, Monk, Mottle(d), Spot, Stain

Blouse Choli, Garibaldi, Gimp, Guimpe, Middy, Sailor, Shell, Shirtwaist, Smock, Tunic, Waist(er), Windjammer

Blow(er), Blown Bang, Bash, Bat, Bellows, Biff, Billow, Blip, Bloom, Body, Box, Brag, Breeze, Buffet, Bump, Burst, Buster, Calamity, Chop, Clap, Clat, Claut, Clip, Clout, Clump, Conk, Coup, Cuff, Dad, Daud, Dawd, Dev(v)el, Dint, Dod, Douse, Dowse, Etesian, Exsufflate, Facer, Fan, Fillip, Finisher, Fisticuffs, Fuse, Gale, Grampus, Gust, Hammer, Hander, Haymaker, Headwind, Hit, Hook, Hurricane, Ictus, Impact, Insufflate, Karate, Kibosh, Knuckle sandwich, KO,

Lame, Lander, Left-hander, Lick, Montant(o), Muff, Muzzler, Northerly, Noser, Oner, One-two, Paddywhack, Pash, Peise, Peyse, Phone, Piledriver, Plague, Plug, Plump(er), Polt, Pow, Puff, Punch, Purler, Raft, Rats, Rattler, Rib-roaster, Roundhouse, Sas(s)arara, Scat, Settler, Short, Sideswipe, Side-winder, Sis(s)erary, Skiff, Skite, Skyte, Slat, Slog, Slug, Smack, Snell, Snot, Sock, Sockdolager, Southwester, Spanking, Spat, Spout, Squall, Squander, Squelcher, Stripe, Stroke, Stunning, Sufflate, Supercharger, Swash, Swat, Swinger, Swipe, Tap, Telephone, Thump, Thwack, Tingler, Tootle, Triple whammy, Trump(et), Tuck, Twister, Undercut, Upper-cut, Waft, Wallop, Wap, Waste, Welt, Whammy, Whang, Whap, Wheeze, Whiffle, Whirret, Whistle, → **WIND**, Winder, Windswept, Wipe

Blow-out Binge, Bloat, Blowhole, Exhale, Feast, Feed, Flat, Fulminate, Lava, Nosh-up, Snuff, Spiracle, → **SPREAD**

Bludgeon Bulldoze, Bully, Club, Cosh, Cudgel, Life-preserver, Sap

Blue(s), Bluesman Adult, Aqua, Aquamarine, Azure, Azurn, Beard, Berlin, Bice, Bleuâtre, Blow, Boogie, Bottle, Butterfly, Caesious, Cambridge, Cantab, Celeste, Cerulean, City, Clair de lune, Classic, Cobalt, Copenhagen, Cornflower, Country, Coventry, Cyan, Danish, Danube, Dejected, Dirty, Disconsolate, Doldrums, → **DOWN**, Duck-egg, Eatanswill, Eggshell, Electric, Erotica, Firmament, Fritter, Gentian, Germander, Glaucous, Glum, Heliotrope, Hump, Ice, Indecent, Indigo, Indol(e), Iron, Isatin(e), Lapis lazuli, Lavender, Leadbelly, Lewd, Lionel, Low, Mazarine, Methylene, Midnight, Mope, Morose, Murder, Nattier, Naughty, Navy, Nile, Obscene, Ocean, Off-colour, Oxford, Peacock, Periwinkle, Perse, Petrol, Porn, Powder, Prussian, Rabbi, Racy, Ribald, Riband, Right, Ripe, Robin's egg, Royal, Sad, Sapphire, Saxe, Saxon(y), Scurrilous, → **SEA**, Shocking, → **SKY-TINCTURED**, Slate, Smalt(o), Smutty, Sordid, Spirit, Splurge, Squander, Stafford, Steel, Stocking, Teal, Thenard's, Tony, Top shelf, Tory, Trist, True, Turquoise, Ultramarine, Unhappy, Urban, Washing, Watchet, Wedgwood®, Welkin, Woad

▷**Blue** *may indicate* an anagram

Bluebell Blawort, Blewart, Campanula, Harebell, Hyacinth

Bluebottle Blawort, Blewart, Blowfly, Blowie, Brommer, Brummer, Cop, Cornflower, Fly, Officer, Policeman

Blueprint Cyanotype, Design, Draft, Drawing, Plan, Recipe

Bluff(ing) Blunt, Cle(e)ve, Cliff, Clift, Crag, Double, Escarpment, Fake, Flannel, Four-flush, Frank, Hal, Headland, Height, Hoodwink, Kidology, Pose, Precipice, Scarp, Steep, Trick

Blunder(er), Blundering Barry (Crocker), Betise, Bévue, Bish, Bloomer, Blooper, Boner, Boob, Bull, Bumble, Bungle, Clanger, Clinker, Cock-up, Crass, Err, Fault, Faux pas, Floater, Flub, Fluff, Gaff(e), Goof, Howler, Inexactitude, Inexpert, Josser, Malapropism, → **MISTAKE**, Mumpsimus, OG, Oversight, Ricket, Slip, Slip up, Solecism, Stumble, Trip

Blunt(ed), Bluntly Abrupt, Alleviate, Bald, Bate, Bayt, Brash, Brusque, Candid, Deaden, Disedge, Downright, Dull, Explicit, Forthright, Frank, Hebetate, Home truth, Mole, Morned, Obtund, Obtuse, Outspoken, Plainspoken, Pointblank, Pointless, Rebate, Retund, Retuse, Roundly, Snub, Straight-out, Stubby

Blur(red), Blurring, Blurry Cloud, Confuse, Daze, Fog, Fuzz, Halation, Mackle, Macule, Muzzy, Stump, Tortillon, Unfocussed

Blush(ing) Colour, Cramoisy, Crimson, Erubescent, Erythema, Incarnadine, → **REDDEN**, Rosy, Rouge, Ruby, Rutilant

Bluster(ing), Blusterer, Blustery Arrogance, Bellow, Blore, Brag, Fanfaronade, Hector, Huff-cap, Rage, Rant, Rodomontade, Roister, Sabre-rattler, Squally, Squash, Swagger, Swashbuckler, Vapour, Wuthering

Boar Barrow, Calydonian, Erymanthian, Hog, Pentheus, Sanglier, Sounder, Tusker

Board(s), Boarding Abat-voix, Admiralty, Aquaplane, Baffle, Banker, Barge, Bd, Beaver, Billet, Bristol, Bulletin, Catchment, Centre, Cheese, Chevron, Circuit, Committee, Counter, Cribbage, Dagger, Dam, Dart, Daughter, Deal, Directors, Diving, Draft, Draining, Drawing, Duck, Embark, Embus, Emery, Enter, Entrain, Expansion, Fa(s)cia, Fare, Farm out, Featheredge, Fibro, Fibrolite®, Food, Full, Gib(raltar), Groaning, Gunwale, Gutter, Hack, Half, Half-royal, Hawk, Hoarding, Idiot, Instrument, Insulating, Ironing, Kip, Lag, Lap, Leader, Ledger, Lee, Lodge, Magnetic, Malibu, Management, Marketing, Masonite®, Match, Message, Mill, Monkey, Mortar, Moulding, Muft(i)at, Notch, Notice, Otter, Ouija, Paddle, Palette, Pallet, Panel, Paper, Parochial, Particle, Patch, Pedal, Peg(board), Pension, Planch(ette), Plank, Plug, Ply(wood), Punch, Quango, Ribbon-strip, Roof, Running, Sandwich, Sarking, Scale, Scaleboard, School, Score, Scraper, Scratch, Screen, Sheathing, Shelf, Shifting, Shingle, Shooting, Side-table, Sign, Skim, Skirting, Sleeve, SMART®, Smoke, Snow, Sounding, Splasher, Spring, Stage, Stretcher, Strickle, Stringboard, Supervisory, Surf, Switch, →**TABLE**, Teeter(-totter), Telegraph, Thatch, Theatre, Timber, Tray, Trencher, Tribunal, Verge, Wainscot, Wobble, Wokka, Wood chip

▷**Board** *may refer to* chess or draughts

Boarder Interne, Pensioner, PG, Roomer

Boarding house Digs, Kip, Lodgings, Pension

Boast(er), Boastful, Boasting Bigmouth, Big-note, Blew, Blow, Blowhard, Bluster, Bobadil, Bounce, Brag, Braggadocio, Bravado, Breeze, Bull, Cock-a-hoop, Crake, Crow, Fanfaronade, Gas, Gascon(nade), Glory, Hot air, Jact(it)ation, Line, Loudmouth, Ostent(atious), Prate, Rodomontade, Scaramouch, Self-glorious, Show-off, Skite, Spread-eagle, Swagger, Swank, Tall, Thrasonic, Vainglory, Vapour, Vaunt, Yelp

Boat(s) Ark, Barge, Bark, Cat, Flagship, Fly(ing), Fore-and-after, Goldie, Isis, Keel, Kit, Lugger, Privateer, She, →**SHIP**, →**VESSEL**

Boatman Bargee, Charon, Cockswain, Coxswain, George, Gondolier, Harris, Hoveller, Legger, Noah, Phaon, Punter, Voyageur, Waterman, Wet-bob

Bob Acres, Beck, Curtsey, Deaner, Dip, Dock, Dop, Duck, Dylan, Eton crop, Float, Haircut, Hairdo, Hod, Hog, Jerk, Major, Maximus, Minor, Nod, Page-boy, Peal, Plain, Plumb, Plummet, Popple, Rob, Royal, S, Shingle, Skeleton, Skip

Bobby Bluebottle, Busy, Copper, Flatfoot, Patrolman, Peeler, Pig, →**POLICEMAN**, Rosser, Wolly

Body, Bodies, Bodily Administration, Amount, Anatomic, Astral, Barr, Board, Bouk, Buke, Bulk, Cadaver, Cadre, Carcase, Carnal, Caucus, Chapel, Chapter, Chassis, Clay, Cohort, Column, Comet, Committee, Contingent, Corpora, Corpor(e)al, Corps, Corpse, Corpus, Corse, Cytode, Detail, Earth, Elaiosome, Establishment, Flesh, Frame, Fuselage, Gate, Goner, →**GROUP**, Hull, Immune, Inclusion, Kenning, Lich, Lifting, Like, Lithites, →**MASS**, Militia, Mitochondrion, Moit, Mote, Mummy, Nacelle, Nave, Nucleole, Nucleolus, Olivary, Orb, Order, Pack, Personal, Phalanx, Pineal, Plant, Platelet, Platoon, Politic, Posse, Purview, Quango, Relic(t), Remains, Review, Ruck, Satellite, Sect, Senate, Shaft, Solid, Soma(tic), Sound-box, Spinar, Spore, Squad(ron), Square, Staff, Stiff, Strobila, Syndicate, Systemic, Torso, Trunk, Turm, Ulema, Uvula, Vase

▷**Body** *may indicate* an anagram

Bodyguard Amulet, Beefeater, →**ESCORT**, Gentleman-at-arms, House-carl, Minder, Praetorian, Protector, Retinue, Schutzstaffel, →**SHIELD**, SS, Sun cream, Switzer, Triggerman, Varangian, Yeomen

Boffin Brain, Egghead, Expert

Bog(gy) Allen, Can, Carr, Clabber, Fen, Gents, Glaur, Hag, Lair, Lerna, Lerne, Letch, Loo, Machair, Marish, Marsh, Mire, Moory, Morass, Moss(-flow), Moss-hag, Mud, Muskeg, Peat, Petary, Quag, Serbonian, Slack, Slade, Slough, Spew, Spouty, Stodge, Sump, Swampland, Urinal, Vlei, Washroom, WC, Yarfa, Yarpha

Bog(e)y, Bogeyman Boggart, Bug(aboo), Bugbear, Chimera, Colonel, Eagle, Gremlin, Ogre, Poker, Scarer, Siege, Spectre, Troll

Bohemian Arty, Beatnik, Boho, Calixtin(e), Demi-monde, Gypsy, Hippy, Zingara, Zingaro

Boil(er), Boiled, Boiling (point) Aleppo, Anthrax, Blain, Botch, Brew, Bubble, C, Coction, Cook, Copper, Cree, Dartre, Decoct, Ebullient, Foam, Furuncle, Gas-fired, Gathering, Hen, Herpes, Hijinks, Kettle, Laddish, Leep, Ligroin, Pimple, Poach, Poule, Rage, Reflux, Rowdy, Samovar, Seethe, Set pot, Simmer, Sod, Sore, Stew, Stye, Tea-kettle, Water tube

Boisterous(ly), Boisterousness Ariot, Gilp(e)y, Gusty, Hoo, Knockabout, Ladette, Noisy, Rambunctious, Randy, Riotous, Rollicking, Rorty, Rough, Rounceval, Splurge, Stormy, Tearer, Termagant, Tomboy, Turbulent, Wild

Bold(ly), Boldness Audacious, Brash, Brass, Bravado, Bravery, Bravura, Brazen, Confident, Crust, Daredevil, Dauntless, Defiant, Derring-do, Familiar, Forward, Free, Gutsy, Hard-edge, Hardihood, Heroics, High-spirited, Impudent, Intrepid, Malapert, Manful, Mature, Mettle, Minx, Outspoken, Pert, Plucky, Presumptive, Rash, Sassy, Stout, Temerity, Unabashed, Unshrinking, Valiant

Bolt Arrow, Captive, Carriage, Cuphead, Dash, Dead, Do a runner, Eat, Elope, Fasten, Flee, Gobble, Gollop, Gorge, Gulp, Hurtle, Latch, Levant, Levin, Lightning, Lock, Missile, Pig, Pintle, Ragbolt, Rivet, Roll, Scoff, Slot, Snib, Sperre, Through, Thunder, Toggle, U, Wolf, Wring

Bomb(ed), Bomber, Bombing, Bombshell Atom, Attack, B, Benny, Blast, Blockbuster, Borer, Bunkerbuster, Buzz, Car, Carpet, Cluster, Daisycutter, Deterrent, Doodlebug, Drogue, Egg, Fission, Flop, Flying Fortress, Fusion, Grenade, H, Hand grenade, Homicide, Hydrogen, Lancaster, Land-mine, Letter, Liberator, Logic, Mail, Megaton, Mills, Minnie, Mint, Molotov cocktail, Mortar, Nail, Napalm, Necklace, Neutron, Nuclear, Nuke, Packet, Parcel, Petar, Petard, Petrol, Pineapple, Pipe, Plaster, Plastic, Prang, Ransom, Robot, Sex, Shell, Smash, Smoke, Stealth, Stick, Stink, Stuka, Suicide, Tactical, Tank, Terrorist, Thunderbolt, Time, Torpedo, V1, Vulcan

Bombard(ment) Attack, Battery, Blitz, Cannonade, Crossfire, Drum-fire, Mortar, Pelt, Shell(fire), Stone, Stonk, Strafe, Straff

Bond(s), Bondage, Bonding, Bondsman Adhesive, Affinity, Afrikander, Agent, Baby, Bail, Bearer, Cement, Chain, Chemical, Compact, Connect, Consols, Coordinate, Copula, Corporate, Covalent, Covenant, Daimyo, Dative, Debenture, Deep-discount, Double, Duty, Electrovalent, English, Enslave, Ernie, Escrow, Esne, Fetter, Fleming, Flemish, Geasa, Gilt, Glue, Granny, Heart, Herringbone, Hydrogen, Hyphen, Income, Investment, Ionic, James, Junk, Knot, Liaise, Ligament, Ligature, Link(age), Long, Manacle, Managed, Metallic, Mortar, Multicentre, Municipal, Nexus, Noose, Obligation, Pair, Peptide, Performance, →**PLEDGE**, Post-obit, Premium, Property, Rapport,

Recognisance, Relationship, Revenue, Running, Samurai, Savings, Security, Semipolar, Serf, Servitude, Shackle, Shogun, Single, Singlet, Sinter, Slave, Solder, Stacked, Starr, Subjection, Superglue, Surety, Thete, Three-per-cent, →TIE, Tiger, TIGR, Treasury, Triple, Trivalent, Tusking, Valence, Valency, Vassal, Vinculum, Yearling, Yoke, Zebra

Bone(s), Bony Angular, Atlas, Axis, Busk, Caluarium, Cannon, Capitate, Carpal, Carpus, Cartilage, Catacomb, Centrum, Chine, Chordate, Clavicle, Cly, Coccyx, Coffin, Concha, Coral, Costa, Coxa, Crane, Cranium, Cuboid, Cuneiform, Cuttlefish, Dib, Dice, Diploe, Doctor, Dolos, Endosteal, Femur, Fetter, Fibula, Fillet, Fossil, Frontal, Funny, Gaunt, Hamate, Hammer, Haunch, Hause-bane, Horn, Humerus, Hyoid, Ilium, Incus, Interclavicle, Ivory, Kneecap, Knuckle, Lacrimal, Long, Lunate, Luz, Malar, Malleus, Mandible, Marrow, Mastoid, Maxilla, Medulla, Membrane, Metacarpal, Metatarsal, Nasal, Occipital, Orthopaedics, Os, Ossicle, Osteo-, Palatine, Parasphenoid, Parietal, Patella, Pecten, Pectoral, Pedal, Pelvis, Pen, Percoid, Petrous, Phalanx, Ploughshare, Prenasal, Pterygoid, Pubis, Rack, Radiale, Radius, Relic, Rib, Rump-post, Sacrum, Scapula, Sclere, Sepium, Sequestrum, Share, Shin, Skeleton, Skull, Spade, Splint, Splinter, Spur, Stapes, →STEAL, Sternum, Stifle, Stirrup, T, Talus, Tarsometatarsus, Tarsus, Temporal, Tibia, Tibiotarsus, Tot, Trapezium, True-rib, Turbinate, Tympanic, Ulna, Vertebrae, Whirl, Wish

Bonfire Bale-fire, Beltane, Blaze, Clavie, Pyre

Bonny Blithe, Gay, Merry, Sonsy, Weelfar'd

Bonus Bisque, Bounty, Braata, Bye, Dividend, Hand-out, Icing, Lagniappe, No-claim, →PREMIUM, Reward, Scrip, Signing, Spin-off, Windfall

Book(s), Bookish, Bookwork Abcee, Absey, Academic, Adversaria, Album, Appointment, Audio, B, Backlist, Bedside, Bestiary, Bestseller, Black, Block, Blockbuster, Blotter, Blue, Cash, Chick, Classic, Closed, Codex, Coffee-table, Diary, Digest, Directory, Diurnal, Eightvo, Engage(ment), Enter, Erudite, Exercise, Folio, Fortune, Garland, Good, Gradual, Guide, Hardback, Hymnal, Imprint, Index, Issue, Lectionary, Ledger, Lib, Liber, Literary, Livraison, Manual, Memorandum, Missal, Monograph, Muster, Octavo, Office, Open, Order, Page-turner, Paperback, Pass, Pedantic, Peerage, Phrase, Pica, Plug, Polyglot, Potboiler, Pseudepigrapha, Publication, Puzzle prize, Quarto, Quire, →RESERVE, Road, Roman-a-clef, Script, Sealed, Sext, Sexto, Sixmo, Sketch, Softback, Source, Spelling, Spine-chiller, Statute, Studious, Study, Style, Swatch, Symbolical, Table, Tablet, Talking, Tall copy, Te igitur, Text(ual), Thirty-twomo, Thriller, Title, Titule, Tome, Trade, Transfer, Twelvemo, Twenty-fourmo, Unputdownable, Visiting, Visitor's, Vol(ume), Waste, White, Whodunit, Work, Year

Bookbinder, Bookbinding Fanfare, Grolier, Mutton-thumper, Organdie

Book-case Credenza, Press, Satchel

Bookie(s), Bookmaker Binder, John, Layer, Librettist, Luke, Mark, Matthew, Printer, Ringman, Roget, To-bit, Turf accountant

Bookkeeper, Bookkeeping Clerk, Double entry, Librarian, Posting, Recorder, Satchel, Single-entry

Booklet B, Brochure, Folder, Inlay, Pamphlet

Boom(ing) Baby, Beam, Boost, Bowsprit, Bump, Gaff, Increase, Jib, Loud, Orotund, Plangent, Prosper, Resonance, Roar, Sonic, Spar, Thrive, Thunder, Wishbone

Boon Asset, Bene, Benefit, Blessing, Bounty, Cumshaw, Gift, Godsend, Mills, Mitzvah, Prayer, Windfall

Boor(ish) Borel, Bosthoon, Chuffy, Churl, Clodhopper, Crass, Curmudgeon, Goth, Grobian, Hog, Ill-bred, Jack, Jungli, Keelie, Kern(e), Kernish, Kill-courtesy, Lob, Lout, Lumpen, Lumpkin, Ocker, Oik, Peasant, Philistine, Pleb, Trog, Uncouth, Unmannerly, Yahoo, Yob

Boost(er) Adrenalin, Afterburner, Amplify, Augment, Bolster, Eik, Eke, Elevate, Encourage, Fillip, Help, Hoist, Impetus, Increase, Injection, Invigorate, Lift, Perk up, Promote, Raise, Reheat, Reinforce, Reinvigorate, Spike, Steal, Step up, Steroid, Supercharge, Tonic

Boot(s) Addition, Adelaide, Avail, Balmoral, Beetle-crushers, Benefit, Blucher, Bottine, Bovver, Brogan, Brogue, Buskin, Chelsea, Chukka, Cold, Combat, Concern, Cowboy, Daisy roots, Denver, Derby, Desert, Dismiss, Field, Finn(e)sko, Finsko, Fire, Galage, Galosh, Gambado, Go-go, Granny, Gum, Heave-ho, Hessian, Hip, Jack, Jemima, Kick-start, Kinky, Lace-up, Last, Mitten, Muchie, Muc(k)luc(k), Pac, Para, Profit, Sabot, **→ SACK**, **→ SHOE**, Shoepac(k), Skivvy, Stogy, Surgical, Tackety, Toe, Tonneau, Tops, Trunk, Ugg, Vibs, Wader, Walking, Warm, Weller, Wellie, Wellington, Welly

Booth Assassin, Crame, Cubicle, Kiosk, Polling, Stall, Stand, Tolsel, Tolsey, Voting

Bootleg(ger) Cooper, Coper, Pirate, Runner

Booty Creach, Creagh, Haul, Loot, Prey, Prize, Rump, Spoil(s), Spolia optima, Swag

Booze(r) **→ DRINK**, Inn, Liquor, Spree, Tipple

Border(s), Borderland, Borderline Abut, Adjoin, Apron, Bed, Bind, Bound, Boundary, Brush, Checkpoint, Coast, Cot(t)ise, Dado, Dentelle, **→ EDGE**, Enclose, Engrail, Fimbria, Frieze, Fringe, Frontier, Furbelow, Head-rig, Hedgerow, Hem, Herbaceous, Impale, Kerb, Limb, Limbate, Limbo, Limes, Limit, Line, Lip, List, March, Marchland, **→ MARGIN**, Mat, Mattoid, Meith, Mete, Mount, Neighbour, Orle, Outskirts, Pale, Pand, Pelmet, Perimeter, Purfle, Purlieu, Rand, Rim, Rio Grande, Roadside, Roon, Royne, Rund, Screed, Selvage, Side, Skirt, Splenium, Strand, Strip, Surround, Swage, T(h)alweg, The Marches, Trench, Valance, Valence, **→ VERGE**, Wayside

▷**Borders** *may indicate* first and last letters

Bore(d), Boredom, Borer, Boring Aiguille, Airshaft, Anorak, Apathy, Auger, Awl, Beetle, Bind, Bit, Blasé, Broach, Brog, Bromide, Calibre, Cataclysm, Chamber, Deadly, Def(fed), Drag, **→ DRILL**, Dry, Dullsville, Eagre, Eat, Eger, Elshin, Elsin, Endured, Ennui, Ennuye, Fag, Flat, Foozle, Gasbag, Gim(b)let, Gouge, Gribble, Grind, Had, Heigh-ho, Ho-hum, Irk, Jack, Land, Listless, Longicorn, Longueur, Meh, Menial, Mind-numbing, Miser, Mole, Mopoke, Motormouth, Nerd, Nuisance, Pall, Penetrate, Perforate, Pest, Pierce, Pill, Platitude, Possessed, Probe, Prosaic, Prosy, Punch, Ream(ingbit), Rifle, Rime, Saddo, Sat, Screw, Severn, Snooze, Snore, Sondage, Spleen, Spod, Spudding-un, Sting, Stob, Tedious, Tedium, Termes, Termite, Thirl, Tidal wave, Tire, Trocar, Tunnel, Turn-off, Underwent, Uninterested, Vapid, **→ WEARY**, Well, Wimble, Windbag, Wonk, Woodworm, Workaday, Worldweary, Yawn

Born B, Begun, Free, Great, Nascent, Nat(us), Né(e)

Borneo Dyak, Kalimantan, Sabahan

Borough Borgo, Brooklyn, Close, Pocket, Port, Quarter, Queens, Rotten, Township, Wick

Borrow(ed), Borrowing Adopt, Appropriate, Cadge, Copy, Eclectic, George, Hum, Scrounge, Scunge, Stooze, Straunge, **→ TAKE**, Touch

Boss(ed), Bossy Alder(man), Big White Chief, Blooper, Burr, Cacique, Capo, Cazique, Cow, Dictate, Director, Dominate, Domineer, Gadroon, Gaffer, Guv, Headman, Honcho, Hump, Inian, Inion, Jewel, Kingpin, Knob, Knop, Knot, Maestro, →**MANAGER**, Massa, MD, →**MISTAKE**, Mistress, Netsuke, Noop, Nose-led, Omphalos, Oubaas, Overlord, Overseer, Owner, Padrone, Pellet, Protuberance, Ruler, Run, Stud, Superintendent, Superior, Supervisor, Supremo, Taskmaster, Top banana, Umbo(nate)

Bother(some) Ado, Aggro, Annoy, Brush, Care, Deave, Deeve, Disturb, Drat, Fash, Fluster, Fracas, Fuss, Get, Harassment, Harry, Hector, Hoot-toot, Incommode, Irritate, Moither, Nag, Nark, Nonplus, Nuisance, Palaver, Perturb, Pest(er), Pickle, Reke, Rile, Shtuck, Todo, →**TROUBLE**, Vex

Bottle(s) Ampul(la), Balthasar, Balthazar, Belshazzar, Blackjack, Bravado, Bundle, Carafe, Carboy, Case, Chapine, Cock, Cork, Costrel, Courage, Cruet, Cruse, Cucurbital, Cutter, Dead-man, Decanter, Demijohn, Fearlessness, Feeding, Fiasco, Filette, Flacket, Flagon, Flask, Glass can, Goatskin, Gourd, Grit, Hen, Imperial, Jeroboam, Junk, Klein, Lachrymal, Lagena, Magnum, Matrass, Medicine, Melchior, Methuselah, Mettle, Middy, Nebuchadnezzar, Phial, Pig, Pitcher, Rehoboam, Resource, Retort, Salmanazar, Scent, Siphon, Split, Stubby, Vial, Vinaigret(te), Wad, Wallop, Water, Water bouget, Winchester, Woulfe

▷**Bottle(d)** *may indicate* an anagram or a hidden word

Bottom Anus, Aris, Arse, Ass, Base, Batty, Beauty, Bed, Benthos, Bilge, Booty, Breech, Bum, Butt, Buttocks, Coit, Croup(e), Croupon, Demersal, Derrière, Doup, Dowp, Duff, Fanny, Floor, Foot, Foundation, Fud, Fundus, Ground, Haunches, Hunkers, Hurdies, Jacksy, Keel(son), Kick, Minimus, Nadir, Planning, Podex, Posterior, Pottle-deep, Prat, Pyramus, Quark, Rear, Rock, Root, Rump, Seat, Ship, Sill, Sole, Staddle, Stamina, Tail, Tush, Weaver

Bounce(r), Bouncing, Bouncy Ananias, Ball, Bang, Blague, Bound, Bumper, Caper, Convention, Dandle, Dap, Dead-cat, Doorman, Dop, Dud, Eject, Evict, Jounce, Kite, Lie, Lilt, Muscleman, Resilient, Ricochet, Spiccato, Spring, Stot, Tale, Tamp, Tigger, Trampoline, Valve, Verve, Vitality, Yorker, Yump

▷**Bouncing** *may indicate* an anagram

Bound(er), Boundary Adipose, Apprenticed, Articled, Bad, Barrier, Beholden, Border, Bourn(e), Cad, Cavort, Certain, Circumference, Curvet, Dart, Decreed, Demarcation, Demarkation, Divide, Duty, End, Engirt, Entrechat, Erub, Eruv, Extent, Fence, Finite, Four, Frontier, Galumph, Gambado, Gambol, Girt, Goal, Hedge, Heel, Held, Hoarstone, Hops, Hourstone, Interface, Jump, Kangaroo, →**LEAP**, Liable, Limes, Limit, Linch, Lollop, Lope, Mason-Dixon line, Meare, Meer, Mere, Merestone, Mete, Milestone, Muscle, Obliged, Outedge, Outfield, Outward, Pale, Parameter, Perimeter, Periphery, Plate, Prance, Precinct, Purlieu, Quickset, Redound, Ring-fence, Roller, Roo, Roped, Rubicon, Scoundrel, Scoup, Side, Sideline, Six(er), Skip, Spang, Spring, Sten(d), Stoit, Sure, T(h)alweg, Tide, Tied, Touchline, Tramline, Upstart, Vault, Verge, Wallaby, Wound

Boundless Illimited, Unlimited, Vast

▷**Bounds** *may indicate* outside letters

Bounty, Bountiful Aid, Bligh, Boon, Christian, Generosity, →**GIFT**, Goodness, Grant, Head money, Honorarium, Largess(e), Lavish, Philanthropy, Queen's, Reward

Bouquet Aroma, Attar, Aura, Compliment, Congratulations, Corsage, Fragrancy, Garni, Nose, Nosegay, Odour, Perfume, Plaudit, Posy, Pot pourri, Scent, Spiritual, Spray

Bout Bender, Binge, Bust, Contest, Dose, Go, Jag, Match, Spell, Spree, Turn, Venery, Venewe, Venue

Bow(ing), Bower, Bowman Accede, Alcove, Arbour, Arc, Arch, → **ARCHER**, Arco, Arson, Beck, Bend, Boudoir, Buckle, Capitulate, Cellist, Clara, Congé(e), Crescent, Crook, Cupid, → **CURVE**, Defer, Dicky, Droop, Duck, East end, Eros, Eyes, Fiddle(r), Fiddlestick, Foredeck, Halse, Hawse, Headgear, Honour, Incline, Inswing(er), Jouk, Kneel, Kotow, Lean, Londoner, Loof, Lout, Luff, Menuhin, Nock, Nod, Nutate, Oar, Obeisance, Outswing, Paganini, Pergola, Quarrel, Reverence, Salaam, Seamer, Shelter, Slope, Spiccato, Staccato, Stick, → **SUBMIT**, Swing, Throw, Tie, Torrent, Tureen, Weather, Yew, Yield

Bowels Entrails, Guts, Innards, Melaena, Viscera

▷**Bower** *may indicate* using a bow

Bowl(ing), Bowler, Bowl over, Bowls B, Basin, Begging, Bicker, Bodyline, Bool, Bosey, Bouncer, Cage-cup, Calabash, Caldera, Cap, Carpet, Caup, Chalice, Cheese, Chinaman, Christie, Christy, Cog(g)ie, Concave, Crater, Cup, Derby, → **DISH**, Dismiss, Dome, Doosra, Drake, Dumbfound, Dust, Ecuelle, End, Finger, Font, Goblet, Goldfish, Googly, Grail, Grub, Headgear, Hog, Hoop, Inswing(er), Jack, Jeroboam, Jorum, Lavabo, Laver, Leg-spin, Lightweight, Lob, Locke, Monteith, Night, Offbreak, Off-cutter, Old, Outswing, Over-arm, Overpitch, Pace(man), Pan, Pétanque, Pitch, Porringer, Pot-hat, Pottinger, Punch, Raku, Rink, Roll, Roundarm, Seam(er), Skip, Skittle(s), Spare, Spinner, Stadium, Stagger, Super, Swing, Ten-pin, Throw, Tom, Tureen, Underarm, Underhand, Voce, Washbasin, Wassail, Wood, York(er)

Box(ing) ABA, Alert, Ark, Baignoire, Ballot, Bandbox, Bareknuckle, Bento, Bijou, Bimble, Binnacle, Black, Blow, Blue, Bonk, Booth, Bunk, Bush, Caddy, Call, Camera, Canister, Cardboard, Case, Cash, Casket, Cassette, Chest, Chinese, Chocolate, Christmas, Clog, Coach, Coffer, Coffin, Coffret, Coin, Commentary, Compartment, Confessional, Cool, Crash, Crate, Cuff, Dabba, Dead-letter, Deed, Dialog(ue), Dispatch, Ditty, Dog, Drawer, Earpiece, Egg, Encase, Enclose, Etui, → **FIGHT**, File, Fist, Fund, Fuse, Fuzz, Gear, Glory, Glove, Go-kart, Grass, Hat, Hay, Hedge, Hive, Honesty, Horse, Humidor, Hutch, Ice, Idiot, Inherce, Inro, Inter, Jewel, Journal, Juke, Junction, Jury, Keister, Kick, Kiosk, Kite, Knevell, Knowledge, Ladle, Letter, Light, Live, Locker, Lodge, Loge, Loose, Lug, Lunch, Match, Message, Mill, Mitre, Mocuck, Money, Musical, Nest(ing), Noble art, Noble science, Omnibus, Orgone, Out, Package, Packing, Paint, Pandora's, Patch, Pattress, Peepshow, Peg, Pen, Penalty (area), Petara, Pew, Phylactery, Piggybank, Pill, Pillar, Pitara, Pix, Poor, Post, Powder, Press, Prize fight, Prompt, Protector, Puff, Pugilism, Punnet, Pyxis, Red, Register, Resonance, Ring, Rope-a-dope, Royal, Safe-deposit, Saggar(d), Sagger, Sand, Savate, Scent, Scrap, Scrine, Seggar, Sentry, Set-top, Shadow, Shoe, Shooting, Side, Signal, Skinner, Skip(pet), Slipcase, Smudge, Sneeshin-mull, Sneeze, Soap, Solander, Sound, Sound body, → **SPAR**, Spice, Spit, Spring, Squawk, Squeeze, Stock, Strong, Stuffing, Swell, Tee, Telephone, Telly, Tick, Tin, Tinder, Tivo, Tool, Touch, Trunk, Tube, Tuck, TV, Urn, Vanity, Vinaigrette, Voice, Weather, Window, Wine, Witness

Boxer(s) Ali, Bantamweight, Bruiser, Bruno, Canine, Carnera, Carpentier, Carthorse, Chinaman, Cooper, Corbett, Crater, Cruiserweight, Darcy, Dempsey, Dog, Eryx, Farr, Featherweight, Flyweight, Foreman, Ham, Heavyweight, Middleweight, Pandora, Pug, Pugil(ist), Rebellion, Rocky, Shadow, Shorts, Sparrer, Sugar Ray Robinson, Welterweight

Boy(s) Anchor, Apprentice, Ball, Bevin, Blue-eyed, Bovver, Bub(by), Cabin, Callant, Champagne, Chiel(d), →**CHILD**, Chummy, Cub, Galopin, Garçon, Groom, Grummet, Ha, I say, Jack, Kid, Klonkie, Knave, Lackbeard, →**LAD**, Loblolly, Loon(ie), Minstrel, Nibs, Nipper, Page, Poster, Prentice, Principal, Putto, Rent, Roaring, Rude, Shaver, Ship's, Son, Spalpeen, Sprig, Stripling, Swain, Tad, Ted(dy), Tiger, Toxic, Toy, Urchin, Whipping, →**YOUTH**
▷**Boy** *may indicate* an abbreviated name

Boycott Avoid, Bat, Black, Blacklist, Exclude, Geoff(rey), Hartal, Isolate, Ostracise, Shun

Brace(s), Bracing Accolade, Clamp, Couple, Crosstree, Gallace, Gallows, Gallus(es), Gird, Hound, Invigorate, Ozone, Pair, Pr, Rear-arch, Rere-arch, Sea air, Skeg, Splint, Stage, Steady, Stiffener, Strut, →**SUPPORT**, Suspenders, Tauten, Tone, Tonic, Two(-hander)

Bracelet Armil(la), Armlet, Bangle, Cuff, Darbies, Handcuff, Manacle, Manilla

Bracken Brake, Fern, Pteridium, Tara

Bracket Ancon, Angle-iron, Bibb, Brace, Cantilever, Console, Corbel, Couple, Cripple, Gusset, Hanger, Misericord(e), Modillion, Mutule, Parenthesis, Potence, Pylon, Rigger, Round, Sconce, Straddle, Strata, Trivet, Truss

Brag(gart), Bragging Birkie, Bluster, Boast, Bobadil, Boister, Bombastic, Braggadocio, Bull, Cockalorum, Crow, Falstaff, Fanfaronade, Gab, Gascon, Hot-air, Loudmouth, Mouth off, Puff, Rodomontader, Skite, Slam, Swagger, Upstart, Vainglorious, Vapour, Vaunt

Braid A(i)glet, Aiguillette, Enlace, Frog, Galloon, Lacet, Plait, Plat, Rickrack, Ricrac, Scrambled eggs, Seaming-lace, Sennet, Sennit, Sinnet, Soutache, Tress, Trim, Twist, Weave

Brain(box), Brain disease, Brain-power, Brain problem, Brains, Brainstorm, Brainy Appestat, Bean, Boffin, Bright, Brilliant, Cerebellum, Cerebrum, Contravene, Cortex, Crane, Cranium, Dura mater, Egghead, Encephalon, Fornix, Genius, Gliosis, Grey matter, Gyrus, Harn(s), Head, Headpiece, Hippocampus, Hypothalamus, Inspiration, Insula, Intelligence, IQ, Loaf, Lobe, Lobule, Mater, Medulla, Mind, Noddle, Noesis, Nous, Peduncle, Pericranium, Pia mater, Pons, Pontile, Quick, Ringleader, Sconce, Sense, Sensorium, Smarty pants, Striatum, Subcortex, Sulcus, Thalamus, Vortex
▷**Brain(s)** *may indicate* an anagram

Brake, Braking Adiantum, Aerodynamic, Air, Anchors, Bracken, Centrifugal, Curb, Disc, Drag, Drum, Estate car, Fern, Fly, Grove, Hub, Hydraulic, Nemoral, Overrun, Ratchet, Rein, Rim, Shoe, →**SLOW**, Spinney, Sprag, Tara, Thicket, Vacuum

Bramble, Brambly Batology, Blackberry, Boysenberry, Brier, Cloudberry, Rubus, Thorn, Wait-a-bit

Bran Cereal, Chesil, Chisel, Oats, Pollard

Branch(ed), Branches, Branching, Branch office Affiliate, Antler, Arm, BO, Bough, Chapel, Cladode, Cow, Dendron, Dept, Diversify, Diverticulum, Divide, Filiate, Fork, Grain, Jump, Kow, Lateral, Limb, Lobe, Lobus, Loop, Lye, Lylum, Offshoot, Olive, Patulous, Phylloclade, Prong, Rachilla, Raguly, Ramate, Ramulus, Reis, Rice, Shroud, Special, Spray(ey), Sprig, Spur, Stirpes, Tributary, Turning, Turn-off, Twig, Wattle, Whip, Yard

Brand(ing) Broadsword, Buist, Burn, Cauterise, Chop, Class, Dealer, Denounce, Earmark, Ember, Excalibur, Falchion, Faulchin, Faulchion, Flambeau, Home, Idiograph, Ilk, Iron, Label, Line, →**MARK**, Marque, Name, Neckverse, Sear, Stigma, Sweard, Sword, Torch, Trade name, Wipe

Brandy Aguardiente, Applejack, Aqua vitae, Armagnac, Bingo, Calvados, Cape smoke, Cherry bounce, Cognac, Cold without, Dop, Eau de vie, Fine, Fine champagne, Framboise, Grappa, Kirsch, Mampoer, Marc, Mirabelle, Nantes, Nantz, Napoleon, Quetsch, Slivovic(a), Slivovitz, Smoke, VSOP

Brash Cocky, Flashy, Impudent, Jack-the-lad, Pushy, Rain, Rash, Uppity

Brass(y), Brassware Alpha-beta, Althorn, Benares, Brazen, Bugle, Cheek, Corinthian, Cornet, Cornopean, Dinanderie, Effrontery, Face, Front, Harsh, Horn, Horse, Latten, Lip, Lolly, Loot, Lota(h), Loud, Matrix, →MONEY, Moola(h), Palimpsest, Pyrites, Sass, Snash, Sopranino, Talus, Top, Trombone, Tuba, White, Yellow metal

Brat Bairn, Bra(t)chet, Gait(t), Gamin, Get, Horror, Imp, Lad, Perisher, Terror, Tyke, Urchin

Bravado, Brave(ry) Amerind, Apache, Bold, Conan, Corragio, Courage, Creek, Dare, Derring-do, Doughty, Dress, Face, Gallant, Game, Gamy, Gutsy, Hardy, Heroism, Impavid, Indian, Injun, Intrepid, →LION, Lion-hearted, Lionly, Manful, Manly, Nannup, Plucky, Prow(ess), Redskin, Russian roulette, Sannup, Stalwart, Stout, Uncas, Valiant, Valour, Venturesome, Wight, Withstand, Yeoman

Bravo Acclaim, Bandit, Bully, Desperado, Euge, Murderer, Olé, Shabash, Spadassin, Villain

Brawl(er) Affray, Bagarre, Bicker, Brabble, Donnybrook, Dust, Dust-up, Fight, Flite, Flyte, Fracas, Fratch, Fray, Free-for-all, Melee, Prawl, Punch up, Rammy, Roughhouse, Ruck, Scold, Scrap, Scuffle, Set-to, Shindig, Slugfest, Stoush, Tar, Troublesome, Wrangle

Brawn Beef, Burliness, Headcheese, He-man, Muscle, Power, Rillettes, Sinew

Bray Cry, Heehaw, Stamp, Vicar, Whinny

Brazen Blatant, Bold, Brash, Brassy, Flagrant, Forward, Impudent, Shameless, Unabashed

Breach Affray, Assault, Break, Chasm, Cleft, Foul, Gap(e), Great schism, Gulf, Infraction, Redan, Rift, Rupture, Saltus, Schism, Solecism, Solution, Trespass, Violate

Bread, Bread crumbs Azym(e), Bagel, Baguette, Bannock, Bap, Barmbrack, Barm cake, Batch, Baton, Black, Bloomer, Brewis, Brioche, Brown, Brownie, Bun, Cash, Chal(l)ah, Chametz, Chapati, Cheat, Ciabatta, Cob, Coburg, Compone, Corn (pone), Corsned, Croissant, Crostini, Croute, Crouton, Crumpet, Crust, Currency, Damper, Dibs, Dika, Doorstep, Eucharist, Fancy, Flatbread, Focaccia, Fougasse, French (stick), Funds, Garlic, Gluten, Graham, Granary, Grissini, Guarana, Hallah, Horse, Host, Indian, Jannock, Johnny-cake, Kaffir, Lavash, Laver, Leavened, Loaf, Long tin, Manchet, Maori, Matzo, Milk loaf, Milk-sop, →MONEY, Monkey, Na(a)n, Pain, Panada, Panary, Pane, Paneity, Panini, Panko, Paratha, Pay, Petit pain, Pikelet, Pit(t)a, Pone, Poori, Popover, Poppadom, Poultice, Prozymite, Pumpernickel, Puree, Puri, Quick, Raspings, Ravel, Roll, Rooty, Roti, Round, Rusk, Rye, Sally Lunn, Shewbread, Simnel, Sippet, Smor(re)brod, Soda, Soft-tommy, Sop, Sourdough, Split tin, Staff of life, Standard, Stollen, Stottie, Sugar, Sweet, Tartine, Tea, Tommy, Twist, Wastel, White, Wrap

Break, Break-down, Break down, Break-in, Break-up, Break up, Broken Adjourn, Analyse, Apn(o)ea, Bait, Biodegrade, Breach, Breather, Burst, Bust, Caesura, Caesure, Cantle, Career, Cark, Cesure, Chance, Chinaman, Chip, Cleave, Coffee, Comb, Comma, Commercial, Comminute, Compost,

Compurgatory, Conk, Contravene, Crack, Crock, Crumble, Dash, Debacle, Decompose, Demob, Destroy, Detach, Diaresis, Diffract, Disband, Disintegrate, Disperse, Disrupt, Dissect, Duvet day, Elevenses, Erumpent, Erupt, Exeat, Fast, Fault, Flaw, Four, → **FRACTURE**, Fragment, Fritter, Frush, Gaffe, Gap, Give, Haematolysis, Half-term, Half-time, Harm, Hernia, Hiatus, Holiday, Hydrolyse, Infringe, Interim, Interlude, Intermission, Interrupt, Interspace, → **INTERVAL**, Irrupt, Kark, Knap, Lacuna, Lapse, Layover, Leave, Moratorium, Natural, Outage, Parse, Part, Pause, Playtime, Poach, Polarise, Price, Reave, Recess, Relief, Rend, Resolve, Respite, Rest, Rift, Rise, Ruin, Rupture, Saltus, Schism(a), Secede, Service, Shatter, Shear, Shiver, Smash, Snap, Split, Start, Stave, Stop, Stop-over, Stove, Sunder, Take five, Take ten, Tame, Tea-ho, Tear, Tenderise, Time-out, Torn, Transgress, Truce, Twist, Vacation, Violate, Watergate, Weekend

Breakable Brittle, Delicate, Fissile, Fragile, Frail, Friable

Breakdown Abruption, Analyse, Autolysis, Cataclasm, Collapse, Conk, Crack-up, Glitch, Glycolosis, Glycolysis, Haematolysis, Histolysis, Lyse, Lysis, Ruination

Breaker Billow, Circuit, Comber, Ice, Roller, Smasher, Surf

Breakfast B, Brunch, Chota-hazri, Continental, Deskfast, Disjune, Kipper, Wedding

Breakwater Groyne, Jetty, Mole, Pier, Tetrapod

Bream Fish, Porgy, Sar(gus), Sea, Silver, Tai, White

Breast(s), Breastbone, Breastwork Bazuma, Boob, Bosom, Brave, Brisket, Bristols, Bust, Chimney, Clean, Counter, Diddy, Duddy, Dug, Garbonza, Gazunga, Heart-spoon, Jubbies, Jugs, Knockers, Norg, Nork, Rampart, Redan, Sangar, Stem, Sternum, Stroke, Sungar, Supreme, Tit, Xiphisternum

Breastplate Armour, Byrnie, Curat, Curiet, Pectoral, Plastron, Rational, Rest, Shield, Thorax, Xiphiplastron

Breath(e), Breathing, Breather Aerobe, Air-sac, Apneusis, Aqualung, Aspirate, Bated, Buteyko method, Exhalation, Expiration, Flatus, Gasp, Gill, H, Halitosis, Hauriant, Inhale, Inspiration, Interval, Knee, Lenticellate, Lung, Nares, Nostril, Oxygenator, Pant, Plosion, Pneuma, Prana, Pulmo, Rale, Respire, Respite, Rest, Rhonchus, Scuba, Sigh, Smooth, Snorkel, Snotter, Snuffle, Souffle, Spiracle, Spirit, Suspire, Tachypnoea, Trachea, Vent, Wheeze, Whiff, Whift, Whisper, Whist, Wind, Windpipe

Breathless(ness) Anhelation, Apnoea, Asthma, Dyspnoea, Emphysema, Orthopnoea, Puffed-out, Purfled, Tachypnoea, Wheezing

Breech(es) Bible, Buckskin, Chaps, Chausses, Flog, Galligaskins, Hose, Jodhpurs, Kneecords, Knickerbockers, Pantaloons, Petticoat, Plushes, Smallclothes, Smalls, Trews, Trouse(rs), Trunk hose, Trusses

Breed(er), Breeding(-place) Bear, Beget, Digoneutic, Engender, Eugenics, Fancier, Gentility, Line, Lineage, → **MANNERS**, Origin, Procreate, Pullulate, Race, Rear, Savoir vivre, Seminary, Sire, Species, Stirpiculture, Stock, Strain, Stud, Tribe

Breeze, Breezy Air, Breath, Brisk, Cakewalk, Catspaw, Chipper, Doctor, Draught, Fresh, Gentle, Gust, Land, Light, Mackerel, Moderate, Piece of cake, Pushover, Sea, Slant, Sniffler, Snifter, Strong, Tiff, Zephyr

Brew(er), Brewery, Brewing Afoot, Ale, Billycan, Boutique, Brose, Browst, Bummock, Contrive, Dictionary, Elixir, Ferment, Infusion, Liquor, Malt, Percolate, Perk, Potion, Scald, Steep, Yeast, Yill, Zymurgy

Bribe(ry) Backhander, Barratry, Barretry, Bonus, Boodle, Bung, Buy, Carrot, Dash, Douceur, Embracery, Get at, Gift, Graft, Grease, Hamper, Hush-money, Insult, Kickback, Lubricate, Oil, Palm, Palm-grease, Palm-oil, Payola, Schmear, Slush, Soap, Sop, Square, Straightener, Suborn, Sweeten(er), Tamper, Tempt, Tenderloin, Vail, Vales

Brick(s), Brickwork Adobe, Bat, Bath, Bonder, Bondstone, Boob, Breeze(-block), Bristol, Bullnose, Bur(r), Clanger, Clinker, Closer, Course, Fletton, Gaffe, Gault, Good egg, Header, Ingot, Klinker, Lateritious, Lego®, Malm, Nog(ging), Opus latericium, Red, Rubber, Rubble, Soldier, Spawn, Sport, Stalwart, Stretcher, Terra-cotta, Testaceous, Tile, Trojan, Trump

Bride(s) Bartered, Danaides, Ellen, Mail-order, Newlywed, Spouse, War, Wife, Ximena

Bridge(head), Bridge player Acol, Air, Aqueduct, Auction, Australian, Avignon, Ba(u)ck, Bailey, Balance, Barre, Bascule, Bestride, Board, Brig, Brooklyn, Cable-stayed, Cantilever, Capo, Capodastro, Capotasto, Catwalk, Chicago, Chicane, Clapper, Clifton, Contract, Counterpoise, Cross, Cut-throat, Deck, Declarer, Drawbridge, Duplicate, Flying, Flyover, Foot, Forth, Four-deal, Gangplank, Gangway, Gantry, Girder, Golden Gate, Hog's back, Humber, Humpback, Humpbacked, Ice, Irish, Jigger, Land, Lattice, Leaf, Lifting, Ligger, Link, London, Menai, Millau, Millennium, Murray, Overpass, Pivot, Pons, Pontifice, Pont levis, Pontoon, Raft, Rainbow, Rialto, Rubber, Severn, Sighs, Skew, Snow, →SPAN, Spanner, Stamford, Straddle, Suspension, Swing, Tay, Temper, Tête-de-pont, Through, Tide over, Transporter, Traversing, Trestle, Truss, Turn, Vertical lift, Viaduct, Waterloo, Weigh, Wheatstone, Wire

Bridle Bit, Branks, Bridoon, Bristle, Browband, Curb, Double, Hackamore, Halter, Headstall, Musrol, Noseband, Rein

Brief(s), Briefing, Briefly, Brevity Acquaint, Advocate, Aphoristic, Attorney, Awhile, Bluette, Brachyology, Breviate, Cape, Compact, →CONCISE, Counsel, Curt, Dossier, Ephemeral, Fleeting, In a word, Inform, Instruct, King's, Laconic, Lawyer, Legal eagle, Nearly, Nutshell, Pants, Papal, Pennorth, Pithy, Precise, Prime, Scant, →SHORT(EN), Short-term, Short-winded, Sitrep, Sparse, Succinct, Summing, Tanga, Terse, Transient, Undershorts, Undies, Update, Watching

Brigade Anchor Boys, Boys', Corps, Fire, International, Red, Troop

Bright(ness) Afterglow, Alert, Bertha, Brainbox, Brainy, Breezy, Brilliant, Brisk, Cheery, Chiarezza, Chipper, Clara, Cla(i)re, Clear, Clever, Cuthbert, Danio, Effulgent, Eileen, Elaine, Ellie, Fair, Floodlit, Florid, Garish, Gay, Glad, Glary, Glow, Hono(u)r, Hubert, Light, Lit, Loud, Lucent, Lucid, Luculent, Luminous, Lustre, Net(t), Nit, Nitid, Radiant, Roarie, Ro(a)ry, Rosy, Scintillating, Sematic, Sharp, Sheeny, Sheer, Shere, Skyre, Smart, Splendour, Starry, Stilb, Sunlit, Sunny, Vive, Vivid, White, Zara

Brilliant, Brilliance Ace, Aine, Blaze, Brainy, Bravura, Bright, Def, Effulgent, Eurian, Fantastic, Flashy, Galaxy, Gay, Gemmy, Gifted, Glitter, Glossy, High flyer, Humdinger, Inspired, Irradiance, Lambent, Leam, Lustre, Masterstroke, Mega-, Meteoric, Nitid, Pear, →RADIANT, Refulgent, Resplendent, Shiny, Spangle, Splendid, Splendour, Star, Superb, Virtuoso, →VIVID, Water

Brim Edge, Lip, Rim, Ugly

Brine Muriatic, Ozone, Pickle, Saline, Salt

Bring Afferent, Bear, Carry, Cause, Conduct, Convey, Deploy, Earn, Evoke, Fet, Fetch, Hatch, Induce, Land, Precipitate, Produce, Wreak, Yield

Bring up Breed, Educate, Exhume, Foster, Nurture, Raise, → **REAR**

Brisk(ly), Briskness Active, Alacrity, Alert, Allegro, Breezy, Busy, Cant, Chipper, Con moto, Crank, Crisp, Crouse, Fresh, Gaillard, Galliard, Jaunty, Kedge, Kedgy, Kidge, Lively, Nippy, Perk, Pert, Rattling, Roaring, Scherzo, Sharp, Skelp, Smacking, Smart, Snappy, Spanking, Spirited, Sprightly, Vivace, Yare, Zippy

Bristle, Bristling, Bristly Arista, Awn, Barb, Bewhiskered, Birse, Bridle, Chaeta, En brosse, Flurry, Fraught, Frenulum, Gooseflesh, Hackles, Hair, Hérissé, Horripilation, Seta, Setose, Striga, Strigose, Stubble, Vibraculum, Villus, Whisker

Brit(ish), Briton(s) Anglo, Herring, Iceni, Insular, Isles, Limey, Pict, Pom, Rooinek, Rosbif, Saxon, Silt, Silurian, UK

Britain Alban(y), Albion, Old Dart

Brittle Bruckle, Crackly, Crimp, Crisp, Delicate, Edgy, → **FRAGILE**, Frangible, Frush, Redsear, Shivery, Spall, Spalt

▷**Brittle** *may indicate* an anagram

Broach Approach, Open, Raise, Spit, Suggest, Tap, Widen

Broad(ly) Beamy, Cheesy, Crumpet, Dame, Doll, Doxy, Drab, Eclectic, Gaping, General, Generic, Hippy, Largo, Latitudinous, Loose, Outspoken, Ovate, Pro, Roomy, Spatulate, Tart, Thick, Tolerant, Wide, Woman

Broadcast(er), Broadcasting Ad(vertise), Air, Announce, Beam, Breaker, Broadband, CB, Disclose, Disperse, Disseminate, DJ, Emission, Ham, IBA, Joyce, Monophonic, Multicast, Narrowband, OB, On, Outside, Pirate, Programme, Promulgate, Public address, Put out, Radiate, Radio, Reith, Relay, RTE, Run, → **SCATTER**, Scattershot, Screen(ed), SECAM, Seed, Send, Sky, Sow, Sperse, Sportscast, Spread, Sprinkle, Stereophonic, Telebridge, Telethon, Transmission, Veejay, Ventilate, Wavelength, Wireless

Brochure Booklet, Leaflet, Pamphlet, Prospectus, Throwaway, Tract, Travelogue

Broke(n) Badly off, Bankrupt, Boracic, Bust(ed), Duff, Evans, Fragmentary, Fritz, Insolvent, Kaput, Puckeroo, Shattered, Skint, Stony, Stove, Strapped

▷**Broken** *may indicate* an anagram

Broker Agent, Banian, Banyan, Discount, Go-between, Government, Insurer, Jobber, Mediator, → **MERCHANT**, Power, Shadchan, Uncle

Bronze(d), Bronze age Aeneous, Aluminium, Bell, Bras(s), Brown, Corinthian, Gunmetal, Hallstatt(ian), Helladic, Minoan, Mycenean, Ormolu, Phosphor, Schillerspar, Sextans, Suntanned, Talos, Tan, Third, Torso

Brooch Breastpin, Cameo, Clasp, Fibula, Luckenbooth, Ouch, Owche, Pin, Plaque, Preen, Prop, Spang, Sunburst

Brood(y) Clecking, Clock, Clutch, Cogitate, Contemplate, Cour, Cover, Covey, Dwell (on), Eyas, Eye, Eyrie, Hatch, Hover, Incubate, Introspect, Kindle, Litter, Meditate, Mill, Mope, Mull, Nest, Nid, Nyas, Perch, Pet, → **PONDER**, Repine, Roost, Sit, Sulk, Team

Brook Babbling, Beck, Branch, Burn, Countenance, Creek, Endure, Ghyll, Gill, Kerith, Kill, Pirl, Purl, Rill(et), River, Rivulet, Runlet, Runnel, Springlet, Stand, Stomach, Stream, Suffer, Thole, Tolerate, Wear

Broom Besom, Brush, Butcher's, Cow, Genista, Gorse, Greenweed, Hog, Knee-holly, Kow, Orobranche, Plantagenet, Retama, Spart, Sweeper, Whisk

Broth Bouillon, Bree, Brew(is), Court bouillon, Cullis, Dashi, Gruel, Kail, Kale, Muslin-kale, Pottage, Ramen, Scotch, Skilly, → **SOUP**, Stock

Brothel Bagnio, Bawdy-house, Bordel(lo), Cathouse, Corinth, Crib, Den, Honkytonk, Hothouse, Kip, Knocking shop, Leaping-house, Seraglio, Sporting house, Stew

Brother(s), Brotherhood Ally, Bhai, Billie, Billy, Blood, Brer, Brethren, Bro, Bud, Comrade, Félibre, Fellow, Fra, Freemason, Grimm, Guild, Lay, Marx, →**MONK**, Moose, My, Plymouth, Sib(ling), Theatine, Trappist, Worker

Brow Crest, Forehead, Glabella, Knitted, Ridge, Sinciput, Superciliary, Tump-line

Brown(ed) Abram, Adust, Amber, Auburn, Bay, Biscuit, Bisque, Bister, Bistre, Bole, Br, Braise, Brindle, Bronzed, Brunette, Bruno, Burnet, Camel, Capability, Caramel, Caromel, Centennial, Chocolate, Cinnamon, Cocoa, Cook, Coromandel, Drab, Dun, Duncan, Fallow, Filemot, Fulvous, Fusc(ous), Grill, Hazel, Ivor, John, Khaki, Liver, Meadow, Mocha, Mousy, Mulatto, Mushroom, Nut, Oatmeal, Philamot, Pygmalion, Rufous, Rugbeian, Russet, Rust, Sallow, Sand, Scorch, Sepia, Sienna, Snuff, Soare, Sore, Sorrel, Spadiceous, Tan, Tawny, Tenné, Tenny, Terracotta, Testaceous, Toast, Tom, Umber, Vandyke, Wallflower, Walnut, Wholemeal, Windsor

Browse(r) Eland, Graze, Mouch, Pasture, Read, Scan, Stall-read, Surf, Tapir

Bruise Black eye, Clour, Contund, Contuse, Crush, Damage, Ding, Ecchymosis, Frush, Golp(e), Haematoma, Hurt, Intuse, Livedo, Lividity, Mark, Mouse, Pound, Purpure, Rainbow, Shiner, Ston(n), Stun, Surbate, Vibex

Brush (off), Brushed, Brushwood Bavin, Brake, Broom, Carbon, Caudate, Chaparral, Clash, Clothes, Dandy, Dismiss, Dust, Encounter, Fan, Filbert, Filecard, Firth, Fitch, Foxtail, Frith, Grainer, Hag, Hagg, Hair-pencil, Hog, Kiss, Liner, Lip, Loofa(h), Mop, Paint, Pallet, Pig, Pope's head, Putois, Rebuff, Rice, Rigger, Sable, Scrap, Scrub, Scuff, Shaving, Skim, Skirmish, Striper, Sweep, Tail, Thicket, Touch, Undergrowth, Wipe

Brutal(ity), Brute Animal, Atrocity, Beast, Bestial, Bête, Caesar, Caliban, Cruel, Down and dirty, Gorilla, Hun, Iguanodon, Inhuman, Nazi, Nero, Ostrogoth, Pitiless, Quagga, Rottweiler, Roughshod, Ruffian, Stupid, Thresher-whale, Torture, Yahoo

Bubble(s), Bubbly Aeration, Air-bell, Air-lock, Air pocket, Barmy, Bead(ed), Bell, Bleb, Blister, Boil, Bright, Buller, Cavitate, Champagne, Champers, Cissing, Ebullition, Effervesce, Embolus, Enthuse, Espumoso, Fizz, Foam, →**FROTH**, Gassy, Globule, Gloop, Gurgle, Head, Mantle, Mississippi, Moet, Perrier, Popple, Rale, Reputation, Roundel, Rowndell, Seed, Seethe, Simmer, Soap, South Sea, Vesicle, Widow

Buck (up) Bongo, Brace, Cheer, Dandy, Deer, Dollar, Elate, Encheer, Hart, Jerk, Leash, Male, Ourebi, Pitch, Pricket, Ram, Rusa, Sore, Sorel(l), Sorrel, Spade, Spay(a)d, Staggard, Stud, Wheel

Bucket(s) Bail, Bale, Clamshell, Dipper, Ice, Kibble, Ladle, Noria, Pail, Pelt, Piggin, Rain, Scuttle, Situla, Stoop(e), Stope, Stoup, Tub

Buckle Artois, Bend, Clasp, Contort, Crumple, Deform, Dent, Fasten, Give, Warp

▷**Buckle** *may indicate* an anagram

▷**Bucks** *may indicate* an anagram

Bucolic Aeglogue, Eglogue, Idyllic, Pastoral, Rural, Rustic

Bud(ding), Buddy Botoné, Bottony, Bulbil, Burgeon, Cacotopia, Caper, Clove, Cobber, Deb, Eye, Gem(ma), Germinate, Hibernaculum, Knosp, Knot, Nascent, Pal, Scion, Serial, Shoot, Sprout, Statoblast, Taste, Turion

Buddha, Buddhism, Buddhist Abhidhamma, Ahimsa, Amitabha, Anata, Anicca, Arhat, Asoka, Bardo, Bodhisattva, Dalai Lama, Gautama, Hinayana, Jain, Jataka, Jodo, Mahatma, Mahayana, Maitreya, Maya, Pali, Pitaka, Pure Land, Sakya-muni, Satori, Sila, Sima, Soka Gakkai, Sutra, Tantric, Theravada, Tripitaka, Triratna, Zen(o)

Budge Jee, Move, Shift, Stir, Submit

Budget(ary) Allot, Cheap, Estimate, Fiscal, Plan, Programme, Rudder, Save, Shoestring

Buff Altogether, Beige, Birthday suit, Blind man's, Cineaste, Eatanswill, Expert, Fan, Fawn, Maven, Mavin, Nankeen, Natural, Nude, Nut, Polish, → **RUB**, Streak

Buffalo African, Anoa, Arna, Asiatic, Bison, Bonasus, Bugle, Cap, Cape, Carabao, Obstinacy, Ox, Perplex, Takin, Tamarao, Tamarau, Timarau, Water, Zamouse

Buffer Bootblack, Cofferdam, Cutwater, Fender

Buffet Bang, Blow, Box, Counter, Cuff, Fork luncheon, Fork-supper, Hit, Lam, Maltreat, Meal, Perpendicular, Shove, Sideboard, Smorgasborg, Strike, Strook(e), Thwack

Bug(s) Ambush, Annoy, Antagonise, Arthropod, Assassin, Bacteria, Beetle, Bishop's mitre, Bunny, Cabbage, Capsid, Chinch, Cicada, Cimex, Cockchafer, Creepy-crawly, Croton, Damsel, Debris, Demon, Dictograph®, Eavesdrop, E-coli, Entomology, Error, Exasperate, Flea, Get at, Gremlin, Harlequin, Hassle, → **INSECT**, Irritate, Jitter, June, Kissing, Lace, May, Mealy, Micrococcus, Microphone, Midge, Mike, Milkweed, Millennium, Mite, Nark, Pest(er), Rile, Sow, Squash, Tap, Termite, Vex, Virus, Water-measurer, Wheel, Wiretap

Buggy Beach, Car, Cart, Inside-car, Shay, Tipcart, Trap

Bugle, Bugle call Boots and saddles, Chamade, Clarion, Cornet, Flugelhorn, Hallali, Kent, Last post, Ox, Reveille, Taps, → **TRUMPET**, Urus

Build (up), Building(s), Building site, Build-up Accrue, Aggrade, Ar(a)eostyle, Assemble, Barn, Basilica, Bathhouse, Big, Boathouse, Brick-laying, Bricks and mortar, Capitol, Chapterhouse, Cob, Colosseum, Commons, Construction, Containment, Corncrib, Cot, → **CREATE**, Cruck, Curia, Days' house, Develop, Dome, Drystone, Duplex, Ectomorph, Edifice, Edify, Endomorph, Erect, Exchange, Fabric, Gain, Gatehouse, Gazebo, Granary, Guildhall, Hangar, Heapstead, High-rise, Hut, Infill, Insula, Kaaba, Ken, Linhay, Listed, Lodge, Low-rise, Lyceum, Malting, Mansion, Mesomorph, Minaret, Mosque, Mould, Observatory, Odeon, Odeum, Outhouse, Palace, Palazzo, Pataka, Pavilion, Pentagon, Pentastyle, Phalanx, Physique, Pile, Plaque, Portakabin®, Premises, Quonset®, Raise, Rectory, Ribbon, Rotunda, Shippen, Skyscraper, Somatotype, Squat, Stance, Statehouse, Stature, Structure, Summerhouse, Suspension, Synthesis, System, Systyle, Tectonic, Telecottage, Temple, Tenement, Terrapin®, Tower, Tower block, Town hall, Whata, Wheelhouse

▷**Building** *may indicate* an anagram

Bulb Camas(h), Chive, Cive, Corm, Garlic, Globe, Lamp, Light, Pearl, Scallion, Set, Shallot, Squill

Bulge, Bulging Astrut, Bag, Bias, Biconvex, Bug, Bulbous, Bunchy, Cockle, Entasis, Expand, Exsert, Inion, Node, Prolate, Protrude, Relievo, Rotund, Shoulder, Strout, Strut, → **SWELL**, Torose, Tumid

Bulk(y) Aggregate, Ample, Big, Body, Bouk, Coerce, Corpulent, Domineer, Edict, Extent, Gross, Hull, Immensity, Lofty, Massive, Peak, Pester, Preponderance, Roughage, Scalar, → **SIZE**, Stout, Threaten, Vol(ume), Voluminous, Weight

Bull(s), Bullock, Bully(ing) Abuser, Anoa, Apis, Beef, Blarney, Bluster, Bouncer, Bovine, Brag, Brave, Browbeat, Bucko, Centre, Cuttle, Despot, Dragoon, Drawcansir, Englishman, Fancyman, Farnese, Flashman, Flatter, Gold, Gosh, Hapi, Harass, Haze(r), Hector, Hibernicism, Hogwash, Hoodlum, Huff, Intimidate, Investor, Irish(ism), John, Killcow, Lambast, Maltreat, Menace, Mick(e)(y), Mistake, Mithraism, Mohock, Neat, Oppressor, Ox, Papal, Pennalism, Piker, Pistol, Placet, Poler, Pussy-whip, Railroad, Rhodian, Roarer, Rot, Ruffian, Sitting, Stag, Strong-arm, Swash-buckler, Taurine, Taurus, Tommy-rot, Tosh, Trash, Tripe, Twaddle, Tyran(ne), Tyrannise, Tyrant, Victimise, Zo(bo)

Bulldoze(r) Coerce, Earthmover, Flatten, Leveller, Overturn, Raze

Bullet Balata, Ball, Biscayan, Blank, Dumdum, Fusillade, Lead towel, Minié, Minié ball, Missile, Pellet, Plastic, Round, Rubber, Shot, Slug, Tracer

Bulletin All points, Memo, Newscast, Newsletter, News sheet, Report, Summary, Update

Bull-fight(er), Bull-fighting Banderillero, Banderillo, Corrida, Cuadrilla, Encierro, Escamillo, Faena, Mano a mano, Matador, Picador, Rejoneador, Tauromachy, Toreador, Torero

Bulwark Bastion, Defence, Rampart, Resistor

Bum Ass, Beg, Beggar, Cadge, Deadbeat, Prat, Scrounge, Sponge, Thumb, Tramp, Vagabond

Bump(er), Bumps, Bumpy Barge, Big, Blow, Bouncer, Bucket, Bustle, Cannon, Clour, Collide, Dunch, Fender, Hillock, Immense, Impact, Inian, Inion, Jo(u)le, Joll, Jolt, Jostle, Jowl, Keltie, Kelty, Knar, Knock, Large, Mamilla, Mogul, Nudge, Organ, Phrenology, Reveille, Rouse, Speed, Supernaculum, Thump, Twitter, Uneven

Bumpkin Bucolic, Bushwhacker, Clodhopper, Hawbuck, Hayseed, Hick, Jock, Lout, Oaf, Peasant, Put(t), Rube, Rustic, Yokel, Zany

Bun Barmbrack, Bath, Chelsea, Chignon, Chou, Cookie, Hot-cross, Huffkin, Mosbolletjie, Roll, Teacake, Toorie, Wad

Bunch Acinus, Anthology, Bob, Botryoid, Cluster, Fascicle, Finial, Flock, Gang, → GROUP, Hand, Handful, Ilk, Lot, Lump, Panicle, Posy, Raceme, Spray, Staphyline, Tassel, Tee, Truss, Tuft, Tussie-mussie, Tussock

Bundle(d) Axoneme, Bale, Bavin, Bluey, Bottle, Byssus, Desmoid, Dorlach, Drum, Fag(g)ot, Fascicle, Fasciculate, Fascine, Fibre, Fibrovascular, Kemple, Knitch, Lemniscus, Matilda, → PACK(AGE), Parcel, Sack, Sheaf, Shiralee, Shock, Shook, Stela, Stook, Swag, Tie, Top, Trousseau, Truss, Vascular, Wad, Wadge, Wap, Yealm

Bungle(r), Bungled, Bungling Awkward, Blunder, Blunk, Bodge, Boob, Boss shot, Botch, Bumble, Bummle, Duff, Fluff, Foozle, Foul, Goof, Gum up, Maladroit, Mess, Mis(h)guggle, Muddle, Muff, Mull, Prat, Screw, Spoil, Tinker

Bunk(er), Bunk off, Bunkum Abscond, Absquatulate, Balderdash, Baloney, Berth, Blah, Bolt, Casemate, Claptrap, Clio, Decamp, Entrap, Flit, Guff, Guy, Hazard, History, Hogwash, Hokum, Hooey, Humbug, Malarky, Moonlight flit, Moonshine, Rot, Scuttle, Skive, Tommy-rot, Tosh, Trap, Tripe, Truant, Twaddle

Bunting Bird, Cirl, Flag, Fringilline, Ortolan, Pennant, Snow, Streamer, Tanager, Towhee, Yellow-hammer, Yowley

Buoy (up) Bell, Breeches, Can, Dan, Daymark, Dolphin, Float, Marker, Nun, Raft, Reassure, Ring, Seamark, Sonar, Sustain

Buoyancy, Buoyant Blithe, Floaty, Mae West, Resilient

Burden Albatross, Beare, Bob, Brunt, Cargo, Cark, Chant, Chorus, Cross, Cumber, Drone, Droore, Encumber, Encumbrance, Fa-la, Fardel, Folderol, Fraught, Freight, Gist, Handicap, Hardship, Hum, Lade, →**LOAD**, Lumber, Millstone, Monkey, Oercome, Onus, Oppress, Payload, Put-upon, Refrain, Rumbelow, Saddle, Servitude, Shanty, Substance, Task, Tax, Tenor, Theme, Torch, Tote, Trouble, Weight, White man's, Woe, Yoke

Burdensome Deere, Irksome, Onerous, Oppressive, Weighty

Bureau Agency, Agitprop, Breakfront, Cominform, Davenport, Desk, Interpol, Kominform, Marriage, →**OFFICE**, Weather

Bureaucracy, Bureaucrat(ic) Apparatchik, Bean-counter, Bumbledom, CS, Functionary, Impersonal, Jack-in-office, Mandarin, Red tape, Tapist, Technocrat, Wallah

Burgeon(ing) Asprout, Bud, Grow, Sprout, Swell

Burgh Burrowstown, Parliamentary, Police, Royal

Burglar(y), Burgle Aggravated, Area-sneak, Break-in, Cat, Crack(sman), Intruder, Peterman, Picklock, Raffles, Robber, Screw, Thief, Yegg

Burial (place) Catacomb, Charnel, Committal, Crypt, Darga(h), Funeral, Golgotha, Grave, Green, Interment, Kurgan, Lair, Last rites, Pyramid, Sepulture, Speos, Tholos, Tomb, Vault, Vivisepulture, Zoothapsis

Burlesque Caricatura, Caricature, Comedy, Farce, Heroicomical, Hudibrastic(s), Hurlo-thrumbo, Lampoon, Macaronic, Parody, Satire, Skimmington, Skit, Spoof, Travesty

Burma, Burmese Karen(ni), Mon(-Khmer), Myanmar, Naga, Shan

Burn(ed), Burner, Burning, Burnt Ablaze, Adust, Afire, Alow(e), Ardent, Argand, Arson, Ash, Auto-da-fé, Back, Bake, Bats-wing, Beck, Bishop, Blaze, Blister, Blowlamp, Blush, Brand, Brazier, Brent, Brook(let), Bunsen, Caustic, Cauterise, Char, Chark, Chinese, Cinder, Clavie, Coal, Coke, Combust, Conflagration, Cremate, Crucial, Destruct, Effigy, Eilding, Ember, Emboil, Fervid, →**FIRE**, First degree, Fishtail, Flagrant, Flambe, Flare, Flash, Frazzle, Fresh(et), Gleed, Gut, Holocaust, Ignite, In, Incendiary, Incinerate, Intense, Inure, Inust(ion), Itch, Kill, Lean, Live, Lunt, Moorburn, Muirburn, Offering, On, Phlogiston, Pilot, Raster, Rill, Runnel, Sati, Scald, Scaud, Scorch, Scouther, Scowder, Scowther, Sear, Sienna, Singe, Smart, Smoulder, Sore, Stake, Suttee, Swale, Thurible, Torch, Umber, Urent, Ustion, Wick, Ybrent

Burrow(er), Burrowing Dig, Earth, Earthworm, Fossorial, Gopher, Groundhog, Hole, Holt, How, Howk, Mine, Mole, Nuzzle, Sett, Terricole, Tunnel, Viscacha, Warren, Wombat, Worm

Bursar(y) Camerlengo, Camerlingo, Coffers, Grant, Purser, Scholarship, Tertiary, Treasurer

Burst(ing), Bursts Blowout, Bout, Brast, Break, Dehisce, Disrupt, Dissilient, Ebullient, Erumpent, Erupt, →**EXPLODE**, Fits and starts, Fly, Gust, Implode, Pop, Salvo, Sforzato, Shatter, Spasm, Spirt, Split, Sprint, Spurt, Stave, Tetterous

Bury Conceal, Cover, Eard, Earth, Embowel, Engrave, Enhearse, Entomb, Graff, Graft, Imbed, Inhearse, Inherce, Inhume, Inter, Inurn, Landfill, Repress, Sepulture, Sink, Ye(a)rd, Yird

Bus Aero, Bandwagon, Car, Charabanc, Coach, Crew, Double-decker, Highway, Hondey, Hopper, ISA, Jitney, Mammy-wagon, Purdah, Rattletrap, Single-decker, Tramcar, Trolley, Trunk

Bush(es), Bush-man, Bushy Aloe, Bitou, Bramble, Brier, Bullace, Busket, Calico, Clump, Cotton, Creosote, Dumose, Firethorn, Furze, Glib, Greasewood,

Hawthorn, Hedge, Hibiscus, Ivy-tod, Jaborandi, Kapok, Kiekie, Mallee, Matagouri, Mulberry, Outback, Pachysandra, Poinsettia, Poly-poly, President, Prostanthera, Sallee, San, Scrog, Shepherd, Shrub, Sloe, Sloethorn, Sugar, Thicket, Tire, Tod(de), Tumatakuru

Bushel Co(o)mb, Homer, Peck, Weight, Wey

Business Affair, Agency, Biz, Bricks and clicks, Brokerage, Bus, Cahoot, Cartel, Cerne, Chaebol(s), Co, Commerce, Company, Concern, Conglomerate, Corporate, Craft, Custom, Dealership, Duty, Enterprise, Ergon, Establishment, Exchange, Fasti, Field, Firm, Funny, Game, Gear, Goings on, Hong, Industry, Kaizen, Lifestyle, Line, Métier, Monkey, Office, Palaver, Pidgin, Pi(d)geon, Practice, Professional, Racket, Shebang, Shop, Show, Thick, To-do, Trade, Traffic, Transaction, Tread, Turnover, Unincorporated, Vocation, Wall Street, Zaibatsu, Zaikai

Businessman Babbitt, Baron, City, Dealer, Fat-cat, Realtor, Taipan, Trader, Tycoon

Busk(er) Bodice, Corset, Entertainer, German-band

Bust Beano, Boob, Brast, Break, Chest, Dollarless, Falsies, Fold, Herm(a), Kaput, Mamma, Penurious, Raid, Rupture, Sculp, Shatter(ed), Skint, Spree, Statue, Swoop, Term(inus), To-tear, To-torne, Ups(e)y

▷**Bust** *may indicate* an anagram

Bustle Ado, Do, Flap, Fuss, Pad, Scurry, → **STIR**, Swarm, To-do, Tournure, Whew

Busy Active, At (it), Deedy, → **DETECTIVE**, Dick, Doing, Eident, Employ, Engaged, Ergate, Eventful, Eye, Goer, Hectic, Hive, Hot spot, Humming, Manic, Occupied, Operose, Ornate, Prodnose, Stir, Stirabout, Tec, Throng, Worksome

Busybody Bee, Bustler, Meddler, Pantopragmatic, Snooper, Trout, Yenta

But Aber, Algates, Bar, Except, However, Merely, Nay, Only, Save, Sed, Simply, Tun, Without, Yet

Butcher(s), Butchery Cumberland, Decko, Dekko, Eyeful, Flesher, Gander, Glimpse, Ice, Kill, Killcow, Look, Looksee, Mangle, Massacre, Ovicide, Peek, Sever, Shambles, Shochet, Shufti, Slaughter, Slay, Slink

Butler Bedivere, Bread-chipper, Crichton, Jeeves, RAB, Rhett, Samuel, Servant, Sewer, Sommelier, Steward

Butt (in) April fool, Aris, Arse, Ass, Barrel, Buns, Bunt, Clara, Dout, Dowt, Enter, Geck, Glasgow kiss, Goat, Header, Horn, Interject, Jesting-stock, Laughing-stock, Mark, Outspeckle, Pantaloon, Pipe, Push, Ram, Roach, Scapegoat, Snipe, Straight man, Stump, Target, Tun, Ups

Butter Adulation, Apple, Beurre, Billy, Blandish, Brandy, Butyric, Cacao, Cocoa, Coconut, Drawn, Flatter, Galam, Garcinia, Ghee, Ghi, Goat, Illipi, Illupi, Kokum, Malua, Mahwa, Mow(r)a, Nutter, Palm, Pat, Peanut, Print, Ram, Rum, Scrape, Shea, Spread

▷**Butter** *may indicate* a goat or such

Buttercup Crowfoot, Crow-toe, Goldilocks, Ranunculus, Reate, Thalictrum

Butterflies, Butterfly Apollo, Argus, Birdwing, Blue, Brimstone, Brown, Cabbage white, Camberwell beauty, Cardinal, Chequered skipper, Cleopatra, Clouded yellow, Collywobbles, Comma, Common blue, Copper, Dilettante, Eclosion, Elfin, Emperor, Fritillary, Gate-keeper, Gatemen, Grayling, Hair-streak, Heath, Hesperid, Imaginal, Kaleidoscope, Kallima, Large copper, Large white, Leaf, Marbled-white, Meadow brown, Metalmark, Milk-weed, Monarch, Morpho, Mountain ringlet, Nerves, Orange-tip, Owl, Painted lady,

Peacock, Pieris, Psyche, Purple emperor, Red admiral, Ringlet, Scotch argus, Silverspot, Skipper, Small white, Snake's head, Speckled wood, Stamper, Stroke, Sulphur, Swallow-tail, Thecla, Thistle, Tiger swallowtail, Tortoiseshell, Two-tailed pasha, Umber, Vanessa, Wall brown, White admiral

Buttocks Aristotle, Arse, Ass, Bahookie, Bottom, Buns, Cheeks, Coit, Derrière, Doup, Duff, Fud, Fundament, Gluteus maximus, Heinie, Hinderlan(d)s, Hunkers, Hurdies, Jacksie, Jacksy, Keester, Keister, Nates, Posterior, Prat, Quatch, Quoit, Seat

Button(s) Barrel, Bellboy, Buzzer, Fastener, Frog, Hold, Hot, Knob, Mescal, Mouse, Netsuke, Olivet, Page(boy), Panic, Pause, Press, Snooze, Stud, Switch, Toggle, Toolbar

Buttonhole Accost, Carnation, Detain, Doorstep, Eye, Flower

Buttress Brace, Counterfort, Pier, Prop, Reinforce, Stay, Support

Buy(ing), Buyer, Buy off Accept, Believe, Bribe, Coemption, Coff, Corner, Customer, Emption, Engross, Monopsonist, Munich, Purchase, Redeem, Shop, Shout, Spend, Take, Trade, Treat, Vendee

▷**Buyer** *may indicate* money

Buzz(er) Bee, Birr, Bombilate, Bombinate, Button, Drone, Fly, Hum, Kazoo, Kick, Rumour, Scram, Whirr, Whisper, Zed, Zing, Zoom

Buzzard Bee-kite, Bird, Buteo, Hawk, Honey, Pern, Puttock, Turkey, Vulture

By Alongside, At, Beside, Gin, Gone, In, Near, Neighbouring, Nigh, Of, On, Past, Per, Through, With, X

Bye-bye Adieu, Farewell, Tata

Bygone Dead, Departed, Past, Yore

Bypass Avoid, Beltway, Circuit, Coronary, →**DETOUR**, Dodge, Evade, Ignore, Omit, Ring-road, Shunt, Skirt

By-product Epiphenomenon, Spill-over, Spin-off

Byre Cowshed, Manger, Stable, Trough

Byway Alley, Lane, Path

Byword Ayword, Nayword, Phrase, Proverb, Slogan

▷**Byzantine** *may indicate* an anagram

Cc

C Around, Caught, Celsius, Cent, Centigrade, Charlie, Conservative, San

Cab Boneshaker, Crawler, Drosky, Fiacre, Growler, Hackney, Hansom, Mini, Noddy, Taxi, Vettura

Cabbage(-head), Cabbage soup Black, Bok choy, Borecole, Brassica, Castock, Cauliflower, Chinese (leaf), Chinese leaves, Chou, Choucroute, Cole, Collard, Crout, Gobi, Kohlrabi, Kraut, Loaf, Loave, Mibuna, Mizuna, Pak-choi, Pamphrey, St Patrick's, Sauerkraut, Savoy, Sea-kale, Thieve, Turnip, Wort

Cabin Berth, Bibby, Bothy, Box, Cabana, Caboose, Camboose, Coach, Cottage, Crannog, Crib, Cuddy, Den, Gondola, Hovel, Hut, Izba, Lodge, Long-house, Room, Roundhouse, Saloon, Shack, Shanty, Signal box, Stateroom

Cabinet Armoire, Bahut, Cabale, Case, Cellaret, Chiffonier, Chill(er), Closet, Commode, Console, Cupboard, Display, Encoignure, Kitchen, Locker, Ministry, Nest, Official family, Repository, Secretaire, Shadow, Shrinal, Unit, Vitrine

Cable(way), Cable-car Arrester, Choucroute, Coax(ial), Extension, Flex, Halser, Hawser, Jump leads, Junk, Kissagram, Landline, Lead, Lead-in, Lifeline, Outhaul, Outhauler, Rope, Shroud, Slatch, Téléférique, →**TELEGRAM**, Telpher(age), Towrope, Vine, Wire

Cackle Cluck, Gaggle, Gas, Haw, Horse laugh, Snicker, Titter

Cactus, Cactus-like Alhagi, Barel, Cereus, Cholla, Christmas, Dildo, Easter, Echino-, Hedgehog, Jointed, Jojoba, Maguey, Mescal, Mistletoe, Nopal, Ocotillo, Ombrophobe, Opuntia, Organ-pipe, Peyote, Pita(ha)ya, Prickly pear, Retama, Saguaro, Schlumbergera, Star, Torch-thistle, Tuna, Xerophytic

Cad Base, Boor, Bounder, Churl, Cocoa, Heel, Oik, Rascal, Rotter, Skunk, Varlet

Cadaver(ous) Body, Corpse, Emaciated, Ghastly, Haggard, Stiff

Cadence Authentic, Beat, Close, Fa-do, Flow, Interrupted, Lilt, Meter, Plagal, Rhythm

Cadet(s) Junior, OTC, Plebe, Recruit, Rookie, Scion, Snooker, Space, Syen, Trainee

Café, Cafeteria Automat, Bistro, Brasserie, Buvette, Canteen, Carvery, Commissary, Diner, Dinette, Donko, Estaminet, Filtré, Greasy spoon, Juke joint, Netcafé, Noshery, Pizzeria, Pull-in, Snackbar, Tearoom, Tea-shop, Transport, Truckstop

Cage Aviary, Bar, Battery, Box, Cavie, Confine, Coop, Corf, Dray, Drey, Enmew, Faraday, Fold, Frame, Grate, Hutch, Mew, Mortsafe, Pen, →**PRISON**, Roll, Trave

Cake Agnus dei, Angel, Baba, Babka, Baklava, Banbury, Bannock, Bara brith, Barm(brack), Battenberg, Bhaji, Biffin, Birthday, Black bun, Brandy snap, Brioche, Brownie, Buckwheat, Bun, Carcake, Cattle, Chapat(t)i, Chillada, Chupati, Chupattie, Chupatty, Clapbread, Clot, Coburg, Cookie, Corn dodger, Cotton, Croquante, Croquette, Cruller, Crumpet, Currant, Dainty, Devil's food, Drizzle, Dundee, Eccles, Eclair, Falafel, Fancy, Farl(e), Filter, Fish, Flapjack,

Frangipane, Frangipani, Fritter, Galette, Gateaux, Genoa, Gingerbread, Girdle, Griddle, →**HARDEN**, Hockey, Hoe, Idli, Jaffa, Jannock, Johnny, Jumbal, Jumbles, Koeksister, Kruller, Kuchen, Kueh, Lady's finger, Lamington, Lardy, Latke, Layer, Linseed, Macaroon, Madeira, Madeleine, Maid of honour, Marble, Meringue, Millefeuille, Moon, Mooncake, Mud, Muffin, Napoleon, Nut, Oatmeal, Oil, Pan, Panettone, Paratha, Parkin, Parliament, Pastry, Pat, Patty, Pavlova, Pepper, Petit four, Pikelet, →**PLASTER**, Pomfret, Pone, Pontefract, Poori, Popover, Potato, Pound, Profiterole, Puff, Puftaloon(a), Puri, Queencake, Ratafia, Ready-mix, Religieuse, Rice, Rock, Rosti, Roti, Rout, Rum baba, Rusk, Sachertorte, Saffron, Sally Lunn, Salt, Sandwich, Savarin, Scone, Seed, Set, Simnel, Singing-hinny, Slab, Slapjack, Soap, Soul, Spawn, Spice, Sponge, Stollen, Stottie, Sushi, Swiss roll, Tablet, Tansy, Tea(bread), Tipsy, Torte, Tortilla, Twelfth, Upside down, Vetkoek, Wad, Wafer, Waffle, Wedding, Wonder, Yeast, Yule log
▷**Cake** *may indicate* an anagram

Calculate(d), Calculation, Calculator Abacus, Actuary, Arithmetic, Comptometer, Compute(r), Cost, Design, Estimate, Extrapolate, Four-function, Log, Number-crunch, Prorate, Quip(p)u, Rate, →**RECKON**, Slide-rule, Sofar, Soroban, Tactical, Tell

Calendar Advent, Agenda, Almanac, Chinese, Diary, Dies fasti, Fasti, Gregorian, Intercalary, Jewish, Journal, Julian, Luach, Menology, Newgate, New Style, Ordo, Perpetual, Planner, Revolutionary, Roman, Sothic

Calf Ass, Bobby, Box, Cf, Deacon, Divinity, Dogie, Dogy, Fatted, Freemartin, Golden, Law, Leg, Mottled, Poddy, Slink, Smooth, Stirk, Sural, Tollie, Tolly, Veal, Vitular

Call(ed), Call (for), Calling, Call on, Call up Adhan, Ahoy, Alew, Appeal, Arraign, Art, Awaken, Azan, Banco, Bawl, Beck(on), Behote, Bevy, Bid, Boots and saddles, Bugle, Business, Buzz, Career, Chamade, Cite, Claim, Clang, Clarion, Cleep, Clepe, Close, Cold, Conference, Conscript, Convene, Convoke, Coo, Cooee, Cry, Curtain, Denominate, Dial, Drift, Dub, Duty, Effectual, Entail, Evoke, First post, Game, Go, Hail, Hallali, Halloa, Halloo, Haro, Heads, Heave-ho, Hech, Heckle, Hete, Hey, Hight, Ho, Hot(e), Howzat, Huddup, Hurra(h), Invocation, Job, Junk, Last (post), Levy, Line, Local, Look in, Margin, Métier, Misère, Mobilise, Mot, Name, Nap, Need, Nemn, Nempt, Niche, Nominate, No trumps, Nuisance, Olé, Page, Phone, Photo, Pop in, Post, Profession, Proo, Pruh, Pursuit, Rechate, Recheat, Retreat, Reveille, Ring, Roll, Rort, Rouse, Route, Sa-sa, Scream, See, Sennet, →**SHOUT**, Shut-out, Slam, Slander, Slogan, Soho, Sola, SOS, STD, Style, Subpoena, Summon(s), Tails, Tally ho, Tantivy, Taps, Telephone, Term, Toho, Toll, Trumpet, Trunk, Turn, Tweet, Visit, Vocation, Waken, Wake-up, War cry, Whoa-ho-ho, Wo ha ho, Yell, Yo, Yodel, Yodle, Yo-ho(-ho), Yoicks, Yoo-hoo

Caller Fresh, Guest, Herring, Inspector, Muezzin, Rep, Traveller, →**VISITOR**

Calm Abate, Allay, Allege, Appease, Assuage, Ataraxy, Composed, Cool, Dead-wind, Dispassionate, Doldrums, Easy, Easygoing, Equable, Equanimity, Even, Eye, Flat, Glassy, Halcyon, Level, Loun(d), Lown(d), Lull, Mellow, Mild, Milden, Millpond, Mollify, Nonchalant, Pacify, Patient, Peaceable, Peaceful, Philosophical, Phlegmatic, Placate, Placid, Quell, Quiet, Raise, Relax(ed), Repose, Restful, Restrained, Sedate, Self-possessed, Seraphic, Serena, Serene, Settle, Sleek, Sober, →**SOOTHE**, Steady, Still(ness), Stilly, Subside, Supercool, Tame, Tranquil(lise), Unruffled, Windless

Camel, Camel train Arabian, Artiodactyla, Bactrian, Beige, Caisson, Colt, Dromedary, Kafila, Llama, Oont, Sopwith, Tulu

Camera, Camera man All-round, Box, Brownie®, Camcorder, Candid, Chambers, Cine, Compact, Digicam, Disc, Dolly, Flash, Gamma, Gatso®, Iconoscope, Image orthicon, Imager, Instant, Kodak®, Lucida, Nannycam, Obscura, Orthicon, Palmcorder, Panoramic, Pantoscope, Periphery, Phone-cam, Pinhole, Point and shoot, Polaroid®, Projectionist, Reflex, Schmidt, SLR, Somascope, Speed, Spycam, Steadicam®, Subminiature, Swing-back, Video

Camouflage(d) Battledress, Conceal, →**DISGUISE**, Mark, Maskirovka, Secret, Unnoticeable, War-dress

▷**Camouflaged** *may indicate an anagram*

Camp(er) Affectation, Aldershot, Auschwitz, Banal, Base, Belsen, Bivouac, Boma, Boot, Buchenwald, Caerleon, Cantonment, Castral, Colditz, Concentration, Coterie, Dachau, David, Death, Depot, D(o)uar, Dumdum, Epicene, Faction, Fat, Flaunt, Gay, Gulag, Happy, Health, High, Holiday, Labour, Laer, La(a)ger, Lashkar, Leaguer, Low, Manyat(t)a, Motor, Nudist, Oflag, Outlie, Peace, Prison, Sect, Side, Site, Siwash, Stagey, Stalag, Stative, Summer, Swagman, Tent, Theatrical, Transit, Treblinka, Valley Forge, Work, Zare(e)ba, Zariba, Zereba, Zeriba

Campaign(er) Activist, Agitate, Barnstorm, Battle, Blitz, Blitzkrieg, Canvass, Crusade, Drive, Enterprise, Field, Gallipoli, Hustings, Jihad, Lobby, Mission, Offensive, Pankhurst, Promotion, Real Ale, Roadshow, Run, Satyagraha, Smear, Stint, Stopes, Strategist, Suffragette, The stump, Vendetta, Venture, Veteran, War, War horse, Warray, Warrey, Whistle-stop, Women's Lib

Can(s) Able, Aerosol, Billy, Bin, Bog, Capable, Churn, Cooler, Dow, Dyke, Gaol, Gents, Headphones, Is able, Jail, John, Jug, Karsy, Kazi, Lav(atory), Loo, May, Nick, Pail, Pitcher, Pot, Preserve, →**PRISON**, Privy, Six-pack, Stir, Tin, Tube

Canada, Canadian Abenaki, Acadian, Bella Bella, Bella Coola, Beothuk, Bois-brûlé, .ca, Canuck, Che(e)chako, Coureur de bois, Dakotan, Dene, Habitans, Heiltsuk, Herring choker, Inuit, Johnny Canuck, Joual, Manitoban, Metis, Micmac, Quebeccer, Quebecker, Québecois, Salishan, Saulteaux

Canal Alimentary, Ampul, Anal, Birth, Caledonian, Channel, Conduit, Corinth, Cruiseway, Da Yunhe, Duct, Duodenum, Ea, Ear, Enteron, Erie, Foss(e), Gota, Grand (Trunk), Grande Terre, Grand Union, Groove, Gut, Haversian, Houston Ship, Kiel, Klong, Labyrinth, Lode, Manchester Ship, Meatus, Midi, Mittelland, Moscow, Navigation, New York State Barge, Oesophagus, Panama, Pharynx, Pipe, Pound, Regent's, Resin, Rhine-Herne, Ring, Root, Sault Sainte Marie, Scala, Schlemm's, Semi-circular, Ship, Shipway, Soo, Spinal, Stone, Suez, Suo, Urethra, Vagina, Vertebral, Waterway, Welland, Zanja

Canal-boat Barge, Fly-boat, Gondola, Vaporetto

Canary Bird, Grass, Prisoner, Roller, Serin, Singer, Yellow

Cancel(led) Abort, Abrogate, Adeem, Annul, Axe, Counteract, Countermand, Cross, Delete, Destroy, Erase, Kill, Negate, Nix, Nullify, Obliterate, Override, Rained off, Red line, Remit, Repeal, Rescind, Retract, Retrait, Revoke, Scratch, Scrub, Undo, Unmake, Void, Wipe

Cancer(ian), Cancerous Big C, Carcinoma, Crab, Curse, Hepatoma, Kaposi's sarcoma, Leukaemia, Lymphoma, Marek's disease, Moon child, Oat-cell, Oncogenic, Tropic, Tumour, Wolf

Candid, Candour Albedo, Blunt, Camera, Forthright, Franchise, Frank, Honesty, Ingenuous, Man-to-man, Open, Round, Straight, Upfront

Candidate(s) Agrege, Applicant, Aspirant, Contestant, Entrant, Field, Literate, Maybe, Nomenklatura, Nominee, Office-seeker, Ordinand, Postulant, Running mate, Short list, Slate, Spoiler, Stalking-horse, Testee

Candied, Candy Angelica, Caramel, Cotton, Eryngo, Eye, Glace, Maple, Rock, Snow, Succade, Sucket, Sugar, →**SWEET**

Candle(stick), Candelabra, Candles Amandine, Bougie, C(i)erge, Chanukiah, Corpse, Dip, Fetch, Girandole, Hanukiah, Jesse, Lampadary, Light, Menorah, New, Padella, Paschal, Pricket, Roman, Rushlight, Sconce, Serge, Shammash, Shammes, Shammosim, Shortsix, Slut, Sperm, Tace, Tallow, Tallow-dip, Taper, Tea-light, Torchère, Tricerion, Vigil light, Wax

▶**Candy** see **CANDIED**

Cane, Caning Arrow, Baculine, Bamboo, Baste, Beat, Birk, Dari, Dhurra, Doura, Dur(r)a, Ferula, Ferule, Goor, Gur, Jambee, Malacca, Narthex, Penang-lawyer, Pointer, Rat(t)an, Rod, Six of the best, Split, Stick, Sugar, Swagger-stick, Swish, Switch, Sword, Swordstick, Tan, Tickler, Vare, Wand, Whangee, Wicker(-work)

Canine Biter, C, Dhole, Dog, Eye-tooth

Cannibal Anthropophagus, Heathen, Long pig, Ogre, Thyestean

Cannon Amusette, Barrage, Basilisk, Bombard, Breechloader, Carom, Carronade, Cascabel, Chaser, Collide, Criterion, Culverin, Demi-culverin, Drake, Falcon, Gun, Howitzer, Kiss, Long-tom, Monkey, Nursery, Oerlikon, Saker, Stern-chaser, Trunnion, Water, Zamboorak, Zomboruk, Zumbooru(c)k

Canny Careful, Frugal, Prudent, Scot, Shrewd, Slee, Sly, Thrifty, Wice, Wily, Wise

Canoe(ist) Bidarka, Bidarkee, Canader, Canadian, Dugout, Faltboat, Kayak, Monoxylon, Montaria, Oomiack, Paddler, Piragua, Pirogue, Rob Roy, Woodskin

Canon(ise) Austin, Brocard, Camera, Chapter, Chasuble, Code, Crab, Criterion, Decree, Honorary, Isidorian, →**LAW**, Line, Mathurin(e), Nocturn, Nursery, Pitaka, Polyphony, Prebendary, Precentor, Premonstrant, Premonstratensian, Regular, Residential, Rota, Round, Rule, Secular, Square, Squier, Squire, Standard, Tenet, Unity, Vice-dean

Canopy Awning, Baldachin, Baldaquin, Chuppah, Ciborium, Dais, Gore, He(a)rse, Huppah, Majesty, Marquee, Marquise, Parapente, Pavilion, Shamiana(h), State, Tabernacle, Tent, Tester, Veranda(h), Virando

Canticle Benedictus, Carol, Nunc dimittis

Canton(ese) Basil, District, Quarter, Tanka

Canvas Awning, Big top, Binca®, Burlap, Drab(b)ler, Found, Lug-sail, Mainsail, Maintopsail, Marquee, Oil-cloth, Paint, Raven's-duck, Reef, →**SAIL**, Square-sail, Staysail, Stuns(ai)l, Tarp(aulin), Tent(age), Trysail, Wigan, Woolpack

Canvass(er), Canvassing Agent, Doorstep, Drum, Electioneer, Mainstreeting, Poll, Press flesh, Solicit

▷**Canvasser** *may indicate* a painter or a camper

Canyon Arroyo, Box, Canada, Coprates, Defile, Grand, Kings, Nal(l)a, Nallah, Ravine

Cap(ped) Abacot, Amorce, Balaclava, Balmoral, Barret, Baseball, Bathing, Bellhop, Bendigo, Ber(r)et, Better, Biggin, Biretta, Black, Blakey, Blue, Blue-bonnet, Bonnet-rouge, Bycoket, Call, Calotte, Calpac(k), Calyptrate, Capeline, Caul, Chaco, Chape, Chapeau, Chaperon, Chapka, Charge, Chechia, Cheese-cutter, Cloth, Cockernony, Coif, College, Coonskin, Cope, Cornet, Cowl, Cradle, Crest, →**CROWN**, Czapka, Davy Crockett, Deerstalker, Dunce's, Dutch, Excel, Fatigue, Ferrule, Filler, Flat, Fool's, Forage, Gandhi, Garrison, Gimme,

Glengarry, Gorblim(e)y, Grannie, Granny, →**HAT**, Havelock, Hummel bonnet, Hunting, Iceberg, International, Jockey, Juliet, Kalpak, Kepi, Kilmarnock (cowl), Kippa, Kippoth, Kipput, Kiss-me(-quick), Knee, Legal, Liberty, Lid, Maintenance, Mob, Monmouth, Monteer, Montero, Mor(r)ion, Mortar-board, Muffin, Mutch, Newsboy, Night, Old wife, Outdo, Pagri, Patella(r), Percussion, Perplex, Petrol, Phrygian, Pile, Pileus, Pinner, Polar, Puggaree, Quoif, Rate, Root, Schapska, Shacko, Shako, Skullcap, Square, Squirrel-tail, Statute, Stocking, Summit, →**SURPASS**, Taj, Tam(-o'-shanter), Thimble, Thinking, Thrum, Toe, Toorie, Top, Toque, Toy, Trenchard, Trencher, Truck, Tuque, Turk's, Watch, Wishing, Yarmulka, Yarmulke, Zuchetto

Capable, Capability Able, Brown, Capacity, Competent, Deft, Effectual, Efficient, Firepower, Intelligent, Qualified, Reach, Skilled, Susceptible, Up to, Viable

Capacitance, Capacious, Capacity Ability, Ample, Aptitude, C, Cab, Calibre, Carrying, Co(o)mb, Competence, Content, Cor, Cubic, Endowment, Full, Function, Legal, Limit, Log, Mneme, Potency, Potential, Power, Prowess, Qua, Rated, Receipt, Roomy, Scope, Size, Tonnage, Valence, Vital, Volume

Cape(s) Agulhas, Almuce, Athlete, Beachy Head, Blanc(o), Bon, Burnouse, Byron, C, Calimere Point, Canaveral, Canso, Cardinal, Chelyuskin, Cloak, Cod, Comorin, Delgado, Dezhnev, Domino, Dungeness, East(ern), Fairweather, Faldetta, Fanion, Fanon, Farewell, Fear, Fichu, Finisterre, Flattery, Gallinas Point, Good Hope, Guardafui, Harp, Hatteras, Head(land), Helles, Hoe, Hogh, Hook of Holland, Horn, Inverness, Kennedy, Leeuwin, Lindesnes, Lizard, Mantilla, Mantle, Mant(e)let, Mantua, Matapan, May, Miseno, Moz(z)etta, Muleta, Naze, Ness, Nordkyn, North, Northern, Ortegal, Palatine, Palliser, Parry, Pelerine, Peninsula, Point, Poncho, Race, Ras, Ray, Reinga, Roca, Ruana, Runaway, Sable, St Vincent, Sandy, Scaw, Skagen, Skaw, Sontag, Southwest, Talma, Tippet, Trafalgar, Ushant, Verde, Vert, Waterproof, Western, Wrath, York

Capital(s) A1, Assets, Block, Boodle, Bravo, Cap, Chapiter, Chaptrel, Circulating, Doric, Equity, Euge, Excellent, Fixed, Flight, Float, Floating, Fonds, Great, Helix, Human, Initial, Ionic, Lethal, Lulu, Metropolis, Principal, Refugee, Risk, Rustic, Seat, Seed, Share, Social, Splendid, Sport, Stellar, Stock, Super, Topping, UC, Upper case, Venture, Wealth, Working

▷**Capitalist** *may indicate* a citizen of a capital

▷**Capless** *may indicate* first letter missing

▷**Capriccioso** *may indicate* an anagram

Caprice, Capricious Arbitrary, Boutade, Capernoitie, Cap(p)ernoity, Conceit, Desultory, Eccentric, Elf(in), Erratic, Fancy, Fickle, Fitful, Freak, Humoresk, Humoresque, Irony, Migraine, Mood, Perverse, Quirk, Vagary, Wayward, Whim(sy)

Capsize Keel, Overbalance, Overturn, Purl, Tip, Turn turtle, Upset, Whemmle, Whomble

▷**Capsized** *may indicate* a word upside down

Capsule Amp(o)ule, Boll, Bowman's, Cachet, Habitat, Nidamentum, Ootheca, Orbiter, Ovisac, Pill, Pyxidium, Spacecraft, Spermatophore, Time, Urn

Captain Ahab, Bligh, Bobadil, Bones, Bossyboots, Brassbound, Capt, Chief, Cid, Commander, Condottiere, Cook, Copper, Cuttle, Flint, Group, Hardy, Hook, Hornblower, Kettle, Kidd, Leader, Macheath, Master, Nemo, Oates, Old man, Owner, Patroon, Post, Privateer, Protospatharius, Pugwash, Rittmaster, Skip(per), Standish, Subah(dar), Subedar, Swing, Trierarch

Caption Heading, Headline, Inscription, Masthead, Sub-title, Title

Captivate(d), Captivating Beguile, Bewitch, Charm, Enamour, Enthrall, Epris(e), Rapt, Take, Winsome

Captive, Captivity Babylonish, Bonds, Chains, Duress, Hostage, POW, Prisoner, Slave, Thrall

Capture Abduct, Annex, Bag, Catch, Collar, Cop, Data, Entrance, Grab, Land, Nail, Net, Prize, Rush, Seize, Snabble, Snaffle, Snare, → **TAKE**, Trap

Car(s) Alvis, Aston Martin, Astra, Audi, Austin, Auto(matic), Banger, Beemer, Beetle, Benz, Berlin, Biza, BL, Bluebird, Bomb, Boneshaker, Brake, Bubble, Buffet, Bugatti, Buick, Bumper, Bus, Cab(riolet), Cadillac, Catafalco, Catafalque, Chariot, Chelsea-tractor, Chorrie, Citroen, Classic, Clunker, Coach, Compact, Company, Concept, Convertible, Cortina, Coupé, Courtesy, Crate, Daimler, Diesel, Diner, Dodgem®, Drag(ster), Drophead, Dual control, Dunger, Elf, Estate, E-type, Fastback, Ferrari, Fiat, Fleet, Flivver, Ford, Formula, Freight, Friday, Gas guzzler, Getaway, Ghost, Gondola, Gran turismo, Griddle, GT, Gyrocar, Hardtop, Hatchback, Heap, Hearse, Hillman, Horseless carriage, Hot hatch, Hot-rod, Irish, Jag(uar), Jalop(p)y, Jamjar, Jammy, Jam sandwich, Jaunting, Jim Crow, Kart, Kia, Kit, Knockabout, Lada, Lagonda, Lancia, Landaulet, Landrover, Lexus, Lift-back, Limo, Limousine, Lincoln, Merc(edes), MG, Mini, Model T, Morgan, Morris, Motor, Muscle, Nacelle, Notchback, Observation, Opel, Pace, Palace, Panda, Parlo(u)r, Patrol, Pimpmobile, Popemobile, Production, Prowl, Pullman, Racer, Ragtop, Railroad, Rattletrap, Restaurant, Roadster, Roller, Rolls (Royce), Rover, RR, Runabout, Runaround, Rust bucket, Saloon, Scout, Seat, Sedan, Service, Shooting-brake, Skoda, Sleeper, Sleeping, Soft-top, Speedster, Sports, Squad, Station wagon, Steam, Stock, Stretch-limo, Subcompact, Sunbeam, Supermini, SUV, Tank, Taxi, Telepherique, Telpher, Three-wheeler, Tin Lizzie, Tonneau, Tourer, Touring, Tram, Triumph, Trolley, Tumble, Turbo, Two-seater, Vehicle, Veteran, Vintage, Voiture, Volvo, VW, Wheeler, Wheels

Caravan(ner) Caf(f)ila, Convoy, Fleet, Kafila, Motor home, Safari, Trailer, Trailer trash, Winnebago®

Carbohydrate Agar, Agarose, Callose, Carrageenan, Cellulose, Chitin, Dextran, Disaccharide, Glycogen, Heptose, Hexose, Inulin, Ketose, Laminarin, Mannan, Pectin, Pentene, Pentose, Pentylene, Polysaccharide, Saccharide, Sorbitol, Starch, Sucrose, Sugar

Carcase, Carcass Body, Cadaver, Carrion, Corpse, Cutter, Krang, Kreng, Morkin, Mor(t)ling

Card(s), Cardboard, Carding Accelerator, Access, Ace, Affinity, Amex®, Arcana, Baccarat, Basto, Bill, Birthday, Blue Peter, Boarding, Bower, Business, Calling, Canasta, Cartes, Cash, Caution, Charge, Chicane, Club, Comb, Communion, Community, Compass, Court(esy), Credit, Cue, Dance, Debit, Deck, Deuce, Diamond, Doffer, Donor, Ecarté, Eccentric, Euchre, Expansion, Flaught, Flop, Flush, Fourchette, → **GAME**, Goulash, Graphics, Green, Guide, Hand, Heart, Honour, Humorist, Identity, Idiot, Jack, Jambone, Joker, Kanban, Key, King, Knowing, Loo, Loyalty, Manille, Matador, Meishi, Menu, Mise, Mistigris, Mogul, Mournival, Natural, Notelet, Oddity, Ombre, Original, Pack, Pasteboard, PC, Phone, Picture, Piquet, Placard, Plastic, Playing, Postal, Proximity, Quatorze, Queen, Quiz, Ration, Red, Rippler, Rove, Royal marriage, Score, Scratch, Scream, Screwball, Scribble, Singleton, Smart, Soda, Solo, Sound, Spade, Spadille, Squeezer, Store, Strawboard, Sure, Swab, Swipe, Swish, Switch, Swob, Swot, Talon, Tarok, Tarot, Tease(r), Tenace, Test, Thaumatrope,

Ticket, Top-up, Tose, Toze, Trading, Trey, Trump, Two-spot, Valentine, Visiting, Wag, Warrant, Weirdie, Whitechapel, Wild, Wit, Yellow, Zener

Cardigan Ballet-wrap, Jacket, Lumber jacket, Wampus, Wam(m)us, Woolly

Cardinal Apostolic vicar, Camerlingo, Chief, College, Eight, Eminence, Eminent, Grosbeak, Hat, HE, Hume, Legate, Manning, Mazarin, Medici, Newman, Nine, Number, Pivotal, Polar, Prefect, Prelate, Radical, Red, Red-hat, Richelieu, Sacred college, Seven, Sin, Spellman, Ten, Virtue, Vital, Ximenes

Care(r), Caring Attention, Befriend, Burden, Cark, Caution, Cerne, Cherish, →CONCERN, Cosset, Doula, Exactitude, Grief, Guard, Heed, Intensive, Kaugh, Keep, Kiaugh, Maternal, Mind, Mother, Pains, Palliative, Parabolanus, Primary, Reck(e), Regard, Reke, Respite, Retch, Rought, Shared, Solicitude, →TEND, Tenty, Thought, Trouble, Ts(o)uris, Ward, Worry

Career Course, Hurtle, Life, Line, Profession, Run, Rush, Scorch, Speed, Start, Tear, Vocation

▷**Career** *may indicate* an anagram

Careful(ly) Canny, Chary, Delicate, Diligent, Discreet, Gentle, Heedy, Hooly, Leery, Meticulous, Mindful, Penny-pinching, Penny-wise, Pernickety, Provident, Prudent, Scrimp, Scrupulous, Softly-softly, Studious, Tentie, Tenty, Thorough, Thrifty, Vigilant, Ware, Wary

Careless(ness), Careless(ly) Anyhow, Casual, Cavalier, Cheery, Debonair, Easy, Free-minded, Gallio, Improvident, Imprudent, Inadvertent, Inattention, Inconsiderate, Insouciance, Lax, Lighthearted, Négligé, →NEGLIGENT, Nonchalant, Oversight, Raffish, Rash, Remiss, Resigned, Riley, Slam-bang, Slapdash, Slaphappy, Slipshod, Sloppy, Sloven(ly), Slubber, Taupie, Tawpie, Unguarded, Unmindful, Untenty, Unwary

▷**Carelessly** *may indicate* an anagram

Caress Bill, Coy, Embrace, Feel, Fondle, Kiss, Lallygag, Lollygag, Noursle, Nursle, Pet, Straik, Stroke, Touch

Caretaker Acting, Charge d'affaires, Concierge, Curator, Custodian, Dvornik, Guardian, Janitor, Nightwatchman, Sexton, Shammash, Shammes, Superintendent, Verger, Warden

Careworn Haggard, Lined, Tired, Weary

Cargo Boatload, Bulk, Burden, Fraught, Freight, Lading, Last, →LOAD, Navicert, Payload, Shipment

Caribbean Belonger, Cuban, Puerto Rican, Soca, Sokah, Spanish Main, Taino, WI

Caricature, Caricaturist Ape, Beerbohm, Burlesque, Caran d'Ache, Cartoon, Cruikshank, Doyle, Farce, Gillray, Mimicry, Rowlandson, Scarfe, Skit, Spy, Toon, Travesty

Carnation Dianthus, Malmaison, Picotee, Pink

Carnival Fair, Festival, Fete, Mardi Gras, Moomba, Rag, Revelry, Surf

Carol(ler) Noel, Sing, Song, Wait, Wassail, Yodel

Carousal, Carouse Bend, Birl(e), Bouse, Bride-ale, Compotation, Drink, Mallemaroking, Mollie, Orge, Orgy, →REVEL, Roist, Screed, Spree, Upsee, Upsey, Upsy, Wassail

Carp(er) Beef, Cavil, Censure, Complain, Crab, Critic, Crucian, Crusian, Fault, Gibel, Goldfish, Gripe, Id(e), Kvetch, Mirror, Mome, Nag, Nibble, Niggle, Prussian, Roach, Roundfish, Scold, Snipe, Twitch, Whine, Yerk, Yirk

Carpenter Beveller, Bush, Cabinet-maker, Carfindo, Chippy, Chips, Fitter, Joiner, Joseph, Menuisier, Quince, Sawyer, Shipwright, Tenoner, Wright

▷**Carpenter** *may indicate* an anagram

Carpet(ing) Admonish, Aubusson, Axminster, Beetle, Berate, Bessarabian, Body, Broadloom, Brussels, Castigate, Chide, Drugget, Durrie, Excoriation, Kali, Kelim, Khilim, Kidderminster, Kilim, Kirman, Lecture, Lino, Mat(ting), Moquette, Persian, Rate, Red, Reprimand, Reproach, Roast, Rug, Runner, Shagpile, Shark, Turkey, Wall-to-wall, What for, Wig, Wilton

Carriage Air, Ar(a)ba, Aroba, Bandy, Barouche, Bearing, Berlin(e), Bier, Brake, Brit(sch)ka, Britska, Britzka, Brougham, Buckboard, Buggy, Cab, Calash, Calèche, Car, Cariole, Caroche, Carriole, Carryall, Cartage, Chaise, Charabanc, Charet, Chariot, Chassis, Chay, Clarence, Coach, Coch, Composite, Conveyance, Coupé, Curricle, Demeanour, Dennet, Deportment, Désobligeante, Diner, Dormeuse, Dormitory-car, Dos-a-dos, Do-si-do, Drag, Dros(h)ky, Ekka, Equipage, Fiacre, Fly, Four-in-hand, Freight, Gait, Gig, Gladstone, Go-cart, Growler, Gun, Haulage, Herdic, Horseless, Howdah, Hurley-hacket, Jampan, Job, Landau(let), Landing, Limber, Mien, Non-smoker, Norimon, Observation-car, Phaeton, Pick-a-back, Pochaise, Pochay, Poise, Port(age), Portance, Postchaise, Posture, Poyse, Pram, Pullman, Purdah, Railcar, Railway, Random, Rath(a), Remise, Ricksha(w), Rig, Rockaway, Set-up, Shay, Sled, Sleeper, Smoker, Sociable, Spider, Spider phaeton, Stanhope, Sulky, Surrey, Tarantas(s), Taxi, T-cart, Tender, Tenue, Tilbury, Tim-whiskey, Tonga, Trail, Trap, Van, Vetture, Victoria, Voiture, Wagonette, Waterage, Whirligig, Whisk(e)y, Whisky gig

Carrier Aircraft, Airline, Arm, Baldric, Barkis, Barrow, Bomb-ketch, Briefcase, Bulk, Cacolet, Caddy, Cadge, Camel, Charon, Coaster, Common, Conveyor, Donkey, Escort, Fomes, Fomites, Frog, Grid, Hamper, Haversack, Hawker, Hod, Janker, Jill, Majority, Minority, Nosebag, Noyade, Obo, Omnibus, Packhorse, Personnel, Pigeon, Porter, Rucksack, Satchel, Schistosoma, Semantide, Sling, Spore, Straddle, Stretcher(-bearer), Tiffin, Tranter, → **TRAY**, Trug, TWA, Vector, Wave

Carrion Cadaver, Carcase, Carcass, Flesh, Ket, Stapelia

Carry(ing), Carry over Asport, Bear, Chair, Convey, Enlevé, Escort, Ferry, Frogmarch, Hawk, Hent, Humf, Hump, Humph, Kurvey, Land, Move, Pack, Pickaback, Port, Reappropriate, Stock, Sustain, Tide over, Tote, → **TRANSPORT**, Trant, Waft, Wage, With, Yank

Cart(er) Bandy, Barrow, Bogey, Buck, Cape, Car(r)iole, Chapel, Dandy, Democrat, Democrat wagon, Dog, Dolly, Dray, Egyptologist, Float, Furphy, Gambo, Gill, Golf, Governess, Gurney, Hackery, Jag, Jill, Lead, Mail(-gig), Night, Pie, Pram, Rickshaw, Scot, Scotch, Shandry, T, Tax(ed), Telega, Trolley, Tumbrel, Tumbril, Village, Wag(g)on, Wain, Water, Wheelbarrow, Whitechapel

Cartel Duopoly, Firms, Ring, Syndicate, Zaibatsu

Cartilage Chondral, Ensiform, Gristle

Carton Box, Case, Crate, Sydney, Tub

Cartoon(ist) Andy Capp, Animated, Bateman, Caricature, Comic, Comic strip, Disney, Drawn, Emmet, Garland, Lancaster, Leech, Low, Manga, Mel, Partridge, Popeye, Schulz, Short, Shrek, Spy, Strip, Superman, Tenniel, Tintin, Trog

Cartridge Ball, Blank, Bullet, Cartouche, Crystal, Doppie, Live, Magnetic, Magnum, Rim-free, Shell, Spent

Carve(d), Carver, Carving Abated, Apsaras, Bas relief, Cameo, Chair, Chip, Chisel, Cilery, Crocket, Cut, Dismember, Doone, Emboss, Enchase, Engrave, Entail, Entayle, Fiddlehead, Gargoyle, Gibbons, Glyphic, Glyptic, Hew, Incise, Inscribe, Insculp, Intaglio, Netsuke, Nick, Petroglyph, Scrimshaw, Sculp(t), Slice, Tondo, Trophy, Truncheon, Tympanum, Whakairo, Whittle

Cascade Cataract, Fall, Lin(n), Stream, Waterfall

Case(s), Casing Ablative, Accusative, Action, Allative, Altered, Appeal, Aril, Ascus, Assumpsit, Attaché, Basket, Beer, Bere, Bin, Bittacle, Blimp, Box, Brief, Bundwall, Burr, Burse, C, Ca, Cabinet, Cachet, Calyx, Canister, Canterbury, Capsule, Cartouch(e), Cartridge, Cask(et), Cause celebre, Cellaret, Chase, Chitin, Chrysalis, Cocoon, Coffin, Comitative, Compact, Crate, Croustade, Crust, Cyst, Dative, Declension, Detinue, Digi-pack, Dispatch, Dossier, Dressing, Elytron, Enclose, Ensheath, Ergative, Etui, Etwee, Event, Example, Flan, Flapjack, Flask, Frame, Gearbox, Genitive, Grip, Hanaper, Hard, Hatbox, Helmet, Hold-all, Housewife, Hull, Humidor, Husk, Illative, Imperial, Index, Indusium, Instance, Kalamdan, Keg, Keister, Locative, Locket, Lorica, Manche, Matchbox, Matter, Mermaid's purse, Mezuzah, Music, Nacelle, Nominative, Non-suit, Nutshell, Objective, Oblique, Ochrea, Ocrea, Outpatient, Packing, Pair, Papeterie, Patient, Peapod, Pencil, Penner, Phylactery, Plight, Plummer-block, Pod, Port, Portfolio, Possessive, Prima facie, Puparium, Quiver, Recce, Reconnoitre, Red box, Sabretache, Sad, Scabbard, Seashell, Sheath(e), Shell, Situation, Six-pack, Sleeve, Sporocyst, Sporran, Stead, Straitjacket, Subjective, Suit, Tantalus, Tea-chest, Telium, Test, Theca, Tichborne, Toolbox, Trial, Trunk, Valise, Vanity bag, Vasculum, Vitrine, Vocative, Volva, Walise, Walking, Wallet, Wardian, Wing, Worst, Writing

Cash Blunt, Bonus, Bounty, Bread, Change, Coin, Digital, Dosh, Dot, Float, Funds, Idle money, Imprest, Liquid, Lolly, → **MONEY**, Needful, Ochre, Oof, Pence, Petty, Ready, Realise, Redeem, Rhino, Spondulicks, Stumpy, Tender, Tin, Wampum, Wherewithal

Cashier, Cash machine Annul, ATM, Break, Depose, Disbar, Dismiss, Displace, Teller, Treasurer

Cask(et) Armet, Barrel, Barrico, Bas(i)net, Box, Breaker, Butt, Cade, Casque, Cassette, Drum, Firkin, Galeate, Harness, Heaume, Hogshead, Keg, Leaguer, Octave, Pin, Pipe, Puncheon, Pyxis, Run(d)let, Salade, Sallet, Sarcophagus, Shook, Shrine, Solera, Tierce, Tun

Casserole Diable, Hotpot, Osso bucco, Pot, Salmi, Terrine, Tzimmes

Cassette Cartridge, Tape, Video

Cast (down, off, out), Casting Abattu, Actors, Add, Angle, Appearance, Bung, Cire perdue, Dash, Death mask, Die, Discard, Ecdysis, Eject, Emit, Exorcise, Exuviae, Exuvial, Fling, Form, Found, Fusil, Hawk, Heave, Hob, Horoscope, Hue, Hurl, Impression, Ingo(w)es, Keb, Look, Lose, Lost wax, Mew, Mo(u)lt, Moulage, Mould, Plaster(stone), Plastisol®, Players, Print, Put, Reject, Sand, Sculptured, Sent, Shed, Shoot, Shy, Sling, Slive, Slough, Spoil, Stamp, Stookie, Swarm, Tailstock, Terracotta, → **THROW**, Toss, Tot, Warp, Wax, Worm, Ytost

▷**Cast** *may indicate* an anagram or a piece of a word missing

Castaway Adrift, Crusoe, Gunn, Left, Man Friday, Outcast, Robinson, Selkirk, Stranded

▷**Cast by** *may indicate* surrounded by

Caste Burakumin, Class, Dalit, Group, Harijan, Hova, Kshatriya, Rajput, Rank, Sect, Shudra, Sudra, Untouchable, Varna

Castle(d) Barbara, Bouncy, Broch, C, Casbah, Chateau, Citadel, Fastness, Fort, Kasba(h), Man, Mot(t)e, Motte and bailey, Move, Palace, Rook, Stronghold, Villa

Casual(ly), Casuals Accidental, Adventitious, Airy(-fairy), Blasé, Chance, Chav(ette), Flippant, Grass, Haphazard, Idle, Incidental, Informal, Jaunty,

Lackadaisical, Leisurewear, Nonchalant, Odd(ment), Odd-jobber, Offhand, Off-the-cuff, Orra, Overly, Passing, Promiscuous, Random, Scratch, Shoe, Slaphappy, Slipshod, Sporadic, Stray, Temp, Throwaway

Cat Ailuro-, Barf, Boat, Boke, Bush, Catamount, Dandy, Egurgitate, Fat, Felid, Feline, Foss, Garfield, Glaring, Gossip, Grimalkin, Gus, Hipster, Jazzer, Lair, Lash, Mewer, Mog, Native, Neuter, Nib, Painter, Pardal, Practical, Puss, Queen, Regurgitate, Scourge, Sick, Spew, Spue, Swinger, Vomit, Whip

Catalogue(r) Categorise, Dewey, Durchkomponi(e)rt, Index, Inventory, Itemise, K(ochel), List, Litany, Magalog, MARC, Messier, Ragman, Ragment, Raisonné, Record, Register, Roll, Star, Table, Tabulate, Thematic

Catalyst Accelerator, Agent, Aldol, Chemical, Enzyme, Erepsin, Impetus, Influence, Kryptonite, Stereospecific, Unicase, Ziegler

Catapult Ballista, Ging, Launch, Mangon(el), Perrier, Petrary, Propel, Scorpion, Shanghai, Sling, Slingshot, Stone-bow, Tormentum, Trebuchet, Wye, Y

Catastrophe, Catastrophic Calamity, Damoclean, →**DISASTER**, Doom, Epitasis, Fiasco, Meltdown, Ruinous, Tragedy

Catch(y), Catcher, Catching, Caught Air, Apprehend, Arrest, Attract, Backstop, Bag, Benet, Bone, C, Capture, Chape, Clasp, Cog, Collar, Conquest, Contagious, Contract, Cop, Corner, Ct, Deprehend, Detent, Dolly, Engage, Enmesh, Ensnare, Entoil, Entrap, Fang, Fastener, Field, Fish, Fumble, Gaper, Get, Glee(some), Grasp, Had, Hank, Haud, Haul, Hear, Hold, Hook, Inmesh, Keddah, Keight, Kep(pit), Kheda, Kill, Land, Lapse, Lasso, Latch, Lazo, Lime, Lock, Morse, Nab, Nail, Net, Nick, Nim, Nobble, Noose, Overhear, Overhent, Overtake, Parti, Pawl, Rap, Release, Rope, Round, Rub, Safety, Save, Sean, Sear, See(n), Seize, →**SNAG**, Snap, Snare, Snig(gle), →**SONG**, Stop, Surprise, Swindle, Tack, Taen, Take, Tane, Trammel, Trap, Trawl, Trick, Tripwire, Troll, Twenty two, Twig, Understand, Wrestle

Categorise, Categories, Category →**CLASS**, Classify, Etic, Genera, Genus, Infraclass, Infraorder, Label, Order, Pigeonhole, Range, Specie, Stereotype, Taxon, Triage, Type

Cater(er) Acatour, Cellarer, Feed, Manciple, →**PROVIDE**, Serve, Steward, Supply, Victualler, Vivandière

Caterpillar Aweto, Boll worm, Cabbageworm, Cotton-worm, Cutworm, Eruciform, Geometer, Grub, Hop-dog, Hornworm, Inchworm, Larva, Looper, Osmeterium, Palmer, Silkworm, Tent, Webworm, Woolly-bear

Cathedral Amiens, Basilica, Birmingham, Burgos, Chartres, Chester, →**CHURCH**, Cologne, Cortona, Dome, Duomo, Durham, Ely, Evreux, Exeter, Gloucester, Hereford, Hertford, Huesca, Kirkwall, Lateran, Lugo, Minster, Mullingar, Notre Dame, Rheims, Rochester, St Albans, St Davids, St Paul's, Santiago de Compostela, Sens, Teruel, Viseu, Wakefield, Wells, Westminster, Winchester

Catholic Assumptionist, Broad, Christian Socialism, Comprehensive, Defenders, Doolan, Ecumenical, Fenian, General, German, Irvingism, Jebusite, Latin, Lazarist, Left-footer, Liberal, Marian, Old, Ostiary, Papalist, Papaprelatist, Papist, Recusant, Redemptionist, Roman, Romish, Salesian, Spike, Theatine, Thomist, Tory, Tridentine, Uniat, Universal, Ursuline, Wide

Cattle(pen) Aberdeen Angus, Africander, Ankole, Aver, Ayrshire, Beefalo, Belgian Blue, Belted Galloway, Black, Brahman, British White, Buffalo, Carabao, Charbray, Charolais, Chillingham, Dexter, Drove, Durham, Fee, Friesian, Friesland, Galloway, Gaur, Gayal, Guernsey, Gyal, Heard, Herd, Hereford, Highland, Holstein (Friesian), Illawarra, Jersey, Kerry, Kine, Kouprey, Kraal,

Ky(e), Kyloe, Lairage, Limousin, Lincoln, Longhorn, Luing, Neat, Nout, Nowt, Owsen, Oxen, Piemontese, Rabble, Redpoll, Rother, Santa Gertrudis, Shorthorn, Simment(h)al, Soum, South Devon, Sowm, Steer, Stock, Store, Stot, Sussex, Tamarao, Tamarau, Teeswater, Wagyu, Welsh Black

Caucus Assembly, Cabal, Cell, Gathering, Race

Caulk Fill, Pay, Pitch, Snooze

Causation, Cause(d), Causes Aetiology, Agent, Bandwagon, Beget, Breed, Bring, Célèbre, Common, Compel, Create, Crusade, Determinant, Due, Effect, Efficient, Encheason, Engender, Entail, Evoke, Expedite, Factor, Final, First, Flag-day, Formal, Gar(re), Generate, Ideal, Incur, Induce, Inspire, Lead, Lost, Make, Material, Motive, Movement, Natural, → **OCCASION**, Parent, Pathogen, Precipitate, Probable, Prompt, Provoke, Proximate, Reason, Root, Sake, Secondary, Show, Source, Teleology, Topic, Trigger, Ultimate, Wreak

Caustic Acid, Acrimonious, Alkaline, Burning, Common, Erodent, Escharotic, Lunar, Moxa, Potash, Pungent, Sarcastic, Scathing, Seare, Soda, Tart, Vitriol, Waspish, Withering

Caution, Cautious (person) Achitophel, Admonish, Ahithophel, Alert, Amber, Awarn, Beware, Cagey, Card, Care, Cave, Caveat, Chary, Circumspect, Credence, Cure, Defensive, Deliberate, Discretion, Fabian, Forewarn, Gingerly, Guard(ed), Hedger, Heedful, Leery, Prudent, Rum, Scream, Skite, Tentative, Timorous, Vigilant, Ware, → **WARN**, Wary, Yellow card

▷**Cavalier** *may indicate* an anagram

Cave(rn), Caves, Cave-dwelling, Cave in, Cavernous Acherusia, Aladdin's, Altamira, Antar, Antre, Beware, Bone, Capitulate, Cellar, Cheddar, Collapse, Corycian, Deep, Den, Domdaniel, Erebus, Fingal's, Fore, Grot(to), Hollow, Jenolan, Lascaux, Look-out, Lupercal, Mammoth, Mind out, Nix, Pot-hole, Proteus, Sepulchre, Spel(a)ean, Speleology, Spelunker, Speos, Tassili, Trophonian, Vault, Waitomo, Ware, Weem, Wookey Hole

Caveman Adullam, Aladdin, Fingal, Neanderthal, Primitive, Troglodyte, Troll

Caviare Beluga, Osietra, Roe, Sevruga, Sturgeon

Cavity Acetabulum, Amygdale, Antrum, Archenteron, Atrial, Atrium, Body, Camera, Celom, Chamber, Cisterna, Coelom(e), Conceptacle, Concha, Countermark, Crater, Crypt, Cyst, Dent, Druse, Enteron, Follicle, Foss, Gap, Geode, Glenoid, Gloryhole, Hold, Hole, Lacuna, Locule, Mediastinum, Mialoritic, Orbita, Orifice, Pelvis, Pleural, Pocket, Pothole, Pulp, Sinus, Stomod(a)eum, Tartarus, Tear, Thunderegg, Tympanum, Vacuole, Vein, Ventricle, Vesicle, Vitta, Vomica, Vug, Well

Cease(fire) Abate, Blin, Cut, Desist, Devall, Die, Disappear, Halt, Ho, Intermit, Leese, Lin, Lose, Pass, Refrain, Sessa, → **STOP**, Truce

Cedar(wood) Arolla, Atlas, Barbados, Cryptomeria, Deodar, Incense, Jamaica, Toon

Ceiling Absolute, Barrel, Coffered, Cove, Cupola, Dome, Glass, Lacunar, Laquearia, Limit, Plafond, Roof, Silver, Soffit, Stained glass

Celebrate(d), Celebration, Celebrity Ale, A-list, All-star, Beanfeast, Beano, Besung, Big name, Bigwig, Binge, B-list, Brat-packer, Carnival, Chant, Commemorate, Distinguished, Do, Eclat, Emblazon, Encaenia, Epithalamion, Epithalamium, Fame, Feast, Fest(al), Festivity, Fete, Fiesta, First-footing, Gala, Gaudeamus, Gaudy, Glitterati, Glorify, Grog-up, Harvest home, Headliner, Hold, Holiday, Honour, Hoop-la, Jamboree, Jol, Jollifications, Jollities, Joncanoe, Jubilee, Junkanoo, Keep, Large it, Laud, Legend, Limelight, Lion, Loosing,

Lowsening, Maffick, Mardi Gras, Mawlid al-Nabi, Monstre sacre, Name, Noted, Nuptials, Observe, Occasion, Orgy, Panathenaea, Party, Personage, Personality, Pinata, Praise, Randan, Rave-up, Record, Rejoice, Renown, Repute, Revel, Rite, Roister, Sangeet, Saturnalia, See in, Sex symbol, Shindig, Sing, Spree, Star, Storied, Sung, Supermodel, Tet, Triumph, Wassail, Wet, Whoopee

Celestial Chinese, Cosmic, Divine, Ethereal, Heavenly, Supernal, Uranic

Celibate, Celibacy Bachelor, Chaste, Nun, Paterin(e), Priest, Rappist, Rappite, Shakers, Single, Spinster

Cell(s), Cellular Amyloidal, Battery, Black hole, Bullpen, Cadre, Chamber, Chapel, Crypt, Cubicle, Death, Dungeon, Group, Laura, Lock up, Padded, Peter, Priesthole, →**PRISON**, Proviral, Safety, Unit

Cellar Basement, Coalhole, Salt, Shaker, Storm, Vault, Vaultage, Vaut

Celt(ic) Archdruid, Breton, Brython, Cornish, Druid, Gadhel, Gael(dom), Goidel, Helvetii, Kelt, La Tène, Manx, P, Q, Welsh

Cement Araldite®, Asbestos, Blast-furnace, Compo, Concrete, Fix, Flaunch, Glue, Granolithic, Grout, Gunite, Lute, Luting, Maltha, Mastic, Mastich, Mortar, Paste, Pointing, Portland, Putty, Rubber, Screed, →**STICK**, Trass

Cemetery Aceldama, Arenarium, Arlington, Boneyard, Boot Hill, Campo santo, Catacomb, God's Acre, Golgotha, Graveyard, Musall, Necropolis, Père Lachaise, Saqqara, Urnfield

Censor(ious), Censorship, Censure Abridge, Accuse, Admonition, AD notice, Airbrush, Animadvert, Appeach, Ban, Banner, Berate, Blame, Blue-pencil, Bowdler, Braid, Cato, Chasten, Comstockery, →**CONDEMN**, Critical, Criticise, Cut, Damn, Dang, Decry, Dispraise, Edit, Excommunicate, Excoriate, Expurgate, Gag, Obloquy, Rap, Rebuke, Redact, Repress, Reprimand, Reproach, Reprobate, Reprove, Satirise, Slam, Slate, Suppress, Tax, Tear into, Tirade, Traduce, Wig

Cent(s) Bean, Coin, Ct, Penny, Red, Zack

Central(ly), Centre Active, Amid, Assessment, Attendance, Axis, Battlebus, Broca's, Bunt, Call, Cardinal, Chakra, Civic, Community, Contact, Core, Cost, Crisis, Day, Daycare, Dead, Design, Detention, Detoxification, Deuteron, Deuton, Downtown, Drop-in, Epergne, Eye, Field, Focus, Foyer, Frontal, Garden, Health, Heart, Heritage, Hotbed, Hothouse, Hub, Incident, Inmost, Inner, Internal, Interpretive, Juvenile, Juvie, Kernel, Kingpin, Law, Leisure, Lincoln, Live, Main, Mecca, Median, Medulla, Mid(st), Midpoint, Midway, Mission, Music, Nave, Navel, Nerve, Nucleus, Omphalus, Pompidou, Profit, Property, Reception, Rehabilitation, Remand, Respiratory, Service, Shopping, Social Education, Storm, Teachers', Trauma, Visitor, Waist, Weather, Youth custody

Central American Mangue, Miskito, Olmec, Otomi, Pueblo, Totomac, Zapotec

▷**Centre** *may indicate* middle letters

Century Age, C, Eon, Era, Magdeburg, Period, Siècle, Ton

Ceramic(s) Arcanist, Cermet, China, Earthen, Ferrite, Ferronneries, Porcelain, Pottery, Sialon, Syalon®, Tiles

Cereal Amelcorn, Barley, Blé, Bran, Bread-basket, Buckwheat, Bulgar, Bulg(h)ur, Cassava, Corn, Couscous, Emmer, Farina, Gnocchi, Grain, Granola, Hominy, Maize, Mandioc(a), Mandiocca, Manihot, Mani(h)oc, Mealie, Millet, Muesli, Oats, Paddy, Popcorn, Rye(corn), Sago, Samp, Seed, Semolina, Sorghum, Spelt, Tapioca, Tef(f), Triticale, Wheat, Zea

Ceremonial, Ceremony Aarti, Amrit, Asperges, Baptism, Barmitzvah, Chado, Chanoyu, Commemoration, Common Riding, Coronation, Dedication, Doseh,

Durbar, Encaenia, Enthronement, Etiquette, Eucharist, Flypast, Form(al),
Formality, Function, Gongyo, Habdalah, Havdalah, Havdoloh, Heraldry,
Investiture, Koto(w), Matsuri, Maundy, Mummery, Nipter, Observance,
Occasion, Official, Ordination, Pageantry, Parade, Pomp, Powwow, Protocol,
Rite, Rite of passage, Ritual, Sacrament, Sado, Seder, Service, State, Sun dance,
Tea, Topping-out, Trooping (the Colour), Unveiling, Usage

Cert(ain), Certainty Absolute, Actual, Assured, Banker, Bound, Cast-iron,
Cinch, Cocksure, Confident, Conviction, Convinced, Decided, Definite,
Doubtless, Exact, Fact, Fate, Foolproof, Indubitable, Inevitable, Infallible, Lock,
Monte, Nap, Needly, One, Positive, Poz, Precise, Racing, Red-hot, Shoo-in,
Siccar, Sicker, Snip, Some, Stiff, → **SURE**, Sure-fire, Truth, Type, Unerring, Yes

Certificate, Certified, Certify Accredit, Affirm, Assure, Attest, Bene decessit,
Birth, Bond, Chit, Cocket, Confirm, Credential, Death, Debenture, Depose,
Diploma, Docket, Document, End-user, Enseal, Gold, Guarantee, Landscrip,
Licence, Lines, Medical, MOT, Notarise, Paper, Patent, Proven, Savings, School,
Scrip, Scripophily, Security, Share, Smart-ticket, Stamp note, Stock, Sworn,
Talon, Testamur, Testimonial, Treasury, U, Unruly, Voucher, Warrant

Chafe(r), Chafing Chunter, Fray, Fret, Gall, Harass, Intertrigo, Irritate, Pan,
Rankle, → **RUB**, Scuff, Seethe, Worry

Chain(s), Chained Acre's-breadth, Albert, Anklet, Bicycle, Bind, Bond,
Bracelet, Bucket, Cable, Catena, Check, Choke, Cistron, Closed, Daisy, Decca,
Drive, Dynasty, Engineer's, Esses, Fanfarona, Fetter, Fob, Food, Furlong,
Gleipnir, Gunter's, Gyve, Human, Light, Line, Lockaway, Markov, Mayor,
Micella(r), Micelle, Noria, Pennine, Pitch, Range, Rode, Roller, Seal, → **SERIES**,
Shackle, Sierra, Slang, Snow, Span, Sprocket, String, Strobila, Team, Trace,
Tug, Watch

Chair Balloon-back, Basket, Bath, Bench, Bentwood, Berbice, Bergère, Birthing,
Bosun's, Butterfly, Camp, Cane, Captain's, Carver, Club, Curule,
Deck, Dining, Director's, Easy, Elbow, Electric, Estate, Fauteuil, Fiddle-back,
Folding, Frithstool, Garden, Gestatorial, Guérite, High, Jampan, Jampanee,
Jampani, Ladder-back, Lounger, Love-seat, Lug, Merlin, Morris, Nursing, Pew,
Preside, Professorate, Reader, Recliner, Rocker, Ruckseat, Rush-bottomed,
Sedan, Settee, Steamer, Stool, Straight, Sugan, Swivel, Throne, Wainscot,
Wheel, Windsor, Wing

Chairman Convener, Emeritus, Humph, Mao, MC, Pr(a)eses, Prof, Prolocutor,
Sheraton, Speaker

Chalk(y) Black, Calcareous, Cauk, Cawk, Crayon, Credit, Cretaceous, Dentin,
French, Soapstone, White(n), Whit(en)ing

Challenge(r), Challenging Accost, Acock, Assay, Call, Cartel, Champion,
Charge, Claim, Confront, Contradict, Contest, Dare, Daur, Defy, Dispute,
Face, Gage, Gainsay, Gauntlet, Glove, Hazard, Hen(ner), Iconoclasm, Impugn,
Insubordinate, Opponent, Oppose, Oppugn, Provoke, Query, Question, Recuse,
Remonstrate, Rival, Sconce, Shuttle, Tackle, Taker, Tall order, Tank, Threat,
Tongue-twister, Vie, Whynot

Chamber(s) Anteroom, Atrium, Auricle, Bladder, Camarilla, Camera, Casemate,
Cavern, Cavitation, Cavity, Cell(a), Chanty, Cloud, Cofferdam, Columbarian,
Combustion, Commons, Cubicle, Decompression, Dene-hole, Dolmen, Echo,
Float, Fogou, Fume, Gas, Gazunder, Hall, Hopper, Horrors, Hyperbaric,
Hypogea, Ionization, Jerry, Jordan, Kiva, Lavatory, Lethal, Locule, Manhole,
Manifold, Mattamore, Naos, Po(t), Priest('s)-hole, Privy, Room, Roum, Serdab,

Silo, Spark, Star, Stateroom, Steam-chest, Swell-box, Synod, Thalamus, Undercroft, Upper, Utricle, Vault, Ventricle, Zeta

Champ(er), Champers Bite, Chafe, Chew, Chomp, Eat, Fume, Gnash, Gnaw, Ivories, Mash, Morsure, Munch

Champagne Boy, Brut, Bubbly, Charlie, Fizz, Gigglewater, Krug, Mumm, Pop, Sillery, Simkin, Simpkin, Stillery, Troyes, Widow

Champion(s) Ace, Adopt, Ali, Apologist, Apostle, Artegal, Assert, Back, Belt, Brill(iant), Campeador, Cid, Cock, Defend, Don Quixote, Doucepere, Douzeper, Dymoke, Endorse, Enoch, Espouse, Gladiator, Gun, Harry, → **HERO**, Herodotus, Horse, Kemp, Kemper(yman), King, Knight, Maestro, Maintain, Matchless, Messiah, Messias, Neil, Paladin, Palmerin, Partisan, Peerless, Perseus, Promachos, Proponent, Protagonist, Roland, St Anthony, St David, St Denis, St George, St James, St Patrick, Seven, Spiffing, Spokesman, Star, Support, Tiro, Title-holder, Torch-bearer, Tribune, Upholder, Victor, Wardog, → **WINNER**, World-beater, Yokozuna

Chance (upon), Chancy Accident, Adventitious, Aleatory, Aunter, Bet, Break, Buckley's, Cast, Casual, Cavel, Contingent, Dice, Earthly, Even, → **FATE**, Fluke, Fortuitous, Fortuity, Fortune, → **GAMBLE**, Game, Hap, Happenstance, Hit and miss, Hobnob, Iffy, Kevel, Light, Look-in, Lot, → **LOTTERY**, Luck, Meet, Mercy, Occasion, Occur, Odds, Opening, Opportunity, Peradventure, Posse, Potluck, Prayer, Probability, Prospect, Random, Rise, Risk, Serendipity, Shot, Slant, Snip, Spec, Stake, Stochastic, Stray, Sweep, Toss-up, Treble, Turn, Tychism, Ventre, Venture, Wager, Wild card

Change(able), Changes, Changing About-face, Adapt, Adjust, Agio, Aleatoric, → **ALTER**, Amendment, Amoeba, Attorn, Backtrack, Barter, Become, Bob-major, Budge, Capricious, Cash, Catalysis, Cent, Channel-hop, Chop, Chump, Climacteric, Climate, Cline, Codicil, Commute, Convert, Coppers, Covary, Cut, Denature, Departure, Development, Differentiate, Dissolve, Diversion, Ectopia, Edit, Embellish, Emend, Enallage, Eustatic, Evolution, Exchange, Find, Flighty, Float, Fluctuate, Fluid, Flux, Gradate, Grandsire, Guard, Gybe, Histogen, Holiday, Inflect, Innovate, Instead, Kaleidoscope, Killcrop, Labile, Make-over, Mercurial, Metabolic, Metabolise, Metamorphosis, Metathesise, Mew, Mobile, Modify, Modulate, Morph, Mutable, Mutation, Ontogeny, Parallax, Paraphrase, Peal, Pejoration, Permute, Prisere, Protean, Quarter, Rat, Realise, Recant, Reconstruct, Rectify, Redact, Redo, Refine, Reform, Refraction, Regeneration, Reset, Reshuffle, Rest, Revise, Rework, Sandhi, Sd, Seasonal, Seesaw, Shake-out, Shake-up, Shift, Shrapnel, Shuffle, Silver, Small, Substitute, Supervene, Swap, Sweeping, Swing, Switch, Toggle, Tolsel, Tolsey, Tolzey, Transfer, Transfiguration, Transform, Transition, Translate, Transmute, Transpose, Transubstantial, Triple, Turn (about), Tweak, Uncertain, Upheaval, U-turn, Vagary, Variant, Variation, Vary, Veer, Versatile, Volatile, Volte-face, Weathercock, Wheel, Wow

▷**Change(d)** *may indicate* an anagram

Channel Access, Airwave, Al Jazeera, Aqueduct, Artery, Beagle, Bed, Billabong, Binaural, Bristol, Canal, Chimb, Chime, Chine, Chute, Conduit, Course, Creek, Culvert, Cut, Cutting, Datagram, Distribution, Ditch, Drain, Duct, Dyke, Ea, Eau, English, Estuary, Euripus, Fairway, Feeder, Floodway, Flume, Foss, Funnel, Furrow, Gat, Gate, Geo, Gio, Glyph, Groove, Gully, Gut, Gutter, Head-race, Ingate, Katavothron, Khor, Kill, Kos, Kyle, Lake, La Manche, Lane, Latch, Leat, Lee-lane, Leet, Limber, Major, Meatus, Medium, Minch, Moat, Mozambique,

Multiplex, Narrows, North, Nulla(h), Offtake, Penstock, Pentland Firth, Pescadores, Pipeline, Qanat, Race, Raceway, Rean, Rebate, Rigol(l), Rigolets, Rivulet, Run, Sea-gate, Seaway, Sewer, Shatt-el-Arab, Shunt, Side, Sinus, Sky, Sloot, Sluice, Sluit, Sny(e), Solent, Solway Firth, Sound, Source, Sow, Spillway, Sprue, Strait, Suez, Sure, Swash, Tailrace, Tideway, Trough, Ureter, Vein, Wasteweir, Watercourse, Waterspout, Yucatan

Chant Anthem, Antiphon, Cantillate, Cantus, Chaunt, Decantate, Euouae, Evovae, Gregorian, Haka, Harambee, Hymn, Incantation, Intone, Introit, Mantra(m), Motet, Pennillion-singing, Proper, Psalm, Sing, Slogan, Te Deum, The Reproaches, Yell

Chaos, Chaotic Abyss, Anarchy, Confusion, Disorder, Disorganised, Fitna, Fractal, Goat fuck, Havoc, Helter-skelter, Hun-tun, Jumble, Maelstrom, Mayhem, Mess, Muddle, Muss, Pandemonium, Shambles, Snafu, Tohu bohu, Turmoil

▷**Chaotic** *may indicate* an anagram

Chapel Alamo, Bethel, Bethesda, Beulah, Cha(u)ntry, Chevet, Ebenezer, Feretory, Galilee, Lady, Oratory, Proprietary, Sacellum, Sistine

▷**Chaps** *may indicate* an anagram

Chapter Accidents, C, Canon, Cap, Capitular, Ch, Chap, Cr, Division, Episode, Lodge, Phase, Section, Social, Sura(h), Verse

Character(s) Aesc, Agma, Alphabet, Ampersand, Ampussyand, Antihero, Aura, Backbone, Backslash, Brand, Calibre, Case, Cipher, Clef, Cliff, Climate, Complexion, Contour, Credit, Digamma, Domino, Dramatis personae, Emoticon, Ess, Essence, Eta, Ethos, →**FEATURE**, Fibre, Fish, Fist, Form, Grain, Grass, Grit, Hair, Heart, Her, Hieroglyphic, Him, Hue, Ideogram, Ideograph, Italic, Kern, Kind, La(m)bda, Letter, Logogram, Make-up, Mark, Mettle, Mu, Nagari, →**NATURE**, Nu, Ogam, Ogham, Pahlavi, Pantaloon, Part, Pehlevi, Person(a), Personage, →**PERSONALITY**, Phonogram, Physiognomy, Protagonist, Psi, Reference, Reference-mark, Repute, Rho, Role, Rune, Runic, Sampi, San, Script, Sel(f), Sigma, Sign, Sirvente, Slash, Sonancy, Sort, Stamp, Subscript, Superhero, Superscript(ion), Swung dash, Syllabary, Symbol, Tab, Temperament, Testimonial, Ton(e), Trait, Uncial, Vav, Vee, Waw, Wen

Characterise(d), Characterism, Characteristic(s) Attribute, Aura, Cast, Colour, Distinctive, Earmark, Ethos, Example, Facies, Feature, Hair, Hallmark, Has, Headmark, Idiomatic, Idiosyncrasy, Jizz, Keystroke, Lineament, Mark, Metamorphism, Mien, Nature, Notate, Note, Peculiar, Persona, Point, Property, Quality, Stigma, Strangeness, Streak, Style, Trademark, Typical, Vein, Way

Charge(s), Charged, Charger Access, Accusal, Accuse, Aerate, Agist, Allege, Anchorage, Anion, Annulet, Arraign, Ascribe, Assault, Baton, Battery, Bear, Behest, Blame, Book, Brassage, Brush, Buckshot, Bum rap, Burden, Care, Carrying, Cathexis, Cellarage, Command, Commission, Community, Complaint, Congestion, Corkage, Cost, Count, Cover, Criminate, Damage, Debit, Delate, Delf, Delph, Demurrage, Depth, Depute, Directive, Dittay, Dockage, Due, Duty, Dynamise, Electric, Electron, Entrust, Entry, Exit, Expense, Fare, Fee, Fill, Fixed, Flag fall, Fleur-de-lis, Floating, Flock, Freight, Fullage, Fuse, Fusil, Fuze, Gazump, Giron, Gravamen, Gyron, →**HERALDIC**, Horse, Hot, Hypothec, Impeach, Impute, Incriminate, Indict, Inescutcheon, Inform, Instinct, Ion, Isoelectric, Laid, Last, Levy, Lien, Lioncel(le), Lionel, Live, Load, Lozenge, Mandate, Metage, Mine, Mob, Mount, Mulct, Nuclear, Objure, Obtest, Onrush, Onslaught, Onus, Ordinary, Orle, Overhead, Pastoral, Pervade, Pew-rent, Plaint,

Positive, Postage, Premium, Prime, Prix fixe, Q, Quayage, Rack-rent, Rampage, Rap, Rate, Recrimination, Red-dog, Rent, Report, Reprise, Reverse, Roundel, Run, →**RUSH**, Saddle, Service, Specific, Stampede, Steed, Storm, Supplement, Tariff, Tax(ation), Tear, Terms, Tilt, Toll, Tonnage, →**TRAY**, Tressure, Trickle, Trust, Tutorage, Upfill, Vaire, Vairy, Verdoy, Vigorish, Ward, Warhead, Warhorse, Wharfage, Yardage

Charitable, Charity Aid, Alms, Alms-deed, Awmous, Benign, Breadline, Caritas, Chugger, Dole, Dorcas, Eleemosynary, Glove money, Good works, Kiwanis, Largesse, Leniency, Liberal, Lion, Love, Mercy, Oddfellow, Openhanded, Outreach, Oxfam, Pelican, Philanthropic, Rotarian, Samaritan, Zakat

Charm(er), Charmed, Charming Abracadabra, Abrasax, Abraxas, Agacerie, Allure, Amulet, Appeal, Aroma, Attraction, Bangle, Beguile, Bewitch, Bracelet, Captivate, Charisma, Chocolate box, Circe, Comether, Cramp-bone, Cute, Cutie, Debonair, Delight(ful), Emerods, Enamour, Enchant, Engaging, Ensorcell, →**ENTRANCE**, Fascinate, Fay, Fetching, Fetish, Grace, Greegree, Gri(s)gris, Hand of glory, Horseshoe, Houri, Incantation, Juju, Magnetic, Mascot, Mojo, Nice, Obeah, Obi(a), Periapt, Personal, Phylactery, Porte-bonheur, Prince, Pull, Purty, Quaint, Quark, Ravish, Siren, Smoothie, Spellbind, Suave, Sweetness, Taking, Talisman, Telesm, Temptress, Tiki, Trinket, Unction, Voodoo, Winsome
▷**Charming** *may indicate* an anagram

Chart(ed), Charting Abac, Alignment, Bar, Breakeven, Card, Diagram, Draw, Eye, Flip, Flow, Gantt, Graph, Histogram, Histograph, Horoscope, Hydrography, Isogram, Isopleth, List, Log, Magna Carta, →**MAP**, Mappemond, Movement, Nomogram, Plot, Portolano, Rating, Ringelmann, Run, Snellen, Social, Sociogram, Table, Test, Timetable, Waggoner, Weather

Charta, Charter Book, Covenant, Freedom, Hire, Lease, Let, Novodamus, Rent

Chase(d), Chaser, Chasing Cannock, Chace, Chevy, Chivy, Ciseleur, Ciselure, Course, Cranbome, Decorate, Drink, Game, Harass, Hound, →**HUNT**, Inlaid, Inscribe, Jumper, Oxo, Pursuit, Race, Scorse, Sic(k), Snag, Steeple, Sue, Suit, Toreutic, Venery, Wild-goose

Chasm Abyss, Fissure, Gap, Gorge, Gulf, Hiatus, Ravine, Rent, Schism, Yawn

Chaste, Chastity Aggie, Agnes, Attic, Celibate, Classic, Clean, Continent, Fatima, Florimell, Ines, Innocent, Modesty, Nessa, Nunlike, Platonic, →**PURE**, Vestal, Virginal, Virtue

Chat, Chatter(box), Chatterer Babble, Bavardage, Bird, Blab(ber), Blatherskite, Blether, Campanero, Causerie, Chelp, Chew the fat, Chinwag, Clack, Clishmaclaver, Confab(ulate), Converse, Cosher, Coze, Crack, Dialogue, Froth, Gab(ble), Gas, Gibble-gabble, Gossip, Gup, Hobnob, Jabber, Jargon, Jaw, Kilfud, Liaise, Madge, Mag(pie), Nashgab, Natter, Patter, Pie, Pourparler, Prate, Prattle, Rabbit, Rabble, Rap, Rattle, Schmooze, Scuttlebutt, Shmoose, Shoot the breeze, Stone, Talk, Talkee-talkee, Talky-talky, Tattle, Twattle, Waffle, Whin, Windbag, Witter, Wongi, Yacketyyak, Yad(d)a-yad(d)a-yad(d)a, Yak, Yarn, Yatter, Yellow-breasted, Yoking

Cheap A bon marché, Bargain, Base, Budget, Catchpenny, Cheesy, Chintzy, Cut-price, Downmarket, Gimcrack, Giveaway, Jitney, Kitsch, Knockdown, Low, Off-peak, Poor, Sacrifice, Shoddy, Steerage, Stingy, Tarty, Tatty, Tawdry, Ticky-tacky, Tinpot, Tinselly, Trashy, Trivial, Twopenny-halfpenny, Undear, Vile
▷**Cheap** *may indicate* a d- or p- start to a word

Cheat(ers), Cheating Bam, Bamboozle, Bedswerver, Beguile, Bilk, Bite(r), Bob, Bonnet, Bubble, Bucket, Bullock, Bunce, Burn, Cabbage, Cardsharp(er),

Charlatan, Chiaus, Chicane(ry), Chisel, Chouse, Clip, Cod, Cog(ger), Colt, Con, Cony-catcher, Cozen, Crib, Cross, Cross-bite(r), Cuckold, Cully, Defraud, Delude, Diddle, Dingo, Dish, Do, Do down, Doublecross, Double-dealer, Duckshove, Dupe, Escroc, Faitor, Fiddle, Finagle, Fix, Flam, Flanker, Fleece, Fob, Foister, Fox, Fraud, Gaff, Gamesmanship, Gip, Glasses, Gudgeon, Gum, Gyp, Hoax, Hocus, Hoodwink, Hornswoggle, Horse, Intake, Jockey, Magsman, Mulct, Mump, Nick, Nobble, Pasteboard, Picaro(on), Plagiarist, Poop, Queer, Rib, Rig, Rogue, Rook, Rush, Scam, Screw, Screw over, Sell, Shaft, Sharper, Sharpie, Sharp practice, Short-change, Slur, Smouch, Snap, Specs, Stack, Stiff, Sting, Swindle, Take-in, Thimble-rigging, Trepan, Trick(ster), Trim, Twister, Two-time, Welch, Welsh, Wheedle

Check(ed) Abort, Anchor, Arrest, Audit, Ba(u)lk, Bauk, Bill, Block, Bridle, Collate, Compesce, Confirm, Control, Count, Counterroll, Cramp, Cross-index, Curb, Dam, Damp, Detain, Detent, Discovered, Ditch, Dogs-tooth, Examine, Foil, Forestall, Frisk, Frustrate, Gingham, Halt, Hamper, Hobble, Houndstooth, Inhibit, Inspect, Jerk, Jerque, Let, Limit(ation), Mate, Measure, Medical, Meter, Monitor, Nip, Observe, Obstacle, Overhaul, Parity, Perpetual, Prevent, Rain, Reality, Rebuff, Rebuke, Rein, Repress, Reprime, Repulse, Reread, Resist, → **RESTRAIN**, Retard, Revoke, Saccade, Screen, Service, Setback, Shepherd's, Shorten, Sit-upon, Sneap, Sneb, Snib, Snub, Sound, Spongebag, Spot, Standard, Std, → **STEM**, Stent, Stint, Stocktake, Stop(-go), Stunt, Style, Subdue, Suppress, Tab, Tally, Tartan, Tattersall, Test, Thwart, Tick, Trash, Verify, Vet

Cheek(y) Alforja, Audacity, Brash, Buccal, Chap, Chit, Chollers, Chutzpah, Crust, Cub, Flippant, Fresh, Gall, Gena(l), Gobby, Gum, Hussy, Insult, Irreverent, Jackanapes, Jowl, Lip, Malapert, Malar, Masseter, Neck, Nerve, Noma, Pert, Presumption, Quean, Sass, Sauce, Sideburns, Uppity, Upstart, Wang, Whippersnapper, Yankie, Zygoma

Cheer(s), Cheerful(ness), Cheering Acclaim, Agrin, Applaud, Arrivederci, Banzai, Barrack, Blithe, Bonnie, Bravo, Bright, Bronx, Bubbly, Buck, Buoy(ant), Cadgy, Canty, Carefree, Cherry, Chin-chin, Chipper, Chirpy, Chirrupy, → **COMFORT**, Consolate, Console, Convivial, Crouse, Debonair, Drink, Ease, Elate, Elevate, Encourage, Enliven, Exhilarate, Exuberant, Festive, Genial, Gladden, Goodbye, Happy-go-lucky, Hearten, Hilarity, Holiday, Hooch, Hoorah, Hurra(h), Huzzah, Insouciance, Joco, Jocund, Jovial, Kia-ora, L'allegro, Light-hearted, Lightsome, Lively, Meal, Olé, Optimistic, Ovate, Peart, Perky, Please, Praise, Prosit, Rah, Riant, Rivo, Roar, Root, Rosy, Rumbustious, Shout, Sko(a)l, Slainte, Smiley, Sonsie, Sunny, Ta, Tata, Thanks, Three, Tiger, Tiggerish, Toodle-oo, Up, Upbeat, Uplift, Warm, Winsome, Yell

Cheese, Cheesy American, Amsterdam, Appenzell, Asiago, Au gratin, Bel Paese, Blue, Blue vein, Boc(c)oncini, Boursin, Brie, Caboc, Caerphilly, Cambazola, Camembert, Cantal, Casein, Caseous, Cheddar, Cheshire, Chessel, Chèvre, Colby, Comte, Cottage, Coulommiers, Cream, Crowdie, Curd, Damson, Danish blue, Derby, Dolcelatte, Double Gloucester, Dunlop, Dutch, Edam, Emmental(er), Emmenthal(er), Ermite, Esrom, Ewe, Fet(a), Fontina, Fromage frais, Fynbo, Gloucester, Goat, Gorgonzola, Gouda, Grana Padano, Green, Gruyère, Halloumi, Hard, Havarti, Huntsman, Ilchester, Islay, Jarlsberg®, Junket, Kebbock, Kebbuck, Kenno, Killarney, Lancashire, Leicester, Lemon, Limburg(er), Lymeswold®, Macaroni, Manchego, Mascarpone, Monterey Jack, Mousetrap, Mozzarella, Mu(e)nster, Mycella, Neufchatel, Numero uno, Oka, Orkney, Paneer, Parmesan, Pecorino, Pont l'Eveque, Port Salut, Pot, Provolone,

Quark, Raclette, Rarebit, Reblochon, Red Leicester, Rennet, Ricotta, Romano, Roquefort, Sage Derby, Samso, Sapsago, Skyr, Stilton®, Stone, Stracchino, Swiss, Taleggio, Tilsit, Tofu, Truckle, Vacherin, VIP, Wensleydale, Whey, Yarg

Chef Commis, Escoffier, Oliver, Ramsay

Chelsea Bun, Pensioner, Tractor

Chemical Acid, Acrolein, Adrenalin®, Alar, Aldehyde, Alkali, Alum(ina), Amide, Amino-group, Avertin, Barilla, Bromic, Bute, Camphene, Camphor, Carbide, Caseose, Catalyst, Cephalin, Coal tar, Co-factor, Developer, Dopamine, Encephalin, Ethanal, Ethoxy, Ethyl, Fixer, Fluoride, Formyl, Fungicide, Furosemide, Gibbsite, Glutamine, Glycol, Halide, Halon, Harmin, Heptane, Hexylene, Histamine, Hormone, Hypo, ICI, Imine, Indican, Inositol, Interleukin, Lewisite, Limonene, Lipid, Masking-agent, Massicot, Naioxone, Napalm, Naphtha, Natron, Neurotransmitter, Nitre, Nitroluene, Nonylphenol, Oestrogen, Olefin, Olein, Oxide, Oxysalt, Paraben, Pentane, Pentene, Pentyl, Peptide, Phenol, Phenyl, Pheromone, Potash, Potassa, Ptomaine, Reagent, Resorcin, Sequestrant, Soup, Stearate, Steroid, Strontia, Styrene, Sulphide, Terpene, Thio-salt, Toluol, Trimer, Tritide, Urethane, Weedkiller, Xylol

Chemist Analyst, Apothecary, Dispenser, Druggist, Drugstore, FPS, Pharmacist, Pothecary

Chemistry Alchemy, Alchymy, Inorganic, Organic, Physical, Radiation, Spageric, Spagiric, Spagyric, Stinks, Stoecheometry, Stoechiometry

Cheque Blank, Bouncer, Giro, Gregory, Stumer, Tab, Traveller's

Cherry (tree) Amarelle, Amazon, Ball, Barbados, Bigaroon, Bigarreau, Blackheart, Bladder, Cerise, Choke, Cornelian, Gean, Ground, Heart, Jerusalem, Kearton, Kermes, Kermesite, Malpighia, Marasca, Maraschino, May-duke, Maz(z)ard, Merry, Morel(lo), Prunus, Red, Whiteheart

Chessman Bishop, Black, Castle, Cheque, Horse, King, Knight, Pawn, Pin, Queen, Rook, White

Chest(y) Ark, Bahut, Bosom, Box, Breast, Buist, Bunker, Bureau, Bust, Caisson, Cap-case, Case, Cassone, Chapel, Charter, Chiffonier, Coffer, Coffin, Coffret, Commode, Cub, Girnel, Hope, Hutch, Inro, Kist, Larnax, Locker, Lowboy, Medicine, Ottoman, Pectoral, Pereion, Pigeon, Pleural, Ribcage, Safe, Scrine, Scryne, Shrine, Sternum, Tallboy, Tea, Thorax, Toolbox, Treasure, Trunk, Wangun, Wanigan, War

Chestnut Aesculus, Auburn, Badious, Ch, Chincapin, Chinese, Chinkapin, Chinquapin, Cliché, Conker, Favel(l), Hoary, Marron, Marron glacé, Moreton Bay, Roan, Russet, Saligot, Soare, Sorrel, Spanish, Sweet, Water

Chew(ing) Bite, Champ, Chaw, Chomp, Crunch, Cud, Gnaw, Gum, Manducate, Masticate, Maul, Meditate, Moop, Mou(p), Munch, Ruminate, Siri(h), Spearmint

Chic Dapper, Debonair, Elegant, Heroin, In, Kick, Modish, Posh, Smart, Soigné, Stylish, Swish, Tonish, Trim

Chick(en) Battery, Biddy, Broiler, Cheeper, Chittagong, Chuckie, Clutch, Cochin(-China), Coward, Cowherd, Craven, Drumstick, Eirack, Gutless, Hen, Howtowdie, Kiev, Layer, Marengo, Minorca, Niderling, Pavid, Poltroon, Poot, Pope's nose, Poult, Pout, Prairie, Precocial, Quitter, Roaster, Scaredy-cat, Spatchcock, Spring, Squab, Supreme, Sussex, Timorous, Unheroic, Unmanly, Wimp, Windy, Wishbone, Wyandotte, Yellow

Chief(tain) Ag(h)a, Arch, Ardrigh, Boss, Caboceer, Cacique, Calif, Caliph, Capital, Capitan, Capitayn, Capo, Caractacus, Caradoc, Cazique, Ch, Chagan, Coriolanus, Dat(t)o, DG, Dominant, Duke, Eleutherarch, Emir, Figurehead, First,

Foremost, Geronimo, Grand, Haggis, →**HEAD**, Hereward, Jarl, Kaid, Keystone, King, Leader, MacDuff, →**MAIN**, Mass, Mocuddum, Mokaddam, Mugwump, Muqaddam, Nawab, Nizam, Nkosi, Oba, Overlord, Pendragon, Predominant, Premier, Primal, Prime, Principal, Provost-marshal, Quanah, Raja(h), Rajpramukh, Rangatira, Ratoo, Ratu, Sachem, Sagamore, Sardar, Sarpanch, Sea-king, Sheikh, Sirdar, Staple, Sudder, Supreme, Tanist, Tank, Taxiarch, Thane, Top

Child(ren), Childhood, Childish Aerie, Alannah, Auf, Babe, Baby, Bach(ch)a, Badger, Bairn, Bambino, Bantling, Boy, Brat, Brood, Butter-print, Ch, Changeling, Cherub, Chick, Chickabiddy, Chit, Collop, Cub, Dream, Duddie weans, Elfin, Eyas, Feral, Foundling, Gangrel, Ge(i)t, Girl, Guttersnipe, Gyte, Heir, Hurcheon, Imp, Infant, Issue, It, Jailbait, Jejune, Juvenile, Kid, Kiddie(wink), Kiddy, Kidult, Kinder, Lad, Lambkin, Limb, Litter, Littlie, Mamzer, Minion, Minor, Mite, Moppet, Munchkin, Naive, Nipper, Nursling, Offspring, Pantywaist, Papoose, Petty, Pickin, Problem, Progeny, Puerile, Puss, Putto, Ragamuffin, Rip, Romper, Rug rat, Scion, Seed, Siblings, Smout, Smowt, Sprog, Street arab, Subteen, Ted, Tike, Toddle(r), Tot(tie), Totty, Trot, Tweenie, Tyke, Urchin, Wean, Weanel, Weanling, Weeny-bopper, Whelp, Young, Youngster, Younker, Youth

Chill(er), Chilly Bleak, →**COLD**, Cool, Cryogen, Flu, Frappé, Freeze, Freon®, Frigid, Frosty, Gelid, Ice, Iciness, Laze, Mimi, Oorie, Ourie, Owrie, Parky, Raw, Refrigerate, Relax, Rigor, Scare

Chime(s) Agree, Bell, Clam, Cymar, Jingle, Peal, Rhime, Ring, Semantron, Tink, →**TOLL**

Chimney (pot), Chimney corner Can, Cow(l), Femerall, Flare stack, Flue, Funnel, Lug, Lum, Smokestack, Stack, Stalk, Tallboy, Tunnel

China(man), Chinese Ami, Amoy, Bone, Boxer, Bud(dy), Cameoware, Cantonese, Catayan, Cathay, Celestial, Ch, Chelsea, Chow, Coalport, Cochin, Cock, Colleague, Confucius, Crackle, Crockery, Cully, Delft, Derby, Dresden, Eggshell, Etrurian, Goss, Hakka, Han, Hard paste, Hizen, Hmong, Imari, Ironstone, Kanji, Kaolin, Kuo-yu, Limoges, Macanese, Manchu, Manchurian, Mandarin, Mangi, Maoist, Mate, Meissen, Middle kingdom, Min, Ming, Minton, Oppo, Pal, Pareoean, Pekingese, Pe-tsai, Pinyin, Porcelain, →**POTTERY**, Putonghua, Queensware, Quina, Rockingham, Royal Worcester, Rusticware, Semiporcelain, Seric, Sèvres, Shanghai, Sinaean, Sinic, Sino-, Soft paste, Spode®, Sun Yat-sen, Tai-ping, Taiwanese, Taoist, Teng, Tocharian, Tungus, Uigur, Wal(l)y, Ware, Wedgwood®, Whiteware, Willow pattern, Willowware, Worcester, Wu, Yao, Yellow peril

Chip(s) Blitter, Bo(a)st, Carpenter, Counter, Cut, Deep-fried, Fish, Flake, Fragment, French fry, Hack, Knap, Micro, Microchip, Nacho(s), Nick, Pin, Shaving, Silicon, Spale, Spall, Splinter, Tease, Tortilla, Transputer, Virus
▷**Chip** *may indicate* an anagram

Chirp(y), Chirrup Cheep, Cherup, Chirm, Chirr, Cicada, Peep, Pip, Pipe, Pitter, Stridulate, Trill, Tweet, Twitter

Chisel(ler), Chisel-like Bam, Boaster, Bolster, Bur, Burin, Carve, Cheat, Clip, Drove, Firmer, Gad, Mason, Scalpriform, Scauper, Scorper, Sculpt, Slick, Sting

Chit Docket, Girl, Memo, Note, Voucher

Chivalry, Chivalrous Brave, Bushido, Courtly, Datin, Gallant, Gent, Grandisonian

Chocolate Aero, Brown, Cacao, Carob, Cocoa, Dragee, Ganache, Neapolitan, Noisette, Pinole, Praline, Rolo®, Truffle, Vermicelli

Choice, Choose, Choosy, Chosen Adopt, Anthology, Appoint, Aryan, Ballot, Capped, Cherry-pick, Cull, Dainty, Decide, Druthers, Eclectic, Elect, Elite, Esnecy, Fine, Fork, Free will, Hercules, Hobson's, Leet, Leve, Lief, List, Opt, Option, Or, Ossian, Peach, Peacherino, Peculiar, → PICK, Picking, Plum(p), Precious, Predilect, Prefer, Proairesis, Rare, Recherché, → SELECT, Single out, Superb, Try(e), Via media, Volition, Wale

Choir, Choral, Chorister, Chorus Antiphony, Antistrophe, Anvil, Apse, Bass, Burden, Chant, Chorister, Choryphaeus, Dawn, Decani, Faburden, Fauxbourdon, Glee, Glee club, Group, Hallelujah, Harmony, Hymeneal, Motet, Parabasis, Precentor, Quirister, → REFRAIN, Reprise, Schola cantorum, Serenata, Singing, Strophe, Treble, Triad

Choke(r) Accloy, Block, Clog, Die, Gag, Silence, Smoor, Smore, Smother, Stifle, Stop, Strangle(hold), Strangulate, → THROTTLE, Warp

Chop, Chops, Chopper(s), Choppy Adze, Air tax, Ax(e), Cakehole, Celt, Charge, Cheek, Chump, Cleave, Côtelette, Cuff, Curtail, Cutlet, Dice, Dismissal, False teeth, Fell(er), Flew, Hack, Hash, Helicopter, Hew, Ivory, Karate, Lop, Mince, Mouth, Rotaplane, Rough, Split, Standing, Suey, Teeth, Underhand, Wang

Chord(s) Altered, Arpeggio, Barré, Common, Diameter, Harmony, Intonator, Nerve, Sixth, Triad, Vocal

Christ Ecce homo, Lamb of God, Logos, Messiah, Paschal Lamb, Saviour, Son (of God), Son of Man, X

Christen(ing) Baptise, Launch, Name-day

Christian(ity) Adventist, Albigenses, Antioch, Baptist, Beghard, Believer, Cathar(ist), Colossian, Coptic, Dior, Donatist, D(o)ukhobor, Ebionite, Eucharistic, Fletcher, Galilean, Giaour, Gilbertine, Gnostic, Goy, Holy roller, Homo(i)ousian, Jehovah's Witness, Maronite, Marrano, Melchite, Melkite, Molinism, Monarchian, Monophysite, Moral, Mozarab, Mutineer, Nazarene, Nestorian, Phalange, Pilgrim, Protestant, Quartodeciman, RC, Sabotier, Scientist, SCM, Solifidian, Traditor, Uniat(e), Unitarian, Waldensian, Wesleyan, Xian, Zwinglian

Christmas(time) Advent, Beetle, Box, Cactus, Card, Carol, Chrissie, Day, Dec, Island, Nativity, Noel, Nowel(l), Pudding, Stocking, Xmas, Yuletide

Chronicle(r) Anglo-Saxon, Annal, Brut, Calendar, Diary, Froissart, Hall, Historiographer, History, Holinshed, Logographer, Narrative, Paralipomena, Parian, → RECORD, Register, Stow

Church Abbey, Armenian, Auld Licht, Autocephalous, Basilica, Bethel, Bethesda, Brood, Byzantine, → CATHEDRAL, CE, Ch, Chapel, Chevet, Classis, Clergy, Collegiate, Congregational, Coptic, Decanal, Delubrum, Easter (Orthodox), EC, Ecumenical, Episcopal, Episcopalian, Established, Faith, Fold, Free, High, Institutional, Kirk, Lateran, Low, Lutheran, Maronite, Melchite, Methodist, Minster, Moonie, Moravian, Mormon, Mother, National, Nazarene, Nestorian, Notre Dame, Old Light, Oratory, Orthodox, Parish, Peculiar, Prebendal, Presbyterian, Ratana, RC, Reformed, Rome, Schism house, Schism shop, Secession, Shrine, Smyrna, Stave, Steeple, Steeplehouse, Tabernacle, Temple, Title, Titular, Transept, Unification, United Free, Wee Free, Western

Churchgoer, Churchman, Churchwarden Anglican, Azymite, Barnabite, Cameronian, Cantor, High, Marrowman, Moonie, Pew-opener, Predicant, Predikant, Racovian, Romanist, Ruridecanal, Socinian, Spike, Subchanter, Subdeacon, Succentor, Ubiquitarian, Verger, Vestryman

Ciao Adieu, Adios, Aloha

Cider Drink, Hard, Perry, Scrumpy, Sweet

Cigar(ette), Cigarette cards Beedi(e), Bidi, Biftah, Bifter, Bumper, Burn, Camberwell carrot, Cancer stick, Caporal, Cartophily, Cheroot, Cigarillo, Claro, Coffin nail, Conch, Concha, Corona, Dog-end, Doob, Durry, Fag, Filter-tip, Gasper, Giggle(-stick), Havana, Joint, Locofoco, Long-nine, Loosies, Low-tar, Maduro, Manilla, Number, Panatella, Paper-cigar, Perfecto, Puritano, Reefer, Regalia, Roach, Roll-up, Segar, Smeek, Smoke, Snout, Splif(f), Stogie, Stog(e)y, Stompie, Tab, Twist, Weed, Whiff, Woodbine, Zol

Cinch Doddle, Duck soup, Easy, Stroll

Cinema(s) Art house, Big screen, Biograph, Bioscope, Circuit, Drive-in, Films, Fleapit, Flicks, Grindhouse, IMAX®, Megaplex, Movies, Multiplex, Multiscreen, Mutoscope, New Wave, Nickelodeon, Nouvelle Vague, Odeon, Picture palace, Pictures, Plaza, Scope, Silver-screen, Theatre, Tivoli

Cinnamon, Cinnamon stone Canella, Cassia (bark), Essonite, Hessonite, Saigon, Spice

Circle Almacantar, Almucantar, Annulet, Antarctic, Arctic, Circassian, Co, Colure, Company, Compass, Cordon, Corn, Corolla, Coterie, Cromlech, Crop, Cycloid, Cyclolith, Dip, Disc, Dress, Druidical, Eccentric, Ecliptic, Embail, Enclose, Engird, Epicyclic, Equant, Equator, Equinoctial, Euler's, Fairy ring, Family, Fraternity, Full, Galactic, Girdle, Gloriole, Great, Gyrate, Gyre, Halo, Henge, Hoop, Horizon, Hour, Hut, Inner, Inorb, Lap, Longitude, Loop, Magic, Malebolge, Mandala, Meridian, Mohr's, Mural, Nimbus, O, Orb, Orbit, Parhelic, Parquet, Parterre, Penannular, Peristalith, Pitch, Polar, Quality, Red-line, Rigol, →**RING**, Rondure, Rotate, Roundel, Roundlet, Seahenge, Sentencing, Set, Setting, Small, Sphere, Stemme, Stone, Stonehenge, Striking, Surround, Tinchel, Tondino, Traffic, Transit, Tropic, Turning, Umbel, Upper, Vertical, Vicious, Vienna, Virtuous, Volt, Wheel, Whorl

Circuit(-board), Circuitous Ambit, AND, Autodyne, Bridge, Bus, Bypass, Chipset, Closed, Comparator, Daughterboard, Diocese, Discriminator, Dolby®, Electrics, Equivalent, Eyre, Feedback, Gate, Gyrator, Half-adder, Highway, IC, Indirect, Integrated, Interface, Lap, Le Mans, Limiter, Live, Logic, Loop, Microchip, Microprocessor, Monza, Motherboard, NAND, NOR, NOT, Open, OR, Orbital, Perimeter, Phantom, Phase, Preamp, Printed, Push-pull, Quadripole, Racetrack, Reactance, Ring main, Round, Roundure, Rubber-chicken, Scaler, Series, Short, Silverstone, Smoothing, Sound card, Squelch, Stage, Three-phase, Tour, Trunk, Windlass, XNOR, XOR

Circular Annular, Brochure, Court, Disc(al), Endless, Flysheet, Folder, Leaflet, Mailshot, Orby, Round, Spiral, Unending, Vertical, Wheely

Circulate, Circulation, Circulatory Ambient, Astir, Bandy, Bloodstream, Cyclosis, Disseminate, Eddy, Flow, Gross, Gyre, Issue, Mingle, Mix, Orbit, Out and about, Pass, Publish, Report, Revolve, Rotate, Scope, Send round, Spread, Stir, Treadmill, Troll, Utter

▷**Circulating** *may indicate* an anagram

Circumference Boundary, Girth, Perimeter, Size

Circumstance(s), Circumstantial Case, Concept, Detail, Event, Fact, Formal, →**INCIDENT**, Mitigating, Precise, Shebang, Situation, Stede

Circus, Circus boy Arena, Big top, Flea, Flying, Hippodrome, Marquee, Maximus, Media, Monty Python, Oxford, Piccadilly, Ring, Three-ring

Citation, Cite Adduce, Allegation, Instance, Mensh, Mention, Name, Quote, Recall, Reference, Repeat, Sist, Summon

Citizen(s), Citizenship Burgess, Burgher, Civism, Cleruch, Denizen, Dicast, Ephebe, Franchise, Freeman, Jus sanguinis, Jus soli, Kane, Keelie, National, Oppidan, Patrial, People, Proletarian, Propr(a)etor, Quirites, Resident, Roman, Second-class, Senior, Snob, Subject, Townspeople, Trainband, Trierarch, Venireman, Vigilante, Voter

Citrus Acid, Calamondin, Cedrate, Hesperidium, Lemon, Lime, Mandarin, Min(n)eola, Orange, Pomelo, Tangerine, Ugli

City Agra, Astrakhan, Athens, Atlantis, Babylon, Burgh, Cardboard, Carthage, Cosmopolis, Ctesiphon, EC, Empire, Eternal, Forbidden, Gath, Heavenly, Holy, Inner, LA, Leonine, Medina, Megalopolis, Metropolis, Micropolis, Mother, Municipal, Mycenae, Nineveh, NY, Petra, Pompeii, Rhodes, See, Smoke, Sparta, Square mile, Tech, The Big Smoke, Town, Ur, Urban(e), Vatican, Weltstadt, Yonkers

Civil(ian), Civilisation, Civilised, Civility Amenity, Amicable, Christian, Citizen, Civ(vy), Comity, Courtesy, Culture, Fertile crescent, Humane, Humanised, Indus Valley, Maya, Minoan, Mufti, Municipal, Nok, Paramilitary, Plain clothes, Polite, Politesse, Push-button, Respectful, Secular, Temporal, Urbane

Claim(s) Allege, Appeal, Arrogate, Assert, Bag, Challenge, Charge, Crave, Darraign(e), Darrain(e), Darrayn, Demand, Deraign, Droit, Encumbrance, Exact, Haro, Harrow, Insist, Lien, List, Maintain, Nochel, Plea, Pose, Posit, Postulate, Predicate, Pretence, Pretend, Profess, Pulture, Purport, Puture, Rank, Revendicate, Right, Set-off, Small, Sue, Title

Claimant Irredentist, Petitioner, Pot-waller, Pretender, Prospector, Tichborne, Usurper

Clam Bivalve, Chowder, Cohog, Geoduck, Giant, Gweduc, Hardshell, Littleneck, Mollusc, Mya, Quahang, Quahog, Razor(-shell), Round, Steamer, Tridacna, Venus, Vongole

Clammy Algid, Damp, Dank, Moist, Sticky, Sweaty

Clamp(er) Chuck, Clinch, Denver boot, Fasten, Grip, Haemostat, Holdfast, Jumar, Pinchcock, Potato-pit, Stirrup, Tread, Vice, Wheel

Clan(sman) Brood, Cameron, Campbell, Clique, Gens, Gentile, Group, Horde, Kiltie, Kindred, Name, Ngati, Nomen, Phratry, Phyle, Sect, Sept, Society, Stewart, Stuart, Tribe

Clap(per), Clapping Applaud, Blow, Castanet, Chop, Crotal, Dose, Jinglet, Peal, Plaudit(e), Stroke hands, Thunder, Tonant

Clarify, Clarified, Clarifier Clear, Despumate, Dilucidate, Elucidate, Explain, Explicate, Fine, Finings, Ghee, Purge, Refine, Render, Simplify, Tease out

Clash(ing) Bang, Clangour, Clank, Claver, Coincide, Collide, Conflict, Dissonant, Friction, Gossip, →IMPACT, Incident, Jangle, Jar, Loud, Missuit, Riot, Shock, Showdown, Strike, Swash, Tilt

Clasp(ing) Adpress, Agraffe, Barrette, Brooch, Button, Catch, Chape, Clip, Embrace, Fibula, Grasp, Hasp, Hesp, Hook, Hug, Link, Morse, Netsuke, Ochreate, Ouch, Peace, Press, Slide, Tach(e), Unite

Class(ification), Classify, Classified, Classy Acorn, Arrange, Assort, Bourgeois(ie), Bracket, Brand, Breed, Business, Cabin, Canaille, Caste, →CATEGORY, Chattering, Cheder, Cl, Cladistics, Clan, Clerisy, Clinic, Club, Composite, Course, Criminal, Dalit, Dewey, Digest, Division, Economy, Establishment, Estate, Evening, Faction, First, Folksonomy, Form, Genera, Genre, Gentry, Genus, →GRADE, Group, Harvard, Haryan, Heder, Hubble,

Ilk, Keep-fit, Kidney, Kohanga reo, League, Lesson, Life, Linn(a)ean, List, Lower, Mammal, Master, Meritocracy, Middle, Night, Number, Nursery, Order, Peasantry, Petit bourgeois, Phenetics, Phylum, Pigeon-hole, Pleb(eian), Posh, Proletariat, Proper, Race, Range, Rank, Rate, Rating, Raypoot, Raypout, Reception, Remove, Ruling, Salariat, Second, Secret, Seminar, Shell, Siege, Social, Sort(ation), Spectral, Sphere, Standard, Steerage, Stratum, Stream, Syntax, Taxonomy, Teach-in, Third, Tony, Tourist, Tribe, Tutorial, →**TYPE**, U, Universal, Upper, Varna, Water, Working, World, Year

Classic(al), Classics, Classicist Ageless, Ancient, Basic, Derby, Elzevir, Epic, Grecian, Greek, Humane, Leger, Literature, Oldie, Pliny, Purist, Roman, Standard, Traditional, Vintage

Clause Acceleration, Adjunct, Apodosis, Article, Complement, Condition, Escalator, Escape, Filioque, Four, Golden parachute, Grandfather, Member, Noun, Novodamus, Object, Poison-pill, Predicator, Protasis, Proviso, Reddendum, Relative, Reservation, Reserve, Rider, Salvo, Sentence, Subject, Subordinate, Sunset, Tenendum, Testatum

Claw Chela, Claut, Cloye, Crab, Dewclaw, Edate, Falcula, Grapple, Griff(e), Hook, Insessorial, Lark-heel, Nail, Nipper, Pounce, Scrab, Sere, Talent, Tear, Telson, Unguis

Clay Ali, Argil, Blaes, Blaise, Blaize, Blunge, Bole, Boulder, Calm, Cam, Cassius, Caum, Ceramic, Charoset(h), China, Cloam, Clunch, Cob, Earth, Engobe, Fango, Figuline, Fuller's earth, Gault, Glei, Gley, Hardpan, Haroset(h), Illite, Kaolin, Kokowai, Laterite, Lithomarge, Loam, London, Lute, Malm, Marl, Meerschaum, Mire, Mortal, Mud, Oxford, Papa, Pipeclay, Pise, Potter's, Pottery, Pug, Saggar(d), Sagger, Seggar, Slip, Slurry, Terra sigillata, Thill, Till(ite), Varve, Warrant, Warren, Wax

Clean(er), Cleaning, Cleanse Abrasive, Absterge, Ammonia, Besom, Bidet, Blanco, Bleach, Blue flag, Boots, Bream, Breast, Broom, Careen, Catharise, Catharsis, Chamois leather, Char(e), Chaste, Clear, Cottonbud, Daily, Debride, Depurate, Deterge(nt), Dhobi, Dialysis, Dishrag, Disinfect, Do, Douche, Dredge, Dust(er), Dyson®, Eluant, Emunge, Enema, Epurate, Erase, Ethnic, Evacuant, Evacuate, Expurgate, Fay, Fettle, Fey, Floorcloth, Floss, Flush, Full, Grave, Groom, Gut, Heels, Home help, Hoover®, House-trained, Hygienic, Immaculate, Innocent, J-cloth, Kosher, Launder, Lave, Linish, Lustrum, Lye, Mouthwash, Mrs Mop(p), Mundify, Net, Nipter, Overhaul, Porge, Prophylaxis, Pull-through, Pumice, Pure, Purgative, Purge, Ramrod, Rebite, Rub, Rump, Sanitize, Scaffie, Scavenge, Scour, Scrub, Shampoo, Shot-blast, Snow-white, Soap, Soogee, Soogie, Soojey, Sponge, Spotless, Square, Squeaky, Squeegee, Squilgee, Sterile, Sujee, Swab, Sweep, Syringe, Tissue, Turpentine, Uproot, Vac(uum), Valet, →**WASH**, Whistle, Whiter, Wipe, Zamboni

Clear(ance), Cleared, Clearer, Clearly Absolve, Acquit, Allow, Aloof, Apparent, Articulate, Assart, Bald, Bell, Berth, Bold, Bore, Brighten, Bus, Clarify, Cloudless, Cogent, Comprehensive, Concise, Consomme, Crystal, Daylight, Decode, Decongest, Definite, De-ice, Demist, Diaphanous, Disafforest, Dispel, Distinct, Downright, Eidetic, Evacuate, Evident, Exculpate, Exonerate, Explicit, Express, Fair, Flagrant, Gain, Get over, Headroom, Highland, Hyaline, Intelligible, Iron, Laund, Leap, Leapfrog, Legible, Limpid, Lucid, Luculent, Manifest, Mop, Neat, Negotiate, Net(t), No brainer, Observable, Obvious, Ope(n), Overleap, Overt, Palpable, Patent, Pay, Pellucid, Perspicuous, Plain, Play, Pratique, Predy, Pure, Purge, Quit, Rack, Realise, Reap, Remble, Rid, Ripple,

Serene, Sheer, Shere, Silvery, Slum, Snowplough, Specific, Stark, Straight, Strip, Succinct, Sweep, Swidden, Thro(ugh), Thwaite, Transire, Translucent, Transparent, Unambiguous, Unblock, Unclog, Uncork(ed), Unequivocal, Unstop, Vault, Vindicate, Vivid, Void, Well, Whiten, Windage, Wipe

Clearing Assart, Glade, Opening, Shire, Slash

Cleft Crevice, Fissirostral, Notch

Clench Close, Double, Grip, Grit, Squeeze, Stiffen, Tense

Clergy(man), Cleric(al) Abbé, Abbot, Archdeacon, Ayatollah, Canon, Cantor, Cardinal, Chancellor, Chaplain, Chapter, Circuit rider, Cleric, Clerk, Cloth, Curate, Curé, Deacon, Dean, Ecclesiast(ic), God-botherer, Goliard, Holy Joe, Incumbent, Josser, Levite, Ministerial, Ministry, Minor canon, Non-juror, Non-usager, Notarial, Padre, Parson, Pastor, Pontifex, Pontiff, Preacher, Prebendary, Precentor, Prelate, Presbyter, Presenter, Priest, Primate, Prior, Proctor, Rabbi, Rector, Red-hat, Reverend, Rome-runner, Scribal, Secretarial, Secular, Shaveling, Shepherd, Slope, Spin-text, Squarson, Subdeacon, Theologian, Vartabed, Vicar

Clerk(s) Actuary, Articled, Baboo, Babu, Basoche, Circar, Cleric, Cratchit, Cursitor, Enumerator, Limb, Notary, Paper-pusher, Penman, Penpusher, Petty Bag, Poster, Protocolist, Prot(h)onotary, Quill-driver, Recorder, St Nicholas's, Scribe, Secretariat, Sircar, Sirkar, Tally, Town, Vestry, Vicar, Writer

Clever(ness) Able, Accomplished, Adroit, Astute, Brainy, Bright, Canny, Cool, Cunning, Cute, Daedal(e), Deft, Genius, Gleg, Habile, Ingenious, Intellectual, Know-all, Natty, Nimblewit, Resourceful, Sage(ness), Shrewd, Skeeley, Skilful, Smart(y), Smarty-pants, Souple, Subtle

Cliché Banality, Boilerplate, Commonplace, Corn, Journalese, Platitude, Saying, Tag

Click(er), Clicking Castanet, Catch, Forge, Implosive, Pawl, Ratch(et), Snick, Succeed, Tchick, Ticktack

Client Account, Customer, End-user, Fat, Gonk, John, Patron, Thin, Trick

Cliff(s) Beachy Head, Bluff, Cleve, Crag, Craig, Escarp, Lorelei, Palisade(s), Precipice, Promontory, Sca(u)r

Climate Ambience, Atmosphere, Attitude, Continental, Mood, Saharan, Sun, Temperament, Temperature, Weather

Climax Apex, Apogee, Catastasis, Come, Crescendo, Crest, Crisis, Culminate, Edaphic, End, Head, Height, Heyday, Moment of truth, Orgasm, Payoff, Selling, Top, Zenith

Climb(er), Climbing Aid, Alpinist, Aralia, Aristolochia, Artificial, Ascend, Bignonian, Bougainvillaea, Breast, Briony, Bryony, Clamber, Clematis, Clusia, Cowage, Cowhage, Cowitch, Crampon, Creeper, Cubeb, Cucumber, Dodder, Eglatere, Ers, Heart-pea, Hedera, Honeysuckle, Ibex, Ivy, Jamming, Kie-kie, Kudzu, Lawyer, Layback, Liana, Liane, →MOUNT, Pareira, Parvenu, Pea, Peg, Poison oak, Prusik, Rat(t)an, Rhoicissus, Rise, Rope, Scale, Scan, Scandent, Scansores, Sclim, Shin, Shinny, Sklim, Smilax, Social, Speel, Steeplejack, Stegophilist, Sty(e), Swarm, Timbo, Tuft-hunter, Udo, Up(hill), Uprun, Upstart, Vetch, Vine, Vitaceae, Wistaria, Wisteria, With(y)wind, Zoom

Clinch Attach, Determine, Ensure, Fix, Rivet, Secure, Settle

Cling(er), Clinging Adhere, Barnacle, Bur(r), Cherish, Cleave, Embrace, Hold, Hug, Limpet, Ring, Suctorial, Tendril

Clinic Abortuary, Antenatal, Dispensary, Hospital, Hospitium, Mayo

Clip(ped), Clipper, Clipping Alberta, Banana, Barrette, Bicycle, Brash, Bulldog, Butterfly, Cartridge, Chelsea, Clasp, Crocodile, Crop-ear, Crutch,

Curt, Curtail, Cut, Cutty Sark, Dag, Dock, Dod, Excerpt, Film, Fleece, Hairslide, Jubilee, Jumar, Krab, Lop, Money, Mow, Nail, Outtake, Pace, Paper, Pare, Pedicure, Peg, Prerupt, Prune, Roach, Scissel, Secateur, Shear, Ship, Shore, Shorn, Shorten, Snip, Spring, Staccato, Terse, Tie, Tie-tack, Tinsnips, Toe, Tonsure, Topiarist, Trim, Trot

Clique Cabal, Clan, Club, Coterie, Elite, Faction, Four Hundred, Gang, Incrowd, Ring, Sect, Set, Tribe

Cloak(room), Cloaks Aba, Abaya, Abba, Abolla, Amice, Anonymity, Bathroom, Burnous, Capa, Cape, Capote, Caracalla, Cardinal, Cassock, Chasuble, Chimer(e), Chlamydes, Chlamys, Chuddah, Chuddar, Cocoon, Conceal, Cope, Cover, Disguise, Dissemble, Djellaba(h), Domino, Gabardine, Gaberdine, Gal(l)abea(h), Gal(l)abi(y)a(h), Gal(l)abi(y)eh, Gentlemen, Gents, Hall-robe, Heal, Hele, Himation, Hood, Inverness, Jelab, Jellaba, Joseph, Kaross, Korowai, Ladies, Manta, Manteau, Manteel, Mantle, Mant(e)let, →**MASK**, Mousquetaire, Mozetta, Paenula, Paletot, Pallium, Paludamentum, Pelisse, Pilch, Poncho, Rail, Revestry, Rocklay, Rokelay, Roquelaure, Sagum, Sarafan, Scapular, →**SCREEN**, Shroud, Swathe, Talma, Toga, Vestiary, Vestry, Visite

Clock Alarm, Ammonia, Analogue, Astronomical, Atomic, Beetle, Big Ben, Biological, Blowball, Body, Bracket, Bundy, Caesium, Carriage, Cartel, Clepsydra, Cuckoo, Dandelion, Dutch, Floral, Grandfather, Grandmother, Hit, Knock, Long case, Meter, Paenula, Puss, Repeater, Settler's, Solarium, Speaking, Speedo, Strike, Sundial, Taximeter, Tell-tale, Time(r), Travelling, Wag at the wa', Water

Clog(gy) Ball, Block, Clam, Congest, Crowd, Dance, Fur, Galosh, Golosh, Hamper, Jam, Lump, Mire, Obstruct, Overshoe, Patten, Stickjaw

Close(d), Closing, Closure Adjacent, Adjourn, Agree, Airless, Alongside, Anigh, Atresia, Block, Boon, By, Cadence, Cap, Clammy, Clap, Clench, Collapse, Compact, Complete, Concentration, Cone off, Court, Crown cap, Curtain, Dear, Debar, Dense, Dissolve, →**END**, Epilogue, Ewest, Eye to eye, Finale, Forby, Gare, Grapple, Handy, Hard, Hard by, Hot, Humid, Imminent, Inbye, Infibulate, Intent, Intimate, Local, Lock, Lucken, Marginal, Mean, Miserly, Muggy, Mure, Narre, Narrow, Near, Nearhand, Neck and neck, Neist, Next, Nie, Niggardly, Nigh, Nip and tuck, Obturate, Occlude, Occlusion, Oppressive, Parochial, Penny-pinching, Photo-finish, Placket, Precinct, Reserved, Reticent, Seal, Secret, Serre, Serried, Serry, Shet, Shut(ter), Shutdown, Silly, Slam, Snug, Stap, Sticky, Stifling, Stuffy, Sultry, Tailgate, Temenos, Terminate, Tight(knit), Uproll, Wafer, Wanr, Warm, Yard

Closet Cabinet, Confine, Cubicle, Cupboard, Earth, Locker, Safe, Wardrobe, WC, Zeta

Close-up Detail, Fill, Shut, Stop, Zoom

Clot(ting) Bozo, Clump, Coagulate, Duffer, Heparin, Moron

Cloth Aba, Abaya, Abba, Bandanna, Bearing, Bib, Bribe, Carmelite, Clergy, Cloot, Clout, Communion, Corporal(e), →**FABRIC**, →**FELT**, Frocking, Frontal, Gremial, G-string, Habit-cloth, Interfacing, Jharan, Kerchief, Loin, Lungi, Manta, →**MATERIAL**, Mercery, Meshing, Nap, Napery, Napje, Napkin, Nappie, Neckerchief, Needlework, Netting, Pack, Painted, Pall, Pane, Pilch, Priesthood, Pull-through, Rag, Raiment, Roll, Roon, Runner, Sashing, Scarlet, Serviette, Sheet, Sheeting, Shirting, Shoddy, Stock, Stripe, Stupe, Tapestry, Tea, Throw, Tissue, Toilet, Veronica

Clothe(s), Clothing, Clothed Accoutrements, Ao dai, Apparel, Array, Attire, Baggies, Battledress, Besee, Cape, Casuals, Chino, Choli, Cits, Clad,

Clericals, Clobber, Combinations, Confection, Coordinates, Costume, Cour, Cover, Croptop, Cruisewear, Culottes, Deck, Diffusion line, Dight, Don, Drag, →**DRESS**, Duds, Dungarees, Emboss, Endue, Fig leaf, Finery, Foot muff, Frippery, Garb, Garments, Gear, Gere, Get-up, Glad rags, Gymslip, Gyves, Habit, Haute couture, Hejab, Hot pants, Hug-me-tight, Innerwear, Judogi, Jump (suit), Layette, Leathers, Lederhosen, Leisurewear, Long-togs, Menswear, Mitumba, Muff, Nebris, Nightdress, Outfit, Overalls, Pannicle, Pantsuit, Pareu, Pea-coat, Pea-jacket, Pin-striped, Playsuit, Plus fours, Raiment, Rami, Rigout, Robes, Rompers, Samfoo, Samfu, Sayon, Scapulary, Schmutter, Scrubs, Scungies, Shell suit, Shirtwaister, Shroud, Slops, Stomacher, Strip, Sundress, Sunsuit, Swaddling, Swathe, Swothling, Tackle, Things, Toggery, Togs, Tracksuit, Trappings, Trews, Trousseau, Tube top, Tweeds, Unitard, Veiling, Vernicle, Vestiary, Vestiture, Vestment, Wardrobe, Watteau, Wear, Weeds, Wetsuit, Workwear, Yclad, Ycled, Y-fronts

Clothier Dresser, Dressmaker, Tailor

Cloud(ing), Clouded, Cloudiness, Cloudy Altocumulus, Altostratus, Benight, Cirrocumulus, Cirrostratus, Cirrus, Coalsack, Coma, Crab Nebula, Cumulonimbus, Cumulus, Dim, Dull, Emission nebula, Fog, Fractocumulus, Fractostratus, Funnel, Goat's hair, Haze, Horsehead Nebula, Infuscate, Magellanic, Mammatus, Mare's tail, Milky, Mist, Mushroom, Nacreous, Nephele, Nephelometer, Nepho-, Nimbostratus, Nimbus, Nubecula, Nubilous, Nuée ardente, Obnubilation, Obscure, Oort, Overcast, Pall, Pother, Protostar, Rack, Roily, Smoor, Stain, Storm, Stratocumulus, Strat(o)us, Thunder(head), Turbid, Unclear, Virga, War, Water-dog, Weft, Woolpack, Zero-zero

Clove Chive, Eugenia, Garlic, Rose-apple, Split, Yrent

Clover Alfalfa, Alsike, Berseem, Calvary, Cinque, Cow-grass, Dutch, Hare's-foot, Hop, Hop-trefoil, Japan, Ladino, Lespedeza, Medic(k), Melilot, Owl's, Rabbit-foot, Serradella, Serradilla, Shamrock, Souple, Sucklers, Suckling, Trefoil, Trilobe, Truelove

Clown(ish) Airhead, Antic, Antick, August(e), Boor, Bor(r)el, Buffoon, Carl, Chough, Chuff, Clout-shoe, Coco, →**COMEDIAN**, Comic, Costard, Daff, Feste, Froth, Girner, Gobbo, Goon, Gracioso, Grimaldi, Harlequin, Hob, Jack-pudding, Jester, Joey, Joker, Joskin, Leno, Merry Andrew, Mountebank, Nedda, Nervo, Patch(c)ocke, Peasant, Pickle-herring, Pierrot, Put, Rustic, Slouch, Thalian, Touchstone, Trinculo, Wag, Zany

Club(s), Club-like Adelphi, Airn, Alloa, Almack's, Alpeen, Apex, Army and Navy, Arsenal, Artel, Association, Athen(a)eum, Baffy, Band(y), Basto, Bat, Bath, Beefsteak, Blackjack, Blaster, Bludgeon, Boodles, Bourdon, Brassie, Breakfast, Brook's, Bulger, C, Caman, Card, Carlton, Caterpillar, Cavalry, Chapter, Chartered, Chigiriki, Cleek, Clip-joint, Combine, Compassion, Conservative, Constitutional, Cordeliers, Cosh, Cotton, Country, Crockford's, Cudgel, Devonshire, Disco(theque), Dive, Driver, Driving iron, Drones, Fan, Farm team, Fascio, Fellowship, Fleshpot, Garrick, Glee, Golf, Guards, Guild, Hampden, Health, Hell-fire, Hercules', Hetairia, Honky-tonk, Indian, Investment, Iron, Jacobin, Jigger, Job, Jockey, Junior Carlton, Kennel, Kierie, Kiri, Kitcat, Kiwanis, Knobkerrie, Landsdowne, Laughter, League, Leander, Lions, Lofter, Luncheon, Mace, Mallet, Mashie, Maul, Mell, Mere, Meri, Mess, Midiron, Minor suit, Monday, National Liberal, Niblick, Night(stick), Niterie, Nitery, Oddfellows, Paris, Patu, Polt, Pregnant, Priest, Provident, Pudding, Putter, Putting-cleek, RAC, R & A, Reform, Ring, Rota, Rotarian, Rotary, Sap, Savage,

Savile, Shillelagh, Slate, Society, Soroptimist, Sorority, Sorosis, Spoon, Spot, Spurs, Strike, Strip, Stunner, Suicide, Supper, Texas wedge, Thatched House, Tong, Travellers, Trefoil, Truncheon, Trunnion, Union, United Services, Variety, Waddy, Warehouse, Wedge, White's, Wood, Yacht, Youth

Clue 1ac, Across, Acrostic, Anagram, Aradne, Ball, Charade, Clavis, Dabs, Down, → **HINT**, Inkling, Key, Lead, Light, Rebus, Scent, Signpost, Thread, Tip

Clump Cluster, Finial, Knot, Mass, Mot(te), Patch, Plump, Sock, Tread, Tuft, Tump, Tussock

▷**Clumsily** *may indicate* an anagram

Clumsy Artless, Awkward, Bauchle, Blunderbuss, Bungling, Butterfingers, Calf, Chuckle, Clatch, Clodhopper, Cumbersome, Dub, Dutch, Galoot, Galumphing, Gauche, Gimp, Gink, Ham(-fisted), Heavy-handed, Hulk, Inapt, Inelegant, Inept, Inexpert, Klutz, Lob, Loutish, Lubbard, Lubber, Lumbering, Lummox, Lumpish, Maladdress, Maladroit, Mauther, Mawr, Mawther, Messy, Mor, Nerd, Nurd, Oafish, Overhasty, Palooka, Plonking, Rough, Schlemihl, S(c)hlemiel, Squab, Stot, Stumbledom, Swab, Swob, Two-fisted, Unco, Ungain, Unskilful, Unsubtle, Unwieldy, Wooden

Clutch(es) Battery, Brood, Chickens, Clasp, Cling, Eggs, Glaum, Grab, → **GRASP**, Gripe, Hold, Nest, Net, Seize, Sitting, Squeeze

Clutter Confusion, Impedimenta, Litter, Mess, Rummage

Coach(es) Autodidact, Battlebus, Berlin, Bogie, Bus, Car, Carriage, Chara(banc), Clerestory, Crammer, Diligence, Dilly, Double-decker, Drag, Edifier, Fiacre, Fly, Gig, Griddle car, Groom, Hackney, Handler, Landau(let), Microbus, Mourning, Phaeton, Pullman, Railcar, Rattler, Repetiteur, Rolling stock, Saloon, Shay, Sleeper, Stage, Surrey, Tally(-ho), Teach(er), Thoroughbrace, Train(er), Transport, Tutor, Voiture

Coal Anthracite, Bituminous, Block, Burgee, Caking, Cannel, Char, Cherry, Clinker, Coking, Coom, Crow, Culm, Day, Edge, Eldin, Ember, Fusain, Gathering, Indene, Jud, Knob, Lignite, Open-cast, Parrot, Pea, Purse, Sapropelite, Score, Sea, Slack, Splint, Stone, Surtarbrand, Surturbrand, Vitrain, Wallsend

Coalition Alliance, Bloc, Fusion, Janata, Merger, Tie, Union

Coarse(ness) Base, Bawdy, Blowzy, Bran, Broad, Chav, Common, Crude, Earthy, Fisherman, Foul, Gneissose, Grained, Gross, Gruff, Ham, Illbred, Indelicate, Low-bred, Plebeian, Rank, Raunchy, Ribald, Rough, Rudas, Rude, Russet, Sackcloth, Schlub, Slob, Sotadic, Vulgar, Yahoo

Coast(al) Barbary, Beach, Cape, Causeway, Coromandel, Costa, Dalmatian, Drift, Freewheel, Glide, Hard, Heritage, Ivory, Littoral, Longshore, Maritime, Med, Orarian, Riviera, Scrieve, Seaboard, Seafront, Seashore, Seaside, → **SHORE**, Sledge, Strand, Sunshine, Toboggan, Trucial

Coaster Beermat, Drog(h)er, Mat, Ship, Smack

Coat(ed), Coating Ab(b)a, Abaya, Achkan, Acton, Admiral, Afghan, Anarak, Anodise, Anorak, Balmacaan, Barathea, Basan, Bathrobe, Belton, Benjamin, Blazer, Bloomed, Bolero, Box, British warm, Buff, Buff-jerkin, Car, Chesterfield, Cladding, Claw-hammer, Clearcole, Cloak, Clutch, Cocoon, Coolie, Cover, Covert, Creosote, Crust(a), Cutaway, Dip, Doggett's, Drape, Dress, Duffel, Duster, Enamel, Encrust, Envelope, Ermelin, Ermine, Extine, Fearnought, Film, Finish, Fleece, Frock, Fur, Gabardine, Galvanise, Gambeson, Glaze, Grego, Ground, Hair, Happi, Ha(c)queton, Icing, Impasto, Inverness, Iridise, Jack(et), Jemmy, Jerkin, Jodhpuri, Joseph, Jump, Jupon, Lacquer, Lammie, Lammy, Lanugo, Layer, Laying, Lerp, Limewash, Loden, Lounge, Mac, Mackinaw,

Matinee, Metallise, Mink, Morning, Newmarket, Paint, Paletot, Palla, Paper, Parka, Parkee, Patina(te), Pebbledash, Pelage, Pelisse, Perfuse, Petersham, Phosphor, Pitch, Pla(i)ster, Plate, Plumage, Polo, Pos(h)teen, Primer, Prince Albert, Raglan, Redingote, Resin, Resist, Riding, Roquelaure, Sable, Sack, Salband, Saque, Sclerotic, Scratch, Seal, Sheepskin, Shellac, Sherwani, Silver, Spencer, Sports, Stadium, Surtout, Swagger, Swallowtail(ed), Tabard, Taglioni, Tail, Tar, Teflon, Tent, Testa, Top, Trench, Truss, Trusty, Tunic, Tuxedo, Ulster(ette), Varnish, Veneer, Verdigris, Warm, Wash, Weasel, Whitewash, Windjammer, Wool, Wrap-rascal, Zamarra, Zamarro, Zinc

Coax Blandish, Blarney, Cajole, Carn(e)y, Collogue, Cuittle, Entice, Flatter, Lure, Persuade, Tempt, Wheedle, Whillywha(w)

Cobble(s), Cobbled, Cobbler(s), Cobblestone Bunkum, Clicker, Coggle, Cosier, Cozier, Dessert, Guff, Mend, Patch, Pie, Rot, Snob, Soutar, Souter, Sowter, Stone, Sutor, Twaddle, Vamp

Cobweb(by) Arachnoid, Araneous, Gossamer, Snare, Trap

Cock(y), Cockerel Alectryon, Ball, Brash, Capon, Chanticleer, Chaparral, Confident, Erect, Flip, Fowl, France, Fugie, Half, Hay, Henny, Jack-the-lad, Jaunty, Penis, Perk, Roadrunner, Robin, Rooster, Snook, Strut, Sunshine, Swaggering, Tap, Tilt, Turkey, Twaddle, Vain, Valve, Vane, Weather-vane

Cockatoo Bird, Corella, Galah, Major Mitchell, Parrot

▷**Cockle(s)** *may indicate* an anagram

Cockney 'Arriet, 'Arry, Bow, Londoner, Londonese

▷**Cockney** *may indicate* a missing h

Cocktail Alexander, Aperitif, Atomic, Bellini, Between the sheets, Black Russian, Black Velvet, Bloody Mary, Brandy Alexander, Buck's fizz, Bullshot, Bumbo, Caipirinha, Champagne cocktail, Cobbler, Cold duck, Crusta, Daiquiri, Egg-flip, Fruit, Fustian, Gibson, Gimlet, Grasshopper, Harvey Wallbanger, Highball, Horse's neck, Julep, Kir Royale, Mai-Tai, Manhattan, Margarita, Martini®, Mix, Molotov, Moscow mule, Negroni, Old-fashioned, Piña colada, Pink lady, Pisco Sour, Planter's punch, Prairie oyster, Prawn, Punch, Rickey, Rusty nail, Sangaree, Sangria, Sazerac®, Screwdriver, Sea Breeze, Sherry cobbler, Side-car, Singapore sling, Slammer, Snakebite, Snowball, Sour, Spritzer, Stengah, Stinger, Swizzle, Tequila sunrise, Tom Collins, Twist, Whiskey Sour, White-lady, White Russian

Cod Bag, Cape, Coalfish, Fish, Gade, Gadus, Haberdine, Hoax, Keeling, Kid, Lob, Man, Morrhua, Saith, Spoof, Stockfish, Take in, Tease, Torsk, Tusk, Whiting

Code, Coding, Codification Access, Alphanumeric, Amalfitan, Area, Bar, Barred, Binary, Brevity, Bushido, Canon law, Character, Cheat, Cipher, City, Civil, Clarendon, Codex, Colour, Computing, Condition, Cookie, Country, Cryptogram, Cryptograph, Da Vinci, Dialling, Disciplinary, Dogma, Dress, DX, Easter egg, EBCDIC, Encipher, Enigma, Error, Escape, Ethics, Etiquette, Fuero, Genetic, Gray, Green Cross, Hammurabic, Highway, Justinian, MAC, Machine, Morse, Napoleon(ic), National, Netiquette, Object, Omerta, Opcode, Penal, PGP, PIN, Pindaric, Postal, Price, Protocol, Reflective binary, Rulebook, Scytale, Sharia, Shulchan Aruch, Signal, Sort, Source, STD, Talmud, Time, Twelve Tables, Zip

Coffee, Coffee beans, Coffee pot Americano, Arabica, Bean, Black, Brazil, Cafetiere, Cappuccino, Decaff, Demi-tasse, Espresso, Expresso, Filter, Frappuccino, Gaelic, Gloria, Granules, Grounds, Instant, Irish, Java, Latte, Mocha, Peaberry, Percolator, Robusta, Skinny latte, Tan, Triage, Turkish, White

Coffin Bier, Box, Casket, Hearse, Pall, Sarcophagus, Shell

Cog(ged) Contrate, Mitre-wheel, Nog, Pinion, Tooth, Wheel
Cogent Compelling, Forceful, Good, Sound, Telling
Cohere(nt) Agglutinate, Clear, Cleave, Cling, Logical, Stick
Cohort Colleague, Crony, Soldier
Coil(s), Coiled Bight, Bought, Choke, Choking, Circinate, Clew, Clue, Convolute(d), Convolve, Curl, Current, Fake, Fank, Field, Flemish, Furl, Hank, Helix, Induction, Loop, Mortal, Mosquito, Resistance, Rouleau, Scorpioid, Solenoid, Spark, Spiral, Spiraster, Spire, Tesla, Tickler, Toroid, Twine, Twirl, →**WIND**, Wound, Wreath, Writhe
Coin(er) Base, Bean, Bit, Broad(piece), Cash, Change, Contomiate, Copper, Create, Doctor, Dosh, Dump(s), Fiddler's money, Fiver, Han(d)sel, Imperial, Invent, Lucky piece, Makc, Mint, Mintage, →**MONEY**, Neologist, Neoterise, Numismatic, Nummary, Piece, Plate, Pocket-piece, Proof, Shiner, Slip, Specie, Stamp, Strike, Subsidiary, Sum, Tenner, Token, Unity
Coincide(nt), Coincidence Accident, Agree, Chance, Consilience, Conterminous, Fit, Fluke, Overlap, Rabat(to), Simultaneous, Synastry, Synchronise, Tally
Cold(-blooded), Cold(ness) Ague, Algid, Aloof, Apathetic, Arctic, Asocial, Asperity, Austere, Baltic, Biting, Bitter, Bleak, Blue, Brr(r), C, Catarrh, Cauld(rife), Chill(y), Clinical, Colubrine, Common, Coryza, Coy, Dead, Distant, Ectotherm, Emotionless, Fish, Frappé, Frem(d), Fremit, Frigid, Frost(y), Gelid, Glacial, Hiemal, Icy, Impersonal, Jeel, Nippy, Nirlit, Parky, Passionless, Perishing, Poikilotherm(ic), Polar, Psychro-, Remote, Rheumy, Rigor, Rume, Shivery, Siberia, Snap, Snell, Sour, Starving, Streamer, Subzero, Taters, Unmoved, Weed, Wintry
Collapse, Collapsing Apoplexy, Breakdown, Burn out, Cave, Conk, Crash, Crumble, Crumple, Debacle, Deflate, Disintegrate, Downfall, Fail(ure), Fall (in), Flake out, Fold, Founder, Give, Go phut, Implode, Inburst, Landslide, Meltdown, Phut, Purler, Rickety, Rockfall, Rot, Ruin, Scat(ter), Sink, Slump, Snap, Stroke, Subside, Sunstroke, Swoon, Telescope, Tumble, Tumbledown, Wilt, Zonk
▷**Collapsing** *may indicate* an anagram
Collar(ed) Arrest, Astrakhan, Band, Bermuda, Bertha, Berthe, Bib, Bishop, Blue, Brecham, Buster, Butterfly, Button-down, Buttonhole, Capture, Carcanet, Chevesaile, Choke(r), Clerical, Collet, Dog, Esses, Eton, Falling-band, Flea, Gorget, Grandad, Hame, Head(stall), Holderbat, Horse, Jabot, Jampot, Karenni, Lapel, Mandarin, Moran, Mousquetaire, Nab, Nail, Neckband, Necklet, Ox-bow, Peter Pan, Piccadell, Piccadillo, Piccadilly, Pikadell, Pinch, Pink, Polo, Puritan, Rabatine, Rabato, Rebater, Rebato, Revers, Rollneck, Roman, Romance, Ruff, Sailor, Seize, Shawl, Steel, Storm, Tackle, Tappet, Tie-neck, Torque, Turndown, Turtleneck, Vandyke, Whisk, White, Wing, Yoke
Colleague(s) Accomplice, Associate, Bedfellow, Co-host, Confrère, Fellow, Mate, Mentor, Oppo, Partner, Sociate, Team mate, Workmate
Collect(ion), Collectable, Collected, Collective(ly), Collectivism, Collector Accrue, Agglomerate, Aggregate, Album, Alms, Amass, Ana, Anthology, Artel, Assemble, Bank, Bow, Budget, Bundle, Burrell, Bygones, Caboodle, Calm, Cap, Clan, Clowder, Compendium, Compile, Composed, Congeries, Conglomerate, Cool-headed, Covey, Cull, Dossier, Dustman, Earn, Egger, Exaltation, Exordial, Eyrie, Farrago, Fest, Fetch, Fleet, Gaggle, Garbo, Garner, Gather, Get, Gilbert, Glean, Glossary, Grice, Harvest, Heap, Herd, Hive, Idant, Jingbang, Kit, Kitty, Levy, Library, Magpie, Meal, Meet, Menagerie,

Miscellany, Mish-mash, Montem, Munro-bagger, Murmuration, Museum, Muster, Nide, Offertory, Olio, Omnibus, Pack, Paddling, Pile, Plate, Pod, Poor box, Post, Poste restante, Prayer, Quest, Raft, Ragbag, Raise, Rammle, Recheat, Rhapsody, Rouleau, Sangfroid, Scramble, Sedge, Self-possessed, Serene, Set, Shoe, Siege, Skein, Smytrie, Sord, Sottisier, Sounder, Spring, Stand, Team, Together, Toolkit, Tronc, Troop, Ujamaa, Unkindness, Uplift, Watch, Wernher, Whipround, Wisp

▷**Collection** *may indicate* an anagram

College(s) Academy, All Souls, Ampleforth, Balliol, Brasenose, Business, C, Caius, Campus, CAT, Cheltenham, Clare, Classical, Commercial, Community, Conservatoire, Corpus (Christi), Downing, Dulwich, Electoral, Emmanuel, Eton, Exeter, Foundation, Freshwater, Girton, Grande école, Hall, Heralds', Institute, Institution, Ivy League, Jail, Keble, King's, Lancing, Linacre, Lincoln, LSE, Lycée, Lyceum, Madras(s)a(h), Madressah, Magdalen(e), Marlborough, Medresseh, Merton, Newnham, Nuffield, Oriel, Pembroke, Poly, Polytechnic, Protonotariat, Queen's, Ruskin, St Johns, Saliens, Selwyn, Seminary, Sixth-form, Somerville, Sorbonne, Staff, Tech(nical), Tertiary, Theologate, Training, Trinity, Tug, UMIST, Up, Village, Wadham, Winchester, Yeshiva(h)

Collide(r), Collision Afoul, Barge, Bird-strike, Bump, Cannon, Carom(bole), Clash, Conflict, Dash, Elastic, Fender-bender, Foul, Hadron, Head-on, Hurtle, Impact, Inelastic, Into, Kiss, Meet, Pile-up, Prang, Ram, Smash-up, Strike, Thwack

Colony Acadia, Aden, Bermuda, Burkina Faso, Cape, Cleruchy, Crown, Dependency, Elea, Gibraltar, Halicarnassian, Heronry, Hongkong, Kaffraria, Nudist, Penal, Plymouth, Presidio, Proprietary, Rookery, Senegal, Settlement, Swarm, Termitarium, Zambia, Zimbabwe

Colour(ed), Colouring, Colours Achromatic, Bedye, Blanco, Blee, Blush, C, Cap, Chromatic, Chrome, Complementary, Complexion, Crayon, Criant, Cross, Distort, Dye, False, Film, Flag, Florid, Flying, Garble, Gouache, Haem, → **HUE**, Imbue, Ink, Irised, Kalamkari, Leer, Livor, Local, Lutein, Metif, Nankeen, Opalescence, Orpiment, Palette, Pantone®, Pastel, Pied, Pigment, Pochoir, Polychrome, Primary, Prism, Prismatic, Process, Queen's, Raddle, Reddle, Regimental, Rinse, Riot, Ruddle, Secondary, Sematic, Shade, Shot, Slant, Solid, Spectrum, Stain, Startle, Tertiary, Tie-dye, Tinc(ture), Tinctorial, Tinge, Tint, Tone, Uvea, Wash

▷**Coloured** *may indicate* an anagram

Colourful Abloom, Brave, Exotic, Flamboyant, Flowery, Gay, Iridescent, Kaleidoscope, Opalescent, Showy, Splashy, Vivid

Colourless Albino, Bleak, Drab, Dull, Faded, Flat, Hyalite, Pallid, Pallor, Wan, White

Column(s), Column foot Agony, Anta, Architrave, Atlantes, Commentary, Corinthian, Correspondence, Cylinder, Decastyle, Diastyle, Distillation, Doric, Editorial, Eustyle, Fifth, File, Flying, Fractionating, Gossip, Hypostyle, Impost, Lat, Lonelyhearts, Monolith, Nelson's, Newel, Notochord, Obelisk, Pedestal, Pericycle, Peripteral, Peristyle, Persian, Personal, Pilaster, → **PILLAR**, Pilotis, Plume, Prostyle, Pycnostyle, Rachis, Rouleau, Row, Sheet pile, Spina, Spinal, Spine, Stalactite, Stalagmite, Steering, Stylobate, Systyle, Tabulate, Telamone, Third, Tige, Tore, Torus, Trajan's

Comb(er), Combed, Combing Afro, Alveolate, Beehive, Breaker, Card, Copple, Crest, Ctenoid, Curry, Dredge, Fine-tooth, Hackle, Heckle, Hot, Kaim,

Kame, Kangha, Kemb, Noils, Parter, Pecten, Pectinal, Rake, Rat-tail, Red(d), Ripple(r), Rose, Scribble, Search, Side, Smooth, Tease(l), Toaze, Tose, Toze, Trawl, Tuft, Wave

Combination, Combine(d), Combining Accrete, Aggregate, Alligate, Ally, Amalgam, Associate, Axis, Bloc, Cartel, Cleave, Clique, Coalesce, Coalition, Concert, Concoction, Conflated, Conglomerate, Consolidate, Consortium, Coordinate, Crasis, Fuse, Group, Harvester, Incorporate, Integration, Interfile, Join, Junta, Kartell, League, Meld, Merge(r), Mingle, Mixture, Monogram, Motor cycle, One, Perm(utation), Piece, Pool, Quill, Ring, Solvate, Splice, Syncretize, Synthesis, Terrace, Trivalent, Trona, Unify, Unite, Valency, Wed

▷**Combustible** *may indicate* an anagram

Come, Coming (back), Coming out Accrue, Advent, Anear, Anon, Appear, Approach, Ar(r), Arise, Arrive, Attend, Debouch, Derive, Emanate, Future, Happen, Iceman, In store, Issue, Millenarian, Orgasm, Parousia, Pass, Pop, Reach, Respond, Second, Via

Comedian Benny, Buffoon, Chaplin, →**CLOWN**, Comic, Durante, Emery, Farceur, Gagman, Goon, Groucho, Hardy, Harpo, Joe Miller, Joker, Jokesmith, Karno, Keaton, Laurel, Leno, Punster, Quipster, Riot, Robey, Scream, Screwball, Stand-up, Starr, Tate, Tati, Wag, Wise(cracker), Witcracker, Yell

Comedy Alternative, Blackadder, Com, Custard-pie, Drama, Ealing, Errors, Farce, Humour, Improv(ised), Millamant, Romantic, Romcom, Screwball, Sitcom, Situation, Slapstick, Stand-up, Thalia, Travesty

Comet Chiron, Geminid, Halley's, Kohoutek, Meteor

Comfort(able), Comforter, Comforting, Comfy Affluent, Amenity, Analeptic, Balm, Bein, Bildad, Calm, Canny, Cheer, Cherish, Cherry, Cocoon, Cold, Consolation, Console, Convenience, Cose, Cosh, Cosy, Couthie, Couthy, Creature, Crumb, Cushy, Dummy, Dutch, Ease, Easy, Eliphaz, Featherbed, Gemutlich, Heeled, Homely, Homy, Hottie, Job's, Legroom, Luxury, Mumsy, Noah, Reassure, Relaxed, Relief, Relieve, Rosewater, Rug, Scarf, Sinecure, Snug, Solace, Soothe, Stay, Succour, Tosh, Trig, Warm, Wealthy, Well, Well-to-do, Zofar, Zophar

Comic(al) Beano, Buff, Buffo(on), Bumpkin, Buster, Chaplin, Clown, →**COMEDIAN**, Dandy, Drag, Droll, Eagle, Emery, Facetious, Fields, →**FUNNY**, Gagster, Hardy, Horror, Humorist, Jester, Knock-about, Laurel, Leno, Mag, Manga, Quizzical, Robey, Stand up, Strip, Tati, Trial, Wag, Zany

Command(eer), Commanding, Commandment(s) About face, Attention, Behest, Bid, Categorical imperative, Charge, Coerce, Control, Decalogue, Declare, Direct, Direction, Dominate, Easy, Edict, Expertise, Fiat, Fiaunt, Fighter, Firman, Grip, Haw, Hest, Hijack, Imperious, Injunction, Instruction, Jussive, Lead, Magisterial, Mandate, Mastery, Mitzvah, Obtest, →**ORDER**, Peremptory, Precept, Press, Query language, Requisition, Rule, Seize, Shun, Ukase, Warn, Warrant, Will, Wish, Writ

Commander Ag(h)a, Agamemnon, Ameer, Barleycorn, Bey, Bloke, Blucher, Boss, Brennus, Brig, Caliph, Centurion, Cid, Decurion, Dreyfus, Emir, Emperor, Encomendero, Exon, Field cornet, Garibaldi, Generalissimo, Hetman, Hipparch, Imperator, Killadar, Kitchener, Leader, Manager, Marshal, Master, Meer, Moore, Mr Big, Officer, Overlord, Pendragon, Polemarch, Pr(a)efect, Raglan, Shogun, Sirdar, Supreme, Taxiarch, Trierarch, Warlord

Commemorate, Commemoration Encaenia, Epitaph, Eulogy, Keep, Memorial, Month's mind, Monument, Plaque, Remember, Saint's day, Trophy, Year's mind

Comment(ary), Commentator Analyst, Animadvert, Annotate, Barb, Comm, Coryphaeus, Coverage, Critic, Descant, Discuss, Editorial, Essay, Exegete, Explain, Exposition, Expound, Fair, Footnote, Gemara, Gloss(ographer), Glossator, Glosser, Hakam, Kibitz, Margin, Marginalia, Midrash(im), Narration, Noise, Note, Obiter dictum, Observation, Par, Platitude, Play-by-play, Postil, Remark, Rider, Scholiast, Scholion, Scholium, Sidenote, Voice-over

Commerce, Commercial Ad, Adland, Barter, Business, Cabotage, Jingle, Marketable, Mercantile, Mercenary, Merchant, Retail, Shoppy, Simony, Tele-ad, Trade, Traffic, Wholesale

Commission(er), Commissioned Agio, Audit, Bonus, Boundary, Brevet, Brokage, Brokerage, Charge, Charity, Competition, Contango, Contract, Countryside, Delegation, Depute, ECE, Employ, Engage, Envoy, Errand, Factor, Gosplan, High, Husbandage, Interpol, Job, Kickback, Magistrate, Mandate, Office(r), Official, Ombudsman, Order, Oyer and terminer, Percentage, Perpetration, Place, Poundage, Rake-off, Roskill, Shroffage, Task, Task force, Trust

Commit(tal), Committed, Commitment Allegiance, Aret(t), Consign, Contract, Decision, Dedication, Delegate, Devotion, Devout, Do, Engage, Entrust, Enure, Paid up, Perpetrate, Pledge, Position, Promise, Rubicon, Staunch, Toe

Committee ACRE, Audit, Board, Body, Cabinet, COBR(A), Collegium, Commission, Commune, Council, Delegacy, Group, Hanging, Joint, Junta, Politburo, Presidium, Propaganda, Riding, Samiti, Select, Standing, Steering, Syndicate, Table, Think tank, Vigilance, Watch, Ways and means

Common(ly), Commoner, Commons Alike, Average, Cad, Cheap, Clapham, Conventional, Diet, Dirt, Ealing, Eatables, Enclosure, Endemic, Epicene, Everyday, Familiar, Fare, Folk, Frequent, General, Green, Gutterblood, House, Law, Lay, Low, Mark, Mere, MP, Mutual, Naff, Non-U, Normal, People, Pleb, Plebe(i)an, Prevalent, Prole, Public, Ragtag, Related, Rife, Roturier, Ryfe, Scran, Sense, Shared, Stock, Stray, Tarty, The mob, Tie, Trite, Tritical, Tuft, Two-a-penny, Tye, Use, → **USUAL**, Vile, Vul(gar), Vulgo, Vulgus, Widespread, Wimbledon, Working-class

Commonsense Gumption, Mother wit, Nous, Savoir-faire, Smeddum, Wit

Communal, Commune Agapemone, Collective, Com, Meditate, Menage, Mir, Phalanstery, Public, Talk, Township

Communicate, Communication Ampex, Anastomosis, Announce, Appui, Aviso, Baud, Bluetooth, Boyau, Braille, Cable, Cellnet, Channelling, Citizen's band, Conversation, Convey, Cybernetic, E-mail, ESP, Expansive, Exude, Impart, Infobahn, Inform, Infrastructure, Intelsat, Internet, Liaison, Lifeline, Memoranda, Message, Mime, Multichannel, Multimedia, Note, Open letter, Oracy, Oralism, Paralanguage, Prayer, Prestel®, Proxemics, Put across, Reach, Reportage, Revelation, Road, Semaphore, Semiotics, Signal, Sitrep, Syncom, Talkback, Tannoy®, Telecom, Telepathy, Telephony, Teletex, Telex, Telstar, Tieline, Transmit, Utraquist, Webmail, Wire, Word of mouth

Communism, Communist Apparat(chik), Aspheterism, Bolshevist, Brook Farm, Cadre, Castroism, Com, Comecon, Cominform, Comintern, Commo, Comsomol, Deviationist, Engels, Essene, Fourier, Fraction, Khmer Rouge, Komsomol, Leninite, Maoist, Marxist, Menshevist, Nomenklatura, Ossi, Perfectionist, Pinko, Politburo, Red (Guard), Revisionism, Second World, Soviet, Spartacist, Tanky, Titoist, Trot, Vietcong, Vietminh

Communities, Community Agapemone, Alterne, Ashram, Association, Biome, Body, Brotherhood, Clachan, Climax, Closed, Coenobitism, Coenobium, Colonia, Colony, Consocies, Constituency, District, EC, Ecosystem, EEC, Enclave, Etat, Ethnic, European, Faith, Frat(e)ry, Gated, Hamlet, Kahal, Kibbutz, Mesarch, Mir, Neighbourhood, Pantisocracy, People, Phalanx, Phyle, Preceptory, Public, Pueblo, Republic, Sarvodaya, Seral, Sere, Settlement, Shtetl, Sisterhood, Sociation, Society, Speech, Street, Town, Tribe, Ujamaa, Ummah, Village, Virtual, Zupa

Commute(r) Change, Convert, Reduce, Shuttle, Standee, Straphanger, Travel

Compact Accord, Agreement, Bargain, Cement, Centralise, Concise, Conglobe, Covenant, Covin, Coyne, Dense, Entente, Fast, Firm, Flapjack, Hard, Knit, League, Match, Neat, Pledge, Powder, Solid, Tamp, Terse, Tight, Treaty, Well-knit

Companion(able) Achates, Arm candy, Associate, Attender, Barnacle, Bedfellow, Bonhomie, Brolga, Bud(dy), Butty, CH, China, Comate, Compadre, Compeer, Compotator, Comrade, Consort, Contubernal, Crony, Cupman, Duenna, Ephesian, Escort, Feare, Felibre, → **FELLOW**, Fere, Franion, Furked, Handbook, Man Friday, Mate, Native, Oliver, Pal, Pard, Pheer(e), Pot, Roland, Shadow, Sidekick, Stablemate, Thane, Thegn, Vade-mecum, Wag, Walker

Company, Companies Actors, Along, Artel, Ass, Assembly, Band, Bank, Battalion, Bevy, Brigade, → **BUSINESS**, Bv, Cahoot, Cartel, Cast, Cavalcade, Chartered, Chirm, CIA, Circle, City, Close, Club, Co, Conger, Consort, Cordwainers, Core, Corporation, Corps, Coy, Crew, Crowd, Crue, Decury, Dotcom, East India, Enterprise, Entourage, Faction, Finance, Fire, → **FIRM**, Flock, Free, Gang, Garrison, Ging, Guild, Haberdashers, Heap, Holding, Hudson's Bay, ICI, Inc, Indie, In-house, Intercourse, Investment, Joint-stock, Limited, Listed, Livery, Management, Maniple, Muster, Order, Organisation, Parent, Plc, Present, Pride, Private, Public, Public limited, Push, Quoted, Rep(ertory), Room, SA, Sedge, Set, Set out, Shell, Siege, Sort, SpA, Stationers', Stock, Studio, Subsidiary, Syndicate, Table, Team, Touring, Troop, Troupe, Trust, Twa, Two(some), UPS, Visitor, White, Yfere

Compare(d), Comparable, Comparison Analogy, Beside, Bracket, Collate, Confront, Contrast, Correspond, Cp, Equate, Liken, Match, Odious, Parallel, Relation, Similar, Simile, Synonymous, Weigh

Compartment Alcove, Bay, Booth, Box, Cab, Carriage, Casemate, Cell, Chamber, Cockpit, Cubbyhole, Cubicle, Dog box, Glove, Locellate, Locker, Loculament, Loculus, Pane, Panel, Partition, Pigeonhole, Pocket, Room(ette), Severy, Sleeper, Smoker, Stall, Till, Trunk, Wind chest

Compass Ambit, Area, Beam, Bounds, Bow, Dividers, Extent, Gamut, Goniometer, Gyro, Gyroscope, Infold, Magnetic, Needle, Orbit, Pencil, Perimeter, → **RANGE**, Reach, Rhumb, Room, Scale, Trammel

Compassion(ate) Aroha, Clemency, Commiseration, Empathy, Goodwill, Heart, Humane, Kindliness, Kuan Yin, Kwan Yin, Loving kindness, Mercy, Pity, Remorse, Samaritan, Sympathy, Tender, Ubuntu

Compel(ling), Compelled, Compulsion, Compulsive, Compulsory Addiction, Coact, Coerce, Cogent, Command, Constrain, Dragoon, Driving, Duress, Enforce, Exact, Extort, Fain, → **FORCE**, Force majeure, Gar, Habit-forming, Hypnotic, Insistent, Make, Mandatory, Obligate, Oblige, Pathological, Steamroller, Strongarm, Tyrannise, Urge, Walk Spanish

Compensate, Compensation Amend(s), Balance, Boot, Bote, Comp, Consideration, Counterbalance, Counterpoise, Damages, Demurrage, Guerdon,

Indemnity, Offset, Payment, Recoup, Redeem, Redress, Reparation, Reprisal, Requital, Restitution, Restore, Retaliation, Salvage, Satisfaction, Solatium, Wergild, X-factor

Compete Contend, Dog eat dog, Enter, Match, Play, Rival, Run, Vie

Competence, Competent Ability, Able, Adequate, Can, Capable, Capacity, Dab, Dow, Efficient, Fit, Proficient, Responsible, Sui juris, Worthy

Competition, Competitive, Competitor Agonist, Antitrust, Arch rival, Autotest, Battle, Bee, Biathlon, Buckjumping, Checks and balances, Concours, Contender, Contention, Contest, Cook off, Cup, Dog eat dog, Drive, Entrant, Entry, Event, Field, Finals, Gamesman, Grand Prix, Gymkhana, Head over heels, Heptathlon, Iron woman, Jump off, Keen, Match, Monopolistic, Olympiad, Open, Opponent, Outsider, Pairs, Panellist, Pentathlon, Player, Pools, Premiership, Puissance, Race, Rally, Rat race, Repechage, Rival(ise), Rodeo, Run, Runner-up, Show-jumping, Slam, Spelldown, Sporty, Stableford, Starter, Tenson, Test, Three-day event, Tiger, Tournament, Tourney, Track meet, Trial, Triallist, Wap(p)enshaw, Wild card

Compile(r), Compilation Anthology, Arrange, Collect, Cross, Doxographer, Edit, Prepare, Setter, Synthesis, Zadkiel

Complain(t), Complainer Ache, Acne, Adenoids, Affection, Affliction, Alas, Alopecia, Anaemia, Angina, Anorexia, Arthritis, Asthma, Barrack, Beef, Bellyache, Bewail, Bitch, Bleat, BSE, Carp, Charge, Chorea, Colic, Crab, Cramp, Criticise, Croup, Diatribe, Disorder, Distemper, Dropsy, Epidemic, Ergot, Exanthema, Fever, Girn, Gout, Gravamen, Grievance, Gripe, Groan, Grouch, Grouse, Growl, Grudge, Grumble, Grutch, Harangue, Hives, Hone, Hypochondria, Ileitis, →**ILLNESS**, Jeremiad, King's evil, Lament, Lumbago, Lupus, Malady, Mange, Mean(e), Mein, Mene, Moan, Morphew, Mump(s), Murmur, Nag, Natter, Neuralgia, Orchitis, Peeve, Peritonitis, Pertussis, Plica, Poor-mouth, Protest, Pyelitis, Quibble, Rail, Remonstrate, Repine, Report, Rhinitis, Rickets, Ringworm, Sapego, Sciatica, Scold, Scream, Sequacious, Sigh, Silicosis, Snivel, Squawk, Squeal, Staggers, Tennis Elbow, Thrush, Tic, Tinea, Upset, Whimper, Whine, Whinge, Yammer, Yaup, Yawp

▷**Complement** *may indicate* a hidden word

Complete(d), Completely, Completion Absolute, Accomplish, All, Altogether, Arrant, Attain, Clean, Congenital, Consummate, Crashing, Crown, Dead, Do, Downright, End, Entire, Finalise, Finish, Flat, Foregone, Fruition, Fulfil, Full, Full-blown, Head over heels, Hollow, Incept, Integral, In toto, Neck and crop, One, Out, Out and out, Perfect, Plenary, Plum, Prolative, Pure, Quite, Radical, Rank, Root and branch, Rounded, Self-contained, Sheer, Spang, Sum, Teetotal, Thorough(going), Total, Unabridged, Unbroken, Uncensored, Uncut, Unequivocal, Unmitigated, Utter, Whole (hog), Wrap

Complex(ity) Abstruse, Advanced, Compound, Daedal, Developed, Difficult, Electra, Fancy, Hard, Inferiority, Intricate, Intrince, Involute, Knot, Manifold, Megalopolis, MHC, Military-industrial, Mixed, Multinucleate, Nest, Network, Obsession, Oedipus, Overwrought, Paranoid, Phaedra, Plexiform, Ramification, Subtle, Superiority, Syndrome, System, Tangle, Thick, Web

Complexion Aspect, Blee, Hue, Leer, Permatan, Temper, Tint, View

Compliance, Compliant, Comply Abet, Agree, Amenable, Assent, Aye-aye, Conform, Deference, Hand-in-glove, Obedience, Obey, Observe, Orchitis, Plastic, Sequacious, Surrender, Wilco

Complicate(d), Complication Bewilder, Complex, Deep, Elaborate, Embroil, Entangle, Implex, Intricate, Involution, Involve, Inweave, Knot, Node, Nodus, Perplex, Ramification, Rigmarole, Tangle, Tirlie-wirlie, Tricky

▷**Complicated** *may indicate* an anagram

Compliment(s), Complimentary Backhanded, Baisemain, Bouquet, Congratulate, Devoirs, Douceur, Encomium, Esteemed, Flatter, Flummery, Freebie, Glowing, Greetings, Left-handed, Praise, Soap, Tribute

Compose(d), Composure Aplomb, Appeased, Arrange, Calm, Collected, Consist, Cool, →**CREATE**, Equable, Equanimity, Equilibrium, Even, Face, Improvise, Indite, Level-headed, Lull, Notate, Patience, Pen, Phlegm, Placid, Poise, Produce, Reconcile, Sangfroid, Score, Sedate, Serenity, Settle, Soothe, Thorough, Tranquil

Composer Contrapunt(al)ist, Inventor, Maker, Melodist, Minimalist, Musician, Musicker, Psalmist, Serialist, Songsmith, Symphonist, Triadist, Troubadour, Tunesmith, Writer

▷**Composing** *may indicate* an anagram

Composition, Compositor Aleatory, Beaumontage, Capriccio, Caprice, Cob, Concerto, Concertstuck, Concetto, Creation, Dite, Essay, Etude, Fantasia, Inditement, Ingredient, Literature, Loam, Met, Montage, Morceau, Nonet(te), Nonetto, Opus, Oratorio, Organum, Pastiche, Piece, Poem, Polyphony, Polyrhythm, Port, Printer, Quartette, Raga, Repoussage, Rhapsody, Setting, Ship, Sing, Smoot, Smout, Sonata, Sonatina, Structure, Study, Symphony, Synthesis, Terracotta, Texture, Toccata, Treatise, Trio, Typesetter, Work

Compound (stop), Compound word Addition, Aggravate, Amalgam, Anti-inflammatory, Anti-knock, Blend, →**CAMP**, Composite, Constitute, Cpd, Derivative, Dibasic, Mix, Multiply, Oxidant, Sodaic, Synthesise, Tatpurusha, Type, Ureic

▷**Compound(ed)** *may indicate* an anagram

Comprehend, Comprehensive All-in, Broad-brush, Catch-all, Catholic, Compass, Compendious, Contain, Encyclopaedic, Exhaustive, Fathom, Follow, General, Global, Grand, Grasp, Include, In depth, Ken, Large, Omnibus, Overall, Panoptic, Panoramic, Perceive, School, Sweeping, Thoroughgoing, Tumble, →**UNDERSTAND**, Wide

Compress(ed), Compression, Compressor Astrict, Axial-flow, Bale, Coarctate, Contract, Pump, Shoehorn, Solidify, Squeeze, Stupe, Thlipsis, Tourniquet

Compromise, Compromising Avoision, Brule, Commit, Concession, Endanger, Fudge, Golden mean, Halfway house, Honeytrap, Involve, Middleground, Modus vivendi, Negotiate, Settlement, Time-server, Trade off, Via media

Computation, Compute(r) Analog(ue), Animatronics, Apple (Mac)®, Botnet, Calcular, Desknote, Desktop, Digital, Eniac, Fifth generation, Front-end, Host, IALI, Laptop, Mainframe, Micro, Multiuser, Network, Notepad, Number-cruncher, Palmtop, Personal, Proxy server, Reckon, TALISMAN, Voice response, WIMP

Computer hardware, Computer memory Busbar, Chip, Dataglove®, Docking station, DRAM, EAROM, EPROM, Floptical, IDE, Modem, Neurochip, Pentium®, Platform, Plug'n'play, Processor, PROM, RAM, ROM, Router, Tower, Track(er)ball

Computer language Acrobat®, ADA, ALGOL, APL, ASCII, Assembly, AWK, Basic, C, COBOL, COL, Computerese, CORAL, Fortran, High-level, ICL, Java®,

Java script®, LISP, LOGO, Low-level, OCCAM, PASCAL, PROLOG, Python, Scratchpad, Scripting, Small-talk, SNOBOL, SQL, Visual Basic, Weblish

Computer network, Computer systems ARPANET, BIOS, Cambridge ring, Darknet, ERNIE, Evernet, Executive, Extranet, Fileserver, Freenet, HOLMES, Hypermedia, Internet, Intranet, JANET, LAN, MIDI, Multipoint, Neural, Stand-alone, TALISMAN, Tally, TAURUS, Telnet, Token ring, Unix, Usenet, VAN, WAN, Wide-area, WIMP

Computer program(s), Computer programmer, Computer programming, Computer software Abandonware, Acrobat, ActiveX, Address harvester, Adware, Agent, App(let), Application, Assembler, Auto-responder, Bot, Browse, CADMAT, Cancelbot, Careware, Case, Casemix, Chatbot, Checksum, Choiceboard, Client, Closed-loop, Columbus, Courseware, CU See Me, Datel®, Debugger, Demo, Device-driver, Diagnostic, Dictionary, Disassembler, Emacs, Enterprise, ERP, Est, Extreme, Facemail, Flash, Formatter, Free-to-air, Freeware, Groupware, HAL, Hard card, Heuristic, ITunes®, Linker, Loader, Logic bomb, Macro, Mail-merge, Malware, Mmorpg, Module, Neural net, Object, OCR, Plug-in, Powerpoint, Relocator, Ripper, Rootkit, Screensaver, Servlet, Shareware, Shell, Shopping agent, Shovelware, Spam killer, Spellchecker, Spider, Spreadsheet, Spyware, Stiffware, TELNET, Text editor, Translator, Trialware, Uninstaller, Utility, Vaccine, Vaporware, Virus, Warez, Web browser, Webcast, Web crawler, Wiki, Windows®, Word processor, Worm

Computer term(s) Address bus, Alert box, Authoring, Autosave, Backslash, Bank-switching, Bitmap, Blog(ging), Blogroll, Bookmark, Boot, Boot-virus, Bot army, Breakpoint, Broadband, Calculate, Calculus, Cascade, Chatroom, Choke route, Clickstream, Client-server, Cobweb site, Coder, Cold boot, Conf, Core(dump), Counter, Cron, Cuspy, Cyber(netics), Cybercafe, Cyberslacking, Dataglove, Daughterboard, Defrag(ment), Dial-up, DIF, Disk drive, Domain name, Dotcom, Earcon, Enqueue, Estimate, FAT, FIFO, Figure, Flash ROM, Floptical, GIGO, Greybarland, Half-adder, Hardwire, Hashing, Hotlist, Hypertext, Inbox, Inputter, Integrator, Interface, IT, Joypad, Kludge, Linear, List serv, Logic, Measure, Meatspace, Memory stick, Moblog, Motherboard, Mouseover, Mouse potato, Mung, Non-volatile, Notwork, Numlock, Nybble, Nyetwork, Object, On-line, Outbox, Package, Packet sniffer, Pageview, Patch, Path name, Peer-to-peer, Pel, Permalink, Pharming, Phishing, Phreak, Pixel, Plug and play, Podcast, Podcatcher, Point and click, Poke, Popunder, Pop-up, Pseudocode, Pseudorandom, Public-key, Pushdown, Reader farm, README file, Read-out, Realtime, Reboot, Reckoner, Report program, Rogue dialler, Rogue site, Rootserver, Router, Screensaver, Screen turtle, Scriptkiddie, Search engine, Serial port, Server farm, Shared logic, Shell, Shovelware, Sim, Smart, Smurfing, Soft copy, Soft return, Source, Spam, Spigot, Splog, Spreadsheet, Sprite, Style sheet, Superserver, Swap file, Systems, Telecottage, Time slice, Toggle, Token ring, Triple, Turnkey, Turtle graphics, ULA, Unicode, Username, Utility program, Vaccine, Vlog, Vodcast, Voice response, Voxel, Wave file, Webbie, WebBoard, Webfarm, Wideband, Wi-fi, Wiki, WIMAX, Wordwrap, WORM, Wysiwyg, Yottabyte, Zettabyte, Zmodem

Computer user(s) Alpha geek, Brain, Cast(er), Chiphead, Cybernaut, Cyberpunk, Cybersurfer, Digerati, Hacker, Liveware, Nethead, Netizen, Nettie, Onliner, Pumpking, Surfer, Tiger team, Troll, Webhead, White hat

Con(man) Against, Anti, Bunco, Defraudment, Diddle, Dupe, Enveigle, Gyp, Inveigle, Jacob, Learn, Peruse, Pretence, Read, Scam, Scan, Screw, Shark, Steer, Sucker, Swindle

Concede, Concession Acknowledge, Admit, Allow, Appeasement, Carta, Charter, Compromise, Confess, Favour, Forfeit, Franchise, Grant, Munich, Ou, Ow, Owe, Own, Privilege, Sop, Synchoresis, Yield

Conceit(ed) Arrogant, Bumptious, Caprice, Carriwitchet, Cocky, Concetto, Crank, Crotchet, Device, Dicty, Egoist, Egomania, Fancy, Fastuous, Fop, Fume, Hauteur, Idea, Notion, Podsnappery, Popinjay, Pretentious, Prig, Princock, Princox, Puppyism, Quiblin, Side, Snotty, Stuck-up, Swellhead, Swollenhead, Toffee-nose, Vain(glory), Wind

Conceive, Conceivable Beget, Create, Credible, Imagine, Possible, Surmise

Concentrate(d), Concentration Abridge, Address, Aim, Apozem, Application, Attention, Bunch, Centre, Collect, Condense, Dephlegmate, Distil, Elliptical, Essence, Extract, Focalise, Focus, Geographical, Intense, Listen, Major, Mantra, Mass, Molality, Molarity, Pithy, Pore, Potted, Reduce, Rivet, Samadhi, Strong, Thick, Titrate, Titre, Undiluted, Undivided

Concern(ed), Concerning About, Affair, After, Agitation, Ail, Alarm, Altruism, Anent, As to, Bother, Business, Care, Cerne, Company, Disturb, Dot com, Firm, Going, Heed, Hereof, House, Humanitarian, In re, Intéressé, Interest, Into, Involve, Lookout, → **MATTER**, Mell, Misease, Moment, Over, Part, Pidgin, Pigeon, Re, Reck, Regard, Reke, Relevant, Respect, Retch, Shake, Solicitous, Solicitude, Touch, Trouble, Versant, Wirra, Worry

▷**Concerned** *may indicate an anagram*

Concert (place) Agreement, Ballad, Barbicon, Benefit, Chamber, Charivari, Cooperation, Device, Dutch, Gig, Hootanannie, Hootananny, Hootenanny, Hootnannie, Hootnanny, League, Odeon, Odeum, Open-air, Pop, Prom(enade), Recital, Singsong, Smoker, Smoking, Subscription, Symphony, The Proms, Together, Unison, Unity, Wit

Concise Brief, Compact, Curt, Laconic, Short, Snappy, Succinct, Telegraphic, Terse, Tight

Conclude(d), Conclusion, Conclusive Achieve, A fortiori, Afterword, Amen, Binding, Button-up, Cease, Clinch, Close, Complete, Consectary, Dead, Decide, Deduce, Demise, Diagnosis, → **END**, End-all, Endwise, Envoi, Epilogue, Explicit, Finality, Finding, Fine, Finis, → **FINISH**, Foregone, Gather, Illation, Infer, Lastly, Limit, Non sequitur, Omega, Outro, Over, Peroration, Point, Postlude, Punchline, Realise, Reason, Resolve, Settle, Showdown, Summary, Terminate, Upshot, Uptie, Verdict, Wind up

Concrete, Concretion Actual, Aggregate, Beton, Bezoar, Breeze, Cake, Calculus, Caprolite, Clot, Dogger, Gunite, Hairball, Hard, Laitance, Mass, Minkstone, No-fines, Pile-cap, Positive, Real, Reify, Siporex, Solid, Tangible, Tremie, Vacuum

Condemn(ation) Abominate, Beknave, Blame, Blast, Cast, Censor, Censure, Convict, Damn, Decry, Denounce, Deprecate, Doom, Judge, Kest, Obelise, Obloquy, Prejudge, Proscribe, Reprove, Sentence, Theta, Upbraid

Condense(d), Condenser Abbreviate, Abridge, Capacitator, Compress, Contract, Distil, Encapsulate, Epitomise, Liebig, Précis, Rectifier, Reduce, Shorten, Shrink, Summarise, Surface

Condescend(ing) De haut en bas, Deign, Patronise, Snobbish, Stoop, Superior, Vouchsafe

Condiment Caraway, Catsup, Cayenne, Chutney, Flavour, Kava, Ketchup, Mustard, Paprika, Pepper, Relish, Salt, Sambal, Sauce, Seasoning, Spice, Tracklement, Turmeric, Vinegar, Zedoary

Condition(al), Conditioning Acathisia, Akathisia, Autism, Calvities, Case, Cense, Cinchonism, Circ(s), Circumstance, Classical, Climate, Congenital, Connote, Contingent, Disease, Disomy, Dropsy, Experimental, Feather, Fettle, Finite, Going, Hammertoe, Health, Hood, Hunk, If, Indoctrinate, Kelter, Kernicterus, Kilter, Latah, Necessary, Nick, Order, Parole, Pass, Pavlovian, Plight, Pliskie, Ply, Point, Position, Predicament, Premise, Premiss, Prepare, Prerequisite, Presupposition, Protasis, Proviso, Provisory, Repair, Reservation, Reserve, Rider, Ropes, Sine qua non, Sis, Spina bifida, Standing, State (of play), Status quo, Sted, Stipulation, String, Sufficient, Term, Tid, Tox(a)emia, Trim, Trisomy, Understanding, Unless, Vir(a)emia, Weal, White finger

Condom(s) Cap, Gumboot, Johnny, Letter, Prophylactic, Rubber, Rubber goods, Safe, Sheath

Conduct(or), Conductance, Conductress Abbado, Accompany, Administer, Anode, Ansermet, Antipode, Arm, Arrester, Barenboim, Bearing, Behaviour, Bernstein, Bohm, Boult, Bus-bar, Cad, Capellmeister, Clippie, Clippy, Coil, Comport, Demean(our), Deportment, Direct, Drive, Editor, Electrode, Escort, Fetch, G, Guide, Hallé, Ignitron, Kappellmeister, Klemperer, Lark, Lead, LED, Liber, Lightning, Mackerras, Maestro, Mantovani, Mho, Microchip, Nerve, Officiate, Ormandy, Outer, Ozawa, Parts, → **PILOT**, Previn, Prosecute, Psychagogue, Rattle, Safe, Sargent, Scudaller, Scudler, Silicon, Solicit, Solti, Stokowski, Strauss, Szell, Tao, Thermal, Thermistor, Thyristor, Toscanini, Transact, → **USHER**, Von Karajan, Walter, Wire, Wood

▷**Conducting** *may indicate* an '-ic' ending

Conduit Aqueduct, Canal, Carrier, Channel, Culvert, Duct, Main, Pipe, Sewer, Tube, Wireway

Cone(s), Conical, Cone-shaped Alluvial, Cappie, Conoidal, Egmont, Ellipse, Fir, Ice-cream, Monticule, Moxa, Pastille, Peeoy, Pineal, Pingo, Pioy(e), Pottle, Puy, Pyramid, Pyrometric, Shatter, Spire, Storm, Strobilus, Taper, Tee, Traffic, Volcanic, Windsock

Confederal, Confederacy, Confederate, Confederation Accessory, Alliance, Ally, Association, Body, Bund, Bunkosteerer, Cover, Creek, Dixie, F(o)edarie, Gueux, Illinois, League, Partner, Union

Confer(ence) Bestow, Cf, Collogue, Colloqium, Colloquy, Congress, Convention, Council, Diet, Do, Dub, Fest, Forum, Grant, Huddle, Imparlance, Indaba, Intercommune, Lambeth, Meeting, Munich, Negotiate, Palaver, Parley, Pawaw, Pear, Potsdam, Pourparler, Powwow, Press, Pugwash, Quadrant, Seminar, Settle, Summit, Symposium, Synod, → **TALK**, Tete-a-tete, Vouchsafe, Yalta

Confess(ion), Confessor Acknowledge, Admit, Agnise, Avowal, Concede, Confiteor, Cough up, Declare, Disclose, Edward, Helvetic, Own, Recant, Shema, Shrift, Shriver, Sing, Tetrapolitan, Verbal, Whittle

Confide(nce), Confident(ial), Confidant Aplomb, Aside, Assertive, Assured, Authoritative, Bedpost, Belief, Bottle, Bouncy, Brash, Can do, Certitude, Chutzpah, Cocksure, Cocky, Cred, Crouse, Egoistical, Entre nous, Entrust, Extravert, Extrovert, Faith, Favourite, Fearless, Feisty, Gatepost, Hardy, Hope, Hubris, Hush-hush, Intimate, Morale, Nerve, Pack, Panache, Positive, Presumptuous, Private, Privy, QT, Reliance, Sanguine, Secret, Secure, Self-assured, Self-possessed, Self-trust, Suavity, Sub rosa, Sure(ness), Sure-footed, Tell, Together, Top secret, Trust, Unabashed, Unbosom, Under the rose, Unselfconscious, Vaulting

Confine(d), Confines, Confinement Ambit, Bail, Bale, Cage, CB, Chain, Closet, Constrain, Contain, Coop, Cramp, Crib, Detain, Down-lying, Emmew,

Encase, Enclose, Endemic, Enmew, Ensheath, Gate, Gender-moon, Hem
in, Housebound, Immanacle, Immew, Immure, Impound, →**IMPRISON**,
Incommunicado, Inertial, Inhoop, Intern, Kettle, Limit, Local, Lying in, Mail,
March, Mew, Mure, Narrow, Pen, Pent, Pinion, Poky, Quarantine, Restrict,
Rules, Solitary, Trammel

Confirm(ed), Confirmation Addict, Approve, Assure, Attest, Bear
(out), Certify, Check, Chris(o)m, Christen, Chronic, Clinch, Corroborate,
Dyed-in-the-wool, Endorse, Homologate, Ink in, Obsign, Official, OK, Qualify,
Ratify, Reassure, Sacrament, Sanction, Seal, Strengthen, Substantiate, Ten-four,
Tie, True, Validate, Vouch

Conflict(ing) Agon, Ambivalence, Antinomy, Armageddon, At odds,
Battle(ground), Boilover, Camp, Casus belli, Clash, Contend, Contravene,
Controversy, Disharmony, Diverge, Encounter, Feud, Fray, Inconsistent,
Internecine, Jar, Lists, Mêlée, Muss, Off-key, Oppose, Psychomachia, Rift,
Shoot-out, Strife, →**STRUGGLE**, Tergiversate, War

Conform(ist), Conformity Accord, Adjust, Agreement, Comply, Conservative,
Consistence, Correspond, Hew to, Keep step, Normalise, Obey, Observe,
Procrustean, Propriety, Quadrate, Standardize, Stereotype(d), Suit, Time-server,
Toe, Trimmer, Yield

Confound(ed) Abash, Amaze, Astound, Awhape, Baffle, Bewilder, Blamed,
Blasted, Blest, Bumbaze, Contradict, Darn, Dash, Deuce, Devastate, Dismay,
Drat, Dumbfound, Elude, Floor, Jigger, Mate, Murrain, Nonplus, Perishing,
Perplex, Rabbit, Spif(f)licate, Stump, Throw

▷**Confound** *may indicate* an anagram

Confront(ation) Appose, Beard, Breast, Brush, Cross, Eyeball, Face (off), Face
down, Head on, Head-to-head, Impasse, Incident, Mau-Mau, Meet, Militance,
Nose, Oppose, Outface, Showdown, Smackdown, Tackle, Toe-to-toe, War

Confuse(d), Confusedly, Confusion Addle, Adrift, Anarchy, Astonishment,
At sea, Babel, Baffle, Bamboozle, Bedevil, Befog, Befuddle, Bemuse, Bewilder,
Blur, Burble, Bustle, Callaloo, Chaos, Cloud, Clutter, Cobweb, Complicate,
Consternation, Debacle, Désorienté, Didder, Disarray, Disconcert, Disorient,
Distract, Dither, Dizzy, Doubting, Dudder, Dust, Dwaal, Embrangle, Embroglio,
Embroil, Entanglement, Farrago, Flap, Flummox, Flurry, Fluster, Fog, Fox,
Fubar, Fuddle, Gaggle, Galley-west, Garble, Guddle, Hash, Havoc, Hazy,
Hirdy-girdy, Huddle, Hugger-mugger, Hurly-burly, Hurry-skurry, Imbrangle,
Imbroglio, Inchoate, Incoherent, →**IN CONFUSION**, Indistinct, Litter, Lost,
Lurry, Maelstrom, Maffled, Maving, Mayhem, Maze, Melange, Melee, Mess,
Mingle, Mish-mash, Misorder, Mither, Mixter-maxter, Mixtie-maxtie, Mizzle,
Moider, Moither, Moonstruck, →**MUDDLE**, Mudge, Muss(e), Muzzy, Mystify,
Obfuscate, Overset, Pellmell, Perplex, Pi(e), Pig's ear, Pose, Puzzle head, Ravel,
Razzle-dazzle, Razzmatazz, Rout, Rummage, Rumpus, Snafu, Spaced out, Spin,
Stump, Stupefy, Surprise, Swivet, Tangle, Tapsalteerie, Throw, Topsy-turvy,
Toss, Turbulence, Turmoil, Tzimmes, Upside down, Welter, Whomble,
Woolly, Woozy

▷**Confuse(d)** *may indicate* an anagram

Congratulate, Congratulation Applaud, Felicitate, Laud, Mazeltov, Preen,
Salute

Congregate, Congregation(alist) Assembly, Barnabite, Body, Brownist,
Class, Community, Conclave, Ecclesia, Flock, Fold, For(e)gather, Gathering,
Group, Host, Laity, Oratory, Propaganda, Synagogue

Congress(man) Assembly, Capitol, Conclave, Council, Eisteddfod, Intercourse, Legislature, Rally, Senator, Solon, Synod, Vienna

Conjunction Alligation, Ampersand, And, Combination, Consort, Coordinating, Inferior, Subordinating, Superior, Synod, Syzygy, Together, Union, Unition

Connect(ed), Connection, Connector Accolade, Adaptor, Affiliate, Affinity, Agnate, Ally, Anastomosis, And, Associate, Attach, Band, Bind, Bridge, Bridle, Cable, Chiasm, Clientele, Cognate, Coherent, Colligate, Conjugate, Correlate, Couple, Cross-link, Delta, DIN, Dovetail, Downlink, Drawbar, Earth, Enlink, Fishplate, Fistula, Hydrant, Interlink, Interlock, Interrelation, Join, Jumper, Kinship, Liaison, Lifeline, Link(age), Linkup, Marry, Merge, Neck, Network, Nexus, Nose, On, Online, Pons, Raphe, Rapport, Relate, Relative, Relevant, Respect, Sentence, Shank, Socket, Splice, S-R, Tendon, Through, Tie, Tie-in, Twin, Unction, Union, Yoke, Zygon

Connive, Connivance Abet, Cahoots, Collude, Condone, Conspire, Lenocinium, Plot

Connoisseur Aesthete, Barista, Cognoscente, Epicure, Expert, Fancier, Gourmet, Judge, Oenophil(e)

Conquer(or), Conquering, Conquest Alexander, Beat, Caesar, Conquistador, Cortes, Crush, Debel, Defeat, Genghis Khan, Hereward, →**MASTER**, Moor, Norman, Ostrogoth, Overcome, Overpower, Overrun, Pizarro, Saladin, Subjugate, Tame, Tamerlane, Vanquish, Victor, Vincent, Win

Conscience, Conscientious Casuistic, Dutiful, Heart, Inwit, Morals, Painstaking, Pang, Remorse, Scruple(s), Scrupulous, Sense, Superego, Syneidesis, Synteresis, Thorough, Twinge

Conscious(ness) Awake, Aware, Black, Deliberate, Limen, Sensible, Sensitivity, Sentient, Witting

Consent Accord, Affo(o)rd, Agree, Approbate, Assent, Comply, Concur, Grant, Homologate, Informed, Permit, Ratify, Submit, Una voce, Volens, Yes-but, Yield

Consequence(s), Consequent(ial), Consequently After effect, Aftermath, Consectaneous, Corollary, Effect, End, Implication, Importance, Issue, Karma, Knock-on, Moment, Outcome, Out-turn, Party game, Ramification, Repercussion, →**RESULT**, Sequel, Thence, Threat, Thus

Conservative Blimpish, Blue, C, Cautious, Diehard, Disraeli, Fabian, Hard-hat, Hunker, Misoneist, New Right, Old guard, Old School, Reactionary, Rearguard, Right(-wing), Square, Thatcherite, Thrifty, Tory, True blue, Unionist, Verkrampte, Young Fogey

Conserve, Conservation(ist) Comfiture, Game warden, Greenpeace, Husband(ry), Jam, Jelly, Maintain, Maintenance, NT, Protect, Save

Consider(able), Considerate, Consideration Ad referendum, Animadvert, Attention, Avizandum, By-end, Case, Cogitate, Contemplate, Count, Courtesy, Debate, Deem, Deliberate, Entertain, Envisage, Factor, Fair, Feel, Gay, Gey, Heed, Importance, Inasmuch, Judge, Kind, Many, Materially, Measure, Meditate, Much, Mull, Muse, Pay, Perpend, Poise, Ponder, Pretty, Priority, Pro and con, Rate, Reck, Reckon, Reflect, Regard, Respect, Scruple, See, Sensitive, Several, Solicitous, Song, Speculate, Steem, Study, Substantial, Think, Tidy, Vast, View, Ween, Weigh

Consign(ment) Allot, Award, Batch, Bequeath, Delegate, Deliver, Entrust, Freight, Lading, Ship, Shipment, Transfer

Consist(ent), Consistency Changeless, Coherent, Comprise, Concordant, Enduring, Liaison, Rely, Sound, Steady, Texture, Uniform

Consolation, Console Ancon, Appease, Balm, Cheer, Comfort, Games, Panel, Play, Prize, Reassure, Relief, Solace, Station

Conspicuous Arresting, Blatant, Bold, Clear, Eminent, Eye-catching, Glaring, Kenspeck(le), Landmark, Light, Manifest, Patent, Radiant, Salient, Shining, Showy, Signal, Striking

Conspiracy, Conspirator, Conspire, Conspiring Brutus, Cabal, Cartel, Casca, Cassius, Catiline, Cato St, Cinna, Collaborate, Colleague, Collogue, Collude, Complot, Connive, Covin, Covyne, Guy Fawkes, In cahoots, Intrigue, Oates, Omerta, → **PLOT**, Practisant, Ring, Scheme

Constable High, Hog, Lord High, Petty, → **POLICEMAN**, Uniformed

Constancy, Constant Abiding, Boltzmann, C, Changeless, Chronic, Coefficient, Cosmic, Cosmological, Decay, Devotion, Dielectric, Diffusion, Dilys, Dirac, Eccentricity, Equilibrium, Eternal, Faith, Firm, Fixed, Frequent, Fundamental, G, Gas, Gravitational, H, Honesty, Hubble's, Incessant, K, Lambert, Leal(ty), Logical, Loyal, Magnetic, Nonstop, Often, Parameter, Pi, Planck's, Pole star, Rate, Regular, Relentless, Resolute, Sad, Solar, Stable, Staunch, Steadfast, Steady, Time, True, Unceasing, Unfailing, Uniform, Usual

Constellation Andromeda, Antlia, Apus, Aquarius, Aquila, Ara, Argo, Aries, Auriga, Bootes, Caelum, Camelopardalis, Camelopardus, Canes Venatici, Canis Major, Canis Minor, Carina, Cassiopeia, Centaurus, Cepheus, Cetus, Cham(a)eleon, Circinus, Columba, Coma Berenices, Coma Cluster, Corvus, Crater, Cygnus, Cynosure, Delphinus, Delta, Dolphin, Dorado, Draco, Equuleus, Eridanus, Fornax, Galaxy, Gemini, Great Bear, Gru(i)s, Hercules, Horologium, Hydra, Hydrus, Indus, Lacerta, Leo, Leo Minor, Lepus, Libra, Little Bear, Little Dipper, Lupus, Lynx, Lyra, Mensa, Microscopium, Monoceros, Musca, Norma, Octans, Ophiuchus, Orion, Pavo, Pegasus, Perseus, Phoenix, Pictor, Piscis Austrinus, → **PLANET**, Puppis, Pyxis, Reticulum, Sagitta, Sagittarius, Scorpius, Sculptor, Scutum, Serpens, Sextans, Southern Cross, Spica, → **STAR**, Telescopium, The Rule, Triangulum (Australe), Tucana, Twins, Unicorn, Vela, Vilpecula, Virgin, Virgo, Volans, Vulpecula, Wag(g)oner, Whale, Zodiacal

Constituency, Constituent Agglutinogen, Borough, Component, Element, Part, Seat, Staple, Sub unit, Ultimate, Voter

▷**Constituents** *may indicate* an anagram

Constitute, Constitution(al) Appoint, Character, Charter, Clarendon, Compose, Comprise, Congenital, Creature, Establishment, Form, Fuero, Health, Physique, Policy, Polity, Seat, State, Stroll, Synthesis, Trek

Constrain(ed), Constraint Bind, Bondage, Coerce, Confine, Coop, Curb, Dragoon, Duress(e), Force, Hard, Impel, Limit, Localise, Oblige, Pressure, Repress, Stenosis, Taboo, Tie

Constrict(ed), Constriction Bottleneck, Cage, Choke, Coarctate, Contract, Cramp, Hour-glass, Impede, Isthmus, Limit, Narrow, Phimosis, Squeeze, Stegnosis, Stenosis, Stifle, Strangle, Thlipsis, Tighten, Venturi

Construct(ion), Constructor, Constructive Architect, Assemble, Build, Cast, Compile, Engineer, Erect, Fabricate, Facture, Fashion, Form, Frame, Make, Manufacture, Meccano, Partners, Seabee, Stressed-skin, Tectonic, Weave

Consult(ant), Consultation Avisement, Confer, Deliberate, Discuss, Holmes, Imparl, Peritus, See, Sexpert, Shark watcher, Surgery

Consume(r), Consumption, Consumptive Bolt, Burn, Caterpillar®, Conspicuous, Decay, Devour, Diner, Eat, End-user, Engross, Exhaust, Expend,

Feed, Glutton, Hectic, Intake, Mainline, Preoccupy, Scoff, Spend, Swallow, TB, Use, Waste, Wear

Contact Abut, Adpress, Contingence, Electrode, Eye, Fax, Hook-up, Lens, Liaise, Liaison, Meet, Outreach, Radio, Reach, Shoe, Telephone, → **TOUCH**

Contagious, Contagion Infection, Noxious, Poison, Psora, Taint, Variola, Viral

Contain(er) Amphora, Ampoule, Ampulla, Aquafer, Aquifer, Ashcan, Barrel, Basket, Bass, Beaker, Bidon, Billy(-can), Bin, Boat, Bottle, Bowl, Box, Brazier, Buddle, Bunker, Butt, Butter-boat, Cachepot, Can, Canakin, Canikin, Canister, Cannikin, Cantharus, Capsule, Carafe, Carboy, Carry, Carton, Cartridge, Case, Cask, Cassette, Censer, Chase, Chest, Chilly bin, Churn, Clip, Coffer, Coffret, Comprise, Coolamon, Crate, Crater, Crib, Crucible, Cup, Cupel, Cuvette, Decanter, Dracone, Dredger, Encircle, Enclose, Encompass, Enseam, Esky®, Feretory, Flagon, Flask, Flat, Gabion, Gallipot, Gourd, Growler, → **HOLD**, House, Humidor, Igloo, Include, Incubator, Inseam, Intray, Jar, Jeroboam, Jerrican, Jerrycan, Jug, Keg, Kettle, Kirbeh, Leaguer, Lekythos, Locker, Magnox, Melting-pot, Monkey, Monstrance, Mould, Muffineer, Nosebag, Olpe, Ostensorium, Out-tray, Packet, Pail, Percolator, Pinata, Piscina, Pitcher, Pithos, Pocket, Pod, Poke, Pottle, Punnet, Pyxis, Receptacle, Reliquary, Repository, Restrain, Sac(k), Sachet, Safe, Saggar, Scrip, Scuttle, Scyphus, Shaker, Sheath, Silo, Situla, Skin, Skip, Snaptin, Solander, Spittoon, Stamnos, Stillage, Tank, Tantalus, Tea kettle, Terrarium, Tinaja, Trough, Trug, Tub, Tun, Tupperware®, Urn, Valise, Vase, Vat, Vessel, Vinaigrette, Wardian case, Wineskin, Woolpack, Workbag

Contaminate(d), Contaminant, Contamination Corrupt, Defile, Flyblown, Impure, Infect, Moit, Mysophobia, Salmonella, Soil, Spike, Stain, Tarnish, Toxic

Contemporary AD, Coetaneous, Coeval, Concomitant, Current, Equal, Fellow, Modern, Modish, Present, Topical, Verism

Contempt(ible), Contemptuous Abject, Ageism, Aha, Arsehole, Bah, Base, BEF, Blithering, Cheap, Contumely, Crud, Crumb, Crummy, Cullion, Cur, Cynical, Derision, Diddy, Dis(s), Disdain, Dismissive, Disparaging, Disrespect, Dog-bolt, Dusty, Fico, Fig, Figo, Flouting, Foh, Git, Ignominious, Jive-ass, Lousy, Low, Mean, Measly, Misbegotten, Misprision, Och, Paltry, Pelting, Pfui, Pho(h), Phooey, Pipsqueak, Pish, Poof, Poxy, Pshaw, Rats, Razoo, Scabby, Scarab, Scofflaw, → **SCORN**, Scumbag, Scurvy, Sdeign, Sexism, Shabby, Shitface, Shithead, Sneer, Sneeze, Sniffy, Snook, Snooty, Snot, Snotty, Soldier, Sorry, Sprat, Squirt, Squit, Supercilious, Toad, Toerag, Tossy, Turd, Tush, Weed, Wretched

Contend(er) Allege, Athlete, Candidate, Claim, Clash, Compete, Cope, Debate, Dispute, Fight, Grapple, Oppose, Rival, Stickle, → **STRIVE**, Struggle, Submit, Tussle, → **VIE**, Wrestle

Content(ed), Contentment Apaid, Apay, Appay, Arcadia, Blissful, Calm, Happy, Inside, Matter, Please, Raza, Reza, Satiate, Satisfy, Subject matter, Volume

▷**Content** *may indicate* a hidden word

Contention, Contentious Argument, Bellicose, Cantankerous, Case, Combat, Competitive, Logomachy, Perverse, Polemical, Rivalry, Strife, Struggle, Sturt

Contest(ant) Agon, Battle (royal), Beauty, Beetle drive, Biathlon, Bout, Catchweight, Challenge, Championship, Combat, Competition, Concours, Darraign, Decathlon, Defend, Deraign, Dogfight, Duathlon, Duel(lo), Entrant,

Eurovision, Event, Examinee, Finalist, Free-for-all, Fronde, Handicap,
Heptathlon, Joust, Kemp, Kriegspiel, Lampadephoria, Match, Matchplay,
Olympiad, Pancratium, Panel-beater, Par, Paralympics, Pentathlon, Pingle,
Play-off, Prizer, Race (meeting), Rat race, Rival, Roadeo, Rodeo, Scrap,
Scrum, Set-to, Skirmish, Slam, Slugfest, Strife, Struggle, Tenson, Tetrathlon,
Tournament, Triathlon, Tug-of-war, Tussle, Vie, War, With

Continent(al) Abstinent, Asia, Atlantis, Austere, Chaste, Epeirogeny, Euro,
Gallic, Gondwanaland, Greek, Landmass, Laurasia, Lemuria, Mainland,
Moderate, NA, Oceania, Pang(a)ea, Shelf, Teetotal, Temperate, Walloon

Continual(ly), Continuous Adjoining, At a stretch, Away, Ceaseless, Chronic,
Connected, Durational, Eer, Endlong, Eternal, Eterne, Ever, Forever, Frequent,
Incessant, On(going), Perpetual, Unbroken, Unceasing

Continue, Continuation, Continuing, Continuity Abye, Drag on,
Duration, Dure, During, Enduring, Enjamb(e)ment, Hold, Keep, Last, Link,
Onward, Perpetuate, Persevere, Persist, Proceed, Prolong, Push on, Resume,
Sequel, Sequence, Stand, Subsist, Survive, Sustain, Tenor

▷**Continuously** *may indicate* previous words to be linked

Contraception, Contraceptive Billings method, Cap, Coil, Condom,
Depo-Provera®, Diaphragm, Etonogestrol, IU(C)D, Legonorgestrel, Lippes
loop, Loop, Minipill, Oral, Pessary, Pill, Precautions, Prophylactic, Sheath,
Spermicide, Vimule®

Contract(ion), Contractor Abbreviate, Abrege, Abridge, Affreightment,
Agreement, Astringency, Bargain, Biceps, Binding, Bridge, Builder, Catch,
Champerty, Charter (party), Clench, Clonus, Concordat, Condense, Constringe,
Contrahent, Convulsion, Covenant, Cramp, Curtail(ment), Debt, Develop, Dwindle,
Engage, Entrepreneur, Escrow, Extrasystole, Fibrillation, Forward, Gainsay,
Gooseflesh, Guarantee, Hedge, Hire, Incur, Indenture, Jerk, Knit, Labour, Lease,
Lessen, Levator, Make, Mandate, Miosis, Myosis, Narrow, Outsource, Party,
Policy, Privilege, Promise, Pucker, Purse, Restriction, Shrink, Shrivel, Sign,
Slam, Slim, Social, Spasm, Specialty, Squinch, Stenosis, Stipulation, Straddle,
Supplier, Swap, Sweetheart, Synaloepha, Systole, Taper off, Telescope, Tender,
Tense, Tetanise, Tetanus, Tic, Tighten, Tittle, Tonicity, Tontine, Treaty, Triceps,
Trigger-finger, Trismus cynicus, Undertaker, Wrinkle, Yellow-dog, Z

▷**Contract** *may indicate* a bridge call, e.g. 1S, 1C, 1D

Contradict(ion), Contradictory Ambivalent, Antilogy, Antinomy, Bull,
Contrary, Counter, Dementi, Deny, Disaffirm, Disprove, Dissent, Negate,
Oxymoron, Paradox, Perverse, Sot, Stultify, Sublate, Threap, Threep, Traverse

Contraption Contrivance, Doodah, Scorpion

Contrarily, Contrary Adverse, A rebours, Arsy-versy, But, Captious, Converse,
Counter, Crosscurrent, Froward, Heretic, Hostile, Inverse, Mary, Opposite,
Oppugnant, Ornery, Perverse, Rebuttal, Retrograde, Wayward, Withershins

Contrast Chiaroscuro, Chiasmus, Clash, Compare, Differ, Foil, Relief

Contribute, Contribution Abet, Add, Assist, Conduce, Donate, Dub, Furnish,
Go, Help, Input, Mite, Offering, Share, Sub, Subscribe, Whack

▷**Contributing to** *may indicate* a hidden word

Contrivance, Contrive(r), Contrived Art, Artificial, Cam, Chicaner,
Contraption, Cook, Deckle, Deus ex machina, Device, Devise, Dodge, Engine,
Engineer, Finesse, Frame, Gadget, Gimmick, Gin, Hatch, Hokey, Intrigue,
Invention, Machinate, Manage, Manoeuvre, Page, Plan, Plot, Procure, Rest,
Rowlock, Scheme, Secure, Shift, Stage, Trump, Wangle, Weave

Control(ler), Controllable, Controlled Ada, Aircon, Appestat, Atorvastatin, Autopilot, Ballcock, Bias, Big Brother, Birth, Boss, Boundary layer, Bridle, Cabotage, Camshaft, Chair, Check, Choke(hold), Christmas tree, Contain, Corner, Correct(ion), Corset, Curb, Cybernetics, Damage, Descendeur, Dirigible, Dirigism(e), Dominate, Dominion, Driving seat, Duopsony, Dynamic, Elevon, Etatiste, Fader, Fast-forward, Fet(ch), Finger, Flood, Fly-by-wire, Gain, Gar, George, Gerent, Govern, Ground, Gubernation, Hae, Handle, Harness, Have, Heck, Helm, Hog, Influence, Influx, Inhibitor, Interchange, Joystick, Keypad, Knee-swell, Lead, Lever, Limit, Line, → MANAGE, Martinet, Mastery, Moderate, Mouse, Nipple, Noise, Nozzled, Numerical, Operate, Override, Pacemaker, Pilot, Placebo, Police, Population, Possess, Power, Preside, Price, Process, Puppeteer, Quality, Radio, Referee, Regime(nt), Regulate, Regulo®, Rein, Remote, Rent, Repress, Restrain, Restrict, Rheostat, Ride, Ripple, Rule, Run, School, Servo, Slide(r), Snail, Solion, Spoiler, Stage-manage, Steady, Steer, Stop, Stopcock, Stranglehold, Stringent, Subdue, Subject, Subjugate, Supervise, Suzerain, Svengali, Sway, Switch, Takeover, Tame, Tap, Temperate, Thermostat, Throttle, Tie, Tiller, Tone, Traction, Umpire, Upper hand, Valve, Weld, Wield, Zapper

Controversial, Controversy Argument, Cause celebre, Contention, Debate, Dispute, Emotive, Eristic(al), Furore, Heretical, Hot potato, Moot point, Quarrel

▷**Contuse** *may indicate* an anagram

Convenience, Convenient Behoof, Cosy, Easy, Eft, Ethe, Expedient, Facility, Gain, Gents, Handsome, → HANDY, Hend, Lav, Leisure, Men's room, Near, Opportune, Pat, Privy, Public, Suitable, Toilet, Use, Well

Convent Abbatial, Cloister, Fratry, Friary, House, Motherhouse, Nunnery, Port-royal, Priory, Retreat

Convention(al) Academic, Accepted, Babbitt, Blackwood, Bourgeois, Caucus, Code, Conclave, Conformity, → CUSTOMARY, Decorous, Diet, Done, Formal, Geneva, Habitude, Hidebound, Iconic, Lame, Lingua franca, Mainstream, Meeting, Middlebrow, Middle-of-the-road, More, National, Nomic, Normal, Orthodox, Ossified, Pompier, Pooterish, Proper, Propriety, Readymade, Schengen, Square, Staid, Starchy, Stereotyped, Stock, Straight, Stylebook, Synod, The thing, Uptight, Usage, Warsaw

Conversation(al), Conversationalist, Converse, Conversant Abreast, Antithesis, Antitype, Aware, Board, Buck, Cackle, Causerie, Chat, Chinwag, Chitchat, Colloquy, Commune, Convo, Crack, Crossfire, Deipnosophist, Dialogue, Discourse, Eutrapelia, Eutraply, Exchange, Facemail, Hobnob, Interlocution, In tune with, Jaw-jaw, Natter, Opposite, Palaver, Parley, Rap, Rhubarb, Shop, Shoptalk, Sidebar, Small talk, Socialise, → TALK, Transpose, Trialogue, Wongi, Word

Conversion, Converter, Convert(ible) Adapt, Alter, Assimilate, Bessemer, Cabriolet, Cash, Catalytic, Catechumen, Change, Commutate, Commute, Cyanise, Damascene, Diagenesis, Disciple, Distil, Encash, Evangelize, Exchange, Expropriate, Fixation, Goal kick, Ismalise, Landau, Liquid(ate), Marrano, Metamorphosis, Metanoia, Missionary, Neophyte, Noviciate, Novitiate, Persuade, Proselyte, Put, Ragtop, Realise, Rebirth, Reclamation, Recycle, Revamp, Romanise, Sheik(h), Soft-top, Souper, Tablet, Transduce, Transmute, Try, Vert

▷**Conversion, Converted** *may indicate* an anagram

Convey(ance) Assign, BS, Carousel, Carry, Carrycot, Cart, Chaise, Charter, Coach, Conduct, Cycle, Deed, Deliver, Eloi(g)n, Enfeoffment, Esloyne, Exeme,

Grant, Guide, Lease, Litter, Lorry, Mailcar(t), Pirogue, Re-lease, Sac, Sled, Soc, Tip, Title deed, Tote, Tram, Transfer, Transit, Transmit, Transport, Trolley, Vehicle

Convict(ion) Attaint, Belief, Botany Bay, Bushranger, Canary, Certitude, Cockatoo, Cogence, Crawler, Credo, Creed, Crime, Criminal, Demon, Dogma, Emancipist, Faith, Felon, Forçat, Gaolbird, Government man, Jailbird, Lag, Magwitch, → **PERSUASION**, Plerophory, Previous, Prisoner, Record, Ring, Trusty, Vehemence, Yardbird

Convince(d), Convincing Assure, Certain, Cogent, Conclusive, Credible, Doubtless, Luculent, Persuade, Plausible, Satisfy, Sold, Sure

Convulse, Convulsion(s), Convulsive Agitate, Clonic, Clonus, Commotion, Disturb, DT, Eclampsia, → **FIT**, Galvanic, Grand mal, Paroxysm, Petit mal, Seizure, Shudder, Sob, Spasm, Throe, Tic

Cook(s), Cooker(y), Cooking Aga®, Babbler, Babbling brook, Bain marie, Bake, Balti, Barbecue, Beeton, Benghazi, Bhindi, Bouche, Braise, Broil, Cacciatore, Calabash, Captain, Casserole, Charbroil, Chargrill, Chef, Coction, Coddle, Concoct, Cordon bleu, Costard, Creole, Cuisine, Cuisinier, Delia, Devil, Do, Doctor, Dumple, Easy over, Edit, En papillote, Escoffier, Explorer, Fake, Falsify, Fiddle, Fireless, Fix, Flambé, Forge, Fricassee, Fry, Fudge, Fusion, Gastronomy, Gratinate, Greasy, Griddle, Grill, Haute cuisine, Haybox, Hibachi, Hot plate, Jackaroo, Kiln, Lyonnaise, Marengo, Marinière, Meunière, Microwave, Mount, Poach, Prepare, Pressure, Range, Ring, Roast, Roger, Sauté, Short-order, Silver, Sous-chef, Spit, Steam, Stew, Stir-fry, Stove, Tandoori, Tire, Toast

▷**Cook** *may indicate* an anagram

Cookie Biscuit, Fortune, Rye-roll

Cool(er), Coolant, Cooling, Coolness Ace, Aloof, Aplomb, Calm, Can, Chill, Chokey, Collected, Composed, Cryogen, Cryostat, Defervescence, Dignified, Dispassionate, Distant, Esky®, Fan, Frappé, Fridge, Frigid, Frosty, Gaol, Goglet, Heat sink, Hip, Ice(box), Imperturbable, In, Jail, Jug, Keel, Lubricating oil, Maraging, Nervy, Nonchalant, Offish, Phlegm, Poise, Prison, Quad, Quod, Radiator, Refresh, Reserved, Sangfroid, Serene, Shady, Skeigh, Splat, Stir, Super-duper, Sweat, Temper(ate), Thou(sand), Unruffled

Coop Cage, Cavie, Confine, Gaol, Hutch, Mew, Pen, Rip

Cooperate, Cooperation, Cooperative Accommodate, Ally, Artel, Bipartisan, Collaborate, Combine, Conspire, Contribute, Coop, Credit union, Liaise, Pitch in, Tame, Teamwork, Together

Coordinate(s), Coordinated, Coordination Abscissa, Abscisse, Agile, Arrange, Cartesian, Del, Ensemble, Harmony, Nabla, Orchestrate, Ordonnance, Peer, Polar, Synergy, Tight, Twistor, Waypoint, X, Y, Z

Cop(s) Bag, Bull, Catch, Copper, Dick, Flic, Keystone, Peeler, Peon, → **POLICEMAN**

Cope Chlamys, Deal, Face, Fare, Handle, Hood, → **MANAGE**, Mantle, Meet, Negotiate, Pallium, Poncho, Scrat(ch)

Copy(ing), Copier, Copyist, Copywriter Adman, Aemule, Ape, Apograph, Association, Autotype, Calk, Calque, Carbon, Clerk, Clone, Counterpart, Crib, Cyclostyle, Diazo, Ditto, Double, Duplicate, Dyeline, Echo, Echopraxia, Ectype, Edition, Eidograph, Electro, Emulate, Engross, Estreat, Example, Facsimile, Fair, Fax, Flimsy, Forge, → **IMITATE**, Issue, Knockoff, Manifold, Manuscript, Match, Me-tooer, Microdot, Milline, Mimeograph®, Mimic, Mirror, MS, Ozalid,

Pantograph, Parrot, Photostat®, Pirate, Plagiarism, Read-out, Repeat, Replica, Reprint, Repro, Reproduce, Rip, Roneo®, Scanner, Scribe, Script, Scrivener, Sedulous, Simulate, Skim, Soft, Spit, Stat, Stencil, Stuff, Tall, Telefax, Tenor, Tenure, Trace, Transcribe, Transume, Transumpt, Typescript, Vidimus, Xerox®

Coral (reef) Alcyonaria, Aldabra, Atoll, Brain, Gorgonia(n), Laccadives, Madrepore, Millepore, Organ-pipe, Pink, Reef, Sea fan, Sea ginger, Sea-pen, Sea whip, Staghorn, Zoothome

Cord, Cord-like Achilles tendon, Aiguillette, Band, Bedford, Bind, Boondoggle, Cat-gut, Chenille, Clew, Communication, Creance, Cybernaculum, Drawstring, Elephant, Flex, Fourragère, Funicle, Gasket, Heddle, Laniard, Lanyard, Ligature, Line, Moreen, Myelon, Nerve, Net, Ocnus, Picture, Piping, Quipo, Quipu, Rep(s), Restiform, Rip, Rope, Sash, Sennit, Service, Sinew, Sinnet, Spermatic, Spinal, Static line, →**STRING**, Tendon, Tie, Tieback, Twine, Twitch, Umbilical, Vocal

Cordon Band, Beltcourse, Picket, Police, Ring, Surround

Core Barysphere, Calandria, Campana, Centre, Essence, Filament, Heart, Hub, Magnetic, Nife, Plerome, Quintessence, Runt

Cork(ed), Corker Balsa, Bouché, Bung, Float(er), Humdinger, Oner, Periderm, Phellem, Phellogen, Plug, Seal, Shive, Stopper, Suber(ate)

Corkscrew Bore, Opening, Spiral, Twine

Cormorant Duiker, Duyker, Scart(h), Shag, Skart(h)

Corn(y) Bajr(a), Banal, Blé, Callus, Cereal, Cob, Dolly, Durra, Emmer, Epha, Flint, Gait, Graddan, Grain, Grist, Hokey, Icker, Indian, Kaffir, Kanga pirau, Mabela, Maize, Mealie, Muid, Nubbin, Pickle, Pinole, Posho, Rabi, Shock, Stitch, Straw, Tail ends, Thrave, Trite, Zea

Corner Amen, Angle, Bend, Canthus, Cantle, Canton, Chamfer, Cranny, Dangerous, Diêdre, Dominate, Elbow, Entrap, Hog, Hole, Hospital, Inglenook, Long, Lug, Monopoly, NE, Niche, Nook, NW, Predicament, Quoin, SE, Speakers', Spot, SW, Tack, Tattenham, Trap, Tree, Vertex

Corporation Alvine, Beer gut, Belly, Body, Breadbasket, Commune, Company, Conglomerate, Guild, Kite, Kyte, Paunch, Pot(-belly), Public service, Stomach, Swag-belly, Tum, Wame, Wem

Corps Body, C, Cadet, Crew, Diplomatic, Marine, Peace, RAC, RE, REME, Unit

Corpse(s) Blob, Body, Cadaver, Carcass, Carrion, Deader, Dust, Goner, Like, Mort, Quarry, Relic, Remains, Stiff, Zombi(e)

Correct(ive), Correcting, Correctly, Correctness, Correction, Corrector About east, Accepted, Accurate, Alexander, Align, Amend, Aright, Bodkin, Castigate, Chasten, Chastise, Check, Cheese, Comme il faut, Decorous, Diorthortic, Discipline, Edit, Emend, Epanorthosis, Ethical, Exact, Fair, Fix, Grammatical, Kosher, Legit, Letter perfect, Mend, Orthopaedic, Precise, Preterition, Probity, Proofread, Proper, Propriety, Punctilious, Punish, Rebuke, Rectify, Red pencil, Redress, Reform, Remedial, Reprove, Revise, Right(en), Scold, Spinning-house, Spot-on, Straighten, Sumpsimus, Tickety-boo, Tippex®, Trew, True, Twink, U, Yep, Yes

▷**Corrected** *may indicate* an anagram

Correspond(ence), Correspondent, Corresponding Accord, Agree, Analogy, Assonance, Coincident, Communicate, Congruence, Correlate, Counterpart, Cynghanedd, Epistolist, Equate, Eye-rhyme, Fit, Homolog(ue), Identical, Isomorph, Lobby, Match, On all fours, One-one, One to one, Par, Parallel, Parity, Pen-friend, Penpal, Post(bag), Relate, Symmetry, Sync, Tally, Veridical, Write

Corridor Air, Aisle, Gallery, Greenway, Lobby, Passage(-way), Penthouse

Corrode(d), Corrosion, Corrosive Acid, Acid rain, Brinelling, Burn, Canker, Caustic, Decay, Eat, Erode, Etch, Fret, Gnaw, Hydrazine, Mordant, **→ ROT**, Rubiginous, Rust, Waste

Corrupt(er), Corrupting, Corruption Abuse, Adulterate, Bastardise, Bent, Canker, Cesspit, Contaminated, Debase, Debauch, Decadent, Defile, Degenerate, Depravity, Dishonest, Dissolute, Dry rot, Emancipate, Embrace(o)r, Embrasor, Empoison, Enseam, Etch, Evil, Fester, Gangrene, Graft(er), Immoral, Impaired, Impure, Infect, Inquinate, Jobbery, Leprosy, Malversation, Mar, Nefarious, Obelus, Payola, Perverse, Poison, Pollute, Power, Putrefaction, Putrid, Rakery, Ret(t), Rigged, Rot, Scrofulous, Seduce, Sepsis, Septic, Sleaze, Sodom, Sophisticate, Spoil, Stench, Suborn, Taint, Tammany, Twist, Ulcered, Venal, Vice, Vitiate

Cosmetic Aloe vera, Beautifier, Blusher, Bronzer, Chapstick, Conditioner, Detangler, Eye-black, Eyeliner, Eye-shadow, Face-lift, Face-pack, Foundation, Fucus, Highlighter, Kohl, Lightener, Liner, Lip gloss, Lip liner, Lippie, Lipstick, Lotion, Maquillage, Mascara, Moisturizer, Mousse, Mudpack, Nail polish, Paint, Panstick, Pearl-powder, Pearl-white, Powder, Q-tip, Reface, Rouge, Talcum, Toner, Warpaint

Cosmos, Cosmic Globe, Heaven, Infinite, Mundane, Nature, Universe, World

Cost(s), Costly Be, Bomb, Carriage, Charge, Current, Damage, Disadvantage, Earth, Escuage, Estimate, Exes, **→ EXPENSE**, Fetched, Hire, Historic(al), Legal, Loss, Marginal, Outlay, Overhead, Precious, Price, Quotation, Rate, Rent, Running, Sacrifice, Standard, Storage, Sumptuous, Tab, Toll, Unit, Upkeep, Usurious

Costume(s) Apparel, Attire, Camagnole, Cossie, Dress, Ensemble, Garb, Get-up, Gi(e), Guise, Judogi, Livery, Maillot, Motley, National, Nebris, Polonaise, Rig, Ruana, Surcoat, Tanga, Trollopee, Tutu, Uniform, Wardrobe

Cosy Cosh, Gemutlich, Intime, Snug

Cottage(r) Bach, Batch, Bordar, Bothie, Bothy, Bower, Box, Bungalow, Cabin, Cape Cod, Chalet, Cot, Crib, Da(t)cha, Dove, Gite, Hut, Lodge, Mailer, Thatched

Cotton Absorbent, Agree, AL, Alabama, Balbriggan, Batiste, Batting, Calico, Candlewick, Ceiba, Chambray, Cheesecloth, Chino, Chintz, Collodion, Coutil(le), Cretonne, Denim, Dho(o)ti, Dimity, Ducks, Fustian, Galatea, Gingham, Gossypine, Gossypium, Humhum, Ihram, Jaconet, Kapok, Lawn, Lea, Lille, Lint, Lisle, Longcloth, Madras, Manchester, Marcella, Muslin, Nainsook, Nankeen, Nankin, Nap, Percale, Pongee, Sateen, Sea-island, Seersucker, Silesia, Stranded, Surat, T-cloth, Thread, Twig, Upland, Velveteen

Couch Bed, Davenport, Daybed, Express, Grass, Lurk, Palanquin, Palkee, Palki, Quick, Recamier, Sedan, Settee, Sofa, Studio, Triclinium, Vis-à-vis, Word

Cough(ing) Bark, Chin, Croup, Expectorate, Hack, Harrumph, Hawk, Hem, Hoast, Kink, Rale, Tisick, Tussis, Ugh, Whooping

Council (meeting), Councillor, Counsel(lor), Counselling Achitophel, Admonish, Admonitor, Advice, Advocate, Ahithophel, Alderman, Alfred, Aread, Assembly, Attorney, Aulic, Board, Body, Boule, Bundesrat, Burgess, Cabal, Cabinet, Casemate, Committee, Consistory, Corporation, County, Cr, Decurion, Defending, Devil, Divan, Douma, Duma, Ecofin, Egeria, Europe, Exhort, General, Greenbag, Hebdomadal, Indaba, Induna, Info, Jirga, Junta, Kabele, Kebele, Kite, Landst(h)ing, Lateran, Latrocinium, Leader, Legislative, Majlis, Mentor, Nestor, Nicene, Panchayat, Parish, Powwow, Privy, Prosecuting,

Provincial, Rede, Reichsrat, Relate, Runanga, Samaritan, Sanhedrim, Sanhedrin, Security, Senate, Shura, Sobranje, Sobranye, Soviet, States, Syndicate, Synod, Thing, Tradeboard, Trent, Tridentine, Trullan, Unitary, Volost, Whitley, Witan, Witenagemot, Works, Zila, Zila parishad, Zillah

Count(ed), Counter(balance), Counting Abacus, Add, Algoriam, Anti, Aristo, Balance, Bank, Bar, Basie, Buck, Buffet, Calculate, Calorie, Cavour, Census, Check, Chip, Compute, Coost, Crystal, Cuisenaire rods, Deem, Depend, Desk, Disc, Dracula, Dump, Earl, Enumerate, Fish, Geiger, Geiger-Muller, Graf(in), Grave, Itemise, Jet(t)on, Landgrave, Margrave, Matter, Meet, Merel(l), Meril, Milton work, Number, Numerate, Obviate, Olivia, Oppose, Outtell, Palatine, Palsgrave, Paris, Pollen, Presume, Rebut, →RECKON, Refute, Rejoinder, Rely, Resist, Respond, Retaliate, Retort, Rhinegrave, Riposte, Scaler, Scintillation, Score, Shopboard, Sperm, Squail, Statistician, Stop, Sum, Table, Tally, Tell, Tiddleywink, Tolstoy, Ugolino, Walk, Weigh, Zeppelin, Zinc

Counterfeit(er) Bastard, Belie, Bogus, Boodle, Brum, Coiner, Doctor, Duffer, Dummy, Fain, Fantasm, Fayne, Feign, Flash, Forge, Fraudster, Imitant, Paperhanger, Phantasm, Phoney, Pseudo, Queer, Rap, Schlenter, Sham, Shan(d), Simular, Simulate, Skim, Slang, Slip, Smasher, Snide, Spurious

Counties, County Co, Comital, Comitatus, District, Hundred, Metropolitan, Palatine, Parish, Seat, Shire, Six

Countless Infinite, Innumerable, Myriad, Umpteen, Unending, Untold

Country(side), Countries, Countrified Agrest(i)al, Annam, Arcadia, Bangladesh, Bolivia, Boondocks, Bucolic, Champaign, Clime, Colchis, Edom, Enchorial, Farmland, Fatherland, Georgic, Inland, Jordan, Karoo, Karroo, →LAND, Lea, Lee, Macedonia, Mongolia, Motherland, Nation, Nature, Oman, Outback, Parish, Paysage, People, Province, Rangeland, Realm, Region, Republic, Rural, Rustic, Satellite, Scythia, Soil, Statal, State, The sticks, Tundra, Veld, Venezuela, Weald, Wold, Yemen

Coup Blow, Deal, KO, Masterstroke, Move, Putsch, Scoop, Stroke, Treason

Couple(r), Coupling Acoustic, Ally, Attach, Band, Brace, Bracket, Connect, Duet, Duo, Dyad, Enlink, Fishplate, Gemini, Geminy, Hitch, Interlock, Item, →JOIN, Marry, Mate, Meng(e), Ment, Ming, Pair, Pr, Relate, Shackle, Tenace, Tie, Tirasse, Turnbuckle, Tway, Twosome, Union, Unite, Universal, Voltaic, Wed, Yoke

Coupon(s) Ration, Ticket, Voucher

Courage(ous) Balls, Ballsy, Bottle, Bravado, Bravery, Bulldog, Daredevil, Daring, Derring-do, Dutch, Fortitude, Gallantry, Game, Gimp, Grit, Gumption, Guts, Hardy, Heart, Heroism, Indomitable, Lion-heart, Macho, Manful, Mettle, Moral, Moxie, Nerve, Pluck, Resolve, Rum, Spirit, Spirited, Spunk, Stalwart, Steel, Stomach, Valiant, Valour, Wight

Course(s) Afters, Aim, Aintree, Antipasto, Appetiser, Arroyo, Ascot, Assault, Atlantic, Back straight, Bearing, Beat, Campaign, Canal, Career, Channel, Chantilly, Chase, Circuit, Civics, Consommé, Conversion, Correspondence, Crash, Current, Curriculum, Cursus, Damp(-proof), Dessert, Diadrom, Dish, Dromic, Easting, Entrée, Fish, →FOOD, Foundation, Furrow, Gleneagles, Going, Goodwood, Greats, Gut, Heat, Hippodrome, Hors d'oeuvres, Induction, Lacing, Lane, Lap, Layer, Leat, Leet, Line, Lingfield, Links, Longchamp, Meal, Meat, Mess, Mizzen, Newbury, Newmarket, Nine-hole, Northing, Nulla, Obstacle, →OF COURSE, Orbit, Orthodromic, Period, Policy, PPE, Practicum, Procedure, Process, Programme, Progress, Pursue, Race, →RACETRACK, Raik, Ravioli,

Refresher, Regimen, Rhumb, Ride, Ring, Rink, Road, Rota, Route, Routine, Run, Rut, Sandown, Sandwich, Semester, Series, Slalom, Soup, Southing, Span, Starter, Stearage, Steerage, Step(s), Straight, Stratum, Streak, Stream, Stretch, String, Syllabus, Tack, Tanride, Tenor, Track, Trade, Trail, Trajectory, Troon, Way, Westing

Court(ier), Courtship, Courtyard Ad(vantage), Address, Admiralty, Appellate, Arbitration, Arches, Atrium, Attention, Audience, Audiencia, Aula, Banc, Bar, Basecourt, Bench, Beth Din, Bishop's, Boondock, Caerleon, Camelot, Canoodle, Caravanserai, Cassation, Centre, Chancery, Chase, Clay, Cloister-garth, Commercial, Commissary, Commission, Conscience, Conservancy, Consistory, County, Criminal, Crown, CS, Ct, Curia, Curia Regis, Curtilage, Damocles, Date, Dedans, Deuce, Diplock, District, Divisional, Doctor's Commons, Domestic, Duchy, Durbar, Dusty Feet, En tout cas, Eyre, Faculties, Federal, Fehm(gericht), Fiars, Fifteen, Forensic, Forest, Forum, Fronton, Galleria, Garth, Go steady, Grass, Guildenstern, Halimot(e), Hampton, Hard, High, High Commission, Hof, Holy See, Hustings, Inferior, Innyadr, Intermediate, Invite, Jack, Judicatory, Justice, Juvenile, Kacheri, Kangaroo, Keys, King, King's Bench, Kirk Session, Knave, Law, Law Lords, Leet, Lobby, Lyon, Magistrate's, Majlis, Marshalsea, Mash, Moot, Old Bailey, Open, Osric, Palace, Parvis, Patio, Peristyle, Petty Sessions, Philander, Piepowder, Police, Porte, Prerogative, Presbytery, Prize, Probate, Provincial, Provost, Quad, Quarter Sessions, Queen, Queen's Bench, Racket, Request, Retinue, Romance, Rosenkrantz, Royal, St James's, Sanhedrin, Scottishland, See, Seek, Service, Session, Sheriff, Shire-moot, Shoe, Small-claims, Spoon, Stannary, Star Chamber, Sudder, Sue, Suitor, Superior, Supreme, Swanimote, Sweetheart, Synod, Thane, Thegn, Traffic, Trial, Tribunal, Vehm, Vestibulum, Walk out, Ward, Wardmote, Wench, Woo, World, Wow, Yard, Youth

Courteous, Courtesy Affable, Agreement, Bow, Comity, Debonair, Devoir, Etiquette, Fair, Genteel, Gentilesse, Gentility, Gracious, Hend, Obliging, Polite, Politesse, Refined, Strain, Urbanity, Well-mannered

Courtly Aulic, Chivalrous, Cringing, Dignified, Flattering, Refined

Courtyard Area, Atrium, Close, Cortile, Marae, Patio, Quad(rangle)

Cousin(s) Bette, Cater, Country, Coz, Cross, First, German, Kin, Kissing, Parallel, Robin, Second, Skater

Cover(ed), Coverage, Covering Adventitia, Air, A l'abri, Amnion, Antependium, Antimacassar, Apron, Aril, Armour, Attire, Awning, Bandage, Barb, Bard(s), Bark, Bathrobe, Bed linen, Bedspread, Bestrew, Bind, Blanket, Bodice, Bonnet, Brood, Bubblewrap, Burka, Bury, Cache-sex, Camouflage, Canopy, Cap, Caparison, Cape, Capsule, Carpet, Cartonnage, Casing, Casque, Catch-all, Caul, Ceil, Ciborium, Ciel, Cladding, Clapboard, Cleithral, Clithral, Cloak, Cloche, Coat, Cocoon, Coleorhiza, Conceal, Cope, Copyright, Cosy, Cot, Counterpane, Cour, Covert, Cowl, Crust, Curtain, Deadlight, Debruised, Deck, Deputise, Dividend, Dome, Drape(t), Dripstone, Duchesse, Dusting, Dust-sheet, Duvet, Eiderdown, Encase, Endue, Enguard, Enlace, Ensheathe, Enshroud, Envelop(e), Enwrap, Exoderm(is), Exoskeleton, Exposure, Extra, Eyelid, Eye patch, Face, Falx, Fanfare, Fascia, Felting, Fielder, Figleaf, Fingerstall, First-day, Flashing, Flown, Fother, Front, Gaiter, Gambado, Gift wrap, Gild, Glove, Gobo, Grolier, Ground, Groundsheet, G-string, Guarantee, Hap, Harl, Hat, Hatch, Havelock, Heal, Heather, Heel, Hejab, Hele, Hell, Helmet, Hide, Hijab, Hood, Housing, Hubcap, Husk, Ice, Immerse, Incase, Include, Indument,

Indusium, Inmask, Insulate, Insurance, Insure, Jacket, Lag, Lambrequin, Laminate, Lampshade, Lay, Leap, Leep, Legging, Legwarmer, Lid, Ligger, Liner, Loincloth, Loose, Manche, Mantle, Mask, Mat, Membrane, Metal, Mort-cloth, Mount, Muffle, Mulch, Notum, Numnah, Obscure, OC, Occlude, On, Oose, Operculum, Orillion, Orlop, Overgrown, Overlap, Overlay, Overnet, Overwrap, Pad, Palampore, Palempore, Pall, Pand, Panoply, Parcel, Partlet, Pasties, Patch, Patent, Pave, Pavilion, Pebbledash, Pelmet, Periderm, Perigone, Pillow sham, Pinny, Plaster, Plate, Pleura, Plumage, Pod, Point, Pseudonym, Pullover, Quilt, Radome, Redingote, Regolith, Report, Riza, Robe, Roof, Roughcast, Rug, Run, Sally, Sarafan, Scabbard, Screen, Serviette, Setting, Shagpile, Sheath, Sheet, Shell, Shelter, Shield, Shower, Shrink-wrap, Shroud, Shuck, Skin, Slipcase, Smokescreen, Solleret, Span, Spat, Splashback, Spread, Stand-by, Stand-in, Stifle, Stomacher, Strew, Strow, Superfrontal, Superimpose, Surplice, Swathe, Tampian, Tampion, Tapadera, Tapis, Tarmac, Tarp(aulin), Teacosy, Tectorial, Tectum, Tegmen, Tegument, Tent, Terne, Test(a), Tester, Thatch, Thimble, Thumbstall, Tick(ing), Tidy, Tile, Tilt, Tonneau, Tinfoil, Top, Trapper, Trench, Trip, Turtleback, Twill, Twilt, Umbrella, Up, Upholster, Valance, Veale, Veil, Vele, Veneer, Ventail, Vert, Vesperal, Vest, Vestiture, Visor, Volva, Wainscot, Warrant, Waterdeck, Weeper, Whelm, Whemmle, Whitewash, Whomble, Whommle, Whummle, Wrap, Wrappage, Wrapper, Wreathe, Yapp, Yashmak

Covet(ed), Covetous Avaricious, Crave, Desiderata, Desire, Eager, Envy, Greedy, Hanker, Yearn

Cow(s) Adaw, Alderney, Amate, Appal, Awe, Belted Galloway, Boss(y), Bovine, Browbeat, Cash, Cattle, Charolais, Colly, Crummy, Dant(on), Daunt, Dexter, Dsomo, Dun, Friesian, Galloway, Gally, Goujal, Guernsey, Hawkey, Hawkie, Heifer, Hereford, Intimidate, Jersey, Kouprey, Kyloe, Lea(h), Mart, Milch, Milker, Mog(gie), Moggy, Mooly, Muley, Mulley, Neat, Oppress, Overawe, Ox-eyed, Redpoll, Red Sindhi, Rother(-beast), Runt, Sacred, Santa Gertrudis, Scare, Simmental, Slattern, Steer, Step on, Stirk, Subact, Subjugate, Teeswater, Threaten, Unnerve, Vaccine, Zebu, Z(h)o

Coward(ice), Cowardly Bessus, Cat, Chicken, Cocoa, Craven, Cuthbert, Dastard, Dingo, Dunghill, Faint-heart, Fraidy-cat, Fugie, Funk, Gutless, Hen, Hilding, Lily-livered, Mangy, Meacock, Nesh, Niddering, Nidderling, Nidering, Niderling, Niding, Nithing, Noel, Panty-waist, Poltroon, Pusillanimous, Recreant, Scaramouch(e), Scaredy cat, Sganarelle, Sissy, Slag, Sook, Viliaco, Viliago, Villagio, Villiago, Weak-spirited, White feather, Yellow, Yellow-belly, Yellowstreak

Cowboy, Cowgirl Buckaroo, Gaucho, Inexpert, Io, Jerrybuilder, Leger, Llanero, Neatherd, Puncher, Ranchero, Ritter, Roper, Shoddy, Vaquero, Waddy, Wrangler

Coy Arch, Coquettish, Mim, Modest, Nice, Shamefast, →**SHY**, Skittish

Crab(by), Crablike, Crabwise Apple, Attercop, Boston, Cancer, Cancroid, Cantankerous, Capernoity, Cock, Coconut, Daddy, Decapoda, Diogenes, Dog, Ethercap, Ettercap, Fiddler, Ghost, Grouch, Hard-shell, Hermit, Horseman, Horseshoe, King, Land, Limulus, Mantis, Mitten, Nebula, Ochidore, Oyster, Pagurian, Partan, Perverse, Podite, Roast, Robber, Rock, Saucepan-fish, Scrawl, Scrog, Sentinel, Sidewards, Sidle, Soft-shell, Soldier, Spider, Std, Stone, Velvet-fiddler, Xiphosura, Zoea

▷**Crab** may indicate an anagram

Crack(ed), Cracker(s), Cracking A1, Ace, Ad-lib, Admirable, Attempt, Bananas, Beaut, Biscuit, Bonbon, Break, Cat, Catalytic, Chap, Chasm, Chat,

Cradle Chink, Chip, Chop, Clap, Cleave, Cleft, Cloff, Confab, Cranny, Craquelure, Craqueture, Craze, Cream, Crepitate, Crevasse, Crevice, Crispbread, Dawn, Decipher, Decode, Def, Doom, Dunt, Elite, Expert, Fab, Fatiscent, Fent, Firework, First-rate, Fisgig, Fissure, Fizgig, Flake, Flaw, Flip-flop, Fracture, Gem, Gibe, Go, Graham, Grike, Gryke, Gully, Hairline, Hit, Insane, Jest, Jibe, Joint, Joke, Leak, Liar, Little-endian, Lulu, Matzo, Mot, Moulin, One-liner, Oner, Perlite, Peterman, Pleasantry, Pore, Praise, Prawn, Quip, Rap, Report, Rhagades, Rictus, Rift, Rille, Rima, Rime, Rimous, Rive, Rock, Saltine, Seam, Shatter, Snap, Soda, Solve, Split, Spring, Squib, Sulcus, Super, Top, Try, Waterloo, Wind shake, Witticism, Yegg

Cradle Bassinet, Berceau, Book rest, Cat's, Cot, Crib, Cunabula, Hammock, Knife, Nestle, Rocker

Craft(y), Craftwork Adroitness, Aerostat, Arch, Art, Aviette, Barbola, Batik, Boat, Canal boat, Canny, Cautel, Crochet, Cunning, Disingenuous, Expertise, Finesse, Flotilla, Fly, Foxy, Guile, Hydroplane, Ice-breaker, Insidious, Knack, Kontiki, Landing, Lifeboat, Loopy, Machiavellian, Marquetry, Mister, Mystery, Oomiack, Pedalo, Pirogue, Powerboat, Reynard, Saic, Shallop, Ship, Shrewd, Shuttle, →**SKILL**, Slee, Sleeveen, Slim, Slippy, Sly, Slyboots, Sneaky, State, Subdolous, Subtil(e), Subtle, Surface, Suttle, Tender, Trade, Triphibian, Umiak, Underhand, Versute, →**VESSEL**, Wicker, Wile, Workmanship

Craftsman AB, Artificer, Artisan, Artist, Cabinet maker, Chippy, Coppersmith, Cutler, Ebonist, Enameller, Fabergé, Finisher, Gondolier, Guild, Hand, Joiner, Journeyman, Mason, Mechanic, Morris, Opificer, Potter, Saddler, Stonemason, Tinsmith, Wainwright, Wright

Cram(mer), Crammed Bag, Bone up, Candle-waster, Chock-a-block, Cluster, Craig, Fill, Gag, Gavage, Mug up, Neck, Pang, Prime, Revise, Rugged, Scar(p), Spur, Stap, Stodge, Stow, Swat, Tuck

Cramp(ed) Agraffe, Charleyhorse, Claudication, Confine, Constrict, Crick, Hamper, Hamstring, Incommodious, Musician's, Myalgia, Narrow, Pinch, Poky, Potbound, Restrict, Rigor, Sardines, Scrivener's palsy, Squeeze, Stunt, Tenesmus, Tetany, Writer's

Crane, Crane-driver Adjutant-bird, Australian, Cherry picker, Container, Davit, Demoiselle, Derrick, Dogman, Gantry, Herd, Heron, Hooper, Ichabod, Jenny, Jib, Jigger, Native companion, Numidian, Rail, Sandhill, Sarus, Sedge, Seriema, Shears, Sheer, Siege, Stork, Stretch, Whooper, Winch

Crash Accident, Bingle, Collapse, Ditch, Dush, Fail, Fall, Fragor, Frush, Intrude, Linen, Meltdown, Nosedive, Plough into, Prang, Rack, Ram, Rote, Shock, Shunt, Slam, Smash, South Sea Bubble, Thunderclap, Topple, Wham, Wrap

▷**Crashes** *may indicate* an anagram

Crate Banger, Biplane, Box, Case, Ceroon, Crib, Hamper, Jalopy, Langrenus, Petavius, Purbach, Rustbucket, Tea chest, Tube

Crave, Craving Appetent, Appetite, Aspire, Beg, Beseech, Covet, Desire, Entreat, Hanker, Hunger, Itch, Libido, Long, Lust, Malacia, Methomania, Orexis, Pica, Polyphagia, Sitomania, The munchies, Thirst, Yearn, Yen

Crayfish Astacology, Gilgie, Jilgie, Marron, Yabbie, Yabby

Crayon Chalk, Colour, Conté®, Pastel, Pencil

Craze(d), Crazy Absurd, Ape, Apeshit, Avid, Barking, Barmy, Bats, Batty, Berserk, Bonkers, Break, Cornflake, Crack(ers), Crackpot, Cult, Daffy, Dement, Derange, Dingbats, Dippy, Distraught, Doiled, Doilt, Doolally, Doolally tap, Dottle, Dotty, Fad, Flaky, Flaw, Folie, Frantic, Furious, Furore, Furshlugginer,

Gaga, Geld, Gonzo, Gyte, Haywire, Headbanger, Insane, Loco, Loony, Loopy, Lunatic, Madden, Maenad(ic), Mania, Manic, Mattoid, Meshug(g)a, Moonstruck, Nuts, Odd, Out to lunch, Porangi, Potty, Psycho(path), Rage, Ramp, Rave, Round the bend, Round the twist, Scatty, Screwball, Skivie, Stunt, Thing, Troppo, Typomania, Unhinge, Wacko, W(h)acky, Wet, Whim, Wowf, Zany
▷**Crazy** *may indicate* an anagram

Creak(y) Cry, Grate, Grind, Rheumatic, Scraich, Scraigh, Scroop, Seam, Squeak

Cream(y) Barrier, Bavarian, Best, Chantilly, Cherry-pick, Cleansing, Cold, Crème fraîche, Devonshire, Double, Elite, Flower, Foundation, Frangipane, Ganache, Glacier, Heavy, Lanolin, Liniment, Lotion, Mousse, Off-white, Ointment, Opal, Paragon, Pastry, Peppermint, Pick, Ream, Rich, Salad, Shaving, Single, Skim, Unguent, Vanishing

Crease(d) Bowling, Crinkle, Crumple, →**FOLD**, Goal, Lined, Lirk, Pitch, Pleat, Ply, Popping, Ridge, Ruck(le), Ruga, Rugose, Wreathe, Wrinkle

Create, Creation, Creative Brainstorm, Build, Cause, Coin, Compose, Craft, Devise, Dreamtime, Engender, Establish, Fabricate, Forgetive, Form, Found, Generate, Genesis, Godhead, Hexa(h)emeron, Ideate, →**INVENT**, Kittle, Knit, Nature, Omnific, Originate, Produce, Promethean, Shape, Synthesis, Universe

Creature Animal, Ankole, Basilisk, Beast, Being, Bigfoot, Chevrotain, Cratur, Critter, Crittur, Indri, Mammal, Man, Moner(on), Nekton, Organism, Sasquatch, Sphinx, Whiskey, Wight, Zoon

Credibility, Credible, Credit(or), Credits Ascribe, Attribute, Belief, Billboard, Brownie points, Byline, Carbon, Catholic, Crawl, Easy terms, Esteem, Extended, Family, Ghetto, Honour, HP, Kite, Kudos, LC, Lender, Mense, Never-never, On the nod, Post-war, Probable, Reliable, Renown, Repute, Revolving, Shylock, Social, Strap, Tally, Tax, Tick, Title, Trust, Weight, Youth

Creep(er), Creeping, Creeps, Creepy Ai, Aseismic, Cleavers, Crawl, Eery, Function, Grew, Grovel, Grue, Heebie-jeebies, Heeby-jeebies, Herpetic, Inch, Insect, Ivy, Nerd, Nuthatch, Periwinkle, Pussyfoot, Repent, Reptant, Sarmentous, Sidle, Silverweed, Sinister, Sittine, Skulk, Slink, Snake, Sobole(s), Speedwell, Steal, Toad, Truckle, Uncanny, Vine, Virginia, Willies

Crepe Blini, Blintz(e), Canton, Pancake

Crescent Barchan(e), Bark(h)an, Fertile, Lune(tte), Lunulate, Lunule, Meniscus, Moon, Red, Sickle, Waxing

Crest(ed) Acme, Brow, Chine, Cimier, Cockscomb, Comb, Copple, Cornice, Crista, Height, Kirimon, Knap, Mon, Peak, Pileate, Pinnacle, Plume, Ridge, Rig, Summit, Tappit, Tee, →**TOP**, Wreath

Crevice Chine, Cranny, Fissure, Interstice, Ravine, Vallecula

Crew Boasted, Company, Complement, Co-pilot, Core, Deckhand, Eight, Four, Ground, Lot, Manners, Men, Oars, Sailors, Salts, Seamen, Ship men, Team

Crib Aid, Cheat, Cot, Cowhouse, Cradle, Cratch, Filch, Horse, →**KEY**, Manger, Pony, Purloin, Putz, Shack, Stall, Steal, Trot

Cricket ground Edgbaston, Lord's, The Oval

Crikey Argh, Gosh, I say

Crime ABH, Attentat, Barratry, Bias, Caper, Car jack, Chantage, Chaud-mellé, Computer, Corpus delicti, Ecocide, Embracery, Fact, Felony, Fraud, GBH, Graft, Heist, Iniquity, Insider trading, Malefaction, Malfeasance, Mayhem, Misdeed, Misdemeanour, →**OFFENCE**, Organised, Ovicide, Peccadillo, Perjury, Pilferage, Public wrong, Rap, Rape, Rebellion, →**SIN**, Snaffling-lay, Stranger, Theft, Thievery, Tort, Transgression, Treason, Villa(i)ny, White-collar, Wrong

Criminal Accessory, Arsonist, Bandit, Bent, Bigamist, Bushranger, Chain gang, Chummy, Con, Cosa Nostra, Counterfeiter, Crack-rope, →**CROOK**, Culpable, Culprit, Delinquent, Desperado, Escroc, Fagin, Felon, Flagitious, Forensic, Fraudulent, Gangster, Goombah, Hard men, Heavy, Heinous, Highbinder, Highwayman, Hitman, Hood(lum), Illegal, Jailbird, Ladrone, Lag, Larcener, Lifer, Looter, Lowlife, Maf(f)ia, Malefactor, Maleficent, Malfeasant, Mens rea, Miscreant, Mob(ster), Molester, Ndrangheta, Nefarious, Nefast, Offender, Outlaw, Peculator, Pentito, Perp(etrator), Peterman, Prohibited, Racketeer, Ram raider, Receiver, Recidivist, Reprehensible, Rogue, Rustler, Safe blower, Sinner, Snakehead, Terrorist, Thief, Thug, Triad, Triggerman, Underworld, Villain, Wicked, Wire, Yakuza, Yardie, Yegg
▷**Criminal** *may indicate* an anagram
Cringe, Cringing Cower, Creep, Crouch, Cultural, Fawn, Grovel, Recoil, Shrink, Sneaksby, Sycophantic, Truckle, Wince
Cripple(d) Damage, Disable, Game, Hamstring, Handicap, Injure, →**LAME**, Lameter, Lamiter, Maim, Paralyse, Polio, Scotch, Spoil
Crisis Acme, Craunch, Crunch, Drama, Emergency, Exigency, Fastigium, Fit, Flap, Head, Identity, Make or break, Panic, Pass, Shake-out, Solution, Suez, Test, Turn, Turning-point
Crisp(ness) Brisk, Clear, Crimp, Crunchy, Fire-edge, Fresh, Sharp, Short, Succinct, Terse
Critic(al), Criticise, Criticism Acute, Agate, Agee, Armchair, Arnold, Attack, Backbite, Badmouth, Barrack, Belabour, Berate, Bird, Blame, Boileau, Boo, Bottom line, Brickbat, Bucket, Captious, Carp, Castigate, Cavil, Censor(ious), →**CENSURE**, Clobber, Comment, Condemn, Connoisseur, Crab, Crossroads, →**CRUCIAL**, Crunch, Dangle, Decisive, Denigrate, Denounce, Deprecate, Desperate, Diatribe, Diss, Do down, Dress down, Earful, Exacting, Excoriate, Exegesis, Fastidious, Fateful, Fault-finder, Flak, Flay, Fulminous, Hammer, Harrumph, Hatchet job, Higher, Iconoclast, Ideal, Important, Impugn, Inge, Inveigh, Judge, Judgemental, Judicial, Knife-edge, Knock(er), Lambast, Lash, Leavis, Lecture, Life and death, Literary, Lower, Masora(h), Mas(s)orete, Nag, Nasute, Nibble, Nice, Niggle, Nitpicker, Obloquy, Overseer, Pan, Pater, Peck, Potshot, Puff, Pundit, Quibble, Rap, Rebuke, Reprehend, Reproach, Review(er), Rip, Roast, Ruskin, Savage, Scalp, Scarify, Scathe, Scorn, Second guess, Serious, Severe, Sharp-tongued, Shaw, Sideswipe, Slag, Slam, Slashing, Slate, Slaughter, Sneer, Snipe, Spray, Stick, Stricture, Strop, Swipe, Tense, Textual, Thersitic, Threap, Tipping-point, Touch and go, Trash, Turning-point, Upbraid, Urgent, Vet, Vital, Vitriol, Vivisect, Watershed, Zoilean
Croak(er), Croaky Caw, Creak, Crow, Die, Grumble, Gutturalise, Hoarse, Perish, Sciaena
Crockery Ceramics, China, Dishes, Earthenware, Service, Ware
▷**Crocks** *may indicate* an anagram
Crocodile Bask, Cayman, Dundee, File, Garial, Gavial, Gharial, Gotcha lizard, Line, Mugger, River-dragon, Saltie, Saltwater, Sebek, Teleosaur(ian)
Crook(ed), Crookedness Adunc, Ajee, Angle, Asymmetric, Awry, Bad, Bend, Bow, Cam, Camsheugh, Camsho(ch), Cock-eyed, Criminal, Cromb, Crome, Crosier, Crummack, Crummock, Crump, Curve, Dishonest, Elbow, Flex, Fraud, Heister, Hook, Ill, Indirect, Kam(me), Kebbie, Lituus, Lowlife, Malpractitioner, Obliquity, Shank, Sheep-hook, Shyster, Sick, Skew(whiff), Slick(er), Staff, Swindler, Thraward, Thrawart, Thrawn, Twister, Wonky, Wrong'un, Wry, Yeggman

▷**Crooked** *may indicate* an anagram

Crop(ped), Cropping, Crops, Crop up Abridge, Basset, Befall, Browse, Cash, Catch, Cereal, Clip, Craw, Cut, Distress, Dock, Emblements, Emerge, Epilate, Eton, Foison, Forage, Grain, Graze, →**HAIRCUT**, Harvest, Hog, Ladino, Lop, Not(t), Plant, Poll, Produce, Prune, Rawn, Reap, Riding, Rod, Root, Scythe, Shave, Shear, Shingle, Sithe, Standing, Stow, Strip, Succession, Top, Trim, Truncate, →**VEGETABLE**

Cross(ing), Crossbred, Crossbreed Angry, Ankh, Ansate, Archiepiscopal, Banbury, Bandog, Basta(a)rd, Baster, Beefalo, Bestride, Boton(n)e, Brent, Bridge, Bristling, Buddhist, Burden, Calvary, Cancel, Cantankerous, Canterbury, Capital, Capuchin, Cat(t)alo, Cattabus, Celtic, Channel, Charing, Chi, Chiasm(a), Choleric, Clover-leaf, Cocktail, Compital, Constantine, Crosslet, Crosswalk, Crotchety, Crucifix, Crux, Cut, Decussate, Demi-wolf, Dihybrid, Double, Dso(mo), Dzobo, Eleanor, Encolpion, Faun, Fiery, Fitché, Fleury, Foil, Footbridge, Ford, Frabbit, Fractious, Frampold, Franzy, Funnel, Fylfot, Geneva, George, Grade, Greek, Hinny, Holy rood, Hybrid, Ill, Imp, Indignant, Interbreed, Intersect, Intervein, Iona, Iracund, Irascible, Irate, Irked, Iron, Jersian, Jerusalem, Jomo, Jumart, King's, Kiss, Ladino, Latin, Level, Liger, Lorraine, Lurcher, Maltese, Mameluco, Market, Mermaid, Military, Misfortune, Mix, Moline, Mongrel, Mule, Narky, Nattery, Node, Norman, Northern, Nuisance, Oblique, Obverse, Ordinary, Orthodox, Overpass, Overthwart, Papal, Pass, Patonce, Patriarchal, Pattée, Pectoral, Pedestrian, Pelican, Percolin, Perverse, Plus, Pommé, Potence, Potent, Preaching, Puffin, Quadrate, Railway, Ratty, Reciprocal, Red, Riled, Roman, Rood, Rose, Rosy, Rouen, Rouge, Rubicon, Sain, St Andrew's, St Anthony's, St George's, St Patrick's, St Peter's, Saltier, Saltire, Sambo, Satyr, Shirty, Sign, Snappy, Southern, Span, Splenetic, Strid, Svastika, Swastika, T, Tangelo, Tau, Tayberry, Ten, Testy, Thraw, Thwart, Tiglon, Tigon, Times, Toucan, Transit, Transom, Transverse, Traverse, Tree, Unknown, Urdé, Vexed, Vext, Victoria, →**VOTE**, Weeping, Whippet, Wholphin, Wry, X, Zebra(ss), Zhomo, Z(h)o, Zobu

▷**Cross** *may indicate* an anagram

Cross-examination, Cross-examine Elenctic, Grill, Interrogate, Question, Targe

Crossword Cruciverbal, Cryptic, Grid, Puzzle, Quickie

Crouch Bend, Cower, Cringe, Falcade, Fancy, Lordosis, Ruck, Set, Squat, Squinch

Crow Big-note, Bluster, Boast, Brag, Carrion, Chewet, Chough, Corbie, Corvus, Crake, Currawong, Daw, Gab, Gloat, Gorcrow, Hooded, Hoodie, Huia, Jackdaw, Jim(my), Ka(e), Murder, Raven, Rook, Scald, Skite, Squawk, Swagger, Vaunt

Crowd(ed) Abound, Army, Bike, Boodle, Bumper, Bunch, Busy, Byke, Caboodle, Clutter, Compress, Concourse, Congest(ed), Cram, Cramp, Crush, Crwth, Dedans, Dense, Doughnut, Drove, Fill, Flock, Galere, Gang, Gate, Gathering, Herd, Horde, →**HOST**, Huddle, Hustle, Jam, Jam-packed, Lot, Many, Meinie, Mein(e)y, Melee, Menyie, Mob, Mong, Multitude, Ochlo-, Pack, Pang, Populace, Prease, Press, Rabble, Raft, Ragtag, Ram, Ratpack, Ring, Roll-up, Rout, Ruck, Scrooge, Scrouge, Scrowdge, Scrum, Serr(é), Shoal, Shove, Slew, Slue, Squash, Squeeze, Stuff, Swarm, Swell, Thick, Thrang, Three, Throng, Trinity, Varletry

Crown Acme, Apex, Apogee, Bays, Bull, Camp, Cantle, Cap, Capernoity, Cidaris, Civic, Coma, Corona, Cr, Diadem, Ecu, Engarland, Enthrone, Fillet, Garland, Gloria, Haku, Head, Headdress, Instal, Iron, Ivy, Krans, Krantz,

Laurel, Monarch, Mural, Naval, Nole, Noll, Northern, Noul(e), Nowl, Olive, Ore, Ovation, Pate, Peak, Pediment, Pschent, Sconce, Stephen's, Summit, Taj, Thick'un, Tiar(a), → **TOP**, Treetop, Triple, Triumphal, Trophy, Vallary, Vertex

Crucial Acute, Bottom line, Critical, Decider, Essential, Indispensable, Key, Kingpin, Linchpin, Momentous, Paramount, Pivotal, Vital, Watershed

Crude(ness) Bald, Brash, Brute, Coarse, Earthy, Halfbaked, Ill-bred, Immature, Incondite, Lewd, No tech, Oil, Primitive, Rabelaisian, Raunch, Raw, Rough, Rough and ready, Rough-hewn, Rough-wrought, Tutty, Uncouth, Unrefined, Vulgar, Yahoo

Cruel(ty) Barbarous, Bloody, Brutal, Cold-blooded, Cut-throat, Dastardly, De Sade, Draconian, Fell, Fiendish, Flinty, Hard, Heartless, Immane, Inhuman(e), Machiavellian, Neronic, Pitiless, Raw, Remorseless, Stern, Tiger, Tormentor, Tyranny, Unmerciful, Vicious, Violence, Wanton

▷**Cruel** *may indicate* an anagram

Cruise(r) Busk, Cabin, Coast, Nuke, Orientation, Prowl, Sail, Sashay, Search, Ship, Tom, Travel, Trip, Voyager

Crumb(le), Crumbly, Crumbs Coo, Cor, Decay, Derelict, Disintegrate, Ee, Fragment, Friable, Fritter, Golly, Law, Leavings, Moulder, Mull, Murl, Nesh, Nirl, Ort, Panko, Particle, Ped, Pulverise, Raspings, Rot, Tumbledown

Crunch(y), Crunching Abdominal, Acid test, Chew, Craunch, Credit, Crisis, Crisp, Gnash, Grind, Munch, Number, Occlude, Scranch, Shoot-out

Crush(ed), Crusher, Crushing Acis, Anaconda, Annihilate, Beetle, Bow, Breakback, Careworn, Champ, Comminute, Conquer, Contuse, Cram(p), Cranch, Crunch, Defeat, Demoralise, Destroy, Graunch, Grind, Hug, Humble, Jam, Knapper, Levigate, Liquidise, Litholapaxy, Mangle, Mash, Mill, Molar, Mortify, Nib, Oppress, Overcome, Overpower, Overwhelm, Pash, Policeman, Pound, Press, Pulp, Pulverise, Quash, Quell, Ruin, Schwarmerei, Scotch, Scrum, Scrumple, Scrunch, Smash, Squabash, Squash, Squeeze, Squelch, Squidger, Squish, Stamp, Stave, Steam-roll, Step on, Stove, Stramp, Suppress, Swot, Telescope, Trample, Tread, Vanquish

Crust(y) Argol, Beeswing, Cake, Caliche, Coating, Coffin, Continental, Cover, Crabby, Craton, Fur, Geogeny, Geosphere, Gratin, Heel, Horst, Ice fern, Kissing, Kraton, Lithosphere, Orogen, Osteocolla, Pie, Reh, Rind, Rine, Sal, Salband, Scab, Scale, Shell, Sial, Sima, Sinter, Surly, Tartar, Teachie, Tectonics, Terrane, Tetchy, Upper, Wine-stone

Crustacea(n) Acorn-shell, Amphipod, Barnacle, Cirriped, Copepod, Crab, Crayfish, Cyclops, Cyprid, Cypris, Daphnia, Decapod(a), Entomostraca, Fishlouse, Foot-jaw, Gribble, Isopod, Krill, Limulus, Lobster, Marine borer, Maron, Nauplius, Nephrops, Oniscus, Ostracoda, Prawn, Red seed, Sand flea, Sand-hopper, Sand-skipper, Scampi, Shrimp, Slater, Squilla, Woodlouse

Cry(ing) Aha, Alalagmus, Alew, Baa, Banzai, Bark, Battle, Bawl, Bay, Bell, Bemoan, Bill, Bingo, Blat, Bleat, Bleb, Blub(ber), Boo, Boohoo, Boom, Bray, Bump, Caramba, Caw, Cheer, Chevy, Chirm, Chivy, Clang, Cooee, Crake, Croak, Crow, Dire, Euoi, Eureka, Evoe, Evoke, Exclaim, Eye-water, Fall, Field-holler, Gardyloo, Gathering, Geronimo, Gowl, Greet, Halloo, Harambee, Haro, Harrow, Havoc, Heave-ho, Heigh, Hemitrope, Herald, Hey presto, Hinny, Hoicks, Holler, Honk, Hoo, Hoop, Hosanna, Hout(s)-tout(s), Howl, Howzat, Humph, Hunt's up, Hurra(h), Io, Kaw, Low, Mewl, Miaou, Miau(l), Miserere, Mourn, Night-shriek, Nix, O(c)hone, Oi, Olé, Ow, Pugh, Rabbito(h), Rallying, Rivo, Sab, Scape, Scream, Screech, Sell, Sese(y), Sessa, → **SHOUT**, Shriek, Slogan, Snivel, Snotter, Sob,

Soho, Sola, Squall, Squawk, Street, Sursum corda, Tally-ho, Tantivy, Umph, Vagitus, View-halloo, Vivat, Vociferate, Wail, War, War whoop, Watchword, Waterworks, Waul, Wawl, Weep, Westward ho, Whammo, Whee(ple), Whimper, Whine, Whinny, Whoa, Whoop, Winge, Wolf, Yammer, Yawl, Yelp, Yicker, Yikker, Yip, Yippee, Yodel, Yo-heave-ho, Yo-ho-ho, Yoick, Yoop, Yowl

Crypt(ic) Catacomb, Cavern, Chamber, Crowde, Encoded, Enigmatic, Esoteric, Favissa, Grotto, Hidden, Mystic, Obscure, Occult, Secret, Sepulchre, Short, Steganographic, Tomb, Unclear, Undercroft, Vault

Crystal(s), Crystal-gazer, Crystalline, Crystallise Allotriomorphic, Baccara(t), Beryl, Candy, Clear, Cleveite, Copperas, Coumarin, Cumarin, Cut-glass, Dendrite, Druse, Enantiomorph, Epitaxy, Form, Geode, Glass, Hemitrope, Ice-stone, Jarosite, Lase, Lead, Liquid, Love-arrow, Macle, Melamine, Needle, Nematic, Niacin, Nicol, Orthogonal, Palace, Pellucid, Penninite, Pericline, Phenocryst, Piezo, Pinacoid, Pinakoid, Prism, Pseudomorph, Purin(e), Quartz, R(h)aphide, R(h)aphis, Rhinestone, Rock, Rotenone, Rubicelle, Scawtite, Scryer, Shoot, Silica, Skatole, Skryer, Snowflake, Sorbitol, Spar, Spherulite, Table, Tina, Tolan(e), Trichite, Triclinic, Trilling, Wafer, Watch-glass, Xenocryst, Yag

Cub(s) Baby, Kit, Lionet, Novice, Pup, Sic, Whelp, Youth

Cubicle Alcove, Booth, Carrel(l), Compartment, Stall

Cuckoo Ament, Ani, April fool, Bird, Chaparral cock, Dotty, Gouk, Gowk, Inquiline, Insane, Koekoea, Koel, → **MAD**, Mental, Piet-my-vrou, Stupid, Zany
▷**Cuckoo** *may indicate* an anagram

Cuddle, Cuddly Canoodle, Caress, Clinch, Embrace, Fondle, Hug, Inarm, Nooky, Pet, Smooch, Smuggle, Snog, Snuggle, Spoon, Zaftig

Cue Billiard, Cannonade, Catchword, Feed, Half-butt, Hint, Mace, Pool, → **PROMPT**, Reminder, Rod, Sign, Signal, Wink

Cuisine Balti, Cookery, Food, Menu, Nouvelle, Tex-Mex

Cult Cabiri, Cargo, Creed, Moony, New Age, Sect, Snake, Voodoo, Worship

Cultivate(d), Cultivation, Cultivator Agronomy, Arty, Breed, Civilise, Developed, Dig, Dress, Farm, Garden, Genteel, Grow, Hoe, Hydroponics, Improve, Labour, Plough(man), Polytunnel, Pursue, Raise, Reclaim, Refine, Sative, Sophisticated, Tame, Tasteful, Till, Tilth, Wainage, Woo, Work

Culture(d), Cultural Abbevillean, Acheulean, Acheulian, Agar, Art(y), Aurignacian, Azilian, Bacterian, Bel esprit, Brahmin, Broth, Canteen, Capsian, Civil(isation), Clactonian, Club, Compensation, Dependency, Enterprise, Ethnic, Experiment, Explant, Fine arts, Folsom, Gel, Gravettian, Grecian, Halafian, Hallstatt, Hip-hop, Humanism, Intelligentsia, Kultur(kreis), La Tène, Learning, Levallois, Madelenian, Magdalenian, Meristem, Minimalism, Monolayer, Mousterian, New Age, Polish, Polite, Refinement, Solutrean, Sophisticated, Strepyan, Tissue, Well-read

Cunning Arch, Art, Artifice, Astute, Cautel, Craft(y), Deceit, Deep, Devious, Down, Finesse, Foxy, Guile, Insidious, Knacky, Leary, Leery, Machiavellian, Quaint, Ruse, Scheming, Skill, Slee(kit), Sleight, Slim, Sly(boots), Smart, Sneaky, Stratagem, Subtle, Vulpine, Wheeze, Wile, Wily

Cup(s), Cupped Aecidium, America's, Beaker, Bledisloe, Calcutta, Calix, Calyculus, Cantharus, Ca(u)p, Chalice, Claret, Communion, Cotyle, Cruse, Cupule, Cyathus, Cylix, Davis, Demitasse, Dish, Dop, European, Eyebath, FA, Fairs, Final, Fingan, Finjan, Glenoid, Goblet, Grace, Gripe's egg, Hanap, Horn, Kylix, Loving, Melbourne, Merry, Monstrance, Moustache, Mug, Noggin, Nut,

Optic, Pannikin, Paper, Planchet, Plate, Pot, Procoelous, Quaich, Quaigh, Rhyton, Rider, Ryder, Sangrado, Scyphus, Sippy, Stirrup, Suction, Tantalus, Tass(ie), Tastevin, Tazza, Tea-dish, Tig, Tot, →**TROPHY**, Tyg, Volva, World

▷**Cup** *may indicate* a bra size

Cupboard Airing, Almery, Almirah, A(u)mbry, Armoire, Beauf(f)et, Cabinet, Chiffonier, Chiff(o)robe, Closet, Coolgardie safe, Court, Credenza, Dresser, Encoignure, Locker, Press, Unit

Cupid Amoretto, Amorino, Archer, Blind, Cherub, Dan, Eros, Love, Putto

Curb Bit, Brake, Bridle, Check, Clamp, Coaming, Constraint, Dam, Edge, Puteal, Rein, Restrain, Restringe, Rim, Snub, Stifle

Cure(d), Curative Amend, Antidote, Antirachitic, Bloater, Cold turkey, Dry-salt, Euphrasy, Faith, Fix, Flue, Ginseng, Heal, Heal-all, Heat treatment, Hobday, Jadeite, Jerk, Kipper, Magic bullet, Medicinal, Nostrum, Panacea, Park-leaves, Pickle, Posset, →**PRESERVE**, Reck, Recover, Recower, Reest, Relief, Remede, Remedy, Re(i)st, Restore, Salt, Salve, Save, Serum, Smoke, Smoke-dry, Snakeroot, Tan, →**TREATMENT**, Tutsan

▷**Cure** *may indicate* an anagram

Curfew Bell, Gate, Prohibit, Proscribe

Curio, Curiosity, Curious Agog, Bibelot, Bric a brac, Collector's item, Esoteric, Ferly, Freak, Inquisitive, Interesting, Meddlesome, Nos(e)y, Objet d'art, Objet de vertu, Oddity, Peculiar, Prurience, Quaint, Rarity, Rum, Spectacle, →**STRANGE**, Wondering

▷**Curious(ly)** *may indicate* an anagram

Curl(s), Curler, Curling, Curly Ailes de pigeon, Bonspiel, Cirrus, Cockle, Coil, Crimp, Crimple, Crinkle, Crisp, Crocket, Earlock, Eddy, Favourite, Frisette, Friz(z), Frizzle, Heart-breaker, Hog, Inwick, Kiss, Leaf, Loop, Love-lock, Outwick, Perm, Pigeon's wing, Pin, Quiff, Repenter, Ringlet, Roll, Roulette, Shaving, Spiral, Spit, Tress, Twiddle, →**TWIST**, Undée, Wave, Wind

Currant Berry, Raisin, Rizard, Rizzar(t), Rizzer

Currency Cash, Circulation, →**COIN**, Coinage, Decimal, Euro(sterling), Finance, Hard, Jiao, Kip, Koruna, Managed, Monetary, →**MONEY**, Petrodollar, Prevalence, Tender

▷**Currency** *may indicate* a river

Current Abroad, AC, Actual, Alternating, Amp(ere), Amperage, California, Canary, Contemporaneous, Cromwell, Dark, DC, Direct, Draught, Drift, Dynamo, Ebbtide, Electric, El Nino, Emission, Equatorial, Euripus, Existent, Faradic, Flow, Foucault, Galvanic(al), Going, Headstream, Hot button, Humboldt, I, Immediate, Inst, Intermittent, In vogue, Japan, Jet stream, Kuroshio, Labrador, Live, Maelstrom, Millrace, Modern, Newsy, Now, Ongoing, Present, Present day, Prevalent, Race, Rapid, Recent, Rife, Rip, Roost, Running, Ryfe, Stream, Thames, Thermal, Thermionic, Tide, Topical, Torrent, Turbidity, Underset, Undertow, Up-to-date

Curry Bhuna, Brush, Comb, Cuittle, Dhansak, Dress, Favour, Fawn, Groom, Ingratiate, Korma, Ruby (Murray), Skater, Spice, Tan, Turmeric, Vindaloo

Curse(d) Abuse, Anathema, Badmouth, Ban, Bane, Beshrew, Blast, Bless, Chide, Dam(me), Damn, Dee, Drat, Ecod, Egad, Evil, Excommunicate, Execrate, Heck, Hex, Hoodoo, Imprecate, Jinx, Malediction, Malgre, Malison, Maranatha, Mau(l)gré, Mockers, Moz(z), Mozzle, Nine (of diamonds), Oath, Paterson's, Pize, Plague, Rant, Rats, Scourge, 'Snails, Spell, Star-crossed, Swear, Tarnation, Upbraid, Vengeance, Vituperate, Wanion, Weary, Winze, Wo(e)

Curtain(s), Curtain raiser, Curtain-rod Air, Arras, Backdrop, Bamboo, Café, Canopy, Casement, Caudle, Cloth, Death, Demise, Drape, Drop, Dropcloth, Dropscene, Fatal, Hanging, Iron, Lever de rideau, Louvre, Net, Pall, Portière, Purdah, Rag, Safety, Scene, Screen, Scrim, Swag, Tab, Tableau, Tormentor, Tringle, Vail, Valance, Veil, Vitrage

Curtsey Bob, Bow, Dip, Dop, Honour

Curve(d), Curvaceous, Curvature, Curving, Curvy Aduncate, Arc, Arch, Archivolt, Assurgent, Axoid, Bend, Bezier, Bow, Brachistochrone, Camber, Catacaustic, Catenary, Caustic, Chordee, Cissoid, Conchoid, Contrapposto, Crescent, Cycloid, Demand, Dowager's hump, Ellipse, Entasis, Epinastic, Ess, Evolute, Exponential, Extrados, Felloe, Felly, Freezing point, Geodesic, Gooseneck, Growth, Hance, Harmonogram, Helix, Hodograph, Hyperbola, Inswing, Intrados, Invected, Isochor, J, Jordan, Laffer, Learning, Lemniscate, Limacon, Linkage, Lissajous figure, Lituus, Lordosis, Loxodrome, Meniscus, Nowy, Ogee, Parabola, Pothook, Rhumb, RIAA, Roach, Rondure, Rotundate, Scolioma, Scoliosis, Sheer, Sigmoid flexure, Sinuate, Sonsie, Spiral, Spiric, Strophoid, Supply, Swayback, Tie, Trajectory, Trisectrix, Trochoid, Twist, Witch (of Agnesi)

Cushion(s) Air, Allege, Bank, Beanbag, Bolster, Buffer, Bustle, Hassock, King's, → **PAD**, Pillow, Pouf(fe), Pulvinus, Soften, Squab, Tyre, Upholster, Whoopee

Custodial, Custodian, Custody Care, Claviger, Curator, Guard, Hold, Incarceration, Janitor, Keeping, Protective, Retention, Sacrist, Steward, Trust, Ward, Wardship

Custom(ised), Customs (officer), Customs house, Customary Agriology, Chophouse, Coast-waiters, Cocket, Consuetude, Conventional, Couvade, Culture, De règle, Douane, Exciseman, Familiar, Fashion, Folklore, → **HABIT**, Lore, Manner, Montem, Mores, Nomic, Obsequy, Octroi, Ordinary, Perfunctory, Practice, Praxis, Protocol, Regular, Relic, Rite, Routine, Rule, Set, Sororate, Sunna, Tax, Thew, Tidesman, Time-honoured, Tradition, Trait, Unwritten, Usance, Used, Usual, Won, Wont, Woon, Zollverein

Customer(s) Client, Cove, End user, Footfall, Gate, Patron, Prospect, Punter, Purchaser, Shillaber, Shopper, Smooth, Trade, Trick, User, Vendee

Cut(ter), Cutdown, Cutting Abate, Abbreviate, Abjoint, Ablate, Abridge, Abscond, Acute, Adeem, Adze, Aftermath, Ali Baba, Amputate, Apocopate, Axe, Bang, Bisect, Bit, Bite, Bowdlerise, Boycott, Brilliant, Broach, Caesarean, Caique, Canal, Cantle, Caper, Carver, Castrate, Caustic, Censor, Chap, Cheese, Chisel, Chopper, Circumscribe, Cleaver, Clinker-built, Clip, Clod, Colter, Commission, Concise, Coulter, Coupé, Crew, Crop, Cruel, Cube, Curtail, Deadhead, Decrease, Diamond, Dicer, Die, Diminish, Discide, Discount, Disengage, Dismember, Dissect, Division, Divorce, Dock, Dod, Edge, Edit, Embankment, Engraver, Entail, Entrecote, Epistolary, Epitomise, Escalope, Eschew, Etch, Excalibur, Excide, Excise, Exscind, Exsect, Exude, Fashion, Fell, Filet mignon, Fillet, Flench, Flense, Flinch, Flymo®, Form, Framp, Froe, Frow, Garb, Gash, Grater, Graven, Gride, Groove, Gryde, Hack, Hairdo, Handsaw, Harvest, Hew(er), Ignore, Incision, Incisor, Indent, Insult, Intersect, Jigsaw, Joint, Junk, Kerf, Kern, Kirn, Lacerate, Lance, Lase(r), Leat, Lesion, Limit, Loin, Lop, Math, Medaillon, Medallion, Microtome, Milling, Minimise, Minish, Mohel, Mordant, Mortice, Mortise, Mower, Nick, Not, Notch, Nott, Occlude, Omit, Open, Operate, Oxyacetylene, Padsaw, Pare, Pink, Plant, Pliers, Ploughshare, Poll, Pollard, Pone, Power, Precisive, Proin, Quota, Race, Rake off, Rase, Razee, Razor, Reap,

Rebate, Reduction, Re-enter, Resect, Retrench, Revenue, Ring, Ripsaw, Roach, Rose, Rout, Saddle, Sarcastic, Saw(n), Saw-tooth, Scaloppine, Scarf, Scarify, Scathing, Scion, Scission, Scissor, Score, Scrap, Sculpt, Scye, Scythe, Secant, Secateurs, Sect, Set, Sever, Sey, Share (out), Shaver, Shears, Shingle, Ship, Shive, Shorn, Short, Shred, Shun, Sickle, Side, Sirloin, Skip, Slane, Slash, Slice(r), Slight, Slip, Slit, Sloop, Sned, Snee, Snib, Snick, Snip, Snippet, Snub, Spade, Spin, Spud, Stall, Steak, Stencil, Stir, Stramazon, Strim, Style, Sunder, Surgeon, Tailor(ess), Tap, Tart, Tenderloin, Tomial, Tonsure, Tooth, Topside, Tournedo, Transect, Trash, Trench, Trenchant, Trepan, Trim, Truant, Truncate, Urchin, Vivisection, Whang, Whittle

▷**Cut** *may indicate* an anagram

▷**Cutback** *may indicate* a reversed word

Cute Ankle, Canny, Dinky, Perspicacious, Pert, Pretty, Taking

Cutlery Canteen, Eating irons, Flatware, Fork, Knife, Service, Setting, Silver, Spoon, Spork, Sunbeam, Tableware, Trifid

Cycle, Cyclist, Cycling Anicca, Arthurian, Bike, Biorhythm, Biospheric, Born-Haber, Business, Cal(l)ippic, Calvin, Carbon, Carnot, Cell, Circadian, Citric acid, Closed, Daisy, Eon, Era, Fairy, Frequency, Heterogony, Indiction, Keirin, Ko, Krebs, Life, Lytic, Madison, Metonic, Minibike, Natural, Oestrus, Operating, Orb(it), Otto, Pedal, Peloton, Period, Product life, Repulp, Revolution, Ride, Roadman, Roadster, Rota, Round, Samsara, Saros, Scorch, Series, Sheng, Solar, Song, Sonnet, Sothic, Spin, TCA, Trike, Turn, UCI, Vicious, Water, Wheeler, Wheelman, Wu

Cyclone Storm, Tornado, Tropical, Typhoon, Willy-willy

Cylinder, Cylindrical Air, Capstan, Clave, Column, Dandy-roll, Drum, Licker-in, Magic, Nanotube, Pipe, Roll, Rotor, Siphonostele, Slave, Spool, Steal, Stele, Swift, Terete, Torose, Treadmill, Tube, Vascular

Cyst Atheroma, Bag, Blister, Chalazion, Dermoid, Ganglion, Hydatid, Impost(h)ume, Meibomian, Ranula, Sac, Vesicle, Wen

Dd

Dab(s) Bit, Blob, Daub, Fish, Flounder, Lemon, Pat, Print, Ringer, Smear, Smooth, Spot, Stupe, Whorl

Dad(dy) Blow, Dev(v)el, Father, Generator, Hit, Male, Pa(pa), Pater, Polt, Pop, Slam, Sugar, Thump

Daffodil Asphodel, Jonquil, Lent-lily, Narcissus

Daft Absurd, Crazy, Potty, Ridiculous, Silly, Simple, Stupid

Dagga Cape, Red, True

Dagger(s) An(e)lace, Ataghan, Baselard, Bayonet, Bodkin, Crease, Creese, Da(h), Diesis, Dirk, Double, Dudgeon, Hanger, Han(d)jar, Jambiya(h), Katar, Kindjahl, Kirpan, Kreese, Kris, Lath, Misericord(e), Obelisk, Obelus, Poi(g)nado, Poniard, Puncheon, Sgian-dubh, Shank, Skean, Skene(-occle), Stiletto, Whiniard, Whinyard, W(h)inger, Yatag(h)an, Yuc(c)a

Daily Adays, Broadsheet, Char(lady), Circadian, Cleaner, Diurnal, Domestic, Guardian, Help, Journal, Le Monde, Mail, Mirror, Mrs Mopp, →**NEWSPAPER**, Paper, Per diem, Quotidian, Rag, Regular, Scotsman, Sun, Tabloid

Dainty, Daintiness Cate(s), Cute, Delicacy, Dinky, Elegant, Elfin, Entremesse, Entremets, Exquisite, Genty, Junket, Lickerish, Liquorish, Mignon(ne), Minikin, →**MORSEL**, Neat, Nice, Particular, Petite, Precious, Prettyism, Pussy, Sunket, Titbit, Twee

Dairy Creamery, Days' house, Loan, Parlour, Springhouse

Daisy African, Aster, Bell, Boneset, Cineraria, Felicia, Gerbera, Gowan, Groundsel, Hardheads, Hen and chickens, Livingstone, Michaelmas, Ox-eye, Ragweed, Saw-wort, Shasta, Transvaal

Dale(s) Dell, Dene, Diarist, Dingle, Glen, Nidder, Ribbles, Swale, Vale, Valley, Wensley, Wharfe

Dam An(n)icut, Arch, Aswan, Aswan High, Bar, Barrage, Barrier, Block, Boulder, Bund, Cabora Bassa, Cauld, Check, Dental, Grand Coulee, Grande Dixence, Gravity, Hoover, Kariba, Kielder, Ma, Mangla, Mater, Nile, Obstacle, Obstruct, Pen, Sennar, Stank, →**STEM**, Sudd, Tank, Three Gorges, Turkey nest, Volta River, Weir, Yangtze

Damage(d), Damages, Damaging Accidental, Appair, Bane, Banjax, Blight, Bloody, Blunk, Bruise, Buckle, Burn, Charge, Contuse, Cost, Cripple, Defame, Dent, Desecrate, Detriment, Devastate, Devastavit, Discredit, Distress, Estrepe, Expense, Fault, Flea-bite, Harm, Havoc, Hedonic, Hit, Hole, Hurt, Impair, Injury, Lacerate, Lesion, Loss, Mar, Mayhem, Moth-eaten, Nobble, Opgefok, Pair(e), Prang, Price, Reparation, Retree, Ruin, Sabotage, Scaith, Scath(e), Scotch, Scratch, Shop-soiled, Skaith, Smirch, Solatium, →**SPOIL**, Tangle, Tear, Tigger, Toll, Toxic, Unsound, Value, Vandalise, Violate, Wear and tear, Wing, Wound, Wreak, Wreck, Write off

▷**Damage(d)** *may indicate* an anagram

Dame Crone, Dowager, Edna (Everage), Gammer, Lady, Matron, Nature, Naunt, Partlet, Peacherino, Sis, Title(d), Trot, Woman

Damn(ation), Damnable, Damned Accurst, Attack, Blame, Blast, Blinking, Censure, Condemn, Cotton-picking, Curse, Cuss, D, Darn, Dee, Doggone, Drat, Execrate, Faust, Heck, Hell, Hoot, Jigger, Malgre, Perdition, Predoom, Ruddy, Sink, Swear, Very

Damp(en), Damping, Dampness Aslake, Black, Blunt, Check, Choke, Clam(my), Dank, Dewy, Fousty, Humid(ity), Hydric, Mesarch, Moch, Moist(ure), Muggy, Raw, Retund, Rheumy, Rising, Roric, Soggy, Sordo, Sultry, Unaired, → **WET**

Dance(r), Dancing Alma(in), Astaire, Avignon, Baladin(e), Balanchine, Ballabile, Ballant, Ballerina, Ballroom, Baryshnikov, Bayadère, Bob, Body-popping, Bump and grind, Caper, Ceili(dh), Chorus-girl, Comprimario, Contredanse, Corp de ballet, Corybant, Coryphee, Dervish, De Valois, Diaghilev, Dinner, Dolin, Exotic, Figurant, Figure, Fooling, Foot, Foot-it, Gandy, Gigolo, Groove, Hetaera, Hetaira, Hoofer, Isadora Duncan, Kick-up, Knees-up, Leap, Lope, Maenad, Majorette, Markova, Matachina, Modern, Nautch-girl, Night, Nijinsky, Nod, Number, Nureyev, Oberek, Old-time, Orchesis, Partner, Pavlova, Peeler, Petipa, Pierette, Prom(enade), Pyrrhic, Rambert, Raver, Reindeer, Ring, Romp, St Vitus, Salome, Saltant, Saltatorious, Shearer, Skank, Skipper, Slammer, Spring, Step(per), Strut, Table, Tea, Terpsichore, Thé dansant, Tread, Trip(pant), Vogue(ing), Whirl, Wire-walker

Dance hall Disco, Juke-joint, Palais

▷**Dancing** *may indicate* an anagram

Danger(ous) Apperil, Black spot, Breakneck, Crisis, Critical, Dic(e)y, Dire, Emprise, Fear, Hairy, Hazard, Hearie, Hero, Hot, Hotspot, Icy, Insecure, Jeopardy, Lethal, Menace, Mine, Minefield, Nettle, Nocuous, Parlous, Pitfall, Plight, Precarious, Quicksand, Risk, Rock, Serious, Severe, Sicko, Snag, Tight, Tight spot, Trap, Treacherous, Ugly

Dangle A(i)glet, Aiguillette, Critic, Flourish, Hang, Loll, Swing

Dank Clammy, Damp, Humid, Moist, Wet, Wormy

Dare, Dare-devil, Daring Adventure, Audacious, Aweless, Bold, Brave, Bravura, Challenge, Courage, Dan, Da(u)nton, Defy, Durst, Emprise, Face, Foolhardy, Gallant, Gallus, Groundbreaking, Hardihood, Hazard, Hen, Prowess, Racy, Risk, Swashbuckler, Taunt, Venture

Dark(en), Darkness Aphelia, Aphotic, Apophis, Black(out), Blind, Byronic, Caliginous, Cimmerian, Cloud, Colly, Crepuscular, Depth, Dim, Dingy, Dirk(e), Dour, Dusky, Eclipse, Egyptian, Embrown, Erebus, Evil, Gloom, Glum, Grim, Inky, Inumbrate, Jet, Kieran, Low-key, Mare, Maria, Melanous, Mirk, Murk(y), Negro, Night(time), Obfuscate, Obnubilation, Obscure, Obsidian, Ominous, Ousel, Ouzel, Overcast, Pall, Phaeic, Pitch-black, Pit-mirk, Rooky, Sable, Sad, Saturnine, Secret, Shades, Shady, Shuttered, Sinister, Solein, Sombre, Sooty, Sphacelate, Starless, Sullen, Sunless, Swarthy, Tar, Tenebrose, Tenebr(i)ous, Unfair, Unlit, Woosel

Darling Acushla, Alannah, Asthore, Beloved, Charlie, Cher, Chéri(e), Chick-a-biddy, Chick-a-diddle, Chuck-a-diddle, Dear, Dilling, Do(a)ting-piece, Duck(s), Favourite, Grace, Honey, Idol, Jarta, Jo(e), Lal, Love, Luv, Mavourneen, Mavournin, Minikin, Minion, Oarswoman, Own, Peat, Pet, Poppet, Precious, Squeeze, Sugar, Sweetheart, Sweeting, Yarta, Yarto

Dart(s), Darter Abaris, Arrow, Banderilla, Beetle, Dace, Dash, Deadener, Dodge, Fleat, Fléchette, Flirt, Flit, Harpoon, Javelin, Launch, Leap, Lunger, Pheon, Race, Scoot, Shanghai, Skrim, Speck, Spiculum, Strike, Thrust, Wheech

Dash(ing), Dashed Backhander, Bally, Blade, Blight, Blow, Bribe, Buck, Charge, Collide, Cut, Dad, Dah, Damn, Dapper, Dart(le), Daud, Dawd, Debonair, Ding, Dod, Doggy, Elan, Em (rule), En (rule), Flair, Fly, Gallop, Go-ahead, Hang, Hurl, → **HURRY**, Hustle, Hyphen, Impetuous, Jabble, Jaw, Jigger, Lace, Leg it, Line, Minus, Modicum, Morse, Natty, Nip, Panache, Pebble, Race, Raffish, Rakish, Ramp, Rash, Rule, Run, Rush, Sally, Scamp(er), Scapa, Scarper, Scart, Scoot, Scrattle, Scurry, Scuttle, Shatter, Showy, Skitter, Skuttle, Soupçon, Souse, Spang, Speed, Splash, Splatter, Sprint, Strack, Streak, Strike, Stroke, → **STYLE**, Swashbuckling, Swung, Throw, Tinge, Touch, Treacherous, Ugly

Data(base), Datum Archie, Evidence, Factoid, Facts, Fiche, File, Floating-point, Garbage, Gen, Griff, Hard copy, Info, Input, IT, Material, Matrix, Newlyn, News, Ordnance, Read-out, Statistic, Table, Triple

Date(d), Dates, Dating AD, Age, AH, Almanac, Appointment, Blind, Boyfriend, Calendar, Carbon, Carbon-14, Computer, Court(ship), Deadline, Engagement, Epoch, Equinox, Era, Escort, Exergue, Expiry, Fission-track, Fixture, Girlfriend, Ides, Julian, Meet, Obsolescent, Outmoded, Passé, Past, Radio-carbon, Rubidium-strontium, See, Speed, System, Target, Ult(imo), Uranium-lead

Daunt Adaw, Amate, Awe, Deter, Dishearten, Intimidate, Overawe, Quail, Stun, Stupefy, Subdue

Dawdle(r) Dally, Draggle, Drawl, Idle, → **LOITER**, Malinger, Potter, Shirk, Slowcoach, Snail, Troke, Truck

Dawn(ing) Aurora, Cockcrow, Daw, Daybreak, Day-peep, Dayspring, Early, Enlightenment, Eoan, Eos, False, French, Half-light, Light, Morning, Morrow, Occur, Prime, Sparrowfart, Spring, Start, Sunrise, Sun up

Day(s) Account, Ahemeral, All Fools', All Hallows', All Saints', All Souls', Anniversary, Annunciation, Anzac, April Fool's, Arbor, Armistice, Ascension, Australia, Bad hair, Baker, Banian, Banyan, Barnaby, Bastille, Borrowing, Box, Boxing, Broad, Calendar, Calends, Calpa, Canada, Canicular, Childermas, Civil, Columbus, Commonwealth, Contango, Continental, Continuation, D, Daft, Date, Decoration, Degree, Derby, Der Tag, Dismal, Distaff, Dog, Dominion, Double, Dress down, Dressed, Duvet, Early, Ember, Empire, Epact, Fast, Fasti, Father's, Feast, Ferial, Field, Fiesta, Flag, Fri, Gang, Gaudy, Glory, Groundhog, Guy Fawkes', Halcyon, Hey, High, Hogmanay, Holocaust, Holy, Holy Innocents', Holy-rood, Hundred, Ides, Inauguration, Independence, Intercalary, Jour, Judgment, Juridical, Kalends, Kalpa, Labo(u)r, Lady, Lammas, Last, Law(ful), Lay, Leap, Mardi, Market, May, Memorial, Michaelmas, Midsummer, Mon, Morrow, Mother's, Muck-up, Mufti, Mumping, Name, Ne'erday, New Year's, Nones, Oak-apple, Octave, Off, Open, Orangeman's, Palmy, Pancake, Paper, Pay, Poppy, Post, Pound, Present, Press(ed), Primrose, Pulvering, Quarter, Rag, Rainy, Red-letter, Remembrance, Rent, Rest, Robin, Rock, Rogation, Rood(-mas), Rosh Chodesh, Sabbath, St John's, Saint's, St Swithin's, St Thomas's, St Valentine's, Salad, Sansculotterie, Sat, Scambling, Settling, Sexagesima, Show, Sidereal, Snow, Solar, Solstice, Speech, Sports, Station, Sun, Supply, Tag, Term, Thanksgiving, Thurs, Ticket, Time, Transfer, Trial, Triduum, Tues, Twelfth, Utas, Valentine's, Varnishing, VE, Vernissage, Veterans', Victoria, Visiting, VJ, Wash, Wed, Wedding, Working

Daydream(er), Daydreaming Brown study, Castle(s) in the air, Dwam, Dwaum, Fancy, Imagine, Lose oneself, Muse, Reverie, Rêveur, Walter Mitty, Woolgathering

Daze(d) Amaze, Bemuse, Confuse, Dwaal, Gally, Muddle, Muzzy, Petrify, Reeling, → **STUN**, Stupefy, Stupor, Trance

Dazzle(d), Dazzler, Dazzling Bewilder, Blend, Blind, Bobby, Eclipse, Foudroyant, Glare, Larking glass, Meteoric, Outshine, Radiance, Resplendent, Splendour, Yblent

Dead(en) Abrupt, Accurate, Alamort, Asgard, Asleep, Bang, Blunt, Bung, Cert, Cold, Complete, D, Deceased, Defunct, Dodo, Doggo, Expired, Extinct, Flatliner, Gone(r), Inert, Infarct, Late, Lifeless, Muffle, Mute, Napoo, Numb, Obsolete, Obtund, Ringer, Sequestrum, She'ol, Smother, Stillborn, True, Under hatches, Utter, Waned

Dead end, Deadlock Cut-off, Dilemma, Impasse, Logjam, Stalemate, Stoppage

Deadline Date, Epitaph, Limit

Deadly Baleful, Dull, Exact, Fell, Funest, Internecine, →LETHAL, Malign, Monkshood, Mortal, No more, Pestilent, Stone, Thanatoid, Unerring, Venomous

Deal(er), Dealership, Dealing(s), Deal with Act, Address, Agent, Agreement, Allot(ment), Arb, Arbitrageur, Bargain, Biz, Breadhead, Brinjarry, Broker, Bulk, Business, Cambist, Candyman, Chandler, Chapman, Clocker, Commerce, Connection, Contract, Cope, Coup, Cover, Croupier, Dispense, Distributor, Do, Dole, Done, East, Eggler, Exchange, Fir, Franchise, Fripper, Front-running, Goulash, Hack, Hand(le), Help, Inflict, Insider, Interbroker, Jiggery-pokery, Jobber, Lashing, Lay on, Lay out, Loads, Lot, Manage, Mercer, Merchandise, Merchant, Mickle, Middleman, Monger, Mort, Negotiate, New, North, Operator, Package, Pine, Plain, Post, Productivity, Pusher, Racketeer, Raft, Raw, Red, Relations, Sale, Scrap merchant, See to, Serve, Side, Sight, Simoniac, Slanger, Sort, South, Spicer, Spiv, Square, Stapler, Stockbroker, Stockist, Stockjobber, Takeover, Tape, Timber, Totter, Tout(er), →TRADE, Trade in, Trade off, Tradesman, Traffic, Traffick, Transaction, Treat, Truck, West, Wheeler, White, Wholesaler, Wield, Woolstapler, Yarborough, Yardie

Dear(er), Dearest, Dear me Ay, Bach, Beloved, Cara, Caro, Cher(e), Cherie, Chuckie, Darling, Duck(s), Expensive, High, Honey(bun), Joy, Lamb, Leve, Lief, Lieve, Loor, Love, Machree, Mouse, My, Pet, Soote, Steep, Sugar, Sweet, Sweeting, Toots(ie), Unreasonable, Up

Death(ly) Abraham's bosom, Bane, Bargaist, Barg(h)est, Black, Carnage, Cataplexis, Charnel, Commorientes, Curtains, Cypress, Demise, Deodand, Departure, Dormition, End, Eschatology, Euthanasia, Exit, Expiry, Extinction, Fatality, Fey, Funeral, Gangrene, Grim Reaper, Hallal, Infarction, Jordan, King of Terrors, Lethee, Leveller, Loss, Mortality, Necrosis, Nemesis, Night, Obit, Passing, Quietus, Reaper, Sati, Sergeant, SIDS, Small-back, Sorry end, Strae, Sudden, Suttee, Terminal, Thanatism, Thanatology, Thanatopsis, Thanatos, Yama

Deathless(ness) Athanasy, Eternal, Eterne, Immortal, Struldberg, Timeless, Undying

Debase(d) Adulterate, Allay, Bemean, Corrupt, Demean, Depreciate, Dialectician, Dirty, Grotesque, Hedge, Lower, Pervert, Traduce, Vitiate

Debate(r) Adjournment, Argue, Casuist, Combat, Contention, Contest, Controversy, Deliberate, Dialectic, Discept, Discourse, Discuss(ion), →DISPUTE, Flyte, Forensics, Moot, Paving, Polemics, Reason, Teach-in, Warsle, Wrangle, Wrestle

Debris Bahada, Bajada, Detritus, Eluvium, Flotsam, Jetsam, Moraine, Moslings, Pyroclastics, Refuse, Ruins, Sawdust, Shrapnel, Tel, Tephra, Waste, Wreckage

▷**Debris** *may indicate* an anagram

Debt(or) Abbey-laird, Alsatia, Arrears, Arrestee, Bankrupt, Bonded, Dr, Due, Floating, Funded, Insolvent, IOU, Liability, Moratoria, National, Obligation,

Obligor, Outstanding, Oxygen, Poultice, Public, Queer Street, Red, Score, Senior, Subordinated, Tick, Tie, Unfunded

Debt-collector Bailiff, Forfaiter, Remembrancer

Decadence, Decadent Babylonian, Decaying, Degeneration, Dissolute, Effete, Fin-de-siècle, Libertine

▷**Decapitated** *may indicate* first letter removed

Decay(ed), Decaying Alpha, Appair, Beta, Biodegrade, Blet, Canker, Caries, Caseation, Crumble, Decadent, Declension, Decline, Decompose, Decrepit, Dieback, Disintegrate, Doat, Doddard, Doddered, Dote, Dricksie, Druxy, Dry rot, Ebb, Fail, F(o)etid, Forfair, Gamma, Gangrene, Heart-rot, Impair, Moulder, Pair(e), Plaque, Ptomaine, Putrefy, Ret, Rot, Rust, Saprogenic, Sap-rot, Seedy, Senility, Sepsis, Spoil, Tabes, Thoron, Time-worn, Wet-rot

Decease(d) Death, Decedent, Demise, Die, Stiff

Deceit(ful), Deceive(r) Abuse, Ananias, Artifice, Bamboozle, Befool, Bitten, Blag, Blind, Bluff, →**CHEAT**, Chicane, Chouse, Cozen, Cuckold, Decoy, Defraud, Deke (out), Delude, Diddle, Dissemble, Double-cross, Double-dealing, Dupe, Duplicity, False(r), Fast-talk, Fiddle, Fineer, Flam, Fool, Four-flusher, Fox, Fraud, Gag, Guile, Gull, Hoax, Hoodwink, Humbug, Hype, Hypocritical, Imposition, Inveigle, Invention, Jacob, Kid, Lead on, Liar, Mamaguy, Misinform, Mislead, Patter, Perfidy, Poop, Poupe, Pretence, Prevaricate, Punic, Rig, Ruse, Sell, Sham, Shifty, Sinon, Spruce, Stall, Stratagem, String along, Swindle, Swizzle, Take in, Trick, Trump, Trumped up, Two-time, Weasel, Wile

Decency, Decent Chaste, Decorum, Fitting, Godly, Healsome, Honest, Honourable, Kind, Mensch, Modest, Moral, Presentable, Respectable, Salubrious, Seemly, Sporting, Straight, Wholesome, Wise-like

Deception, Deceptive Abusion, Artifice, Bluff, Catchpenny, Catchy, Cheat, Chicanery, Codology, →**DECEIT**, Decoy, Disguise, Dupe, Duplicity, Elusive, Eyewash, Fallacious, False, Feigned, Fineer, Flam, Fraud, Fubbery, Gag, Gammon, Guile, Gullery, Have-on, Hocus-pocus, Hokey-pokey, Hum, Hunt-the-gowks, Hype, Ignes-fatui, Ignis-fatuus, Illusion, Insidious, Jiggery-pokery, Kidology, Legerdemain, Lie, Mamaguy, Moodies, Phantasmal, Runaround, Ruse, Scam, Sciolism, Sell, Sleight, Smoke and mirrors, Specious, Sting, The moodies, Thimblerig, →**TRICK**, Trompe l'oeil, Two-timing, Underhand

Decide(r), Decided, Decisive Addeem, Adjudge, Agree, Arbitrate, Ar(r)e(e)de, Ballot, Barrage, Bottom-line, Call, Cast, Clinch, Conclude, Conclusive, →**DECISION**, Deem, Definite, Determine, Distinct, Draw lots, Effectual, Fatal, Firm, Fix, Foregone, Jump-off, Mediate, Opt, Parti, Predestination, Pronounced, Rescript, Resolute, →**RESOLVE**, Result, Rule, Run-off, Seal, See, Settle, Split, Sure, Tiebreaker, Try

Decipher(ing) Cryptanalysis, Decode, Decrypt, Descramble, Discover, Explain, Interpret

▷**Decipher(ed)** *may indicate* an 'o' removed

Decision Arbitrium, Arrêt, Bottom line, Crossroads, Crunch, Crux, Decree, Fatwa, Fetwa, Firman, Judg(e)ment, Parti, Placit(um), Referendum, Resolution, Resolve, Responsa, Ruling, Sentence, Split, Verdict

Decisive Climactic, Clincher, Crisis, Critical, Crux, Definite, Final, Pivotal

Deck Adonise, Adorn, Angled, Array, Attrap, Bejewel, Boat, Canted, Cards, Clad, Clothe, Daiker, Daub, Decorate, Dizen, Embellish, Equip, Flight, Focsle, Forecastle, Garland, Hang, Helideck, Hurricane, Lower, Mess, Orlop, Pack, Pedestrian, Platform, Poop, Prim, Promenade, Quarter, Sun, Tape, Upper, Void, Weather

Declare, Declaration, Declaim, Decree Absolute, A(r)e(e)de, Affidavit, Affirm, Air, Allege, Announce, Aread, Assert, Asseverate, Aver, Avow, Balfour, Bann(s), Bayyan, Breda, Call, Canon, Dictum, Diktat, Doom, Edict, Emit, Enact, Fatwa(h), Fiat, Firman, Go, Grace, Harangue, Improbation, Indiction, Insist, Interlocutory, Irade, Law, Mandate, Manifesto, Meld, Mou(th), Nisi, Noncupate, Novel(la), Nullity, Orate, Ordain, Order, Ordinance, Parlando, Petition of Right, Pontificate, Present, Proclaim, Profess, Promulgate, Pronounce, Protest, Publish, Rant, Read, Recite, Remark, Rescript, Resolve, Restatement, Rights, Rule, Ruling, SC, Sed, Senatus consultum, Signify, Speak, Spout, Statement, Swear, Testament-dative, Testify, Testimony, UDI, Ukase, Ultimatum, Unilateral, Vie, Voice, Vouch, Will, Word
▷**Declaring** *may indicate* a word beginning 'Im'

Decline, Declination, Declining Abate, Abstain, Age, Ail, Atrophy, Catabasis, Comedown, Decadent, Degeneration, Degringoler, Deny, Descend, Deteriorate, Devall, Die, Diminish, Dip, Dissent, Downhill, Downtrend, Downturn, Droop, Drop, Dwindle, Ebb, Elapse, Escarpment, Fade, Fall, Flag, Forbear, Lapse, Magnetic, Opt out, Paracme, Pejoration, Peter, Plummet, Quail, Recede, Recession, Reflow, Refuse, Relapse, Retrogression, Rot, Ruin, Rust, Sag, Senile, Set, Sink, Slide, Slump, Slumpflation, Stoop, Subside, Sunset, Tumble, Twilight, Wane, Welke, Withdraw, Wither

Decorate(d), Decoration, Decorative Adorn, Aiguilette, Angelica, Applique, Attrap, Award, Bard, Bargeboard, Baroque, Bauble, Beaux-arts, Bedeck, Bedizen, Bells and whistles, Bordure, Braid, Breastpin, Brooch, Cartouche, Centrepiece, Chain, Champlevé, Chinoiserie, Christingle, Cinquefoil, Cloisonné, Coffer, Crocket, Croix de guerre, Daiker, Decoupage, Dentelle, Dentil, Diamante, Distemper, Doodad, Doodah, Do over, Dragée, Emblazon, Emboss, Embrave, Enrich, Epaulet, Epergne, Etch, Fancy, Festoon, Filigree, Fillet, Finery, Finial, Fleuron, Floriated, Fob, Frieze, Frill, Frog, Frost, Furbish, Gadroon, Garniture, Gaud, Gilt, Glitter, Godroon, Goffer, Gradino, Grotesque, Guilloche, Ice, Illuminate, Impearl, Inlay, Intarsia, Intarsio, Interior, Jabot, Jari, Kalambari, Knotwork, Leglet, Linen-fold, Marquetry, MC, Medal(lion), Moulding, Oath, OBE, Ogee, Openwork, Order, →**ORNAMENT**, Ornate, Orphrey, Overglaze, Ovolo, Paint, Paper, Parament, Pattern, Photomural, Pokerwork, Polychromy, Prettify, Prink, Purfle, Rag-rolling, Rangoli, Repoussé, Ribbon, Rich, Ric(k)-rac(k), Ruche, Scallop, Scrimshaw, Set-off, Sgraffito, Soutache, Spangle, Staffage, Stipple, Stomacher, Strapwork, Stucco, Tailpiece, Tart up, Tassel, Tattoo, TD, Titivate, Tool, Topiary, Tracery, Trim, Trinket, Vergeboard, Wallpaper, Wirework, Zari

Decoy Allure, Attract, Bait, Bonnet, Button, Call-bird, Coach, Crimp, Entice, Lure, Piper, Q-ship, Roper, Ruse, Shill, Stale, Stalking-horse, Stall, Stoolie, Stool-pigeon, Tame cheater, Tice, Tole, Toll, Trap, Trepan

Decrease Cut back, Decrew, Diminish, Dwindle, Fall, Iron, Lessen, Press, Ramp down, Reduce, Rollback, Step-down, Subside, Wane, Wanze

Decrepit Dilapidated, Doddery, Doitit, Failing, Feeble, Frail, Moth-eaten, Spavined, Tumbledown, Warby, Weak

Dedicate(d), Dedication Allot, Corban, Determination, Devote, Dinah, Endoss, Hallow, Inscribe, Oblate, Patriotism, Pious, Sacred, Single-minded, Votive, Work ethic

Deduce, Deduction, Deductive Allowance, A priori, Assume, Conclude, Consectary, Corollary, Derive, Discount, Draw, Gather, Illation, Infer(ence), Natural, Reason, Rebate, Recoup, Reprise, Stoppage, Surmise, Syllogism

Deed(s) Achievement, Act(ion), Atweel, Backbond, Back letter, Charta, Charter, Defeasance, Derring-do, Escrol(l), Escrow, Exploit, Fact(um), Indeed, Indenture, Manoeuvre, Mitzvah, Muniments, Settlement, Specialty, Starr, → **TITLE**, Work

Deep(en), Deeply Abstruse, Abysmal, Bass(o), Brine, Briny, Enhance, Excavate, Grum, Gulf, Hadal, Intense, Low, Mindanao, Mysterious, → **OCEAN**, Profound, Re-enter, Rich, Sea, Sonorous, Sunk(en), Throaty, Upsee, Ups(e)y

Deer(-like) Axis, Bambi, Barasing(h)a, Barking, Brocket, Buck, Cariacou, Carjacou, Cervine, Chevrotain, Chital, Doe, Elaphine, Elk, Fallow, Gazelle, Hart, Irish elk, Jumping, Moose, Mouse, Mule, Muntjac, Muntjak, Musk, Père David's, Pricket, Pudu, Red, Rein, Roe, Rusa, Sambar, Sambur, Selenodont, Sika, Sorel(l), Spade, Spay(d), Spayad, Spitter, Spottie, Stag(gard), Tragule, Ungulate, Virginia, Wapiti

▷**Defaced** *may indicate* first letter missing

Defame, Defamatory, Defamation Abase, Blacken, Calumny, Cloud, Denigrate, Detract, Dishonour, Impugn, In rixa, Libel, Mud, Mudslinging, Obloquy, Sclaunder, Scurrilous, Slander, Smear, Stigmatise, Traduce, Vilify

Default(er) Absentee, Bilk, Dando, Delinquent, Flit, Levant, Neglect, Omission, Renegue, Waddle, Welsh

Defeat(ed), Defeatist Beat, Best, Bowed, Caning, Capot, Cast, Checkmate, Clobber, Codille, Conquer, Counteract, Cream, Debel, Defeasance, Demolish, Destroy, Discomfit, Dish, Ditch, Donkey-lick, Drub, Fatalist, Floor, Foil, Foyle, Hammer, Hiding, Kippered, Laipse, Lick, Loss, Lurch, Marmelize, Master, Mate, Moral, Negative, Out, Outclass, Outdo, Outfight, Outfox, Outgeneral, Outgun, Outplay, Outvote, Outwit, → **OVERCOME**, Overmarch, Overpower, Overreach, Overthrow, Overwhelm, Pip, Plaster, Pulverise, Quitter, Rebuff, Repulse, Reverse, Rout, Rubicon, Scupper, Set, Shellacking, Sisera, Skunk, Squabash, Stump, Tank, Thrash, Thwart, Toast, Tonk, Trounce, Undo, Vanquish, War, Waterloo, Whap, Whip, Whitewash, Whop, Whup, Wipe-out, Worst

Defect(ion), Defective, Defector Abandon, Amateur, Apostasy, Blemish, Bug, Coma, Crawling, Deficient, Desert, Dud, Failing, Faulty, Flaw, Frenkel, Halt, Hamartia, Hiatus, Kink, Low, Manky, Mass, Mote, Natural, Renegade, Renegate, Ridgel, Ridgil, Rig, Rogue, Runagate, Shortcoming, Spina bifida, Stammer, Substandard, Terrace, Treason, Trick, Want, Wanting, Weakness

Defence, Defended, Defend(er), Defensible, Defensive Abat(t)is, Advocate, Alexander, Alibi, Antibody, Antidote, Antigenic, Antihistamine, Anti-predator, Apologia, Apologist, Arm, Back, Bailey, Barbican, Barmkin, Barricade, Bastion, Battery, Battlement, Berm, Bodyguard, Bridgehead, Bulwark, Calt(h)rop, Castling, CD, Champion, Civil, Counter-measure, Curtain, Demibastion, Ditch, Embrasure, Enguard, Estacade, Goalie, Guard, Hedgehog, Herisson, Hold, Immunity, J(i)u-jitsu, Justify, Kaim, Keeper, Kraal, Laager, Laer, Libero, Maginot-minded, Mail, Maintain, Martello tower, Moat, Motte and bailey, Muniment, Outwork, Palisade, Parapet, Pentagon, Protect, Quinte, Rampart, Redan, Redoubt, Refute, Resist, Ringwall, Roman wall, Sandbag, Sangar, Scarecrow, Seawall, → **SHELTER**, Shield(wall), Sicilian, Stonewall, Strategic, Support, Tenail(le), Testudo, Tower, Trench, Trou-de-loup, Uphold, Vallation, Vallum, Vindicate, Wall, Warran(t)

Defenceless Helpless, Inerm, Insecure, Naked, Sitting duck, Vulnerable

Defendant Accused, Apologist, Respondent, Richard Roe

Defer(ence), Deferential, Deferring Bow, Curtsey, Delay, Dutiful, Homage, Moratory, Morigerous, Obeisant, Pace, Polite, Postpone, Procrastinate, Protocol, Respect, Roll over, Shelve, Spaniel, Stay, Submit, Suspend, Waive, Yield

Defiance, Defiant, Defy Acock, Bite the thumb, Bold, Brave, Brazen, Cock a snook, Dare, Daring, Disregard, Do or die, Flaunt, Insubordinate, Kembo, Kimbo, Outbrave, Outdare, Rebellion, Recalcitrant, Recusant, Scab, Stubborn, Titanism, Truculent, Unruly, Yahboo

Deficiency, Deficient Absence, Acapnia, ADA, Anaemia, Anoxia, Aplasia, Beriberi, Dearth, Defect, Failing, Hypinosis, Inadequate, Incomplete, Lack, Scant, Scarcity, SCID, Shortage, Spanaemia, Want
▷**Deficient** *may indicate* an anagram

Deficit Anaplerotic, Arrears, Defective, Gap, Ischemia, Loss, Overdraft, Poor, Shortfall

Define(d), Definition, Definitive Classic, Clear-cut, Decide, Demarcate, Determine, Diorism, Distinct, Explain, Fix, Limit, Parameter, Pinpoint, Set, Sharp, Specific, Tangible, Term

Definite(ly) Categorically, Cert(ainty), Classic, Clear (cut), Concrete, Deffo, Emphatic, Firm, Hard, Indeed, Positive, Precise, Sans-appel, Specific, Sure, Tangible, Unquestionably, Yes

Deflate Burst, Collapse, Flatten, Lower, Prick, Squeeze

Deflect(or), Deflection Avert, Back-scatter, Bend, Detour, Diverge, Divert, Glance, Head off, Holophote, Otter, Paravane, Parry, Refract, Snick, Swerve, Throw, Trochotron, Veer, Windage

Deform(ed), Deformity Anamorphosis, Blemish, Boutonniere, Contracture, Crooked, Disfigure, Distort, Freemartin, Gammy, Hammer-toe, Harelip, Miscreated, Misfeature, Mishapt, Mutilate, Polt-foot, Splay feet, Stenosed, Talipes, Valgus, Warp
▷**Deformed** *may indicate* an anagram

Defraud Bilk, Cheat, Cozen, Gyp, Lurch, Mulct, Skin, Sting, Swindle, Trick

Degrade, Degradation Abase, Brutalise, Cheapen, Culvertage, Debase, Demission, Demote, Diminish, Disennoble, Humble, Imbase, Imbrute, Lessen, Lower, →**SHAME**, Sink, Waterloo

Degree(s) Aegrotat, As, Attila (the Hun), Azimuthal, BA, Baccalaureate, BCom, BD, Bearing, B ès S, C, Carat, Class, D, Doctoral, Double first, Engler, Extent, External, F, First, Forbidden, Foundation, Geoff (Hurst), German, Gradation, Grade, Grece, Gree(s), Greece, Gre(e)se, Grice, Griece, Grize, Incept, Incidence, K, Lambeth, Latitude, Letters, Level, Licentiate, Longitude, MA, Master's, Measure, Mediant, Nuance, Order, Ordinary, Pass, Peg, PhD, Pin, Poll, Rate, Reaumur, Remove, Second, Stage, Status, Step, Submediant, Subtonic, Supertonic, Third, Water

Deject(ed), Dejection Abase, Abattu, Alamort, Amort, Cast down, Chap-fallen, Chopfallen, Crab, Crestfallen, Despondent, Discouraged, Dismay, Dispirited, Downcast, Gloomy, Hangdog, Humble, Low, Melancholy, Spiritless, Wae

Delay(ed), Delaying Adjourn(ment), After-effect, Ambage, Avizandum, Await, Backlog, Behindhand, Belated, Bottleneck, Check, Cunctator, Dawdle, Defer, Demurrage, Detention, Dilatory, Fabian, Filibuster, Forsloe, For(e)slow, Frist, Hangfire, Hesitate, Hinder, Hitch, Hold up, Hysteresis, Impede, Laches, Lag, Late, Laten, Let, Linger, Mora(torium), Obstruct, Pause, Procrastinate, Prolong, Prorogue, Remanet, Reprieve, Respite, Retard, Rollover, Setback, Slippage, Sloth, Slow, →**STALL**, Stand-over, Stay, Stonewall, Suspend, Tarry, Temporise, Time-lag, Wait

Delegate, Delegation Agent, Amphictyon, Apostolic, Appoint, Assign, Commissary, Decentralise, Depute, Devolution, Mission, Nuncio, Offload, Outsource, Representative, Secondary, Transfer, Vicarial, Walking

Delete Adeem, Annul, Axe, Cancel, Cut, Erase, Expunge, Purge, Rase, Scratch, Scrub, Strike

Deliberate(ly), Deliberation Adagio, Calculated, Conscious, Consider, Debate, Intentional, Measured, Meditate, Moderate, Muse, On purpose, Overt, Plonking, Pointedly, Ponder, Prepensely, Purposely, Ruminate, Studied, Thought, Voulu, Weigh, Witting

Delicacy, Delicate Airy-fairy, Beccafico, Canape, Cate, Caviare, Dainty, Difficult, Discreet, Dorty, Ectomorph, Eggshell, Elfin, Escargot, Ethereal, Fairy, Fastidious, Filigree, Fine, Finespun, Finesse, Flimsy, Foie-gras, Fragile, → **FRAIL**, Friand, Gentle, Goody, Gossamer, Guga, Hothouse, Inconie, Incony, Lac(e)y, Ladylike, Light(weight), Lobster, Nesh, Nicety, Niminy-piminy, Oyster, Pastel, Reedy, Roe, Sensitive, Slight, Soft(ly-softly), Subtle(ty), Sunket, Tactful, Taste, Tender, Tenuous, Ticklish, Tidbit, Titbit, Trotter, Truffle, Wispy

Delicious Ambrosia, Delectable, Exquisite, Fragrant, Goloptious, Goluptious, Gorgeous, Lekker, Lip-smacking, Mor(e)ish, Mouthwatering, Savoury, Scrummy, Scrumptious, Tasty, Toothsome, Yummy, Yum-yum

Delight(ed), Delightful Bewitch, Bliss, Charm, Chuff, Coo, Delice, Dreamy, Ecstasy, Edna, Elated, Enamour, Enchant, Enjoyable, Enrapture, Exhilarate, Exuberant, Exultation, Felicity, Fetching, Frabjous, Gas, Glad, Glee, Glorious, Gorgeous, Gratify, Honey, Joy, Lap up, Love, Overjoy, Please, Pleasure, Precious, → **RAPTURE**, Regale, Rejoice, Revel, Scrummy, Super, Sweet, Taking, Turkish, Whacko, Whee, Whoopee, Yippee, Yum-yum

▷**Delight** *may indicate* 'darken'

Delinquent Bodgie, Criminal, Halbstarker, Hoody, Law-breaker, Negligent, Offender, Ted

Delirious, Delirium Deranged, DT, Fever, Frenetic, Frenzy, Insanity, Jimjams, Mania, Phrenetic, Phrenitis, Rambling, Spaced out, Wild

Deliver(ance), Delivered, Deliverer, Delivery(man) Accouchement, Air-drop, Air-lift, Bailment, Ball, Birth, Born, Bowl, Caesarean, Consign, Convey, Courier, Deal, Doosra, Escape, Exorcise, Give, Googly, Lead, Leg-spin, Liberate, Mail drop, Messiah, Midwifery, Orate, Over, Pronounce, Punch-line, Ransom, Receipt, Recorded, Redeem, Refer, Release, Relieve, Render, Rendition, → **RESCUE**, Rid, Round(sman), Salvation, Save, Say, Seamer, Sell, Service, Shipment, Soliloquy, Speak, Special, Spell, Tice, Transfer, Underarm, Underhand, UPS, Utter, Ventouse extraction, Wide, Yorker

Dell Dale, Dargle, Dene, Dimble, Dingle, Dingl(e)y, Glen, Valley

Delude, Delusion Bilk, Cheat, Deceive, Dupe, Fallacy, Fool, Hoax, Megalomania, → **MISLEAD**, Myth, Trick, Zoanthropy

Delve Burrow, Dig, Excavate, Exhume, Explore, Mine, Probe, Rummage, Search

Demand(ing), Demanded Appetite, Ball-buster, Call, Choosy, Claim, Cry, De rigueur, Derived, Difficult, Dun, Exact, Exigent, Fastidious, Final, Gruelling, Heavy, Herculean, Hest, → **INSIST**, Market, Necessitate, Need, Onerous, Order, Postulate, Pressure, Pushy, Ransom, Request, Requisition, Rigorous, Rush, Sale, Severe, Stern, Stipulate, Stringent, Summon, Tax, Ultimatum, Want

Demean(ing) Comport, Debase, Degrade, Lower, Maltreat

Dement(ed) Crazy, Frenetic, Hysterical, Insane, Mad, Possessed

Demo March, Parade, Protest, Rally, Sit-in

Democracy, Democrat, Democratic D, Liberal, Locofoco, Menshevik, Montagnard, People's, Popular, Republic, Sansculotte, Social, Tammany

Demolish, Demolition Bulldoze, Devastate, Devour, Floor, KO, Level, Rack, Rase, Smash, Tear down, Wreck

▶**Demon** *see* **DEVIL(ISH)**

Demonstrate, Demonstration, Demonstrator Agitate, Barrack, Dharma, Display, Endeictic, Évènement, Evince, Explain, Gesture, Maffick, Manifest, March, Morcha, Ostensive, Peterloo, Portray, Present, Proof, Protest, Prove, Provo, →**SHOW**, Sit-in, Touchy-feely, Verify, Vigil

Demoralise, Demoralisation Bewilder, Corrupt, Depths, Destroy, Dishearten, Shatter, Unman, Weaken

Demote, Demotion Comedown, Degrade, Disbench, Embace, Embase, Reduce, Relegate, Stellenbosch

Demure Coy, Mim, Modest, Prenzie, Primsie, Sedate, Shy

Den Dive, Domdaniel, Earth, Hell, Hide-away, Holt, Home, Lair, Lie, Lodge, Room, Shebeen, Spieler, Study, Sty, Wurley

Denial, Deny, Denier Abnegate, Antinomian, Aspheterism, Bar, Belie, Contradict, Controvert, Démenti, Disavow, Disclaim, Disenfranchise, Disown, Forswear, Nay, Negate, Nick, Nihilism, Protest, Refuse, Refute, Renague, Renay, Reneg(e), Renegue, Reney, Renig, Renounce, Reny, Repudiate, Sublate, Withhold

Denote Import, Indicate, Mean, Signify

Denounce, Denunciation Ban, Commination, Condemn, Criticise, Decry, Diatribe, Execrate, Fulminate, Hatchet job, Hereticate, Proclaim, Proscribe, Rail, Shop, Stigmatise, Thunder, Upbraid

Dense, Density B, Buoyant, Charge, Compact, Critical, D, Firm, Intense, Opaque, Packing, Rank, Relative, Single, Solid, Spissitude, Tesla, Thick, Woofy

Dent(ed) Batter, Dancette, Depress, Dimple, Dinge, Dint, Nock, Punctate, Punt, V

Dental (problem), Dentist(ry) DDS, Extractor, Kindhart, LDS, Malocclusion, Odontic, Paedodontics, Periodontic, Toothy

▶**Deny** *see* DENIAL

Depart(ed), Departing, Departure Abscond, Absquatulate, Apage, Bunk, D, Dead, Death, Decamp, Decession, Defunct, Demise, Die, Digress, Divergence, Egress, Exception, Exit, Exodus, Expire, Flight, French leave, →**GO**, Imshi, Late, Leave, Lucky, Moonlight flit, Obiter dicta, Outbound, Remue, Scat, Send-off, Swan off, Vacate, Vade, Vamoose, Walkout

Department Achaea, Ain, Aisne, Allier, Alpes de Provence, Alpes-Maritimes, Angers, Arcadia, Ardeche, Ardennes, Argo, Arrondissement, Arta, Attica, Aube, Aude, Belfort, Bell-chamber, Branch, Bureau, Calvados, Cantal, Casualty, Charente-Maritime, Cher, Cleansing, Commissariat, Cote d'Or, Cotes d'Armor, Cotes du Nord, Creuse, Deme, Deuxième Bureau, Deux-Sevres, Division, Domain, Dordogne, Essonne, Extramural, Faculty, Finistere, FO, Foggy Bottom, Gard, Gironde, Greencloth, Guadeloupe, Gulag, Haberdashery, Hanaper, Hautes-Pyrenees, Helpdesk, Inspectorate, Isere, Jura, Loire, Loiret, Lot, Lot-et-Garonne, Marne, Martinique, Menswear, Ministry, Nome, Nomos, Office, Oise, Ordnance, Orne, Portfolio, Province, Puy de Dôme, Region, Savoie, Secretariat(e), Section, Somme, Sphere, State, Treasury, Tuscany, Unit, Var, Vienne, Wardrobe, Yonne

Depend(ant), Dependence, Dependency, Dependent Addicted, Child, Client, Colony, Conditional, Contingent, Count, Dangle, E, Fief, Habit, Hang, Hinge, Icicle, Lean, Lie, Lippen, Minion, Pensioner, Relier, Rely, Retainer, Sponge, Stalactite, Statistical, Subject, Subordinate, Trust, Turn on, Vassal, Virgin Islands, Ward

Dependable Empirical, Reliable, Reliant, Rock, Safe, Secure, Solid, Sound, Staunch, Stolid, Sure, →**TRUSTWORTHY**

▷**Deploy(ment)** *may indicate* an anagram

Deport(ation), Deportment Address, Air, Banish, → BEARING, Carriage, Demeanour, Dressage, Mien, Renvoi, Renvoy, Repatriation

Depose, Deposition Affirm, Banish, Dethrone(ment), Displace, Dispossess, Hoard, Inqueen, Overthrow, Pieta, Testify

Deposit(s), Depository Aeolian, Alluvial, Alluvium, Aquifer, Arcus, Argol, Arles, Atheroma, Bank, Bathybius, Bergmehl, Calc-sinter, Calc-tuff, Caliche, Cave-earth, Coral, Crag, Crystolith, Delta, Depone, Diatomite, Diluvium, Dust, Evaporite, Fan, File, Firn, Fort Knox, Fur, Glacial, Gyttja, Hoard, Icing, Illuvium, Kieselguhr, Land, Laterite, Lava, Lay, Lay away, Lay-by, Laydown, Lead tree, Limescale, Limonite, Lode, Lodge(ment), Loess, Löss, Measure, Natron, Outwatch, Park, Pay in, Phosphorite, Placer, Plank, Plaque, Put, Repose, Residuum, Saburra, Salamander, Sandbank, Saprolite, Saturn's tree, Scale, Sea dust, → SEDIMENT, Silt, Sinter, Sludge, Soot, Speleothem, Stalagmite, Stockwork, Storeroom, Stratum, Surety, Tartar, Terramara, Terramare, Tophus, Tripoli, Turbidite, Warehouse

Depot Barracoon, Base, Camp, Coach station, Depository, Etape, Station, Terminus, Treasure-city, Warehouse

Deprave(d), Depravity Bestial, Cachexia, Cachexy, Caligulism, → CORRUPT, Dissolute, Evil, Immoral, Low, Outrage, Rotten, Sodom, Subhuman, Turpitude, Ugly, Unholy, Vice, Vicious, Vile

Depress(ed), Depressing, Depression Agitated, Alamort, Amort, Black dog, Blight, Blue devils, Blues, Cafard, Canada, Canyon, Cheerless, Chill, Col, Combe, Couch, Crab, Crush, Cyclone, Dampen, Deject, Dell, Demission, Dene, Dent, Despair, Dimble, Dip, Dismal, Dispirit, Ditch, Doldrums, Drear, Drere, Dumpish, Exanimate, Flatten, Foss(ula), Fossa, Glen, Gloom, Ha-ha, Hammer, Heart-spoon, Hilar, Hilum, Hilus, Hollow, Howe, Hyp, Hypothymia, Indentation, Joes, Kettle, Kick(-up), Lacuna, Leaden, Low(ness), Low-spirited, Megrims, Melancholy, Mood, Moping, Morose, Neck, Pit, Postnatal, Postpartum, Pothole, Prostrate, Punt, Recession, Re-entrant, Retuse, Sad, Saddle, Sag, Salt-cellar, Salt-pan, Sink, Sinkhole, Sinus, Slot, Slough, → SLUMP, Soakaway, Spiritless, Sump, Swag, Swale, Trench, Trough, Vale, Valley, Wallow

Deprivation, Deprive(d) Amerce, Bereft, Deny, Disenfranchise, Disfrock, Dispossess, Disseise, Disseize, Expropriate, Geld, Ghetto, Have-not, Hunger, Reduce, Remove, Rob, Sensory, Starve, Strip, Withhold

Depth F, Fathom, Gravity, Intensity, Isobath, Pit, Profundity

Deputise, Deputy Act, Agent, Aide, Assistant, Commis(sary), Delegate, Legate, Lieutenant, Locum, Loot, Number two, Pro-chancellor, Proxy, Represent, Secondary, Sidekick, Standby, Stand-in, Sub, Subchanter, Substitute, Succentor, Surmistress, Surrogate, Tanaiste, Vicar, Vice, Viceregent, Vidame

Derange(d), Derangement Craze, Détraqué, Disturb, Flipped, Insane, Loopy, Manic, Skivie, Trophesy, Troppo, Unhinge, Unsettle

Derelict Abandoned, Broken-down, → DECREPIT, Deserted, Disused, Negligent, Outcast, Ramshackle, Tramp

Deride, Derision, Derisive Contempt, Gup, Guy, Hiss, Ho-ho, Hoot, Jeer, Jibe, Mock, Nominal, Pigs, Raspberry, → RIDICULE, Sardonic, Scoff, Scorn, Sneer, Snifty, Snort, Ya(h)boo (sucks), Yah

Derive, Derivation, Derivative Amine, Ancestry, Apiol, Creosote, Deduce, Descend, Extract, Get, Kinone, Of, Offshoot, Origin, Pedigree, Picoline, Saponin, Secondary, Taurine, Tyramine

Descend(ant), Descent Abseil, Ancestry, Avail, Avale, Bathos, Blood, Cadency, Catabasis, Chute, Cion, Decline, Degenerate, Dégringoler, Derive, Dismount,

Dive, Drop, Epigon, Extraction, Heir, Heraclid, Offspring, Pedigree, Posterity, Progeny, Prone, Purler, Rappel, Said, Say(y)id, Scarp, Scion, Seed, Shelve, Sien(t), Sink, Spearside, Stock, Syen, Vest, Volplane

Describe, Describing, Description, Descriptive Account, Blazon, Blurb, Define, Delineate, Depict, Designate, Draw, Epithet, Exposition, Expound, Graphic, Job, Label, Liken, Narrate, Outline, Paint, Portray, Rapportage, Recount, Relate, Report, Sea-letter, Semantic, Signalment, Sketch, Specification, Sum up, Synopsis, Term, Thumbnail, Trace, Vignette, Write-up

▷**Describing** *may indicate* 'around'

Desecrate, Desecration Abuse, Defile, Dishallow, Profane, Sacrilege, Unhallow

▷**Desecrated** *may indicate* an anagram

Desert(er), Deserted, Deserts Abandon, Absquatulate, Apostasy, Arabian, Arid, Arunta, Atacama, AWOL, Badland, Barren, Bug, Bunk, D, Defect, Desolate, Dissident, Ditch, Drop, Due, Empty, Eremic, Factious, Fail, Foresay, Forhoo, Forhow, Forlorn, Forsake, Forsay, Gibson, Gila, Gobi, Great Basin, Great Sandy, Great Victoria, Heterodox, Kalahari, Karma, Libyan, Lurch, Merit, Mojave, Nafud, Namib, Negev, Nubian, Ogaden, Painted, Patagonian, Pindan, Rat, Refus(e)nik, Reg, → **RENEGADE**, Reward, Run, Sahara(n), Sands, Secede, Sertao, Simpson, Sinai, Sonoran, Sturt, Syrian, Tergiversate, Turncoat, Void, Wadi, Waste(land), Wild, Worthiness

Deserve(d) Condign, Earn, → **MERIT**, Rate, Well-earned, Worthy

Design(er) Adam, Aim, Amies, Arabesque, Architect(ure), Argyle, Armani, Ashley, Batik, Between-subjects, Broider, Cable stitch, Calligram(me), Cameo, Cardin, Cartoon, Chequer, Chop, Cloisonné, Courreges, Couturier, Create, Cul de lampe, Damascene, Decor, Deep, Depict, Device, Devise, Dévoré, Dior, Draft, Eiffel, Embroidery, End, Engine(r), Engineer, Erté, Etch, Fashion, Flanch, Format, Former, Fretwork, Hepplewhite, Hitech, Iconic, Imagineer, Impresa, Imprese, Inlay, Intaglio, Intend(ment), Intent(ion), Interior, Invent, Klein, Layout, Le Corbusier, Limit-state, Linocut, Logo, Marquetry, Matched pairs, McCartney, Mean, Meander, Mehndi, Modiste, Monogram, Morris, Mosaic, Motif, Multifoil, Nailhead, Nissen, Paisley, → **PLAN**, Plot, Propose, Prostyle, Pyrography, Quant, Ruse, Schema, Scheme, Schiaparelli, Seal, Sheraton, Sketch, Sopwith, Spatterwork, Specification, Sprig, Stencil, Stubble, Tatow, Tattoo, Tatu, Think, Tooling, Townscape, Trigram, Tupelov, Vignette, Watermark, Weiner, Werkstalte, Whittle, Within-subjects

Desirable, Desire, Desirous Ambition, Aphrodisia, Appetite, Aspire, Avid, Best, Cama, Conation, Concupiscence, Covet, Crave, Cupidity, Des, Dreamboat, Earn, Eligible, Epithymetic, Esurience, Fancy, Gasp, Greed, Hanker, Hope, Hots, Hunger, Impulse, Itch, Kama(deva), Le(t)ch, Libido, List, Long, Luscious, Lust, Mania, Month's mind, Notion, Nymphomania, Orectic, Owlcar, Pica, Pleasure, Plum, Provocative, Reak, Reck, Request, Residence, Salt, Slaver, Spiffing, Streetcar, Thirst, Urge, Velleity, Vote, Wanderlust, Want, Whim, Will, Wish, Yearn, Yen

Desk Almemar, Ambo, Bonheur-du-jour, Bureau, Carrel(l), Cash, Check-in, Cheveret, City, Copy, Davenport, Desse, Devonport, E(s)critoire, Enquiry, Faldstool, Lectern, Lettern, Litany, Pay, Pedestal, Prie-dieu, Pulpit, Reading, Roll-top, Scrutoire, Secretaire, Vargueno, Writing

Desolate, Desolation Bare, Barren, Desert, Devastate, Disconsolate, Forlorn, Gaunt, Gousty, Lonesome, Moonscape, Stark, Waste, Woebegone

Despair, Desperate, Desperation Acharne, Dan, De profundis, Despond, Dire, Drastic, Extreme, Forlorn hope, Frantic, Gagging, Giant, Gloom, Hairless, Headlong, Hopelessness, Reckless, Unhopeful, Urgent, Wanhope

▶**Despatch** *see* **DISPATCH**

Despise(d) Condemn, Conspire, Contemn, Forhow, Futz, Hate, Ignore, Scorn, Spurn, Vilify, Vilipend

Despite For, Malgré, Notwithstanding, Pace, Though, Venom

Despot(ism) Autarchy, Autocrat, Bonaparte, Caesar, Darius, Dictator, Little Hitler, Martinet, Monocrat, Napoleon, Nero, Satrap, Soldan, Stratocrat, Tsar, Tyrant, Tzar

Dessert Afters, Apple charlotte, Baclava, Baked Alaska, Baklava, Banana split, Bavarian cream, Bavarois, Blancmange, Bombe, Cannoli, Charlotte, Charlotte russe, Cheesecake, Clafoutis, Cobbler, Compote, Coupe, Cranachan, Cream, Crème brulée, Crème caramel, Crepe Suzette, Dulce de leche, Entremets, Eve's pudding, Floating Island, Flummery, Fool, Granita, Jelly, Junket, Kissel, Knickerbocker glory, Kulfi, Marquise, Melba, Mousse, Mud pie, Nesselrode, Pannacotta, Parfait, Pashka, Pavlova, Peach Melba, → **PUDDING**, Rasmalai, Roulade, Rum baba, Sabayon, Sawine, Semifreddo, Shoofly pie, Sorbet, Split, Spumone, Strudel, Sundae, Syllabub, Tapioca, Tart, Tarte tatin, Tartufo, Tiramisu, Tortoni, Trifle, Vacherin, Whip, Zabaglione

Destine(d), Destination Born, Design, End, Fate, Foredoom, Goal, Gole, Home, Intend, Joss, Port, Purpose, Vector, Weird

Destiny Doom, → **FATE**, Karma, Kismet, Lachesis, Lot, Manifest, Moira, Portion, Yang, Yin

Destroy(er) Annihilate, Apollyon, Atomise, Blight, Bulldoze, Can, Canker, Crush, D, Decimate, Deface, Delete, Demolish, Demyelinate, Denature, Destruct, Devastate, Dish, Dismember, Dissolve, Eat, Efface, End, Eradicate, Erase, Exterminate, Extirpate, Fordo, Graunch, Harry, Iconoclast, Incinerate, Invalidate, → **KILL**, KO, Lay waste, Locust, Murder, Obliterate, Overkill, Perish, Predator, Pulverize, Q-ship, Ravage, Raze, Ruin, Saboteur, Sack, Scuttle, Siva, Slash, Smash, Spif(f)licate, Sterilize, Stew-can, Stonker, Stultify, Subvert, Undo, Uproot, Vandal, Vitiate, Waste, Whelm, Wreck, Zap

Destruction, Destructive Adverse, Bane, Can, Catabolism, Collapse, Deathblow, Deleterious, Desecration, Devastation, Doom, Downfall, Ecocide, End, Götterdämmerung, Grave, Havoc, Holocaust, Hunnish, Iconoclasm, Insidious, Internecine, Kali, Lethal, Loss, Maelstrom, Maleficent, Malignant, Moorburn, Nihilistic, Pernicious, Pestilential, Pogrom, Rack, Ragnarok, Ravage, Ruination, Sabotage, Stroy, Wrack, Wreckage

Detach(ed), Detachment Abeigh, Abstract, Alienate, Aloof, Apart, Body, Calve, Clinical, Cut, Detail, Discrete, Disinterested, Dispassionate, Distinct, Garrison, Isolate, Loose, Outlying, Outpost, Patrol, Separate, Sever, Staccato, Stoic, Unfasten, Unhinge, Unit, Unpick, Withdrawn

Detail(s), Detailed Annotate, Circumstances, Depict, Dock, Elaborate, Embroider, Expatiate, Explicit, Exploded, Expound, Instance, Intricate, → **ITEM**, Itemise, Minutiae, Narrate, Nicety, Nitty-gritty, Nuts and bolts, Particular(ise), Pedantry, Point, Recite, Recount, Relate, Respect, Send, Spec, Special, Specific, Specification, Technicality, Touch

▷**Detailed** *may indicate* last letter missing

Detain(ee), Detention (centre) Arrest, Buttonhole, Collar, Custody, Delay, Demurrage, Detinue, Gate, Glasshouse, Hinder, Imprison, Intern, Juvie, Keep, POW, Retard, Sin bin, Stay, → **WITHHOLD**

Detect(or), Detective Agent, Armchair, Arsène, Asdic, Bergerac, Bloodhound,
Brown, Bucket, Busy, Catch, Chan, Chlorometer, CIB, CID, Cuff, Det, Dick, Discern,
Discover, Divine, Doodlebug, Dupin, Enquiry agent, Espy, Eye, Father Brown, Fed,
Find, Flambeau, Flic, Fortune, French, Galvanoscope, Geigercounter, Geophone,
G-man, Gumshoe, Hanaud, Hercule, Holmes, Interpol, Investigator, Jack,
Lecoq, Lupin, Maigret, Methanometer, Minitrack®, Morse, Nail, Nose, Peeper,
PI, Pinkerton, Plant, Poirot, Private, Private eye, Prodnose, Radar, Reagent,
Retinula, Rumble, Scent, Scerne, Sense, Sensor, Shadow, Shamus, Sherlock,
Sleuth-hound, Smell out, Snooper, Sofar, Solver, Sonar, Sonobuoy, Spot, Store,
Tabaret, Take, Tec, Thorndyke, Toff, Trace, Trent, Vance, Wimsey, Yard(man)
Deter(rent) Block, Check, Daunt, Dehort, Delay, Disincentive, Dissuade, Faze,
Prevent, Restrain, Scare, Trident, Turn-off, Ultimate
Detergent Clean(s)er, Non-ionizing, Solvent, Sujee, Surfactant, Syndet, Tepol,
Whitener
Deteriorate, Deterioration Decadence, Degenerate, Derogate, Go to pot,
Pejoration, Perish, Relapse, Retrograde, Rust, Worsen
▷**Deterioration** *may indicate* an anagram
▷**Determination** *may indicate* 'last letter'
Determine(d), Determination Adamant, All-out, Appoint, Arbitrament,
Ardent, Ascertain, Assign, Assoil, Bent, Causal, Choose, Condition, Dead-set,
→ **DECIDE**, Define, Dictate, Doctrinaire, Dogged, Do-or-die, Dour, Drive,
Earnest, Fix, Govern, Granite, Grim, Grit(ty), Headstrong, Hell-bent,
Indomitable, Influence, Intent, Ironclad, Judgement, Law, Liquidate, Orient,
Out, Point, Pre-ordain, Purpose, Quantify, → **RESOLUTE**, Resolve, Rigwiddie,
Rigwoodie, Self-will, Set, Settle, Set upon, Shape, Single-minded, Soum, Sowm,
Stalwart, Steely, Stout, Tenacious, Type, Valiant, Weigh
Detest(able), Detested Abhor, Abominate, Anathema, Despise, Execrable,
Execrate, Hate, Loathsome, Pestful, Vile
Detonate, Detonator Blast, Explode, Fire, Fuse, Fuze, Ignite, Kindle, Plunger,
Primer, Saucisse, Saucisson, Spring, Tetryl, Trip-wire
Detour Bypass, Deviate, Divert
Detract Belittle, Decry, Diminish, Discount, Disparage
Devalue Cheapen, Debase, Impair, Reduce, Undermine
Devastate, Devastation Demolish, Destroy, Ground zero, Gut, Overwhelm,
Ravage, Sack, Waste, Wrack
Develop(er), Developed, Developing, Development Advance, Age, Agile,
Apotheosis, Arise, Breed, Build, Cutting edge, Dark room, Educe, Elaborate,
Enlarge, Escalate, Evolve, Expand, Expatriate, Fixer, Fulminant, Germinate,
Gestate, Grow, Hatch, Hothouse, Hypo, Imago, Immature, Improve, Incubate,
Larva, Mature, Metamorphose, Metol, Morphosis, Mushroom, Nascent,
Nurture, Offshoot, Ongoing, Pathogeny, Pullulate, Pupa, Pyro, Quinol, Ribbon,
Ripe(n), Sarvodaya, Sensorimeter, Separate, Shape, Soup, Sprawl, Subtopia,
Technography, Twist, Unfold, Upgrow
▷**Develop** *may indicate* an anagram
Deviant, Deviate, Deviation Aberrance, Abnormal, Anomaly, Blip, Brisure,
Deflect, Deflexure, Depart, Derogate, Detour, Digress, Discrepant, Diverge, Divert,
Drift, Error, Fade, Kurtosis, Masochist, Pervert, Quartile, Sadist, Sheer, Solecism,
Sport, Stray, Swerve, → **TURN**, Valgus, Varus, Veer, Wander, Wend, Yaw
Device Allegory, → **APPARATUS**, Appliance, Artifice, Bush, Contraption,
Contrivance, Dodge, Emblem, Expedient, Gadget, Gimmick, Gismo, Gubbins,

Instrument, Logo, Mnemonic, Motto, Plan, Pointing, Ruse, Safeguard,
→ **STRATAGEM**, Subterfuge, Tactic, Tag, Thing, Tool, Trademark, Trick, Wile

Devil(ish), Demon Abaddon, Afrit, Apollyon, Archfiend, Asmodeus, Auld
Hornie, Beelzebub, Belial, Buckra, Cacodemon, Cartesian, Clootie, Cloots, Deev,
Deil, Demon, Deuce, Diable, Diabolic, Dickens, Div, Drudge, Duende, Eblis,
Familiar, Fiend, Ghoul, Hornie, Iblis, Imp, Incubus, Infernal, Knave, Lucifer,
Mahoun(d), Man of Sin, Mephisto(pheles), Mischief, Nick, Nickie-ben, Old Nick,
Ragman, Rahu, Ralph, Satan, Satyr, Scratch, Succubine, Succubus, Tasmanian,
Tempter, Unholy, Wicked, Worricow

Devious Braide, Cunning, Deep, Eel(y), Erroneous, Evasive, Heel, Implex,
Indirect, Insincere, Meandering, Scheming, Shifty, Sly, Sneaky, Stealthy, Subtle,
Tortuous, Tricky, Twisting, Two-faced

Devise(d) Arrange, Coin, Comment, Concoct, Contrive, Cook up, Decoct,
Hit-on, Imagine, Invenit, Invent, Plan, Plot

Devote(e), Devotion(al), Devoted Addiction, Adherent, Aficionado,
Âme damnée, Angelus, Attached, Bhakti, Buff, Bunny, Commitment,
Consecrate, Consign, Corban, Dedicate, Employ, Enthusiast, Fan, Fervid,
Fetishism, Fidelity, Fiend, Gallantry, Grebo, Holy, Hound, Lapdog, Loyalty,
Mariolate, Novena, Nut, Partisan, Passion, Piety, Pious, Puja, Religioso,
Sacred, Saivite, Sanctity, Savoyard, Sivaite, Solemn, Sworn, True, Voteen,
Zealous

Devour(ing) Consume, Eat, Engorge, Engulf, Manducate, Moth-eat, Scarf,
Scoff, Snarf, → **SWALLOW**

▷**Devour** *may indicate* one word inside another

Devout God-fearing, Holy, Pious, Religiose, Reverent, Sant, Sincere, Solemn

Dew(y) Bloom, Gory, Moist, Mountain, Rime, Roral, Roric, Rorid, Roscid,
Serene, Tranter

Diagnose, Diagnosis, Diagnostic Amniocentesis, Findings, Identify,
Iridology, Pulse, Radionics, Scan, Scintigraphy, X-ray

Diagonal(ly) Bias, Cater(-corner), Counter, Oblique, Principal, Slant, Solidus,
Speed, Twill

Diagram Argand, Bar chart, Bar graph, Butterfly, Chart, Chromaticity,
Cladogram, Compass rose, Decision tree, Drawing, Feynman, Figure, Graph,
Graphics, Grid, Map, Phase, Plan, Plat, Scatter, Schema, Schematic, Scintigram,
Stemma, Stereogram, Topo, Tree, Venn

Dial(ling) Card, Face, Mug, Phiz, Phone, Ring, Speed, STD, Visage

Dialect Acadian, Accent, Amoy, Anglican, Burr, Castilian, Damara, Eldin, Epic,
Erse, Eye, Franconian, Galician, Gascon, Geordie, Hassaniya, Idiom, Ionic,
Isogloss, Jargon, Jockney, Ladin, Lallans, Landsmaal, Langue d'oui, Ledden,
Lingo, Low German, Min, Norman, Norn, Occitan, Old Icelandic, Old North
French, Parsee, Parsi, Patavinity, Patois, Pedi, Picard, Prakrit, Rhaeto-Romance,
Rhotic, Rock English, Romans(c)h, Ruthenian, Salish, Savoyard, Scouse, Taal,
Tadzhik, Ta(d)jik, Talky-talky, Tongue, Tuscan, Tyrolese, Umbrian, Vaudois,
Walloon, West Saxon, Yenglish, Yinglish

Dialogue Colloquy, Conversation, Critias, Discussion, Exchange, Imparl, Lazzo,
Pastourelle, Repartee, Speech, Stichomythia, Talk, Upspeak

Diameter Breadth, Calibre, Gauge, Width

Diamond(s), Diamond-shaped Adamant, Black, Boart, Brilliant, Bristol,
Carbon, Carbonado, Cullinan, D, DE, Delaware, Eustace, False, Florentine,
Hope, Ice, Isomer, Jewel, Jim, Koh-i-Noor, Lasque, Lattice, Lozenge,

Minor suit, Off-colour(ed), Paragon, Pick, Pitch, Pitt, Reef, Rhinestone, Rhomb, Rock, Rose-cut, Rosser, Rough, Sancy, Solitaire, Spark, Sparklers, Squarial, Suit

Diary, Diarist Adrian Mole, Blogger, Burney, Chronicle, Crossman, Dale, Day-book, Evelyn, Frank, Hickey, Journal, Journal intime, Kilvert, Log, Mole, Nobody, Noctuary, Pepys, Personal organiser, Planner, Pooter, Record

Dice(r), Dicey Aleatory, Astragals, Bale, Bones, Chop, Craps, Cube, Dodgy, Fulham, Fullams, Fullans, Gourd(s), Hash, Highman, Jeff, Mince, Novum, Shoot, Smalto, Snake-eyes, Tallmen

▷**Dick** *may indicate* a dictionary

▷**Dicky** *may indicate* an anagram

Dictate, Dictator(ial) Amin, Autocrat, Bonaparte, Caesar, Castro, Cham, Command, Czar, Decree, Demagogue, Despot, Duce, Franco, Fu(e)hrer, Gaddafi, Gauleiter, Hitler, Idi, Impose, Indite, Lenin, Mussolini, Ordain, Peremptory, Peron, Pol Pot, Salazar, Shogun, Stalin, Tell, Tito, Totalitarian, Trujillo, Tsar, Tyrant, Tzar

Dictionary Alveary, Calepin, Chambers, Etymologicon, Fowler, Gazetteer, Glossary, Gradus, Hobson-Jobson, Idioticon, Johnson's, Larousse, Lexicon, Lexis, OED, Onomasticon, Thesaurus, Webster, Wordbook

Die(d), Dying Ache, Buy the farm, Calando, Cark, Choke, Conk out, Crater, Croak, Cube, D, Decadent, Desire, End, Evanish, Exit, Expire, Fade, Fail, Forfair, Fulham, Fulhan, Fullam, Go, Hallmark, Hang, Highman, Hop, Hop the twig, Infarct, Kark, Long, Morendo, Moribund, Ob(iit), Orb, Pass, Perdendosi, Perish, Peter, Pop off, Pop one's clogs, Slip the cable, Snuff, Solidum, Sphacelation, Stagheaded, Stamp, Sterve, Succumb, Suffer, Swage, Swelt, Terminal, Tessera, Tine, Touch, Wane

Diet(er), Dieting Assembly, Atkins, Augsburg, Bant(ing), Congress, Council, Dail, Eat, Fare, Feed, Hay, Intake, Knesset, Landtag, Lent, Macrobiotic, Parliament, Reduce, Regimen, Reichstag, Short commons, Slim, Solid, Sprat, Staple, Strict, Tynwald, Vegan, Vegetarian, Weightwatcher, Worms, Yo-yo

Differ(ence), Differing, Different(ly) Afresh, Allo, Alterity, Anew, Barney, Change, Cline, Contrast, Contretemps, Deviant, Diacritic, Diesis, Disagree, Discord, Discrepant, Disparate, Dispute, Dissent, Distinct, Diverge, Diverse, Else, Elsewise, Epact, Exotic, Gulf, Heterodox, Loggerheads, Nonconformist, Nuance, Omnifarious, Other, Othergates, Otherguess, Otherness, Otherwise, Poles apart, Quantum, Separate, Several, Spat, Special, Tiff, Unlike, Variform, Various, Vary

Difficult(y), Difficult person Abstruseness, Ado, Adversity, Aggro, Aporia, Arduous, Augean, Badass, Balky, Ballbuster, Bitter, Block, Bolshie, Bother, Cantankerous, Catch, Choosy, Complex, Complication, Contretemps, Corner, Cough drop, Crisis, Crotchety, Deep, Delphic, Depth, Dysphagia, Embarrassment, Enigma, Extreme, Fiddly, Formidable, Gnomic, Gordian, →**HARD**, Hassle, Hazard, Hiccough, Hiccup, Hobble, Hole, Hoor, Hump, Ill, Impasse, Inconvenient, Indocile, Inscrutable, Intractable, Intransigent, Jam, Jawbreaker, Kink, Kittle, Knot, Lob's pound, Lurch, Matter, Mulish, Net, Nodus, Obdurate, Obstacle, Parlous, Perverse, Pig, Pitfall, Plight, Predicament, Pretty pass, Quandary, Queer St, Recalcitrant, Rough, Rub, Scabrous, Scrape, Scrub, Scruple, Setaceous, Shlep, Snag, Soup, Steep, Stey, Stick, Sticky, Stiff, Stinker, Strait, Stubborn, Stymie, Swine, Tall order, Testing, Thorny, Ticklish, Tight spot, Tough, Trial, Tricky, Troublous, Trying, Une(a)th, Unwieldy, Uphill, Via dolorosa, Woe

Diffuse, Diffusion Disperse, Disseminate, Endosmosis, Exude, Osmosis, Permeate, Pervade, Radiate, Run, Sperse, Spread, Winnow

Dig(s), Digger, Digging, Dig up Admire, Antipodean, Australian, Backhoe, Barb, Beadle, Bed(e)ral, Billet, Bore, Bot, Burrow, Costean, Delve, Deracinate, Enjoy, Excavate, Flea-bag, Flophouse, Fork, Fossorial, Gaulter, Get, Gibe, Gird, Graft, Graip, Grub, Hoe, Howk, Into, Jab, Kip, Lair, Like, Lodgings, Luxor, Mine, Navvy, Nervy, Nudge, Pad, Pioneer, Probe, Prod, Prospect(ing), Raddleman, Resurrect, Root(le), Ruddleman, Sap, See, Sneer, Spade, Spit, Spud, Star-nose, Taunt, Till, Tonnell, Trench, Tunnel, Undermine, Unearth

Digest(ible), Digestion, Digestive Abridgement, Absorb, Abstract, Aperçu, Archenteron, Assimilate, Beeda, Bile, Bradypeptic, Brief, Codify, Concoct, Endue, Epitome, Eupepsia, Eupepsy, Fletcherism, Gastric, Indew, Indue, Insalivate, Light, Pandect, Pem(m)ican, Pepsin(e), Peptic, Précis, Salt-cat, Steatolysis, →SUMMARY

Dignified, Dignify August, Elevate, Ennoble, Exalt, Grace, Handsome, Honour, Imposing, Lordly, Maestoso, Majestic, Manly, Proud, Stately, Statuesque

Dignity Aplomb, Bearing, Cathedra, Decorum, Face, Glory, Grandeur, Gravitas, High horse, Majesty, Nobility, Poise, Presence, Scarf

Digress(ion) Aside, Deviate, Diverge, Ecbole, Episode, Excurse, Excursus, Maunder, Sidetrack, Vagary, Veer, Wander

Dilate, Dilation, Dilatation, Dilator Amplify, Develop, Diastole, Ecstasis, Enlarge, Expand, Increase, Mydriasis, Nitro, Sinus, Tent, Varix

Dilemma Casuistry, Choice, Cleft(stick), Double-bend, Dulcarnon, Fix, Horn, Jam, Predicament, Quandary, Stymie, Teaser, Why-not

Diligence, Diligent Active, Application, Assiduous, Coach, Conscience, Eident, Hard-working, Industry, Intent, Painstaking, Sedulous, Studious

Dilute(d), Dilution Adulterate, Allay, Cut, Deglaze, Delay, Diluent, Lavage, Qualify, Simpson, Thin, Water, Weaken, Wishy-washy

Dim(ness), Dimming, Dimwit(ted) Becloud, Blear, Blur, Brownout, Caligo, Clueless, Crepuscular, Dense, Dumbo, Dusk, Eclipse, Fade, Faint, Feint, Fozy, Gormless, Ill-lit, Indefinable, Indistinct, Mist, Nebulous, Ninny, Obliterate, Obscure, Overcast, Owl, Pale, Purblind, Shadow, Stupid, Unclear, Unsmart

Dimension(s) Area, Breadth, Extent, Height, Length, Linear, Measure, New, Scantling, Size, Space, Third, Volume, Width

Diminish(ed), Diminishing, Diminuendo, Diminution, Diminutive Abatement, Allay, Assuage, Attenuate, Baby, Calando, Contract, Cot(t)ise, Deactivate, Decline, Decrease, Détente, Detract, Disparage, Dissipate, Dwarf, Dwindle, Erode, Fourth, Hypocorism(a), Impair, Lessen, Lilliputian, Little, Minify, Minus, Mitigate, Petite, Pigmy, Ritardando, Scarp, Small, Stultify, Subside, Taper, Toy, Trangle, Wane, Whittle

Dingy Crummy, Dark, Dirty, Drear, Dun, Fleapit, Fusc(ous), Grimy, Isabel(la), Isabelline, Lurid, Oorie, Ourie, Owrie, Shabby, Smoky

Dining-room Cafeteria, Cenacle, Commons, Frater, Hall, Langar, Mess hall, Refectory, Restaurant, Triclinium

Dinner Banquet, Collation, Feast, Hall, Kail, Kale, Meal, Prandial, Repast

Dinosaur Aepyornis, Allosaurus, Archosaur, Atlantosaurus, Baryonyx, Brachiosaurus, Brontosaurus, Ceratosaurus, Ceteosaurus, Compsognathus, Diplodocus, Galeopithecus, Hadrosaur, Ichthyosaur(us), Iguanodon, Megalosaur, Microraptor, Odontornithes, Pachycephalosaur, Perissodactyl, Plesiosaur, Pliosaur, Prehistoric, Pterodactyl, Pterosaur, Pythonomorpha,

Raptor, Rhynchocephalian, Sauropod, Sauropterygian, Smilodon, Square, Stegosaur, Teleosaurus, Titanosaurus, T-rex, Triceratops, Tyrannosaurus

Diocese Bishopric, District, Eparchate, Eparchy, See

Dip(per), Dippy Baptise, Basin, Bathe, Bob, Brantub, Dabble, Dap, Dean, Dib, Diver, Dop, Duck, Dunk, Fatuous, Foveola, Geosyncline, Guacamole, Houmous, H(o)ummus, Humus, Immerge, Immerse, Intinction, Ladle, Lucky, Ousel, Ouzel, Paddle, Plough, Rinse, Rollercoaster, Salute, Sheep-wash, Star, Submerge, Tzatziki, Ursa

Diploma Bac, Cert(ificate), Charter, Parchment, Qualification, Scroll, Sheepskin

Diplomacy, Diplomat(ic) Alternat, Ambassador, Attaché, Career, CD, Chargé d'affaires, Consul, DA, Dean, Discretion, Doyen, El(t)chi, Emissary, Envoy, Fanariot, Fetial, Finesse, Gunboat, Legation, Lei(d)ger, Metternich, Negotiator, Phanariot, Suave, →TACT

▷**Dippy** *may indicate* a bather

Dire Dreadful, Fatal, Fell, Grim, Hateful, Ominous, Urgent

Direct(or), Directed, Directly Ad hominem, Administer, Advert, Agonothetes, Aim, Airt, Air-to-air, Auteur, Beeline, Board, Boss, Cann, Cast, Chairperson, Channel, Charge, Chorus-master, Command, Compere, Con(n), Conduct, Control, Cox, Dead, Dean, Due, Dunstable road, Enjoin, Explicit, Face to face, Fair, First-hand, Forthright, Frontal, Full, Guide, Helm, Immediate, Impresario, Instruct, Kapellmeister, Lead, Manager, Navigate, Outright, Oversee, Person to person, Pilot, Plain-spoken, Play, Point-blank, Ready, Refer, Régisseur, Regulate, Rudder, Send, Set, Signpost, Slap-bang, Stear, →STEER, Straight, Superintend, Supervise, Teach, Telic, Tell, Train, Vector

Direction, Directive Address, Aim, Airt, Arrow, Astern, Bearings, Course, Cross-reference, E, End-on, Guidance, Guide, Heading, Keblah, L, Line, N, Orders, Orientation, Passim, Quarter, R, Recipe, Route, Rubric, S, Sanction, Send, Sense, Side, Slap, Sub-heading, Tacet, Tack, Tenor, Thataway, Trend, W, Way

Directory Crockford, Data, Debrett, Encyclop(a)edia, Folder, French, Herbal, Kelly, List, Red book, Register, Root, Search, Web

Dirge Ballant, Coronach, Dirige, Epicedium, Knell, Monody, Requiem, Song, Threnody

Dirigible Airship, Balloon, Blimp, Zeppelin

Dirk Dagger, Skean, Whinger, Whiniard, Whinyard

Dirt(y) Augean, Bed(r)aggled, Begrime, Bemoil, Chatty, Clag, Clarty, Colly, Contaminate, Coom, Crock, Crud, Defile, Distain, Draggle, Dung, Dust, Earth, Filth, Foul, Gen, Gore, Grime, Grubby, Grufted, Grungy, Impure, Manky, Moit, Mote, Muck, Obscene, Ordure, Pay, Pick, Ray, Scandal, Scody, Sculdudd(e)ry, Scum, Scuttlebutt, Scuzzy, Skulduddery, Slattery, Smirch, Smut(ch), Soil, Sordor, Squalid, Squalor, Stain, Stuff, Substrata, Sully, Tidemark, Trash, Unclean, Unwashed, Yucky, Yukky

Disability, Disable(d) Cripple, Crock, Gimp, Handicapped, Hors de combat, Invalid, Kayo, Lame, Maim, Paralyse, Scotch, Scupper, Supercrip, Wreck

Disadvantage Detriment, Disamenity, Drawback, Flipside, Handicap, Mischief, Out, Own goal, Penalise, Penalty, Prejudice, Shortcoming, Snag, Supercherie, Upstage, Wrongfoot, Zugswang

Disagree(ing), Disagreeable, Disagreement Altercation, Argue, Argy-bargy, Bad, Clash, Conflict, Contest, Contradict, Debate, Demur, Differ, Discrepant, Dispute, Dissent, Dissonant, Evil, Fiddlesticks, Flak, Friction,

Heterodoxy, Inharmonious, Onkus, Pace, Rank, Rift, Testy, Troll, Uh-uh, Uncongenial, Vary

Disappear(ing) Cook, Dispel, Evanesce, Evanish, Evaporate, Fade, Fizzle out, Kook, Latescent, Melt, Occult, Pass, Skedaddle, Slope, → **VANISH**

Disappoint(ment), Disappointed, Disappointing Anticlimax, Balk, Baulk, Blow, Chagrin, Choked, Comedown, Crestfallen, Delude, Disgruntle, Fizzer, Frustrate, Gutted, Heartsick, Lemon, Letdown, Mislippen, Off, Regret, Sell, Setback, Shucks, Sick, Suck-in, Sucks, Swiz(zle), Thwart, Tsk, Underwhelm

Disapproval, Disapprove(d) Ach, Animadvert, Boo, Catcall, Censure, Condemn, Deplore, Deprecate, Expostulate, Fie, Frown, Harrumph, Hiss, Mal vu, Napoo, Object, Pejorative, Po-faced, Pshaw, Raspberry, Reject, Reproach, Reprobate, Slow handclap, Squint, Tush, Tut, Umph, Veto, Whiss

Disarm(ament), Disarming Bluff, Defuse, Demobilise, Mutilate, Nuclear, Winsome

Disarray Disorder, Mess, Rifle, Tash, Tousle, Undress

Disaster, Disastrous Accident, Adversity, Apocalypse, Bale, Calamity, Cataclysm(ic), Catastrophe, Chernobyl, Crash, Crisis, Debacle, Dire, Doom, Evil, Fatal, Fiasco, Flop, Impostor, Meltdown, Mishap, Pandemic, Pitfall, Providence, Quake, Rout, Ruin, Shipwreck, Titanic, Tragedy, Train wreck, Wipeout

Disbelief, Disbelieve(r) Acosmism, Agnosticism, Anythingarian, Atheism, Cor, Doubt, Huh, Incredulity, Mistrust, Nothingarianism, Occamist, Pfui, Phew, Phooey, Puh-lease, Puh-leeze, Question, Sceptic, Stroll on, Voetsak

Disc, Disk Accretion, Bursting, Button, CD, Chart-buster, Cheese, Clay pigeon, Compact, Coulter, Counter, Diaphragm, Dogtag, EP, Epiphragm, Fla(w)n, Flexible, Floppy, Frisbee®, Gold, Gong, Granum, Grindstone, Hard, Hard card, Harrow, Impeller, Intervertebral, Laser, LP, Magnetic, Mono, O, Optic(al), Parking, Paten, Patin, Planchet, Plate, Platinum, Platter, Puck, RAID, RAM, Rayleigh, Record, Reflector, Rosette, Roundel, Rowel, Rundle, Sealed unit, Silver, Slipped, Slug, Stereo, Sun, Swash plate, System, Tax, Thylacoid, Tiddl(e)ywink, Token, Video, Wafer, Wharve, Whorl, Winchester, Wink, WORM, Zip®

Discard(ed) Abandon, Crib, Dele, Jettison, Kill, Leave, Minimise, Obsolete, Off, Offload, Oust, Outtake, → **REJECT**, Scrap, Shuck, Slough, Sluff, Supersede, Throw over

Discern(ing), Discernment Acumen, Acute, Astute, Clear-eyed, Descry, Detect, Discrimination, Flair, Insight, Intuition, Perceive, Percipient, Perspicacity, Quick-sighted, Realise, Sapient, Scry, See, Skry, → **TASTE**, Tell, Wate, Wise

Discharge Absolve, Acquit, Arc, Assoil, Blow off, Boot, Brush, Cashier, Catarrh, Conditional, Conge, Corona, Corposant, Deliver, Demob, Depose, Disembogue, Disgorge, Dishono(u)rable, Dismiss, Disruptive, Drain(age), Dump, Efflux, Effusion, Egest, Ejaculate, Eject, Emission, Emit, Enfilade, Evacuate, Excrete, Execute, Exemption, Expectorate, Expel, Expulsion, Exude, Fire, Flashover, Flower, Flux, Free, Fusillade, Glow, Honourable, Issue, Jaculatory, Lava, Lay off, Leak, Let off, Liberate, Loose, Maturate, Menses, Muster out, Mute, Offload, Oust, Outfall, Pass, Pay, Perform, Period, Pour, Purulence, Pus, Pyorrhoea, Quietus, Redeem, Release, Rheum, Run, Sack, Salvo, Sanies, Secretion, Seepage, Show, Shrive, Smegma, Snarler, Spark, Spill(age), Static, Suppurate, Teem, Unload, Unloose, Vacuate, Vent, Void, Water

Disciple(s) Adherent, Apostle, Babi, Catechumen, Chela, Dorcas, Follower, John, Judas, Luke, Mark, Matthew, Peter, Simon, Son, Student, Thomist, Votary

Disciplinarian, Disciplinary, Discipline(d) Apollonian, Ascesis, Chasten, Chastise, Constrain, Correct, Despot, Dressage, Drill, Exercise, Feng shui, Inure, Judo, Martinet, Mathesis, Penal, Phonetics, Punish, Punitive, Ramrod, Regimentation, Regulate, School, Science, Sergeant major, Spartan, Stickler, Subject, Train, Tutor, Yoga

Disclaim(er) Deny, Disown, No(t)chel, Recant, Renounce, → **REPUDIATE**, Voetstoots

Disclose, Disclosure Apocalypse, Confess, Divulge, Expose, Impart, Leak, Manifest, Open, Propale, → **PUBLISH**, Report, Reveal, Showdown, Spill, Tell, Unheal, Unhele, Unrip, Unveil

Discomfort(ed), Discompose Ache, All-overish, Angst, Dysphoria, Gyp, Heartburn, Pain, Purgatory, Ravel, Unease, Wedgie

Disconcert(ing), Disconcerted Abash, Astound, Confuse, Disturb, Embarrass, Faze, Feeze, Flurry, Nonplus, Phase, Pheese, Pheeze, Phese, Put off, → **RATTLE**, Red-faced, Shatter, Startle, Tease, Throw, Unnerve, Upset, Wrong-foot

▷**Disconcert(ed)** *may indicate* an anagram

Disconnect(ed) Asynartete, Decouple, Detach, Disassociate, Disjointed, Off-line, Segregate, Sever, Staccato, Trip, Uncouple, Undo, Ungear, Unplug

Discontent(ed) Disquiet, Dissatisfied, Repined, Sour

Discord(ant) Absonant, Ajar, Charivari, Conflict, Din, Dispute, Eris, Faction, Hoarse, Inharmonious, Jangle, Jar(ring), Raucous, Ruction, Strife

▷**Discord(ant)** *may indicate* an anagram

Discount Agio, Cashback, Cut-rate, Deduct, Disregard, Forfaiting, Invalidate, Leave, Quantity, → **REBATE**, Trade

Discourage(ment) Caution, Chill, Dampen, Dash, Daunt, Deject, Demoralise, Deter, Dishearten, Disincentive, Dismay, Dispirit, Dissuade, Enervate, Frustrate, Intimidate, Opposition, Stifle

Discourse Address, Argument, Colloquy, Conversation, Descant, Diatribe, Dissertate, Eulogy, Expound, Homily, Lecture, Lucubrate, Orate, Philippic, Preach, Recount, Relate, Rigmarole, Sermon

Discover(y), Discoverer Amundsen, Anagnorisis, Ascertain, Betray, Breakthrough, Columbus, Cook, Descry, Detect, Determine, Discern, Discure, Esery, Espy, Eureka, Expiscate, → **FIND**, Heureka, Heuristic, Hit on, Learn, Locate, Manifest, Moresby, Protegé, Rumble, Serendip, Serendipity, Spy, Sus, Tasman, Trace, Trouvaille, Unearth, Unhale, Unmask, Unveil

▷**Discovered in** *may indicate* an anagram or a hidden word

Discredit(able) Debunk, Decry, Disbelieve, Disgrace, Explode, Infamy, Negate, Scandal, Slur, Stigmatise, Unworthy

Discreet, Discretion Cautious, Circumspect, Finesse, Freedom, Judicious, Option, Polite, Politic, Prudence, Prudent, Trait, Unobtrusive, Wise

Discrepancy Difference, Gap, Lack, Shortfall, Variance

Discriminate, Discriminating, Discrimination Ag(e)ism, Colour bar, Diacritic, Differentiate, Discern, Distinguish, Elitism, Fastidious, Handism, Invidious, Lookism, Nasute, Racism, Rankism, Reverse, Secern, Segregate, Select, Sexism, Siz(e)ism, Speciesism, Subtle, Taste

Discuss(ed), Discussion Agitate, Air, Bandy, Bat around, Canvass, Commune, Confer(ence), Consult, Corridor work, Debate, Deliberate, Dialectic, Dialog(ue), Dicker, Disquisition, Emparl, Examine, Gabfest, Handle, Heart-to-heart, Hob and nob, Imparl, Interlocution, Interplead, Issue, Kick-about, Korero, Moot,

Negotiation, Over, Palaver, Parley, Pourparler, Prolegomenon, Quodlibet, Rap, Re, Round table, Symposium, Talk, Talkathon, Talkboard, Tapis, Treatment, Trialogue, Words

Disdain(ful) Belittle, Contempt, Coy, Deride, Despise, Geck, Poof, Pooh-pooh, Pugh, Puh, Rats, Sassy, Scoffer, →**SCORN**, Scout, Sneering, Sniffy, Sour grapes, Spurn, Stuffy, Supercilious

Disease(d) Affection, Ailment, Bug, Communicable, Comorbid, Complaint, Deficiency, Defluxion, Dunt, Epidemic, Epidemiology, Fever, Infection, Malady, Notifiable, Occupational, Rot, Scourge, Sickness, Wildfire

▷**Diseased** *may indicate* an anagram

Disengage(d), Disengagement Breach of promise, Clear, Detach, Divorce, Liberate, Loosen, Neutral, Release, Untie

▷**Disfigured** *may indicate* an anagram

Disgrace, Disgraceful Atimy, Attaint, Baffle, Blot, Contempt, Contumely, Degrade, Discredit, Dishonour, Dog-house, Embace, Embase, Ignoble, Ignominious, Ignominy, Indign, Indignity, Infamous, Infamy, Mean, Notorious, Obloquy, Opprobrium, Pity, Reprehensible, Scandal, Scandalous, Shame, Shameful, Shend, Slur, Soil, Stain, Stigma, Turpitude, Yshend

▷**Disgruntled** *may indicate* an anagram

Disguise(d) Alias, Belie, Blessing, Camouflage, Cloak, Colour, Conceal, Cover, Covert, Dissemble, Hide, Hood, Incog(nito), Mantle, Mask, Masquerade, Obscure, Peruke, Pretence, Pseudonym, Ring, Stalking-horse, Travesty, Veil, Vele, Veneer, Visagiste, Vizard

▷**Disguised** *may indicate* an anagram

Disgust(ing) Ach-y-fi, Ad nauseam, Aversion, Aw, Bah, Cloy, Discomfort, Execrable, Faugh, Fie, Foh, Fulsome, Grisly, Grody, Icky, Irk, Loathsome, Manky, Nauseous, Noisome, Obscene, Odium, Offputting, Oughly, Ouglie, Pah, Pho(h), Pip, Pish, Repel, Repugnant, Repulse, →**REVOLT**, Revulsion, Scomfish, Scumfish, Scunner, Scuzz, →**SICKEN**, Sir-reverence, Slimeball, Slimy, Squalid, Turn off, Tush, Ugh, Ugly, Ugsome, Vile, Yech, Yu(c)k

Dish(y), Dish out Adonis, Allot, Apollo, Ashet, Basin, Belle, Bowl, Butterboat, Chafing, Charger, Cocotte, Compotier, Concoction, Cook-up, Crockery, Cutie, Dent, Diable, Dreamboat, Epergne, Flasket, Grail, Kitchen, Laggen, Laggin, Lanx, Looker, Luggie, Pan, Pannikin, Paten, Patera, Patin(e), Pay, Petri, Plate, Platter, Porringer, Ramekin, Ramequin, Receptacle, Rechauffé, Remove, Sangraal, Sangrail, Sangreal, Satellite, Saucer, Scorifier, Scupper, Scuttle, Serve, Service, Sexpot, Side (order), Smasher, Special(ty), Stunner, Watchglass

Dishevel(led) Bedraggled, Blowsy, Blowzy, Daggy, Mess, Rumpled, Scraggly, Touse, Tousle, Touzle, Towse, Tumble, Uncombed, Unkempt, Untidy, Windswept

Dishonest(y) Bent, Crooked, Cross, Dodgy, False, Fraud, Graft, Hooky, Hot, Ill-gotten, Knavery, Light-fingered, Malpractice, Malversation, Maverick, Ringer, Rort, Shonky, Sleazy, Snide, Stink, Twister, Underhand, Venal, Wrong'un

Dishonour(able) Abatement, Caddish, Defile, Disgrace, Disparage, Ignom(in)y, Indignity, Infame, Scandal, Seduce, →**SHAME**, Violate, Wrong

Disinfect(ant) Acriflavin(e), Carbolic, Carvacrol, Cineol(e), Cleanse, Cresol, Dip, Eucalyptole, Formalin, Fuchsine, Fumigate, Lysol®, Orcein, Phenol, Purify, Sheep-dip, Sheep-wash, Terebene

Disjoint(ed) Bitty, Dismember, Incoherent, Rambling, Scrappy

▶**Disk** *see* **DISC**

Dislike(d) Abhor, Allergy, Animosity, Animus, Antipathy, Aversion, Bete noire, Derry, Detest, Disesteem, Displeasure, Distaste, Gross out, Hate, Lump, Mind, Odium, Resent, Ug(h)

Dislocate, Dislocation Break, Diastasis, Displace, Fault, Luxate, Slip, Subluxate

Dislodge Budge, Displace, Evict, Expel, Oust, Rear, Shift, Untenant, Uproot

Disloyal(ty) Blue, False, Recreant, Renegade, Treacherous, Treason, Unfaithful, Untrue

Dismal Black, Bleak, Blue, Cheerless, Dark, Dowie, Drack, Dreary, Funereal, →**GLOOMY**, Grey, Grim, Morne, Obital, Sepulchral, Sombre, Sullen, Trist(e), Wae, Woebegone, Wormy

Dismantle(d), Dismantling Derig, Divest, Get-out, Sheer-hulk, Strike, Strip, Unpin, Unrig

Dismay(ed) Aargh, Aghast, Alarm, Amate, Appal, Caramba, Confound, Consternation, Coo, Criv(v)ens, Daunt, Discourage, Dispirit, Dread, Fear, Ha, Hah, Horrify, Lordy, Lumme, Nonplus, Qualms, Strewth, Uh-oh

Dismiss(al), Dismissive Airy, Annul, Ax, Banish, Boot, Bounce, Bowl(er), Brush off, Bum's rush, Can, Cancel, Cashier, Catch, Chuck, Congé, Daff, Discard, Discharge, Dooce(d), Eject, Expulsion, Fire, Forget, Golden bowler, Heave-ho, Lay off, License, Marching orders, Mitten, Och, Oust, Pink-slip, Pooh-pooh, Prorogue, Push, Recall, Red card, Reform, Reject, Remove, Road, Sack, Scorn, Scout, Send, Shoo, Shrug off, Skittle out, Spit, Stump, Suka wena, Turn out, Via, Walking papers, Wicket, York

Disobedience, Disobedient, Disobey Contumacy, Defy, Flout, Insubordination, Rebel, Sit-in, Unruly, Wayward

Disorder(ly), Disordered Acidosis, Affective, Ague, Ailment, Anarchy, Ariot, Asthma, Ataxia, Bear garden, Betumbler, Catatonia, Chaos, Clutter, Collywobbles, Conduct, Confuse, Consumption, Contracture, Conversion, Defuse, Derange, Deray, Diabetes, Dishevel, DT's, Dyslexia, Dystrophy, Echolalia, Entropy, Farrago, Folie a deux, Greensickness, Grippe, Haemophilia, Heartburn, Huntingdon's chorea, Hypallage, Inordinate, Irregular, Mare's nest, ME, Mess, Misrule, Mistemper, →**MUDDLE**, Muss(y), Neurosis, Oncus, Onkus, Overset, Pandemonium, Para-, Phenylketonuria, Priapus, Psychomatic, Psychoneurosis, Psychopathic, Psychosis, Rile, Rumple, SAD, Schizothymia, Seborrh(o)ea, Shambolic, Shell-shock, Sickness, Slovenly, Snafu, Thalass(a)emia, Thought, Tobacco-heart, Tousle, Turmoil, Ulcer, Unhinge, Unrest, Unruly, Upheaval, Uproar, Upset, Virilism

▷**Disorder(ed)** *may indicate* an anagram

Dispatch Bowl, Celerity, Consign, Destroy, Dismiss, Epistle, Expede, Expedite, Export, Express, Gazette, Kibosh, Kill, Letter, Message, Missive, Note, Post, Pronto, Remit, Report, →**SEND**, Shank, Ship, Slaughter, Slay, Special

Dispensation, Dispense(r), Dispense with Absolve, Administer, Ax(e), Cashpoint, Chemist, Chop, Container, Distribute, Dose, Dropper, Exempt, Fountain, Handout, Hole in the wall, Indult, Inhaler, MPS, Optic, Pour, Scrap, Siphon, Soda fountain, Spinneret, Vendor

Displace(ment), Displaced Antevert, Blueshift, Chandler's wobble, Depose, Dethrone, Disturb, Ectopia, Ectopy, Evacuee, Fault, Heterotopia, Load, Luxate, Move, Oust, Proptosis, Ptosis, Reffo, Stir, Subluxation, Unsettle, Uproot, Upthrow, Valgus, Varus

Display, Display ground Air, Array, Blaze, Blazon, Brandish, Bravura, Dangle, Depict, Eclat, Epideictic, Etagere, Etalage, Evidence, Evince, Exhibition,

Exposition, Express, Extend, Extravaganza, Exude, Fanfare, Fireworks, Flash, Flaunt, Float, Flypast, Gala, Glitz, Gondola, Hang, Head-down, Head-up, Heroics, HUD, Iconic, Lay out, LCD, LED, Lek, Liquid crystal, Manifest, Motorcade, Mount, Muster, Ostentation, Outlay, Overdress, Pageant, Parade, Paraf(f)le, Peepshow, Pixel, Pomp, Post, Present(ation), Propale, Pyrotechnics, Rode, Rodeo, Roll-out, Ruffle, Scene, Screensaver, Scroll, Set piece, Shaw, →**SHOW**, Showcase, Sideshow, Sight, Spectacle, Splash, Splurge, Sport, Spree, State, Stunt, Swank, Tableau, Tattoo, Tournament, Turn out, Up, Vaunt, Wear, Window dressing

Displease(d), Displeasure Anger, Dischuffed, Humph, Irritate, Provoke, Umbrage
Dispose(d), Disposal, Disposition Arrange, Bestow, Bin, Cast, Despatch, Dump, Eighty-six, Ethos, Incline, Kybosh, Lay(-out), Mood, Prone, Riddance, Sale, Sell, Service, Settle, Spirit, Stagger, Throwaway, Will
▷**Disposed, Disposition** *may indicate* an anagram
Disposition Affectation, Attitude, Bent, Bias, Humour, Inclination, Kidney, Lie, Nature, Penchant, Propensity, Talent, Temper(ament), Trim
Disprove, Disproof, Disproval Debunk, Discredit, Invalidate, Negate, Rebut, Redargue, Reductio ad absurdum, Refel, Refute
Dispute(d), Disputant Altercation, Argue, Argy-bargy, At odds, Barney, Brangle, Brawl, Cangle, Case, Chaffer, Chorizont(ist), Contend, Contest, Contretemps, Controversy, Debate, Demarcation, Deny, Differ, Discept, Discuss, Eristic, Feud, Fracas, Fray, Gainsay, Haggle, Issue, Kilfud-yoking, Lock-out, Loggerheads, Militate, Moot, Ob and soller, Odds, Oppugn, Plea, Polemic, Pro-and-con, Quarrel, Query, →**QUESTION**, Rag, Resist, Run in, Skirmish, Slanging-match, Spar, Spat, Stickle, Stoush, Threap(it), Threep(it), Tiff, Tissue, Tug-of-love, Variance, Vendetta, Wrangle
Disqualify Debar, Incapacitate, Recuse, Reject, Unfit
Disregard(ed) Anomie, Anomy, Contempt, Disfavour, Flout, Forget, Ignore, Neglect, Oblivion, Omit, Overlook, Oversee, Pass, Pretermit, Slight, Spare, Violate, Waive
Disreputable, Disrepute Base, Black sheep, Bowsie, Disgrace, Grubby, Ill fame, Ken, Louche, Low, Lowlife, Notorious, Raffish, Ragamuffin, Ratbag, Reprobate, Rip, Scuzz(ball), Scuzzbag, Scuzzbucket, Seamy, Seamy side, Shady, Shameful, Shy, Shyster, Sleazy
Disrespect(ful) Contempt, Discourtesy, Impiety, Impolite, Irreverent, Levity, Naughty, Profane, Sacrilege, Slight, Uncivil, Violate
Disrupt(ion) Breach, Cataclasm, Dislocate, Disorder, Distract, Hamper, Hiatus, Interrupt, Jetlag, Mayhem, Perturb, Quonk, Ruffle, Sabotage, Screw, Upheaval
▷**Disruption** *may indicate* an anagram
Dissatisfaction Displeasure, Distaste, Humph, Umph
Dissent(er), Dissension, Dissenting Contend, Demur, Differ, Disagree, Discord, Dissident, Divisiveness, Faction, Flak, Friction, Heretic, Holmes, Jain, Leveller, Lollard, Maverick, Methodist, Negation, Noes, Non-CE, Non-con(formist), Occasional conformist, Old Believer, Pantile, Protest, Raskolnik, Recusant, Remonstrant, Sectary, Splinter group, →**STRIFE**, Vary, Wesleyan
Dissertation Essay, Excursus, Lecture, Paper, Thesis, Treatise
Dissipate(d) Debauch, Decadent, Diffuse, Dispell, Disperse, Dissolute, Gay, Revel, Scatter, Shatter, Squander, Waste
▷**Dissipated** *may indicate* an anagram

Dissolute Decadent, Degenerate, Hell, Immoral, Lax, Libertine, Licentious, Loose, Rake-helly, Rakish, Rip, Roué

▷**Dissolute** *may indicate* an anagram

Dissolve Deliquesce, Digest, Disband, Disunite, Lap, Liquesce, Melt, Terminate, Thaw

Distance Absciss(a), Afield, Apothem, Apse, Apsos, Breadth, Coss, Declination, Eloi(g)n, Elongation, Farness, Focal, Foot, Headreach, Height, Ice, Intercalumniation, Interval, Klick, Kos(s), Latitude, League, Length, Long-haul, Maintenance, Mean, Middle, Mileage, Ordinate, Parasang, Parsec, Range, Reserve, Rod, Skip, Span, Spitting, Stade, Step, Striking, Way, Yardage, Yojan

Distant Aloof, Chilly, Cold, Far, Frosty, Icy, Long (view), Offish, Outremer, Remote, Tele-, Timbuctoo, Timbuktu, Unfriendly, Yonder

Distaste(ful) Dégoût, Gory, Grimace, Repellent, Repugnant, Ropy, Scunner, Sour, Unpalatable, Unpleasant, Unsavoury

Distil(late), Distillation, Distiller, Distilling Alcohol, Alembic, Anthracine, Azeotrope, Brew, Cohobate, Condense, Destructive, Drip, Essence, Ethanol, Extract, Fractional, Naphtha, Paraffin wax, Pelican, Pyrene, Pyroligneous, Rosin, Turps, Vacuum, Vapour

▷**Distillation** *may indicate* an anagram

Distinct(ive) Apparent, Beside, Characteristic, Clear, Different, Discrete, Evident, Grand, Idiosyncratic, Individual, Peculiar, Plain, Separate, Several, Signal, → **SPECIAL**, Stylistic, Trenchant, Vivid

Distinction Beaut(y), Blue, Cachet, Class, Credit, Diacritic, Difference, Dignity, Diorism, Disparity, Division, Double-first, Eclat, Eminence, Entelechy, Honour, Laurels, Lustre, Mark, Mystique, Nicety, Note, Nuance, OM, Prominence, Quiddity, Rank, Renown, Speciality, Style, Title

Distinguish(ed), Distinguishable, Distinguishing Classify, Contrast, Demarcate, Denote, Diacritic, Different(iate), Discern, Discriminate, Distinct, Divide, Elevate, Eminent, Ennoble, Especial, Eximious, Mark, Nameworthy, Notable, Perceive, Pick out, Prestigious, Prominent, Rare, Renowned, Scerne, Secern, Special, Tell, VIP

Distort(ion), Distorted Anamorphosis, Bend, Bias, Caricature, Colour, Contort, Deface, Deform, Dent, Foreshorten, Fudge, Harmonic, Helium speech, Jaundiced, Mangle, Misshapen, Pervert, Rubato, Skew, Stretch, Thraw, Time-warp, Twist, → **WARP**, Wow, Wrest, Wring, Writhe, Wry

▷**Distort(ed)** *may indicate* an anagram

Distract(ed), Distraction Absent, Agitate, Amuse, Avocation, Bewilder, Divert, Éperdu, Forhaile, Frenetic, Loon, Lost, Madden, Mental, Nepenthe, Perplex, Red herring, Scatty, Upstage

▷**Distract(ed)** *may indicate* an anagram

Distress(ed), Distressing Afflict, Aggrieve, Agony, Ail, Alack, Alopecia, Anger, Anguish, Antique, Crise, Cut up, Desperation, Distraint, Dolour, Exigence, Extremity, Fraught, Fret, Gnaw, Grieve, Harass, Hardship, Harrow, Hurt, Ill, → **IN DISTRESS**, Irk, Misease, Misfortune, Need, Oppress, Pain, Poignant, Prey, Privation, Sad, Shorn, Sore, SOS, Straiten, Straits, Suffering, Tole, Torment, Tragic, Traumatic, → **TROUBLE**, Une(a)th, Unstrung, Upset, Wound

▷**Distress** *may indicate* a haircut

Distribute(d), Distribution, Distributor Allocate, Allot, Binomial, Busbar, Carve, Chi-square, Circulate, Colportage, Deal, Deliver(y), Deploy, Dish, Dispense, Dispose, Dissemination, Geographical, Issue, Ladle out, Lie, Lot,

Mete, Out(let), Pattern, Poisson, Prorate, Renter, Repartition, Send out, Serve, Share, Strew

▷**Distributed** *may indicate* an anagram

District Alsatia, Amhara, Arcadia, Ards, Area, Attica, Bail(l)iwick, Banat, Banate, Bannat, Barrio, Belt, Canton, Cantred, Circar, Classis, Community, Congressional, Diocese, Encomienda, End, Exurb, Falernian, Federal, Fitzrovia, Gaeltacht, Gau, Ghetto, Hundred, Land, Lathe, Liberty, Locality, Loin, Manor, Metropolitan, Nasik, →**NEIGHBOURHOOD**, Oblast, Pachalic, Pale, Pargana, Parish(en), Paroch, Pashalik, Patch, Peak, Pergunnah, Precinct, Province, Quarter, Quartier, Rape, →**REGION**, Reserve, Ride, Riding, Ruhr, Sanjak, Section, Sheading, Sircar, Sirkar, Soc, Soke(n), Stake, Stannary, Suburb, Sucken, Talooka, Taluk, Tenderloin, Township, Urban, Venue, Vicinage, Visne, Walk, Wapentake, Ward, Way, Zila, Zillah, Zone

Disturb(ance), Disturbed, Disturbing Ado, Aerate, Affray, Aggrieve, Agitate, Alarm, Atmospherics, Autism, Betoss, Brabble, Brainstorm, Brash, Brawl, Broil, Carfuffle, Choppy, Clatter, Collieshangie, Concuss, Delirium, Dementia, Derange, Desecrate, Disconcert, Disquiet, Dust, Eat, Feeze, Firestorm, Fray, Fret, Harass, Hoopla, Incident, Incommode, Infest, Interference, Interrupt, Intrude, Jee, Kerfuffle, Kick-up, Kurfuffle, Macabre, Molest, Muss, Neurosis, Outbreak, Prabble, Ramp, Riot, Ripple, Rock, Roil, Romage, Roughhouse, Rouse, Ruckus, Ruction, Ruffle, Rumpus, Shake, Shindig, Shindy, Shook-up, Stashie, Static, Steer, Stir, Stress, Sturt, Tremor, Troppo, Trouble, Turbulent, Turmoil, Unquiet, Unrest, Unsettle, Upheaval, Uproot, →**UPSET**, Vex, Whistler

▷**Disturb(ed)** *may indicate* an anagram

Ditch Abandon, Abolish, Barathron, Barathrum, Cast aside, Channel, Chuck, Cunette, Delf, Delph, Dike, Discard, Donga, Drainage, Drop, Dyke, Eliminate, Euripus, Foss(e), Graft, Grip, Gully, Ha(w)-ha(w), Jettison, Khor, Last, Level, Lode, Moat, Nal(l)a(h), Nulla(h), Rean, Reen, Rhine, Rid, Sea, Sheuch, Sheugh, Sike, Sloot, Sluit, Spruit, Stank, Sunk-fence, Syke, Tenail(le), Trench

Dive, Diver(s), Diving Armstand, Backflip, Belly-flop, Crash, Dart, Den, Didapper, Duck, Embergoose, File, Flop, Free-fall, Frogman, Full-gainer, Gainer, Grebe, Guillemot, Half-gainer, Header, Honkytonk, Jackknife, Joint, Ken, Loom, Loon, Lungie, Merganser, Night club, Nitery, Nose, Pass, Pearl, Pickpocket, Pike, Plong(e), Plummet, Plunge, Plutocrat, Pochard, Poker, Power, Puffin, Saturation, Sawbill, Scoter, Scuba, Skin, Snake-bird, Sound, Speakeasy, Stage, Step-to, Stoop, Submerge, Swallow, Swan, Swoop, Tailspin, Urinant, Urinator, Zoom

Diverge(nce), Divergent Branch, Deviate, Heterochrony, Spread, Swerve, Variant, Veer

Divers(e), Diversify Alter, Branch out, Dapple, Different, Interlard, Intersperse, Manifold, Many, Mixed, Motley, Multifarious, Separate, Sundry, Variegate, Various, Vary

Diversion, Divert(ing) Amuse, Avocation, Beguile, Cone, Deflect, Detour, Disport, Dissuade, Distract, Droll, Entertain, Game, Hare, Hijack, Hive off, Hobby, Interlude, Pastime, Pleasure, Prolepsis, Ramp, Red-herring, Reflect, Refract, Reroute, Ruse, Shunt, Sideline, Sideshow, Sidetrack, Siphon, Smokescreen, Sport, Stalking-horse, Steer, Stratagem, Sublimation, Sway, Switch, Syphon, Tickle, Upstage, Yaw, Zany

▷**Diverting** *may indicate* an anagram

Divide(d), Divider, Dividing, Division Abkhazia, Adzharia, Apportion, Balkanise, Band, Bifurcate, Bipartite, Bisect, Branch, Cantle, Chancery, Cleave, Cleft, Comminute, Commot(e), Continental, Counter-pale, Cusp, Cut, Deal, Demerge, Dimidiate, Discide, Dismember, Estrange, Fork, Furcate, Great, Indent, Isere, Lot, Montgomery, Parcel, Part, Partite, Partition, Party wall, Pentomic, Plebs, Polarise, Potential, Precisive, Quotient, Ramify, Rend, Rift, Sectionalise, Separate, Sever, Share, →**SPLIT**, Stanza, Sunder, Transect, Tribalism, Trisect, Twixt, Utgard, Voltage, Watershed, Zone

Dividend Bonus, Contango, Div, Interim, Into, Numerator, Share

Divine, Divine presence, Divinity Acoemeti, Aitu, Ambrose, Atman, Avatar, Beatific, Blessed, Celestial, Chaplain, Clergyman, Conjecture, Curate, DD, Deduce, Deific, Deity, Douse, Dowse, Ecclesiastic, Empyreal, Forecast, Foretell, Fuller, →**GOD**, →**GODDESS**, Godhead, Godlike, Guess, Hallowed, Hariolate, Heavenly, Holy, Hulse, Immortal, Inge, Isiac, Mantic, Numen, Olympian, Pontiff, Predestinate, Predict, Presage, Priest, Prophesy, RE, Rector, RI, Rimmon, Scry, Sense, Seraphic, Shechinah, Shekinah, Spae, Supernal, Theandric, Theanthropic, Theologise, Theology, Triune

Division, Divisible Arcana, Arm, Arrondissement, Banat(e), Bar, Branch, Caesura, Canto, Canton, Cantred, Cantref, Caste, Category, Chapter, Classification, Cleft, Cloison, Clove, Commune, Compartment, Corps, County, Crevasse, Curia, Department, Dichotomy, Disagreement, Disunity, Div, Fork, Fragmentation, Glires, Grisons, Gulf, Hapu, Hedge, Hide, Holland, Hotchpot, Hundred, Inning, Lathe, Leet, Legion, List, Lobe, Mannion, Maturation, Nome, Oblast, Over, Part, Partition, Period, Pipe, Pitaka, Platoon, Polarisation, Presidency, Province, Quartering, Quotition, Rape, Region, Reservation, Riding, Schism, Section, Sector, Segment, Sept(ate), Sever, Share, Shed, Shire, Stage, Stake, Subheading, Suborder, Tahsil, Theme, Trichotomy, Trio, Troop, Unit, Wapentake, Ward

Divorce(d) Alienate, Apart, Diffarreation, Dissolution, Dissolve, Disunion, Div, Estrange, Get(t), Isolate, Part, Put away, Reno, Separate, Sequester, →**SUNDER**, Talak, Talaq, Unhitch

Divulge Confess, Disclose, Expose, Publish, Reveal, Split, Tell, Unveil, Utter

Dizziness, Dizzy Beaconsfield, Ben, Blonde, Capricious, Dinic, Disraeli, Giddy, Giglot, Lightheaded, Mirligoes, Scotodinia, Scotomania, Swimming, Vertiginous, →**VERTIGO**, Woozy

Do(es), Doing Accomplish, Achieve, Act, Anent, Barbecue, Bash, Beano, Blow-out, Char, Cheat, Chisel, Cod, Con, Cozen, Deed, Defraud, Dich, Diddle, Dish, Div, Doobrie, Doth, Dupe, Effectuate, Enact, Event, Execute, Fare, Fleece, Function, Fuss, Gull, Handiwork, Hoax, Imitate, Jamboree, Measure up, Mill, Occasion, Perform, Perpetrate, Provide, Rip off, Rook, Same, Serve, Settle, Shindig, Soiree, Spif(f)licate, Suffice, Swindle, Thrash, Thrive, Tonic, Up to, Ut

▷**Do** *may indicate an anagram*

Dock(er), Docked, Docks Abridge, Barber, Basin, Bistort, Bob, Camber, Canaigre, Clip, Crop, Curta(i)l, Cut, Deduct, De-tail, Dry, Floating, Grapetree, Knotweed, Lay-up, Longshoreman, Lop, Lumper, Marina, Monk's rhubarb, Moor, Off-end, Pare, Patience, Pen, Pier, Quay, Rhubarb, Rumex, Rump, Seagull, Shorten, Snakeweed, Sorrel, Sourock, Stevedore, Tilbury, Watersider, Wet, Wharf, Yard

Doctor(s) Alter, Arnold, Barefoot, Barnardo, Bleeder, BMA, Bones, Breeze, Bright, Brighton, Brown, Caius, Castrate, Clinician, Cook, Crocus, Cup(per),

Cure(r), Dale, Death, Diagnose, Dolittle, Dr, Erasmus, Extern(e), Fake, Falsify, Family, Faustus, Fell, Fiddle, Finlay, Flying, Foster, Fu manchu, Galen, GP, Guillotin(e), Healer, Homeopath, Houseman, Hyde, Intern, Internist, Jekyll, Jenner, Johnson, Juris utriusque, Kildare, Lace, Leach, Leech, Linacre, Load, Locum, Luke, Manette, Manipulate, Massage, MB, MD, Medicate, Medico, Mganga, Minister, Misrepresent, MO, MOH, Molla(h), Moreau, Mulla(h), Myologist, Neuter, No, Ollamh, Ollav, Paediatrician, Panel, Pangloss, Paracelsus, Paramedic, Pedro, PhD, Physician, Pill(s), Practitioner, Quack, Quacksalver, Rabbi, RAMC, Registrar, Resident, Rhinologist, Rig, Rorschach, Salk, Saw, Sawbones, School, Script, Seraphic, Seuss, Slammer, Slop, Spay, Spin, Surgeon, Syn, Therapist, Thorne, Treat, Vet, Water, Watson, Who, Wind, Witch

▷**Doctor(ed)** *may indicate* an anagram

Doctrine Adamitism, Adoptionism, Archology, Blairism, Cab(b)ala, Cacodoxy, Calvanism, Catastrophism, Chiliasm, Credo, Creed, Diabology, Ditheism, Divine right, Dogma, Doxie, Doxy, Dualism, Dysteleology, Encratism, Eschatology, Esotery, Eutychian, Evangel, Febronianism, Federalism, Gnosticism, Gospel, Henotheism, Hesychasm, Holism, Idealism, Illuminism, Immaterialism, Immersionism, Indeterminism, Islam, Ism, Jansenism, Lore, Machtpolitik, Malthusian, Materialism, Modalism, Monadism, Monothel(et)ism, Monroe, Neomonianism, Panentheism, Pantheism, Pelagianism, Personalism, Physiocracy, Pluralism, Pragmatism, Premillennialism, Preterition, Probabilism, Psilanthropism, Quietism, Real presence, Reformism, Scotism, Secularism, Sheria, Shibboleth, Solidism, Soteriology, Subjectivism, Substantialism, Syndicalism, Synergism, System, Theory, Thomism, Transubstantiation, Trialism, Tridentine, Universalism

Document(s), Documentary Archive, Blog, Brevet, Bumph, Carta, Certificate, Charge sheet, Charter, Chop, Contract, Conveyance, Copy, Covenant, Daftar, Deed, Diploma, Docket, Doco, Dompass, Dossier, E-journal, Elegit, Escrol(l), Escrow, Fieri Facias, Fly-on-the-wall, Form, Green paper, Holograph, Indenture, Latitat, Logbook, Mandamus, Papers, Permit, Policy, Production, Pro forma, Ragman, Ragment, Roll, Roul(e), Screed, Scroll, Sea brief, Statute, Voucher, Waybill, Weblog, Webpage, White paper, Writ

Dodge(r), Dodgy Artful, Avoid, Column, Elude, Evade, Evasion, Evite, Idler, Jink, Jook, Jouk, Malinger, Racket, Ruse, Scam, Shirk, Sidestep, Skip, Slalom, Slinter, Tip, Trick, Twist, Urchin, Weave, Welsh, Wheeze, Wire, Wrinkle

Dog(s), Doglike Assistance, Attack, Bowwow, Canes, Canidae, Canine, Cynic, Dropper, Feet, Hearing, Hot, Huntaway, Isle, Kennel, Native, Pursue, Ranger, Ratter, Shadow, Sleuthhound, Sniffer, Stalk, Strong-eye, Tag, Tail, Therapy, Toby, Top, Toto, Tracker, Trail, Truffle, Tumbler, Water dog, Working

Dogma(tic), Dogmatist Assertive, Belief, Bigot, Bigotry, Conviction, Creed, Doctrinal, En tête, Ewe, Fundamental, Ideology, Literal, Opinionative, Pedagogic, Peremptory, Pontifical, Positive

Dole Alms, Batta, B(u)roo, Give, Grief, Maundy, Mete, Payment, Pittance, Ration, → **SHARE**, Tichborne, UB, Vail, Vales

Doll(y) Barbie®, Bimbo, Bobblehead, Common, Corn, Crumpet, Dress, Dutch, Ewe, Girly, Golliwog, Kachina, Kewpie®, Maiden, Marionette, Matryoshka, Maumet, Mommet, Moppet, Mummet, Ookpik®, Ornament, Parton, Pean, Peen, Peggy, Pein, Pene, Poppet, Puppet, Ragdoll, Russian, Sindy®, Sis(ter), Sitter, Tearsheet, Toy, Trolley, Varden, Washboard

Dollar(s) Balboa, Boliviano, Buck, Cob, Euro, Fin, Greenback, Iron man, Peso, Piastre, Pink, S, Sand, Sawbuck, Sawhorse, Scrip, Smacker, Spin, Wheel

▷**Dolly** *may indicate* an anagram

Dolphin Amazon, Arion, Beluga, Bottlenose, Cetacean, Coryphene, Delphinus, Grampus, Lampuka, Lampuki, Mahi-mahi, Meer-swine, Porpess(e), Porpoise, Risso's, River, Sea-pig

Dome(-shaped) Bubble, Cap, Cupola, Dagoba, Geodesic, Head, Imperial, Louvre, Millennium, Onion, Periclinal, Pleasure, Rotunda, Stupa, Tee, Tholobate, Tholos, Tholus, Tope, Vault

Domestic(ate) Char, Cinderella, Cleaner, Dom, Esne, Familiar, Fireside, Homebody, Home-keeping, Homely, House, Housetrain, Humanise, In-service, Interior, Internal, Intestine, Maid, Menial, →**SERVANT**, Swadeshi, Tame, Woman

Dominate, Dominance, Dominant, Domination Alpha, Ascendancy, Baasskap, Bethrall, Boss, Clou, Coerce, Control, Enslave, Henpeck, Maisterdome, Master, Mesmerise, Momism, Monopolise, O(v)ergang, Overmaster, Override, Overshadow, Power, Preponderant, Preside, Rule, Soh, →**SUBDUE**, Subjugate, Top dog, Tower

Dominion Canada, Dom, Empire, Khanate, NZ, Realm, Reame, Reign, →**RULE**, Supremacy, Sway, Territory

Domino(es) Card, Fats, Mask, Matador

Don(s) Academic, Address, Assume, Caballero, Capo, Endue, Faculty, Fellow, Garb, Giovanni, Grandee, Indew, Juan, Lecturer, Prof, Quixote, Reader, Señor, Spaniard, Tutor, Wear

Donate, Donation Aid, Bestow, Contribution, Gift, Give, Offertory, Tribute

Done Achieved, Complete, Crisp, Ended, Executed, Had, Over, Spitcher, Tired, Weary

Donkey Ass, Burro, Cardophagus, Cuddie, Cuddy, Dapple, Dick(e)y, Eeyore, Engine, Funnel, Fussock, Genet(te), Ignoramus, Jackass, Jacket, Jennet, Jenny, Jerusalem pony, Kulan, Modestine, Moke, Mule, Neddy, Onager, Stupid, Years

Donor Benefactor, Bestower, Blood, Settlor

Doom(ed) Condemned, Date, Destine, Destiny, →**FATE**, Fay, Fey, Fie, Goner, Ill-fated, Ill-omened, Ill-starred, Lot, Predestine, Preordain, Ragnarok, Ruined, Sentence, Spitcher, Star-crossed, Weird

Door(s), Doorstep, Doorway Aperture, Communicating, Drecksill, Dutch, Elephant, Entry, Exit, Fire, Folding, French, Front, Gull-wing, Haik, Hake, Hatch, Heck, Ingress, Jib, Lintel, Louver, Louvre, Muntin, Oak, Open, Overhead, Patio, Portal, Postern, Revolving, Rory, Screen, Sliding, Stable, Stage, Storm, Street, Swing, Tailgate, Trap, Up and over, Vomitory, Wicket, Yett

Doorkeeper, Doorman Bouncer, Commissionaire, Concierge, Dvornik, Guardian, Janitor, Nab, Ostiary, Porter, Tiler, Tyler, Usher

Dope Acid, Amulet, Bang, Coke, Crack, Datum, →**DRUG**, Dunderhead, Facts, Fuss, Gen, Goose, Info, Latest, Narcotic, Nitwit, Nobble, Rutin, Sedate, →**STUPID PERSON**

Doppelganger Double, Look-alike, Ringer

Dormitory Barrack, Bunkhouse, Dorter, Dortour, Hall, Hostel, Quarters

Dosage, Dose Absorbed, Administer, Aperient, Cascara, Draught, Drug, Fix, Kilogray, Lethal, →**MEASURE**, Permissible, Physic, Posology, Potion, Powder, Standing off

Dot(s), Dotted, Dotty Absurd, Blip, Bullet (point), Criblé, Dieresis, Dit, Dower, Dowry, Engrailed, Intersperse, Leader, Lentiginous, Limp, Micro, Occult, Or,

Particle, Pinpoint, Pixel, → **POINT**, Pointillé, Polka, Precise, Punctuate, Punctulate, Punctum, Schwa, Semé(e), Set, Speck, Spot, Sprinkle, Stigme, Stipple, Stud, Tap, Tittle, Tocher, Trema, Umlaut

Dote, Dotage, Doting, Dotard Adore, Anile, Anility, Cocker, Dobbie, Idolise, Imbecile, Pet, Prize, Senile, Spoon(e)y, Tendre, Twichild

Double(s) Alter-ego, Amphibious, Ancipital, Bi-, Bifold, Binate, Counterpart, Crease, Dimeric, Doppel-ganger, Dual, Duo, Duple(x), Duplicate, Equivocal, Fetch, Fold, Foursome, Geminate, Gimp, Image, Ingeminate, Ka, Look-alike, Loop, Martingale, Pair, Parlay, Polyseme, Reflex, Replica, Ringer, Run, Similitude, Spit, Stuntman, Trot, Turnback, Twae, → **TWIN**, Two(fold), Two-ply

Doubt(s), Doubter, Doubtful Agnostic, Ambiguous, Aporia, Askance, But, Debatable, Discredit, Distrust, Dubiety, Dubitate, Erm, Hesitate, Hum, Iffy, Incertitude, Misgiving, Mistrust, Or, Precarious, Qualm, Query, → **QUESTION**, Rack, Reservation, Scepsis, Sceptic, Scruple, Second thoughts, Shady, Shy, Sic, Skepsis, Sus, Suspect, Suss, Thomas, Thos, Umph, Uncertain, Unsure, Waver

Dough(y) Boodle, Cake, Calzone, Cash, Duff, Dumpling, Gnocchi, Hush-puppy, Knish, Loot, Magma, Masa, Money, Pasta, Paste, Polenta, Pop(p)adum, Ready, Sad, Spondulicks

Doughnut Bagel, Cruller, Fried cake, Knish, Sinker, Torus

Dour Glum, Hard, Mirthless, Morose, Reest, Reist, Sinister, Sullen, Taciturn

Douse Dip, Drench, Extinguish, Snuff, Splash

Dove Collared, Columbine, Culver, Cushat, Diamond, Doo, Ground, Ice-bird, Mourning, Pacifist, → **PIGEON**, Ring, Rock, Stock, Turtle

Dowdy Frumpish, Mopsy, Mums(e)y, Plain Jane, Shabby, Sloppy, Slovenly

Down(s), Downbeat, Downsize, Downward, Downy A bas, Abase, Abattu, Alow, Amort, Bank, Below, Blue, Cast, Catabasis, Chapfallen, Comous, Cottony, Crouch, Darling, Dejected, Demoralised, Descent, Disconsolate, Dowl(e), Drink, Duck, Epsom, Feather, Fledge, Floccus, Flue, Fluff, Fly, Fuzz, Glum, Goonhilly, Ground, Hair, Hangdog, Hill, Humble, Humiliate, Lanate, Lanugo, Latitant, Losing, Low, Lower, Miserable, Moxa, Nap, Neck, North Wessex, Oose, Ooze, Owing, Pappus, Pennae, Pile, Plumage, Quark, Quash, Repress, Scuttle, Sebum, Sussex, Swallow, Thesis, Thistle, Tomentum, Under, Vail, Watership, Wretched

Downcast Abject, Chapfallen, Dejected, Despondent, Disconsolate, Dumpish, Glum, Hopeless, Melancholy, Woebegone

Downfall, Downpour Brash, Cataract, Collapse, Deluge, Doom, Fate, Flood, Hail, Onding, Overthrow, Plash, Rain, Rainstorm, Ruin, Shower, Soak, Thunder-plump, Torrent, Undoing, Waterspout

Downright Absolute, Arrant, Bluff, Candid, Clear, Complete, Flat, Plumb, Plump, Pure, Rank, Sheer, Stark, Utter

Downturn Decrease, Recession, Slump

Dowry Dot, Dower, Lobola, Lobolo, Merchet, Portion, Settlement, Tocher

Doze, Dozy Ca(u)lk, Catnap, Dove(r), Nap, Nod, Semi-coma, Sleep, Sleepyhead, Slip, Slumber

Drab Cloth, Dell, Dingy, Dowdy, Dreary, Dull, Dun, Ecru, Hussy, Isabel(line), Lifeless, Livor, Olive, Prosaic, Pussel, Quaker-colour, Rig, Road, Scarlet woman, Slattern, Sloven, Strumpet, Subfusc, Tart, Taupe, Trull, Wanton, Whore

Draft Bank, Bill, Cheque, Conscript, Draw, Ebauche, Essay, Landsturm, Minute, MS, Outline, Paste up, Plan, Press, Protocol, Recruit, Rough, Scheme, Scroll, Scrowle, → **SKETCH**

Drag Car, Cigarette, Clothing, Drail, Dredge, Drogue, Elicit, Eonism, Epicene, Extort, Gender-bender, Hale, Hang, Harl, → **HAUL**, Keelhaul, La Rue, Liability, Lug, Nuisance, Puff, Pull, Rash, Sag, Schlep, Shockstall, Shoe, Skidpan, Sled, Snake, Snig, Sweep, Toke, Tote, Tow, Trail, Trailing vortex, Train, Travail, Travois, Trawl, Treck, Trek, Tug, Tump

Dragon Aroid, Basilisk, Bel, Bellemère, Chaperon(e), Chindit, Draco, Drake, Komodo, Kung-kung, Ladon, Lindworm, Opinicus, Python, Rouge, Serpent, Wantley, Wivern, Worm, Wyvern, Yacht

Drain(ed), Drainage, Drainer, Draining, Drainpipe Bleed, Brain, Buzz, Can(n)ula, Catchment, Catchwater, Channel, Cloaca, Colander, Condie, Culvert, Cundy, Cunette, Delf, Delph, Dewater, Ditch, Dry, Ea(u), → **EMPTY**, Emulge(nt), Enervate, Exhaust, Fleet, Gargoyle, Grating, Grip, Gully, Gutter, Ketavothron, Kotabothron, Lade, Leach, Leech, Limber, Lose, Lymphatic, Milk, Nalla(h), Pump, Rack, Rone, Sanitation, Sap, Scalpins, Scupper, Seton, Sew(er), Sheuch, Sheugh, Shore, Silver, Sink, Siver, Sluice, Sluse, Small-trap, Soakaway, Sough, Spend, Spunge, Stank, Suck, Sump, Sure, Syver, Tile, Trench, Trocar, Unwater, Ureter, U-trap

Dram Drink, Drop, Portion, Snifter, Tickler, Tiff, Tot, Wet

Drama(tic), Drama school Azione, Charade, Comedy, Costume, Epic, Eumenides, Farce, Heroic, Histrionic, Kabuki, Kathakali, Kitchen sink, Legit, Legitimate, Mask, Masque, Mime, Moralities, Music, No, Nogaku, Noh, Oresteia, Piece, Play, RADA, Sangeet, Scenic, Screenplay, Sensational, Serial, Singspiel, Soap, Spinto, Stagy, Striking, Sudser, Tetralogy, Theatric, The Birds, Thespian, Tragedy, Unities, Wagnerian, Wild

Drape(ry) Adorn, Coverlet, Coverlid, Curtain, Festoon, Fold, Hang, Lambrequin, Swag, Swathe, Valance, Veil, Vest

Draught(s), Draughtsman(ship) Aloetic, Apozem, Breeze, Checkers, Chequer, Dam, Dams, Design, Dose, Drench, Drink, Fish, Gulp, Gust, Haal, Hippocrene, King, Line, Men, Nightcap, Outline, Plan, Potation, Potion, Puff, Pull, Quaff, Sketch, Sleeping, Slug, Swig, Tracer, Veronal, Waft, Waucht, Wind

▷**Draught** *may refer to* fishing

Draw (off), Drawer(s), Drawing, Drawn Adduct, Allure, Attract, Attrahent, Blueprint, Bottom, Cartoon, Charcoal, Cityscape, Cock, Crayon, Dead-heat, Delineate, Dentistry, Derivation, Describe, Detail, Diagram, Doodle, Dr, Draft, Drag, Dress, Educe, Elevation, Elicit, Elongate, Entice, Equalise, Escribe, Evaginate, Even-steven, Eviscerate, Extract, Fet(ch), Freehand, Fusain, Gather, Gaunt, Glorybox, Goalless, Graffiti, Graphics, Gravitate, Gut, Haggard, Hale, Halve, Haul, Identikit, Indraft, Induce, Indue, Inhale, Isometric, Lead, Lengthen, Limn, Line, Longbow, Lots, Lottery, Magnet, Mechanical, Monotint, No-score, Orthograph, Pantalet(te)s, Panty, Pastel(list), Pen and ink, Perpetual check, Petroglyph, Profile, Protract, Pull, RA, Rack, Raffle, Realize, Reel, Remark, Scenography, Scent, Seductive, Sepia, Sesquipedalian, Shottle, Shuttle, Silverpoint, Siphon, Sketch, Slub, Snig, Spin, Stalemate, Stretch, Study, Stumps, Sweepstake, Syphon, Tap, Taut, Technical, Tempera, Tempt, Tenniel, Tie, Till, Toke, Tole, Tombola, Top, Tose, Tow(age), Toze, Trace, Traction, Trice, Troll, Tug, Unsheathe, Uplift, Visual, Wash, Working

▷**Draw** *may indicate* something to smoke

▷**Drawn** *may indicate* an anagram

Dread(ed), Dreadful Angst, Anxiety, Awe, Awful, Chronic, Dearn, Dern, Dire, Fear, Formidable, Funk, Ghastly, Horrendous, → **HORROR**, Nightmare,

Nosophobia, Penny, Redoubt, Shocking, Sorry, Terrible, Thing, Tragic, Unholy, Willies

Dream(er), Dream home, Dreamland, Dreamlike, Dream state, Dreamy Absent, Aisling, Alchera, Alcheringa, Ambitious, American, Aspire, Desire, Drowsy, Dwa(u)m, Fantast, Fantasy, Faraway, Fugue, Idealise, Illusion, Imagine, Joseph, Languor, Mare, Mirth, Moon, Morpheus, Muse, Nightmare, On(e)iric, Pensive, Phantom, Pipe, Rêveur, Romantic, Somniate, Stargazer, Surreal, Sweven, Trance, Trauma, Utopia, Vague, Vision, Walter Mitty, Wet, Wool-gathering

Dreary Bleak, Desolate, Dismal, Doleful, Dreich, Dull, Gloom, Gousty, Gray, Grey, Oorie, Ourie, Owrie, Sad

Dress(ing), Dressed Adjust, Adorn, Align, Apparel, Array, Attire, Attrap, Bandage, Boast, Clad, →**CLOTHING**, Comb, Compost, Compress, Curry, Decent, Deck, Deshabille, Dink, Don, Dub, Dubbin, Enrobe, Fertiliser, French, Frou-frou, Garnish, Gauze, Get-up, Girt, Gussy up, →**HABIT**, Immantle, Italian, Jaconet, Ketchup, Line, Lint, Livery, Marie Rose, Mayonnaise, Mulch, Oil, Pad, Patch, Plaster, Pledget, Pomade, Potash, Poultice, Prank, Preen, Prepare, Rational, Rehearsal, Rémoulade, Rig, Salad, Salad cream, Sartorial, Sauce, Sterile, Tartare, Taw, Thousand Island, Tiff, Tire, Toilet, Treat, Trick, Trim, Vinaigrette, Wear, Wig, Window

▷**Dressed up, Dressing** *may indicate* an anagram

Dresser Adze, Almery, Bureau, Chest, Costumier, Couturier, Deuddarn, Dior, Lady's maid, Lair, Lowboy, Sideboard, Transvestite, Tridarn, Welsh

Dribble Drip, Drivel, Drop, Slaver, Slop, Trickle

Drift(ing), Drifter Becalmed, Continental, Crab, Cruise, Current, Digress, Drumlin, Float, Flow, Heap, Impulse, Maunder, Nomad, North Atlantic, Plankton, Purport, Rorke, Sail, Slide, Swan, Tendence, Tendency, →**TENOR**, Tramp, Waft, Wander

Drill(ing) Archimedean, Auger, Bore, Burr, Close order, Educate, Exercise, Form, Hammer, Inculcate, Jackhammer, Jerks, Kelly, Monkey, Pack, PE, Pierce, Pneumatic, PT, Reamer, Ridge, Rig, Rock, Rope, Seeder, Sow, Square-bashing, Teach, Train, Twill, Twist, Usage, Wildcat

Drink(er), Drinking, Drunk(enness) AA, Absorb, Alky, A pip out, Bacchian, Bat, Bender, Beverage, Bev(v)y, Bibber, Binge, Bladdered, Blind, Blitzed, Bloat, Blootered, Blotto, Bombed, Boose, Booze, Borachio, Bosky, Bottled, Bouse, Bowsey, Bowsie, Bracer, Brahms and Liszt, Brew, Bucket, Bumper, CAMRA, Capernoitie, Cap(p)ernoity, Carafe, Carousal, Cat-lap, Chaser, Chota peg, Corked, Cot case, Crapulous, Crocked, Cuppa, Cut, Demitasse, Dionysian, Dipsomaniac, Discombobulated, Double, Down, Drain, Draught, Drop, Ebriate, Elixir, Energy, Entire, Eye-opener, Feni, Feny, Finger, Flush, Fou, Fuddled, Full, Gnat's piss, Grog, Half-cut, Half-seas-over, Happy, Heavy wet, High, Hobnob, Hogshead, Hooker, Hophead, Imbibe, In-cups, Indulge, Infusion, Inked, In liquor, Insulse, Intemperate, Irrigate, Jag, Jakey, Jar, Kaylied, Lager lout, Langered, Lap, Legless, Lethean, →**LIQUOR**, Lit, Loaded, Lord, Lower, Lush(y), Maggoty, Mallemaroking, Maudlin, Mellow, Merry, Moon-eyed, Mops and brooms, Mortal, Mug, Mullered, Neck, Nog(gin), Obfuscated, Ocean, Oiled, On, One, Overshot, Paid, Paint, Paralytic, Partake, Particular, Pickled, Pick-me-up, Pie-eyed, Pint(a), Piss-artist, Pissed, Pisshead, Pisspot, Piss-up, Pixil(l)ated, Pledge, Potion, Primed, Quaff, Quencher, Quickie, Rat-arsed, Ratted, Refreshment, Rolling, Rotten, Rummer, St Martin's evil, Screamer, Screwed,

Sea, Shebeen, Shotover, Sink, Sip(ple), Skinned, Slake, Slewed, Sloshed, Slug, Slurp, Smashed, Snort, Soak, Soused, Sponge, Squiffy, Stewed, Stimulant, Stinko, Stoned, Stukkend, Sucker, Suckle, Suiplap, Sup, Swacked, Swallow, Swig, Swill, Tank, Tanked up, Tape, Tiddl(e)y, Tiff, Tight, Tincture, Tipple, Tipsy, Tope, Toss, Tot, Two-pot, Under the weather, Upsey Dutch, Up the pole, Usual, Wash, Wat, Well away, Well-oiled, Wet, Winebag, Wine bibber, Wino, Wish-wash, Woozy, Wrecked, Zonked

Drip Bore, Dribble, Drop, Gloop, Gutter, IV, Leak, Milksop, Seep, Splatter, Stillicide, Trickle, Wimp

Drive(r), Driving, Drive out AA, Actuate, Ambition, Aroint, Automatic, Backseat, Banish, Battue, Beetle, Belt, Ca', Cabby, Campaign, Carman, Carriage, Charioteer, Chauffeur, Coachee, Coachy, Coact, Coerce, Countershaft, Crankshaft, Crew, Crowd, Disk, Dislodge, Dr, Drover, Drum, Dynamic, Economy, Eject, Emboss, Energy, Enforce, Engine, Exorcise, Faze, Ferret, Fire, Flash, Fluid, Force, Four-wheel, Front-wheel, Fuel, Goad, Golfer, Hack, Hammer, Haste, Heard, Helmsman, Herd, Hie, Hish, Hiss, Hoon, Hoosh, Hot-rod, Hoy, Hunt, Hurl, Hydrostatic, Impel, Impetus, Impinge, Impulse, Instinct, Jehu, Jockey, Juggernaut, Key(ring), Lash, Libido, Lunge, Mahout, Make, Mall, M(a)cGuffin, Micro, Motor, Motorman, Muleteer, Offensive, Oomph, Peg, Penetrate, Piston, Pocket, Power, P-plater, Propel, Push, Put, Quill, RAC, Rack, Rally(e), Ram, Rear-wheel, Rebut, Ride, Road, Roadhog, Run, Sales, Scorch, Screw, Scud, Senna, Sex, Shepherd, Shoo, Shover, Spank, Spin, Spur, Start, Steer, Stroke, Sunday, Sweep, Swift, Task-master, Teamster, Tee, Test, Testosterone, Thrust, Thumb, Toad, Toe and heel, Tool, Tootle, Trot, Trucker, Truckie, Truckman, Turn, Twoccer, Two-stroke, Urge, Urgence, USB, Wagoner, Warp, Wood, Wreak, Zest

Drivel Balderdash, Blather, Blether(skate), Drip, Drool, Humbug, Nonsense, Pap, Rot, Salivate, Slabber, Slaver, Trash

Drizzle Dew, Drow, Haze, Mist, Mizzle, Roke, Scotch mist, Scouther, Scowther, Serein, Skiffle, Smir(r), Smur, Spit, Sprinkle

Droop(y), Drooping Cernuous, Decline, Epinasty, Flabby, Flag, Jowled, Languish, Lill, Limp, Lob, Loll, Lop, Nutate, Oorie, Ourie, Owrie, Peak, Pendulous, Ptosis, Slink, Slouch, Slump, Weeping, Welk(e), Wilt, Wither

Drop(s), Dropping Acid, Airlift, Apraxia, Asperge, Bag, Bead, Beres, Blob, Butter, Cadence, Calve, Cascade, Cast, Chocolate, Cowpat, Dap, Decrease, Delayed, Descent, Deselect, Dew, Dink, Dip, Downturn, Drappie, Drib(let), Ean, Ease, Ebb, Escarp(ment), Fall, Floor, Flop, Fruit, Fumet, Gallows, Glob(ule), Gout(te), Guano, Gutta, Guttate, Ha-ha, Heel-tap, Instil, Knockout, Land, Lapse, Minim, Modicum, Muff, Mute, Omit, Pilot, Plap, Plonk, Plop, Plummet, Plump, Plunge, Plunk, Precepit, Precipice, (Prince) Rupert's, Rain, Relegate, Scat, Scrap, Scrub, Shed, Sip, Skat, Slurry, Spat, Spill, Splash, Spraint, Stilliform, Tass, Taste, Tear, Thud, Trapdoor, Turd, Virga, Wrist

Drop-out Beatnik, Hippie, Hippy

Drought Dearth, Drouth, Lack, Thirst

Drove(r) Band, Crowd, Flock, Herd, Host, Masses, Mob, Overlander, Puncher

Drown(ed), Drowning Drook, Drouk, Engulf, Inundate, Noyade, Overcome, Sorrows, Submerge

Drudge(ry) Boswell, Devil, Dogsbody, Fag, Grind, Hack, Hackwork, Hireling, Jackal, Johnson, Menial, Plod, Scrub, Slave(y), Snake, Spadework, Stooge, Sweat, Thraldom, Toil, Trauchle, Treadmill

Drug(ged) Anorectic, Antabuse®, Antarthritic, Anti-depressant, Antimetabolite, Antipyrine, Antiviral, Bag, Base, Blow, Blue devil, Bolus, Bomber, Boo, Cathartic, Chalybeate, Clofibrate, Clot buster, Contraceptive, Corrigent, Custom, Dadah, Deck, Depot, Designer, Dope, Dose, Downer, Elixir, Fantasy, Fertility, Fig, Gateway, Gear, Generic, Hallucinogen, Hard, High, Hocus, Hypnotic, Indinavir, Joint, Lifestyle, Line, Load, Mainline, Medicine, Mercurial, Mind-expanding, Miracle, Modified release, Monged, Nervine, Nobble, Nootropic, Obstruent, Opiate, Orphan, Painkiller, Paregoric, Parenteral, Pharmaceutics, Pharmacology, Pharmacopoeia, Poison, Prophylactic, Proprietary, Psychedelic, Psychodelic, Purgative, Sedate, Sedative, Shit, Shot, Skin-pop, Smart, Snort, Soft, Specific, Spike, Stimulant, Street name, Stupefy, Styptic, Substance, Sudorific, Suppressant, Toot, Tout, Truth, Upper, Vasoconstrictor, Vasodilator, Vermifuge, Weed, White stuff, Wonder, Zonked

Drum(mer), Drumming, Drumbeat Arête, Atabal, Barrel, Bass, Beatbox, Bodhran, Bongo, Brake, Carousel, Chamade, Conga, Cylinder, Cymograph, Daiko, Dash-wheel, Devil's tattoo, Dhol, Dr, Droome, Drub, Ear, Flam, Kettle, Kymograph, Lambeg, Mridamgam, Mridang(a), Mridangam, Myringa, Naker, Pan, Percussion, Rappel, Rataplan, Reel, Rep, Ridge, Rigger, Ringo, Roll, Ruff, Ruffle, Salesman, Side, Snare, Steel, Tabla, Tabour, Tabret, Taiko, Tambour, Tambourin(e), Tam-tam, Tap, Tattoo, Tenor, Thrum, Timbal, Timp(ano), Tom-tom, Touk, Traps, Traveller, Tuck, Tymbal, Tympanist, Tympano, Whim, Work

▷**Drunken** *may indicate* an anagram

Dry(ing), Drier, Dryness Abstinent, Air, Anhydrous, Arefaction, Arefy, Arid, Blot, Bone, Brut, Corpse, Crine, Dehydrate, Demist, Desiccate, Detox, Drain, Droll, Dull, Eild, Evaporate, Exsiccator, Firlot, Fork, Harmattan, Hasky, Hi(r)stie, Humidor, Jejune, Jerk, Juiceless, Khor, Kiln, Mummify, Oast, →**PARCH**, Plate rack, Prosaic, Reast, Rehab, Reist, Rizzar, Rizzer, Rizzor, Scarious, Sciroc, Scorch, Sear, Season, Sec(co), Seco, Sere, Shrivel, Siccative, Silical gel, Siroc(co), Sober, Sponge, Squeegee, Squeeze, Steme, Sterile, Stove, Ted, Teetotal, Thirsty, Thristy, Toasted, Torrefy, Torrid, Towel, Tribble, Trocken, TT, Tumbler, Turgid, Unsod, Unwatery, Watertight, Welt, Wilt, Win(n), Windrow, Wipe, Wither, Wizened, Wring, Wry, Xeransis, Xerasia, Xero(sis), Xeroderma, Xerophthalmia, Xerostomia

Dual Double, Twin, Twofold

Dubious Arguable, Backscratching, Doubtful, Elliptic, Equivocal, Fishy, Fly-by-night, Hesitant, Iffy, Improbable, Left-handed, Questionable, Scepsis, Sceptical, Sesey, Sessa, →**SHADY**, Shifty, Suspect, Trumped up, Unclear, Unlikely, Unsure

▷**Dubious** *may indicate* an anagram

Duck(ling), Ducked Amphibian, Avoid, Aylesbury, Bald-pate, Bargander, Bathe, Bergander, Blob, Blue, Bob, Bombay, Bufflehead, Bum(m)alo, Burrow, Butterball, Canard, Canvasback, Dead, Dearie, Decoy, Dip, Dodge, Dodo, Douse, Drook, Drouk, Dunk(er), Eider, Elude, Enew, Escape, Evade, Ferruginous, Flapper, Gadwall, Garganey, Garrot, Golden-eye, Goosander, Greenhead, Hareld, Harlequin, Heads, Herald, Immerse, Jook, Jouk, King-pair, Long-tailed, Mallard, Mandarin, Muscovy, Musk, Nil, O, Oldsquaw, Paddling, Pair of spectacles, Palmated, Paradise, Pekin(g), Pintail, Plunge, Pochard, Poker, Putangitangi, Ring-bill, Ruddy, Runner, Rush, St Cuthbert's, Scaup, Scoter, Sheld(d)uck, Shieldrake, Shirk, Shovel(l)er, Shun, Sitting, Smeath, Smee(th), Smew, Sord,

Souse, Sowse, Spatula, Sprigtail, Surf(scoter), Teal, Team, Tufted, Tunker, Velvet scoter, Whio, Whistling, Whitewing, Widgeon, Wigeon, Wild, Wood, Zero

Duct Bile, Canal(iculus), Channel, Conduit, Epididymus, Fistula, Flue, Gland, Lachrymal, Laticifer, Mesonephric, Pancreatic, Passage, Pipe, Tear, Thoracic, Tube, Ureter, Vas deferens, Wolffian

Due(s) Accrued, Adequate, Annates, Arrearage, Attributable, Claim, Debt, Deserts, Expected, Fit(ment), Forinsec, Geld, Heriot, Inheritance, Just, Lot, Mature, Needful, Offerings, Offload, Owing, Reddendo, Rent, Right, →**SUITABLE**, Thereanent, Toll, Tribute, Worthy

Dug-out Canoe, Shelter, Trench, Trough

Duke(dom) Albany, Alva, Chandos, Clarence, D, Duc, Ellington, Fist, Iron, Milan, Orsino, Peer, Prospero, Rohan, Wellington

Dull(ard), Dullness Anodyne, Anorak, Bald, Banal, Barren, Beef-witted, Besot, Blah, Bland, Blear, Blockish, Blunt, Boeotian, Boring, Cabbage, Cloudy, Colourless, Commonplace, Dead (and alive), Deadhead, Dense, Dim, Dinge, Dingy, Ditchwater, Doldrums, Dowf, Dowie, Drab, Drear, Dreich, Dry, Dunce, Faded, Fadeur, Flat, Fozy, Gray, Grey, Heavy, Hebetate, Hebetude, Himbo, Ho-hum, Humdrum, Illustrious, Insipid, Insulse, Jejune, Lacklustre, Lifeless, Log(y), Lowlight, Mat(t), Matte, Monochrome, Monotonous, Mopish, Mull, Mundane, Nondescript, Obtund, Obtuse, Opacity, Opiate, Ordinary, Overcast, Owlish, Pall, Pedestrian, Perstringe, Plodder, Podunk, Prosaic, Prose, Prosy, Rebate, Rust, Saddo, Slow, Solein, Sopite, Staid, Stick, Stodger, Stodgy, Stolid, Stuffy, Stultify, →**STUPID**, Sunless, Tame, Tarnish, Tedious, Ticky-tacky, Toneless, Torpor, Treadmill, Trite, Tubby, Unimaginative, Unresponsive, Vapid, Witless, Wonk, Wooden, Zoid

Dumb(ness) Alalia, Aphonic, Blonde, Crambo, Hobbididance, Inarticulate, Mute, Mutism, Shtum, Silent, Speechless, Stumm, Stupid, Thunderstruck

Dummy Clot, Comforter, Copy, Effigy, Lummox, Mannequin, Meatball, Mock-up, Model, Pacifier, Table, Waxwork

Dump(ing), Dumps Abandon, Ammunition, Blue, Core, Dispirited, Ditch, Doldrums, Empty, Eyesore, Hole, Jettison, Jilt, Junk, Laystall, Offload, Pigsty, Scrap, Scrapyard, Screen, Shed, Shoot, Store(house), Thud, Tip, Toom, Unlade, Unload

Dumpling(s) Clootie, Dim sum, Dough(boy), Gnocchi, Gyoza, Knaidel, Knish, Norfolk, Perogi, Pi(e)rogi, Quenelle, Suet, Won ton

Dune Areg, Bar, Barchan(e), Bark(h)an, Erg, Sandbank, Seif, Star, Whaleback

Dungeon Bastille, Cell, Confine, Donjon, Durance, Keep

Dupe Catspaw, Chiaus, Chouse, Cony, Cull(y), Delude, Easy game, Easy mark, Easy meat, Geck, Gull, Hoax, Hoodwink, Mug, Pawn, Pigeon, Plover, Sitter, Soft mark, Sucker, Swindle, →**TRICK**, Victim

Durable, Durability Enduring, Eternal, Eterne, Hardy, Lasting, Permanent, Stamina, Stout, Tough

Duration Extent, Lifetime, Limit, Period, Span, Timescale

Duress Coercion, Pressure, Restraint

During Amid, Dia-, For, In, Live, Over, Throughout, While, Whilst

Dusk(y) Dark, Dewfall, Dun, Eve, Eventide, Gloaming, Gloom, Half-light, Owl-light, Phaeic, Puliginous, Twilight, Umbrose

Dust(y) Arid, Ash, Bo(a)rt, Calima, Clean, Coom, Cosmic, Derris, Devil, Dicht, Duff, Earth, Fuss, Gold, Khak(i), Lemel, Limail, Limit, Lo(e)ss, Miller, Nebula, Pollen, Pother, Pouder, Poudre, Powder, Pozz(u)olana, Pudder, Rouge, Sea, Seed, Shaitan, Slack, Springfield, Stour, Talc, Timescale, Volcanic, Wipe

▷**Dusted** *may indicate* an anagram

Duster Cloth, Feather, Talcum, Torchon

Dutch(man), Dutchwoman Batavian, Boor, Butterbox, Cape, Courage, D(u), Double, Elm, Erasmus, Fri(e)sian, Frow, German, Kitchen, Knickerbocker, Meneer, Missis, Missus, Mynheer, Patron, Sooterkin, Taal, Vrouw, Wife

Dutiful, Duty Active, Ahimsa, Allegiance, Attentive, Average, Blench, Bond, Charge, Corvee, Countervailing, Customs, Death, Debt, Deontology, Detail, Devoir, Docile, Drow, Due, Duplicand, End, Estate, Excise, Export, Fatigue, Feu, Filial, Function, Heriot, Homage, Import, Imposition, Impost, Incumbent, Lastage, Legacy, Likin, Mission, Mistery, Mystery, Obedient, Obligation, Octroi, Office, Onus, Pia, Picket, Pious, Point, Preferential, Prisage, Probate, Rota, Sentry-go, Shift, Stamp, Stillicide, Stint, Succession, Tariff, →**TASK**, Tax, Toll, Transit, Trap, Trow, Watch, Zabeta

Dwarf(ism) Achondroplasia, Agate, Alberich, Andvari, Ateleiosis, Bashful, Belittle, Bes, Black, Bonsai, Brown, Doc, Dopey, Droich, Drow, Durgan, Elf, Gnome, Grumpy, Happy, Hobbit, Homuncule, Hop o' my thumb, Knurl, Laurin, Leetle, Little man, Man(n)ikin, →**MIDGET**, Mime, Minikin, Minim, Nanism, Nectabanus, Ni(e)belung, Nurl, Outshine, Overshadow, Pacolet, Pigmy, Pipsqueak, Pygmy, Red, Regin, Ront, Rumpelstiltskin, Runt, Skrimp, Sleepy, Sneezy, →**STUNT**, Tiddler, Titch, Tokoloshe, Tom Thumb, Toy, Troll, Trow, White

Dwindle Decline, Diminish, Fade, Fail, Lessen, Peter, Shrink, Wane

Dye(ing), Dyestuff, Dye-seller Alkanet, Anil, Anthracene, Anthraquinone, Archil, Arnotto, Aweto, Azo(benzine), Bat(t)ik, Benzidine, Camwood, Canthaxanthin, Carthamine, Catechin, Chay(a), Chica, Choy, Cinnabar, Cobalt, Cochineal, Colour, Congo, Coomassie blue, Corkir, Crocein, Crotal, Crottle, Cudbear, Dinitrobenzene, Direct, Embrue, Engrain, Envermeil, Eosin, Flavin(e), Fuchsin(e), Fustet, Fustic, Fustoc, Gambi(e)r, Grain, Henna, Hue, Ice colours, Ikat, Imbrue, Imbue, Incarnadine, Indamine, Indican, Indigo, Indigotin, Indirubin, Indoxyl, Indulin(e), Ingrain, Kamala, Kermes, Kohl, Korkir, Lightfast, Madder, Magenta, Mauvein(e), Mauvin(e), Myrobalan, Nigrosin(e), Orcein, Orchel(la), Orchil, Orseille, Para-red, Phenolphthalein, Phthalein, →**PIGMENT**, Ponceau, Primuline, Puccoon, Purple, Purpurin, Pyronine, Quercitron, Quinoline, Raddle, Resorcinol, Rhodamine, Rosanilin(e), Safranin(e), Salter, Shaya, →**STAIN**, Stilbene, Stone-rag, Stone-raw, Sumac(h), Sunfast, Tannin, Tartrazine, Tie-dye, Tinct, Tint, Tropaeolin, Trypan blue, Turmeric, Turnsole, Ultramarine, Valonia, Vat, Wald, Weld, Woad, Woald, Wold, Xanthium, Xylidine

▶**Dying** see **DIE(D)**

Dyke Aboideau, Aboiteau, Bund, Devil's, Ditch, Gall, Offa's, Ring, Sea-wall

Dynamic(s) Ballistics, Ball of fire, Driving, Energetic, Forceful, High-powered, Kinetics, Potent, Vibrant, Whizz kid

Dynamite Blast, Explode, Gelignite, Giant powder, TNT, Trotyl

Dynasty Abbasid(e), Angevin, Bourbon, Capetian, Carolingian, Chen, Chin(g), Ch'ing, Chou, Era, Fatimid, Frankish, Habsburg, Han, Hanoverian, Hapsburg, Holkar, Honan, House(hold), Hyksos, Khan, Manchu, Maurya, Merovingian, Ming, Omayyad, Osman, Pahlavi, Plantagenet, Ptolemy, Qajar, Q'in(g), Rameses, Romanov, Rule, Safavid, Saga, Sassanid, Seleucid, Seljuk, Shang, Song, Sui, Sung, Tai-ping, Tang, Tudor, Umayyad, Wei, Yi, Yuan, Zhou

Ee

E Boat, East, Echo, Energy, English, Spain

Each All, Apiece, A pop, Ea, → **EVERY**, Ilka, Per (capita), Respective, Severally

Eager(ly) Agog, Animated, Antsy, Ardent, Avid, Beaver, Bore, Bright-eyed, Dying, Earnest, Enthusiastic, Fain, Fervent, Fervid, Fidge, Frack, Game, Greedy, Gung-ho, Hot, Intent, → **KEEN**, Motivated, Perfervid, Prone, Race, Raring, Rath(e), Ready, Roost, Sharp-set, Sore, Spoiling, Thirsty, Toey, Wishing, Yare, Zealous

Eagle(s) Al(l)erion, Altair, American, Aquila, Bald, Bateleur, Berghaan, Convocation, Eddy, Ensign, Erne, Ethon, Gier, Golden, Harpy, Legal, Lettern, Ossifrage

Ear(drum), Ear problem Ant(i)helix, Attention, Audience, Auricle, Cauliflower, Cochlea, Concha, Deafness, External, Glue, Hearing, Inner, Jenkins, Listen, Lug, Otalgia, Otalgy, Otic, Otocyst, Parotic, Pinna, Presby(a)c(o)usis, Shell-like, Souse, Spikelet, Stapes, Tragus, Utricle

Earlier, Early Above, Ago, Ahead, AM, Auld, Betimes, Cockcrow, Daybreak, Ex, Foretaste, Germinal, In advance, Incipient, Matin, Matutinal, Preceding, Precocious, Precursor, Prehistoric, Premature, Premie, Prevernal, Previous, Primeur, Primeval, Primordial, Prior, Rear, Rough, Rudimentary, Small hours, Soon, Timely, Tim(e)ous

▷**Early** *may indicate* belonging to an earl

▷**Early stages of** *may indicate* first one or two letters of the words following

Earmark Allocate, Bag, Book, Characteristic, Flag, → **RESERVE**, Tag, Target, Ticket

Earn(er), Earning(s) Achieve, Addle, Breadwinner, Cash cow, Curdle, Deserts, Deserve, Ern, Gain, Make, Merit, Pay packet, Reap, Rennet, Runnet, Win, Yearn

Earnest(ly) Agood, Ardent, Arle(s)(-penny), Deposit, Devout, Fervent, Imprest, Intent, Promise, Serious, Sincere, Token, Wistly, Zealous

Earring Drop, Ear bob, Hoop, Keeper, Pendant, Sleeper, Snap, Stud

Earth(y), Earthling Antichthon, Art, Barbados, Bury, Capricorn, Carnal, Clay, Cloam, Clod, Cologne, Den, Dirt, Drey, Dust, Eard, Epigene, Foxhole, Friable, Fuller's, Gaea, Gaia, Gault, Ge, Globe, Green, Ground, Heavy, Horst, Kadi, Lair, Loam, Malm, Mankind, Mantle, Mools, Mould, Mouls, Papa, Pise, Planet, Podsol, Racy, Rare, Raunchy, Red, Samian, Seat, Sett, Sod, → **SOIL**, Surcharge, Taurus, Telluric, Tellus, Terra, Terrain, Terramara, Terran, Terra rossa, Terrene, Tilth, Topsoil, Virgo, Ye(a)rd, Yird

Earthquake Aftershock, Aseismic, Bradyseism, Mercalli, Richter, Seism, Shake, Shock, Temblor, Trembler

Ease, Easing, Easygoing Alleviate, Assuage, Carefree, Clear, Clover, Comfort, Content, Defuse, Deregulate, Détente, Easy-osy, Facility, Genial, Hands down,

Informal, Laid back, Lax, Lenify, Mellow, Mid(dy), Mitigate, Otiosity, Palliate, Peace, Quiet, Relieve, Reposal, Repose, Resilient, Soothe

East(erly), Eastward Anglia, Asia, Chevet, E, Eassel, Eassil, Eothen, Eurus, Far, Levant, Morning-land, Orient, Ost, Sunrise

Easter Festival, Island, Pace, Pasch(al), Pasque

Easy, Easily ABC, Amenable, Approachable, Cakewalk, Carefree, Cinch, Comfortable, Comfy, Crispy, Cushy, Doddle, Doss, Duck soup, Effortless, Facile, Fluent, Free, Gift, Glib, Gravy train, Jammy, Kid's stuff, Lax, Light, Natural, No-brainer, Picnic, Pie, Plain sailing, Pushover, Romp, Scoosh, Simple, Skoosh, Snap, Snotty, Soft, Spoon fed, Tolerant, Turkey shoot, Walk-over, Yare

▷**Easy** *may indicate* an anagram

Eat(able), Eater, Eating Bite, Bolt, Break bread, Chomp, Chop, Consume, Corrode, Cram, Devour, Dig in, Dine, Edible, Erode, Esculent, Etch, Fare, Feast, →**FEED**, Fret, Gnaw, Go, Gobble, Gourmand, Gourmet, Graze, Grub, Guts, Have, Hoe into, Hog, Hyperorexia, Mess, Muckamuck, Munch, Nosh, Nutritive, Omnivore, Partake, Phagomania, Refect, Scoff, Slurp, Snack, Stuff, Sup, Swallow, Take, Taste, Trencherman, Tuck away, Tuck into, Twist

Eating problem Anorexia, Bulimia, Cachexia

Eavesdrop(per) Detectophone, Earwig, Listen, Overhear, Snoop, Spy, Tap

Ebb(ing) Abate, Decline, Recede, Sink

Eccentric Abnormal, Antic, Atypical, Cam, Card, Character, Crackpot, Crank, Curious, Dag, Deviant, Dingbat, Ditsy, Ditzy, E, Farouche, Fay, Fey, Fie, Flaky, Freak, Geek, Gonzo, Iffish, Irregular, Kinky, Kook(y), Loon, Madcap, Mattoid, Monstre sacré, Nutcase, Odd(ball), Offbeat, Off-centre, Off the rails, Original, Outré, →**PECULIAR**, Pixil(l)ated, Queer, Quirky, Quiz, Rake, Raky, Recondite, Rum, Scatty, Screwball, Screwy, Spac(e)y, Wack(y), W(h)acko, Way-out, Weird(o), Weirdie

▷**Eccentric** *may indicate* an anagram

Ecclesiast(es), Ecclesiasticus, Ecclesiastical Abbé, Clergyman, Clerical, Lector, Secular, Sir(ach), Theologian, The Preacher, Vatican

Echinoderm Asteroidea, Basket-star, Brittle-star, Comatulid, Crinoid, Ophiurid, Sea-egg, Sea-lily, Sea-urchin, Starfish

Echo, Echoing, Echo-sounder Angel, Answer, Ditto, E, Fathometer®, Imitate, Iterate, Mirror, Phonocamptic, Rebound, Recreate, Repeat, Repercussion, Reply, Resemble, Resonant, Respeak, Reverb(erate), Ring, Rote, Sonar

Eclipse Annular, Block, Cloud, Deliquium, Excel, Hide, Lunar, Obscure, Occultation, Outjump, Outmatch, Outshine, Outweigh, Overshadow, Penumbra, Rahu, Solar, Total, Transcend, Upstage

Economise Budget, Conserve, Eke, Finance, Husband, Pinch, Retrench, Scrimp, Skimp, Spare, Whip the cat

Economy, Economic(al), Economics Agflation, Agronomy, Autarky, Black, Brevity, Careful, Cheap rate, Chrematistics, Cliometrics, Conversation, Cut, Domestic, Frugal, Hidden, Home, Husband(ry), Informal, Lean-burn, LSE, Market, Mitumba, Neat, Parsimony, Provident, Pusser's logic, Retrenchment, Shadow, Shoestring, Sparing, Stumpflation, Thrift

Ecstasy, Ecstatic Bliss, Delight, Dove, E, Enrapt, Exultant, Joy, Lyrical, Pythic, Rapture, Sent, Trance, Transport, Utopia

Edda Elder, Legend, Prose, Younger

Eden Bliss, Fall, Heaven, Paradise, PM, Utopia

Edge, Edging, Edgy Advantage, Arris, Bleeding, Border, Bordure, Brim, Brink, Brittle, Brow, Burr, Chamfer, Chimb, Chime, Chine, Coaming, Costa, Creston, Cutting, Dag, Deckle, Ease, End, Flange, Flounce, Frill, Fringe, Frontier, Furbelow, Gunnel, Gunwale, Hem, Hone, Inch, Inside, Kerb, Knife, Leading, Leech, Limb(ate), Limbus, Limit, Lip, List, Lute, Marge(nt), Margin, Neckline, Nosing, Orle, Outside, Parapet, Periphery, Picot, Pikadell, Piping, Rand, Reeding, Rim, Rund, Rymme, Selvage, Selvedge, Side, Sidle, Skirt, Strand, Surbed, Tense, Tomium, Trailing, Trim, Twitchy, Tyre, Uneasy, Uptight, Verge, Wear, Whet

▶**Edible** *see* **EAT(ABLE)**

Edict(s) Ban, Bull, Clementines, Decree, Decretal, Extravagantes, Fatwa, Interim, Irade, Nantes, Notice, Order, Pragmatic, Proclamation, Pronouncement, Sext, Ukase

Edit(or), Editorial Abridge, Amend, Article, City, Cut, Dele, Desk, Dramaturg(e), Ed, Emend, Expurgate, Footsteps, Garble, Leader, Manipulate, Overseer, Recense, Redact, Revise, Reword, Rewrite, Seaman, Tweak

▷**Edited** *may indicate* an anagram

Edition Aldine, Ed, Extra, Facsimile, Hexapla(r), Issue, Limited, Number, Omnibus, Re-issue, Variorum, Version

Educate(d) Academic, Baboo, Babu, Cultured, Enlighten, Evolué, Informed, Instruct, Learned, Lettered, Literati, Nourish, Noursle, Nousell, Nousle, Nurture, Nuzzle, Polymath, Preppy, Progressive, Scholarly, School, → **TEACH**, Train, Yuppie

Education(alist) Adult, Basic, B.Ed, Classical, D.Ed, Didactics, Estyn, Froebel, Heurism, Learning, Literate, Mainstream, Montessori, Oxbridge, Pedagogue, Pestalozzi, Piarist, Primary, Schooling, Special, Teacher, Tertiary, Tutelage, Upbringing

Edward Confessor, Ed, Elder, Lear, Longshanks, Martyr, Ned, Ted

Eel Conger, Electric, Elver, Hagfish, Lamprey, Launce, Moray, Olm, Salt, Sand(ling), Snake

Efface Cancel, Delete, Dislimn, → **ERASE**, Expunge, Obliterate

Effect(s), Effective(ness), Effectual Achieve, Acid trip, Acting, Alienation, Auger, Bags, Barnstorming, Belongings, Binaural, Bit, Bite, Border edge, Bystander, Causal, Coastline, Competent, Consequence, Do, Domino, Doppler, Edge, Efficacious, Electro-optical, Enact, End, Enforce, Estate, Execute, Fet, Functional, Fungibles, Furnishing(s), Fx, Gangbuster, Gear, General, Goods, Greenhouse, Hall, Hangover, Home, Impact, Implement(al), Impression, Influence, Knock-on, Magneto-optical, Militate, Moire, Mutual, Neat, Net, Nifty, Nisi, Operant, Outcome, Personal, Phi, Position, Potent, Practical, Prevailing, Promulgate, Punchy, Reaction, Redound, Repercussion, → **RESULT**, Ripple, Shadow, Shore, Side, Slash-dot, Sound, Special, Spectrum, Spin-off, Stage, Striking, Subsidiary, Tableau, Telling, Therapeutic, Upshot, Viable, Virtual, Well, Whammy, Work

Effervescence, Effervescent Bubbling, Ebullient, Fizz

▷**Effervescent** *may indicate* an anagram

Efficiency, Efficient Able, Businesslike, Capable, Competent, Despatch, Ecological, Ergonomics, Expeditious, High-powered, Lean, Productivity, Smart, Spectral luminous, Streamlined, Strong

Effigy Buddha, Figure, Guy, Idol, Image, Statua, Statue

Effluence, Effluent, Effluvia, Effluvium Air, Aura, Billabong, Discharge, Fume, Gas, Halitus, Miasma, Odour, Outflow, Outrush, Reek

Effort Achievement, All-out, Attempt, Best, Conatus, Concerted, Damnedest, Drive, Endeavour, Essay, Exertion, Fit, Frame, Hardscrabble, Herculean, Joint, Labour, Legwork, Molimen, Nisus, Pull, Rally, Shy, Spurt, Stab, Strain, Struggle, Team, Travail, → TRY, Work, Yo

Effrontery Audacity, Backchat, Brass, Cheek, Face, Gall, Neck, Nerve, Temerity

Effuse, Effusion, Effusive Emanate, Exuberant, Exude, Gush, Lyric, Ode, Outburst, Prattle, Rhapsody, Screed, Spill

Egg(s), Egg on Abet, Addled, Benedict, Berry, Blow, Bomb, Caviar(e), Cavier, Chalaza, Cheer, Cleidoic, Clutch, Cockney, Collop, Coral, Curate's, Darning, Easter, Edge, Encourage, Fabergé, Fetus, Flyblow, Foetus, Free-range, Glair(e), Goad, Goog, Graine, Hoy, Incite, Instigate, Isolecithal, Layings, Mine, Nit, Oocyte, Oophoron, Ova, Ovum, Pasch, Prairie oyster, Press, Prod, Raun, Roe, Rumble-tumble, Scotch, Seed, Setting, Spat, Spawn, Spur(ne), Tar(re), Tempt, Tooth, Tread(le), Urge, Yelk, Yolk

Egghead Brainbox, Don, Highbrow, Intellectual, Mensa, Pedant

Ego(ism), Egoist, Egotist(ical) Che, Conceit, I, Narcissism, Not-I, Pride, Self, Self-seeker, Solipsism, Tin god, Vanity

Egypt(ian), Egyptologist Arab, Cairene, Carter, Cheops, Chephren, Cleopatra, Copt(ic), ET, Goshen, Imhotep, Nasser, Nefertiti, Nilote, Nitrian, Old Kingdom, Osiris, Potiphar, Ptolemy, Rameses, Syene, Theban, Wafd

Eight(h), Eighth day Acht, Byte, Crew, Cube, Isis, Nundine, Oars, Octa, Octad, Octal, Octant, Octastrophic, Octave, Octet, Octonary, Octuor, Ogdoad, Okta, Ottava, Ure, Utas

Either Also, Both, O(u)ther, Such

Ejaculate Blurt, Discharge, Emit, Exclaim

Eject Belch, Bounce, Defenestrate, Disgorge, Dismiss, Emit, Erupt, Evict, Expel, Oust, Propel, Spew, Spit, Spue, Turf out, Vent, Void

Eke Augment, Eche, Enlarge, Husband, Supplement

Elaborate Baroque, Creation, Detail, Develop, Embroider, Enlarge, Fancy, Flesh out, Florid, Intricate, Magnificent, Opulent, Ornate, Spectacular

Elan Dash, Drive, Esprit, → FLAIR, Gusto, Lotus, Spirit, Style, Vigour

Elastic(ity) Adaptable, Buoyant, Dopplerite, Elater, Flexible, Give, Lithe(some), Resilient, Rubber, Scrunchie, Scrunchy, Spandex®, Springy, Stretchy, Tone, Tonus

Elate(d), Elation Cheer, Cock-a-hoop, Euphoric, Exalt, Exhilarate, Gladden, Hault, High, Lift, Rapture, Ruff(e), Uplift

Elbow, Elbow tip Akimbo, Ancon, Angle, Bender, Cubital, Hustle, Joint, Jolt, Jostle, Kimbo, Noop, Nudge, Olecranon, Tennis

Elder(ly), Eldest Ainé(e), Ancestor, Ancient, Bourtree, Chief, Classis, Coffin dodger, Eigne, Geriatric, Greying, Guru, Kaumatua, OAP, Presbyter, → SENIOR, Sire, Susanna, Wallwort

Elect(ed), Election(eer), Elective, Elector(al) Ballot, Choice, Choose, Chosen, Constituent, Co-opt, Eatanswill, Elite, Gerrymander, Hustings, In, Israelite, Khaki, Member, Opt, Optional, Pick, PR, Predetermine, Primary, Psephology, Rectorial, Return, Select, Stump, Vote in

Electricity Galvanism, Grid, HT, Inductance, Juice, Power, Static, Utility

Electrify Astonish, Fire, Galvanise, Startle, Stir, Thrill

Elegance, Elegant Artistic, Bijou, Chic, Chichi, Classy, Concinnity, Dainty, Daynt, Debonair, Dressy, Fancy, Finesse, Gainly, Galant, Grace, Luxurious, Natty, Neat, Poise, Polished, Refined, Ritzy, → SMART, Soigné(e), Style, Svelte, Swish, Tall, Tasteful, Urbane

Element(s), Elementary Abcee, Abecedarian, Absey, Barebones, Chromosome, Detail, → **ESSENCE**, Essential, Ether, Factor, Feature, Fuel, Heating, Hot-plate, Ideal, Identity, Insertion, Logical, M(a)cGuffin, Milieu, Non-metal, Peltier, Pixel, Primary, Principle, Radio, Rare earth, Rudimental, Sieve, Simple, Simplex, Stabial, Strand, Superheavy, Trace(r), Tramp, Transition, Transuranic, Weather

Elephant(ine) African, Bull, Calf, Cow, Indian, Jumbo, Mammoth, Mastodon, Oliphant, Pachyderm, Rogue, Stegodon, Tusker, White

Elevate(d), Elevation, Elevator Aerial, Agger, Aggrandise, Attitude, Aweight, Bank, Cheer, Eminence, Ennoble, Euphuism, Glabella, Haute, Heighten, Hoist, Jack, Lift, Lob, Lofty, Pitch, Promote, → **RAISE**, Random, Relievo, Ridge, Rise, Sublimate, Up(lift)

Eleven Elf, Legs, O, Side, Team, XI

Eligible Available, Catch, Fit, Nubile, Parti, Qualified, Worthy

Eliminate, Elimination Cull, Cure, Deep-six, Delete, Discard, Exclude, Execute, Extirpate, Knock out, Liquidate, Omit, Preclude, Purge, Rid, Weed out, Zap

Elite Best, Choice, Crachach, Crack, → **CREAM**, Crème (de la crème), Egalitarian, Elect, Flower, Gentry, Meritocracy, Plutocracy, Ton, Top drawer, Twelve pitch, U, Zaibatsu

Elm Nettle-tree, Rock, Slippery, Wich, Wych

Elongate Extend, Lengthen, Protract, Stretch

Eloquence, Eloquent Articulate, Blarney stone, Demosthenic, Facundity, Fluent, Honey-tongued, Oracy, Oratory, Rhetoric, Silver-tongued, Speaking, Vocal

Else(where) Absent, Alibi, Aliunde, Et al, Other

Elude, Elusion, Elusive Avoid, Dodge, Eel, Escape, → **EVADE**, Evasive, Foil, Intangible, Jink, Pimpernel, Sliddery, Slippy, Subt(i)le, Will o' the wisp

Emaciated, Emaciation Atrophy, Erasmus, Gaunt, Haggard, Lean, Skeleton, Skinny, Sweeny, Tabid, Thin, Wanthriven, Wasted

Email Flame, Online, Spam, Spim

Emancipate(d), Emancipation Catholic, Deliver, Forisfamiliate, Free, → **LIBERATE**, Manumission, Uhuru

Embankment Bund, Causeway, Dam, Dyke, Earthwork, Levee, Mattress, Mound, Rampart, Remblai, Stopbank

Embargo → **BAN**, Blockade, Boycott, Edict, Restraint

Embark Begin, Board, Enter, Inship, Launch, Sail

Embarrass(ed), Embarrassing, Embarrassment Abash, Ashamed, Awkward, Besti, Buttock-clenching, Colour, Crimson, Cringe-making, Cringe-worthy, Disconcert, Discountenance, Encumber, Mess, Plethora, Pose, Predicament, Scundered, Scunnered, Shame, Sheepish, Squirming, Straitened, Tongue-tied, Whoopsie

▷**Embarrassed** *may indicate* an anagram

Embassy Chancery, Consulate, Embassade, Legation, Mission

Embellish(ed), Embellishment Adorn, Beautify, Bedeck, Curlicue, Deck, Decór(ate), Embroider, Enrich, Fioritura, Garnish, Garniture, Grace note, Melisma(ta), → **ORNAMENT**, Ornate, Overwrought, Prank, Prettify, Story, Twist

Ember(s) Ash, Cinder, Clinker, Gleed

Emblem(atic) Badge, Bear, Colophon, Daffodil, Device, Figure, Fleur-de-lis, Golp(e), Hammer and sickle, Ichthys, Impresa, Insignia, Kikumon, Leek, Lis,

Logo, Maple leaf, Mon, Oak, Pip, Rose, Roundel, Shamrock, Sign, Spear-thistle, → **SYMBOL**, Tau-cross, Thistle, Token, Totem(ic), Triskelion, Wattle, Wheel

Emboss(ed) Adorn, Chase, Cloqué, Engrave, Pounce

Embrace(d) Accolade, Arm, Bear hug, Canoodle, Clasp, Clinch, Clip, Coll, Complect, Comprise, Cuddle, Embosom, Encircle, Enclasp, Enclose, Enfold, Envelop, Espouse, Fold, Grab, Grip, Hug, Include, Inlace, Kiss, Lasso, Neck, Overarch, Press, Snog, Snug(gle), Twine, Welcome, Wrap

▷**Embraces, Embracing** *may indicate* a hidden word

Embroider(y) Add, Appliqué, Arpillera, Braid, Brede, Colour, Couching, Crewellery, Crewel-work, Cross-stitch, Cutwork, Embellish, Exaggerate, Fag(g)oting, Fancywork, Featherstitch, Gros point, Handiwork, Lace(t), Laid work, Needlecraft, Needlepoint, Needlework, Orfray, Ornament, Orphrey, Orris, Petit point, Pinwork, Purl, Queen-stitch, Sampler, Sew, Smocking, Spider-wheel, Stitch, Stitchery, Stumpwork, Tent, Zari

Embryo(nic), Embryologist Anlage, Archenteron, Blastocyst, Blastospore, Blastula, Egg, Fo(e)tus, Gastrula, Germ, Mesoblast, Origin, Rudiment, Undeveloped, Wolff

Emend Adjust, Alter, Edit, Reform

Emerge(ncy), Emerging Anadyomene, Arise, Craunch, Crise, Crisis, Crunch, Debouch, Emanate, Erupt, Exigency, Flashpoint, Hard-shoulder, Issue, Last-ditch, Need, Outcrop, Pinch, SOS, Spare, Spring, Stand-by, Strait

▷**Emerge from** *may indicate* an anagram or a hidden word

Eminence, Eminent Altitude, Cardinal, Celebrity, Distinguished, Grand, Greatness, Height, Hill, Hywel, Illustrious, Light, Lion, Lofty, Luminary, Noble, → **NOTABLE**, Prominence, Renown, Repute, Stardom, Stature, Tor, → **VIP**

Emirate Abu Dhabi, Dubai, Qatar, Sharjah

Emission, Emit Discharge, Emanate, Give, Issue, Radiate, Utter, Vent

Emolument Income, Perk, Remuneration, Salary, Stipend, Tip, Wages

Emotion(s), Emotional Anger, Anoesis, Breast, Cathartic, Chord, Ecstasy, Excitable, Feeling, Flare up, Freak-out, Gushing, Gut-wrenching, Hate, Heartstrings, Hippocampus, Histrionics, Hoo, Hysteria, Intense, Joy, Limbic, Maenad, Nostalgia, Nympholepsy, Passion, Poignant, Reins, Rhapsodic, Roar, Sensibility, Sensitive, Sentiment, Soulful, Spirit, Stormy, Teary, Theopathy, Transport, Weepy, Wigged out

Empathy Rapport, Rapprochement, Sympathy

Emperor Agramant(e), Akbar, Akihito, Antoninus, Augustus, Aurelian, Babur, Bao Dai, Barbarossa, Bonaparte, Caesar, Caligula, Caracalla, Charlemagne, Claudius, Commodus, Concerto, Constantine, Diocletian, Domitian, Ferdinand, Flavian, Gaius, Galba, Genghis Khan, Gratian, Great Mogul, Hadrian, Haile Selassie, Heraclius, Hirohito, HRE, Imp, Inca, Jimmu, Justinian, Kaiser, Keasar, Kesar, King, Kubla(h) Khan, Manuel I Comnenus, Maximilian, Meiji, Menelik, Mikado, Ming, Mogul, Montezuma, Mpret, Napoleon, Negus, Nero, Nerva, Otho, Otto, Penguin, Peter the Great, Purple, Pu-yi, Rastafari, Rex, Rosco, Ruler, Severus, Shah Jahan, Shang, Sovereign, Sultan, Tenno, Theodore, Theodosius, Tiberius, Titus, Trajan, Tsar, Valens, Valentinian, Valerian, Vespasian, Vitellius

Emphasis(e), Emphasize, Emphatic(ally) Accent, Birr, Bold, Dramatise, Ek se, Forcible, Foreground, Forzando, Forzato, Hendiadys, Highlight, In spades, Italic, Marcato, Point up, Positive, Resounding, Risoluto, Sforzando, Sforzato, Sublineate, Underline, Underscore, Vehement

Empire Assyria, British, Byzantine, Domain, Empery, French, Kingdom, Latin, Osmanli, Ottoman, Realm, Reich, Roman

Employ(ment) Appoint, Bestow, Business, Calling, Engage, Hire, Occupy, Pay, Post, Practice, Pursuit, Retain, Task, Usage, Use, Using, Utilise, Vocation

Employee(s) Barista, Casual, Clock-watcher, Earner, Factotum, Full-timer, Hand, Help, Minion, Part-timer, Payroll, Personnel, Salariat, Servant, Staff, Staffer, Worker, Workforce, Workpeople

Employer Baas, Boss, Governor, Guv, Master, Padrone, Taskmaster, User

▷**Employs** *may indicate* an anagram

Empress Eugenie, Josephine, Matilda, Messalina, Sultana, Tsarina, VIR

Empty Addle, Bare, Barren, Blank, Buzz, Clear, Deplete, Deserted, Devoid, Disembowel, Drain, Evacuate, Exhaust, Expel, Forsaken, Futile, Gut, Hent, Hollow, Inane, Jejune, Lave, Meaningless, Null, Pump, Shallow, Space, Teem, Toom, Tum(e), Unfurnished, Uninhabited, Unlade, Unoccupied, Vacant, Vacate, Vacuous, Vain, → **VOID**

▷**Empty** *may indicate* an 'o' in the word or an anagram

Emulate Ape, Copy, Envy, Equal, Imitate, Match

Enable Authorise, Capacitate, Empower, Permit, Potentiate, Qualify, Sanction

Enamel(led), Enamel work Aumail, Champlevé, Cloisonné, Della-robbia, Dentine, Fabergé, Ganoin(e), Lacquer, Mottled, Nail, Polish, Porcelain, Schwarzlot, Shippo, Smalto, Stoved, Vitreous

Encampment Bivouac, Castrametation, Douar, Dowar, Duar, Laager, Laer, Settlement

Encase(d), Encasement Box, Crate, Emboîtement, Encapsulate, Enclose, Obtect, Sheathe

Enchant(ing), Enchanted, Enchantment Captivate, Charm, Delight, Gramary(e), Incantation, Magic, Necromancy, Rapt, Sirenize, Sorcery, Spellbind, Thrill

Enchanter, Enchantress Archimage, Archimago, Armida, Circe, Comus, Faerie, Fairy, Houri, Lorelei, Magician, Medea, Mermaid, Prospero, Reim-kennar, Sorcerer, Vivien, Witch

Encircle(d), Encirclement Besiege, Enclose, Encompass, Enlace, Entrold, Gird, Hoop (la), Inorb, Introld, Orbit, Pale, Ring, Siege, Stemme, → **SURROUND**

Enclose(d), Enclosing, Enclosure Aviary, Bawn, Beset, Boma, Bower, Box, Bullring, Cage, Carol, Carrel, Case, Circumscribe, Cockpit, Common, Compound, Corral, Court, Cubicle, Embale, Embower, Embrace, Enceinte, Enchase, Encircle, Enclave, Engirt, Enhearse, Enlock, Enshrine, Fence, Fold, Garth, Haining, Haw, Hem, Henge, Hope, Impound, In, Incapsulate, Inchase, Include, Inhoop, Inlock, Insert, Interclude, Interlude, Lairage, Obvolute, Paddock, Pale, Parrock, Peel, Pele, Pen(t), Pin, Pinfold, Playpen, Plenum, Pocket, Radome, Rail, Rath, Recluse, Ree(d), Ring, Run, Saleyard, Seal, Sekos, Sept, Seraglio, Serail, Sin bin, Steeld, Stell, Stive, Stockade, Sty, → **SURROUND**, Tatt(ersall)s, Terrarium, Tine, Vibarium, Ward, Wrap, Yard, Zareba

Encompass Bathe, Begird, Beset, Cover, Environ, Include, Surround

Encounter Battle, Brush, Close, Combat, Contend, Cope, Experience, Face, Hit, Incur, Interview, → **MEET**, Rencontre, Ruffle, Skirmish

Encourage(ment), Encouraging Abet, Acco(u)rage, Alley-oop, Attaboy, Barrack, Bolster, Boost, Buck, Cheer, Chivy, Clap, Coax, Cohortative, Come-on, Commend, Countenance, Dangle, Egg, Embolden, Exhort, Fillip, Fire, Fortify, Foster, Fuel, Gee, Hearten, Heigh, Help, Heuristic, Hortatory, Incite, Inspire,

Invite, Lift, Nourish, Nurture, Ole, Pat, Patronise, Pep talk, Prod, Promote, Push, Reassure, Root, Seed, Spur, Steel, Stimulate, Stoke, Support, Tally-ho, Uplift, Urge, Yay, Yo, Yoicks

Encroach(ment) Eat out, Impinge, Infringe, Intrude, Invade, Overlap, Overstep, Poach, Trample, Trespass, Usurp

Encumber, Encumbrance Accloy, Burden, Clog, Dead weight, Deadwood, Dependent, Embarrass, →**HANDICAP**, Impede, Liability, Load, Obstruct, Saddle

End(ing) Abolish, Abort, Abrogate, Abut, Aim, Ambition, Amen, Anus, Arse, Big, Bitter, Bourn(e), Butt, Cease, Cessation, Cesser, Climax, Close, Closure, Cloture, Coda, Conclude, Crust, Culminate, Curtain, Curtains, Cut off, Dead, Death, Decease, Demise, Denouement, Desinence, Destroy, Determine, Dissolve, Domino, Effect, Envoi, Envoy, Epilogue, Exigent, Expire, Explicit, Extremity, Fade, Fatal, Fattrels, Feminine, Ferrule, Fin, Final(e), Fine, Finis, →**FINISH**, Finite, Gable, Grave, Heel, Ice, Ish, Izzard, Izzet, Kill, Kybosh, Lapse, Last, Let up, Limit, Little, Loose, Masculine, Mill, Nirvana, No side, Ort, Out, Outrance, Outro, Period, Peter, Pine, Point, Pole, Purpose, Quench, Receiving, Remnant, Rescind, Result, Roach, Round off, Runback, Scotch, Scrag, Shank, Slaughter, Sopite, Split, Sticky, Stub, Surcease, Swansong, Tag, Tail, Tailpiece, Telic, Telos, Term, Terminal, Terminate, Terminus, Thrum, Tip, Toe, Top, Ultimate, Up, Upshot, Utterance, West, Z

Endeavour Aim, Attempt, Effort, Enterprise, Essay, Strain, Strive, Struggle, Try, Venture

Endless Aeonian, Continuous, Cornucopia, Ecaudate, Eternal, Eterne, Infinite, Interminable, Perpetual, Undated

▷**Endlessly** *may indicate* a last letter missing

Endorse(ment) Adopt, Affirm, Approve, Assurance, Back, Certify, Confirmation, Docket, Initial, Okay, Oke, Ratify, Rubber stamp, Sanction, Second, Sign, →**SUPPORT**, Underwrite, Visa

Endow(ment) Assign, Bequeath, Bestow, Bless, Cha(u)ntry, Dotation, Enrich, Foundation, Gift, Leave, Patrimony, Vest

Endurance, Endure(d), Enduring Abide, Bear, Bide, Brook, Dree, Dure, Face, Fortitude, Granite, Have, Hold, →**LAST**, Livelong, Lump, Marathon, Patience, Perseverance, Persist, Pluck, Ride, Stamina, Stand, Stay, Stomach, Stout, Substantial, Sustain, Swallow, Thole, Timeless, Tolerance, Undergo, Wear, Weather

Enemy Adversary, Antagonist, Boer, Devil, Fifth column, Foe(n), Fone, Opponent, Public, Time

Energetic, Energise, Energy Active, Amp, Animation, Arduous, Barnstorming, Battery, Binding, Bond, Brisk, Cathexis, Chakra, Chi, Dark, Dash, Doer, Drive, Dynamic, Dynamo, E, Enthalpy, Entropy, EV, Feng shui, Fermi, Fireball, Force, Fructan, Fuel, Fusion, Ginger, Gism, Go, Go ahead, Goer, Hartree, Hearty, Horme, Hustle, Hyper, Input, Instress, Internal, Isotonic, →**JET**, Jism, Jissom, Joie de vivre, Joule, Kerma, Kinetic, Kundalini, Libido, Life, Live wire, Luminous, Magnon, Moxie, Nuclear, Orgone, Pep, Phonon, Pithy, Pizzazz, Potency, Potential, →**POWER**, Powerhouse, QI, Quantum, Quasar, Rad, Radiant, Radiatory, Rydberg, S(h)akti, Sappy, Second-wind, Solar, Steam, Thermodynamics, Trans-uranic, Verve, Vibrancy, Vigour, Vim, Vital, Vivo, Wave, Whammo, Whirlwind, Zealous, Zero point, Zestful, Zing, Zip

Enforce(ment) Administer, Coerce, Control, Exact, Implement, Impose

Engage(d), Engagement, Engaging Absorb, Accept, Adorable, Appointment, Attach, Battle, Bespoken, Betrothal, Bind, Book, Busy, Contract,

Courtship, Date, Embark, Employ, Engross, Enlist, Enmesh, Ensure, Enter, Fiance(e), Fight, Gear, Gig, Hire, Hold, In gear, Interest, Interlock, Lock, Mesh, Met, Occupy, Pledge, Promise, Prosecute, Rapt, Reserve, Residency, Rope in, Sapid, Skirmish, Sponsal, Sponsion, Spousal, Trip, Wage, Winsome

▷**Engagement** *may indicate* a battle

Engine, Engine part Air, Analytical, Appliance, Atmospheric, Banker, Banking, Beam, Bricole, Carburettor, Catapult, Compound, Dashpot, Diesel, Dividing, Donkey, Dynamo, Fan-jet, Fire, Four-cycle, Gas, Humdinger, ICE, Internal combustion, Ion, Iron horse, Ivor, Jet, Lean-burn, Light, Little-end, Loco(motive), Machine, Mangonel, Mogul, →**MOTOR**, Nacelle, Oil, Orbital, Otto, Outboard, Overhead valve, Petrol, Pilot, Plasma, Podded, Pony, Puffer, Pug, Pulp, Pulsejet, Push-pull, Radial, Ramjet, Reaction, Reciprocating, Retrorocket, Rocket, Rose, Rotary, RR, Scramjet, Search, Side-valve, Sleeve valve, Stationary, Steam, Sustainer, Tank, Testudo, Thermometer, Thruster, Top-end, Traction, Turbine, Turbofan, Turbojet, Turboprop, Turbo-ram-jet, Two-stroke, V, Vernier, V-type, Wankel, Water, Wildcat, Winding

Engineer(ing), Engineer(s) Aeronautical, AEU, Arrange, Badge, Chartered, Concurrent, Contrive, Greaser, Human, Interactive, Knowledge, Liability, Manhattan District, Manoeuvre, Marine, Mastermind, Operator, Organise, Paper, Planner, Repairman, Reverse, Sales, Sanitary, Sapper, Scheme, Software, Sound, Stage, Usability, Wangle

▷**Engineer** *may indicate* an anagram

England Albany, Albion, Blighty, John Bull, Merrie

English(man) Ang(le), Anglican, Brit, Bro talk, Canajan, E, Ebonics, Eng, Estuary, Gringo, Hiberno, John Bull, King's, Limey, Middle, Modern, Morningside, New Zealand, Nigerian, Norman, Officialese, Old, Oxford, Pidgin, Plain, Pom(my), Pommie, Pongo, Queen's, Rosbif, Sassenach, Saxon, Scotic, Scottish, Seaspeak, Shopkeeper, Singlish, Southron, Southroun, Spanglish, Standard, Wardour Street, Whingeing Pom, World

Engrave(r), Engraving Aquatint, Blake, Bury, Carve, Cerotype, Chalcography, Chase, Cut, Dry-point, Durer, Enchase, Etch, Glyptic, Glyptograph, Heliogravure, Hogarth, Impress, Inchase, Inciser, Inscribe, Intagliate, Lapidary, Mezzotint, Niello, Photoglyphic, Photogravure, Plate, Scrimshandy, Scrimshaw, Steel, Stillet, Stipple, Stylet, Stylography, Toreutics, Xylographer

Engross(ed) Absorb, Engage, Enwrap, Immerse, Inwrap, Monopolise, →**OCCUPY**, Preoccupy, Prepossess, Rapt, Rivet, Sink, Thrill, Transfix, Writ large

Enhance(r) Add, Augment, Better, Catalyst, Embellish, Exalt, Heighten, Improve, Intensify, Supplement

Enigma(tic) Charade, Conundrum, Cryptic, Dilemma, Gioconda, Gnomic, Mystery, Oracle, Poser, Problem, →**PUZZLE**, Quandary, Question, Rebus, Recondite, Riddle, Secret, Sphinxlike, Teaser

Enjoy(able), Enjoyment Apolaustic, Appreciate, Ball, Brook, Delectation, Delight, Fruition, Glee, Groove, Gusto, Have, High jinks, Lap up, Lekker, Like, Own, Palate, Pleasance, Pleasing, Possess, Relish, Ripping, Sair, Savour, Stonking, Taste, Wallow

Enlarge(ment), Enlarger Accrue, Acromegaly, Add, Aneurism, Aneurysm, Augment, Blow-up, Diagraph, Dilate, Exostosis, Expand, Expatiate, Explain, Hypertrophy, Increase, Jumboise, →**MAGNIFY**, Pan, Piece, Ream, Rebore, Sensationalize, Spavin, Swell, Telescope, Tumefy, Varicosity, Zoom

Enlighten(ed), Enlightenment Aha, Aufklarung, Awareness, Disabuse, Edify, Educate, Explain, Illumine, Instruct, Liberal, Luce, Nirvana, Relume, Revelation

Enlist Attest, Conscript, Draft, Engage, Enrol, Induct, Join, Levy, Prest, Recruit, Rope in, Roster, Sign on, Volunteer

Enliven(ed) Animate, Arouse, Brighten, Cheer, Comfort, Exhilarate, Ginger, Invigorate, Juice, Merry, Pep, Refresh, Warm

Enmity Animosity, Aversion, Bad blood, Feud, Hatred, Nee(d)le, Rancour

Ennoble(ment) Dub, Elevate, Exalt, Honour, Raise

Enormous Colossal, Exorbitant, Gargantuan, Giant, Gigantic, Googol, Hellacious, Huge, Humongous, Humungous, →IMMENSE, Jumbo, Mammoth, Mega, Untold, Vast, Walloper, Walloping

Enough Adequate, →AMPLE, Anow, Appreciable, Basta, Belay, Do(eth), Enow, Fill, Geyan, Nuff, Pax, Plenty, Qs, Sate, Satis, Sese, Sessa, Suffice, Sufficient, Via

Enquire, Enquiring, Enquiry Ask, Case, Check, Curious, Eh, Inquire, Organon, Probe, Public, Request, Research, Scan, Seek, Trial

Enrage(d) Bemad, →INCENSE, Inflame, Irate, Livid, Madden, Wild

Enrich Adorn, Endow, Enhance, Fortify, Fructify, Oxygenate

Enrol(ment) Attest, Conscribe, Conscript, Empanel, Enlist, Enter, Incept, →JOIN, List, Matriculate, Muster, Recruit, Register

Ensign Ancient, Badge, Banner, Duster, Ens, →FLAG, Gonfalon, Officer, Pennon, Pistol, Red, White

Enslave(ment) Bondage, Captivate, Chain, Yoke

Ensue, Ensuing Et sequens, Follow, Result, Succeed, Transpire

Entangle(ment) Amour, Ball, Elf, Embroil, Encumber, Ensnarl, Entrail, Fankle, Hank, Implicate, →KNOT, Liaison, Mat, Ravel, Retiarius, Trammel

Enter, Entry Admit, Broach, Come, Enrol, Field, Infiltrate, Ingo, Insert, Intromit, Invade, Item, Key in, Lodge, Log, Penetrate, Pierce, Post, Record, Slate, Submit, Table, Wild card

Enterprise, Enterprising Adventure, Ambition, Aunter, Dash, Emprise, Forlorn hope, Free, Goey, Go-getter, Gumption, Indie, Industry, Initiative, Plan, Private, Project, Public, Push, Spirit, Stunt, Venture

Entertain(er), Entertaining, Entertainment Acrobat, Afterpiece, All-dayer, All-nighter, Amphitryon, Amuse, Apres ski, Balladeer, Ballet, Barnum, Beguile, Belly dancer, Bread and circuses, Bright lights, Burlesque, Busk, Cabaret, Carnival, Cater, Charade, Cheer, Circus, Comedian, Comic, Concert (party), Conjure, Consider, Cottabus, Crack, Craic, Cuddy, Distract, Divert, · Divertissement, ENSA, Extravaganza, Fairground, Fete (champetre), Fleshpots, Floorshow, Foy, Friendly lead, Fun, Gaff, Gala, Gas, Gaudy, Geisha, Gig, Harbour, Harlequin, Have, Hospitality, Host(ess), Houdini, Impresario, Impressionist, Infotainment, Interest, Interlude, Intermezzo, Jester, Juggler, Karaoke, Kidult, Kursaal, Lap-dancer, Lauder, Leg-show, Levee, Liberace, Light, Masque, Melodrama, Mind candy, Minstrel, Movieoke, Musical, Music hall, Niterie, Olio, Opera, Palladium, Panto, Pap, Party, Peepshow, Performer, Piece, Pierrot, Play, Pop singer, Reception, Recreation, Redcoat, Regale, Review, Revue, Rice, Ridotto, Rinky-dink, Roadshow, Rodeo, Rush, Serenade, Showbiz, Showgirl, Sideshow, Simulcast, Singer, Sitcom, Slapstick, Snake-charmer, Soirée, Son et lumière, Street theatre, Striptease, Table, Tamasha, Tattoo, Treat, Tumbler, Tummler, Variety, Vaudeville, Ventriloquist

Enthuse, Enthusiasm, Enthusiast(ic) Ardour, Avid, Buff, Bug, Cat, Cheerleader, Devotee, Ebullience, Ecstatic, Empresse, Energy, Faddist, Fancier, Fervid, Fiend, Fire, Flame, Freak, Furor(e), Geek, Get-up-and-go, Gung-ho, Gusto, Hearty, Hype, Into, Keen, Lyrical, Mad, Mane, Mania, Motivated, Muso,

Oomph, Outpour, Overboard, Passion, Perfervid, Petrolhead, Rah-rah, Raring, Rave, Relish, Rhapsodise, Sold, Spirit, Turfite, Verve, Warmth, Whacko, Whole-hearted, Young gun, Zealot, Zest, Zing

Entice(ment), Enticing Allure, Angle, Cajole, Carrot, Dangle, Decoy, Draw, Lure, Persuade, Seductive, →TEMPT, Tole, Toll, Trap, Trepan

Entire(ly), Entirety Absolute, All, Complete, Genuine, Intact, Integral, In toto, Lot, Purely, Root and branch, Systemic, Thorough, Total, Undivided, →WHOLE

Entity Being, Body, Existence, Holon, Tao, Tensor, Thing, Transfinite

Entrail(s) Bowels, Giblets, Gralloch, Guts, Ha(r)slet, Humbles, Lights, Numbles, Offal, Tripe, Umbles, Viscera

Entrance(d), Entrant, Entry Access, Adit, Admission, Anteroom, Arch, Atrium, Attract, Avernus, Bewitch, Cat flap, Charm, Closehead, Contestant, Door, Doorstop, Double, Eye, Fascinate, Foyer, Frawbridge, Gate(way), Ghat, Hypnotise, Illegal, In-door, Infare, Inflow, Ingate, Ingress, Inlet, Jaws, Mesmerise, Mouth, Pend, Porch, Porogamy, Portal, Postern, Propylaeum, Propylon, Reception, Record, Registration, Single, Spellbound, Starter, Stem, Stoa, Stoma, Stulm, Throat

Entreat(y) Appeal, Ask, Beg, Beseech, Flagitate, Impetrate, Orison, Petition, Plead, Pray, Precatory, Prevail, Prig, Rogation, Solicit, Sue, Supplicate

Entrepreneur Branson, Businessman, E-tailer, Wheeler-dealer, Yettie

▶**Entry** see **ENTRANCE(D)**

Entwine Complect, Impleach, Intervolve, Lace, Twist, Weave

Enumerate, Enumeration Catalogue, Count, List, Tell

Envelop(e), Enveloping Corolla, Corona, Cover(ing), Enclose, Enshroud, Entire, Flight, Flown cover, Invest, Involucre, Muffle, Nuclear, Perianth, Round, Sachet, Serosa, Shroud, Skin, Smother, Surround, Swathe, Wrap

Environment(s), Environmental(ist) ACRE, Ambience, Cyberspace, Ecology, Entourage, Green(ie), Habitat, Hothouse, Milieu, SEPA, Setting, Sphere, Surroundings

Envoy Agent, Diplomat, Hermes, Legate, Missioner, Plenipo(tentiary)

Epic Aeneid, Ben Hur, Beowulf, Blockbuster, Calliope, Colossal, Dunciad, Edda, Epopee, Eyeliad, Gilgamesh, Homeric, Iliad, Kalevala, Lusiad(s), Mahabharata, Mock-heroic, Nibelungenlied, Odyssey, Ramayana, Saga

Epicure(an) Apicius, Connoisseur, Gastronome, Glutton, →GOURMAND, Gourmet, Hedonist, Sybarite

Epidemic Asian flu, Enzootic, Outbreak, Pandemic, Pestilence, Plague, Prevalent, Rampant, Rife

Epilogue Appendix, Coda, End, Postlude, Postscript

Episode(s), Episodic Bipolar, Chapter, Incident, Instalment, Microsleep, Page, Picaresque, Scene, Serial

Epistle(s) Catholic, Dispatch, General, Lesson, Letter, Missive, Pastoral

Epitome, Epitomise Abridge, Abstract, Avowal, Digest, Exemplar, Image, Model, Summary, Typify

Epoch Age, Era, Holocene, Miocene, Oligocene, Palaeocene, Period, Pleistocene, Pl(e)iocene

Equable, Equably Calm, Just, Placid, Smooth, Tranquil

Equal(ly), Equality, Equal quantities Across the board, Alike, All square, As, Balanced, Commensurate, Compeer, Co-partner, Egal(ity), Emulate, Equinox, Equiparate, Equity, Even, Even-steven, Ex aequo, Fair, Feer, Fe(a)re, Fiere, Fifty-fifty, For, Identical, Identity, Is, Iso-, Isocracy, Level, Level-pegging,

Make, Match, Par, Parage, Parallel, Parametric, Parity, Peregal, Rise, Rival, →**SO**, Square

Equate, Equation(s) Arrhenius, Balance, Chemical, Defective, Differential, Dirac, Identity, Nernst, Parametric, Quadratic, Reduce, Relate, Simultaneous

Equestrian Dressage, Eventer, Turfite

Equilibrium Balance, Composure, Homeostasis, Instable, Isostasy, Poise, Stasis, Tautomerism

Equip(ment), Equipage, Equipped Accoutrement, Accustrement, Adorn, Apparatus, Apparel, Appliance, Arm, Array, Attire, Blender, Carriage, Chequerboard, Clobber, Clothe, Deck, Dight, Expertise, Fortify, →**FURNISH**, Gear, Get-up, Graith, Hamper, Hand-me-up, Hardware, Headset, Hi-tech, Impedimenta, Implement, Incubator, iPod®, Kit, Lie-detector, Log-reel, Material, Matériel, Monitor, Muniments, Outfit, Pile-driver, Plant, Projector, Receiver, Refit, Retinue, Rig, Scrambler, Sonobuoy, Stapler, Stereo, Stock, Stuff, Tabulator, Tack(le), Tenderiser, Tool, Transformer, Turn-out, Vision-mixer, Wakeboard, Webcam, Well-appointed

Equitable Even-handed, Fair, Just

Equivalence, Equivalent Akin, Amounting to, Correspondent, Counterpart, Dose, Equal, Same, Tantamount, Version

Equivocate Flannel, Lie, Palter, Prevaricate, Quibble, Tergiversate, Weasel

Era Age, Archaean, C(a)enozoic, Christian, Common, Cretaceous, Decade, Dynasty, Ediocaron, Epoch, Hadean, Hegira, Hej(i)ra, Hijra, Jurassic, Lias, Mesozoic, Oligocene, Period, Precambrian, Proterozoic, Torridonian

Eradicate, Erase Abolish, Delete, Demolish, Destroy, Dislimn, Efface, Expunge, Exterminate, Extirp, Obliterate, Purge, Root, Scratch, Strike out, Uproot, Wipe

Erect(ion), Erector Boner, Build, Construct(ion), Elevate, Exalt, Hard-on, Perpendicular, Priapism, Prick, Rear, Upend, Upright, Vertical, Wall

Ergo Argal, Hence, Therefore

Erode, Erosion Ablate, Appair, Corrasion, Degrade, Denude, Destroy, Deteriorate, Detrition, Etch, Fret, Hush, Peneplain, Wash, Wear, Yardang

Eros, Erotic(a) Amatory, Amorino, Amorous, Aphrodisiac, Carnal, Cupid, Lascivious, Philtre, Prurient, Salacious, Steamy

Err(or), Errant Aliasing, Anachronism, Bish, Blip, Blooper, Blunder, Boner, Boob(oo), Botch, Bug, Clanger, Comedy, Corrigendum, Execution, Fat-finger, Fault, Fluff, Glaring, Heresy, Hickey, Howler, Human, Inaccuracy, Inherited, K'thibh, Lapse, Lapsus, Literal, Misgo, Misprint, Misprise, Misprize, Misstep, →**MISTAKE**, Out, Paladin, Parachronism, Probable, Recoverable, Rounding, Rove, Runtime, Sampling, Semantic, Sin, Slip, Slip-up, Solecism, Standard, Stray, Trip, Truncation, Type I, Type II, Typo, Typographical, Unforced

Errand Ance, Chore, Commission, Message, Mission, Once, Sleeveless, Task

Erratic Haywire, Planetary, Spasmodic, Temperamental, Vagary, Vagrant, Wayward, Whimsical

Erroneous False, Inaccurate, Mistaken, Non-sequitur, Untrue

Erudite, Erudition Academic, Learned, Literosity, Well-bred, Wisdom

Erupt(ion), Erupture Belch, Brash, Burst, Eject, Emit, →**EXPLODE**, Fumarole, Hives, Lichen, Mal(l)ander, Mallender, Outbreak, Outburst, Papilla, Plinian, Pustule, Quat, Rash, Sneeze

Escape(e), Escapade, Escapist Abscond, Adventure, Avoid, Bale out, Bolt, Bolthole, Breakout, Caper, Close call, Eject, Elope, Elude, Elusion, Esc,

Eschewal, Evade, Exit, Fire, Flee, Flight, Fredaine, Frolic, Fugacity, Gaolbreak, Get-out, Hole, Hoot, Houdini, Houdini act, Hout, Lam, Lark, Leakage, Leg-it, Let-off, Levant, Lifeline, Loop(-hole), Meuse, Mews, Miss, Muse, Narrow, Near thing, Outlet, Prank, Refuge, Runaway, Scarper, Seep(age), Shave, Slip, Splore, Squeak, Stunt, Vent, Walter Mitty

Escort Accompany, Arm candy, Attend, Beard, Beau, Bodyguard, Bring, Chaperone, Comitatus, Conduct, Convoy, Cortège, Corvette, Date, Destroyer, Entourage, Frigate, Gallant, Gigolo, Guard, Guide, Lead, Outrider, Protector, Retinue, See, Squire, Take, Tend, Usher, Walker

Esoteric Abstruse, Hermetic, Orphic, Rarefied, Recondite, Secret

Especial(ly) Chiefly, Esp, Espec, Outstanding, Particular

Espionage Industrial, Spying, Surveillance

Esprit Cameraderie, Insight, Spirit, Understanding, Wit

Essay(s) Article, Attempt, Critique, Disquisition, Dissertation, Endeavour, Paper, Sketch, Stab, Study, Thesis, Tractate, Treatise, Try

Essayist Addison, Bacon, Columnist, De Quincey, Elia, Ellis, Emerson, Hazlitt, Holmes, Hunt, Huxley, Lamb, Locke, Montaigne, Pater, Prolusion, Ruskin, Scribe, Steele, Temple, Tzara, → **WRITER**

Essence Alma, Atman, Attar, Aura, Being, Bergamot, Core, Crux, Element, Entia, Esse, Extract, Fizzen, Flavouring, Flower, Foison, Gist, Heart, Hom(e)ousian, Inbeing, Inscape, Kernel, Marrow, Mauri, Mirbane, Myrbane, Nature, Nub, Nutshell, Ottar, Otto, Perfume, Per-se, Petrol, Pith, Quiddity, Ratafia, Saul, Soul, Substance, Sum, Ylang-ylang

Essential(ly), Essentials Arabin, At heart, Bare, Basic, Central, Crucial, Entia, Formal, Fundamental, Imperative, In, Inbred, Indispensable, Inherent, In se, Integral, Intrinsic, Kernel, Key, Lifeblood, Linch-pin, Main, Marrow, Material, Mun, Must, Necessary, Need, Nitty-gritty, Nub, Nuts and bolts, Part-parcel, Per-se, Pith, Prana, Prerequisite, Quintessence, Radical, Requisite, Sine qua non, Skeleton, Soul, Vital, Whatness

Establish(ed) Abide, Anchor, Appoint, Ascertain, Base, Bred-in-the-bone, Build, Chronic, Confirm, Conform, Conventional, Create, Deep-seated, Deploy, Embed, Enact, Endemic, Ensconce, Entrench, Erect, Evidence, Fix, → **FOUND**, Haft, Honoured, Imbed, Ingrain, Instal(l), Instate, Instil, Institute, Inveterate, Legislate, Ordain, Pitch, Pre-set, Prove, Radicate, Raise, Redintegrate, Root(ed), Secure, Set, Stable, Standing, State, Stell, Substantiate, Trad(itional), Trite, Valorise, Verify

Establishment Building, Business, CE, Church, Co, Concern, Conformation, Creation, Hacienda, Household, Instauration, Institution, Lodge, Proving ground, Salon, School, Seat, Succursal, System, Traditional

Estate, Estate-holder Acres, Allod(ium), Alod, Assets, Campus, Car, Commons, Dais, Demesne, Domain, Dominant, Dowry, Est, Estancia, Fazenda, Fee-simple, Fee-tail, Fen, First, Fourth, General, Hacienda, Hagh, Haugh, Having, Hay, Housing, Industrial, Jointure, Land-living, Latifundium, Legitim, Life, Longleat, Manor, Messuage, Odal, Patrimony, Pen, Personal(ity), Plantation, Press, Princedom, → **PROPERTY**, Real, Runrig, Situation, Spiritual, Standing, Talooka, Taluk(a), Temporal, Termer, Termor, Thanage, Trading, Udal

Esteem(ed), Estimable Account, Admiration, Appreciation, Count, Credited, Have, Honour, Izzat, Los, Precious, Prestige, Price, Pride, Prize, Rate, → **REGARD**, Respect, Revere, Store, Value, Venerate, Wonder, Worthy

▶**Estimable** *see* **ESTEEM(ED)**

Estimate, Estimation Appraise, Assess, Calculate, Carat, Conceit, Cost, Esteem, Extrapolation, Figure, Forecast, Gauge, Guess(timate), Measure, Opinion, Projection, Quotation, Rate, Rating, Reckon, Regard, Value, Weigh

Etch(ing) Aquafortis, Aquatint(a), Bite, → **ENGRAVE**, Erode, Incise, Inscribe

Eternal(ly), Eternity Aeonian, Ageless, All-time, Amarantine, Endless, Everlasting, Evermore, Eviternal, Ewigkeit, Forever, Immortal, Infinity, Never-ending, Perdurable, Perpetual, Sempiternal, Tarnal, Timeless, Triangle, Unending

Ether Air, Atmosphere, Ch'i, Gas, Sky, Yang, Yin

Ethereal Airy, Delicate, Fragile, Heavenly, Nymph

Ethic(al), Ethics Deontics, Ideals, Marcionite, Moral, Principles, Situation

Ethiopia(n) African, Amharic, Asmara, Cushitic, Falasha, Geez, Kebele, Ogaden

Etiquette Code, Conduct, Decorum, → **MANNERS**, Propriety, Protocol, Ps and Qs, Punctilious, Table manners

Eucalyptus Blackbutt, Bloodwood, Cadaga, Cadagi, Coolabah, Gum-tree, Ironbark, Mallee, Marri, Morrell, Red gum, Sallee, Sally, Stringybark, Tallow wood, Tewart, Tooart, Tuart, Wandoo, White gum, Woolly butt

Euphoria, Euphoric Buzz, Cock-a-hoop, Elation, High, Jubilation, Nirvana, Rapture, Rush

Europe(an) Andorran, Aryan, Balt, Bohunk, Bosnian, Catalan, Community, Continent, Croat, E, Esth, Estonian, Faringee, Faringhi, Feringhee, Fleming, Hungarian, Hunky, Icelander, Japhetic, Lapp, Lett, Lithuanian, Magyar, Maltese, Monagesque, Palagi, Polack, Ruthene, Ruthenian, Serb, Slavonian, Slovak, Slovene, Topi-wallah, Transleithan, Tyrolean, Ugrian, Vlach, Wessi, Yugoslav

Evacuate, Evacuation Dunkirk, Escape, Excrete, Expel, Getter, Medevac, Movement, Planuria, Planury, Retreat, Scramble, Stercorate, Stool, Vent, Void, Withdraw

Evade, Evasion, Evasive Abscond, Ambages, Avoid, Circumvent, Cop-out, Coy, Dodge, Duck, Elude, Escape, Fence, Fudge, Hedge, Jink, Loophole, Parry, Prevaricate, Quibble, Quillet, Quirk, Salvo, Scrimshank, Shifty, Shirk, Shuffling, Sidestep, Skive, Stall, Subterfuge, Tergiversate, Waive, Weasel, Whiffler

Evaluate, Evaluation Appraise, Assess, Estimate, Gauge, Measure, Ponder, Rate, Review, Try, Waid(e), Weigh

Evangelical, Evangelist(ical) Bible-thumper, Buchman, Clappy-doo, Converter, Crusader, Fisher, Godsquad, Gospeller, Graham, Happy-clappy, Hot gospeller, Jansen, Jesus freak, John, Luke, Marist, Mark, Matthew, Missioner, Moody, Morisonian, Peculiar, Preacher, Propagandist, Revivalist, Salvo, Sim(eonite), Stundist, Wild

Evaporate, Evaporation Angel's share, Condense, Dehydrate, Desorb, Disappear, Exhale, Steam, Steme, Ullage, Vaporise

Eve(ning) First lady, First mate, Nightfall, Postmeridian, Soirée, Subfusk, Sunset, Tib(b)s, Twilight, Vesperal, Vespertinal, Vigil, Watch night, Yester

Even(ly), Evenness Aid, Albe(e), Albeit, All, Average, Balanced, Clean, Drawn, Dusk, Een, Ene, Equable, Equal, Erev, Fair, Fair play, Flush, Gradual, Iron, Level, Meet, Nay, Pair, Par, Parallel, Plain, Plane, Plateau, Quits, Rib, Smooth, Square, Standardise, Still, Temperate, Tie(d), Toss-up, Uniform, Well-balanced, Yet

Event(ing) All-nighter, Bash, Case, Circumstance, Cross-country, Discus, Dressage, Encaenia, Episode, Fest, Field, Fiesta, Function, Grand Prix, Gymkhana, Happening, Heat, Incident, Landmark, Leg, Liquidity, Media, Meeting, Milestone, Occasion, Occurrence, Ongoing, Outcome, Pass, Rag-day,

Regatta, Result, Shot put, Show-jumping, Soirée, Telethon, Three-ring circus, Time trial, Tour de France, Track

Eventual(ity), Eventually Case, Contingent, Finally, Future, In time, Later, Nd, Ultimate

Ever Always, Ay(e), Constantly, Eternal, Eviternity

Evergreen Abies, Ageless, Arbutus, Cembra, Cypress, Fir, Gaultheria, Golden lie, Holly, Ivy, Myrtle, Oleander, Olearia, Periwinkle, Pinaster, Privet, Thuja, Thuya, Washington, Winterberry

Everlasting Cat's ear, Changeless, Enduring, Eternal, Immortal, Immortelle, Perdurable, Perennial, Recurrent, Tarnal, Undying

Every(one), Everything All, Apiece, A'thing, Catch-all, Complete, Each, Et al, Ilk(a), Sub chiz, Sum, The full monty, The works, Tout, Tout le monde, Universal, Varsal

Everyday Informal, Mundane, Natural, Ordinary, Plain, Routine, Year round

Everywhere Ambient, Omnipresent, Passim, Rife, Throughout, Thru, Ubique, Ubiquity, World

Evidence, Evident(ly) Adminicle, Apparent, Argument, Axiomatic, Circumstantial, Clear, Compurgation, Confessed, Credentials, Deposition, Direct, Distinct, DNA, Document, Empirical, Exemplar, Flagrant, Forensic, Hearsay, Indicate, Internal, King's, Manifest, Marked, Material, Naked, Obvious, Ostensibly, Overt, Plain, Premise, Prima facie, Probable, Proof, Queen's, Record, Sign, Smoking gun, State's, Surrebuttal, Tangible, Testimony, Understandable

Evil Ahriman, Alastor, Amiss, Bad, Badmash, Bale, Beelzebub, Budmash, Corrupt, Curse, Depraved, Eale, Falling, Guilty, Harm, Hydra, Ill, Iniquity, Loki, Malefic, Malign, Mare, Mischief, Monstrous, Nasty, Necessary, Night, Perfidious, Pestilence, Rakshas(a), Satanic, Shrewd, Sin, Theodicy, Turpitude, Vice, Villainy, Wicked

Evince Disclose, Exhibit, Indicate, Show

Evolution(ary) Clade, Convergent, Countermarch, Darwin, Development, Growth, Holism, Lamarck, Lysenkoism, Moner(on), Phylogeny, Turning

▷**Evolution** *may indicate* an anagram

Ex Former, Late, Old flame, Quondam, Ten

Exacerbate Aggravate, Embitter, Exasperate, Inflame, Irritate, Needle

Exact(ing), Exactitude, Exactly Accurate, Authentic, Bang on, Careful, Dead, Definite, Due, Elicit, Estreat, Even, Exigent, Extort, Fine, Formal, It, Jump, Literal, Literatim, Mathematical, Meticulous, Minute, Nice(ty), On the nail, Pat, Plumb, Point-device, → **PRECISE**, Require, Slap-bang, Spang, Specific, Spot-on, Strict, Sweat, T, Verbatim

Exaggerate(d), Exaggeration Agonistic, Amplify, Boast, Brag, Camp, Caricature, Colour, Distend, Dramatise, → **EMBROIDER**, Exalted, Goliathise, Hype, Hyperbole, Inflate, Magnify, Overdo, Overegg, Overpaint, Overpitch, Overplay, Oversell, Overstate, Overstate, Overstretch, Over-the-top, Play up, Shoot a line, Stretch, Theatrical, Writ large

Exalt(ed), Exaltation Attitudes, Deify, Dignify, Elation, Enhance, Ennoble, Ensky, Enthrone, Erect, Extol, Glorify, High, Jubilance, Larks, Laud, Lofty, → **PRAISE**, Raise, Rapture, Sublime

Exam(ination), Examine, Examinee, Examiner A-level, Alnage, Analyse, Analyst, Anatomise, Assess, Audit, Audition, Autopsy, Baccalauréat, Biopsy, Case, Check-out, Check-up, Collate, Comb, Common Entrance, Concours, Consideration, Cross-question, CSE, Deposal, Depose, Disquisition, Dissect,

Edexcel, Eleven plus, Entrance, Explore, Eyeball, Finals, GCE, GCSE, Going-over, Grade(s), Great-go, Greats, Gulf, Hearing, Higher, Inspect, Inter, Interrogate, Interview, Introspection, Jury, Laparoscopy, Local, Look, Mark, Matriculation, Medical, Mocks, Mod(erations), Moderator, Mods, Mug, Multiple choice, O-level, Once-over, Oral, Ordeal, Overhaul, Palp(ate), Paper, Peruse, Physical, Post-mortem, Prelims, Probe, Professional, Pry, Psychoanalyse, Pump, →**QUESTION**, Quiz, Ransack, Recce, Reconnaissance, Resit, Review, Sayer, Scan, Schools, Scope, Screen, Scrutineer, Scrutinise, Search, Seek, Sift, Sit, Smalls, Strip search, Study, Survey, Sus(s), Test, Trial, Tripos, Try, Vet, Viva

Example Byword, Epitome, Erotema, Foretaste, →**FOR EXAMPLE**, Illustration, Instance, Lead, Lesson, Model, Monument, Paradigm, Paragon, →**PATTERN**, Praxis, Precedent, Prototype, Quintessence, Say, Shining, Showpiece, Specimen, Standard, Touchstone, Type, Typify

Excavate, Excavation, Excavator Bore, Burrow, Catacomb, Crater, Delf, Delph, →**DIG**, Dike, Ditch(er), Dredge, Drift, Graft, Heuch, Heugh, Hollow, JCB, Mine, Moat, Pioneer, Pioner, Power shovel, Quarry, Shaft, Sink, Sondage, Spade, Stope, Well

Excel(lence), Excellency, Excellent A1, Ace, Admirable (Crichton), Awesome, Bangin(g), Bang on, Beat, Beaut, Beezer, Better, Blinder, Bodacious, Boffo, Bonzer, Booshit, Boss, Bravo, Brill, Bully, Capital, Champion, Cheese, Choice, Class(y), Classical, Cool, Corking, Crack, Crackajack, Crackerjack, Crucial, Cushty, Daisy, Def, Dic(k)ty, Dilly, Dominate, Doozy, Dope, Elegant, Excelsior, Exemplary, Eximious, Exo, Exquisite, Fab, Fabulous, Fantastic, First-class, First rate, Five-star, Goodly, Goodness, Great, HE, Hellacious, High, Humdinger, Hunky(-dory), Inimitable, Jake, Jammy, Kiff, Knockout, Laudable, Matchless, Mean, Mega-, Merit, Neat, Noble, Nonesuch, Olé, Out and outer, Outdo, Outgeneral, Outrank, Outstanding, Outstrip, Overdo, Overpeer, Paragon, Peachy, Peerless, Perfection, Prime, Pure, Quality, Rad, Rare, Rattling, Ring, Rinsin', Ripping, Ripsnorter, Shagtastic, →**SHINE**, Sick-dog, Sik, Slammin(g), Socko, Sound, Spanking, Spiffing, Stellar, Stupendous, Sublime, Superb, Super-duper, Superior, Supernal, Supreme, Surpass, Swell, Terrific, Tip-top, Top flight, Top-hole, Topnotch, Topping, Tops, Virtue, Virtuoso, Wal(l)y, War, Way-out, Whizzo, Whizzy, Wicked, Worth

Exceptional Abnormal, Anomaly, Doozy, Egregious, Especial, Ever so, Extraordinary, Extreme, Inimitable, Odd, Rara avis, Rare, Ripsnorter, Singular, Spanking, Special, Super(normal), Unco(mmon), Unusual, Zinger

Excess(ive), Excessively All-fired, Almighty, Basinful, Binge, De trop, Epact, Exaggeration, Exorbitant, Extortionate, Extravagant, Flood, Fulsome, Glut, Hard, Indulgence, Inordinate, Intense, Lake, →**LAVISH**, Mountain, Needless, Nimiety, OD, Old, OTT, Outrage, Over, Overabundance, Overage, Overblown, Overcome, Overdose, Over-indulgence, Overkill, Overmuch, Overspill, Oversupply, Over-the-top, Owercome, Plethora, Preponderance, Profuse, Salt, Satiety, Spate, Spilth, Staw, Steep, Superabundant, Superfluity, Superplus, Surfeit, Surplus, Terrific, Thundering, Too, Troppo, Ultra, Undue, Unequal, Unnecessary, Woundily

Exchange Baltic, Bandy, Banter, Barter, Bourse, Cambist, Cash, Catallactic, Change, Chop, Commodity, Commute, Confab, Contango, Convert, Cope, Corn, Crossfire, Ding-dong, Discourse, Employment, Enallage, Excambion, Foreign, Gematria, Global, Inosculate, Intercooler, Interplay, Ion, Job centre, Labour, Logroll, →**MARKET**, Mart, Needle, Niffer, Paraphrase, PBX, Post, Quid pro quo, Rally, Rate, RE, Recourse, Redeem, Rialto, Royal, Scorse, Scourse, Sister-chromated, Spoonerism, Stock (market), Swap, Switch, Switchboard, Swop (shop), Telephone, Tolsel, Tolsey, Tolzey, → **TRADE**, Trade in, Traffic, Transfusion, Transpose, Trophallaxis, Truck

Excite(ment), Excitable, Excitability, Excited, Exciting Ablaze, Abuzz, Action-packed, Aerate, Aflutter, Agog, Amove, Amp, Animate, Apeshit, Aphrodisiac, Arouse, Athrill, Atwitter, Awaken, Brouhaha, Bubbly, Buck-fever, Buzzing, Climactic, Combustible, Commotion, Delirium, Dither, Electrify, Emove, Enthuse, Erethism, Eventful, Feisty, Fever (pitch), Fire, Flap, Frantic, Frenzy, Frisson, Furore, Fuss, Galvanise, Gas, Headiness, Heat, Hectic, Het, Hey-go-mad, Highly-strung, Hilarity, Hobson-Jobson, Hoopla, Hothead, Hyped, Hyper, Hypomania, Hysterical, Impel, Incite, Inebriate, Inflame, Intoxicate, Jimjams, Kick, Kindle, Liven, Maenad, Mania, Metastable, Must, Nappy, Nervous, Neurotic, Oestrus, On fire, Orgasm, Overheat, Overwrought, Panic, Passion, Pride, Provoke, Psyched up, Racy, Radge, Red-hot, Rile, Roil, Ruff(e), Rut, Salutation, Send, Shivering, Spin, Splash, Spur, Startle, Stimulate, Stir(e), Suscitate, Suspense, Swashbuckling, Tense, Tetanoid, Tetany, Tew, Thrill, Tickle, Titillate, Turn-on, Twitter, Upraise, Waken, Whee, Whoopee, Work up, Yahoo, Yerk, Yippee, Yirk, Yoicks, Zest

▷**Excite(d)** *may indicate* an anagram

Exclaim, Exclamation (mark) Ahem, Arrah, Aue, Begorra, Bliksem, Blurt, Bo, Ceas(e), Crikey, Criv(v)ens, Dammit, Ecphonesis, Eina, Eish, Ejaculate, Eureka, Expletive, Fen(s), Good-now, Haith, Heigh-ho, Hem, Hosanna, Inshallah, Interjection, Moryah, Omigod, Oof, Oops, Phew, Pish, Pow, Protest, Pshaw, Push, Strewth, Uh-oh, Uh-uh, Unberufen, Voila, Whoopee, Whoops, Wirra, Yay, Yeehaw, Yippee, Yo-ho-ho, Yummy, Zounds

Exclude, Excluding, Exclusion Ban, Banish, Bar, Berufsverbot, Block, Competitive, Corner, Debar, Disbar, Eliminate, Ex, Except, Excommunicate, Ice out, Omit, Ostracise, Proscribe, Rule out, Upmarket

Excursion Airing, Alarum, Cruise, Dart, Day tour, Day trip, Digression, Jaunt, Junket, Outing, Pleasure-trip, Road, Sally, Sashay, Sortie, Tour, Trip, Vagary

Excuse, Excusable Absolve, Alibi, Amnesty, Condone, Cop-out, Evasion, Exempt, Exonerate, Explain, Forgive, Gold brick, Hook, Justify, Let off, Mitigate, Occasion, Out, Overlook, Palliate, → **PARDON**, Plea, Pretext, Release, Venial, Viable, Whitewash

Execute(d), Executioner, Executive, Executor Accomplish, Administrate, Behead, Discharge, Finish, Fry, Gar(r)otte, Guardian, Hang, Headsman, Implement, Ketch, Kill, Koko, Literary, Lynch, Management, Martyr, Monsieur de Paris, Noyade, Official, Perform, Perpetrate, Pierrepoint, Politburo, Top, Tower Hill, Trustee

Exempt(ion) Aegrotat, Dispensation, Exclude, Free, Immune, Impunity, Indemnity, Indulgence, Quarter, Spare, Tyburn ticket

Exercise(s) Aerobics, Apply, Athletics, Bench press, Burpee, Buteyko method, Cal(l)isthenics, Callanetics®, Chi kung, Chin-up, Circuit training, Cloze, Constitutional, Dancercise, Drill, Employ, Enure, Eurhythmics, Exert, Falun dafa, Falun gong, Fartlek, Feldenkrais method, Five-finger, Floor, Gradus, Gymnastics, Hatha yoga, Inure, Isometrics, Kata, Keepy-uppy, Lat spread, Lesson, Limber, Medau, Op, Operation, PE, Ply, Plyometrics, Practice, Practise, Preacher curl, Press-up, Problem, Prolusion, PT, Pull-up, Push-up, Qigong, Sadhana, Scales, Shintaido, Sit-up, Solfege, Solfeggi(o), Step (aerobics),

Tae-Bo®, Tai chi (ch'uan), Task, Thema, Theme, Thesis, Train, Treadmill, Trunk curl, Use, Warm-down, Warm-up, Wield, Work, Work-out, Xyst(us), Yogalates, Yomp

▷**Exercise(d)** *may indicate* an anagram

Exert(ion) Conatus, →**EFFORT**, Exercise, Labour, Operate, Strain, Strive, Struggle, Trouble, Wield

Exhaust(ed), Exhausting, Exhaustion, Exhaustive All-in, Backbreaking, Beaten, Beggar, Bore, Burn, Burn-out, Bushed, Clapped out, Collapse, Consume, Deadbeat, Debility, Deplete, Detailed, Dissipate, Done, Drain, Effete, Emission, Empty, End, Enervate, Euchred, Fatigue, Finish, Flue, Fordo, Frazzle, Gruelling, Haggard, Heat, Heatstroke, Jet-lagged, Jet-stream, Jiggered, Knacker, Mate, Milk, Out, Outspent, Overtax, Peter, Play out, Poop, Powfagged, Prostrate, Puckerood, Rag, Ramfeezle, Rundown, Sap, Sell out, Shatter, Shot, Shotten, Spend, Spent, Stonkered, Tailpipe, Tax, Tedious, Tire, Up, Use (up), Used up, Washed-up, Wasted, Waygone, Weak, →**WEARY**, Wind, Worn, Zonked

Exhibition (centre), Exhibit(ing), Exhibitioner, Exhibitionism, Exhibitionist Aquashow, Bench, Circus, Concours, Demo, Demonstrate, Demy, Diorama, Discover, Display, Earls Court, ENC, Endeictic, Evince, Expo, Expose, Extrovert, Fair, Hang, Indicate, Installation, Lady Godiva, NEC, Olympia, Pageant, Panopticon, Parade, Poseur, Present, Retrospective, Rodeo, Salon, Scene, Show(piece), Showman, Show-off, Showplace, Sideshow, Sight, Spectacle, Sport, Stand, Streaker, Viewing, Waxworks, Zoo

Exigency, Exigent Demanding, Emergency, Pressing, Taxing, Urgent, Vital

Exile Adam, Babylon, Ban, Banish, Deport, Deportee, Eject, Emigré, Eve, Expatriate, Exul, Galut(h), Ostracise, Outlaw, Relegate, Siberia, Tax, Wretch

Exist(ence), Existing Be(ing), Corporeity, Dwell, Enhypostasia, Entelechy, Esse, Extant, Haeccity, Identity, Inbeing, Inherent, Life, Lifespan, Live, Ontology, Perseity, Solipsism, Status quo, Substantial, Ubiety

Exit Débouché, Door, Egress, Emergency, Exhaust, Gate, Leave, Outgate, Outlet, Swansong, Trapdoor, Vent, Vomitory

Exodus Book, Departure, Flight, Hegira, Hejira, Passover

Exorbitant Excessive, Expensive, Nimiety, Slug, Steep, Tall, Undue

Exotic Alien, Chinoiserie, Ethnic, Foreign, Outlandish, Strange

Expand(able), Expanse, Expansion Acreage, Amplify, Boom, Bulking, Develop, Diastole, Dilate, Distend, Ectasis, Elaborate, →**ENLARGE**, Escalate, Grow, Increase, Inflate, Magnify, Ocean, Outstretch, Sheet, Snowball, Sprawl, Spread, Stretch, Swell, Tensile, Vastitude, Wax, Wire-draw

Expatiate Amplify, Descant, Dwell, Enlarge, Perorate

Expect(ant), Expectation, Expected, Expecting Agog, Anticipate, Ask, Await, Due, En l'air, Foresee, Gravid, Hope, Imminent, Intend, Lippen, Look, Natural, On cue, Par, Pip, Predict, Pregnant, Presume, Probable, Prognosis, Prospect, Require, →**SUPPOSE**, Tendance, Think, Thought, Usual, Ween

Expedient Advisable, Artifice, Contrivance, Dodge, Fend, Make-do, Makeshift, Measure, Politic, Resort, Resource, Salvo, Shift, Stopgap, Suitable, Wise

Expedite, Expedition, Expeditious Advance, Alacrity, Anabasis, Celerity, Crusade, Dispatch, Excursion, Field trip, Hasten, Hurry, Kon-Tiki, Mission, Pilgrimage, Post-haste, Rapidity, Safari, Speed, Trek, Trip, Voyage, Warpath

Expel Amove, Blow, Deport, Dispossess, Egest, Evacuate, Evict, Excommunicate, Excrete, Exile, Exorcize, Hoof, Oust, Out(cast), Spit, Suspend, Turn forth, Void

Expend(iture) Budget, Consume, Cost, Dues, Oncost, Outgo(ing), Outlay, Poll, Squander, Tithe, Toll, Use

Expense(s) Boodle, Charge, Cost, Exes, Fee, Housekeeping, Law, Oncost, Outgoing, Outlay, Overhead, Price, Sumptuary

Expensive Chargeful, Costly, Dear, Executive, Precious, Pricey, Ruinous, Salt, Steep, Top dollar, Upmarket, Valuable

Experience(d) Accomplished, A posteriori, Assay, Blasé, Come up, Dab (hand), Discovery, Dree, Empiric, Encounter, Expert, → **FEEL**, Felt, Foretaste, Freak-out, Gust, Hands-on, Hard way, Have, Incur, Know, Learn, Level, Live, Mature, Meet, Mneme, Occlude, Old hand, Pass, Plumb, Seasoned, See, Senior, Sense, Sensory, Sophisticated, Spin, Stager, Stand, Street-smart, Streetwise, Taste, Transference, Trial, Trip, Tirocinium, Try, Undergo, Versed, Veteran, Work, Worldly wise

Experiment(al) Attempt, Aufgabe, Avant-garde, Ballon d'assai, Double blind, Empirical, Essay, Gedanken, → **JET**, Michelson-Morley, Peirastic, Pilot, Sample, Shy, Single-blind, Taste, Tentative, → **TRIAL**, Trial balloon, Try, Venture

Expert(ise), Experts Able, Accomplished, Ace, Adept, Adroit, Arch, Artistry, Astacologist, Au fait, Authority, Boffin, Buff, Cambist, Cocker, Cognoscente, Competent, Connoisseur, Crack, Dab(ster), Dab hand, Dan, Deft, Demon, Diagnostician, Digerati, Don, Egghead, Fancier, Fundi, Gourmet, Grand master, Gun, Guru, Hotshot, Karateka, Know-all, Know-how, Learned, Luminary, Maestro, Masterly, Mastery, Maven, Mavin, Meister, Nark, Nohow, Old hand, Oner, Oneyer, Oneyre, Oracle, Past master, Peritus, Practised, Pro, Proficient, Pundit, Ringer, Rubrician, Savant, Savvy, Science, Skill(y), Sly, Specialist, Techie, Technique, Technocrat, Technofreak, Technophile, Think tank, Tipster, Ulema, Used, Whizz, Wireman, Wisard, W(h)iz, Wizard, Wonk

Expire(d), Expiry Blow, Collapse, Croak, → **DIE**, End, Exhaust(ed), Exhale, Go, Invalid, Ish, Lapse, Neese, Pant, → **PERISH**, Sneeze, Terminate

Explain(able), Explanation Account, Annotate, Aperçu, Appendix, Clarify, Conster, Construe, Decline, Define, Describe, Eclaircissement, Elucidate, Epexegesis, Expose, Expound, Extenuate, Gloss, Glossary, Gloze, Justify, Outline, Parabolize, Salve, Solve, Tell, Upknit, Why

Explanation, Explanatory Apology, Commentary, Definition, Exegesis, Exegetic, Exposition, Farse, Gloss, Gloze, Hypothesis, Interpret, Key, Note, Preface, Rationalise, Reading, Rigmarole, Solution, Theory, Translate

Expletive Arrah, Darn, Exclamation, Oath, Ruddy, Sapperment

Explicit Clean-cut, Clear(-cut), Definite, Express, Frank, Graphic, Open, Outspoken, → **PRECISE**, Specific, Unequivocal

Explode, Explosion, Explosive Aerobomb, Agene, Airburst, Amatol, Ammonal, Aquafortis, Atishoo, Backfire, Ballistic, Bang(er), Bangalore torpedo, Big bang, Blast, Blow-out, Booby-trap, Burst, C4, Cap, Cheddite, Chug, Clap, Controlled, Cordite, Cramp, Crump, Cyclonite, Debunk, Demolitions, Depth bomb, Detonate, Dualin, Dunnite, Dust, Erupt, Euchlorine, Fiery, Fireball, Firecracker, Firedamp, Firework, Flip, Fulminant, Fulminate, Gasohol, Gelatine, Gelignite, Glottal stop, Grenade, Guncotton, Gunpaper, Gunpowder, Hand grenade, HE, Initiator, Jelly, Landmine, Low, Megaton, Melinite, Mine, Nail-bomb, Napalm, Nitre, Nitro(glycerine), Nitrobenzene, Nitrocotton, Outburst, Payload, Petar(d), Petre, Phreatic, Plastic, Plastique, Pop, Pow, Propellant, Roburite, SAM, Saucisse, Semtex®, Sheet, Shrapnel, Snake, Squib, TATP, Tetryl, Thermite, Thunderflash, Tinderbox, TNT, Tonite, Trident, Trinitrobenzene, Trotyl, Volatile, Volcanic, Warhead, Xyloidin(e)

Explore(r), Exploration Bandeirante, Caver, Chart, Discover, Dredge, Examine, Feel, Investigate, Map, Navigator, Oceanaut, Pathfinder, Pioneer, Potholer, Probe, Prospect, Research, Scout, Search, Spaceship, Voyageur

▷**Explosive** *may indicate* an anagram

Exponent Advocate, Example, Index, Interpreter, Logarithm

Expose(d), Exposure Adamic, Air, Anagogic, Apparent, Bare, Bleak, Blot, Blow, Burn, Crucify, Debag, Debunk, Denounce, Denude, Desert, Disclose, Double, Endanger, En prise, Exhibit, Flashing, Glareal, Imperil, Indecent, Insolate, In the buff, Liable, Moon, Nail, Naked, Nude, Object, Open, Out, Over, Paramo, Propale, Reveal, Showdown, Snapshot, Starkers, Streak, Strip, Subject, Sun, Time, Uncover, Unmask, Unrip, Unshroud, Whistle-blow, Windswept

Expound(er) Discourse, Discuss, Exegete, Explain, Open, Prelict, Red, Scribe

Express(ed), Expression, Expressionism, Expressive Abstract, Air, Alas, APT, Arrah, Articulate, Aspect, Breathe, Cacophemism, Circumbendimus, Cliché, Colloquialism, Conceive, Concetto, Couch, Countenance, Crumbs, Declare, Denote, Desorb, Diction, Eloquent, Embodiment, Epithet, Estafette, Explicit, Face, Fargo, Flying Scotsman, Formulate, Frown, Function, Gesticulate(d), Godspeed, Good-luck, Gotcha, Graphic, Gup, Hang-dog, Hech, Heck, Hell's bells, Idiom, Isit, Limited, Locution, Lyrical, Manifest, Metonym, Mien, Mot (juste), Neologism, Non-stop, Orient, Paraphrase, Phrase, Pleonasm, Pony, Precise, Pronouncement, Pronto, Put, Quep, Rapid, Register, Rhetoric, Say(ne), Shade, Show, Sigh, Soulful, → **SPEAK**, State, Strain, Succus, Sumpsimus, Taxeme, Term, Token, Tone, Topos, Trope, Utterance, Vent, → **VOICE**, V-sign

Expressionless Blank, Deadpan, Glassy, Impassive, Inscrutable, Po(ker)-faced, Vacant, Wooden

Expulsion Abjection, Discharge, Eccrisis, Ejection, Eviction, Exile, Pride's Purge, Removal, Sacking, Synaeresis

Extempore, Extemporise(d) Ad lib, Autoschediasm, Improvise, Pong

Extend(ed), Extension Aggrandise, Annexe, Aspread, Augment, Cremaster, Dendrite, Draw, Drop-leaf, Ecarté, Eke, Elapse, Elongate, Enlarge, Escalate, Expand, Exsert, Extrapolation, Fermata, Grow, Increase, Lanai, Leaf, Length, Long, Long-range, Long-stay, Long-term, Offer, Outgrowth, Outspread, Overbite, Overlap, Pong, Porrect, Proffer, Prolong, Protract, Reach, Renew, Retrochoir, Span, Spread, Steso, Stilt, → **STRETCH**, Substantial, Vert, Widen, Widespread, Yonks

Extensive, Extent Acre, Ambit, Area, Capacious, Catch-all, Compass, Comprehensive, Degree, Distance, Far-reaching, Large, Length, Limit, Measure, Outspread, Panoramic, Range, Reach, Scale, Scope, Size, Spacious, Sweeping, Wholesale, Wide, Widespread

Exterior Aspect, Crust, Derm, Exoteric, Facade, Outer, → **OUTSIDE**, Shell, Surface, Veneer

External Exoteric, Exterior, Extraneous, Foreign, Outer, Outward

Extinguish(er) Douse, Dout, Dowse, Extirpate, Obscure, Quash, Quell, Quench, Slake, Slo(c)ken, Snuff, Sprinkler, Stifle, Suppress

Extra Accessory, Addendum, Additament, Addition(al), Additive, Adjunct, And, Annexe, Appendix, Attachment, Bisque, Bonus, By(e), Codicil, Debauchery, Else, Encore, Etcetera, Frill, Further, Gash, Lagniappe, Left-over, Leg bye, Make-weight, Mo, More, Nimiety, No ball, Odd, Optional, Out, Over, Perk, Plus, Plusage, Reserve, Ripieno, → **SPARE**, Spilth, Staffage, Sundry, Super, Superadd,

Supernumerary, Supplementary, Suppletive, Surcharge, Surplus, Top up, Trop, Undue, Walking-gentleman, Walking-lady, Wide, Woundy

Extract(ion), Extractor Bleed, Breeding, Catechu, Clip, Corkscrew, Decoction, Derive, Descent, Distil, Draw, Educe, Elicit, Episode, Essence, Excerpt, Extort, Formyl, Gist, Gobbet, Insulin, Ionone, Liebig, Malta, Parentage, Passage, Pick, Piece, Prize, Pry, Quintessence, Quotation, Render, Retrieve, Smelt, Snippet, Soundbite, Succus, Suck, Summary, Tap, Tincture, Trie, Try, Vanilla, Vegemite®, Winkle, Withdraw, Worm, Wrest, Wring

Extraordinary Amazing, Egregious, Fabulous, Humdinger, Important, Non(e)such, Phenomenal, Preternatural, Rare, Remarkable, Signal, Singular, Sorter, Startling, Stellar, Strange, Unusual

Extrasensory Clairaudience, Clairvoyance, ESP

Extravagance, Extravagant, Extravaganza Bizarre, Dissipation, Elaborate, Enthusiasm, Excessive, Fancy, Feerie, Flamboyant, Grotesque, Heroic, High-flown, High roller, Hyperbole, Immoderate, Lavish, Lush, Luxury, OTT, Outré, Prodigal, Profuse, Rampant, Reckless, Riotise, Splash, Splurge, Squander, Sumptuous, Superfluous, Waste, Wasterfulness

Extreme(s), Extremely, Extremist, Extremity Acute, All-fired, Almighty, Butt, Desperate, Die-hard, Drastic, Edge, Exceptional, Farthermost, Fascist, Gross, In spades, → **INTENSE**, Leveller, Major, Maximum, Mega-, Merveilleux, Militant, Minimum, Much, National Front, Not half, Opposite, OTT, Over the top, Parlous, Pretty, Radical, Remote, So, Solstice, Sublime, Tendency, Terminal, Terrorist, The last cast, Tip, Too, Tremendous, Ultimate, Ultra, Utmost, Utter(ance), → **VERY**, Violent, Vitally, Wing

▷**Extreme** *may indicate* a first or last letter

Exuberance, Exuberant Abundant, Brio, Bushy, Copious, Ebullient, Effusive, Feisty, Flamboyant, Gleeful, Gusto, Hearty, Joie de vivre, Lavish, Mad, Overflowing, Profuse, Rumbustious, Skippy, Streamered

Exult(ant), Exultation Cock-a-hoop, Crow, Elated, → **GLOAT**, Glorify, Glory be, Jubilant, Paeonic, Rejoice, Tripudiate, Triumphant, Whoop

Eye(d), Eyes, Eye-ball, Eyeful, Eye movement, Eyepiece Aperture, Detective, Evil, Glass, Goggles, Iris, Jack, Keek, Klieg, Lamp, Lazy, Lens, Magic, Mincepie, Mind's, Naked, → **OBSERVE**, Ocellar, Ogle, Optic, Orb, Peeper, PI, Pupil, Regard, Retina, Roving, Saccade, Saucer, Sheep's, Sight, Spy, Stemma, Tiger, Uvea, Watch, Weather, Windows

Eyesore Blot, Carbuncle, Disfigurement, Sty(e)

Eye trouble, Eye-problem Amblyopia, Ametropia, Anirida, Aniseikonia, Anisomatropia, Asthenopia, Astigmatism, Cataract, Ceratitis, Coloboma, Comae, Conjunctivitis, Detached retina, Diplopia, Ectropion, Ectropium, Entropion, Exophthalmus, Glaucoma, Hemeralopia, Hemi(an)op(s)ia, Hypermetropia, Iritis, Keratitis, Leucoma, Lippitude, Micropsia, Miosis, Mydriasis, Myosis, Nebula, Nyctalopia, Nystagmus, Presbyopia, Proptosis, Ptosis, Retinitis, Scotoma(ta), Stigmatism, Strabismus, Synechia, Teichopsia, Trachoma, Tritanopia, Tylosis, Wall-eye, Xeroma, Xerophthalmia

Ff

F Fahrenheit, Fellow, Feminine, Fluorine, Following, Force, Foxtrot

Fable(s) Aesop, Allegory, Apologue, Exemplum, Fiction, Hitopadesa, La Fontaine, Legend, Lie, Marchen, Milesian, Myth, Panchatantra, Parable, Romance, Tale

Fabric Acetate, Cheesecloth, →**CLOTH**, Dévoré, Evenweave, Felt, Framework, Hessian, Interfacing, Interlining, Interlock, Lycra, Orlon®, Plissé, Ratteen, Ripstop, Spandex, Stretch-knit, Textile, Velour

Fabricate, Fabrication Artefact, Concoct, Confabulate, Construct, Contrive, Cook, Fake, Figment, Forge, →**INVENT**, Lie, Make up, Porky, Trump, Weave, Web

Fabulous (beast), Fabulous place Chimera, Cockatrice, Eldorado, Fictitious, Fung, Gear, Incredible, Jabberwock(y), Legendary, Magic, Manticore, Merman, Mythical, Orc, Phoenix, Roc, Romantic, Sphinx, Unicorn, Unreal, Wyvern

Face, Facing Abide, Affront, Ashlar, Ashler, Aspect, Audacity, Beard, Bide, Bold, Brave, Brazen, Caboched, Caboshed, Cheek, Chiv(v)y, Cliff, Coal, Confront, Countenance, Culet, Dalle, Dare, Dartle, Daur, Deadpan, Dial, Eek, Elevation, Encounter, Expression, Facade, Fat, Favour, Features, Fineer, Fortune, →**FRONT**, Gardant, Girn, Gonium, Grid, Groof, Groue, Grouf, Grufe, Gurn, Hatchet, Head-on, Jib, Kisser, Light, Lining, Look, Lore, Map, Mascaron, Meet, Metope, Moe, Mug, Mush, Obverse, Oppose, Opposite, Outstare, Outward, Pan, Paper tiger, Pavilion, Phisnomy, Phiz(og), Physiognomy, Poker, Puss, Revet, Revetment, Roughcast, Rud, Rybat, Side, Snoot, Socle, Straight, Stucco, Tallow, Three-quarter, Times Roman, Type, Veneer, Vis(age), Visnomy, Wall, Withstand, Zocco(lo)

Facetious Frivolous, Jocose, Jocular, Waggish, Witty

Facile Able, Adept, Complaisant, Ductile, Easy, Fluent, Glib, Trite

Facilitate, Facilities, Facility Agrement, Amenity, Assist, Benefit, Bent, Capability, Committed, →**EASE**, Expedite, Fluency, Gift, ISO, Knack, Lavatory, Loo, Provision, Skill

Fact(s), Factual Actual, Brass tacks, Case, Correct, Data, Datum, Detail, Eo ipso, Evidence, French, Gospel, In esse, Info, Information, Literal, Mainor, Material, Nay, Poop, Really, Stat, Statistics, Truism, Truth, Veridical, Yes

Faction Bloc, Cabal, Camp, Caucus, Clique, Contingent, Gang of four, Group(let), Junta, Junto, Party, Schism, Sect, Tendency, Wing

Factor(s) Agent, Aliquot, Amildar, Broker, Cause, Chill, Clotting, Coagulation, Co-efficient, Common, Divisor, Edaphic, Element, F, Feedback, Feel-bad, Feel-good, Fertility, Growth, House, Imponderabilia, Institorial, Intrinsic, Judicial, Load, Modulus, Moment, Multiple, Power, Pull, Q, Quality, Reflection, Representative, Rh, Rhesus, Risk, Safety, Sex, Steward, Transfer, Unit, Utilization, Wind chill, X

Factory Ashery, Bakery, Brickworks, Cannery, Creamery, Etruria, Gasworks, Glassworks, Hacienda, Ironworks, Maquiladora, Mill, Plant, Refinery, Sawmill, Shot tower, Steelworks, Sugarhouse, Sweatshop, Tanyard, Tinworks, Wireworks, Works, Workshop

Faculty Aptitude, Arts, Capacity, Department, Ear, Ease, Flair, Hearing, Indult, Knack, Lavatory, Loo, Moral, Power, School, Sense, Speech, → **TALENT**, Teachers, Uni(versity), Wits

Fad(dish) Crank, Craze, Cult, Fashion, Foible, Ismy, Thing, Vogue, Whim

Fade(d), Fading Blanch, Decrescendo, Die, Diminuendo, Dinge, Disperse, Dwindle, Elapsion, Etiolate, Evanescent, Fall, Filemot, Fizzle, Lessen, Mancando, Miffy, Pale, Passé, Perdendo(si), Peter, Pine, Smorzando, Smorzato, Stonewashed, Vade, Vanish, Wallow, Wilt, Wither

Fag(ging) Chore, Cigarette, Drag, Drudge, Fatigue, Gasper, Inconvenience, Menial, Reefer, Snout, Tire, Toil, Weary

Fail(ing), Failure Achalasia, Ademption, Anile, Anuria, Awry, Backfire, Bankruptcy, Blemish, Blow, Bomb, Bummer, Burst-up, Cark, Chicken, → **COLLAPSE**, Common-mode, Conk, Crack up, Crash, Cropper, Damp squib, Debacle, Decline, Defalcation, Default, Defeat, Defect, Demerit, Demise, Die, Disaster, Dog, Down the tubes, Dry, Dud, Fatigue, Fault, Feal, Fiasco, Fink out, Flame out, Flivver, Flop, Flow, Flunk, Fold, Footfault, Founder, Frost, Futility, Glitch, Goner, Go phut, Gutser, Impotent, Infraction, Isn't, Lapse, Lemon, Lose, Lossage, Malfunction, Manqué, Meltdown, Mis-, Miscarry, Misfire, Misprision, Miss, Muff, Nerd, No-hoper, No-no, No-show, Omission, Omit, Outage, Oversight, Pip, Plough, Plow, Pluck, Pratfall, Reciprocity, Refer, Refusal, Relapse, Respiratory, Shambles, Short(coming), Short circuit, Shortfall, Sink, Slippage, Smash, Spin, Stumer, Tank, Turkey, Vice, Wash-out, Waterloo, Weakness, White elephant, Wilt, Wipeout

Faint(ness) Black-out, Conk, Darkle, Dim, Dizzy, Dwalm, Fade, Giddy, Lassitude, Pale, Stanck, Subtle, Swarf, Swarve, Swelt, Swerf, Swerve, Swoon, Swound, Syncope, Unclear, Wan, Whitish

Fair, Fairground Aefauld, Aefwld, A(e)fald, Barnet, Bartholomew, Bazaar, Beauteous, Belle, Big dipper, Blond, Bon(n)ie, Bonny, Brigg, Clean, Clement, Decent, Donnybrook, Eirian, Equal, Equitable, Evenhanded, Exhibition, Fancy, Feeing-market, → **FESTIVAL**, Fête, Fine, Fiona, Funfair, Gaff, Gay, Gey, Goose, Gwyn, Handsome, Hiring, Honest, Hopping, Isle, Isold(e), → **JUST**, Kermess, Kermis, Kirmess, Light, Market, Mart, Mediocre, Mela, Mop, Nundinal, Objective, OK, Paddington, Passable, Play, Pro rata, Rag, Rosamond, Sabrina, Second rate, So-so, Sportsmanlike, Square, Statute, Straight, Tavistock, Tidy, Tolerable, Tow-headed, Trade, Tryst, Unbias(s)ed, Vanity, Wake, Widdicombe, Xanthe

Fairly Clearly, Enough, Evenly, Midway, Moderately, Pari passu, Pretty, Properly, Quite, Ratherish, So-so

Fairy, Fairies Banshee, Befana, Brownie, Cobweb, Dobbie, Dobby, Elf(in), Fay, Gloriana, Good neighbour, Hob, Hop o' my thumb, Leprechaun, Lilian, Mab, Morgane(tta), Morgan le Fay, Moth, Mustardseed, Nis, Oberon, Peri, Pigwidgin, Pigwiggen, Pisky, Pixie, Pouf, Puck, Punce, Queen Mab, Sandman, Spirit, Sprite, Sugar-plum, Tink(erbell), Titania, Tooth, Urchin-shows

Faith(ful) Accurate, Achates, Adam, Belief, Constant, Creed, Cupboard, Devoted, Doctrine, Faix, Fay, Feal, Fegs, Fideism, Fiducial, Haith, Implicit, Islam, Lay, Liege, Loyal, Pantheism, Plerophory, Puritanism, Quaker, Reliance,

Religion, Shema, Solifidian, Staunch, Strict, Troth, →**TRUE**, True-blue, Trust, Truth, Umma(h), Vera

Fake(d), Faker, Faking Bodgie, Bogus, Charlatan, Cod, Copy, Counterfeit, Duff(er), Ersatz, False, Feign, Fold, Forgery, Fraud, Fudge, Imitation, Imposter, Impostor, Inauthentic, Paste, Phoney, Pirate(d), Postiche, Pretend, Pseudo, Quack, Sham, Spurious, Straw man, Toy, Trucage, Trumped up, Truquage, Truqueur, Unreal, Untrue

Falcon Cast, Gentle, Hawk, Hobby, Kestrel, Lanner(et), Merlin, Nankeen kestrel, Nyas, Peregrine, Prairie, Saker, Sakeret, Sparrow-hawk, Stallion, Staniel, Stannel, Stanyel, Stone, Tassel-gentle, Tassell-gent, Tercel-gentle

Fall(s), Fallen, Falling, Fall out Abate, Accrue, Alopecia, Angel, Anticlimax, Arches, Astart, Autumn, Boyoma, Cadence, Caducous, Cascade, Cataract, Chute, Collapse, Crash, Cropper, Cross press, Declasse, Declension, Decrease, Degenerate, Deluge, Descent, Dip, Domino effect, Douse, Downpour, Downswing, Dowse, →**DROP**, Ebb, End, Firn, Flop, Flump, Folding press, Free, Grabble, Gutser, Gutzer, Horseshoe, Idaho, Iguaçu, Incidence, Kabalega, Kaieteur, Keel over, Lag, Landslide, Lapse, Lin(n), Montmorency, Mtarazi, Niagara, Oct(ober), Overbalance, Owen, Perish, Plonk, Plummet, Plump, Plunge, Precipitance, Prolapse, Ptosis, Purl(er), Rain, Reaction, Relapse, Ruin, Season, Sheet, Sin, Sleet, Slide, Slip, Snow, Spill, Sutherland, Swallow, Tailor, Takakkau, Teem, Topple, Toss, Trip, Tugela, Tumble, Victoria, Voluntary, Wipeout, Yosemite

Fallacious, Fallacy Elench(us), Error, Idolon, Idolum, Illogical, Illusion, Pathetic, Sophism, Unsound

▷**Falling** *may indicate* an anagram or a word backwards

False, Falsify, Falsification, Falsehood Adulterate, Assumed, Bastard, Bodgie, Bogus, Braide, Bricking, Bum, Calumny, Canard, Cavil, Charlatan, Cook, Counterfeit, Deceitful, Disloyal, Dissemble, Doctor, Façade, Fake, Faux, Feigned, Fiddle, Forge, Illusory, Inexact, Insincere, Knave, Leasing, Lying, Masquerade, Meretricious, Misconception, Misrepresented, Misstatement, Mock, Mooncalf, Mooncall, Myth, Obreption, Perjury, Phoney, Pinchbeck, Postiche, Pretence, Prosthesis, Pseudo, Refute, Roorback, Sham, Specious, Spoof, Spurious, Strumpet, Suspect, Treacherous, Trumped-up, Two-faced, Untrue

Fame, Famous A-list, All-star, Bruit, Cause célèbre, Celebrity, Distinguished, Eminent, Five, Glitterati, Gloire, Glory, Greatness, History, Humour, Illustrious, Known, Kudos, Legendary, Luminary, Luminous, Lustre, Megastar, Mononym, Name, Noted, Notorious, Prestige, Reclamé, Renown, Repute, Robert, Rumour, Splendent, Spotlight, Spur, Stardom, Word

Familiar(ise), Familiarity Accustom, Acquaint, Assuefaction, Au fait, Auld, Chummy, Comrade, Consuetude, Conversant, Couth, Crony, Dear, Demon, Easy, Free, Fresh, Friend, Habitual, Hailfellow, Homely, Homey, Incubus, Intimate, Known, Liberty, Maty, Old, Old-hat, Privy, Public, Python, Streetwise, Used, Versant, Versed, Warhorse

Family Ainga, Ancestry, Bairn-team, Blood, Breed, Clan, Class, Cognate, Consanguine, County, Descent, Dynasty, Extended, Eye, Hapsburg, House(hold), Issue, Kin, Kind, Kindred, Line, Mafia, Medici, Name, Nuclear, Orange, People, Phratry, Progeny, Quiverful, Race, Roots, Sept, Sib(b), Sibship, Single-parent, Stem, Stirps, Storge, Strain, Sub-order, Syndyasmian, Taffy, Talbot, Totem, Tribe

Famine Dearth, Lack, Scarcity

▷**Famished** *may indicate* an 'o' in the middle of a word

Fan(s), Fan-like Addict, Adherent, Admirer, Aficionado, Alligator, Alluvial, Arouse, Bajada, Barmy-army, B-boy, Blow, Cat, Cheer-leader, Clapper, Claque, Colmar, Cone, Cool, Cuscus, Devotee, Diadrom, Dryer, Ducted, Enthusiast, Extractor, Fiend, Flabellum, Following, Goth, Grebo, Groupie, Groupy, Headbanger, Hepcat, Khuskhus, Muso, Outspread, Partisan, Popette, Propellor, Public, Punka(h), Radiate, Rhipidate, Ringsider, Rooter, Rotary, Sail, Splay, Spread, Supporter, Tail, Tartan army, Teenybopper, Tifosi, Trekkie, Ventilate, Votary, Voteen, Washingtonia, Wing, Winnow, Zealot, Zelant

▷**Fan** *may indicate* an anagram

Fanatic(al) Bigot, Boatie, Devotee, Energumen, Enthusiastic, Extremist, Fiend, Frenetic, Glutton, Idolater, Mad, Maniac, Nut, Partisan, Phrenetic, Picard, Rabid, Santon, Ultra, Workaholic, Wowser, Zealot

Fancy, Fancies, Fanciful Adore, Caprice, Chim(a)era, Conceit, Concetto, Crotchet, Daydream, Dream, Dudish, Elaborate, Embellishment, Fangle, Fantasy, Fit, Flam, Flash, Florid, Flowery, Frilly, Frothy, Guess, Hallo, Idea(te), Idolon, →**IMAGINE**, Inclination, I say, Itch, Lacy, Liking, Maggot, Maya, Metaphysical, Mind, Mirage, Moonshine, My, Nap, Notion, Opine, Ornamental, Ornate, Passing, Petit four, Picture, Pipe dream, Predilection, Preference, Reverie, Rococo, Romanticise, Suppose, Thought, Unreal, Urge, Vagary, Visionary, Ween, Whigmaleerie, Whigmaleery, Whim(sy), Woolgather

▷**Fancy** *may indicate* an anagram

Fanfare Flourish, Sennet, Show, Tantara, Trump, Tucket

Fantasist, Fantasy, Fantastic Absurd, Amazing, Antic, Bizarre, Brilliant, Caprice, Centaur, Chimera, Cloud-cuckoo land, Cockaigne, Cockayne, Daydream, Dream world, Escapism, Fab, Fanciful, First class, Grotesque, Hallucination, Idola, Illusion, Kickshaw(s), Lucio, Make believe, Mega, Myth, Outré, Phantasmagoria, Pipe-dream, Queer, Reverie, Romance, Schizoid, Surreal, Transcendent, Unreal, Untrue, →**WHIM**, Whimsical, Wild, Wishful thinking, Wonderland, Wuxia

Far Apogean, Away, Distal, Distant, Eloi(g)n, Extreme, Outlying, Remote, Thether, Thither

Fare Apex, Charge, Cheer, Commons, Do, Eat, →**FOOD**, Go, Passage, Passage money, Passenger, Rate, Saver, Table, Traveller

Farewell Adieu, Adios, Aloha, Apopemptic, Bye, Cheerio, Departure, Godspeed, →**GOODBYE**, Leave, Prosper, Sayonara, Send off, So long, Toodle-oo, Toodle-pip, Totsiens, Vale, Valediction

Farm(ing), Farmhouse Agronomy, Animal, Arable, Bender, Bowery, Cold Comfort, Collective, Croft, Cultivate, Dairy, Deep-litter, Emmerdale, Estancia, Extensive, Factory, Fat, Fish(ery), Funny, Geoponical, Grange, Grow, Hacienda, Health, Home, Homestead, Husbandry, Intensive, Kibbutz, Kolkhoz, Land, Ley, Loaf, Location, Mains, Mas, Mixed, No-tillage, Onstead, Orley, Oyster, Pen, Poultry, Ranch, Render, Rent, Set-aside, Sewage, Shamba, Sheep run, Smallholding, Sovkhoz, Station, Stead(ing), Sted(d), Stedde, Steed, Stock, Stud, Subsistence, Tank, Till, Toon, Toun, Town, Trout, Wick, Wind

Farmer Boer, Campesino, Carl, Cockatoo, Cocky, Collins Street, Colon, Crofter, Dairy, Estanciero, Gebur, George, Giles, Hick, Husbandman, Macdonald, Metayer, Nester, NFU, Peasant, Pitt Street, Publican, Rancher(o), Reaper, Ryot, Share-cropper, Sodbuster, Squatter, Tax, Tenant, Tiller, Whiteboy, Yeoman, Zeminda(r)

Farmhand Cadet, Churl, Cottar, Cotter, Cottier, Cowman, Ditcher, Goat herd, Hand, Harvester, He(a)rdsman, Hind, Land girl, Neat herd, Orraman, Peon, Ploughman, Ranchero, Redneck, Rouseabout, Roustabout, Shearer, Sheepo, Stockman, Swineherd, Thresher, Vaquero

▶**Farmhouse** *see* FARM(ING)

Farthing Brass, F, Fadge, Har(r)ington, Mite, Q, Quadragesimal, Rag

Fascinate(d), Fascinating, Fascinator Allure, Attract, Bewitch, →CHARM, Dare, Enchant, Engross, Enrapt, Ensorcell, Enthral(l), Fetching, Hypnotise, Inthral, Into, Intrigue, Jolie laide, Kill, Mesmeric, Rapt, Rivet, Sexy, Siren, Sirenic, Spellbounding, Witch

Fascist Blackshirt, Blue shirt, Brownshirt, Dictator, Falange, Falangist, Iron Guard, Lictor, National Front, Nazi, Neo-Nazi, NF, Phalangist, Rexist, Sinarchist, Sinarquist

Fashion(able), Fashioned, Fashion house Adapt, Aguise, À la (mode), Alta moda, Armani, Bristol, Build, Chic, Construct, Convention, Cool, Corinthian, Craze, Create, Cult, Custom, Cut, Design, Directoire, Du jour, Elegant, Entail, Fabricate, Fad, Fantoosh, Feat, Feign, Fly, Forge, Form, Garb, Genteel, Go, Hew, Hip, In, Invent, Kick, Kitsch, Look, →MAKE, Manière, Manners, Method, Mode, Mondain(e), Mould, Newgate, New Look, Pink, Prada, Preppy, Rage, Rate, Sc, Shape, Sloane, Smart, Smith, Snappy, Snazzy, Soigne, Stile, Stylar, Style, Swish, Tailor, Ton, Ton(e)y, →TREND(Y), Trendsetter, Turn, Twig, U, Vogue, Waif, Way, Wear, Wise, With-it, Work, Wrought

Fast(ing), Faster Abstain, Apace, Ashura, Breakneck, Brisk, Citigrade, Clappers, Clem, Clinging, Daring, Double-quick, Elaphine, Express, Fizzer, Fleet, Hypersonic, Immobile, Lent, Lightning, Loyal, Maigre, Meteoric, Moharram, Muharram, Muharrem, Nippy, Pac(e)y, Posthaste, Presto, Promiscuous, Pronto, Quadragesimal, Quick, Raffish, Raking, Ramadan, Ramadhan, Rash, Rathe, Sehri, Smart, Spanking, Speedy, Stretta, Stretto, Stuck, Supersonic, Sure, Swift, Tachyon, Thick, Tied, Tisha b'Av, Whistle-stop, Xerophagy, Yarer, Yom Kippur, Zippy

Fasten(er), Fastening Anchor, Attach, Bar, Belay, Belt, Bind, Bolt, Buckle, Button, Chain, Clamp, Clasp, Click, Clinch, Clip, Cramp, Cufflink, Dead-eye, Diamond-hitch, Dome, Espagnolette, Eye-bolt, Frog, Gammon, Hasp, Hesp, Hitch, Hook, Infibulation, Lace, Latch, Lock, Moor, Morse, Nail, Netsuke, Nip, Nut, Padlock, Parral, Patent, Pectoral, Pin, Preen, Press stud, Reeve, Rivet, Rope, Rove, Safety pin, Screw, Seal, →SECURE, Sew up, Shut, Spar, Sprig, Staple, Steek, Stitch, Strap, Stud, Suspender, Swift(er), Tach(e), Tag, Tape, Tassel, Tether, Thong, Tintack, Toggle, Twist-tie, U-bolt, Velcro®, Wedge, Zip

Fat(s), Fatted, Fatten, Fatty Adipic, Bard, Batten, Battle, Beefy, Blubber, Bunter, Butter, Calf, Calipash, Chubby, Corpulent, Curd, Deutoplasm, Dripping, Embonpoint, Endomorph, Ester, Flab, Flesh, Frank, Grease, Gross, Lanolin, Lard, Lard-ass, Love handles, Margarine, Mart, Moti, Motu, Obese, Oil, Olein, Oleomargarine, Olestra, Plump, Podgy, Polyunsaturated, Portly, Pudgy, Puppy, Rich, Rolypoly, Rotund, Saturated, Seam(e), Shortening, Stearic, Steatosis, Suet, Tallow, Tomalley, Trans, Tub, Unsaturated, Well-padded

Fatal(ism), Fatality, Fate(s), Fated, Fateful Apnoea, Atropos, Cavel, Chance, Clotho, Deadly, Death (blow), Decuma, Destiny, Doom, End, Fay, Fell, Joss, Karma, Kismet, Lachesis, Lethal, Lethiferous, Loss, Lot, Meant, Moera(e), Moira, Morta, Mortal, Mortiferous, Nemesis, Nona, Norn(a), Parca, Pernicious, Portion, Predestination, Pre-ordain, Skuld, Urd, Verdande, Waterloo, Weird

Father(s), Fatherly Abba, Abbot, Abuna, Adopt, Agnation, Apostolic, Bapu, Begetter, Breadwinner, Brown, City, Conscript, Curé, Da, Dad, Engender, Founding, Fr, Generator, Genitor, Getter, Governor, Male, NASCAR dad, Pa, Padre, Papa, Pappy, Parent, Pater(nal), Paterfamilias, Patriarch, Patroclinic, Père, Pop(pa), Popper, Priest, Rev, Seraphic, Sire, Stud, Thames, Tiber, William

Fathom Delve, Depth, Dig, F, Plumb, Plummet, Understand

Fatigue(d) Battle, Bonk, Chore, Compassion, Exhaust, Fag, Jade, Jet lag, ME, Neurasthenia, Overdo, Overwatch, Swinked, Time-zone, Tire, Weariness, Weary

Fault(y), Fault-finding Arraign, Bad, Beam, Blame(worthy), Blunder, Bug, Cacology, Captious, Carp, Compound, Culpa, Culpable, Defect, Demerit, Dip, Dip-slip, Down to, Drop-out, Dud, Duff, → **ERROR**, Expostulate, Failing, Flaw, Foot, Frailty, Gall, Glitch, Gravity, Henpeck, Hitch, Impeach, Imperfect, Knock, Literal, Massif, → **MISTAKE**, Mortal sin, Nag, Nibble, Niggle, Nit-pick, Oblique, Oblique-slip, Out, Outcrop, Overthrust, Pan, Para, Peccadillo, Pre-echo, Quibble, Rate, Red eye, Reprehend, Rift, Rupes Recta, San Andreas, Sclaff, Set-off, Short, Slip, Snag, Step, Strike, Strike-slip, Technical, Thrust, Trap, Trough, Underthrust, Upbraid, Vice

Faux pas Blunder, Boner, Conversation stopper, Gaffe, Leglen-girth, Solecism

Favour(able), Favoured, Favourite, Favouritism Advance, Advantage(ous), Aggrace, Agraste, Alder-liefest, Anne, Approval, Auspicious, Aye, Back, Befriend, Behalf, Benefit, Benign, Bias, Bless, Blue-eyed, Boon, Bribe, Cert, Chosen, Cockade, Condescend, Conducive, Countenance, Curry, Darling, Elitist, Ewe lamb, Ex gratia, Fancy, Favonian, Firm, Front runner, Grace, Gracioso, Graste, Gratify, Gree, Hackle, Hot, In, Indulge, Intend, Kickback, Lean, Minion, Nepotism, Nod, Odour, Optimal, Particular, Peat, Persona grata, Pet, Pettle, Popular, → **PREFER**, Promising, Propitious, Resemble, Rib(b)and, Roseate, Rose-knot, Rosette, Side, Smile, Successful, Toast, Token, White boy, White-headed

Fawn(er), Fawning Adulate, Bambi, Beige, Blandish, Brown-nose, Camel, Crawl, Creep, Cringe, Deer, Ecru, Elaine, Flatter, Fleech, Footlick, Grovel, Ko(w)tow, Lickspittle, Obsequious, Servile, Slavish, Smarm, Smoo(d)ge, Subservient, Sycophant, Tasar, Toady, Truckle, Tussah, Tusseh, Tusser, Tussore

Fear Angst, Apprehension, Astra(po)phobia, Awe, Bathophobia, Bugbear, Claustrophobia, Cold sweat, Crap, Cyberphobia, Dismay, Doubt, Drad, Dread, Dromophobia, Ecophobia, Foreboding, Fright, Funk, Genophobia, Hang-up, Horripilation, Horror, Kenophobia, Monophobia, Mysophobia, Nostopathy, Nyctophobia, Ochlophobia, Panic, Redoubt, Revere, Taphephobia, Taphophobia, Terror, Trepidation, Willies

Fearful Afraid, Cowardly, Cowering, Dire, Horrific, Nervous, Pavid, Rad, Redoubtable, Sinister, Timorous, Tremulous, Windy

Fearless Bold, Brave, Courageous, Daring, Gallant, Impavid, Intrepid, Proud, Unafraid

Feast(s) Adonia, Agape, Assumption, Banquet, Barmecide, Beano, Belshazzar's, Blow-out, Candlemas, Carousal, Celebration, Convive, Dine, Do, Double, Eat, Encaenia, Epiphany, Epulation, Festival, Fleshpots, Folly, Fool's, Gaudeamus, Gaudy, Hakari, Hallowmas, Heortology, Hockey, Hogmanay, Holy Innocents, Id-al-Adha, Id-al-Fitr, Immaculate Conception, Ingathering, Isodia, Junket, Kai-kai, Lady Day, Lamb-ale, Lammas, Luau, Martinmas, Michaelmas, Movable, Name days, Noel, Passover, Pentecost, Pesach, Pig, Potlatch, Purim, Regale, Repast, Revel, Roodmas, Seder, Shavuot(h), Shindig, Spread, Succoth, Sukkot(h), Tabernacles, Trumpets, Tuck-in, Wayzgoose, Weeks, Yule, Zagmuk

Feat Achievement, Deed, Effort, Exploit, Gambado, Heroic, Stunt, Tour de force, Trick

Feather(s), Feathered, Feather-star Aigrette, Alula, Barbicel, Boa, Braccate, Cock, Contour, Covert, Crinoid, Crissum, Down, Duster, Egret, Eiderdown, Filoplume, Fledged, Fletch, Flight, Gemmule, Hackle, Harl, Hatchel, Herl, Lure, Macaroni, Oar, Ostrich, Pen(na), Pin, Pinna, Pith, Plumage, Plume, Plumule, Prince's, Pteryla, Ptilosis, Rectrix, Remex, Remiges, Rocket-tail, Rotate, Saddle-hackle, Scapular, Scapus, Semiplume, Sickle, Standard, Stipa, Swansdown, Tail covert, Tectrix, Tertial, Tippet, Tuft, Vibrissa, White, Wing covert

Feature(s) Amenity, Appurtenance, Article, Aspect, Attribute, Brow, Character, Chin, Contour, Depict, Eye, Eyebrow, Face, Facet, Figure, Fronton, Gable(t), Hallmark, Highlight, Item, Jizz, Landmark, Lineament, Neotery, Nose, Nucleus, Overfold, Phiz(og), Physiognomy, Signature, Snoot, Spandrel, Star, Temple, Topography, Touch, Trait, Underlip

Federal, Federation Alliance, Axis, Bund, Commonwealth, Interstate, League, Solidarity, Statal, Union

Fee(s) Appearance money, Base, Bench, Capitation, Charge, Conditional, Consideration, Consultation, Corkage, Corporation, Dues, Duty, Emolument, Entrance, Entry, Faldage, Fine, Great, Hir(e)age, Hire, Honorarium, Kill, Kitchen, Mortuary, Mouter, Multure, Obvention, Pay, Pierage, Premium, Ransom, Refresher, Retainer, Search, Sub, Transfer, Tribute

Feeble(ness) Banal, Characterless, Daidling, Debile, Decrepit, Dotage, Droob, Effete, Faint, Feckless, Flabby, Flaccid, Footling, Fragile, Geld, Ineffective, Infirm, Jessie, Lame, Limp, Milk and water, Mimsy, Namby-pamby, Pale, Pathetic, Puny, Rickety, Sickly, Silly, Sissy, Slender, Slight, Soppy, Tailor, Tame, Thin, Tootle, Unmanly, Wallydrag, Wallydraigle, Wan, Washy, Wastrel, Weak, Weak-kneed, Weak-minded, Weed, Weedy, Wersh, Wet, Wimpish, Worn

Feed(er), Feeding Battle, Bib, Browse, Cake, Cater, Chicken, Cibation, Clover, Diet, Dine, Drip, → EAT, Fatten, Fire, Fishmeal, Fodder, Food, Gavage, Graze, Hay, Input, Intravenous, Line, Lunch, Meal, Munch, Nourish, Nurse, Paid, Pecten, Picnic, Provender, Refect, Repast, Sate, Soil, Stoke, Stooge, Storer, Stover, Stuff, Suckle, Sustain, Tire, Tractor, Wean

Feel(ingly), Feeling(s) Aesthesia, Affetuoso, Afterglow, Algesis, Angst, Animus, Ardour, À tâtons, Atmosphere, Compassion, Conscience, Darshan, → EMOTION, Empathy, Empfindung, Euphoria, → EXPERIENCE, Fellow, Finger, Flaw, Frisk, Fumble, Grope, Groundswell, Handle, Hard, Heart, Heartstrings, Hunch, Intuit, Knock, Know, Mondayish, Mood, Palp(ate), Passible, Passion, Pity, Premonition, Presentiment, Probe, Realise, Sensate, Sensation, → SENSE, Sensible, Sensitive, Sentiency, Sentiment, Spirit, Sprachgefühl, Tactual, Tingle, Touch, Turn, Undercurrent, Vehemence, Vibes, Zeal

▶**Feet** *see* **FOOT(ING)**

Feign Act, Affect, Assume, Colour, Fake, Malinger, Mime, Mock, → PRETEND, Sham, Simulate

▶**Feline** *see* **CAT**

Fell Axe, Chop, Cruel, Cut down, Deadly, Dire, Dread, Fen, Fierce, Floor, Hew, Hide, Hill, Inhuman, Knock-down, KO, Lethal, Lit, Log, Moor, Pelt, Poleaxe, Ruthless, Sca, Shap, Skittle

Fellow(s), Fellowship Academic, Associate, Bawcock, Birkie, Bloke, Bo, Bro, Buck(o), Buffer, Callan(t), Carlot, Cat, Chal, Chap(pie), Chi, China, Chum, Co,

Cock, Cod(ger), Collaborator, Colleague, Co-mate, Communion, Companion, Compatriot, Comrade, Confrère, Cove, Cully, Cuss, Dandy, Dean, Dog, Don, Dude, Equal, F, Fogey, Fop, Gadgie, Gadje, Gaudgie, Gauje, Gink, Guy, Housemate, Joe (Soap), Joker, Josser, Lad, Like, M, Mall, Man, Match, Mate, Member, Mister, Mun, Odd, Partner, Peare, Peer, Professor, Rival, Sister, Skate, Sociate, Society, Sodality, Stablemate, Swab, Teaching, Twin, Waghalter, Wallah, Workmate

Fel(d)spar Adularia, Albite, Amazon-stone, Anorthite, Bytownite, Gneiss, Hyalophane, Labradorite, Microcline, Moonstone, Orthoclase, Peristerite, Petuntse, Petuntze, Plagioclase, Sanidine, Saussurite, Sun-stone

Felt Baize, Bat(t), Drugget, Knew, Met, Numdah, Numnah, Pannose, Roofing, Sensed, Tactile, Underlay, Velour

Female (bodies), Feminine, Feminist Anima, Bint, Bit, Dame, Distaff, Doe, F, Fair sex, Filly, Girl(y), Greer, Harem, Hen, Her, Kermes, Lady(like), Libber, Maiden, Pen, Petticoated, Pistillate, Riot girl, Sakti, Shakti, She, Sheila, Shidder, Soft, Spindle, Thelytoky, -trix, →**WOMAN**, Womens' libber, Yin

▷**Female, Feminine** *may indicate* an -ess ending

Fence(r), Fencing (position) Appel, Bar, Barrier, Botte, Carte, Deer, Dogleg, Electric, Encase, Enclose, Épée, Fight, Flanconade, Foils, Fraise, Haha, Hay, Hedge, Hurdle, Iaido, Imbroccata, Kendo, Kittle, Line, Link, Mensur, Netting, Obstacle, Oxer, Pale, Paling, Palisade, Passado, Pen, Picket, Quart(e), Quinte, Rabbit-proof, Raddle, Rail, Rasper, Receiver, Reset, Ring, Scrimure, Seconde, Sepiment, Sept(um), Septime, Singlestick, Sixte, Snake, Stacket, Stockade, Stramac, Stramazon, Sunk, Swordplay, Tac-au-tac, Trellis, Virginia, Wattle, Wear, Weir, Wire, Zigzag

Fend(er), Fend off Buffer, Bumper, Cowcatcher, Curb, Mudguard, Parry, Provide, Resist, Skid, Stiff-arm, Ward, Wing

Fennel Finnochio, Finoc(c)hio, Florence, Herb, Love-in-a-mist, Narthex, Ragged lady

Ferment(ation) Barm, Brew, Enzym(e), Leaven, Mowburn, Must, Protease, Ptyalin, Seethe, Solera, Stum, Trypsin, Turn, Vinify, Working, Ye(a)st, Zyme, Zymolysis, Zymosis, Zymotic, Zymurgy

Fern Acrogenous, Adder's-tongue, Adiantum, Archegonial, Asparagus, Aspidium, Asplenium, Azolla, Barometz, Beech, Bird's nest, Bladder, Bracken, Brake, Buckler, Ceterach, Cinnamon, Cryptogam, Cyathea, Cycad, Dicksonia, Elkhorn, Filicales, Filices, Filmy, Grape, Hard, Hart's-tongue, Holly, Isoetes, Lacy, Maidenhair, Man, Mangemange, Marsh, Marsilea, Marsilia, Meadow, Miha, Moonwort, Mosquito, Mulewort, Nardoo, Nephrolepis, Northern, Ophioglossum, Osmunda, Para, Parsley, Peppergrass, Pepperwort, Pillwort, Polypody, Ponga, Pteridology, Pteris, Punga, Rachilla, Rockbrake, Royal, Rusty-back, Scale, Schizaea, Scolopendrium, Silver, Soft tree, Spleenwort, Staghorn, Sweet, Sword, Tara, Tree, Venus's hair, Whisk, Woodsia

Ferry(man) Charon, Convey, Flying bridge, Harper's, Hovercraft, Passage, Plier, Roll-on, RORO, Sea-cat, Sealink, Shuttle, Traject, Tranect

Fertile, Fertility (symbol), Fertilisation Arable, Ashtoreth, Battle, Cleistogamy, Fat, Fecund, Fruitful, Green, Linga, Oasis, Priapus, Productive, Prolific, Rhiannon, Rich, Uberous

Fertilise(r), Fertilisation Ammonia, Auxin, Bee, Bone-ash, Bone-earth, Bone-meal, Caliche, Caprify, Compost, Dress, Fishmeal, Guano, Heterosis, Humogen, Humus, In-vitro, IVF, Kainite, Krilium®, Lime, Manure, Marl,

Night soil, Nitrate, Nitre, Pearl-ash, Phallus, Phosphate, Pollen, Potash, Seaware, Self, Sham, Side dressing, Stamen, Superfetation, Superphosphate, Tankage, Top dressing, Treat

Fervent, Fervid, Fervour Ardent, Burning, Earnest, Gusto, Heat, Hot, Hwyl, Intense, Into, Keen, Passionate, White-hot, Zeal, Zeloso

Festival, Festive, Festivity Anniversary, Beano, Carnival, Celebration, Commemoration, Convivial, En fête, → FAIR, Feast, Feis, Fête, Gaff, Gaudy, High day, → HOLIDAY, Lemural, Play, Revel, Semi-double, Wake, Wassail

Fête Bazaar, Champêtre, Entertain, → FESTIVITY, Gala, Honour, Mela, Tattoo

Fetish(ist) Charm, Compulsion, Idol, Ju-ju, Obeah, Obi(a), Talisman, Totem, Voodoo

Fetter Anklet, Basil, Bilboes, Chain, Gyve, Hamshackle, Hobble, Hopple, Iron, Leg-iron, Manacle, Shackle

Feud Affray, Clash, Dissidence, Feoff, Fief, Quarrel, Strife

Fever(ish) Ague, Biliary, Brain, Cabin, Camp, Childbed, Dandy, Dengue, Enteric, Febrile, Ferment, Frenetic, Glandular, Heatstroke, Hectic, Jungle, Kissing disease, Malaria, Marsh, Milk, Parrot, Passion, Phrenitis, Pyretic, Rheumatic, Scarlatina, Scarlet, Ship, Splenic, Spring, Stage, Sunstroke, Swine, Trench, Typhoid, Valley, Weed, Yellow(jack)

Few(er) Handful, Infrequent, → LESS, Limited, RAF, Scarce, Several, Some, Wheen

Fiancé(e) Betrothed, Intended, Promised

Fiasco Bomb, Debacle, Disaster, Failure, Flask, Flop, Lash-up, Turkey, Wash-out

Fibre, Fibrous Abaca, Abroma, Acrilan®, Acrylic, Aramid, Arghan, Backbone, Bass, Bast, Buaze, Bwazi, Cantala, Cellulose, Coir, Constitution, Corpus Callosum, Cotton, Courtelle®, Crimple, Cuscus, Desmosome, Dralon®, Elastane, Filament, Filasse, Flax, Funicle, Giant, Glass, Gore-Tex®, Guncotton, Hair, Harl, Hemp, Henequen, Henequin, Herl, Istle, Ixtle, Jipyapa, Jute, Kapok, Kenaf, Kevlar®, Kittul, Laps, Ligament, Maguey, Monkey-grass, Monofil, Monomode, Moorva, Moral, Murva, Natural, Noil(s), Nub, Nylon, Oakum, Orlon®, Peduncle, Piassaba, Piassava, Pine-wool, Pita, Pons, Pontine, Pulu, Raffia, Ramee, Rami, Ramie, Rayon, Rhea, Roughage, Shoddy, Sinew, Sisal, Slub(b), Spherulite, Staple, Stepped-index, Strick, Sunn-hemp, Tampico, Tencel®, Toquilla, Tow, Towy, Viver, Watap, Whisker, Wood pulp

Fickle(ness) Capricious, Change, False, Flibbertigibbet, Inconsistent, Inconstant, Kittle, Light, Mutable, Protean, Shifty, Varying, Volatile, Wind-changing

Fiction(al), Fictitious Airport, Bogus, Chick-lit, Cyberpunk, Fable, Fabrication, Myth, Pap, Phoney, Pulp, Romance, Science, Sex and shopping, Speculative, Splatterpunk, → STORY, Sword and sorcery, Transgressive, Whole cloth

Fiddle(r), Fiddlesticks, Fiddlestring, Fiddling Amati, Bow, Calling-crab, Cello, Cheat, Con, Crab, Cremona, Croud, Crouth, Crowd, Crwth, Do, Fidget, Fix, Gju, Ground, Gu(e), Gut-scraper, Jerrymander, Kit, Launder, Nero, Peculate, Petty, Potter, Racket, Rebec(k), Rig, Rote, Sarangi, Saw, Sawah, Scam, Scrape, Scrapegut, Second, Sharp practice, Short change, Spiel, Strad, Sultana, → TAMPER, Thimblerig, Tinker, Trifle, Tweedle(-dee), Twiddle, Viola, → VIOLIN, Wangle

Fidget(y) Fantad, Fanteeg, Fantigue, Fantod, Fike, Fuss, Fyke, Hirsle, Hotch, Impatient, Jimjams, Jittery, Niggle, Restive, Trifle, Twiddle, Twitch, Uneasy

Field(er), Fielding, Fields(man) Aalu, Aaru, Abroad, Aceldama, Aerodrome, Agrestic, Airstrip, Area, Arena, Arish, Arpent, Arrish, Bailiwick, Baseman, Battleground, Bocage, Campestral, Campestrian, Catch, Champ(s), Chief, Close, Colour, Coulomb, Cover, Cover-point, Diamond, Discipline, Domain, Electric, Electromagnetic, Electrostatic, Elysian, Entry, Extra cover, Fid, Fine leg, Flodden, Flying, Force, Forte, Fylde, Glebe, Gracie, Gravitational, Grid(iron), Gull(e)y, Hop-yard, Ice, Keep wicket, Killing, Land, Landing, Lare, Lay, Lea(-rig), Leg slip, Ley, Line, Long leg, Long-off, Long-on, Longstop, Lord's, Magnetic, Mead(ow), Mid-off, Mid-on, Mid-wicket, Mine, Oil, Padang, Paddock, Paddy, Parrock, Pasture, Peloton, Pitch, Playing, Point, Potter's, Province, Quintessence, Realm, Reame, Runners, Salting, Sawah, Scarecrow, Scope, Scout, Shamba, Short leg, Short stop, Silly, Slip, Sphere, Square leg, Stage, Stray, Stubble, Territory, Third man, Tract, Unified, Vector, Visual, W.C., World
▷**Field** *may indicate* cricket
Field marshal Allenby, Bulow, French, Haig, Ironside, Kesselring, Kitchener, Montgomery, Roberts, Robertson, Rommel, Slim, Wavell
Fiend Barbason, Buff, Demon(ic), → **DEVIL**, Enthusiast, Flibbertigibbet, Frateretto, Fresh air, Hellhound, Hellion, Hobbididance, Mahn, Modo, Obidicut, Smulkin, Succubus
Fierce(ly) Amain, Billyo, Breem, Breme, Cruel, Draconic, Dragon, Fell, Grim, Hard-fought, Lorcan, Ogreish, Rampant, Renfierst, → **SAVAGE**, Severe, Tigrish, Tranchant, Violent, Wild, Wood, Wrathy, Wud
Fiery Abednego, Ardent, Argand, Aries, Con fuoco, Dry, Eithna, Fervent, Flambeau, Hot, Hotspur, Idris, Igneous, Impassioned, Leo, Mettlesome, Phlogiston, Piri-piri, Sagittarius, Salamander, Zealous
Fiesta Carnival, Festival, Fête, Gala, Holiday
Fifth Column, Diapente, Hemiol(i)a, Nones, Quentin, Quint(ile), Sesquialtera
Fig Bania, Banyan, Benjamin-tree, Caprifig, Fico, Figo, Footra, Fouter, Foutra, Foutre, Hottentot, Moreton Bay, Sycamore, Sycomium, Sycomore, Trifle
Fight(er), Fighting Achilles, Action, Affray, Aikido, Alpino, Altercate, Arms, Bandy, Bare-knuckle, Barney, → **BATTLE**, Battle royal, Bicker, Biffo, Blue, Bout, Box, Brave, Brawl, Bruiser, Bush-whack, Camp, Campaign, Chetnik, Chindit, Combat, Compete, Conflict, Contest, Contra, Crusader, Defender, Digladiation, Ding-dong, Dog, Dreadnought, Duel, Ecowarrior, Encounter, Engagement, Extremes, F, Faction, Fence, Fisticuffs, Fray, Freedom, Free-for-all, Fund, Gamecock, Garibaldi, Gladiator, Grap(p)le, Green beret, Grudge, Guerilla, Gunslinger, Gurkha, Handicuffs, Hurricane, J(o)ust, Karate, Kendo, Kite, Lapith, Maquis, Marine, Med(d)le, Medley, Mêlée, Mercenary, MIG, Mill, Mujahideen, Night, Ninja, Partisan, Pellmell, Pillow, PLO, Press, Pugilist, Pugnacity, Punch up, Rapparee, Rejoneo, Repugn, Resist, Ring, Rough and tumble, Ruck, Ruction, Rumble, Run-in, Running, Savate, Scold, Scrap, Scrape, Scrimmage, Scuffle, Set-to, Shadow, Shine, Shoot-out, Skirmish, Slam, Slugger, Soldado, Soldier, Spar, Spat, Spitfire, Squabble, Stealth, Straight, Strife, Struggle, Sumo, Swordsman, Tar, Tatar, Terrier, Tilt, Toreador, Torero, Tornado, Tussle, Ultimate, Umbrella, War(-dog), War-horse, War-man, Warplane, Warrior, Wrangle, Wrestle
Figure(d), Figures, Figurine, Figurative Action, Allegoric, Arabic, Aumail, Bas-relief, Body, Build, Cartouche, Caryatid, Cast, Cinque, Cipher, Cone, Cube, Cypher, Decahedron, Digit, Ecorché, Effigy, Eight, Ellipse, Enneagon, Equiangular, Father, → **FORM**, Fret, Fusil, Gammadion, Giosphinx, Girth, Graph,

Hexagram, Hour-glass, Icon, Idol, Ikon, Image, Insect, Intaglio, Integer, Lay, Manaia, Mandala, Monogram, Motif, Nonagon, Number, Numeral, Numerator, Numeric, Octagon, Octahedron, Ornate, Outline, Ovoid, Parallelepiped, Parallelogram, Pentacle, Polygon, Polyhedron, Prism, Puppet, Pyramid, Reckon, Repetend, Rhombus, Sector, See, → **SHAPE**, Simplex, Staffage, Stat(istic)s, Statue(tte), Stick, Table, Tableau, Telamon, Tetragon, Tetrahedron, Topical, Torus, Triangle, Trigon, Triskelion, Trisoctahedron, Tropology, Undecagon, Waxwork

Figure of speech Abscission, Allegory, Analogy, Antimask, Antimasque, Antimetabole, Antithesis, Antithet, Antonomasia, Assonance, Asyndeton, Catachresis, Cataphora, Chiasmus, Deixis, Diallage, Ellipsis, Euphemism, Hypallage, Hyperbaton, Hyperbole, Hysteron proteron, Irony, Litotes, Meiosis, Metalepsis, Metaphor, Metonymy, Oxymoron, Paral(e)ipsis, Prolepsis, Prosopopoeia, Siddhuism, Simile, Syllepsis, Synecdoche, Taxeme, Tmesis, Trope, Zeugma

Filament Barbule, Byssus, Cirrus, Fibre, Fibrilla, Fimbria, Floss, Gossamer, Hair, Hormogonium, Hypha, Mycor(r)hiza, Myofibril, Paraphysis, Protonema, Stand, → **THREAD**

File(s), Filing(s) Abrade, Archive, Bastard, Batch, Binary, Binder, Box, Burr, Circular, Clyfaker, Coffle, Croc(odile), Crosscut, Data set, Dead-smooth, Directory, Disc, Disk, Dossier, Download, Enter, Floatcut, Folder, Generation, In-box, Index, Indian, Lemel, Lever-arch, Limail, Line, Nail, Out-box, Packed, Pickpocket, Pigeon-hole, Podcast, Pollute, Quannet, Rank, Rasp, Rat-tail, README, Riffler, Risp, Rolodex®, Row, Scalprum, Scratch, Signature, Single, String, Swap, Swarf, Text, Tickler, TIF(F)

Filibuster Freebooter, Hinder, Obstruct, Pirate, Run on, Stonewall

Fill(ing), Filler Anaplerosis, Balaam, Banoffee, Banoffi, Beaumontag(u)e, Beaumontique, Billow, Bloat, Brick-nog, Brim, Bump, Caulk, Centre, Charge, Cram, Debone, Ganache, Gather, Gorge, Heart, Imbue, Implete, Impregn(ate), Inlay, Inspirit, Jampack, Line, Load, Magma, Mastic, Mincemeat, Nagging, Occupy, Pabulous, Packing, Permeate, Plug, Replenish, Repletive, Salpicon, Sate, Satisfy, Sealant, Shim, Slush, Stack, Stock, Stocking, Stopgap, Stopping, → **STUFF**, Tales, Tampon, Teem, Ullage

Fillet(s) Anadem, Annulet, Band, Bandeau, Bandelet, Bone, Cloisonné, Flaunching, Fret, Goujons, Grenadine, Headband, Infula, Label, Lemniscus, List(el), Mitre, Moulding, Reglet, Regula, Ribbon, Rollmop, Slice, Snood, Sphendone, Stria, Striga, Taeniate, Tape, Teniate, Tournedos, Vitta

Film(s), Filmmaker, Filmy, Filming Acetate, Animatronics, Anime, Biopic, Blockbuster, Bollywood, Bubble, Buddy, Cartoon, Caul, Cel, Chopsocky, Cine, Cinerama®, Cliffhanger, Cling, Clip, Colour, Conjunctiva, Deepie, Dew, Diorama, Docudrama, Documentary, Dramedy, Dust, Epic, ET, Exposure, Fantasia, Feature, Featurette, Fiche, Flick, Floaty, Footage, Gauze, Genevieve, Gigi, Gossamer, Hammer, Haze, Hollywood, Horror, Ident, Jaws, Kell, Lacquer, Lamella, Layer, Limelight, Loid, Machinima, Mask, Membrane, Microfiche, Mist, Monochrome, Montage, Mylar®, Newsreel, Noir, Oater, Outtake, Ozacling®, Panchromatic, Pathé, Patina, Pellicle, Photo, Plaque, Prequel, Projection, Psycho, Quickie, Reel, Release, Rockumentary, Rush, Scale, Scenario, Screen, Scum, Sepmag, Short, Shot, Silent, Skin, Skin flick, Slashfest, Slick, Slo-mo, Snuff, Spaghetti western, Splatter, Star Wars, Studio, Super 8, Suspensor, Sword and sandal, Take, Talkie, Tear-jerker, Technothriller, Toon,

Trailer, Two-shot, Ultrafiche, Ultra-rapid, Vertigo, Vicenzi, Video, Videogram, Video-nasty, Wardour St, Web, Weepie, Weepy, Western, Wuxia

Filter(ing) Bo(u)lt, Clarify, Dialysis, High-pass, Leach, Luxiviation, Percolate, Perk, Polarizing, Refine, Seep, Sieve, Sile, Skylight, Strain, Trickle

Filth(y) Addle, Augean, Bilge, Bogging, Colluvies, Crock, Crud, Defile, Dirt, Dung, Foul, Grime, Hard core, Litter, Lucre, Mire, Muck, Nasty, Obscene, Ordure, Pythogenic, Refuse, Sewage, Slime, Smut(ch), Soil, Squalor, Stercoral, Unwashed, Yuck

Final(e), Finalise, Finally Absolute, Apogee, At last, Closing, Closure, Coda, Conclusive, Cup, Decider, Denouement, End, End-all, Epilogue, Eventual, Exam, Extreme, Grand, Last, Last gap, Last resort, Net(t), Peremptory, Sew up, Swansong, Tailpiece, Terminal, Ultimate, Utter

Finance, Financial, Financier Ad crumenam, Angel, Back, Banian, Banker, Bankroll, Banyan, Bay Street, Cambism, Chrematistic, City (man), Exchequer, Fiscal, Forfaiting, Gnome, Grubstake, Monetary, Moneyman, Patronise, Revenue, Sponsor, Subsidise, Treasurer, Underwrite, Wall Street

Finch Bird, Brambling, Bunting, Canary, Cardinal bird, Charm, Chewink, Conirostral, Crossbill, Darwin's, Fringillid, Linnet, Marsh-robin, Peter, Serin, Siskin, Spink, Twite, Weaver-bird

Find(er), Finding Ascertain, Come across, Detect, Dig up, Direction, Discover(y), Get, Gobind, Govind, Hit, Inquest, → LOCATE, Meet, Minitrack®, Provide, Rake up, Rarity, Rumble, Trace, Track down, Trouvaille, Unearth, Verdict

Fine, Fine words A1, Admirable, Amerce(ment), Arts, Assess, Bawcock, Beau(t), Bender, Boss, Brandy, Brave, Braw, Bully, Buttock-mail, Capital, Champion, Clear, Clement, Cloudless, Cobweb(by), Dainty, Dandy, Donzie, Dry, End, Eriach, Eric(k), Estreat, F, Fair, Famous, Forfeit, Godly, Good(ly), Gossamer, Gradely, Grand, Hair, Hairline, Handsome, Heriot, Hunkydory, Ideal, Idle, Immense, Issue, Keen, Log, Mulct, Nice, Nifty, Niminy-piminy, Noble, OK, Okay, Oke, Okey-doke(y), Penalise, → PENALTY, Precise, Pretty, Pure, Relief, Righto, Safe, Sconce, Scratch, Sheer, Sicker, Slender, Smart, Spanking, Subtle, Summery, Super, Sure, Take, Tax, Terrific, Ticket(t)y-boo, Tiptop, Topping, Transmission, Triff, Wally, Waly, Well, Wispy

Finery Braws, Caparison, Fallal, Frills, Frippery, Gaudery, Glad rags, Ornament, Trinket, Wally, Warpaint

Finger(s), Fingernail Annular, Dactyl, Digit, Fork, Handle, Idle worms, Index, Lunula, Medius, Name, Nip, Piggy, Pinky, Pointer, Prepollex, Pusher, Ring(man), Shop, Talaunt, Talon, Tot, Trigger, White

Fingerprint(ing) Arch, Dabs, Dactylogram, Genetic, Loop, Whorl

Finish(ed), Finishing (touch), Finish off Arch, Blanket, Cadenza, Calendar, Close, Coating, Coda, Complete, → CONCLUDE, Crown, Dénouement, Die, Dish, Do, Dope, Dress, Eggshell, → END, Epilog(ue), Epiphenomena, Eradicate, Exact, Fine, Full, Gloss, Grandstand, Ice, Intonaco, Kibosh, Lacquer, Log off, Mat(t), Mirror, Napoo, Neat, Outgo, Outwork, Pebbledash, Peg out, Perfect, Photo, Picking, Polish off, Refine, Ripe, Round, Satin, Settle, Shellac, Shot, Spitcher, Surface, Terminate, Through, Top out, Up (tie), Varnish, Veneer, Washed-up, Wau(l)k, Wind-up, Wrap (up)

Finland, Finn(ish) Esth, Esthonian, Huck(leberry), Karelian, Mickey, Mordvin, Suomic, Udmurt, Votyak

Fire(side), Firing Accend, Agni, Aidan, Aiden, Animate, Anneal, Ardour, Arouse, Arson, Atar, Awaken, Axe, Bake, Bale, Barbecue, Barrage, Beacon,

Behram, Belting, Biscuit, Blaze, Boot, Brand, Brazier, Brush, Burn, Bush, Cashier, Central, Chassé, Conflagration, Corposant, Counterbattery, Covering, Cremate, Delope, Discharge, Dismiss, Élan, Electric, Element, Embolden, Ena, Energy, Enfilade, Enkindle, Enthuse, Flak, Flame, Friendly, Furnace, Glost, Greek, Gun, Hearth, Heater, Hob, Ignite, Inferno, Ingle, Inspire, Kentish, Kiln, Kindle, Launch, Let go, Let off, Light, Liquid, Lowe, Oust, Pop, Prime, Prometheus, Pull, Pyre, Pyromancy, Quick, Radiator, Rake, Rapid, Red, Red cock, Sack, St Anthony's, St Elmo's, Salvo, Scorch, Shell, Shoot, Smudge, Spark, Spirit, Spunk, Stoke, Stove, Strafe, Torch, Tracer, Trial, Trigger, Wake, Watch, Wisp, Zeal, Zip

▶**Firearm** *see* GUN(FIRE)

Fireplace Chiminea, Chimney, Grate, Hearth, Hob, Ingle, Loop-hole, Range

Fireproof Abednego, Asbestos, Incombustible, Inflammable, Meshach, Salamander, Shadrach, Uralite

Firewood Billet, Faggot, Kindling, Knitch, Tinder

Firework(s) Banger, Bengal-light, Bunger, Catherine wheel, Cherry bomb, Cracker, Devil, Feu d'artifice, Firedrake, Fisgig, Fizgig, Fountain, Gerbe, Girandole, Golden rain, Indian fire, Iron sand, Jumping jack, Maroon, Pastille, Peeoy, Petard, Pinwheel, Pioy(e), Pyrotechnics, Realgar, Rocket, Roman candle, Serpent, Set piece, Skyrocket, Slap-bang, Sparkler, Squib, Tantrum, Throwdown, Tourbill(i)on, Volcano, Waterloo cracker, Wheel, Whizzbang

Firm, Firmness Adamant, Agency, Al dente, Binding, Business, Collected, Compact, Company, Concern, Concrete, Consistency, Constant, Crisp, Decided, Definite, Determined, Duro, Establishment, Faithful, Fast, Fixed, Hard, House, Inc, Inelastic, Insistent, Loyal, Marginal, Oaky, Obdurate, Obstinate, Partnership, Persistent, →RESOLUTE, Robust, Sclerotal, Secure, Set, Siccar, Sicker, →SOLID, Sound, Stable, Stalwart, Staunch, Steady, Ste(a)dfast, Steely, Steeve, Stern, Stieve, Stiff, Strict, Sturdy, Tenacious, Tight, Tough, Unflinching, Unshakeable, Well-knit

First 1st, Ab initio, Alpha, Arch, Archetype, Best, Calends, Champion, Chief, Curtain raiser, Earliest, Eldest, E(a)rst, Foremost, Former, Front, Head, I, Ideal, Imprimis, Initial, Kalends, Led, Maiden, No 1, One, Opener, Or, Ordinal, Original, Pioneer, Pole, Premier, Première, Prima, Primal, Prime, Primo, Primordial, Principal, Priority, Prototype, Rudimentary, Scoop, Senior, Starters, Top, Victor, Yama

First class, First rate A1, Capital, Crack, Plump, Prime, Pukka, Slap up, Super-duper, Supreme, Tiptop, Top(notch)

First man Adam, Ask, Premier, President, Yama

▶**First rate** *see* FIRST CLASS

First woman Embla, Eve, Pandora, Premier

Firth Dornoch, Estuary, Forth, Inlet, Moray, Tay

Fish(ing) Angle, Bob, Cast, Catch, Chowder, Coarse, Counter, Cran, Creel, Deep-sea, Dib, Dredge, Dry-fly, Episcate, Fighting, Fly, Flying, Fry, Gefilte, Gefulte, Goujons, Guddle, Halieutics, Haul, Hen, Ledger, Mess, Net, Odd, Offshore, Oily, Otterboard, Overnet, Piscary, Piscine, Poisson, Roe, Runner, Sacred, Sashimi, Shoal, Skitter, Sleeper, Snigger, Sniggle, Spin, Spot, Surfcasting, Surimi, Trawl, Troll, Trotline, Tub, White

Fisher(man) Ahab, Andrew, Angler, Black cat, Caper, Heron, Herringer, High-liner, Liner, Pedro, Peter (Grimes), Piscator, Rodster, Sharesman, Walton

▶**Fisherwoman** *see* FISH-SELLER

Fish-seller, Fisherwoman Fishwife, Molly Malone, Ripp(i)er, Shawley, Shawlie

Fissure Chasm, Cleft, Crack, Crevasse, Crevice, Gap, Grike, Gryke, Lode, Rent, Rift, Rille, Sand-crack, Scam, Swallet, Swallow hole, Vallecula, Vein, Zygon

Fist Clench, Dukes, Hand, Iron, Join-hand, Mailed, Neaf(f)e, Neif, Neive, Nief, Nieve, Pud, Punch, Thump, Writing

Fit(s), Fitful, Fitter, Fitting(s), Fitness Able(-bodied), Access, Adapt, Ague, Align, Aline, Apoplexy, Appointment, Apposite, Appropriate, Apropos, Apt(itude), A salti, Athletic, Attack, Bayonet, Becoming, Belong, Beseemly, Bout, Canto, Capable, Competent, Condign, Congruous, Convulsion, Decent, Decorous, Dod, Dove-tail, Due, Eligible, Ensconce, Epilepsy, Equip, Expedient, Fairing, Fiddle, Form, Furnishing, Gee, Germane, Glove, Gusty, Hale, Handsome, Hang, Health, Hissy, Huff, Hysterics, In-form, Jactitation, Jag, Just, Like, Lune, Mate, Meet, Mood, Nest, Opportune, Paroxysm, Pertinent, Pet, Prepared, → **PROPER**, Ready, Relevant, Rig, Rightful, Rind, Ripe, Roadworthy, Rynd, Seemly, Seizure, Serving, Set, Sit, Sliding, Slot, Snit, Snug, Sort, Sound, Spasm, Spell, Start, Stroke, Suit(able), Tailor, Tantrum, Tenoner, Throe, Tide, Tref(a), Treif, Trim, Turn, Unit, Up to, Well, Worthy, Wrath

▷**Fit(ting)** *may indicate* a 't'

Five(s), Fiver Cinque, Flim, Mashie, Pallone, Pedro, Pentad, Quinary, Quincunx, Quintet, Sextan, Towns, V

Fix(ation), Fixed, Fixer, Fixative Affeer, Anchor, Appoint, → **ARRANGE**, Assess, Assign, Attach, Bed, Bind, Brand, Cement, Clamp, Clew, Clue, Confirm, Constant, Cure, Decide, Destine, Determine, Do, Embed, Engrain, Establish, Fast, Fasten, Fiddle, Firm, Fit, Freeze, Hard and fast, Hold, Immutable, Impasse, Imprint, Inextensible, Ingrain, Iron on, Jag, Jam, Locate, Lodge, Mend, Mount, Nail, Name, Narcotic, Nitrogen, Nobble, Odd-job man, Orientate, Peen, Peg, Permanent, Persistent, Pin, Place, Point, Repair, Resolute, Rig, Rigid, Rivet, Rut, Screw, Seat, Seize, Set, Settle, Shoo, Skewer, Splice, Square, Stable, Staple, Steadfast, Steady, Step, Stereotype, Swig, Swing, Tie, To, Toe, Unchangeable, Weld

Fixture Attachment, Away (game), Event, Home, Match, Permanence, Unit

Fizz(ed), Fizzy Bubbles, Buck's, Effervesce, Gas, Hiss, Pop, Sherbet, Sod, Soda

Flab(by) Flaccid, Lank, Lax, Limp, Pendulous, Saggy, Tubby

Flabbergast(ed) Amaze, Astound, Floor, Thunderstruck

Flag(gy), Flagging, Flags Acorus, Ancient, Ashlar, Banderol, Banner, Black, Blue Peter, Bunting, Burgee, Chequered, Colour(s), Decline, Droop, Duster, Ensign, Fail, Faint, Falter, Fane, Fanion, Gladdon, Gonfalon, Hail, Hoist, House, Iris, Jack, Jade, Jolly Roger, Kerbstone, Languish, Lis, Maple leaf, Old Glory, Orris, Pave(ment), Paviour, Pennant, Pennon, Peter, Pin, Rag, Rainbow, Red, Red Duster, Red Ensign, Repeater, Royal standard, Sag, Semaphore, Sett, Sink, Slab(stone), Slack, Stand, Standard, Stars and Bars, Stars and Stripes, Streamer, Substitute, Sweet, Tire, Tricolour, Union (Jack), Vane, Waft, Wasting, Weaken, Whiff, Whift, White (ensign), Wilt, Wither

Flagon Bottle, Carafe, Ewer, Jug, Pitcher, Stoop, Stoup, Vessel

Flagrant Blatant, Egregious, Glaring, Gross, Heinous, Patent, Rank, Shameless, Wanton

Flail Beat, Drub, Swingle, Threshel

Flair Art, Artistic, Bent, Élan, Gift, Instinct, Knack, Nose, Panache, Style, → **TALENT**

Flake Chip, Flame, Flaught, Flaw, Floccule, Flocculus, Fragment, Peel, Scale, Smut, Snow, Spark

Flamboyant Baroque, Brilliant, Flame-tree, Florid, Garish, Grandiose, Jazzy, Loud, Ornate, Ostentatious, Panache, Paz(z)azz, Piz(z)azz, Pzazz, Showoff, Swash-buckler

Flame, Flaming Ardent, Blaze, Fire, Flake, Flambé, Flammule, Flareback, Glow, Kindle, Leman, Lover, Lowe, Naked, Oxyacetylene, Reducing, Sweetheart

Flank(s) Accompany, Anta, Flange, Flitch, Ilia, Lisk, Loin, Side, Spur

Flannel Blather, Canton, Cloth, Flatter, Soft-soap, Waffle, Washrag, Zephyr

Flap(ped), Flapper, Flapping Ado, Aileron, Alar, Alarm(ist), Bate, Beat, Bird, Bobbysoxer, Bustle, Chit, Deerstalker, Dither, Earcap, Elevon, Epiglottis, Epiploon, Flag, Flaught, Flutter, Fly, Fuss, Giglet, Hover, → **IN A FLAP**, Labrum, Lapel, Loma, Loppet, Luff, Lug, Omentum, Panic, Shirt-tail, Spin, Spoiler, State, Tab, Tag, Tailboard, Tailgate, Tiswas, To-do, Tongue, Wave, Whisk

Flare(d), Flares, Flare up Bell, Bell-bottoms, Fishtail, Flame, Flanch, Flaunch, Godet, Magnesium, Scene, Signal, Skymarker, Spread, Spunk, Ver(e)y (light), Widen

Flash(y), Flasher, Flashpoint Bling, Bluette, Brainstorm, Brash, Bulletin, Emicant, Exposure, Flare, Flaught, Fulgid, Garish, Gaudy, Gleam, Glent, Glint, Glisten, Glitter, Glitzy, Instant, Lairy, Levin, Lightning, Loud, Lurex, Mo, Moment, Nanosecond, News, Pyrotechnic, Raffish, Rakish, Ribbon, Roary, Scintillation, Sec(ond), Sequin, Showboater, Showy, Snazzy, Spark, Sparkle, Sport, Streak, Strobe, Swank(e)y, Thunderbolt, Tick, Trice, Tulip, Twinkle, Vivid, Wink, Wire

▷**Flashing** *may indicate* an anagram

Flask(-shaped) Ampulla, Aryballos, Bottle, Canteen, Carafe, Cask, Coffin, Costrel, Cucurbit, Decanter, Dewar, Erlenmeyer, Fiasco, Flacket, Flacon, Florence, Goatskin, Hip, Lekythos, Livery pot, Matrass, Mick(e)(y), Moon, Pycnidium, Reform, Retort, Thermos®, Vacuum, Vial

Flat(s), Flatness, Flatten(ed), Flattener Adobe, Alkali, Amaze, Ancipital, Apartment, Bachelor, Bald, Banal, Beat, Bed-sit, Blow-out, Bulldoze, Callow, Cape, Compress, Condominium, Cottage, Court, Dead, Demolish, Diageotropic, Double, Dress, Dry, Dull, Even, Feeble, Flew, Floor, Flue, Fool, Gaff, Garden, Granny, High-rise, Home-unit, Horizontal, Insipid, Ironed, Jacent, Key, KO, Law, Lay, Level, Lifeless, Llano, Lodge, Maderised, Maison(n)ette, Marsh, Monotonous, Mud, Nitwit, Obcompressed, Oblate, Ownership, Pad, Pancake, Pedestrian, Penthouse, Pied-à-terre, Plain, Plane, Plap, Plat, Plateau, Platitude, Press, Prone, Prostrate, Puncture, Recumbent, Rooms, Salt, Scenery, Service, Smooth, Spread-edged, Squash, Stale, Studio, Tableland, Tame, Tasteless, Tedious, Tenement, Time-share, Trample, True, Uniform, Unimaginative, Unsensational, Vapid, Walk-up

Flatter(er), Flattering, Flattery Adulate, Beslaver, Blandish, Blarney, Bootlick, Butter, Cajole, Candied, Carn(e)y, Claw(back), Complimentary, Court-dresser, Damocles, Fawn, Flannel, Flummery, Foot-licker, Fulsome, Grease, Honey, Imitation, Lip-salve, Moody, Palaver, Palp, Poodle-faker, Puffery, Sawder, Smarm, Soap, Soother, Spaniel, Stroke, Sugar, Sweet talk, Sycophant, Taffy, Toady, Treacle, Unction, Wheedle

Flatulence, Flatulent Belch, Borborygmus, Burp, Carminative, Colic, Gas, Tympanites, Ventose, Wind, Wind dropsy

Flaunt Brandish, Flourish, Gibe, Parade, Skyre, Sport, Strout, Strut, Wave

Flavour(ed), Flavouring, Flavoursome Absinth(e), Alecost, Amaracus, Anethole, Angostura, Anise, Aniseed, Aroma, Bergamot, Body, Bold, Borage, Bouquet garni, Chil(l)i, Clove, Coriander, Cumin, Dill, Essence, Eucalyptol, Fenugreek, Flor, Garni, Marinate, Mint, Orgeat, Potherb, Quark, Race, Ratafia, Relish, Sair, Sapor, Sassafras, Season, Spearmint, Spice, Tack, Tang, Tarragon, → TASTE, Tincture, Twang, Umami, Vanilla, Yummy

Flaw(ed) Blemish, Brack, Bug, Chip, Crack, Defect, Fallacy, → FAULT, Gall, Hamartia, Imperfection, Infirmity, Kink, Knar, Lophole, Misspent, Nick, Rima, Spot, Stain, Taint, Tear, Thief, Windshake

Flax(en) Allseed, Blonde, Codilla, Harakeke, Harden, Hards, Herden, Herl, Hurden, Line, Linseed, Lint, Linum, Mill-mountain, Poi, Tow

Flea Aphaniptera, Chigger, Chigoe, Chigre, Daphnid, Hopper, Itch-mite, Lop, Pulex, Sand, Water

Flee(ing) Abscond, Bolt, Decamp, Escape, Eschew, Fly, Fugacity, Lam, Loup, Run, Scapa, Scarper, Scram

Fleece(d), Fleecy Bilk, Bleed, Coat, Con, Despoil, Flocculent, Golden, Lambskin, Lambswool, Lanose, Nubia, Overcharge, Pash(i)m, Pashmina, Plo(a)t, Pluck, Rifte, Ring, Rob, Rook, Shave, Shear, Sheepskin, Shorn, Skin, Skirtings, Sting, → SWINDLE, Toison, Wool

Fleet(ing) Armada, Brief, Camilla, Caravan, Convoy, Ephemeral, Evanescent, Fast, Flit, Flota, Flotilla, Fugacious, Fugitive, Glimpse, Hasty, Hollow, Lightfoot, Navy, Pacy, Passing, Prison, Spry, Street, Swift, Transient, Velocipede, Volatile

Flesh(y) Beefy, Body, Carnal, Carneous, Carrion, Corporeal, Corpulent, Creatic, Digastric, Finish, Gum, Hypersarcoma, Joint, Jowl, Ket, Long pig, Love handles, Lush, Meat, Mole, Mons, Muffin top, Muscle, Mutton, Pulp, Quick, Sarcous, Spare tyre, Succulent, Tissue, Wattle

Flex(ible), Flexibility Adaptable, Bend(y), Elastic, Genu, Leeway, Limber, Lissom(e), Lithe, Pliant, Rubbery, Springy, Squeezy, Tensile, Tolerant, Tonus, Tractile, Versatile, Wieldy, Willing, Willowy, Wiry

▷**Flexible, Flexuous** *may indicate* an anagram

Flick(er), Flicks Bioscope, Cinema, Fillip, Film, Flip, Flirt, Flutter, Glimmer, Gutter, Kinema, Movie, Movy, Riffle, Snap, Snow, Spark, Switch, Talkie, Twinkle, Waver, Wink, Zap

Flier Airman, Alcock, Amy, Aviator, → BIRD, Blimp, Brown, Crow, Daedalus, Erk, Fur, George, Gotha, Handout, Icarus, Insert, Leaflet, Lindbergh, Pegasus, Pilot, RAF, Scotsman, Spec, Speedy

Flight(y), Flight path Aeronautical, Aerospace, Air corridor, Backfisch, Birdbrain, Bolt, Bubble-headed, Capricious, Charter, Contact, Dart, Dash, Departure, Escalate, Escalier, Escape, Exaltation, Exodus, Fast, Fickle, Flapper, Flaught, Flibbertigibbet, Flip, Flock, Flyby, Fly-past, Free, Fugue, Getaway, Giddy, Grece, Grese, Gris(e), Guy, Hegira, Hejira, Hejira, Hellicat, Hijra, Lam, Loup-de-dyke, Mercy, Milk-run, Mission, Moonshot, Open-jaw, Pair, Parabola, Proving, Redeye, R(a)iser, Rode, Ro(a)ding, Rout, Runaway, Skein, Sortie, Stairs, Stayre, Steps, Swarm, Test, Top, Tower, Trap, Vol(age), Volageous, Volatile, Volley, Whisky-frisky, Wing

▷**Flighty** *may indicate* an anagram

Flimsy Airy-fairy, Delicate, Finespun, Fragile, Gimcrack, Gossamer, Jimcrack, Paper thin, Sleazy, Sleezy, Tenuous, Thin, Weak, Wispy

Flinch Blench, Cringe, Funk, Quail, Recoil, Shrink, Shudder, Start, Wince

Fling Affair, Amour, Dance, Flounce, Heave, Highland, Hurl, Lance, Pitch, Shy, Slat, Slug, Slump, Spanghew, Spree, Throw, →**TOSS**

Flint Chert, Eolite, Firestone, Granite, Hag-stone, Hornstone, Microlith, Mischmetal, Pirate, Rock, Silex, Silica, Stone, Touchstone, Tranchet

Flip(pant), Flippancy, Flipping Airy, Bally, Brash, Cocky, Facetious, Flick, Frivolous, Go postal, Impudent, Jerk, Nog, Overturn, Persiflage, Pert, Purl, Ruddy, Sassy, Saucy, Toss, Turn, Upend

Flirt(ation), Flirtatious, Flirting Bill, Buaya, Carve, Chippy, Cockteaser, Come-hither, Come-on, Coquet(te), Dalliance, Demivierge, Fizgig, Footsie, Gallivant, Heart-breaker, Kittenish, Mash, Minx, Neck, Philander(er), Pickeer, Prick-teaser, Prink, Rig, Spark, Toy, Trifle, Vamp, Wow

Float(er), Floating, Flotation Ark, Balsa, Bidarka, Bob, Bubble, Buoy(ant), Caisson, Camel, Carley, Clanger, Drift, Fleet, Flotsam, Flutterboard, Froth, Fucus, Jetsam, Jetson, Levitate, Lifebuoy, Milk, Natant, Neuston, Oropesa, Outrigger, Paddle, Planula, Pontoon, Pram, Quill, Raft, Ride, Sail, Skim, Sponson, Stick, Trimmer, Vacillate, Waft, Waggler, Waterwings, Weightless

Flock(s) Assemble, Bevy, Charm, Chirm, Company, Congregation, Dopping, Drove, Flight, Fold, Forgather, Gaggle, Gather, Gregatim, Herd, Mob, Paddling, Parishioners, Rally, Rout, School, Sedge, Sord, Spring, Trip, Tuft, Vulgar, Walk, Wing, Wisp, Wool

Flog(ger), Flogging Baculine, Beat, Birch, Breech, Cane, Cat, Clobber, Exert, Flay, Hawk, Hide, Horsewhip, Knout, Lace, Lambast, Larrup, Lash, Lather, Lick, Orbilius, Retail, Rope's end, Scourge, Sell, Strap, Tan, Tat, Taw, →**THRASH**, Thwack, Tout, Vapulate, Welt, Whip, Whipping-cheer

Flood(ed) Avalanche, Bore, Cataclysm, Deluge, Deucalion's, Diluvium, Dump, Eger, Flash, Freshet, Gush, Inundate, Irrigate, Noachic, Ogygian deluge, Outpouring, Overflow, Overswell, Overwhelm, Pour, Rage, Smurf, Spate, Speat, Suffuse, Swamp, Tide, Undam, Washland, Waterlog

Floor(ing) Area, Astonish, Astound, Baffle, Barbecue, Beat, Bemuse, Benthos, Chess, Deck(ing), Dev(v)el, Down, Entresol, Étage, Fell, Flags(tone), Flatten, Flight, Gravel, Ground, Kayo, KO, Mezzanine, Mould loft, Orlop, Paralimnion, Parquet, Pelvic, Piano nobile, Pit, Planch, Platform, Puncheon, Screed, Shop, Siege, Sole, Stage, Stagger, Story, Stump, Terrazzo, Tessella, Tessera, Thill, Throw, Trading, Woodblock

Flop(py) Belly-landing, Bomb(shell), Collapse, Dud, Failure, Fizzer, Fosbury, Limp, Lollop, Mare's-nest, Misgo, Phut, Plump, Purler, Turkey, Washout, Whap, Whitewash

Florid Asian, Baroque, Coloratura, Cultism, Flamboyant, Fresh, Gongorism, High, Red, Rococo, Rubicund, Ruddy, Taffeta

Flotsam Detritus, Driftwood, Flotage, Waift, Waveson, Weft, Wreckage

Flounce Falbala, Frill, Furbelow, Huff, Prance, Ruffle, Sashay, Toss

Flounder Blunder, Flail, Fluke, Pitch, Reel, Sandsucker, Slosh, Struggle, Stumble, Tolter, Toss, Wallop, Wallow

Flour Buckwheat, Cassava, Couscous(ou), Cribble, Crible, Farina, Graham, Gram, Kouskous, Meal, Middlings, Pinole, Powder, Red-dog, Rice, Strong, Wheatmeal, Wholegrain, Wholemeal, Wholewheat

Flourish(ed), Flourishing Blague, Bless, Bloom, Blossom, Boast, Boom, Brandish, Bravura, Burgeon, Cadenza, Dow well, Epiphonema, Fanfare, Fiorita, Fl, Flare, Florescent, Green, Grow, Kicking, Lush, Melisma, Mort, Palmy, Paraph, Pert, Prosper, Rubric, Ruderal, Scroll, Serif, Swash, Tantara, Thrive, Tucket, Veronica, Vigorous, Wampish, Wave, Welfare

Flow(ing) Abound, Afflux, Cantabile, Cantilena, Cash, Circumfluence, Current, Cursive, Cusec, Data, Distil, Ebb, Emanate, Estrang(h)elo, Fleet, Fluent, Fluid, Flush, Flux, Freeform, Gush, Indraft, Issue, Knickpoint, Lahar, Laminar, Liquid, Loose-bodied, Mane, Nappe, Nickpoint, Obsequent, Onrush, Ooze, Popple, Pour, Purl, Rail(e), Rayle, Rill, Rin, Run, Rush, Scapa, Seamless, Seep, Seton, Setter, Slur, Spate, Stream, Streamline, Teem, Tidal, Torrent, Wash, Well

Flower (part), Flowering, Flowers, Flower bed Best, Bloom, Bloosme, Blossom, Composite, Cream, Develop, Disc, Ecblastesis, Efflorescence, Elite, Fiori, Imperfect, Inflorescence, Parterre, Pick, Plant, Pre-vernal, Prime, Quatrefeuille, Quatrefoil, → **RIVER**, Rogation, Serotine, Spray, Stalked, Stream, Thyrse, Trefoil, Verdoy, Vernal, Wreath

▷**Flower** *may indicate* a river

Flu Bird, Fujian, Gas(tric), → **INFLUENZA**, ME, Wog, Yuppie

Fluctuate(r), Fluctuating, Fluctuation Ambivalence, Balance, Irregular, Seasonal, Seiche, Trimmer, Unsteady, Vacillate, Vary, Waver, Yo-yo

Flue Chimney, Duct, Funnel, Pipe, Recuperator, Tewel, Uptake, Vent

Fluent(ly) Eloquent, Facile, Flowing, Glib, Liquid, Oracy, Verbose, Voluble

Fluff(y) Blow, Bungle, Candyfloss, Dowl(e), Down, Dust, Dust bunny, Feathery, Fleecy, Flocculent, Floss, Flue, Fug, Fuzz, Girl, Lint, Muff, Noil, Oose, Ooze, Plot, Thistledown

Fluid Aldehyde, Amniotic, Anasarca, Ascites, Bile, Broo, Chyle, Cisterna, Colostrum, Condy's, Correcting, Dewdrop, Enema, Erf, Fixative, Fl, Glycerin, Humoral, Humour, Juice, → **LIQUID**, Lymph, Mucus, Oedema, Perilymph, Plasma, Pus, Sap, Serum, Shifting, Succus, Synovia, Transudate, Vitreum, Vril, Water

▷**Fluid** *may indicate* an anagram

Fluke Accident, Anchor, Chance, Fan, Flounder, Ga(u)nch, Grapnel, Killock, Liver, Lobe, Redia, Scratch, Spud, Trematoid, Upcast

Flush(ed) Affluent, Beat, Bloom, Crimson, Even, Ferret, Florid, Flow, Gild, Hectic, Hot, Level, Red, Rolling, Rosy, Royal, Rud, Scour, Sluice, Spaniel, Start, Straight, Sypher, Thrill, Tierce, Vigour, Wash, Wealthy, Well-heeled

Fluster(ed) Befuddle, Confuse, Disconcert, Faze, Flap, Jittery, Panic, Pudder, Rattle, Shake

Flute (player) Bellows-mender, Bohm, Channel, Claribel(la), Crimp, English, Fife, Fipple, Flageolet, Glass, Glyph, Groove, Kaval, Marsyas, Nose, Ocarina, Octave, Piccolo, Pipe, Poogye(e), Quena, Shakuhachi, Sulcus, Thisbe, Tibia, Toot, Transverse, Whistle, Wineglass, Zuf(f)olo

Flutter Bat, Bet, Fan, Fibrillate, Flacker, Flaffer, Flap, Flaught, Flichter, Flicker, Flitter, Fly, → **GAMBLE**, Hover, Palpitate, Pitapat, Play, Pulse, Sensation, Twitter, Waft, Wave, Winnow

Fly(ing), Flies Abscond, Agaric, Airborne, Alder, Alert, Antlion, Arch, Assassin, Astute, Aviation, Awake, Aware, A-wing, Baker, Bedstead, Bee, Black, Blister, Blowfly, Blue-arsed, Bluebottle, Bolt, Bot, Breese, Breeze, Brize, Brommer, Bulb, Bush, Cab, Caddis, Canny, Carriage, Carrot, Cecidomyia, Chalcid, Cheesehopper, Cheese skipper, Cleg, Cluster, Cock-a-bondy, Crane, Cuckoo, → **CUNNING**, Damsel, Dash, Decamp, Deer, Diptera, Dobson, Doctor, Dolphin, Doodlebug, Dragon, Drake, Drone, Drosophila, Dry, Dung, Dutchman, Escape, Face, Fiacre, Flee, Flesh, Flit, Fox, Frit, Fruit, Gad, Glide, Glossina, Gnat, Goutfly, Grannom, Greenbottle, Greenhead, Hackle, Hairy Mary, Harl, Harvest, Hedge-hop, Herl, Hessian, Homoptera, Hop, Horn, Horse, Hover, Hurtle, Ichneumon, Instrument, Jenny-spinner, Jock Scott, Lace-wing, Lamp, Lantern, Laputan,

March brown, Midge, Mosquito, Mossie, Moth, Motuca, Murragh, Musca, Mutuca, Namu, Needle, New Forest, Nymph, Onion, Opening, Ox-warble, Palmer, Para, Pilot, Pium, Plecopteran, Pomace, Race, Rapid, Robber, Sacrifice, Saucer, Sciaridae, Sciurus, Scorpion, Scotsman, Screwworm, Scud, Sedge, Sheep ked, Silverhorn, Simulium, Smart, Smother, Snake, Snipe, Soar, Spanish, Speed, Spinner, Stable, Stone, Stream, Streetwise, Syrphidae, Tabanid, Tachina, Tag, Tail, Tear, Thrips, Tipula, Trichopteran, Tsetse, Tube, Turkey brown, Turnip, Vamoose, Vinegar, Volatic, Volitate, Warble, Watchet, Water, Welshman's button, Wet, Wheat, Wide-awake, Willow, Wily, Wing (over), Yellow Sally, Yogic, Zebub, Zimb, Zipper, Zoom

Fly-catcher Attercop, Clamatorial, Cobweb, Darlingtonia, Dionaea, King-bird, Phoebe, Spider, Tanrec, Tentacle, Tyrant, Yellowhead

Foam(ing) Aerogel, Barm, Bubble, Froth, Head, Lather, Mousse, Oasis®, Polystyrene, Ream, Scum, Seethe, Spindrift, Spooming, Spume, Sud(s), Surf, Yeast, Yest

Focal, Focus(sed) Anal, Centre, Centrepiece, Clou, Concentrate, Converge, Epicentre, Fix, Hinge, Hub, Narrow, Nub, Pinpoint, Pivot, Point, Pressure point, Real, Spotlight, Train, Zoom

Fodder Alfalfa, Browsing, Buckwheat, Cannon, Clover, Eatage, Ensilage, Fescue, Foon, Forage, Gama-grass, Grama, Guar, Hay, Lucerne, Maize, Mangle, Mangold, Oats, Pasture, Provender, Rye-grass, Sainfoin, Silage, Stover, Straw, Ti-tree, Vetch, Yarran

Foe Anti, Arch, Contender, → ENEMY, Opponent, Rival

Fog Aerosol, Blur, Brume, Cloud, Damp, Fret, Haar, Miasm(a), Mist, Murk, Obscure, Pea-soup(er), Roke, Sea-fret, Sea-haar, Smog, Smoke, Soup, Thick, Vapour, Yorkshire

Foil(ed) Ba(u)lk, Chaff, Counterpoint, Cross, Dupe, Epée, Fleuret(te), Frustrate, Gold leaf, Lametta, Leaf, Offset, Paillon, Pip, Scotch, Silver, Stime, Stooge, Stump, Stymie, Sword, Thwart, Tinsel, Touché

Fold(er), Folding, Folded, Folds Camp bed, Close, Collapse, Concertina, Corrugate, Crease, Crimp, Crinkle, Cristate, Fan, Fourchette, Frill, Furl, Gather, Geanticline, Inflexure, Intussuscept, Jacket, Jack-knife, Mantle, Mitre, Monocline, Nappe, Pintuck, → PLEAT, Ply, Pound, Ruck(le), Sheep-pen, Syncline, Tuck, Wrap

Foliage Canopy, Coma, Finial, Frond, Frondescence, Greenery, Leafage, Leaves

Follow(er), Following Acolyte, Acolyth, Adhere, Admirer, After, Agree, Amoret, Anthony, Attend(ant), Believer, Chase, Clientele, Consequence, Copy, Dangle, Disciple, Dog, Echo, Ensew, Ensue, Entourage, Epigon(e), Equipage, F, Fan, Groupie, Heel(er), Henchman, Hereon, Hunt, Imitate, Jacob, Man, Merry men, Mimic, Minion, Muggletonian, Myrmidon, Neist, Next, Obey, Pan, Post, Prosecute, Pursue, Rake, Retinue, Road, Run, Satellite, School, Sectary, Secundum, Seewing, Segue, Sequel, Sequential, Seriation, Shadow, Sheep, Sidekick, S(h)ivaite, So, Stag, Stalk, Stear, Steer, Subsequent, Succeed, Sue, Suivez, Supervene, Tag, Tail, Tantony, Trace, Track, Trail, Train, Use, Vocation, Votary, Yesman

▷**Follower** *may indicate* B

Folly Absurd, Antic, Bêtise, Idiocy, Idiotcy, Imprudence, Inanity, Lunacy, Madness, Mistake, Moria, Niaiserie, Stupidity, Unwisdom, Vanity

Fond(ness) Amatory, Ardour, Attachment, Dote, Keen, Loving, Partial, Tender, Tendre

Fondle Canoodle, Caress, Dandle, Grope, Hug, Nurse, Pet, Snuggle, Stroke

Food Aliment, Ambrosia, Bait, Bento, Board, Broth, Bully, Burger, Bush-tucker, Canape, Carry-out, Cate, Cereal, Cheer, Cheese, Chometz, Chop, Chow (mein), Clio, Collation, Comestible, Commons, Cook-chill, Course, Crab, Cud, → **DISH**, Doner kebab, Eatage, Eats, Famine, Fare, Fodder, Forage, Formula, Fritter, Fuel, Giffengood, Gobi, Grillade, Grub, Gruel, Hamburger, Keep, Lasagne, Makan, Maki, Manna, Meat (loaf), Nosh, Nourishment, Oats, Obento, Opsonium, Ort, Pasta, Pasture, Pilaf, Pilau, Provand, Provender, Provision, Pu(l)ture, Real, Refreshment, Risotto, Roughage, Royal jelly, Samosa, Sandwich, Schri, Scoff, Scran, Scroggin, Skran, Snack, Soft meat, Square meal, Staple, Stir fry, Stodge, Swill, Table, Tack, Takeaway, Tempeh, Tex-Mex, Trimmings, Tripe, Tsamba, Tuck(er), Viand, Victuals, Vivres, Waffle

Fool(hardy), Fooling, Foolish(ness) April, Asinico, Asinine, Baloney, Beef-witted, Berk, Blithering, Booby, Bottom, Buffoon, Chump, Clot, Clown, Cockeyed, Cockscomb, Con, Coney, Coof, Coxcomb, Cuif, Delude, Desipience, Dilly, Dipstick, Divvy, Doat, Doilt, Dote, Dummy, Dunce, Dweeb, Flannel(led), Folly, Gaby, Gaga, Git, Goat, Goon, Goose, Gormless, Gubbins, Gull, Halfwit, Have, Haverel, Hoax, Horseplay, Idiotic, Imbecile, Inane, Insensate, Jest, Jester, Joke, Kid, Lark, Madcap, Maffin, Misguide, Mislead, Moron, Muggins, Nelly, Nerk, Ni(n)compoop, Ninny, Noodle, Nose-led, Nut, Nutmeg, Pea-brained, Prat, Preposterous, Rhubarb, Senseless, S(c)hmo, Silly billy, Simpleton, Soft, Sot, Stultify, → **STUPID**, Sweet, Thicko, Trifle, Turkey, Unredy, Vacuous, Yap, Zany

Foot(ing), Footwork, Feet Anap(a)est, Athlete's, Base, Board, Choliamb, Choreus, Choriamb, Club, Dactyl, Dance, Dipody, Flat, Ft, Hoof, Iamb(us), Infantry, One-two, Pad, Paeon, Paw, Pedal, Penthemimer, Pettitoes, Podiatry, Podium, Shanks's pony, Socle, Splay, Standing, Tarsus, Terms, Tootsie, Tread, Trench, Trochee, Trotter, Ungula, Zocco(le)

Football(er), Football club American, Association, Back, Banyana-banyana, Barbarian, Ba'spiel, Best, Camp, Centre, Double header, Dynamo, Fantasy, FIFA, Flanker(back), Futsal, Gaelic, Gazza, Goalie, Gridder, Half, Hooker, Juventus, Keeper, Kicker, Libero, Linebacker, Lineman, Lock, Midfield, Moore, National code, Nickelback, Pack, Pele, Pigskin, Ranger, RU, Rugby, Rugger, Rules, Safety, Soccer(oos), Sport, Striker, Superbowl, Sweeper, Table, Total, Touch(back), Wing

Footman Attendant, Flunkey, Hiker, Lackey, Ped(estrian), Pompey, Valet de chambre, Yellowplush

Footpath, Footway Banquette, Catwalk, Causeway, Clapper, Track

Footprint Carbon, Electronic, Ichnite, Ichnolite, Ornithichnite, Pad, Prick, Pug, Seal, Slot, Trace, Track, Vestige

Footwear Espadrille, Gumboot, Jackboot, Sandshoe, → **SHOE**, Slipper, Sock, Spats, Stocking

Fop(pish) Apery, Barbermonger, Beau, Buck, Cat, Coxcomb, Dandy, Dude, Exquisite, Fallal, Fantastico, Finical, La-di-da, Macaroni, Monarcho, Muscadin, Petit maître, Popinjay, Skipjack, Swell, Toff

For Ayes, Because, Concerning, Cos, Pro, Since, To

Forage Alfalfa, Etape, Fodder, Graze, Greenfeed, Lucern(e), Pickeer, Prog, Raid, Rummage, Sainfoin, Scavenge, Search

Forbear(ance), Forbearing Abstain, Clement, Endure, Indulgent, Lenience, Lineage, Longanimity, Mercy, Overgo, Pardon, Parent, Patient, Quarter, → **REFRAIN**, Suffer, Tolerant, Withhold

Forbid(den), Forbidding Aversive, Ban, Bar, City, Denied, Don't, Dour, Enjoin, For(e)speak, Gaunt, Grim, Haram, Hostile, Illicit, Loury, NL, Prohibit, Proscribe, Sinister, Stern, Taboo, Tabu, Tapu, Tref(a), Verboten, Veto

Force(d), Forceful(ly), Forces, Forcible, Forcing Agency, Armada, Army, Assertive, Back emf, Bludgeon, Body, Brigade, Bring, Brunt, Brute, Bulldoze, Capillary, Centrifugal, Coerce, Coercive, Commando, Compel, Con brio, Conscript, Constabulary, Constrain, Contingent, Cops, Cram, Detachment, Domineer, Dragoon, Drive, Duress(e), Edge, Electromotive, Emphatic, Energetic, Exact, Exchange, Expeditionary, Fifth, Fire brigade, Foot-pound, Foot-ton, Foss, Frogmarch, Full-line, Garrison, Gendarmerie, Gravitational, Great Attractor, High-powered, Host, Hunter-killer, Impetus, Impose, Impress, Impulsion, Inertial, Interpol, Juggernaut, Kinetic, Kundalini, Labour, Land, Landsturm, Landwehr, Legion, Leverage, Life, Lift, Live load, Magnetomotive, Make, Manpower, Market, Met, Muscle, Nature-god, Oblige, Od, Old Contemptibles, Orotund, Personnel, Physical, Pierce, Plastic, Police, Polis, Posse, Potent, Pound, Power, Press(gang), Pressure, Prise, Propel, Psyche, Psychic, Pull, Punchy, Pushy, Railroad, Ram, Rape, Ravish, Reave, Red Army, Require, Robust, SAS, Shoehorn, Spent, Squad, Squeeze, Steam(roller), Steem, Stick, Stiction, Sting and ling, Strength, Strong-arm, Subject, Sword, TA, Task, Teeth, Territorial, The Bill, The Great Attractor, Thrust, Torque, Tractive, Troops, Upthrust, Vehement, Vigorous, Vim, Violence, Vis major, Vis visa, Vital, Vociferous, Weak, Wedge, Wrench, Wrest, Wring, Zap
▷**Force(d)** *may indicate* an anagram
▶**Forebear** *see* **FORBEAR(ANCE)**

Foreboding Anxiety, Augury, Cloudage, Croak, Feeling, Freet, Hoodoo,
→**OMEN**, Ominous, Premonition, Presage, Presentient, Presentiment, Sinister, Zoomantic

Forecast(er), Forecasting Aeromancy, Augury, Auspice, Divine, Estimate, Extrapolation, Glass, Horoscope, Long-range, Metcast, Metman, Omen, Perm, Precurse, Predicate, Predict, Presage, Prescience, Prevision, Prognosis, Prognosticate, Projection, Prophesy, Quant, Rainbird, Scry, Shipping, Skry, Soothsay, Spae, Tip, Weather

Forehead Brow, Front(let), Frontal, Glabella(r), Metopic, Nasion, Sincipitum, Temple

Foreign(er) Adventitious, Alien, Arab, Auslander, Barbarian, Easterling, Eleanor, Ethnic, Étranger, Exclave, Exotic, External, Extraneous, Extrinsic, Forane, Forinsecal, Forren, Fraim, Fremit, Gaijin, German, Gringo, Gweilo, Malihini, Metic, Moit, Mote, Outlander, Outlandish, Outside, Oversea, Peregrine, Remote,
→**STRANGE**, Stranger, Taipan, Tramontane, Uitlander, Unfamiliar
▷**Foreign** *may indicate* an anagram

Foreman Baas, Boss, Bosun, Chancellor, Clicker, Gaffer, Ganger, Manager, Overseer, Steward, Straw boss, Superintendent, Supervisor, Tool pusher, Topsman, Walla(h)

Foremost First, Front, Leading, Number one, Primary, Prime, Salient, Supreme, Upfront, Van
▷**Foremost** *may indicate* first letters of words following

Forerunner Augury, Harbinger, Herald, Messenger, Omen, Pioneer, Precurrer, Precursor, Trailer, Vaunt-courier

Foreshadow Adumbrate, Augur, Bode, Forebode, Hint, Portend, Pre-echo, Prefigure, Presage, Type

Foresight Ganesa, Prescience, Prophecy, Prospect, Providence, Prudence, Taish, Vision

Forest(ry), Forested Arboreal, Arden, Ardennes, Argonne, Ashdown, Black, Bohemian, Brush, Bush, Caatinga, Charnwood, Chase, Cloud, Cranborne Chase, Dean, Deer, Elfin, Epping, Firth, Gallery, Gapo, Glade, Greenwood, Igapo, Jungle, Katyn, Monte, Nandi, Nemoral, New, Nottingham, Savernake, Selva, Sherwood, Taiga, Teutoburg, Urman, Virgin, Wealden, →**WOOD**, Woodland

Forestall Anticipate, Head-off, Obviate, Pip, Pre-empt, Prevent, Queer, Scoop

Foretaste Antepast, Antipasto, Appetiser, Avant-goût, Pregustation, Prelibation, Sample, Trailer

Foretell(ing), Forewarn Augur, Bode, Caution, Divine, Fatidic, Forecast, Portend, Predict, Premonish, Presage, Previse, Prognosticate, Prophecy, Soothsay, Spae, Weird

Forethought Anticipation, Caution, Prometheus, Provision, Prudence

Forever All-time, Always, Amber, Ay(e), Constant, Eternal, Evermore, Keeps, Permanent

▶**Forewarn** *see* **FORETELL(ING)**

Foreword Introduction, Preamble, Preface, Proem, Prologue

For example Eg, Say, Vg, ZB

Forfeit(ed) Confiscated, Deodand, Fine, Forgo, →**PENALTY**, Phillepina, Phillepine, Philop(o)ena, Relinquish, Rue-bargain, Sconce

Forge(d), Forger(y) Blacksmith, Copy, Counterfeisance, Counterfeit, Drop(-hammer), Dud, Excudit, Fabricate, Fake, Falsify, Fashion, Foundry, Hammer, Heater, Horseshoe, Ireland, Ironsmith, Lauder, Mint, Nailery, Paper-hanger, Pigott, Proceed, Progress, Rivet head, Smith(y), Smithery, Spurious, Stiddie, Stiff, Stithy, Stumer, Tilt, Trucage, Truquage, Utter, Valley, Vermeer, Vulcan, Weld

Forget(ful), Forget-me-not, Forgetting Amnesia, Dry, Fluff, Infonesia, Lethe, Lotus, Myosotis, Neglect, Oblivious, Omit, Overlook, Senior moment, Unlearn, Wipe, Write off

Forgive(ness), Forgiving Absolution, Amnesty, Clement, Condone, Divine, Excuse, Lenity, Merciful, Overlook, Pardon, Placable, Remission, Remittal, Reprieve, Tolerant

Forgo(ne) Abstain, Cut and dried, Expected, Refrain, Renounce, Waive

Fork(ed), Fork out Angle, Bifurcate, Biramous, Branch, Caudine, Cleft, Crotch, Divaricate, Forficate, Fourchette, Grain, Graip, Morton's, Osmeterium, Pastry, Pay, Pickle, Prong, Runcible, Slave, Split, Tine, Toaster, Toasting, Tormenter, Tormentor, Trident, Trifid, Tuner, Tuning, Y

Form(s) Allotropic, Alumni, Archetypal, Bench, Body, Bumf, Cast, Ceremonial, Charterparty, Class(room), Clipped, Constitute, Coupon, Create, Document, Draw up, Dress, Etiquette, Experience, Fashion, Feature, Fig, →**FIGURE**, Formula, Frame, Free, Game, Generate, Gestalt, Group, Hare, Idea, Image, Inscape, Keto, Lexicalise, Life, Logical, Mode, Mood, Morph(ic), Morphology, Mould, Nucleate, Order, Originate, P45, Penitent, Physique, Protocol, Questionnaire, Redia, Remove, Rite, Ritual, Schedule, Sculpt, Shape, Shell, Sonata, Song, Stage, Stamp, State, Stem, Stereotype, Structure, Style, Symmetry, Talon, Ternary, Version

▷**Form** *may indicate* a hare's bed

Formal, Formality Amylum, Black tie, Ceremony, Conventional, Dignified, Dressy, Dry, Exact, Fit, Ice, Literal, Mannered, Methodic, Official, Pedantic,

Pedantry, Perfunctory, Pomp, Precise, Prim, Protocol, Punctilio, Reserved, Routine, Set, Starch, Starched, Starchy, Stiff, Stiff-necked, Stodgy, Stuffed shirt, Tails, Uptight, White tie

Formation Battalion, Brown, Catenaccio, Configuration, Diapyesis, Echelon, Eocene, Fours, Growth, Layout, Line (out), Manufacture, Origin, Pattern, Phalanx, Potence, Prophase, Reticular, Riss, Series, Serried, Shotgun, Testudo, Wedge

Former(ly) Ance, Auld, Before, Ci-devant, Earlier, Ere-now, Erst(while), Ex, Late, Maker, Matrix, Old(en), Once, One-time, Past, Previous, Prior, Pristine, Quondam, Sometime, Then, Umquhile, Umwhile, Whilere, Whilom, Yesterday

▷**Former** *may indicate* something that forms

Formidable Alarming, Armipotent, Battleaxe, Fearful, Forbidding, Gorgon, Grande dame, Powerful, Redoubtable, Shrewd, Stoor, Stour, Stowre, Sture, Tall order, Terrible, Tiger

▷**Form of, Forming** *may indicate* an anagram

Formula(te) Conceive, Define, Devise, Doctrine, Empirical, Equation, Frame, Graphic, Incantation, Invent, Kekule, Lurry, Molecular, Paternoster, Prescription, Protocol, Prunes and prisms, Reduction, Rite, Ritual, Spell, Stirling's, Structural

Fort(ification), Fortress Abatis, Acropolis, Alamo, Bastel-house, Bastide, Bastille, Battlement, Berchtesgaden, Blockhouse, Burg, Casbah, Castle, Citadel, Counterscarp, Earthwork, Fastness, Fieldwork, Garrison, Gatehouse, Grenada, Haven, Hill, Kasba(h), Keep, La(a)ger, Legnaga, Line, Mantua, Moat, Pa(h), Peel, Peschiera, Przernysl, Rampart, Ravelin, Redan, Redoubt, Salient, Stavropol, Stockade, Stronghold, Ticonderoga, Tower, Tower of London, Vallum, Verona

Forthright(ness) Blunt, Candid, Direct, Four-square, Frank, Glasnost, Outspoken, Prompt, Vocal

Fortify Arm, Augment, Brace, Casemate, Defend, Embattle, Lace, Munify, Soup up, Steel, →**STRENGTHEN**

Fortitude Endurance, Grit, Guts, Mettle, Patience, Pluck, →**STAMINA**

Fortune, Fortunate, Fortuitous Auspicious, Blessed, Blest, Bomb, Bonanza, Chance, Coincident, Godsend, Happy, Killing, →**LUCKY**, Madoc, Opportune, Pile, Providential, Sonce, Tyche, Up, Well, Well off

Fortune teller, Fortune-telling Auspicious, Bonanza, Bumby, Cartomancy, Chaldee, Cha(u)nce, Chiromancy, Destiny, Diviner, Dukkeripen, Fame, Fate, Felicity, Forecast, Genethliac, Geomancy, Hap, Hydromancy, I Ching, Lot, Luck, Mint, Motser, Motza, Oracle, Packet, Palmist, Peripety, Pile, Prescience, Pyromancy, Sibyl, Soothsayer, Sortilege, Spaewife, Success, Taroc, Tarok, Tarot, Tyche, Wealth, Windfall

Forum Arena, Assembly, Debate, Platform, Synod, Tribunal

Forward (looking), Forward(s) Accede, Advanced, Ahead, Along, Arch, Assertive, Assuming, Avanti, Bright, Cheeky, Early, Flanker, Forrad, Forrit, Forth, Fresh, Front-row, Future, Hasten, Hooker, Immodest, Impudent, Insolent, Lock, Malapert, Minx, Number eight, On(wards), Pack, Pert, Petulant, Porrect, Precocious, Prescient, →**PROGRESS**, Promote, Prop, Readdress, Redirect, Saucy, Scrum, Send, Stem, Striker, To(ward), Van, Wing

Fossil(ised), Fossils Amber, Ammonite, Baculite, Belemnite, Blastoid(ea), Calamite, Ceratodus, Chondrite, Conodont, Corallite, Cordaites, Creodont, Crinite, Derived, Dolichosauria, Encrinite, Eohippus, Eozoon, Eurypterus, Exuviae, Fogy, Goniatite, Graptolite, Hippurite, Hominid, Ichnite, Ichnolite,

Ichnology, Ichthyodurolite, Ichthyolite, Index, Kenyapithecus, Lingulella, Mosasauros, Nummulite, Olenellus, Olenus, Orthoceras, Osteolepis, Ostracoderm, Petrifaction, Phytolite, Plesiosaur, Pliohippus, Pliosaur, Pterygotus, Pythonomorph, Relics, Reliquiae, Remanié, Sigillaria, Sinanthropus, Snakestone, Stigmaria, Stromatolite, Taphonomy, Tentaculite, Thunderegg, Titanotherium, Trace, Trilobite, Uintatherium, Wood-opal, Zinganthropus, Zone, Zoolite

Foster (child, mother), Fostering Adopt, Cherish, Da(u)lt, Develop, Feed, Fornent, Further, Harbour, Incubation, Metapelet, Metaplot, Nourish, Nourse(l), Noursle, Nousell, Nurse, Nurture, Nuzzle, → REAR

Foul, Foul-smelling Base, Bastardise, Bedung, Beray, Besmirch, Besmutch, Bewray, Bungle, Contaminate, Dirty, Dreggy, Drevill, Dunghole, Enseam, Evil, Feculent, Gross, Hassle, Hing, In-off, Mephitic, Mud, Noisome, Old, Osmeterium, Paw(paw), Personal, Professional, Putid, Putrid, → RANK, Reekie, Reeky, Rotten, Sewage, Soiled, Squalid, Stagnant, Stain, Stapelia, Technical, Unclean, Unfair, Vilde, Vile, Violation, Virose

▷**Foul** *may indicate* an anagram

Found (in) Among, Base, Bed, Bottom, Build, Cast, Emong, Endow, → ESTABLISH, Eureka, Institute, Introduce, Met, Occur, Plant, Recovered, Rest, Stablish, Start, Table

Found(ation), Foundations Base, Basis, Bedrock, Cribwork, Establishment, Fond, Footing, Girdle, Grillage, Ground, Grounding, Groundwork, Hard-core, Infrastructure, Initiate, Institution, Matrix, Mattress, Pile, Pitching, Roadbed, Rockefeller, Scholarship, Stays, Subjacent, Substrata, Substructure, Trackbed, Underlie, Underlinen

▷**Foundations** *may indicate* last letters

Founder Author, Beginner, Bell, Crumple, Fail, Inventor, Iron-master, Miscarry, Oecist, Oekist, Patriarch, Perish, Progenitor, Settle, Sink, Stumble

Fountain Acadine, Aganippe, Bubbler, Castalian, Cause, Conduit, Drinking, Fauwara, Forts, Gerbe, Head, Hippocrene, Jet, Pant, Pirene, Salmacis, Scuttlebutt, Soda, Spring, Trevi, Well-spring, Youth

Four(times), Foursome, Four-yearly Boundary, Cater, Georges, Horsemen, IV, Mess, Mournival, Penteteric, Quartet, Quaternary, Quaternion, Reel, Tessara, Tessera, Tetrad, Tetralogy, Tiddy, Warp

Fourth Deltaic, Estate, Fardel, Farl(e), Forpet, Forpit, July, Martlet, Quartet, Quaternary, Quintan, Sesquitertia, Tritone

Fowl Barnyard, Biddy, Boiler, Brahma, Brissle-cock, Burrow-duck, Capon, Chicken, Chittagong, Cob, Cock, Coot, Duck, Ember, Gallinaceous, Gallinule, Game, Guinea, Hamburg(h), → HEN, Houdan, Jungle, Knob, Kora, Leghorn, Moorhen, Papageno, Partridge, Pheasant, Pintado, Poultry, Pullet, Quail, Rooster, Rumkin, Rumpy, Scrub, Solan, Spatchcock, Spitchcock, Sultan, Sussex, Teal, Turkey, Wyandotte

Fox(y) Alopecoid, Arctic, Baffle, Bat-eared, Bewilder, Blue, Canid, Charley, Charlie, Corsac, Crafty, Cunning, Desert, Discolour, Fennec, Floor, Fool, Friend, Fur, Grey, Kit, Lowrie(-tod), Outwit, Pug, Puzzle, Quaker, Red, Reynard, Rommel, Russel, Silver, Skulk, → SLY, Spot, Stump, Swift, Tod, Uffa, Uneatable, Vixen, White, Zerda, Zoril(le), Zorro

Fracas Brawl, Dispute, Mêlée, Prawle, Riot, Rumpus, Shindig, Uproar

Fraction Complex, Decimal, Improper, Ligroin, Mantissa, Mixed, Mole, Part, Piece, Proper, Quarter, Scrap, Simple, Some, Tithe, Vulgar

Fracture Break, Colles, Comminuted, Complicated, Compound, Crack, Fatigue, Fault, Fissure, Gap, Greenstick, Hairline, Impacted, Incomplete, Oblique, Pathological, Platy, Pott's, Rupture, Shear, Simple, Spiral, Splintery, Split, Stress, Transverse

Fragile Brittle, Crisp, Delicate, Flimsy, Frail, Frangible, Nesh, Slender, Tender, Vulnerable, Weak

Fragment(s) Agglomerate, Atom, Bit, Bla(u)d, Brash, Breccia, Brockage, Brockram, Cantlet, Clastic, Crumb, Disjecta membra, End, Flinder, Fritter, Frust, Graile, Lapilli, Mammock, Morceau, Morsel, Ort, →**PARTICLE**, Piece, Piecemeal, Potshard, Potsherd, Relic, Rift, Rubble, Scrap, Scree, Segment, Shard, Shatter, Sheave, Shiver, Shrapnel, Skerrick, Sliver, Smithereens, Smithers, Snatch, Snippet, Splinter

▷**Fragment of** *may indicate a hidden word*

Fragrance, Fragrant Aromatic, Attar, Balsam, Bouquet, Conima, Lavender, Nosy, Odiferous, Odour, Olent, Otto, →**PERFUME**, Pot-pourri, Redolent, →**SCENT**, Sent, Spicy, Suaveolent

Frail Brittle, Creaky, Delicate, Feeble, Flimsy, →**FRAGILE**, Nice, Puny, Rushen, Slight, Slimsy, Tottery, Weak

Frame(work) A, Angle, Babywalker, Bier, Body, Build, Bustle, Cage, Case, Casement, Casing, Chassis, Cloche, Coaming, Cold, Cradle, Crinoline, Dutchwife, Easel, Espalier, Fabric, Falsework, Fender, Fit-up, Form, Gantry, Haik, Hake, Hem, Hovel, Husk, Incriminate, Lattice, Louvre, Monture, Pack, Pergola, Pumphead, Punchboard, Quilting, Rack, Reading, Roof rack, Scaffold, Screen, Setting, Skeleton, Spider, Stand, Stern, Stitch up, →**STRUCTURE**, Substructure, Swift, Tabouret, Timeline, Tympan, Zimmer®

Franchise Charter, Concession, Contract, Liberty, Pot-wall(op)er, Privilege, Right, Suffrage, Vote, Warrant

Frank(ish), Frankly Bluff, Blunt, Cancel, →**CANDID**, Diarist, Direct, Easy, Eye-to-eye, Forthcoming, Four square, Free, Free-spoken, Guileless, Honest, Ingenuous, Man-to-man, Merovingian, Natural, Open, Outspoken, Plain-spoken, Postage, Postmark, Raw, Ripuarian, Salian, Sinatra, Sincere, Squareshooter, Stamp, Straight, Sty, Upfront, Vocal

Frantic Demoniac, Deranged, Distraught, Drissy, Frenzied, Hectic, Mad, Overwrought, Phrenetic, Rabid, Violent, Whirl(ing)

▷**Frantic** *may indicate an anagram*

Fraternise, Fraternity Affiliate, Brotherhood, Burschenschaft, Consort, Elk, Fellowship, Lodge, Mingle, Moose, Order, Shriner, Sodality

Fraud(ulent) Barratry, Bobol, Bogus, Bubble, Chain-letter, Charlatan, Cheat, Chisel, Collusion, Covin, Cronk, Deceit, Diddle, Dishonesty, Do, Fake, Fiddle, Fineer, Grift, Gyp, Humbug, Hypocrite, →**IMPOSTOR**, Imposture, Jiggery-pokery, Jobbery, Kite, Liar, Peculator, Phishing, Phon(e)y, Piltdown, Pious, Pseud(o), Put-up, Quack, Ringer, Rip-off, Roguery, Rort, Salami technique, Scam, Shoulder surfing, South Sea Bubble, Stellionate, Sting, Stumer, Supercherie, Swindle, Swiz(z), Swizzle, Tartuffe, Trick, Vishing, Wire

Fray(ed), Frayer Bagarre, Brawl, Contest, Feaze, Frazzle, Fret, Fridge, Ravel, Raw, Riot, Scrimmage, Wigs on the green

Freak(ish) Bizarre, Cantrip, Caprice, Chimera, Control, Deviant, Geek, Lusus naturae, Mutant, Sport, Teras, Vagary, Weirdo, Whim, Whimsy

Free(d), Freely Absolve, Abstrict, Acquit, Assoil, At large, Blank, Buckshee, Candid, Canny, Church, Clear, Complimentary, Cuffo, Dead-head, Deliver,

Deregulate, Detach, Devoid, Disburden, Disburthen, Disembarrass,
Disembroil, Disengage, Disentangle, Eleutherian, Emancipate, Enfranchise,
Enlarge, Excuse, Exeem, Exeme, Exempt, Exonerate, Extricate, Familiar,
Footloose, Frank, French, Generous, Gratis, Hand, House, Idle, Immune,
Indemnify, Independent, Kick, Large, Lavish, Lax, Leisure, Let, Liberal,
Liberate, Loose, Manumit, Open, Parole, Pro bono, Pure, Quit(e), Range,
Ransom, Redeem, →**RELEASE**, Relieve, Requiteless, Rescue, Reskew, Rick,
Rid, Sciolto, Scot, Solute, Spare, Spring, Stald, Stall, Trade, Unbowed,
Unhampered, Unhitch, Unlace, Unlock, Unloosen, Unmew, Unmuzzle, Unpen,
Unshackle, Unsnarl, Unstick, Untangle, Untie, Untwine, Untwist, Vacant,
Verse, Voluntary

▷**Free** *may indicate* an anagram

Freedom Abandon, Autonomy, Breadth, Carte blanche, Eleutherian, Exemption,
Fear, Fling, Four, Immunity, Impunity, Independence, Latitude, Leeway, Leisure,
Liberty, Licence, Magna Carta, Play, Recourse, Releasement, Speech, Uhuru,
UNITA, Want, Wiggle room, Worship

Freehold(er) Enfeoff, Franklin, Frank tenement, Seisin, Udal(ler), Yeoman

▷**Freely** *may indicate* an anagram

Freemason(ry), Freemason's son Craft, Lewis, Lodge, Moose, Templar

Freeze(s), Freezer, Freezing Alcarrazo, Arctic, Benumb, Congeal, Cool,
Cryogenic, Eutectic, Freon®, Frost, Geal, Harden, Ice, Ice cold, Lyophilize, Nip,
Numb, Paralyse, Pause, Peg, Regelate, Riss, Stiffen, Subpolar, Tense, Zero

Freight(liner) Cargo, Carriage, Fraught, Goods, Goods train, Lading, Load

French(man), Frenchwoman Alain, Alsatian, Anton, Basque, Breton,
Crapaud, Creole, Dawn, Emil(e), Frog(-eater), Gallic(e), Gascon, Gaston, Gaul,
Gombo, Grisette, Gumbo, Homme, Huguenot, Joual, M, Mamselle, Marianne,
Midi, Mounseer, Neo-Latin, Norman, Parleyvoo, René, Rhemish, Richelieu,
Savoyard, Yves

Frenzied, Frenzy Agitato, Amok, Berserk, Corybantic, Deliration, Delirium,
Demoniac, Dionysiac, Enrage, Enrapt, Euhoe, Euoi, Evoe, Fever, Fit, Frenetic,
Fury, Hectic, Hysteric, Lune, Maenad, Mania, Must, Nympholepsy, Oestrus,
Phrenetic, Rage, Tantrum, Vehement

Frequency, Frequent(er), Frequently Attend, Audio, Channel, Common,
Constant, Familiar, Formant, FR, Fresnel, Habitué, Hang-out, Haunt, Hertz,
High, Incidence, Kilocycle, L-band, Low, Megahertz, Mode, Often, Oft-times,
Passband, Penetrance, Pulsatance, Radio, Recurrent, Spectrum, Superhigh,
Terahertz, Thick, Waveband

Fresh(en), Freshness Anew, Aurorean, Brash, Caller, Chilly, Clean, Crisp,
Deodorise, Dewy, Entire, Evergreen, Fire-new, Forward, Green, Hot, Insolent,
Live(ly), Maiden, Mint, Nas(s)eem, New, Novel, Quick, Rebite, Recent, Roral,
Roric, Rorid, Rub up, Smart, Span-new, Spic(k), Sweet, Tangy, Uncured,
Verdure, Vernal, Virent, Virescent

Fret(ful) Chafe, Filigree, Fractious, Fray, Gnaw, Grate, Grecque, Haze, Impatient,
Irritate, Key, Mist, Ornament, Peevish, Repine, Rile, Ripple, Roil, Rub, Tetchy,
Tracery, Whittle, Worry

Friar(s) Augustinian, Austin, Bacon, Barefoot, Black, Bonaventura, Bonaventure,
Brother, Bungay, Capuchin, Carmelite, Conventual, Cordelier, Crutched, Curtal,
Dervish, Dominican, Fra(ter), Franciscan, Frate, Jacobin, Laurence, Limiter,
Lymiter, Minim, Minorite, →**MONK**, Observant, Observantine, Preaching,
Predicant, Recollect, Recollet, Rush, Tuck, White

Friction Attrition, Conflict, Detrition, Dissent, Drag, Massage, Rift, Rub, Stridulation, Tribology, Tripsis, Wear, Windblast, Xerotripsis

Friend(ly), Friends Ally, Alter ego, Ami(cable), Amie, Amigo, Bach, Benign, Bosom, Bra, Bro, Bru, Bud(dy), China, Chommie, Chum, Cobber, Companion, Comrade, Confidant, Cordial, Cotton, Couthy, Crony, Damon, Dog, Ehoa, Familiar, Folksy, Gossip, Homeboy, Informal, Intimate, Kidgie, Lover, Mate, McKenzie, Mutual, Next, Oppo, Pal, Pard(ner), Pen, Platonic, Playmate, Quaker, Sidekick, Sociable, Sport, Steady, Thawing, Thick, Type B, User, Well-disposed, Yaar

Friendliness, Friendship Amity, Bonhomie, Camaraderie, Contesseration, Entente, Goodwill, Platonic, Rapprochement, Sodality

Fright(en), Frightened, Frightening, Frightful Afear, Affear(e), Agrise, Agrize, Agryze, Alarm, Aroint, Aroynt, Ashake, Chilling, Cow, Da(u)nt, Dare, Deter, Eek, Eerie, Eery, Faceache, Fear(some), Flay, Fleg, Fleme, Fley, Flush, Gallow, Gally, Ghast, Gliff, Glift, Grim, Grisly, Hairy, Horrid, Horrific, Intimidate, Menace, Nightmare, Ordeal, Panic, Petrify, Scar, Scarre, Scaur, Schrecklich, Sight, Skear, Skeer, Skrik, Spook, Stage, Startle, Terrible, Terrify, Terror, Tirrit, Ugly, Unco, Unease, Unman, Windy

Frill(y) Armil, Armilla, Bavolet, Chidlings, Chitlings, Falbala, Flounce, Furbelow, Jabot, Lacy, Lingerie, Newgate, Ornament, Papillote, Ruche, Ruff(le), Shirt, Tucker, Valance

▷**Frilly** *may indicate* an anagram

Fringe(s), Fringed Bang, Border, Bullion, Celtic, Ciliated, Ciliolate, Edge, Fall, Fimbria, Frisette, Furbelow, Laciniate, Loma, Lunatic, Macramé, Macrami, Newgate, Pelmet, Peripheral, Robin, Ruff, Run, Thrum, Toupee, Toupit, Tzitzit(h), Valance, Verge, Zizith

Frisk(y) Caper, Cavort, Curvet, Fisk, Flimp, Frolic, Gambol, Search, Skip, Skittish, Wanton

Fritter Batter, Beignet, Dribble, Dwindle, Fragment, Fribble, Pakora, Potter, Puf(f)taloon, Squander, Waste, Wonder

Frivolity, Frivolous Butterfly, Empty(-headed), Etourdi(e), Facetious, Featherbrain, Flighty, Flippant, Footling, Frippet, Frothy, Futile, Giddy, Idle, Inane, Levity, Light, Lightweight, Moth, Persiflage, Playboy, Shallow, Skittish, Trifling, Trivial

Frog Amphibian, Anoura, Anura, Arrow poison, Batrachia(n), Braid, Breton, Bullfrog, Cape nightingale, Depression, Fourchette, Frenchman, Frush, Goliath, Hairy, Hyla, Kermit, Leopard, Marsupial, Mounseer, Nic, Nototrema, Paddock, Paradoxical, Peeper, Pelobatid, Platanna, Puddock, Puttock, Rana, Ranidae, Spring peeper, Tree, Wood, Xenopus

Frolic(some) Bender, Bust(er), Cabriole, Caper, Disport, Escapade, → **FRISK(Y)**, Fun, Galravage, Galravitch, Gambol, Gammock, Gil(l)ravage, How's your father, Jink, Kittenish, Lark, Play, Prank, Rag, Rand, Rant, Rig, Romp, Scamper, Skylark, Splore, Sport, Stooshie, Tittup, Wanton

From A, Against, Ex, For, Frae, Of, Off, Thrae

Front(al), Frontman Antependium, Anterior, Bow, Brass, Brow, Cold, Cover, Dead, Dickey, Dicky, Esplanade, Facade, Face, Fore(head), Forecourt, Fore end, Foreground, Groof, Grouf, Grufe, Head, Home, Insolence, Metope, National, Newscaster, Nose, Occluded, Paravant, People's, Plastron, Polar, Popular, Pose, Preface, Presenter, Pro, Prom, Prow, Rhodesian, Sector, Sinciput, Spearhead, Stationary, Tabula, Temerity, Van, Vaward, Ventral, Warm, Western

Frost(ing), Frosty, Frostbite Air, Alcorza, Black, Chill, Cranreuch, Cryo-, Freon®, Frigid, Frore(n), Frorne, Glacé, Ground, Hoar, Hore, Ice, Icing, Jack, Mat, Rime, Silver, Trench foot, White

Froth(y) Barm, Bleb, Bubble, Chiffon, Despumate, Foam, Frogspit, Gas, Head, Lather, Nappy, Off-scum, Ream, Saponin, Scum, Seethe, Shallow, Spittle, Spoom, Spoon, Spume, Sud, Toadspit, Yeasty, Yest

Frugal Meagre, Parsimonious, Provident, Prudent, Scant, Skimpy, Spare, Spartan, Thrifty

Fruit(ing), Fruit tree, Fruity Accessory, Achaenocarp, Achene, Akene, Allocarpy, Apothecium, Autocarp, Bacciform, Catapult, Cedrate, Coccus, Compot(e), Confect, Conserve, Cremocarp, Crop, Dessert, Drupe, Eater, Encarpus, Etaerio, First, Follicle, Forbidden, Fritter, Harvest, Issue, Multiple, Orchard, Output, Pericarp, Primeur, Primitiae, Product(ion), Pseudocarp, Regma(ta), Replum, Result, Return, Rich, Ripe, Schizocarp, Seed, Silicle, Siliqua, Silique, Soft, Sorosis, Stoneless, Succade, Sweetie, Sweety, Syconium, Syncarp, Utricle, Valve, Wall, Xylocarp, Yield

Fruitcake Dundee, Madman, Nutter

Fruitful(ness) Calathus, Ephraim, Fat, Fecund, Feracious, Fertile, Productive, Prolific, Teeming, Uberty, Worthwhile

Frustrate(d), Frustration Baffle, Ba(u)lk, Beat, Blight, Bugger, Check, Cheesed off, Confound, Countermine, Dash, Defeat, Discomfit, Dish, Disillusionment, Foil, Forestall, Hamper, Hogtie, Outwit, Scotch, Snooker, Spike, Stymie, Thwart

Fry, Fried, Fries Blot, Brit, French, Fricassee, Fritter, Frizzle, Parr, Sauté, Skirl-in-the-pan, Small, Spawn, Whippersnapper, Whitebait

Fuddle(d) Drunk, Fluster, Fuzzle, Maudlin, Ta(i)vert, Tosticated, Woozy

▷**Fuddle(d)** *may indicate* an anagram

Fudge Cook, Doctor, Dodge, Drivel, Evade, Fiddlesticks, Nonsense, Rot, Stop-press, Sweet(meat)

Fuel Alternative, Anthracite, Argol, Astatki, Avgas, Benzene, Benzine, Benzol, Biodiesel, Biogas, Borane, Briquet(te), Brown coal, Bunker, Butane, Candle-coal, Cannel, Coal, Coalite®, Coke, Derv, Diesel, Eilding, Eldin(g), Faggot, Feed, Fire(wood), Fossil, Gasahol, Gasohol, Gasoline, Hexamine, Hydrazine, Hydyne, Ignite, Jud, Kerosene, Kerosine, Kindling, Knitch, Lead-free, Lignite, Lox, Mox, Multigrade, Napalm, Naphtha, Nuclear, Oilgas, Outage, Paraffin, Peat, Propane, Propellant, Smudge, Sterno®, Stoke, SURF, Synfuel, Tan balls, Triptane, Yealdon

Fugitive Absconder, Defector, Ephemeral, Escapee, Fleeting, Hideaway, Lot, Outlaw, Refugee, Runagate, Runaway, Runner, Transient, Vagabond

Fulfil(ment), Fulfilled Accomplish, Come true, Complete, Consummate, Fruition, Honour, Meet, Pass, Realise, →**SATISFY**, Serve, Steed

Full(est), Fullness, Fully Abrim, Ample, Arrant, Bouffant, Capacity, Chock-a-block, Chocker, Complete, Copious, Embonpoint, Engorged, Entire, Fairly, Fat, Fed, Fou, Frontal, German, High, Hoatching, Hotch, Jam-packed, Mill, Orotund, Plein, Plenary, Plenitude, Pleroma, Plethora, Plump, Replete, Rich, Rotund, Sated, Satiated, Thorough, Thronged, Torose, Torous, Toss, Turgid, Turgor, Ullage, Uncut, Up, Wau(l)k, Whole hog, Wholly

Fulminate, Fulmination Chastise, Detonate, Explode, Levin, Lightning, Rail, Renounce, Thunder

Fumble Blunder, Faff, Grope, Misfield, Muff

Fume(s) Bluster, Gas, Halitus, Incense, Nidor, Rage, Reech, Reek, Settle, Smoke, Stum, Vapours

Fun(ny), Funny bone Amusing, Antic, Boat, Buffo, Caper, Clownery, Comedy, Comic(al), Crack, Craic, Delight, Droll, Frolic, Gammock, Gas, Gig, Giocoso, Glaik, Guy, Hilarity, Hoot, Horseplay, Humerus, Humorous, Hysterical, Ironic, Jest, Jokey, Jouisance, Jouysaunce, Kicks, Killing, Lark, Pleasure, Priceless, Rag, Rib-tickling, Rich, Rummy, Scream, Sidesplitting, Skylark, Slap and tickle, Sport, Strange, Suspect, Unwell, Weird(o), Whoopee, Wisecrack, Wit, Yell

Function(al), Functioning, Functions Act, Antilog, Arccos, Arcsin(e), Arctan, Assignment, Behave, Bodily, Business, Ceremony, Circular, Cosec, Cosh, Cot(h), Cotangent, Dance, Discriminant, Do, Dynamic, Exponential, Gibbs, Hamilton(ian), Helmholtz, Hyperbolic, Integral, Integrand, Inverse, Job, Logarithm, Nutracentrical, →**OPERATE**, Periodic, Practicable, Purpose, Quadric, Quantical, Quartic, Reception, Role, Run, Sec(h), Sensation, Service, Sin(e), Sinh, Ste(a)d, Stedde, Step, Surjection, Tan(h), Tangent, Tick, Tool bar, Truth, Up and running, Use, Wave, Wingding, →**WORK**

Fund(ing), Fund raiser, Fundraising, Funds -athon, Bank, Bankroll, Barrel, Capital, Chest, Coffers, Consolidated, Emendals, Endow, Evergreen, Finance, Fisc, Fisk, Focus, Gap, Gild, Green, Hedge, Imprest, Index, Jackpot, Kail, Kale, Kitty, Lend, Maestro®, Managed, Means, Mutual, Nest-egg, Onlend, Pension, Pool, Pork-barrel, Pot, Prebend, Private, Public, Purse, Rest, Revolving, Roll-up, Sinking, Slush, Social, Sou-sou, Stabilisation, Stock, Store, Subsidise, Sustentation, Susu, Telethon, -thon, Tracker, Treasury, Trust, Vulture, Wage(s), War chest, Wherewithal

Fundamental(ist) Basic(s), Bedrock, Bottom (line), Cardinal, Essence, Grass-roots, Hamas, Integral, Nitty-gritty, Organic, Prime, Principle, Radical, Rudimentary, Taleban, Ultimate

Funeral, Funereal Charnel, Cortege, Dismal, Exequy, Feral, Interment, Obit, Obital, Obsequy, Sad-coloured, Solemn, Tangi

Fungicide Benomyl, Biphenyl, Bordeaux mixture, Captan, Diphenyl, Ferbam, Menadione, Pentachlorophenol, Resveratrol, Thiram, Zineb

Fungoid, Fungus Dry rot, Endophyte, Enoki, Flor, Pest, Wet rot

Funnel Buchner, Chimney, Choana, Cross, Flue, Hopper, Infundibulum, Smokestack, Stack, Stovepipe, Tun-dish, Tunnel

Fur(ry) Astrakhan, Astrex, Atoc, Beaver(skin), Boa, Broadtail, Budge, Calabre, Caracul, Castor, Chinchilla, Civet, Coati, Cony-wool, Coonskin, Crimmer, Deposit, Ermelin, Ermine, Fitchew, Flix, Flue, Fun, Galyac, Galyak, Genet, Genette, Kolinsky, Krimmer, Lettice, Marten, Minever, Miniver, Mink, Mohair, Mouton, Musquash, Neckpiece, Ocelot, Otter, Palatine, Pane, Pashm, Pean, Pekan, Rac(c)oon, Roskyn, Sable, Sealskin, Sea-otter, Stole, Stone-marten, Tincture, Tippet, Vair(e), Victorine, Wolverine, Zibeline, Zorino

Furl Clew up, Fold, Roll, Stow, Wrap

Furnace Arc, Athanor, Blast, Bloomery, Bosh, Breeze, Calcar, Cockle, Cremator, Cupola, Destructor, Devil, Finery, Firebox, Forge, Gas, Glory-hole, Incinerator, Kiln, Lear, Lehr, Lime-kiln, Oast, Oon, Oven, Producer, Reverberatory, Scaldino, Stokehold, Stokehole

Furnish(ing) Appoint, Array, Deck, Decorate, Endow, Endue, Equip, Feed, Fledge, Gird, Lend, Nourish, Produce, Provision, Purvey, Soft, Stock, Suit, Supply, Tabaret, Upholster

Furniture, Furniture designer Armoire, Bahut, Biedermeier, Bombe, Chattels, Chippendale, Couch, Dresser, Encoignure, Escritoire, Flatpack, Fyfe,

Hallstand, Hatstand, Hepplewhite, Highboy, IKEA, Insight, Lowboy, Lumber, Moveable, Screen, Sheraton, Sideboard, Sticks, Stoutherie, Tire, Unit, Whatnot

Furrow(ed) Channel, Crease, Feer, Feerin(g), Frown, Furr, Groove, Gutter, Knit, Plough, Pucker, Rabbet, Ridge, Rill(e), Rugose, Rut, Stria, Sulcus, Vallecula, Wrinkle

Further, Furthermore, Furthest Additional, Advance, Again, Aid, Also, Apolune, Besides, Deeper, Else, Enable, Expedite, Extend, Extra, Extreme, Fresh, Infra, Longer, Mo(e), Mow, Onwards, Other, Outermost, Promote, Serve, Speed, Then, To boot, Yet

Furtive(ly) Clandestine, Covert, Cunning, Hangdog, Secret, Shifty, Sly, Sneaky, Stealthy, Stowlins, Stownlins, Weaselly

Fury, Furies, Furious Acharné, Agitato, Alecto, → **ANGER**, Apoplexy, Atropos, Avenger, Demonic, Eriny(e)s, Eumenides, Exasperation, Frantic, Frenzied, Furor, Hairless, Hot, Incandescent, → **IRE**, Livid, Maenad, Manic, Megaera, Paddy, Rabid, Rage, Red, Ripsnorter, Savage, Spitting, Tisiphone, Virago, Wood, Wrath, Yond

Fuse(d), Fusion Anchylosis, Ankylosis, Arthrodesis, Blend, Coalesce, Cohere, Colliquate, Conflate, Consolidate, Converge, Encaustic, Endosmosis, Flow, Flux, Igniter, Integrate, Knit, Match, Melt, Merge, Merit, Nuclear, Plasmogamy, Portfire, Proximity, Rigelation, Run, Sacralization, Saucisse, Saucisson, Slow-match, Solder, Symphytic, Syncretism, Syngamy, Tokamak, Union, Unite, Weld

Fuss(y) Ado, Agitation, Anal, Anile, Ballyhoo, Bobsie-die, Bother, Br(o)uhaha, Bustle, Carfuffle, Carry on, Chichi, Coil, Commotion, Complain, Cosset, Create, Cu(r)fuffle, Dust, Elaborate, Faddy, Faff, Fantad, Fantod, Fiddle-faddle, Finical, Finicky, Finikin, Folderol, Futz, Hairsplitter, Hoohah, Hoopla, Mither, Mother, Niggle, Nit-pick, Noise, Old-womanish, Ostentation, Overnice, Palaver, Particular, Pedantic, Perjink, Pernickety, Picky, Pother, Precise, Prejink, Primp, Prissy, Pudder, Puristical, Racket, Raise cain, Razzmatazz, Rout, Song, Song and dance, Spoffish, Spoffy, Spruce, Stashie, Stickler, → **STIR**, Stishie, Stooshie, Stushie, Tamasha, To-do, Tracasserie

Futile Empty, Feckless, Hopeless, Idle, Inept, No-go, Nugatory, Null, Otiose, Pointless, Sleeveless, Stultified, Trivial, → **VAIN**

Future(s), Futurist Again, Avenir, Be-all, By and by, Coming, Demain, Hence, Hereafter, Horoscope, Later, Long-range, Offing, Ovist, Prospect, To-be, To come, Tomorrow, Vista

Gg

Gad(about), Gadzooks Fisk, Gallivant, Lud, Rover, Sbuddikins, Sdeath, Traipse, Trape(s), Viretot

Gadget Adaptor, Appliance, Artifice, Device, Dingbat, Dingus, Doodad, Doodah, Doofer, Doohickey, Gismo, Gizmo, Gubbins, Hickey, Jiggumbob, Jimjam, Notion, Possum, Toy, Utility, Widget

Gag Brank, Chestnut, Choke, Estoppel, Joke, Pong, Prank, Scold's bridle, Silence(r), Smother, Wheeze, Wisecrack

Gain(s), Gained Acquire, Appreciate, Attain, Avail, Boot, Bunce, Carry, Catch, Chevisance, Clean-up, Derive, Earn, Edge, Fruit, → GET, Good, Gravy, Ill-gotten, Land, Lucre, Net, Obtain, Paper, Payment, Plus, Profit, Purchase, Rake-off, Reap, Thrift, Unremittable, Use, Velvet, Wan, Win, Windfall, Winnings

Gait Bearing, Canter, → CHILD, Pace, Piaffer, Rack, Trot, Volt(e)

Galaxy, Galaxies Blazar, Elliptical, Heaven, Irregular, Local group, Magellanic cloud, Milky Way, Radio, Regular, Seyfert, Spiral, Stars, Universe

Gale(s) Backfielder, Near, Peal, Ripsnorter, Sea turn, Snorter, Squall, Storm, Strong, Tempest, Winder

Gallant(ry) Admirer, Amorist, Beau, Blade, Buck, Cavalier, Chevalier, Cicisbeo, Courtliness, Lover, Prow, Romeo, Sigisbeo, Spark, Valiance

Gallery Accademia, Amphitheatre, Arcade, Balcony, Belvedere, Burrell (Collection), Catacomb, Cupola, Gods, Hayward, Hermitage, ICA, Loft, Loggia, Louvre, Mine, Minstrel, National, Picture, Prado, Press, Rogues', Scaffolding, Shooting, Singing, Strangers', Tate, Traverse, Uffizi, Veranda(h), Whispering

Galley Bireme, Bucentaur, Caboose, Drake, Galliot, Kitchen, Lymphad, Penteconter, Proof, Trireme

Gallows Dule-tree, Gibbet, Nub, Stifler, Tree, Tyburn, Tyburn-tree, Woodie

Gambit Manoeuvre, Overture, Ploy, Stratagem

Gamble(r), Gambling(-house), Gambling place Amber, Back, Bet, Bouillotte, Casino, Chance, Dice(-play), Double or quits, Flutter, Hell, Irish sweep, Lotto, Mise, Pari-mutuel, Parlay, Piker, Policy, Punt(er), Raffle, Risk, Roulette, Scratch card, Spec, Speculate, Speculator, Sweep(stake), Throw(ster), Tinhorn, Tombola, Tontine, Two-up, → WAGER, Wheeze

Game (birds) Bag, Colin, Covey, Fowl, Grouse, Guan, Hare, Meat, Partridge, Pheasant, Prairie chicken, Preserve, Ptarmigan, Quail, → QUARRY, Rype(r), Snipe, Spatchcock, Venery, Wildfowl, Woodcock

Game(s) Away, Caper, Circensian, Closed, Commonwealth, Computer, Console, Decider, Easy, Electronic, Elis, Exhibition, Fair, Final, Frame, Gallant, Gammy, Ground, Gutsy, High-jinks, Highland, Home, Intrepid, Isthmian, Jeu, → LAME, Lark, Match, Middle, Mind, MUD, Needle, Nemean, Net, Numbers, Olympic, On, Open, Panel, Paralympic, Parlour, Perfect, Platform, Play, Plaything, Ploy,

Plucky, Preference, Preserve, Pythian, Raffle, Ready, Road, Role-playing, Round, Rubber, Saving, Scholar's, Secular, Sport, Square, Strategy, String, Table, Test, Tie-break, Tournament, Up for, Video, Vie, Waiting, Willing

Gang Baader-Meinhof, Band(itti), Bevy, Bikers, Bing, Cadre, Canaille, Chain, Coffle, Core, Crew, Crue, Elk, Go, Group, Hell's Angels, Horde, Massive, Mob, Nest, Outfit, Pack, Posse, Press, Push, Ratpack, Rent-a-mob, Ring, Shearing, Tribulation, Troop, Tsotsi, Yardie

Gangster Bandit, Capone, Crook, Goodfella, Hatchet-man, Highbinder, Home boy, Homey, Homie, Hood, Mafioso, Ochlocrat, Skinhead, Skollie, Skolly, Yakuza, Yardie

▶**Gaol(er)** *see* JAIL(ER)

Gap Breach, Chasm, Chink, Cleavage, Credibility, Cumberland, Day, Distance, Embrasure, F-hole, Flaw, Fontanel(le), Generation, Hair-space, Hiatus, Hole, Interlude, Interstice, Lacunae, Leap, Loophole, Node of Ranvier, Opening, Outage, Pass, Rest, Rift, Shard, Sherd, Slap, → SPACE, Spark, Spread, Street, Synapse, Time lag, Vacancy, Vent, Window

Garb Apparel, Burqa, Costume, Gear, Gere, Guise, Ihram, Invest, Leotard, Raiment, Toilet, Uniform

Garbage Bunkum, Junk, Refuse, Rubbish, Trash

▷**Garble** *may indicate* an anagram

Garden(ing), Gardens Arboretum, Arbour, Area, Babylon(ian), Bear, Beer, Botanic, Container, Cottage, Covent, Dig, Eden, Floriculture, Gethsemane, Hanging, Heligan, Herb(ar), Hesperides, Hoe, Horticulture, Italian, Japanese, Kew, Kitchen, Knot, Landscape, Lyceum, Market, Nursery, Orchard, Orchat, Ornamental, Paradise, Parterre, Physic, Plantie-cruive, Pleasance, Plot, Potager, Rockery, Roof, Rosarium, Stourhead, Tea, Topiary, Truck-farm, Tuileries, Vauxhall, Vegetable, Walled, Window, Winter, Zoological

Gardener Adam, Capability Brown, Hoer, Hoy, Jekyll, Landscape, Mary, Nurseryman

Garibaldi Biscuit, Blouse, Red Shirt

Garland Anadem, Anthology, Chaplet, Coronal, Crants, Festoon, Lei, Stemma, Toran(a), Vallar(y), Wreath

Garment → DRESS, Habit, Vestment, Vesture

Garnish Adorn, Attach, Cress, Crouton, Decorate, Enarm, Engild, Gremolata, Lard, Parsley, Sippet, Staffage

Gas(sy) Blah(-blah), Blather, Blether, Blow off, Bottle(d), Chat, Emanation, Exhaust, Flatulence, Gabnash, Jaw, Meteorism, Prate, → TALK, Waffle, → WIND, Yackety-yak

Gash Incise, Rift, Rip, Score, Scotch, → SLASH

Gasp(ing) Anhelation, Apn(o)ea, Breath, Chink, Exhale, Kink, Oh, Pant, Puff, Singult, Sob

Gast(e)ropod Ataata, Cowrie, Cowry, Doris, Euthyneura, Glaucus, Harp-shell, Helmet-shell, Limpet, Mollusc, Money cowry, Murex, Nerita, Nerite, Nudibranch, Opisthobranch, Ormer, Pennywinkle, Periwinkle, Purpura, Sea-ear, Sea-hare, Slug, Snail, Spindle-shell, Streptoneura, Stromb, Top shell, Unicorn, Whelk, Winkle

Gate(s), Gateway Alley, Arch, Bill, Brandenburg, Caisson, Corpse, Crowd, Decuman, Entry, Erpingham, Five-barred, Golden, Head, Iron, Kissing, Lych, Menin, Moon, NOR, Payment, Pearly, Port, Portal, Portcullis, Postern, Propylaeum, Propylon, Pylon, Sallyport, Silver, Sluice, Starting, Toran(a), Torii, Traitor's, Turnstile, Vimana, Wicket, Yate, Yet(t)

▷**Gateshead** *may indicate* 'g'

Gather(ed), Gatherer, Gathering Accrue, Aggregate, AGM, Amass, Army, Assemble, Bee, Boil, Braemar, Ceilidh, Clambake, Cluster, Collate, →COLLECT, Colloquium, Concentration, Concourse, Conglomerate, Congregate, Convene, Conventicle, Conversazione, Corral, Corroboree, Crop, Crowd, Cull, Cut, Derive, Eve, Fester, Frill, Function, Gabfest, Galaxy, Get together, Glean, Glomerate, Hangi, Harvest, Hear, Hive, Hoard, Hootenanny, Hotchpot, Hui, Hunter, Husking, In, Infer, Jamboree, Kommers, Learn, Lek, Lirk, Love-in, Mass, Meinie, Menyie, Multitude, Pleat, Plica, Plissé, Pluck, Pucker, Purse, Raft, Raising-bee, Rake, Rally, Rave, Reap, Reef, Reunion, Round-up, Rout, Ruche, Ruck, Ruff(le), Salon, Scrump, Sheave, Shindig, Shir(r), Shoal, Shovel, Singsong, Social, Spree, Stockpile, Suppurate, Swapmeet, Take, Tuck, Vindemiate, Vintage, Wappensc(h)aw, Witches' sabbath

Gauche Awkward, Clumsy, Farouche, Graceless, Tactless

Gaudy Classy, Criant, Fantoosh, Flash, Garish, Glitz(y), Meretricious, Tacky, Tawdry, Tinsel

Gauge Alidad(e), Anemometer, Assay, →ASSESS, Block, Bourdon, Broad, Calibre, Denier, Depth, Estimate, Etalon, Evaluate, Feeler, Hydrometer, Judge, Loading, Manometer, Marigraph, Measure, Meter, Narrow, Nilometer, Oil, Ombrometer, Oncometer, Pressure, Rate, Scantle, Size, Standard, Steam, Strain, Tape, Tonometer, Tram, Tread, Udometer, Yardstick

Gaunt Cadaverous, Haggard, Lancaster, Lean, Peaked, Randletree, Ranneltree, Rannletree, Rantletree, Rawbone, →THIN, Wasted

Gauze, Gauzy Dandy-roll, Gas mantle, Gossamer, Illusion, Muslin, Sheer, Tiffany

Gear(ing), Gearbox Alighting, Angel, Apparatus, Arrester, Attire, Bags, Bevel, Capital, Clobber, Dérailleur, Designer, Differential, Draw, Duds, Eccentric, Engrenage, Epicyclic, Fab, Finery, Granny, G-suit, Harness, Helical, Herringbone, High, Hypoid, Idle wheel, Involute, Kit, Landing, Lay-shaft, Low, Mesh, Mess, Mitre, Neutral, Notchy, Overdrive, Planetary, Ratio, Reduction, Reverse, Rig, Riot, Rudder, Running, Spur, Steering, Stickshift, Straight, Sun and planet, Switch, Synchromesh, →TACKLE, Timing, Tiptronic®, Top, Trim, Tumbler, Valve, Variable, Worm(-wheel)

Geek Creep, Nerd, Nurd, Uncool

Geld(ing) Castrate, Lib, Neuter, Sort, Spado

Gem Intaglio, →JEWEL, Stone

Gene(tics) Allel(e), Allelomorph, Anticodon, Codominant, Codon, Control, Creation, Disomic, Dysbindin, Episome, Exon, Factor, Genome, Hereditary, Heterogamy, Homeobox, Homeotic, Intron, Mendel, Muton, Operon, Orthologue, Paralogue, Plasmon, Promoter, Proteome, Recessive, Reporter, Reverse, Selfish, STR, Suppressor, Synteny, Terminator, Testcross

Genealogist, Genealogy Armory, Cadency, Family, Heraldry, Line, Pedigree, Seannachie, Seannachy, Sennachie, Whakapapa

General(ly) At large, Average, Broad, Common, Communal, Current, Eclectic, Ecumenical, Election, Endemic, Five-star, Gen, Hoi polloi, Inspector, In the main, In the mass, Main, Omnify, On average, Overall, Overhead, Prevailing, Public, Rife, Rough, Strategist, Sweeping, Tactician, →UNIVERSAL, Usual, Vague, Wide(spread)

Generate, Generation, Generator Abiogenetic, Age, Beat, Beget, Breeder, Charger, Cottonwool, Create, Dynamo, Epigon, Father, Fuel-cell, House, Kipp, Loin, Lost, Magneto, Me, Olds, Sire, Spawn, Stallion, Stonewall, Tesla coil, Turbine, Van de Graaff, Wind farm, Yield

Generosity, Generous Ample, Benign, Bounty, Charitable, Expansive, Free-handed, Handsome, Kind, Large, Largess(e), →LAVISH, Liberal, Magnanimous, Munificent, Noble(-minded), Open, Open-handed, Open-hearted, Philanthropic, Plump, Profuse, Public-spirited, Round, Sporting, Tidy, Unselfish

Genesis Cause, Episome, Seed

▶**Genetic** *see* GENE(TICS)

Genial(ity) Affable, Amiable, Benign, Bluff, Bonhomie, Convivial, Cordial, Expansive, Hearty, Human, Mellow

Genius Agathodaimon, Bel esprit, D(a)emon, Einstein, Engine, Flash, Ingine, Inspiration, Ka, Maestro, Mastermind, Michaelangelo, Numen, Prodigy, Spirit

Genre Splatterpunk, Tragedy, Variety

Gentle(ness) Amenable, Amenage, Assuage, Bland, Clement, Delicate, Gradual, Grub, Kind, Lamb, Light, Linda, Lynda, Maggot, Mansuete, Mansuetude, Mild, Soft, Sordamente, Tame, Tender

Gentry County, Landed, Quality, Squir(e)age

Genuflexion Bend, Curts(e)y, Knee, Kowtow, Salaam

Genuine Artless, Authentic, Bona-fide, Dinkum, Dinky-di, Earnest, Echt, Entire, Fair dinkum, Frank, Heartfelt, Intrinsic, Jonnock, Kosher, Legit(imate), Nain, Pucka, Pukka, Pure, Pusser, →REAL, Real McCoy, Right, Simon-pure, Sincere, Square, Sterling, True, Unfeigned, Unsophisticated, Veritable

Germ(s) Bacteria, Bug, Klebsiella, Ovule, Salmonella, Seed, Sperm, Spirilla, Staph(ylococcus), Strep, Swarm-cell, Swarm-spore, Virus, Wog, Zyme

German(y), Germanic Angle, Anglo-Saxon, Bavarian, Berliner, Boche, Denglish, Franconian, Frank, Fritz, G, Goth, Habsburg, Hans, Hapsburg, Herr, Hun, Jerry, Jute, Kaiser, Kraut, Ludwig, Pennsylvania, Prussian, Rolf, Salic, Saxon, Squarehead, Teuton(ic), Visigoth, Volsungs, Wolfgang

Gesticulate, Gesticulation, Gesture(s) Air quotes, Backslap, Beck(on), Chirology, Ch(e)ironomy, Fig, Mannerism, Mime, Motion, Nod, Pass, Salaam, Salute, →SIGN, Signal, Token, V-sign, Wave, Wink

Get(ting), Get back, Get off, Get(ting) by, Get(ting) on, Get out Acquire, Advance, Aggravate, Annoy, Attain, Become, Becoming, Brat, Bring, Buy, Capture, Catch on, Click, Come by, Compare, Cop, Cope, Debark, Derive, Draw, Escape, Fathom, Fet(ch), Fette, Gain, Gee, Land, Learn, Make, Manage, Milk, Net, Niggle, Noy, →OBTAIN, Pass, Peeve, Procure, Progress, Reach, Realise, Recure, Rile, Roil, Secure, See, Shift, Sire, Twig, Understand, Win

▷**Getting** *may indicate* an anagram

Getting better Convalescing, Improving, Lysis

Ghastly Charnel, Gash, Grim, Gruesome, Hideous, Lurid, Macabre, Pallid, Spectral, Welladay, White

Ghost(ly) Acheri, Apparition, Apport, Banquo, Caddy, Chthonic, Duende, Duppy, Eerie, Eery, Fantasm, Fetch, Gytrash, Haunt, Hint, Jumbie, Jumby, Larva(e), Lemur, Malmag, Manifestation, Marley, Masca, No'canny, Paraclete, Pepper's, Phantasm(agoria), Phantom, Poe, Revenant, Sampford, Shade, Shadow, Spectre, Spectrology, →SPIRIT, Spook, Trace, Truepenny, Umbra, Unearthly, Vision, Visitant, Waff, Wraith

Giant(ess) Alcyoneus, Alifanfaron, Anak, Antaeus, Archiloro, Argus, Ascapart, Balan, Balor, Bellerus, Blunderbore, Bran, Briareus, Brobdingnagian, Cacus, Colbrand, Colbronde, Colossus, Coltys, Cormoran, Cottus, Cyclop(e)s, Despair, Drow, Enceladus, Ephialtes, Eten, Ettin, Ferragus, Gabbara, Galligantus, Gargantua, Géant, Gefion, Geirred, Gentle, Gigantic, Gog, Goliath, Great, Grim,

Harapha, Heimdal(l), Hrungnir, Hymir, Idris, Jotun(n), Jumbo, Krasir, Large, Lestrigon, Leviathan, Magog, Mammoth, Mimir, Monster, Oak, Og, Ogre, Orion, Otus, Pallas, Pantagruel, Patagonian, Polyphemus, Pope, Red, Rounceval, Skrymir, Slaygood, Talos, Talus, Thrym, Titan, Tityus, Tregeagle, Triton, Troll, Tryphoeus, Typhon, Urizen, Utgard, Ymir, Yowie

Gibberish Claptrap, Double Dutch, Drivel, Greek, Jargon, Mumbo-jumbo, Scat

Gibe Barb, Brocard, Chaff, Fleer, Glike, Jeer, Jibe, Quip, Shy, Slant, Wisecrack

Gift(s), Gifted Ability, Alms, Aptitude, Bef(f)ana, Bequest, Blessing, Blest, Bonbon, Bonsel(l)a, Boon, Bounty, Cadeau, Charism(a), Congiary, Corban, Covermount, Cumshaw, Dash, Deodate, → **DONATION**, Endow, Etrenne, Fairing, Fidecommissum, Flair, Foy, Free, Freebie, Frumentation, Gab, Garnish, Give, Godsend, Goody-bag, Grant, Gratuity, Handout, Han(d)sel, Hogmanay, Indian, Knack, Koha, Kula, Lagniappe, Largesse, Legacy, Manna, Mystique, Ne'erday, Nuzzer, Oblation, Offering, Parting, Potlatch, → **PRESENT**, Presentation, Prezzie, Propine, Reward, Sop, Stocking-filler, Talent, Theosophy, Tip, Tongues, Tribute, Windfall

Gigantic Atlantean, Briarean, Colossal, Goliath, → **HUGE**, Immense, Mammoth, Rounceval, Titan

Giggle, Giggling Cackle, Fou rire, Ha, Ha-ha, He-he, Simper, Snicker, Snigger, Tehee, Titter

Gild(ed), Gilding Checklaton, Embellish, Enhance, Inaurate, Ormolu, S(c)hecklaton, Vermeil

Gill(s) Beard, Branchia, Cart, Ctenidium, Dibranchiate, Jill, Noggin, Spiracle, Trematic

Gimmick Doodad, Doodah, Hype, Novelty, Ploy, Ruse, Stunt

Gin Bathtub, Blue ruin, Geneva, Genever, Hollands, Illaqueable, Juniper, Lubra, Max, Noose, Old Tom, Ruin, Schiedam, Schnapp(s), Sling, Sloe, Snare, Springe, Square-face, Toil, Trap, Trepan, Twankay

Gingerbread D(o)um-palm, Lebkuchen, Parkin, Parliament(-cake)

▶**Gipsy** *see* **GYPSY**

Girder Beam, Binder, Box, I-beam, Loincloth, Spar

Girdle Baldric, Cestus, Chastity, Cincture, Cingulum, Corset, Equator, Hippolyte, Hoop, Mitre, Panty, Ring, Sash, Surcingle, Surround

Girl(s), Girly Backfisch, Ball, Bimbo, Bint, Bird, Bit, Bluebell, Blushet, Bobby-dazzler, Bohemian, Bondmaid, Broad, Burd, Calendar, Call, Charlie, Chick, Chit, Chorus, Coed, Colleen, Crumpet, Cutey, Cutie, Deb, Demoiselle, Dish, Doll, Dollybird, Essex, Filly, Flapper, Flower, Fluff, Fraulein, Frippet, Gaiety, Gal, Geisha, Gibson, Giselle, Good-time, Gouge, Grisette, Hen, Hoiden, Hoyden, Hussy, It, Judy, Kimmer, Ladette, Land, Lass(ock), Maid(en), May, Midinette, Miss(y), Moppet, Muchacha, Niece, Nymph(et), Nymphette, Peach, Peacherino, Popsy, Poster, Puss, Quean, Queyn, Riot, Señorita, Sheila, Shi(c)ksa, Shi(c)kse, Sis(s), Tabby, Teenybopper, Tootsie, Totty, Trull, Vi, Wench, Wuss

▷**Girl** *may indicate* a female name

Gist Drift, Essence, Kernel, → **NUB**, Pith, Substance

Give(r), Give up, Giving Abandon, Abstain, Accede, Accord, Administer, Afford, Award, Bend, Bestow, Buckle, Cede, Confiscate, Consign, Contribute, Dative, Dispense, Dole, → **DONATE**, Drop, Duck, Elasticity, Enable, Endow, Forswear, Gie, Hand, Impart, Indian, Jack, Largition, Present, Provide, Render, Resign, Reward, Sacrifice, Sag, Sent, Spring, Stop, Tip, Vacate, Yeve, Yield

Give out Belch, Bestow, Dispense, Emit, Exude, Peter

Glacier Aletsch, Crevasse, Drumlin, Fox, Franz-Josef, Iceberg, Ice-cap, Icefall, Moraine, Moulin, Muir, Riss, Serac, Stoss, Stoss and lee, Tasman

Glad(ly), Gladden, Gladness Cheer, Fain, →HAPPY, Lettice, Lief, Willing

Glamour, Glamorise, Glamorous Charm, Glitter(ati), Glitz, Halo, It, Prestige, Ritz, SA, Sex up, Spell, Swanky, Tinseltown

Glance Allusion, Blink, Browse, Copper-head, Coup d'oeil, Deflect, Dekko, Glad eye, Glimpse, Lustre, Oeillade, Once-over, Peek, →PEEP, Ray, Ricochet, Scan, Sheep's eyes, Shufti, Shufty, Side, Silver, Skellie, Skelly, Slant, Snick, Squint, Squiz, Tip, Vision, Waff

Gland(s) Adenoid, Adrenal, Apocrine, Bartholin's, Bulbourethral, Clitellum, Colleterial, Conarium, Cowper's, Crypt, Dart-sac, Digestive, Eccrine, Endocrine, Epiphysis, Exocrine, Goitre, Green, Holocrine, Hypophysis, Ink-sac, Lachrymal, Lacrimal, Liver, Lymph, Mammary, Melbomian, Musk-sac, Nectary, Oil, Osmeterium, Ovary, Pancreas, Paranephros, Parathyroid, Parotid, Parotis, Pineal, Pituitary, Pope's eye, Prostate, Prothoracic, Racemose, Salivary, Salt, Scent, Sebaceous, Sericterium, Silk, Spermary, Suprarenal, Sweat, Tarsel, Testicle, Testis, Third eye, Thymus, Thyroid, Tonsil, Udder, Uropygial, Vesicle, Vulvovaginal

Glare, Glaring Astare, Blare, Blaze, Dazzle, Egregious, Flagrant, Garish, Gleam, Glower, Gross, Holophotal, Iceblink, Lour, Low(e), Notorious, Shine, Stare, Vivid, Whally

Glass(es), Glassware, Glassy Amen, Ampul(la), Aneroid, Avanturine, Aventurine, Aviator, Baccara(t), Balloon, Barometer, Bell, Bifocals, Bin(ocular)s, Bock, Borosilicate, Bottle, Brimmer, Bumper, Burmese, Burning, Calcedonio, Case, Cheval, Claude Lorraine, Cloche, Cocktail, Cooler, Copita, Cordial, Coupe, Cover, Crookes, Crown, Crystal, Cullet, Cupping, Cut, Dark, Delmonico, Dildo, Diminishing, Eden, Euphon, Favrile, Fibre, Field, Flint, Float, Flute, Foam, Frigger, Frit, Fulgurite, Gauge, Glare, Goblet, Goggles, Granny, Green, Ground, Hand, Handblown, Highball, Horn-rims, Humpen, Hyaline, Iceland agate, Jar, Jena, Jigger, Keltie, Kelty, Lace, Lacy, Lalique, Laminated, Lanthanum, Larking, Latticinio, Lead, Lead crystal, Lens, Liqueur, Liquid, Log, Looking, Lorgnette, Loupe, Lozen(ge), Lunette, Magma, Magnifying, Metal, Mica, Middy, Milk, Millefiori, Minimizing, Mirror, Moldavite, Monocle, Mousseline, Multiplying, Murr(h)ine, Muscovy, Musical, Nitreous, Object, Obsidian, One-way, Opal(ine), Opera, Optical, Ovonic, Pane, Parison, Paste, Pearlite, Pebble, Peeper, Pele, Pele's hair, Perlite, Perspective, Pier, Pince-nez, Pinhole, Pinta, Pitchstone, Plate, Pocket, Pon(e)y, Pressed, Prism, Prospective, Prunt, Psyche, Pyrex®, Quarrel-pane, Quarry, Quartz, Reducing, Roemer, Ruby, Rummer, Safety, Schmelz, Schooner, Seam, Seidel, Shard, Sheet, Silex, Silica, Sleever, Slide, Sliver, Smalt(o), Snifter, Soluble, Specs, →SPECTACLES, Spun, Stained, Stein, Stem, Stemware, Stone, Storm, Strass, Straw, Sun, Supernaculum, Tachilite, Tachylite, Tachylyte, Tektite, Telescope, Tiffany, Tiring, Toilet, Trifocals, Triplex®, Tumbler, Uranium, Varifocals, Venetian, Venice, Vernal, Vita, Vitrail, Vitreous, Vitreous silica, Vitrescent, Vitro-di-trina, Volcanic, Watch, Water, Waterford, Weather, Window (pane), Wine, Wire, Yard of ale

Gleam(ing) Aglow, Blink, Flash, Glint, Glitter, Gloss, Leme, Light, Lustre, Ray, Relucent, Sheen, Shimmer, →SHINE, Spotless

Glee Delight, Exuberance, Hysterics, Joy, Madrigal, Mirth, Song

Glide(r), Glideaway, Gliding Aquaplane, Aviette, Chassé, Coast, Elapse, Float, Illapse, Lapse, Luge, Microlight, Monoplane, Parascend, Portamento, Sail,

Sailplane, Sashay, Scorrendo, Scrieve, Skate, Ski, Skim, Skite, Skyte, Sleek, Slide, Slip, Swim, Volplane

Glimpse Aperçu, Flash, Fleeting, Glance, Gledge, Glisk, Peep, Stime, Styme, Waff, Whiff

Glint Flash, Shimmer, → **SPARKLE**, Trace, Twinkle

Glisten(ing) Ganoid, Glint, Sheen, Shimmer, → **SHINE**, Sparkle

Glitter(ing) Asterism, Clinquant, Garish, Gemmeous, Paillon, Scintillate, Sequin, Spang(le), Sparkle, Tinsel

Gloat(ing) Crow, Drool, Enjoy, Exult, Schadenfreude

Globe, Global, Globule Ball, Bead, Celestial, Drop, Earth, Orb, Pandemic, Pearl, Planet, Shot, Sphear, Sphere, Tectonic, Terrestrial, Ubiquitous, World

Gloom(y) Atrabilious, Blues, Cheerless, Cimmerian, Cloud, Crepuscular, Damp, Dark, → **DESPAIR**, Dingy, Dire, Disconsolate, Dismal, Dool(e), Drab, Drear, Drumly, Dump(s), Dyspeptic, Erebus, Funereal, Glum, Grey, Grim, Half light, Louring, Lowery, Mirk, Misery, Mopish, Morbid, Morne, Morose, Murk(y), Night(fall), Obscurity, Overcast, Sable, Sad, Saturnine, Sepulchral, Shadow, Solemn, → **SOMBRE**, Sourpuss, Stygian, Subfusc, Surly, Tenebrious, Tenebrose, Tenebrous, Wan

Glorification, Glorify Aggrandise, Apotheosis, Avatar, Bless, → **EXALT**, Halo, Laud, Lionise, Praise, Radiance, Roose, Splendour

Glorious, Gloria, Glory Chorale, Crow, Crowning, Grand, Halo, Hosanna, Ichabod, Kudos, Lustre, Magnificent, Nimbus, Signal, Sublime

Gloss(y) Enamel, Gild, Glacé, Interpret, Japan, Lip, Lustre, Mag, Patina, → **POLISH**, Postillate, Sheen, Sleek, Sleekit, Slick, Slide, Slur, Veneer, Whitewash

Glove Boxing, Cestus, Chevron, Dannock, Gage, Gauntlet, Kid, Mitten, Oven, Rubber, Velvet

Glow(er), Glowing, Glowworm Aflame, Aura, Bloom, Burn, Candescence, Candlelight, Corona, Emanate, Fire, Flush, Foxfire, Gleam, Glimmer, Glisten, Halation, Incandescence, Lambent, Lamp-fly, LED, Luculent, Luminesce, Lustre, Noctilucent, Phosphorescence, Radiant, Radiate, Ruddy, Rutilant, Shine, Sullen, Translucent, → **WARMTH**

Glue(y) Affix, Araldite®, Bee, Cement, Colloidal, Epoxy, Fish, Gelatin(e), Gunk, Hot-melt, Ichthyocolla, Isinglass, Paste, Propolis, Resin, Rice, Size, Solvent, Spetch, Uhu®

Glum Dour, Livery, Lugubrious, Moody, Morose, Ron, Solemn, Sombre

Glut Choke, Gorge, Plethora, Sate, Satiate, Saturate, Surfeit

Glutton(ous), Gluttony Bellygod, Carcajou, Cormorant, Edacity, Feaster, Free-liver, Gannet, Gorb, Gourmand, Gulosity, Gutsy, Hog, Lurcher, Pig, Ratel, Scoffer, Sin, Trencherman, Trimalchio, Wolverine

Gnat Culex, Culicidae, Midge, Mosquito

Gnaw(ing) Corrode, Erode, Fret, Lagomorph, Rodent

Gnome Adage, Bank-man, Chad, Cobalt, Epigram, Europe, Financier, Garden, Hobbit, Kobold, Maxim, Motto, Proverb, Saw, Sprite, Zurich

Go, Going (after, ahead, away, back, for, off, on, through, up, etc) Advance, Afoot, Anabasis, Animation, Apage, Ascent, Assail, Attempt, Attend, Bash, Begone, Bing, Bout, Brio, Choof, Chunter, Clamber, Comb, Continuance, Deal, Depart, Die, Do, Effort, Energy, Fare, Function, Gae, Gang, Gaun, Gee, Green (light), Hamba, Hark, Heavy, Hence, Hie, Hup, Imshi, Imshy, Ish, Kick, → **LEAVE**, March, Match, Move, Off, OK, Path, Pee, Pep, Perpetual, Ply, Quit,

Raik, Repair, Resort, Resume, Run, Satanas, Scat, Scram, Segue, Shoo, Shot, Skedaddle, Snick-up, Sour, Spank, Spell, Square, Stab, Success, Tag along, Traipse, Transitory, Travel, Trine, Try, Turn, Vamo(o)se, Vanish, Verve, Via, Viable, Vim, Wend, Work, Yead, Yede, Yeed, Zap, Zest, Zing, Zip

Goad Ankus, Brod, Gad, Incite, → NEEDLE, Prod, Provoke, Spur, Stimulate, Stimulus, Taunt

Goal(posts) Aim, Ambition, Basket, Bourn(e), Cage, Decider, Destination, Dream, Drop, End, Field, Grail, Mark, Mission, Net, Own, Score, Silver, Target, Ultima Thule

Goat(-like) Angora, Billy, Bucardo, Buck, Caprine, Cashmere, Cilician, Hircine, Ibex, Kashmir, Kid, Markhor, Nan(ny), Roue, Ruminant

Gobble Bolt, Devour, Gorge, Gulch, Gulp, Scarf, Slubber, Wolf

Go-between Agency, Broker, Factor, Intermediate, Link, Mediate, Middleman, Pandarus, Pander, Shuttle

Goblin Banshee, Bargaist, Barg(h)est, Bodach, Bogey, Bogle, Bogy, Bucca, Bull-beggar, Croquemitaine, Empusa, Erl-king, Genie, Gnome, Gremlin, Knocker, Kobold, Lob-lie-by-the-fire, Lubberfiend, Lutin, Nis(se), Phooka, Phynnodderree, Pooka, Pouke, Puca, Puck, Pug, Red-cap, Red-cowl, Shellycoat, Troll, Trow

God(s) Amen, Ancient of Days, Deus, Di, Divine, First Cause, Gallery, Gracious, Inner Light, Light, Maker, Od(d), Principle, Shechina, Soul, Supreme Being, Tin, Trinity, Truth, Unknown, Vanir, Water

Goddess(es) Divine, Muse, Sea nymph

Godless Agnostic, Atheistic, Atheous, Impious, Profane, Unholy

▷**Going wrong** *may indicate* an anagram

Gold(en) Age, Amber, Apple, Ass, Au, Auriel, Auriferous, Auriol, Aurum, Bough, Bull, Bullion, Bull's eye, California, Chryselephantine, Doubloon, Dutch, Eagle, Electron, Electrum, Emerods, Fairy, Fiftieth, Filigree, Fleece, Fool's, Gate, Gilden, Handshake, Hind, Horde, Horn, Ingot, King of metals, Kolar, Leaf, Lingot, Moidore, Mosaic, Muck, Nugget, Oaker, Obang, Ochre, Ophir, Or, Oreide, Ormolu, Oroide, Pistole, Placer, Pyrites, Red, Reef, Rolled, Silence, Sol, Soneri, Standard, Stubborn, Taelbar, Talent, Talmi, Thrimsa, Tolosa, Treasury, Wash-up, White, Xanthe, Yellow

Golfer Alliss, Braid, Cotton, Faldo, Hogan, Lyle, Pivoter, Rees, Roundsman, Seve, Snead, Teer, Texas scramble, Tiger Woods, Trevino, Wolstenholme, Yipper

Gone Ago, Dead, Defunct, Deid, Extinct, Napoo, Out, Past, Ygo(e), Yod

▷**Gone off** *may indicate* an anagram

Good(ness), Goody(-goody) Agatha, Agathodaimon, Altruism, Angelic, Ascertained, Bad, Banner, Behoof, Bein, Benefit, Blesses, Blinder, Bon(ism), Bonzer, Bosker, Bounty, Braw, Brod, Budgeree, By George, Canny, Castor, Civil, Classy, Clinker, Common, Coo, Cool, Corker, Crack(ing), Credit, Crikey, Dab, Dandy, Def, Divine, Dow, Enid, Estimable, Fancy that, Fantabulous, Favourable, Finger lickin', First-class, G, Gear, Giffen, Glenda, Gold, Gosh, Guid, Holy cow, Hooray, Humdinger, Lekker, Lois, Lor, Ma foi, Mega, Merchandise, Merit, Moral, Neat, Nobility, Pi, Plum, Prime, Proper, Pucka, Pukka, Purler, Rattling, Rectitude, Riddance, Right(eous), Rum, St, Sake, Salutary, Samaritan, Sanctity, Slap-up, Smashing, Sound, Spiffing, Splendid, Suitable, Super, Superb, Taut, Teacher's pet, Tollol, Topping, Valid, Virtue, Virtuous, Weal, Welfare, Whacko, Wholesome, Worthy

Goodbye Addio, Adieu, Adios, Aloha, Arrivederci, Cheerio, Cheers, Ciao, Farewell, Haere ra, Hamba kahle, Later, Sayonara, See-you, So long, Tata, Toodle-oo, Toodle-pip, Vale

Goods Brown, Cargo, Commodities, Consumer, Disposable, Durable, Durables, Fancy, Flotsam, Freight, Gear, Hardware, Line, Luxury, Merchandise, Piece, Products, Property, Schlock, Soft, Stock, Wares, White

Goodwill Amity, Bonhom(m)ie, Favour, Gree

Goose, Geese Anserine, Barnacle, Bernicle, Blue, Brent, Canada, Cape Barren, Colonial, Daftie, Ember, Gaggle, Gander, Gannet, Golden, Greylag, Grope, Harvest, Hawaiian, Idiot, Iron, Juggins, MacFarlane's, Magpie, Michaelmas, Mother, Nana, Nene, Pink-footed, Pygmy, Quink, Roger, Saddleback, Silly, Simpleton, Skein, Snow, Solan, Strasbourg, Stubble, → **STUPID PERSON**, Swan, Team, Wav(e)y, Wawa, Wedge, Whitehead

Goosefoot Allgood, Amaranthaceae, Beet, Blite, Fat-hen, Mercury, Orache, Quinoa, Saltbush

Gorge(s) Abyss, Barranca, Barranco, Canyon, Carnarvon, Chasm, Cheddar, Cleft, Couloir, Cram, Defile, Donga, Flume, Gap, Ghyll, Glut, Grand Canyon, Gulch, Ironbridge, Katherine, Khor, Kloof, Lin(n), Nala, Nalla(h), Nulla(h), Olduvai, Overeat, Pass, Pig, Ravine, Staw, → **STUFF**, Throat, Tire, Tums, Valley, Valley of the Kings, Yosemite

Gorgeous Dishy, Dreamboat, Eye-candy, Grand, Ravishing, Splendid, Superb

Gorilla Heavy, → **MONKEY**, Silverback, Whoop

Gosh Begad, Begorra, Blimey, Cor, Crumbs, Ecod, Fancy, Gadzooks, Gee, Golly, Gracious, Gum, Lor, My, Odsbobs, Odso, Phew, Really, Shucks

Gossip Ana(s), Aunt, Backbite, Cackle, Cat, Causerie, Chat, Chin-wag, Chitchat, Clash, Clash-me-clavers, Claver, Cleck, Clish-clash, Clishmaclaver, Clype, Confab, Cosher, Crack, Dirt, Flibbertigibbet, Furphy, Gab(nash), Gabfest, Gas, Gash, Hearsay, Jaw, Loose-tongued, Maundrel, Moccasin telegraph, Natter, Newsmonger, Noise, Pal, Prate, Prattle, Prose, Quidnunc, Rumour(monger), Scandal(monger), Schmooze, Scuttlebutt, Shmoose, Shmooze, Talk(er), Tattle, Tattletale, Tittle(-tattle), Twattle, Whisper, Yak, Yatter

Gourmand, Gourmet Aesthete, Apicius, Chowhound, → **EPICURE**, Free-liver, Gastronome, Gastrosopher, Lickerish, Table, Trencherman, Ventripotent

Govern(or), Government Administer, Alderman, Andocracy, Archology, Aristocracy, Autarchy, Autocrat, Autonomy, Bashaw, Bencher, Board, Bureaucracy, Cabinet, Caciquism, Caliphate, Caretaker, Cassio, Clive, Coalition, Command, Condominium, Congress, Consistorian, Constitution, Despotocracy, Diarchy, Dinarchy, Domain, Dominate, Dominion, Duarchy, Dulocracy, Dyarchy, Ecclesiarchy, Eminent domain, Federal, G, Gerontocracy, Gov, Gubernator, Guv, Gynarchy, Hagiarchy, Hagiocracy, Helm, Heptarchy, Hierocracy, Inspector, Isocracy, Kakistocracy, Kawanatanga, Kremlin, Legate, Matriarchy, Monarchy, Monocracy, Nawab, Nomocracy, Ochlocracy, Oligarchy, Patriarchism, Petticoat, Plutocracy, Politics, Polyarchy, Power, Raj, Regency, Regime(n), Regulator, Reign, Republican, → **RULE**, Senate, Soviet, Stear, Steer, Stratocracy, Subah(dar), Sway, Technocracy, Thalassocracy, Thalattocracy, Thearchy, Theocracy, Third Republic, Timocracy, Triarchy, Vaivode, Vichyssois(e), Voivode, Whitehall, Woiwode

Governess Duenna, Eyre, Fraulein, Griffin, Mademoiselle, Prism, Vicereine

Grab Accost, Annexe, Areach, Bag, Clutch, Cly, Collar, Glaum, Grapnel, Hold, Holt, Nab, Rap, Reach, Seise, Seize, Snaffle, Swipe, Usurp

Grace(s), Graceful Aglaia, Amazing, Amnesty, Anna, Beauty, Become, Benediction, Ben(t)sh, Blessing, Charis(ma), Charites, Charity, Cooperating, Darling, Dr, Elegance, Eloquent, Euphrosyne, Fluent, Gainly, Genteel, Genty, Godliness, Handsome, Honour, Mense, Mercy, Mordent, Omnium, Ornament, Plastique, Poise, Polish, Prayer, Sacrament, Spirituelle, Streamlined, Style, Svelte, Thalia, Thanks, Thanksgiving, Tuesday, Willowy

Gracious Benign, By George, Charismatic, Gee, Generous, Good, Handsome, Hend, Mamma mia, Merciful, Polite

Grade, Gradient Alpha, Analyse, Angle, Assort, Beta, Bubs, Class(ify), Conservation, Dan, Degree, Delta, Echelon, Etat, Gamma, Gon, Gride, Hierarchy, Inclination, Kyu, Lapse, Measure, Order, Ordinary, Rank, Reserve, Score, Seed, Slope, Stage, Standard, Status, Thermocline, Tier

Graduate, Graduation Alumnus, BA, Bachelor, Calibrate, Capping, Incept, Laureateship, Licentiate, LlB, MA, Master, Nuance, Optime, Ovate

Graft Anaplasty, Autoplasty, Boodle, Bribery, Bud, Cion, Cluster, Dishonesty, Ditch, Dub, Enarch, Enrace, Heteroplasty, Imp, Implant, Inarch, Inoculate, Payola, Pomato, Racket, Scion, Shoot, Sien(t), Slip, Syen, Transplant, Ympe

Grain(y), Grains Bajra, Bajree, Bajri, Barley(corn), Bear, Bere, Boll, Bran, Cereal, Corn, Couscous, Crop, Curn, Curn(e)y, Cuscus, D(o)urra, Dye, Extine, Floor, Frumentation, Gr, Graddan, Granule, Grit(s), Groats, Grout, Grumose, Intine, Kaoliang, Knaveship, Malaguetta, Malt, Mashlam, Mashlin, Mashloch, Mashlum, Maslin, Mealie, Millet, Milo, Minim, Mongcorn, Oats, Orzo, Pickle, Pinole, Pollen, Polynology, Popcorn, Proso, Psyllium, Puckle, Quinoa, Rabi, Raggee, Raggy, Ragi, Rhy, Rye, Sand, Scruple, Seed, Semolina, Semsem, Sorghum, Spelt, Statolith, Tef(f), Tola, Touch, Wheat, Wholemeal

▷**Grain** *may indicate* wood

Grand(eur), Grandiose Big, Canyon, Concert, Epical, Flugel, G, Gorgeous, Guignol, High-faluting, Hotel, Imposing, K, La(h)-di-da(h), Lordly, Magnificent, Majestic, Noble, Overblown, Palatial, Piano(forte), Pompous, Regal, Splendid, Stately, Stoor, Stour, Stowre, Sture, Sublime, Superb, Swell, Tour

Granite Aberdeen, Chinastone, Greisen, Luxul(l)ianite, Luxulyanite, NH, Pegmatite, Protogine

Grant(ed) Accord, Aid, Allot, Allow, Award, Benefaction, Bestow, Block, Bounty, Bursary, Carta, Cary, Cede, Charta, Charter, Concession, →**CONFER**, Cy, Datum, Endow, Enfranchise, Feoff, General, Hugh, Lend, Let, License, Munich, Patent, President, Scholarship, Send, Sop, Subsidy, Subvention, Supply, Ulysses, Ure, Vouchsafe, Yeven, Yield

Grape(s) Aligoté, Botros, Botryoid, Bullace, Cabernet, Cabernet Sauvignon, Carmenère, Catawba, Cépage, Chardonnay, Chenin blanc, Colombard, Concord, Cot, Delaware, Fox, Gamay, Garnacha, Gewurztraminer, Haanepoot, Hamburg(h), Hanepoot, Honeypot, Hyacinth, Lambrusco, Malbec, Malmsey, Malvasia, Malvesie, Malvoisie, Marsanne, Merlot, Montepulciano, Muscadel, Muscadine, Muscat(el), Nebbiolo, Noble rot, Pinot, Pinotage, Primitivo, Racemose, Raisin, Rape, Riesling, Sangiovese, Sauvignon, Scuppernong, Sémillon, Sercial, Shiraz, Sour, Sultana, Sweet-water, Sylvaner, Syrah, Tokay, Uva, Verdelho, Véronique, Vino, Vognier, Zinfandel

Graph, Graphic(s) Avatar, Bar, Chart, Clip art, Computer, Contour, Diagram, Histogram, Ogive, Picturesque, Pie (chart), Plot, Profile, Raster, Sine curve, Sonogram, Table, Turtle, Vivid, Waveform, Waveshape

Grapple Clinch, Close, Hook, Lock, Struggle, Wrestle

Grasp(ing) Apprehend, Catch, Clat, Claut, Claw, Clench, → **CLUTCH**, Compass, Comprehend, Fathom, Get, Go-getting, Grab, Grapple, Greedy, Grip(e), Hend, Hold, Hug, Knowledge, Prehend, Prehensile, Purchase, Raptorial, Reach, Realise, Rumble, Seize, Sense, Snap, Snatch, Squeeze, Twig, Uptak(e)

Grass(land), Grass roots, Grassy Agrostology, Alang, Alfa(lfa), Arrow, Avena, Bahia, Bamboo, Bang, Barbed wire, Barley, Barnyard, Beard, Bennet, Bent, Bermuda, Betray, Bhang, Blade, Blady, Blue(-eyed), Blue moor, Bristle, Brome-grass, Bromus, Buffalo, Buffel, Bunch, Bush, Campo, Canary, Cane, Canna, Cannach, Carpet, Cat's tail, Cheat, Chess, China, Citronella, Cleavers, Clivers, Clover, Cochlearia, Cocksfoot, Cockspur, Cogon, Cord, Cortaderia, Cotton, Couch, Cow, Crab, Culm, Cuscus, Cutty, Dactylis, Danthonia, Dari, Darnel, Deergrass, Dhur(r)a, Diss, Divot, Dogstail, Dog's tooth, Dogwheat, Doob, Doura, Dura, Durra, Eddish, Eel, Eelwrack, Elephant, Emmer, Ers, Esparto, Feather, Fescue, Finger, Fiorin, Flag, Flinders, Floating, Flote, Fog, Foggage, Foxtail, Gage, Gama-grass, Ganja, Gardener's garters, Glume, Glumella, Goose, Grama, Gramineae, Green(sward), Hair, Halfa, Harestail, Hashish, Hassock, Haulm, Hay, Haycock, Heath(er), Hemp, Herbage, High veld, Holy, Indian corn, → **INFORM**, Jawar(i), Job's tears, Johnson, Jowar(i), Kangaroo, Kans, Kentucky blue, Khuskhus, Kikuyu, Knoll, Knot, Lalang, Laund, Lawn, Lay, Lea, Lee, Lemon, Llano, Locusta, Lolium, Lop, Lucern(e), Lyme, Mabela, Machair, Maize, Manna, Marram, Marrum, Mary Jane, Mat, Materass, Matweed, Mead, Meadow(-fescue), Mealies, Melic, Melick, Millet, Milo, Miscanthus, Monkey, Moor, Moss-crop, Nark, Nassella tussock, Nature strip, Nit, Nose, Nut, Oat, Orange, Orchard, Oryza, Painted, Palet, Pamir, Pampas, Panic, Paspalum, Pasturage, Peach, Pennisetum, Pepper, Persicaria, Phleum, Pilcorn, Plume, Poa, Porcupine, Pot, Purple moor, Puszta, Quack, Quaking, Quick, Quitch, Ramee, Rami(e), Rat, Rat on, Redtop, Reed, Rescue, Rhodes, Rib, Ribbon, Rice, Rips, Roosa, Rotgrass, Rough, Rumble(r), Rusa, Rush, Rye(-brome), Sacaton, Sago, Salt, Savanna(h), Saw, Scorpion, Scraw, Scurvy, Scutch, Sea-reed, Sedge, Seg, Sesame, Shave, Sheep's fescue, Shop, Sing, Sinsemilla, Sisal, Sneak(er), Snitch, Snout, Snow, Sorghum, Sour-gourd, Sourveld, Spanish, Spear, Spelt, Spike, Spinifex, Splay, Split, Squeal, Squirrel-tail, Squitch, Stag, Star(r), Stipa, Stool-pigeon, Storm, Sudan, Sugar, Sward, Swath(e), Sword, Tape, Taramea, Tath, Tea, Tef(f), Tell, Teosinte, Timothy, Toad, Toetoe, Toitoi, Triticale, Triticum, True-love, Tuffet, Turf, Tussac, Tussock, Twitch, Veld(t), Vernal, Vetiver, Viper's, Whangee, Wheat, Wheatgrass, Whistleblower, Whitlow, Wild oat, Windlestraw, Wire, Witch, Wood melick, Worm, Yard, Yellow-eyed, Yorkshire fog, Zizania, Zostera, Zoysia

Grasshopper Cicada, Cricket, Katydid, Locust, Reeler, Short-horned

Grate(r), Grating Abrade, Burr, Cancelli, Chafe, Chain, Chirk, Crepitus, Diffraction, Erosure, → **FRET**, Graticule, Grid, Grill, Guichet, Guttural, Hack, Haik, Hake, Harsh, Hearth, Heck, Hoarse, Ingle, Iron, Jar, Lattice, Nag, Portcullis, Rasp, Risp, Rub, Ruling, Scrannel, → **SCRAPE**, Scrat, Scratchy, Scroop, Shred, Siver, Strident, Syver

Gratuitous, Gratuity Baksheesh, Beer-money, Bonsella, Bonus, Bounty, Cumshaw, Dash, Free, Glove-money, Gratis, Lagn(i)appe, Mag(g)s, Tip

Grave(yard) Accent, Arlington, Austere, Barrow, Bass, Bier, Burial, Carve, Charnel, Chase, Count, Critical, Darga, Demure, Dignified, Dust, Eorl, God's acre, Heavy, Heinous, Important, Ingroove, Kistvaen, Kurgan, Lair, Mool,

Mould, Mound, Passage, Pit, Sad, Saturnine, Serious, Sober, Solemn, Sombre, Speos, Staid, Stern, Tomb, Watery

Gravel(ly) Calculus, Channel, Glareous, Grail(e), Grit, Hard, Hoggin(g), Murram, Nonplus, Shingle

Gravity Barycentric, Downforce, G, Geotaxis, Geotropism, Magnitude, Mascon, Specific, Weight(iness)

▶**Gray** *see* GREY(ING)

Grease, Greasy Bribe, Creesh, Dope, Dubbing, Elaeolite, Elbow, Enlard, Enseam, Glit, Lanolin, Lard, Oil, Ointment, Pinguid, Rich, Saim, Seam(e), Shearer, Sheep-shearer, Smarm, Smear, Suint, Unctuous

Greater, Greatest, Great(ly), Greats Alfred, Ali, A majori, Astronomical, Brilliant, Bully, Capital, Classical, Colossus, Cosmic, Enorm(ous), Ever so, Excellent, Extreme, Fantastic, Gargantuan, Gatsby, Gran(d), Gt, Guns, Hellova, Helluva, Humdinger, Immense, Immortal, Important, Intense, Jumbo, Large, Lion, Macro, Magic, Magnus, Main, Major, Massive, Mega, Mickle, Modern, Much, Muckle, No end, OS, Preponderant, Profound, Rousing, Smashing, Splendiferous, Stupendous, Sublime, Super, Superb, Superduper, Swingeing, Tall, Thrice, Titan(ic), Top notch, Tremendous, Unco, Untold, Utmost, Vast, Voluminous, Wide, Zenith

Greed(y) Avarice, Avid, Bulimia, Bulimy, Cupidity, Edacious, Esurient, Gannet, Gare, Grabby, Grip(ple), Gulosity, Guts(e)y, Hungry, Insatiable, Killcrop, Lickerish, Liquorish, Mercenary, Money-grubbing, Piggery, Pleonexia, Rapacity, Selfish, Shark's manners, Solan, Voracity, Wolfish

Greek(s) Achaean, Achaian, Achilles, Aeolic, Agamemnon, Ajax, Ancient, Aonian, Arcadia, Archimedes, Argive, Aristides, Athenian, Attic, Boeotian, Byzantine, Cadmean, Cleruch, Corinthian, Cretan, Delphian, Demotic, Demotike, Ding, Diomedes, Dorian, Doric, Elea, Eoka, Eolic, Epaminondas, Ephebe, Epirus, Euclid, Evzone, Fanariot, Gr, Helladic, Hellene, Hellenic, Hesychast, Homer, Hoplite, Ionian, Isocrates, Italiot(e), Javan, Katharev(o)usa, Klepht, Koine, Lapith, Late, Leonidas, Linear B, Locrian, Lucian, Lysander, Macedonia, Medieval, Milesian, Momus, Nestor, Nike, Nostos, Orestes, Paestum, Patroclus, Pelasgic, Pelopid, Perseus, Phanariot, Pythagoras, Romaic, Samiot, Seminole, Spartacus, Spartan, Stagirite, Strabo, Sybarite, Tean, Teian, Theban, Thersites, Theseus, Thessal(on)ian, Thracian, Timon, Typto, Uniat, Xenophon, Zorba

Green(ery) Apple, Bleaching, Bottle, Callow, Celadon, Cerulein, Chartreuse, Chlorophyll, Chrome, Common, Copper, Crown, Eau de nil, Eco-, Ecofreak, Ecofriendly, Ecologic, Econut, Emerald, Emerande, Envious, Environmentalist, Erin, Fingers, Foliage, Forest, Fuchsin, Fundie, Fundy, Glaucous, Goddess, Gretna, Herbage, Immature, Inexpert, Jade, L, Lawn, Leafage, Lime, Lincoln, Loden, Lovat, Moss, Naive, Neonate, New, Nile, Olive, Organic, Pea, Peridot, Pistachio, Putting, Raw, Realo, Reseda, Rifle, Rink, Rookie, Sage, Sap, Scheele's, Seasick, Shaw, Sludge, Sward, Teal, Tender, Tiro, Tyro, Unfledged, Uninitiated, Unripe, Unsophisticated, Untrained, Uranite, Verdant, Verdigris, Verdure, Vert, Vir(id)escent, Viridian, Wide-eyed, Yearn

Greens Broccoli, Cabbage, Calabrese, Castor, Sprout, Vegetable(s)

Greet, Greeting(s) Accost, Air-kiss, Aloha, Banzai, Benedicite, Bid, Bonsoir, Ciao, Curtsey, Den, G'day, Glad hand, Gorillagram, Hail, Hallo, Handshake, Heil, Herald, Hi, High-five, Hiya, How, Howsit, Jambo, Kia ora, Kiss, Mwah, Respects, Salaam, Salue, Salute, Salve, Save you, Shalom, Shalom aleichem,

Sorry, Tena koe, Tena korua, Tena koutou, Wave, Weep, →**WELCOME**, Wellmet, Wotcha, Wotcher, Yo

▶**Gremlin** *see* **GOBLIN**

Grenadine(s) Bequia, Canounan, Mustique, Union Island

Grey(ing), Gray, Greybeard Argent, Ashen, Ashy, Battleship, C(a)esius, Charcoal, Cinereous, Clair de lune, Dapple, Dorian, Dove, Drab, Earl, Elegist, Glaucous, Gloomy, Gr, Gridelin, Grise, Grisy, Grizzled, Gunmetal, Hoary, Hore, Iron, Leaden, Lipizzaner, Lloyd, Mouse-coloured, Oldster, Pearl, Putty, Slaty, Steel

Greyhound Grew, Lapdog, Longtail, Ocean, Saluki, Sapling, Whippet

Grid(dle), Gridiron Bar, Barbecue, Brandreth, Cattle, Dot matrix, Grate, Graticule, Grating, Lattice, Network, Reseau, Reticle, Roo-bar, Schema, Tava(h), Tawa, Windscale

Grief, Grievance, Grieve, Grievous Anguish, Axe, Bemoan, Bitter, Complaint, Condole, Cry, Dear(e), Deere, Distress, Dole, Dolour, Eyedrop, Gram(e), Gravamen, Grudge, Heartbreak, Hone, Illy, Io, Lamentation, →**MISERY**, Monody, Noyous, O(c)hone, Overset, Pain, Pathetic, Peeve, Pity, Plaint, Plangent, Rue, Sorrow, Tears, Teen, Tene, Tragic, Wayment, Weeping, Woe, Wrong

Grill(er), Grilling Barbecue, Braai, Brander, Broil, Carbonado, Crisp, Cross-examine, Devil, Gridiron, Inquisition, Interrogate, Kebab, Mixed, Pump, Question, Rack, Reja, Siver, Yakimona

Grim Austere, Dire, Dour, Forbidding, Gaunt, Glum, Grysie, Gurly, Hard, Hideous, Reaper, Stern

▷**Grim** *may indicate* an anagram

Grimace Face, Girn, Moe, Mop, Moue, Mouth, Mow, Murgeon, Pout, Wince

Grime(s), Grimy Colly, Coom, Dirt, Grunge, Peter, Reechie, Reechy, Soil, Sweep, Tash

Grin Cheesy, Fleer, Girn, Leer, Risus, Simper, Smirk, Sneer

Grind(er), Grinding Bray, Bruxism, Chew, Crunch, →**CRUSH**, Droil, Drudgery, Gnash, Grate, Graunch, Grit, Kern, Kibble, Labour, Levigate, Mano, Mill, Mince, Molar, Muller, Offhand, Powder, Pug, Pulpstone, Pulverise, Slog, Stamp, Triturate

Grip(ping), Gripper Absorb, Adhesion, Arm lock, Ascendeur, Bite, Chuck, Clam, Clamp, Cleat, Clip, Clutch, Craple, Dog, Duffelbag, Embrace, Engrasp, Enthral, Foothold, Get, Grapple, →**GRASP**, Haft, Hairpin, Handbag, Handhold, Headlock, Hend, Hold, Hug, Interesting, Jaw, Kirby®, Lewis, Obsess, Pincer, Pinion, Prehensile, Purchase, Raven, Rhine, Sally, Sipe, Strain, Streigne, Thrill, Traction, Valise, Vice, Walise, Wrestle

Gripe(s) Beef, Colic, Complain, Ditch, Grasp, Griffin, Ileus, Pain, Tormina, Whine

Grit(s), Gritty Blinding, Clench, Fibre, Gnash, Granular, Grate, Guts, Mattress, Millstone, Pennant, Pluck, Resolution, Sabulose, Sand, Shingle, Swarf, Tenacity, Toughness

Groin Gnarr, Inguinal, Lisk

▷**Groom** *may indicate* an anagram

Groove(d), Grooves, Groovy Bezel, Canal, Cannelure, Chamfer, Channel, Chase, Clevis, Cool, Coulisse, Croze, Dièdre, Exarate, Fissure, Flute, Fuller, Furr, Furrow, Glyph, Gouge, Hill and dale, Kerf, Key-seat, Keyway, Nock, Notch, Oche, Pod, Quirk, Rabbet, Race(way), Raggle, Rare, Rebate, Rif(f)le, Rifling, Rigol(l), Rout, →**RUT**, Scrobe, Scrobiculate, Sipe, Slot, Striate, Sulcus, Throat, Track, Trough, Vallecula

Grope(r) À tâtons, Feel, Fumble, Grabble, Hapuka, Ripe, Scrabble

Gross All-up, Coarse, Coarse-grained, Complete, Crass, Dense, Earthy, Flagrant, Frankish, Giant, Gr, Material, Obese, Obscene, Outsize, Overweight, Pre-tax, Rank, Ribald, Rough, Stupid, Whole

▷**Gross** *may indicate* an anagram

Grotesque Antic, Bizarre, Fantastic, Fright, Gargoyle, Macaroni, Magot, Mascaron, Outlandish, Rabelaisian, Rococo

Ground(ed), Grounds Acreage, Arena, Astroturf, A terre, Basis, Bottom, Breeding, Campus, Cause, Chewed, Clod, Common, Criterion, Crushed, Deck, Dregs, Eard, Earth, Epig(a)eal, Epig(a)ean, Epigene, Epig(a)eous, Estate, Etching, Footing, Forbidden, Grated, Grist, Grouts, Happy hunting, Headingley, Home, Justification, Lees, Leeway, Lek, Lord's, Lot, Marl, Meadow, Mealed, Motive, Neutral, Occasion, Oval, Parade, Pitch, Plat, Plot, Policy, Proving, Quad, → **REASON**, Rec(reation), Réseau, Ring, Sandlot, Sediment, Slade, Soil, Solum, Stadium, Strand, Terra, Terrain, Tiltyard, Tract, Turf, Udal, Venue, Waste(land), Yard, Yird

▷**Ground** *may indicate* an anagram

Group(ie), Grouping Affinity, Age, Al Fatah, Align, Apparat, Bananarama, Band, Batch, Battle, Beatles, Bee, Bevy, Bloc(k), Board, Body, Break-out, Bunch, Camp, Cartel, Category, Cell, Choir, Circle, Clan, Class(is), Clique, Clump, Cluster, Clutch, Coachload, Colony, Committee, Commune, Community, Complex, Confraternity, Conglomerate, Congregation, Consort(ium), Constellation, Contingent, Coterie, Crew, Decile, Dectet, Delegation, Department, Detachment, Division, Draft, Drove, En bloc, Ensemble, Faction, Family, Fauna, Fleet, Flora, Follower, Functional, Gaggle, Generation, Genotype, Genus, Guild, Hardcore, Herd, Household, In-crowd, Intake, Interest, Junction, Keiretsu, Knob, Komsomol, League, Led Zeppelin, Lichfield, Linkage, Lobby, Local, Lot, Lumpenproletariat, Machine, Minority, Minyan, Movement, Nest, Network, Oasis, Octuor, Order, Outfit, Panel, Party, Peer, Phalanx, Platoon, PLO, Plump, Posse, Powerbase, Retinue, Ring, Salon, School, Sector, Seminar, Senate, Septet, Series, Set, Several, Shoal, Social, Society, Sort, Species, Squad(ron), Stick, Subclass, Subculture, Subfamily, Sub-order, Subphylum, Subset, Subspecies, Swarm, Symbol, Syndicate, Synectics, Syntagm, System, Team, The few, Topological, Triad, Tribe, Trio, Troika, Troop, Troupe, Umbrella, Undecimole, Unit, Usenet®, Vertical, Wing

Grouse Bellyache, Blackcock, Bleat, Caper(caillie), Capercailzie, Covey, Game, Gorcock, Greyhen, Gripe, Growl, Grumble, Hazel-hen, Heath-cock, Heathfowl, Heath-hen, Jeremiad, Kvetch, Moan, Moorcock, Moorfowl, Moor-pout, Muir-poot, Muir-pout, Mutter, Natter, Peeve, Pintail, Prairie chicken, Prairie-hen, Ptarmigan, Red game, Resent, Rype(r), Snarl, Spruce, Squawk, Twelfth, Wheenge, Willow, W(h)inge

Grove Academy, Arboretum, Bosk, Bosquet, Copse, Glade, Hurst, Lyceum, Nemoral, Orchard, Orchat, Silva, Tope

Grow(ing), Grow out, Growth Accrete, Accrue, Acromegaly, Adenoma, Aggrandisement, Angioma, Apophysis, Arborescence, Auxesis, Bedeguar, Boom, Braird, Breer, Burgeon, Bushiness, Carcinoma, Car(b)uncle, Chancre, Cholelith, Chondroma, Compensatory, Condyloma, Corn, Crescendo, Crescent, Crop, Culture, Cyst, Down, Dysplasia, Ectopia, Edema, Ellagic, Enate, Enchondroma, Enlarge, Epiboly, Epinasty, Epitaxy, Excrescence, Exostosis, Expansion, Fibroid, Flor, Flourish, Flush, Gain, Gall, Germinate,

Get, Glareal, Goitre, Groundswell, Hair, Hepatocele, Hummie, Hyperostosis, Hypertrophy, Hyponasty, Increase, Involucrum, Keloidal, Knee, Knur(r), Lichen, Lipoma, Monopodial, Moss, Mushroom, Myoma, Neoplasia, Nur(r), Oak-nut, Oedema, Oncology, Osselet, Osteoma, Pharming, Polyp, Polypus, Proleg, Proliferate, Rampant, Scirrhus, Scopa, Septal, Snowball, Spavin, → **SPROUT**, Stand, Stipule, Sympodial, Tariff, Thigmotropism, Thrive, Trichome, → **TUMOUR**, Tylosis, Upsurge, Vegetable, Wart, Wax, Weed, Witches'-broom, Wox, Zeatin

▷**Grow(n)** *may indicate* an anagram

Growl(er), Growling Fremescent, Gnar, Groin, Grr, Gurl, Iceberg, Knar, Roar(e), Roin, Royne, Snar(l)

Grub(by) Assart, Bardie, Bardy, Caddis, Caterpillar, Cheer, Chow, Chrysalis, Deracinate, Dig, Eats, Fare, Fodder, → **FOOD**, Gentle, Groo-groo, Gru-gru, Larva, Leatherjacket, Maggot, Mawk, Mess, Nosh, Palmerworm, Peck, Pupa, Root(le), Rout, Rowt, Sap, Shopsoiled, Slave, Stub, Tired, Wireworm, Witchetty, Worm, Wroot

Gruesome Ghastly, Grisly, Grooly, Horror, Macaberesque, Macabre, → **MORBID**, Sick

Grumble Beef, Bellyache, Bitch, Bleat, Chunter, Croak, Girn, Gripe, Grizzle, Groin, Growl, Moan, Mump, Murmur, Mutter, Nark, Natter, Repine, Rumble, Whinge, Yammer

Grump(y) Attercop, Bearish, Crabby, Cross, Curmudgeon, Ettercap, Grouchy, Moody, Ogre(ish), Sore-headed, Surly, Testy

Grunt Groin, Grumph, Humph, Oink, Pigfish, Ugh, Wheugh

Guarantee(d) Accredit, Assure, Attest, Avouch, Certify, Cheque card, Collateral, Ensure, Fail-safe, Gage, Hallmark, Insure, Mainprise, Money-back, Pignerate, Pignorate, → **PLEDGE**, Plight, Promise, Seal, Secure, Sponsion, Surety, Underwrite, → **VOUCHSAFE**, Warn, Warrandice, Warrant(y)

Guard(ed), Guards Advance, Apron, Beefeaters, Blues, Bouncer, Centinel(l), Centry, Chamfrain, Colour, Conductor, Cordon, Crinoline, Custodian, Defend, Duenna, Ensure, Escort, Fender, Gaoler, Gateman, Gauntlet, Hedge, Home, Horse, Insure, Irish, Iron, Jailer, Keep, Life, Look out, Mask, Militia, Muzzle, National, Nightwatch(man), Noncommital, Old, Palace, Patrol, Picket, Point, Policeman, → **PROTECT**, Provost, Rail, Ride, Roof, Scots, Screw, Secure, Security, Sentinel, Sentry, Shadow, Shield, Shin, Shopping, Shotgun, Sky marshal, Splashback, Splashboard, Splasher, SS, Switzer, Turnkey, Vambrace, Vigilante, Visor, Ward, Warder, Watch (and ward), Watchdog, Watchman, Wire, Yeoman

Guardian(ship) Agathodaimon, Altair, Angel, Argus, Caretaker, Chaperone, Curator, Custodian, Custos, Dragon, Gemini, Granthi, Griffin, Griffon, Gryfon, Gryphon, Hafiz, Janus, Julius, Miminger, Patron, Protector, Templar, Trustee, Tutelage, Tutelar(y), Tutor, Warder, Watchdog, Xerxes

Guer(r)illa Bushwhacker, Chetnik, Comitadji, Contra, ETA, Fedayee, Gook, Haiduk, Heyduck, Irregular, Khmer Rouge, Komitaji, Maquis, Mujahadeen, Mujahedeen, Mujahed(d)in, Mujahideen, Partisan, Phalanx, Red Brigade, Tamil Tiger, Terrorist, Tupamaro, Urban, Viet Cong, Zapata, Zapatista

Guess Aim, Aread, Arede, Arreede, Assume, Augur, Conjecture, Divine, Educated, Estimate, Harp, Hazard, Hunch, Imagine, Infer, Inspired, Level, Mor(r)a, Mull, Psych out, Reckon, Shot, Speculate, Stab, Suppose, Surmise, Theorise, Venture

Guest(s) Caller, Company, Invitee, Parasite, Paying, PG, Resident, Symbion(t), Symphile, Synoecete, Visitant, →**VISITOR**, Xenial

Guidance, Guide, Guiding, Guideline Advice, Aunt, Baedeker, Befriend, Bradshaw, Cicerone, Clue, Code, Command, Conduct, Counsel, Courier, Cox, Cybrary, Director(y), Engineer, →**ESCORT**, Form, Homing, Index, Inspire, Itinerary, Key, Landmark, Mahatma, Manoeuvre, Map, Mark, Mentor, Michelin, Missile, Mitre box, Model, Navigate, Nose, Pilot, Pointer, Providence, Rainbow, Ranger, Reference, Rudder, Rule of thumb, Satnav, Sea Ranger, Shepherd, Sign, Sixer, Standard, Steer, Target, Template, Terminal, Train, Usher(ette), Waymark

Guild Artel, Basoche, Company, Gyeld, Hanse(atic), Hoastman, League, Society, Tong, Union

Guillotine Closure, Decapitate, Louisiette, Maiden, Marianne

Guilt(y) Affluenza, Angst, Blame, Cognovit, Contrite, Flagitious, Hangdog, Nocent, Peccavi, Proven, Redhanded, Remorse, Wicked

Guitar(ist) Acoustic, Axe(man), Bass, Bottleneck, Cithern, Cittern, Dobro®, Fender®, Fretman, Gittern, Guthrie, Hawaiian, Humbucker, Lute, Plankspanker, Samisen, Sancho, Sanko, Segovia, Shamisen, Sitar, Spanish, Steel, Uke, Ukulele

Gulf Aden, Anadyr, Aqaba, Bay, Bothnia, California, Cambay, Campeche, Carpentaria, Chasm, Chihli, Darien, Exmouth, Finland, Fonseca, G, Hauraki, Honduras, Iskenderun, Isthmus, Izmit, Lepanto, Lingayen, Lions, Mannar, Martaban, Maw, Mexico, Ob, Oman, Patras, Persian, Pozzuoli, Queen Maud, Rapallo, Riga, St Lawrence, St Vincent, Salerno, Salonika, Saronic, Saros, Sidra, Spencer, Taranto, Thailand, Tonkin, Trieste, Tunis, Venice

Gull(s) Bamboozle, Bonxie, Cat's paw, Cheat, Cob(b), Cod, Cozen, Cull(y), Dupe, Easy game, Fool, Geck, Glaucous, Haglet, Hoodwink, Hum, Laridae, Larus, Lie to, Maw, Mew, Noodle, Pickmaw, Pigeon, Queer, Ring-billed, Rook, Scaury, Scourie, Scowrie, Sea-cob, Sea-mew, Sell, Simp, Skua, Sucker, Tern, Tystie, Xema

Gullet Crop, Enterate, Maw, Throat, Weasand-pipe

Gully Couloir, Donga, Fielder, Geo, Gio, Goe, Grough, Gulch, Infielder, Pit, Rake, Ravine, Sloot, Sluit, Wadi

Gulp Bolt, Draught, Gollop, Quaff, Slug, Sob, →**SWALLOW**, Swipe, Wolf

Gum (tree) Acacia, Acajou, Acaroid, Agar, Algin, Angico, Arabic, Arabin, Arar, Arctic, Asafoetida, Bablah, Balata, Balm, Bandoline, Bdellium, Benjamin, Benzoin, Bloodwood, Boot, Bubble, Cerasin, Chicle, Chuddy, Chutty, Coolabah, Courbaril, Dextrin(e), Dragon's-blood, Ee-by, Eucalyptus, Frankincense, Galbanum, Gamboge, Gingival, →**GLUE**, Goat's-thorn, Gosh, Guar, Ironbark, Juniper, Karri, Kauri, Lac, La(b)danum, Lentisk, Mastic(h), Mucilage, Myrrh, Nicotine, Olibanum, Opopanax, Oshac, Resin, River red, Sagapenum, Sarcocolla, Scribbly, Size, Sleep, Spearmint, Spirit, Sterculia, Stringybark, Sugar, Tacamahac, Tragacanth, Tupelo, Xanthan

Gun(fire), Guns, Gunfight Amusette, Archibald, Archie, Arquebus, Automatic, Barker, Baton, Bazooka, Beanbag, Beretta, Big Bertha, Biscayan, Blunderbuss, Bofors, Bombard, Breech(-loader), Bren, Broadside, Brown Bess, Browning, Bulldog, Bullpup, Bundook, Burp, Caliver, Cannonade, Carbine, Carronade, Cement, Chokebore, Chopper, Coehorn, Colt®, Dag, Derringer, Electron, Elephant, Escopette, Falcon(et), Field, Fieldpiece, Firearm, Fire lock, Flame, Flash, Flintlock, Four-pounder, Fowler, Fowlingpiece, Full-bore, Fusil, Garand, Gas, Gat(ling), Gingal(l), Grease, HA, Hackbut, Half-cock, Harquebus,

Heater, Hired, Howitzer, Jezail, Jingal, Kalashnikov, Lewis, Long Tom, Luger®, Machine, Magazine, Magnum, Maroon, Martini-Henry®, Matchlock, Mauser®, Maxim, Metal, Minnie, Minute, Mitrailleuse, Mons Meg, Mortar, Musket(oon), Muzzle-loader, Nail, Needle, Neutron, Noonday, Oerlikon, Ordnance, Over and under, Owen, Paderero, Paterero, Ped(e)rero, Pelican, Perrier, Persuader, Petronel, Piece, Pistol(et), Pompom, Pump (action), Punt, Purdey®, Quaker, Radar, Ray, Repeater, Rev, Revolver, Riot, Rod, Roscoe, Saker, Sarbacane, Saturday night special, Scatter, Self-cocker, Shooter, Shooting iron, Shoot-out, Sidearm, Siege, Smoothbore, Snapha(u)nce, Spear, Speed, Spray, Squirt, Staple, Starting, Sten, Sterculia, Sterling, Stern-cannon, Stern-chaser, Stun, Swivel, Taser®, Tea, Thirty eight, Thompson, Three-pounder, Tier, Time, Tire, Tommy, Tool, Tupelo, Turret, Uzi, Walther, Wesson, Wheel-lock, Young, Zip

Gunner, Gunner's assistant Arquebusier, Arsenal, Artillerist, Cannoneer, Cannonier, Culverineer, Gr, Matross, RA

Gunpowder Charcoal, Saltpetre, Saucisse, Saucisson

Gurgle Burble, Clunk, Gollar, Goller, Guggle, Ruckle, Squelch

Gush(er), Gushing Blether, Effusive, → **FLOOD**, Flow, Fountain, Jet, Oil well, Outpour, Rail, Regurgitate, Scaturient, Spirt, Spout, Spurt, Surge, Too-too

Gust Blast, Blore, Flaught, Flaw, Flurry, Puff, Sar, Squall, Waff

Gut(s), Gutty Abdomen, Archenteron, Balls, Beer, Bowel(s), Chitterlings, Cloaca, Colon, Disembowel, Draw, Duodenum, Enteral, Enteron, Entrails, Fore, Gill, Hind, Ileum, Innards, Insides, Kyle, Mesaraic, Mesenteron, Mid, Omental, Omentum, Remake, Sack, Sand, Snell, Stamina, Staying-power, Strip, Thairm, Tripe, Ventriculus, Viscera

Gutta-percha Jelutong, Pontianac, Pontianak

Gutter(ing) Channel, Conduit, Cullis, Grip, Gully, Kennel, Rhone, Rigol(l), Roan, Rone, Runlet, Runnel, Sough, Spout, Strand, Swale, Swayl, Sweal, Sweel

Guy Backstay, Bo, Burgess, Buster, Cat, Chaff, Clewline, Decamp, Deride, Dude, Effigy, Fall, Fawkes, Fellow, Gibson, Gink, Josh, Mainstay, Mannering, Parody, Rag, Rib, Ridicule, Rope, Scarecrow, Send up, Stay, Taunt, Tease, Vang, Wise

Gym(nasium), Gymnast(ic) Acrobat, Akhara, Arena, Dojo, Exercise, Jungle, Korbut, Lyceum, Palaestra, PE, PT, Real, Rhythmic, Sokol, Trampolinist, Tumbler

Gypsum Alabaster, Gesso, Plaster, Satin spar, Satin-stone, Selenite

Gypsy, Gipsy Bohemian, Cagot, Caird, Caqueux, Chai, Chal, Chi, Collibert, Egyptian, Esmeralda, Faw, Gipsen, Gitana, Gitano, Hayraddin, Lavengro, Meg, Pikey, Rom(any), Rye, Scholar, Siwash, Tinker, Traveller, Travelling folk, Tsigane, Tzigane, Tzigany, Vagabond, Vlach, Walach, Wanderer, Zigan, Zigeuner, Zincala, Zincalo, Zingaro

Gyrate Revolve, Rotate, → **SPIN**, Twirl

Hh

H Ache, Aitch, Aspirate, Height, Hospital, Hotel, Hydrant, Hydrogen, Zygal

Habit(s), Habitual, Habituate, Habitué Accustom, Addiction, Apparel, Assuetude, Bent, Chronic, Clothes, Coat, Consuetude, Cowl, Custom, Dependency, Dress, Ephod, Frequenter, Garb, Garment, Hand-me-down, Inure, Inveterate, Motley, Mufti, Nature, Outfit, Practice, Quirk, Raiment, Regular, Riding, Robe, Routine, Scapular, Schema, Season, Second nature, Set, Soutane, Suit, Surplice, Toge, Trait, Trick, Usual, Way, Won, Wont

Habitable, Habitat(ion) Ecad, Element, Environment, Haunt, Home, Locality, Niche, Pueblo, Refugium, Station, Tel

Hack(er), Hacking Blackhat, Chip, Chop, Cough, Cut, Cypherpunk, Drudge, Garble, Gash, Ghost, Grub-Street, Hag, Hash, Hedge-writer, Heel, Hew, Horse, Ink-slinger, Jade, Mangle, Mutilate, Nag, Nerd, Notch, Pad, Paper-strainer, Penny-a-liner, Phreak, Pick, Plater, Pot-boiler, Rosinante, Script kiddie, Slash, Spurn, Tadpole, Taper, Tap into, Tiger team, Tussis, Unseam, Warchalking

Hackney(ed) Banal, Cab, Cliché, Corny, Percoct, Stale, Threadbare, Tired, Trite, Twice-told, Worn

Haddock Arbroath smokie, Finnan, Whitefish

Hades Dis, Hell, Orcus, Pit, Tartarus

Hag(-like) Anile, Beldame, Besom, Carlin(e), Crone, Harpy, Harridan, Hell-cat, Hex, Moss, Rudas, Runnion, Sibyl, Trot, Witch

Haggard Drawn, → GAUNT, Pale, Rider

Haggle Argue, Badger, → BARGAIN, Barter, Chaffer, Dicker, Horse-trade, Jew, Niffer, Palter, Prig

Hail(er) Acclaim, Acco(a)st, Ahoy, Ave, Bull-horn, Cheer, Fusillade, Graupel, Greet, Gunfire, Hi, Ho, Megaphone, Salue, Salute, Shower, Signal, Skoal, Skol, Sola, Stentor, Storm, What ho, Whoa-ho-ho

Hair(y), Haircut, Hairlike, Hair problem/condition, Hair style Afro, Angora, Backcomb, Bang, Barnet, Beard, Bob, Bouffant, Braid, Bristle, Bun, Bunches, Bush, Capillary, Chignon, Coiffure, Combings, Comose, Cowlick, Crew-cut, Crinigerous, DA, Dicey, Dreadlocks, Ear-lock, Excrement, Eyelash, Fibril, Follicle, Fringe, Fur, Goatee, Hippy, Lanate, Lock, Mane, Mohawk, Mohican, Mop, Mophead, Pageboy, Peekabo(o), Perm(anent), Pigtail, Pincurl, Plait, Plica Polonica, Pompadour, Ponytail, Precarious, Prison crop, Rug, Rush, Scaldhead, Sericeous, Shingle, Shock, Sideburns, Switch, Tache, Thatch, Tonsure, Toorie, Topknot, Tour(ie), Tress, Trichosis, Ulotrichous, Updo, Whisker, Wig, Wiglet

Hairdresser Barber, Coiffeur, Comb, Crimper, Friseur, Marcel, Salon, Stylist, Trichologist

Hairless Bald, Callow, Glabrate, Glabrous, Irate

Hairpiece Merkin, Strand, Toupee, →**WIG**

Halcyon Calm, Kingfisher, Mild

Half, Halved Bifid, Demi, Dimidiate, Divide, Hemi, Moiety, Semi, Share, Split, Stand-off, Term

Half-wit Changeling, Mome, Numbskull, Simpleton, →**STUPID**

Hall Anteroom, Assembly, Atrium, Auditorium, Aula, Bachelor's, Basilica, Bingo, Carnegie, Chamber, Citadel, City, Concert, Crosby, Dance, Divinity, Dotheboys, Festival, Foyer, Guild, Hostel, Ivied, Judgement, Liberty, Lobby, Music, Odeon, Palais, Passage, Rideau, Salle, Saloon, Study, Tammany, Town, Trullen, Vestibule, Wildfell

Hallucinate, Hallucinating, Hallucination, Hallucinatory, Hallucinogen Autoscopy, Fantasy, Freak, Illusion, Image, Mandrake, Mirage, Negative, Peyote, Psychedelic, Psychotic

Halo Antheolion, Areola, Aura, Aureola, Corona, Gloria, Gloriole, Mandorla, Nimbus, Rim, Vesica

Halt(er), Halting Abort, Arrest, Avast, Block, Brake, Bridle, Cavesson, Cease, Cesse, Check, Deactivate, End, Full stop, Game, Hackamore, Heave-to, Hilch, Inarticulate, Lame(d), Limp, Moratorium, Noose, Paralyse, Prorogue, Rope, Stall, Standstill, →**STOP**, Stopover, Suspend, Toho, Whoa, Widdy

Ham(s) Amateur, Barnstormer, Flitch, Gammon, Haunch, Hock, Hoke, Hough, Hunker, Jambon, Jamon serrano, Jay, Mutton, Nates, Overact, Overplay, Parma, Pigmeat, Prat, Prosciutto, Serrano, Spe(c)k, Tiro, Westphalian, York

Hamlet(s) Aldea, Auburn, Cigar, Dane, Dorp, Hero, Kraal, Stead, Thorp(e), Tower, Vill(age), Wick

Hammer(ed), Hammerhead, Hammering Atmospheric, Ballpeen, Ballpein, Beetle, Bone, Bully, Bush, Celt, Claw, Dolly, Flatten, Fuller, Gavel, Hack, Incuse, Kevel, Knap, Madge, Mall(et), Malleate, Martel, Maul, Mjol(l)nir, Nevel, Ossicle, Pane, Pean, Peen, Pein, Pene, Percussion, Percussor, Piledriver, Plessor, Plexor, Rawhide, Rout, Shingle, Sledge, Strike, Tenderizer, Tilt, Trip, Trounce, Umbre, Water

▷**Hammered** *may indicate* an anagram

▷**Hammy** *may indicate* an anagram

Hamper Basket, Cabin, Cramp, Cumber, Delay, Encumber, Entrammel, Hamstring, Handicap, Hobble, Hog-tie, Impede, Obstruct, Pad, Pannier, Restrict, Rub, Shackle, Tangle, Trammel, Tuck

Hand(s), Hand over, Hand down, Hand-like, Handwriting Applause, Assist(ance), Bananas, Bequeath, Charge, Clap(ping), Club, Clutch, Copperplate, Court, Crabbed, Crew, Cursive, Dab, Deal, Deck, Deliver, Devolve, Dukes, Dummy, Extradition, Fin, Fist, Flipper, Flush, Free, Full (house), Glad, Graphology, Half-text, Help, Helping, Hidden, Impart, L, Laydown, Loof, Man, Manual, Mitt(en), Mutton-fist, Nap, Operative, Ovation, Pad, Palaeography, Part, Pass, Paw, Post, Present, Pud, R, Royal flush, Running, Script, Secretary, Signature, Span, Straight, Text, Uncial, Upper, Whip, Worker

Handbag Caba(s), Grip, Indispensable, Pochette, Purse, Reticule, Valise

Handbook Baedeker, Companion, Enchiridion, Guide, Manual, Vade-mecum

Handcuff(s) Bracelet, Darbies, Irons, Manacle, Mittens, Nippers, Shackle, Snaps

Handicap Burden, Disable, Encumber, Half-one, Hamper, Hunchback, Impede, Impost, Lame, Liability, →**OBSTACLE**, Off, Penaliser, Restrict, Scratch, Weigh(t), Welter-race

Handkerchief, Hanky Bandan(n)a, Clout, Curch, Kleenex®, Napkin, Nose-rag, Orarium, Tissue, Wipe(r)

Handle(d), Handler Ansate, Bail, Bale, Bitstock, Brake, Broomstick, Cope, Crank, Dead man's, Deal, Doorknob, Dudgeon, Ear, Feel, Field, Finger, Forename, Gaum, Gorm, Grip, Gunstock, Haft, Helve, Hilt, Hold, Knob, Knub, Lug, → MANAGE, Manipulate, Manubrium, Maul, Name, Nib, Palp, Paw, Pistol-grip, Pommel, Port-crayon, Process, Roadie, Rounce, Shaft, Snath(e), Snead, Sneath, Sned, Staff, Staghorn, Stale, Starting, Steal(e), Steel, Steil, Stele, Stilt, Stock, Sweep, Tiller, Title, To-name, Touch, Treat, Use, Whipstock, Wield, Winder, With(e)

Hand-out Alms, Charity, Dole, Gift, Issue, Release, Sample

Handsome Adonis, Apollo, Attractive, Beefcake, Bonny, Brave, Comely, Dishy, Featuous, Fine, Gracious, Kenneth, Liberal, Lush, Resplendent, Rugged, Seemly, Shapely, Tidy

▶**Handwriting** *see* **HAND(S)**

Handy(man) Accessible, Close, Convenient, Deft, Dext(e)rous, Digit, Factotum, Gemmy, Get-at-able, Jack(-of-all-trades), Jemmy, Near, Nigh, Of use, On site, Palmate, Palmist, Ready, Skilful, Spartan, Useful

Hang(er), Hanging(s), Hang up Append, Arras, Aweigh, Chick, Chik, Curtain, Dangle, Darn, Depend, Dewitt, Dorser, Dossal, Dossel, Dosser, Drape, Droop, Execute, Exhibit, Frontal, Gobelin, Hinge, Hoove, Hove(r), Icicle, Kakemono, Kilt, Lobed, Loll, Lop, Lynch, Mooch, Noose, Nub, Obsession, Oudenarde, Overarch, Pend(ant), Pothook, Preoccupation, Sag, Scenery, Scrag, Set, Sit, Sling, String up, Suspend, Suspercollate, Swag, Swing, Tapestry, Tapet, Tapis, The rope, Toran(a)

Hanger-on Bur(r), Camp-follower, Dewdrop, Lackey, Leech, Limpet, Liripoop, Parasite, Satellite, Sponge(r), Sycophant, Tassel, Toady

Hangman, Hangmen Bull, Calcraft, Dennis, Derrick, Executor, Gregory, Ketch, Lockman, Marwood, Nubbing-cove, Pierrepoint, Topsman, Word game

Hangover Canopy, Cornice, Crapulence, Drape, DT's, Eaves, Executer, Head, Hot coppers, Katzenjammer, Mistletoe, Relic, Tester, Valance

Hanker(ing) Desire, Envy, Hunger, Itch, Long, Yearn, Yen

Haphazard Aimless, Anyhow, Casual, Chance, Higgledy-piggledy, Promiscuous, → RANDOM, Rough and tumble, Scattershot, Slapdash, Willy-nilly

Happen(ing), Happen to Afoot, Are, Be, Befall, Befortune, Betide, Chance, Come (about), Crop up, Event(uate), Fall-out, Incident, → OCCUR, Pan, Pass, Phenomenon, Prove, Thing, Tide, Transpire, Worth

Happiness, Happy Apposite, Ave, Beatific, Beatitude, Blessed, Bliss, Bonny, Carefree, Cheery, Chirpy, Chuffed, Cloud nine, Cock-a-hoop, Content, Dwarf, Ecstatic, Elated, Eud(a)emony, Felicity, Felix, Fortunate, Glad(some), Gleeful, Golden, Goshen, Gruntled, Halcyon, Half-cut, Hedonism, High-feather, Inebriated, Jovial, Joy, Jubilant, Kvell, Larry, Light-hearted, Mellow, Merry, Opportune, Radiant, Rapture, Sandboy, Seal, Seel, Sele, Serendipity, Serene, Slap, Squiffy, Sunny, Tiddl(e)y, Tipsy, Trigger, Warrior

Harangue Declaim, Diatribe, Laisse, Lecture, Oration, Perorate, Philippic, Sermon, Speech, Spruik, Tirade

Harass(ed) Afflict, Annoy, Badger, Bait, Bego, Beleaguer, Beset, Bother, Chivvy, Distract, Dun, Gall, Hassle, Heckle, Hector, Henpeck, Hound, Importune, Irritate, Molest, Nettle, Overdo, Persecute, Pester, Pingle, Plague, Press, Sekuhara, Stalk, Tailgate, Torment, Vex

Harbour(ed) Anchorage, Basin, Brest, Cherish, Deep water, Dock, Entertain, Gosport, Haven, Heard, Herd, Hide, Incubate, Kaipara, Macquarie, Marina, Mole, Mulberry, Nurse, Pearl, PLA, Port, Quay, Reset, Seaport, →**SHELTER**, Waitemata, Waterfront

Hard(en), Hardened, Hardness Abstruse, Adamant(ine), Arduous, Armour-plated, Austere, Billy-o, Bony, Brittle, Bronze, Cake, Calcify, Callous, Cast-iron, Compact, Crusty, Diamond, Difficult, Dour, Ebonite, Emery, Endure, Enure, Exacting, Fiery, Firm, Flint(y), Geal, Granite, Gruelling, H, Hawkish, HH, Horny, Inure, Inveterate, Iron(y), Knotty, Metallic, Mohs, Murder, Nails, Obdurate, Osseous, Ossify, Permafrost, Petrify, Raw, Rugged, Ruthless, Scirrhus, Set, Severe, Solid, Sore, Steel(y), Steep, Stern, Sticky, Stiff, Stoic, Stony, Strongly, Teak, Temper, Temporary, Tough, Uneasy, Unyielding, Wooden

Hardship Adversity, Affliction, Austerity, Grief, Mill, Mishap, Ordeal, Penance, Privation, Rigour, Trial, Trouble

Hardy Brave, Gritty, Manful, Oliver, Ollie, Rugged, Sturdy, Thomas

Hare Arctic, Belgian, Body-snatcher, Dash, Doe, Down, Electric, Jugged, Jumping, Leporine, Malkin, Mouse, Piping, Scut, Snowshoe

Harm(ed), Harmful Aggrieve, Bane, Blight, Damage, Deleterious, Dere, Detriment, Discredit, Disfigure, E-coli, Evil, Hip, Hurt, Hyp, Inimical, Injury, Insidious, Maim, Maleficent, Malignant, Maltreat, Mischief, Noisome, Noxious, Pernicious, Scathe, Sinister, Spoil, Unwholesome, Wroken, Wrong

Harmless Benign, Canny, Drudge, Informidable, Innocent, Innocuous, Innoxious, Inoffensive

Harmonious, Harmonise, Harmonist, Harmony Accord, Agree(ment), Alan, Allan, Allen, Alternation, Assort, Atone, Attune, Balanced, Barbershop, Blend, Chord, Community, Concent, Concentus, Concert, Concinnity, Concord, Congruous, Consonant, Consort, Correspondence, Counterpoint, Descant, Détente, Diapason, Diatessaron, Doo-wop, Euphony, Eur(h)ythmy, Faburden, Feng-shui, In step, Integrate, Jibe, Keeping, Key, Melody, Musical, Overblow, Overtone, Rapport, Salve, Solidarity, Suit, Symmetry, Sympathy, Sync, Thorough-bass, Tone, Tune, Unanimity, Union, Unison

Harness(maker) Breeching, Bricole, Bridle, Cinch, D-ring, Equipage, Frenum, Gear, Gere, Girth, Hitch, Inspan, Lorimer, Loriner, Pad-tree, Partnership, Tack(le), Team, Teme, Throat-stop, Tie, Trace, Trappings, Tug, Yoke

Harp(sichord) Aeolian, Cembalo, Clairschach, Clarsach, Clavier, Drone, Dwell, Irish, Jew's, Kora, Lyre, Nebel, Trigon, Triple, Virginal, Welsh, Zither

Harridan Hag, Harpy, Shrew, Termagant, Xantippe, Zantippe, Zentippe

Harris Boatman, Cloth, Island, Isle, Rolf

Harry Aggravate, Badger, Bother, Champion, Chase, Chivvy, Coppernose, Dog, Dragoon, Flash, Fret, Hal, Harass, Hassle, Hector, Herry, Houdini, Hound, Lauder, Lime, Maraud, Molest, Nag, Pester, Plague, Rag, Ravage, Reave, Reive, Rieve, Rile, Tate, Tchick, Torment

▷**Harry** *may indicate* an anagram

Harsh(ness) Acerbic, Asperity, Austere, Barbaric, Biting, Brassy, Coarse, Cruel, Desolate, Discordant, Dissonant, Draconian, Glary, Grating, Gravelly, Grim, Gruff, Guttural, Hard, Hoarse, Inclement, Oppressive, Raucid, Raucle, Raucous, Raw, Rigour, Risp, Rude, Ruthless, Scabrid, Scrannel, Screechy, →**SEVERE**, Sharp, Spartan, Stark, Stern, Stoor, Stour, Stowre, Strict, Strident

Hart Deer, Spade, Spay, Spay(a)d, Venison

Harvest(er), Harvest home Combine, Crop, Cull, Fruit, →**GATHER**, Glean, Hairst, Hawkey, Hay(sel), Hockey, Horkey, In(ning), Ingather, Kirn, Lease, Nutting, Pick, Produce, Rabi, Random, Reap, Seed-time, Shock, Spatlese, Spider, Tattie-howking, Thresh, Vendage, Vendange

Hash(ish) Benj, Bungle, Charas, Discuss, Garble, Garboil, Hachis, Lobscouse, Mess, Mince, Pi(e), Ragout
▷**Hashed** *may indicate* an anagram

Haste(n), Hastening, Hastily, Hasty Amain, Cursory, Despatch, Elan, Express, Festinately, Fly, Hare, Headlong, Helter-skelter, Hie, Hotfoot, →**HURRY**, Impetuous, Precipitant, Race, Ramstam, Rash, Run, Rush, Scuttle, Speed, Spur, Stringendo, Subito, Sudden, Tear, Tilt, Whistle-stop

Hat Broad-brim, →**CAP**, Cocked, →**HEADDRESS**, Head-rig, Lid, Lum, Nab, Red, Tit(fer)

Hatch(ment), Hatching Achievement, Altricial, Booby, Breed, Brew, Brood, Cleck, Clutch, Companion, Concoct, Conspire, Cover, Devise, Eclosion, Emerge, Escape, Incubate, Serving, Set, Trap-door
▷**Hatching** *may indicate* an anagram

Hate(d), Hateful, Hatred Abhor, Abominable, Abominate, Animus, Antipathetic, Aversion, Bugbear, Cursed, Detest, Enmity, Haterent, Loathe, Misogyny, Odium, Pet, Phobia, Racism, Resent, Sacred, Spite, Toad, Ug(h), Vitriol

Haughty, Haughtiness Aloof, Aristocratic, Arrogant, Disdainful, Dorty, Fastuous, High, Hogen-mogen, Hoity-toity, Hye, Imperious, Lofty, Morgue, Paughty, →**PROUD**, Scornful, Sniffy, Stiff-necked, Toffee-nosed, Upstage

Haul(age), Haulier Bag, Bouse, Bowse, Brail, Capstan, Carry, Cart, Catch, Drag, Heave, Hove, Kedge, Long, Loot, Plunder, Pull, Rug, Sally, Scoop, Snake, Snig, Tote, Touse, Touze, Tow(se), Towze, Transporter, Winch, Yank

Haunt(s), Haunting Catchy, Den, Dive, Evocative, Frequent, Ghost, Hang-out, Honky-tonk, Houf(f), Howf(f), Obsess, Possession, Purlieu, Resort, Spot

Have, Having Bear, Ha(e), Han, Hoax, Hold, Hoodwink, Know, Of, →**OWN**, Possess, Sell, With

Haven Asylum, Harbour, Hithe, Hythe, Nature reserve, Oasis, Port, Refuge, Refugium, Retreat, Safe, Sekos, Shelter, Tax

Havoc Desolation, Devastation, Hell, Mayhem, Ravage, Waste
▷**Havoc** *may indicate* an anagram

Hawk(er), Hawkish Accipitrine, Auceps, Austringer, Badger, Bastard, Buzzard, Caracara, Cast, Cheapjack, Cooper's, Cry, Eagle, Elanet, Eyas, Falcon, Gerfalcon, Goshawk, Haggard, Hardliner, Harrier, Hobby, Keelie, Kestrel, Kight, Kite, Lammergeier, Lanner(et), Marsh, Merlin, Monger, Musket, Night, Nyas, Osprey, Ossifrage, Passage(r), Pearly, Peddle, Pedlar, Peregrine, Privet, Ringtail, Sell, Slab, Soar(e), Sorage, Sore(-eagle), Sparrow, Spiv, Staniel, Stone, Tallyman, Tarsal, Tarsel(l), Tassel(l), Tercel(et), Tiercel, Tote, Tout, Trant(er), Warlike, Warmonger

Hawthorn Albespine, Albespyne, May(flower), Quickset, Quickthorn

Hay(cock), Hey, Haybox Antic, Bale, Cock, Contra-dance, Fodder, Goaf, Hi, Kemple, Math, Mow, Norwegian nest, Norwegian oven, Pleach, Salt, Stack, Straw, Truss, Windrow

Hazard(ous) Bet, Booby trap, Breakneck, Bunker, Chance, Danger, Dare, Die, Dye, Estimate, Game, Gremlin, Guess, Hero, Hornet's nest, Ice, Imperil, In-off, Jeopardy, Losing, Main, Minefield, Mist, Moral, Nice, Niffer, Occupational, Perdu(e), Peril, Pitfall, Play, Pothole, Queasy, Razor-edge, →**RISK**, Risque, Stake, Thread, Trap, Venture, Vigia, Wage, Winning

Haze, Hazy Blear, Cloud, Filmy, Fog, →**MIST**, Mock, Muzzy, Nebulous, Pea-souper, Smog, Tease

▷**Haze** *may indicate* an anagram

Head(s), Head for, Heading, Headman, Head shaped, Heady Abuna, Apex, Beachy, Bean, Behead, Bill, Block, Bonce, Boss, Bound, Brain, Brow, But(t), Byline, Cabbage, Can, Cape, Capo, Captain, Caudillo, Cauliflower, Chief, Chump, Coarb, Coconut, Coma, Comarb, Commander, Conk, Cop, Coppin, Costard, Crest, Crisis, Crown(ed), Crumpet, Crust, Dateline, Dean, Director, Dome, Each, Ear, Figure, Flamborough, Foam, Froth, Hoe, Huff-cap, Inion, Jowl, Keyword, Knob, Knowledge-box, Lead(er), Lemma, Lid, Lizard, Loaf, Loo, Lore, Manager, Mayor, Maz(z)ard, Morne, Mull, Nab, Nana, Napper, Ness, Nob, Noddle, Noggin, Noll, Noup, Nowl, Nut, Obelion, Obverse, Occiput, Onion, Panorama, Pate, Pater(familias), Patriarch, Point, Poll, Pow, Prefect, President, Principal, Promontory, Provost, Ras, Ream, Rector, Repair, Ringleader, Scalp, Sconce, Short, Sinciput, Skull, Source, Squeers, Stad(t)holder, Strapline, Subject, Superior, Supervisor, Talking, Tete, Throne, Tight, Tintagel, Tip, Title, Toilet, Top, Topic, Zero in

▷**Head** *may indicate* the first letter of a word

Head cover, Headdress, Head gear Aigrette, Alice band, Ampyx, Balaclava, Bandeau, Bas(i)net, Bearskin, Bonnet, Bridle, Burnous(e), Busby, Calotte, Caul, Chaplet, Circlet, Comb, Commode, Cor(o)net, Cowl, Coxcomb, Crownet, Curch, Diadem, Doek, Dopatta, Dupatta, Fascinator, Feather bonnet, Fontange, Hat(tock), Helm(et), Joncanoe, Juliet cap, Kaffiyeh, Kell, Kepi, Kerchief, Kuffiyeh, Kufiah, Kufiya(h), Madras, Mantilla, Mitre, Mobcap, Modius, Mortarboard, Nubia, Periwig, Pill-box, Plug-hat, Porrenger, Porringer, Quoif, Romal, Rumal, Sakkos, Skid lid, Skullcap, Sphendone, Taj, Tarbush, Tiara, Tire-vallant, Topi, Tower, Tulban, Turban, War bonnet, Wig, Wimple, Wreath

Headland Bill, Cape, Foreland, Head-rig, Hoe, Hogh, Land's End, Morro, Naze, Ness, Noup, Point, Ras, Ross, Scaw, Skaw

Headline Banner, Caption, Frown, Majuscular, Scare-head, Screamer, Splash, Strapline, Streamer, Title

Headlong Breakneck, Helter-skelter, Pell-mell, Plummet, Precipitate, Ramstam, Reckless, Steep, Sudden, Tantivy, Tearaway

▶**Headman** *see* **HEAD(S)**

Headphone(s) Cans, Earpiece, Walkman®

Headquarters Base, Command, Command post, Depot, Guardhouse, Pentagon, Praetorium, Station, Torshavn, Valley Forge

▷**Heads** *may indicate* a lavatory

Headstrong Obstinate, Rash, Stubborn, Unruly, Wayward

Headway Advancement, Headroom, Progress

Heal(ing) Absent, Aesculapian, Ayurveda, Balsam, Chiropractic, Cicatrise, Cleanse, Curative, Cure, Distant, Esculapian, G(u)arish, Hele, Knit, Mend, Naturopathy, Olosis, Osteopathy, Recuperation, Restore, Sain, Salve, Sanative, Sanitary, Styptic, Therapeutic, Time

Healer Althea, Asa, Doctor, Homeopath, Medicine man, Naturopath, Osteopath, Sangoma, Shaman, Time

Health(y) Aglow, Aseptic, Bottoms up, Bracing, Cheerio, Chin-chin, Constitution, Cosy, Doer, Environmental, Fat-free, Fit(ness), Flourishing, Gesundheit, Hail, Hale, Hartie-hale, Heart, Holism, Hygeian, Kia-ora, L'chaim, Lustique, Lusty, Medicaid, Medicare, Piert, Pink, Prosit, Public, Robust, Ruddy,

Salubrious, Sane, Slainte, Sound, Toast, Tope, Valentine, Valetudinarian, Vigour, Welfare, Well, Wellbeing, WHO, Wholesome

Heap(ed), Heaps Acervate, Agglomerate, Amass, Bing, Bulk, Car, Clamp, Cock, Compost, Congeries, Cumulus, Drift, Hog, Jalopy, Lot, Molehill, Pile, Pyre, Rattletrap, Rick(le), Ruck, Scads, Scrap, Shell, Slag, Stash, Toorie

Hear(ing), Hearing problem Acoustic, Attend, Audience, Audile, Avizandum, Captain's mast, Catch, Clairaudience, Dirdum, Ear, Glue ear, Harken, Learn, List(en), Oyer, Oyez, Panel, Pick up, Session, Subpoena, Tin ear, Tinnitus

▷**Hear(say)** *may indicate* a word sounding like one given

Hearsay Account, Anecdotal, Gossip, Report, Rumour, Second-hand, Surmise

Heart(en), Heartily, Hearty, Heart-shaped AB, Agood, Auricle, Backslapping, Beater, Bleeding, Bluff, Bosom, Bradycardia, Buoy, Cant, Cardiac, Centre, Cheer, Cockles, Columella, Cordate, Cordial, Core, Courage, Crossed, Daddock, Embolden, Encourage, Essence, Fatty, Floating, Gist, H, Hale, Herz, Hub, Inmost, Jarta, Kernel, Lepid, Lonely, Lusty, Memoriter, Mesial, Mid(st), Middle, Nub, Nucleus, Obcordate, Pericardium, Pith, Purple, Reassure, Robust, Root, Sacred, Sailor, Seafarer, Seaman, Sinoatrial, Staunch, Tachycardia, Tar, Ticker, Tweedy, Yarta, Yarto

Hearth Cupel, Finery, Fireside, Home, Ingle

Heartless Callous, Cored, Cruel, Inhumane, Three-suited

Heart-throb Idol, Ladies' man, Valentino

Heat(ed), Heater, Heating Anneal, Ardour, Arousal, Atomic, Background, Bainite, Barrage, Blood, Brazier, Calcine, Calescence, Caloric, Calorifier, Central, Chafe, Chip, Convector, Dead, Decay, Dielectric, Dudgeon, Element, Eliminator, Emotion, Estrus, Etna, Excite, Fan, Ferment, Fever, Fire, Fluster, Fug, Furnace, Gat, Gleed, Gun, Het, Hyperthermia, Hypocaust, Immersion, Incalescence, Induction, J, Kettle, Kindle, Latent, Lust, Mowburn, Normalise, Oestrus, Panel, Passion, Prelim, Pre-warm, Prickly, Pyrolysis, Q, Quartz, Radiant, Radiator, Red, Render, Rut, Salamandrian, Salt, Scald, Sizzle, Smelt, Solar, Space, Specific, Spice, Stew, Storage, Stove, Swelter, Temperature, Thermotics, Tind, Tine, Torrefy, Total, Underfloor, Verve, Warming-pan, Warmth, White, Zip®

Heathen(s) Ethnic, Gentile, Godless, Idolator, Infidel, Litholatrous, Pagan, Pa(i)nim, Paynim, Philistine, Primitive, Profane, Ungodly

▷**Heating** *may indicate* an anagram

Heave(d), Heaving Cast, Emesis, Fling, Heeze, Hoise, Hoist, Hump, Hurl, Popple, Retch, Shy, Sigh, Vomit

▷**Heave** *may indicate* 'discard'

Heaven(s), Heavenly Air, Aloft, Ama, Ambrosial, Arcady, Asgard, Bliss, Celestial, Celia, Divine, Ecstasy, Elysian, Elysium, Empyrean, Ethereal, Euphoria, Fiddler's Green, Firmament, Hereafter, Himmel, Hog, Holy, Hookey Walker, Lift, Mackerel, New Jerusalem, Olympus, On high, Paradise, Pole, Seventh, Shangri-la, Sion, Sky, Sublime, Supermundane, Supernal, Svarga, Swarga, Swerga, Tir na n'Og, Upper region, Uranian, Utopia, Welkin, Zion

Heavy(weight), Heavily, Heaviness Ali, Biased, Bodyguard, Bouncer, Close, Dutch, Elephantine, Embonpoint, Endomorph, Gorilla, Gothic, Grave, Hefty, Last, Leaden, Muscleman, Onerous, Osmium, Pesante, Ponderous, Roughneck, Sad, Scelerate, Stodgy, Stout, Torrential, Upsee, Ups(e)y, Weighty, Wicked

Heckle Badger, Gibe, Harass, Jeer, Needle, Spruik

Hedge, Hedging Box, Bullfinch, Enclosure, Equivocate, Evade, Haw(thorn), Hay, Lay off, Meuse, Mews, Muse, Ox-fence, Pleach, Prevaricate, Privet,

Pussyfoot, Quickset, Raddle, Sepiment, Shield, Stall, Stonewall, Temporise, Thicket

Hedgehog Erinaceous, Gymnure, Hérisson, Tenrec, Tiggywinkle, Urchin

Heed(ed), Heedful Attend, Cavendo tutus, Gaum, Gorm, Listen, →**MIND**, Notice, Obey, Observe, Rear, Reck, Regard(ant), Respect, Rought, Tent, Tinker's cuss

Heedless Blithe, Careless, Inattentive, Incautious, Rash, Scapegrace, Scatterbrain, Unaware

Heel Cad, Calcaneum, Cant, Careen, Cuban, Dogbolt, Foot, French, Incline, Kitten, List, Louse, Parliament, Rat, Rogue, Seel, Spike, Stacked, Stiletto, Tilt, Wedge, Wedgie

Height(en), Heights Abraham, Altitude, Cairngorm, Ceiling, Dimension, Elevation, Embroider, Eminence, Enhance, Eye-level, Giddy, Golan, H, Hem, Hill, Ht, Hypsometry, Level, Might, Mount, Peak, Procerity, Roof, Shap, Stature, Stud, Sum, →**SUMMIT**, Tallness, Tor, Zenith

Heir Alienee, Atheling, Claimant, Coparcener, Dauphin, Devisee, Eigne, Institute, Intitule, Legatee, Parcener, Scion, Sprig, Successor, Tanist

▷**Held by** *may indicate* a hidden word

Hell(ish) Abaddon, Ades, Agony, Amenthes, Annw(yf)n, Avernus, Below, Blazes, Bottomless pit, Chthonic, Dis, Erebus, Furnace, Gehenna, Hades, Heck, Inferno, Malebolge, Naraka, Netherworld, Orcus, Pandemonium, Perditious, Pit, Sheol, Stygian, Tartar(ean), Tartaric, Tartarus, Tophet, Torment

Hello, Hallo, Hullo Aloha, Chin-chin, Ciao, Dumela, G'day, Hi, Ho(a), Hoh, Howdy, Howzit, Wotcha, Wotcher, Yoo-hoo

Helmet Armet, Balaclava, Basinet, Bearskin, Beaver, Brain bucket, Burganet, Burgonet, Cask, Casque, Comb, Crash, Galea, Gas, Hard hat, Heaume, Knapscal, Knapscull, Knapskull, Montero, Mor(r)ion, Nasal, Pickelhaube, Pith, Plumed, Pot, Salade, Sal(l)et, Shako, Skid-lid, Tin hat, Topee, Topi

Help(er), Helping, Helpful Abet, Accommodate, Accomplice, Adjuvant, Advantage, Aid(ance), Aidant, Aide, Alexis, Alleviate, Ally, →**ASSIST**, Avail, Back, Befriend, Benefit, Bestead, Boon, Brownie, Carer, Char(woman), Charity, Coadjutor, Collaborate, Complice, Daily, Dollop, Dose, Ezra, Forward, Further(some), Go, Godsend, Hand, Handyman, Hint, Hyphen, Instrumental, Intercede, Kind, Leg-up, Maid, Mayday, Obliging, Ophelia, Order, Patronage, Pitch in, Promote, Prompt, Quantity, Ration, Recourse, Relieve, Samaritan, Servant, Serve, Service, Slice, SOS, Stead, Sted, Subserve, Subvention, Succour, Taste, Therapeutic, Use

Helpless(ness) Anomie, Downa-do, Feeble, High and dry, Impotent, Incapable, Incapacity, Paralytic, Prostrate

Hen(s) Ancona, Andalusian, Australorp, Biddy, Buff Orpington, Chock, Clocker, Cochin, Deep litter, Dorking, Eirack, Fowl, Houdan, Langshan, Layer, Leghorn, Mother, Orpington, Partlet, Pertelote, Plymouth Rock, Poulard, Poultry, Pullet, Ree(ve), Rhode Island red, Sitter, Spanish fowl, Speckled, Sultan, Tappit, Welsummer, Wyandotte

Hence Apage, Avaunt, Ergo, Go, Hinc, Scram, So, Therefore, Thus

Herald(ic), Heraldry Crier, Earl Marshal, Hermes, Messenger

Herb(aceous), Herbs Bouquet garni, Garnish, Maror, Oleraceous, Seasoning, Simple, Suffruticose, Weed

Herd(er), Herding, Herdsman Band, Buffalo, Byreman, Corral, Cowpuncher, Drive, Drover, Flock, Gang, Lowing, Meinie, Mein(e)y, Menyie, Mob, Pod, Rabble, Raggle-taggle, Round-up, Shepherd, Tail, Vaquero, Wrangling

Here Adsum, Hi, Hic, Hither, Kilroy, Local, Now, Oy, Present

Hereditary, Heredity Ancestry, Blood, Breeding, Codon, Eugenics, Genetics, Id(ant), Idioplasm, Inborn, Mendelism, Panagenesis

▷**Herein** *may indicate* a hidden word

Heresy, Heretic(al) Agnoitae, Albi, Albigensian, Apostasy, Arian, Arius, Bogomil, Bugger, Cathar, Docete, Dulcinist, Encratite, Errant, Eudoxian, Giaour, Gnosticism, Heresearch, Heterodoxy, Lollard, Montanism, Nestorian, Non-believer, Nonconformist, Origen, Patarin(e), Pelagius, Phrygian, Racovian, Rebel, Revisionist, Unitarian, Zendik

Hermaphrodite Androgynous, Bi-, Gynandromorph, Monochinous, Monoccious, Prot(er)andry, Protogyny

Hermit(age), Hermit-like Anchoret, Anchorite, Ascetic, Ashram(a), Augustinian, Austin, Cell, Cloister, Crab, Eremite, Grandmontine, Hieronymite, Loner, Marabout, Monk, Museum, Nitrian, Pagurid, Peter, Recluse, Retreat, Sannyasi, Solitary, Troglodyte

Hero(es), Heroic Asgard, Brave, Champ(ion), Couplet, Derring-do, Eidola, Epic, Eponym, Folk, God, Goody, Great, Ideal, Idol, Lion, Noble, Olitory, Priestess, Principal, Resolute, Tragic, Valiant, VC, White knight

Heroine Andromeda, Ariadne, Candida, Cleopatra, Darling, Demigoddess, Electra, Eurydice, Hedda, Heidi, Imogen, Isolde, Judith, Juliet, Leda, Leonora, Lulu, Manon, Mimi, Nana, Norma, Pamela, Star, Tess, Tosca, Una

Herring Bloater, Brisling, Caller, Glasgow magistrate, Kipper, Red, Rollmop, Sild, Silt

Hesitant, Hesitate, Hesitation Balance, Boggle, Cunctation, Delay, Demur, Dicker, Dither, Doubtful, Dwell, Erm, Falter, Halting, Haver, Haw, Mammer, Mealy-mouthed, → **PAUSE**, Qualm, Scruple, Shillyshally, Shrink, Stagger, Stammer, Stutter, Swither, Tarrow, Teeter, Tentative, Think twice, Um, Um and ah, Ur, Vacillate, Wait, Waver

Hew(er) Ax, Chop, Cut, Gideon, Hack, Sever

▶**Hey** *see* **HAY(COCK)**

Hiatus Caesura, Gap, Hernia, Interregnum, Lacuna, Lull, Respite

Hibernal, Hibernate, Hibernating Estivate, Hiemal, Latitant, Sleep, Winter

Hiccup Blip, Glitch, Hitch, Singultus, Snag, Spasm, Yex

Hidden Buried, Cabalistic, Covert, Cryptic, Delitescent, De(a)rn, Doggo, Eclipsed, Healed, Hooded, Latent, Obscure, Occult, Recondite, Screened, Secret, Shuttered, Sly, Subterranean, Ulterior, Unseen, Veiled, Wrapped

▷**Hidden** *may indicate* a concealed word

Hide, Hiding (place) Abscond, Babiche, Basan, Befog, Bield(y), Blind, Box-calf, Burrow, Bury, Butt, Cache, Camouflage, Cane, Ceroon, Coat, Coonskin, Cootch, Cordwain, Couch, Cour, Crop, Curtain, Cwtch, Dea(r)n, Deerskin, Derm, Dissemble, Doggo, Earth, Eclipse, Encave, Ensconce, Enshroud, Envelop, Epidermis, Fell, Flaught, Flay, Fur, Gloss over, Harbour, Heal, Heel, Hele, Hell, Hibernate, Hole-up, Hoodwink, Incave, Inter, Kip, Kipskin, Lair, Leather, Lie doggo, Mai-mai, Mask, Mew, Mobble, Morocco, Nebris, → **OBSCURE**, Paper over, Parfleche, Pell, Pelt, Plank, Plant, Priest's hole, Repress, Robe, Saffian, Screen, Secrete, Sequester, Shadow, Shellac(k), Shroud, Skin, Smuggle, Spetch, Squirrel, Stash, Strap-oil, Tappice, Thong, Thrashing, Trove, Veil, Wallop, Whang, Wrap

Hideous(ness) Deform(ed), Enormity, Gash, Ghastly, Grotesque, Horrible, Monstrous, Odious, Ugly, Ugsome

High(er), Highly, Highness Alt(a), Altesse, Alteza, Altissimo, Altitudinous, Apogee, Atop, Brent, Climax, Culminant, Doped, Drugged, E-la, Elation, Elevated, Eminent, Euphoria, Exalted, Excelsior, Exhilarated, Five, Frequency, Gamy, Half seas over, Haut(e), Intoxicated, Jinks, Lofty, Mind-blowing, Orthian, Prime, Rancid, Ripe, School, Senior, Sent, Shrill, So, Spaced out, Steep, Stenchy, Stoned, Stratospheric, String-out, Strong, Superior, Swollen, Tall, Tension, Tipsy, Topmost, Treble, Turned on, Ultrasonic, Up(per), Very, Wired, Zonked
▷**High** *may indicate* an anagram

Highbrow Brain, Egghead, Intelligentsia, Long-hair, Third programme

Highest Apotheosis, Best, Cacumen, Climax, Culminant, Maximum, Ne plus ultra, Supreme

Highland(er), Highlands Black Forest, Blue-bonnet, Blue-cap, Cameron, Cat(h)eran, Down, Dun(n)i(e)wassal, Gael, Gaelic, Irish Scot, Kiltie, Nepalese, Plaid(man), Redshank, Riff, Scot, Seaforth, Shire, Teuchter

▶**High-pitched** *see* **HIGH(ER)**

Highway Alaska, Alcan, Autobahn, Autopista, Autostrada, Bus, Camino Real, Flyover, Freeway, Information, Interstate, King's, Motorway, Overpass, Parkway, Pass, Thoroughfare, Tightrope, Tollway, Watling St

Highwayman, Highway robber(y) Bandit, Bandolero, Duval, Footpad, Gilderoy, Jack Sheppard, Latrocinium, Scamp, Skyjacker, Toby, Turpin

Hike(r) Backpack, Bushbash, Bushwalk, Raise, Rambler, Ramp, Rise, Traipse, Tramp, Trape(s), Up(raise)

Hill(ock), Hills, Hillside Ant, Antidine, Arafar, Areopagus, Aventine, Barrow, Beacon, Ben, Bent, Berg, Beverly, Blackdown, Bluff, Brae, Brew, Broken, Bunker, Butte, Caelian, Calvary, Capitol(ine), Cheviots, Chiltern, Chin, Cleve, Coast, Cone, Coolin, Coteau, Cotswolds, Crag-and-tail, Crest, Cuillin, Damon, Djebel, Drumlin, Dun(e), Eminence, Esquiline, Fell, Gebel, Golan Heights, Golgotha, Gradient, Grampians, Hammock, Height, Helvellyn, Highgate, Horst, How, Howe, Hummock, Incline, Inselberg, Janiculum, Jebel, Kip(p), Knap, Knoll, Knot, Kop(je), Koppie, Lammermuir, Lavender, Law, Loma, Low, Ludgate, Majubar, Malvern, Mamelon, Man, Marilyn, Mendip, Merrick, Mesa, Monadnock, Monticule, Morro, Mound, Mount Lofty Ranges, Nab, Nanatak, North Downs, Otway Ranges, Palatine, Pap, Pennines, Pike, Pingo, Pnyx, Quantocks, Quirinal, Rand, Range, Saddleback, Scaur, Silbury, Sion, Steep, Stoss, Strawberry, Tara, Tel(l), Toft, Toot, Tor, Toss, Tump, Tweedsmuir, Vatican, Viminal, Wolds, Wrekin, Zion

Hilt Basket, Coquille, Haft, Handle, Hasp, Shaft

Hind(er), Hindering, Hindrance, Hindsight Back, Bar, Block, Check, Counteract, Cramp, Crimp, Cumber, Debar, →**DELAY**, Deter, Encumber, Hamper, Handicap, Harass, Hitch, Holdback, Imbar, Impeach, Impede, Inconvenience, Inhibit, Liability, Obstacle, Obstruct, Porlock, Posterior, Preclusion, Rear, Rein, Remora, Retard, Retral, Retrospect, Rump, Rumple, Set back, Shackle, Slow, Stonewall, Stunt, Stymie, Taigle, Thwart, Trammel

Hind(most) Back, Deer, Lag, Rear, Starn, Stern

Hindi, Hindu(ism) Arya Samaj, Babu, Bania(n), Banyan, Brahman, Brahmin, Dalit, Gentoo, Gurkha, Harijan, Jain(a), Kshatriya, Maharishi, Pundit, Rajpoot, Rajput, Rama, Sad(d)hu, Saiva, S(h)akta, Saktas, Sankhya, Shaiva, Sheik(h), Shiv Sena, Shudra, Sivaite, Sudra, Swami, Trimurti, Untouchable, Urdu, Vais(h)ya, Varna, Vedanta, Vedism

Hinge(d) Axis, Butt, Cardinal, Cross-garnet, Garnet, Gemel, Gimmer, Gullwing, Joint, Knee, Piano, Pivot

▷**Hinge(s)** *may indicate* a word reversal

Hint Allude, Clew, Clue, Cue, Echo, Element, Gleam, Hunch, Imply, Inkle, Inkling, Innuendo, Insinuate, Intimate, Key, Mint, Nod, Nuance, Office, Overtone, Pointer, Preview, Ray, Reminder, Scintilla, Shadow, Soupçon, →**SUGGEST**, Tang, Tip, Touch, Trace, Trick, Wind, Wink, Wisp, Word, Wrinkle

▷**Hint** *may indicate* a first letter

Hip(pie), Hippy, Hips Beatnik, Cafard, Cheer, Coxa(l), Drop-out, Flower-power, Huck(le), Hucklebone, Hunkers, Ilium, In, Informed, Ischium, Pubis, Sciatic

Hire(d), Hiring Affreightment, Charter, Engage, Fee, Freightage, Job, Lease, Merc(enary), Never-never, Rent, Shape-up, Ticca, Wage

▷**His** *may indicate* greetings

Hiss(ing) Boo, Fizzle, Goose, Hish, Sibilant, Siffle, Sizzle, Static, Swish

Historian Acton, Antiquary, Archivist, Arrian, Asellio, Bede, Biographer, Bryant, Buckle, Camden, Carlyle, Chronicler, Du Bois, Etain, Eusebius, Froude, Genealogist, Gibbon, Gildas, Green, Griot, Herodotus, Knickerbocker, Livy, Macaulay, Oman, Pliny, Plutarch, Ponsonby, Procopius, Read, Renan, Roper, Rowse, Sallust, Starkey, Strabo, Strachey, Suetonius, Tacitus, Taylor, Thiers, Thucydides, Toynbee, Trevelyan, Wells, Xenophon

History, Historic(al) Account, Age, Anamnesis, Annal, Bunk, Case, Chronicle, Clio, Diachronic, Epoch(a), Epoch-making, Ere-now, Ever, Heredity, Heritage, Legend, Life, Meiji, Mesolithic, Natural, Ontogency, Past, Record, Relie, Retroactive, Story, Track record, Yesterday

Hit Attain, Bang, Bash, Baste, Bat, Bean, Belt, Bepat, Best seller, Blip, Blockbuster, Bloop, Blow, Bludgeon, Boast, Bolo, Bonk, Bump, Bunt, Catch, Chip, Clip, Clobber, Clock, Clout, Club, Collide, Cuff, Dot, Flail, Flick, Flip, Foul, Fourpenny-one, Fungo, Fustigate, Get, Hay, Head-butt, Home(-thrust), Ice-man, Impact, Inner, Knock, Lam, Lob, Magpie, Mug, Outer, Pandy, Paste, Pepper, Pinch, Pistol-whip, Polt, Prang, Punto dritto, Ram, Roundhouse, Sacrifice, Score, Sensation, Six, Skier, Sky, Slam, Slap, Slosh, Smash(eroo), Smit(e), Sock, Spank, Spike, Stoush, Straik, Stricken, Strike, Strook, Struck, →**SUCCESS**, Swat, Switch, Thwack, Time-thrust, Tip, Tonk, Touché, Twat, Undercut, Venewe, Venue, Volley, Wallop, Whack, Wham, Wing, Ythundered, Zap, Zonk

Hitch(ed) Catch, Cat's paw, Clove, Contretemps, Edge, Espouse, Harness, Hike, Hirsle, Hoi(c)k, Hotch, Jerk, Kink, Knot, Lorry-hop, Rope, Rub, Setback, Sheepshank, Sheet bend, Shrug, Snag, Technical, Thumb

Hitman Assassin, Eliminator, Gun

Hoard(ing) Accumulate, Amass, Bill, Cache, Coffer, Eke, Heap, Hog, Hoord, Husband, Hutch, Mucker, Plant, Pose, Save, Sciurine, Snudge, Squirrel, Stash, Stock, Stockpile, Store, Treasure

Hoarse(ness) Croupy, Frog, Grating, Gruff, Husky, Raucous, Roar(er), Roopit, Roopy, Roup, Throaty

Hoax Bam, Canard, Cod, Do, Doff, Fub, Fun, Gag, Gammon, Gowk, Gull, Have on, Hum, Huntie-gowk, Josh, Kid, Leg-pull, Piltdown, Quiz, Sell, Sham, Skit, Spoof, String, Stuff, →**TRICK**

Hob Ceramic, Cooktop, Ferret, Goblin, Lout

Hobble, Hobbling Enfetter, Game, Hamshackle, Hilch, Hitch, Impair, Lame, Limp, Pastern, Picket, Shackle, Spancel, Stagger, Tether

Hobby Avocation, Fad, Falcon, Interest, Pastance, Predator, Pursuit, Recreation, Scrimshaw

Hock Cambrel, Dip, Gambrel, Gambril, Gammon, Ham, Heel, Hough, Hypothecate, Pawn, Pledge, Rhenish, Wine

Hoe Claut, Draw, Dutch, Grub, Grubbing, Jembe, Nab, Pecker, Rake, Weed

Hog Babiroussa, Babirusza, Boar, Glutton, Guttle, Mexican, Peccary, Pig, Porker, Puck, Road, Shoat, Shott, Whole

Hoist(ing) Boom, Bouse, Bunk-up, Crane, Davit, Derrick, Garnet, Gin, Heave, Heft, Hills, Jack, Lewis, Lift, Raise, Shearlegs, Shears, Sheerlegs, Sheers, Sway, Teagle, Trice, Whip-and-derry, Wince, Winch, Windas, Windlass

Hold(er), Holding, Hold back, out, up, etc Absorb, Airlock, Allege, Alow, Anchor, Apply, Argue, Asset, Belay, Believe, Boston crab, Cachepot, Caesura, Canister, Cease, Cement, Cinch, Clamp, Clasp, Cling, Clip, Clutch, Contain, Corral, Cresset, Defer, Delay, Detain, Display, Document, Dog, Embrace, Engage, Engross, Er, Farm, Fast, Fistful, Frog, Full nelson, Garter, →**GRASP**, Grip, Half-nelson, Hammerlock, Handle, Have, Headlock, Heft, Heist, Hinder, Hitch, Ho(a), Hoh, Hoy, Hug, Impedance, Impede, Impediment, In chancery, Incumbent, Inhibit, Intern, Keep, Keepnet, Lease, Lifebelt, Maintain, Nef, Nelson, Nurse, Oasis, Obstacle, Occupant, Own, Port, Proffer, Purchase, Rack, Reach, Reckon, Reserve, Restrain, Retain, Rivet, Rob, Save, Scissors, Shelve, Shore, Sleeve, Sostenuto, Stand, Stock, Suspend, Take, Tenancy, Tenure, Territory, Toehold, Tripod, Trivet, Wait, →**WRESTLING**, Wristlock, Zarf

Hole(s), Holed, Holey Ace, Albatross, Antrum, Aperture, Beam, Birdie, Black, Bogey, Bolt, Bullet, Burrow, Cat, Cave, Cavern, Cavity, Cissing, Coal, Coalsack, Collapsar, Cove, Crater, Cubby, Cup, Dell, Den, Dene, Dog-leg, Dormie, Dormy, Dreamhole, Dry, Dugout, Eagle, Earth, Eye(let), Finger, Foramen, Funk, Gap, Geat, Glory, Gore, Gutta, Hag(g), Hideout, Kettle, Knot, Lill, Limber, Loop, Loup, Maar, Moulin, Nineteenth, Oillet, →**OPENING**, Orifice, Ozone, Perforate, Pierce, Pigeon, Pinprick, Pit, Pocket, Pore, Port, Pot, Potato, Priest's, Punctuate, Puncture, Rabbit, Rivet, Rove, Scupper, Scuttle, Sinus, Situation, Slot, Snag, Snow, Soakaway, Socket, Sound, Spandrel, Spider, Starting, Stead, Stew, Stop, Stove, Swallow, Tear, Thumb, Tight spot, Touch, Trema, Vent, Voided, Watering, Weep(er), Well, White, Wookey

Holiday(s), Holiday maker Away, Bank, Benjo, Break, Camper, Carnival, Childermas, Days of Awe, Easter, Ecotour, Ferial, Festa(l), →**FESTIVAL**, Fête, Fiesta, Fly-drive, French leave, Furlough, Gala, Half(term), High, Kwanzaa, Laik, Leasure, Leave, Leisure, Long, Minibreak, Outing, Pace, Packaged, Pink-eye, Playtime, Recess, Repose, Rest, Roman, Schoolie, Seaside, Shabuoth, Shavuot, Stay, Sunday, Time off, Trip, →**VACATION**, Villeggiatura, Wake(s), Weekend, Whitsun, Xmas

Hollow(ed) Aeolipile, Alveary, Antar, Antre, Armpit, Boss, Bowl, Cave(rn), Cavity, Chasm, Cirque, Comb(e), Concave, Coomb, Crater, Cup(mark), Dean, Dell, Delve, Den(e), Dent, Dimple, Dingle, Dip, Dish(ing), Empty, Groove, Grot(to), Hole, How, Howe, Igloo, Incavo, Insincere, Intaglio, Keck(sy), Kettle(hole), Kex, Lap, Mortise, Niche, Orbita, Pan, Philtrum, Pit, Playa, Punchbowl, Punt, Rut, Scoop, Sinus, Sleepy, Slot, Slough, Socket, Trough, Vacuous, Ventricle, Vesicle

Holy(man), Holiness Adytum, Alliance, Ariadne, Blessed, →**DIVINE**, Godly, Grail, Halidom, Hallowed, Helga, Hery, Inner sanctum, Khalif, Loch, Mountain, Olga, Orders, Pious, Sacred, Sacrosanct, Sad(d)hu, Saintdom, Saintly, Sanctitude, Sannayasi(n), Santon, Sekos, Sepulchre, Shrine, Starets, Staretz, SV, Tirthankara, War

Holy books, Holy writing Adigranth, Atharvaveda, Bible, Gemara, Granth, Hadith, Hagiographa, Koran, Mishnah, NT, OT, Pia, Purana, Rigveda, Sama-Veda, → **SCRIPTURE**, Shaster, Shastra, Smriti, Sura(h), Tanach, Writ

Holy building, Holy city, Holy place Chapel, Church, Kaaba, Kirk, Mashhad, Mecca, Medina, Meshed, Najaf, Penetralia, Sanctum, Station, Synagogue, Temenos, Temple

Homage Bow, Cense, Honour, Kneel, Obeisance, Tribute

Home(land), Homeward Abode, Apartment, Base, Blighty, Bro, Broken, Burrow, Cheshire, Chez, Clinic, Community, Convalescent, Crib, Domal, Domicile, Dwelling, Earth, Eventide, Family, Fireside, Flat, Funeral, Gaff, Goal, Habitat, Harvest, Heame, Hearth, Heme, Hospice, House, In, Lair, Libken, Lockwood, Lodge, Maisonette, Mental, Mobile, Montacute, Motor, Nest, Nursing, Old sod, Orphanage, Pad, Penny-gaff, Pied à terre, Pile, Pit dwelling, Plas Newydd, Remand, Res(idence), Rest, Semi, Starter, Stately, Tepee, Turangawaewae, Up-along, Villa, Warren

Homespun Cracker-barrel, Folksy, Plain, Raploch, Russet, Simple

Homicidal, Homicide Chance-medley, Killing, Manslaughter

Homily Lecture, Pi, Postil, Prone, Sermon

▷**Homing** *may indicate* coming back

Honest(y), Honestly Aboveboard, Afauld, Afawld, Amin, Candour, Clean, Faith, Four square, Frank, Genuine, Incorruptible, Injun, Jake, Jannock, Jonnock, Legitimate, Lunaria, Lunary, Mensch, Open-faced, Penny, Probity, Realtie, Rectitude, Reputable, Righteous, Round, Sincere, Soothfast, Square, Squareshooter, Straight, Straightforward, Straight-out, Trojan, → **TRUE**, Truepenny, Upright, Upstanding

Honey(ed) Comb, Flattery, Hybla(ean), Hymettus, Mel, Melliferous, Mellifluous, Nectar, Peach, Popsy-wopsy, Sis, Sugar, Sweetheart, Sweetie (pie), Virgin, Wild

Honeysuckle Lonicera, Twinflower, Woodbind, Woodbine

Honour(able), Honorary, Honoured, Honorific, Honours A, Acclaim, Accolade, Ace, Adward, Birthday, Blue, Bow, CBE, Commemorate, Credit, Crown, Curtsey, Dan, Elate, Emeritus, Ennoble, → **ESTEEM**, Ethic, Face-card, Fame, Fête, Gloire, Glory, Grace, Greats, Homage, Insignia, Invest, J, Jack, K, King, Knave, Knight, Kudos, Laudation, Laureate, Laurels, MBE, Mensch, Mention, OBE, Optime, Order, Pundonor, Q, Queen, Regius, Remember, Repute, Respect, Revere, Reward, Salute, Straight, Ten, Tenace, Titular, Tribute, Tripos, Venerate, White, Worship, Wranglers

Hood(ed) Almuce, Amaut, Amice, Amowt, Apache, Balaclava, Bashlik, Biggin, Blindfold, Calash, Calèche, Calyptra, Capeline, Capuccio, Capuche, Chaperon(e), Coif, Cope, Cowl, Cucullate(d), Faldetta, Fume, Gangster, Headdress, Jacobin, Kennel, Liripipe, Liripoop, Mantle, Mazarine, Nithsdale, Pixie, Robin, Rowdy, Snood, Trot-cosey, Trot-cozy, Visor

Hook(ed), Hooker, Hooks Addict, Adunc, Aduncous, Aquiline, Arrester, Barb(icel), Barbule, Becket, Butcher's, Cant(dog), Catch, Chape, Claw, Cleek, Clip, Clove, Cocotte, Corvus, Crampon, Cromb, Crome, Crook, Crotchet, Cup, Drail, Duck, Fish, Floozy, Gaff, Grap(p)le, Grapnel, Grappling, Gripple, Hamate, Hamose, Hamulus, Hanger, Heel, Hitch, Inveigle, Kype, Meat, Picture, Pot, Prostitute, Punch, Sickle, Snare, Snell, Sniggle, Solicit, Tala(u)nt, Tenaculum, Tenter, Tie, Trip, Uncus, Wanton

Hooligan Apache, Bogan, Casual, Desperado, Droog, Goonda, Hobbledehoy, Hoon, Keelie, Larrikin, Lout, Ned, Rough(neck), Ruffian, Skollie, Skolly, Tearaway, Ted, Tityre-tu, Tough, Tsotsi, Vandal, Yahoo, Yob(bo)

Hoop(s) Bail, Band, Circle, Farthingale, Garth, Gird, Girr, Hula®, O, Pannier, →RING, Sleeper, Tire, Trochus, Trundle

Hoot(er) Deride, Honk, Madge, Nose, Owl, Riot, Screech-owl, Siren, Ululate

Hop(per) An(o)ura, Ball, Bin, Cuscus, Dance, Flight, Jeté, Jump, Kangaroo, Leap, Lilt, Long, Opium, Pogo, Roo, Saltate, Scotch, Skip, Tremié, Vine

Hope(ful) Anticipate, Aspirant, Auspicious, Bob, Combe, Comer, Contender, Daydream, Desire, Dream, Esperance, Evelyn, Expectancy, Forlorn, Gleam, Great white, Inshallah, Pipe-dream, Pray, Promising, Prospect, Ray, Roseate, Rosy, Sanguine, Trust, Upbeat, Valley, Wannabe, White, Wish

Hopeless(ness), Hopeless quest Abattu, Anomie, Anomy, Black, Buckley's chance, Dead duck, Despair, Despondent, Forlorn, Gloom, Goner, Lost cause, Non-starter, No win, Perdu, Pessimist

Hophead Drinker, Lush, Sot

Horizon A, Apparent, Artificial, Event, Scope, Sea-line, Sensible, Skyline, Visible

Horn(s), Horny Acoustic, Advancer, Amalthea, Antenna(e), Baleen, Basset, Beeper, Bez, Brass, Buck, Bugle, Bur(r), Cape, Ceratoid, Cor, Cornet, Cornett, Cornopean, Cornu(a), Cornucopia, Cromorna, Cromorne, Cusp, Dilemma, English, Flugel-horn, French, Frog, Gemshorn, Golden, Gore, Hooter, Hunting, Ivory, Keratin, Klaxon, Lur, Morsing, Mot, Oliphant, Parp, Periostracum, Plenty, Post, Powder, Pryse, Saddle, Shoe, Shofar, Shophor, Spongin, Tenderling, Trey, Trez, Trumpet, Tusk, Vulcan's badge, Waldhorn

Horrible, Horror Appalling, Aw(e)some, Beastly, Brat, Creepy, Dire, Distaste, Dread(ful), Execrable, Gashful, Ghastly, Grand Guignol, Grisly, Grooly, Gruesome, Grysie, Hideous, Minging, Nightmare, Odious, Panic, Rascal, Shock, Shudder, Stupefaction, Terror, The creeps, Ugh

Horrid, Horrific, Horrified, Horrify(ing) Aghast, Agrise, Appal, Chill, Dire, Dismay, Dreadful, Frightful, Ghastly, Gothic, Grim, Grisly, H, Loathy, Odious, Shock, Spine-chilling, Spiteful, Ugly

Hors d'oeuvres Antipasto, Canapé, Carpaccio, Ceviche, Hoummos, Houmus, Hummus, Mez(z)e, Pâté, Smorgasbord, Starter, Tapas, Zak(o)uski

Horse(s) Abasta, Airer, Bidet, Bloodstock, Carriage, Cut, Cutting, Dark, Doer, Dray, Drier, Drug, Equine, Eye-necked, Form, H, High, Hobby, Iron, Knight, Kt, Light, Lot, Maiden, Malt, Non-starter, Outsider, Pack, Pantomime, Plug, Ride, Rocking, Sawbuck, Scag, Screen, Selling-plater, Sense, Stable, Stalking, Standard-bred, Starter, Stayer, Steeplechaser, Stiff, Stock, Teaser, Trestle, Vanner, Vaulting, White, Willing, Wooden

Horse complaint, Horse disease, Horse problem, Horse trouble Blood spavin, Bogspavin, Bot(t)s, Broken wind, Canker, Capel(l)et, Cratches, Curb, Deer-neck, Dourine, Drepance, Equinia, Eweneck, Farcin, Farcy, Fives, Frush, Glanders, Gourdy, Grape, Grass-sickness, Head staggers, Heaves, Hippiatric, Hoof rot, Malander, Megrims, Moon blindness, Mooneye, N(a)gana, Parrot mouth, Poll-evil, Quartercrack, Quitter, Quittor, Ringbone, Roaring, Sallenders, Sand crack, Scratches, Seedy-toe, Shaft, Spavie, Spavin, Springhalt, Staggers, Strangles, Stringhalt, Surra, Sween(e)y, Thorough-pin, Thrush, Tread, Vives, Weed, Weid, Whistling, Windgall, Wire-heel, Yellows

Horseman Ataman, Caballero, Cavalry, Centaur, Conquest, Cossack, Cowboy, Death, Dragman, Famine, Farrier, Hobbler, Hussar, Knight, Lancer, Nessus, Ostler, Parthian, Picador, Pricker, Quadrille, Revere, →RIDER, Slaughter, Spahi, Stradiot, Tracer, Wrangler

Horseplay Caper, Polo, Rag, Rant, Romp

Horseshoe(-shaped) Henge, Hippocrepian, King-crab, Lophophorate, Lunette, Manilla, Oxbow, Plate

Hose Chausses, Fishnet, Galligaskins, Gaskins, Hydrant, Lisle, Netherstock(ing), Nylons, Panty, Sock, Sox, Stockings, Tights, Trunk, Tube, Wet

Hospice, Hospital Almshouse, Ambulance, Asylum, Barts, Base, Bedlam, Booby hatch, Bughouse, Clinic, Cottage, Day, Dressing station, ENT, Field, Foundation, Guest-house, Guys, H, Home, Hôtel dieu, Imaret, Infirmary, Isolation, Karitane, Lazaretto, Leprosarium, Leprosery, Lock, Loony bin, MASH, Mental, Nosocomial, Nuthouse, Nuttery, Pest-house, Polyclinic, Rathouse, San, Scutari, Sick bay, Spital, Spittle, Teaching, Trauma centre, UCH

Hospitable, Hospitality Cadgy, Convivial, Corporate, Entertainment, Euxine, Kidgie, Lucullan, Open house, Philoxenia, Social, Xenial

Host(s), Hostess Alternate, Amphitryon, Anchorman, Army, Barmecide, Bunny girl, Chatelaine, Commerce, Compere, Crowd, Definitive, Emcee, Entertainer, Geisha, Hirsel, Hotelier, Innkeeper, Inviter, Laban, Landlady, Landlord, Legend, Legion, Licensee, Lion-hunter, Lot, Maitre d', Mass, Mavin, MC, Number, Presenter, Publican, Quickly, Quizmaster, Speakerine, Swarm, Taverner, Throng, Torrent, Trimalchio, Wafer, Winfrey

Hostile, Hostility Adverse, Aggressive, Alien, Anger, Animus, Anti, Arms, Aversion, Bad blood, Bellicose, Bitter, Currish, Diatribe, Enemy, Feud, Forbidding, Hating, Ho, Icy, Ill, Ill-will, Inimical, Inveterate, Opposed, Oppugnant, Pugnacity, Unfriendly, Virulent, Vitriolic, War

Hot(spot), Hot (tempered) Aboil, Aetnean, Aflame, Ardent, Baking, Big, Blistering, Breem, Breme, Cajun, Calid, Candent, Cayenne, Chilli, Dog days, Enthusiastic, Erotic(al), Etnaen, Facula, Fervid, Feverish, Fiery, Fuggy, Gospeller, Het, In, Incandescent, Irascible, Ireful, Latest, Lewd, Live, Mafted, Mirchi, Mustard, Nightclub, Pepper, Piping, Potato, Quick, Randy, Red, Roaster, Scalding, Scorcher, Sexpot, Sexy, Sizzling, Spicy, Spitfire, Steamy, Stewy, Stifling, Stolen, Sultry, Sweaty, Sweltering, Sweltry, Tabasco®, Thermidor, Torrid, Toustie, Tropical, Zealful

Hotchpotch Bricolage, Farrago, Mish-mash, Pot pourri, Powsowdy, Welter

Hotel, Hotelkeeper Bo(a)tel, Boutique, Commercial, Flophouse, Gasthaus, Gasthof, H, Hilton, Hydro(pathic), Inn, Internet, Khan, Military, Motel, Parador, Pension, Posada, Ritz, Roadhouse, Savoy, Tavern, Telco, Waldorf, Watergate

Hothead(ed) Impetuous, Madcap, Rash, Spitfire, Volcano

Hot-house Conservatory, Forcing-house, Nursery, Orangery, Vinery

Hotspot Bricolage, Farrago, Mish-mash, Powsowdy, Suntrap, Welter

Hound(s) Afghan, Badger, Basset, Beagle, Bellman, Brach, Cad, Canine, Cry, →DOG, Entry, Gaze, Harass, Harrier, Hen-harrier, Importune, Javel, Kennet, Lurcher, Lyam, Lym(e), Mute, Otter, Pack, Persecute, Pursue, Rache, Ranter, Reporter, Saluki, Scoundrel, Talbot, True, Tufter

Hour(s) Canonical, Complin(e), Daylight, Elders', Flexitime, H, Happy, Holy, Hr, Literacy, None(s), Office, Orthros, Peak, Prime, Rush, Sext, Small, Terce, Tide, Time, Undern, Unearthly, Unsocial, Vespers, Visiting, Witching, Zero

House(s), Housing, Household(er) Abode, Accepting, Adobe, Aerie, Aery, Astrology, Audience, Auditorium, Billet, Bingo, Black, Brick veneer, Broiler, Cinema, Clan, Co, Coffee, Cottage (orné), Counting, Country, Crankcase, Death, Discount, Disorderly, Domestic, Domicile, Drostdy, Dynasty, Establishment, Estate, Eyrie, Finance, Firm, Forcing, Fraternity, Free, Gambling, Gazebo, Gemini, Government, Grace and favour, Guest, Habitation, Hall, Hearth,

Homestead, Ice, Infill, Inner, Issuing, Joss, Libken, Lodge, Lofted, Loose, Lot(t)o, Malting, Meiney, Ménage, Menyie, Mobility, Monastery, Nacelle, Node, Open(-plan), Outer, Picts, Picture, Pilot, Pleasure, Pole, Post, Prefab, Printing, Public, Radome, Ranch, Register, Residence, Rooming, Root, Rough, Sacrament, Saltbox, School, Sheltered, Show, Social, Software, Spec-built, Sporting, State, Station, Steeple, Storey, Succession, Tea, Tenement, Third, Treasure, Tree, Trust, Try, Upby, Vaulting, Villa(-home), Wash, Watch, Weather, Weigh, Wheel, Work, Zodiac

Housing Case, Crankcase, Shabrack, Shelter, Slum, Tenement

Hovel Cru(i)ve, Den, Pigsty, Shack, Shanty

However Although, As, But, Even-so, Leastwise, Sed, Still, Though, Yet

Howl(er) Banshee, Bawl, Bay, Bloop, Clanger, Hue, Mycetes, Slip up, Tornado, Ululate, War whoop, Wow, Yawl, Yowl

Hub Boss, Boston, Centre, Focus, Hob, Nave, Nucleus, Pivot, Tee

Hubbub Charivari, Chirm, Coil, Din, Level-coil, Palaver, Racket, Row, Stir

Huckster Hawker, Kidd(i)er, Pedlar

Huddle Cringe, Gather, Hunch, Nestle, Ruck, Shrink

Hue Chrome, Colour, Dye, Outcry, Proscription, Steven, Tincture, Tinge, Umbrage, Utis

Huff Dudgeon, Hector, Pant, Pet, Pique, Strunt, Umbrage, Vex

Huge (number) Astronomical, Brobdingnag, Colossal, Elephantine, Enorm(ous), Epic, Gargantuan, Giant, →**GIGANTIC**, Gillion, Ginormous, Humongous, Humungous, Immane, Immense, Leviathan, Lulu, Mega-, Milliard, Monumental, Octillion, Socking, Stupendous, Thumping, Titanian, Tremendous, Voluminous, Whacking, Whopping

Hull Bottom, Framework, Husk, Inboard, Monocoque, Pod, Sheel, Shell, Shill

▶**Hullo** *see* **HELLO**

Hum(ming) BO, Bombilate, Bombinate, Bum, Buzz, Chirm, Chirr, Drone, Eident, Lilt, Moan, Murmur, Nos(e)y, Odorate, Odorous, Pong, Rank, Reek, Sough, Sowf(f), Sowth, Stench, Stink, Stir, Whir(r), Zing

Human(e), Humanist, Humanitarian, Humanity, Humanoid Anthropoid, Anthropology, Bang, Colet, Earthling, Earthman, Erasmus, Hominid, Homunculi, Incarnate, Kindness, Mandom, Meatbot, Merciful, Mortal, Philanthropic, Species, Sympathy, Ubuntu, Unpaid

Humble Abase, Abash, Afflict, Baseborn, Chasten, Conquer, Cow, Degrade, Demean, Demiss(ly), Grovel, Lower, Lowly, Mean, Mean-born, →**MEEK**, Modest, Morigerate, Obscure, Poor, Rude, Small, Snub, Truckle

Humbug Berley, Blague, Blarney, Burley, Claptrap, Con, Delude, Eyewash, Flam, Flummery, Fraud, Fudge, Gaff, Gammon, Gas, Guff, Gum, Hoax, Hoodwink, Kibosh, Liar, Maw-worm, Nonsense, Prig, Shenanigan, Tosh, Wind

Humdrum Banal, Boredom, Bourgeois, Monotonous, Mundane, Ordinary, Prosaic, Routine, Tedious, Uninspiring

Humiliate(d), Humiliation, Humility Abase(ment), Abash, Baseness, Comedown, Debag, Degrade, Disbench, Eating crow, Fast, Indignity, Laughing stock, Lose face, Lowlihead, Mortify, Put-down, →**SHAME**, Skeleton, Take-down, Wither

Humorist Cartoonist, Comedian, Jester, Leacock, Lear, Punster, Thurber, Twain, Wodehouse

Humour, Humorous Aqueous, Bile, Blood, Bonhomie, Caprice, Cardinal, Chaff, Choler, Coax, Cocker, Coddle, Cosher, Cuiter, Cuittle, Custard-pie,

Daut, Dawt, Droll, Dry, Facetious, Fun, Gallows, Ichor, Indulge, Irony, Jocose, Jocular, Juice, Kidney, Lavatorial, Levity, Light, Melancholy, →**MOOD**, Observe, One-liner, Pamper, Phlegm, Pun, Pythonesque, Ribaldry, Salt, Satire, Serum, Sick, Temper, Trim, Vein, Vitreous, Vitreum, Whim, Whimsy, Wit, Wry

Hump(ed), Humping Boy, Bulge, Dorts, Dowager's, Gibbose, Gibbous, Hog, Huff, Hummock, Hunch, Pip, Protrusion, Ramp, Sex, Sleeping policeman, Tussock

▶**Humpback** *see* **HUNCH(ED)**

Humus Compost, Leafmould, Moder, Mor, Mull

Hunch(ed), Hunchback Camel, Chum, Crookback, Hump, Intuition, Kyphosis, Premonition, Presentiment, Quasimodo, Roundback, Squat, Urchin

Hundred(s), Hundredfold, Hundredth Burnham, C, Cantred, Cantref, Cent, Centum, Centuple, Century, Chiltern, Commot, Desborough, Host, Northstead, Shire, Stoke, Tiyin, Ton, Tyiyn, Wapentake

Hungarian, Hungary Bohunk, Csardas, Magyar, Nagy, Szekely, Tzigane, Ugric, Vogul

Hunger (strike), Hungry Appestat, Appetite, Bulimia, Bulimy, Clem, →**CRAVE**, Desire, Edacity, Emaciated, Empty, Esurient, Famine, Famish, Fast, Hanker, Hunter, Insatiate, Itch, Orectic, Pant, Peckish, Pine, Pyne, Rapacious, Raven, Ravin, Sharp-set, Starve, Unfed, Unfuelled, Yaup, Yearn

▷**Hungry** *may indicate* an 'o' in another word

Hunt(er), Hunting, Huntress, Huntsman Beachcomb, Blood sport, Bushman, Chasseur, Chiv(vy), Comb, Corner, Dog, Drag(net), Gun, Horse, Hound, Kennet, Letterbox, Lurcher, Mouser, Nimrod, Poacher, Predator, Prowl, Pursue, Quest, Quorn, Ride, Run, Safari, San, Scavenge(r), Scout, Sealer, →**SEARCH**, Seek, Stalk, Ticker, Trap, Venerer, →**WATCH**, Whipper-in, Woodman, Yager

Hunting-call Rechate, Recheat, Tally-ho, View-halloo

Hurdle(r) Barrier, Doll, Fence, Flake, Gate, Hemery, Jump, Obstacle, Raddle, Snag, Sticks, Wattle

Hurl(ing) Camogie, Cast, Dash, →**FLING**, Heave, Put(t), Sling, Throw, →**TOSS**

Hurry, Hurried Belt, Bustle, Chivvy, Chop-chop, Dart, Dash, Drive, Expedite, Festinate, Fisk, Frisk, Gad, Gallop, Giddap, Giddup, Giddy-up, Hadaway, Hare, Haste, Hie, Hightail, Induce, Mosey, Pop, Post-haste, Press (on), Push, Race, Railroad, →**RUSH**, Scamper, Scoot, Scramble, Scur(ry), Scutter, Scuttle, Skelter, Skurry, Spank, Speed, Streak, Sudden, Tear, Whirr, Zip

Hurt(ful) Abuse, Ache, Adverse, Aggrieve, Ake, Bruise, Damage, De(a)re, Detriment, Disservice, Harm, Harrow, Hit, →**INJURE**, Lesion, Maim, Nocent, Nocuous, Noisome, Noxious, Noyous, Offend, Pain, Pang, Prick(le), Scaith, Spite, Sting, Trauma, Wring

Husband(ry), Husbands Add, Baron, Betty, Breadwinner, Conserve, Consort, Darby, Ear, Eche, Economy, Eke, Ere, Farm, Gander(-mooner), Georgic, Goodman, Groom, H, Hoddy-doddy, Hodmandod, Hubby, Ideal, Lord and master, Man, Manage, Mate, Partner, Polyandry, Reserve, Retrench, Save, Scrape, Scrimp, Spouse, Squirrel, →**STORE**, Tillage

Husk(s), Husky Acerose, Bran, Draff, Eskimo, Gruff, Hoarse, Hull, Malemute, Seed, Sheal, Shiel, Shuck, Throaty

Hustle(r) Fast talk, Frogmarch, Jostle, Pro, Push, Railroad, Shoulder, Skelp

Hut(s) Banda, Booth, Bothie, Bothy, Bustee, Cabin, Chalet, Choltry, Gazebo, Gunyah, Hogan, Humpy, Igloo, Mia-mia, Nissen, Pondok(kie), Quonset®,

Rancheria, Rancho, Rondavel, Shack, Shanty, Sheal(ing), Shebang, Shed, Shiel(ing), Skeo, Skio, Succah, Sukkah, Tilt, Tolsel, Tolsey, Tolzey, Wan(n)igan, Wigwam, Wi(c)kiup, Wil(t)ja, Wurley

Hybrid Amerasian, Bigener, Bois-brûlé, Cama, Catalo, Centaur, Chamois, Chichi, Citrange, Cross, Dso, Funnel, Geep, Graft, Incross, Interbred, Jomo, Jumart, Lurcher, Mameluco, Mermaid, Merman, Metif, Métis, Mongrel, Mule, Mutation, Noisette, Onocentaur, Ox(s)lip, Percolin, Plumcot, Pomato, Ringed, Single-cross, Tangelo, Tiglon, Tigon, Topaz, Ugli, Werewolf, Zedonk, Zho(mo)
▷**Hybrid** *may indicate* an anagram

Hydrocarbon Acetylene, Aldrin, Alkane, Alkene, Alkyl, Alkyne, Amylene, Arene, Asphaltite, Benzene, Butadiene, Butane, Butene, Camphane, Camphene, Carotene, Cetane, Cubane, Cumene, Cyclohexane, Cyclopropane, Decane, Diene, Dioxin, Diphenyl, Ethane, Ethylene, Gutta, Halon, Hatchettite, Heavy oil, Heptane, Hexane, Hexene, Hexyl(ene), Indene, Isobutane, Isoprene, Ligroin, Limonene, Mesitylene, Methane, Naphtha, Naphthalene, Naphthalin(e), Nonane, Octane, Olefin(e), Paraffin, Pentane, Pentene, Pentylene, Phenanthrene, Phene, Picene, Pinene, Polyene, Propane, Pyrene, Pyridine, Pyrimidine, Retene, Squalene, Stilbene, Styrene, Terpene, Toluene, Triptane, Wax, Xylene, Xylol

Hydrogen Deut(er)on, Diplon, Ethene, H, Heavy, Protium, Tritium

Hyena Aard-wolf, Cackle, Earthwolf, Nandi bear, Strand-wolf, Tiger-wolf

Hymn(s) Amazing Grace, Anthem, Benedictine, Bhajan, Canticle, Carol, Cathisma, Choral(e), Coronach, Dies Irae, Dithyramb, Doxology, Epithalamia, Gloria, Hallel, Introit(us), Ithyphallic, Lay, Magnificat, Mantra, Marseillaise, Nunc Dimittis, Ode, P(a)ean, Praise, Processional, Psalm, Psalmody, Recessional, Rigveda, Sanctus, Sequence, Stabat Mater, Sticheron, Tantum Ergo, Te Deum, Trisagion, Troparion, Veda

Hymnographer, Hymnologist Cowper, David, Faber, Heber, Moody, Neale, Parry, Sankey, Watts

Hype(d) Aflutter, Ballyhoo, Blurb

Hypnosis, Hypnotise, Hypnotic, Hypnotism, Hypnotist Braidism, Chloral, Codeine, Entrance, Fluence, Magnetic, Magnetise, Mesmerism, Psychognosis, Svengali

Hypocrisy, Hypocrite, Hypocritical Archimago, Bigot, Byends, Cant, Carper, Chadband, Creeping Jesus, Deceit, Dissembler, Dissimulating, Double standards, False-faced, Heep, Holy Willie, Humbug, Mucker, Nitouche, Pecksniff, Pharisaic, Pharisee, Piety, Plaster saint, Prig, Sepulchre, Tartuf(f)e, Two-faced, Whited sepulchre

Hypothesis, Hypothesize, Hypothetic, Hypothetical Avogadro, Biophor, Conditional, Gaia, Gluon, Graviton, Micella, Nostratic, Suppose, Suppositious, Theory, Virtual, Whorf

Hysteria, Hysteric(al) Conniption, Crazy, Delirium, Frenzy, Meemie, Panic

Ii

I A, Ch, Cham, Che, Dotted, Ego, Element, Ich, Indeed, India, Iodine, Italy, J, Je, Me, Myself, Self, Yours truly

Ice(d), Ice-cream, Icing, Icy A la mode, Alcorza, Anchor, Arctic, Ballicatter, Banana split, Berg, Black, Brainstorm, Brash, Camphor, Cassata, Coconut, Cone, Cool, Cornet, Coupe, Cream, Crystal, Diamonds, Drift, Dry, Field, Floe, Frappé, Frazil, Freeze, Frigid, Frore, Frosting, Frosty, Gelato, Gelid, Gems, Glacé, Glacial, Glacier, Glare, Glaze, Glib, Granita, Graupel, Ground, Hailstone, Hok(e)y-pok(e)y, Intention, Kitty-benders, Knickerbocker glory, Kulfi, Lolly, Marzipan, Neapolitan, Neve, Oaky, Pack, Pancake, Pingo, Polar, Popsicle®, Rime, Rink, Rivière, Ross, Royal, Sconce, Serac, Shelf, Sherbet, Slay, Slider, Slob, Sludge, Slush, Sorbet, Spumone, Spumoni, Stream, Sugar, Sundae, Theme, Tickly-benders, Topping, Tortoni, Tutti-frutti, Verglas, Wafer, Water, Wintry

Iceberg Calf, Floe, Growler, Lettuce

▶**Ice-cream** *see* **ICE(D)**

ID Dog-tag, Microchip, PIN

Idea(s) Archetype, Brainstorm, Brainwave, Clou, Clue, Conceit, Concept, Fancy, Figment, Germ, Hunch, Idée fixe, Idolum, Image, Inkling, Inspiration, Intention, Interpretation, Light, Meme, Motif, → **NOTION**, Obsession, Plan, Plank, Rationale, Recept, Theme, Theory, Thought, Zeitgeist

Ideal(ise) A1, Abstract, At best, Cat's pyjamas, Dream, Eden, Erewhon, Goal, Halo, Hero, Model, Monist, Mr Right, Nirvana, Notional, Paragon, Pattern, → **PERFECT**, Perfet, Prince Charming, Role-model, Rose, Siddhi, Sidha, Sublime, Utopian, Vision

Identical Alike, Carbon copy, Clone, Congruent, Double, Indistinguishable, One, Same, Selfsame, Verbatim

Identification, Identify Armband, Codeword, Cookie, Credentials, Designate, Detect, Diagnosis, Differentiate, Discern, Document, Dog-tag, Earmark, E-fit, Empathy, Espy, Finger(print), ID, Identikit®, Know, Label, Mark, Monomark, Name, Nameplate, Name-tape, Password, Photofit®, Pin, Pinpoint, Place, Point up, Recognise, Registration, Reg(g)o, Specify, Spot, Swan-upping, Verify

Identity Alias, Appearance, Corporate, Credentials, Ego, Equalness, Likeness, Mistaken, Numerical, Oneness, Personal, Qualitative, Seity, Self, Selfhood

Idiom Argot, Cant, Dialect, Expression, Jargon, Language, Pahlavi, Parlance, Pehlevi, Persism, Scotticism, Slavism, Syri(a)cism, Syrism

Idiot(ic), Idiocy Airhead, Congenital, Dingbat, Dipstick, Dolt, Dotard, Dumbo, Eejit, Fatuity, Fool, Git, Goose, Half-wit, Headbanger, Imbecile, Inane, Klutz, Maniac, Moron, Nana, Natural, Nerk, Nidget, Noncom, Numpty, Oaf, Ouph(e), Stupe, → **STUPID**, Tony, Twit, Village, Whacko, Zany

Idle(ness), Idler Beachcomber, Bum, Couch potato, Deadbeat, Dilly-dally, Drone, Eric, Farnarkel, Fester, Flaneur, Frivolous, Gold brick, Groundless,

Indolent, Inert, Lackadaisical, Layabout, Laze, Lazy, Lead-swinger, Lie,
Lig, Linger, Loaf, Loll, Lollard, Lollop, Lounge, Mooch, Neet, Potato, Ride,
Scapegrace, Shiftless, Skive, Slob, Sloth, Sluggard, Spiv, Stagnate, Stock-still,
Stooge, Sweirt, Tarry, Tick over, Trifle, Truant, Twiddle, Unemployed,
Unoccupied, Vacuity, Vain, Vegetate, Wait, Waste, Whip the cat, Workshy

Idol(ise) Adore, Adulate, Baal(im), Baphomet, Bel, Crush, Eikon, E(i)luned, Fetich(e),
Fetish, God, Graven image, Hero, Icon, Image, Joss, Juggernaut, Lion, Mammet,
Manito, Manitou, Matinee, Maumet, Mawmet, Molech, Moloch, Mommet,
Mumbo-jumbo, Pagoda, Swami, Teraph(im), Termagant, Vision, Wood, Worship

Idyll(ic) Arcady, Eclogue, Eden, Paradise, Pastoral, Peneian, Xanadu

Ignite, Ignition Coil, Flare, Flash-point, Glow plug, Kindle, Lightning, Spark,
Spontaneous, Starter

Ignominious, Ignominy Base, Dishonour, Fiasco, Humiliation, Infamous,
Scandal, →SHAME

Ignorance, Ignorant 404, Agnoiology, Analphabet, Anan, Artless, Benighted,
Blind, Clueless, Darkness, Green, Hick, Illiterate, Inerudite, Ingram, Ingrum,
Inscient, Irony, Know-nothing, Lewd, Lumpen, Misken, Nescience, Night,
Oblivious, Oik, Philistine, Purblind, Red-neck, Unaware, Uneducated,
Unlessoned, Unlettered, Unread, Unschooled, Untold, Unversed, Unwist

Ignore(d) Alienate, Ba(u)lk, Blink, Bypass, Connive, Cut, Discount, Disregard,
Forget, Leave, Neglect, Omit, Overlook, Overslaugh, Pass, Pass up, Scrub round,
Slight, Snub, Tune out, Unheeded

Ill(ness) Access, Adverse, All-overish, Awrong, Bad, Bilious, Cronk, Disorder, Evil,
Gout, Grotty, Income, Indisposed, Infection, Labyrinthitis, Laid up, Lovesick,
Misorder, Off-colour, Poorly, Pox, Queer, Ropy, Rough, Rubella, SARS,
Schistosomiasis, Scrofula, Sea-sick, →SICK, Strongylosis, Strung out,
Unpropitious, Unweal, Unwell, Valetudinarian, Vomito, Wog, Wrong, Yuppie flu

▷**Ill** *may indicate an anagram*

Ill-advised Foolish, Imprudent, Redeless

Ill-bred Carl, Churlish, Plebeian, Uncouth, Unmannerly

▷**Ill-composed** *may indicate an anagram*

Illegal, Illicit Adulterine, Black, Bootleg, Breach, Contraband, Furtive,
Ill-gotten, Malfeasance, Misbegotten, Pirated, Shonky, Unlawful, Wrong(ous)

Illegitimate Baseborn, Bastard, By-blow, Come-o'-will, Fitz, Irregular, Natural,
Scarp, Slink, Spurious, Unlawful

Ill-feeling, Ill-humour, Ill-will Acrimony, Animosity, Bad blood, Bile,
Complaint, Curt, Dudgeon, Enmity, Gall, Glum, Grudge, Hate, Hostility, Malice,
Mau(l)gre, Miff, Peevish, Pique, Rheum(atic), Spite, Spleen, Tantrum

▶**Illicit** *see* ILLEGAL

Ill-mannered, Ill-natured, Ill-tempered Acid, Attercop, Cad, Coarse,
Crabby, Crotchety, Curst, Ethercap, Ettercap, Gnarly, Goop, Gurrier, Guttersnipe,
Huffy, Lout, Mean, Splenetic, Stingy, Sullen, Surly, Ugly, Unkind

Illness Aids, Ailment, Attack, Autism, Brucellosis, Chill, Complaint, Croup,
Diabetes, Disease, DS, Dwalm, Dwaum, Dyscrasia, Eale, Eclampsia, Grippe,
Hangover, Hypochondria, Malady, ME, SAD, Scarlatina, Sickness, Toxaemia,
Urosis, Weed, Weid, Wog

▶**Ill-tempered** *see* ILL-MANNERED

Ill-treat Harm, Hurt, Shaft

Illuminate(d), Illumination, Illuminating Ambient, Aperçu, Brighten,
Bright-field, Candlelight, Clarify, Cul-de-lampe, Daylight, Decorate, Educative,

Enlighten, Floodlit, Lamplight, Langley, Lantern, Light, Limbourg, Limelight, Limn, Miniate, Moonlight, Nernst, Phot, Pixel, Radiate, Rushlight, Spotlight, Starlight

Illusion(ary), Illusionist, Illusory, Illusive Air, Apparition, Barmecide, Chimera, Deception, Escher, Fallacy, Fancy, Fantasy, Fata morgana, Hallucination, Ignis-fatuus, Indian rope trick, Mare's-nest, Maya, Mirage, Optical, Phantasmal, Phantom, Size-weight, Specious, Transcendental, Will o'the wisp

Illustrate(d), Illustration, Illustrator Artwork, Attwell, Bleed, Case, Centrefold, Collotype, Demonstrate, Dore, Drawing, Eg, Elucidate, Epitomise, Exemplify, Explain, Figure, Frontispiece, Grangerize, Graphic, Half-tone, Heath Robinson, Hors texte, Illume, Illumin(at)e, Instance, Instantiate, Keyline, Limner, Line-engraver, Plate, Rackham, Rockwell, Show, Sidelight, Spotlight, Tenniel, Vignette, Visual, Woodcut

▶**Ill-will** *see* ILL-FEELING

Image(s), Imaging Atman, Blip, Brand, Corporate, Dead ringer, Discus, Effigy, E-fit, Eidetic, Eidolon, Eikon, Emoticon, Emotion, Favicon, Fine-grain, Gift, Graphic, Graven, Hologram, Icon, Iconograph, Ident(ikit), Idol, Invultuation, Joss, Latent, Likeness, Litho, Matte, Mirror, Morph, Murti, Paraselene, Persona, Photogram, Photograph, Pic(ture), Pieta, Pixel(l)ated, Pixil(l)ated, Poetic, Print, Profile, Public, Radionuclide, Real, Recept, Reflectogram, Reflectograph, Representation, Scintigram, Search, Shrine, Simulacrum, Sonogram, Species, Spectrum, Spitting, Split, Stereotype, Symbol, Teraph(im), Thermal, Thermogram, Thumbnail, Tiki, Totem, Vectograph, Venogram, Video, Virtual, Waxwork

Imagine(d), Imaginary (land), Imagination, Imaginative Assume, Bandywallop, Believe, Bullamakanka, Cloud-cuckoo-land, Conceive, Conjure, Create, Cyborg, Dystopia, Envisage, Erewhon, Faery, Faine, Fancy, Feign, Fictional, Fictitious, Fictor, Figment, Figure, Hallucinate, Hobbit, Ideate, Invent, Moral, Narnia, Never-never-land, Non-existent, Notional, Otherworldly, Oz, Picture, Poetical, Prefigure, Propose, Recapture, Replicant, Scotch mist, →SUPPOSE, Surmise, Think, Tricorn, Tulpa, Unreal, Vision, Visualise, Whangam, Wonderland

▷**Imbecile** *may indicate* an anagram

Imbibe Absorb, Drink, Lap, Quaff, Suck, Swallow

Imitate, Imitation, Imitator Act, Ape, Burlesque, Caricature, Clone, Copy(cat), Counterfeit, Crib, Dud, Echo, Echopraxia, Emulate, Epigon(e), Ersatz, Facsimile, Fake, False, Faux, Hit off, Marinist, Me-too, Mime, Mimesis, Mimetic, Mimic(ry), Mini-me, Mockery, Monkey, Onomatopoeia, Parody, Parrot, Paste, Paste grain, Pastiche, Pinchbeck, Potichomania, Recreate, Repro, Rhinestone, Rip-off, Sham, Simulate, Skeuomorphism, Stumer, Take-off, Travesty, Unreal

Immaculate Conception, Flawless, Impeccable, Lily-white, Perfect, Pristine, Spotless, Virgin

Immature(ly), Immaturity Adolescent, Babyish, Beardless, Blast, Callow, Childish, Crude, Embryo, Ergate(s), Green, Imago, Inchoate, Larval, Neotenic, Nymph, Peter Pan, Puberal, Pupa, Raw, Rudimentary, Sophomoric, Tender, Unbaked, Underage, Unformed, Unripe, Young

▷**Immature** *may indicate* a word not completed

Immediate(ly) Anon, At once, Direct, First-time, Forthwith, Go on, Imminent, Incontinent, Instantaneous, Lickety-split, Near, Next, →NOW, Now-now, On the knocker, Outright, Posthaste, Present, Pronto, Ready, Right-off, Short-term, Slapbang, Spontaneous, Stat, Statim, Straight, Straight off, Sudden, Then, Thereupon

Immense Astronomical, Brobdingnag, Cosmic, Enormous, →**GIGANTIC**, Huge, Vast

Immerse Baptise, Demerge, Demerse, Drench, Emplonge, Enew, Engage, Plunge, Soak, Steep, Submerge

Immobility, Immobile, Immobilise(r) Akinesia, Cataplexy, Catatonia, Ecstasis, Hamstring, Hog-tie, Inertia, Pinion, Rigidity, Taser, Tether

Immodest(y) Brash, Brazen, Forward, Impudicity, Indelicate, Unchaste

Immoral(ity) Corrupt, Degenerate, Dissolute, Evil, Lax, Libertine, Licentious, Misconduct, Nefarious, Peccable, Reprobate, Scarlet, Sleazebag, Sleazeball, Sleazy, Turpitude, Unchaste, Unclean, Unholy, Unprincipled, Unsavoury, Vice, Vicious, Wanton

Immortal(ity) Agelong, Amarant(h), Amritattva, Athanasy, →**DIVINE**, Endless, Enoch, Eternal, Famous, Godlike, Hera, Memory, Sin, Struldbrug, Timeless, Undying

Immune, Immunisation, Immunise(r), Immunity Acquired, Active, Amboceptor, Anamnestic, Anergy, Antiserum, Bar, Cree, Diplomatic, Dispensation, Exempt, Free, Humoral, Inoculate, Klendusic, Natural, Non-specific, Passive, Pasteurism, Pax, Premunition, Properdin, Serum, Tachyphylaxis, Vaccine

Imp(ish) Devilet, Elf, Flibbertigibbet, Gamin(e), Gremlin, Hobgoblin, Leprechaun, Limb, Lincoln, Litherly, Monkey, Nickum, Nis(se), Puck, Rascal, Spright, Sprite

Impact Astrobleme, Bearing, Brunt, Bump, Chase, Clash, Collision, Feeze, Glance, Head-on, High, Impinge, Imprint, Jar, Jolt, Pack, Percuss, Pow, Slam, Souse, Strike home, Tell, Weight, Wham, Whammo

Impartial(ity) Candid, Detached, Disinterest, Dispassionate, Equitable, Equity, Even-handed, Fair, Just, Neutral, Unbiased

Impasse, Impassable Deadlock, Dilemma, Invious, Jam, Log jam, Mexican standoff, Snooker, Stalemate, Stand off, Zugzwang

Impatience, Impatient Agog, Chafing, Champ, Chut, Dysphoria, Dysthesia, Eager, Fiddle-de-dee, Fiddlesticks, Fidgety, Fretful, Hasty, Hoot(s), Irritable, Och, Peevish, Peremptory, Petulant, Pish, Pshaw, Restless, Tilly-fally, Till(e)y-vall(e)y, Tut

Impedance, Impede, Impediment Block, Burr, Clog, Dam, Encumber, Halt, Hamper, Hamstring, Handicap, →**HINDER**, Hog-tie, Let, Log, Obstacle, Obstruct, Reactance, Rub, Shackle, Slur, Snag, Speed bump, Stammer, Tongue-tie, Trammel, Veto, Z

Imperative Dire, Hypothetical, Jussive, Mood, Need-be, Pressing, Vital

Imperfect(ion) Aplasia, Aplastic, Blotch, Defect, Deficient, Faulty, Flawed, Half-pie, Kink, Lame, Poor, Rough, Second

Imperial(ist), Imperious Adroit, Beard, Commanding, Dictatorial, Flag-waver, Haughty, Lordly, Majestic, Masterful, Mint, Peremptory, Regal, Rhodes, Royal

Imperishable Eternal, Immarcescible, Immortal, Indestructible

Impersonal Abstract, Cold, Dehumanised, Detached, Inhuman, Institutional

Impersonate(d), Impersonation, Impersonator Amphitryon, Ape, As, Drag queen, Echo, Imitate, Imposter, Impostor, Impression, Mimic, Pose

Impertinence, Impertinent Backchat, Crust, Flip(pant), Fresh, Impudent, Irrelevant, Nos(e)y, Rude, Sass, Sauce

Impetuous, Impetuosity Birr, Brash, Bullheaded, Careless, Élan, Harum-scarum, →**HASTY**, Headstrong, Heady, Hothead, Impulsive, Rash, Rees, Rhys, Tearaway, Vehement, Violent

Impetus Birr, Drift, Drive, Incentive, Momentum, Propulsion, Slancio

Implant(ation) AID, Cochlear, Embed, Engraft, Enrace, Enroot, Graft, Inset, Instil, Microchip, Silicone, Sow, Stent

Implement Agent, Apply, Backscratcher, Biffer, Breast plough, Caman, Curette, Do, Enforce, Flail, Fork, Grater, Grubber, Hacksaw, Harrow, Hayfork, Mezzaluna, Mop, Muller, Neolith, Pin, Pitchfork, Plectrum, Plough, Pruning-bill, Rest, Ricker, Ripple, Scuffler, Seed drill, Snuffer, Spatula, Spork, Squeegee, Straw-cutter, Sucket fork, Sucket spoon, Tongs, → **TOOL**, Toothpick, Tribrach, Utensil, Wheelbrace

Implicate, Implication Accuse, Concern, Connotation, Drift, Embroil, Incriminate, Innuendo, → **INVOLVE**, Overtone

Imply, Implied Connote, Hint, Insinuate, Intimate, Involve, Predicate, Signify, → **SUGGEST**, Tacit, Unstated, Unwritten

Importance, Important (person) Account, Acute, A-list, Big, Big cheese, Big pot, Big-time, Big wheel, Billing, Calibre, Capital, Cardinal, Central, Cheese, Chief, Cob, Coming, Consequence, Considerable, Core, Cornerstone, Count, Critical, Crucial, Crux, Earth-shaking, Earth-shattering, Ego-trip, Eminent, Epochal, Essential, Flagship, Focal, Grandeur, Grave, Gravitas, Gravity, Greatness, Heavy, High, High-profile, His nibs, Historic, Honcho, Hotshot, Huzoor, Indispensable, Instrumental, Key, Keystone, Leading, Life and death, Macher, Magnitude, Main, Major, Material, Matters, Megastar, Mighty, Milestone, Moment(ous), Nabob, Nawab, Nib, Note, Numero uno, Obbligato, Outbalance, Overriding, Paramount, Personage, Pivotal, Pot, Preponderate, Prime, Principal, Red-carpet, Red-letter, Salient, Seismic, Seminal, Senior, Serious, Signal, Significant, Something, Special, Stature, Status, Stress, Substantive, Supreme, Tuft, Urgent, VIP, Visiting fireman, Vital, Weight, Weighty, Worth

Importune, Importunate Beg, Coax, Flagitate, Pester, Press(ing), Pressgang, Prig, Solicit, Urgent

Impose(r), Imposing, Imposition Allocate, Assess, August, Burden, Charge, Diktat, Dread, Enforce, Enjoin, Epic, Fine, Flam, Foist, Fraud, Grand(iose), Handsome, Hidage, Homeric, Hum, Impot, Inflict, Kid, Lay, Levy, Lofty, Lumber, Majestic, Noble, Obtrude, Penance, Pensum, Pole, Scot, Sponge, Statuesque, Stonehand, Sublime, Titan, Try-on, Whillywhaw

Impossible Can't, Hopeless, Inconceivable, Incorrigible, Insoluble, Insurmountable, Irreparable, No can do, No-no, Unacceptable, Unachievable

Imposter, Impostor Bunyip, Charlatan, Disaster, → **FAKE**, Fraud, Idol, Phantasm, Pretender, Ringer, Sham, Triumph, Warbeck

Impotent Barren, Helpless, Powerless, Spado, Sterile, Weak

Impoverish(ed) Bankrupt, Bare, Beggar, Exhaust, Needy, Poor, Skint, Straiten

Impractical Abstract, Absurd, Academic, Blue-sky, Chim(a)era, Crackpot, Dreamer, Idealist, Laputan, Non-starter, Not on, Other-worldly, Quixotic, Theoretic, Useless

Imprecise Approximate, Inaccurate, Indeterminate, Intangible, Loose, Nebulous, Rough, Sloppy, Vague

Impregnable, Impregnate Conceive, Embalm, Imbue, Inexpugnable, Inseminate, Milt, Permeate, Virtue-proof, Watertight

Impress(ive), Impression(able) Affect, Appearance, Astonish, August, Awe(struck), Class act, Description, Draft, Effect, Engrain, Etch, Eye-catching, Feel(ing), Glorious, Grandstand, Greeking, Idea, Imitation, Impact, Imposing, Imprint, Indent, Ingrain, Magnificent, Majestic, Mould, Name-drop, Pit, Pliable,

Powerful, Press(gang), Print, Prodigious, Proof, Register, Resplendent, Signet, Stamp, Stately, Stonker, Strike, Stunning, Stupendous, Take, Type, Watermark, Whale, Woodcut

Imprison(ment) Cage, Cape, Confine, Constrain, Custody, Durance, Emmew, Gherao, Hitch, Immure, Incarcerate, Inside, Intern, Jail, Lock-up, Quad, Quod, Stretch, Time

Impromptu Ad lib(itum), Extempore, Improvised, Offhand, Pong, Spontaneous, Sudden, Unrehearsed

Improper, Impropriety Abnormal, Blue, Demirep, False, Indecent, Indecorum, Naughty, Outré, Prurient, Solecism, Undue, Unmeet, Unseemly, Untoward

▷**Improperly** *may indicate* an anagram

Improve(ment), Improver, Improving Advance, Airbrush, Ameliorate, Amend, Beat, Benefit, Bete, Better, Boost, Break, Buck, Cap, Chasten, Conditioner, Convalesce, Defrag, Détente, Didactic, DIY, Ease, Edify, Embellish, Embroider, Emend, Enhance, Enrich, Eugenic, Euthenics, File, Gentrify, J-curve, Kaizen, Meliorate, Mend, Modernise, Polish, Potentiate, Progress, Promote, Rally, Refine, Reform, Resipiscence, Retouch, Revamp, Slim, Surpass, Tart, Tatt, Titivate, Top, Touch-up, Turn round, Upgrade, Upswing, Uptrend, Upturn, Vernissage

Improvise(d), Improvisation Ad hoc, Adlib, Break, Busk it, Contrive, Devise, Extemporise, Gorgia, Invent, Jury-rig, Knock-up, Lash-up, Noodle, On the fly, Play by ear, Pong, Ride, Scat, Scratch, Sodain, Stopgap, Sudden, Tweedle, Unscripted, Vamp, Wing it

Impudence, Impudent Audacious, Backchat, Bardy, Barefaced, Bold, Brash, Brassy, Brazen, Cheeky, Cool, Crust, Effrontery, Forward, Gall, Gallus, Gobby, Hussy, Impertinent, Insolent, Jackanapes, Jack-sauce, Lip, Malapert, Neck, →**NERVE**, Pert, Sass(y), Sauce, Saucebox, Saucy, Skipjack, Slack-jaw, Temerity, Whippersnapper, Yankie

Impulse, Impulsive Acte gratuit, Beat, Compelling, Conatus, Dictate, Drive, Efferent, Flighty, Foolhardy, Headlong, Horme, Ideopraxist, Impetus, Instigation, →**INSTINCT**, Madcap, Nisus, Precipitant, Premature, Premotion, Send, Signal, Snap, Spontaneous, Tearaway, Tendency, Thrust, Tic, Urge, Whim

Impure, Impurity Adulterated, Contaminated, Donor, Faints, Feints, Indecent, Lees, Lewd, Regulus, Scum, Unchaste, Unclean

In A, Amid, Amidst, Amongst, At, Batting, Chic, Current, Fashionable, Hip, Home, Hostel, I', Indium, Inn, Intil, Occupying, Pop(ular), Pub, Trendy, Within

Inaccurate Distorted, Erroneous, Faulty, Imprecise, Inexact, Misquote, Out, Overestimate, Rough, Slipshod

Inactive, Inaction, Inactivity Acedia, Anestrum, Anoestrus, Cabbage, Canicular day, Comatose, Dead, Dormant, Extinct, Fallow, Hibernate, Idle, Inert, Languor, Lotus-eater, Masterly, Moratorium, Non-term, Passive, Quiescent, Racemic, Recess, Rusty, Sluggish, Stagnation, Stasis, Torpid, Vacancy, Veg(etate)

Inadequate, Inadequacy Derisory, Feeble, Hopeless, Inapt, Inferior, Joke, Lean, Meagre, Measly, Pathetic, Poor, Ropy, Slender, Slight, Thin, Unable, Unequal, Want

▷**In a flap** *may indicate* an anagram

Inane Empty, Fatuous, Foolish, Imbecile, Silly, Vacant

Inappropriate Amiss, Ill-timed, Incongrous, Infelicitous, Malapropos, Off-key, Out of place, Pretentious, Unapt, Unbecoming, Undue, Unmeet, Unsuitable, Untoward

Inattentive, Inattention Absent, Abstracted, Asleep, Careless, Deaf, Distrait, Dwaal, Dwa(l)m, Dwaum, Heedless, Listless, Loose, Slack, Unheeding, Unobservant

Inaugurate Dedicate, Han(d)sel, Initiate, Install, Introduce, Swear in

Inauspicious Adverse, Ominous, Sinister

▷**In a whirl** *may indicate* an anagram

▷**In a word** *may indicate* two clue words linked to form one

Inborn, Inbred Inherent, Innate, Native, Selfed, Sib

Incandescent Alight, Bright, Brilliant, Excited, Radiant

Incantation Chant, Charm, Magic, Mantra, Spell

Incendiary Arsonist, Firebug, Fire-lighter, Greek fire, Napalm, Thermite

Incense(d), Incenser Anger, Aroma, Elemi, Enfelon, Enrage, Homage, Hot, →**INFLAME**, Infuriate, Irate, Joss-stick, Mosquito coil, Navicula, Onycha, Outrage, Pastil(le), Provoke, Stacte, Thurible, Thus, Vex, Wrathful

Incentive Carrot, Feather-bed, Fillip, Impetus, Inducement, Motive, Spur, Stimulus

Inch(es) Ait, Edge, Isle(t), Miner's, Sidle, Uncial

Incident(al) Affair, Baur, Bawr, Byplay, Carry-on, Case, Chance, Circumstance, Episode, Event, Facultative, Negligible, Occasion, Occurrent, Page, Peripheral, Scene

Incinerate, Incinerator Burn, Combust, Cremate

Incise(d), Incision, Incisive(ness) Bite, Cut, Edge, Engrave, Enterotomy, Episiotomy, Intaglio, Mordant, Phlebotomy, Pleurotomy, Pungent, Rhizotamy, Slit, Surgical, Thoracotomy, Tracheotomy, Trenchant

Incite(ment) Abet, Agitate, Drive, Egg, Enrage, Fillip, Goad, Hortative, Hoy, Impassion, Inflame, Instigate, Kindle, Motivate, Onsetting, Prod, Prompt, Provoke, Put, Rabble-rouse, Rouse, Sa sa, Sedition, Set, Sic(k), Sool, →**SPUR**, Stimulus, Sting, Suborn, Suggest, Tar, Urge

Incline(d), Inclination Acclivity, Angle, Aslant, Aslope, Atilt, Bank, Batter, Bent, Bevel, Bias, Bow, Camber, Cant, Clinamen, Cock, Crossfall, Declivity, Dip, Disposed, Drift, Enclitic, Escarpment, Glacis, →**GRADIENT**, Grain, Habitus, Hade, Heel, Hill, Italic, Kant, Kip, Lean, Liable, Liking, List, Maw, Minded, Nod, On, Partial, Partisan, Peck, Penchant, Proclivity, Prone, Propensity, Rake, Ramp, Ready, Rollway, Set, Sheer, Shelve, Slant, →**SLOPE**, Steep, Steeve, Stomach, Supine, Sway, Tend, Tilt, Tip, Trend, Upgrade, Uptilt, Velleity, Verge, Weathering, Will

Include(d), Inclusion, Inclusive Add, All-told, Bracket, Compass, Comprise, Connotate, Contain, Cover, Embody, Embrace, Enclose, Encompass, Involve, Short-list, Social, Therein

Incognito Anonymous, Disguised, Faceless, Secret, Unnamed, Unobserved

Income Annates, Annuity, Discretionary, Disposable, Dividend, Earned, Entry, Living, Meal-ticket, Milch cow, Notional, Penny-rent, Prebend, Primitiae, Proceeds, Rent(al), Rent-roll, Returns, Revenue, Salary, Stipend, Take, Unearned, Wages

Incomparable Disparate, Par excellence, Supreme, Unequalled, Unique, Unlike, Unmatched

Incompatible, Incompatibility Clashing, Contradictory, Dyspathy, Inconsistent, Mismatched, Unsuited

Incompetent(ly) Blind Freddie, Bungler, Deadhead, Helpless, Hopeless, Ill, Inefficient, Inept, Nebbich, Not for nuts, Palooka, Rabbit, Shlepper, Shower, Slouch, Unable, Unfit, Useless

Incomplete Cagmag, Catalectic, Deficient, Inchoate, Lacking, Partial, Pendent, Rough, Sketchy, Unfinished

▷**In confusion** *may indicate* an anagram

Incongruous, Incongruity Absurd, Discordant, Irish, Ironic, Sharawadgi, Sharawaggi, Solecism

Inconsiderate Asocial, High-handed, Lairy, Light-minded, Petty, Presumptuous, Roughshod, Thoughtless, Unkind, Unthinking

Inconsistency, Inconsistent Alien, Anacoluthon, Anomaly, Clashing, Contradictory, Discrepant, Fitful, Illogical, Jar(ring), Oxymoronic, Paradoxical, Patchy, Variance

Inconvenience, Inconvenient Awkward, Bother(some), Disadvantageous, Discommode, Fleabite, Incommodious, Inopportune, Put out, →**TROUBLE**, Ungain(ly)

Incorporate(d), Incorporation Absorb, Embody, Hard wire, Inc(lude), Inorb, Integrate, Introgression, Introject, Join, Merge, Subsume

Incorrect Catachresis, Erroneous, False, Improper, Naughty

Incorruptible Honest, Immortal, Pure, Sea-green

Increase(s), Increasing Accelerando, Accelerate, Accession, Accretion, Accrew, Accrue, Add, Additur, Aggrandise, Amplify, Amp up, Appreciate, Approve, Augment, Auxetic, Bolster, Boost, Build up, Bulge, Burgeon, Charge, Crank up, Crescendo, Crescent, Crescive, Cumulate, Deepen, Dilate, Double, Ech(e), Eech, Eik, Eke, Enhance, Enlarge, Enliven, Escalate, →**EXPAND**, Explosion, Extend, Gain, Gather, Greaten, →**GROW**, Heighten, Hike, Ich, Increment, Interbreed, Irrupt, Jack, Jack up, Joseph, Lengthen, Lift, Magnify, Mark up, Mount, Multiply, Plus, Proliferate, Prolong, Propagate, Ramp up, Redshift, Reflation, Regrate, Resurgence, Rise, Snowball, Speed up, Supercharger, Surge, Swell, Thrive, Up, Upload, Upsize, Upswell, Upswing, Up the ante, Wax, Write up

Incredible Amazing, Astonishing, Cockamamie, Extraordinary, Fantastic, Preposterous, Staggering, Steep, Stey, Tall, Theeing, Unbelievable, Unreal

Incredulity, Incredulous As if, Distrust, Sceptic, Suspicion, Thunderstruck

Incriminate Accuse, Implicate, Inculpate, Stitch up

Incumbent Lying, Obligatory, Occupier, Official, Resident

Incursion Foray, Inroad, Invasion, Raid, Razzia

Indecent Bare, Blue, Free, Immodest, Immoral, Improper, Indelicate, Lewd, Obscene, Racy, Scurril(e), Uncomely, Unnatural, Unproper, Unseem(ly)

Indecision, Indecisive Demur, Dithery, Doubt, Hamlet, Hesitation, Hung jury, Irresolute, Shilly-shally, Suspense, Swither, Weakkneed, Wishy-washy

Indecorous Graceless, Immodest, Outré, Unbecoming, Unseemly

Indefinite(ly) A, An, Any, Evermore, Hazy, Nth, Sine die, Some, Uncertain, Undecided, Vague

Indelicate Broad, Coarse, Improper, Sultry, Vulgar, Warm

Indent(ed), Indentation Apprentice, Contract, Crenellate, Dancetty, Dimple, Impress, Niche, Notch, Order, Prophet's thumbmarks, Subentire

Independence, Independent Apart, Autocephalous, Autogenous, Autonomy, Crossbencher, Detached, Extraneous, Free(dom), Free-lance, Freethinker, I, Individual, Liberty, Mana motuhake, Maverick, Mugwump, Perseity, Self-contained, Self-sufficient, Separate, Separatist, Swaraj, Udal, UDI, Uhuru, Viscosity

Indestructible Enduring, Impenetrable, Inextirpable

Index Alidad(e), All-Ordinaries, Catalogue, Cephalic, Colour, Concordance, Cranial, Cross, DAX, Dial, Dow Jones, Exponent, Facial, Finger, Fist, Fog, Footsie, Forefinger, FTSE, Gazetteer, Glycaemic, Hang Seng, Kwic, Margin, Misery, Mitotic, Nasal, Nikkei, Power, Price, Refractive, → **REGISTER**, Rotary, Share, Stroke, Table, Therapeutic, Thumb, TPI, UV, Verborum, Zonal

India(n) Adivisi, Apache, Assamese, Ayah, Baboo, Babu, Bharat(i), Canarese, Chin, Crazy Horse, Dard, Dravidian, East, File, Gandhi, Goanese, Gond(wanaland), Gujarati, Harijan, Harsha, Hindu, .in, Ink, Jain, Jat, Jemadar, Jewel in the crown, Kanarese, Kannada, Khalsa, Kisan, Kolarian, Kshatriyas, Lepcha, Mahatma, Maratha, Ma(h)ratta, Maya, Mazhbi, Mishmi, Mission, Mofussil, Mogul, Munda, Munshi, Nagari, Nair, Nasik, Nation, Nayar, Ocean, Oriya, Pali, Parsee, Parsi, Pathan, Peshwa, Poppadom, Prakrit, Punjabi, Ravi, Red, Redskin, Sanskrit, Sepoy, Shri, Sikh, Sind(h), Sowar, Subcontinent, Summer, Swadeshi, Taino, Tamil, Telegu, Treaty, Vakeel, Vakil, West, Ynd

Indicate, Indication, Indicative, Indicator Adumbrate, Allude, Argue, Barcode, Bespeak, Betoken, Cite, Clue, Convey, Cursor, → **DENOTE**, Design, Designate, Desine, Dial, Dial gauge, Endeixis, Evidence, Evince, Extort, Finger, Gesture, Gnomon, Guideline, Hint, Imply, Litmus, Manifest, Mean, Mood, Nod, Notation, Pinpoint, Plan-position, Point, Portend, Proof, Ray, Register, Remarque, Representative, Reveal, → **SIGN**, Signal, Signboard, Signify, Specify, Speedo, Spell, Symptom, Tip, Token, Trace, Trait, Winker

Indifference, Indifferent Adiaphoron, Aloof, Apathetic, Apathy, Blasé, Blithe, Callous, Cauld, Cavalier, Cold, Cool(th), Dead, Deaf, Detached, Disdain, Easy-osy, Empty, Fico, Incurious, Insouciant, Jack easy, Lax, Lukewarm, Mediocre, Neutral, Nonchalant, Perfunctory, Phlegm, Pococurante, Sangfroid, So-so, Stoical, Supercilious, Supine, Tepid, Thick-skinned, Third-rate, Unconcerned

Indignant, Indignation Anger, Annoyed, Bridling, Incensed, Irate, Outrage, Resentful, Steamed up, Umbrage, Wrathful

Indigo Anil, Blue, Bunting, Carmine, Indole, Isatin(e), Wild

Indirect Aside, Back-handed, By(e), Bypath, Circumlocution, Devious, Evasive, Implicit, Mediate, Oblique, Remote, Roundabout, Second-hand, Sidelong, Sly, Subtle, Vicarious, Zig-zag

Indiscreet, Indiscretion Folly, Gaffe, Imprudence, Indelicate, Injudicious, Lapse, Loose cannon, Rash, Tactless, Unguarded

Indiscriminate Haphazard, Random, Scattershot, Sweeping, Wholesale

Indispensable Basic, Essential, King-pin, Linch-pin, Necessary, Requisite, Vital

Indispose(d), Indisposition Adverse, Disincline, Ill, Incapacitate, Loth, Reluctant, Sick, Unwell

Indistinct Ambiguous, Bleary, Blur, Bumble, Bummle, Faint, Filmy, Fuzzy, Grainy, Hazy, Misty, Mumbling, Mush-mouthed, Nebulous, Neutral, Nondescript, Pale, Sfumato, Slurred, Smudged, Unincorporate, → **VAGUE**

▷**In distress** *may indicate* an anagram

Indite Compose, Pen, Write

Individual(ist), Individuality Apiece, Being, Discrete, Exclusive, Free spirit, Gemma, Haecceity, Hand-crafted, Identity, Ka, Libertarian, Loner, Man, Man-jack, Morph, One-to-one, Original, Own, Particular, Person(al), Poll, Respective, Seity, Self, Separate, Single, Singular, Solo, Soul, Special, Unique, Unit, Zoon

Indolence, Indolent Bone idle, Fainéance, Inactive, Languid, Lazy, Lentor, Lotus-eater, Otiose, Purposeless, Shiftless, Sloth, Sluggish, Supine

Indomitable Brave, Dauntless, Invincible

Indubitably Certainly, Certes, Manifestly, Surely

Induce(ment) Bribe, Carrot, Cause, Coax, Draw, Encourage, Entice, Evoke, Get, Inveigle, Invite, Lead, Motivate, →**PERSUADE**, Prevail, Suasion, Suborn, Tempt, Urge

Induct(ion), Inductance Epagoge, Henry, Inaugurate, Initiate, Install, L, Logic, Mutual, Ordain, Prelude, Remanence

Indulge(nce), Indulgent Absolution, Aristippus, Binge, Coddle, Cosset, Debauchery, Dissipation, Drink, Favour, Fond, Gentle, Gratify, Humour, Lie-in, Luxuriate, Oblige, Orgy, Pamper, Pander, Pardon, Partake, Permissive, Pet, Pettle, Pig-out, Please, Plenary, →**SATISFY**, Splurge, Spoil, Spoonfeed, Spree, Surfeit, Sybarite, Tolerant, Venery, Voluptuous, Wallow

Industrial, Industrious, Industry Appliance, Application, Basic, Black Country, Business, Busy, Commerce, Cottage, Deedy, Diligence, Eident, Energetic, Growth, Heavy, Heritage, Labour, Legwork, Millicent, Ocnus, Process, Ruhr, Service, Technical, Technics, Tertiary, Tourism, Zaibatsu

▶**Inebriate** *see* INTOXICATE(D)

Ineffective, Ineffectual Chinless wonder, Clumsy, Deadhead, Drippy, Droob, Dud, Empty, Eunuch, Fainéant, Feeble, Fruitless, Futile, Idle, Ill, Impotent, Invalid, Lame, Mickey Mouse, Milksop, Neuter, Neutralised, Otiose, Powerless, Resty, Sterile, Stumbledown, Toothless, Unable, →**USELESS**, Void, Weak, Weenie, Wet, Wimp

Inefficient Clumsy, Incompetent, Lame, Shiftless, Slack, Slouch

Inept Absurd, Amateurish, Anorak, Farouche, Flaky, Fumbler, Galoot, Loser, Maladjusted, Nerd, Otaku, Plonker, Sad sack, Schlimazel, Schmo, Unskilled, Wet

Inert(ia) Catatonia, Comatose, Dead, Dull, Excipient, Inactive, Krypton, Languid, Leaden, Mollusc, Motionless, Neon, Oblomovism, Potato, Rigor, Sluggish, Stagnant, Stagnation, Thowless, Torpid, Turgid

Inevitable, Inevitably Automatic, Certain, Fateful, Inescapable, Inexorable, Infallible, Necessary, Needs, Perforce, TINA, Unavoidable

Inexact(itude) Cretism, Imprecise, Incorrect, Terminological, Wrong

Inexpedient Impolitic, Imprudent, Unwise

Inexpensive Bargain, Cheap, Dirt-cheap, Economic

Inexperience(d), Inexpert Amateur, Awkward, Callow, Colt, Crude, Fledgling, Fresh, →**GREEN**, Ham, Ingénue, Jejune, Newbie, Put(t), Raw, Rookie, Rude, Tender, Unseasoned, Untried, Unversed, Waister, Wide-eyed, Youthful

Inexplicable Magical, Mysterious, Paranormal, Supernatural, Unaccountable

Infamous, Infamy Base, Ignominious, Notorious, Opprobrium, Shameful, Villainy

Infant, Infancy Babe, Baby, Innocent, Lamb, Minor, Nurs(e)ling, Oral, Rug rat, The cradle

Infantry(man) Buff, Foot, Grunt, Jaeger, Phalanx, Pultan, Pulto(o)n, Pultun, →**SOLDIER**, Tercio, Turco, Twenty, Voetganger

▷**Infantry** *may refer to* babies

Infatuate(d), Infatuating, Infatuation Assot, Besot, Crush, Enamoured, Engou(e)ment, Entêté, Epris, Fanatic, Foolish, Lovesick, Mash, →**OBSESSION**, Pash, Rave, Turn

Infect(ed), Infecting, Infection, Infectious Adenoviral, Angina, Anthrax, Babesiasis, Babesiosis, Canker, Carrier, Catching, Catchy, Cholera, Communicable, Contagious, Contaminate, Corrupt, Cowpox, Cryptococcosis, Cryptosporidiosis, Dermatophytosis, Diseased, E-coli, Fester, Gonorrhoea, Herpes, Impetigo, Listeria, Lockjaw, Mycetoma, Opportunistic, Overrun, Poison, Polio(myelitis), → **POLLUTE**, Pyoderma, Rife, Ringworm, Roseola, Roup, Salmonella, SARS, Scabies, Secondary, Septic, Shingles, Strep throat, Strongyloidiasis, Taint, Taking, Tetanus, Thrush, Tinea, Toxoplasmosis, Transfection, Tryp, Typhoid, Typhus, Varroa, Vincent's angina, Viral pneumonia, Virulent, Whitlow, Zoonosis

Infer(ence), Inferred Conclude, Construe, Deduce, Divine, Educe, Extrapolate, Generalise, Guess, Illation, Imply, Judge, Surmise

▷**Infer** *may indicate* 'fer' *around another word*

Inferior Base, Bodgier, Cheap-jack, Cheesy, Coarse, Crummy, Degenerate, Dog, Epigon, Ersatz, Gimcrack, Grody, Grub-Street, Impair, Indifferent, Infra, Jerkwater, Less, Lo-fi, Lousy, Lower, Low-grade, Mediocre, Minor, Naff, Nether, One-horse, Ornery, Paravail, Petty, Poor, Rop(e)y, Schlock, Second, Second-best, Shilpit, Shlock, Shoddy, Shonky, Slopwork, Sprew, Sprue, Subjacent, Subordinate, Substandard, Surat, Tatty, Third-rate, Tinpot, Trashy, Underdog, Underneath, Untermensch, Waste, Worse

Infest(ed), Infestation Beset, Blight, Dog, Hoatching, Overrun, → **PLAGUE**, Swamp, Swarm, Taeniasis, Torment, Trypanosomiasis

Infidel Atheist, Caffre, Heathen, Heretic, Kafir, Miscreant, Pagan, Saracen

Infiltrate(d), Infiltration, Infiltrator Encroach, Enter, Entryist, Fifth columnist, Gatecrash, Instil, Intrude, Mole, Pervade, Trojan horse

Infirm(ity) Decrepit, Doddery, Feeble, Frail, Frailness, Lame, Shaky, Sick

▷**Infirm** *may indicate* 'co' *around another word*

Inflame(d), Inflammable, Inflammation Afire, Anger, → **AROUSE**, Bloodshot, Enamoured, Enchafe, Enfire, Enkindle, Fever, Fire, Gleet, Ignite, Incense, Infection, Ire, Kindle, Methane, Napalm, Naphtha, → **RED**, Rouse, Stimulate, Swelling, Touchwood

Inflate(d), Inflation Aerate, Aggrandise, Balloon, Bloat, Bombastic, Bracket-creep, Demand-pull, Dilate, Distend, Distent, Increase, Pneumatic, Pompous, Pump, Raise, Remonetise, RPI, Spiral, Stagnation, Swell, Wage-push

Inflexible, Inflexibility Adamant(ine), Authoritarian, Byzantine, Doctrinaire, Hard-ass, Hard-liner, Iron, Obstinate, Ossified, Ramrod, Relentless, Resolute, Rigid, Rigour, Set, Staid, Steely, Stiff, Stubborn

Inflict(ion) Force, Give, Impose, Subject, Trouble, Visit, Wreak

Inflorescence Bostryx, Catkin, Ci(n)cinnus, Drepanium, Glomerule, Monochasium, Panicle, Pleiochasium, Raceme, R(h)achis, Umbel

Influence(d), Influential Act, Affect, After, Amenable, Backstairs, Bias, Brainwash, Catalyse, Charm, Clamour, Clout, Colour, Credit, Determine, Dominant, Drag, Earwig, Eclectic, Embracery, Éminence grise, Factor, Force, Govern, Guide, Hegemony, Hold, Impact, Impinge, Impress, Incubus, Inspire, Interfere, Jinx, Lead, Leverage, Lobby, Mastery, Militate, Mogul, Mould, Nobble, Octopus, Operation, Outreach, Outweigh, Panjandrum, Power, Preponderant, Pressure, Prestige, → **PULL**, Push, Reach, Rust, Say, Securocrat, Seminal, Significant, Star, Star-blasting, Stimulus, String-pulling, Suggest, Svengali, Sway, Swing, Telegony, Thrall, Undue, Weigh with, Will, Work, Wull

Influenza Asian, Equine, Flu, Gastric, Grippe, Lurgi, Spanish, Wog, Yuppie

Inform(ation), Informant, Informed, Informer Acquaint, Advise, Agitprop, Apprise, Arise, Au fait, Aware, Beagle, Bit, Blow, Briefing, Burst, Callboard, Canary, Ceefax®, Clype, Contact, Database, Datum, Debriefing, Deep throat, Delate, Diane, Dicker, Dob(ber), Dobber-in, Dope, Download, Education, Facts, FAQs, Feedback, Fink, Fisgig, Fiz(z)gig, Gen, Genome, Good oil, Grapevine, Grass, Griff, Gunsel, Hep, Hip, Immersive, Input, Inside, Instruct, Izvesti(ya)a, Light, Literate, Little bird, Lowdown, Media, Metadata, Microdot, Moiser, Nark, Nepit, News, Nit, Nose, Occasion, Output, Peach, Pem(m)ican, Pentito, Pointer, Poop, Post, Prestel®, Prime, Promoter, Propaganda, Prospectus, Rat, Read-out, Relator, Report, Revelation, Rheme, Rumble, Shelf, Shop, Sidelight, Sing, Sneak, Snitch, Snout, SP, Squeak, Squeal, Stag, Stoolie, Stool-pigeon, Supergrass, Sycophant, Tell, Throughput, Tidings, Tip-off, Up, Up to speed, Whistle(-blower), Wire, Witting

Informal Bat, Casual, Cosy, Free and easy, Go-as-you-please, Intimate, Irregular, Outgoing, Rough and ready, Unofficial

Infuriate(d) Anger, Apoplectic, Bemad, Bepester, Enrage, Exasperate, Gall, Incense, Livid, Madden, Pester, Provoke

Ingenious, Ingenuity Acumen, Adept, Adroit, Art, Artificial, Clever, Cunning, Cute, Inventive, Natty, Neat, Resourceful, Smart, Subtle, Trick(s)y, Wit

Ingenuous Artless, Candid, Green, Innocent, Naive, Open, Transparent

Ingle Bardash, Hearth, Nook

Ingot Bar, Billet, Bullion, Lingot, Sycee, Wedge

Ingratiate, Ingratiating Bootlick, Butter, Court, Flatter, Greasy, Oily, Pick-thank, Smarm(y)

Ingredient(s) Additive, Admixture, Asafoetida, Basis, Content, Element, Factor, Formula, Makings, Mincemeat, Staple

Inhabit(ant), Inhabitants Affect, Children, Denizen, Dweller, Indweller, Inholder, Inmate, Live, Native, Occupant, People, Populate, Population, Populous, Resident, Towny

Inhale(r), Inhalation Aspirate, Breath(e), Draw, Gas, Inbreathe, Inspire, Intal, Sniff, Snort, Snuff, Take, Toot, Tout

Inherit(ance), Inherited, Inheritor Accede, Ancestral, Birthright, Congenital, Esnecy, Gene, Genom, Heirloom, Heritage, Inborn, Legacy, Legitim, Meek, Patrimony, Portion, Succeed

Inhibit(ing), Inhibition, Inhibitor ACE, Antihistamine, Anuria, Captopril, Chalone, Chalonic, Deter, Donepezil, Enalapril, Etanercept, Feedback, Finasteride, Forbid, Hang-up, Indinavir, Protease, Restrain, Retard, Retroactive, Stunt, Suppress, Tightass

Initial Acronym, First, Inaugural, Letter, Monogram, Paraph, Prelim(inary), Primary, Rubric

▷**Initially** *may indicate* first letters

Initiate(d), Initiating, Initiation, Initiative Begin, Bejesuit, Blood, Bora, Bring, Ceremony, Debut, Enter, Enterprise, Epopt, Esoteric, Gumption, Induct, Instigate, Instruct, **→ LAUNCH**, Neophyte, Nous, Onset, Open, Proactive, Spark, **→ START**, Tyro

Inject(or), Injection Antiserum, Bang, Blast, Bolus, Booster, Collagen, Direct, Enema, Epidural, Epipen®, Fuel, Hypo, Immit, Implant, Innerve, Inoculation, Instil, Introduce, Jab, Jack up, Jag, Lidocaine, Mainline, Pop, Reheat, Serum, Shoot, Shoot up, Skin-pop, Solid, Spike, Syringe, Transfuse, Venipuncture

Injunction Command, Embargo, Freezing, Mandate, Mareva, Quia timet, Writ

Injure(d), Injury, Injurious, Injustice ABH, Abuse, Accloy, Aggrieve, Bale, Barotrauma, Bled, Bruise, Casualty, Contrecoup, Contuse, Crick, Damage, De(a)re, Disservice, Frostbite, Gash, GBH, Harm, → **HURT**, Ill-turn, Impair, Industrial, Iniquity, Lesion, Malign, Mar, Mayhem, Mistreat, Mutilate, Needlestick, Nobble, Nocuous, Non-accidental, Noxal, Nuisance, Occupational, Oppression, Outrage, Packet, Paire, Prejudice, Rifle, RSI, Scaith, Scald, Scath(e), Scotch, Shend, Shiner, Sore, Sprain, Tene, Tort, Trauma, Umbrage, Whiplash, Wound, Wrong

▶**Injury** *see* **AFTER INJURY**

Ink(y), Inker Black, Copying, Cyan, Indian, Invisible, Marking, Monk, Printing, Sepia, Stained, Tattooist, Toner

Inlaid, Inlay(er) Boulle, Buhl, Clear, Compurgation, Crustae, Damascene, Emblemata, Empaestic, Enamel, Enchase, Incrust, Intarsia, Intarsio, Marquetrie, Marquetry, Piqué, Set, Tarsia, Unsuspecting, Veneer

Inlet Arm, Bay, Cook, Cove, Creek, Entry, Fiord, Firth, Fjord, Fleet, Flow, Geo, Gio, Golden Horn, Gulf, Gusset, Hope, Infall, Jervis Bay, Loch, Port Phillip Bay, Puget Sound, Ria, Rio de la Plata, Sogne Fjord, Strait, Sullom Voe, Table Bay, The Wash

▷**Inlet** *may indicate* 'let' *around another word*

Inn(s), Innkeeper Albergo, Alehouse, Auberge, Barnard's, Boniface, Caravanserai, Coaching, Gastropub, Gray's, Halfway-house, Host(ry), Hostelry, Hotel(ier), House, Imaret, In, Inner Temple, Khan, Kneipe, Ladin(ity), Law, Licensee, Lincoln's, Lodging, Luckie, Lucky, Maypole, Middle Temple, Padrone, Parador, Patron, Porterhouse, Posada, Posthouse, Pothouse, Publican, Roadhouse, Ryokan, Serai, Stabler, Tabard, Tavern(er), Victualler

▷**Inn** *may refer to* the law

Innards Entrails, Giblets, Gizzard, Guts, Harigals, Harslet, Haslet, Omasa, Rein, Viscera

▶**Innkeeper** *see* **INN(S)**

Innocent Absolved, Angelic, Arcadian, Babe, Blameless, Canny, Chaste, Cherub, Childlike, Clean, Clear, Compurgation, Dewy-eyed, Doddypoll, Dodipoll, Dove, Encyclical, Green, Guileless, Idyllic, Inadvertent, Ingenue, Lamb, Lily-white, Maiden, Naive, Opsimath, Pope, Prelapsarian, → **PURE**, Sackless, St, Seely, Simple, Unsuspecting, White

Innuendo Hint, Insinuation, Overtone, Slur

Inoperative Futile, Nugatory, Silent, Void

Inordinate Excessive, Irregular, Undue

▷**Inordinately** *may indicate* an anagram

In place of For, Qua, Vice, Vise, With

Inquest Debriefing, Hearing, Inquiry, Investigation

Inquire, Inquiring, Inquiry Ask, Demand, Investigation, Nose, Organon, Probe, Public, Query, Question, See, Speer, Speir

Inquisition, Inquisitive, Inquisitor Curious, Interrogation, Meddlesome, Nosy, Prying, Rubberneck, Snooper, Stickybeak, Torquemada

▷**In revolt, In revolution** *may indicate* an anagram

Insane, Insanity Absurd, Batty, Berserk, Crazy, Dementia, Deranged, Loco, Looniness, Mad, Manic, Mental, Paranoia, Pellagra, Psycho, Schizo, Troppo

Inscribe(d), Inscription Chisel, Colophon, Dedicate, Emblazon, Endoss, Engrave, Enter, Epigraph, Epitaph, Graffiti, Hic jacet, Hierograph, Lapidary, Legend, Lettering, Ogham, Pen, Writ

Insect(s) Entomic, Nonentity, Non-person, Stridulator, Wax

Insectivore Agouta, Desman, Donaea, Drongo, Drosera, Hedgehog, Jacamar, Nepenthaceae, Shrew, Tanrec, Tenrec(idae), Tupaia, Venus flytrap, Zalambdodont

Insecure Infirm, →LOOSE, Needy, Precarious, Shaky, Unsafe, Unstable, Unsteady, Vulnerable

Insert(ed), Insertion, Inset Anaptyxis, Cue, Empiecement, Enchase, Enter, Entry, Epenthesis, Foist, Fudge, Godet, Gore, Graft, Gusset, Immit, Imp, Implant, Inchase, Inject, Inlay, Input, Interject, Interpolate, Interpose, Intersperse, Introduce, Intromit, Intubate, Mitre, Pin, Plant, Punctuate, Sandwich

Inside(r) Content, Core, Entrails, Gaol, Giblets, Heart, Indoors, Interior, Internal, Interne, Inward, Inwith, Mole, Tum, →WITHIN

Insignia Armour, Arms, Badger, Charge, Chevron, Club tie, Crest, Eagle, Mark, Order, Regalia, Ribbon, Roundel, Tab

Insignificant (person) Bobkes, Bubkis, Bupkes, Bupkis, Chickenfeed, Cog, Dandiprat, Fico, Fiddling, Flea-bite, Fractional, Gnat, Inconsiderable, Insect, Jerkwater, Mickey Mouse, Minimus, Miniscule, Minnow, Nebbich, Nickel and dime, Nobody, Nominal, Nondescript, Nonentity, Non-event, Non-person, No one, One-eyed, Paltry, Peanuts, Petit, Petty, Piddling, Pipsqueak, Pissant, Quat, Rabbit, Scoot, Scout, Scrub, Shrimp, Slight, Small beer, Small potatoes, Small-time, Squirt, Squit, Tenuous, Trifling, Trivial, Two-bit, Unimportant, Venial, Warb, Whiffet, Whippersnapper, Wind

Insincere, Insincerity Affected, Artificial, Barmecide, Cant, Crocodile tears, Disingenuous, Double, Double-faced, Duplicity, Empty, Factitious, Faithless, False, Forced, Glib, Greenwash, Hollow, Janus-faced, Lip service, Mealy-mouthed, Meretricious, Mouth-made, Pseudo, Shallow, Superficial, Synthetic, Tongue-in-cheek, Two-faced, Unnatural

Insipid Banal, Blah, Bland, Fade, Flat, Insulse, Jejune, Lash, Mawkish, Milk and water, Shilpit, Spiritless, Tame, Tasteless, Vapid, Weak, Wearish

Insist(ent) Adamant, Assert, Clamant, Demand, Dogmatic, Exact, Press, Require, Stickler, →STIPULATE, Stress, Swear, Threap, Threep, Urge

Insolence, Insolent Attitude, Audacity, Bardy, Brassy, Cheek, Contumely, Cub, Effrontery, Gum, Hectoring, Hubris, Hybris, Impudence, Lairy, Lip, Mouth, Rude, Snash, Snide, Stroppy, Wanton

Insolvent Bankrupt, Broke, Destitute, Penniless

Inspect(ion), Inspector Ale-conner, Alnage(r), Auditor, Check(er), Comb, Conner, Cook's tour, Examine, Exarch, Government, Investigator, Jerque, Keeker, Look over, Maigret, Muster, Once-over, Peep, Perlustrate, Proveditor, Rag-fair, Recce, Review, School, Scrutinise, Searcher, Shufti, Supervisor, Survey, Test, Vet, Vidimus, Visitation

Inspire(d), Inspiration, Inspiring Actuate, Aerate, Afflatus, Aganippe, Animate, Brainstorm, Brainwave, Breath(e), Castalian, Draw, Elate, Encourage, Estro, Exalt, Fire, Flash, Geist, Hearten, Hunch, Hwyl, Idea, Illuminate, Imbue, Impress, Impulse, Indrawn, Induce, Inflatus, Infuse, Inhale, Invention, Messianic, Motivate, Move, Muse, Pegasus, Pig's whisper, Plenary, Prompt, Prophetic, Reassurance, Satori, Sniff(le), Stimulus, Stoke, Taghairm, Theopneust(y), Uplift, Vatic

Install(ation) Elect, Enchase, Enthrone, Inaugurate, Induction, Infrastructure, Insert, Invest, Put (in)

Instalment Call, Episode, Fascicle, Heft, Livraison, Never-never, Part, Piecemeal, Serial, Tranche

Instance, Instant(aneous) As, Case, Example, Flash, Jiffy, Moment, Present, Say, Shake, Snappy, Spur, Tick, Trice, Twinkling, Urgent, Yocto-second

Instead (of) Deputy, For, Lieu, Locum, Vice

Instigate, Instigating, Instigator Arouse, Foment, Impel, Incite, Proactive, Prompt, Ringleader, Spur

Instinct(ive) Automatic, Conation, Flair, Gut, Herd, Id, Impulse, Inbred, Ingenerate, Innate, Intuition, Knee-jerk, Life, Nature, Nose, Prim(a)eval, Reflex, Second nature, Sense, Talent, Tendency, Visceral

Institute, Institution Academy, Activate, Asylum, Bank, Begin, Bring, Centre, Charity, College, Collegiate, Create, Erect, Found(ation), Halls of ivy, Hospital, I, Impose, Inaugurate, Mechanics, MORI, Organise, Orphanage, Poorhouse, Raise, Redbrick, Retraict, Retrait(e), Retreat, Smithsonian, Start, Technical, University, Varsity, WI, Women's, Workhouse

Instruct(ed), Instruction, Instructor Advice, Algorithm, Apprenticeship, Brief, Catechism, Chautauquan, Clinic, Coach, Course, Didactic, Direct(ive), Document, Drill, Edify, Educate, Ground(ing), Guide, How-to, Inform, Lesson, Maharishi, Mandate, Manual, Master class, Mentor, MIPS, Notify, Order, Patch, Pedagogue, Precept, RE, Recipe, RI, Rubric, Sensei, Statement, Stet, Swami, → **TEACH**, Train, Tutelage, Tutorial, Up

Instrument(al) Ablative, Act, Agent, Helpful, Mean(s), Measure, Negotiable, → **RESPONSIBLE**, → **TOOL**, → **UTENSIL**, Weapon

Insubordinate Contumacious, Faction, Mutinous, Rebel, Refractory

Insubstantial Airy, Brief, Flimsy, Frail, Frothy, Illusory, Jackstraw, Light, Scotch mist, Slender, Slight, Spectre, Syllabub, Thin, Wispy, Ye(a)sty

Insult(ing) Abuse, Affront, Aspersion, Barb, Becall, Contumely, Cut, Derogatory, Diatribe, Dyslogistic, Effrontery, Embarrass, Facer, Fig, Gibe, Lese-majesty, Mud, Mud-pie, Offend, Opprobrious, Ronyion, Runnion, Scurrilous, Skit, Slagging, Sledge, Slight, Slur, Snub, Trample, Trauma, Uncomplimentary, Verbal, Wazzock, Yenta, Yente

Insure(r), Insurance Abandonee, Accident, Actuarial, Comprehensive, Cover, Coverage, Death futures, Endowment, Fire, Group, Guarantee, Hedge, Indemnity, Knock-for-knock, Life, Lloyds, Medibank, Medicaid, Medicare, Mutual, Name, National, Policy, Public liability, Reversion, Safety net, Security, Third party, Tontine, Travel, Underwrite

Insurgent, Insurrect(ion) Cade, Mutiny, Outbreak, Rebel, Revolt, Riot, Rising, Sedition, Terrorist, Uprising

▷**Insurgent** *may indicate* 'reversed'

Intact Complete, Entire, Inviolate, Unused, Whole

Integrate(d), Integration Amalgamate, Assimilate, Combine, Coordinate, Fuse, Harmonious, Mainstream, Merge, Postural, Synergism, Vertical

Integrity Honesty, Honour, Principle, Rectitude, Strength, Uprightness, Whole, Worth

Intellect, Intellectual(s) Academic, Aptitude, Belligerati, Brain (box), Cerebral, Chattering class, Cultural, Dianoetic, Egghead, Eggmass, Erudite, Far-out, Genius, Grey matter, Highbrow, Intelligent, Intelligentsia, -ist, Learned, Literati, Luminary, Mastermind, Mental(ity), Mind, Noesis, Noetic, Noology, Nous, Pointy-headed, Profound, Reason, Sublime, Titan

Intelligence, Intelligent Advice, Artificial, Boss, Brainiac, Brain-power, Brains, Bright, Cerebral, CIA, Discerning, Dope, Eggmass, Emotional, Esprit, G, Gifted, Grey matter, GRU, Guile, Humint, Info, Ingenious, IQ, Knowledgeable,

Machiavellian, Machine, MI, Mossad, Mother wit, News, Pate, Perspicacity, Pointy-headed, Rational, Sconce, Sense, Sharp(-witted), Shrewd, Smart, Spetsnaz, Spetznaz, Tidings, Wit

Intend(ed), Intending Allot, Contemplate, Deliberate, Design, Destine, Ettle, Fiancé(e), Going, →**MEAN**, Meditate, Planned, Propose, Purpose, Think

Intense, Intensify, Intensity, Intensive Acute, Aggravate, Ardent, Compound, Crash, Crescendo, Deep, Earnest, Earthquake, Edgy, Emotional, Enhance, Escalate, Excess, Extreme, Fervent, Fully, Hot up, Keen, Luminous, Might, Profound, Radiant, Redouble, Saturation, Sharpen, Strong, Towering, Vehement, Vivid, Warmth

Intent, Intention(al) À dessein, Aim, Animus, Deliberate, Design, Dole, Earmark, Earnest, Ettle, Hellbent, Manifesto, Mens rea, Mind, Prepense, Purpose, Rapt, Resolute, Set, Special, Studious, Systematic, Thought, Wilful, Witting, Yrapt

Interaction Enantiodromia, Solvation, Symbiosis, Synergy

Intercede, Intercession Mediate, Negotiate, Plead, Prayer

Interdict Ban, Forbid, Prohibit, Taboo, Veto

Interest(ed), Interesting Amusive, APR, Attention, Behalf, Benefit, Care, Clou, Compound, Concern, Contango, Controlling, Coupon, Dividend, Double-bubble, Ear-grabbing, Engage, Engross, Enthusiasm, Fad, Fascinate, Fee-simple, Fee-tail, Grab, Hot, Human, Import, Income, Insurable, Int(o), Intrigue, Juicy, Landed, Life, Line, Meaty, Negative, Newsworthy, Nibble, Part, Partisan, Percentage, Public, Readable, Rente, Respect, Return, Revenue, Reversion, Riba, Riding, Scene, Sepid, Share, Side, Sideline, Simple, Spice, Stake, Tasty, Tickle, Titillate, Topical, Usage, Usance, Use, Usure, Usury, Vested, Vig(orish), Warm

Interface Centronics, Modium, Spigot

Interfere(r), Interference Atmospherics, Busybody, Clutter, Crackle, Disrupt, Disturb, Hamper, Hinder, Hiss, Intrude, Mar, Molest, Noise, Nose, Officious, Pry, Shash, Shot noise, Static, Tamper, Teratogen

Interim Break, Meanwhile, Temporary

Interior Backblocks, Cyclorama, Domestic, Innards, Innate, Inner, Inside, Outback, Plain, Up-country, Vitals

Interject(ion) Ahem, Begorra(h), Chime-in, Doh, Duh, Haith, Hoo-oo, Interpolate, Lackaday, Lumme, Nation, Sese(y), Sessa, 'Sheart, 'Slid, Tarnation, Tush

Interlace Mingle, Weave, Wreathe

Interloper Cowan, Gate-crasher, Intruder, Trespasser

Interlude Antimask, Antimasque, Divertimento, Entr'acte, Interruption, Kyogen, Lunch-hour, Meantime, Pause, Verset

Intermediary, Intermediate, Intermediatory Agent, Bardo, Between, Bytownite, Cat's paw, Comprador(e), Contact man, Go-between, Hypabyssal, In-between, Instar, Mean, Medial, Mesne, Mezzanine, Middleman, Middle-of-the-road, Negotiant, Transitional

Intermission Apyrexia, Break, Interval, Pause, Recess

Intermittent Broken, Episodic, Fitful, Periodic, Random, Spasmic, Spasmodic, Sporadic

Intern(e) Confine, Doctor, Impound, Restrict, Trainee

Internal Domestic, Inner, Internecine, Inward, Within

International Cap, Cosmopolitan, Fourth, Lion, Second, Trotskyist, UN, Universal

Interpret(er) Aread, Ar(r)e(e)de, Conster, Construe, Decipher, Decode, Dragoman, Exegete, Explain, Exponent, Expositor, Expound, Glossator,

Hermeneutist, Jehovist, Linguistic, Linkster, Lipreader, Medium, Moralise, Oneiroscopist, Polyglot, Prophet, Rabbi, Rationalise, Read, Rede, Reed(e), Render, Represent, Spokesman, Subjectivity, Textualist, → **TRANSLATE**, Ulema

Interpretation Anagoge, Anagogy, Analysis, Cabbala(h), Construction, Copenhagen, Diagnosis, Dittology, Eisegesis, Exegesis, Exegete, Gematria, Gloss(ary), Gospel, Halacha(h), Halakah, Hermeneutics, Kabbala(h), Midrash, Oneirocriticism, Portray, Reading, Rede, Rendition, Targum, Translation, Zohar

Interrogate, Interrogation, Interrogator Catechism, Corkscrew, Cross-question, Debrief(ing), Enquire, Examine, Grill, Inquisitor, Pump, → **QUESTION**, Quiz, Quiz-master

Interrupt(ion), Interrupter Ahem, Blip, Break, Butt, Chequer, Chip in, Cut in, Disturb, Entr'acte, Heckle, Hiatus, Intercept, Interfere, Interject, Interlard, Interpellate, Interpolate, Interpose, Interregnum, Intrusion, Pause, Portage, Punctuate, Rheotome, Stop, Suspend, Tmesis, Waylay

Intersect(ion), Intersecting Carfax, Carfox, Chiasm(a), Clover-leaf, Compital, Cross, Crunode, Cut, Decussate, Divide, Groin, Metacentre, Node, Orthocentre, Quadrivium, Trace, Vertex

Intersperse Dot, Interlard, Interpose, Scatter, Sprinkle

Intertwine Braid, Knit, Lace, Plait, Splice, Twist, Wreathe, Writhe

Interval Between, Break, Breather, Class, Closed, Comma, Confidence, Diesis, Distance, Duodecimo, Entr'acte, Episodic, Fifth, Gap, Half-step, Half-time, Harmonic, Hiatus, Hourly, Imperfect, Interim, Interlude, Interregnum, Interruption, Interspace, Interstice, Leap, Limma, Lucid, Lull, Meantime, Meanwhile, Melodic, Minor third, Ninth, Octave, Open, Ottava, Parenthesis, Pycnon, QT, Regular, Respite, Rest, Schisma, Semitone, Seventh, Sixth, Space, Span, Spell, Third, Thirteenth, Time lag, Twelfth, Wait

Intervene, Intervening, Intervention Agency, Arbitrate, Expromission, Hypothetical, Interfere, Interjacent, Interrupt, Intromit, Mediate, Mesne, Reprieve, Step in, Theurgy, Up

Interview Audience, Audition, Conference, Debriefing, Examine, Hearing, Oral, Press conference, See, Vox pop

Interweave, Interwoven, Interwove Complect, Entwine, Interlace, Monogram, Plait, Plash, Pleach, Raddle, Splice, Wreathed

Intestinal, Intestine(s) Bowel, Chit(ter)lings, Derma, Duodenum, Enteric, Entrails, Gastric, Guts, Harigals, Innards, Jejunum, Kishke, Large, Mesenteron, Omenta, Rectum, Small, Splanchnic, Thairm, Tripes, Viscera

In the club Gravid, Pregnant, Up the spout

Intimacy, Intimate(ly) Achates, À deux, Arm-in-arm, Boon, Bosom, Close, Communion, Confidante, Connote, Familiar, Far ben, Friend, Hint, Imply, Inmost, Innuendo, Intrigue, Nearness, Opine, Pack, Private, Signal, Special, Thick, Throng, Warm, Well

Intimidate, Intimidating Browbeat, Bulldoze, Bully, Cow, Daunt, Dragon, Harass, Hector, Menace, Overawe, Psych, Scare, Threaten, Unnerve

Intolerant, Intolerable Allergic, Bigotry, Egregious, Excessive, Illiberal, Impatient, Impossible, Insupportable, Ombrophobe, Redneck, Self-righteous

Intoxicate(d), Intoxicant, Intoxicating, Intoxication Bhang, Blasted, Crink, Ethanol, Half-cut, Incite, Ivresse, Krunk, La-la land, Methystic, Narcotise, Nitrogen narcosis, Potent, Rapture of the deep, Shroom, Swacked, The narks, Trolleyed, Zonked

Intractable Disobedient, Kittle, Mulish, Obdurate, Perverse, Surly, Unruly, Wilful

Intransigent Adamant, Inflexible, Rigid, Uncompromising

Intrepid(ity) Aweless, Bold, Bottle, Brave, Dauntless, Doughty, Fearless, Firm, Plucky, → **RESOLUTE**, Stout, Unafraid, Undaunted, Valiant

Intricate Complex, Crinkum-crankum, Daedal(ian), Daedale, Dedal, Gordian, Intrince, Involute, Knotty, Parquetry, Pernickety, Tricky, Vitruvian

Intrigue(r), Intriguing Affaire, Artifice, Brigue, Cabal, Camarilla, Cloak and dagger, Collogue, Conspiracy, Fascinate, Hotbed, Ignatian, Interest, Jesuit, Jobbery, Liaison, Machinate, Plot, Politic, Rat, → **SCHEME**, Stairwork, Strategy, Traffic, Trinketer, Web

▷**Intrinsically** *may indicate* something within a word

Introduce(r), Introduction, Introductory Acquaint, Alap, Anacrusis, Cataphoresis, Code name, Curtain-raiser, Debut, Emcee, Enseam, Entrée, Exordial, Foreword, Immit, Import, Induct, Initiate, Inject, Insert, Instil(l), Institutes, Intercalate, Interpolate, Introit, Isagogic, Lead-in, Lead up, Opening, Overture, Plant, Preamble, Precede, Preface, Preliminary, Prelude, Prelusory, Preparatory, Present, Primer, Proem, Prolegomena, Prolegomenon, Prolog, Prologue, Prooemium, Proponent, Raise, Referral, Start, Usher

▷**Introduction** *may indicate* a first letter

▷**In trouble** *may indicate* an anagram

Intrude(r), Intrusion, Intrusive Abate, Aggress, Annoy, Bother, Burglar, Derby dog, → **ENCROACH**, Gatecrash, Impinge, Inroad, Interloper, Invade, Lopolith, Meddle, Nosey, Personal, Porlocking, Presume, Raid, Sorn, Trespass

Intuition, Intuitive Apercu, Belief, ESP, Hunch, Insight, Instinct, Noumenon, Premonition, Seat-of-the-pants, Sixth sense, Telepathy

▷**In two words** *may indicate* a word to be split

Inundate(d), Inundation Awash, Engulf, Flood, Overflow, Overwhelm, Submerge, Swamp

Inure Acclimatise, Accustom, Harden, Season, Steel

Invade(r), Invasion Aggressor, Angle, Attack, Attila, Cortes, Dane, Descent, Encroach, Goth, Hacker, Hengist, Horsa, Hun, Incursion, Infest, Inroad, Intruder, Jute, Lombard, Martian, Norman, Norsemen, Occupation, Ostrogoth, Overrun, Permeate, Pict, Raid, Trespass, Vandal, Viking

Invalid(ate), Invalidation Annul(led), Bad, Bogus, Bunbury, Cancel, Chronic, Clinic, Defunct, Diriment, Erroneous, Expired, False, Inauthentic, Inform, Inoperative, Irritate, Lapsed, Negate, Nugatory, Null, Nullify, Overturn, Quash, Refute, Shut-in, Terminate, Vitiate, Void

Invaluable Essential, Excellent, Precious, Useful

Invariable, Invariably Always, Consistent, Constant, Eternal, Habitual, Perpetual, Steady, Uniform

Invective Abuse, Billingsgate, Diatribe, Philippic, Reproach, Ribaldry, Tirade

Inveigle Charm, Coax, Entice, Persuade, Subtrude

Invent(ion), Inventive Adroit, Babe, Baby, Brainchild, Chimera, Coin, Concept, Contrive, Cook up, → **CREATE**, Creed, Daedal, Design, Device, Dream up, Embroider, Excogitate, Fabricate, Fain, Fantasia, Feign, Fiction, Figment, Imaginary, Improvise, Independent, Ingenuity, Make up, Mint, Myth, Originate, Patent, Plateau, Pretence, Resourceful, Synectics, Trump up, Whittle, Wit

Inventor Artificer, Author, Coiner, Creator, Designer, Engineer, Idea-hamster, Mint-master, Patentee

Inventory Account, Index, Itemise, List, Record, Register, Scroll, Stock, Terrier

Inverse, Inversion, Invert(ed) Arch, Back to front, Capsize, Chiasmus, Entropion, Entropium, Lid, Opposite, Overset, Reciprocal, Retrograde, Reverse, Turn, Upset, Upside down

Invertebrate Acanthocephalan, Annelida, Anthozoan, Arthropod, Brachiopod, Chaetognath, Crinoid, Ctenophore, Decapod, Echinoderm, Echinoid, Entoprocta, Euripterid, Feather star, Gast(e)ropod, Globigerina, Holothurian, Hydrozoan, Lobopod, Mollusc, Nacre, Onychophoran, Parazoan, Pauropod, Peritrich, Platyhelminth, Polyp, Poriferan, Protostome, Rotifer, Roundworm, Scyphozoan, Sea-cucumber, Sea-lily, → **SHELLFISH**, Slug, Spineless, Sponge, Spoonworm, Starfish, Tardigrade, Trepang, Trochelminth, Trochophore, Water bear, Worm, Zoophyte

Invest(or), Investment Ambient, Angel, Assiege, Beleaguer, Beset, Besiege, Bet, Blockade, Blue-chip, Bond, Bottom-fisher, Capitalist, Clothe, Contrarian, Debenture, Dignify, Dub, Embark, Enclothe, Endow, Endue, Enrobe, Ethical, Financier, Flutter, Gilt, Girt, Gross, Holding, Infeft, Install, Inward, On, Pannicle, Parlay, Place, Portfolio, Put, Retiracy, Ring, Robe, Saver, Share(holder), Siege, Sink, Smart money, Spec, Speculation, Stag, Stake, Stock(holder), Tessa, Tie up, Trochophore, Trojan War, Trust, Trustee, Venture (capital), With profits

▷**Invest** *may indicate* one word surrounding another

Investigate, Investigation, Investigative, Investigator Analyse, Audit, Canvass, Case, CID, Delve, DI, Enquire, Examine, Explore, Fact-find, Fed, Fieldwork, Going over, Gumshoe, Heuristic, Hunt, Inquest, Inquirendo, Inquiry, Inquisition, Kinsey, McCarthyism, Nose, Organon, Organum, Probe, Prodnose, Pry, Quester, Rapporteur, Recce, Research, Scan, Scrutinise, Search, Sleuth, Snoop, Study, Suss, Tec, Test, T-man, Track, Try, Zetetic

Inveterate Chronic, Dyed-in-the-wool, Habitual, Hardened

Invidious Harmful, Hostile, Malign

Invigorate, Invigorating, Invigoration Analeptic, Animate, Brace, Brisk, Cheer, Crispy, Elixir, Energise, Enliven, Exhilarate, Fortify, Insinew, Inspirit, Pep, Refresh, Renew, Stimulate, Tonic, Vital

Invincible Almighty, Brave, Stalwart, Valiant

Invisible Blind, Hidden, Imageless, Infra-red, Secret, Tusche, Unseen

Invite, Invitation, Inviting Ask, Attract, Bid, Call, Card, Overture, → **REQUEST**, Solicit, Stiffie, Summons, Tempt, Woo

Invocation, Invoke Appeal, Begorra, Call, Conjure, Curse, Entreat, Epiclesis, Imprecate, Solicit, White rabbits

Invoice Account, Bill, Itemise, Manifest, Pro forma

Involve(d), Involvement Active, Close knit, Commitment, Complicate, Complicit, Concern, Deep, Embroil, Engage, Enlace, Entail, Entangle, Envelop, Imbroglio, Immerse, → **IMPLICATE**, Include, Intervene, Into, Intricate, Knee-deep, Meet, Necessitate, Tangle, Tortuous, Tricksy

▷**Involved** *may indicate* an anagram

Inward(s) Afferent, Homefelt, Introrse, Mental, Private, Varus, Within

Iota Atom, Jot, Subscript, Whit

IOU Cedula, Market, PN, Vowels

Iran(ian) Babist, Kurd, Mede, Pahlavi, Parsee, Pehlevi, Persic

Irascible Choleric, Crusty, Fiery, Grouchy, Peevish, Quick-tempered, Short-tempered, Snappy, Tetchy

Irate Angry, Cross, Infuriated, Wrathful

Ire Anger, Cholera, Fury, Rage, Wrath

Iridescence, Iridescent Chatoyant, Opaline, Reflet, Shimmering, Shot, Water-gall

Iris Areola, Eye, Flag, Fleur-de-lis, Florence, Gladdon, Gladioli, Ixia, Lily, Lis, Orris, Rainbow, Sedge, Seg, Sunbow, Triandria, Uvea, Water flag

Irish(man) Bark, Boy, Bucko, Celt(ic), Clan-na-gael, Declan, Defender, Dermot, Dubliner, Eamon(n), Eirann, Eoin, Erse, Feargal, Fenian, Fionn, Gaeltacht, Goidel, Greek, Hibernian, Jackeen, Keltic, Kern(e), Mick(e)(y), Milesian, Mulligan, Neil, Ogamic, Orange(man), Ostmen, Paddy(-whack), Partholon, Pat(rick), Rapparee, Redshank, Reilly, Riley, Rory, Sean, Shoneen, UDA, Ultonian

Iron(s), Ironstone, Ironwork(s) Airn, Alpha, Angle, Barking, Beta, Bloom, Branding, Carron, Cast, Cautery, Chains, Chalybeate, Chancellor, Channel, Climbing, Coquimbite, Corrugated, Cramp(on), Crimp, Cross, Curling, Curtain, Delta, Derringer, Dogger, Dogs, Driving, Eagle-stone, Even, Fayalite, Fe, Ferredoxin, Ferrite, Fetter, Fiddley, Flatten, Flip-dog, Galvanised, Gamma, Gem, Golfclub, Goose, Grappling, Grim, Grozing, →**GUN**, Gyve, Haematite, Horse, Ingot, Italian, Kamacite, Laterite, Lily, Lofty, Long, Maiden, Malleable, Marcasite, Mars, Martensite, Mashie, Mashy, Merchant, Meteoric, Mitis (metal), Pea, Pig, Pinking, →**PRESS**, Pro-metal, Rabble, Rations, Rod, Sad, Scrap, Shooting, Short, Smoother, Soft, Soldering, Spathic, Specular, Speeler, Spiegeleisen, Steam, Stirrup, Stretching, Strong, Taconite, Taggers, Terne, Tin terne, Toggle, Tow, Turfing, Wafer, Waffle, Wear, Wedge, White, Wrought

Ironic, Irony Antiphrasis, Asteism, Dramatic, Ferrous, Meiosis, Metal, Ridicule, Sarcasm, Satire, Socratic, Tongue-in-cheek, Tragic, Trope, Wry

▶**Ironwork(s)** *see* IRON(S)

Irrational Absurd, Brute, Delirious, Doolally, Foolish, Illogical, Pi, Squirrelly, Superstitious, Surd, Wild, Zany

Irregular(ity) Abnormal, Anomaly, A salti, Asymmetric, Bashi-bazouk, Blotchy, Carlylean, Casual, Crazy, Eccentric, Ectopic, Episodic, Erratic, Evection, Fitful, Flawed, Formless, Glitch, Guerilla, Heteroclitic, Higgledy-piggledy, Incondite, Inordinate, Intermittent, Jitter, Kink, Occasional, Orthotone, Para-military, Partisan, Patchy, Random, Rough, Scalene, Scraggy, Sebundy, Solecism, Spasmodic, Sporadic, Strange, TA, Turbulence, Uneven, Unorthodox, Unsteady, Variable, Wayward, Zigzag

▷**Irregular** *may indicate* an anagram

Irrelevant Digression, Gratuitous, Immaterial, Inapplicable, Inconsequent, Inept, Pointless, Ungermane

Irreproachable Blameless, Spotless, Stainless

Irresistible Almighty, Endearing, Inevitable, Mesmeric, Overwhelming

Irresolute, Irresolution Cliffhanger, Doubtful, Faltering, Hesitant, Timid, Unsure, Wavery

Irresponsible Capricious, Feckless, Flighty, Free spirit, Gallio, Reckless, Skittish, Slap-happy, Strawen, Trigger-happy, Wanton, Wildcat

Irreverent, Irreverence Disrespectful, Godless, Impious, Profane, Sacrilege

Irrigate, Irrigation Colonic, Drip, Enema, Flood, Water

Irritable, Irritability, Irritant, Irritate(d), Irritation Abrasive, Acerbate, Anger, Annoy, Antagonise, Bête noire, Bile, Blister, Bother, Bug, Chafe, Chauff, Chippy, Chocker, Choleric, Crabbit, Crabby, Cross-grained, Crosspatch, Crotchety, Crusty, Dod, Dyspeptic, Eat, Eczema, Edgy, Emboil, Enchafe, Erethism, Ewk, Exasperate, Eyestrain, Fantod, Feverish, Fiery, Fleabite, Frabbit,

Fractious, Fraught, Fretful, Gall, Get (to), Gnat, Goad, Grate, Gravel, Hasty, Heck, Hoots, Humpy, Impatience, Intertrigo, Irk, Itch, Jangle, Jar, Livery, Mardy, Molest, Narky, Needle, Nerk, Nettle, Niggly, Nudnik, Ornery, Peckish, Peevish, Peppery, Pesky, Pestilent(ial), Pet, Petulance, Pinprick, Pique, Prickly, Provoke, Rag'd, Ragde, Rankle, Rash, Rasp, Rattle, Ratty, Rile, Riley, Roil, Rub, Ruffle, Savin(e), Scratchy, Shirty, Smart, Snappy, Snit, Snitchy, Sore, Splenetic, Sting, Tease, Techy, Testy, Tetchy, Thorn, Tickle, Tiff, Tift, Tingle, Tiresome, Toey, Touchy, Uptight, → **VEX**, Waspish, Waxy, Windburn, Wind-up

▷**Irritated** *may indicate* an anagram

Islam(ic) Crescent, Druse, Druz(e), Kurd(ish), Muezzing, Pillars, Salafism, Sanusi, Senus(si), Sheriat, Shia(h), Shiite, Sufism, Wah(h)abi

Island, Isle(t) Ait, Archipelago, Atoll, Cay, Char, Desert, Eyot, Floating, Heat, Holm, I, Inch, Is, Key, Lagoon, Motu, Refuge, Traffic

Isn't Aint, Nis, Nys

Isolate(d), Isolation Alienate, Ancress, Backwater, Cone off, Cut off, Desolate, Dissociate, Enclave, Enisle, Exclude, Incommunicado, Inisle, In vacuo, Island, Lone, Lonely, Maroon, Outlying, Pocket, Quarantine, Sea-girt, Seclude, Secret, Segregate, Separate, Sequester, Sequestration, Set apart, Siege, Six-finger country, Solitary, Sporadic, Stray

Isotope Actinon, Cobalt-60, Deuterium, Muonium, Protium, Radiothorium, Strontium-90, Thoron, Tritium

Issue(s) Army, Bonus, Capitalization, Children, Come, Crux, Daughter, Debouch, Denouement, Derive, Disclose, Dispense, Edition, Effluence, Egress, Embryo, Emerge, Emission, Emit, Escape, Exit, Exodus, Family, Feigned, Fiduciary, Flotation, Fungible, General, Government, Gush, Handout, Hiccup, Immaterial, Ish, Litter, Material, Matter, Mise, Number, Offspring, Outcome, Outflow, Part, Point, Privatization, Proof, Publish, Release, Result, Rights, Sally, Scion, Scrip, Seed, Share, Side, Son, Spawn, Special, Spring, Stream, Subject, Topic, Turn, Utter, Yearbook

Isthmus Darien, Karelian, Kra, Neck, Panama, Suez

It A, Chic, Hep, Hip, Id, Italian, Oomph, SA, Same, Sex appeal, 't, Vermouth

Italian, Italy Alpini, Ausonian, Bolognese, Calabrian, Chian, Ding, Este, Etnean, Etrurian, Etruscan, Faliscan, Florentine, Garibaldi, Genoese, Ghibelline, Guelf, Guelph, Hesperia, Irredentist, It, Latian, Latin, Lombard, Marconi, Medici, Milanese, Moro, Neapolitan, Oscan, Paduan, Patarin(e), Roman, Sabine, Samnite, Sicel, Sienese, Signor(i), Sikel, Tuscan, Umbrian, Venetian, Vermouth, Volscian

Itch(ing), Itchiness Annoy, Burn, Cacoethes, Dhobi, Heat rash, Hives, Prickle, Prickly heat, Prurience, Prurigo, Pruritis, Psora, Scabies, Scrapie, Seven-year, Swimmer's, Tickle, → **URGE**, Yen

Item(ise) Also, Article, Bulletin, Couple, Detail, Entry, Equipment, Exhibit, Flash, Line, List, Note, Number, Pair, Particular, Piece, Point, Product, Spot, Talking point, Too, Topic, Twosome, Unit

Itinerant, Itinerary Ambulant, Didakai, Didakei, Did(d)icoy, Dusty Feet, Gipsy, Gypsy, Journey, Log, Pedlar, Peripatetic, Pie-powder, Roadman, Roamer, Romany, Rootless, Route, Stroller, Traveller, Vagrom, Wayfarer

Ivory (tower) Bone, Chryselephantine, Dentine, Distant, Eburnean, Impractical, Incisor, Key, Molar, Solitude, Teeth, Tusk, Vegetable

Ivy Ale-hoof, Aralia, Boston, Bush, Climber, Creeper, Grape, Hedera, Helix, Japanese, Poison, Rhoicissus, Shield, Sumac, Sweetheart, Weeping

Jj

Jab(ber) Chatter, Foin, Gabble, Immunise, Immunologist, Inject, Jaw, Jook, Lunge, Nudge, Peck, Poke, Prattle, Prod, Proke, Punch, Puncture, Sook, Sputter, Stab, Thrust, Venepuncture, Yak

Jack(s) AB, Apple, Ass, Ball, Boot, Bowl(s), Boy, Cade, Card, Cheap, Coatcard, Crevalle, Deckhand, Dibs(tones), Five stones, Flag, Frost, Giant-killer, Hoist, Honour, Horner, Hydraulic, Idle, J, Jock, Jumping, Ketch, Kitty, Knave, Lazy, London, Loord, Lout, Lumber, Maker, Mark, Matlow, Mistress, Nob, Noddy, Pilot, Point, Pot, Pur, Rabbit, Raise, Rating, Ripper, Roasting, Robinson, Russell, Sailor, Salt, Screw, Sea-dog, Seafarer, Seaman, Sprat, Spring-heeled, Springtail, Steeple, Sticker, Straw, Tar, Tee, Tradesman, Turnspit, Union, Uplift, Wood, Yellow

Jacket Acton, Afghanistan, Air, Amauti(k), Anorak, Atigi, Baju, Bania(n), Banyan, Barbour®, Basque, Battle, Bed, Biker, Blazer, Blouse, Blouson, Body-warmer, Bolero, Bomber, Brigandine, Bumfreezer, Bush, Cagoul(e), Camisole, Cardigan, Carmagnole, Casing, →**COAT**, Combat, Cosy, Cover, Dinner, Dolman, Donkey, Doublet, Drape, Dressing, Dressing-sack, Duffel coat, Duffle coat, Dust-cover, Dustwrapper, Duvet, Fearnought, Flak, Fleece, Gambeson, Gendarme, Grego, Habergeon, Hacking, Half-kirtle, Ha(c)queton, Hoodie, Hug-me-tight, Jerkin, Jupon, Kagool, Life, Life preserver, Lumber, Mackinaw, Mae West, Mandarin, Mao, Matinée, Mess, Monkey, Nehru, Newmarket, Norfolk, Parka, Pea, Pilot, Polka, Potato, Pyjama, Reefer, Roundabout, Sackcoat, Safari, Shell, Shooting, Shortgown, Simar(re), Slip-cover, Smoking, Spencer, Sports, Steam, Strait, Sweatshirt, Tabard, Tailcoat, Toreador, Tunic, Tux(edo), Tweed, Vareuse, Waistcoat, Wampus, Wam(m)us, Water, Waxed, Windbreaker®, Windcheater, Windjammer, Wrapper, Zouave

Jackknife Dive, Fold, Jockteleg, Pike

Jacob Epstein, Ladder, Sheep

Jade(d) Axe-stone, Cayuse, Cloy, Crock, Exhaust, Fatigue, Greenstone, Hack, Hag, Horse, Hussy, Limmer, Minx, Nag, Nephrite, Passe, Sate, Screw, Slut, Stale, Tired, Trite, Weary, Yu(-stone)

Jag(ged) Barbed, Cart, Drinking, Erose, Gimp, Hackly, Injection, Laciniate, Ragde, Ragged, Sawtooth, Serrate, Snag, Spree, Spur, Tooth

Jaguar Car, Caracal, Cat, E-type, Ounce, Tiger

Jail(er) Adam, Alcatraz, Bastille, Bedford, Bin, Can, Clink, Cooler, Gaol, Hoosegow, Imprison, Incarcerate, Jug, Keeper, Limbo, Lockup, Marshalsea, Newgate, Nick, Pen, Pokey, Porridge, →**PRISON**, Screw, Shop, Stir, Strangeways, Turnkey, Warder

Jailbird Con, Lag, Lifer, Life server, Trusty

Jalopy Banger, Boneshaker, Buggy, Car, Crate, Heap, Stock-car

Jam(my) Block, Bottleneck, Choke, Clog, Confiture, Crowd, Crush, Cushy, Damson, Dilemma, Extra, Fix, Gridlock, Hold-up, Hole, How d'ye do, Imbroglio, Improvise, Jeelie, Jeely, Lock, Log, Pack, Paper, Pickle, Plight, →**PREDICAMENT**, Preserve, Press, Quince, Rat run, Rush hour, Seize, Snarl-up, Spot, Squeeze, Standstill, Stick, Tailback, Traffic, Vice, Vise, Wedge

Jamb Doorpost, Durn, Sconcheon, Scontion, Scuncheon, Upright

Jane Austen, Calamity, Eyre, Seymour, Shore, Sian

Jangle Clank, Clapperclaw, Clash, Rattle, Wrangle

Japan(ese), Japanese drama Ainu, Burakumin, Daimio, Eta, Finish, Geisha, Genro, Gloss, Haiku, Heian, Hondo, Honshu, Issei, Japlish, Kabuki, Kami, Kana, Kirimon, Lacquer, Mandarin, Mikado, Mousmé, Mousmee, Nihon, Nippon, Nisei, No(h), Resin, Sansei, Satsuma, Shinto, Shogun, Taisho, Togo, Tycoon, Yamato, Yellow peril

Jar(ring) Albarello, Amphora, Bell, Canopus, Churr, Clash, Crock, Cruet, Din, Dolium, Enrough, Gallipot, Gas, Grate, Greybeard, Gride, Grind, Gryde, Humidor, Hydria, →**JOLT**, Kalpis, Kang, Kilner®, Leyden, Mason, Monkey, Off-key, Olla, Pint, Pithos, Pot(iche), Rasp, Rock, Screwtop, Shake, Shelta, Shock, Stamnos, Start, Stave, Stean, Steen, Stein, Tankard, Terrarium, Tinaja, Turn, Untune, Vessel, Water-monkey

Jargon Argot, Babble, Baragouin, Beach-la-mar, Buzzword, Cant, Chinese, Chinook, Cyberspeak, Eurobabble, Eurospeak, Geekspeak, Gobbledegook, Gobbledygook, Greenspeak, Jive, Kennick, Legalese, Lingo, Lingoa geral, Lingua franca, Mumbo-jumbo, Netspeak, Newspeak, Parlance, Patois, Patter, Shelta, Shoptalk, →**SLANG**, Sociologese, Technospeak, Telegraphese, Vernacular

Jaundice(d) Cholestasis, Cynical, Icterus, Prejudiced, Sallow, Yellow

Jaunt Journey, Outing, Sally, Stroll, Swan, Trip

Jaunty Airy, Akimbo, Chipper, Debonair, Perky, Rakish

▷**Jaunty** *may indicate* an anagram

Javelin Dart, Gavelock, Harpoon, Jereed, Jerid, Pile, Pilum, Spear

Jaw(s), Jawbone Blab, Chaft, Chap, Chat, Chaw, Cheek, Chide, Chin, Confab, Entry, Gills, Glass, Gnathite, Gonion, Imparl, Jabber, Jobe, Kype, Lantern, Mandible, Maw, Maxilla, Mesial, Muzzle, Mylohyoid, Natter, Opisthognathous, Overbite, Overshot, Phossy, Pi, Premaxillary, Prognathous, Ramus, Shark, Stylet, Underhung, Undershot, Wapper-jaw, Ya(c)kety-Ya(c)k

Jazz(er), Jazzman Acid, Afro-Cuban, Barber, Barrelhouse, Bebop, Blues, Boogie, Boogie-woogie, Bop, Cat, Coleman, Cool, Count Basie, Dixieland, Enliven, Free, Funky, Gig, Gutbucket, High life, Hipster, Jam, Jive, Kansas City, Latin, Lick, Mainstream, Modern, New Wave, Nouvelle Vague, Progressive, Ragtime, Riff, Scat, Skiffle, Slap base, Stomp, Stride, Swinger, Tailgate, Trad, Traditional, Waller

Jealous(y) Envious, Green(-eyed), Grudging, Zelotypia

Jeer(ing) Barrack, Belittle, Birl, Boo, Burl, Deride, Digs, Fleer, Flout, Frump, Gird, Heckle, Hoot, Jape, Jibe, →**MOCK**, Rail, Razz, Ridicule, Scoff, Sneer, Taunt

Jehovah God, Lord, Yahve(h), Yahwe(h)

Jell(y) Agar(-agar), Aspic, Brawn, Calf's foot, Chaudfroid, Comb, Cranberry, →**EXPLOSIVE**, Flummery, Gel, Isinglass, Jam, K-Y®, Liquid paraffin, Meat, Medusa, Mineral, Mould, Napalm, Petrolatum, Petroleum, Royal, Set, Sterno®, Vaseline®

▷**Jelly** *may indicate* an anagram

Jellyfish Aurelia, Box, Cnidaria, Hydrozoa, Medusa, Nettlefish, Physalia, Portuguese man-of-war, Sea-blubber, Sea-nettle, Sea-wasp

Jenny Ass, Lind, Mule, Spinner, Spinster, Wren

Jeopardise, Jeopardy Danger, Expose, Hazard, Imperil, Peril, Risk

Jerk(y), Jerkily, Jerking, Jerks Aerobics, A salti, Bob, Braid, Bump, Cant, Diddle, Ebrillade, Flirt, Flounce, Gym(nastics), Half-wit, Hike, Hitch, Hoi(c)k, Idiot, Jigger, Jolt, Jut, Kant, PE, Peck, Physical, Saccade, Shove, Shrug, Spasm, Start, Surge, Switch, Sydenham's chorea, Tic, Toss(en), Tweak, →TWITCH, Wrench, Yank

Jerry, Jerry-built Boche, Flimsy, Fritz, Hun, Kraut, Lego, Mouse, Po(t), Slop-built

Jersey(s) Bailiwick, Cow, Football, Frock, Gansey, Guernsey, Kine, Lily, Maillot, Polo, Potato, Roll-neck, Rugby, Singlet, →SWEATER, Sweatshirt, V-neck, Yellow, Zephyr

Jest(er), Jesting Badinage, Barm, Buffoon, Clown, Cod, Comic, Droll, Gleek, Humorist, Jape, Joculator, Joker, Josh, Miller, Mot, Motley, Patch, Quip, Raillery, Ribaldry, Ribaudry, Rigoletto, Sport, Toy, Wag, Waggery, Wit, Yorick

Jesus →CHRIST, Emmanuel, IHS, INRI, Jabers, Lord

Jet, Jet lag Airbus®, Aircraft, Beadblast, Black, Bubble, Burner, Chirt, Douche, Executive, Fountain, Geat, Harrier, Jumbo, Plane, Pump, Sable, Sandblast, Sloe, Soffione, Spirt, Spout, Spray, Spurt, Squirt, Stream, Time-zone disease, Time-zone fatigue, Turbine, Turbo, Vapour

Jettison Discard, Dump, Flotsam, Jetsam, Lagan, Ligan, Offload

Jew(ish), Jews Ashkenazi, Chas(s)id, Diaspora, Essene, Falasha, Has(s)id, Haskala(h), Hebraic, Hebrew, Hellenist, Hemerobaptist, Kahal, Karaite, Ladino, Levite, Lubavitch, Maccabee, Mitnag(g)ed, Nicodemus, Pharisee, Sadducee, Semite, Sephardim, Shemite, Shtetl, Tobit, Wandering, Yiddish

Jeweller(y), Jewel(s) Agate, Aigrette, Almandine, Artwear, Beryl, Bijou(terie), Bling(-bling), Brilliant, Cameo, Cartier, Chrysoprase, Cloisonné, Coral, Cornelian, Costume, Crown, Diamond, Earbob, Ear-drop, Emerald, Ewe-lamb, Fabergé, Fashion, Ferron(n)ière, Finery, Garnet, →GEM, Girandole, Gracchi, Jade, Junk, Lherzolite, Locket, Marcasite, Medallion, Navette, Olivine, Opal, Parure, Paste, Pavé, Pearl, Pendant, Peridot, Rivière, Rock, Rubin(e), Ruby, Sapphire, Sard, Scarab, Showpiece, Smaragd, Solitaire, Stone, Sunburst, Taonga, Tiara, Tiffany, Tom, Tomfoolery, Topaz, Torc, Treasure, Trinket, Zircon

Jib Ba(u)lk, Boggle, Face, Foresail, Genoa, Milk, Reest, Reist, Sideswipe, Stay-sail

Jibe Barb, Bob, Correspond, Crack, Fling, Gleek, →JEER, Mock, Sarcasm, Slant, Taunt

Jig(gle) Bob, Bounce, Dance, Fling, Frisk, Hornpipe, Jog, Juggle, Shake

Jilt(ed) Abandon, Discard, Lorn, Reject, Shed, Throw-over

Jingle(r) Clerihew, Clink, Ditty, Doggerel, Rhyme, Tambourine, Tinkle

Jinx(ed) Curse, Hex, Hoodoo, Jonah, Kibosh, Spoil, Unlucky, Voodoo, Whammy

Jitter(s), Jittery Coggly, DT, Fidgets, Funk, Jumpy, Nervous, Willies

▷**Jitter(s)** *may indicate* an anagram

Job(bing), Jobs Appointment, Assignment, Berth, Calling, Career, Chore, Comforter, Crib, Darg, Desk, Duty, Earner, Errand, Gig, Gut, Homer, Inside, Line, Métier, Mission, Occupation, Oratorio, Paint, Parergon, Patient, Pensum, Plum, Position, Post, Problem, Put-up, Role, Sinecure, Situation, Spot, Steady, →TASK, Ticket, Trade, Trotter, Truck, Undertaking, Work

▷**Job** *may indicate* the biblical character

Jockey Carr, Cheat, Diddle, Eddery, Horseman, Jostle, Jump, Lester, Manoeuvre, Mouse, Piggott, Rider, Steve, Swindle, Trick, Video, Vie, Winter
▷**Jockey** *may indicate* an anagram

Jocose, Jocular(ity), Jocund Badinage, Cheerful, Debonair, Facete, Facetious, Jesting, Lepid, Scurril(e), Waggish

Joe(y), Joseph Addison, Dogsbody, GI, Kangaroo, Pal, Public, Roo, Sloppy, Stalin, Surface, Trey

Jog(ger), Joggle, Jog-trot Arouse, Canter, Dunch, Dunsh, Heich-how, Heigh-ho, Hod, Jiggle, Jolt, Jostle, Mnemonic, Mosey, Nudge, Prompt, Ranke, Refresh, Remind, Road-runner, Run, Shake, Shog, Tickle, Trot, Whig

Join(er), Joined, Joining Accompany, Add, Affix, Alligate, Amalgamate, Annex, Associate, Attach, Bond, Brad, Cabinet-maker, Carpentry, Club, Cold-well, Combine, Confluent, Conglutinate, Conjunct, Connect, Converge, Cope, →**COUPLE**, Dovetail, Engraft, Enlist, Enrol, Enter, Entrant, Entrist, Fay, Fuse, Glue, Graft, Include, Inosculate, Interconnect, Link, Marry, Meet, Member, Merge, Mix, Pin, Push fit, Rabbet, Regelation, Rivet, Seam, Sew, Solder, Splice, Staple, Stick, Stitch, Tack-weld, Tenon, Toenail, Together, Unite, Wed, Weld, Wire, Yoke

Joint(ed) Ankle, Bar, Butt, Capillary, Carpus, Chine, Clip, Co, Cogging, Collaborative, Collar, Colonial goose, Compression, Conjunction, Coursing, Cuit, Cup and ball, Cut, Dive, Dovetail, Drumstick, Elbow, Entrecôte, False, Fetlock, First, Fish, Flitch, Genu, Gigot, Haunch, Heel, Hinge, Hip, Hough, Housing, Huck, Inseam, J, Joggle, Jolly, Junction, Knee, Knuckle, Loin, Marijuana, Meat, Mitre, Mortise, Mutton, Node, Phalange, Phalanx, Pin, Push-fit, Rabbet, Rack, Reefer, Ribroast, Roast, Saddle, Scarf, Scarph, Seam, Second, Shoulder, Silverside, Sirloin, Soaker, Splice, Stifle, Straight, Strip, Synchondrosis, Syndesmosis, T, Tarsus, T-bone, Teamwork, Temperomandibular, Tenon, Together, Toggle, Tongue and groove, Topside, Trochite, Undercut, Union, Universal, Water, Wedging, Weld, Wrist

Joist Bar, Beam, Dormant, Ground plate, Groundsill, I-beam, Rib, Sleeper, Solive, String

Joke(r), Joke-book, Joking Banter, Bar, Baur, Bawr, Boff, Booby-trap, Card, Chaff, Chestnut, →**CLOWN**, Cod, Comedian, Comic, Corn, Crack, Cut-up, Facete, Farceur, Farceuse, Fool, Fun, Funster, Gab, Gag(ster), Gamester, Gleek, Glike, Guy, Have-on, Hazer, Hoax, Hum, Humorist, In fun, Jape, Jest, Jig, Jocular, Josh, Knock-knock, Lark, Legpull, Merry-andrew, Merryman, One-liner, Practical, Prank(ster), Pun, Punchline, Quip, Rag, Raillery, Rib-tickler, Rot, Sally, Scherzo, Scream, Sick, Skylark, Squib, Standing, Throwaway, Tongue-in-cheek, Wag, Wheeze, Wild, Wisecrack, Wit

Jollity, Jolly, Jollification 'Arryish, Bally, Beano, Bright, Cheerful, Convivial, Cordial, Dashed, Do, Festive, Galoot, Gaucie, Gaucy, Gawcy, Gawsy, Gay, Hilarious, Jocose, Jovial, Marine, Mirth, Rag, Revel, RM, Roger, Sandboy, Sight, Tar, Trip, Very

Jolt(ing) Bump, Jar, Jig-a jig, Jog(gle), Jostle, Jounce, Jumble, Shake, Shog, Start
▶**Joseph** *see* **JOE(Y)**

Josh Chaff, Kid, Rib, Tease

Jostle Barge, Bump, Compete, Elbow, Hustle, Jockey, Push, Shoulder, Throng

Journal Band(e), Blog, Chronicle, Daily, Daybook, Diary, E-zine, Gazette, Hansard, Lancet, Log, Mag, Organ, Paper, Periodical, Pictorial, Punch, Rag, Record, Reuter, Trade, Waste book, Webzine

Journalism, Journalist Cheque-book, Columnist, Commentariat, Contributor, Diarist, Ed, Fleet St, Freelance, (GA) Sala, Gazetteer, Gonzo, Grub Street, Hack, Hackery, Hackette, Interviewer, Investigative, Keyhole, Leader-writer, Lobby, Marat, Muckraker, Newshound, Newsman, Northcliffe, NUJ, Penny-a-liner, Pepys, Press(man), Reporter, Reviewer, Scribe, Sob sister, Stead, Stringer, Wireman, → **WRITER**, Yellow

Journey Bummel, Circuit, Cruise, Errand, Expedition, Eyre, Foray, Hadj, Jaunce, Jaunse, Jaunt, Lift, Long haul, Mush, Nestos, Odyssey, Passage, Peregrination, Periegesis, Pilgrimage, Ply, Raik, Rake, Red-eye, Ride, Round trip, Route, Run, Sabbath's-day, Sentimental, Soup run, Step, Swag, Tour, Travel, Trek, Trip, Voyage, Walkabout, Wend

Journeyman Artisan, Commuter, Craftsman, Sterne, Trekker, Yeoman

Joust Pas d'armes, Tilt, Tiltyard, Tournament, Tourney

Jovial Bacchic, Boon, Convivial, Cordial, Festive, Genial, Jolly, Merry

Joy(ful), Joyous Ah, Beatific, Blithe, Charmian, Cheer, → **DELIGHT**, Dream, Ecstasy, Elation, Exhilaration, Exulting, Fain, Felicity, Festal, Frabjous, Glad, Glee, Gloat, Groove, Hah, Happy, Hey, Joie de vivre, Jubilant, Nirvana, Rapture, Schadenfreude, Sele, Tra-la, Transport, Treat, Yahoo, Yay, Yippee

Jubilant, Jubilation, Jubilee Celebration, Cock-a-hoop, Diamond, Ecstatic, Elated, Holiday, Joy, Triumphant

Judas Double-crosser, Traitor, Tree

Judder Put-put, Shake, Vibrate

Judge(ment), Judges Absolute, Adjudicator, Appraise, Arbiter, Arbitrate, Assess, Assize, Award, Believe, Bench, Calculate, Chancellor, Chief Justice, Commonsense, Connoisseur, Consider, Coroner, Court, Criterion, Critic(ise), Dayan, Decide, Dempster, Depth, Determine, Dies irae, Dies non, Doom(ster), Esteem, Estimate, Evaluate, Faisal, Faysal, Gauge, Guess, Hearing, Honour, Interlocutor, J, Justice, Kadi, Line, Lord Chief Justice, Opinion, Provisional, Puisne, Ragnarok, Rate, Reckon(ing), Recorder, Ref(eree), Regard, Second guess, Sentence, Sheriff, Sizer, Sober, Solomon, Stipendiary, Suppose, Think, Touch, Try, Umpire, Verdict, Ween, Wig, Wine-taster, Wisdom, Worship

Judicious Critical, Diplomatic, Discreet, Politic, Rational, Sage, Sensible, Shrewd, Sound

Jug(s) Amphora, Aquamanale, Aquamanile, Bird, Blackjack, Can, Cooler, Cream(er), Crock, Ewer, Flagon, Gaol, Gotch, Jar, Pitcher, Pound, Pourer, Pourie, → **PRISON**, Quad, Quod, Sauceboat, Shop, Slammer, Stir, Toby

Juice, Juicy Aloe vera, Bacca, Cassareep, Cassaripe, Cremor, Current, Fluid, Fruity, Gastric, Hypocist, Ichor, La(b)danum, Laser, Latex, Lush, Must, Nectar, Oil, Pancreatic, Perry, Petrol, Ptisan, Rare, Sap, Snake, Soma, Spanish, Stum, Succulent, Succ(o)us, Thridace, Vril, Zest

Jumble Cast offs, Chaos, Conglomeration, Farrago, Gallimawfry, Garble, Hodge-podge, Huddle, Jabble, Lumber, Mass, Medley, Mingle-mangle, Mish-mash, Mixter-maxter, Mixture, Pasticcio, Pastiche, Praiseach, Raffle, Ragbag, Scramble, Shuffle, Wuzzle

▷**Jumbled** *may indicate* an anagram

Jumbo Aircraft, Colossal, Elephant, Huge, Jet, Large-scale, Mammoth, OS, Plane, Vast

Jump(er), Jumping, Jumpy Ambush, Antelope, Aran, Assemble, Axel, Base, Batterie, Bean, Boomer, Bound, Broad, Bungee, Bungy, Bunny-hop, Caper, Capriole, Cicada, Cicata, Crew-neck, Cricket, Croupade, Daffy,

Desultory, Entrechat, Euro, Eventer, Flea, Fosbury flop, Frog, Gansey, Gazump, Gelande(sprung), Grasshopper, Guernsey, Halma, Handspring, Helicopter, High, Hurdle, Impala, Itchy, Jersey, Joey, Jolly, Kangaroo, Katydid, Kickflip, Knight, Lammie, Lammy, Leap(frog), Lep, Long, Loop, Lope, Lutz, Nervous, Nervy, Ollie, Pallah, Para, Parachute(r), Pig, Pogo, Polo-neck, Pounce, Prance, Prank, Pronking, Puissance, Quantum, Quersprung, Rap, Roo, Salchow, Saltatory, Saltigrade, Saltus, Scissors, Scoup, Scowp, Shy, Skip, Skipjack, Skydiver, → **SPRING**, Star, Start, Steeplechaser, Straddle, Sweater, Tanktop, Toe(-loop), Trampoline, Triple, Turtle-neck, Vau(l)t, V-neck, Volatile, Water, Western roll

Junction Abutment, Alloyed, Box, Bregma, Carfax, Circus, Clapham, Clover-leaf, Connection, Crewe, Crossroads, Intersection, Joint, Josephson, Knitting, Meeting, Node, Point, Raphe, Rhaphe, Roundabout, Spaghetti, Stage, Suture, Synapse, T, Turn off, Union

Jungle Asphalt, Blackboard, Boondocks, Bush, Concrete, Forest, Maze

Junior Cadet, Dogsbody, Filius, Fils, Gofer, Office, Petty, Scion, Second fiddle, Sub(ordinate), Underling, Younger

Junk(ie), Junkshop Addict, Bric-à-brac, Fiddle-de-dee, Glory hole, Glue-sniffer, Jettison, Litter, Lorcha, Lumber, Refuse, Schmeck, Ship, Shmek, Spam, Tatt, Trash, Tripe, User

▷**Junk** *may indicate* an anagram

Junket(ing) Beano, Celebration, Creel, Custard, Feast, Picnic, Rennet, Spree

Jurisdiction Authority, Bailiwick, Domain, Pashalic, Pashalik, Province, Soke(n), Sucken, Verge

Juror(s), Jurist, Jury Array, Assize, Blue-ribbon, Dicast, Grand, Hung, Inquest, Judges, Man, Mickleton, Old Fury, Pais, Panel, Panellist, Party, Petit, Petty, Sail, Savigny, Special, Strike, Tales, Talesman, Tribunal, Venire, Venireman, Venue

Just(ice) Adeel, Adil, Alcalde, All, Aristides, Astraea, Balanced, Barely, By a nose, Condign, Cupar, Deserved, E(v)en, Equal, Equity, Ethical, Even-handed, Exactly, Fair, Fair-minded, Forensic, Hardly, Honest, Impartial, Incorruptible, J, Jasper, Jeddart, Jethart, Jurat, Kangaroo, Legitimate, Mere(ly), Moral, Natural, Nemesis, Newly, Nice, Only, Palm-tree, Piso, Poetic, Precisely, Provost, Puisne, Pure and simple, Quorum, Reasonable, Recent, Restorative, Right(ful), Righteous, Rightness, Rough, Shallow, Silence, Simply, Solely, Sommer, Street, Themis, Tilt, Unbiased, Upright

Justifiable, Justification, Justify Apology, Autotelic, Avenge, Aver, Avowry, Clear, Darraign(e), Darrain(e), Darrayn, Defend, Deraign, Deserve, Excusable, Explain, Grounds, Merit, Pay off, Raison d'être, Rationale, Reason, Vindicate, Warrant

Jut(ting) Beetle, Bulge, Condyle, Overhang, Project, Protrude, Sail

Juvenile Childish, Pupa, Teenage(r), Yonkers, Young, Younkers, Youth

Kk

K Kelvin, Kilo, King, Kirkpatrick

Kangaroo Bettong, Boodie-rat, Boomer, Boongary, Bounder, Cus-cus, Diprotodont, Euro, Forester, Joey, Macropodidae, Nototherium, Old man, Potoroo, Rat, Steamer, Tree, Troop, Wallaby, Wallaroo

Karate (costume) Gi(e), Kung Fu, Shotokan, Wushu

Karma Destiny, Fate, Predestination

Kebab Cevapcici, Gyro, Impale, Satay, Sate, Shashli(c)k, Souvlakia

Keel Bilge, Bottom, Carina, Centreboard, Cheesecutter, Daggerboard, Even, Faint, False, Fin, List, Overturn, Skeg(g), Sliding

Keen(ness), Keener Acid, Acuity, Acute, Agog, Ardent, Argute, Aspiring, Astute, Athirst, Avid, Aygre, Bemoan, Bewail, Breem, Breme, Cheap, Coronach, Cutting, Dash, Devotee, Dirge, Eager, Edge, Elegy, Enthusiastic, Fanatical, Fell, Game, Gleg, Greet, Grieve, Hone, Hot, Howl, Into, Itching, Lament, Mourn, Mustard, Mute, Narrow, Nuts, Ochone, Ohone, Overfond, Partial, Peachy, Penetrating, Perceant, Persant, Pie, Raring, Razor, Ready, Red-hot, Rhapsodic, Sharp, Shrewd, Shrill, Slavering, Snell, Thirsting, Threnodic, Thrillant, Trenchant, Ululate, Wail, Whet, Zeal(ous)

Keep(er), Keeping, Kept Ames, Armature, Austringer, Caretaker, Castellan, Castle, Celebrate, Chatelain(e), Citadel, Conceal, Conserve, Curator, Custodian, Custody, Custos, Depositary, Depository, Detain, Donjon, Escot, Fastness, Finder, Fort, Gaoler, Goalie, Guard(ian), Harbour, Have, Hoard, → **HOLD**, Maintain, Nab, Net, Observe, On ice, Ostreger, Own, Park, Perpetuate, Pickle, Preserve, Retain, Safe, Safeguard, Save, Stay, Stet, Stock, Store, Stow, Stronghold, Stumper, Support, Sustain, Tower (of London), Warden, Withhold

Keepsake Memento, Relic, Souvenir, Token

Keg(s) Barrel, Cask, Ks, Tub, Tun, Vat

Kennel(s) Guard, Home, House, Shelter

Kerb Edge, Gutter, Roadside

Kernel Copra, Core, Grain, Nucleus, Pistachio, Praline, Prawlin

Kestrel Bird, Hawk, Keelie, Stallion, Staniel, Stannel

Kettle Boiler, Caldron, Cauldron, Dixie, Dixy, Drum, Fanny, Pot, Turpin

Key(s), Keyhole A, Ait, Answer, Ash, Atoll, B, Backspace, Black, C, Cardinal, Cay, Chief, Claver, Clue, Command, Cornerstone, Cryptographer, D, Del(ete), E, Essential, F, Flat, Function, G, Grecque, Ignition, Important, Inch, Index, Insert, Isle(t), Ivory, Largo, Linchpin, Major, Minor, Natural, Note, Opener, Open sesame, Shift, Signature, Skeleton, Space bar, Subdominant, Swipecard, Tuning-hammer, Type, USB, West, White, Yale®

Keyboard, Keypad Azerty, Calliope, Console, Digitorium, Dvorak, Manual, Martenot, Numeric(al), Piano, Pianola®, Qwerty, Spinet

Kick(ing) Abandon, Back-heel, Banana, Bicycle, Boot, Buzz, Corner, Dribble, Drop, Fling, Flutter, Fly, Free, Frog, Garryowen, Goal, Grub, Hack, Heel, High, Hitch, Hoof, Lash, Nutmeg, Pause, Penalty, Pile, Place, Punce, Punt, Recalcitrate, Recoil, Recoyle, Renounce, Savate, Scissors, Shin, Sixpence, Speculator, Spice, Spot, Spur, Spurn, Squib, Stab, Tanner, Tap, Thrill, Toe, Up and under, Vigour, Volley, Wince, Yerk, Zip

Kid(s) Arab, Bamboozle, Befool, Billy, Brood, Chaff, Cheverel, Cheveril, Chevrette, Child, Chit, Con, Delude, Doeskin, Fox, Giles, Goat, Hoax, Hocus, Hoodwink, Hum, Joke, Josh, Leather, Mag, Minor, Misguide, Nappe, Nipper, Offspring, Pretend, Rag, Rib, Small fry, Spoof, Sprig, Suede, Sundance, →**TEASE**, Tot, Trick, Whiz(z), Wiz

Kidnap(per), Kidnapped Abduct, Captor, Enleve, Hijack, Nobble, Plagium, Snatch, Spirit, Steal

Kill(ed), Killer, Killing Asp, Assassin, Axeman, Bag, Behead, Booth, Bump off, Butcher, Carnage, Category, Choke, Coup de grâce, Croak, Crucify, Cull, Curiosity, Cut-throat, Deep six, Despatch, Destroy, Do in, Electrocute, Eradicate, Euthanasia, Execute, Exhibition, Exterminate, Fallen, Garotte, Gun(man), Handsel, Hara kiri, Hatchet man, Hilarious, Homicide, Honour, Howitzer, Humane, Ice, Infanticide, Insecticide, Jugulate, Knacker, Knock off, Liquidate, Lynch, Mactation, Mercy, Misdo, Mortify, Murder, Necklace, Penalty, Pesticide, Pick off, Pogrom, Predator, Put down, Quell, Sacrifice, Serial, Shoot up, Slaughter, Slay(er), Slew, Smite, Spike, Strangle, Take out, Thagi, Thug(gee), Top, Toreador, Total, Vandal, Veto, Waste, Written off, Zap

Kilt Drape, Filabeg, Fustanella, Plaid, Tartan

Kin(ship), Kin(sman) Ally, Family, Kith, Like, Nearest, Phratry, Relation

Kind(ly) Akin, Amiable, Avuncular, Benefic, Benevolent, Benign, Boon, Breed, Brood, Brotherly, Category, Class, Clement, Considerate, Doucely, Favourable, Gender, Generic, Generous, Genre, Gentle, Genus, Good, Good-natured, Gracious, Human, Humane, Ilk, Indulgent, Kidney, Kin, Lenient, Manner, Merciful, Modal, Nature, Sisterly, Species, Strain, Strene, Thoughtful, Trine, Type, Understanding, Variety, Well-disposed, Ylke

Kindle, Kindling Accend, Fire, Ignite, Incense, Incite, Inflame, Kitten, →**LIGHT**, Litter, Lunt, Spark, Stimulate, Teend, Tind, Tine

King(s), Kingly Ard-ri(gh), Butcher, Card, Cobra, Csar, English, ER, Evil, Face card, Highness, Kong, Ksar, Majesty, Monarch, Negus, Pearly, Peishwa(h), Penguin, Peshwa, Pharaoh, Philosopher, Potentate, R, Raja, Ransom, Reigner, Rex, Rial, Roi, Royalet, Ruler, Ryal, Sailor, Seven, Shah, Shepherd, Shilling, Sophy, Sovereign, Stork, Tsar, Tzar

Kingdom, Kingship An(n)am, Animal, Aragon, Arles, Armenia, Ashanti, Assyria, Austrasia, Babylonia, Barataria, Belgium, Bhutan, Bohemia, Brandenburg, Brunel, Buganda, Burgundy, Dahomey, Darfur, Denmark, Domain, Dominion, Edom, Elam, Fife, Galicia, Gwynedd, He(d)jaz, Heptarchy, Hijaz, Jordan, Kongo, Latin, Lydia, Lyonnesse, Macedon(ia), Media, Mercia, Meroe, Mineral, Moab, Murcia, Naples, Navarre, Nepal, Noricum, Nubia, Numidia, Parthia, Phyla, Pontic, Protista, Pruce, Prussia, Rayne, Realm, Reich, Reign, Royalty, Sardinia, Saul, Siam, Sphere, Sweyn, Throne, Tonga, UK, Ulster, Vegetable, Wessex, Westphalia, World

Kink(y) Bent, Buckle, Crapy, Enmeshed, Flaw, Gasp, Knurl, Null, Nurl, Odd, Perm, Perverted, Quirk, SM, Twist, Wavy

▷**Kink(y)** *may indicate* an anagram

Kiosk Booth, Call-box, Stall, Tollbooth

Kip(per) At, Cure, Dosser, Doze, Limey, Nap, Nod, → SLEEPER, Sleepyhead, Smoke, → TIE

Kish Rubbish, Scum, Tat

Kiss(er), Kissing Air, Baisemain, Buss, Butterfly, Caress, Contrecoup, Cross, French, Graze, Lip, Mwah, Neck, Osculate, Pax(-board), Pax-brede, Peck, Pet, Plonker, Pree, Salue, Salute, Smack(er), Smooch, Smouch, Snog, Spoon, Suck face, Thimble, Tonsil hockey, Tonsil tennis, Trap, X, Yap

Kitchen Caboose, Chuck-wagon, Cookhouse, Cookroom, Cuisine, Dinette, Galley, Percussion, Scullery, Soup

Kitty Ante, Cat, Fisher, Float, Fund, Jackpot, Pool, Pot, Puss, Tronc

Knack Art, Facility, Faculty, Flair, Forte, Gift, Hang, Instinct, Nose, → TALENT, Trick

Knead Massage, Mould, Pug, Pummel, Work

Kneel(er) Defer, Genuflect, Hassock, Kowtow, Truckle

Knicker(bockers), Knickers Bloomers, Culottes, Directoire, Irving, Panties, Plus-fours, Rational dress, Shorts, Trousers

Knick-knack Bagatelle, Bibelot, Bric-à-brac, Gewgaw, Pretty(-pretty), Quip, Smytrie, Toy, Trangam, Trifle, Victoriana

Knife, Knife edge Anelace, Athame, Barlow, Barong, Bistoury, Blade, Boline, Bolo, Bolster, Bowie, Bread, Bush, Butterfly, Canelle, Carver, Carving, Case, Catling, Chakra, Chiv, Clasp, Cleaver, Couteau, Cradle, Cuttle, Cutto(e), Da(h), Dagger, Dirk, Fleam, Flick, Fruit, Gamma, Gulley, Gully, Hay, Hunting, Jockteleg, Kard, Keratome, Kukri, Lance(t), Machete, Matchet, Moon, Near thing, Oyster, Palette, Panga, Paper, Parang, Paring, Peeler, Pen, Pigsticker, Pocket, Putty, Scalpel, Scalping, Sgian-dhu, Sgian-dubh, Sheath, Shiv, Simi, Skean-dhu, Slash, Snee, Snickersnee, Spade, Stab, Stanley, Steak, Sticker, Stiletto, Swiss army, Switchblade, Table, Toothpick, Tranchet, Trench

Knight(hood) Accolon, Aguecheek, Alphagus, Artegal, Banneret, Bayard, Bedivere, Black, Bliant, Bors, Britomart, Caballero, Calidore, Cambel, Caradoc, Carpet, Cavalier, Chevalier, Chivalry, Companion, Crusader, Douceper, Douzeper, Dub, Equites, Errant, Galahad, Gallant, Gareth, Garter, Gawain, Giltspurs, Gladys, Guyon, Hospitaller, Jedi, Kay, KB, KBE, KG, King's, Lamorack, La(u)ncelot, Launfal, Lionel, Lochinvar, Lohengrin, Maecenas, Malta, Mark, Medjidie, Melius, Modred, N, Noble, Orlando, Paladin, Palmerin, Palomides, Papal, Paper, Parsifal, Perceforest, Perceval, Percival, Pharamond, Pinel, Queen's, Red Cross, Ritter, Samurai, Sir, Tannhauser, Templar, Teutonic, Tor, Trencher, Tristan, Tristram, Valvassor, Vavasour, White

Knit(ting), Knitter, Knitwear Cardie, Cardigan, Contract, Crochet, Entwine, Hosiery, Intarsia, Intertwine, Jersey, Jumper, Marry, Mesh, Porosis, Pullover, Purl, Seam, Set, Stockinet, Sweater, Tricoteuse, Unite, Weave, Woolly, Wrinkle

Knob(by) Berry, Boll, Boss, Botoné, Bottony, Bouton, Bur(r), Cam, Caput, Cascabel, Croche, Handle, Heel, Hill, Inion, Knur(r), Mouse, Mousing, Node, Noop, Pellet, Pommel, Protuberance, Pulvinar, Snib, Snub, Snuff, Stud, Torose, Trochanter, Tuber, Tuner, Wildfowl

Knock(er), Knockabout, Knocked, Knock(ed) down, (off, out), Knockout Aunt Sally, Bang, Beaut, Biff, Blow, Bonk, Bump, Ca(a), Chap, Chloroform, Clash, Clour, Collide, Con, Criticise, Dad, Daud, Dawd, Degrade, Denigrate, Dent, Deride, Dev(v)el, Ding, Dinnyhauser, Dod, Elimination, Etherise, Eyeful, Floor, Grace-stroke, → HIT, Innings, KD, King-hit, Knap, KO,

Lowse, Lowsit, Manhandle, Mickey Finn, Mud-slinger, Pan, Pink, Quietus, Rap, Rat-tat, Semi-final, Skittle, Socko, Spat, Steal, Stop, Stoun, Strike, Stun(ner), Sucker punch, Tap, Technical, Thump, Tit(s), Wow

Knot(ted), Knotty Apollo, Baff, Band, Bend, Bind, Blackwall hitch, Bow, Bowline, Bur(r), Burl, Carrick-bend, Cat's paw, Clinch, Clove hitch, Cluster, Crochet, Diamond hitch, Englishman's, Entangle, Figure of eight, Fisherman's (bend), Flat, French, Geniculate, Gnar, Gordian, Granny, Half-hitch, Harness hitch, Hawser-bend, Herculean, Hitch, Interlace, Knag, Knap, Knar, Knob, Knur(r), Loop, Love(r's), Macramé, Macrami, Magnus hitch, Marriage-favour, Matthew Walker, Mouse, Nirl, Node, Nowed, Nub, Nur(r), Overhand, Peppercorn, Picot, Porter's, Problem, Prusik, Quipu, Reef, Rolling hitch, Root, Rosette, Running, Seizing, Sheepshank, Sheetbend, Shoulder, Shroud, Sleave, Slip, Slub, Spurr(e)y, Square, Stevedore's, Surgeon's, Sword, Tangle, Tat, Thumb, Tie, Timberhitch, Torose, Truelove, True lover's, Tubercle, Turk's head, Virgin, Wale, Wall, Weaver's (hitch), Windsor, Witch

Know(how), Knowing(ly), Knowledge(able), Known Acquaintance, Aptitude, Au fait, Autodidactic, Aware, Cognition, Compleat, Comprehend, Cred, Cum-savvy, Epistemics, Erudite, Experience, Expertise, Famous, Fly, Gnosis, Gnostic, Have, Hep, Hip, Info, Information, Insight, Intentional, Intuition, Jnana, Ken(t), Kith, Kydst, Lare, Light, Lore, Mindful, Omniscience, On, Pansophy, Party, Polymath, Positivism, Privity, Realise, Recherché, →**RECOGNISE**, Resound, Sapient, Savvy, Science, Scilicet, Sciolism, Sciosophy, Shrewd, Smartarse, Smattering, Suss, Technology, Telegnosis, Understand(ing), Up, Versed, Wat(e), Weet(e), Well-informed, Well-read, Wis(dom), Wise(acre), Wist, Wit, Wonk, Wost, Wot

Ll

L Latitude, League, Learner, Left, Length, Liberal, Lima, Litre, Long, Luxembourg, Pound

Label Band, Book-plate, Brand, Care, Designer, Docket, File, Indie, Mark, Name tag, Own, Seal, Sticker, Style, Tab, Tag, Tally, Ticket, Trace

Laboratory Elaboratory, Lab, Language, Skunkworks, Skylab, Space-lab, Studio, Workshop

Labour(er), Laboured, Laborious Agonise, Apronman, Arduous, Begar, Birth, Bohunk, Carl, Casual, Childbirth, Chore, Churl, Confinement, Corvée, Cottager, Cottar, Culchie, Dataller, Donkey work, Dwell, Effort, Emotional, Farmhand, Gandy-dancer, Ganger, Gibeonite, Grecian, Grind, Grunt, Hard, Hercules, Hod carrier, Hodge, Ida, Job, Journeyman, Kanaka, Katorga, Leaden, Manpower, Moil, Navvy, Nemean, New, Okie, Operose, Pain, Peon, Pioneer, Prole, Redneck, Roll, Roustabout, Rouster, Seagull, Serf, Sisyphean, Slave, Stertorous, Stint, Strive, Struggle, Sudra, Sweated, Task, Tedious, Tiresome, →**TOIL(S)**, Toss, Travail, Uphill, Vineyard, Wetback, →**WORK(ER)**, Workforce, Workmen

Labyrinth Daedalus, Maze, Mizmaze, Warren, Web

▷**Labyrinthine** *may indicate* an anagram

Lace, Lacy Alençon, Babiche, Beat, Blonde, Bobbin, Bone, Bourdon, Brussels, Chantilly, Cluny, Colbertine, Dash, Dentelle, Drug, Duchesse, Embraid, Entwine, Filet, Galloon, Guipure, Honiton, Inweave, Irish, Jabot, Lash, Macramé, Malines, Mechlin, Mignonette, Mode, Net, Orris, Pearlin, Picot, Pillow, Point, Queen Anne's, Reseau, Reticella, Ricrac, Rosaline, Seaming, Shoestring, Shoe-tie, Spiderwork, Spike, Stay, Tat(ting), Tawdry, Thrash, Thread, Tie, Torchon, Trim, Troll(e)y, Truss, Tucker, Valenciennes, Venise, Weave, Welt, Window-bar

Lack(ing), Lacks Absence, Ab(o)ulia, Aplasia, Bereft, Catalexis, Dearth, Decadent, Devoid, Famine, Gap, Ha'n't, Manqué, Meagre, Minus, →**NEED**, Paucity, Poor, Poverty, Privation, Remiss, Sans, Shortage, Shortfall, Shy, Sterile, Void, Want

Lackey Boots, Doormat, Flunkey, Lapdog, Moth, Page, Poodle, Stooge, Underling

Lacquer Coromandel, Enamel, Japan, Shellac, →**VARNISH**

Lad Boy(o), Bucko, Callan(t), Chiel(d), Child, Geit, Gyte, Knight, Loonie, Master, Nipper, Shaver, Stableman, Stripling, Tad, Whipper-snapper

Ladder(y) Accommodation, Bucket, Companion, Companionway, Etrier, Extension, Jack, Jacob's, Pompier, Potence, Rope, Run, Salmon, Scalado, Scalar, Scaling, Step, Stie, Sty, Stye, Trap, Turntable

▶**Lade** *see* **LOAD(ED)**

Ladle Bail, Dipper, Divider, Scoop, Toddy

Lady, Ladies Baroness, Bevy, Bountiful, Burd, Chatelaine, Dame, Dark, Don(n)a, Duenna, Female, Frau, Frow, Gemma, Godiva, Hen, Khanum, Lavatory, Leading, Loo, Luck, Maam, Madam(e), Martha, Memsahib, Nicotine, Palsgravina, Peeress, Powder room, Señ(h)ora, Signora, Slate, Tea, WC, Windermere

▷**Lady** *may indicate* an '-ess' ending

▷**Ladybird** *may indicate* a female of a bird family

Lair Couch, Den, Earth, Haunt, Hideaway, Holt, Kennel, Lodge, Spiv, Warren

Lake(s) Alkali, Basin, Bayou, Carmine, Crater, Crimson, Epilimnion, L, Lacustrine, Lagoon, Lagune, Limnology, →**LOCH**, Lochan, Lode, Lough, Madder, Meer, Mere, Natron, Nyanza, Ox-bow, Poets, Pond, Pool, Pothole, Red, Reservoir, Salt, Shott, Tank, Tarn, Vlei, Zee

Lamb(skin) Baa, Barometz, Beaver, Budge, Bummer, Cade, Canterbury, Caracul, Cosset, Ean(ling), Elia, Fell, Innocent, Keb, Larry, Noisette, Paschal, Persian, Poddy, Rack, Shearling, Target, Yean(ling)

Lame(ness) Accloy, Claude, Cripple, Crock, Game, Gammy, Gimp(y), Halt, Hamstring, Hirple, Hors de combat, Maim, Main, Spavined, Springhalt, Stringhalt, Useless, Weak

Lament(able), Lamentation, Lamenter Bemoan, Bewail, Beweep, Boo-hoo, Complain, Croon, Cry, Deplore, Dire, Dirge, Dumka, Elegy, Funest, Jeremiad, Jeremiah, Keen, Meane, Mein, Mene, Moon, Mourn, Ochone, Paltry, Piteous, Plain(t), Regret, Repine, Sorry, Threne, Threnody, Ululate, →**WAIL**, Wel(l)away, Welladay, Yammer

Lamina(te), Laminated Film, Flake, Folium, Formica®, Lamella, Layer, Plate, Scale, Table, Tabular, Veneer

Lamp(s) Aladdin's, Aldis, Anglepoise, Arc-light, Argand, Blow, Bowat, Bowet, Buat, Cru(i)sie, Crusy, Davy, Daylight, Discharge, Diya, Eye, Eyne, Flame, Fluorescent, Fog, Gas, Geordie, Girandole, Glow, Head, Hurricane, Incandescent, Induction, Kudlik, Lampion, Lantern, Lava, Lucigen, Mercury vapour, Miner's, Moderator, Neon, Nernst, Nightlight, Padella, Pendant, Photoflood, Pilot, Platinum, Quartz, Reading, Riding, Safety, Sanctuary, Scamper, Searchlight, Signal, Sodium, Sodium-vapour, Spirit, Standard, Street, Stride, Striplight, Strobe, Stroboscope, Sun, Tail, Tantalum, Tiffany, Tilley, Torch, Torchier(e), Tungsten, Uplight(er), Veilleuse, Xenon

Lampoon Caricature, Parody, Pasquil, Pasquin(ade), Satire, Send-up, Skit, Spoof, Squib

Lance Dart, Harpoon, Impale, Morne, Pesade, Pike, Prisade, Prisado, Rejôn, Sand-eel, Spear, Speisade, Thermic

Land(s), Landed Acreage, Alight, Alluvion, Bag, Beach, Brownfield, Byrd, Common, Corridor, Country, Croft, Crown, Curtilage, Debatable, Demain, Demesne, Disbark, Disembark, Ditch, Dock, Earth, Enderby, Estate, Fallow, Farren, Farthingland, Fee, Feod, Feoff, Feud, Fief, Freeboard, Gair, Glebe, Gore, Graham, Greenfield, Ground, Hide, Holding, Holm, Holy, Horst, Ind, Innings, Isle, Isthmus, Kingdom, La-la, Lathe, Lea, Leal, Ley, Light, Link, Maidan, Manor, Marginal, Marie Byrd, Mesnalty, Moose pasture, Mortmain, Nation, Net, Never-never, Nod, No man's, Odal, Onshore, Oxgang, Oxgate, Pakahi, Palmer, Panhandle, Parcel, Pasture, Peneplain, Peneplane, Peninsula, Piste, Plot, Point, Polder, Premises, Private, Promised, Property, Public, Purlieu, Queen Maud, Real estate, Realm, Realty, Reservation, Run, Runrig, Rupert's, Ruritania, Seigniory, Set-aside, Settle, Several, Smallholding, Soil, Spit, Splash down, Tack, Tenement, Terra(e), Terra-firma, Terrain, Territory, Tie, Touchdown, Udal, Unship, Ure, Van Diemen's, Veld(t), Victoria, Waste, Wilkes

Landing (craft, gear, stair, system) Autoflare, Duck, Forced, Gha(u)t, Halfpace, LEM, Module, Oleo, Omaha, Pancake, Pier, Quay, Quayside, Roman candle, Soft, Solar, Sol(l)er, Sollar, Splashdown, Three-point, Touchdown, Undercarriage

Landlord, Land owner Absentee, Balt, Boniface, Copyholder, Fiar, Franklin, Herself, Host, Innkeeper, Junker, Laird, Lessor, Letter, Owner, Patron, Proprietor, Publican, Rachman, Rentier, Squatter, Squattocracy, Squire, Yeoman

Landscape Karst, Paysage, Picture, Saikei, Scene, Stoss and lee

Landslide, Landfall Avalanche, Earthfall, Éboulement, Lahar, Scree

Lane(s) Alley, Bikeway, Boreen, Bus, Carriageway, Corridor, Crawler, Drury, Express, Fast, Fetter, Gut, La, Loan, Lois, Loke, Lovers', Memory, Middle, Mincing, Nearside, Offside, Passage, Passing, Petticoat, Pudding, Ruelle, Sea-road, Twitten, Twitting, Vennel, Wynd

Language(s) Argot, Armoric, Artificial, Assembly, Auxiliary, Backslang, Basic, Body, Cant, Centum, Clinic, Community, Comparative, Computer, →**COMPUTER LANGUAGE**, Demotic, Descriptive, Dialect, Estem, Georgian, Gothic, Heritage, High-level, Humanities, Idioglossia, Idiom, Inclusive, Jargon, Legalese, Lingo, Lingua franca, Macaronic, Median, Meta-, Mobspeak, Neutral, Newspeak, Object, Parlance, Patois, Penutian, PERL, Pidgin, Plain, Pragmatics, Procedural, Programming, Prose, Rabbinic, Register, Rhetoric, Satem, Semitic, Sign, Slanguage, →**SPEECH**, Strong, Style, Symbolic, Target, Technobabble, Telegraphese, Terms, Tone, →**TONGUE**, Tropology, Tushery, Verbiage, Vernacular, Vocabulary, Wawa, Words, World

Languid, Languish Die, Divine, Droop, Feeble, Flagging, Listless, Lukewarm, Lydia, Melancholy, Mope, Quail, Torpid, Wilt, Wither

Lanky Beanpole, Gangly, Gawky, Lean(y), Spindleshanks, Windlestraw

Lantern Aristotle's, Bowat, Bowet, Buat, Bull's eye, Chinese, Dark(e)y, Epidiascope, Episcope, Glim, Jaw, Lanthorn, Magic, Sconce, Stereopticon, Storm

Lap Drink, Gremial, Leg, Lick, Lip, Luxury, Override, Pace, Sypher

▷**Lapdog** *may indicate* 'greyhound'

Lapse Aberration, Drop, Error, Expire, Fa', Failure, Fall, Nod, Sliding, Trip

Large(ness), Largest Ample, Astronomical, Big, Boomer, Bulky, Bumper, Buster, Colossus, Commodious, Considerable, Decuman, Enormous, Epical, Extensive, Gargantuan, →**GIGANTIC**, Ginormous, Gog, Great, Grit, Gross, Handsome, Hefty, Helluva, Huge, Hulking, Humdinger, Humongous, Humungous, Kingsize, L, Labour intensive, Lg, Lunker, Macrocephaly, Magog, Man-sized, Massive, Maximin, Maximum, Mega, Outsize, Plethora, Prodigious, Rotund, Rounceval, Rouncival, Scrouger, Skookum, Slew, Slue, Snorter, Sollicker, Spacious, Spanking, Stonker, Stout, Swingeing, Tidy, Titanic, Vast, Voluminous, Well-endowed, Whopping

Largess Alms, Charity, Frumentation

Lark Adventure, Aunter, Caper, Dido, Dunstable, Exaltation, Fool, Gammock, Giggle, Guy, Laverock, Mud, Pipit, Prank, Spree

Larva Amphibiotic, Amphiblastule, Apteral, Army-worm, Axolotl, Bagworm, Bipinnaria, Bloodworm, Bookworm, Bot(t), Budworm, Caddice, Caddis(-worm), Cankerworm, Caterpillar, Chigger, Chigoe, Corn borer, Corn earworm, Cysticercoid, Doodlebug, Glass-crab, Grub, Jigger, Jointworm, Leather-jacket, Maggot, Mealworm, Measle, Microfilaria, Muckworm, Mudeye, Naiad, Nauplius, Neoteny, Ox-bot, Planula, Pluteus, Polypod, Shade, Silkworm, Spat, Tadpole, Warble, Wireworm, Witchetty, Woodworm, Xylophage, Zoea

Lascivious(ness) Crude, Drooling, Goaty, Horny, Lewd, Lubric, Paphian, Raunch(y), Satyric, Sotadic, Tentigo

Lash(ed), Lashing(s) Cat, Cilium, Firk, Flagellum, Flay, Flog, Frap, Gammon, Gripe, Knout, Mastigophora, Mousing, Oodles, Oup, Quirt, Riem, Rope's end, Scourge, Secure, Sjambok, Stripe, Swinge, Tether, Thong, Trice, Whang, →**WHIP**, Wire

Lass(ie) Colleen, Damsel, Maid, Quean, Queyn, Quin(i)e

Lasso Lariat, Lazo, Reata, Rope

Last(ing) Abide, Abye, Aft(er)most, →**AT LAST**, Boot-tree, Bottom, Cargo, Chronic, Dernier, Dure, Dying, Eleventh, Endmost, Endurance, Endure, Epilogue, Exist, Extend, Extreme, →**FINAL**, Finale, Hinder, Hindmost, Hold out, In extremis, Keep, Latest, Latter, Linger, Live, Load, Long-life, Model, Nightcap, Outstay, Perdure, Permanent, Perpetuate, Persist, Rearmost, Spin, Stable, Stamina, Stand, Stay, Supper, Survive, Swan-song, Tag end, Tail-ender, Thiller, Thule, Tree, Trump, Ult(imate), Ultima, Ultimo, Utmost, Uttermost, Wear, Weight, Whipper-in, Z

Last word(s) Amen, Envoi, Farewell, L'envoy, Ultimatum, Zythum

Latch Bar, Clicket, Clink, Espagnolette, Lock, Sneck, Thumb, Tirling-pin

Late(r), Latest After(wards), Afterthought, Anon, Behindhand, Brand-new, Chit-chat, Dead, Delayed, Eventual, Ex, Former, Gen, In arrears, Infra, Lag, Lamented, Manana, New(s), Overdue, Owl-car, Past, PM, PS, Recent, Serotine, Sine, Slow, Stop-press, Syne, Tardive, Tardy, Trendy, Umquhile, Update

Latent Concealed, Delitescent, Dormant, Maieutic, Potential

Lateral Askant, Edgeways, Sideways

Lathe Capstan, Mandrel, Mandril, Turret

Lather Flap, Foam, Froth, Sapples, Suds, Tan

Latin(ist) Biblical, Classical, Clausula, Criollo, Dog, Erasmus, High, Humanity, Italiot, L, Late, Law, Low, Medieval, Mexican, Middle, Modern, Neapolitan, New, Pig, Quarter, Rogues', Romanic, Romish, Scattermouch, Silver, Thieves', Uruguayan, Vulgar

Latitude Breadth, Celestial, Free hand, Horse, L, Leeway, Liberty, Licence, Meridian, Parallel, Play, Roaring forties, Scope, Tropic, Width, Wiggle room

Latrine Ablutions, Benchhole, Bog, Cloaca, Furphy, Garderobe, Loo, Privy, Rear

Lattice Bravais, Cancelli, Clathrate, Crystal, Espalier, Grille, Matrix, Pergola, Red, Treillage, Treille, Trellis

Laugh(ing), Laughable, Laughter Belly, Boff, Cachinnate, Cackle, Canned, Chortle, Chuckle, Cod, Corpse, Democritus, Deride, Derision, Fit, Fou rire, Gas, Gelastic, Giggle, Goster, Guffaw, Ha, He-he, Ho-ho, Homeric, Hoot, Horse, Hout, Howl, Irrision, Isaac, Jackass, Jocular, Lauch, Leuch, Levity, Mock, Nicker, Peal, Present, Riancy, Riant, Rich, Rident, Ridicule, Risus, Scream, Snigger, Snirt(le), Snort, Stitches, Tehee, Titter, Yo(c)k

Launch(ing), Launcher, Launch pad Bazooka, Begin, Blast-off, Catapult, Chuck, Countdown, Debut, Fire, Float, Hurl, Initiate, Introduce, Lift-off, Pioneer, Presentation, Release, Rolling, Send, Shipway, Shot, Slipway, →**TOSS**, Unstock, Upsend, VTO

Launder, Laund(e)rette, Laundress, Laundry Bagwash, Blanchisseuse, Clean, Clear starcher, Coin-op, Lav, Linen, Steamie, Tramp, Transfer, Wash(ery), Washhouse, Whites

Laurel(s) Aucuba, Bay, Camphor, Daphne, Kalmia, Kudos, Pichurim, Sassafras, Spicebush, Spurge, Stan, Sweet-bay

Lava Aa, Bomb, Coulée, Cysticercus, Dacite, Lahar, Lapilli, Magma, Mud, Nuée ardente, Pahoehoe, Palagonite, Pitchstone, Pumice, Pyroclast, Scoria, Tephra, Toadstone

Lavatory Ajax, Bogger, Brasco, Can, Carsey, Carzey, Cludgie, Comfort station, Convenience, Cottage, Dike, Draught, Dunnakin, Dunny, Dyke, Earth closet, Elsan®, Facilities, Forica, Furphey, Gents, Heads, Jakes, Jane, John, Kars(e)y, Karzy, K(h)azi, Kleinhuisie, Kybo, Ladies, Lat(rine), Loo, Necessary, Netty, Office, Outhouse, Pissoir, Portaloo®, Privy, Rear(s), Reredorter, Shithouse, Shouse, Siege, Smallest room, Superloo, Throne, Thunderbox, Toilet, Toot, Tout, Urinal, Washroom, WC

Lavish Barmecidal, Copious, Excessive, Expensive, Extravagant, Exuberant, Flush, Free, Fulsome, Generous, Lordly, Lucullan, Lush, Palatial, Prodigal, Profuse, Regal, Shower, Sumptuous, Unsparing, Wanton, Waste

Law(ful), Laws Act, Agrarian, Anti-trust, Ass, Association, Avogadro's, Bar, Barratry, →**BILL**, Biogenetic, Blue-sky, Bonar, Bourlaw, Boyle's, Bragg's, Brewster's, Brocard, Byelaw, Byrlaw, Cain, Canon, Capitulary, Case, Chancery, Charles's, Civil, Code, Combination, Common, Constitution, Corn, Coulomb's, Criminal, Cupar, Curie's, Cy pres, Dalton's, Dead-letter, Decree, Decretum, De Morgan's, Dharma, Dictate, Digest, Din, Distributive, Dry, Edict, Einstein's, Enact, Excise, Fiqh, Forensic, Forest, Fundamental, Game, Gas, Graham's, Gresham's, Grimm's, Grotian, Halal, Halifax, Henry's, Hess's, Homestead, Hooke's, Hubble's, Hudud, Hume's, International, Irade, Iure, Joule's, Jura, Jure, Jus, Kain, Kepler's, Kirchhoff's, Labour, Land, Lay, Legal, Leibniz's, Lemon, Lenz's, Licit, Lien, Liquor, Lor(d), Losh, Lydford, Lynch, Magdeburg, Mariotte's, Martial, May, Megan's, Mendel's, Mercantile, Military, Moral, Mosaic, Murphy's, Natural, Newton's, Nomistic, Nomology, Octave, Ohm's, Oral, Ordinance, Parity, Parkinson's, Pass, Penal, Periodic, Planck's, Plebiscite, Plod, Poor, Principle, Private, Public, Rape shield, Regulation, Rhodian, Roman, Rubric, Rule, Salic, Salique, Scout, Sharia(h), Sheria(t), Shield, Shulchan Aruch, Snell's, Sod's, Statute book, Stefan's, Stokes, Sumptuary, Sunna, Sus(s), Sword, Table, Talmud, Tenet, The (long) robe, Thorah, Thorndike's, Torah, Tort, Tradition, Twelve Tables, Ulema, Unwritten, Use, Valid, Verner's, Vigilante, Written

Lawmaker, Lawman, Lawyer Alfaqui, Att(orney), AV, Avocat, Avvogadore, Barrack room, Barrister, Bencher, BL, Bluebottle, Bramble, Brief, Bush, Cadi, Coke, Counsel, DA, Decemvir, Deemster, Defence, Dempster, Doge, Draco, Eagle(t), Enactor, Fiscal, Greenbag, Grotius, Hammurabi, Jurisconsult, Jurist, Juvenal, Legist, Mooktar, Moses, MP, Mufti, Mukhtar, Nomothete, Notary, Penang, Pettifoggers, Rabbi, Sea, Shirra, Shyster, Silk, Solicitor, Spenlow, Stratopause, Talmudist, Templar, Writer

Lawn Cambric, Cloth, Grass, Green, Linen, Ruche, Sward, Turf

Lawsuit Action, Case, Cause, Plea, Trover

▶**Lawyer(s), Lawman** *see* **LAWMAKER**

Lax(ity) Freedom, Inexact, Laissez-aller, Latitude, Lenience, Loose, Remiss, →**SLACK**, Wide

▷**Lax** *may indicate* an anagram

Lay(ing), Layman, Laic, Laid, Laity Air, Antepost, Aria, Ballad, Bed, Bet, Blow, Chant, Christian Brothers, Ditty, Drop, Earthly, Egg, Embed, Fit, Impose, Impropriator, Lied, Lodge, Man, Minstrel, Oat, Oblate, Ode, Outsider, Oviparous, Oviposit, Parabolanus, Pose, Secular, Set, Sirvente, →**SONG**, Songsmith, Sypher, Temporalty, Tertiary, Tribal, Untrained, Wager, Warp

Layer(s) Abscission, Aeuron(e), Ancona, Appleton, Battery, Bed, Boundary, Cake, Caliche, Cambium, Canopy, Chromosphere, Cladding, Coating, Crust, D, Depletion, E, Ectoplasm, Ectosarc, Ekman, Epiblast, Epilimnion, Epitaxial, Epitheca, Epithelium, Erathem, E-region, Exine, Exocarp, F, Film, Flake, Friction, Ganoin, Germ, Gossan, Gozzan, Granum, Ground, Heaviside, → **HEN**, Herb, Hypotheca, Intima, Inversion, Kennelly(-Heaviside), Kerf, Lamella, Lamina, Lap, Leghorn, Lenticle, Lie, Malpighian, Media, Mesoblast, Miocene, Ozone, Palisade, Pan, Patina, Paviour, Photosphere, Ply, Retina, Reversing, Rind, Scale, Scattering, Sclerite, Screed, Shrub, Skim, Skin, Skiver, Sliver, Spathic, Stratify, Stratopause, Stratum, Substratum, Tabular, Tapetum, Tier, Tremic, Trophoblast, Trophoderm, Uvea, Varve, Vein, Velamen, Veneer

Lay-off Dismiss, Hedge, Redundance, Suspend

Lay-out Ante, Design, Expend, Fell, Format, Map, Mise, Pattern, Spend, Spreadsheet, Straucht, Straught, Streak, Streek, Stretch

Laze, Laziness, Lazy (person), Lazybones Bed-presser, Bone idle, Bummer, Cabbage, Couch potato, Faineant, Grunge, Hallian, Hallion, Hallyon, Indolent, Inert, Lackadaisical, Laesie, Languid, Layabout, Lie-abed, Lig(ger), Lime, Lither, Loaf, Lotus-eater, Lusk, Shiftless, Sleepyhead, Sloth, Slouch, Slug(-a-bed), Sluggard, Susan, Sweer, Sweir, Timeserver, Underactive, Veg, Workshy

▷**Lazily** *may indicate* an anagram

Lead(er), Leading, Leadership Ag(h)a, Ahead, Akela, Amakosi, Arch, Article, Atabeg, Atabek, Ayatollah, Bab, Bear away the bell, Bellwether, Black, Bluey, Bodhisattva, Bonaparte, Brand, Cable, Cade, Calif, Caliph, Came, Capitano, Capo, Captain, Castro, Caudillo, Centre, Chair, Cheer, Chief, Chieftain, Chin, China white, CO, Codder, Concert-master, Condottiere, Conducive, Conduct, Corporal, Coryphaeus, Coryphee, Czar, Dalai Lama, De Gaulle, Demagogue, Dictator, Director, Dominant, Drail, Duce, Dux, Editorial, Element, Escort, Ethnarch, Extension, Figurehead, First, Flagship, Flake-white, Floor, Foreman, Foremost, Franco, Front man, Frontrunner, Fu(e)hrer, Gaffer, Gandhi, Garibaldi, General, Gerent, Go, Graphite, Guide(r), Halter, Hand, Head, Headman, Headmost, Headnote, Hegemony, Hero, Hetman, Hiawatha, Hierarch, Honcho, Idi, Imam, Imaum, Induna, Ink(h)osi, Inveigle, Jason, Jeune premier(e), Jump, Juve(nile), King, Ksar, Leam, Leash, Livid, Loss, Lost, Lyam, Lym(e), Mahatma, Mahdi, Main, Market, Marshal, Massicot, Mayor, Meer, Mehdi, Minium, Mir, Mussolini, No 1, Nomarch, Nose, Numero uno, Open, Pace car, Pacemaker, Pacesetter, Padishah, Panchen Lama, Patriarch, Pb, Petain, Pilot, Pioneer, Pit, Plummet, PM, Pointer, Precede, Precentor, Premier(e), President, Price, Primo, Rangitara, Ratoo, Rebbe, Rebecca, Red, Role, Ruler, Sachem, Sagamore, Saturn, Saturn's tree, Scotlandite, Scout, Scudler, Senior, Shaper, Sharif, Sheik(h), Sixer, Skipper, Skudler, Soaker, Soul, Sounding, Spearhead, Stalin, Staple, Star, Start, Sultan, Supremo, Taoiseach, Tenno, Tetraethyl, Top banana, Top dog, Trail(blazer), Tribune, Tsar, Up, Usher, Vaivode, Van(guard), Va(u)nt, Vaunt-courier, Voivode, Waivode, Wali, Warlord, Whip, White, Whitechapel, Wulfenite, Yeltsin, Youth

▷**Lead(s), Leaders** *may indicate* first letters of words

Leaf(y), Leaves Acanthus, Acrospire, Amphigastrium, Amplexicaul, Ascidia, At(t)ap, Baccy, Betel, Blade, Bract, Carpel, Cataphyll, Cladode, Compound, Consent, Corolla, Costate, Cotyledon, Crocket, Drop, Duff, Dutch, Fig, Finial, Foil, Foliage, Foliar, Folio(se), Folium, Frond, Frondose, Glume, Gold, Green, Holiday, Induviae, Jugum, K(h)at, Lattice, Lilypad, Lobe, Lobulus, Megaphyll,

Microphyll, Needle, Nervate, Out, P, Pad, Page, Paper, Phyllid, Phyllode, Phyllome, Pot, Qat, Recto, Repair, Riffle, Rosula, Salad, Scale, Sclerophyll, Secede, Sepal, Sheet, Siri(h), Skim, Skip, Spathe, Stipule, Succubus, Tea, Ternate, Tobacco, TTL, Unicostate, Valve, Verso, Vert, Withdraw

Leaflet At(t)ap, Bill, Bracteole, Circular, Dodger, Flier, Fly-sheet, Foliolose, Handbill, Hand-out, Pinna, Pinnula, Prophyll, Stipel, → **TRACT**

League Alliance, Amphictyony, Band, Bund, Compact, Decapolis, Delian, Denominal, Entente, Federation, Gueux, Guild, Hanse(atic), Holy, Ivy, L, Land, Little, Major, Muslim, Parasang, Primrose, Redheaded, Rugby, Solemn, Super, Union, Zollverein, Zupa

Leak(y) Bilge, Drip, Escape, Extravasate, Gizzen, Holed, Holey, Ooze, Pee, Porous, Run, Seepage, Sype, Transude, Trickle, Urinate, Wee, Weep

Lean(ing) Abut, Aslope, Atilt, Barren, Batter, Bend, Cant, Careen, Carneous, Carnose, Griskin, Heel, Hike up, → **INCLINE**, Lie, Lig(ge), List, Minceur, Partiality, Propend, Rake, Rawboned, Rely, Rest, Scraggy, Scrawny, Skinny, Spare, Stoop, Taste, Tend, Thin, Tilt, Tip, Walty, Wiry

Leap(ing), Leapt Assemblé, Bound, Brisé, Cabriole, Caper, Capriole, Cavort, Clear, Croupade, Curvet, Echappé, Entrechat, Falcade, Fishdive, Flying, Frisk, Gambade, Gambado, Gambol, Jeté, Jump, Loup, Luppen, Over, Pounce, Pronk, Quantum, Sally, Salto, Somersa(u)lt, Somerset, → **SPRING**, Transilient, Vault, Volte

Learn(ed), Learner, Learning Associative, Beginner, Blended, Blue, Bluestocking, Chela, Classical, Con, Cram, Culture, Discipline, Discover, Distance, Doctor, Don, Erudite, Erudition, Gather, Get, Glean, Greenhorn, Hear, Insight, Instrumental, Kond, L, Lear(e), Leir, Lere, Letters, Lifelong, Literate, Literati, Literato, Lore, Lucubrate, Master, Memorise, Mirza, Mug up, → **NOVICE**, Opsimath(y), Pandit, Programmed, Pundit, Pupil, Rep, Rookie, Savant, Scan, Scholar(ship), See, Sleep, Starter, Student, → **STUDY**, Tiro, Trainee, Tutee, Tyro, Visile, Wise, Wit

Lease(-holder) Charter, Farm, Feu, Gavel, Hire, Let, Long, Novated, → **RENT**, Set(t), Sublet, Subtack, Tack, Tacksman

Leash Lead, Lyam, Lym(e), Slip, Tether, Three, Trash, Triplet

Leather(s), Leather-worker, Leathery Aqualeather, Artificial, Bouilli, Bouilly, Box-calf, Brail, Buckskin, Buff, Cabretta, Calf, Capeskin, Chammy, Chamois, Chaps, Checklaton, Cheverel, Chevrette, Chrome, Cordovan, Cordwain, Corium, Counter, Cowhide, Crispin, Crocodile, Cuir(-bouilli), Currier, Deacon, Deerskin, Diphthera, Doeskin, Dogskin, Durant, Fair, Foxing, Goatskin, Grain, Hide, Hog-skin, Horsehide, Japanned, Kid, Kip(-skin), Labretta, Lacquered, Lamp, Levant, Marocain, Maroquin, Mocha, Morocco, Mountain, Nap(p)a, Neat's, Nubuck®, Oak, Ooze, Oxhide, Paste-grain, Patent, Pigskin, Plate, Rand, Rawhide, Rexine®, Riem(pie), Roan, Rock, Rough-out, Russet, Russia, Saffian, Shagreen, Shammy, Sharkskin, Shecklaton, Sheepskin, Shoe, Skiver, Slinkskin, Snakeskin, Spetch, Split, Spruce, Spur, Spur-whang, Stirrup, Strand, Strap, Strop, Suede, Tan, Taw, Thong, Upper, Wallop, Wash, Waxed, Welt, White, Whitleather, Yuft

Leave(r), Leaving(s), Leave off Abandon, Abiturient, Abscond, Absit, Absquatulate, Acquittal, Adieu, Annual, Avoid, Bequeath, Betake, Blessing, Blow, Broken meats, Bug, Compassionate, Congé, Congee, Days off, Debris, Decamp, Depart, Desert, Devisal, Devise, Ditch, Evacuate, Except, Exeat, Exit, Exodus, Extrude, Flit, Forego, Forget, Forgo, Forsake, French, Furlough, Gardening, Garlandage, Get out, → **GO**, Holiday, Inspan, Ish, Legate, Licence,

Log off, Maroon, Mass, Mizzle, Nick, Omit, Orts, Pace, Parental, Park, Part, → **PERMISSION**, Permit, → **QUIT**, Repair, Residue, Resign, Retire, Sabbatical, Scapa, Scat, Scram, Shore, Sick(ie), Skedaddle, Strand, Vacate, Vade, Vamo(o)se

Leaven Barm, Ferment, Yeast

Lecher(ous), Lechery Gate, Goaty, Lascivious, Libertine, Lickerish, Lustful, Profligate, Rake, Randy, Roué, Salaciousness, Satirisk, Satyr, Silen, Wolf

Lecture(r), Lectures, Lecturing Address, Aristotelian, Course, Creed, Curtain, Dissert(ator), Docent, Don, Earful, Erasmus, Expound, Harangue, Homily, Hulsean, Jaw, Jawbation, Jobe, L, Lantern, Lector, Moralise, Orate, Prelect, Prone, Rate, Read(er), Rede, Reith, Reprimand, Roasting, Rubber chicken circuit, Sententious, → **SERMON**, Spout, Take to task, Talk, Teacher, Teach-in, Tongue-lashing, Wigging, Yaff

Ledge Altar, Berm, Buttery-bar, Channel, Fillet, Linch, Miserere, Misericord(e), Nut, Rake, Scarcement, Settle, Sill, Subsellium

Ledger Book, General, Purchase, Register

Left (hand), Left-handed, Left-hander, Left-wing(er) Abandoned, Avoided, Balance, Bolshy, Commie, Corrie-fisted, Fellow traveller, Forsaken, Haw, Hie, High, L, Laeotropic, Laevorotation, Larboard, Links, Loony, Lorn, Marxist, Militant, Near(side), Other, Over, Pink, Pinko, Port, Prompt side, Quit, Rad, Red (Brigade), Relic, Residuum, Resigned, Secondo, Set out, Sinister, Soc(ialist), Southpaw, Split, Stage right, Thin, Titoism, Trot, Unused, Verso, Vo, Went, West, Wind, Yet

Leg(s), Leggings, Leggy, Leg-wear Antigropelo(e)s, Bandy, Barbados, Bow, Breeches, Cabriole, Cannon, Chaparajos, Chaparejos, Chaps, Crural, Crus, Cuisse, Cush, Dib, Drumstick, Fine, Gaiter, Galligaskins, Gam(b), Gamash, Gambado, Garter, Gaskin, Gigot, Gramash, Gramosh, Haunch, Hexapod, Jamb, Jambeaux, Limb, Long, Member, Milk, Myriapod, Oleo, On(side), Peg, Peraeopod, Periopod, Peroneal, Pestle, Pin, Podite, Proleg, Puttees, Pylon, Relay, Sea, Section, Shanks, Shanks's pony, Shaps, Shin, Short, Spats, Spatterdash, Spindleshanks, Square, Stage, Stifle, Stump, Thigh, Tights

Legacy Bequest, Dowry, Endowment, Entail, Heirloom

Legal(ism), Legally, Legitimate Above board, Bencher, Decriminalised, De regle, Forensic, Halacha, Halaka(h), Halakha, Lawful, Licit, Nomism, Scienter

Legend(ary) Arthurian, Caption, Edda, Fable, Folklore, Hadith, Motto, Myth, Saga, Story, Urban, Yowie

▷**Legend** *may indicate* leg-end, e.g. foot, talus

Legible Clear, Lucid, Plain

Legion(ary), Legionnaire Alauda, Army, Brigade, British, Cohort, Countless, Deserter, Foreign, Geste, Honour, → **HOST**, Maniple, Many, Throng, Zillions

Legislate, Legislation, Legislator, Legislature Assemblyman, Backbencher, Congress, Decemvir, Decree, Delegated, Diet, MP, Nomothete, Oireachtas, → **PARLIAMENT**, Persian, Senator, Supreme soviet, Thesmothete

Legume, Leguminous Bean, Guar, Lentil, Lomentum, Pea, Peanut, Pod, Pulse, Vetch

Leisure(ly) Adagio, Andantino, Bytime, Ease, Liberty, Moderato, Off day, Otium, Respite, Rest, Vacation

Lemon Answer, Cedrate, Citron, Citrus, Dud, Twist, Yellow

Lemur Angwantibo, Aye-aye, Babacoote, Bush-baby, Colugo, Cynocephalus, Galago, Half-ape, Indri(s), Loris, Macaco, Malmag, Mongoose, → **MONKEY**, Nagapie, Potto, Ringtail, Sifaka, Tana, Tarsier

Lend(er) Advance, Library, Loan, Prest, Sub, Swap line, Usurer, Vaunce

Length(y), Lengthen(ing), Lengthwise Archine, Arsheen, Arshin(e), Aune, Cable, Chain, Cubit, Distance, Eke, Ell, → **ELONGATE**, Endways, Ennage, Epenthetic, Expand, Extensive, Foot, Footage, Furlong, Inch, Ley, Longitudinal, Mile, Nail, Parsec, Passus, Perch, Piece, Plethron, Pole, Prolix, Prolong, Protract, Reach, Remen, Rigmarole, Rod, Rope, Slow, Span, Stadium, Toise, Vara, Verbose, Yard

Lenient, Lenience, Leniency Clement, Exurable, Lax, Mild, Permissive, Quarter, Soft line, Tolerant

Lens Achromatic, Acoustic, Anamorphic, Anastigmat, Bifocal, Bull's eye, Condenser, Contact, Corneal, Crookes, Crown, Crystalline, Dielectric, Diopter, Dioptre, Diverging, Electron, Eye, Eyeglass, Eye-piece, Field, Fish-eye, Gas-permeable, Gravitational, Hard, Lentil, Macro, Magnetic, Metallic, Mirror, Object(ive), Optic, Pantoscope, Soft, Stanhope, Sunglass, Telephoto, Toric, Trifocal, Wide-angle, Zoom

Leopard Catamountain, Clouded, Cougar, Jaguar, Leap, Libbard, Oceloid, Ocelot, Ounce, Panther, Pard, Snow, Spots, Tiger

Lesbian Boi, Diesel, Homophile, Lipstick, Sapphist, Tribade

Lesion Cut, Gash, Scar, Serpiginous, Sore, Ulcer, Wheal, Whelk

Less(en), Lesser, Lessening Abate, Alaiment, Attenuate, Bate, Comedown, Contract, Deaden, Decline, Deplete, Derogate, Dilute, → **DWINDLE**, Extenuate, Fewer, Junior, Littler, Meno, Minus, Play down, Reduce, Relax, Remission, Sen, Shrink, Subordinate, Subsidiary, Tail, Under

Lesson Class, Example, Lear(e), Lection, Leir, Lere, Liripipe, Masterclass, Moral, Object, Period, Sermon, Tutorial

Let (go, off, out), Letting Allow, Cap, Charter, Conacre, Displode, Divulge, Enable, Entitle, Explode, Hire, Impediment, Indulge, Leak, Lease, Litten, Loot(en), Luit(en), Lutten, Obstacle, Obstruct, → **PERMIT**, Rent, Reprieve, Sett, Unhand, Warrant

Lethal Deadly, Fatal, Fell, Mortal

Lethargic, Lethargy Accidie, Apathy, Coma, Comatose, Drowsy, Ennui, Hebetude, Inactive, Inertia, Lassitude, Limp, Listless, Logy, Passive, Sleepy, Sluggish, Stagnant, Stupor, Supine, Torpid, Turgid, Weariness

Letter(s) Ache, Aerogram, Aesc, Airgraph, Aleph, Alif, Alpha, Aspirate, Bayer, Begging, Beta, Beth, Block, Breve, Canine, Capital, Capon, Chain, Cheth, Chi, Chitty, Circular, Col, Collins, Consonant, Covering, Credentials, Cue, Cuneiform, Dead, Dear John, Delta, Digamma, Digraph, Dispatch, Dog, Dominical, Edh, Ef(f), E-mail, Emma, Encyclical, Ep(isemon), Epistle, Epistolet, Epsilon, Eta, Eth, Fan, Favour, Form, French, Gamma, Gimel, He, Heth, Hieratic, Initial, Iota, Izzard, Jerusalem, Juliet, Kaph, Kappa, Koppa, Labda, Lambda, Lamed(h), Landlady, Landlord, Lessee, Lessor, Literal, Love, Mail, Mail-shot, Majuscule, Mem, Memo, Message, Missive, Monogram, Mu, Nasal, Night, Note, Notelet, Nu, Nun, Og(h)am, Omega, Omicron, Open, Ou, Pacifical, Paragoge, Pastoral, Patent, Pe(h), Phi, Pi, Plosive, Poison-pen, Polyphone, Postbag, Psi, Pythagorean, Qof, Realtor, Rho, Rhyme, Rom, Romeo, Runestave, Sad(h)e, Samian, Sampi, San, Scarlet, Screed, Screeve, Screwtape, Script, See, Shin, Ship, Sick-note, Sigma, Sign, Signal, Sin, Sort, Stiff, Swash, Tau, Tav, Taw, Teth, Theta, Thorn, Toc, Typo, Uncial, Upsilon, Vau, Vav, Versal, Vowel, Waw, Wen, Xi, Yod(h), Yogh, Ypsilon, Zed, Zeta

Lettuce Batavia, Chicon, Corn-salad, Cos, Iceberg, Lactuca, Lamb's, Lollo rosso, Mache, Radicchio, Romaine, Salad, Sea, Thridace

Level(ler) A, Abney, Abreast, Aclinic, Aim, Bargaining, Base, Break even, Champaign, Confidence, Countersink, Degree, Dumpy, Echelon, Equal, → **EVEN**, Extent, Eye, Flat, Flush, Grade, Horizontal, Impurity, Infill, Meet, O, Par, Plain, Planation, Plane, Plat(eau), Point, Race, Rank, Rase, Raze, Savanna, Spirit, Split, Springing, → **SQUARE**, Status, Step, Stor(e)y, Stratum, Strew, Strickle, Summit, Tear-down, Tier, Trophic, Water, Wye

Lever(age) Backfall, Bell-crank, Brake, Cock, Crampon, Crowbar, Dues, Gear, Handspike, Jaw, Jemmy, Joystick, Key, Knee-stop, Landsturm, Pawl, Peav(e)y, Pedal, Pinch, Prise, Prize, Pry, Purchase, Stick, Sweep, Swipe, Tappet, Throttle, Tiller, Treadle, Treddle, Tremolo arm, Trigger, Tumbler, Typebar, Whipstaff

Levy Impose, Imposition, Leave, Militia, Octroi, Raise, Scutage, Stent, Talliate, Tax, Tithe

Lewd(ness) Bawd(r)y, Blue, Cyprian, Debauchee, Impure, Libidinous, Lubricity, Obscene, Priapism, Prurient, Raunchy, Silen(us), Tentigo, Unclean

Lexicographer, Lexicon Compiler, Craigie, Drudge, Etymologist, Florio, Fowler, Grove, Johnson(ian), Larousse, Liddell, Murray, OED, Thesaurus, Vocabulist, Webster, Words-man

Liability, Liable Anme, Apt, Chance, Debt, Incur, Limited, Open, Prone, Subject, Susceptible, White elephant

Liaison Affair, Contact, Link

Libel(lous) Blasphemous, Defamatory, Malign, Sclaunder, Slander, Smear, Sully, Vilify

Liberal(ity) Abundant, Adullamites, Ample, Besant, Bounteous, Bountiful, Breadth, Bright, Broad(minded), Catholic, Enlightened, Free(hander), Free-hearted, → **GENEROUS**, Giver, Grey, Grimond, Handsome, Indulgent, L, Largesse, Latitudinarian, Lavish, Limousine, Munificent, Octobrist, Open, Permissive, → **PROFUSE**, Rad(ical), Right on, Samuelite, Simonite, Spender, Steel, Tolerant, Trivium, Unstinted, Verlig, Verligte, Whig

Liberate(d), Liberation, Liberator Bolivar, Deliver, Dissimure, Emancipate, Fatah, → **FREE**, Gay, Inkatha, Intolerant, Messiah, Nick, PLO, Redeem, Release, Risorgimento, Save, Steal, Sucre, Unfetter, UNITA, Women's

Liberty Bail, Discretion, Franchise, Freedom, Hall, Ish, Latitude, Licence, Mill, Presumption, Sauce

Library, Librarian Bibliothecary, BL, Bodleian, Bookmobile, British, Chartered, Copyright, Cottonian, Dewey, Genomic, Harleian, Laurentian, Lending, Mazarin, Public, Radcliffe, Reference, Rental, Tauchnitz

Licence, License Abandon, Allow, Authorisation, Carnet, Charter, Dispensation, Driving, Enable, Exequatur, Fling, Franchise, Free(dom), Gale, Import, Imprimatur, Indult, → **LATITUDE**, Let, Marriage, Occasional, Passport, Patent, → **PERMIT**, Poetic, Pratique, Provisional, Road-fund, Rope, Slang, Special, Table, Ticket of leave

Lichen Apothecia, Archil, Corkir, Crotal, Crottle, Epiphyte, Epiphytic, Graphis, Korkir, Lecanora, Litmus, Moss, Oakmoss, Orcein, Orchel, Orchil(la), Orcine, Orseille, Parella, Parelle, Roccella, Rock tripe, Soredium, Stone-rag, Stone-raw, Tree-moss, Usnea, Wartwort

Lick(ing) Bat, Beat, Deer, Felch, Lambent, Lap, Leather, Rate, Salt, Slake, Speed, Trounce, Whip

Lid(ded) Cloche, Cover, Crust, Hat, Kid, Maximum, Opercula, Screwtop, Stegocarpus, Twist-off

Lie(s), Liar, Lying Abed, Accubation, Accumbent, Ananias, Bam, Bare-faced, Bask, Billy, Bounce(r), Braide, Cau(l)ker, Cellier, Clipe, Clype, Concoction, Consist, Contour, Couch(ant), Cracker, Cram(mer), Cretism, Cumbent, Deception, Decubitous, Decumbent, Direct, Doggo, Fable, Fairytale, False(r), Falsehood, Falsify, Falsity, Fib, Fiction, Figment, Flam, Gag, Gonk, Hori, Incumbent, Invention, Inveracity, Kip, Lair, Leasing, Lee(ar), Lig(ge), Lurk, Mythomania, Nestle, Obreption, Oner, Perjury, Plumper, Porky (pie), Procumbent, Prone, Prostrate, Pseudologia, Recline, Recumbent, Repent, Repose, Reptant, Ride, Romance(r), Sham, Sit, Sleep, Strapper, Stretcher, Supine, Swinger, Tale, Tappice, Tar(r)adiddle, Thumper, Tissue, Try, Untruth, Whacker, Whid, White, Whopper, Yanker

Lieutenant Flag, Loot, Lt, No 1, Sub(altern)

Life Age, Animation, Being, Bio, Biog(raphy), Biota, Breath, Brio, Chaim, Clerihew, Energy, Esse, Eva, Eve, Existence, Good, Heart, Memoir, Mortal coil, Nellie, Nelly, Night, Non-fiction, Plasma, Public, Quick, Riley, Span, Spirit, Still, Subsistence, Time, Vita, Vitality, Zoe

Lifeless(ness) Abiosis, Algidity, Amort, Arid, Azoic, Barren, Cauldrife, → **DEAD**, Dull, Flat, Inanimate, Inert, Key-cold, Log, Mineral, Possum, Stagnant, Sterile, Stonen, Vapid, Wooden

Lift(ed), Lifter, Lifting Araise, Arayse, Arsis, Attollent, Bone, Cable-car, Camel, Chair, Clean and jerk, Cly, Copy, Crane, Davit, Dead, Dumb waiter, Elate, Elevator, Enhance, Exalt, Extol, Filch, Fillip, Greaten, Heave, Heeze, Heezie, Heft(e), Heighten, Heist, Hitch, Hoise, Hoist, Hove, Jack, Jigger, Kleptomania, Leaven, Lefte, Lever, Lewis, Nab, Nap, Nim, Otis®, Paternoster, Pilfer, Pulley, → **RAISE**, Ride, Rotor, Scoop, Service, Shearlegs, Ski, Sky, Snatch, Sneak, Spout, Steal, Surface, T-bar, Thumb, Topping, Up, Winch, Windlass

Light(en), Lighter, Light holder, Lighting, Lights Aerate, Afterglow, Airglow, Airy, Albedo, Ale, Alleviate, Alow, Alpenglow, Amber, Ancient, Ans(wer), Arc, Arson, Aurora, Back-up, Barge, Batement, Beacon, Beam, Bengal, Beshine, Bezel, Birlinn, Black, Bleach, Blond(e), Brake, Breezy, Bulb, Bull's eye, Buoyant, Calcium, Candle, Canstick, Casco, Casement, Chandelier, Chiaroscuro, Cierge, Clue, Courtesy, Day(time), Dewali, Dewbow, Diffused, Direct, Diwali, Dormer, Drop, Ease, Eddystone, Electrolier, Ethereal, Eulachon, Fair, Fairy, Fall, Fan, Fantastic, Fastnet, Feathery, Fetch-candle, Fill, Filter, Fire, First, Fixed, Flambeau, Flame, Flare, Flicker, Flimsy, Flippant, Flit(t), Floating, Flood, Fluorescent, Fog (lamp), Frothy, Fuffy, Gas-poker, Glare, Gleam, Glim(mer), Glow, Gossamer, Green, Guiding, Halation, Hazard, Head, House, Idiot, Ignite, Illum(in)e, Incandescence, Indirect, Induction, Inner, Irradiate, Junior, Keel, Key, Kindle, Kiran, Klieg, Lamp, Lampadary, Lampion, Land, Lantern, Lanthorn, Laser, Leading, LED, Leerie, Lenient, Levigate, Lime, Link, Linstock, Loadstar, Lodestar, Lucarne, Lucigen, Luminaire, Lumine, Luminescence, Luminous, Lunt, Lustre, Lux, Mandorla, Match, Menorah, Mercurial, Mithra(s), Moon, Naphtha, Navigate, Navigation, Neon, New, Nit, Northern, Obstruction, Od(yl), Optics, Pale, Pane, Parhelion, Pavement, Pennyweight, Phosphorescence, Phot(ic), Photon, Photosphere, Pilot, Pipe, Polar, Pontoon, Portable, Porthole, Pra(a)m, Rainbow, Range, Rear, Red, Reflex, Relieve, Rembrandt, Reversing, Riding, Robot, Rocket, Running, Rush, Safe(ty), St Elmo's fire, Scoop, Scow, Sea-dog, Sea fire, Search, Shine, Shy, Signal, Solid-state, Southern, Southern-vigil, Sparse, Spill, Spot, Spry, Star, Steaming, Strip, Strobe, Stroboscope, Subtle, Sun (lamp), Sunshine, Svelte, Tail, Tally, Taper, Taps,

Tead, Threshold, Tind, Tine, Torch, Torchère, Touchpaper, Track, Traffic, Trivial, Ultraviolet, Unchaste, Unoppressive, UV, Ver(e)y, Vesica, Vesta, Vigil, Watch, Wax, Welsbach burner, White, → **WINDOW**, Winker, Zippo, Zodiacal

▷**Light** *may indicate* an anagram

Light-headed Captious, Dizzy, Kicksin

Lighthouse Beacon, Caisson, Eddystone, Fanal, Fastnet, Needles, Phare, Pharos, Signal, Spurn

Lightning Ball, Bolt, Catequil, Éclair, Enfouldered, Forked, Fulmination, Levin, Sheet, Summer, Thunderbolt, Wildfire, Zigzag

Like(ness), Liking Affinity, À la, Analogon, As, Assimilate, Attachment, Broo, Care, Corpse, Dig, Duplicate, Effigy, Eg, Egal(ly), Enjoy, Equal, Fancy, Fellow, Guise, Lich, Palate, Parallel, Peas, Penchant, -philus, Please, Predilection, Resemblance, Semblant, Shine, Similar, Simile, Simulacrum, Smaak, Sort, Speaking, Taste, Tiki, Uniformity

Likely, Likelihood Apt, Fair, Liable, Odds-on, On, Plausible, Possible, Probable, Probit, Prone, Prospective

Lily African, Agapanthus, Aloe, Amaryllis, Annunciation, Arum, Asphodel, Aspidistra, Belladonna, Calla, Camas(h), Camass, Canada, Candock, Chincherinchee, Colchicum, Colocasia, Convallaria, Corn, Crinum, Dale, Day, Easter, Elaine, Endogen, Fawn, Fleur de lys, Fritillary, Funkia, Galtonia, Haemanthus, Hellebore, Hemerocallis, Herb-Paris, Jacobean, Jacob's, Kniphofia, Laguna, Lent, Leopard, Lote, Lotus, Madonna, Martagon, Nelumbo, Nenuphar, Nerine, Nuphar, Nymphaea, Padma, Phormium, Plantain, Quamash, Regal, Sarsa, Scilla, Sego, Skunk cabbage, Smilax, Solomon's seal, Spider, Star of Bethlehem, Stone, Sword, Tiger, Trillium, Tritoma, Tuberose, Turk's cap, Victoria, Water, Water maize, Yucca, Zephyr

Limb Arm, Bough, Branch, Crural, Exapod, Flipper, Forearm, Hindleg, Imp, Leg, Leg-end, Member, Proleg, Ramus, Scion, Shin, Spald, Spall, Spaul(d), Wing

Lime Bass(wood), Beton, Bird, Calc, Calcicolous, Caustic, Lind(en), Malm, Mortar, Slaked, Soda, Teil, Tilia, Trap, Viscum, Whitewash

Limit(ation), Limited, Limiting Ambit, Asymptote, Basebound, Bind, Border, Bound, Boundary, Bourn(e), Brink, Cap, Cash, Ceiling, Circumscribe, Climax, Compass, Confine, Constrain, Constrict, Credit, Curb, Cut-off, Deadline, Define, Demark, Determine, Earshot, Eddington, Edge, Edition, End, Entail, Esoteric, → **EXTENT**, Extreme, Finite, Fraenum, Frontier, Gate, Goal, Height, Hourlong, Impound, Insular, Limes, Line, Lite, Lynchet, March, Maximum, Mete, Minimum, Narrow, Nth, Outedge, Pale, Parameter, Perimeter, Periphery, Predetermine, Qualify, Range, Rate-cap, Ration, Reservation, Restrict, Rim, Roof, Saturation point, Scant, Scrimp, Shoestring, Short-term, Sky, Somedeal, Somedele, Speed, Stint, String, Tail(lie), Tailye, Term(inus), Tether, Three-mile, Threshold, Thule, Tie, Time, Tramline, Tropic, Twelve-mile, Ultimate, Utmost, Utter, Verge

▷**Limit** *may indicate* 'surrounding'

Limp Claudication, Dot, Droopy, Flabby, Flaccid, Flaggy, Flimsy, Floppy, Gimp, Hamble, Hobble, Hop, Lifeless, Spancel, Tangle, Wilting

Line(d), Lines, Lining Abreast, Agate, Agonic, Allan, → **ANCESTRY**, Anent, Angle, Apothem, Arew, Assembly, Attention, Axis, Bakerloo, Bar, Barcode, Baton, Battle, Baulk, Becket, Bikini, Bluebell, Bob, Body, Bombast, Bottom, Boundary, BR, Brail, Branch, Bread, Building, Bush, By, Canal, Carriage, Casing, Cathetus, Ceil, Cento, Central, Ceriph, Chord, Ciel, Circle, Clew,

Club, Coach, Colour, Column, Command, Conga, Contour, Cord(on), Course, Crease, Credit, Crib, Crocodile, Crosshatch, Crowfoot, Crow's feet, Cunard, Curve, Cushion, Dancette, Danger, Date, Datum, Dead-ball, Decidua, Delay, Descent, DEW, Diagonal, Diameter, Diffusion, Distaff, District, Dochmiachal, Dotted, Downhaul, Dress, Dynasty, Earing, El, E-la-mi, Encase, End, Equator, Equinoctial, Equinox, Faint, Fall(s), Fathom, Fault, Feint, Fess(e), Fettle, File, Finishing, Firing, Firn, Fixed, Flex, Flight, Frame, Front, Frontier, Frost, Furr(ow), Geotherm, Germ, Gimp, Giron, Goal, Graph, Grass, Green, Gridiron, Gymp, Gyron, Hachure, Halyard, Hard, Hatching, Hawser, Header, Hemistich, Heptameter, Hexameter, High-watermark, Hockey, Hot, House, Impot, Inbounds, Inbred, Incase, Inhaul(er), Insole, Intima, Isallobar, Isobar, Isobath, Isochron(e), Isoclinic, Isoclude, Isogloss, Isogonal, Isogonic, Isogram, Isohel, Isohyet, Isomagnetic, Isometric, Isonome, Isophote, Isopiestic, Isopycnic, Isopyenal, Isotherm, Jubilee, Kill, Knittle, L, Land, Lane, Lansker, Lap, Lariat, Lasso, Lateral, Latitude, Lead, Leash, Le(d)ger, Length, Ley, Lie, Ling, LMS, Load, Log, Longitude, Lossy, Loxodrome, Lubber, Lugger, Lye, Macron, Maginot, Main, Mainsheet, Mark, Marriage, Mason-Dixon, Median, Meridian, Mesal, Metropolitan, Monofilament, Monorail, Nacre, Naman, Noose, Norsel, Northern, Number, Oche, Octastichon, Ode, Oder-Neisse, Og(h)am, Omentum, Onedin, Ordinate, Orphan, Orthostichy, Painter, Panty, Parallel, Parameter, Parastichy, Party, Paternoster, Path, Penalty, Pencil, Phalanx, Piccadilly, Picket, Pinstripe, Pipe, Plasterboard, Pleuron, Plimsoll, Plumb, Poetastery, Polar, Police, Policy, Popping-crease, Potichomania, Poverty, Power, Princess, Procession, Product(ion), Profession, Punch, Pure, Queue, Race, Radial, Radius, Rail, Rank, Raster, Ratlin(e), Ratling, Rattlin, Ray, Receiving, Red, Reticle, Retinue, Rew, Rhumb, Ripcord, Rope, Route, Row, Rule, Ry, Scazon, Score, Scotch, Scratch, Scrimmage, Script, Secant, Seperatrix, Serif, Seriph, Service, Set, Shielded, Shore, Shout, Shroud, Siding, Siegfried, Sight, Silver, Six-yard, Slur, Snow, Soft, Solidus, Sounding, Specialty, Spectral, Spider, Spilling, Spring, Spunyarn, Squall, SR, Staff, Stance, Stanza, Starting, Static, Stave, Stean, Steen, Stein, Stem, Stich(os), Stock, Story, Strain, Strap, Streak, Strene, Stretch mark, Striate, String, Stripe, Stuff, Subject, Swap, Symphysis, Tag, Tailback, Talweg, Tangent, Teagle, Tea lead, Terminator, Tetrameter, Thalweg, Thin blue, Thin red, Thread, Throwaway, Tidemark, Tie, Tier, Tiercet, Timber, Touch, Tow, Trade, Transmission, Transoceanic, Transversal, Tree, Trimeter, Tropic, Trot, Trunk, Try, Tudor, Twenty-five, Twenty-two, Upstroke, Variety, Verse, Victoria, Virgule, Wad, Wallace's, Washing, Water(shed), Waterloo, White, Widow, Windrow, Wire, World, Wrinkle, Z, Zag, Zip

Linen Amice, Amis, Barb, Bed, Byssus, Cambric, Crash, Damask, Dornick, Dowlas, Duck, Ecru, Harn, Lawn, Line, Lint, Napery, Percale, Seersucker, Sendal, Silesia, Snow, Table, Toile, Undies

Liner Artist, Bin-bag, RMS, Rule(r), Ship, Sleeve, Steamer, Steen, Titanic

Linger(ing) Dawdle, Dwell, Hang, Hove(r), Lag, Loaf, → **LOITER**, Straggle, Taigle, Tarry, Tie

Linguist(ic), Linguistics Clitic, Comparative, Descriptive, Glottic, Onomastics, Philological, Phonemics, Polyglot, Pragmatics, Semantics, Stylistics, Taxeme

Link(ed), Linking, Links Associate, Between, Bond, Bridge, Chain, Cleek, Close knit, Colligate, Concatenation, Conjunction, Connect, Copula, Couple, Course, Cuff, Desmid, Drag, Draw-gear, Ess, Flambeau, Golf (course), Hookup,

Hotline, Hyphen, Incatenation, Index, Interconnect, Interface, Internet, Interrelation, Intertwine, Karabiner, Krab, Ley-line, Liaise, Machair, Missing, Modem, Nexus, On-line, Pons, Preposition, Reciprocal, Relate, Ring, Tead(e), Terrestrial, →**TIE**, Tie-in, Tie-line, Torch, Twin, Unite, Wormhole, Yoke

Lion(ess) Androcles, Aphid, Aslan, Chindit, Elsa, Glitterati, Hero, Leo, Leopard, Literary, Maned, Nemean, Opinicus, Personage, Pride, Simba

Lip(py), Lips Backchat, Cheek, Cupid's bow, Fat, Fipple, Flews, Helmet, Jib, Labellum, Labial, Labiate, Labret, Labrum, Ligula, Muffle, Philtrum, →**RIM**, Rubies, Sass, Sauce, Slack-jaw, Spout, Submentum

Lipid Ganglioside, Inositol, Sphingarine

Liqueur, Liquor Bree, Brew, Broo, Broth, Creature, Elixir, Fumet, Hard stuff, Hooch, Lap, Mother, Ooze, Pot, Potation, Stock, Stuff, Vat

Liquid(ate), Liquidise(r), Liquidity, Liquids, Liquefaction Acetal, Amortise, Annihilate, Apprize, Aqua-regia, Bittern, Bouillon, Bromine, Cash, Condenser, Court-bouillon, Creosol, Decoction, Dope, Eluate, Erase, Ethanal, Ethanol, Ether, Eucalyptol, Fluid, Fural, Furfural, Guaiacol, Indisputable, Ink, Isoprene, Jaw, Log, Lye, Mess, Minim, Nebula, Pipe, Potion, Protoplasm, PSL, Ptisan, Purge, Quinoline, Semen, Serum, Smectic, Solution, Solvent, Syrup, Titre, Triptane, Tuberculin, Ullage, Unset, Washing-up, Whey, Wind up

List(s), Listing A, Active, Agenda, Antibarbarus, Appendix, Arena, Army, Atilt, B, Barocco, Barrace, Bead-roll, Bibliography, Border, British, Calendar, Canon, Cant, Catalog(ue), Categorise, Catelog, Cause, Check, Choice, Civil, Class, Compile, Credits, Danger, Debrett, Docket, Empanel, Entry, Enumerate, Front, Glossary, Hark, Hearken, Heel, Hit, Hit-parade, Honours, Incline, Index, Indian, Interdiction, Inventory, Itemise, Laundry, Lean, Leet, Line-up, Linked, Litany, Lloyds, Mailing, Manifest, Menu, Navy, Notitia, Official, Panel, Paradigm, Party, Payroll, Price, Prize, Register, Repertoire, Reserved, Retired, Roin, Roll, Roon, Roster, Rota, Rund, Schedule, Script, Short, Sick, Slate, Slope, Strip, Syllabary, Syllabus (of Errors), Table, Tariff, Tick, Ticket, Tilt, Timetable, Tip, To-do, Transfer, Union, Waiting, Waybill, White, Wine, Wish

▷**List** *may indicate* 'listen'

Listen(er) Attend, Auditor, Auscultate, Bug, Ear, Earwig, Eavesdropper, Gobemouche, Hark, →**HEED**, List, Lithe, Lug, Monitor, Oyez, Simon, Stethoscope, Tune-in, Wire-tap

▷**Listen to** *may indicate* a word sounding like another

Listless(ness) Abulia, Accidie, Acedia, Apathetic, Atony, Dawney, Ex-directory, Indolent, Lackadaisical, Languor, Mooning, Mope, Mopus, Sloth, Thowless, Torpor, Upsitting, Waff

▷**Lit** *may indicate* an anagram

Literary Academic, Bas bleu, Booksie, Erudite, Lettered

Literature Agitprop, Belles lettres, Comparative, Corpus, Edda, Fiction, Gongorism, Hagiology, Midrash, Musar, Page, Picaresque, Prose, Responsa, Samizdat, Sci-fi, Sturm und Drang, Wisdom

Litter Bed, Brancard, Brood, Cacolet, Cat, Cubs, Debris, Deep, Doolie, Emu-bob, Farrow, Jampan, Kago, Kajawah, Kindle, Mahmal, Nest, Norimon, Palankeen, Palanquin, Palkee, Palki, Pup, →**REFUSE**, Scrap, Sedan, Stretcher, Team, Whelp

Little Beans, Bijou, Brief, Chicken feed, Chota, Curn, Diddy, Dorrit, Drib, Drop, Fewtrils, Fraction, Haet, Hait, Hate, Ickle, Insect, Iota, John, Jot, Leet, Lilliputian, Limited, Lite, Lyte, Manikin, Means, Mini, Miniscule, Minnow, Minuscule, →**MINUTE**, Modicum, Morceau, Nell, Paltry, Paucity, Paul, Petite,

Pink, Scant, Scut, Shade, Shoestring, Short, Shred, Shrimp, Slight, Sliver, Sma', →SMALL, Smattering, Smidge(o)n, Smidgin, Smout, Smowt, Some, Soupçon, Spot, Tad, Teensy(-weensy), Tich, Tiddly, Tine, Titch, Touch, Tyne, Unimportant, Vestige, Wee, Weedy, Whit, Women

Live(d), Livelihood, Living, Liveliness, Lively, Lives Active, Advowson, Alert, Allegro, Animated, Animation, Animato, Are, AV, Awake, Be, Benefice, Biont, Boisterous, Bouncy, Bread, Breezy, Brio, Brisk, Canonry, Cant(y), Cheery, Chipper, Chirpy, Cohabit, Con moto, Con spirito, Crouse, Crust, Dash, Durante vita, Dynamic, Ebullient, Entrain, Esprit, Exist, Extant, Exuberant, Feisty, Frisky, Gamy, Gay, Giocoso, Glebe, Hang-out, Hard, High jinks, Hijinks, Indwell, Inquiline, Is, Jazz, Kedge, Lad, Lead, Lodging, Mercurial, Merry, Mouvementé, Organic, Outgo, Pacey, Peart, Pep, Perky, Piert, Quick, Quicksilver, Rackety, Racy, Reside, Resident, Rousing, Salt, Saut, Scherzo, Simony, Skittish, Smacking, Spanking, Sparky, Spiritoso, Spirituel(le), Sprack, Sprightly, Spry, Spunky, Subsist, Subsistence, Swinging, Symbiotic, Thrive, Unrecorded, Up tempo, Vibrant, Vicarage, Vital(ity), Vive, →VOLATILE, Wick, Zappy, Zingy, Zippy

▶**Livelihood** *see* LIVE(D)

▶**Living** *see* LIVE(D)

Lizard Abas, Agama, American chameleon, Amphisbaena, Anguis, Anole, Basilisk, Bearded, Blindworm, Blue-tongued, Brontosaurus, Chameleon, Chuckwalla, Dinosaur, Draco, Dragon, Eft, Evet, Frilled, Galliwasp, Gecko(ne), Gila, Gila monster, Glass snake, Goanna, Guana, Hatteria, Hellbender, Horned, Iguana, Jew, Kabaragoya, Komodo (dragon), Lacerta, Legua(a)n, Lounge, Malayan monitor, Mastigure, Menopome, Mokomoko, Moloch, Monitor, Mosasaur(us), Newt, Ngarara, Perentie, Perenty, Reptile, Rock, Sand, Sauria, Scincoid, Seps, Skink, Slow-worm, Snake, Sphenodon, Stellio(n), Sungazer, Swift, Tegu(exin), Teiid, Tokay, Tuatara, Tuatera, Varan, Wall, Whiptail, Worm, Worral, Worrel, Zandoli

Load(ed), Loader, Loading, Loads Accommodation, Affluent, Amass, Back-end, Ballast, Base, Biased, Boot-strap, Boozy, Burden, Cargo, Charge, Cobblers, Dead weight, Disc, Dope, Drunk, Dummy, Fardel, Fork-lift, Fother, Frau(gh)tage, Freight, Front-end, Fulham, Full, Gestant, Glyc(a)emic, Heap, Input, Install, Jag, Lade, Lard, Last, Live, Onus, Opulent, Pack, Packet, Pay, Peak, Power, Prime, Raft, Rich, Scads, Seam, Shipment, Shoal, Some, Span, Stow, Super, Surcharge, →TIGHT, Tipsy, Tod, Traction, Ultimate, Useful, Wealthy, Weight, Wharfinger, Wing

Loaf(er), Loaves Baguette, Bannock, Barmbrack, Baton, Beachbum, Beachcomber, Bloomer, Bludge, Bonce, Boule, Bread, Brick, Bum, Bu(r)ster, Cad, Cob, Coburg, Cottage, Currant, Farmhouse, Hawm, Head, Hoe-cake, Idle, Layabout, →LAZE, Lazybones, Long tin, Lusk, Manchet, Meat, Miche, Milk, Mooch, Mouch, Pan(h)agia, Plain, Roll, Roti, Shewbread, Shoe, Showbread, Sliced, Slosh, Split tin, Stollen, Stotty, Sugar, Tin, Vantage, Yob

Loan(s) Advance, Balloon, Benevolence, Bottomry, Bridging, Call, Consolidation, Debenture, Demand, Imprest, Lane, Mutuum, Omnium, Out, Prest, Respondentia, Roll-over, Start-up, Student, Sub, Top-up

Loathe, Loathing, Loathsome Abhor(rent), Abominate, Carrion, Despise, Detest, Execrate, Hate, Keck, Nauseate, Odious, Reptilian, Scunner, Ug(h)

Lobby Demo, Entry, Foyer, Gun, Hall, Press, Pressure group, Urge

Lobster Cock, Crawfish, Crayfish, Crustacean, Decapoda, Langouste, Macrura, Norway, Pereion, Pot, Scampo, Spiny, Squat, Thermidor, Tomalley

Local(ity) Area, Boor, Bro, Close, Des(h)i, Endemic, Home, Inn, Landlord, Native, Near, Nearby, Neighbourhood, Number, Parochial, Provincial, Pub, Regional, Resident, Tavern, Topical, Vernacular, Vicinal

▷**Local** *may indicate* a dialect word

Locate(d), Location Address, Connect, Echo, Emplacement, Find, Fix, Lay, Milieu, Pinpoint, Pitch, Place, Placement, Plant, Post, Put, Recess, Sat, Scene, Set-up, Site, Situate, Situation, Sofar, Spot, Theatre, Trace, Ubiety, Venue, Website, Where(abouts), Workplace, Zone

Loch, Lough Ashie, Awe, Derg, Earn, Eil, Erne, Etive, Fine, Gare, Garten, Glen Lyon, Holy, Hourn, Katrine, →**LAKE**, Larne, Leven, Linnhe, Lomond, Long, Moidart, Morar, More, Na Keal, Neagh, Ness, Rannoch, Ryan, Sea, Shiel, Strangford, Tay, Torridon

Lock(ing), Locker, Locks, Lock up Bar, Barnet, Bolt, Canal, Central, Chain, Chubb®, Clap-sill, Clinch, Combination, Cowlick, Curlicue, Davy Jones, Deadbolt, Detent, Drop, Fastener, Fermentation, Foretop, Gate, Haffet, Haffit, Handcuff, Hasp, Hold, Intern, Key, Kiss curl, Latch, Lazaretto, Man, Mane, Mortise, Percussion, Prison, Quiff, Ragbolt, Rim, Ringlet, Safety, Sasse, Scalp, Scissors, →**SECURE**, Sluice, Snap, Spring, Staircase, Sta(u)nch, Stock, Strand, Tag, Talon, Tetanus, Time, Trap, Tress, Tuft, Tumbler, Vapour, Villus, Ward, Watergate, Wheel, Wrestle, Yale®

▷**Lockkeeper** *may indicate* a hairnet

Locomotive Banker, Bogie, Bul(l)gine, Engine, Iron horse, Mobile, Mogul, Rocket, Steamer, Train

Locust, Locust tree Acacia, Anime, Carob, Cicada, Hopper, Nymph, Robinia, Seventeen-year, Voetganger

Lodge(r) Bestow, Billet, Board(er), Box, Chalet, Cosher, Deposit, Dig, Doss, Encamp, Entertain, Freemason, Grange, Grove, Guest, Harbour, Host, Hunting, Inmate, Inquiline, Instal, Layer, Lie, Masonic, Nest, Orange, Parasite, PG, Porter's, Put up, Quarter, Rancho, Resident, Room(er), Roommate, Stay, Storehouse, Stow, Tenant, Tepee, Up-put, Wigwam

Lodging(s) Abode, B and B, Chummage, Dharms(h)ala, Diggings, Digs, Dosshouse, Ferm, Grange, Grove, Hospitium, Hostel, Inquiline, Kip, Minshuku, Pad, Pension, Pied-à-terre, Quarters, Resiant, Rooms, Singleen, Sponging-house, Spunging-house, YHA

Loft(iness), Lofty Aerial, Airy, Arrogant, Attic, Celsitude, Chip, Exalted, Garret, Garryowen, Grand, Haymow, High, Hoity-toity, Jube, Lordly, Magniloquent, Noble, Organ, Rarefied, Rigging, Rood, Roost, Sky(ish), Sublime, Tallat, Tallet

Log(ging), Logs Billet, Black box, Cabin, Chock, Deadhead, Diarise, Diary, Enter, Hack, Key(stroke), Lumber, Mantissa, Minutes, Nap(i)erian, Neper, Patent, Poling, Raft, →**RECORD**, Stock, Tachograph, Yule

Logic(al) Alethic, Analytical, Aristotelian, Boolean, Chop, Cogent, Coherent, Deontic, Dialectic(s), Digital, Doxastic, Elench(us), Epistemics, Hardhead(ed), Modal, Organon, Ramism, Ratiocinate, Rational(e), Reason, Sane, Sequacious, Shared, Sorites, Syllogism, Symbolic, Trivium, Vienna circle

Loiter(ing) Dally, Dare, Dawdle, Dilatory, Dilly-dally, Idle, Lag, Lallygag, Leng, Lime, →**LINGER**, Loaf, Lollygag, Mike, Mooch, Mouch, Potter, Saunter, Scamp, Suss, Taigle, Tarry

London(er) 'Arry, Big Smoke, Cockaigne, Cockney, Co(c)kayne, East-ender, Flat-cap, Jack, Port, Roseland, Smoke, Town, Troynovant, Wen

Lone(r), Lonely Anchoret, Bereft, Eremite, Grass widow, Hermit, Isolated, Recluse, Remote, Rogue, Saddo, Secluded, Sole, Solitary, Unked, Unket, Unkid

Long(er), Longing, Longs Ache, Aitch, Ake, Appetent, Appetite, Aspire, Brame, Covet, Crave, Desire, Die, Earn, Erne, Eternal, Far, Gasp, Greed, Green, Grein, → **HANKER**, Huey, Hunger, Island, Itch, L, Lanky, Large, Lengthy, Longa, Lust, Macron, Marathon, Miss, More, Nostalgia, Option, Pant, Parsec, → **PINE**, Prolix, Side, Sigh, Tall, Thirst, Trews, Weary, Wish, Wist, Yearn, Yen

Longshoreman Hobbler, Hoveller, Wharfinger

Loo Ajax, Bog, Can, Chapel, Dike, Game, Gents, Jakes, John, Latrine, Privy, Toilet

Look(s), Look at After-eye, Air, Aspect, Await, Behold, Belgard, Blink, Bonne-mine, Browse, Busk, Butcher's, Butcher's hook, Case, Clock, Close-up, Countenance, Crane, Daggers, Decko, Deek, Dekko, Demeanour, Ecce, Ecco, Expression, Eye, Eyeball, Eye-glance, Face, Facies, Gander, Gawp, Gaze, Geek, Glad-eye, Glance, Glare, Gleam, Gledge, Glimpse, Glom, Glower, Goggle, Good, Grin, Hallo, Hangdog, Hey, Hippocratic, Iliad, Inspect, Keek, La, Leer, Lo, Mien, New, Ogle, Old-fashioned, Peek, Peep, Peruse, Prospect, Ray, Recce, Refer, → **REGARD**, Scan, Scowl, Scrutinise, Search, See, Seek, Seem, Shade, Sheep's eyes, Shufti, Shufty, Spy, Squint, Squiz, Stare, Survey, Toot, V, Vista, Wet

Look-out (man) Achtung, Cockatoo, Crow's nest, Huer, Mirador, Nit, Pas op, Picket, Prospect, Sangar, Scout, Sentry, Spotter, Sungar, Tentie, Toot(er), Watch, Watchtower

▷**Look silly** *may indicate* an anagram

Loom Beamer, Dobby, Emerge, Impend, Jacquard, Lathe, Lease-rod, Menace, Overhang, Picker, Temple, Threaten, Tower

Loop(ed), Loophole, Loopy Becket, Bight, Billabong, Bouclé, Carriage, Chink, Closed, Coil, Eyelet, Eyesplice, Fake, Feedback, Frog, Frontlet, Grom(m)et, Grummet, Hank, Heddle-eye, Henle's, Hysteresis, Infinite, Kink, Knop, Lasket, Local, Lug, Noose, Oillet, Parral, Parrel, Pearl(-edge), Picot, Purl, Riata, Squiggle, Staple, Stirrup, Swag, Terry, Toe, Twist

Loose(n), Loose woman Absolve, Abstrict, Adrift, Afloat, Anonyma, Baggage, Bail, Besom, Bike, Bunter, Chippie, Chippy, Clatch, Cocotte, Demi-mondaine, Demirep, Desultory, Dissolute, Dissolve, Doxy, Draggletail, Dratchell, Drazel, Ease, Emit, Flabby, Flipperty-flopperty, Flirt-gill, Floosie, Floozie, Floozy, Floppy, Franion, Free, Gangling, Gay, Geisha, Hussy, Insecure, Jade, Jay, Jezebel, Lax, Limp, Loast, Loon, Loste, Mob, Mort, Painted, Pinnace, Profligate, Promiscuous, Quail, Ramp, → **RELAX**, Sandy, Scrubber, Shaky, Slack, Slag, Slapper, Slipshod, Slut, Streel, Strumpet, Tart, Tramp, Trull, Unhasp, Unhitch, Unlace, Unlash, Unleash, Unpin, Unreined, Unscrew, Unstuck, Untie, Vague, Wappend, Whore

Loot Berob, Boodle, Booty, Cragh, Creach, Foray, Haul, Mainour, Oof, Peel, Pillage, Pluck, → **PLUNDER**, Ransack, Rape, Reave, Reif, Rieve, Rob, Sack, Smug, Spoils, Spoliate, Stouth(e)rie, Swag, Treasure, Waif

Lop Behead, Clip, Clop, Curtail, Detruncate, Droop, Shroud, Sned, Snee, Trash

Lord(s), Lordship, Lordly Adonai, Ahura Mazda, Anaxandron, Arrogant, Boss, Byron, Cardigan, Chatelain, Cripes, Dieu, Dominate, Domineer, Dominical, Drug, Duc, Earl, Elgin, Gad, Gilded Chamber, God, Haw-haw, Herr, Idris, Imperious, Jim, Justice, Kami, Kitchener, Land, Landgrave, Law, Ld, Liege, Lonsdale, Losh, Lud, MCC, Meneer, Misrule, Mynheer, Naik, Oda Nobunaga, Omrah, Ordinary, Ormazd, Ormuzd, Palsgrave, Peer, Second chamber, Seigneur, Seignior, Shaftesbury, Sire, Spiritual, Taverner, Temporal, Tuan, Ullin

Lore Cab(b)ala, Edda, Lair, Lare, Riem, Upanis(h)ad

Lorry, Lorries Artic(ulated), Camion, Carrier, Crummy, Double-bottom, Drag, Drawbar outfit, Dropsided, Flatbed, Juggernaut, Low-loader, Rig, Road train, Tipper, Tonner, →**TRUCK**, Wagon

Lose(r) Also-ran, Decrease, Drop, Elude, Fail, Forfeit, Leese, Misère, Mislay, Misplace, No-no, Nowhere, Saddo, Spread, Stiff, Tank, Throw, Tine(r), Tyne, Underdog, Unsuccessful, Waste, Weeper

Loss, Lost Angel's share, Anosmia, Aphesis, Aphonia, Apocope, Apraxia, Astray, At sea, Attainder, Boohai, Chord, Cost, Dead, Decrease, Depreciation, Detriment, Disadvantage, Elision, Extinction, Foredamned, Forfeited, Forgotten, Forlorn, Gone, Hurtful, Lore, Lorn, Lurch, Missing, Omission, Outage, Pentimento, Perdition, Perdu, Perished, Preoccupied, Privation, Psilosis, Shrinkage, Stray, Tine, Tinsel, Tint, Toll, Traik, Tribes, Tyne(d), Ullage, Unredeemed, Wastage, Will, Wull

▷**Lost** *may indicate* an anagram or an obsolete word

Lot(s) Abundant, Amount, Aret(t), Badly, Bags, Batch, Boatload, Bomb, Caboodle, Cavel, Chance, Deal, Destiny, Dole, Doom, Due, →**FATE**, Fortune, Hantle, Hap, Heaps, Horde, Host, Item, Job, Kevel, Kismet, Lank, Lashings, Legion, Loads, Loadsa, Luck, Manifold, Many, Mass, Moh, Moira, Mony, Mort, Much, Myriad, Oceans, Often, Omnibus, Oodles, Oodlins, Pack, Parcel, Plenitude, Plenty, Plethora, Portion, Power, Purim, Raft, Scads, Set, Shedload, Sight, Slather, Slew, Slue, Sortilege, Stack, Sum, Tall order, Tons, Vole, Wagonload, Weird

Lothario Lady-killer, Libertine, Rake, Womaniser

Lotion After-shave, Blackwash, Calamine, Collyrium, Cream, Emollient, Humectant, Suntan, Unguent, Wash

Lottery, Lotto Bingo, Cavel, Draw, Gamble, Pakapoo, Pools, Punchboard, Raffle, Rollover, Scratchcard, Sweepstake, Tombola

Loud(ness), Loudly Bel, Big, Blaring, Booming, Brassy, Clarion, Decibel, Ear-splitting, F, FF, Flashy, Forte, Fracas, Full-mouthed, Garish, Gaudy, Glaring, Hammerklavier, High(pitched), Jazzy, Lumpkin, Noisy, Orotund, Plangent, Raucous, Roarie, Siren, Sone, Stentor(ian), Strident, Vocal, Vociferous, Vulgar

Loudspeaker Action, Boanerges, Bullhorn, Hailer, Megaphone, PA, Squawk box, Stentor, Subwoofer, Tannoy®, Tweeter, Woofer

Lounge(r) Couch potato, Daiker, Da(c)ker, Departure, Doze, Executive, Hawm, Idle, Laze, Lie, Lizard, Loaf, Loll, Lollop, Parlour, Recline, Settee, Slouch, Sun, Sunbed, Transit, Transitive

Louse (up), Lousy, Lice Acrawl, Argulus, Bolix, Bollocks, Chat, Chicken, Cootie, Crab, Crawling, Crummy, Head, Isopod(a), Kutu, Mallophaga, Nit, Oniscus, Pedicular, Phthiriasis, Psocid, Psocoptera, Psylla, Pubic, Slater, Snot, Sowbug, Sucking, Vermin

Lout(ish) Auf, Clod(hopper), Coof, Cuif, Galere, Hallian, Hallion, Hallyon, Hick, Hob, Hobbledehoy, Hooligan, Hoon, Jack, Jake, Keelie, Lager, Larrikin, Lob(lolly), Loord, Lubber, Lumpkin, Lycra, Oaf, Oik, Rube, Swad, Tout, Ungallant, Yahoo, Yob(bo)

Love(d), Lovable, Lover Abelard, Admire, Adore, Adulator, Affection, Agape, Alma, Amabel, Amanda, Amant, Amateur, Ami(e), Amoret, Amoroso, Amour, Angharad, Antony, Ardour, Ariadne, Aroha, Aucassin, Beau, Bedfellow, Bidie-in, Blob, Brotherly, Calf, Care, Casanova, Chamberer, Cicisbeo, Concubine, Coquet, Court, Courtly, Cupboard, Cupid, Dear, Dotard, Dote, Doxy, Duck(s),

Ducky, Dulcinea, Eloise, Eloper, Emotion, Enamorado, Eros, Esme, Fan(boy), Flame, Frauendienst, Free, Gal(l)ant, Goose-egg, Hon(ey), Idolise, Inamorata, Inamorato, Iseult, Isolde, Item, Jo, Lad, Lancelot, Leander, Leman, Like, Lochinvar, Loe, Loo, Lurve, Man, Mistress, Nada, Nihility, Nil, Nothing, Nought, Nut, O, Pairs, Paramour, Pash, Passion, Pet, Phaedra, Philander, Philtre, Platonic, Precious, Protestant, Psychodelic, Puppy, Revere, Rhanja, Romance, Romeo, Sigisbeo, Smitten, Spark, Spooner, Stale, Storge, Suitor, Swain, Thisbe, Toyboy, Treasure, Tristan, Troilus, True, Turtle(-dove), Valentine, Venus, Virtu, Woman, Zap, Zeal, Zero

Lovely Adorable, Belle, Cute, Dishy, Dreamy, Fair, Gorgeous, Looker, Super

Love-making Kama Sutra, Sex, Slap and tickle, Snog

Low(est), Low-born, Low-cut, Lower(ing), Low-key Abase, Abate, Abysmal, Amort, Area, Avail(e), Avale, B, Basal, Base(-born), Bass(o), Beneath, Blue, Calf, Canaille, Cartoonist, Cheap, Church, Cocktail, Condescend, Contralto, Couch, Cow, Crestfallen, Croon, Crude, Darken, Debase, Declass, Décolleté, Deepen, Degrade, Deign, Demean, Demit, Demote, Depress, Despicable, Devalue, Dim, Dip, Dishonourable, Dispirited, Doldrums, Downbeat, Downmarket, Drawdown, Drop, Early, Embase, Flat, Foot, Frown, Gazunder, Glare, Guernsey, Gurly, Gutterblood, Hedge(-hopping), Hidalgo, Humble, Ignoble, Imbase, Inferior, Jersey, Laigh, Lallan, Law, Lessen, Mass, Mean(born), Menial, Moo, Mopus, Morose, Nadir, Net, Nether, Nett, Non-U, Ornery, Ostinato, Paravail, Plebeianise, Profound, Prole, Relegate, Ribald, Rock-bottom, Sad, Scoundrel, Scowl, Secondo, Shabby, Short, Soft, Stoop, Subordinate, Subscript, Sudra, Sunken, Undermost, Unobtrusive, Vail, Vulgar, Weak, Wretched

▷**Lower** *may refer to* cattle

Loyal(ty) Adherence, Allegiant, Brand, Brick, Clanship, Dependable, Diehard, Faithful, Fast, Fealty, Fidelity, Firm, Gungho, Leal, Liegedom, Liegeman, Patriotic, Pia, Stalwart, Staunch, Tribalism, Troth, →**TRUE**, Trusty

Lozenge Cachou, Catechu, Coughdrop, Fusil, Jujube, Mascle, Pastille, Pill, Rhomb, Rustre, Tablet, Troche, Voided

Lubricant, Lubricate, Lubrication Carap-oil, Coolant, Derv, Fluid, Grease, Oil, Petrolatum, Sebum, Synovia, Unguent, Vaseline®, Wool-oil

Lucid Bright, Clear, Perspicuous, Sane

Lucifer Devil, Match, Proud, Satan, Venus

Luck(y) Amulet, Auspicious, Beginner's, Blessed, Bonanza, Break, Caduac, Canny, Cess, Chance, Charmed, Chaunce, Daikoku, Dip, Fat, Fate, Fluke, →**FORTUNE**, Godsend, Hap, Heather, Hit, Jam(my), Jim, Joss, Lady, Lot, Mascot, Mercy, Mozzle, Prosit, Providential, Pudding-bag, Purple passage, Purple patch, Seal, Seel, Sele, Serendipity, Sess, Sonsie, Sonsy, Spawny, Star(s), Streak, Success, Talisman, Tinny, Tough, Turn-up, White rabbits, Windfall, Wishbone, Worse

Ludicrous Absurd, Bathetic, Bathos, Crackpot, Farcical, Fiasco, Inane, Jest, Laughable, Risible

Luggage Bags, Carryon, Cases, Dunnage, Excess, Grip, Hand, Kit, Petara, Samsonite®, Suiter, Traps, Trunk

Lull, Lullaby Berceuse, Calm, Cradlesong, Hushaby, Respite, Rock, Sitzkreig, Soothe, Sopite

Lumber(ing) Clump, Galumph, Jumble, Pawn, Ponderous, Raffle, Saddle, Scamble, Timber

Luminance, Luminous, Luminosity, Luminescence Aglow, Arc, Candela, Dayglo, Glow, Hero, Ignis-fatuus, L, Light, Meteor, Nit, Phosphorescent, Scintillon, Sea-dog, Wildfire, Will o' the wisp

Lump(ectomy), Lump(s), Lump(y) Adam's apple, Aggregate, Bolus, Bubo, Bud, Bulge, Bur(r), Caruncle, Chuck, Chunk, Clat, Claut, Clod, Clot, Cob, Combine, Da(u)d, Dallop, Dollop, Enhydros, Epulis, Flocculate, Ganglion, Geode, Gnarl, Gob(bet), Goiter, Goitre, Goop, Grape, Grip, Grumose, Hunch, Hunk, Inium, Knarl, Knob, Knub, Knur(r), Knurl, Lob, Lunch, Malleolus, Mass, Mastoid, Moss-litter, Mote, Mott, Myxoma, Neuroma, Nibble, Nirl, Node, Nodule, Nodulus, Nub(bin), Nubble, Nugget, Nur(r), Nurl, Osteophyte, Plook, Plouk, Quinsy, Raguly, Sarcoma, Scybalum, Sitfast, Slub, Strophiole, Tragus, Tuber(cle), Tumour, Tylectomy, Wart, Wodge

Lunacy, Lunatic Bedlam, Dementia, Demonomania, Folly, Insanity, Mad(ness), Madman, Maniac, Nutter, Psychosis
▷**Lunatic** *may indicate* an anagram

Lunch(time) Bait, Box, Crib, Dejeune, Déjeuner, Fork, L, Liquid, Nacket, Nuncheon, Packed, Piece, Ploughman, Pm, Tiff(in), Working

Lung(s) Alveoli, Bellows, Book, Breather, Coalminer's, Farmer's, Iron, Lights, Pleural, Pulmo, Pulmonary, Soul

Lunge Breenge, Breinge, Dive, Stab, Thrust, Venue

Lurch Reel, Slew, Stagger, Stoit, Stumble, Swee, Toss

Lure Bait, Bribe, Carrot, Decoy, Entice, Horn, Inveigle, Jig, Judas, Loss leader, Plug, Roper, Spinner, Spoon, Squid, Stale, Temptation, Tice, Tole, Train, Trepan

Lurk(ing) Dare, Latitant, Skulk, Slink, Snoke, Snook, Snowk

Lush Alcoholic, Alkie, Alky, Dipso(maniac), Drunk, Fertile, Green, Juicy, Lydian, Soak, Sot, Succulent, Toper, Tosspot, Verdant

Lust(ful), Lusty Cama, Concupiscence, Corflambo, Desire, Eros, Frack, Goatish, Greed, Kama, Lech(ery), Lewd, Libertine, Libido, Obidicut, Prurience, Radge, Randy, Rank, Raunchy, Salacious, Steamy, Venereous

Lustre, Lustrous Brilliance, Census, Chatoyant, Galena, Gaum, Gilt, Gloss, Gorm, Inaurate, Lead-glance, Lovelight, Pearlescent, Pearly, Pentad, Reflet, Satiny, Schiller, Shellac, Water

Lute, Lutist Amphion, Chitarrone, Cither, Dichord, Orpharion, Pandora, Pandore, Pipa, Theorbo, Vielle

Luxuriant, Luxuriate, Luxurious, Luxury (lover) Apician, Bask, Clover, Cockaigne, Cockayne, Comfort, Copious, Delicate, Deluxe, Dolce vita, Extravagant, Exuberant, Five-star, Fleshpots, Lavish, Lotus-eating, Lucullan, Lush, Milk and honey, Mollitious, Opulence, Ornate, Palatial, Pie, Plush(y), Posh, Rank, →**RICH**, Ritzy, Sumptuous, Sybarite, Wallow

▶**Lying** *see* **LIE(S)**

Lyre Box, Cithern, Harp, Psaltery, Testudo, Trigon

Lyric(s), Lyrical, Lyricist, Lyrist Awdl, Cavalier, Dit(t), Epode, Gilbert, Hammerstein, Melic, Ode, Orphean, Paean, Pean, Poem, Poetic, Rhapsodic, Song, Spinto, Words

Mm

M Married, Member, Metre, Mike, Mile, Thousand

Macabre Gothic, Grotesque, Morbid, Sick

Machine(ry) Apparat(us), Appliance, Bathing, → **DEVICE**, Facsimile, Fax, Fruit, Infernal, Instrument, Life-support, Party, Plant, Propaganda, Rowing, Sausage, Sewing, Slot, Spin, Tape, Teaching, Time, Vending, Virtual, War, Washing, Weighing

Mackintosh Burberry®, Mac, Mino, Oilskin, Slicker, Waterproof

Mad(den), Madman, Madness Angry, Apoplectic, Balmy, Bananas, Barking, Barmy, Bedlam, Berserk, Besotted, Bonkers, Crackbrained, Crackpot, Crazy, Cuckoo, Cupcake, Delirious, Dement, Deranged, Détraqué, Distract, Dotty, Enrage, Fay, Fey, Fie, Folie, Folly, Frantic, Frenetic(al), Fruitcake, Furioso, Fury, Gelt, Gyte, Harpic, Hatter, Idiotic, Insane, Insanie, Insanity, Into, Irate, Ireful, Irritate, Kook, Livid, Loco, Lunatic, Lycanthropy, Madbrained, Maenad, Mango, Mania, Mental, Meshug(g)a, Metric, Midsummer, Moonstruck, Mullah, Nuts, Porangi, Provoke, Psycho, Rabid, Raving, Redwood, Redwud, Scatty, Screwy, Short-witted, Starkers, Tonto, Touched, Troppo, Unhinged, Wood, Wowf, Wrath, Wud, Xenomania, Yond, Zany

▷**Mad(den)** *may indicate* an anagram

▷**Madly** *may indicate* an anagram

Madonna Lady, Lily, Mary, Pietà, Virgin

Mafia, Mafioso Camorra, Capo, Cosa Nostra, Godfather, Goombah, Mob, Ndrangheta, Omerta, Padrone, Pentito, Sicilian, Triad

Magazine Arsenal, Clip, Colliers, Cornhill, Cosmopolitan, Digizine, Economist, E-zine, Field, Girlie, Glossy, Granta, House organ, Journal, Ladmag, Lady, Lancet, Life, Listener, Little, Magnet, New Yorker, Organ, Paper, Part work, Periodical, Pictorial, Playboy, Powder, Private Eye, Pulp, Punch, She, Slick, Spectator, Store, Strand, Tatler, Time, Vogue, Warehouse, Weekly, Yoof, Zine

Magic(al), Magician, Magic square Alchemy, Art, Black, Charm, Conjury, Diablerie, Diablery, Druid, Enchanting, Fabulous, Faust, Fetish, Genie, Goetic, Goety, Gramary(e), Hey presto, Houdini, Illusionist, Incantation, Makuto, Math, Medea, Medicine man, Merlin, Mojo, Moly, Morgan le Fay, Necromancer, Occult, Powwow, Prospero, Rhombus, Sorcery, Spell, Speller, Stardust, Supernatural, Talisman, Voodoo, Warlock, White, Witch-doctor, Wizard

Magistracy, Magistrate Aedile, Alcalde, Amman, Amtman, Archon, Avoyer, Bailie, Bailiff, Bailli(e), Beak, Bench, Boma, Burgess, Burgomaster, Cadi, Censor, Consul, Corregidor, Curule, Decemvirate, Demiurge, Dictator, Doge(ate), Edile, Effendi, Ephor, Field cornet, Finer, Foud, Gonfalonier, JP, Judiciary, Jurat, Justice, Kotwal, Landamman(n), Landdrost, Maire, Mayor, Mittimus, Novus homo, Pilate, Podesta, Portreeve, Pr(a)efect, Pr(a)etor, Prior, Proconsul, Propraetor,

Provost, Qadi, Quaestor, Recorder, Reeve, Shereef, Sherif, Stad(t)holder, Stipendiary, Syndic, Tribune, Trier, Worship

Magnate Baron, Beaverbrook, Bigwig, Industrialist, Mogul, Tycoon, VIP, Zillionaire

Magnet(ic), Magnetism Animal, Artificial, Attraction, Bar, Charisma, Field, Gauss, Horseshoe, Induction, It, Loadstone, Lodestone, Maxwell, Od, Oersted, Oomph, Permanent, Personal, Polar, Pole, Pole piece, Poloidal, Pull, Remanence, Retentivity, Slug, Solenoid, Terrella, Terrestrial, Tesla, Tole, Weber

Magnificence, Magnificent Epic, Fine, Gorgeous, Grandeur, Imperial, Laurentian, Lordly, Noble, Pride, Regal, Royal, Splendid, State, Sumptuous, Superb

Magnifier, Magnify(ing) Aggrandise, Augment, Binocle, →**ENLARGE**, Exaggerate, Extol, Increase, Loupe, Microscope, Praise, Teinoscope, Telescope

Magnolia An(n)ona, Beaver-tree, Champac, Champak, Mississippi, Sweet bay, Umbrella-tree, Yulan

Magpie Bell, Bird, Bishop, Chatterer, Hoarder, Madge, Mag, Margaret, Outer, Pica, Piet, Pyat, Pyet, Pyot

Maid(en), Maidenly Abigail, Aia, Amah, Biddy, Bonibell, Bonne, Bonnibell, Burd, Chamber, Chaste, Chloe, Clothes-horse, Damoisel, Dam(o)sel, Debut, Dell, Dey, Dresser, First, Girl, Guillotine, Ignis-fatuus, Imago, Inaugural, Io, Iras, Iron, Lorelei, M, Marian, May, Miss, Nerissa, Nymph, Opening, Over, Pucelle, Racehourse, Rhian, Rhine, Scullion, Skivvy, Soubrette, Stillroom, Suivante, Tabby, Table, Thestylis, Tirewoman, Tweeny, Valkyrie, Virgin, Wench

Mail Air, →**ARMOUR**, Byrnie, Cataphract, Chain, Da(w)k, E(lectronic), Epistle, Express, Fan, Gusset, Habergeon, Hate, Hauberk, Helm, Junk, Letter, Media, Panoply, Pony express, Post, Ring, Send, Snail, Spam, Surface, Tuille(tte), Voice

Main(s) Brine, Briny, Bulk, →**CENTRAL**, Chief, Cockfight, Conduit, Essential, Foremost, Gala, Generally, Grid, Gross, Head, →**KEY**, Lead(ing), Ocean, Palmary, Predominant, Prime, Principal, Ring, →**SEA**, Sheer, Spanish, Staple, Star, Water

Maintain(er), Maintenance Alimony, Allege, Ap(p)anage, Argue, Assert, Aver, Avouch, Avow, Claim, Conserve, Contend, Continue, Defend, Escot, Insist, Lengthman, Preserve, Retention, Run, Serve, Service, Sustain, Upbear, Uphold, Upkeep

Maize Corn, Hominy, Indian, Mealie, Milo, Polenta, Popcorn, Samp, Sweetcorn

Majestic, Majesty August, Britannic, Dignity, Eagle, Grandeur, Imperial, Maestoso, Olympian, Regal, Royal, SM, Sovereign, Stately, Sublime, Tuanku

Major (domo) Drum, Great, →**IMPORTANT**, Lulu, Momentous, PM, Read, Seneschal, Senior, Sergeant, Signal, Star, Trumpet, Wig

Majority Absolute, Age, Body, Eighteen, Landslide, Latchkey, Maturity, Moral, Most, Preponderance, Relative, Silent, Working

Make(r), Make do, Making Amass, Assemble, Brand, Build, Cause, Clear, Coerce, Coin, Compel, Compulse, Concoct, Creant, Create, Devise, Earn, Execute, Fabricate, Factive, Fashion, Faute de mieux, Fet(t), Forge, Form, Gar(re), God, Halfpenny, Increate, Mail(e), Manage, Marque, Meg, Name, Nett, Prepare, Production, Reach, Render, Shape, Sort, Turn

▷**Make** *may indicate* an anagram

Make believe Fantasy, Fictitious, Pretend, Pseudo

Make up, Make-up artist Ad lib, Compensate, Compose, Concealer, Constitute, Constitution, Cosmetics, Eye-liner, Fard, Gaud, Gawd, Gene, Genome, Genotype, Identikit®, Kohl, Liner, Lipstick, Maquillage, Mascara,

Metabolism, Moistener, Orchel, Paint, Pancake, Panstick, Powder, Prime, Reconcile, Rouge, Slap(stick), Tidivate, Titivate, Toiletry, White-face

Male Alpha, Arrhenotoky, Buck, Bull, Dog, Ephebe, Ephebus, Gent, Hob, John Doe, Macho, Mansize, Masculine, Patroclinous, Ram, Rogue, Spear(side), Stag, Stamened, Telamon, Tom, Worthiest of the blood

Malfunction Act up, Glitch, Hiccup

Malice, Malicious Acid, Bitchy, Catty, Cruel, Despiteous, Envy, Grudge, Hatred, Ill-will, Malevolent, Malign, Mudslinger, Narquois, Schadenfreude, Serpent, Snide, Spite, Spleen, Venom, Viperish, Virulent

Malign(ant), Malignity Asperse, Backbite, Badmouth, Baleful, Bespatter, Defame, Denigrate, Detract, Evil, Gall, Harm, Hate-rent, Hatred, Libel, Sinister, Slander, Spiteful, Swart(h)y, Toxin, Traduce, Vicious, Vilify, Vilipend, Viperous, Virulent

Malleable Clay, Ductile, Fictile, Pliable

▷**Malleable** *may indicate* an anagram

Mallet Beetle, Club, Gavel, Hammer, Mace, Maul, Stick, Tenderizer

Mammoth Epic, Gigantic, Huge, Jumbo, Mastodon, Whopping, Woolly

Man(kind), Manly, Manliness Adam, Advance, Andrew, Ask(r), Belt, Best, Betty, Bimana(l), Biped, Bloke, Bo, Boxgrove, Boy, Boyo, Bozo, Cad, Cairn, Calf, Castle, Cat, Chal, Chap, Checker, Chequer, Chiel, Cockey, Cod, Contact, Continuity, Crew, Cro-Magnon, Cuffin, Cully, Dog, Don, Draught, Dude, Emmanuel, Essex, Everyman, Family, Fancy, Fella, Feller, Fellow, Folsom, Friday, Front, G, Gayomart, Geezer, Gent, Gingerbread, Grimaldi, Guy, He, Heidelberg, Himbo, Hombre, Hominid, Homme, Homo, Homo sapiens, Inner, IOM, Iron, Isle, It, Jack, Java, Joe (Bloggs), Joe Blow, Joe Sixpack, Joe Soap, John(nie), John Doe, Josser, Limit, Link, Lollipop, M, Mac, Male, Medicine, Microcosm, Mister, Mon, Mondeo, Mr, Muffin, Mun, Neanderthal, Numbers, Nutcracker, Oreopithecus, Organisation, Ou, Paleolithic, Party, Pawn, Peking, Person, Piece, Piltdown, Pin, Pithecanthropus, Property, Raff, Ray, Remittance, Renaissance, Resurrection, Rhodesian, Right-hand, Rook, Sandwich, Servant, Servitor, Ship, Sinanthropus, Sir, Sodor, Soldier, Solo, Spear, Staff, Stag, Standover, Straw, Terran, Third, Thursday, Trinil, Twelfth, Tyke, Type, Utility, Valet, Vir(ile), Vitality, White van, Wight

Manage(r), Manageable, Management, Managing Administer, Amildar, Anger, Attain, Aumil, Behave, Board, Boss, Chief, Conduct, Contrive, Control, Cope, Crisis, Darogha, Direct, Docile, Eke, Exec(utive), Fare, Find, Govern, Grieve, Handle, Honcho, Husband(ry), IC, Impresario, Intendant, Logistical, MacReady, Maître d('hotel), Make do, Manipulate, Manoeuvre, Operate, Proctor, Procurator, Régisseur, Rig, Road(ie), → **RUN**, Scrape, Shift, Steward, Strategy, Subsist, Succeed, Suit, Superintend, Supervisor, Sysop, Tawie, Tractable, Treatment, Trustee, Wangle, Webmaster, Wield(y), Yare

Mandate, Mandatory Authority, Decree, De rigueur, Fiat, Incumbent, Order

Mangle Agrise, Butcher, Distort, Garble, Hack, Hackle, Haggle, Mammock, Wring(er)

▷**Mangle** *may indicate* an anagram

Mania Cacoethes, Craze, Frenzy, Lunacy, Paranoia, Passion, Rage

Manifesto Communist, Plank, Platform, Policy, Pronunciamento

Manipulate, Manipulative, Manipulator, Manipulation Bend, Card-sharp, Chiropractor, Control, Cook, Demagogic, Diddle, Fashion, Finesse, Gerrymander, Handle, Hellerwork, Jerrymander, Juggle, Logodaedalus,

Massage, Master-slave, McTimoney chiropractic, Milk, Osteopath, Physiotherapist, Ply, Rig, Spin, Svengali, Swing, Tong, Tweeze, Use, Wangle

▷**Manipulate** *may indicate* an anagram

Manner(ism), Mannerly, Manners Accent, Airs, À la, Appearance, Attitude, Bedside, Behaved, Behaviour, Bon ton, Breeding, Carriage, Comportment, Conduct, Couth, Crew, Custom, Delivery, Deportment, Ethos, Etiquette, Farand, Farrand, Farrant, Guise, Habit, How, Mien, Mode, Mood, Morality, Mores, Of, Ostent, Panache, Politesse, Presence, Presentation, P's & Q's, Quirk, Rate, Rhetoric, Side, Sort, Style, Thew(s), Thewe(s), Trick, Urbanity, Way, Wise

Manoeuvre(s) Alley-oop, Campaign, Castle, Démarche, Ebrillade, Engineer, Exercise, Faena, Fianchetto, Fork, Gambit, Grey mail, Heimlich, Hot-dog, Jink(s), Jockey, Loop, Manipulate, Op(eration), Pesade, Ploy, Pull out, Ruse, Short cut, Skewer, Steer, Stickhandle, Tactic, Takeover, Telemark, Use, U-turn, Valsalva, Wheel(ie), Whipstall, Wile, Wingover, Zigzag

▷**Manoeuvre** *may indicate* an anagram

Manor (house) Area, Demain, Demesne, Estate, Hall, Schloss, Vill(a)

Mansion Broadlands, Burghley House, Casa, Castle Howard, Chateau, Chatworth House, Chevening, Cliveden, Knole, Luton Hoo, Mentmore, Palace, Penshurst Place, Pile, Queen's House, Seat, Stourhead, Stowe, Waddesdon Manor, Woburn Abbey

Mantle Asthenosphere, Authority, Blanket, Burnous(e), Capote, Caracalla, Cloak, Dolman, Elijah, Gas, Lithosphere, Pall, Pallium, Paludament, Pelisse, Rochet, Shawl, Sima, Toga, Tunic, Vakas, Veil

Manual Blue collar, Bradshaw, Cambist, Console, Enchiridion, Guide, Hand, Handbook, How-to, Portolan(o), Positif

Manure Compost, Dressing, Dung, →**FERTILISER**, Guano, Hen-pen, Lime, Mould, Muck, Sha(i)rn, Tath

Manuscript(s) Codex, Codicology, Folio, Hand, Holograph, Longhand, MS, Opisthograph, Palimpsest, Papyrus, Parchment, Script, Scroll, Scrowl(e), Slush-pile, Uncial, Vellum

▷**Manx** *may indicate* a last letter missing

Many Bags, C, CD, Countless, Crew(e), D, Hantle, Herd, Horde, Host, L, Lot, M, Manifold, Mony, Multi(tude), Multiple, Myriad, Numerous, Oodles, Power, Scad, Scores, Sight, Slew, Stacks, Tons, Umpteen, Untold

▷**Many** *may indicate* the use of a Roman numeral letter

Map(s), Mapping Atlas, A-Z, Bijection, Card, Cartogram, Chart, Chorography, Choropleth, Cognitive, Contour, Face, Genetic, Image, Inset, Key, Loxodromic, Mappemond, OS, Plan(isphere), Plat, Plot, Portolano, Relief, Sea-card, Sea-chart, Site, Star, Topography, Weather

Maple Acer, Bird's-eye, Box elder, Japanese, Mazer, Norway, Plane, Sugar, Sycamore, Syrup

Map-maker Cartographer, OS, Speed

Marble(s), Marbling Agate, All(e)y, Arch, Bonce, Bonduc, Bool, Boondoggle, Bowl, Calcite, Chequer, Devil's, Dump, Elgin, Forest, Humite, Knicker, Languedoc, Marl, Marmoreal, Mind, Mosaic, Mottle, Nero-antico, Nicker, Onychite, Ophicalcite, Paragon, Parian, Petworth, Plonker, Plunker, Purbeck, Rance, Ringer, Ring-taw, Sanity, Scagliola, Taw, Tolley, Variegate, Verd antique, Wits

March(ing), Marcher Abut, Adjoin, Advance, Alla marcia, Anabasis, Border(er), Borderland, Boundary, Colonel Bogey, Dead, Defile, Demo(nstration),

Étape, File, Footslog, Forced, Freedom, Fringe, Galumph, Go, Goosestep, Grand, Hunger, Ides, Jarrow, Lide, Limes, Lockstep, Meare, Music, →**PARADE**, Paso doble, Progress, Protest, Quick, Regimental, Route, Saint, Slow time, Step, Strunt, Strut, Tramp, Trio, Tromp, Troop, Wedding, Yomp

▷**March** *may indicate* 'Little Women' character, Amy, Beth, Jo, Meg

Marge, Margin(al) Andean, Annotate, Bank, Border, Borderline, Brim, Brink, Constructive, Convergent, Curb, Edge, Gross, Hair's breadth, Lean, Limit, Littoral, Neck, Nose, Periphery, Profit, Rand, Repand, →**RIM**, Selvedge, Sideline, Spread, Tail, Term

Marijuana Alfalfa, Bhang, Camberwell carrot, Dagga, Gage, Ganja, Grass, Greens, Hay, Hemp, Herb, J, Jimson weed, Jive, Joint, Kaif, Kef, Kif, Leaf, Lid, Locoweed, Mary-Jane, Pot, Roach, Rope, Shit, Sinsemilla, Splay, Spliff, Tea, Toke, Weed

Mariner AB, Ancient, MN, RM, Sailor, Salt, Seafarer, Tar

Mark(ing), Marked, Marks, Marker Accent, Aesc, Annotate, Anoint, Antony, Apostrophe, Asterisk, Astrobleme, Badge, Banker, Barcode, Bethumb, Birth, Blaze, Blot, Blotch, Brand, Bruise, Bull, Buoy, Butt, Cachet, Calibrate, Caract, Caret, Caste, CE, Cedilla, Celebrate, Characteristic, Chatter, Chequer, Cicatrix, Class, Clout, Colon, Comma, Coronis, Crease, Criss-cross, Cross(let), Cup (and ring), Cursor, Dash, Denote, Dent, Designate, Diacritic, Diaeresis, Dieresis, Distinction, Ditto, DM, Dot, Duckfoot quote, Dupe, Emblem, Endorsement, Enseam, Ensign, Enstamp, Exclamation, Expression, Feer, Flash, Fleck, Fox(ing), Freckle, Genetic, Glyph, Gospel, Grade, Guillemet, Gybe, Hacek, Haemangioma, Hair-line, Hash, Hatch, Heed, Hickey, High water, Hoofprint, Hyphen, Impress(ion), Imprint, Indicium, Ink, Inscribe, Insignia, Interrogation, Keel, Kite, Kumkum, Lentigo, Line, Ling, Livedo, Logo, Lovebite, Low water, M, Macron, Matchmark, Mate, MB, Medical, Merk, Mint, Minute, Mottle, NB, Nick, Nota bene, Notal, Notch, Note, Notice, Obelisk, Observe, Oche, Paginate, Paragraph, Paraph, Peg, Period, Piece together, Pilcrow, Pin, Pinpoint, Pit, Plage, Plimsoll, Pling, Pock, Point(ille), Popinjay, Port wine, Post, Presa, Printer's, Proof, Punctuation, Question, Quotation, Record, Reference, Register, Regulo, Remarque, Rillmark, Ripple, Roundel, Rune, Sanction, Scar, Scorch, Score(r), Scratch, Scribe, Scuff, Section, See, Senora, Service, Shadow, Shelf, Shilling, Shoal, Sigil, Sign(ature), Smit, Smut, Smutch, Soft touch, Sordes, Speck, Splodge, Splotch, Spot, Spousage, Stain, Stamp, Stencil, Stigma(ta), Strawberry, Stress, Stretch, Stripe, Stroke, Sucker, Swan-upping, Swastika, Symbol, Tag, Target, Tarnish, Tatow, Tattoo, Tee, Theta, Thread, Tick, Tide, Tika, Tikka, Tilak, Tilde, Tittle, Token, Touchmark, Trace, Track, Trema, Trout, Tug(h)ra, Twain, Umlaut, Ure, Victim, Wand, Warchalking, Watch, Weal, Welt, Whelk

Market(ing), Market day, Marketeer, Market place Advergaming, Agora, Alcaiceria, Arbitrageur, Available, Baltic, Bazaar, Bear, Billingsgate, Black, Black stump, Borgo, Bull, Buyers', Capital, Captive, Car boot sale, Cattle, Change, Chowk, Cinema, Circular, Cluster, Commodity, Common, Covent Garden, Demo, Denet, Direct, Discount, Dragon, eBay®, EC, Emerging, Emporium, Errand, Exchange, Exhibition, Fair, Farmers', Feeing, Flea, Forum, Forward, Free, Grey, Growth, Insert, Internal, Kerb, Lloyds, Main, Mandi, Mart, Mass, Meat, Mercat, Money, Niche, Nundine, Obigosony, Oligopoly, Open (air), Order-driven, Outlet, Overt, Pamphlet, Perfect, Piazza, Poster, Press, Publicity, Radio, Rag fair, Reach, Relationship, Rialto, Sale, Sell, Sellers', Servqual, Share,

Shop, Single, Social, Societal, Sook, Souk, Spot, Stance, Staple, Stock, Stock Exchange, Suq, Tattersall's, TECHMARK®, Terminal, Test, Third, Tiger, Trade, Tron, Tryst, USP, Vent, Viral, Wall Street, Yard sale

Maroon Abandon, Brown, Castaway, Enisle, Firework, Inisle, Isolate, Strand

Marriage, Marry, Married (woman) →ALLIANCE, Ally, Amate, Arranged, Bed, Beenah, Bigamy, Bridal, Buckle, Cleek(it), Coemption, Combine, Commuter, Companionate, Confarreation, Conjugal, Connubial, Couple, Digamy, Endogamy, Espousal, Espouse, Exogamy, Feme covert, Forsooth, Fuse, Gandharva, Genial, Hetaerism, Hetairism, Hitch, Hymen(eal), Indeed, Join, Jugal, Ketubah, Knit, Knot, Lavender, Levirate, M, Match, Mating, Matrilocal, Matrimony, Matron, Memsahib, Mésalliance, Ming, Missis, Missus, Monandry, Monogamy, Morganatic, Nikah, Noose, Nuptial, Pair, Pantagamy, Pardie, Polygamy, Punalua, Quotha, Sacrament, Sannup, Shidduch, Splice, Tie, Tie the knot, Troggs, Troth, Umfazi, →UNION, Unite, W, Wed, Wedding, Wedlock, Wive

Marrow Courgette, Friend, Gist, Kamokamo, Medulla, Myeloid, Pith, Pumpkin, Spinal, Squash, Vegetable

Marsh(y) Bayou, Bog, Camargue, Chott, Corcass, Emys, Everglades, Fen(land), Hackney, Maremma, Merse, Mire, Morass, Ngaio, Paludal, Palustrine, Plashy, Pontine, Pripet, Quagmire, Rann of Kutch, Romney, Salina, Salt, Shott, Slade, Slough, Sog, Spew, Spue, Swale, Swamp, Taiga, Terai, Vlei, Wetlands

Marshal Arrange, Array, Commander, Earp, Foch, French, Hickok, MacMahon, Muster, Neil, Ney, Order, Pétain, Provost, Shepherd, Sky, Steward, Tedder, Usher, Vauban

Marsupial Bandicoot, Bilby, Cuscus, Dasyure, Dibbler, Didelphia, Diprotodon(t), Dunnart, Euro, Honey mouse, Honey possum, Kangaroo, Koala, Macropod, Metatheria, Notoryctes, Nototherium, Numbat, Opossum, Pademelon, Pad(d)ymelon, Petaurist, Phalanger, Pig-rat, Polyprodont, Possum, Potoroo, Pouched mouse, Pygmy glider, Quokka, Quoll, Roo, Tammar, Tasmanian devil, Theria, Thylacine, Tuan, Wallaby, Wambenger, Wombat, Yapo(c)k

Martial (arts) Aikido, Bellicose, Budo, Capoeira, Capuera, Chopsocky, Dojo, Iai-do, Judo, Ju-jitsu, Karate, Kata, Kendo, Krav Maga, Kumite, Kung fu, Militant, Ninjitsu, Ninjutsu, Sensei, Shintaido, Tae Bo®, Tae kwon do, T'ai chi (chuan), Warlike, Wushu

Martyr(dom), Martyrs Alban, Alphege, Campion, Colosseum, Cranmer, Donatist, Justin, Lara, Latimer, MM, Passional, Persecute, Ridley, Sebastian, Shaheed, Shahid, Stephen, Suffer, Tolpuddle, Wishart

Marvel(lous) Blinder, Brilliant, Épatant, Fab(ulous), Fantabulous, Marl, Miracle, Mirific, Peachy, Phenomenon, Prodigious, Selcouth, Superb, Super-duper, Terrific, Wonder

Marx(ism), Marxist Aspheterism, Chico, Comintern, Commie, Groucho, Gummo, Harpo, Karl, Lenin, Mao, Menshevik

Mary Bloody, Celeste, Contrary, Madonna, Magdalene, Moll, Morison, Tum(my), Typhoid, Virgin

Mascot Charm, Four-leaf clover, Telesm, Token

Masculine, Masculinity Butch, He, He-man, Linga(m), M, Machismo, Macho, Male, Manly, Virile, Yang

Mash(er) Beau, Beetle, Brew, Flirt, Lady-killer, Pap, Pestle, Pound, Puree, Sour, Squash

Mask(ed) Bird cage, Camouflage, Cloak, Cokuloris, Death, Disguise, Dissemble, Domino, Face pack, False face, Front, Gas, Gorgoneion, Hide, Larvated, Life,

Loo, Loup, Mascaron, Matte, Oxygen, Persona, Respirator, Screen, Semblance, Shadow, Ski, Stalking-horse, Stocking, Stop out, Template, Veil, Visor, Vizard

Mass(es) Aggregate, Agnus Dei, Anniversary, Atomic, Banket, Bezoar, Bike, Blob, Body, Bulk, Cake, Canon, Chaos, Clot, Compound, Congeries, Conglomeration, Consecration, Core, Crith, Critical, Crowd, Demos, Density, Dona nobis, Dozens, Flake, Flock, Flysch, Folk, Geepound, Gradual, Gramme, Gravitational, Great, Heap, Herd, High, Horde, Hulk, Inertial, Isobare, Jud, Kermesse, Kermis, Kilo(gram), Kirmess, Low, Lump, M, Magma, Majority, Missa, Missa solemnis, Mob, Molar, Month's mind, Mop, Nelson, Nest, Phalanx, Pile, Plebs, Plumb, Pontifical, Populace, Proper, Raft, Red, Requiem, Rest, Ruck, Salamon, Salmon, Sanctus, Scrum, Sea, Serac, Service, Shock, Sicilian, Size, Slub, Slug, Solar, Solemn, Solid, Stack, Stroma, Sursum Corda, Te Igitur, Tektite, Trental, Vesper, Vigil, Volume, Wad, Weight, Welter

Massacre Amritsar, Battue, Beziers, Blood-bath, Butcher, Carnage, Glencoe, Havock, Kanpur, Lidice, Manchester, Peterloo, Pogrom, Purge, Scullabogue, Scupper, September, Sicilian vespers, Slaughter, Slay, Trounce

Massage, Masseur An mo, Cardiac, Chafer, Chavutti thirumal, Do-in, Effleurage, →KNEAD, Malax, Manipulate, Osteopathy, Palp, Petrissage, Physio, Reiki, Rolf(ing), Rubber, Shampoo, Shiatsu, Swedish, Tapotement, Thai, Tripsis, Tui na

Massive Big, Bull, Colossal, Cyclopean, Gang, Heavy, Herculean, Huge, Monolithic, Monumental, Ponderous, Seismic, Strong, Titan

Mast(ed), Masthead Acorn, Crosstree, Foreyard, Hounds, Jigger, Jury, Mizzen, Pannage, Pole, Racahout, Royal, Ship-rigged, Spar, Top-gallant

Master(ly), Mastery Ace, Adept, Artful, Baalebos, Baas, Beak, Beat, Boss, Buddha, Bwana, Captain, Careers, Checkmate, Choir, Chorus, Conquer, Control, Dan, Dominate, Dominie, Employer, Enslave, Exarch, Expert, Genius, Gov, Grand, Grip, Harbour, Herr, Himself, International, Learn, Lord, MA, Maestro, Magistral, Mas(s), Massa, Maulana, Mes(s), Nkosi, Old, Ollamh, Ollav, Oner, Oppress, Original, Overcome, Overlord, Overpower, Overseer, Passed, Past, Pedant, Question, Rabboni, Schoolman, Seed, Seigneur, Seignior, Signorino, Sir(e), Skipper, →SUBDUE, Subjugate, Superate, Surmount, Swami, Tame, Task, Teach, Thakin, Towkay, Tuan, Usher, Vanquish, Virtuoso

Mat(ted), Matting Bast, Capillary, Coaster, Coir, Doily, Dojo, Doyl(e)y, Dutch mattress, Felt, Inlace, Pad, Paunch, Plat, Rug, Rush, Surf, →TANGLE, Tat(ami), Tatty, Taut, Tautit, Tawt, Tomentose, Web, Welcome, Zarf

Match(ed), Matching Agree, Alliance, Amate, Balance, Besort, Bonspiel, Bout, Carousel, Compare, Compeer, Congreve, Consolation, Contest, Cope, Correlate, Correspond, Counterpart, Cup tie, Doubles, Emulate, Engagement, Equal(ise), Equate, Even, Even Stevens, Exhibition, Fellow, Fit, Fixture, Four-ball, Foursome, Friction, Friendly, Fusee, Fuzee, Game, Go, Greensome, Grudge, International, Joust, Light, Locofoco, Love, Lucifer, Main, Marriage, Marrow, Marry, Meet, Mouse, Needle, ODI, Pair(s), Paragon, Parallel, Parti, Pit, Play-off, Prizefight, Promethean, Quick, Replica, Reproduce, Return, Rival, Road game, Roland, Rubber, Safety, Semifinal, Sevens, Shield, Shoo-in, Shooting, Shouting, Singles, Slanging, Slow, Slugfest, Spunk, Striker, Suit, Sync(h), →TALLY, Team, Test, Texas scramble, Tie, Tone, To scale, Twin, Twosome, Union, Venue, Vesta, Vesuvian, Wedding

Mate, Mating Achates, Adam, Amigo, Amplexus, Assistant, Assortative, Bedfellow, Bo, Breed, Buddy, Buffer, Butty, Chess, China, Chum, Cobber,

Comrade, Consort, Crony, Cully, Digger, Eve, Feare, Feer, Fellow, Fere, Fiere, Fool's, Helper, Husband, Inbreed, Maik, Make, Marrow, Marry, Match, Mister, Mucker, Nickar, Oldster, Oppo, → **PAIR**, Pal, Pangamy, Paragon, Partner, Pheer(e), Pirrauru, Scholar's, Serve, Sex, Skaines, Smothered, Soul, Sport, → **SPOUSE**, Tea, Tup, Wack, Wed, Wife, Wus(s)

Material(ism) Agitprop, Appropriate, Apt, → **CLOTH**, Compo, Composite, Copy, Corporeal, Data, Dialectical, Documentation, Earthling, Earthly, → **FABRIC**, Factual, Fallout, Fertile, Fuel, Germane, Historical, Hylic, Illusion, Infill, Leading, Matter, Pertinent, Physical, Positive, Raw, Real, Reify, Relevant, Repertoire, Substance, Tangible, Thingy, Worldly

Mathematician Optime, Statistician, Wrangler

Mathematics, Mathematical, Maths Algebra, Arithmetic, Arsmetrick, Calculus, Combinatorics, Exact science, Geometry, Haversine, Logarithms, Mechanics, Numbers, Trig

Matter Affair, Alluvium, Bioblast, Biogen, Body, Business, Concern, Condensed, Consequence, Content, Count, Dark, Degenerate, Ejecta, Empyema, Epithelium, Evidence, Flux, Front, Gear, Gluon, Go, Grey, Hyle, Ichor, Impost(h)ume, Issue, Mass, Material, Molecule, Multiverse, Neutrino, Phlegm, Pith, Plasma, Point, Positron, Premise, Protoplasm, Pulp, Pus, Quark, Reading, Reck, Reke, Scum, Sediment, Shebang, Signify, Solid, Sputum, Stereome, Stuff, Subject, → **SUBSTANCE**, Symptom, Theme, Thing, Topic, Tousle, Touzle, Vinyl, White, Ylem

Mattress Air bed, Bed(ding), Biscuit, Foam, Futon, Lilo®, Pallet, Pa(i)lliasse, Tick

Mature, Maturity Adult, Age, Auld, Blossom, Bold, Concoct, Develop, Fully-fledged, Grow (up), Mellow, Metaplasis, Puberty, Ripe(n), Rounded, Seasoned, Upgrow(n)

Maul Hammer, Manhandle, Paw, Rough, Savage, Tear

Maximum All-out, Full, Highest, Limit, Most, Peak, Utmost

May Blossom, Can, Hawthorn, Merry, Might, Month, Mote(n), Quickthorn, Shall, Whitethorn

Maybe Happen, Mebbe, Perchance, Perhaps, Possibly

▷**May become** *may indicate* an anagram

Mayor Alcaide, Burgomaster, Casterbridge, Charter, Councilman, Portreeve, Provost, Syndic, Whittington, Worship, Worthy

Maze Honeycomb, Labyrinth, Meander, Network, Theseus, Warren, Wilderness

MC Announcer, Compere, Host, Ringmaster

Mead(ow) Flood, Grass(land), Haugh, Inch, Ing, Lea(se), Ley, Meath(e), → **PASTURE**, Runnymede, Saeter, Salting, Water

Meagre Arid, Bar, Bare, Exiguity, Exiguous, Insubstantial, Measly, Mingy, Paltry, Pittance, Scant, Scrannel, Scranny, Scrawny, Skimpy, Skinny, Slender, Spare, Stingy, Thin

Meal(s), Mealie, Mealy Allseed, Banquet, Barbecue, Barium, Beanfeast, Blow-out, Board, Breakfast, Brunch, Buffet, Carry out, Cassava, Cereal, Chilled, Cholent, Chota-hazri, Collation, Corn, Cornflour, Cottoncake, Cottonseed, Cou-cou, Couscous, Crib(ble), Dejeune(r), Deskfast, Dinner, Drammock, Ear, Ervalenta, Fare, Farina, Feast, Feed, Flour, Food, Glacier, Grits, Grout, Hangi, High tea, Iftar, Indian, Italian, Kai, Lock, Lunch, Mandioc, Mandioc(c)a, Mani(h)oc, Matzo, Melder, Meltith, Mensal, Mess, Morning, Mush, No-cake, Nosh, Nuncheon, Ordinary, Picnic, Piece, Pizza, Plate, Ploughman's lunch, Poi,

Polenta, Porridge, Prandial, Prix fixe, Rac(c)ahout, Refection, Repast, Revalenta, Rijst(t)afel, Salep, Scambling, Scoff, Seder, Sehri, Slap-up, Smorgasbord, Snack, Sohur, Spread, Square, Suhur, Supper, Table d'hôte, Takeaway, Tamale, Tea, Thali, Tiffin, Tightener, Tousy tea, Twalhours, Undern

Mean(ing), Meant Aim, Arithmetic(al), Average, Base, Betoken, Bowsie, Caitiff, Cheap, Cheeseparing, Close, Connotation, Curmudgeon, Definition, Denotate, Denote, Design, Dirty, Drift, Essence, Ettle, Feck, Footy, Foul, Geometric(al), Gist, Golden, Hang, Harmonic, Humble, Hunks, Ignoble, Illiberal, Imply, Import, Inferior, Insect, Intend, Intermediate, Kunjoos, Lexical, Low(down), Mang(e)y, Marrow, Measly, Medium, Mesquin, Message, Method, Mid, Miserly, Narrow, Near, Niggardly, Nirlie, Norm, Nothing, One-horse, Ornery, Paltry, Par, Penny-pinching, Penurious, Petty, Piker, Pinch-penny, Pith, Point, Purport, →**PURPOSE**, Quadratic, Ratfink, Revenue, Ribald, Roinish, Roynish, Scall, Scrub, Scurvy, Semanteme, Semantic(s), Sememe, Sense, Shabby, Signify, Slight, Slink, Small, Sneaky, Snoep, Snot, Sordid, Sparing, Spell, Squalid, Stingy, Stink(ard), Stinty, Substance, Symbol, Thin, Threepenny, Tight-lipped, Tightwad, Two-bit, Value, Vile, Whoreson

Means Agency, Ample, Dint, Income, Instrumental, Media, Method, Mode, Opulence, Organ, Private, Recourse, Resources, Staple, Substance, Tactics, Visible, Ways

Measure(d), Measuring, Measure(ment) By(e)law, Calibre, Centile, Circular, Corn Law, Crackdown, Customise, →**DANCE**, →**DIMENSION**, Dipstick, Distance, Doggerel, Dose, Dry, →**GAUGE**, Gavotte, Gross, Imperial, →**INSTRUMENT**, IQ, Limit, Linear, Liter, Litre, Meed, Metage, Moratorium, Of, Offset, Plumb, Precaution, Prophylactic, Quickstep, Ration, Remen, Sanction, Sea-level, Share, Short, →**SIZE**, Sound, Standard, Statute, Step, Stichometry, Strike, Struck, Survey, Tachymetry, Timbre, Token, Triangulate, →**UNIT**, Weigh, Wine

Meat(s) Bacon, Bard, Beef, Beefsteak, Biltong, Brawn, Brisket, Brown, Burger, Cabob, Carbonado, Carrion, Charcuterie, Chop, Collop, Confit, Croquette, Cut, Cutlet, Dark, Devon, Dog-roll, Doner kebab, Easy, Edgebone, Entrecôte, Escalope, Essence, Fanny Adams, Fatback, Fillet, Fleishig, Fleishik, Flesh, Flitch, Force, Galantine, Game, Gigot, Gobbet, Gosht, Griskin, Halal, Ham, Haslet, Haunch, Jerky, Joint, Junk, Kabab, Kabob, Kebab, Kebob, Lamb, Loin, Luncheon, Mart, Medaillon, Medallion, Mince, Mutton, Noisette, Offal, Olive, Oyster, Pastrami, Paupiette, Pem(m)ican, Piccata, Pith, Pope's eye, Pork, Processed, Prosciutto, Rack, Red, Rillettes, Roast, Saddle, Sasatie, Satay, Scaloppino, Schnitzel, Scran, Scrapple, Sey, Shank, Shashlik, Shishkebab, Short ribs, Side, Sirloin, Sosatie, Spam®, Spare rib, Spatchcock, Spaul(d), Steak, Strong, Tenderloin, Tiring, Tongue, Variety, Veal, Venison, Vifda, Virgate, Vivda, White, Wiener schnitzel, Wurst

Mechanic(s) Apron-man, Artificer, Artisan, Banausic, Barodynamics, Card, Celestial, Classical, Dynamics, Engineer, Fitter, Fundi, Hand, Journeyman, Kinematics, Kinesiology, Kinetics, Operative, Statics, Technician

▷**Mechanic(al)** *may indicate* characters from 'A Midsummer Night's Dream'

Mechanical, Mechanism Action, Apparatus, Auto, Autodestruct, Automatic, Banausic, Bottom, Chargehand, Clockwork, Dérailleur, Escapement, Foul-safe, Gimmal, Gust-lock, Instrument, Machinery, Movement, Organical, Pulley, Pushback, Rackwork, Regulator, Rigger, Robotic, Rote, Servo, Synchroflash, Traveller, Trippet, Works

Medal(lion) Award, Bar, Bronze, Cameo, Croix de guerre, Decoration, Dickin, DSM, GC, George, Gold, Gong, Gorget, MM, Numismatic, Pan(h)agia, Purple Heart, Putty, Roundel, Silver, Touchpiece, VC, Vernicle

Mediate, Mediator ACAS, Arbitrate, Conciliate, Intercede, Interpose, Intervene, Liaison, Muti, Peacemaker, Referee, Stickler, Thirdsman, Trouble-shooter

Medical, Medicine (chest), Medicament, Medication Aesculapian, Algology, Aloetic, Alternative, Amulet, Analgesic, Anodyne, Antacid, Antibiotic, Antidote, Antisepsis, Antiseptic, Arnica, Arrowroot, Aurum potabile, Aviation, Bariatrics, Bi, Bismuth, Blister, Charm, Chinese, Chiropody, Chlorodyne, Clinician, Complementary, Cordial, Corpsman, Cubeb, Curative, Defensive, Demulcent, Diapente, Discutient, Doctor's stuff, Dosage, Dose, Draught, Drops, →**DRUG**, Dutch drops, Eardrop, Electuary, Elixir, Emetic, Empirics, Enema, Excipient, Expectorant, Fall-trank, Febrifuge, Folk, Forensic, Fringe, Functional, Galen, Galenism, Gelcap, Genitourinary, Gripe water®, Gutta, Haematinic, Haematology, Herb, Herbal, Holistic, Hom(o)eopathy, Hyssop, Iatric(al), Indian, Industrial, Inhalant, Inro, Internal, Iodine, Iron, Ko cycle, Lariam®, Laxative, L-dopa, Leechcraft, Legal, Lime-water, Loblolly, Lotion, Magnesia, Maqui, Menthol, Microbubbles, Mishmi, Mixture, Moxar, Muti, Natural, Naturopathy, Nephritic, Nephrology, Nervine, Neurology, Nosology, Nostrum, Nuclear, Nux vomica, Ob-gyn, Occupational, Officinal, Oncology, Oporice, Orthopoedics, Osteopath, Palliative, Panacea, Paregoric, Patent, Pathology, Pectoral, P(a)ediatrics, Pharmacy, Phlegmagogue, Physic, Physical, Pill, Placebo, Polypill, Potion, Poultice, Preparation, Preventive, Prosthetics, Prozac®, Psionic, Psychiatry, Ptisan, Purgative, Quin(quin)a, Quinine, Qinghaosu, Radiology, Reborant, Red Crescent, Red Cross, Relaxative, →**REMEDY**, Salts, Salve, Sanative, Sebesten, Senna, Serology, Simple, Snake-oil, Space, Specific, Sports, Steel, Stomachic, Stomatology, Stupe, Suppository, Synergast, Syrup, Tablet, Tar-water, Therapeutics, Thimerosal, TIM, Tincture, Tisane, Tocology, Tonic, Totaquine, Trade, Traditional Chinese, Treatment, Trichology, Troche, Valerian, Veronal, Veterinary, Virology, Witchhazel, Wychhazel

Medieval Archaic, Feudal, Gothic, Med, Old, Trecento

Meditate, Meditation, Meditator, Meditative Brood, Chew, Cogitate, Contemplate, Falun gong, Fifteen o's, Insight, Muse, Mystic, Nirvana, Ponder, Reflect, Reverie, Revery, Ruminate, Samadhi, Tantric, Transcendental, Vipassana, Weigh, Yogic flying, Zazen

Medium (A)ether, Agency, Air, Average, Channel, Clairvoyant, Contrast, Culture, Dispersive, Earth, Element, Ether, Even, Fire, Happy, Home, Intermediary, Interstellar, M, Magilp, Mean, Megilp, Midsize, Midway, Milieu, Oils, Organ, Ouija, Planchette, Press, Radio, Regular, Shaman, Spiritist, Spiritualist, Television, Telly, TV, Vehicle, Water

Medley Charivari, Collection, Gallimaufry, Individual, Jumble, Macedoine, Melange, Mishmash, Mix, Pastiche, Patchwork, Pi(e), Pot-pourri, Quodlibet, Ragbag, Salad, Salmagundi, Series

▷**Medley** *may indicate* an anagram

Meek Docile, Griselda, Humble, Milquetoast, Patient, Sheepy, Tame

Meet(ing), Meeting place Abide, Abutment, Achieve, AGM, Appointment, Apposite, Apropos, Apt, Ascot, Assemblage, Assemble, Assembly, Assignation, Audience, Baraza, Bosberaad, Briefing, Cabinet, Camporee, Caucus, Chapterhouse, Chautauqua, Clash, Commissure, Conclave, Concourse, Concur,

Confluence, Confrontation, Congress, Connivance, Conseil d'etat, Consistory, Consult(ation), Contact, Conterminous, Convene, Convent(icle), Convention, Converge, Conversazione, Convocation, Correspond, Crossroads, Cybercafé, Date, Defray, Demo, EGM, Encounter, Ends, Experience, Face, Find, Fit, For(e)gather, Forum, Fulfil, Gala, Gemot, General, Giron, Gorsedd, Greeting, Guild, Gyeld, Gymkhana, Gyron, Hall, Howf(f), Hunt, Hustings, Imbizo, Impact, Indaba, Infall, Interface, Interview, Jamboree, Join, Junction, Kgotla, Korero, Lekgotla, Liaise, Marae, Match, Moot, Mother's, Obviate, Occlusion, Occur, Oppose, Overflow, Partenariat, Pay, Plenary, Plenum, Pnyx, Pow-wow, Prayer, Prosper, Quadrivial, Quaker, Quorate, Quorum, Race, Races, Rally(ing point), Rencontre, Rencounter, Rendezvous, Replay, Reunion, Sabbat(h), Satisfy, Séance, See, Seminar, Session, Sit, Social, Sports, Suitable, Summit, Swap, Symposium, Synastry, Synaxis, Synod, Tackle, Talkfest, Talk-in, Talking-shop, Think-in, Town, Track, Tryst, Venery, Venue, Vestry, Wapinshaw, Wardmote, Wharenui, Wharepuni, Workshop

Mellow Age, Genial, Mature, Ripe, Smooth

Melody, Melodious Air, Arioso, Cabaletta, Canorous, Cantabile, Cantilena, Cantus, Cavatina, Chant, Chopsticks, Conductus, Counterpoint, Descant, Dulcet, Euphonic, Fading, Musical, Orphean, Part-song, Plainsong, Ranz-des-vaches, Strain, Sweet, Theme, Tunable, → **TUNE(S)**

Melon(like) Cantaloup(e), Cas(s)aba, Charentais, Galia, Gourd, Honeydew, Mango, Musk, Nar(r)as, Ogen, Pepo, Persian, Rock

Melt(ed), Melting Ablate, Colliquate, → **DISSOLVE**, Eutectic, Eutexia, Flux, Found, Fuse, Fusil(e), Liquescent, Liquid, Run, Smectic, Syntexis, Thaw, Touch

Member Adherent, Arm, Beam, Branch, Bro(ther), Charter, Chin, Confrère, Cornice, Crossbeam, Crypto, Direction, Felibre, Fellow, Finger, Forearm, Forelimb, Girder, Gremial, Harpin(g)s, Insider, Leg, Limb, Longeron, M, MBE, Montant, MP, Organ, Part, Partisan, Peer, Politicaster, Politician, Private, Tie, Upright

Membrane, Membranous Amnion, Arachnoid, Axilemma, Bilayer, Caul, Chorioallantois, Chorion, Choroid (plexus), Chromoplast, Conjunctiva, Cornea, Decidua, Dissepiment, Dura (mater), Eardrum, Endocardium, Endometrium, Endosteum, Ependyma, Exine, Extine, Fell, Film, Foetal, Frenulum, Haw, Head, Hyaloid, Hymen, Indusium, Intima, Intine, Involucre, Kell, Mater, Mediastinum, Meninx, Mesentery, Mucosa, Mucous, Neurolemma, Nictitating, Nuclear, Parchment, Patagium, Pellicle, Pericardium, Pericarp, Perichondrium, Pericranium, Periost(eum), Periton(a)eum, Pia mater, Plasma, Plasmalemma, Pleura, Putamen, Rim, Sarcolemma, Scarious, Schneiderian, Sclera, Serosa, Serous, Synovial, Tela, Third eyelid, Tissue, Tonoplast, Trophoblast, Tunic, Tympan(ic), Vacuolar, Velum, Vitelline, Web

Memento, Memoir Keepsake, Locket, Relic, Remembrancer, Souvenir, Token, Trophy

Memo(randum) Bordereau, Cahier, Chit, IOU, Jot, Jurat, Minute, Note, Notepad, → **REMINDER**, Slip

Memorable, Memorise, Memory Associative, ATLAS, Bubble, Cache, Catchy, Collective, → **COMPUTER MEMORY**, Con, Core, DIMM, DRAM, Dynamic, Echoic, Elephantine, Engram(ma), Extended, Flash (bulb), Folk, Get, Highlight, Historic, Hypermnesia, Iconic, Immortal, Immunological, Keepsake, Kilobyte, Learn, Living, Long-term, Main, Mainstore, Memoriter, Mind, Mneme, Mnemonic, Mnemosyne, Non-volatile, Noosphere, Notable, Pelmanism, Photographic, Race, Read-write, Recall, Recollection, Recovered, Red-letter day,

→ **REMEMBER**, Retention, Retrospection, ROM, Ro(a)te, Samskara, Screen, Semantic, Short-term, SIMM, Souvenir, Sovenance, Special, Static, Storage, Study, Video, Virtual, Volatile, Word, Working

Memorial Albert, Altar tomb, Brass, Cenotaph, Cromlech, Ebenezer, Gravestone, Hatchment, Marker, Martyr's, Mausoleum, Monument, Mount Rushmore, Obelisk, Pantheon, Plaque, Relic, Relique, Statue, Tomb(stone), Trophy, Wreath

Menace, Menacing Danger, Dennis, Endanger, Foreboding, Intimidate, Jeopardise, Minatory, Ominous, Peril, Pest, Scowl, Sinister, Threat(en)

Mend(er) Beet, Bete, Bushel, Cobble, Correct, Cure, Darn, Fix, Heal, Improved, Mackle, Patch, Piece, Recover, Remedy, → **REPAIR**, Set, Sew, Solder, Tinker, Trouble-shoot

Menial Dogsbody, Drudge, Drug, Eta, Fag, Flunkey, Lackey, Lowly, Scullion, Servile, Toady, Underling, Wood-and-water joey

▷**Mental** *may indicate* the chin

Mention(ed) Advert, Allusion, Bename, Benempt, Bring up, Broach, Bynempt, Citation, Drag up, Hint, Honourable, Hote, Instance, Name(-check), Notice, Quote, Refer, Same, Specify, Speech, State, Suggest, Touch

Menu Card, Carte, Carte du jour, Cascading, Cuisine, Fare, List, Option, Prix fixe, Table d'hôte, Tariff

Mercenary Arnaout, Condottiere, Freelance, Gallo(w)glass, Greedy, Hack, Hessian, Hired gun, Hireling, Landsknecht, Legionnaire, Mean, Money-grubbing, Pindaree, Pindari, Rutter, Sordid, Spoilsman, Swiss Guard, Switzer, Venal, Warmonger, Wildgeese

Merchandise Cargo, Goods, Line, Produce, Ware(s)

Merchant(man) Abbas, Abudah, Antonio, Argosy, Broker, Bun(n)ia, Burgher, Chandler, Chap, Commission, Crare, Crayer, Dealer, Doom, Factor, Flota, Gossip, Hoastman, Importer, Jobber, Magnate, Marcantant, Mercer, Monger, Nathan, Négociant, Pedlar, Polo, Provision, Retailer, Scrap, Seller, Shipper, Speed, Squeegee, Stapler, Trader, Vintner, Wholesaler

Merciful, Mercy Amnesty, Charity, Clement, Compassionate, Corporal, Grace, Humane, Kind, Kyrie, Lenient, Lenity, Miserere, Misericord(e), Pacable, Pity, Quarter, Ruth, Sparing, Spiritual

Merciless Cruel, Hard, Hard-hearted, Inclement, Pitiless, Wanton

Mere(ly) Allenarly, Bare, Common, Lake, Only, Pond, Pool, Poor, Pure, Sheer, Tarn, Ullswater, Very

Merge(r), Merging Amalgamate, Blend, Coalesce, Coalise, Composite, Conflate, Consolidate, Die, Elide, Fusion, Incorporate, Interflow, Interpenetrate, Liquesce, Meld, Melt, Mingle, Symphysis, Syncretism, Synergy, Unify, Unite

Merit(ed) CL, Condign, Deserve, Due, Earn, Found, Lustre, Meed, Rate, Virtue, Worth(iness)

Mess(y), Mess up Anteroom, Balls-up, Bedraggled, Blotch, Boob, Boss, Botch, Canteen, Caudle, Chaos, Clamper, Clutter, Cock-up, Dining-room, Disorganise, Dog's dinner, Failure, Farrago, Fiasco, Flub, Garboil, Glop, G(l)oop, Gory, Guddle, Gunge, Gunk, Gun-room, Hash, Horlicks, Hotch-potch, Hugger-mugger, Imbroglio, Lash-up, Louse, Mash, Meal, Mismanage, Mix, Mixter-maxter, Modge, Muck, Muddle, Muff, Mullock, Muss, Mux, Pi(e), Pig's ear, Piss-up, Plight, Pollute, Pottage, Screw-up, Scungy, Shambles, Shambolic, Shemozzle, Sight, Slaister, Smudge, Snafu, Soss, Sty, Sully, Tinker, Tousle, Trifle, Untidy, Wardroom, Whoopsie, Yuck(y)

Message(s), Messaging Aerogram, Bull, Bulletin, Cable(gram), Caption, Contraplex, Dépêche, Despatch, Dispatch, Epistle, Errand, Fax, Flame, Inscription, Kissagram, Kissogram, Letter, Marconigram, Missive, News, Note, Notification, Pager, Ping, Posting, Postscript, Propaganda, PTO, Radiogram, Radio telegraph, Read-out, Rumour, Signal, Slogan, SMS, SOS, Subtext, Telco, Telegram, Telepheme, Telephone, Teletype®, Telex, Tidings, Toothing, Tweet, Valentine, Voice mail, Wire, → **WORD**

Messenger Angel, Angela, Apostle, Azrael, Beadle, Caddie, Caddy, Carrier pigeon, Chaprassi, Chuprassy, Corbie, Courier, Culver, Despatch-rider, Emissary, Envoy, Errand boy, Gaga, Gillie whitefoot, Hatta, Herald, Hermes, Internuncio, Iris, Ladas, Mercury, Nuncio, Peon, Post, Pursuivant, Runner, Send, Seraph, Valet de place

Messiah Christ, Emmanuel, Immanuel, Mahdi, Mashiach, Prince of Peace, Saviour, Shiloh, Son of Man, Southcott

Metal(s), Metallic, Metalware, Metalwork Aeneous, Antifriction, Base, Death, Expanded, Filler, Fine, Fusible, Heavy, Hot, Jangling, Leaf, Mercuric, Mineral, Noble, Nonferrous, Ore, Perfect, Planchet, Precious, Prince's, Road, Scrap, Sheet(-iron), Sprue, Stannic, Thrash, Torque, Tramp, Transition, Type, White, Yellow

▷**Metamorphosing** *may indicate* an anagram

Metaphor Conceit, Figure, Image(ry), Kenning, Mixed, Symbol, Trope, Tropical

Meteor(ic), Meteorite Achondrite, Aerolite, Aerosiderite, Bolide, Chondrite, Comet, Drake, Fireball, Geminid, Iron, Leonid, Perseid, Siderite, Siderolite, Star(dust), Stony(-iron)

Method(ology), Methodical Art, Billings, Formal, Formula, Gram's, How, Kumon, Line, Manner, Mode, Modus, Modus operandi, Monte Carlo, Montessori, Neat, Orderly, Organised, Organon, Organum, Painstaking, Phonic, Plan, Ploy, Procedure, Process, Stanislavski, Systematic, Tactics, Technique, Way, Withdrawal

Metre, Metrical Alexandrine, Amphibrach, Amphimacer, Anapaest, Antispast, Arsis, Ballad, Cadence, Choliamb, Choree, Choriamb, Common, Dipody, Galliambic, Iambic, Ithyphallic, Long, M, Penthemimer, Prosody, Pyrrhic, Rhythm, Sapphic, Scansion, Scazon, Semeion, Service, Short, Spondee, Strophe, Tribrach, Tripody, Trochee

Microbiologist Fleming, Sabine, Salk

Microphone Bug, Crystal, Directional, Mike, Phonic Ear®, Radio, Throat

Midday Meridian, N, Noon

Middle(way), Middling, Midpoint Active, Ariston metron, Basion, Centre, Core, Crown, Enteron, Epitasis, Equidistant, Eye, Girth, Heart, Innermost, Internal, Loins, Meat, Median, Mediocre, Medium, Meridian, Meseraic, Mesial, Mesne, Meso, Midriff, Moderate, Nasion, Noon, Passive, Turn, Twixt, Undistributed, Via media, Wa(i)st

Middleman Agent, Broker, Centre, Comprador(e), Diaphragm, Interlocutor, Intermediary, Jobber, Median, Navel, Regrater, Regrator

Midget Dwarf, Homunculus, Lilliputian, Pygmy, Shrimp

Might(iness), Mighty Could, Force, Main, Maud, Mote, Muscle, Nibs, Oak, Potence, → **POWER**, Prowess, Puissant, Should, Strength

Migrate, Migration, Migratory Colonise, Diapedesis, Diaspora, Drift, Eelfare, Exodus, Fleet, Run, Tre(c)k

Mild(ly), Mildness Balmy, Benign, Bland, Clement, Euphemism, Genial, Gentle, Lenient, Lenity, Litotes, Mansuete, Meek, →**MODERATE**, Pacific, Patient, Pussycat, Sarcenet, Sars(e)net, Temperate

Mile(r), Miles Admiralty, Coss, Coverdale, Food, Geographical, Hour, Irish, Knot, Kos, League, Li, Mi, Milliary, Nautical, Passenger, Roman, Royal, Scots, Sea, Soldier, Square, Standish, Statute, Swedish, Train

Militancy, Militant, Military Activist, Aggressive, Battailous, Belligerent, Black Power, Commando, Fortinbras, Hawkish, Hezbollah, Hizbollah, Hizbullah, Hostile, Ireton, Janjaweed, Janjawid, Junta, Kshatriya, Landsturm, Landwehr, Leftist, Logistics, Lumper, Mameluke, Martial, Nahal, Naxalite, Presidio, Soldatesque, Stratocracy, Tactical, War machine, War paint, West Point, Zealous

Militia(-man) Band, Guard, Milice, Minuteman, Peshmerga, Reserve, Trainband, Yeomanry

Milk(er), Milky Acidophilus, Beestings, Bland, Bleed, Bonny-clabber, Bristol, Butter, Casein, Certified, Churn, Colostrum, Condensed, Creamer, Crud, Curd, Dairy, Emulge, Evaporated, Exact, Exploit, Extract, Galactic, Glacier, Goat's, Homogenised, Jib, Kefir, Kephir, K(o)umiss, Lactation, Lacteal, Latex, Long-life, Maas, Madafu, Madzoon, Magnesia, Mamma, Matzoon, Mess, Moo-juice, Opaline, Pigeon's, Pinta, Posset, Rice, Sap, Shedder, Skim(med), Soya, Squeeze, Strip(pings), Stroke, Suckle, Town, UHT, Use, Whey, Whig, Yaourt, Yogh(o)urt

Mill(ing), Mills Aswarm, Ball, Barker's, Blag, Boxing, Coffee, Crazing, Economist, Flatford, Flour, Gang, Gastric, Gig, Grind(er), Hayley, Kibble, Knurl, Lumber, Malt, Mano, Melder, Molar, Nurl, Oil, Paper, Pepper, Plunge-cut, Post, Powder, Press, Pug, Pulp, Quartz, Quern, Reave, Rob, Rolling, Rumour, Satanic, Scutcher, Smock, Spinning, Stamp, Stamping, Strip, Sucken, Sugar, Surge, Thou, Tide, Tower, Tuck, Water, Wool(len), Works

Mime, Mimic(ry) Ape, Batesian, Copycat, Echo, Farce, Imitate, Impersonate, Marceau, Mina, Mock, Mullerian, Mummer, Myna, Sturnine, Take-off

Mind(er) Agent, Aide, Baby-sitter, Beware, Bodyguard, Brain, Care, Gaum, Genius, Grasshopper, Grey matter, Handler, Head, →**HEED**, Herd, Id, Ideo-, Intellect, Mentality, Month's, Nous, Open, Psyche, Psychogenic, Resent, Sensorium, Tabula rasa, Tend, Thinker, View, Wit, Woundwort, Year's

Mine, Mining Acoustic, Antenna, Appalachia, Biomining, Bomb, Bonanza, Bord and pillar, Bottom, Bouquet, Burrow, Camouflet, Chemical, Claymore, Coalfield, Colliery, Contact, Creeping, Dane-hole, Data, Dig(gings), Drifting, Egg, Eldorado, Excavate, Explosive, Fiery, Floating, Flooder, Fougade, Fougasse, Gallery, Gob, Golconda, Gold, Gopher, Grass, Homing, Land, Limpet, Magnetic, Microbiological, Naked-light, Nostromo, Open-cast, Open-cut, Ophir, Pit, Placer, Pressure, Prospect, Rising, Sap, Set(t), Show, Silver, Sonic, Stannary, Stope, Strike, Strip, Undercut, Wheal, Win, Workings

Miner, Mine-worker, Mine-working Bevin boy, Butty-gang, Buttyman, Collier, Corporal, Cutter, Digger, Faceworker, Forty-niner, Geordie, Leaf, Molly Maguire, Noisy, NUM, Oncost(man), Pitman, Sapper, Shot-firer, Stall, Tippler, Tributer, Tunneler, UDM, Undersawyer

Mineral(s) Accessory, Index, Ore, Owre

Mineralogy, Mineralogist Haüy, Heuland, Miller-Smithson, Oryctology

Mingle, Mingling Assort, Blend, Commix, Consort, Interfuse, Intermarry, Mell, Merge, →**MIX**, Participate, Socialise, Theocrasy, Unite

Minimise, Minimum (range) Bare, Downplay, Fewest, Floor, Gloze, Least, Neap, Pittance, Quorum, Scant, Shoestring, Stime, Styme, Threshold, Undervalue

▷**Minimum of** *may indicate* the first letter

Minister Ambassador, Attend, Buckle-beggar, Chancellor, Chaplain, Cleric, Coarb, Commissar, Curate, Deacon, Dewan, Diplomat, Divine, Dominee, Dominie, D(i)wan, Envoy, Front Bench, Home Secretary, Mas(s)john, Mes(s)john, Moderator, Nurse, Officiant, Ordinand, Ordinee, Padre, Parson, Peshwa, Preacher, Predikant, Presbyter, Priest, Rector, Richelieu, Secretary, Seraskier, → **SERVE**, Stick, Stickit, Tanaiste, Tend, Visier, Vizier

Ministry Cabinet, Cloth, Defence, Defra, Department, Dept, DoE, MOD, MOT, Orders, Service, Treasury

▷**Ministry** *may indicate* some government department

Minor(ity) Child, Comprimario, Ethnic, Faction, Few, Fractional, Incidental, Infant, Junior, Less(er), Marginal, Minutia, Negligible, Nominal, Nonage, One-horse, Peripheral, Petty, Piffling, Pre-teen, Pupillage, Signed, Slight, Sub(sidiary), Subordinate, Trivial, Ward, Weeny

Mint Aim, Bugle-weed, Bull's eye, Catnip, Coin, Ettle, Fortune, Herb, Horse, Humbug, Labiate, Monarda, Monetise, Nep, New, Penny-royal, Pepper, Pile, Polo®, Poly, Rock, Selfheal, Spear, Stamp, Stone, Strike, Unused, Utter, Water

Minute(s), Minutiae Acta, Alto, Bijou, Degree, Detailed, Diatom, Entry, Infinitesimal, Lilliputian, Little, Mere, Micron, Mo, Mu, Nano-, New York, Resume, Small, Teen(t)sy, Teeny, Tine, Tiny, Trivia, Tyne, Wee

Miracle(s), Miraculous, Miracle worker Cana, Marvel, Merel(l), Meril, Morris, Mystery, Mythism, Phenomenon, Saluter, Thaumatology, Thaumaturgic, Theurgy, Wonder

Mirror(s), Mirrored Alasnam, Antidazzle, Busybody, Cambuscan, Catoptric, Cheval, Claude Lorraine glass, Coelostat, Conde, Conjugate, Dare, Driving, Enantiomorph, Glass, Handglass, Heliostat, Image, Imitate, Keeking-glass, Lao, Magnetic, Merlin, One-way, Pierglass, Primary, Psyche, Rearview, → **REFLECT**, Reynard, Sign, Specular, Speculum, Stone, Tiring-glass, Two-way, Vulcan, Wing

▷**Misalliance** *may indicate* an anagram

Miscellaneous, Miscellany Ana, Assortment, Chow, Collectanea, Diverse, Etceteras, Gallimaufry, Job lot, Misc, Odds and ends, Odds and sods, Olio, Omnium-gatherum, Paraphernalia, Pie, Potpourri, Raft, Ragbag, Sundry, Varia, Variety, Various

Mischief(-maker), Mischievous Ate, Bale, Bane, Cantrip, Cloots, Devilment, Diablerie, Dido, Disservice, Evil, Gallus, Goings on, Gremlin, Hanky-panky, Harm, Hellery, Hellion, Hob, Imp, Injury, Jiggery-pokery, Jinks, Larky, Larrikin, Limb, Make-bate, Malicho, Mallecho, Monkeyshines, Nickum, Owl-spiegle, Pestilent, Pickle, Prank, Puckish, Rascal, Rogue, Scally(wag), Scamp, Scapegrace, Shenanigans, Spalpeen, Spriteful, Tricksy, Varmint, Wag, Wicked

Misconception Delusion, Idol(on), Idolum, Mirage, Misunderstanding

▷**Misdelivered** *may indicate* an anagram

Miser(ly) Carl, Cheapskate, Cheese-parer, Close, Curmudgeon, Flay-flint, Gare, Grasping, Harpagon, Hunks, Marner, Meanie, Mingy, Muckworm, Niggard, Nipcheese, Nipfarthing, Pennyfather, Penny-pincher, Pinch-commons, Puckfist, Runt, Save-all, Scrape-good, Scrape-penny, Screw, Scrimping, Scrooge, Shylock, Skinflint, Snudge, Storer, Tightwad, Timon

Miserable, Misery, Miserably Abject, Bale, Bane, Cut up, Distress, Dog's-life, Dole, Face-ache, Forlorn, Gloom, Grief, Heartache, Hell, Joyless, Killjoy, Lousy,

Mean, Measly, Perdition, Saturnist, Sorry, Sourpuss, Spoilsport, Torture, Tragic, Triste, →**UNHAPPY**, Wet blanket, Woe(begone), Wretched

Misfortune Accident, Adversity, Affliction, Bale, Calamity, Curse, Disaster, Distress, Dole, Harm, Hex, Ill, Ill-luck, Kicker, Mis(c)hanter, Reverse, Rewth, Ruth, Wroath

▷**Misguided** *may indicate* an anagram

Misjudge(ment) Blunder, Misween, Overrate

Mislead(ing) Blind, Con, Cover-up, Deceive, Delude, Dupe, Equivocate, Fallacious, False, Gag, Half-truth, Red herring, Runaround, Snow job

▷**Misled** *may indicate* an anagram

Mismanage Blunder, Bungle, Muddle

Misprint Error, Literal, Literal error, Slip, Typo

Misrepresent(ation) Abuse, Belie, Calumny, Caricature, Colour, Distort, Falsify, Garble, Lie, Slander, Traduce, Travesty

Miss(ing) Abord, Absent, Airshot, Astray, Avoid, Colleen, Desiderate, Dodge, Drib, Err(or), Eschew, Fail, Forego, Gal, →**GIRL**, Kumari, Lack, Lass, Link, Lose, Mademoiselle, Maid, Maiden, Mile, Muff(et), Need, Neglect, Negligence, Omit, Otis, Overlook, Señorita, Skip, Spinster, Unmeet, Wanting

▷**Miss** *may refer to* Missouri

Missile ABM, Air-to-air, ALCM, Ammo, Anti-ballistic, Arrow, Artillery, Atlas, Ball, Ballistic, Beam Rider, Blue streak, Bolas, Bolt, Bomb, Boomerang, Brickbat, Bullet, Condor, Cruise, Dart, Death star, Dingbat, Doodlebug, Dum-dum, Exocet®, Falcon, Fléchette, Genie, Grenade, Guided, HARM, Harpoon, Hawk, Hellfire, Hound Dog, ICBM, Interceptor, Jired, Kiley, Kyley, Kylie, Lance, Mace, MARV, Maverick, Minuteman, MIRV, Missive, Mx, Onion, Patriot, Pellet, Pershing, Phoenix, Polaris, Poseidon, Qual, Quarrel, Rocket, SAM, Scud, Sea Skimmer, Seeker, Sergeant, Shell, Shillelagh, Shot, Shrike, Side-winder, Smart bomb, Snowball, Sparrow, Spartan, Spear, Sprint, SSM, Standard Arm, Standoff, Styx, Subroc, Surface to air, Surface to surface, Talos, Tartar, Terrier, Thor, Titan, Tomahawk, Torpedo, Tracer, Trident, UAM, Warhead

Mission(ary) Aidan, Alamo, Antioch, Apostle, Assignment, Barnabas, Bethel, Boniface, Caravan, Charge, Columba, Cuthbert, Cyril, Delegation, Embassage, Embassy, Errand, Evangelist, Function, Happy-clappy, Iona, Legation, Livingstone, LMS, Message, Missiology, NASA, Neurolab, Op, Paul, Pr(a)efect, Quest, Reclaimer, Silas, Task, Vocation

Mist(y) Aerosol, Australian, Blur, Brume, Cloud, Damp, Dew, Drow, Fog, Fret, Haar, Haze, Hoar, Miasma, Moch, Nebular, Niflheim, Nimbus, Rack, Roke, Scotch, Sfumato, Smir(r), Smog, Smur, Spotted, Spray, Steam, Vapour, Veil

Mistake(n) Aberration, Barry (Crocker), Bish, Bloomer, Blooper, Blue, Blunder, Boner, Boob, Booboo, Boss, Botch, Bull, Category, Clanger, Clinker, Confound, Deluded, Domino, Erratum, Error, Fallacy, Fault, Floater, Flub, Fluff, Folly, Gaffe, Goof, Hash, Horlicks, Howler, Identity, Incorrect, Lapse, Malapropism, Misprision, Miss, Muff, Mutual, Nod, Off-beam, Oops, Oversight, Own goal, Plonker, Pratfall, Ricket, Screw-up, →**SLIP**, Slip-up, Solecism, Stumer, Trip, Typo, Wrongdoing

▷**Mistake(n)** *may indicate* an anagram

Mistress Amie, Aspasia, Canary-bird, Chatelaine, Concubine, Courtesan, Delilah, Goodwife, Herself, Hussif, Inamorata, Instructress, Kept woman, Lady, Leman, Maintenon, Montespan, Mrs, Natural, Paramour, Querida, Stepney, Teacher, Wardrobe, Wife

Mistrust(ful) Doubt, Gaingiving, Suspect, Suspicion

Misunderstand(ing) Cross-purpose(s), Disagreement, Discord, Generation gap, Mistake

Misuse Abuse, Defalcate, Malappropriate, Malapropism, Maltreat, Perversion, Torment

Mix(ed), Mixer, Mixture, Mix-up Allay, Alloy, Allsorts, Amalgam, Ambivalent, Associate, Assortment, Attemper, Balderdash, Bigener, Bittersweet, Bland, Blend, Blunge, Bombay, Bordeaux, Brew, Carburet, Card, Caudle, Chichi, Chow, Cocktail, Co-meddle, Compo, Compound, Conché, Conglomerate, Consort, Cross, Cut, Disperse, Diversity, Dolly, Drammock, Dukkah, Embroil, Emulsion, Eutectic, Farrago, Fold-in, Freezing, Friar's balsam, Garble, Grill, Griqua, Half-breed, Heather, Hobnob, Hodge-podge, Hotchpotch, Hybrid, Imbroglio, Immingle, Interlace, Intermingle, Isomorphous, Jumble, Lace, Lard, Lignin, Linctus, Load, Macedoine, Marketing, Matissé, Meddle, Medley, Meiny, Melange, Mell, Meng(e), Ment, Mess, Mestizo, Métis, Ming(le), Miscellaneous, Miscellany, Mishmash, Mong, Mongrel, Motley, Muddle, Muss(e), Neapolitan, Octaroon, Octoroon, Olio, Olla, Pastiche, Pi(e), Potin, Pousowdie, Powsowdy, Praiseach, Preparation, Promiscuous, Raggle-taggle, Ragtag, Salad, Scramble, Shuffle, Soda, Solution, Spatula, Stew, Stir, Temper, Through-other, Tonic, Trail, Vision, Witches' brew, Yblent

▷**Mixed** *may indicate* an anagram

Moan(ing), Moaner Beef, Bewail, Bleat, Carp, Groan, Grouse, Grumble, Hone, Keen, →**LAMENT**, Meane, Plangent, Sigh, Snivel, Sough, Wail, W(h)inge

Mob(ster) Army, Assail, Canaille, Crew, Crowd, Drove, Flash, Gang, Herd, Hoi-polloi, Hoodlum, Horde, Lynch, Many-headed beast, Mobocrat, Ochlocrat, Press, Rabble, Rabble rout, Raft, Ragtag, Riff-raff, Rout, Scar-face, Throng

Mobile, Mobilise, Mobility Agile, Donna, Fluid, Intergenerational, Movable, Plastic, Rally, Social, Thin, Upward(ly), Vagile, Vertical

Mock(ery), Mocking Ape, Banter, Catcall, Chaff, Chyack, Cod, Cynical, Deride, Derisory, Dor, Ersatz, False, Farce, Fleer, Flout, Gab, Geck, Gibe, Guy, Imitation, Ironise, Irony, Irrisory, →**JEER**, Jibe, Lampoon, Mimic, Narquois, Paraselene, Paste, Pillorise, Piss-taking, Rag, Rail(lery), Ridicule, Sacrilege, Sardonic, Satirise, Scorn, Scout, Send up, Serve, Sham, Simulate, Slag, Sneer, Snide, Sport, Tease, Travesty, Twit, Wry

Mode Authentic, Church, Convention, Fashion, Form, Hyperdorian, Hypo(dorian), Hypolydian, Insert, Manner, Raga, Rate, Step, Style, Ton

Model(ler), Modelling Archetype, Bozzetto, Cast, Clothes horse, Copy, Cover girl, Cutaway, Demonstration, Diorama, Doll, Dress-form, Dummy, Ecorché, Effigy, Epitome, Example, Exemplar, Exemplary, Fashionist, Fictor, Figure, Figurine, Icon, Ideal, Image, Instar, Jig, Last, Lay-figure, Layman, Madame Tussaud, Manakin, Manikin, Mannequin, Maquette, Mark, Matchstick, Mirror, Mock-up, Moulage, →**MOULD**, Norm, Original, Orrery, Papier-mâché, Parade, Paradigm, Paragon, Pattern, Phelloplastic, Pilot, Plasticine, Plastilina, Play-Doh®, Pose(r), Posture-maker, Precedent, Prototype, Replica, Role, Scale, Schema, Sedulous, Sitter, Specimen, Standard, Stereotype, Superwaif, T, Tellurion, Template, Templet, Terrella, Toy, Type, Typify, Version, Waif, Waxwork

▷**Model(s)** *may indicate* an anagram

Moderate(ly), Moderation Abate, Abbreviate, Allay, Alleviate, Attemper, Average, Ca'canny, Centre, Chair, Chasten, Continent, Decent, Diminish,

Discretion, Ease, Gentle, Girondist, Ho(a), Lessen, Lukewarm, Measure, Medium, Menshevik, Mezzo, Middling, Mild, Mitigate, Muscadin, OK, Politique, Pretty, Realo, Reason(able), Relent, Restraint, RR, Slake, So-so, Sparing, Subdue, Temper(ate), Tolerant, Tone (down), Via media, Wet

Modern(ise) AD, Aggiornamento, Contemporary, Fresh, Latter(-day), Millie, Neonomian, Neoterical, → **NEW**, New-fangled, Present-day, Progressive, Recent, Space age, State-of-the-art, Streamline, Swinger, Trendy, Update

Modest(y) Aidos, Blaise, Chaste, Coy, Decent, Demure, Fair, Humble, Humility, Ladylike, Low-key, Lowly, Maidenly, Mim, Mussorgsky, Propriety, Prudish, Pudency, Pudicity, Pure, Reserved, Reticent, Shame, Shamefaced, Shy, Simple, Slender, Unaffected, Unpretending, Unpretentious, Verecund

Modifiable, Modification, Modified, Modifier, Modify Adapt, Adjust, Alter, Backpedal, Change, Enhance, Extenuate, Genetically, H, Hotrod, Leaven, Plastic, Qualify, Restyle, Retrofit, Soup, Streamline, Temper, Top, Trim, Vary

Moist(en), Moisture Baste, Bedew, Damp, Dank, De(a)w, Dewy, Humect, Imbue, Latch, Love-in-a-mist, Madefy, Mesarch, Mesic, Nigella, Precipitation, Soggy, Sponge, Wet

▷**Moither** *may indicate* an anagram

Molecule(s), Molecular Acceptor, Achiral, Aptameter, Atom, Buckyball, Carbene, Cavitand, Chimera, Chiral, Chromophore, Closed chain, Cobalamin, Codon, Coenzyme, Cofactor, Dimer, DNA, Enantiomorph, Footballene, Fullerene, Gram, Hapten, Iota, Isomer, Kinin, Kisspeptin, Ligand, Long-chain, Metabolite, Metameric, Monomer, Nanotube, Nitryl, Oligomer, Peptide, Polymer, Polysaccharide, Quark, Replicon, Semantide, Stereoisomer, Synthon, Triatonic, Trimer, Uridine

Mollusc(s) Bivalve, Malacology, Opisthobranch, → **SHELLFISH**, Tectibranch, Univalve

Moment(s), Momentous Aha, Bit, Blonde, Brief, Eureka, Eventful, Flash(point), Gliffing, Glift, Import, Instant, Jiffy, → **MINUTE**, Mo, Nonce, Point, Pun(c)to, Sagging, Sands, Sec, Senior, Shake, Stound, Stownd, Tick, Time, Trice, Twinkling, Two-ticks, Weighty, Wink

Momentum Angular, Impetus, L, Speed, Steam, Thrust

Monarch(y) Absolute, Autocrat, Britain, Butterfly, Caesar, Cole, Crown, Dual, Emperor, HM, Karling, King, Kuwait, Netherlands, Norway, Oman, Potentate, Queen, Raine, Realm, Realty, Reign, Ruler, Saudi Arabia, Sovereign, Swaziland, Sweden, Tonga, Tsar

Monastery, Monastic Abbey, Abthane, Celibate, Charterhouse, Chartreuse, Cloister, Community, Gompa, Holy, Hospice, Iona, Lamaserai, Lamasery, Laura, Monkish, Oblate, Priory, Retreat, Sangha, Secluded, Tashi, Vihara, Wat

Money, Monetary Ackers, Akkas, Allowance, Annat, Ante, Appearance, Archer, Assignat, Banco, Batta, Beer, Blood, Blue, Blunt, Boodle, Bottle, Brass, Bread, Bread and honey, Broad, Bull's eye, Bunce, Cabbage, Capital, Cash, Caution, Century, Change, Chink, Circulating medium, Cob, Cock, → **COIN**, Collateral, Confetti, Conscience, Crackle, Cranborne, Crinkly, Crust, Currency, Danger, Dib(s), Dingbat, Dollar, Dosh, Dough, Dump, Dust, Earnest, Easy, Escrow, Even, Fat, Fee, Fiat, Finance, Float, Folding, Fonds, Found, Fund, Funny, Gate, Gelt, Gilt, Godiva, Gold, Grand, Grant, Gravy, Greens, Gross, Hard, Head, Heavy sugar, Hello, Hoot, Hot, Housekeeping, Hush, Idle, Ingots, Investment, Jack(pot), Kail, Kale, Kembla, Key, Knife, L, Legal tender, Lolly, Loot, Lucre, M, Mammon, Maundy, Mazuma, Means, Mint, Monkey, Monopoly, Moola(h),

Narrow, Near, Necessary, Needful, Nest-egg, Note, Nugger, Numismatic, Nummary, Oaker, Ocher, Ochre, Offertory, Oof, Option, Outlay, P, Packet, Paper, Passage, Pavarotti, Payroll, Peanuts, Pecuniary, Pelf, Petrodollar, Pin, Pine-tree, Pink, Pittance, Plastic, Plum, Pocket, Pony, Posh, Press, Prize, Proceeds, Profit, Protection, Purse, Push, Quid, Ransom, Ration, Ready, Reap silver, Rebate, Remuneration, Resources, Revenue, Rhino, Ring, Risk, Rogue, Rowdy, Salt(s), Score, Scratch, Scrip, Seed, Settlement, Shekels, Shell, Shin-plaster, Ship, Short, Siller, Silly, Silver, Sinews of war, Slush (fund), Smart, Soap, Soft, Spending, Spondulicks, Stake, Sterling, Stipend, Stuff, Subsidy, Subsistence, Sugar, Sum, Surety, Table, Take, Takings, Tea, Tender, Tin, Toea, Token, Tranche, Treaty, Tribute, Turnover, Viaticum, Wad, Wealth, Windfall, Wonga

Monitor(ing) Dataveillance, Detect, Goanna, Iguana, Komodo dragon, Lizard, Observe, Oversee, Prefect, Preview, Record, Regulator, Ship, Sniffer, Speed trap, Sphygmophone, Surveillance, Tag, Track, Warship, Watchdog, Worral, Worrel

Monk(s) Anchorite, Bodhidharma, Bro, Brother, Frere, General, Order, Provincial, Thelonious, Votary

Monkey Anger, Ape, Aye-aye, Baboon, Bandar, Bobbejaan, Bonnet, Bushbaby, Capuchin, Catar(r)hine, Cebidae, Cebus, Chacma, Coaita, Colobus, Cynomolgus, Diana, Douc, Douroucouli, Drill, Durukuli, Entellus, Galago, Gelada, Gibbon, Gorilla, Grease, Green, Grison, Grivet, Guenon, Guereza, Hanuman, Hoolock, Howler, Hylobates, Imp, Indri, Jacchus, Jackey, Jocko, Kippage, Kipunji, Langur, Leaf, Lemur, Loris, Macaco, Macaque, Magot, Malmag, Mandrill, Mangabey, Marmoset, Meddle, Meerkat, Mico, Midas, Mona, Mycetes, Nala, Nasalis, New World, Old World, Orang-utang, Ouakari, Ouistiti, Phalanger, Platyrrhine, Pongo, Powder, Proboscis, Pug, Puzzle, Rage, Ram, Rapscallion, Rascal, Rhesus, Sago(u)in, Saguin, Sai(miri), Sajou, Saki, Sapajou, Satan, Scamp, Semnopithecus, Siamang, Sifaka, Silen(us), Silverback, Simian, Simpai, Slender loris, Spider, Squirrel, Talapoin, Tamarin, Tamper, Tana, Tarsier, Tee-tee, Titi, Toque, Trip-hammer, Troop, Tup, Uakari, Urchin, Vervet, Wanderoo, White-eyelid, Wilderness, Wistiti, Wou-wou, Wow-wow, Wrath, Zati

Monologue Dramatic, Patter, Rap, Recitation, Soliloquy, Speech

Monopolise, Monopoly Absolute, Appalto, Bloc, Cartel, Coemption, Corner, Engross, Octroi, Régie, Trust

▷**Monsoon** *may indicate* weekend: Mon soon

▷**Monster, Monstrous** Alecto, Asmodeus, Bandersnatch, Behemoth, Bugaboo, Bunyip, Caliban, Cerberus, Cete, Charybdis, Chichevache, Chim(a)era, Cockatrice, Colossal, Cyclops, Dalek, Deform, Dinoceras, Div, Dragon, Echidna, Enormous, Erebus, Erl-king, Eten, Ettin, Fiend, Fire-drake, Frankenstein, Freak, Geryon, Ghost, Giant, Gila, Goblin, Godzilla, Golem, Gorgon, Green-eyed, Grendel, Harpy, Hippocampus, Hippogriff, Hippogryph, Huge, Hydra, Jabberwock, Kraken, Lamia, Leviathan, Mastodon, Medusa, Minotaur, Moloch, Mooncalf, Nessie, Nicker, Nightmare, Ogre, Ogr(e)ish, Opinicus, Orc, Outrageous, Pongo, Prodigy, Sasquatch, Satyral, Scylla, Shadow, Simorg, Simurg(h), Siren, Skull, Snark, Spectre, Sphinx, Spook, Stegodon, Stegosaur, Succubus, Taniwha, Teras, Teratism, Teratoid, Triceratops, Triffid, Troll, Typhoeus, Typhon, Unnatural, Vampire, Vast, Wasserman, Wendego, Wendigo, Wer(e)wolf, Whale, Wivern, Wyvern, Yowie, Ziffius

Month(ly) Ab, Abib, Adar, April, Asadha, Asvina, August, Bhadrapada, Brumaire, Bul, Caitra, Cheshvan, Chislev, December, Dhu-al-Hijjah, Dhu-al-Qadah, Elul, February, Floréal, Frimaire, Fructidor, Gander, Germinal,

Hes(h)van, Iy(y)ar, January, July, Jumada, June, Jyaistha, Karttika, Kisleu, Kislev, Lide, Lunar, Magha, March, Margasirsa, May, Messidor, Mo, Moharram, Moon, Muharram, Muharrem, Nisan, Nivôse, November, October, Ovulation, Periodical, Phalguna, Pluviôse, Prairial, Rabi(a), Rajab, Ramadan, Safar, Saphar, S(h)ebat, September, Sha(a)ban, Shawwal, Sivan, Solar, Tammuz, Tebeth, Thermidor, Tishri, Tisri, Vaisakha, Veadar, Vendémiaire, Ventôse

Monument Ancient, Arch, Archive, Cairn, Cenotaph, Column, Cromlech, Cross, Dolmen, Eugubine, Henge, Megalith, Memorial, Menhir, National, Pantheon, Pyramid, Stele(ne), Stone circle, Stonehenge, Stupa, Talayot, Tombstone, Trilith, Trilithon, Urn

Mood(y) Active, Air, Anger, Atmosphere, Attitude, Aura, Bipolar, Capricious, Dudgeon, Emoticon, Enallage, Fit, Foulie, Glum, Grammar, Huff, Humour, Hump, Imperative, Infinitive, Miff, Morale, Optative, Passive, Peat, Pet, Revivalist, Sankey, Spleen, Strop, Subjunctive, Sulky, Temper, Temperamental, Tid, Tone, Tune, Vein, Vinegar, Whim

Moon(light), Moony Aah, Adrastea, Alignak, Amalthea, Aningan, Apogee, Artemis, Astarte, Blue, Callisto, Calypso, Chandra, Cheese, Crescent, Cynthia, Diana, Epact, Europa, Eye, Flit, Full, Gander, Ganymede, Gibbous, Glimmer, Grimaldi, Harvest, Hecate, Hunter's, Hyperion, Iapetus, Inconstant, Io, Juliet, Leda, Lucina, Luna(r), Mani, Mascon, McFarlane's Buat, Midsummer, Mock, Month, Mooch, Mope, New, Nimbus, Nocturne, Octant, Oliver, Orb, Paddy's lantern, Paraselene, Paschal, Pasiphaë, Phobos, Phoebe, Plenilune, Proteus, Raker, Rear-view, Satellite, Selene, Set, Shepherd, Shot, Sickle, Sideline, Silvery, Sonata, Stargaze, Stone, Syzygy, Thebe, Thoth, Titan, Triton, Umbriel, Wander

Mop(ping) Dwile, Flibbertigibbet, Girn, Glib, Malkin, Shag, Squeegee, Squilgee, Swab, Swob, Thatch, → WIPE

Moral(ity), Morals Apologue, Deontic, Ethic(al), Ethos, Everyman, Fable, Gnomic, High-minded, Integrity, Laxity, Message, Parable, Precept, Principled, Probity, Puritanic, Righteous, Tag, Upright, Virtuous

Morale Ego, Mood, Spirit, Zeal

Morbid(ity) Anasarca, Ascites, Cachaemia, Dropsy, Ectopia, Ghoul(ish), Gruesome, Pathological, Plethora, Prurient, Religiose, Sick, Sombre, Unhealthy

More Additional, Else, Extra, Increase, Intense, Less, Mae, Merrier, Mo(e), Over, Piu, Plus, Rather, Seconds, Stump, Utopia

Morning Ack-emma, Am, Antemeridian, Dawn, Daybreak, Early, Levée, Matin(al), Matutinal, Morrow

Morose Acid, Boody, Churlish, Cynical, Gloomy, Glum, Grum, Moody, Sour-eyed, Sullen, Surly

Morsel Bit, Bite, Bouche, Canape, Crumb, Dainty, Morceau, Ort, Scrap, Sippet, Sop, Tidbit, Titbit

Mortal(ity) Averr(h)oism, Being, Deathly, → FATAL, Grave, Human, Lethal, Yama

Mortgage(e) Balloon, Bond, Cap and collar, Cedula, Debt, Dip, Encumbrance, Endowment, Hypothecator, Loan, Pledge, Repayment, Reverse, Wadset(t)

Mosaic Buhl, Cosmati, Impave, Inlay, Intarsia, Musive, Pietra dura, Screen, Smalto, Terrazzo, Tessella(te), Tessera

▶**Moslem** *see* MUSLIM (RITUAL)

Mosque Dome of the Rock, El Aqsa, Jami, Masjid, Medina, Musjid

Moss(y) Acrogen, Agate, Bryology, Bur(r), Carrag(h)een, Ceylon, Club, Fairy, Fog, Fontinalis, Hag(g), Hypnum, Iceland, Irish, Lecanoram, Lichen, Litmus, Long, Lycopod, Marsh, Musci, Muscoid, Parella, Peat, Polytrichum, Protonema,

Reindeer, Rose, Scale, Selaginella, Spanish, Sphagnum, Staghorn, Usnea, Wolf's claw

Most(ly) Basically, Largest, Major, Maxi(mum), Optimum

Mother Abbess, Bearer, Church, Cognate, Cosset, Courage, Dam(e), Den, Dregs, Ean, Earth, Eoan, Eve, Fecula, Generatrix, Genetrix, Goose, Hubbard, Lees, Ma, Machree, Mam(a), Mamma, Mater, Matroclinic, Maya, Minnie, Mollycoddle, Mom, Multipara, Mum, Mummy, Native, Nature, Nourish, Parent, Parity, Pourer, Prim(o), Progenitress, Reverend, Shipton, Slime, Superior, Surrogate, Theotokos, Venter, Wit

▷**Mother** *may indicate* a lepidopterist; moth-er

Motion Angular, Blocking, Composite, Contrary, Direct, Diurnal, Early day, Fast, Free-fall, Gesture, Harmonic, Impulse, Kepler, Kinematics, Kinetic, Kipp, Link, Move, Oblique, Offer, Parallactic, Parallel, Peculiar, Perpetual, PL, Precession, Proper, Proposal, Rack and pinion, Rider, Sewel, Slow, Spasm, Tide, Wave

Motionless Doggo, Frozen, Immobile, Inert, Quiescent, Stagnant, Standstill, Stasis, Still, Stock-still

Motive, Motivate, Motivation Actuate, Cause, Drive, Ideal, Impel, Impetus, Incentive, Intention, Mainspring, Mobile, Object, → **PURPOSE**, Raison d'être, Rationale, Reason, Spur, Ulterior, Urge

Motor(boat) Auto, Benz, Car, Dynamo, Engine, Hot rod, Hydroplane, Inboard, Induction, Jato, Linear, Mini, Outboard, Paint job, Rocket, Scooter, Series-wound, Servo, Supermini, Sustainer, Thruster, Turbine, Turbo, Vaporetto

Motorway Autobahn, Autopista, Autoput, Autoroute, Autostrada, Expressway, M(1), Orbital, Superhighway

Motto Device, Epigraph, Excelsior, Gnome, Ich dien, Impresa, Imprese, Impress(e), Legend, Maxim, Mot, Poesy, Posy, Saw, Slogan

Mould(ed), Moulder, Mouldable, Moulding, Mouldy Accolade, Architrave, Archivolt, Astragal, Baguette, Bandelet, Beading, Bend, Black, Bread, Briquet(te), Cabling, Casement, Cast(ing), Chain, Chessel, Chill, Cold, Cornice, Coving, Cyma (recta), Dancette, Dariole, Die, Dripstone, Echinus, Egg and dart, Flong, Forge, → **FORM**, Foughty, Fungus, Fust, Gadroon, Geat, Godroon, Gorgerin, Hood-mould, Hore, Humus, Injection, Matrix, Mildew, Model, Mool, Mucedinous, Mucid, Must(y), Mycetozoan, Necking, Noble rot, Ogee, Ovolo, Palmette, Papier-mâché, Penicillin, Phycomycete, Pig, Plasm(a), Plaster, Plastic, Plastisol, Plat, Prototype, Prunt, Reglet, Rib, Rot, Rust, Sandbox, Scotia, Shape, Smut, Soil, Spindle, Stringcourse, Tailor, Talon, Template, Templet, Timbale, Tondino, Torus, Water table

Mound Agger, Bank, Barp, Barrow, Berm, Cahokia, Cone, Dike, Dun, Embankment, Heap, Hillock, Hog, Knoll, Kurgan, Mogul, Monticule, Mote, Motte, Orb, Pile, Pingo, Pome, Rampart, Rampire, Tuffet

Mount(ed), Mounting, Mountain (peak), Mountains, Mountainside Air, → **ALPINE**, Ascend, Back, Barp, Ben, Berg, Board, Breast, Butter, Chain, Charger, Cliff, Clift, → **CLIMB**, Colt, Cordillera, Cradle, Dew, Display, Djebel, Dolly, Eminence, Escalade, Frame, Hinge, Horse, Inselberg, Jebel, Massif, Monture, Mt, Nunatak, Orography, Orology, Passe-partout, Peak, Pike, Pile, Pin, Pownie, Quad, → **RANGE**, Ride, Rosinante, Saddlehorse, Saddle up, Scalado, Scale, Sclim, Set, Soar, Stage, Stie, Strideways, Tel, Tier, Topo, Tor, Turret, Upgo, Volcano, Yaud

Mountaineer(ing) Aaron, Abseil, Alpinist, Arnaut, Climber, Hunt, Sherpa, Smythe, Upleader

Mourn(er), Mournful, Mourning Adonia, Alack, Black, Cypress, Dirge, Dole, Elegiac, Grieve, Grone, Hatchment, Keen, Lament, Mute, Niobe, Omer, Ovel, Plangent, Saulie, Shivah, Shloshim, Sorrow, Tangi, Threnetic, Threnodial, Weeds, Weep, Willow

Mouse(like), Mousy Black eye, Bus, Church, Deer, Dormouse, Dun(nart), Flitter, Harvest, Honey, Icon, Jerry, Jumping, Kangaroo, Meadow, Mechanical, Mickey, Minnie, Mischief, Muridae, Murine, Optical, Pocket, Rodent, Shiner, Shrew, Vermin, Waltzer

Mouth(piece) Aboral, Bazoo, Brag, Buccal, Cakehole, Chapper, Check, Crater, Debouchure, Delta, Embouchure, Estuary, Fauces, Fipple, Gab, Gam, Gills, Gob, Gub, Gum, Hard, Horn, Kisser, Labret, Laughing gear, Lawyer, Lip, Manubrium, Maw, Neb, Orifex, Orifice, Os, Oscule, Ostium, Outfall, Peristome, Port, Potato trap, Speaker, Spokesman, Spout, Stoma, Swazzle, Swozzle, Teat, Trap, Uvula

Move(d), Mover, Movable, Moving Act, Actuate, Affect, Andante, Astir, Aswarm, Budge, Career, Carry, Castle, Catapult, Chattel, Choreic, Circulate, Claw off, Coast, Counter-measure, Coup, Decant, Démarche, Deploy, Displace, Disturb, Ease, Eddy, Edge, Eloign, Evoke, Extrapose, False, Fidget, Flit, Flounce, Fluctuate, Forge, Fork, Forklift, Frogmarch, Galvanise, Gambit, Gee, Give and go, Glide, Go, Gravitate, Haulier, Hustle, Impress, Inch, Inspire, Instigate, Jee, Jink, Jump, Kedge, Kinetic, Knight's progress, Link, Lumber, Lunge, March, Mill, Mobile, Mosey, Motivate, Motor, Mouse, Nip, Opening, Outwin, Overcome, Pan, People, Poignant, Prime, Proceed, Progress, Progressional, Prompt, Propel, Propose, Push, Qui(t)ch, Quicken, Quinche, Rearrange, Redeploy, Relocate, Remuage, Retrocede, Roll, Rollaway, Roller-skate, Rouse, Roust; Sashay, Scamper, Scoot, Scramble, Scroll, Scurry, Scuttle, Sealed, Sell, Shift, Shog, Shoo, Shunt, Sidle, Skelp, Skitter, Slide, Soulful, Spank, Steal, Steer, Step, Stir, Styre, Surf, Swarm, Sway, Swish, Tack, Tactic, Taxi, Teleport, Touch, Transfer, Translate, Translocate, Transplant, Transport, Transpose, Travel, Troll, Trundle, Turn, Undulate, Unstep, Up, Up sticks, Urge, Vacillate, Vagile, Veronica, Vire, Volt(e), Waft, Wag(gle), Wapper, Whirry, Whish, Whisk, Whiz, Whoosh, Wuther, Yank, Zoom, Zwischenzug

Movement(s) Action, Akathisia, Allegro, Allemande, Almain, Andantino, Antic, Antistrophe, Arts and crafts, Bandwagon, Brisé, Buchmanism, Cadence, Capoeira, Cause, Cell, Charismatic, Chartism, Course, Crusade, Dadaism, Diapirism, Diaspora, Diastole, Ecumenical, Enlightenment, Eoka, Epeirogeny, Eurhythmics, Expressionism, Faction, Falange, Feint, Fianchetto, Fris(ka), Gait, Geneva, Gesture, Groundswell, Heliotaxis, Hip-hop, Honde, Imagism, Indraught, Intermezzo, Jor, Kata, Kinematics, Kinesis, Kin(a)esthetic, Kinetic, Kipp, Larghetto, Largo, Lassu, Ligne, Locomotion, Logistics, Maltese cross, Manoeuvre, Men's, Migration, Motion, Mudra, Nastic, Naturalism, Naziism, Neofascism, Neorealism, New Age, New Urbanism, New Wave, Nihilism, Official, Operation, Orchesis, Overspill, Oxford, Oxford Group, Panislamism, Pan-Slavism, Pantalon, Parallax, Pase, Passade, Passage, Photokinesis, Photonasty, Piaffer, Pincer, Plastique, Play, Populist, Port de bras, Poule, Poulette, Procession, Progress, Provisional, Punk, Puseyism, Reconstructionism, Reformation, Regression, REM, Renaissance, Resistance, Revivalism, Ribbonism, Risorgimento, Romantic, Rondo, Scherzo, Scissors, Seismic, Sinn Fein, Spuddle, Stir(e), Strophe, Subsidence, Swadeshi, Swing, Symbolist, Tamil Tigers, Tantrism, Taphrogenesis, Taxis, Tectonic, Telekinesis, Thermotaxis, Thigmotaxis, Tic, Tide, Trend, Ultramontanism, UNITA, Verismo, Veronica, Wave, Wheel, White flight, Women's, Zionism

Mow(er), Mowing Aftermath, Cut, Grimace, Lattermath, Math, Rawing, Reap, Rowan, Rowen, Rowing, Scytheman, Shear, Sickle, Strimmer®, Tass, Trim

MP Backbencher, Commoner, Deputy, Gendarme, Knight of the Shire, Member, Oncer, Provost, Redcap, Retread, Snowdrop, Stannator, Statist, TD

Much Abundant, Considerable, Ever so, Far, Glut, Great, Lots, Mickle, Mochell, Rotten, Scad, Sore, Viel

Muck (up), Mucky Bungle, Dirt, Dung, Grime, Island, Lady, Leep, Manure, Midden, Mire, Rot, Slush, Soil, Sordid, Spoil, Stercoral

Mud(dy) Adobe, Clabber, Clart, Clay, Cutcha, Dirt, Drilling, Dubs, Fango, Glaur, Glob, Gutter, Kacha, Lahar, Lairy, Limous, Lumicolous, Moya, Mudge, Ooze, Peloid, Pise, Poach, Red, Riley, Roily, Salse, Silt, Slab, Slake, Sleech, Slime, Slob, Slobland, Slough, Sludge, Slur(ry), Slush, Slutch, Tocky, Trouble, Turbid, Volcanic

Muddle(d) Addle, Befog, Bemuse, Botch, Chaos, Cock up, Confuse, Disorder, Disorient, Embrangle, Fluster, Gump, Higgledy-piggledy, Jumble, Mare's nest, Mash, Mêlée, Mess, Mess up, Mix, Mull, Pickle, Puddle, Screw up, Shemozzle, Stupefy, Tangle, Ta(i)vert, Tiert

▷**Muddled** *may indicate* an anagram

Muffle(d), Muffler Baffle, Damp, Deaden, Earplug, Envelop, Hollow, Low, Mob(b)le, Mute, Scarf, Silencer, Sourdine, Stifle

Mug(ger), Muggy Assault, Attack, Bash, Beaker, Bock, Can, Club, Con, Croc(odile), Cup, Dial, Do over, Dupe, Enghalskrug, Face, Fool, Footpad, Gob, Humid, Idiot, Latron, Learn, Mou, Noggin, Pan, Pot, Puss, Rob, Roll, Sandbag, Sap, Sconce, Simpleton, Steamer, Stein, Sucker, Swot, Tankard, Tax, Thief, Thug(gee), Tinnie, Tinny, Toby, Trap, Twerp, Ugly, Visage, Yap

Mule, Mulish Ass, Bab(o)uche, Barren, Donkey, Fadda, Funnel, Hemionus, Hybrid, Mocassin, Moccasin, Moyl(e), Muffin, Muil, Obdurate, Rake, Shoe, Slipper, Sumpter

Multiple, Multiplication, Multiplied, Multiplier, Multiply Augment, Breed, Chorisis, Common, Double, Elixir, →INCREASE, Manifold, Modulus, Populate, Product, Proliferate, Propagate, Raise, Severalfold, Square, Triple

Multitude Army, Crowd, Hirsel, Horde, Host, Legion, Populace, Shoal, Sight, Throng, Zillion

Mumble Grumble, Mouth, Mump, Mushmouth, Mutter, Royne, Slur

Munch Champ, Chew, Chomp, Expressionist, Moop, Moup, Scranch

Mundane Banal, Common, Earthly, Nondescript, Ordinary, Prosaic, Quotidian, Routine, Secular, Trite, Trivial, Workaday, Worldly

Munition(s) Arms, Arsenal, Artillery, Matériel, Ordnance

Murder(er), Murderess, Murderous Abort, Aram, Assassin, Blood guilty, Blue, Bluebeard, Bravo, Burke, Butcher, Butler, Cain, Cathedral, Crackhalter, Crippen, Crows, Cutthroat, Danaid(e)s, Dispatch, Do in, Eliminate, End, Filicide, First degree, Fratricide, Genocide, Hare, Hatchet man, Hitman, Homicide, Hyde, Internecine, →KILL, Liquidate, Locusta, Made man, Man-queller, Massacre, Matricide, Modo, Mullah, Muller, Parricide, Patricide, Poison, Red, Regicide, Removal, Ripper, Ritual, Ritz, Rub out, Second degree, Sikes, Slaughter, Slay, Stiff, Strangle(r), Sweeney Todd, Take out, Thagi, Throttle, Thug(gee), Tyrannicide, Ugly man, Vaticide, Whodun(n)it

Murk(y) Black, Dark, Dirk(e), Gloom, Obscure, Rookish, Stygian

Muscle, Muscleman, Muscular Abductor, Abs, Accelerator, Accessorius, Adductor, Agonist, Anconeus, Aristotle's lantern, Aryepiglottic, Arytaenoid, Athletic, Attollens, Azygous, Beef(y), Beefcake, Biceps, Bowr, Brachialus, Brawn,

Buccinator, Buff, Cardiac, Ciliary, Clout, Complexus, Corrugator, Creature, Cremaster, Delt(oid), Depressor, Diaphragm, Digastric, Dilat(at)or, Duvaricator, Écorché, Effector, Elevator, Erecter, Erector, Evertor, Extensor, Eye-string, Flexor, Force, Gastrocnemius, Gemellus, Glute, Glut(a)eus, Gluteus maximus, Gracilis, Hamstring, Heavy, Hiacus, Hunky, Ideomotor, Iliacus, Intrinsic, Involuntary, Kreatine, Lat, Latissimus dorsi, Laxator, Levator, Lumbricalis, Masseter, Mesomorph, Might, Motor, Mouse, Myalgia, Mylohyoid, Myology, Myotome, Myotonia, Nasalis, Obicularis, Oblique, Occlusor, Omohyoid, Opponent, Orbicularis, Pathos, Pec(s), Pectoral, Perforans, Perforatus, Peroneus, Plantaris, Platysma, Popliteus, →**POWER**, Pronator, Protractor, Psoas, Pylorus, Quad(riceps), Quadratus, Rambo, Rectus, Retractor, Rhomboid, Rhomboideus, Ripped, Risorius, Rotator cuff, Sarcolemma, Sarcous, Sartorius, Scalene, Scalenus, Serratus, Sinew, Six-pack, Smooth, Soleus, Sphincter, Spinalis, Splenial, Sthenic, Striated, Striped, Supinator, Suspensory, Temporal, Tenaculum, Tendon, Tensor, Teres, Thenar, Thew, Tibialis, Toned, Tonus, Trapezius, Triceps, Vastus, Voluntary, Xiphihumeralis, Zygomatic

Muse(s), Muse's home, Musing Aglaia, Aonia(n), Attic, Calliope, Clio, Cogitate, Consider, Dream, Dwell, Erato, Euphrosyne, Euterpe, Goddess, Helicon, Inspiration, IX, Laura, Melpomene, Nine, Nonet, Pensée, Pierides, Poly(hy)mnia, Ponder, →**REFLECT**, Ruminate, Study, Teian, Terpsichore, Thalia, Tragic, Urania, Wonder

Museum Ashmolean, BM, British, Fitzwilliam, Gallery, Guggenheim, Hermitage, Kelvingrove, Louvre, Metropolitan, National Gallery, Parnassus, Prado, Repository, Smithsonian, Tate, Te papa Tongarewa, Uffizi, VA, V and A

Mushroom Aecidium, Aedium, Agaric, Ascomycetes, Blewits, Burgeon, Button, Cep, Champignon, Darning, Destroying angel, Enoki, Escalate, Expand, Explode, Field, Fly agaric, →**FUNGUS**, Girolle, Grisette, Gyromitra, Honey fungus, Hypha(l), Ink-cap, Liberty cap, Magic, Matsutake, Meadow, Morel, Oyster, Parasol, Penny-bun, Porcino, Reishi, Russula, Sacred, Scotch bonnet, Shaggy cap, Shaggymane, Shiitake, Shroom, Sickener, Snowball, Spread, Start-up, Straw, Truffle, Upstart, Velvet shank, Waxcap

Music Absolute, A-side, B-side, Classical, Colour, Indeterminate, Lesson, Light, Minstrelsy, Mood, Morceau, Passage work, Phase, Piece, Popular, Programme, Quotation, Recital, Score, Sound, Table, Tremolando

Musical Annie, Arcadian, Azione, Brigadoon, Canorous, Carousel, Cats, Chess, Chicago, Euphonic, Evergreen, Evita, Gigi, Grease, Hair, Half a Sixpence, Harmonious, Kabuki, Kismet, Kiss Me Kate, Les Miserables, Lyric, Mame, Melodic, My Fair Lady, Oliver, →**OPERA**, Operetta, Oratorio, Orphean, Revue, Showboat, South Pacific, Top Hat, Trial by Jury, West Side Story

Musician(s), Musicologist Accompanist, Arion, Arist, Armstrong, Ashkenazi, Bassist, Boy band, Brain, Buononcini, Busker, Carmichael, Casals, Cellist, Chanter, Combo, →**COMPOSER**, Conductor, Crowder, Ellington, Ensemble, Executant, Flautist, Gate, Group, Grove, Guslar, Handel, Jazzer, Jazzman, Joplin, Keyboardist, Klezmer, Labelmate, Luter, Lyrist, Maestro, Mahler, Mariachi, Menuhin, Minstrel, Moke, Muso, Orphean, Percussionist, Peterson, Pianist, Pied Piper, Rapper, Reed(s)man, Répétiteur, Ripienist, Rubinstein, Satchmo, Schonberg, Serenader, Sideman, Soloist, Spohr, String, Tortelier, Trouvère, Trumpeter, Violinist, Waits

Musket Brown Bess, Caliver, Carabine, Eyas, Flintlock, Fusil, Gingal(l), Hawk, Jingal, Nyas, Queen's-arm, Weapon

Muslim (ritual), Moslem Alaouite, Ali, Almohad(e), Balochi, Baluchi, Berber, Caliph, Dato, Dervish, Fatimid, Ghazi, Hadji, Hafiz, Hajji, Hamas, Hizbollah, Hizbullah, Iranian, Islamic, Ismaili, Karmathian, Khotbah, Khotbeh, Khutbah, Mahometan, Mawlawi, Meivievi, Mog(h)ul, Moor, Morisco, Moro, Muezzin, Mufti, Mughal, Mus(s)ulman, Mutazilite, Nawab, Paynim, Pomak, Said, Saladin, Saracen, Say(y)id, Senus(s)i, Shafiite, Shia(h), Shiite, Sofi, Sonnite, Sufi, Sulu, Sunna, Sunni(te), Turk, Wahabee, Wahabi(te), Whirling Dervish

Must(y) Amok, Essential, Foughty, Fousty, Froughy, Frowsty, Frowy, Funky, Fust, Gotta, Man, Maun(na), Mote, Mould, Mucid, Mun, Necessary, Need(s)-be, Obbligato, Shall, Should, Stum, Vinew, Wine

▷**Must** *may indicate* an anagram

Mustard Black, Brown, Charlock, Cress, Dijon, English, Erysimum, French, Garlic, Gas, Nitrogen, Praiseach, Quinacrine, Runch, Sarepta, Sauce-alone, Senvy, Treacle, Wall, White, Wild, Wintercress

Musteline Atoc, Atok, Skunk

▷**Mutation** *may indicate* an anagram

Mute(d) Deaden, Dumb, Mourner, Noiseless, Saulie, Silent, Sorda, Sordino, Sordo, Sourdine, Stifle, Stop

Mutilate(d), Mutilation Castrate, Concise, Deface, Dismember, Distort, Garble, Hamble, Injure, Maim, Mangle, Mayhem, Obtruncate, Riglin, Tear

▷**Mutilate(d)** *may indicate* an anagram

Mutineer, Mutiny Bounty, Caine, Curragh, Indian, Insurrection, Jhansi, Nore, Pandy, Rebel, →**REVOLT**, Rising, Sepoy, Treason

Mutter(ing) Chunter, Drone, Fremescent, Maunder, Mumble, Mump, Murmur, Mussitate, Rhubarb, Roin, Royne, Rumble, Sotto voce, Witter

Muzzle Decorticate, Gag, Gunpoint, Jaw, Mouth, Mute, Restrain, Snout

Mysterious, Mystery Abdabs, Abdals, Acroamatic, Arcane, Arcanum, Cabbala, Closed book, Craft, Creepy, Cryptic, Dark (horse), Deep, Delphic, Eleusinian, Enigma(tic), Esoteric, G(u)ild, Grocer, Incarnation, Inscrutable, Miracle, Mystagogue, Numinous, Occult, Original sin, Orphic, Penetralia, Recondite, Riddle, Sacrament, →**SECRET**, Shadowy, Shady, Spooky, Suspense, Telestic, Thriller, Trinity, UFO, Uncanny, Unearthly, Unexplained, Unknown, Whodunit

▷**Mysterious(ly)** *may indicate* an anagram

Mystic (word), Mystical, Mysticism Abraxas, Agnostic, Cabbala, Cab(e)iri, Eckhart, Epopt, Fakir, Familist, Gnostic, Hesychast, Mahatma, New Age, Occultist, Rasputin, Rosicrucian, Secret, Seer, Sofi, Sufi, Swami, Tantric, Theosophy, Transcendental

Mystify Baffle, Bamboozle, Bewilder, Metagrabolise, Perplex, Puzzle

Myth(ology), Mythological, Mythical (beast) Allegory, Atlantis, Behemoth, Bunyip, Centaur, Cockatrice, Dragon, Dreamtime, Euhemerism, Fable, Fantasy, Fictitious, Folklore, Garuda, Geryon, Griffin, Hippocampus, Impundulu, Kelpie, Kylin, Legend, Leviathan, Lore, Lorelei, Lyonnesse, Otnit, Pantheon, Pegasus, Phoenix, Sasquatch, Sea horse, Sea serpent, Selkie, Solar, Speewah, Sphinx, Sun, Tarand, Therianthropic, Thunderbird, Tokoloshe, Tragelaph, Unicorn, Urban, Wivern, Wyvern, Yale, Yeti

Nn

N Name, Nitrogen, Noon, North, November

Nadir Bottom, Depths, Dregs, Minimum

Nag(ging) Badger, Bidet, Brimstone, Callet, Cap, Captious, Complain, Fret, Fuss, Harangue, Harp, Henpeck, Horse, Jade, Jaw, Keffel, Peck, Pester, Pick on, Plague, Rosinante, Rouncy, → **SCOLD**, Tit, Yaff

Nail(ed) Brad, Brod, Catch, Clinker, Clout, Fasten, Frost, Hob, Horse, Keratin, Onyx, Pin, Rivet, Seize, Sisera, Sixpenny, Sparable, Sparrow-bill, Spick, Spike, Sprig, Staple, Stub, Stud, Tack(et), Talon, Tenterhook, Thumb, Tingle, Toe, Unguis

Naive(té) Artless, Dewy-eyed, Green(horn), Guileless, Ingenuous, Innocence, Open, Simplistic, Starry-eyed, Trusting, Unsophisticated, Wide-eyed

Naked(ness) Adamical, Artless, Bare, Blunt, Buff, Clear, Cuerpo, Defenceless, Encuerpo, Exposed, Gymno-, Nature, Nuddy, Nude, Querpo, Raw, Scud, Simple, Stark(ers), Uncovered

Name(d), Names Agnomen, Alias, Anonym, Appellation, Appoint, Attribute, Badge, Baptise, Byline, Call, Celeb(rity), Christen, Cite, Cleep, Clepe, Cognomen, Day, Designate, Dinges, Dingus, Dit, Domain, Dub, Entitle, Epithet, Eponym, Exonym, Family, First, Font, Generic, Given, Handle, Hete, Hight, Identify, Identity, Label, Maiden, Marque, Masthead, Mention, Metronymic, Middle, Moni(c)ker, Mud, N, Nap, Nemn, Nempt, Nom, Nomen(clature), Noun, Patronymic, Pennant, Personage, Pet, Place, Praenomen, Proper, Proprietary, Pseudonym, Quote, Red(d), Repute, Sign, Signature, Sir, Specify, Stage, Street, Subdomain, Substantive, Tag, Tautonym, Term, → **TITLE**, Titular, Titule, Trade, Trivial, User

Nap(py) Bonaparte, Diaper, Doze, Drowse, Fluff, Forty winks, Frieze(d), Fuzz, Game, Kip, Moze, Nod, Oose, Ooze, Oozy, Put(t), Shag, Shuteye, Siesta, → **SLEEP**, Slumber, Snooze, Tease, Teasel, Teaze, Terry, Tipsy, Tuft

Napkin Cloth, Diaper, Doily, Sanitary, Serviette

▷**Napoleon** *may indicate* a pig

Narcotic Ava, B(h)ang, Benj, Cannabin, Cannabis, Charas, Churrus, Coca, Codeine, Dagga, Datura, Dope, → **DRUG**, Heroin, Hop, Kava, Laudanum, Mandragon, Mandrake, Marijuana, Meconium, Methadone, Morphia, Narceen, Narceine, Nicotine, Opiate, Opium, Pituri, Sedative, Tobacco

Narrate, Narration, Narrative, Narrator Allegory, Anecdote, Cantata, Describe, Diegesis, Fable, History, Ishmael, Periplus, Plot, Raconteur, Récit, Recital, Recite, Recount, Saga, Sagaman, Scheherazade, Splatterpunk, Story, Tell, Thanatography

Narrow(ing), Narrow-minded Alf, Babbitt, Bigoted, Borné, Bottleneck, Close(-run), Constringe, Cramp, Ensiform, Grundy(ism), Hairline, Hidebound,

Illiberal, Insular, Knife edge, Kyle, Limited, Meagre, Nary, One-idead, Parochial, Phimosis, Pinch, Pinch-point, Po(-faced), Prudish, Puritan, Scant, Shrink, Slender, Slit, Specialise, Squeak, Stenosed, Strait, Straiten, Strait-laced, Strict, Suburban, Taper, Verkramp, Wafer-thin, Waist

Nastiness, Nasty Disagreeable, Drevill, Filth, Fink, Ghastly, Lemon, Lo(a)th, Malign(ant), Noisome, Noxious, Obscene, Odious, Offensive, Ogreish, Poxy, Ribby, Scummy, Sif, Sinister, Sordid, Unholy, Vile, Virose

Nation(s), National(ist), Nationalism Anthem, Baathist, Broederbond, Casement, Chetnik, Country, Cuban, Debt, De Valera, Eta, Federal, Folk, Grand, Hindutva, Indian, INLA, IRA, Jingoist, Kuomintang, Land, Malcolm X, Mexican, Oman, Pamyat, Parnell, Patriot, →**PEOPLE**, Polonia, Race, Risorgimento, Scottish, Shiv Sena, Subject, Swadeshi, Timor-Leste, Tonga, Tribespeople, Turk, United, Vanuatu, Vatican City, Wafd, Xenophobe, Yemini, Young Ireland, Young Turk, Zionist

Native(s) Aborigin, Aborigine, African, Amerind, Annamese, Arab, Ascian, Australian, Autochthon, Aztec, Basuto, Belonging, Bengali, Boy, Cairene, Carib, Carioca, Chaldean, Citizen, Colchester, Conch, Creole, Criollo, Domestic, Dyak, Edo, Enchorial, Endemic, Eskimo, Fleming, Genuine, Habitual, Inborn, Indigene, Indigenous, Inhabitant, Intuitive, Libyan, Local, Malay, Maori, Mary, Micronesian, Moroccan, Norwegian, Oyster, Polack, Portuguese, Son, Spaniard, Te(i)an, Thai, Tibetan, Tribesman, Uzbeg, Uzbek, Whitstable, Yugoslav

Natural(ly), Naturalise(d), Naturalism Altogether, Artless, Ass, Easy, Endenizen, Genuine, Green, Gut, Homely, Idiot, Illegitimate, Inborn, Inbred, Indigenous, Ingenerate, Inherent, Innate, Instinctive, Moron, Native, Nidget, Nitwit, Nude, Ordinary, Organic, Prat, Real, Sincere, True, Untaught

Nature Adam, Character, Disposition, Esse(nce), Ethos, Hypostasis, Inbeing, Inscape, Manhood, Mould, Quintessence, Root, Second, SN, Temperament

Naught Cypher, Failure, Nil, Nothing, Zero

Naughty Bad, Girly, Improper, Indecorous, Light, Marietta, Nineties, Offender, Rascal, Remiss, Rudery, Spright, Sprite, Wayward

Nausea, Nauseous Disgust, Dwa(l)m, Dwaum, Fulsome, Malaise, Queasy, Sickness, Squeamish, Wamble, Wambly

Nave Aisle, Apse, Centre, Hub, Modiolus, Nef

Navigate, Navigator Albuquerque, Baffin, Bering, Bougainville, Cabot, Cartier, Columbus, Control, Cook, Da Gama, Davis, Dias, Direct, Drake, Eric the Red, Franklin, Frobisher, Gilbert, Hartog, Haul, Henry, Hudson, Keel, Magellan, Navvy, Neighbour, Orienteer, Pilot, Raleigh, Sail, Star-read, →**STEER**, Weddell

Navy, Naval AB, Armada, Blue, Fleet, French, Maritime, Merchant, N, Red, RN, Wavy, White squadron, Wren

Near(er), Nearest, Nearby, Nearly, Nearness About, Adjacent, All-but, Almost, Anigh, Approach, Approximate, Beside, By, Close, Cy pres, Degree, Even, Ewest, Feckly, Forby, Gain, Handy, Hither, Imminent, Inby(e), Mean, Miserly, Most, Narre, Neist, Next, Nie, Niggardly, Nigh, Oncoming, Outby, Propinquity, Proximity, Short-range, Stingy, Thereabout(s), To, Upon, Warm, Well-nigh

Neat(ly), Neatness Bandbox, Cattle, Clean-cut, Clever, Dainty, Dapper, Deft, Dink(y), Doddy, Donsie, Elegant, Feat(e)ous, Featuous, Gayal, Genty, Gyal, Intact, Jemmy, Jimpy, Kempt, Nett, Nifty, Ninepence, Orderly, Ox(en), Perjink, Preppy, Pretty, Rother, Saola, Shipshape, Short(horn), Smug, Snod, Spick and span, Spruce, Straight, →**TIDY**, Trig, Trim, Uncluttered, Unwatered, Well-groomed

Necessary, Necessarily Bog, Cash, De rigueur, →**ESSENTIAL**, Estovers, Imperative, Important, Indispensable, Intrinsic, Loo, Money, Moolah, Needful, Ought, Perforce, Requisite, Vital, Wherewithal

Necessitate, Necessity Ananke, Compel, Constrain, Cost, Emergency, Entail, Essential, Exigent, Fate, Indigence, Logical, Mathematical, Moral, Must, Natural, Need, Need-be, Oblige, Perforce, Require, Requisite, Staple

Neck(ed) Bottle, Brass, Canoodle, Cervical, Cervix, Channel, Col, Collar, Crag, Craig, Crew, Crop, Embrace, Gall, Gorgerin, Halse, Hause, Hawse, Inarm, Inclip, Isthmus, Kiss, Mash, Nape, Nuzzle, Pet, Polo, Rubber, Scrag, Scruff, Smooch, Snog, Strait, Swan, Swire, Theorbo, Torticollis, Trachelate, Vee, Volcanic

▷**Necking** *may indicate* one word around another

Necklace Afro-chain, Anodyne, Bib, Chain, Choker, Collar, Corals, Hei-tiki, Medallion, Pearls, Rope, Sautoir, String, Torc, Torque

Neckline Boat, Collar, Cowl, Crew, Décolletage, Plunging, Scoop, Sweetheart, Turtle, Vee

Neckwear Ascot, Barcelona, Boa, Bow, Collar, Cravat, Fur, Steenkirk, Stock, Tie

Nectar Ambrosia, Amrita, Honey, Mead

Need(ed), Needy Absence, Ananke, Call, Demand, Desiderata, Egence, Egency, Essential, Exigency, Gap, Gerundive, Impecunious, Indigent, →**LACK**, Mister, Prerequisite, Pressing, PRN, Rainy day, Require, Special, Strait, Strapped, Want

Needle(s) Acerose, Acicular, Aciform, Acupuncture, Anger, Antagonise, Between, Bodkin, Cleopatra's, Darner, Darning, Dip, Dipping, Dry-point, Electric, Etching, Goad, Gramophone, Hagedorn, Hype, Hypodermic, Ice, Icicle, Inoculate, Knitting, Leucotome, Magnetic, Mainline, Miff, Monolith, Neeld, Neele, Netting, Obelisk, Packing, Pine, Pinnacle, Pique, Pointer, Prick, R(h)aphis, Sew, Sharp, Spanish, Spicule, Spike, Spine, Spud, Stylus, Tattoo, Tease, Thorn, Wire

Needlework Applique, Baste, Crewel, Embroidery, Gros point, Lacet, Mola, Patchwork, Piqué, Rivière, Sampler, Tapestry, Tattoo, White-seam

Negation, Negative Anion, Apophatic, Cathode, Denial, Downside, Enantiosis, Infinitant, Ne, No, Non, Nope, Nullify, Photograph, Refusal, Resinous, Unresponsive, Veto, Yin

Neglect(ed), Neglectful, Negligence, Negligent Careless, Casual, Cinderella, Cuff, Default, Dereliction, Disregard, Disuse, Failure, Forget, Forlorn, For(e)slack, G-devant, Heedless, Inattention, Incivism, Laches, Malpractice, Misprision, Omission, Oversight, Pass, Pass-up, Rack and ruin, Scamp, Shirk, Slight, Slipshod, Undone, Unilateral, Unnoticed

▷**Neglected** *may indicate* an anagram

Negligee Déshabillé, Manteau, Mob, Nightgown, Robe

Negotiate, Negotiator Arbitrate, Arrange, Bargain, Barter, Clear, Confer, Deal, Diplomat, Intercede, Interdeal, Intermediary, Liaise, Manoeuvre, Mediator, Parley, Petition, Talk, Trade, Transact, Treat(y), Tret, Weather

Neigh Bray, Hinny, Nicker, Whicker, Whinny

Neighbour(ly), Neighbouring, Neighbours Abut(ter), Alongside, Amicable, Bor, Border, But, Friendly, Joneses, Nearby, Next-door

Neighbourhood(s) Acorn®, Area, Community, District, Environs, Locality, Precinct, Vicinage, Vicinity

Nerve(s), Nervous(ness), Nervure, Nerve centre, Nervy Abdabs, Accessory, Acoustic, Afferent, Aflutter, Afraid, Alveolar, Antsy, Auditory, Autonomic, Axon, Baroreceptor, Bottle, Bouton, Brass neck, Buccal, Butterflies, Chord, Chutzpah,

Collywobbles, Column, Commissure, Cones, Courage, Cranial, Cyton, Dendron, Depressor, Edgy, Effector, Efferent, Electrotonus, Epicritic, Excitor, Facial, Fearful, Fidgety, Gall, Ganglion, Glossopharyngeal, Grit, Guts, Habdabs, Heart-string, High, Highly-strung, Hyp, Impudence, Jitters, Jittery, Jumpy, Median, Mid-rib, Motor, Moxie, Myelon, Nappy, Neck, Neurological, Nidus, Oculomotor, Olfactory, On edge, Optic, Pavid, Perikaryon, Pons, Proprioceptor, Protopathic, Rad, Radial, Receptor, Restiform, Restless, Sacral, Sangfroid, Sass, Sauce, Sciatic, Screaming abdabs, Sensory, Shaky, Solar plexus, Somatic, Splanchnic, Spunk, Stage fright, Steel, Strung-up, Sympathetic, Synapse, Tense, Timorous, Tizzy, Toey, Tongue-tied, Trembler, Tremulous, Trigeminal, Trochlear, Twitchy, Ulnar, Uptight, Vagus, Vapours, Vasodilator, Vestibular, Vestibulocochlear, Wandering, Willies, Windy, Wired (up), Wittery, Yips

▷**Nervously** *may indicate* an anagram

Nest Aerie, Aery, Aiery, Ayrie, Bike, Bink, Brood, Byke, Cabinet, Cage, Caliology, Clutch, Dray, Drey, Eyrie, Eyry, Guns, Hive, Lodge, Nid, Nide, Nidify, Nidus, Sett, Termitarium, Turkey, Wurley

Nestle Burrow, Cose, Cuddle, Nuzzle, Rest, Snug(gle)

Net(ting), Nets, Network(ing), Networker Bamboo, BR, Bunt, Bus, Butterfly, Cast, Casting, Catch, Caul, Clap, Clear, Co-ax(ial), Cobweb, →**COMPUTER NETWORK**, Craquelure, Crinoline, Criss-cross, Crossover, Diane, Drift, Earn, Eel-set, Enmesh, Equaliser, Fetch, File server, Filet, Final, Fish, Fisherman, Flew, Flue, Fret, Fyke, Gain, Gill, →**GRID**, Hammock, Honeycomb, Hose, Insect, Kiddle, Lace, LAN, Land, Landing, Lattice, Leap, Line, Linin, Mains, Mattress, Maze, Mist, Mosquito, Mycelium, Nerve, Neural, Neuropil, Old boys', PCN, Plexus, Portal system, Pound, Pout, Purse-seine, Quadripole, Reseau, Rete, Retiary, Reticle, Reticulate, Reticulum, Ring, Safety, Sagene, Scoop, Screen, Sean, Seine, Senior, Set(t), Shark, Skype®, Snood, Speed, Stake, Symplast, System, Tangle, Tela, Telex, Tissue, Toil, Torpedo, Trammel, Trap, Trawl, Trepan, Tulle, Tunnel, Wire

Nettle(rash) Anger, Annoy, Day, Dead, Hemp, Hives, Horse, Irritate, Labiate, Nark, Ongaonga, Pellitory, Pique, Ramee, Rami, Ramie, Rhea, Rile, Ruffle, Sting, Urtica(ceae), Urticaria

Neuter Castrate, Gib, Impartial, Neutral, Sexless, Spay

Neutral(ise) Alkalify, Buffer zone, Counteract, Degauss, Grey, Impartial, Inactive, Schwa, Sheva, Shiva, Unbiased

Never(more) As if, Nary, Nathemo(re), No more

Nevertheless Algate, All the same, Anyhow, But, Howbeit, However, Still, Yet

New(s), Newborn, News agency Avant garde, Bulletin, Communique, Copy, Coranto, Dope, Euphobia, Evangel, Flash, Forest, Fresh, Fudge, Gen, Green, Griff, Info(rmation), Initiate, Innovation, Intake, Intelligence, Item, Kerygma, Latest, Mint, Modern, N, Novel, Oil(s), Original, PA, Paragraph, Pastures, Pristine, Propaganda, Raw, Reborn, Recent, Report, Reuter, Scoop, Sidebar, Snippet, Span, Splash, Stranger, Tass, Teletext®, Tidings, Ultramodern, Unco, Update, Word, Young

▷**New** *may indicate* an anagram

Newcomer Dog, Freshman, Griffin, Immigrant, Jackaroo, Jackeroo, Jillaroo, Johnny-come-lately, L, Learner, Newbie, Novice, Parvenu, Pilgrim, Settler, Tenderfoot, Upstart

Newsman, News-reader Announcer, Editor, Journalist, Legman, Press, Reporter, Sub, Sysop

Newspaper Beast, Big Issue, Blat(t), Broadsheet, Compact, Courier, Daily, Express, Fanzine, Feuilleton, Freesheet, Gazette, Guardian, Heavy, Herald, Intelligencer, Izvestia, Journal, Jupiter, Le Monde, Mercury, National, Organ, Patent inside, Patent outside, Post, Pravda, Press, Print, Rag, Red-top, Scotsman, Sheet, Spoiler, Squeak, Sun, Tabloid, Today, Yellow Press

Newt(s) Ask(er), Eft, Evet, Swift, Triton, Urodela

New Zealand(er) Aotearoa, Diggers, Enzed, Kiwi, Maori, Moriori, .nz, Pakeha, Pig Island, Ronz(er), Shagroon

Next Adjacent, Adjoining, After, Alongside, Beside, By, Following, Immediate, Later, Nearest, Neighbour, Neist, Proximate, Proximo, Sine, Subsequent, Syne, Then, Thereafter

Nib(s) Cocoa, J, Pen, Point, Tip

Nibble Bite, Brouse, Browse, Byte, Canapé, Crop, Eat, Gnaw, Knap(ple), Moop, Moup, Munch, Nag, Nepit, Nosh, Peck, Pick, Snack

Nice(ly), Nicety Accurate, Amene, Appealing, Dainty, Fastidious, Fine, Finical, Genteel, Lepid, Ninepence, Pat, Pleasant, Precise, Quaint, Rare, Refined, Subtil(e), Subtle, Sweet, T, To a t

Niche Alcove, Almehrahb, Almery, Ambry, Apse, Aumbry, Awmrie, Awmry, Columbarium, Cranny, Exedra, Fenestella, Mihrab, Recess, Slot

Nick(ed) Appropriate, Arrest, Bin, Blag, Can, Chip, Cly, Colin, Copshop, Crib, Cut, Denay, Dent, Deny, → **DEVIL**, Erose, Groove, Hoosegow, Kitty, Knock, Nab, Nap, Nim, Nock, Notch, Pinch, Pocket, Pook, Pouk, Prison, Run in, Scratch, Serrate, Sneak, → **STEAL**, Steek, Swan-upping, Swipe, Thieve, Wirricow, Worricow, Worrycow

Nickname Alias, Byname, Byword, Cognomen, Monicker, So(u)briquet

Night(s), Nightfall Acronical, Acronychal, Arabian, Burns, Darkling, Darkmans, First, Gaudy, Guest, Guy Fawkes, Hen, Leila, Nacht, Nicka-nan, Nutcrack, Nyx, Opening, School, Sleepover, Stag, Twelfth, Twilight, Walpurgis, Watch, White

Night-cap Biggin, Cocoa, Nip, Pirnie, Sundowner

Nightingale Bulbul, Florence, Frog, Jugger, Lind, Philomel, Philomena, Scutari, Swedish, Watch

Nightmare, Nightmarish Cacod(a)emon, Ephialtes, Incubus, Kafkaesque, Oneirodynia, Phantasmagoria

Nightshade Atropin(e), Belladonna, Bittersweet, Circaea, Dwale, Henbane, Morel, Solanum

Nil Nothing, Nought, Zero

Nimble(ness), Nimbly Active, → **AGILE**, Alert, Deft, Deliver, Fleet, Legerity, Light, Light-footed, Lissom(e), Lithe, Quiver, Sciolto, Springe, Spry, Supple, Sure-footed, Swack, Wan(d)le, Wannel, Wight, Ya(u)ld

Nip(per), Nippers Bite, Brat, Check, Chela, Chill, Claw, Cutpurse, Dip, Dram, Foil, Jack Frost, Lad, Lop, Nep, Nirl, Outsiders, Peck, Pickpocket, Pincers, Pinch, Pook, Scotch, Sneap, Susan, Tad, Talon, Taste, Tot, Tweak, Urchin, Vice, Vise

Nipple Dug, Mastoid, Pap, Teat

Nit-picking Carping, Pedantry, Quibble

No Aikona, Denial, Na(e), Nah, Naw, Negative, Nix, Nope, Nyet, O, Refusal

Nob(by) Grandee, Parage, Prince, Swell, Toff

▷**Nobbled** *may indicate* an anagram

Noble(man), Noblewoman, Nobility, Nobly Adela, Adele, Adeline, Aneurin, Aristocrat, Atheling, Baron(et), Baroness, Baronet(ess), Baronne, Bart,

Blue blood, Boyar, Brave, Bt, Burgrave, Childe, Contessa, Count, County, Cousin, Daimio, Datuk, Dauphine, Dom, Don, Doucepere, Douzeper(s), Duc, Duke, Duniwassal, Earl, Empress, Eorl, Ethel, Eupatrid, Fine, Galahad, Gent, Glorious, Graf, Grandee, Grandeur, Great, Heroic, Hidalgo, Highborn, Illustrious, Infant, Jarl, Junker, King, Landgrave, Lofty, Lord, Maestoso, Magnate, Magnificent, Magnifico, Manly, Margrave, Marquis, Mona, Nair, Nawab, Nayar, Palatine, Patrician, Patrick, Peer, Rank, Ritter, Rose, Seigneur, Seignior, Sheik(h), Stately, Sublime, Thane, Thegn, Titled, Toiseach, Toisech, Vavasour, Vicomte, Vidame, Viscount, Waldgrave

Noble gas(es) Argon, Helium, Krypton, Neon, Radon, Xenon

Nobody Diarist, Gnatling, Jack-straw, Nebbish, Nemo, None, Nonentity, Nyaff, Pipsqueak, Pooter, Quat, Schlepp, Scoot, Shlep, Zero

Nod(ding) Agree, Assent, Beck(on), Bob, Browse, Catnap, Cernuous, Dip, Doze, Drowsy, Mandarin, Nutant, Somnolent

Node, Nodular, Nodule Boss, Enhydros, Geode, Knot, Lump, Lymph, Milium, Pea-iron, Ranvier, Septarium, Swelling, Thorn, Tophus

Noise, Noisy Ambient, Babel, Bedlam, Big, Blare, Blat(t), Bleep, Blip, Blue murder, Bobbery, Boing, Boink, Bray, Bruit, Cangle, Charm, Cheep, Chellup, Clam, Clamant, Clamour, Clangour, Clash, Clatter, Clitter, Clutter, Coil, Crackle, Creak, Deen, Din, Dirdum, Discord, Euphonia, Euphony, F, Flicker, Fuss, Hewgh, Howlround, Hubbub, Hue, Hullabaloo, Hum, Hurly-burly, Knocking, Loud, Mush, Obstreperous, Phut, Ping, Plangent, Quonk, Racket, Raucous, Report, Risp, Roar, Roarie, Roary, Robustious, Rorie, Rort, Rory, Row(dow-dow), Rowdedow, Rowdy(dow)(dy), Rucous, Rumble, Schottky, Schottky-Utis, Scream, Screech, Shindig, Shindy, Shot, Shreek, Shreik, Shriech, Shriek, Slosh, Solar, Sone, Sonorous, Sound, Stridor, Surface, Thermal, Thunder, Tinnitus, Top, Trumpet, Tumult, → **UPROAR**, VIP, Visual, Vociferous, Whinny, White, Whoomph, Zoom

Nomad(ic) Bedawin, Bedu, Bed(o)uin, Berber, Chal, Drifter, Edom(ite), Errant, Fula(h), Gypsy, Hyksos, Kurd, Kyrgyz, Lapp, Rom, Rootless, Rover, Saracen, Sarmatian, Strayer, Tsigane, Tsigany, Tuareg, Vagabond, Vagrant, Wanderer, Zigan

Nominate, Nomination Appoint, Baptism, Designate, Elect, Postulate, Present, → **PROPOSE**, Slate, Specify, Term

Nonchalance, Nonchalant Blasé, Carefree, Casual, Cool, Debonair, Insouciant, Jaunty, Poco

Non-conformist, Non-conformity Beatnik, Bohemian, Chapel, Deviant, Dissent(er), Dissident, Drop-out, Ebenezer, Enfant terrible, Heresiarch, Heretic, Maverick, Odd-ball, Outlaw, Pantile, Patarine, Rebel, Recusant, Renegade, Renegate, Sectarian, Wesleyan

None Nada, Nary, Nil, Nought, Zero

Nonentity Cipher, Nebbich, Nebbish(er), Nebish, Nobody, Pipsqueak, Quat, Whippersnapper

▷**Nonetheless** *may indicate* an 'o' to be omitted

Nonsense Absurdity, Amphigory, Balderdash, Baloney, Bilge, Bizzo, Blague, Blah, Blarney, Blat(her), Blatherskite, Blether, Bollocks, Boloney, Borax, Bosh, Bs, Bull, Bulldust, Bullshit, Bull's wool, Buncombe, Bunk, Bunkum, Chaff, Clamjamfr(a)y, Clamjamphrie, Claptrap, Cobblers, Cock, Cockamamie, Cod, Codswallop, Crap, Crapola, Drivel, Dust, Eyewash, Faddle, Fandangle, Farce, Fiddlededee, Fiddle-faddle, Fiddlesticks, Flannel, Flim-flam, Footling, Fudge,

Gaff, Gammon, Gas and gaiters, Get away, Gibberish, Gobbledygook, Guff, Gum, Hanky-panky, Haver, Hogwash, Hokum, Hooey, Hoop-la, Horsefeathers, Humbug, Irishism, Jabberwocky, Jazz, Jive, Kibosh, Kidstakes, Malark(e)y, Moonshine, Mouthwash, Mumbo-jumbo, My eye, Phooey, Piffle, Pshaw, Pulp, Ratbaggery, Rats, Rawmaish, Rhubarb, Rigmarole, Rot, Rubbish, Scat, Shenanigans, Shit(e), Squit, Stuff, Taradiddle, Tom(foolery), Tommy-rot, Tosh, Trash, Tripe, Tush, Twaddle, Unreason, Waffle

Noodle(s) Capellini, Crispy, Daw, Fool, Head, Laksa, Lokshen, Manicotti, Mee, Moony, Ninny, Pasta, Sammy, Simpleton

Nook Alcove, Angle, Corner, Cranny, Niche, Recess, Rookery

Noose Fank, Halter, Hempen caudle, Lanyard, Loop, Necktie, Rebecca, Rope, Rope's end, Snare, Twitch, Widdy

▶**Nor** *see* **NOT**

Norm Canon, Criterion, Rule, Standard

Normal Average, Everyday, Natural, Norm, Ordinary, Par, Perpendicular, Regular, Standard, Straightforward, Usu(al)

North(ern), Northerner Arctic, Boreal, Cispontine, Copperhead, Dalesman, Doughface, Eskimo, Hyperborean, Icelander, Magnetic, N, Norland, Runic, Scotia, Scotsman, Sea, Septentrion, True, Up

North American (Indian) Injun, Papoose, Red(skin), Scalper, Totemist, Tribe

Nose, Nosy A(d)jutage, Aquiline, Beak, Bergerac, Boko, Bouquet, Breather, Conk, Copper, Cromwell, Curious, Desman, Droop(snoot), Fink, Gnomon, Grass, Grecian, Honker, Hooknose, Hooter, Index, Informer, Instinct, Meddle, Muffle, Muzzle, Nark, Neb, Nozzle, Nuzzle, Proboscis, Prying, Pug, Red, Retrousse, Rhinal, Roman, Scent, Schnozzle, Shove, Smelly, Sneb, Sniff, Snoot, Snout, Snub, Squeal, Stag, Stickybeak, Toffee

Nostalgia Longing, Memory lane, Oldie, Retrophilia, Wistfulness, Yearning

Not, Nor Aikona, Dis-, Na(e), Narrow A, Ne, Neither, Never, No, Pas, Polled, Taint

Notable, Notability Conspicuous, Dignitary, Distinguished, Eminent, Especial, Landmark, Large, Lion, Memorable, Personage, Signal, Striking, Unco, VIP, Worthy

▷**Not allowed** *may indicate* a word to be omitted

Notation(al) Benesh, Entry, Formalism, Infix, Memo, Polish, Positional, Postfix, Scientific

Notch(ed) Crena(l), Crenel, Cut, Dent, Erode, Erose, Gain, Gap, Gimp, Indent, Insection, Jag, Kerf, Mush, Nick, Nock, Raffle, Serrate, Serrulation, Sinus, Snick, Tally, Vandyke

Note(s), Notebook, Noted A, Accidental, Advance, Advice, Apostil(le), Apparatus, Arpeggio, Auxiliary, B, Bill(et), Bradbury, Bread and butter letter, Breve, C, Cedula, Chit(ty), Chord, Cob, Comment, Commentary, Conceit, Continental, Cover, Credit, Crotchet, Currency, D, Debit, Delivery, Demand, Dig, Dispatch, Do(h), Dominant, Double-dotted, E, E-la, Entry, F, Fa(h), False, Fame, Fiver, Five-spot, Flag up, Flat, Flim, G, Gamut, Gloss(ary), Gold, Grace, Greenback, Greeny, Gruppetto, Harmonic scale, Heed, Hypate, Identic, Index rerum, IOU, Iron man, Item(ise), Jot(tings), Jug(-jug), Key, Kudos, La, Large, Leading, Letter, Line(r), Log, Long, Longa, Lower mordent, Marginalia, Mark, Masora(h), Masoretic, Me, Mediant, Melisma, Melody, Memo(randum), Mese, Message, Mi, Minim, Minute, Missive, → **MONEY**, Mordent, Music, Muzak®, Natural, NB, Nete, Neum(e), Oblong, Observe, Octave, Oncer, On record, Open,

Ostmark, Outline, Passing, Postal, Post-it®, Pound, Promissory, Prompt, Protocol, PS, Quarter, Quaver, Rag-money, Re, Reciting, Record, Remark, Renown, Request, Right, Root, Scholion, Scotch catch, Scotch snap, Semibreve, Semiquaver, Semitone, Sensible, Septimole, Sextolet, Sharp, Shoulder, Si, Sick, Sixteenth, Sixty-fourth, Sleeve, Smacker, Snuff-paper, So(h), Sol, Some, Stem, Strike, Subdominant, Submediant, Subtonic, Supertonic, Te, Ten(ner), Third, Thirty-second, Tierce, Tonic, Treasury, Treble, Two-spot, Ut, Verbal, Wad, Whole, Wolf, Wood

▷**Notes** *may indicate* the use of letters A–G

Noteworthy Eminent, Extraordinary, Memorable, Particular, Signal, Special

Nothing, Nought Buckshee, Bugger-all, Chargeless, Cipher, Damn-all, Devoid, Diddlysquat, Emptiness, FA, Gratis, Jack, Love, Nada, Naught, Nihil, Niks-nie, Nil, Nix(-nie), Noumenon, Nowt, Nuffin, O, Ought, Rap, Rien, Small beer, Sweet FA, Void, Z, Zero, Zilch, Zip(po)

Notice(able) Ad(vertisement), Advance, Advice, Affiche, Apprise, Attention, Avis(o), Banns, Bill, Blurb, Bold, Bulletin, Caveat, Circular, Clock, Cognisance, Crit, D, DA, Descry, Detect, Discern, Discover, Dismissal, Enforcement, Evident, Gaum, Get, Gorm, Handbill, → **HEED**, Intimation, Marked, Mensh, Mention, Message, NB, No(t)chel, Obit(uary), Observe, Oyez, Perceptible, Placard, Plaque, Playbill, Poster, Press, Proclamation, Prominent, Pronounced, → **REMARK**, Review, See, Short, Signal, Si quis, Spot, Spy, Sticker, Tent, Warning, Whip

Notify, Notification Acquaint, Advise, Apprise, Aviso, Awarn, Inform, Payslip, → **TELL**

Notion(al) Chimera, Conceit, Crotchet, Fancy, Hunch, Idea, Idolum, Inkling, Opinion, Reverie, Vapour, Whim

Notoriety, Notorious Arrant, Byword, Crying, Egregious, Esclandre, Fame, Flagrant, Ill-fame, Infamous, Infamy, Legendary, Proverbial, Réclame, Repute

▶**Nought** *see* **NOTHING**

Noun Agent, Agentive, Aptote, Collective, Common, Concrete, Count, Gerund, Mass, N, Proper, Seg(h)olate, Substantive, Tetraptote, Verbal, Vocative

Nourish(ing), Nourishment Aliment, Cherish, Cultivate, Feed, Grub, Ingesta, Manna, Meat, Nurse, Nurture, Nutrient, Promote, Repast, Replenish, Sustenance, Trophic

Novel(ty) Aga-saga, Airport, Bonkbuster, Book, Campus, Change, Clarissa, Different, Dime, Dissimilar, E-book, Epistolary, Erewhon, Fad, Fiction, Fresh, Gimmick, Gothic, Graphic, Historical, Horror, Idiot, Innovation, Modern, → **NEW**, Newfangled, Novation, Original, Outside, Page-turner, Paperback, Penny dreadful, Picaresque, Pot-boiler, Primeur, Pulp, River, Roman-à-clef, Romance, Roman fleuve, Saga, Scoop, Sex and shopping, She, Shilling-dreadful, Shilling-shocker, Terror, Thesis, Ulysses, Unfamiliar, Unusual, Weepie, Whodun(n)it, Yellowback

▷**Novel** *may indicate* an anagram

▶**Novelist** *see* **WRITE(R)**

Novice Acolyte, Apprentice, Beginner, Chela, Colt, Cub, Green(horn), Griffin, Jackaroo, Jillaroo, Kyu, L, Learner, Neophyte, New chum, Noob, Patzer, Postulant, Prentice, Rabbit, Rookie, Tenderfoot, Trainee

Now(adays) AD, Alate, Anymore, Current, Here, Immediate, Instantaneously, Instanter, Interim, Modish, Nonce, Nunc, Present, Pro tem, This

Nozzle Aerospike, A(d)jutage, Fishtail, Nose, Nose-piece, Rose, Spout, Stroup, Syringe, Tewel, Tuyere, Tweer, Twier, Twire, Twyer(e)

Nuance Gradation, Nicety, Overtone, Shade

Nub Crux, Gist, Knob, Lump, Point

Nuclear, Nucl(e)ide, Nucleus Cadre, Calandria, Centre, Chernobyl, Core, Crux, Daughter, Deuteron, Eukaryon, Euratom, Heartlet, Hub, Isomer, Isotone, Karyon, Kernel, Linin, Mesic, Mesonic, Mushroom, Nuke, Organelle, Pith, Prokaryon, Recoil, Sizewell, Triton

▷**Nucleus** *may indicate* the heart of a word

Nude, Nudism, Nudist, Nudity Adamite, Altogether, Aphylly, Bare, Buff, Eve, Exposed, Godiva, Gymnosophy, → **NAKED**, Nuddy, Scud, Stark, Stripped, Undress

Nudge Dunch, Dunsh, Elbow, Jostle, Knee, Poke, Prod

Nuisance Bore, Bot, Bugbear, Chiz(z), Drag, Impediment, Inconvenience, Mischief, Pest, Plague, Public, Terror, Trial, Trouble-maker, Varment

Null(ification), Nullify Abate, Cancel, Counteract, Defeasance, Destroy, Diriment, Disarm, Invalid(ate), Negate, Neutralise, Overturn, Recant, Terminate, Undo, Veto, Void

Numb(ness) Asleep, Blunt, Dead(en), Stun, Stupor, Torpefy, Torpescent, Torpid, Tranquillise

Number(s) Abundant, Access(ion), Air, Algebraic, Algorithm, Aliquant, Aliquot, Amiable, Amicable, Anaesthetic, Analgesic, Anthem, Antilog, Army, Atomic, Babylonian, Binary, Box, Calculate, Cardinal, Cetane, Chromosome, Cinque, Class, Cocaine, Coefficient, Cofactor, Complex, Composite, Concrete, Constant, Coordination, Count, Cyclic, Decillion, Decimal, Deficient, Deficit, Diapason, Digit, DIN, Drove, E, Edition, Epidural, Ether, Eucaine, Ex-directory, F, Feck, Figurate, Figure, Flock, Folio, Folksong, Fraction, Friendly, Frost(bite), Gas, Gobar, Golden, Googol, Handful, Hash(mark), Hemlock, Host, Hyperreal, Imaginary, Include, Incomposite, Index, Integer, Irrational, Isotopic, Item, Kochel, Lac, Lakh, Legion(s), Lepton, Lignocaine, Livraison, Local, Mach, Magazine, Magic, Mantissa, Mass, Melodic, Milliard, Minyan, Mixed, Mort, Muckle, Multiple, Multiplex, Multiplicity, Multitude, Myriadth, Natural, Neutron, No(s), Nonillion, Nth, Nuclear, Num, Numerator, Numerical, Octane, Octillion, Opiate, Opium, Opposite, Opus, Ordinal, OT, Paginate, Par, Paucal, Peck, Perfect, Pile, PIN, Plural, Polygonal, Prime, Procaine, Production, Proton, Quantum, Quorum, Quota, Quotient, Random, Rational, Real, Reckon, Registration, Regulo®, Root, Scads, Serial, Shedload, Show-stopper, Sight, Slew, Slue, Some, Square, Strangeness, Strength, Summand, Surd, T, Tale, Telephone, Tell, Thr(e)ave, Totient, Totitive, Transcendental, Troop, Turn-out, Umpteen, Umpty, Urethan(e), Verse, Wave, Whole, Wrong

▷**Number** *may indicate* a drug

Numeral(s) Arabic, Chapter, Figure, Ghubar, Gobar, Integer, Number, Roman, Sheep-scoring

Nun(nery) Basilian, Beguine, Bhikkhuni, Cell, Clare, Cloistress, Cluniac, Conceptionist, Dame, Deaconess, Gilbertine, Minim, Minoress, Mother Superior, Outsister, Pigeon, Poor Clare, Religeuse, Salesian, Sister, Sister of Mercy, Top, Trappistine, Vestal, Visitant, Vowess, Zelator, Zelatrice, Zelatrix

▷**Nun** *may indicate* a biblical character, father of Joshua

Nurse(ry), Nursing, Nursemaid Aia, Alice, Amah, Angel, Ant, Au pair, Ayah, Barrier, Bonne, Caledonia, Candy-striper, Care(r), Cavell, Charge, Cherish, Consultant, Cradle, Crèche, Day, Deborah, District, Dry, EN, Flo(rence), Foster, Gamp, Glumdalclitch, Harbour, Health visitor, Karitane, Mammy, Midwife,

Minister, Mother, Mrs Gamp, Nan(n)a, Nanny, Night, Nightingale, Norland, Nourice, Nourish, Parabolanus, Phytotron, Playroom, Playschool, Plunket, Practical, Probationer, RN, School, Scrub, Seminary, SEN, Sister, Staff, Suckle, Tend, Therapist, VAD, Visiting, Wet

Nursery(man) Conservatory, Crèche, Garden, Hothouse, Rhyme, Seedsman, Slope

▷**Nursing** *may indicate* one word within another

Nut(s), Nutcase, Nutshell, Nutter, Nut tree, Nutty Acajou, Acorn, Almond, Amygdalus, Aphorism, Arachis, Areca, Arnut, Babassu, Barcelona, Barking, Barmy, Bats, Beech-mast, Bertholletia, Betel, Bonce, Brazil, Briefly, Buffalo, Butterfly, Butternut, Cashew, Castle, Chock, Coal, Cob, Coco-de-mer, Coffee, Cohune, Coke, Cola, Conker, Coquilla, Coquina, Core, Cranium, Crankpin, Cream, Cuckoo, Dukka(h), En, Filberd, Filbert, Freak, Frog, Gelt, Gilbert, Gland, Glans, Goober, Goober-pea, Gum, Hard, Hazel, Head, Helmet, Hickory, Illipe, Ivory, Kachang puteh, Kernel, Kola, Kooky, Lichee, Li(t)chi, Loaf, Lug, Lunatic, Lychee, Macadamia, Macahuba, Macaw-palm, Macoya, Manic, Marking, Mast, Mockernut, Monkey, Noisette, Noodle, Oak, Oil, Pakan, Palmyra, Para, Pate, Pecan, Pekan, Philippina, Philippine, Philopoena, Physic, Pili, Pine, Pin(y)on, Pistachio, Poison, Praline, Prawlin, Quandang, Quantong, Queensland, Rhus, Sapucaia, Sassafras, Scrotum, Shell, Skull, Slack, Sleeve, Stuffing, Supari, Testicles, Thumb, Tiger, Tough, Walnut, Weirdo, Wing, Zany, Zealot

▷**Nut** *may refer to* Egyptian god, father of Osiris

Nutrient, Nutriment, Nutrition Betacarotene, Dietetics, Eutrophy, Food, Ingesta, Protein, Sitology, Sustenance, Trace element, Trophic, Vitamin

▷**Nuts** *may indicate* an anagram

Nymph(et) Aegina, Aegle, Amalthea, Arethusa, Callisto, Calypso, Camenae, Carme, Clytie, Constant, Cymodoce, Daphne, Doris, Dryad, Echo, Egeria, Eurydice, Galatea, Hamadryad, Hesperides, Houri, Hyades, Ida, Insect, Larva, Liberty, Lolita, Maelid, Maia, Maiden, Mermaid, Naiad, Nereid, Oceanid, Oenone, Oread, Pupa, Rusalka, Sabrina, Satyra, Scylla, Siren, Sylph, Syrinx, Tessa, Tethys, Thetis, Water, Wood

Oo

O Blob, Duck, Nought, Omega, Omicron, Oscar, Oxygen, Spangle, Tan, Zero

Oar(s), Oarsman, Oarsmen Blade, Bow, Ctene, Eight, Galley slave, Leander, Organ, Paddle, Pair, Propel, Rower, Scull, Spoon, Sweep

Oat(meal), Oats Ait, Athole brose, Avena, Brome-grass, Fodder, Grain, Grits, Groats, Gruel, Haver, Loblolly, Parritch, Pilcorn, Pipe, Porridge, Quaker®, Rolled, Wild

Oath Affidavit, Begorrah, Blast, Blimey, Bribery, Burgess, Curse, Damn, Dang, Dash, Demme, Doggone, Drat, Ecod, Egad, Expletive, God-so, Halidom, Hell, Hippocratic, Igad, Imprecation, Jabers, Jesus, Keech, Lumme, Lummy, Nouns, Oons, Promise, Rats, Sacrament, Sal(a)mon, 'Sbodikins, Sbud(dikins), Sheart, Shoot, 'Slife, 'Slight, Snails, Sonties, Strewth, Stygian, Swear, Tarnation, Tennis-court, Voir dire, Vow, Zbud

Obedient, Obedience, Obey Biddable, Bridlewise, Comply, Dutiful, Follow, Good, Hear, Mindful, Obsequious, Observe, Obtemper, Perform, Pliant, Servant, Yielding

Obese, Obesity Bariatrics, Corpulent, Fat, Stout

Object(s), Objection(able), Objective(ness), Objector Ah, Aim, Ambition, Argue, Artefact, Article, Artifact, Bar, Beef, But, Case, Cavil, Challenge, Clinical, Cognate, Complain(t), Conchy, Conscientious, Contest, Cow, Demur, Detached, Direct, Dissent, Doodah, End, Exception, Fetish, Found, Fuss, →**GOAL**, Her, Him, Ifs and buts, Impersonal, Improper, Indifferent, Indirect, Intensional, Intention, It, Item, Jib, Lion, Loathe, Mind, Moral, Near-earth, Niggle, Nimby, Nitpick, Non-ego, Non-partisan, Noumenon, Ob, Obnoxious, Offensive, Oppose, Outness, Perspective, Plan, Plot, Point, Protest, Proximate, Quasi-stellar, Question, Quibble, Quiddity, Rank, Rebarbative, Recuse, Refuse, Relation, Resent, Resist, Retained, Sake, Scruple, Sex, Subject, Sublime, Target, Thing, Transitive, Tut, Ultimate, Unbiased, Unsavoury, Virtu, Wart

▷**Object** *may indicate* a grammatical variant

Oblige(d), Obliging, Obligation, Obligatory Accommodate, Affable, Behold, Binding, Burden, Charge, Coerce, Compel, Complaisant, Compliant, Constraint, Contract, Corvée, Debt, De rigueur, Duty(-bound), Easy, Easygoing, Encumbent, Force, Giri, Gratify, Impel, Incumbent, IOU, Mandatory, Must, Necessitate, Needed, Novation, Obruk, Obstriction, Peremptory, Promise, Responsibility, Sonties, Synallagmatic, Tie, Wattle

Oblique(ly) Askance, Askew, Awry, Cross, Diagonal, Glance, Glancing, Perverse, Separatrix, Skew, Skewwhiff, Slanting, Solidus, Squint, Virgule

▷**Oblique** *may indicate* an anagram

Oblivion, Oblivious Forgetful, Lethe, Limbo, Nirvana, Obscurity, Silence, Unaware

Obnoxious Eyesore, Foul, Horrid, Offensive, Pestilent, Repellent, Repugnant, Unpleasant, Wart

Obscene(ly), Obscenity Bawdy, Blue, Fescennine, Filth, Gross, Hard-core, Indecent, Lewd, Lubricious, Paw(paw), Porn(o), Profane, Raunchy, Ribald, Salacious, Scatology, Smut, Vulgar

Obscure, Obscurity Abstruse, Anheires, Arcane, Becloud, Befog, Black out, Blear, Blend, Blot out, Blur, Break, Cloud, Cobweb, Conceal, Cover, Cryptic, Darken, Deep, Dim, Disguise, Eclipse, Elliptic, Encrypt, Engloom, Envelop, Esoteric, Filmy, Fog, Hermetic, Hide, Indistinct, Inky, Jude, Mantle, Mist, Murk, Mystic(al), Nebular, Night, Nubecula, Obfuscate, Obnubilate, Opaque, Oracular, Overcloud, Overshade, Overshadow, Recherché, Recondite, Shadowy, Tenebrific, Twilit, Unclear, Unobvious, →**VAGUE**, Veil, Vele, Wrap

▷**Obscure(d)** *may indicate* an anagram

Observance, Observant, Observation Adherence, Alert, Aphorism, Attention, Comment, Custom, Empirical, Espial, Experience, Eyeful, Holy, Honour, Hour-angle, Inkhorn, Lectisternium, →**NOTICE**, Obiter dicta, Perceptive, Percipient, Practice, Quip, Ready-eyed, Recce, Remark, Right, Rite, Ritual, Use, Vising

Observe(d), Observer Behold, Bystander, Celebrate, Commentator, Detect, Espy, Eye, Eyeball, Heed, Keep, Mark, Monitor, NB, Note, Notice, Obey, Onlooker, Optic, Pharisee, Regard(er), Remark, Rite, Scry, See, Seer, Sight, Spectator, Spial, Spie, Spot, Spy, Study, Take, Twig, View, Voyeur, Watch, Witness

Obsess(ed), Obsession(al), Obsessive Anal, Anorak, Besot, Bug, Complex, Craze, Dominate, Fetish, Fixation, Hang-up, Haunt, Hobbyhorse, Hooked, Idée fixe, Infatuation, Mania, Monomania, Necrophilia, Nerd, Neurotic, One-track, Paranoic, Preoccupy, Smitten, Thing, Wonk

Obsolete, Obsolescence, Obsolescent Abandoned, Antique, Archaic, Dated, Dead, Defunct, Disused, Extinct, Latescent, Obs, Outdated, Outworn, Passé

Obstacle Barrage, Barrier, Boyg, Cheval de frise, Chicane, Clog, Dam, Drag, Dragon's teeth, Drawback, Gate, Handicap, Hazard, Hindrance, Hitch, Hurdle, Node, Oxer, Remora, Rock, Rub, Sandbank, Snag, Stimie, Stumbling-block, Stymie

Obstinacy, Obstinate Asinine, Bigoted, Bitter-ender, Buckie, Bullheaded, Bullish, Contrarian, Contumacious, Cussed, Dour, Froward, Headstrong, High-stomached, Inflexible, Intractable, Intransigent, Mule, Persistent, Perverse, Pervicacious, Piggish, Pig-headed, Recalcitrant, Refractory, Restive, Rigid, Rusty, Self-will, Stiff(-necked), Strure, Stubborn, Wilful

Obstruct(ion) Airlock, Bar, Barricade, Barrier, Block, Bottleneck, Caltrop, Chicane, Clog, Crab, Cross, Cumber, Dam, Delay, Embolus, Fil(l)ibuster, Gridlock, Hamper, Hand-off, Hedge, Hinder, Hurdle, Ileus, Impede, Let, Obstacle, Occlude, Oppose, Sab(otage), Sandbag, Snarl-up, Snooker, Stall, Stap, Stonewall, Stop, Stymie, Sudd, Thwart, Trammel, Trump

Obtain Achieve, Acquire, Borrow, Buy, Cop, Derive, Exist, Gain, Get, Land, Pan, Prevail, Procure, Realise, Secure, Succeed, Wangle, Win

Obvious Apparent, Axiom, Bald, Blatant, Brobdingnag, Clear, Distinct, Evident, Flagrant, Frank, Inescapable, Kenspeck(le), Manifest, Marked, Needless, Open(ness), Open and shut, Overt, Palpable, Patent, Pikestaff, Plain, Pronounced, Salient, Self-evident, Staring, Stark, Transparent, Truism, Unsubtle, Visible, Writ large

Occasion Call, Cause, Ceremony, Do, Encheason, Engender, Event, Fête, Field day, Nonce, →**OPPORTUNITY**, Reason, Ride, Tide, Time, Treat, Whet

Occasional(ly) At times, Black tie, Casual, Cause, Chance, Daimen, Day, Episode, Ever and anon, Instance, Intermittent, Irregular, Lawful, Motive, Odd, Orra, Periodic, Scattered, Social, Sometimes, Sporadic, While, White tie

Occupant, Occupation, Occupy(ing) Absorb, Acquire, Activity, Amuse, Avocation, Beset, Business, Busy, Career, Denizen, Dwell, Embusy, Employ, Engage, Engross, Hold, In, Incumbent, Indwell, Inhabitant, Inmate, Invade, Involve, Line, Man, Métier, Obsess, Overrun, People, Possess, Profession, Pursuit, Residency, Resident, Runrig, Sideline, Squat, Stay, Tenancy, Tenant, Tenure, Thrift, Trade, Upon, Use, Vocation, Walk of life

Occur(rence) Arise, Be, Betide, Betime, Case, Event, Eventuate, Fall, Happen, Incident, Instance, Outbreak, Outcrop, Pass, Phenomenon

Ocean(ic), Oceania Abundance, Abyssal, Antarctic, Arctic, Atlantic, Blue, Deep, German, Hadal, Herring-pond, High seas, Indian, Melanesia, Micronesia, Millpond, Pacific, Panthalassa, Pelagic, Polynesia, Pond, Sea(way), Southern, Thalassic, Waves, Western

Octopus Cephalopod, Devilfish, Polyact, Scuttle, Squid

Odd (person), Oddity Abnormal, Anomaly, Bizarre, Card, Cure, Curio, Curious, Droll, Eccentric, Eery, Erratic, Fishy, Freaky, Gink, Gonzo, Impair, Imparity, Jimjam, Offbeat, Original, Orra, Outré, Paradox, Parity, Peculiar, Queer, Quirky, Quiz, Random, Rare, Remote, Rum, Screwball, Singular, Spooky, →**STRANGE**, Unequal, Uneven, Unmatched, Unpaired, Unusual, Weird, Whims(e)y, Zany

▷**Odd(s)** *may indicate* an anagram or the odd letters in words

Odds, Oddments Bits, Carpet, Chance, Gubbins, Handicap, Line, Price, SP, Tails, Variance

Ode Awdl, Dit, Epicede, Epicedium, Epinicion, Epinikion, Genethliacon, Horatian, Hymn, Lay, Lyric, Monody, Paeon, Pindaric, Poem, Sapphic, Song, Stasimon, Threne, Threnody, Verse

Odium, Odious Comparison, Disestimation, Disgrace, Foul, Hatred, Heinous, Invidious, Repellent, Repugnant, Stigma

Odorous, Odour Air, Aroma, BO, Flavour, Funk, Hum, Musk, Opopanax, Perfume, Quality, Redolence, Sanctity, Scent, Smell, Stench, Waff, Waft

▷**Of** *may indicate* an anagram

Of course Certainly, Natch, Yes

Off Absent, Agee, Ajee, Away, Discount, Distance, Far, From, High, Inexact, Licence, Odd, Rancid, Reasty, Reesty, Relâche, Start

▷**Off** *may indicate* an anagram

▷**Off-colour** *may indicate* an anagram

Offence Affront, Attack, Crime, Delict, Delinquency, Demerit, Distaste, Fault, Huff, Hurt, Indictable, Lapse, Lese majesty, Malfeasance, Miff, Misdemeanour, Misprision, Odium, Outrage, Peccadillo, Perjury, Pip, Pique, Piracy, Praemunire, Regrate, Sedition, →**SIN**, Summary, Trespass, Umbrage, Violation

Offend(ed), Offender Affront, Anger, Annoy, Bridles, Criminal, Culprit, Default, Delinquent, Disoblige, Displease, Distaste, Hip, Huff, Hurt, Hyp, Infringe, Inveigh, Miffy, Miscreant, Nettle, Nonce, Nuisance, Outrage, Peeve, Perp(etrate), Provoke, Serial, Sin(ner), Sledge, Sting, Stray, Sus, Touchy, Twoccer, Umbrage, Violate, Wrongdoer

Offensive(ness) Affront, Aggressive, Alien, Attack, Bombardment, Campaign, Charge, Charm, Cruel, Derisatory, Derogatory, Dysphemism, Embracery, Euphemism, Execrable, Eyesore, Forbidding, Foul, Gobby, Indecent, Indelicate,

Inroad, Insulting, Invidious, Nasty, Noisome, Obnoxious, Obscene, Odious, Peccant, Personal, Pungent, Push, Putrid, Rank, Repugnant, →**RUDE**, Scandalous, Scurrilous, Sortie, Storm, Ugly, Unbecoming, Unsavoury, War

Offer(ing) Alms, Altarage, Anaphora, Approach, Bargain, Bid, Bode, Bouchée, Cadeau, Corban, Deodate, Dolly, Epanophora, Extend, Ex voto, Gift, Give, Godfather, Heave, Hold, Inferiae, Introduce, Invitation, Libation, Oblation, Overture, Peace, Peddle, Plead, Pose, Potla(t)ch, Present, Propine, →**PROPOSE**, Propound, Sacrifice, Shewbread, Special, S(h)raddha, Stamp, Stand, Submit, Suggestion, Tempting, Tender, Utter, Volunteer, Votive, Wave, Xenium

Offhand Airy, Banana, Brevi manu, Brusque, Casual, Cavalier, Currente calamo, Curt, Extempore, Impromptu, Indifferent, Snappy

Office(s) Abbacy, Agency, Benefice, Booking, Box, Branch, Broo, Bucket shop, Bureau, Buroo, Chair, Chancellory, Chancery, Circumlocution, Clerical, Colonial, Commonwealth, Complin(e), Consulate, Crown, Cube farm, Cutcher(r)y, Dead-letter, Deanery, Decemvirate, Den, Divine, Dogate, Drostdy, Employment, Evensong, Foreign, Front, Function, Holy, Home, Job, Land, Last, Lav(atory), Left luggage, Lieutenancy, Little, Little hours, Loan, Loo, Lost property, Mayoralty, Met(eorological), Ministry, Mistery, Nocturn, Nones, Obit, Oval, Palatinate, Papacy, Patent, Patriarchate, Penitentiary, Personnel, Petty Bag, Pipe, Place, Plum, Portfolio, Position, Post, Prefecture, Prelacy, Press, Prime, Printing, Record, Regency, Register, Registry, Rite, Satrapy, Scottish, Secretarial, Secretariat, See, Sext, Sinecure, Situation, Sorting, Speaker(ship), Stamp, Stationery, Sultanate, Tariff, Terce, Tiara, Ticket, Tierce, Tol(l)booth, Vespers, Vicary, War

Officer(s) Branch, Compliance, Counter-round, Customs, Duty, Engineer, Executive, First, Flag, Flying, Gal(l)ant, Gazetted, Group, Incumbent, Liaison, Non-commissioned, Nursing, Orderly, Peace, Petty, PO, Police, Presiding, Press, Prison, Probation, Radio, Relieving, Returning, Rodent, Safety, Scene-of-crime, Staff, Treasurer, Wardroom, Warrant, Watch

Office-worker Clerk, Peon, Temp, Typist

Official(s), Officiate, Officious Aga, Agent, Aleconner, Amban, Amtman, Apparatchik, Atabeg, Atabek, Attaché, Authorised, Beadle(dom), Borough-reeve, Bossy, Bumble, Bureaucrat, Catchpole, Censor, Chamberlain, Chancellor, Commissar, Commissioner, Consul, Convenor, Coroner, Count, Count palatine, Datary, Dean, Dignitary, Diplomat, Dockmaster, Dogberry, Ephor, Equerry, Escheater, Eurocrat, Executive, Executor, Factotum, →**FORMAL**, Fourth, Functionary, Gauleiter, Governor, Gymnasiarch, Handicapper, Hayward, Hazzan, Incumbent, Inspector, Intendant, Jack-in-office, Jobsworth, Keeper, Landdrost, Lictor, Lifeguard, Line judge, Linesman, Macebearer, Macer, Mandarin, Marplot, Marshal, Mayor, MC, Meddlesome, Mirza, Mueddin, Muezzin, Notary, Notary public, Ombudsman, Palatine, Panjandrum, Paymaster, Placeman, Plenipotentiary, Polemarch, Pontificate, Poohbah, Postmaster, Postulator, Praefect, Pragmatic, Prefect, Proconsul, Proctor, Procurator, Proggins, Proveditor, Provedor(e), Providor, Provost, Purveyor, Recorder, Reeve, Ref(eree), Régisseur, Registrar, Remembrancer, Sachem, Scrutineer, Secretary, Shammash, Shammes, Sherpa, Souldan, Spoffish, Stadtholder, Staff, Standard, Steward, Subdean, Suit, Summoner, Surveyor, Timekeeper, Tipstaff, Touch judge, Tribune, Trier, Trior, Triumvir, Turncock, Umpire, Valid, Valuer General, Verderer, Verger, Vicar-general, Viscount, Vizier, Walla(h), Whip, Yamen, Yeoman

Offset Balance, Cancel, Compensate, Counter(act), Counterbalance, Neutralise

Offspring Boy, Brood, Burd, Chick, Children, Daughter, Descendant, Family, Fruit, Fry, Get, Girl, Heir, Litter, Procreation, Product, Progeny, Seed, Sient, Son, Spawn

Off-white Bone, Cream, Ecru

Often Frequent, Habitual, Repeated

▷**Often** *may indicate* 'of ten'

Oil(s), Oily, Oil producer Anele, Anoint, Balm, Black gold, Bribe, Crab, Crude, Derv, Diesel, Drying, Essence, Essential, Ethereal, Fatty, Fish, Fixed, Frying, Fuel, Good, Grease, Hair, Heavy, Illupi, Joint, Lamp, Landscape, Lipid, Long, Lube, Lubricant, Macaw-tree, Midnight, Mineral, Monounsaturated, Multigrade, Oint, Oleaginous, Polyunsaturated, Pomade, Residual, Seed, Short, Sleek, Slick, Smalmy, Smarmy, Smeary, Sweet, Topped crude, Turps, Unction, Zest

Ointment Balm, Basilicon, Boracic, Boric, Cerate, Collyrium, Cream, Liniment, Lipsalve, Lotion, Nard, Pomade, Pomatum, Rub, Salve, Spikenard, Tiger balm®, Unction, Unguent, Vaseline®, Zinc

OK Agree(d), Approve, Authorise, Clearance, Copacetic, Copesettic, Go-head, Green light, Hunky-dory, Initial, Kosher, Mooi, No sweat, Permissible, Respectable, Right(o), Roger, Sanction, Sound, U, Vet

Old(er), Oldest, Oldie Ae(t), Aged, Aine(e), Ancient, Antique, Auld, Bean, Decrepit, Dutch, Earlier, Elderly, Ex, Fogram, Former, Gaffer, Geriatric, Glory, Golden, Gray, Grey, Hills, Hoary, Immemorial, Major, Mature, Methusaleh, Moore, Nestor, Nick, O, OAP, Obsolete, Off, Ogygian, One-time, Original, Outworn, Palae-, Passé, Primeval, Ripe, Rugose, Sen(escent), Senile, Senior, Shot, Signeur, Stager, Stale, Trite, Venerable, Veteran, Victorian(a), Worn

Old-fashioned Aging, Ancient, Antediluvian, Arch(aic), Arriéré, Back number, Bygone, Corn(y), Dated, Dodo, Dowdy, Dusty, Fogey, Fuddy-duddy, Fusty, Hidebound, Medieval, No tech, Obsolete, Ogygian, Outmoded, Outre, Outworn, Passé, Podunk, Primeval, Quaint, Relic, Retro, Rinky-dink, Schmaltzy, Shot, Square, Steam, Stick-in-the-mud, Traditional, Uncool, Victorian, Vintage

Old man, Old woman Anile, Aunty, Bodach, Buda, Budi, Burd, Cailleach, Carlin(e), Cicerone, Codger, Coniston, Crinkly, Crone, Crow, Crumbly, Fantad, Fantod, Fogey, Fogramite, Fogy, Fussy, Gammer, Geezer, Gramps, Grannam, Greybeard, Greyhen, Husband, Kangaroo, Koro, Kuia, Luckie, Lucky, Matriarch, Methuselah, Mort, Mzee, OAP, Oom, Pantaloon, Patriarch, Presbyte, Roo, Southernwood, Tante, Tripod, Trout, Whitebeard, Wife, Wight, Woopie, Wrinkly

Omelette Crêpe, Foo yong, Foo yung, Frittata, Fu yung, Pancake, Spanish, Tortilla

Omen Abodement, Absit, Augury, Auspice, Foreboding, Forewarning, Freet, Freit, Portent, Presage, Prodrome, Sign, Token, Warning

Ominous Alarming, Baleful, Bodeful, Dire, Dour, Forbidding, Grim, Inauspicious, Menacing, Oracular, Portentous, Sinister, Threatening, Ugly

Omission, Omit Aph(a)eresis, Apocope, Apospory, Apostrophe, Caret, Disregard, Drop, Elide, Elision, Ellipse, Ellipsis, Exception, Failure, Haplography, Haplology, Lipography, Loophole, Miss, Neglect, Nonfeasance, Non-user, Oversight, Paral(e)ipomenon, Pass, Pretermit, Senza, Skip

On (it) Aboard, About, Agreed, Alight, An, An't, At, Atop, By, Game, Gaun, Going, Half-cut, In, Leg, O', Of, Oiled, Over, Pon, Re, Running, Tipsy, Up(on), Viable

▷**On** *may indicate* an anagram

▷**On board** *may indicate* chess, draughts, or 'SS' around another word

Once(r) Ance, As was, Bradbury, Earst, Erst(while), Ever, Ex, Fore, Former, Jadis, Oner, Onst, Secular, Sole, Sometime, Whilom

One(self) A, Ace, Ae, Alike, An(e), Any, Body, Chosen, Digit, Eeny, Ego, Ein, I, Individual, Integer, Lunchtime, Me, Monad, Per se, Person, Single(ton), Singular, Solo, Tane, Un, Unify, Unit(y), Unitary, United, We, Yin, You

Onion(s) Allium, Bengi, Bonce, Bulb, Chibol, Chive, Cibol, Cive, Eschalot, Head, Ingan, Jibbons, Leek, Lyonnaise, Moly, Pate, Pearl, Ramp, Ramson, Rocambole, Ropes, Scallion, Scilla, Shal(l)ot, Spanish, Spring, Squill, Sybo(e), Sybow

Onlooker Beholder, Bystander, Kibitzer, Observer, Rubberneck, Spectator, Witness

Only Allenarly, Anerly, But, Except, Just, Meer, Merely, Nobbut, One, Seul, Singly, Sole, Sommer, Unique

Onward Advance, Ahead, Away, Forth, Forward, Progress

Ooze, Oozy Dowl, Drip, Exhale, Exude, Gleet, Globigerena, Ichorous, Mud, Percolate, Pteropod(a), Radiolarian, Seep, Sew, Sipe, Slime, Slob, Spew, Spue, Sweat, Uliginose, Uliginous

Opaque, Opacity Cloudy, Dense, Dull, Leucoma, Milky, Obscure, Obtuse, Onycha, Onyx, Roil, Thick, Turbid

Open(er), Opening, Openness Adit, Aedicule, Agape, Airhole, Ajar, Anthesis, Anus, Apert(ure), Apparent, Apse, Arch, Armhole, Autopsy, Bald, Bare, Bat, Bay, Begin, Bole, Breach, Break, Broach, Buttonhole, Candid, Candour, Cardia, Cavity, Chance, Chasm, Chink, Clear, Crevasse, Crowbar, Dehisce, Deploy, Dilate, Door(way), Drawbridge, Dup, Embrasure, Exordium, Expansive, Explicit, Eyelet, Fair, Fenestra, Fissure, Fistula, Flue, Fontanel(le), Foramen, Frank, Free, Free-for-all, Funnel, Gambit, Gap, Gaping, Gat, Gate, Give, Glasnost, Glottis, Hagioscope, Hatch, Hatchback, Hatchway, Hiatus, Hilus, → **HOLE**, Ice-breaker, Inaugural, Intake, Interstice, Intro, Key, Kisser, Lacy, Lamp hole, Lance, Latchkey, Lead, Loid, Loophole, Loose, Manhole, Meatus, Mofette, Mouth, Naked, Nare, Natural, Nook, Oillet, Orifice, Os, Oscule, Osculum, Ostiole, Ostium, Ouvert, Overt, Overture, Pandora, Paper knife, Passe partout, Patent, Peephole, Persuadable, Pert, Pervious, Pick(lock), Placket, Plain, Plughole, Pop, Pore, Port(age), Porta, Porthole, Preliminary, Premiere, Prise, Pro-am, Public, Pylorus, Relaxed, Rent, Ring-pull, Room, Scuttle, Sesame, Sicilian, Sincere, Slit, Slot, Spare, Spiracle, Spirant, Squint, Start, Stokehole, Stoma, Stulm, Suasible, Syrinx, Thereout, Thirl, Touchhole, Transparent, Trapdoor, Trema, Trou, Truthful, Unbar, Unbolt, Unbutton, Unclasp, Uncope, Uncork, Undo, Unfurl, Unhasp, Unlatch, Unreserved, Unscrew, Unstop, Unsubtle, Untie, Unwrap, Unzip, Upfront, Vacancy, Vent, Vulnerable, Wide, Window, Yawning

Opera(tic), Opera house, Operetta Aida, Ariadne, Ballad, Boris Godunov, Bouffe, Burletta, Comic, Das Rheingold, Der Rosenkavalier, Die Fledermaus, Die Walküre, Don Carlos, Don Giovanni, ENO, Ernani, Euryanthe, Falstaff, Faust, Fedora, Fidelio, Glyndebourne, Grand, Hansel and Gretel, Horse, Idomeneo, Iolanthe, I Puritani, Kirov, La Bohème, La Donna e Mobile, Lakme, La Scala, Light, Lohengrin, Lulu, Magic Flute, Manon, Merrie England, Met, Musical, Nabucco, Norma, Oater, Oberon, Onegin, Orfeo, Otello, Pag, Parsifal, Pastorale, Patience, Peter Grimes, Pinafore, Porgy and Bess, Rigoletto, Ring, Ruddigore, Rusalka, Salome, Savoy, Seria, Simon Boccanegra, Singspiel, Soap, Space, Sudsen, Tell, The Met, Threepenny, Tosca, Turandot, Verismo, Work, Zarzuela

Operate, Operating, Operation(s), Operative Act(ion), Activate, Actuate, Afoot, Agent, Artisan, Attuition, Barbarossa, Bypass, Caesarean, Campaign, Colectomy, Combined, Conduct, Couching, Current, Desert Storm, Detective, Doffer, Exercise, Function, Game, Hobday, Holding, Hysterectomy, Jejunostomy, Keystroke, Laparotomy, Leucotomy, Liposuction, Lithotomy, Lithotripsy, Lobotomy, Logical, Manipulate, Mechanic, Mules, Nip and tuck, Nose job, Oner, Overlord, Plastic, Practice, Proceeding, Rhytidectomy, Run, Sealion, Shirodkar's, Sortie, Splenectomy, Sting, Strabotomy, Surgery, Titration, Tummy tuck, Unit, Ure, Valid, Wertheim, Work

Operator Agent, Barnard, Camshaft, Conductor, Dealer, Manipulator, Nabla, Sawbones, Sparks, Surgeon, Sysop, System

Opiate, Opium Buprenorphine, Dope, Drug, Hop, Laudanum, Meconin, Meconite, Morphine, Narcotic, Paregoric, Religion, Soporific, Thebaine

Opinion(ated), Opinionative Advice, Attitude, Belief, Bet, Bias, Conjecture, Consensus, Cri, Deem, Diagnosis, Dictum, Dogma, Dogmatic, Doxy, Editorial, Entêté, Esteem, Estimation, Fatwa(h), Feeling, Guess, Heresy, Impression, Judgement, Mind, Mumpsimus, Pious, Prejudice, Private, Public, Pulse, Say, Second, Sense, Sentence, Sentiment, SO, Stand, Syndrome, Take, Tenet, Thought, Utterance, View, Viewpoint, Voice, Vote

Opponent(s) Adversary, Antagonist, Anti, Denier, E-N, Enemy, E-S, Foe, Gainsayer, Mitnaged, N-E, N-W, S-E, Straw-man, S-W, Tiger, W-N, W-S

Opportune, Opportunist, Opportunity Appropriate, Apropos, Break, Buccaneer, Carpetbagger, →**CHANCE**, Day, Equal, Facility, Favourable, Ganef, Ganev, Ganof, Godsend, Godslot, Go-go, Golden, Gonif, Gonof, Heaven-sent, Occasion, Opening, Pat, Photo, Providential, Room, Scope, Seal, Seel, Sele, Snatcher, Sneak thief, Tabula rasa, Tide, Timely, Timous, Vantage, Well-timed, Window

Oppose(d), Opposer, Opposing, Opposite, Opposition Across, Against, Agin, Anti, Antipathy, Antipodes, Antiscian, Antithesis, Antithetic, Antitype, Antonym, Argue, At, Athwart, Au contraire, Averse, Battle, Beard, Black, Breast, Buck, Collision, Colluctation, Combat, Confront, Contradict, Contrary, Converse, Counter(part), Countermove, Diametric, Dissent, Dissident, Distance, E contrario, Face, Foreanent, Fornen(s)t, Gainsay, Hinder, Hostile, Impugn, Inimical, Inverse, Ironic, Meet, Militate, Noes, Object, Obscurant, Overthwart, Polar, Reactance, Reaction, Recalcitrate, Reluct, Repugn, Resist, Retroact, Reverse, Rival, Shadow, Subtend, Synoeciosis, Syzygy, Teeth, Terr, Them, Thereagainst, They, Thwart, Toe to toe, Toto caelo, Traverse, V, Versus, Vice versa, Vis-à-vis, Withstand

Oppress(ion), Oppressive Airless, Bind, Burden, Close, Crush, Dead hand, Despotic, Heavy, Holy cruel, Incubus, Jackboot, Laden, Onerous, Overbear, Overpower, Persecute, Ride, Snool, Stifling, Sultry, Tommy, Totalitarian, Tyrannise, Yoke

Opt, Option(al) Alternative, Call, →**CHOICE**, Choose, Decide, Default, Double zero, Elect(ive), Facultative, Fine, Menu, Naked, Omissible, Pick, Plump, Put, Select, Soft, Swap(tion), Voluntary, Votive, Wale, Zero(-zero)

Optimism, Optimist(ic) Chiliast, Elated, Expectant, Hopeful, Micawber, Morale, Overplay, Pangloss, Pollyanna, Rosy, Sanguine, Starry-eyed, Upbeat

Or Au, Either, Ere, Gold, Ossia, Otherwise, Sol

Orange Agent, An(n)atta, An(n)atto, Apricot, Arnotto, Aurora, Bergamot, Bigarade, Blenheim, Blood, Blossom, Chica, Clockwork, Croceate, Flame,

Flamingo, Fulvous, Genip(ap), Jaffa, Kamala, Kamela, Kamila, Karaka, Mandarin, Methyl, Mock, Naartje, Nacarat, Nartjie, Navel, Ochre, Osage, Petit grain, Pig, Roucou, Ruta, Satsuma, Seville, Shaddock, Tangerine, Tenné, Ugli®, Ulsterman

Orate, Oration, Oratory Address, Chapel, Declamation, Eloge, Elogium, Elogy, Eulogy, Harangue, Panegyric, Speech

Oratorio, Orator(y) Boanerges, Brompton, Brougham, Cantata, Cicero, Creation, Demagogue, Demosthenes, Diction, Elijah, Hwyl, Isocrates, Morin, Nestor, Prevaricator, Proseucha, Proseuche, Rant, Rhetor, Samson, Spellbinder, Stump, Tub-thumper, Windbag

Orbit(al) Apolune, Apse, Apsis, Circuit, Dump, Eccentric, Ellipse, Eye, Lunar, Path, Revolution, Stationary, Subshell

Orchestra(te), Orchestration Brass, Ensemble, Gamelan, Hallé, Instrumentation, LPO, LSO, Percussion, Ripieno, Score, Sinfonietta, Stage-manage, Symphony, Woodwind

Orchid Adam and Eve, Adder's mouth, Arethusa, Bee, Bird's nest, Bog, Burnt-tip, Calanthe, Calypso, Cattleya, Coralroot, Coral wort, Cymbidium, Disa, Epidendrum, Fly, Fragrant, Frog, Helleborine, Hyacinth, Lady, Lady's slipper, Lady's tresses, Lizard, Man, Marsh, Military, Miltonia, Monkey, Musk, Naked lady, Odontoglossum, Oncidium, Phalaenopsis, Puttyroot, Salep, Slipper, Snakemouth, Swamp pink, Swan, Twayblade, Vanda, Vanilla

Ordain Arrange, Command, Decree, Destine, Enact, Induct, Japan, Priest

Ordeal Corsned, Disaster, Preeve, Test, → TRIAL

Order(ed), Orderly, Orders Action, Adjust, Administration, Affiliation, Alphabetical, Anton Piller, Apollonian, Apple-pie, Arrange, Array, ASBO, Attachment, Attendant, Attention, Attic, Augustine, Avast, Bade, Banker's, Bankruptcy, Bath, Batman, Battalia, Batting, Bed, Behest, Benedictine, Bernardine, Bespoke, Bid, Book, Boss, Brotherhood, Buffalo, Call, Camaldolite, Canon, Category, Caveat, CB, Charter, Cheque, Chit, Chronological, Class, Cluniac, Coherent, Command(ment), Committal, Compensation, Composite, Cosmo, Court, Decorum, Decree, Demand, Dictate, Diktat, Direct(ion), Directive, Dispone, Dominican, Doric, Draft, DSO, Edict, Embargo, Enclosed, Enjoin, En règle, Errand, Established, Establishment, Eviction, Exclusion, Fiat, Fiaunt, Firing, Firman, Form(ation), Franciscan, Fraternity, Freemason, Full, Gagging, Garnishee, Garter, Gilbertine, Ginkgo, Good, Grade, Group, Habeas corpus, Hest, Holy, Hospitaller, Indent, Injunction, Insectivora, Instruct, Interdict, In turn, Ionic, Irade, Khalsa, Kilter, Knights Hospitallers, Kosmos, Language, Large, Law, Lexical, Loblolly boy, Loblolly man, Loose, Mail, Major, Mandamus, Mandate, Marching, Marist, Market, Marshal, Masonic, Merit, Methodical, Minor, Monastic, Money, Monitor, Moose, Natural, Neatness, Nunnery, OBE, Oddfellows, Official, OM, Open, Orange, Ord, Ordain, Organic, Organised, Pecking, Plot, Possession, Postal, Precedence, Precept, Premonstrant, Prepare, Prescribe, Preservation, Prioritise, Provisional, Rank, Receiving, Reception, Regiment, Règle, Regular, Regulation, Religious, Requisition, Restraining, Return, Right, Rule, Ruly, Sailing, Sarvodaya, Scale, Sealed, Search, Sequence, Seraphic, Series, Settle, Shipshape, Short, Side, Sisterhood, Sort, Standing, Starter's, State, Statutory, Stop(-loss), Straight, Stratify, Subpoena, Summons, Supervision, System, Tabulate, Tall, Taxis, Tell, Templar, Teutonic, Third, Thistle, Tidy, Trim, Ukase, Uniformity, Warison, Warrant, Word, Working, Writ

▷**Ordering** *may indicate* an anagram

Ordinary Average, Banal, Bog standard, Canton, Chevron, Comely, Common (or garden), Commonplace, Cot(t)ise, Everyday, Everyman, Exoteric, Fess(e), Flanch, Flange, Folksy, Grassroots, Hackneyed, Humdrum, Mass, Mediocre, Middling, Mundane, → **NORMAL**, O, OR, Pedestrian, Plain, Prosy, Pub, Rank and file, Routine, Ruck, Run-of-the-mill, Saltier, Saltire, Scarp, Simple, So-so, Tressure, Trite, Trivial, Undistinguished, Unexceptional, Uninspired, Usual, Vanilla, Workaday, Your

Ore Alga, Babingtonite, Bauxite, Bornite, Braunite, Calamine, Calaverite, Calx, Cerusite, Chalcocite, Chalcopyrite, Chloanthite, Coffinite, Coin, Copper, Crocoite, Dry-bone, Element, Enargite, Galenite, Glance, Haematite, Hedyphane, Horseflesh, Ilmenite, Iridosmine, Ironstone, Limonite, Magnetite, Mat, Melaconite, Middlings, Mineral, Minestone, Morass, Niobite, Oligist, Owre, Peacock, Pencil, Phacolite, Pitchblende, Proustite, Psilomelane, Pyrargyrite, Pyromorphite, Realgar, Ruby silver, Schlich, Seaweed, Slug, Smaltite, Sphalerite, Stephanite, Stilpnosiderite, Stockwork, Stream-tin, Taconite, Tailing, Tenorite, Tetrahedrite, Tin, Wad(d)

Organ(s), Organic Adjustor, Adnexa, American, Antimere, Appendix, Archegonium, Barrel, Biogenic, Biotic, Bladder, Bursa, Calliope, Carbon, Carpel, Carpogonium, Cercus, Chamber, Chemoreceptor, Choir, Chord, Claspers, Clave, Colour, Conch(a), Console, Corti's, Cribellum, Ctene, Ear, Echo, Electric, Electronic, Electroreceptor, Emunctory, End, Epinastic, Essential, Exteroceptor, Eyeball, Feeler, Fin, Flabellum, Fundus, Gall bladder, Gametangium, Gill, Glairin, Gonad, Hammond®, Hand, Hapteron, Harmonica, Harmonium, Haustorium, House, Hydathode, Hydraulos, Imine, Isomere, Kerogen, Kidney, Lien, Light, Liver, Lung-book, Lyriform, Mag(azine), Means, Mechanoreceptor, Media, Medulla, Melodion, Ministry, Modiolus, Nasal, Natural, Nectary, Nematocyst, Nephridium, Newspaper, Nose, Olfactory, Oogonia, Ovary, Ovipositor, Ovotestis, Palp, Pancreas, Paper, Parapodium, Part, Pedal, Photogen, Photophore, Photoreceptor, Physharmonics, Pipe, Pipeless, Placenta, Plastid, Portative, Positive, Procarp, Prothallus, Pudenda, Pulmones, Purtenance, Radula, Receptor, Recit, Reed, Regal, Relict, Rhizoid, Sang, Saprobe, Scent, Sense, Sensillum, Serinette, Serra, Siphon, Spinneret, Spleen, Sporangium, Sporocarp, Sporophore, Stamen, Steam, Swell, Syrinx, Systaltic, Tentacle, Theatre, Theca, Thymus, Tongue, Tonsil, Tool, Trichocyst, Tympanum, Ureic, Uterus, Vegetative, Velum, Verset, Viscera, Viscus, Vitals, Voice, Voluntary, Wing, Womb, Wurlitzer®

Organise(d), Organisation, Organiser Activate, Administer, Agency, Aggregator, Amnesty, Anatomy, Apparat, → **ARRANGE**, Association, Body, Brigade, Broederbond, Caucus, Charter, CIA, Class(ify), Codify, Collect, Comecon, Company, Compile, Configure, Constitution, Coordinate, Design, Direct, Edifice, Embody, Entrepreneur, Eoka, Fascio, Fatah, Firm, Group, Guild, Hamas, Hierarchy, Impresario, Infrastructure, Jaycee, Krewe, Ku Klux Klan, Logistics, Machine, Mafia, Marshal, Mastermind, Mobilise, Movement, NATO, Octopus, Opus Dei, Orchestrate, Orderly, Outfit, Personal, PLO, Promotor, Quango, Rally, Red Crescent, Red Cross, Regiment, Resistance, Rosicrucian, Run, Setup, Sharpbender, Social, Soroptimist, Sort, Stage, Stage manage, Stahlhelm, Steward, Sysop, System, Tidy, Together, UN, UNESCO, Viet Minh
▷**Organise(d)** *may indicate* an anagram

Organism(s) Aerobe, Agamic, Alga, Archaea, Asymmetron, Auxotroph, Being, Biogenic, Biometric, Biont, Biotic, Cell, Chimeric, Ciliate, Clade, Coral,

Detritivore, Diplont, Ecad, Endosymbiont, Entity, Eozoon, Epibenthos, Epizoon, Eurytherm, Extremophile, Germ, Hemiparasite, Incross, Infauna, Infusoria(n), Lichen, Medusa, Meiosis, Metamale, Microaerophile, Microbe, Moneron, Nekton, Neuston, Osmoconformer, Pathogen, Periphyton, Phenetics, Ph(a)enology, Plankton, Pleuston, Poikilotherm, Prokaryote, Protist, Protista, Protozoan, Saprobe, Saprotroph, Schizomycete, Seaslater, Sea spider, Sea squirt, Strĕptococcus, Symbion(t), Teratogen, Thermophile, Trypanosome, Volvox, Vorticella, Zoarium

Orgy Bacchanalia(n), Binge, Bust, Carousal, Dionysian, Feast, Revel, Saturnalia, Spree, Wassail

Orient(al) Adjust, Annamite, Attune, Cantonese, Chinoiserie, Dawn, Dayak, E, East(ern), Far-e(ast), Fu Manchu, Hindu, Laotian, Levant, Leyton, Malay, Mongol, Mongolian, Shan, Sunrise, Tatar, Thai, Tibetan, Turk(o)man

Origin(al), Originate, Originating Abiogenesis, Abo, Adam, Arise, As per, Beginning, Big bang, Birth, Breed, Come, Cradle, Creation, Derive, Editio princeps, Elemental, Emanate, Epicentre, Etymon, Extraction, First, Firsthand, Focus, Found, Generic, Genesis, Genetical, Germ, Grow, Hatch, Imaginative, Incunabula, Ingenious, Innovate, Invent(ive), Master, Mother, Nascence, Natality, New, Novel, Ord, Parentage, Precedent, Primal, Primary, Primigenial, Primitive, Primordial, Pristine, Promethean, Protoplast, Prototype, Provenance, Provenience, Radical, Rise, Root, Seed, Seminal, Source, Spring, Start, Unborrowed, Ur, Urtext, Ylem, Zoism

Orion Alnilam, Alnitak, Ballatrix, Betelgeuse, Hatsya, Lambda, Meissa, Mintaka, Rigel, Saiph

Ornament(al), Ornamentation Additament, Adorn, Aglet, Aiguillette, Anaglyph, Anthemion, Applique, Arabesque, Barbola, Baroque, Barrette, Bead, Bedeck, Billet, Blister, Boss, Bracelet, Broider, Brooch, Bugle, Bulla, Caparison, Cartouche, Charm, Chase, Clock, Cockade, Conceit, Corbeil(le), Cornice, Coromandel work, Crocket, Cross-quarters, Curlicue, Decor, Decorate, Decoration, Diamanté, Die-work, Diglyph, Dog's-tooth, Doodad, Dreamcatcher, Egg and anchor, Egg and dart, Egg and tongue, Embellish, Emblem(a), Embroider, Enrich, Epaulet(te), Epergne, Fallal, Fandangle, Festoon, Fiddlehead, Figuration, Figurine, Filagree, Filigrain, Filigree, Fillagree, Fleur de lis, Fleuret, Fleurette, Fleuron, Florid, Fret, Fretwork, Frill, Frounce, Furbelow, Furnish, Gadroon, Garnish, Gaud, Headwork, Helix, Hip-knob, Honeysuckle, Horse-brass, Illustrate, Inlay, Japanaiserie, Knosp, Knotwork, Labret, Lavalier, Leglet, Lotus, Lunette, Lunula, Macramé, Mantling, Millefleurs, Mordent, Moresque, Motif, Nail-head, Necklet, Netsuke, Nicknackery, Niello, Nose-ring, O, Ouch, Ovolo, Palmette, Paraphernalia, Parure, Patera, Paternoster, Pectoral, Pendant, Picot, Pipe, Piping, Plume, Pompom, Poppyhead, Pounce, Prettify, Prunt, Quatrefoil, Rel(l)ish, Rococo, Rosette, Scalework, Scrollwork, Shell, Shoulder-knot, Snowdome, Snowglobe, Spangle, Spar, Stomacher, Tassel, Tool, Torc, Torque, Torsade, Tracery, Trappings, Tremolo, Trill, Trimming, Trinket, Tsuba, Turn, Twiddle, Versal, Whim-wham

▷**Ornate** *may indicate* an anagram

Orthodox Bien-pensant, Cocker, Conventional, Fundamental, Hardshell, Proper, Sound, Standard

Oscillate, Oscillation, Oscillator Fluctuate, Librate, Local, Relaxation, Ripple, Rock, Seesaw, Seiche, Squeg, Surge, Swing(swang), Vibrate, Waver

Osseous Bony, Hard, Skeletal, Spiny

Ostensibly Apparent, External, Seeming

Ostentation, Ostentatious Camp, Dash, Display, Dog, Dressy, Éclat, Epideictical, Extravagant, Fantoosh, Fastuous, Flamboyant, Flash(y), Flaunt, Florid, Flourish, Garish, Gaudy, Ghetto fabulous, Highfalutin(g), Large, Parade, Pomp, Pretence, Puff, → **SHOW(ING)**, Showboating, Side, Splash, Swank, Tacky, Tulip

Ostracise, Ostracism Banish, Blackball, Blacklist, Boycott, Cut, Exclude, Exile, Potsherd, Proscribe, Snub, Taboo

Other(s), Otherwise Additional, Aka, Alia, Alias, Allo-, Alternative, Besides, Different, Distinct, Else, Et al, Et alli, Etc, Excluding, Former, Further, Hanky-panky, It, Notwithstanding, Rest, Significant, Unlike

▷**Otherwise** *may indicate* an anagram

▶**Ousel** *see* **OUZEL**

Oust Depose, Dislodge, Eject, Evict, Expel, Fire, Supplant, Unseat

Out (of) Absent, Aglee, Agley, Al fresco, Asleep, Aus, Away, Begone, Bowl, Comatose, Dated, En ville, Exposed, External, Forth, From, Furth, Haro, Harrow, Hence, Hors, Inaccurate, In bloom, In blossom, Lent, Oust, Passe, Skittle, Striking, Stump, Taboo, Uit, Unfashionable, Up, York

▷**Out** *may indicate* an anagram

Out and out Absolute, Arrant, Sheer, Stark, Teetotal, Thorough, Totally, Utter

Outbreak Ebullition, Epidemic, Eruption, Explosion, Plague, Putsch, Rash, Recrudescence, Spate

Outburst Access, Blurt, Bluster, Boutade, Brainstorm, Eruption, Evoe, Explosion, Fit, Flaw, Furore, Fusillade, Gale, Gush, Gust, Paroxysm, Passion, Sally, Salvo, Sternutation, Storm, Tantrum, Tirade, Torrent, Tumult, Volley

Outcast Cagot, Discard, Exile, Exul, Ishmael, Leper, Mesel, Pariah, Robinson, Rogue

Outcome Aftermath, Consequence, Decision, Dénouement, Effect, Emergence, End, Event, Issue, Reflection, → **RESULT**, Sequel, Upshot, Wash-up

Outcry Blue murder, Bray, Halloa, Howl, Hue, Humdudgeon, Protest, Racket, Steven, Uproar, Utas

Outdated, Out of date Archaic, Dinosaur, Effete, Feudal, Fossil, Horse and buggy, Obsolete, Old hat, Outmoded, Passé, Square

Outdoor(s) Alfresco, External, Garden, Open air, Outbye, Plein-air

Outer External, Extrogenous, Magpie, Top

Outfit(ter) Arm, Catsuit, Drawbar, Dress, Ensemble, Equipage, Fitout, Furnish, Get-up, Haberdasher, Habit, Kit, Layette, Rig, Samfoo, Samfu, Strip, Suit, Tackle, Team, Trousseau, Turnout, Weed(s), Whites

Outgoing Egression, Exiting, Extrovert, Migration, Open, Rental, Retiring

Outgrowth Ala(te), Appendage, Aril, Bud, Caruncle, Enation, Epiphenomenon, Exostosis, Flagellum, Ligule, Offshoot, Osteophyte, Propagulum, Root-hair, Sequel, Strophiole, Trichome

Outhouse Conservatory, Lean to, Privy, Shed, Skilling, Skipper, Stable

Outing Excursion, Hike, Jaunt, Junket, Picnic, Sortie, Spin, Spree, Treat, Trip, Wayzgoose

Outlandish Alien, Barbarous, Bizarre, Exotic, Foreign, Peregrine, Rum

Outlaw Allan-a-Dale, Attaint, Badman, Ban, Bandit(ti), Banish, Broken man, Bushranger, Desperado, Exile, Forbid, Friar Tuck, Fugitive, Hereward, Hood, Horn, Jesse James, Klepht, Maid Marian, Ned Kelly, Proscribe, Put to the horn, Robin Hood, Rob Roy, Ronin, Tory, Waive

Outlet Débouché, Drain, Egress, Estuary, Exit, Femerall, Market, Opening, Orifice, Outfall, Sluice, Socket, Tuyere, Tweer, Twier, Twire, Twyer(e), Vent

Outline Adumbration, Aperçu, Circumscribe, Configuration, Contorno, Contour, Delineate, Describe, Digest, → **DRAFT**, Draught, Footprint, Layout, Note, Perimeter, Plan, Profile, Projet, Relief, Scenario, Schematic, Shape, Silhouette, Skeletal, Skeleton, Sketch, Summary, Syllabus, Synopsis, T(h)alweg, Trace

Outlook Aspect, Attitude, Casement, Mindset, Perspective, Prospect, View(point), Vista

▷**Out of** *may indicate* an anagram

▷**Out of sorts** *may indicate* an anagram

Output Data, Emanation, Get, Gross, Print out, Produce, Production, Turnout, Yield

▷**Output** *may indicate* an anagram

Outrage(ous) Affront, Apoplectic, Atrocity, Crime, Desecrate, Diabolical, Disgust, Egregious, Enorm(ity), Flagitious, Flagrant, Indignation, Insult, OTT, Rich, Sacrilege, Scandal, Shocking, Ungodly, Unholy, Violate

▷**Outrageously** *may indicate* an anagram

Outright Clean, Complete, Entire, Point-blank, Utter

Outside Ab extra, Crust, Derma, Enthetic, Exterior, External, Extramural, Front, Furth, Hors, Periphery, Plein-air, Rim, Rind, Rine, Shell, Surface

Outsider Alien, Bolter, Bounder, Cad, Extern, Extremist, Foreigner, Incomer, Oustiti, Pariah, Ring-in, Roughie, Stranger, Stumer, Unseeded, Upstart

Outskirts Edge, Fringe, Periphery, Purlieu

Outspoken Bluff, Blunt, Broad, Candid, Explicit, Forthright, Frank, Plain, Rabelaisian, Round, Vocal, Vociferous

Outstand(ing) Ace, Beaut(y), Belter, Billowing, Bulge, Chief, Crack, Crackerjack, Debt, Eminent, Especial, Exceptional, Exquisite, Extant, Extraordinaire, First, Fugleman, Highlight, Humdinger, Impasto, Jut, Left, Lulu, Marked, Masterpiece, Matchless, Oner, Overdue, Owing, Paragon, Paramount, Peerless, Phenom(enal), Pre-eminent, Prince, Prize, Prominent, Promontory, Prosilient, Protrude, Protuberant, Proud, Red letter, Relief, Relievo, Salient, Shining light, Signal, Special, Squarrose, Star, Stellar, Strout, Super(b), Top flight, Tour de force, Unmet, Unpaid, Unsettled, Vocal

Outward Efferent, Extern(e), External, Extrinsic, Extrorse, Extrovert, Posticous, Postliminary, Superficial

Outwit Baffle, Best, Circumvent, Crossbite, Dish, Euchre, Fox, Outthink, Over-reach, → **THWART**, Trick

Ouzel Merle, Ring, Water

Oval(s) Cartouche, Ellipse, Henge, Mandorla, Navette, Ooidal

Oven(-like) Aga®, Calcar, Combination, Convection, Cul-de-four, Dutch, Fan, Furnace, Hangi, Haybox, Horn(it)o, Kiln, Lear, Leer, Lehr, Lime kiln, Microwave, Muffle, Oast, Oon, Rotisserie, Stove, Umu

Over Above, Across, Again, Atop, C, Clear, Done, Finished, Hexad, Left, Maiden, Of, On, Ore, Ort, Owre, Past, Sopra, Spare, Superior, Surplus, Through, Uber, Wicket maiden, Yon

Overcast Cloudy, Dull, Lowering, Sew, Sombre

Overcharge Clip, Extort, Fleece, Gazump, Gyp, OC, Rack-rent, Rook, Rush, Soak, Sting

Overcome Beat, Bested, Conquer, Convince, Dead-beat, Defeat, Expugn, Kill, Master, Mither, Moider, Moither, Prevail, Quell, Speechless, Stun, Subjugate,

Surmount, Survive, Swampt, Underfong, Vanquish, Win

▷**Overdrawn** *may indicate* 'red' outside another word

Overdue Behindhand, Belated, Excessive, Late, Unpaid

Overflow(ing) Abrim, Cornucopia, Lip, Nappe, Ooze, Outpour, Redound, Spillage, Surfeit, Teem

Overhang(ing) Beetle, Bulge, →**JUT**, Loom, Project, Shelvy

Overhaul Bump, Catch, Overtake, Recondition, Refit, Revision, Service, Strip

Overhead(s) Above, Aloft, Ceiling, Cost, Exes, Hair(s), Headgear, Oncost, · Rafter, Upkeep, Zenith

Overhear Catch, Eavesdrop, Tap

Overlap(ping) Correspond, Equitant, Imbricate, Incubous, Kern(e), Limbous, Obvolute, Tace, Tasse

Overlay Ceil, Ciel, Smother, Stucco, Superimpose, Too, Veneer

Overload Burden, Plaster, Strain, Surcharge, Tax

Overlook(ed) Condone, Disregard, Excuse, Forget, Forgive, Indulge, Miss, Neglect, Omit, Pass, Pretermit, Superintend, Unnoticed, Waive

Overpower(ing) Crush, Evince, Mighty, Onerous, Oppress, Outman, Overwhelm, Potent, Profound, Subdue, Surmount, Swelter, Whelm

Override, Overrule Abrogate, Disallow, Outvote, Outweigh, Paramount, Preponderant, Reverse, Talk down, Veto

Overrun Exceed, Extra, Infest, Inundate, Invade, Lip, Swarm, Teem

Overseas Abroad, Colonial, Foreign, Outremer, Transmarine, Ultramarine

Oversee(r) Administer, Baas, Banksman, Boss, Captain, Care, Deputy, Direct, Eyebrow, Foreman, Grieve, Handle, Induna, Mediate, Periscope, Steward, Supercargo, Superintend, Supervise, Survey(or)

Overshadow(ed) Cloud, Dominate, Dwarf, Eclipse, Obscure, Outclass, Umbraculate

Oversight Blunder, Care, Error, Gaffe, Inadvertence, Lapse, Neglect

Overstate(ment), Overstated Embroider, Exaggerate, Hyperbole, Theatral, Theatrical

Overt Manifest, Patent, Plain, Public

Overtake Catch, For(e)hent, Lap, Leapfrog, Overget, Overhaul, →**PASS**, Supersede

Overthrow Dash, Defeat, Demolish, Depose, Dethrone, Down, Labefact(at)ion, Putsch, Ruin, Smite, Stonker, Subvert, Supplant, Unhorse, Unseat, Vanquish, Whemmle, Whommle, Whummle, Worst

Overture Advance, Approach, Carnival, Egmont, Hebrides, Intro, Leonora, Offer, →**OPENING**, Prelude, Propose, Serenade, Sinfonia, Toccata, Toccatella, Toccatina

Overturn(ing) Capsize, Catastrophe, Coup, Cowp, Engulf, Keel, Quash, Rebut, Reverse, Tip, Topple, Up(set), Upend, Whemmle, Whomble, Whommle, Whummle

Overwhelm(ed), Overwhelming Accablé, Assail, Banging, →**CRUSH**, Dearth, Deluge, Engulf, Flabbergast, Inundate, KO, Mind-boggling, Overcome, Plough under, Scupper, Smother, Snow, Submerge, Swamp

Overwork(ed) Fag, Hackneyed, Ornament, Slog, Stale, Supererogation, Tax, Tire, Toil, Travail

Owe(d), Owing Attribute, Due, OD

Owl(s) Barn, Barred, Blinker, Boobook, Brown, Bubo, Bunter, Eagle, Elegant, Fish, Glimmergowk, Grey, Hawk, Hoo(ter), Horned, Jenny, Little, Long-eared,

Longhorn, Madge, Moper, Mopoke, Mopus, Night, Ogle, Parliament, Ruru, Saw-whet, Scops, Screech, Snowy, Spotted, Strich, Striges, Strigiformes, Tawny, Wood

Own(er), Owning, Ownership Acknowledge, Admit, Agnise, Confess, Domain, Dominium, Fess, Have, Hold, Mortmain, Nain, Of, Personal, Possess, Proper, Proprietor, Recognise, Reputed, Title, Tod, Use

Ox(en) Anoa, Aquinas, Aurochs, Banteng, Banting, Bison, Bonas(s)us, Buffalo, Bugle, Bullock, Cat(t)alo, Fee, Gaur, Gayal, Gyal, Kouprey, Mart, Musk, Musk-sheep, Neat, Ovibos, Rother, Saola, Sapi-utan, S(e)ladang, Steare, Steer, Taurus, Ure, Urus, Vu quang, Water buffalo, Yak, Yoke, Zebu

▷**Oxtail** *may indicate* 'x'

Oxygen (and lack of) Aerobe, Anoxia, Epoxy, Liquid, Lox, Loxygen, O, Ozone

Oyster (bed), Oyster disease, Oyster-eater Avicula, Bivalve, Bush, Cul(t)ch, Kentish, Lay, Mollusc, Native, Ostrea, Ostreophage, Pandore, Pearl, Plant, Prairie, Scallop, Scalp, Scaup, Seed(ling), Spat, Spondyl, Stew, Vegetable

Oz Amos, Australia, NSW

Ozone Air, Atmosphere, Oxygen

Pp

Pace, Pacemaker Canter, Clip, Cracking, Dog-trot, Easter, Footstep, Gait, Heel and toe, Jog-trot, Lope, Measure, Pari passu, Pioneer, Prowl, Rack, **→ RATE**, Single-foot, Snail's, Spank, Speed, Step, Stroll, Tempo, Tramp, Tread, Trot

Pacific, Pacify Appease, Bromide, Calm, Conciliate, Dove, Ease, Eirenic, Imperturbable, Irenic, Lull, Mild, Moderate, Ocean, Placid, Quiet, Serene, Soothe, Subdue, Sweeten, Tranquil

Pack(age), Packaging, Packed, Packing, Pack in Back, Bale, Blister, Bobbery, Box, Bubble(wrap), Bundle, Can, Cards, Carry, Cold, Compress, Congest, Cram, Crate, Crowd, Cry, Deck, Dense, Dunnage, Embox, Entity, Everest, Excelsior, Face, Fardel, Flock, Floe, Forswear, Gasket, Gaskin, Glut, Hamper, Hooker, Hunt, Ice, Jam, Kennel, Kitbag, Knapsack, Lies, Load, Matilda, Naughty, Pair, **→ PARCEL**, Pikau, Power, Pun, Ram, Rat, Rout, Ruck, Rucksack, Set, Shiralee, Steeve, Stow, Suits, Sumpter, Tamp, Team, Tread, Troop, Truss, Wad, Wet, Wolf, Wrap

Packet Bindle, Boat, Bomb, Bundle, Cookie, Liner, Mailboat, Mailer, Mint, Parcel, Roll, Sachet, Steamboat, Wage

Pact Agreement, Alliance, Bargain, Bilateral, Cartel, Contract, Covenant, Entente cordiale, Locarno, Stability, **→ TREATY**, Warsaw

Pad(ding) Bachelor, Batting, Bombast, Brake, Bustle, Compress, Condo, Crash, Cushion, Dabber, Damper, Dossil, Earmuff, Enswathe, Expand, Falsies, Filler, Flat, Frog, Gumshield, Hard, Hassock, Horse, Ink, Jotter, Knee, Launch, Leg-guard, Lily, Nag, Note, Numnah, Patch, Paw, Ped, Pillow, Pincushion, Plastron, Pledget, Plumper, Porters' knot, Pouf(fe), Protract, Pudding, Puff, Pulvillus, Pulvinar, Quitting, Scratch, Shoulder, Squab, Stamp, Stuff, Sunk, Swab, Tablet, Thief, Touch, Tournure, Tylopod, Tympan, Velour(s), Velure, Wad, Waffle, Wase, Writing

Paddle, Paddle boat, Paddle-foot Canoe, Dabble, Doggy, Oar, Pinniped, Row, Seal, Side-wheel, Spank, Splash, Wade

Pagan(ism) Animist, Atheist, Baalite, Ethnic, Gentile, Gentoo, Godless, Heathen, Heretic, Idolater, Infidel, Lectisternium, Odinist, Paynim, Saracen, Sun cult, Wicca

Page(s), Pageboy Back, Bastard title, Beep, Bellboy, Bellhop, Bleep, Boy, Buttons, Callboy, Centrefold, Contact, Flyleaf, Fold out, Folio, Foolscap, Front, Gate-fold, Groom, Haircut, Hairdo, Henchman, Home, Hornbook, Leaf, Master, Messenger, Moth, Octavo, Op-ed, P, Pane, PP, Problem, Quarto, Ream, Recto, Ro, Servant, Sheet, Side, Splash, Squire, Tear sheet, Thirty-twomo, Tiger, Title, Varlet, Verso, Web, Yellow

Pageant Antic, Anticke, Antique, Cavalcade, Pomp, Spectacle, Tattoo, Triumph

▶**Paid** see **PAY(MASTER)**

Pain(ful), Pains Ache, Aggrieve, Agony, Ake, Angina, Anguish, A(a)rgh, Bad, Bale, Bitter, Bore, Bot(t), Bother, Causalgia, Colic, Cramp, Crick, CTS, Distress, Dole, Doleur, Dolour, Dool(e), Dysury, Excruciating, Fash, Felon, Gastralgia, Gip, Grief, Gripe, Gyp, Harrow, Heartburn, →**HURT**, Ill, Kink, Laborious, Lancination, Lumbago, Mal, Migraine, Misery, Molimen, Myalgia, Neuralgia, Pang, Persuant, Pest, Phantom, Prick, Pungent, Rack, Raw, Referred, Rick, Sair, Sciatica, Smart, Sore, Sorrow, Sten(d), Sternalgia, Sting, Stitch, Stung, Tarsalgia, Teen(e), Tene, Throe, Torment, Torture, Travail, Twinge, Wo(e), Wrench, Wring
▷**Pain** *may indicate* bread (French)

Painkiller Aminobutene, Analgesic, Bute, Celecoxib, Cocaine, Coxib, Distalgesic, Endorphin, Enkephalin, Meperidine, Metopon, Morphine, Number, Pethidine

Paint(ed), Painting Abstract, Abstract expressionism, Acrylic, Action, Airbrush, Aquarelle, Art autre, Art deco, Artificial, Art nouveau, Ash Can School, Baroque, Battlepiece, Bice, Brushwork, Byzantine, Canvas, Cellulose, Cerograph, Chiaroscuro, Clair-obscure, Clobber, Coat, Colour, Constable, Cubiform, Cubism, Dadaism, Daub, Dayglo, Decorate, Depict, Describe, Diptych, Distemper, Eggshell, Emulsion, Enamel, Expressionist, Fard, Finery, Finger, Flatting, Flemish, Fore-edge, Fresco, Genre, Gild, Gloss, Gothic, Gouache, Graining, Gravure, Grease, Guernica, Hard-edge, Historical, Icon, Impasto, Impressionism, Intumescent, Lead, Limn, Lithochromy, Luminous, Mannerist, Maquillage, Matt, Mehndi, Miniate, Miniature, Modello, Mona Lisa, Monotint, Mural, Naive, Neoclassical, Neo-expressionist, Neo-Impressionism, Neo-Plasticism, Nightpiece, Nocturne, Non-drip, Oaker, Ochre, Oil, Old Master, Oleo(graph), Op art, Orphism, Paysage, Pentimento, Pict, Picture, Pigment, Pinxit, Plein air, Pointillism(e), Polyptych, Pop art, Portray, Poster, Post-Impressionism, Pre-Raphaelite, Primavera, Primitive, Raddle, Rag-rolling, Realist, Renaissance, Rococo, Romantic, Rosemaling, Roughstuff, Sand, Scenography, Scumble, Secco, Semi-gloss, Sfumato, Sien(n)ese, Skyscape, Spray, Stencil, Stereochrome, Still life, Stipple, Surrealist, Tablature, Tableau, Tag, Tempera, Tondo, Townscape, Umber, Umbrian, Undercoat, Underglaze, War, Wax

Painter(s) Animalier, Aquarellist, →**ARTIST**, Ash Can School, Colourist, Cubist, Decorator, Gilder, Illusionist, Impressionist, Lazy, Limner, Little Master, Luminarist, Miniaturist, Modernist, Muralist, Nazarene, Old Master, Paysagist, Plein-airist, Primitive, Sien(n)ese, Vedutista

Pair(ing) A deux, Brace, Couple(t), Doublet, Duad, Duo, Dyad(ic), Electron, Fellows, Geminate, Jugate, Jumelle, King, Link, Lone, Match, Mate, Ocrea, Pigeon, Pr, Span, Spouses, Synapsis, Syndyasmian, Syzygy, Tandem, Thummim, Twa(e), Tway, Twin, Two(some), Urim, Yoke

Pal Ally, Amigo, Bud(dy), China, Chum, Comrade, Crony, Cully, Friend, Mate, Playmate, Roomie, Wus(s)

Palace Alcazar, Alhambra, Basilica, Blenheim, Buckingham, Court, Crystal, Edo, Élysée, Escorial, Escurial, Fontainebleau, Gin, Goslar, Hampton Court, Holyrood, Hotel, Istana, Kensington, Lambeth, Lateran, Louvre, Mansion, Nonsuch, Palatine, Pitti, Pushkin, Quirinal, Sans Souci, Schloss, Seraglio, Serail, Shushan, Topkapi, Trianon, Tuileries, Valhalla, Vatican, Versailles, Winter

Palatable, Palatalized, Palate Dainty, Relish, Roof, Sapid, Savoury, Soft, Taste, Toothsome, Uranic, Uraniscus, Uvula, Velum

Pale, Paling Albino, Ashen, Blanch, Bleach, Cere, Dim, Etiolate(d), Fade, →**FAINT**, Fence, Ghostly, Grey, Haggard, Insipid, Lily (white), Livid, Mealy,

Ox-fence, Pastel, Pasty-faced, Peaky, Peelie-wally, Picket, Sallow, Shilpit, Stang, Verge, Wan, Whey-faced, White, Wishy-washy

Palestine, Palestinian Amorite, Fatah, Gadarene, Galilean, Gaza, Hamas, Holy Land, Intifada, Israel, Pal, Philistine, PLO, Samaria

Pall Bore, Cloy, Curtain, Damper, Glut, Hearse-cloth, Mantle, Satiate, Shroud

Pallet Bed, Cot, Couch, Mattress, Tick

Palm Accolade, Areca, Assai, Atap, Babassu, Betel, Buriti, Burrawang, Bussu, Cabbage, Calamus, Carna(h)uba, Carpentaria, Chamaerops, Chiqui-chiqui, Coco, Conceal, Coquito, Corozo, Corypha, Date (tree), Doom, Doum, Elaeis, Euterpe, Fan, Feather, Fob, Foist, Gomuti, Gomuto, Groo-groo, Gru-gru, Hand, Hemp, Ita, Itching, Ivory, Jip(p)i-Jap(p)a, Jipyapa, Jupati, Kentia, Laurels, Loof, Macahuba, Macaw, Macoya, Miriti, Moriche, Nikau, Nipa, Oil, Palmyra, Paxiuba, Peach, Pupunha, Raffia, Raphia, Rat(t)an, Royal, Sabal, Sago, Saw palmetto, Sugar, Talipat, Talipot, Thatch, Thenar, Toddy, Triumph, Troelie, Troolie, Trooly, Trophy, Vola, Washingtonia, Wax, Wine

Paltry Bald, Cheap, Chickenfeed, Exiguous, Mean, Measly, Mere, Peanuts, Pelting, Petty, Pimping, Poor, Puny, Scalled, Shabby, Shoestring, Sorry, Thingummybob, Tin(-pot), Tinny, Trashy, Trifling, Two-bit, Vile, Waff, Whiffet

Pamper(ed) Baby, Cocker, Coddle, Cosher, Cosset, Cuiter, Feather-bed, Gratify, High-fed, →INDULGE, Mollycoddle, Pet, Pompey, Spoon-fed

Pamphlet(eer) Brochure, Catalogue, Defoe, Leaflet, Notice, Sheet, Tract

Pan Agree, Auld Hornie, Bainmarie, Balit, Basin, Betel(-pepper), Braincase, Chafer, Dent, Dial, Drip, Dripping, Drub, Goat-god, Goblet, God, Hard, Ice-floe, Iron, Jelly, Karahi, Knee, Ladle, Lavatory, Muffin, Nature-god, Non-stick, Oil, Pancheon, Panchion, Patella, Patina, Peter, Plate, Poacher, Preserving, Prospect, Roast, Salt, Search, Skid, Skillet, Slag, Slate, Spider, Steamer, Sweep, Tube, Vacuum, Vessel, Warming, Wo(c)k, Work

Pancake Blin(i), Blintz(e), Burrito, Crêpe (suzette), Crumpet, Drop(ped)-scone, Flam(m), Flapjack, Flaune, Flawn, Fraise, Fritter, Froise, Galette, Latke, Pikelet, Poppadum, Potato, Quesadilla, Ro(e)sti, Slapjack, Suzette, Taco, Tortilla, Tostada, Waffle

Pane Glass, Light, Panel, Quarrel, Quarry, Sheet

Panel(ling) Array, Board, Cartouche, Console, Control, Dashboard, Fa(s)cia, Gore, Hatchment, Inset, Instrument, Jury, Mandorla, Mimic, Mola, Orb, Patch(board), Reredorse, Reredos(se), Rocker, Screen, Skreen, Solar, Stile, Stomacher, Table, Tablet, Tongue and groove, Triptych, Valance, Volet, Wainscot

Pang Achage, Ache, Qualm, Spasm, Stab, Travail, Twinge, Wrench

Panic Alar(u)m, Amaze, Blue funk, Consternation, Fear, Flap, Flat-spin, Flip, Fright, Funk, Guinea-grass, Hysteria, Millet, Raggee, Raggy, Ragi, Scaremonger, Scarre, Stage fright, Stampede, Stampedo, State, Stew, Tailspin

Pannier Basket, Cacolet, Corbeil, Dosser, Skip, Whisket

Panorama, Panoramic Cyclorama, Range, Scenery, Veduta, View, Vista

Pant(s) Bags, Boxer shorts, Breeches, Capri, Cargo, Chaps, Chinos, Culottes, Deck, Dhoti, Drawers, Fatigues, Flaff, Gasp, Gaucho, Harem, Knickers, Long johns, Longs, Parachute, Pech, Pedal-pushers, Pegh, Puff, Rot, Slacks, Smalls, Stirrup, Stovepipe, Sweat, The pits, Throb, Toreador, Trews, Trousers, Trunks, Wheeze, Yearn

Panther Bagheera, Black, Cat, Cougar, Jaguar, Leopard, Pink

Pantomime, Pantomime character Charade, Cheironomy, Cinderella, Dumb-show, Farce, Galanty, Harlequinade, Play

Pantry Buttery, Closet, Larder, Spence, Stillroom

Papa Dad, Father, P

Papal, Papist, Papistry Catholic, Clementine, Concordat, Guelf, Guelph, Holy See, Legation, Pontifical, RC, Roman, Tiara, Vatican

Paper(s), Paperwork, Papery Admin, Antiquarian, Art, Atlas, Ballot, Baryta, Bible, Blat(t), Blotting, Bond, Brief, Broadsheet, Broadside, Bromide, Brown, Building, Bumf, Bumph, Butter, Cap, Carbon, Cartridge, Cellophane®, Chad, Chinese, Chiyogami, Cigarette, Comic, Command, Commercial, Confetti, Corrugated, Cream-laid, Cream-wove, Credentials, Crêpe, Crown, Curl, Daily, Deckle-edge, Decorate, Demy, Docket, Document, Dossier, Eggshell, Elephant, Emery, Emperor, Essay, Exam, File, Filter, Final, Flock, Folio, Foolscap, Form(s), FT, Funny, Furnish, Galley, Garnet, Gazette, Gem, Glass(ine), Government, Grand eagle, Grand Jesus, Graph, Greaseproof, Green, Guardian, Gutter press, Hieratica, ID, Imperial, India, Japanese, Jesus, Journal, Kraft, Lace, Laid, Lavatory, Legal cap, Linen, Litmus, Loo-roll, Mail, Manifold, Manil(l)a, Marble, Mercantile, Mirror, Monograph, MS, Music(-demy), Needle, News(print), → **NEWSPAPER**, Note, Notelet, Oil, Onion-skin, Order, Origami, Packing, Pad, Page, Papillote, Papyrus, Parchment, Pickwick, Plotting, Position, Post, Pot(t), Pravda, Press, Print, Printing, Quair, Quarto, Quire, Rag, Ramee, Rami(e), Ream, Red top, Retree, Rhea, Rice, Rolled, Rolling, Royal, Safety, Satin, Saxe, Scent, Scotsman, Scrip, Script, Scroll, Scrowl, Sheaf, Sheet, Ship's, Silver, Skin, Slipsheet, Spoilt, Stamp, Starch, State, Steamer, Sugar, Sun, Super-royal, Tabloid, Taffeta, Tar, Term, Ternion, TES, Test, Thesis, Thread, Tiger, Tissue, Today, Toilet, Torchon, Touch, Tracing, Tract, Trade, Transfer, Treatise, Treeware, Tri-chad, Turmeric, Two-name, Vellum, Velvet, Voucher, Walking, Wall, Waste, Watch, Wax(ed), Web, Whatman®, White, Willesden, Wirewove, Wood(chip), Woodfree, Worksheet, Wove, Wrapping, Writing

Paper-cutting, Paper-folding Decoupage, Kirigami, Origami, Psaligraphy

Par Average, Equate, Equivalent, → **NORMAL**, Scratch

Parable Allegory, Fable, Proverb

Parachute, Parachutist Aeroshell, Aigrette, Drogue, Float, Freefall, Jump, Pack, Pappus, Para, Parabrake, Parapente, Red Devil, Silk, Skyman, Thistledown, Umbrella

Parade (ground) Air, Arcade, Catwalk, Cavalcade, Ceremony, Church, Display, Dress, Drill, Easter, Emu, Esplanade, Flaunt, Gala, Hit, Identification, Identity, Line-up, Maidan, March-past, Pageantry, Pomp, Prance, Procession, Prom(enade), Show, Sick, Sowarry, Stand-to, Strut, Ticker tape

Paradise Arcadia, Avalon, Bliss, Earthly, Eden, Elysium, Garden, Happy-hunting-ground, Heaven, Idyll(ic), Lost, Malaguetta, Nirvana, Park, Regained, Shangri-la, Sky, Surfer's, Svarga, Swarga, Swerga, → **UTOPIA**

Paradox(ical) Absurdity, Cantor's, Contradiction, Dilemma, Electra, Epimenides, Gilbertian, Irony, Koan, Olbers', Puzzle, Russell's, Zeno's

Paraffin Earthwax, Kerosene, Kerosine, Liquid, Ozocerite, Ozokerite, Photogen(e), Propane

Parallel Analog, Analogy, Arctic circle, Collateral, Collimate, Corresponding, Equal, Even, Forty-ninth, Like, Pattern

Paralysis, Paralyse Akinesia, Apoplexy, Benumb, Cataplexy, Catatonia, Cramp, Curarise, Cycloplegia, Diplegia, Halt, Hemiplegia, Infantile, Monoplegia, Numbness, Ophthalmoplegia, Palsy, Paraplegia, Paresis, Polio, Quadriplegia, Scram, Shock, Shut, Spastic, Spina bifida, Stun, Torpefy, Transfix

Parapet (space) Balustrade, Bartisan, Bartizan, Battlement, Breastwork, Brisure, Bulwark, Crenel, Flèche, Machicolation, Merlon, Rampart, Redan, Surtout, Terreplein, Top, Wall

Parasite, Parasitic Amoeba, Ascarid, Autoecious, Aweto, Babesiasis, Beech-drops, Bilharzia, Biogenous, Biotroph, Bladder-worm, Bloodsucker, Bonamia, Bot, Candida, Chalcid, Chigoe, Coccus, Conk, Copepod, Cosher, Cryptosporidium, Cryptozoite, Dodder, Ectogenous, Ectophyte, Endamoeba, Endophyte, Entophyte, Entozoon, Epiphyte, Epizoon, Filarium, Flea, Freeloader, Giardia, Gregarinida, Guinea worm, Haematozoon, Hair-eel, Hair-worm, Heartworm, Heteroecious, Hook-worm, Ichneumon, Inquiline, Isopod, Kade, Ked, Lackey, Lamprey, Leech, Licktrencher, Liverfluke, Louse, Lungworm, Macdonald, Mallophagous, Measle, Mistletoe, Monogenean, Nematode, Nit, Orobanche, Phytosis, Pinworm, Plasmodium, Puccinia, Quandong, Rafflesia, Rhipidoptera, Rickettsia, Root, Roundworm, Schistosoma, Scrounger, Shark, Smut-fungus, Sponge(r), Sporozoa(n), Strangleweed, Strepsiptera, Strongyle, Strongyloid, Stylops, Sucker, Symphile, Tachinid, Tapeworm, Tick, Toady, Toxoplasma, Trematode, Trencher-friend, Trencher-knight, Trichina, Tryp(anosoma), Vampire, Viscum, Whipworm, Witchweed, Worms

Parcel Allocate, Allot, Aret, Bale, Bundle, Dak, Enwrap, Holding, Inwrap, Lot, Package, Packet, Plot, Sort, Wrap

Parch(ed), Parching Arid, Bake, Dry, Graddan, Hot coppers, Roast, Scorched, Sere, Thirsty, Torrefied, Torrid, Xerotes

Parchment Diploma, Forel, Membrane, Mezuzah, Papyrus, Pell, Pergameneous, Roll, Roule, Scroll, Scrow, Sheepskin, Vellum

Pardon(able), Pardoner Absolution, Absolve, Amnesty, Anan, Assoil, Clear, Condone, Eh, Excuse, →**FORGIVE**, Grace, Mercy, Quaestuary, Qu(a)estor, Release, Remission, Remit, Reprieve, Venial, What

Parent(al) Ancestral, Father, Forebear, Foster, Generant, Genitor, Maternal, Mother, Paternal, Rear, Solo, Storge

Parish District, Flock, Kirkto(w)n, Parischan(e), Parishen, Parochin(e), Peculiar, Province, Title

Park(ing) Amusement, Business, Car, Caravan, Common, Country, Domain, Enclosure, Forest, Fun, Game, Garage, Grounds, Hardstand, Industrial, Lung, Motor, National, Off-street, P, Petrified Forest, Pitch, Pleasure ground, Preserve, Rec, Safari, Sanctuary, Science, Siding, Stand, Stop, Technology, Terrain, Theme, Trailer, Valet, Valley, Water, Wildlife, Wind, Yard

Parliament Addled, Althing, Barebones, Black, Bundestag, Chamber, Commons, Congress, Cortes, Council, Cross-bench, Dail, Diet, Drunken, Eduskunta, Folketing, House, Imperial, Knesset, Lack-learning, Lagt(h)ing, Landst(h)ing, Lawless, Legislature, Lok Sabha, Long, Lords, Majlis, Merciless, Mongrel, Odelst(h)ing, Rajya Sabha, Reichstag, Riksdag, Rump, St Stephens, Sanhedrin, Seanad, Seanad Éireann, Sejm, Short, Stannary, Stirthing, Stormont, Stort(h)ing, The Beehive, Thing, Unicameral, Volkskammer, Westminster

Parliamentarian Cabinet, De Montfort, Fairfax, Ireton, Leveller, Member, MP, Politico, Roundhead, Whip

Parlour Beauty, Funeral, Ice-cream, Lounge, Massage, Salon, Snug, Spence

Parody Burlesque, Lampoon, Mock, Piss-take, Satire, Send-up, Skit, Spoof, Travesty

Parrot Amazon, Ape, Budgerigar, Cockatoo, Conure, Copy, Echo, Emulate, Flint, Green leek, Imitate, Kaka(po), Kea, Lorikeet, Lory, Lovebird, Macaw, Mimic,

Nestor, Owl, Parakeet, Paroquet, Poll(y), Popinjay, Psittacine, Quarrion, Repeat, Rosella, Rote, Shell, Stri(n)gops, T(o)uraco

Parson Clergyman, Cleric, Holy Joe, Minister, Non juror, Pastor, Priest, Rector, Rev, Sky-pilot, Soul-curer, Yorick

Parsonage Glebe, Haworth, Manse, Rectory, Vicarage

Part(s), Parting, Partly Accession, Aliquot, Among, Antimere, Area, Aspect, Aught, Bad, Behalf, Bit, Bite, Bulk, Bye, Cameo, Character, Chunk, Cog, Compartment, Component, Constituent, Crack, Cue, Department, Detail, Dislink, Diverge, Divide, Dole, Element, Episode, Escapement, Farewell, Fascicle, Fork, Fraction, Good, Goodbye, Great, Half, Ill, Imaginary, Ingredient, Instalment, Integrant, Into, Lathe, Lead, Leave, Leg, Lill, Lilt, Lines, List, Livraison, Member, Meronym, Moiety, Morsel, Organ, Parcel, Passus, Percentage, → **PIECE**, Portion, Primo, Principal, Private, Proportion, Pt, Quit, Quota, Rape, Ratio, Real, Region, Rive, Role, Scena, Scene, Secondo, Section, Sector, Segment, Segregate, Separate, Serial, Sever, Shade, Share, Shed, Sleave, Sle(i)ded, Small, → **SOME**, Spare, Split, Stator, Sunder, Synthon, Tithe, To a degree, Tranche, Twin(e), Unit, Vaunt, Voice, Walking, Walk on, Wrench

Partial(ity), Partially Biased, Ex-parte, Fan, Favour, Halflins, Imbalance, Incomplete, Nepotism, One-sided, Predilection, Prejudiced, Slightly, Unequal, Weakness

Particle(s) Alpha, Antielectron, Antineutron, Atom, Baryon, Beta, Bit, Boson, Charmonium, Corpuscle, Cosmic dust, Dander, Delta, Deuteron, Electron, Elementary, Episome, Exchange, Fleck, Floccule, Fragment, Fundamental, Gauge boson, Gemmule, Globule, Gluon, Grain, Granule, Heavy, Ion, J, Jot, J/psi, Laitance, Lambda, Lepton, Lipoplast, Liposome, Meson, Mite, Molecule, Monopole, Mote, Muon, Negatron, Neutralino, Neutretto, Neutrino, Neutron, Nibs, Nucleon, Omega-minus, Parton, Pentaquark, Photon, Pion, Plastisol, Platelet, Positon, Positron, Preon, Proton, Psi(on), Quark, Radioactivity, Scintilla, Shives, Shower, Sigma, Singlet, Sinter, Smithereen, Spark, Speck, Strange, Submicron, Subnuclear, W, Whit, WIMP, XI, Z

Particular Choosy, Dainty, → **DETAIL**, Endemic, Especial, Essential, Express, Faddy, Fastidious, Fiky, Fog, Fussy, Item, Itself, London fog, Minute, Nice, Niffy-naffy, Nipperty-tipperty, Nitpicker, Old-maidish, Own, Pea-souper, Peculiar, Pedant, Pernickety, Pet, Point, Prim, Prissy, Proper, → **RESPECT**, Special, Specific, Stickler, Strict, Stripe

Partisan Adherent, Axe, Biased, Carlist, Champion, Devotee, Factional, Fan, Irregular, Partial, Provo, Queenite, Sider, Spear, Stalwart, Supporter, Tendentious, Yorkist, Zealot

Partition(ed) Abjoint, Bail, Barrier, Brattice, Bretasche, Bulkhead, Cloison, Cubicle, Diaphragm, Dissepiment, Divider, Division, Hallan, Mediastinum, Parpane, Parpen(d), Parpent, Parpoint, Perpend, Perpent, Replum, → **SCREEN**, Scriene, Septum, Skreen, Tabula, Wall, With(e)

Partner(ship) Accomplice, Affiliation, Alliance, Ally, Associate, Butty, Cahoot(s), Coachfellow, Colleague, Comrade, Confederate, Consort, Couple, Date, Dutch, Escort, E-W, Firm, Gigolo, Husband, Limited, Mate, Moll, N-S, Offsider, Other half, Pair, Pal, Pard, Rival, Sidekick, Significant other, Silent, Sleeping, SOP, Sparring, Spouse, Stablemate, Stand, Symbiosis, Wag, Wif(i)e

▷**Part of** *may indicate* a hidden word

Party Acid house, Advance, Aftershow, Alliance, ANC, Apres-ski, Assembly, At-home, Bachelor(ette), Bake, Ball, Band, Barbecue, Bash, Beano, Bee, Binge,

Birthday, Bloc, Blowout, Boarding, Body, Bottle, Buck's, Bunfight, Bust, Caboodle, Camp, Carousal, Carouse, Caucus, Celebration, Clambake, Coach, Cocktail, Colour, Commando, Communist, Concert, Congress, Conservative, Contingent, Cooperative, Coterie, Cult, Democratic, Detail, Ding, Dinner, Disco(theque), Do, Drum, DUP, Faction, Fest, Fianna Fáil, Fiesta, Fine Gael, Firing, Foy, Function, Funfest, Gala, Galravage, Gang, Garden, Ghibel(l)ine, GOP, Green, Greenback, Grumbletonian, Guilty, Hen, Hoedown, Hooley, Hootenanny, House, Housewarming, Hurricane, Inkatha, Jana Sangh, Janata, Jol(lities), Junket, Junto, Kegger, Knees-up, L, Labour, Landing, Launch, Lawn, Levee, Lib, Liberal, Lig, Love-in, Low heels, Mallemaroking, Movement, Musicale, National, Necking, Neck tie, Octobrist, Opposition, Orgy, Peace, People's, Person, Petting, Plaid, Political, Populist, Posse, Progressive, Prohibition, Pyjama, Radical, Rage, Rave, Rave-up, Razzle(-dazzle), Reception, Republican, Reunion, Revel(ry), Ridotto, Roast, Rocking, Roister, Rort, Rout, Scottish Nationalist, SDP, Search, Sect, Set, Shindig, Shindy, Shine, Shiv Sena, Shooting, Shower, Side, Sinn Fein, Slumber, Small and early, Smoker, SNP, Soc(ialist), Social, Social Credit, Social Democratic, Socialise, Soirée, Spree, Squad(rone), Squadrone volante, Stag, Street, Symposium, Tea, Teafight, Third, Thrash, Tory, Treat, UKIP, Unionist, United, Wake, Whig, Wine, Wingding, Working, Wrap

Pass(ed), Passing, Pass on, Past, Pass through Absit, Aforetime, Ago, Agon, Annie Oakley, Aorist, Approve, Arise, Arlberg, Before, Behind, Beyond, Blow over, Boarding, Botte, Brenner, Brief, Burgess, By (the by), Bygone, Caudine Forks, Centre, Cerro Gordo, Chine, Chit(ty), Cicilian Gates, Clear, Col, Cote, Cross, Cursory, Death, Dee, Defile, Delate, Demise, Die, Disappear, Double, Dummy, Dunno, Elapse, Emit, Enact, End, Ensue, Ephemeral, Exceed, Exeat, Flashback, Fleeting, Fob, Foist, Forby, Forgone, Former, Forward, Gap, Gate, Gha(u)t, Give, Glencoe, Glide, Go, Go by, Gorge, Great St Bernard, Gulch, Halse, Hand, Happen, Hause, Hospital, ID, Impart, Impermanent, Interrail, Interval, In transit, Jump, Khyber, Killiecrankie, La Cumbre, Lap, Late, Lead, Legislate, Live, Loss, Migrate, Momentary, Needle, Nek, Nine days' wonder, No bid, Nod through, Notch, Nutmeg, Occur, Oer, O grade, OK, Okay, Oke, Omit, One-time, Overhaul, Overshoot, Overtake, Pa, Palm, Parade, Participle, Perish, Permeate, Permit, Perpetuate, Poll, Poort, Predicament, Pretty, Proceed, Propagate, Pun(c)to, Qualify, Railcard, Ratify, Reach, Reeve, Refer, Relay, Retro, Retroactive, Retrospect, Reverse, Run, Safe conduct, St Gotthard, San Bernardino, Sea-letter, Senile, Serve, Shangri-la, Simplon, Since, Skim, Skip, Skirt, Slap, Sling, Small and early, Snap, Spend, Stab, State, Swipecard, Temporal, Thermopylae, Thread, Through, Thru, Ticket, Time immemorial, Tip, Transient, Transilient, Transitory, Transmit, Transpire, Transude, Travel, Troop, Uspallata, Veronica, Vet, Visa, Visé, Wall, Wayleave, Weather, While, Yesterday, Yesteryear

Passage(way), Passages Abature, Adit, Airshaft, Airway, Aisle, Alley(way), Alure, Apostrophe, Arcade, Archway, Areaway, Arterial, Avenue, Bank, Breezeway, Bridge, Bylane, Cadenza, Canal, Career, Catwalk, Channel, Choana, Chute, Citation, Clarino, Clause, Close, Coda, Condie, Conduit, Corridor, Creep, Crossing, Crush, Dead-end, Defile, Drake, Drift, Duct, Eel-fare, Episode, Epitaph, Excerpt, Extract, Fare, Fat, Fauces, Flat, Flight, Flue, Fogou, Gallery, Gangway, Gap, Gat, Gate, Ghat, Gorgia, Gully-hole, Gut, Hall, Head, Honeycomb, Inlet, Intestine, Journey, Labyrinth, Lane, Lapse, Lick, Lientery, Loan, Lobby, Locus, Meatus, Meridian, Middle, Mine, Mona, Moto perpetuo, Movement, Northeast, Northwest, Para(graph), Parashah, Path, Pend, Phrase,

Pore, Port, Portion, Prelude, Presto, Prose, Purple, Race, Retournelle, Ride, Ripieno, Rite, Road, Rough, Route, Sailing, Screed, Shaft, Shunt, Sinus, Skybridge, Skywalk, Slap, Snicket, Solus, Spillway, Strait, Street, Stretta, Stretto, Subway, Sump, Text, Thorough(fare), Throat, Tour, Trachea, Trance, Transe, Transit(ion), Travel, Tunnel, Tutti, Undercast, Unseen, Ureter, Voyage, Walkway, Way, Windpipe, Windway

▷**Passage of arms** *may indicate* 'sleeve'

Passenger(s) Cad, Commuter, Fare, Parasite, Pax, Pigeon, Pillion, Rider, Slacker, Steerage, Straphanger, Traveller, Voyager, Wayfarer

Passion(ate), Passionately Anger, Appetite, Ardent, Ardour, Con calore, Con fuoco, Crush, Dander, Duende, Emotion, Fervour, Fire, Flame, Frampold, Fury, Gust, Heat, Hot, Hunger, Hwyl, Ileac, Iliac, Infatuation, Intense, Ire, Irish, Kama, Love, Lust, Mania, Messianic, Metromania, Obsession, Oestrus, Polemic, Rage, Sizzling, Steamy, Stormy, Strong, Sultry, Torrid, Vehement, Violent, Warm, Wax, Wrath, Yen, Zeal, Zoolatria

Passive (stage), Passivity Apathetic, Dormant, Drifter, Inaction, Inert, Pathic, Patient, Pupa, Stolid, Supine, Vegetating, Vegetative, Yielding

Passport Access, Clearance, Congé(e), E, Key, Laissez-passer, Nansen, Navicert, Sea-letter, Visa

Password Code, Countersign, Logon, Nayword, Parole, Sesame, Shibboleth, Tessera, Watchword

▶**Past** *see* **PASS(ED)**

Pasta Agnolotti, Al dente, Anelli, Angel hair, Bucatini, Cannelloni, Cappelletti, Carbonara, Conchiglie, Durum, Eliche, Farfal, Farfalle, Farfel, Fedelini, Fettuc(c)ine, Fusilli, Lasagna, Lasagne, Linguini, Macaroni, Maccheroncini, Manicotti, Noodles, Orecchietti, Orzo, Pappardelle, Penne, Perciatelli, Ravioli, Rigatoni, Spaghetti, Spaghettina, Tagliarini, Tagliatelle, Tortelli(ni), Vermicelli, Ziti

Paste, Pasty Almond, Ashen, Batter, Beat, Botargo, Boule, Bridie, Cerate, Clobber, Cornish, Dentifrice, Dough, E, Electuary, Empanada, Fake, Filler, Fondant, Frangipane, Gentleman's Relish®, Glue, Guarana, Harissa, Knish, Lute, Magma, Marchpane, Marzipan, Masala, Mastic, Meat, Miso, Mountant, Pale, Pallid, Panada, Pâté, Patty, Pearl-essence, Pie, Piroshki, Pirozhki, Poonac, Pulp, Punch, Putty, Rhinestone, Rillettes, Sallow, Samosa, Sham, Slip, Slurry, Spread, Strass, Tahina, Tahini, Tan, Tapenade, Taramasalata, Trounce, Wan, Wasabi

Pastor(al) Arcadia, Bucolic, Curé, Eclogue, Endymion, Idyl(l), Minister, Priest, Rector, Rural, Shepherd, Simple

Pastry Baclava, Bakemeat, Baklava, Beignet, Bridie, Brik, Canape, Cannoli, Chausson, Cheese straw, Choux, Coquile, Creamhorn, Cream puff, Croissant, Croustade, Cruller, Crust, Danish, Dariole, Dough, Eclair, Filo, Flaky, Flan, French, Millefeuille, Muffin, Phyllo, Pie, Pie-crust, Profiterole, Puff, Quiche, Raised, Rough-puff, Samosa, Shortcrust, Strudel, Tart, Turnover, Vol-au-vent

Pasture Alp, Eadish, Eddish, Feed, Fell, Fodder, Grassland, Graze, Herbage, Kar(r)oo, Lair, Lare, Lay, Lea, Lease, Leasow(e), Leaze, Lee, Ley, Machair, Mead(ow), Moose, Outrun, Pannage, Pascual, Potrero, Raik, Rake, Sheal(ing), Shiel(ing), Soum, Sowm, Tie, Transhume, Tye

▶**Pasty** *see* **PASTE**

Patch(y) Bed, Bit, Blotchy, Cabbage, Chloasma, Clout, Coalsack, Cobble, Cooper, Court plaster, Cover, Friar, Fudge, Knit, Manor, →**MEND**, Mosaic, Mottled,

Nicotine, Pasty, Piebald, Piece, Plage, Plaque, Plaster, Pot, Purple, Repair, Shinplaster, Shoulder, Solder, Sunspot, Tingle, Tinker, Transdermal, Turf, Uneven, Vamp, Variegated

Path(way) Aisle, Allée, Alley, Arc, Berm, Berme, Boreen, Borstal(l), Bridle, Bridleway, Catwalk, Causeway, Causey, Cinder, Clickstream, Corridor, Course, Cycleway, Downlink, Eclipse, Ecliptic, Eightfold, Flight, Gangway, Gate, Ginnel, Glide, Lane, Ley, Lichwake, Lichway, Locus, Lykewake, Orbit, Packway, Pad, Parabola, Pavement, Peritrack, Primrose, Ride, Ridgeway, Route, Runway, Sidewalk, Slipway, Spurway, Stie, Sty(e), Swath(e), Taxiway, Track, Trail, Trajectory, Trod, Walkway, → **WAY**, Xystus

Pathetic(ally) Abysmal, Derisory, Doloroso, Drip, Forlorn, Piteous, Plaintive, Poignant, Sad, Saddo, Schlub, Sorry, Touching, Wet

Patience Calm, Endurance, Forbearance, Fortitude, Indulgence, Klondike, Klondyke, Monument, Solitaire, Stoicism, Virtue

Patient(s) Calm, Case, Clinic, Cot-case, Forbearing, Grisel(da), Grisilda, Invalid, Job, Long-suffering, Passive, Resigned, Stoic, Subject, Unprotesting, Walking case, Ward

Patriot(ic), Patriotism Cavour, Chauvinist, DAR, Emmet, Flag-waving, Flamingant, Garibaldi, Hereward, Irredentist, Jingoism, Loyalist, Maquis, Nationalist, Tell, Wallace, Zionist

Patrol Armilla, Beat, Coastguard, Guard, Outguard, Picket, Piquet, Prowl-car, Reconnaissance, Round, Scout, Sentinel, Sentry-go, Shark, Shore, Turm

Patron(age), Patroness, Patronise(d), Patronising Advowson, Aegis, Athena, Auspices, Backer, Benefactor, Business, Cavalier, Champion, Client, Condescend, Customer, Donator, Egis, Fautor, Favour, Friend, Lady Bountiful, Maecenas, Nepotic, Protector, Protégé, Provider, Shopper, → **SPONSOR**, Stoop, Stoup

Pattern(ed) Agouti, Agouty, Aguti, Archetype, Argyle, Bird's eye, Blueprint, Branchwork, Candy stripe, Check, Chequer, Chiné, Clock, Crisscross, Design, Diaper, Diffraction, Dog's tooth, Draft, Epitome, Example, Exemplar, Faconné, Fiddle, Figuration, Format, Fret, Grain, Greek key, Greque, Herringbone, Holding, Honeycomb, Hound's tooth, Ideal, Imprint, Intonation, Karman vortex street, Koru, Kowhaiwhai, Matrix, Meander, → **MODEL**, Moire, Moko, Mosaic, Norm, Paisley, Paradigm, Paragon, Pinstripe, Plan, Polka-dot, Pompadour, Precedent, Prototype, Queenstitch, Radiation, Raster, Rat-tail, Rhythm, Ribbing, Rosette, Scansion, Shawl, Starburst, Stencil, Structure, Symmetry, Syndrome, Talea, Tangram, Tarsia, Template, Templet, Tessera, Test, Tracery, Traffic, Tread, Type, Veneration, Vol, Watermark, Whorl, Willow

Pause Break, Breakpoint, Breather, Caesura, Cessation, Cesura, Comma, Desist, Er, Fermata, Hesitate, Hiatus, Interkinesis, Interval, Limma, Lull, Pitstop, Pregnant, Rest, Selah, Stop

Pave(d), Pavement, Paving Causeway, Causey, Clint, Cobble, Desert, Diaper, Flagging, Flagstone, Granolith, Limestone, Moving, Path, Plainstanes, Plainstones, Roadside, Set(t), Sidewalk, Travolator, Trottoir

Pawn(shop), Pawnbroker, Pawnee Agent, Betel, Chessman, Counter, Derby, Dip, Fine, Gage, Gallery, Hanging, Hock, Hockshop, Hostage, Leaving-shop, Lumber, Lumberer, Moneylender, Mont-de-piété, Monte di pietà, Nunky, Pan, Passed, Peacock, Piece, Pignerate, Pignorate, Pledge, Pop, Redeemer, Security, Sheeny, Siri, Spout, Stalking-horse, Three balls, Tiddleywink, Tool, Tribulation, Uncle, Usurer, Wadset, Weed

Pay(master), Payment, Paid, Pay off, Pay out Aby, Advertise, Alimony, Amortise, Annat, Annuity, Ante, Arles, Atone, Backhander, Balloon, Bank draft, Basic, Batta, Blench, Bonus, Bukshee, Cain, Cashier, Cheque, COD, Commute, Compensate, Consideration, Damage, Defray, Disburse, Discharge, Dividend, Down, Dub, E, Earnest, Emolument, Endow, Equalisation, Eric, Escot, Farm, Fee, Feu-duty, Finance, Foot, Fork out, Fund, Gale, Gate, Giro, Give, Gratuity, Grave, Greenmail, Guarantee, Han(d)sel, Hazard, Hire, Honorarium, HP, Imburse, Intown multure, Kain, Kickback, Lin(e)age, Lump sum, Mail, MasterCard®, Meet, Modus, Mortuary, Outcome, Overtime, Palimony, Part exchange, Payola, Pension, Pittance, Pony, Posho, Premium, Primage, Pro, Pro forma, Progress, Purser, Quit(-rent), Ransom, Rate, Reap-silver, Rebate, Rebuttal, Redundancy, Refund, Remittance, Remuneration, Rent, Requite, Residual, Respects, Retainer, Reward, Royalty, Salary, Satisfaction, Scot, Screw, Scutage, Settle, Severance, Shell, Shell out, Shot, Sick, Sink, SO, Sold(e), Soul-shot, →SPEND, Sponsor, Square, Stipend, Strike, Stump, Sub, Subscribe, Sweetener, Table, Take-home, Tar, Tender, Tithe, Token, Tommy, Transfer, Treasure, Treat, Tribute, Truck, Veer, Wage

Pea(s) Carling, Chaparral, Chickling, D(h)al, Desert, Dholl, Garbanzo, Goober, Hastings, Legume, Mangetout, Marrowfat, Mushy, Passiform, Pigeon, Pulse, Rounceval, Snow, Split, Sugar, Sugar snap, Vetch

Peace(ful), Peaceable, Peace-keeper, Peace organisation, Peace symbol Ahimsa, Antiwar, Armistice, Ataraxy, Calm, Douce, Ease, Equilibrium, Frieda, Frith, Halcyon, Harmony, Hush, Interceder, Irenic(on), King's, Lee, Lull, Nirvana, Olive, Pacific, Pax, Queen's, Quiet, Repose, Rest, Rose, Roskilde, Salem, Serene, Sh, Shalom, Siegfried, Siesta, Solomon, Soothing, Still, Tranquil, Truce, UN

Peach Blab, Cling, Clingstone, Dish, Dob, Freestone, Humdinger, Inform, Laetrile, Malakatoone, Melocoto(o)n, Nectarine, Oner, Quandang, Shop, Sing, Sneak, Split, Squeak, Stunner, Tattle, Tell, Victorine

Peacock Coxcomb, Dandy, Fop, Junonian, Muster, Ostentation, Paiock(e), Pajock(e), Pavo(ne), Pawn, Payock(e), Pown, Sashay

Peak(y) Acme, Aiguille, Alp, Ancohuma, Apex, Ben, Chimborazo, Comble, Communism, Cone, Crag, Crest, Darien, Drawn, Eiger, Flower, Gable, Gannett, Garmo, Harney, Horn, Ismail Samani, Kazbek, Matterhorn, Meridian, Mons, →MOUNTAIN, Nib, Nunatak, Optimum, Pale, Pin, Pinnacle, Point, Rainier, Sallow, Snowcap, Snowdon, Spire, Top, Tor, Visor, Widow's, Zenith

Pear Aguacate, Alligator, Anchovy, Anjou, Asian, Asparagus, Avocado, Bartlett, Bergamot, Beurré, Blanquet, Carmelite, Catherine, Choke, Colmar, Comice, Conference, Cuisse-madame, Dutch admiral, Jargonelle, Muscadel, Muscatel, Musk, Nelis, Perry, Poperin, Poppering, Poprin, Prickly, Pyrus, Queez-maddam, Seckel, Seckle, Warden, William

Pearl(s), Pearly Barocco, Barock, Baroque, Cultured, False, Gem, Imitated, Jewel, Mabe, Margaret, Margaric, Nacrous, Olivet, Onion, Orient, Prize, Rope, Seed, Simulated, String, Sulphur, Unio(n)

Peasant Bonhomme, Boor, Bumpkin, Chouan, Churl, Clodhopper, Contadino, Cossack, Cottar, Cott(i)er, Fellah(s), Fellahin, Hick, Jungli, Kern(e), Kisan, Kulak, M(o)ujik, Muzhik, Oik, Raiyat, Roturier, Rustic, Ryot, Swain, Tyrolean, Whiteboy, Yokel

Pebble(s), Pebbly Banket, Calculus, Chuck, Cobblestone, Dreikanter, Gallet, Gooley, Gravel, Psephism, Pumie, Pumy, Scotch, Scree, Shingle

Peck Bill, Bushel, Dab, Forpet, Forpit, Gregory, Job, Kiss, Lip, Lippie, Nibble, Tap

Peculiar(ity) Abnormal, Appropriate, Characteristic, Distinct, Eccentric, Especial, Exclusive, Ferly, Funny, Idiosyncratic, Kink, Kooky, Loopy, Mannerism, Odd, Own, Personal, Proper, Queer, Quirk, Royal, Singular, → **SPECIAL**, Specific, Strange, Unusual

▷**Peculiar** *may indicate* an anagram

Pedal Accelerator, Bike, Brake, Chorus, Clutch, Cycle, Damper, Lever, P, Rat-trap, Soft, Sostenuto, Sustaining, Treddle

Peddle, Pedlar Bodger, Boxwallah, Camelot, Chapman, Cheapjack, Colporteur, Crier, Drummer, Duffer, Hawk, Huckster, Jagger, Packman, Pedder, Pether, Push, Sell, Smouch, Smouse(r), Sutler, Tallyman, Tink(er), Yagger

▷**Peddling** *may indicate* an anagram

Pedestrian Banal, Commonplace, Dull, Ganger, Hack, Hike, Itinerant, Jaywalker, Laborious, Mediocre, Mundane, Ordinary, Ostrich, Trite, Walker

Pedigree(s) Ancestry, Blood(line), Breeding, Descent, Family tree, House, Lineage, Phylogeny, Pure-bred, Stemma(ta), Stirp(s), Thoroughbred

Peel(er) Bark, Bobby, Candied, Constable, Decorticate, Exfoliate, Flype, Grilse, Pare, PC, Potato, Rind, Rine, Rumbler, Scale, Sewen, Shell, Skin, → **STRIP**, Tirr, Zest

▷**Peeled** *may indicate* outside letters to be removed from a word

Peep(er), Peephole Bo, Cheep, Cook, Glance, Gledge, Keek, Kook, Lamp, Nose, Peek, Pink, Pry, Snoop, Spy, Squeak, Squint, Stime, Styme, Voyeur

Peer(age), Peers Coequal, Law Lord, Life, Pry, Representative, Spiritual, Temporal

Peevish(ness) Capernoited, Captious, Crabby, Cross, Doddy, Frabbit, Frampal, Frampold, Franzy, Fretful, Girner, Hipped, Ill, Lienal, Moody, Nattered, Pet, Petulant, Pindling, Protervity, Shirty, Sour, Teachie, Te(t)chy, Testy

Peg(gy) Cheville, Cleat, Clothespin, Cotter-pin, Die, Dowel, Drift-pin, Fix, Freeze, Jukskei, Kabaddi, Knag, Lee, Leg, Margaret, Nail, Nog, Odontoid, Pin(-leg), Piton, Shoe, Snort, Spigot, Spile, Square, Stengah, Stinger, Support, Tap, Tee, Thole, Tholepin, Thowel, Toggle, Tooth, Tot, Woffington

Pelican Alcatras, Bird, Crossing, Golden Hind, LA, Louisiana

Pellet Bolus, Buckshot, Bullet, Pill, Pilula, Pilule, Prill, Shot, Slug, Snow

Pelt Assail, Clod, Fleece, Fur, Hail, Hide, Hie, Lam, Pepper, Random, Shower, Skin, Squail, Stone

Pen Author, Ballpoint, Bamboo, Bic®, Biro®, Cage, Calamus, Can, Cartridge, Catching, Confine, Coop, Corral, Crawl, Crib, Crow-quill, Cru(i)ve, Cub, Cyclostyle, Dabber, Data, Enclosure, Epi®, Fank, Farm, Felt(-tipped), Fold, Fountain, Gaol, Gladius, Hen, Highlighter, Hoosegow, J, → **JAIL**, Keddah, Kraal, Lair, Laser, Light, Magic marker, Marker, Mew, Mure, Music, Piggery, Poison, Pound, Quill(-nib), Rastrum, Ree, Reed, Ring, Rollerball, Scribe, Sheepfold, Stell, Stie, Stir, Stockade, Sty(e), Stylet, Stylo, Stylograph, Stylus, Submarine, Swan, Sweatbox, Tank, Weir, Write, → **WRITER**

▷**Pen** *may indicate* a writer

Penal(ize) Cost, Fine, Gate, Handicap, Huff, Mulct, Punitive, Servitude

Penalty Abye, Amende, Card, Cost, Endorsement, Eriach, Eric, Fine, Foot-fault, Forfeit, Han(d)sel, Huff, Levy, Major, Pain, Price, Punishment, Rubicon, Sanction, Tap, Ticket, Wide

Pencil Beam, Ca(l)m, Caum, Charcoal, Chinagraph®, Crayon, Draft, Draw, Eyebrow, Fusain, Grease, Harmonic, Ink, Keelivine, Keelyvine, Lead, Outline, Propelling, Slate, Stub, Stump, Styptic, Tortillon

Pend(ing) Imminent, In fieri, On hold, Unresolved, Until

Pendant Albert, Chandelier, Drop, Earring, Girandole, Laval(l)ière, Medallion, Necklace, Poffle, Sautoir

Penetrate, Penetrating, Penetration Acumen, Acuminate, Bite, Bore, Cut, Enpierce, Enter, Imbue, Impale, Incisive, Indent, Indepth, Infiltrate, Insight, Into, Intrant, Lance, Permeate, Pierce, Probe, Sagacious, Shear, Shrill, Strike, Thrust, Touch, X-ray

Penguin Adélie, Aeroplane, Anana, Auk, Emperor, Fairy, Gentoo, King, Korora, Macaroni, Rock-hopper

Peninsula Arm, Neck, Promontory, Spit, Spur

Penny Bean, Cartwheel, Cent, Copper, D, Dreadful, New, P, Sen, Sou, Sterling, Stiver, Win(n), Wing

Pension(er) Allowance, Ann(at), Annuitant, Board, Chelsea, Cod, Cor(r)ody, Full-board, Gasthaus, Gratuity, Guest-house, Half-board, Hostel, Hotel, Non-contributory, Occupational, Old-age, Oldster, Payment, Personal, Retire(e), Senior citizen, Serps, SIPP, Stakeholder, Stipend, Superannuation

People(s) Beings, Bods, Body, Chosen, Commonalty, Commons, Demos, Ecology, Electorate, Enchorial, Flower, Folk, Fraim, Gens, Grass roots, Guild, Herd, Human(kind), Inca, Indigenous, Inhabit, Janata, Kin, Land, Lapith, Lay, Man(kind), Masses, Men, Mob, Nair, Nation(s), Nayar, One, Peculiar, Personalities, Phalange, Populace, Proletariat(e), Public, Punters, Quorum, Rabble, Race, Raffle, September, Settle, Society, Souls, They, Tribe, Tuath, Tungus, Volk

Pepper(y) Alligator, All-spice, Ancho, Ava, Bird, Black, Caper, Capsicum, Cayenne, Cherry, Chilli, Chipotle, Condiment, Cubeb, Devil, Dittander, Dittany, Ethiopian, Green, Guinea, Habanero, Jalapeno, Jamaica, Kava, Malaguetta, Matico, Negro, Paprika, Pelt, Pim(i)ento, Piper, Piperine, Piquillo, Red, Riddle, Sambal, Scotch bonnet, Spice, Sprinkle, Szechuan, Szechwan, Tabasco®, Techy, Testy, Water, Yaqona, Yellow

Perceive, Perceptible, Perception, Perceptive Acumen, Acute, Alert, Anschauung, Apprehend, Astute, Clairvoyance, Clear-eyed, Cryptaesthetic, Descry, Dianoia, Discern, Divine, ESP, Extrasensory, Feel, Image, Insight, Intelligence, Intuit(ion), Kinaesthesia, Noesis, Notice, Observe, Pan(a)esthesia, Remark, → **SEE**, Sense, Sensitive, Sentience, Shrewd, Sixth sense, Subjective, Subliminal, Tact, Taste, Understanding, Visual

Percentage Agio, Commission, Contango, Cut, Proportion, Rake off, Royalty, Share, Vigorish

Perch(ing) Aerie, Alight, Anabis, Bass, Comber, Eyrie, Fish, Fogash, Gaper, Insessorial, Lug, Miserere, Ocean, Perca, Pole, Roost, Ruff(e), Seat, Serranid, → **SIT**, Zingel

Percussion (cap) Amorce, Battery, Gong, Idiophone, Impact, Knee, Knock, Spoons, Thump, Timbrel, Traps

Perennial Continual, Enduring, Flower, Livelong, Perpetual, Recurrent

Perfect(ly), Perfection(ist) Absolute, Accomplish, Accurate, Acme, Apple-pie, Bloom, Complete, Consummation, Cross-question, Dead, Develop, Edenic, Fare-thee-well, Faultless, Finish, Flawless, Fulfil, Full, Holy, Hone, Ideal(ist), Impeccable, Intact, It, Letter, Matchless, Mature, Mint, Mr Right, Par, Paradisal, Paragon, Past, Pat, Peace, Pedant, Peerless, Point-device, Practice, Present, Pure, Quintessential, Refine, Salome, Siddha, Soma, Sound, Spotless, Spot-on, Stainless, Stickler, Sublime, The nines, Thorough,

Three-pricker, To a t(ee), Unblemished, Unflawed, Unqualified, Unspoilt, Utopian, Utter, Very, Whole, Witeless

Perform(ed), Performer, Performing Achieve, Acrobat, Act(or), Action, Aerialist, Appear, Artist(e), Barnstorming, Basoche, Busk, Carry out, Chansonnier, Comedian, Contortionist, Discharge, Do, Duo, Effect, Enact, Entertainer, Execute, Exert, Exhibit, Extra, Fancy Dan, Fulfil, Function, Geek, Hand, Headliner, Hersall, Hot dog, Houdini, Implement, Interlocutor, Lion-tamer, Majorette, Make, Mime, Minstrel, Moke, Nonet, Octet, Officiate, On, Operant, Patzer, Player, Praxis, Quartet(te), Quintet, Rap artist, Recite, Render, Represent, Ripieno, Scene-stealer, Septet, Sextet, Showstopper, Soloist, Svengali, Sword-swallower, Throw, Transact, Trio, Troupe, Vaudevillian, Virtuoso, Wire-dancer

Performance Accomplishment, Achievement, Act(ion), Auto, Blinder, Bravura, Broadcast, Chevisance, Command, Concert, Dare, Deed, Demonstration, Discharge, Division, Double act, Enactment, Entr'acte, Execution, Floorshow, Gas, Gig, Hierurgy, Holdover, Hootenanny, House, Karaoke, Masque, Master-class, Masterstroke, Matinee, Mime, Monodrama, Monologue, One-night stand, Operation, Perpetration, Practice, Première, Production, Programme, Recital, Rehearsal, Rendering, Rendition, Repeat, Repertoire, Rigmarole, Roadshow, Scene, Second house, Show (stopper), Showing, Simul, Sketch, Sneak preview, Solo, Specific, Spectacle, Stunt, Theatricals, Track record, Turn, Unicycle

Perfume (box) Abir, Ambergris, Angel water, Aroma, Attar, Bergamot, Cassolette, Chypre, Civet, Cologne, Eau de cologne, Eau de toilette, Enfleurage, Essence, Fragrance, Frangipani, Incense, Ionone, Lavender (water), Linalool, Myrrh, Nose, Opopanax, Orris, Orrisroot, Otto, Patchouli, Patchouly, Pomander, Potpourri, Redolence, Rose water, → SCENT, Smellies, Terpineol, Toilet water, Tonka bean

Perhaps A(i)blins, Belike, Haply, Happen, May(be), Peradventure, Percase, Perchance, Possibly, Relative, Say

▷**Perhaps** *may indicate* an anagram

Perimeter Boundary, Circuit, Circumference, Coastline, Limits

Period(ic) Abbevillian, AD, Aenolithic, Age, Alcher(ing)a, Andropause, Annual, Archaean, Base, Bi-weekly, Bout, Cal(l)ippic, Cambrian, Carboniferous, Chukka, Chukker, Climacteric, Comanchean, Cooling off, Cretaceous, Critical, Curse, Cycle, Day, Decad(e), Devonian, Diapause, Dot, Down, Dreamtime, → DURATION, Eocene, Epoch, Excerpt, Full-stop, Gestation, Glacial, Grace, Great schism, Haute époque, Heyday, Honeymoon, Incubation, Indiction, Innings, Interregnum, Jurassic, Kalpa, Latency, Latent, Lesson, Liassic, Limit, Meantime, Meanwhile, Menopause, Menses, Mesolithic, Mesozoic, Miocene, Mississippian, Moment, Monthly, Moratorium, Neocomian, Neolithic, Octave, Oestrus, Olde-worlde, Oligocene, Ordovician, Palaeogene, Paleolithic, Patch, Payback, Pennsylvanian, Phase, Phoenix, Pre-Cambrian, Proterozoic, QT, Quarter, Quaternary, Recurrent, Reformation, Refractory, Regency, Rent, Riss, Romantic, Saeculum, Safe, Saros, Season, Session, Sidereal, Span, Spasm, Spell, Stage, Stop, Stretch, Synodic, Teens, Term, Tertiary, Time, Trecento, Triassic, Triduum, Trimester, Tri-weekly, Usance, Weekly, Window

Periodic(al) Bi-weekly, Comic, Digest, Economist, Etesian, Journal, Liassic, Listener, Mag, New Yorker, Organ, Paper, Phase, Publication, Punch, Rambler, Regency, Review, Scandal sheet, Spectator, Strand, Stretch, Tatter, Tract

Perish(able), Perished, Perishing Brittle, → DIE, End, Ephemeral, Expire, Fade, Forfair, Fungibles, Icy, Tine, Tint, Transitory, Tyne, Vanish

Perm(anent) Abiding, Durable, Eternal, Everlasting, Fixed, Full-time, Indelible, → LASTING, Marcel, Stable, Standing, Stative, Timeless, Unending, Wave

Permeable, Permeability, Permeate Imbue, Infiltrate, Leaven, Osmosis, Penetrate, Pervade, Poromeric, Porous, Seep, Transfuse

Permission, Permissive, Permit(ted) Allow, Authorise, By-your-leave, Carnet, Chop, Clearance, Congé(e), Consent, Copyright, Easy, Enable, Franchise, Give, Grant, Green light, Indult, Lacet, Laissez-passer, Latitude, Leave, Legal, Legitimise, Let, Liberty, Licence, License, Lief, Loan, Luit, Nihil obstat, Ok(e), Pace, Pass, Placet, Planning, Power, Pratique, Privilege, Remedy, Safe-conduct, Sanction, Stamp-note, Suffer, Ticket, Tolerate, Triptyque, Visa, Vouchsafe, Warrant, Way-leave, Wear

Perpendicular Aplomb, Apothem, Atrip, Cathetus, Erect, Normal, Orthogonal, Plumb, Sheer, Sine, → UPRIGHT, Vertical

Perplex(ed), Perplexity Anan, At a loss, Baffle, Bamboozle, Bemuse, Beset, Bewilder, Bother, Buffalo, Bumbaze, Cap, Confound, Confuse, Embarrass, Feague, Floor, Flummox, Fox, Knotty, Meander, Mystify, Nonplus, Obfuscate, Out, Pother, Pudder, Puzzle, Quizzical, Stump, Tangle, Throw, Tickle, Tostication

Persecute, Persecution Afflict, Annoy, Badger, Bully, Crucify, Dragon(n)ades, Harass, Haze, Intolerant, McCarthyism, Oppress, Paranoia, Pogrom, Ride, Torture, Victimise

Persevere, Perseverance Assiduity, Continue, Fortitude, Hold on, Insist, Jusqu'auboutisme, Patience, Persist, Plug, Press on, Soldier on, Stamina, Steadfastness, Stick, Stickability, Tenacity

Persia(n) Achaemenid, Babee, Babi, Bahai, Cyrus, Dari, Farsi, Iran(ian), Mazdean, Mede, Pahlavi, Parasang, Parsee, Pehlevi, Pushtu, Samanid, Sassanid, Sohrab, Xerxes, Zoroaster

Persist(ence), Persistent Adhere, Assiduity, Chronic, Constant, Continual, Diligent, Doggedness, Endure, Eternal, Hang-on, Importunate, Incessant, Keep at, Labour, Last, Longeval, Lusting, Persevere, Press, Relentless, Sedulous, Sneaking, Stamina, Stick, Stubborn, Tenacity, Unabated, Urgent

Person(s), Personal(ly) Alter, Artificial, Aymaran, Being, Bird, Bod(y), Chai, Chal, Chav, Chi, Cookie, Entity, Everyman, Figure, Fish, Flesh, Ga(u)dgie, Gadje, Gauje, Gut, Head, Human, Individual, Me, Nabs, Natural, Nibs, One, Own, Party, Passer-by, Private, Quidam, Selfhood, Sod, Soul, Specimen, Tales, Type, Wight

Personage, Personality Alter ego, Anima, Celeb(rity), Character, Charisma, Dignitary, Ego, Godhead, Grandee, Identity, Megastar, Noble, Notability, Panjandrum, Presence, Sama, Seity, Sel, Self, Sell, Somatotonia, Star, Temperament, Tycoon

Personified, Personification, Personify Embody, Epitome, Incarnate, Prosopop(o)eia, Represent

Perspective Aerial, Atmospheric, Attitude, Distance, Foreshorten(ed), Point of view, Proportion, Scenography, Take, View, Vista

Persuade(d), Persuasion, Persuasive Brainwash, Cajole, Carrot and stick, Coax, Cogent, Conviction, Convince, Disarm, Eloquent, Exhort, Faith, Feel, Forcible, Geed, Get, Induce, Inveigle, Move, Plausible, → PREVAIL, Religion, Rhetoric, Seduce, Silver-tongued, Smooth-talking, Soft sell, Suborn, Sway, Sweet-talk, Tempt, Truckled, Wheedle, Winning

Pert(ness) Bold, Cocky, Dicacity, Flippant, Forward, Fresh, Impertinent, Insolent, Jackanapes, Minx, Quean, Saucy, Tossy

Pertinent Ad rem, Apropos, Apt, Fit, Germane, Relevant, Timely

Perturb(ation) Aerate, Confuse, Dismay, Disturb, Dither, Faze, Pheese, State, Trouble, Upset, Worry

Pervade, Pervasion, Pervasive(ness) Aroma, Atmosphere, Diffuse, Drench, Immanence, Permeate, Saturate

Perverse, Perversion, Pervert(ed), Perversity Aberrant, Abnormal, Algolagnia, Awkward, Awry, Balky, Cam(stairy), Camsteary, Camsteerie, Cantankerous, →**CONTRARY**, Corrupt, Crabbed, Cussed, Decadent, Deform, Deviate, Distort, Donsie, False, Froward, Gee, Kam(me), Kinky, Licentious, Misinterpret, Misuse, Nonce, Paraphilia, Protervity, Refractory, Sadist, Sicko, Stubborn, Thrawn, Traduce, Travesty, Twist, Unnatural, Untoward, Uranism, Warp(ed), Wayward, Wilful, Wrest, Wry

▷**Perverted** *may indicate* an anagram

Pessimism, Pessimist(ic) Alarmist, Bear, Cassandra, Crapehanger, Crepehanger, Cynic, Defeatist, Dismal Jimmy, Doom merchant, Doomwatch, Doomy, Doubter, Downbeat, Eeyore, Fatalist, Glumbum, Jeremiah, Killjoy, Negative, Weltschmerz

Pest(er) Aggravate, Badger, Bedbug, Beleaguer, Besiege, Blight, Bluebottle, Bombard, Bot, →**BOTHER**, Brat, Breese, Bug, Dim, Disagreeable, Earbash, Fly, Fowl, Fruit fly, Gapeworm, Greenfly, Harass, Hassle, Irritate, Menace, Microbe, Mither, Molest, Mouse, Nag, Nudnik, Nuisance, Nun, Oestrus, Pize, Plague, Rotter, Scourge, Tease, Terror, Thysanoptera, Vermin, Weevil

Pesticide Benomyl, Botanic(al), DDT, Derris, Dichlorvos, Endrin, Glucocorticoid, Glucosinolate, Heptachlor, Mouser, Permethrin, Synergist, Warfarin

Pestilence, Pestilent Curse, Epidemic, Evil, Lues, Murrain, Murren, Noxious, Pernicious, Plague

Pet Aversion, Cade, Canoodle, Caress, Chou, Coax, Cosset, Cuddle, Dandle, Darling, Daut(ie), Dawt(ie), Dear, Dod, Dort, Ducky, Favourite, Fondle, Glumps, Hamster, Huff, Hump, Indulge, Ire, Jarta, Jo, Lallygag, Lapdog, Messan, Miff, Mouse, Neck, Pamper, Pique, Poach, Rabbit, Smooch, Snog, Spat, Stroke, Strum, Sulk(s), Tantrum, Teacher's, Temper, Tiff, Tout, Towt, Umbrage, Virtual, Yarta

Petition(er) Appeal, Beg, Boon, Claimant, Crave, Entreaty, Litany, Millenary, Orison, Plaintiff, Postulant, Prayer, Press, Representation, Request, Round robin, Solicit, Sue, Suit(or), Suppli(c)ant, Supplicat, Vesper

Petrify(ing) Fossilise, Frighten, Lapidescent, Niobe, Numb, Ossify, Scare, Terrify

Petrol(eum) Avgas, Cetane, Diesel, Esso®, Ethyl, Fuel, Gas, High-octane, Leaded, Ligroin, Maz(o)ut, Octane, Olein, Platforming, Refinery, Rock oil, Rock-tar, STP, Styrene, Unleaded

Petticoat Balmoral, Basquine, Crinoline, Female, Filabeg, Fil(l)ibeg, Jupon, Kilt, Kirtle, Phil(l)abeg, Phil(l)ibeg, Placket, Sarong, Shift, Slip, Underskirt, Wylie-coat

Petty, Pettiness Baubling, Bumbledom, Childish, Little, Mean, Minor, Narrow, Niggling, Nyaff, One-horse, Parvanimity, Picayunish, Piffling, Pimping, Puisne, Puny, Shoestring, Small, Small-time, Small town, Stingy, Tin, Trivial, Two-bit

Petty officer Cox, CPO, PO

Petulance, Petulant Fretful, Huff, Mardy, Moody, Peevish, Perverse, Procacity, Sullen, Toutie, Waspish

Phantom Apparition, Bogey, Bugbear, Eidolon, Feature, Idol, Incubus, Maya, Shade, Spectre, Tut, Wild hunt, Wraith

Pharmacist, Pharmacologist Apothecary, → **CHEMIST**, Dispenser, Druggist, Loewi, MPS, Officinal, Preparator

Phase Climacteric, Coacervate, Cycle, Form, Nematic, Period, Post-boost, Primary, REM, Schizont, Stage, State, Synchronise

Phenomenon Blip, Eclipse, Effect, Event, Flying saucer, Geohazard, Hormesis, Marvel, Meteor, Miracle, Mirage, Paranormal, Parascience, Phenology, Phi, Psi, Rankshift, Synergy

Philanthropist, Philanthropy Altruist, Barnardo, Benefactor, Carnegie, Charity, Chisholm, Coram, Donor, Freemason, Geldof, Getty, Guggenheim, Hammer, Lever, Mayer, Nobel, Nuffield, Peabody, Rockefeller, Rowntree, Samaritan, Shaftesbury, Tate, Wilberforce

Philistine, Philistinism Artless, Ashdod, Barbarian, Bigot, Foe, Gath, Gaza, Gigman, Goliath, Goth, Lowbrow, Vandal

Philosopher, Philosophy Academist, Activism, Ahimsa, Analytical, Animism, Anthrosophy, Antinomianism, Antiochian, A priorist, Atomic, Atomist, Attitude, Averr(h)oism, Cartesian, Casuist, Comtism, Conceptualism, Conservatism, Cracker-barrel, Critical, Cynic, Deipnosophist, Deontology, Eclectic, Eleatic, Empiricism, Enlightenment, Epistemology, Ethics, Existentialism, Fatalism, Gnostic, Gymnosophist, Hedonism, Hermeneutics, Hobbism, Holist, Humanism, I Ching, Idealism, Ideology, Instrumentalism, Ionic, -ism, Kaizen, Linguistic, Logical atomism, Logicism, Logos, Maieutic, Marxism, Materialism, Mechanism, Megarian, Metaphysician, Metaphysics, Metempiricism, Monism, Moral(ist), Natural, Neoplatonism, Neoteric, Nihilism, Nominalism, Occamist, Occam's razor, Ockhamist, Opinion, Panhellenism, Peripatetic, Phenomenology, Platonism, Populism, Positivism, Rationalism, Realism, Rosminian, Sage, Sankhya, Sceptic, Schoolman, Scientology, Scotism, Secular-humanism, Sensist, Shankara(-charya), Solipsism, Sophist, Stoic, Synthetic, Taoism, Theism, Theosophy, Thomist, Thought, Transcendentalism, Ultraism, Utilitarianism, Utopianism, Vedanta, Voluntarism, Weltanschauung, Whitehead, Yoga, Yogi

Phone Bell, Blower, Call, Cellular, Clamshell, Dial, Dual band, Flip, Handset, Intercom, Mob(i)e, Mobile, Picture, Ring, Roam, Satellite, Saver, Skype, Talkback, Tel, Text

Phonetic(s) Auditory, Interdental, Oral, Palaeotype, Palato-alveolar, Spoken, Symbol

▷**Phonetically** *may indicate* a word sounding like another

Phon(e)y Bogus, Charlatan, Counterfeit, Ersatz, Faitor, Fake, Impostor, Poseur, Quack, → **SHAM**, Specious, Spurious

▷**Phony** *may indicate* an anagram

Photo(copy), Photograph(y), Photographic, Photo finish Anaglyph, Black and white, Blow-up, Cabinet, Close-up, Composite, Digicam, Duplicate, Dyeline, Exposure, Film, Flash, Half-tone, Headshot, Hologram, Karyogram, Microdot, Microprint, Montage, Mugshot, Negative, Nephogram, Panel, Picture, Polaroid®, Positive, Print, Rotogravure, Sepia, Shoot, Shot, Slide, Snap, Still, Sun-print, Take, Topo, Vignette, X-ray

Phrase Abject, Actant, Buzzword, Cadence, Catch(word), Catchcry, Cliché, Climacteric, Comma, Expression, Hapax legomenon, Heroic, Idiophone, Laconism, Leitmotiv, Lemma, Locution, Mantra, Motto, Phr, Prepositional, Refrain, Riff, Set, Slogan, Soundbite, Tag, Term, Theme, Trope, Verb

Physic(s) Cluster, Cryogenics, Culver's, Cure, Dose, Electronics, Electrostatics, High-energy, Kinematics, Medicine, Nuclear, Nucleonics, Particle, Purge, Remedy, Rheology, Science, Sonics, Spintronics, Statistics, Thermodynamics

Physician Addison, Allopath, Bach, Buteyko, Chagas, Doctor, Erastus, Eustachio, Galen, Gilbert, Graves, Guillotin, Hakim, Hansen, Harvey, Hippocrates, Internist, Jenner, Lamaze, Leech, Linacre, Lister, Medic(o), Menière, Mesmer, Mindererus, Paean, Paian, Paracelsus, Practitioner, Quack, Ranvier, Roget, Russell, Salk, Spiegel, Still, Therapist, Time, Vaidya, Wavell

Pi, Pious Breast-beater, Devotional, Devout, Fraud, Gallio, God-fearing, Godly, Holy, Mid-Victorian, Sanctimonious, Savoury, Smug, Unco guid

Pi(ous) Orant, Reverent, Saintly

Piano Bechstein, Broadwood, Celesta, Celeste, Concert grand, Cottage, Dumb, Flugel, Forte, Grand, Hammerklavier, Honkytonk, Joanna, Keyboard, Mbira, Overstrung, P, Player, Softly, Steinway, Stride, Thumb, Upright

Pick(er), Pickaxe, Picking, Pick out, Pick up Break, Cherry, Choice, Contract, Cream, Cull, Elite, Emu-bob, Evulse, Flower, Gather, Glean, Hack, Holing, Hopper, Mattock, Nap, Nibble, Oakum, Plectrum, Pluck, Plum, Select, Single, Sort, Steal, Strum, Tone arm, Tong, Wale

▷**Picked** *may indicate* an anagram

Pickle(r) Achar, Beetroot, Brine, Cabbage, Caper, Chow-chow, Chutney, Corn, Corner, Cucumber, Cure, Dilemma, Dill, Eisel, Esile, Gherkin, Girkin, Imp, Jam, Kimchi, Marinade, Marinate, Mess, Mull, Olive, Onion, Peculate, Peregrine, Piccalilli, Relish, Rod, Samp(h)ire, Scrape, Souse, Spot, Steep, Trouble, Vinegar, Wolly

Pickpocket(s) Adept, Bung, Cly-faker, Cutpurse, Dip, Diver, Fagin, File, Nipper, Swellmobsman, Whizzer, Wire

Picnic Alfresco, Braaivleis, Clambake, Fun, Junketing, Outing, Push-over, Spread, Tailgate, Valium, Wase-goose, Wayzgoose

Picture(s) Anaglyph, Art, B-movie, Canvas, Caricature, Cartoon, Cinema, Cloudscape, Collage, Cutaway, Decoupage, Depict, Describe, Diptych, Drawing, Drypoint, Emblem, Envisage, Envision, Epitome, Etching, Film, Flick, Fresco, Gouache, Graphic, Histogram, Icon, Iconic, Identikit®, Illusion, Imagery, Inset, Landscape, Lenticular, Likeness, Lithograph, Montage, Mosaic, Motion, Movie, Moving, Movy, Mugshot, Oil, Painture, Photo, Photofit®, Photogram, Photomontage, Pin-up, Pix, Plate, Portrait, Prent, Presentment, Print, Represent, Retrate, Rhyparography, Scene, Semble, Shadowgraph, Shot, Skyscape, Slide, Snapshot, Stereochrome, Stereogram, Stereograph, Stevengraph, Still-life, Table(au), Talkie, Tapestry, Tattoo, Thermogram, Tone, Topo, Transfer, Transparency, Vectograph, Vignette, Vision, Votive, Word, X-ray, Zincograph

Pie(s) Anna, Banoffee, Battalia, Bird, Bridie, Camp, Chewet, Cinch, Cobbler, Cottage, Coulibiac, Curry puff, Custard, Deep-dish, Easy, Flan, Floater, Florentine, Hash, Humble, Koulibiaca, Madge, Meat, Mess, Mince(meat), Mud, Mystery bag, Pandowdy, Pastry, Pasty, Patty, Périgord, Pica, Piet, Pirog, Pizza, Printer's, Pyat, Pyet, Pyot, Quiche, Rappe, Resurrection, Shepherd's, Shoofly, Shred, Spoil, Squab, Stargaz(e)y, Star(ry)-gazy, Sugar, Tart, Tarte tatin, Torte, Tourtière, Turnover, Tyropitta, Umble, Vol-au-vent, Warden

▷**Pie** *may indicate* an anagram

Piece(s) Adagio, Add, Arioso, Bagatelle, Bishop, Bit, Blot, Cameo, Cannon, Cent, Charm, →**CHESSMAN**, Chip, Chunk, Coin, Companion, Component,

Composition, Concerto, Conversation, Counter, Crumb, Domino, End, Entr'acte,
Episode, Extract, Firearm, Fit, Flake, Flitters, Fragment, Gat, Goring, →GUN,
Haet, Hait, Hunk, Item, Join, Mammock, Man, Médaillons, Mite, Money,
Morsel, Museum, Nip, Novelette, Nugget, Oddment, Off-cut, Ort, Part, Party,
Pastiche, Patch, Pawn, Pce, Period, Peso, Pin, Pistareen, Pole, →PORTION,
Recital, Rifle, Rook, Scrap, Section, Sector, Set, Shard, Sherd, Slice, Slip, Sliver,
Snatch, Snippet, Soffit, Sonata, Sou, Spare part, Speck, String, Stub, Swatch,
Tad, Tait, Tate, Tile, Toccata, →WEAPON, Wedge, Wodge

Pier(s) Anta, Chain, Groyne, Jetty, Jutty, Landing, Mole, Plowman, Quay,
Slipway, Swiss roll, Wharf, Wigan

Pierce(d), Piercer, Piercing Accloy, Awl, Bore, Broach, Cleave, Dart, Drill,
Endart, Fenestrate(d), Fulminant, Gimlet, Gore, Gride, Gryde, Hull, Impale,
Jag, Keen, Labret, Lance, Lancinate, Lobe, Move, Needle, Penetrate, Perforate,
Pertusate, Pike, Pink, Poignant, Prince Albert, Punch, Puncture, Riddle, Rive,
Shrill, Skewer, Slap, Sleeper, Spear, Spike, Spit, Stab, Steek, Stilet(to), Sting, Tap,
Thirl, Thrill(ant), Transfix

Pig(s), Piggy, Pigmeat, Pigskin Anthony, Babe, Barrow, Bartholomew,
Bland, Boar, Bush, Cutter, Doll, Elt, Farrow, Fastback, Football, Gadarene, Gilt,
Gloucester Old Spot, Glutton, Greedy guts, Grice, Gryce, Guinea, Gus, Gutzer,
Ham, Hampshire, Hog, Ingot, Iron, Kentledge, Kintledge, Kunekune, Landrace,
Land-shark, Large Black, Large White, Long, Napoleon, Peccary, Policeman,
Porchetta, Pork(er), Raven, Razorback, Rosser, Runt, Saddleback, Shoat, Shot(e),
Shott, Slip, Snowball, Sounder, Sow, Squealer, Suid(ae), Tamworth, Tithe, Toe,
Truffle, Warthog, Yelt

Pigeon Archangel, Barb, Bird, Bronze-winged, Cape, Carrier, Clay, Cropper,
Culver, Danzig, Dove, Fantail, Goura, Ground, Gull, Homer, Homing,
Horseman, Jacobin, Kereru, Kuku, Lahore, Manumea, Mourning dove,
New Zealand, Nun, Owl, Passenger, Peristeronic, Piwakawaka, Pouter,
Ringdove, Rock(er), Roller, Ront(e), Ruff, Runt, Scandaroon, Solitaire, Spot,
Squab, Squealer, Stale, Stock-dove, Stool, Stork, Swift, Talkie-talkee, Tippler,
Trumpeter, Tumbler, Turbit, Wonga(-wonga), Zoozoo

Pigment(s), Pigmentation Accessory, Anthoclore, Anthocyan(in),
Argyria, Betacyanin, Bilirubin, Biliverdin, Bister, Bistre, Cappagh-brown,
Carmine, Carotene, Carotenoid, Carotin, Carotinoid, Chlorophyll, Chrome,
Chromogen, Cobalt, Colcothar, Colour, Curcumin, Dye, Etiolin, Eumelanin,
Flavin(e), Fucoxanthin, Gamboge, Gossypol, Green earth, Haem, Hem(e),
H(a)emocyanin, H(a)emoglobin, Iodopsin, King's yellow, Lake, Lamp-black,
Lipochrome, Lithopone, Liverspot, Lutein, Luteolin, Lycopene, Madder, Madder
lake, Melanin, Mummy, Naevus, Naples yellow, Nigrosine, Oaker, Ochre,
Opsin, Orpiment, Paris-green, Phthalocyanine, Phycocyan, Phycoerythrin,
Phycoxanthin, Phytochrome, Porphyrin, Porphyropsin, Pterin, Puccoon,
Quercetin, Realgar, Retinene, Rhiboflavin, Rhodophane, Rhodopsin, Saffron,
Sepia, Sienna, Sinopia, Sinopsis, Smalt, Tapetum, Tempera, Terre-verte,
Tincture, Turacoverdin, Umber, Urochrome, Verditer, Vermilion, Viridian,
Xanthophyll, Xanthopterin(e), Yellow ochre

Pike Assegai, Crag, Dory, Fogash, Gar(fish), Ged, Gisarme, Glaive, Hie, Holostei,
Javelin, Lance, Langdale, Luce, Partisan, Pickerel, Ravensbill, Scafell, Snoek,
Spear, Speed, Spontoon, Vouge, Walleyed

Pile(d), Piles, Piling Agger, Amass, Atomic, Big, Bing, Bomb, Bubkes,
Camp-sheathing, Camp-shedding, Camp-sheeting, Camp-shot, Clamp, Cock,

Column, Crowd, Deal, Dolphin, Down, Emerods, Farmers, Fender, Fig, Floccus, Fortune, Galvanic, Hair, Haycock, Heap, Hept, Historic, Hoard, Load, Lot, Mansion, Marleys, Mass, Moquette, Nap, Pier, Post, Pyre, Raft, Reactor, Ream(s), Rouleau, Screw, Shag, Sheaf, Sheet, Slush, → **STACK**, Starling, Stately home, Stilt, Toorie, Trichome, Upheap, Velvet, Voltaic, Wad, Wealth, Windrow, Wodge

Pilgrim(age) Aske, Childe Harold, Expedition, Fatima, Gaya, Hadj(i), Hajj(i), Kum, Loreto, Lourdes, Mathura, Mecca, Nasik, Nikko, Palmer, Pardoner, Qom, Questor, Qum, Reeve, Scallop-shell, Shrine, Umra(h), Voyage, Yatra

Pill(s) Abortion, Ball, Beverley, Bitter, Bolus, Cachou, Caplet, Capsule, Chill, Dex, Doll, Dose, Globule, Golfball, Goofball, Lob, Medication, Medicine, Number nine, Peace, Peel, Pellet, Pep, Pilula, Pilule, Placebo, Poison, Protoplasmal, Radio, Sleeping, Spansule, Tablet, Troche, Trochisk, Upper

Pillar(ed), Pillars Anta, Apostle, Atlantes, Baluster, Balustrade, Boaz, Canton, Caryatides, Chambers, Cippus, Columel, Column, Eustyle, Gendarme, Goal, Hercules, Herm, Impost, Islam, Jachin, Lat, Man, Modiolus, Monolith, Newel, Obelisk, Pedestal, Peristyle, Pier, Post, Respond, Saddle, Serac, Stack, Stalactite, Stalagmite, Stanchion, Stoop, Telamon, Trumeau

Pillow(case) Bear, Beer, Bere, Bolster, Cod, Cow, Cushion, Headrest, Hop, Lace, Pad, Pulvinar, Throw

Pilot(s) Ace, Airman, Auto(matic), Aviator, Bader, Biggles, Branch, Bush, Captain, → **CONDUCT**, Experimental, Flier, George, Govern, Guide, Hobbler, Hoveller, Kamikaze, Lead, Lodesman, Palinure, Palinurus, Pitt, Prune, Radar, Red Baron, Shipman, Steer, Test, Tiphys, Trial, Trinity House, Usher, Wingman

Pimpernel Bastard, Bog, Poor man's weatherglass, Scarlet, Water, Wincopipe, Wink-a-peep, Yellow

Pimple, Pimply Blackhead, Botch, Goosebump, Gooseflesh, Grog-blossom, Hickey, Horripilation, Milium, Papilla, Papula, Papule, Plook, Plouk, Pock, Pustule, Quat, Rumblossom, Rum-bud, Spot, Uredinial, Wen, Whelk, Whitehead, Zit

Pin Axle, Bayonet, Belaying, Bolt, Brooch, Candle, Cask, Corking, Cotter, Curling, Dowel, Drawing, Drift, End, Fasten, Fid, Firing, Fix, Gam, Gnomon, Gudgeon, Hair, Hairgrip, Hob, Hook, Joggle, Kevel, King, Leg, Nail, Needle, Nog, Panel, Peg, Pintle, Pivot, Preen, Prick, Rivet, Rolling, Saddle, Safety, Scarf, SCART, Scatter, Shear, Shirt, Skewer, Skittle, Skiver, Spike, Spindle, Split, Staple, Stick, Stump, Swivel, Taper, Tertial, Thole, Thumbtack, Tie, Tietac(k), Tre(e)nail, Trunnion, U-bolt, Woolder, Wrest, Wrist

Pinch(ed) Arrest, Bit, Bone, Chack, Constrict, Cramp, Crisis, Emergency, Gaunt, Misappropriate, Nab, Narrow, Nick, Nim, Nip, Nirlit, Peculate, Peel, Pilfer, Pocket, Pook(it), Pouk, Prig, Pugil, Raft, Raw, Rob, Save, Scrimp, Scrounge, Skimp, Smatch, Snabble, Snaffle, Sneak, Sneap, Sneeshing, Snuff, Squeeze, → **STEAL**, Swipe, Tate, Trace, Tweak, Twinge

Pine(s), Pining Ache, Arolla, Bristlecone, Celery, Cembra, Chile, Cluster, Cone, Conifer, Cypress, Deal, Droop, Dwine, Earn, Erne, Evergreen, Fret, Green, Ground, Hone, Hoop, Huon, Jack, Japanese umbrella, Jeffrey, Kauri, Knotty, Languish, Languor, Loblolly, Lodgepole, Long, Longleaf, Lovelorn, Lovesick, Monkey-puzzle, Monterey, Moon, Norfolk Island, Norway, Nut, Oregon, Parana, Picea, Pinaster, Pitch, Ponderosa, Radiata, Red, Scotch, Scots, Screw, Sehnsucht, Slash, Softwood, Spruce, Starve, Stone, Sugar, Tree, Umbrella, Urman, Waste, White, Yearn, Yellow

Pink Blush, Carnation, Carolina, Castory, Cheddar, Clove, Colour, Coral, Cyclamen, Dianthus, Dutch, Emperce, FT, Fuchsia, Gillyflower, Indian, Knock, Kook, Lake, Lily, Lychnis, Maiden, Moss, Mushroom, Old rose, Oyster, Peach-blow, Peak, Perce, Pierce, Pompadour, Pounce, Rose(ate), Rose-hued, Rose madder, Ruddy, Salmon, Scallop, Sea, Shell, Shocking, Shrimp, Spigelia, Spit, Stab, Tiny

Pin-point Focus, Identify, Isolate, Localise

Pioneer(ing) Alcock, Armstrong, Avant garde, Babbage, Baird, Bandeirante, Blaze, Boone, Brown, Colonist, Emigrant, Explore, Fargo, Fawkner, Fleming, Frontiersman, Ground-breaking, Harbinger, Herodotus, Innovator, Lead, Lister, Marconi, Oecist, Pathfinder, Rochdale, Sandgroper, Settler, Spearhead, Stopes, Trail-blazer, Trekker, Turing, Voortrekker, Wells, Yeager

▶**Pious** see PI

Pipe(s), Piper, Pipeline, Piping Ait, Aorta, Aulos, Balance, Barrel, Blub, Boatswain's, Bong, Briar, Briarroot, Bronchus, Bubble, Calabash, Call, Calumet, Cask, Chanter, Cheep, Cherrywood, Chillum, Churchwarden, Clay, Cob, Conduit, Corncob, Crane, Cutty, Dip, Division, Down, Drain, Drill, Drillstring, Drone, Dry riser, Duct, Escape, Exhaust, Faucet, Feed, Fistula, Flue, Flute, Gage, Gas main, Hawse, Hod, Hogger, Hooka(h), Hose, Hubble-bubble, Hydrant, Ice, Indian, Injection string, Irish, Jet, Mains, Manifold, Meerschaum, Montre, Narghile, Nargile(h), Narg(h)il(l)y, Oat(en), Oboe, Oesophagus, Organ, Ottavino, Outlet, Pan, Peace, Pepper, Pibroch, Piccolo, Pied, Principal, Pule, Quill, Rainwater, Recorder, Ree(d), Rise, Riser, Serpent, Service, Sewer, Sheesha, Shisha, Shoe, Sing, Siphon, Skirl, Sluice, Soil, Spout, Stack, Standpipe, Stopcock, Sucker, Tail, Tee, Throttle, Tibia, Tootle, Trachea, Tremie, Tube, Tweet, U-bend, Union, Uptake, U-trap, Vent, Ventiduct, Volcanic, Waste, Water(-spout), Watermain, Weasand, Whiss, Whistle, Woodcock's head, Woodnote, Worm

Pirate(s), Pirated, Piratical, Piracy Algerine, Barbarossa, Blackbeard, Boarder, Bootleg, Brigand, Buccaneer, Buccanier, Cateran, Condottier, Conrad, Corsair, Crib, Dampier, Fil(l)ibuster, Flint, Gunn, Hijack, Hook, Kidd, Lift, Loot, Morgan, Penzance, Pew, Picaro(on), Pickaroon, Plagiarise, Plunder, Rakish, Rover, Sallee-man, Sallee-rover, Sea-dog, Sea-king, Sea-rat, Sea-robber, Sea-wolf, Silver, Smee, Steal, Teach, Unauthorised, Viking, Water-rat, Water-thief

Pistol Air, Ancient, Automatic, Barker, Captive bolt, Colt®, Dag, Derringer, Gat, →GUN, Hackbut, Horse, Iron, Luger®, Pepperbox, Petronel, Pocket, Revolver, Rod, Shooter, Sidearm, Starter, Starting, Very, Water, Weapon, Zip gun

Pit(ted), Pitting, Pits Abyss, Alveolus, Antrum, Bed, Bottomless, Catch, Cave, Cesspool, Chasm, Cissing, Cloaca, Coalmine, Colliery, Crater, Den, Depression, Depth, Dungmere, Ensile, Fossa, Fougasse, Fovea, Foxhole, Gehenna, Hangi, Heapstead, Heartspoon, Hell, Hillhole, Hole, Hollow, Inferno, Inspection, Khud, Lacunose, Lime, Mark, Match, Measure, →MINE, Mosh, Nadir, Orchestra, Parterre, Pip, Plague, Play, Pock-mark, Potato, Punctate, Putamen, Pyrene, Ravine, Rifle, Salt, Scrobicule, Silo, Slime, Soakaway, Solar plexus, Stone, Sump, Tar, Tartarus, Tear, Trap, Trous-de-loup, Underarm

Pitch(ed) Absolute, Asphalt, Atilt, Attune, Bitumen, Burgundy, Catapult, Coal-tar, Concert, Crease, Diamond, Diesis, Dive, Ela, Elect, Elevator, Encamp, Erect, Establish, Fever, Fling, Fork(ball), French, Ground, Heave, Height, International, Intonation, Key, Knuckleball, Labour, Length, Level, Lurch, Macadam, Maltha, Mineral, Nets, Neume, Outfield, Patter, Peck, Perfect, Philharmonic, Philosophical, Piceous, Pight, Pin, Plong(e), Plunge, Pop, Purl,

Relative, Resin, Rock, Ruff(e), Sales, Scend, Seel, Send, Shape, Sling, Slope, Soprarino, Spiel, Spitball, Stoit, Tar, Tessitura, Tilt, Tone, Tonemic, Tonus, Tremolo, Tune, Unison, Vibrato, Wicket, Wild, Wood

Pith(y) Ambatch, Aphorism, Apo(ph)thegm, Brief, Core, Down, Essence, Gnomic, Hat-plant, Heart, Laconic, Marrow, Meaty, Medulla, Moxa, Nucleus, Rag, Sententious, Succinct, Terse

Pitiless Flint-hearted, Hard, Hard-headed, Relentless, Ruthless

Pity, Piteous, Pitiful, Pitiable Ah, Alack, Alas, Commiseration, →COMPASSION, Hapless, Mercy, Pathos, Pilgarlic, Poor, Quarter, Red-leg, Rue, Ruth(ful), Seely, Shame, Sin, Sympathy, Too bad, Waefu(l), Wretched

Pivot(al) Ax(i)le, Central, Focal, Fulcrum, Gooseneck, Gudgeon, Kingbolt, Marker, Revolve, Rotate, Slue, →SWIVEL, Trunnion, Turn, Wheel

Place(ment) Aim, Allocate, Appoint, Area, Arena, Assisted, Berth, Bro, Decimal, Deploy, Deposit, Dispose, First, Fix, Habitat, Haunt, Hither, Howf, Identify, Impose, →IN PLACE OF, Insert, Install, Job, Joint, Juxtapose, Lay, Lieu, Locality, Locate, Locus, Niche, Parking, Pitch, Plat, Plaza, Point, Posit, →POSITION, Post, Product, Put, Realm, Region, Repose, Room, Rowme, Scene, Second, Set, Sit, Site, Situate, Situation, Slot, Spot, Station, Stead, Sted(e), Stedd(e), Stratify, Third, Toponym, Town, Vendôme

Plagiarise, Plagiarist Copy, Crib, Lift, Pirate, Steal

Plague (spot) Ailment, Annoy, Bane, Bedevil, Black death, Boil, Bubonic, Burden, Curse, Death, Dog, Dun, Epidemic, Frogs, Gay, Goodyear, Goujeers, Harry, Importune, Infestation, Locusts, Lues, Molest, Murrain, Murran, Murrin, Murrion, Nag, Obsess, Pest, Pester, Pox, Press, Scourge, Tease, Token, Torment, Torture, Try, Vex

Plain(s) Abraham, Artless, Ascetic, Au naturel, Bald, Bare, Blatant, Broad, Campagna, Campus Martius, Candid, Ceará, Clear, Dowdy, Downright, Dry, Esdraelon, Evident, Explicit, Flat, Flood, Girondist, Gran Chaco, Great, Homely, Homespun, Inornate, Jezreel, Liverpool, Llano, Lombardy, Lowland, Manifest, Marathon, Mare, Matter of fact, Obvious, Ocean of Storms, Olympia, →ORDINARY, Outspoken, Overt, Packstaff, Palpable, Pampa(s), Patent, Pikestaff, Plateau, Prairie, Prose, Sailing, Salisbury, Savanna(h), Secco, Serengeti, Sharon, Simple, Sodom, Spoken, Staked, Steppe, Tableland, Thessaly, Tundra, Unadorned, Unremarkable, Vanilla, Vega, Veldt, Visible, Walled

Plaint(ive) Complaint, Dirge, Lacrimoso, Lagrimoso, Lament, Melancholy, Sad, Whiny

Plan(s), Planned, Planner, Planning Aim, American, Angle, Architect, Arrange, Atlas, Battle, Blueprint, Brew, Budget, Care, Chart, Commission, Conspire, Contingency, Contrive, Dalton, Dart, Deep-laid, Deliberate, Delors, Design, Device, Devise, Diagram, Draft, Drawing, Elevation, Engineer, European, Family, Figure on, Five-Year, Flight, Floor, Forethought, Format, Galveston, Game, Ground, Hang, Idea, Idée, Initiative, Instal(l)ment, Intent, Itinerary, Lay(out), Leicester, Leicestershire, Logistics, Machinate, Manoeuvre, Map, Marshall, Master, Mastermind, Mean, Meditate, Nominal, Open, Outline, Pattern, Pipe-dream, Plot, Ploy, Policy, Premeditate, Procedure, Programme, Project, Projet, Proposal, Prospectus, Rapacki, Relief map, Road map, Ruse, Scenario, Schedule, Scheme, Schlieffen, Shape, Spec(ification), Stratagem, Strategy, Subterfuge, System, Tactician, Trace, View, Wallchart, Wheeze

Plane(s) Aero(dyne), Air, →AIRCRAFT, Airliner, Airship, Axial, Bandit, Basal, Boeing, Bomber, Bus, Buttock, Camel, Canard, Cartesian, Cessna, Chenar,

Chinar, Comet, Concorde, Crate, Dakota, Datum, Delta-wing, Ecliptic, Even, Facet, Fault, Fillister, Flat, Float, Freighter, Glider, Gliding, Gotha, Hurricane, Icosahedron, Icosohedra, Jack, Jet, Jointer, Jumbo, Level, London, MIG, Mirage, Mosquito, Moth, Octagon, Platan(us), Polygon, Prop-jet, Rocket, Router, Shackleton, Shave, Shuttle, Smooth, Soar, Sole, Spitfire, Spokeshave, STOL, Surface, Sycamore, Taube, Thrust, Trainer, Tree, Trident, Tropopause, Two-seater, Viscount

Planet(s), Planetary Alphonsine, Ariel, Asteroid, Body, Cabiri, Ceres, Chiron, Constellation, Dispositor, Earth, Eros, Extrasolar, Gas giant, Georgian, Giant, House, Hyleg, Inferior, Inner, Jovian, Jupiter, Lucifer, Major, Mars, Mercury, Minor, Moon, Neptune, Outer, Pallas, Pluto, Primary, Psyche, Quartile, Red, Satellitium, Saturn, Sedna, Significator, Sphere, Starry, Sun, Superior, Terra, Terrestrial, Uranus, Venus, Vista, Vulcan, World, Zog

Plank Board, Chess, Duckboard, Garboard, Manifesto, Plonk, Sarking, Slab, Spirketting, Straik, Strake, Stringer, Wood

Plant(s), Plant part Agent, Amphidiploid, Anemochore, Annual, Anther, Aphotoic, Autophyte, Bed, Biennial, Biota, Bloomer, Bonsai, Bryophyte, Chamaephyte, Chomophyte, Conspecific, Creeper, Cropper, Cultigen, Cultivar, Dayflower, Dibble, Ecad, Eccremocarpus, Embed, Endogen, Enemy, Enrace, Epilithic, Epiphyllous, Epiphyte, Establish, Factory, Fix, Flora, Geophyte, Growth, Gymnosperm, Halosere, Herbage, Herbarium, Humicole, Hydrastus, Hydrophyte, Hygrophyte, Hylophyte, Incross, Insert, Instil, Inter, Labiate, Land, Lathe, Legume, Lithophyte, Livelong, Longday, Lurgi, Machinery, Mill, Mole, Monocotyledon, Ornamental, Perennial, Phanerogam, Phloem, Pitcher, Protophyte, Psilophyte, Ramet, Resurrection, Root, Rosin, Saprophyte, Schizophyte, Sciophyte, Sclerophyll, Scrambler, Sere, Shortday, Shrub, Sow, Spermatophyte, Sponge, Spy, Steelworks, Stickseed, Sticktight, Strangler, Streptocarpus, Succulent, Superweed, Thallophyte, Thickleaf, Trailer, →TREE, Trifolium, Trillium, Tropophyte, Twining, Vascular, Washery, Wilding, Works, Zoophyte

Plantation Arboretum, Bosket, Bosquet, Estate, Fazenda, Grove, Hacienda, Pen, Pinetum, Ranch, Tara, Tope, Veticetum, Vineyard

Plaster(ed), Plaster board Artex®, Bandage, Blister, Blotto, Butterfly clip, Cake, Cataplasm, Clam, Clatch, Compo, Court, Daub, Diachylon, Diachylum, Dressing, Drunk, Emplastrum, Fresco, Gesso, Grout, Gyprock®, Gypsum, Intonaco, Laying, Leep, Lit, Mud, Mustard, Oiled, Parge(t), Polyfilla®, Porous, Poultice, Render, Roughcast, Scratch-coat, Screed, Secco, Shellac, Sinapism, Smalm, Smarm, Smear, Sowsed, Staff, Sticking, Stookie, Stucco, Teer, Wattle and daub

Plastic Amex®, Bubblewrap, Ductile, Fibreglass, Fictile, Flexible, Laminate, Loid, Mylar®, Pliant, Polythene, PVC, Supple, Vinyl, Wet-look, Xylonite, Yielding

▷**Plastic** *may indicate* an anagram

Plate(s), Plated, Platelet, Plating Acierage, Ailette, Anchor, Angle, Anode, Armadillo, Armour, Ashet, Baffle, Baleen, Base, Batten, Brass, Butt, Chape, Charger, Chrome, Coat, Communion, Copper, Ctene, Deadman, Denture, Diaphragm, Dinner, Disc, Dish, Echo, Electro, Electrotype, Elytron, Elytrum, Enamel, Equatorial, Escutcheon, Etching, Face, Fashion, Feet, Fine, Fish, Flatware, Foil, Frog, Frontispiece, Gold, Graal, Gravure, Ground, Half, Hasp, Horseshoe, Hot, Hypoplastron, Illustration, Kick, L, Lame, Lamina, Lanx,

Latten, Lead, Licence, Madreporic, Mascle, Mazarine, Nail, Nef, Neural, Nickel, Number, Onycha, P, Paten, Patina, Petri, Phototype, Planometer, Plaque, Plastron, Platter, Poitrel, Print, Pygal, Quarter, Race, Registration, Roof, Rove, Salamander, Scale, Screw, Scrim, Scutcheon, Scute, Scutum, Selling, Sheffield, Shield, Shoe, Side, Sieve, Silver, Slab, Soup, Spacer, Spoiler, Stall, Steel, Stencil, Stereo(type), Sternite, Surface, Swash, T, Tablet, Tace, Tasse(l), Tea, Tectonic, Tergite, Terne, Thali, Theoretical, Tin(ware), Torsel, Touch, Trade, Tramp, Trencher, Trivet, Trophy, Tsuba, Vane, Vanity, Vassail, Vessel, Wall, Water, Web, Wet, Whirtle, Whole, Wobble, Workload, Wrap(a)round, Zincograph

Plateau Altiplano, Anatolian, Barkly Tableland, Central Karoo, Chota Nagpur, Darling Downs, Dartmoor, Deccan, Durango, Ellesworth Land, Fjeld, Fouta Djallon, Highland, Highveld, Horst, Kar(r)oo, Kimberleys, Kurdestan, Kurdistan, La Mancha, Lamington, Langres, Mat(t)o Grosso, Mesa Verde, Meseta, Najd, Nilgiris, Ozark, Paramo, Piedmont, Puna, Shire Highlands, Tableland, Ust Urt

Platform Accommodation, Balcony, Bandstand, Base, Bay, Bema, Bench, Bridge, Catwalk, Crane, Crow's nest, Dais, Deck, Dolly, Drilling, Estrade, Exedra, Exhedra, Fighting top, Flake, Footpace, Footplate, Foretop, Gangplank, Gantry, Gravity, Hustings, Landing stage, Launch-pad, Machan, Maintop, Manifesto, Monkeyboard, Oil, Oil-rig, Pad, Paint-bridge, Pallet, Perron, Plank, Podium, Predella, Production, Programme, Pulpit, Quay, Raft, Rig, Rostrum, Round-top, Scaffold, Shoe, Skidway, Skylab, Soapbox, Space, Sponson, → STAGE, Stand, Stoep, Strandflat, Tee, Terminal, Ticket, Top, Tribunal, Tribune, Turntable, Wave-cut, Wharf

Play(s), Playing Accompany, Active, Amusement, Antic, Assist, At, Caper, Charm, Clearance, Closet, Coriolanus, Curtain-raiser, Dabble, Dalliance, Dandle, Doodle, Drama, Echo, Endgame, Epitasis, Escapade, Everyman, Extended, Fair, Finesse, Freedom, Frisk, Frolic, Fun, Gamble, Gambol, Game, Grand Guignol, Harlequinade, History, Holiday, Inside, Interlude, Jam, Jape, Jest, Jeu, Lake, Lark, Latitude, Lear, Leeway, Licence, Long, Mask, Masque, May, Medal, Melodrama, Miracle, Morality, Mummers, Mysteries, Nativity, Noh, Nurse, Oberammergau, On, Parallel, Passion, Pastorale, Perform, Personate, Peter, Portray, Power, Prank, Pretend, Puppet, Recreation, Represent, Riff, Rollick, Romp, Room, Rope, RUR, Saw, Screen, Show, Shuffle, Sketch, Sport, Squeeze, Stage, Strain, Stroke, Strum, Summerstock, Thrum, Thumb, Tolerance, Tonguing, Toot, Touchback, Toy, Tragedy, Trifle, Triple, Twiddle, Vamp, Word

▷**Play** *may indicate* an anagram

Player(s) Accompanist, Actor, Athlete, Back, Backstop, Black, Brass, Bugler, Busker, Cast, CD, Centre, Centre forward, Centre-half, Colt, Contestant, Cornerback, Cover point, Dealer, Disc, DVD, E, East, ENSA, Equity, Fetcher, Fiddle, Flanker, Fly-half, Flying wing, Fly-slip, Forward, Franchise, Fullback, Ghetto-blaster, Goalie, Goalkeeper, Goaltender, Gramophone, Grand master, Gridder, Guard, Half, Half-back, Half-forward, Hooker, Infielder, iPod®, It, Juke-box, Keg(e)ler, Kest, Kicker, Linebacker, Lineman, Lion, Lock, Long-leg, Longstop, Loose-head, Lutanist, Lutenist, Man, Marquee, Midfield, Mid-on, Mime, Muffin, Musician(er), N, Nickelback, Nightwatchman, North, Nose guard, Nose tackle, Ombre, Onside, Outfielder, Out(side)-half, Participant, Pianola®, Pitcher, Pocket, Pone, Pro, Prop, Quarterback, Receiver, Record, Red shirt, Reliever, Reserve, Rover, S, Safetyman, Scrape, Scratch, Scrum half, Seed, Shamateur, Short-leg, Shortstop, Side, South, Stand-off, Stand-off half,

Stereo, Striker, Strings, Strolling, Substitute, Super, Sweeper, Tabrere, Target man, Team, Thesp(ian), Tight end, Troubador, Troupe, Upright, Utility, Virtuosi, W, Walker-on, Walkman®, West, White, Wide receiver, Wing(back), Winger, Wingman

Playful Arch, Coy, Frisky, Gamesome, Humorous, Impish, Jocose, Kittenish, Ludic, Merry, Piacevole, Scherzo, Skittish, Sportive, Spry, Wanton

Playwright Dramaturge, Dramaturgist, Scriptwriter

Plea(s) Alford, Appeal, Claim, Common, Defence, Entreaty, Essoin, Excuse, Exoration, Orison, Petition, Placit(um), Prayer, Rebuttal, Rebutter, Rogation, Suit

Plead(er), Pleading Answer, Argue, Beg, Entreat, Intercede, Litigate, Moot, Placitory, Solicit, Special, Supplicant, Urge, Vakeel, Vakil

Please(d), Pleasant, Pleasing, Pleasure(-seeker), Pleasurable
Affable, Aggrate, Agreeable, Alcina, Algolagnia, Amenable, Amene, Amiable, Amuse, Apolaustic, Appeal, Arride, Artistic, Be my guest, Beneplacito, Benign, Bitte, Braw, Cheerful, Chuffed, Comely, Comfort, Content, Cordial, Cute, Delectation, Delice, Delight, Divine, Do, Euphonic, Eye candy, Fair, Felicitous, Fit, Flatter, Fun, Genial, Glad, Gladness, Good-o, Gratify, Gusto, Harmonious, Hedonism, Jammy, Joy, Kama, Kindly, Lekker, Lepid, List, Naomi, Oblige, Piacevole, Primrose path, Prithee, Prythee, Purr, Queme, Regale, Sapid, Satisfy, Schadenfreude, Sightly, Suit, Tasty, Thrill, Tickle, Tickle pink, Toothsome, Treat, Vanity, Voluptuary, Wally, Will, Winsome, Wrapped, Xanadu List

Pleat Accordion, Box, Crimp, Crystal, Fold, French, Frill, Goffer, Gusset, Kick, Kilt, Knife, Plait, Pranck(e), Prank, Ruff(le), Sunburst, Sunray

Pledge(r) Abstainer, Affidavit, Arlene, Arles, Band, Betroth, Bond, Borrow, Bottomry, Collateral, Commitment, Dedicate, Deposit, Earnest(-penny), Engage, Fine, Frithborn, Gage, Gilbert, Giselle, Guarantee, Hand, Hock, Hypothecate, Impignorate, Mortgage, Oath, Pass, Pawn, Pignerate, Pignorate, Plight, Pop, Propine, Sacrament, Security, Sponsorship, Stake, Surety, Teetotal, Toast, Troth, Undertake, Vow, Wad, Wage(r), Wed

Plentiful, Plenty Abounding, Abundance, Abundant, Ample, Bags, Copious, Copy, Cornucopia, Easy, Excess, Foison, Fouth, Ful(l)ness, Fushion, Galore, Goshen, Lashings, Loads, Lots, Oodles, Pleroma, Profusion, Quantity, Riches, Rife, Routh, Rowth, Scouth, Scowth, Slue, Sonce, Sonse, Teeming, Umpteen

▶**Pliers** *see* **PLY**

Plimsoll(s) Dap, Gutty, Gym-shoe, Line, Mutton-dummies, Pumps, Sandshoe, Tacky

Plot(s) Allotment, Area, Babington, Bed, Brew, Cabal, Carpet, Chart, Cliché, Collude, Connive, Conspiracy, Conspire, Contrive, Covin, Covyne, Croft, Device, Engineer, Erf, Erven, Frame-up, Graph, Gunpowder, Imbroglio, Intrigue, Lair, Locus, Lot, Machination, Map, Meal-tub, Odograph, Orchard, Pack, Parcel, Patch, Plan, Plat, Rye-house, Scenario, →**SCHEME**, Sect(ion), Shot, Site, Story, Storyline, Taluk, Terf, Turf, Web

Plough(man), Ploughed, Ploughing Arable, Ard, Arval, Big Dipper, Breaker, Bull tongue, Chamfer, Charles's Wain, Contour, Dipper, Disc, Drail, Drill, Ear, Earth-board, Ere, Fail, Fallow, Farmer, Feer, Flunk, Gadsman, Gang, Great Bear, Harrow, Lister, Middlebreaker, Middlebuster, Mouldboard, Piers, Pip, Pleuch, Pleugh, Plodder, Push, Rafter, Rib, Ridger, Rive, Rotary, Rove, Sand, Scooter, Septentrion(e)s, Sill, Sodbuster, Sow, Stump-jump, Swing, The Wagon, Till(er), Tractor, Trench, Triones, Wheel

Ploy Brinkmanship, Dodge, Feint, Finesse, Gambit, Manoeuvre, Stratagem, Strike, Subterfuge, Tactic, Wile

Pluck(ing), Plucky Avulse, Bare, Carphology, Cock, Courage, Deplume, Epilate, Evulse, Floccillation, Gallus, Game, → **GRIT**, Guts, Loot, Mettle, Pick, Pinch, Pip, Pizzicato, Plectron, Plectrum, Ploat, Plot, Plumassier, Plunk, Pook(it), Pouk(it), Pull, Race, Scrappy, Snatch, Spin, Spirit, Spunk, Summon, Tug, Twang, Tweak, Tweeze, Vellicate, Yank

Plug Access eye, Ad, Adapter, Adaptor, Advocate, Banana, Block, Bung, Caulk, Chaw, Chew, Commercial, Dam, DIN, Dook, Dossil, Dottle, Douk, Fipple, Fother, Gang, Glow, Go-devil, Heater, Hype, Jack, Lam, Operculum, Pessary, Phono, Prod, Promote, Publicity, Ram, Rawlplug®, Recommendation, Safety, Salt, Scart, Sealant, Spark(ing), Spigot, Spile, Spiling, Stem, Stop(per), Stopple, Strobili, Suppository, Tampion, Tap, Tent, Tompion, Vent, Volcanic, Wage, Wall, Wander, Wedge

Plum Beach, Bullace, Cherry, Choice, Damson, Drupe, Gage, Greengage, Ground, Jamaica, Japanese, Java, Kaki, Mammee-sapota, Marmalade, Maroon, Mirabelle, Musk, Mussel, Myrobalan, Naseberry, Neesberry, Peach, Persimmon, Proin(e), Pruin(e), Prune(llo), Quetsch, Raisin, Sapodilla, Sebesten, Victoria, Wodehouse

Plumage, Plume Aigrette, Crest, Egret, Feather, Hackle, Panache, Preen, Ptilosis, Quill

Plumb(er), Plumbing Bullet, Dredge, Fathom(eter), Lead(sman), Perpendicular, Plummet, Sheer, Sound, Test, True, U-trap, Vertical

Plump(er) Bold, Bonnie, Bonny, Buxom, Choose, Chopping, Chubbed, Chubby, Cubby, Cuddly, Dumpy, Embonpoint, Endomorph, Fat, Fleshy, Flop, Fubsy, Full, Lie, Matronly, Opt, Pick, Plank, Plonk, Plop, Podgy, Portly, Pudgy, Roll-about, Rolypoly, Rotund, Round(about), Rubenesque, Sonsie, Sonsy, Soss, Souse, Squab, Squat, Stout, Swap, Swop, Tidy, Tubby, Well-covered, Well-fed, Well-padded, Well-upholstered, Zaftig, Zoftig

Plunder(er) Berob, Booty, Brigand, Depredate, Despoil, Devastate, Escheat, Fleece, Forage, Freebooter, Gut, Harry, Haul, Herriment, Herryment, Hership, Loot, Maraud, Peel, Pill(age), Predation, Prey, Privateer, Raid, → **RANSACK**, Rape, Rapparee, Ravine, Reave, Reif, Reive, Rieve, Rifle, Rob, Rummage, Sack, Scoff, Shave, Skoff, Spoil(s), Spoliate, Sprechery, Spuilzie, Spuly(i)e, Spulzie, Swag

Plunge(r) Demerge, Dive, Douse, Dowse, Duck, Enew, Immerge, Immerse, La(u)nch, Nose-dive, Plummet, Raker, Send, Sink, Souse, Swoop, Thrust

Ply, Plier(s) Bend, Birl, Cab, Exercise, Exert, Gondoliers, Importune, Layer, Practise, Run, Trade, Wield

▷ **Plying** *may indicate* an anagram

PM Addington, Afternoon, Attlee, Autopsy, Balfour, Bute, Cabinet-maker, Callaghan, Chamberlain, Disraeli, Gladstone, Major, Melbourne, Peel, Pitt, Portland, Premier, → **PRIME MINISTER**, Salisbury, Taoiseach, Walpole

Pocket Air, Appropriate, Bag, Bin, Breast, Cargo, Cavity, Cly, Cup, Enclave, Fob, Glom, Hideaway, Hip, Jenny, Misappropriate, Patch, Placket, Plaid-neuk, Pot, Pouch, Purloin, Purse, Sac, Sky, Slash, Sling, Slit, Steal, Take, Trouser, Vest, Watch, Whitechapel

Pod(s) Babul, Bean, Belly, Carob, Chilli, Dividivi, Gumbo, Hull, Legume, Lomentum, Neb-neb, Okra, Pipi, Pregnant, Pudding-pipe, Seed, Senna, Siliqua, Tamarind, Vanilla, Vine

Poem(s), Poetry Acmeism, Acrostic, Anthology, Art, A Shropshire Lad, Ballad(e), Bucolic, Canto, Dewan, Dit(t), Dithyramb, Doggerel, Dub, Elegy, Endymion, Epic(ede), Haiku, Heroic, Hokku, Idyl(l), Inferno, Kyrielle, Lay, Limerick, Madrigal, Mahabharata(m), Mahabharatum, Meliboean, Metre, Mock-heroic, Monostrophe, Ode, Odyssey, Pastoral, Pentameter, Performance, Poesy, Prelude, Prose, Punk, Quatorzain, Quatrain, Ramayana, Rhapsody, Rig-Veda, Rime, Rime riche, Rondeau, Sixain, Song, Sonnet, Sound, Stanza, Tetrastich, Thebaid, Title, Vers(e)

Poet(s), Poetic Acmeist, Amorist, Bard(ling), Beatnik, Cumberland, Cyclic, Elegist, Georgian, Iambist, Idyllist, Imagist, Laureate, Layman, Liner, Lyrist, Makar, Maker, Meistersinger, Metaphysical, Metrist, Minnesinger, Minor, Minstrel, Mistral, Monodist, Odist, Parnassian, PL, Pleiad(e), Poetaster, Rhymer, Rhymester, Rhymist, Rymer, Scald, Scop, Silurist, Skald, Smart, Sonneteer, Sound, Spasmodic, Spasmodic School, Te(i)an, Thespis, Tragic, Trench, Troubadour, Trouvère, Trouveur, Verse-monger, Verse-smith, Versifier

▶**Poetry** *see* **POEM(S)**

Point(ed), Pointer, Points Ace, Acnode, Aim, Angular, Antler, Apex, Apogee, Appui, Arrowhead, Ascendant, Bar, Barb, Base, Basis, Boiling, Bradawl, Break(ing), Brownie, Burble, Burbling, Cape, Cardinal, Cash, Catch, Centre, Choke, Clou, Clovis, Clue, Colon, Comma, Cone, Conic, Corner, Cover, Crag, Crisis, Crux, Curie, Cursor, Cusp, Cuss, Danger, Dead, Decimal, Deflater, Deflator, Degree, Descendant, Detail, Di(a)eresis, Direct, Dot, E, Épée, Extremity, Fang, Feature, Fescue, Finger(tip), Fitch(e), Focal, Focus, Foreland, Freezing, Fulcrum, Germane, Gist, Gnomon, Hastate, Head, Hinge, Horn, Hour hand, Icicle, Index, Indicate, Indicator, Ippon, Issue, Jag, Jester, Jog, Juncture, Knub, Lance, Lanceolar, Lead, Limit, Lizard, Locate, Locus, Mark, Melting, Metacentre, Moot, Mull, Muricate, N, Nail, Neb, Needle, Ness, Nib, Node, Now, Nub, Obconic, Obelisk, Opinion, Ord, Organ, Oscillation, Particle, Peak, Periapsis, Periastron, Perigee, Pin, Pinnacle, Pixel, Place, Pour, Power, Pressure, Prong, Prow, Punchline, Punctilio, Punctual, Ras, S, Saturation, Scribe, Seg(h)ol, Selling, Set, Setter, Shaft, Sharpener, Show, Shy, Silly, Socket, Sore, Spearhead, Specie, Spicate, Spick, Spike, Stage, Sticking, Stiletto, Sting, Strong, Sum, Talking, Tang, Taper, Technicality, Tine, →**TIP**, Tongue, Trafficator, Trig, Triple, Turning, Umlaut, Use, Vane, Vantage, Verge, Verse, Vertex, Vowel, W, Waggle-dance, Zenith

Pointless Blunt, Curtana, Flat, Futile, Idle, Inane, Inutile, Muticous, Otiose, Stupid, Vain

Poison(er), Poisoning, Poisonous Bane, Contact, Contaminate, Deleterious, Envenom, Ergotise, Food, Malevolent, Miasma, Noxious, Plumbism, Rankle, Rot, Sausage, Systemic, Taint, Toxic, Toxicology, Toxicosis, Toxin, Toxoid, Venom(ous), Viperous, Virose, Virous, Virulent

Poke, Poky Bonnet, Broddle, Dig, Garget, Itchweed, Jab, Meddle, Mock, Nousle, Nudge, Nuzzle, Ombu, Peg, Pick, Poach, Pote, Pouch, Powter, →**PRISON**, Prog, Proke, Punch, Root(le), Rout, Rowt, Stab, Thrust

Polar, Pole(s), Poler Animal, Anode, Antarctic, Arctic, Boathook, Boom, Bowsprit, Caber, Celestial, Clothes, Crossbar, Electret, Extremity, Fizgy, Flagstaff, Furlong, Gaff, Galactic, Geomagnetic, Greasy, Icy, Lug, Magnetic, Mast, May, N, Nadir, Negative, Nib, North, Oar, Permafrost, Po, Polack, Positive, Punt, Quant, Quarterstaff, Range, Ridge, Rood, Roost, S, Shaft, South, Spar, Spindle, Sprit, Staff, Stake, Stanchion, Starosta, Stilt, Sting, Telegraph, Terrestrial, Tongue, Topmast, Totem, Utility, Zenith

▷**Polar** *may indicate* with a pole

Police(man), Policewoman Beria, Bill, Bluebottle, Blue heeler, Bobby, Boss, Boys in blue, Busy, Catchpole, CID, Commissioner, Constable, Cop(per), Darogha, Detective, DI, Dibble, Europol, Flatfoot, Flying Squad, Force, Fuzz, Garda, Garda Siochana, Gendarme, Gestapo, G-man, Guard, Inspector, Interpol, Jawan, Keystone, KGB, Kitchen, Lawman, Mata-mata, Met(ropolitan), Military, Mobile, Morse, Mountie, MP, Officer, Patrolman, PC Plod, Peeler, Plod, Pointsman, Porn squad, Provincial, Provost, Redcap, Riot, Robert, Roundsman, Rozzer, RUC, Secret, Snatch squad, Special, Special Branch, State Trooper, Super, Superintendent, Sweeney, Texas Rangers, The Bill, The Law, Traffic, Vice squad, Vigilante, Yardie squad, Zabtieh

Police station Copshop, Lock-up, Watchhouse

Policy Assurance, Ballon d'essai, Byline, CAP, Comprehensive, Course, Demesne, Endowment, Expedience, First-loss, Gradualism, Insurance, Keystone, Knock for knock, Laisser-faire, Lend-lease, Line, Manifesto, Method, Open(-sky), Open door, Perestroika, Plank, Platform, Pork-barrel, Practice, Programme, Reaganomics, Revanchism, Scorched earth, Socred, Stop-go, Tack, Tactics, Thatcherism, Third party, Ticket, UDI, White Australia

Polish(ed), Polisher Beeswax, Black(ing), Blacklead, Bob, Buff, Bull, Burnish, Chamois, Complaisant, Edit, Elaborate, Elegant, Emend, Emery, Enamel, Finish, French, Furbish, Gentlemanly, Glass, Glaze, Gloss, Heelball, Hone, Inland, Jeweller's rouge, Lap, Lustre, Nail, Perfect, Pewter-mill, Planish, Polite, Polverine, Refinement, Refurbish, Rottenstone, Rub, Sand, Sandblast, Sandpaper, Scour, Sheen, Shellac, Shine, Sleekstone, Slick, Sophistication, Supercalender, Svelte, Urbane, Veneer, Wax

Polite(ness) Affable, Cabinet, Civil, Courteous, Genteel, Grandisonian, Mannered, Mannerly, Suave, Urbane, Well-bred, Well-mannered

Politic(al), Politics Apparat, Azapo, Body, Chartism, Civic, Diplomacy, Discreet, Dog-whistle, Expedient, Falange, Fascism, Gesture, Leftism, Neoliberalism, New Left, Party, Poujadism, Power, Practical, Public, Radicalism, Rightism, State, Statecraft, Tactful, Wise, Yuppie, Yuppy

Politician(s) Back bench, Bright, Carpet-bagger, Catiline, Centrist, Chancellor, Chesterfield, Christian Democrat, Congressman, Coningsby, Delegate, Demagogue, Demo(crat), Diehard, Disraeli, DUP, Eden, Euro-MP, Eurosceptic, Evita, Front bench, Gladstone, Green, Hardie, Hardliner, Incumbent, Independent, Ins, Isolationist, Laski, Left, Legislator, Liberal, Log-roller, Loony left, MEP, Minister, Moderate, MP, Nationalist, Nazi, Obstructionist, Octobrist, Paisley, Parliamentarian, Parnell, Politico, Pollie, Polly, Poujade, Powell, Puppet, Rad, Rep, Richelieu, Senator, Socialist, Statesman, Statist, Tadpole, Taper, TD, Thatcherite, Tory, Trotsky, Unionist, Veep, Warhorse, Whig, Whip, Wilberforce

Poll(ing) Advance, Ballot, Bean, Canvass, Count, Cut, Deed, Dod, Election, Exit, Gallup, Head count, Humlie, Hummel, MORI, Nestor, Not(t), Opinion, Parrot, Pineapple, Pow, Referendum, Scrutiny, Sondage, Straw, Votes

▷**Poll** *may indicate* a first letter

Pollen, Pollinate(d), Pollination Anemophilous, Beebread, Dust, Entomophilous, Errhine, Ex(t)ine, Farina, Fertilised, Geitonogamy, Intine, Palynology, Sternotribe, Witch-meal, Xenia

Pollute(d), Pollutant, Pollution Acid rain, Adulterate, Atmosphere, Besmear, Contaminate, Defile, Dirty, Feculent, File, Fly ash, Foul, Impure, Infect, Light, Miasma, Nox, Rainout, Smog, Soil, Soilure, Stain, Sully, Taint, Thermal, Violate

Pomp(ous) Aldermanlike, Big, Bloviate, Bombastic, Budge, Ceremonial, Display, Dogberry, Euphuistic, Fustian, Grandiloquent, Grandiose, Heavy, Highfalutin(g), High-flown, High-muck-a-muck, High-sounding, Hogen-mogen, Holier than thou, Inflated, Orotund, Ostentatious, Pageantry, Panjandrum, Parade, Pontificating, Pooh-Bah, Pretentious, Self-important, Sententious, Solemn, Splendour, Starchy, State, Stilted, Stuffed shirt, Stuffy, Turgid

Pond(s) Atlantic, Curling, Dew, Dub, Flash, Hampstead, Lakelet, Oceanarium, Pool, Pound, Puddle, Shield(ing), Slough, Stank, Stew, Tank, Turlough, Vivarium, Viver

Ponder(ous) Brood, Cogitate, Contemplate, Deliberate, Heavy, Laboured, Mull, Muse, Perpend, Poise, Pore, Puzzle, Reflect, Ruminate, →THINK, Vise, Volve, Weigh, Weight(y), Wonder

Pontiff, Pontifical, Pontificate Aaron, Aaronic, Antipope, Dogmatise, Papal, Spout

Pontoon Blackjack, Bridge, Caisson, Chess, Game, Vingt-et-un

Pony Bidet, Canuck, Cayuse, Cow, Dales, Dartmoor, Eriskay, Exmoor, Fell, Garran, Garron, Gen(n)et, GG, Griffin, Griffon, Gryfon, Gryphon, Jennet, Jerusalem, Mustang, New Forest, One-trick, Pit, Polo, Pownie, Sable Island, Shanks', Sheltie, Shetland, Show, Tangun, Tat(too), Timor, Welsh, Welsh Mountain, Western Isles

Pool(s) Backwater, Bank, Bethesda, Billabong, Bogey hole, Cenote, Cess, Collect, Combine, Dub, Dump, Flash, Flow, Fund, Hag, Hot, Infinity, Jackpot, Kitty, Lasher, Lido, Lin(n), Malebo, Meer, Mere, Mickery, Mikvah, Mikveh, Moon, Natatorium, Paddling, Piscina, Piscine, Plash, Plesh, Plunge, →POND, Reserve, Snooker, Spa, Stank, Stanley, Sump, Tank, Tarn, Treble chance, Wading, Wave

Poor(ly) Abysmal, Bad, Bare, Base, Bijwoner, Breadline, Buckeen, Bywoner, Catchpenny, Conch, Cronk, Destitute, Desuetude, Dire, Dirt, Gens de peu, Gritty, Half-pie, Hard-up, Have-nots, Hopeless, Humble, Hungry, Ill(-off), Impecunious, Indigent, Lazarus, Lean, Lo-fi, Lousy, Low, Low-downer, Low-fi, Low-paid, Lumpen, Meagre, Mean, Naff, Needy, Obolary, One-horse, Pathetic, Patzer, Pauper, Peaky, Poxy, Redleg, Roinish, Rop(e)y, Roynish, Sad, Scrub, Second rate, Shabby, Shitty, Shoddy, Sober, Sorry, Strapped, Sub, Tacky, Tatty, Thin, Third-rate, Tinpot, Trashy, Undeserving, Unwell, Useless, Wretched

▷**Poor** *may indicate* an anagram

Pop (off), Popper, Popping Bang, Brit, Burst, Cloop, Cream soda, Crease, Daddy, Die, →DRUG, Each, Father, Fr, Ginger ale, Gingerbeer, Hip-hop, Hock, Iggy, Insert, Lemonade, Lumber, Mineral, Nip, Number, Parent, Party, Pater, Pawn, Pledge, Population, Press-stud, Punk, Rock'n'roll, Scoosh, Sherbet, Slip, Snap fastener, Soda, Splutter, Sputter, Weasel

▷**Pop** *may indicate* an anagram

Pope(s) Adrian, Alexander, Atticus, Boniface, Borgia, Clement, Dunciad, Eminence, Fish, Great Schism, Gregory, Hildebrand, Holiness, Innocent, Joan, Leo, Papa, Pius, Pontiff, Ruff(e), Schism, Sistine, Theocrat, Tiara, Urban, Vatican, Vicar-general of Christ, Vicar of Christ

Poppy Argemone, Bloodroot, California, Chicalote, Coquelicot, Corn, Corydalis, Diacodin, Eschscholtzia, Flanders, Horned, Iceland, Matilija, Mawseed, Opium, Papaver, Ponceau, Prickly, Puccoon, Rhoeadales, Shirley, Tall, Welsh

Popular(ity), Popularly Best-seller, Common, Crowd-pleaser, Democratic, Demotic, Evergreen, Fashionable, General, Heyday, Hit, Hot ticket, In, Laic,

Lay, Mass, Plebeian, Prevalent, Public, Sell-out, Street cred, Successful, Tipped, Trendy, Vogue, Vulgo

Population, Populace Catchment, Census, Closed, Deme, Demography, Inhabitants, Joe Public, Malthusian, Mass, Mob, Optimum, → **PEOPLE**, Public, Universe

Porcelain Arita, Artificial, Bamboo, Celadon, Chantilly, Chelsea, China, Coalport, Crackle(ware), Crouch-ware, Crown Derby, Derby, Dresden, Eggshell, Famille, Famille jaune, Famille noir, Famille rose, Famille verte, Frit, Goss, Hard-paste, Hizen, Imari, Ivory, Jasp, Jasper(ware), Kakiemon, Limoges, Lithophane, Meissen, Minton, Parian, Petuntse, Petuntze, Sèvres, Softpaste, Spode, Sung, Yuan

Pore Browse, Hole, Hydrathode, Lenticel, Muse, Ostiole, Ostium, Outlet, Ponder, Stoma, Study

Pork(y) Bacon, Boar, Brawn, Chap, Char sui, Crackling, Cracknel, Flitch, Griskin, Ham, Lie, Pancetta, Scrapple, Spare-rib, Spek

Porridge Berry, Bird, Brochan, Brose, Busera, Crowdie, Drammach, Drammock, Gaol, Grits, Grouts, Gruel, Hominy, Kasha, Mahewu, Mealie pap, Mielie pap, Oaten, Oatmeal, Parritch, Pease-brose, Polenta, Pottage, Praiseach, Sadza, Samp, Sentence, Skilly, Stirabout, Stretch, Sup(p)awn, Time, Ugali

Port(s) Beeswing, Carry, Cinque, Entrepot, Free, Gate, Gateway, Geropiga, → **HARBOUR**, Haven, Hinterland, Larboard, Left, Manner, Mien, Outport, Parallel, Row, Ruby, Serial, Tawn(e)y, Treaty, USB, VSOP, Wine

Porter Ale, Bearer, Bellboy, Bummaree, Caddie, Caddy, Carrier, Cole, Concierge, Coolie, Door-keeper, Doorman, Dvornik, Entire, Gatekeeper, Ham(m)al, Hamaul, Humper, Janitor, October, Ostiary, Plain, Red-cap, Skycap, Stout, Ticket

Portion Ann(at), Bit, Deal, Distribute, Dole, Dose, Dotation, Endowment, Fragment, Helping, Heritage, Hunk, Jointure, Lot, Lump, Meed, Modicum, Moiety, Nutlet, Ounce, Parcel, → **PART**, Piece, Ratio, Sample, Scantle, Scantling, Section, Segment, Serving, Share, Size, Slice, Something, Tait, Taste, Tate, Tittle, Tranche, Wodge

Portrait(ist) Composite, Depiction, Drawing, Eikon, Icon, Ikon, Image, Kit-cat, Lely, Likeness, Painting, Pin-up, Retraitt, Retrate, Sketch, Vignette

Portray(al) Caricature, Depict, Describe, Feature, Image, Limn, Notate, Paint, Personate, Render, Represent, → **SHOW**

Pose(r), Poseur Aesthete, Affect(ation), Arabesque, Asana, Ask, Contrapposto, Conundrum, Dilemma, Drape, Enigma, Lotus, Masquerade, Model, Place, Plastique, Posture, Pretend, Problem, Propound, Pseud, Puzzle, Sit, Stance, Sticker, Tableau vivant, Tickler

Position Arrange, Asana, Attitude, Bearing(s), Brace, Bridgehead, Case, Close, Codille, Delta, Ecarte, Echelon, Emplacement, Enfilade, False, F(o)etal, Fixure, Foothold, Fowler's, Grade, Honour point, Instal, Lay, Lie, Location, Locus, Lodg(e)ment, Lotus, Missionary, Mudra, Niche, Office, Open, Pass, Peak, Place, Plant, Point, Pole, Port, Possie, Post, Pozzy, Put, Rank, Recovery, Recumbent, Root, Seat, Set(ting), Sextile, Sims, Sinecure, Sit, Site, Situ, Situs, Stance, Standing, Standpoint, Station, Status, Strategic, Syzygy, Tagmeme, Thesis, Tierce, Trendelenburg's, Tuck, Viewpoint

Positive, Positivist Absolute, Actual, Anode, Assertive, Categorical, → **CERTAIN**, Comte, Definite, Emphatic, Plus, Print, Rave, Sure, Thetic, Upbeat, Upside, Utter, Veritable, Yang, Yes

Possess(ed), Possession(s), Possessive Adverse, Apostrophe, Asset, Aver, Bedevil, Belonging(s), Demonic, Driven, Energumen, Estate, Ewe lamb, Have, Haveour, Haviour, Heirloom, His, Hogging, Know, Lares (et) penates, Mad, Obsessed, Occupation, →**OWN**, Proprietorial, Sasine, Seisin, Sprechery, Substance, Tenancy, Usucap(t)ion, Vacant, Worth

Possible, Possibility, Possibly Able, Attainable, Contingency, Could, Feasible, Imaginable, Likely, Maybe, Mayhap, On, Option(al), Oyster, Peradventure, Perchance, Perhaps, Posse, Potential, Prospect, Resort, Viable, Well, Will

▷**Possibly** *may indicate* an anagram

Post(s), Postage Affix, After, Airmail, Appointment, Assign, Billet, Bitt, Bollard, Column, Command, Correspondence, Cossack, Delivery, Durn, Excess, Finger, First(-class), Flagpole, Fly, Goal, Graded, Gradient, Guardhose, Heel, Hitching, Hovel, Jamb, Joggle, Junk, King, Last, Laureate, Listening, Log, Mail, Mast, Newel, Observation, Outstation, Pale, Paling, Parcel, Pendant, Penny, Picket, Pigeon, Pile, Piling, Piquet, Placard, Place, Plant, Plum, Pole, Position, Puncheon, Pylon, Quoin, Registered, Remit, RM, Rubbing, Samson's, Seat, Second-class, Send, Sheriff's, Snubbing, Sound, Staff, Staging, Stake, Stanchion, Stand, Starting, Station, Stud, Tana, Tee, Term(inal), Thanna(h), Tool, Totem pole, Trading, Troll, Upright, Vacancy, Waymark, Winning

Postman, Postmaster, Postwoman Carrier, Courier, Emily, Hill, Messenger, Nasby, Pat, Portionist, Sorter

Postpone(ment), Postponed Adjourn, Backburner, Carryover, Contango, Defer, Delay, Frist, Hold over, Lay over, Long-finger, Moratorium, Mothball, Offput, On ice, Pigeon-hole, Postdate, Prorogue, Put over, Remanet, Reprieve, Respite, Roll back, Shelve, Spike, Stay, Suspend, Withhold

Posture(r), Posturing Affectation, Asana, Attitude, Counter-view, Decubitus, Deportment, Gesture, Mudra, Pose, Pretence, Site, Stance, Swank, Vorlage, Yoga

Pot(s), Potting, Potty Ante, Bankroll, Basil, Belly, Besotted, Billycan, Cafetière, Ca(u)ldron, Cannabis, Cannikin, Casserole, Cast, Ceramic, Chamber, Chanty, Chimney, Close-stool, Cocotte, Coil, Commode, Crewe, Crock(ery), Crucible, Cruse(t), Delf(t), Dixie, Doolally, Ewer, Flesh, Gaga, Gage, Grass, Hash(ish), Helmet, Hemp, Hooped, In off, Kaif, Kef, Kettle, Kitty, Lobster, Loco, Lota(h), Maiolica, Majolica, Marijuana, Marmite, Melting, Ming, Monkey, Olla, Olpe, Pan, Pat, Piñata, Pipkin, Planter, Pocket, Pool, Poot, →**POTTERY**, Pottle, Pout, Prize, Samovar, Shoot, Sink, Skeet, Skillet, Smudge, Steamer, Steane, Stomach, Tea, Terrine, Test, Throw, Trivet, Tureen, Urn, Whitechapel

Potato(es) African, Aloo, Alu, Batata, Chat, Clean, Couch, Datura, Duchesse, Early, Fluke, Hashbrowns, Hog, Hole, Hot, Irish, Jacket, Jersey, Kidney, Kumara, Lyonnaise, Maris piper, Mash, Murphy, Parmentier, Peel-and-eat, Pratie, Praty, Ro(e)sti, Rumbledethump(s), Seed, Small, Solanum, Stovies, Sweet, Tatie, Tattie, Teddy, Tuber, Ware, White, Yam

Potential(ly) Action, Capability, Capacity, Chemical, Latent, Making(s), Manqué, Possible, Promise, Resting, Scope, Viable

▷**Potentially** *may indicate* an anagram

Potter Amble, Cue, Dabbity, Dacker, Daidle, Daiker, Daker, Dibble, Dilly-dally, Dodder, Etruscan, Fettle, Fictor, Fiddle, Footer, Footle, Fouter, Gamesmanship, Idle, Mess, Minton, Muck, Niggle, One-upmanship, Plouter, Plowter, Poke, Spode, Thrower, Tiddle, Tink(er), Troke, Truck, Wedgwood

▷**Potter** *may indicate* a snooker-player

Pottery Agatewear, Bank, Basalt, Bisque, Cameo ware, Celadon, Ceramet, Ceramic, Chelsea, China, Creamware, Crock, Crouch-ware, Dabbity, Delf(t), Dresden, Earthenware, Encaustic, Etruria(n), Faience, Flatback, Gombroon, Granitewear, Hollowware, Ironstone, Jomon, Lustreware, Maiolica, Majolica, Ming, Minton, Pebbleware, Queensware, Raku, Red-figured, Satsuma, Scroddled, Sgraffito, Slab, Slipware, Smalto, Spode, Spongeware, Stoke, Stoneware, Studio, Sung, Terra sigillata, Ware, Wedgwood®, Wemyss, Whieldon, Whiteware

Pouch(ed) Bag, Brood, Bum-bag, Bursa, Caecum, Cheek, Cisterna, Codpiece, Cyst, Diverticulum, Fanny pack, Gill, Jockstrap, Marsupial, Marsupium, Papoose, Pocket, Poke, Posing, Purse, Sac, Saddlebag, Scrip, Scrotum, Snood, Spleuchan, Sporran

Pound(er) Ache, As, Bar, Bash, Batter, Battersea, Beat, Bombard, Bradbury, Bray, Broadpiece, Bruise, Clomp, Contund, Coop, Drub, Embale, Enclosure, Ezra, Fold, Green, Greenie, Greeny, Hammer, Hatter, Imagist, Intern, Iron man, Jail, Jimmy o'goblin, Kiddle, Kidel, Kin, Knevell, L, Lam, Lash, Lb, Lock, Mash, Nevel, Nicker, Oncer, One-er, Oner, Pale, Palpitate, Pen, Penfold, Pestle, Pin, Pindar, Pinfold, Pink, Powder, Pulverise, Pun, Quop, Rint, Scots, Smacker, Sov(ereign), Stalag, Stamp, Sterling, Strum, Throb, Thump, Tower, Troy, Weight

Pour(ing) Affusion, Birl(e), Bucket, Cascade, Circumfuse, Decant, Diffuse, Disgorge, Flood, Flow, Jaw, Jirble, Libate, Rain, Seil, Shed, Sile, Skink, Spew, Stream, Teem, Trill, Turn, Vent, Weep, Well

Poverty Beggary, Dearth, Deprivation, Hardship, Illth, Indigence, →**LACK**, Necessity, Need, Paucity, Pauperism, Penury, Poortith, Squalor, Tobacco Road, Want

Powder(ed), Powdery Allantoin, Alumina, Baking, Bleaching, Boracic, Calamine, Calomel, Chalk, Chilli, Cocoa, Colcothar, Condition, Cosmetic, Culm, Curry, Custard, Cuttlefish, Dentifrice, Dust, Dusting, Eupad, Explosive, Face, Flea, Floury, Fly, Fulminating, Giant, Gregory, Grind, Gun, Hair, Insect, Itching, Kohl, Litmus, Magnesia, Meal, Mepacrine, Mould-facing, Pearl, Percussion, Persian, Plaster of Paris, Plate, Polishing, Pollen, Pounce, Pound, Priming, Prismatic, Projecting, Pulver, Putty, Rachel, Rochelle, Rouge, Seidlitz, Sherbet, Sitosterol, Smokeless, Snuff, Soap, Talc(um), Talcose, Toner, Tooth, Tutty, Washing, Zedoary

Power(ful), Powers Ability, Able, Air, Almighty, Alpha, Arm, Arnold, Athletic, Atomic, Attorney, Audrey, Authority, Axis, Beef, Big, Capability, Cham, Charisma, Clairvoyance, Clout, Cogency, Colossus, Command, Corridor, Cube, Danger, Despotic, Diadem, Dieu, Dominion, Effective, Electricity, Eminence, Éminence grise, Empathy, Energy, Eon, ESP, Exponent, Facility, Faculty, Fire, Flower, Force, Gaddi, Gas, Generator, Geothermal, Grey, Grip, Gutty, Hands, Hefty, Herculean, High, Horse, Hot, Hp, Hydroelectric, Imput, Influence, Juice, Kick, Kilowatt, King, Leccy, Leverage, Locomotion, Log, Logarithm, Mandarin, Mandate, Mastery, Megawatt, Might, Mogul, Motive, Motor, Muscle, Natural, Nature, Nth, Nuclear, Od-force, Oligarch, Omnificent, Omnipotent, Option, P, Panjandrum, People, Pester, Plenary, Posse, Potency, Puissant, Punch, Purchasing, Regime, Resolving, Say-so, Sea, Sinew, Solar, Soup, Stamina, Staying, Steam, Steel, Stiff, Stopping, Stranglehold, Strength, →**STRONG**, Supercharge, Supreme, Sway, Teeth, Telling, Throne, Tidal, Titan, Tycoon, Tyranny, Ulric, Vertu(e), Vigour, Vis, Volt, Vroom, Water, Watt, Wattage, Wave, Weight, Welly, Wheel and axle, Whiphand, Wind, World, Yeast

Practical, Practicable, Practicalities Active, Applied, Brass tacks, Doable, Down-to-earth, Easy-care, Feasible, Hands on, Hard-boiled, Joker, Logistics, Nitty-gritty, No-nonsense, Nuts and bolts, On, Pragmatic, Realist(ic), Realpolitik, Rule of thumb, Sensible, Shrewd, Technical, Useful, Utilitarian, Viable, Virtual

Practice(s), Practise, Practitioner, Practised Abuse, Adept, Custom, Distributed, Do, Drill, Dry run, Dummy run, Enure, Exercise, Fire, General, Graft, Group, Habit, Inure, Ism, Keep, Knock-up, Massed, Meme, Mock, Nets, Operate, Order, Ordinance, Pipe opener, Ply, Policy, Praxis, Private, Prosecution, Pursuit, Rehearsal, Rehearse, Restrictive, Rite, Rule, Rut, Sadhana, Sharp, Sighter, Spanish, System, Target, Teaching, Test-run, Trade, Tradition, Train, Trial, Try out, Ure, Usage, Use, Wage

Prairie IL, Illinois, Llano, Plain, Savanna, Steppe, Tundra, Veldt

Praise(worthy) Acclaim, Accolade, Adulation, Alleluia, Allow, Anthem, Applause, Beatify, Belaud, Bepuff, Bless, Blurb, Bouquet, Bravo, Butter, Carol, Citation, CL, Commend(ation), Compliment, Congratulate, Crack up, Cry up, Dulia, Ego boost, Encomium, Envy, Eulogise, Eulogium, Eulogy, Exalt, Exemplary, Extol, Flattery, Gloria, Glory, Hail, Herry, Hery(e), Hosanna, Hype, Incense, Laud, Laurels, Lip service, Lo(o)s, Meritorious, Paean, Palmary, Palp, Panegyric, Plaudit, Rap, Rave, Recommend, Roose, Talk-up, Thank, Tout, Tribute

Prance Brank, Canary, Caper, Cavort, Galumph, Gambol, Jaunce, Jaunse, Prank(le), Swagger, Tittup, Trounce

Prank(s) Attrap, Bedeck, Bedizen, Caper, Dido, Escapade, Fredaine, Frolic, Gaud, Jape, Lark, Mischief, Pliskie, Rag, Reak, Reik, Rex, Rig, Spoof, Trick, Vagary, Wedgie

Prattle Babble, Blat(her), Chatter, Gab(nash), Gas, Gibber, Gossip, Gup, Lalage, Patter, Yap

Pray(ing) Appeal, Bed, Beg, Beseech, Bid, Daven, →**ENTREAT**, Impetrate, Intercede, Intone, Invoke, Kneel, Mantis, Patter, Solicit, Wrestle

Prayer(s), Prayer book, Prayer wall Acoemeti, Act, Angelus, Ave (Maria), Bead, Beadswoman, Bede, Bene, Bidding, Breviary, Carmelite, Collect, Commination, Common, Cry, Devotion, Eleison, Entreaty, Evensong, Grace, Habdalah, Hail Mary, Intercession, Introit, Invocation, Kaddish, Khotbah, Kol Nidre, Kyrie, Kyrie eleison, Lauds, Litany, Lord's, Loulat-ul-qadr, Ma'ariv, Maiden's, Mani, Mantis, Mat(t)ins, Missal, Morning, Novena, Opus dei, Orant, Orarium, Orison, Our Father, Paternoster, Patter, Petition, Phylactery, Placebo, Plea, Preces, Prime, Requiem, Requiescat, Responses, Rogation, Rosary, Salat, Secret, Shema, State, Suffrage, Terce, Venite, Vesper, Vigils, Wish, Yajur-Veda

▷**Prayer** *may indicate* one who begs

Preach(er) Ainger, Boanerges, Circuit rider, Dawah, Devil-dodger, Donne, Ecclesiastes, Evangelist, Exhort, Gospeller, Graham, Holy Roller, Itinerant, Kerygma, Knox, Lecture, Local, Mar-text, Minister, Missionary, Patercove, Postillate, Predicant, Predicate, Predikant, Priest, Prophet, Pulpiteer, Rant, Revivalist, Sermonise, Soper, Spintext, Spurgeon, Teach, Televangelist, Wesley

Precaution Care, Fail-safe, Guard, In case, Prophylaxis, Safeguard, Safety net

Precede(nce), Precedent Antedate, Example, Forego, Forerun, Herald, Pas, Predate, Preface, Prepotent, Priority, Protocol, Test case, Zeroth

Precinct(s) Ambit, Area, Banlieue, Close, Courtyard, District, Environs, Pedestrian, Peribolos, Region, Shopping, Temenos, Verge, Vihara

Precious Adored, Chary, Chichi, Costly, Dear, Dearbought, Ewe-lamb, La-di-da, Murr(h)a, Nice, Owre, Precise, Priceless, Prissy, Rare, Twee, Valuable

Precipitate, Precipitation, Precipitous, Precipitator Abrupt, Accelerate, Catalyst, Cause, Deposit, Hailstone, Hasty, Headlong, Impetuous, Launch, Lees, Pellmell, Pitchfork, Rash, Sca(u)r, Serein, Serene, Sheer, Shoot, Sleet, Snowfall, Snowflake, Start, →STEEP

Precise(ly), Precisian, Precision Absolute, Accurate, Dry, Exact, Explicit, Fine-drawn, Literal, Minute, Nice(ty), Niminy-piminy, Overnice, Particular, Perfect, Pernickety, Plumb, Point-device, Prig, Prim, Punctilious, Razor, Sharpness, Spang, Specific, Starchy, Stickler, Strict, Stringent, Succinct, Surgical, Tight, To the letter, Very

Predator(y) Carnivore, Condor, Eagle, Eyas, Fox, Glede, Harpy-eagle, Honey badger, Jackal, Kestrel, Kite, Lycosa, Mantis, Marauder, Nyas, Pike, Predacious, Prey, Puma, Skua, Tanrec, Tarantula, Tenrec, Trapper, Wolf

Predecessor Ancestor, Forebear, Foregoer

Predicament Box, Dilemma, Embroglio, Hobble, Hole, In chancery, Jam, Pass, Peril, Pickle, Plight, Quandary, Scrape, Spot

Predict(ion), Predictable, Predicted, Predictor Astrologer, Augur, Belomancy, Bet, Clairvoyance, Damn, Divination, Doomsayer, Doomster, Doomwatch, Ex ante, Far-seeing, Forecast, Foreordain, Foreread, Foresay, Foresee, Foreshadow, Foreshow, Forespeak, Foretell, Formulaic, Forsay, Futurist, Geomancy, Horoscope, Jeremiah, Nap, Necromancy, Omen, Portend, Presage, Previse, Prognosis, Project, Prophecy, Prophesy, Quant, Regular, Second-guess, Soothsayer, Spae, Tip

Pre-eminence, Pre-eminent Arch, Foremost, Monarchic, Palm(ary), Paramount, Primacy, Supreme, Top dog, Topnotch, Unique

Preface Avant-propos, Foreword, Herald, Intro, Preamble, Precede, Proem, Prolegomenon, Prolepsis, Usher

Prefer(ence), Preferred Advance, Better, Choose, Discriminate, Druthers, Elect, Faard, Faurd, Favour, Imperial, Incline, Lean, Liquidity, Predilect(ion), Prefard, Priority, Proclivity, Promote, Rather, Select, Sooner, Stocks, Taste, Will

Pregnancy, Pregnant Big, Clucky, Cyesis, Due (to), Ectopic, Enceinte, Extrauterine, Fertile, F(o)etation, Gestation, Gravid(a), Great, Great-bellied, Heavy, Hysterical, In foal, In pig, In pup, Knocked-up, Molar, Pseudocyesis, Retirement, Significant, Teem, Up the duff, Up the pole, Up the spout, Up the stick

Prehistoric Ancient, Azilian, Beaker Folk, Boskop, Brontosaurus, Cambrian, Clovis, Cro-Magnon, Eocene, Folsom, Primeval, Primitive, Pteranodon, Pterodactyl(e), Pterosaur, Saurian, Sinanthropus, Titanis, Titanosaurus, Trilith(on)

Prejudice(d) Ageism, Bias, Derry, Discrimination, Down, Illiberal, Impede, Inequity, Injure, Insular, Intolerance, Partiality, Parti pris, Preoccupy, Prepossession, Racism, Sexism, Slant, Unfair

Preliminary Curtain-raiser, Draft, Exploration, Heat, Initial, Introductory, Opening, Precursory, Preface, Preparatory, Previous, Prodrome, Proem, Prolusion, Propaedeutic, Rough, Title-sheet

Prelude Entrée, Forerunner, Intrada, Overture, Proem(ial), Ritornell(e), Ritornello, Verset

Premature Early, Precocious, Pre(e)mie, Premy, Pre term, Previous, Slink, Untimely, Untimeous

Premier Chief, Leader, Lenin, Main, PM, → **PRIME MINISTER**, Tojo, Top (drawer)

Premise(s) Assumption, Datum, Epicheirema, Ground, Hypothesis, Inference, Lemma, Licensed, Major, Postulate, Property, Proposition, Reason, Syllogism, Term, Unlicensed

Premium Ap, Bond, Bonus, Discount, Grassum, Pm, Reward, Scarce, Share

Preoccupation, Preoccupied, Preoccupy Absorb, Abstracted, Distrait, Engross, Hang-up, Intent, Obsess, Self-centred, Thing

Prepare(d), Preparation Address, À la, Anticipate, Arrange, Attire, Boun, Bowne, Brilliantine, Busk, Calver, Cock, Concoct, Cook, Cooper, Countdown, Decoct, Did, Do, Dress, Edit, Extract, Forearm, Foundation, Game, Gear (up), Groom, Ground, Groundwork, Inspan, Key, Lay (out), Legwork, Limber (up), Lotion, Measure, Mobilise, Organise, Parasceve, Paste up, Pomade, Poultice, Preliminary, Prime, Procinct, Prothesis, Provide, Psych, Qualified, → **READY**, Redact, Rehearsal, Revise, Ripe, Run up, Scout, Scrub up, Set, Spadework, Stand-to, Suborn, Train, Trim, Truss, Tune up, Type, Up to, Warm-up, Willing, Yare

▷**Prepare(d)** *may indicate* an anagram

Preposterous Absurd, Chimeric, Exorbitant, Foolish, Grotesque, Rich, Tall order, Unreasonable

▷**Preposterous** *may indicate* a word reversed

Prerequisite Condition, Essential, Necessity, Sine qua non

Presbyter(ian) Berean, Blue, Cameronian, Classic, Classis, Covenanter, Elder, Knox, Macmillanite, Moderator, Sacrarium, Seceder, Secesher, Secession Church, Wee Free, Whig(gamore)

Prescribe(d), Prescription Appoint, Assign, Dictate, Enjoin, Impose, Negative, Ordain, Positive, Rule, Scrip, Set, Statutory

Prescription Cipher, Decree, Direction, Formula, Medicine, Placebo, R, Rec, Receipt, Ritual, Specific

Presence Aspect, Bearing, Closeness, Company, Debut, Face, Hereness, Imminence, Mien, Shechinah, Shekinah, Spirit

Present(ation), Presented, Presenter, Presently Advowson, Anchorman, Anon, Assists, Award, Befaba, Bestow, Bonsela, Boon, Bounty, Box, By and by, Cadeau, Congiary, Coram, Current, Debut, Dee-jay, Demo, Deodate, DJ, Donate, Dotal, Douceur, Dower, Endemic, Endew, Endow, Endue, Enow, Étrenne, Exhibit, Existent, Exposition, Fairing, Feature, Format, Free-loader, Front-man, Gie, → **GIFT**, Give, Going, Grant, Gratuity, Hand, Here, Historical, Hodiernal, Holocene, Host(ess), Image, Immediate, Inbuilt, Inst, Introduce, Jock(ey), Largess(e), Linkman, MC, Mod, Newsreader, Nonce, Now, Nuzzer, Offering, Porrect, Pose, Potlach, Pr, Produce, Proffer, Pro-tem, Put, Render, Rendition, Serve-up, Show, Slice, Stage, Study, Submit, Tense, The now, There, Tip, Today, Trojan horse, Vee-jay, Window dressing, Xenium, Yeven

Preserve(d), Preservation, Preservative, Preserver Additive, Bottle, Burnettize, Can, Chill, Chow-chow, Cocoon, Confect, Corn, Creosote, Cure, Damson cheese, Dehydrate, Dry, Eisel, Embalm, Enshield, Enshrine, Fixative, Formaldehyde, Formalin, Freeze, Guard, Hain, Hesperides, Index link, Jam, Jerk, Keep, Kinin, Kipper, Konfyt, Kyanise, Lay up, Lifebelt, → **MAINTAIN**, Marmalade, Mothball, Mummify, National Trust, On ice, Paraben, Pectin, Peculiar, Piccalilli, Pickle, Pot, Powellise, Quince, Quinoline, Salt(petre), Salve, Saut, Season, Souse, Store, Stuff, Sweetmeat, Tanalized, Tar, Tin, Vinegar, Waterglass

Preside(nt) Abe, Adams, Allende, Arthur, Ataturk, Banda, Botha, Buchanan, Bush, Carter, Chair, Chief Barker, Childers, Chirac, Cleveland, Clinton, Coolidge, Coty, Dean, Director, Eisenhower, Fillmore, Ford, Garfield, Grand Pensionary, Grant, Harding, Harrison, Hayes, Hoover, Ike, Jackson, Jefferson, Kennedy, Kruger, Lead, Lincoln, Madison, Mitterand, Moderator, Monroe, Mugabe, Nixon, P, Peron, Polk, Pr(a)eses, Prexy, Reagan, Roosevelt, Sa(a)dat, Speaker, Superintendent, Supervisor, Taft, Taylor, Tito, Truman, Tyler, Van Buren, Vasquez, Veep, Washington, Yeltsin

Press(ed), Pressing, Pressure Acute, Atmospheric, Bar, Barometer, Bench, Blackmail, Blood, Cabinet, Chivvy, Cider, Click, Closet, Clothes, Coerce, Compact, Compression, Copying, Cram, Crease, Crimp, Critical, Crowd, Crush, Cupboard, Cylinder, Dragoon, Drill, Dun, Durable, Duresse, Enforcement, Enslave, Exigent, Filter, Flat-bed, Fleet St, Fluid, Fly, Folding, Force, Fourth estate, Free, Full-court, Goad, Gutter, Hasten, Head, Heat, Herd, Hie, High, Hothouse, Hug, Hurry, Hustle, Hydraulic, Hydrostatic, Impact, Impinge, Important, Importune, Inarm, Instant, Intense, Iron, Jam, Jostle, Knead, Leverage, Lie, Lobby, Low, Make, Mangle, Mill, Minerva, Newspapers, Obligate, Oil, Onus, PA, Palpate, Partial, Pascal, Peer, Permanent, Persist, Ply, Printing, Private, Pump, →**PUSH**, Racket, Ram, Ratpack, Record, Recruit, Reportage, Reporter, Roll, Root, Rotary, Rub, Rush, Sandwich, Screw, Scrum, Serr(e), Sit, Speed, Spur, Squash, Squeeze, Stanhope, Static, Stop, Strain(t), Stress, Tax, Tension, Three-line-whip, Throng, Throttle, Thrutch, Tourniquet, Tread, Turgor, →**URGE**, Urgence, Urgency, Vanity, Vapour, Vice, Wardrobe, Weight, Wine, Wring, Yellow

Prestige, Prestigious Asma, Cachet, Credit, Distinguished, Fame, Influence, Izzat, Kudos, Mana, Notable, Status

Presume, Presumably, Presumption, Presumptuous Allege, Arrogant, Audacity, Believe, Bold, Brass, Cocksure, Cocky, Doubtless, →**EXPECT**, Familiar, Forward, Gall, Impertinent, Insolent, Liberty, Outrecuidance, Overweening, Pert, Probably, Put upon, Suppose, Uppish, Upstart, Whipper-snapper

Pretence, Pretend(er), Pretext Act, Affect(ation), Afflict, Assume, Blind, Bluff, Bogus, Cant, Charade, Charlatan, Claim, Cover, Cram, Dauber(y), Dissemble, Dissimulate, Dive, Excuse, Feign, Feint, Gondolier, Guise, Hokum, Humbug, Hypocrisy, Impersonation, Impostor, Jactitation, Lambert Simnel, Let-on, Make-believe, Malinger, Masquerade, Obreption, Old, Ostensible, Parolles, Perkin Warbeck, Play act, Plea, Pose, Pretension, Profess, Pseud(o), Quack, Sham, Simulate, Stale, Stalking-horse, Subterfuge, Suppose, Swanking, Warbeck, Would-be, Young

Pretentious(ness), Pretension Arty(-farty), Bombast, Fantoosh, Fustian, Gaudy, Grandiose, High-falutin(g), Kitsch, La-di-da, Lady Muck, Orotund, Ostentatious, Overblown, Paraf(f)le, Pompous, Ponc(e)y, Pseud(o), Sciolism, Show, Showy, Snob, Snobbish, Squirt, Tat, Tinhorn, Uppity, Upstart, Vulgar

Pretty Attractive, Becoming, Bobby-dazzler, Chocolate-box, Comely, Cute, Dear, Decorate, Dish, Elegant, Fair(ish), Fairway, Fetching, Inconie, Incony, Keepsaky, Kind of, Looker, Moderately, Pass, Peach, Personable, Picturesque, Primp, Pulchritudinous, Purty, Quite, Rather, Sweet, Twee, Winsome

Prevail(ing) Dominate, Endure, Go, Induce, Outweigh, Persist, Persuade, Predominant, Preponderate, Reign, Ring, Triumph, Victor, Win

Prevalent, Prevalence Catholic, Common, Currency, Dominant, Endemic, Epidemic, Obtaining, Rampant, Rife, Set in, Widespread

Prevent(ion), Prevent(at)ive Avert, Bar, Block, Daidzein, Debar, Deter, Disallow, Dissuade, Embar, Estop, Foil, Foreclose, Forfend, Hamper, Help, Hinder, Hold back, Impound, Inhibit, Keep, Let, Nobble, Obstruct, Obturation, Obviate, Preclude, Prophylactic, Save, Sideline, Stop, Theriac, Thwart, Trammel

Previous(ly) Afore, Already, Antecedent, Backlog, Before, Earlier, Ere(-now), Fore, Former, Hitherto, Old, Once, Prior, Whilom

Prey Booty, Currie, Curry, Feed, Kill, Pelt, Plunder, Predate, Proul, Prowl, Quarry, Raven, Ravin(e), Soyle, Spreagh, Victim

Price(d), Pricing, Price-raising, Pricy Appraise, Asking, Assess, Bride, Charge, Consequence, Contango, →**COST**, Cost-plus, Dearth, Due, Evens, Exercise, Expense, Factory-gate, Fare, Fee, Fiars, Hammer, Hire, Intervention, Issue, Limit, List, Lobola, Loco, Market, Mark up, Offer, Packet, Perverse, Predatory, Prestige, Purchase, Quotation, Quote, Rack, Ransom, Rate, Regrate, Reserve, Sale, Selling, Shadow, Sky high, Song, Spot, Starting, Street value, Striking, Subscription, Toll, Trade, Unit, Upset, Valorise, Value, Vincent, Weregild, Wergeld, Wergild, Worth, Yardage

Priceless Comic, Invaluable, Killing, Unique

Prick(ed), Prickle, Prickly Acanaceous, Acanthus, Accloy, Argemone, Arrect, Bearded, Brakier, Bramble, Brog, Bunya, Cactus, Cloy, Cnicus, Echinate, Goad, Gore, Gorse, Hedgehog, Hedgepig, Impel, Inject, Jab, Jag, Jaggy, Jook, Juk, Kali, Penis, Pierce, Prod, Prog, Puncture, Rubus, Ruellia, Seta, Setose, Smart, Spinate, Stab, Star-thistle, Stimulus, Sting, Tattoo, Tatu, Teasel, Thistle, Thorn, Tingle, Urge, Whin

Pride Arrogance, Bombast, Brag, Conceit, Elation, Esprit de corps, Glory, Hauteur, Hubris, Inordinate, Lions, London, Machismo, Plume, Preen, Purge, Triumphalism, Vainglory, Vanity

Priest(ess), Priests Abbot, Becket, Brahmin, Caiaphas, Cardinal, Celebrant, Clergyman, Cleric, Club, Curé, Dalai Lama, Druid, Exorcist, Father, Flamen, Hierarch, High, H(o)ungan, John, Kohen, Lama, Lazarist, Mage, Mallet, Mass, Mess, Metropolitan, Minister, Missionary, Monsignor, Non-juror, Ordinand, P, Padre, Parish, Parson, Pastor, Père, Pontiff, Pope, Pope's knight, Preacher, Prelate, Presbyter, Prior(ess), Pujari, Pythoness, Rabbi, Rector, Rev, Salian, Samuel, Seminarian, Sir John Lack-Latin, Sky pilot, Spoiled, Turbulent, Usager, Vestal, Vicar, Zymite

Primacy, Primate Angwantibo, Ape, Australopithecus, Aye-aye, Bandar, Bigfoot, Biped, Bishop, Bush baby, Cardinal, Catar(r)hine, Colobus, Ebor, Gibbon, Hanuman, Hominid, Jackanapes, King Kong, Langur, Lemur, Loris, Macaque, Magot, Mammal, Marmoset, →**MONKEY**, Orang, Pongid, Potto, Prosimian, Quadruman, Ramapithecus, Rhesus, Sifaka, Simian, Slender loris, Wanderoo, Zinjanthropus

Prime(r), Primary, Priming Arm, Basic, Bloom, Cardinal, Charging, Chief, Choice, Claircolle, Clearcole, Clerecole, Closed, Detonator, Direct, Donat, Donet, Election, Enarm, Fang, First, Flower, Heyday, Mature, Open, Original, Paint, Paramount, Peak, Principal, Radical, Remex, Sell-by-date, Supreme, Thirteen, Tip-top, Totient, Totitive, Valuable, Windac, Windas, Ylem

Prime Minister Aberdeen, Ahern, Asquith, Attlee, Baldwin, Balfour, Begin, Bute, Callaghan, Campbell-Bannerman, Canning, Chamberlain, Chatham, Churchill, Dewan, Diefenbaker, Disraeli, Diwan, Eden, Gladstone, Grafton, Grand Vizier, Grey, Heath, Home, Iron Duke, Leaderene, Liverpool, Lloyd George, Macdonald, Macmillan, Major, Melbourne, North, Number Ten,

Palmerston, Peel, Perceval, Pitt, PM, Premier, Rockingham, Shastri, Tanaiste, Taoiseach, Thatcher, Trudeau, Walpole, Wilson, Winston

Primitive Aborigine, Amoeba, Antediluvian, Arabic, Archaic, Atavistic, Barbaric, Caveman, Crinoid, Crude, Early, Elemental, Eozoon, Evolué, Feather-star, Fundamental, Hunter-gatherer, Medi(a)eval, Naive, Neanderthal, Neolithic, Oidia, Old, Persian, Prim(a)eval, Primordial, Pro, Prothyl(e), Protomorphic, Protyl(e), Radical, Rudimentary, Savage, Subman, Turkish, Uncivilised, Ur, Zygote

Prince(ly) Albert, Amir, Arjuna, Black, Caliph, Charming, Crown, Donalbain, Elector, Emir, Florizel, Fortinbras, Ganymede, Gospodar, Hamlet, Highness, Igor, Jason, Ksar, Maharaja, Merchant, Noble, Orange, Pantagruel, Paris, Pirithous, Potentate, Rajah, Regal, Rudolph, Serene, Sherif, Student, Tereus, Troilus

Princess Anastasia, Begum, Di(ana), Grace, Helle, Infanta, Isabella, Medea, Palatine, Philomela, Rani, Sadie, Sara(h), Yseult

Principal Arch, Capital, Central, →CHIEF, Decuman, Especial, First, Foremost, Grand, Head, Headmaster, Leading, Lion's share, Main(stay), Major, Mass, Mistress, Protagonist, Ringleader, Special, Staple, Star, Top banana, Uppermost

Principle(s), Principled Accelerator, Animistic, Anthropic, Archimedes, Aufbau, Axiom, Basis, Bernouilli, Brocard, Canon, Carnot, Code, Contradiction, Correspondence, Cosmological, Credo, Creed, Criterion, Cui bono, Cy pres, Doctrine, Dogma, Element, Equivalence, Essential, Estoppel, Ethic, Exclusion, First, Fourier, Geist, Generale, Germ, Greatest happiness, Ground rule, Guideline, Hard line, Heisenberg uncertainty, Hinge, Honourable, Ideal, Indeterminacy, Key, Law, Least time, Lights, Logos, Methodology, Modus, Morality, Object soul, Occam's razor, Organon, Peter, Plank, Platform, Pleasure, Precautionary, Precept, Prescript, Psyche, Purseyism, Rationale, Reality, Reason, Reciprocity, Relativity, Remonstrance, Right-thinking, Rudiment, Rule (of three), Sanction, Scrupulous, Spirit, Standard, Tenet, Theorem, Ticket, Uncertainty, Uti possidetis, Verification, Vital, Weismannism, Word, Yang, Yin

Print(er), Printing A la poupée, Aldine, Baskerville, Batik, Calotype, Caxton, Chain, Chapel, Chromo, Cicero, Collotype, Compositor, Contact, Copperplate, Counter, Creed, Cyclostyle, Dab, Dot matrix, Duotone, Electrostatic, Electrothermal, Electrotint, Electrotype, Elzevir, Engrave, Etching, Ferrotype, Film set, Fine, Font, Gravure, Half-tone, Hard copy, Hectograph, Heliotype, HMSO, Image, Impact, Impress, India, Ink-jet, Intaglio, Italic, Jobbing, Laser, Letterpress, Letterset, Line, Line-engraving, Lino-cut, Lithograph, Logotype, Lower-case, Matrix, Metallographer, Mezzotint, Mimeograph®, Monotype®, Moon, Non-impact, Off-line, Offset, Offset litho, Old-face, Oleo, Oleograph, Opaline, Perfector, Perfect proof, Phototype, Plate, Platinotype, Positive, Press, Process, Publish, Release, Remarque, Report, Reproduction, Retroussage, Reverse, Rotogravure, Run off, Screen, Ship, Shout, Silk-screen, Small, Splash, Spore, Stamp, Stereotype, Stonehand, Strike, Thermal, Three-colour, Thumb, Thumb mark, Trichromatic, Typesetter, Typewriter, Typography, Typothetae, Whorl, Woodburytype, Woodcut, Xylograph

Prior(ity) Abbot, Afore, Antecedent, Earlier, Former, Grand, Hitherto, Monk, Outweigh, Overslaugh, Pre-, Precedence, Prefard, Preference, Previous, Privilege, Triage, Until

Prison Alcatraz, Bastille, Belmarsh, Big house, Bin, Bird, Boob, Bridewell, Brig, Brixton, Bullpen, Cage, Can, Carceral, Cell, Chok(e)y, Clink, Club, College,

Confine, Cooler, Coop, Counter, Dartmoor, Dispersal, Dungeon, Durance, Encage, Fleet, Fotheringhay, Gaol, Glass-house, Gulag, Hokey, Holloway, Hulk(s), Internment, →JAIL, Jug, Kitty, Labour camp, Limbo, Little-ease, Lock-up, Marshalsea, Mattamore, Maze, Newgate, Nick, Oflag, On ice, Open, Parkhurst, Pen, Penitentiary, Pentonville, Pit, Pok(e)y, Porridge, Pound, Princetown, Quad, Quod, Reformatory, Roundhouse, Scrubs, Shop, Sing-Sing, Slammer, Spandau, Stalag, State, Stir, Strangeways, Supermax, Tol(l)booth, Tower, Wandsworth, Wormwood Scrubs

Prisoner Canary-bird, Captive, Collegian, Collegiate, Con(vict), Detainee, Detenu, Inmate, Internee, Lag, Lifer, Parolee, Passman, Political, POW, Rule 43, Trustee, Trusty, Yardbird, Zek

Private(ly), Privacy Ain, Apart, Aside, Atkins, Auricular, Buccaneer, Byroom, Clandestine, Close, Closet, Confidential, Enisle(d), Entre nous, Esoteric, Homefelt, Hush-hush, In camera, Individual, Inmost, Inner, Intimate, Inward, Non-com, Non-governmental, Own, Personal, Piou-piou, Poilu, Postern, Proprietary, Pte, Rank(er), Retired, Retreat, Sanctum, Sapper, Secluded, Secret, Sequestered, Several, Single soldier, →SOLDIER, Sub rosa, Tommy, Under the rose

Privilege(d) Birthright, Blest, Charter, Curule, Enviable, Exempt, Favour, Franchise, Freedom, Haves, Indulgence, Letters patent, Liberty, Mozarab, Nomenklatura, Octroi, Palatine, Patent, Prerogative, Pryse, Regale, Regalia, Right, Sac, Sloane

Privy Apprised, Can, Close-stool, Closet, In on, Intimate, Jakes, John, Loo, Necessary, Reredorter, Secret, Sedge, Siege

Prize(s), Prizewinner, Prized Acquest, Acquisitive, Apple, Archibald, Assess, Award, Best, Booby, Booker, Bravie, Bronze, Capture, Champion, Cherish, Consolation, Creach, Cup, Dux, Efforce, →ESTEEM, Force, Garland, Gold, Goncourt, Grice, Honour, Jackpot, Jemmy, Lever, Loot, Lot, Man Booker, Money, Nobel, Palm, Pay out, Pearl, Pewter, Pie, Plum, Plunder, Pot, Premium, Prix Goncourt, Pulitzer, Purse, Ram, Reprisal, →REWARD, Rollover, Rosette, Russell, Scalp, Ship, Silver, Spreaghery, Sprechery, Stakes, Sweepstake, Tern, Treasure, Trophy, Turner, Value, Win, Wooden spoon

Pro Aye, Coach, For, Harlot, Moll, Paid, Tramp, Yea, Yes

▶**Pro** *see* **PROSTITUTE**

Probable, Probability Apparent, Belike, Classical, Enthymeme, Ergodic, Feasible, Likely, Possible, Prior, Proball

Probe Antenna, Bore, Cassini, Delve, Dredge, Examine, Explore, Fathom, Feeler, Fossick, Gene(tic), Inquire, Investigate, Otoscope, Palpitate, Pelican, Poke, Pump, Ranger, →SEARCH, Seeker, Sound, Space, Stylet, Tent, Thrust, Tracer

Problem(s), Problematic Acrostic, Anuria, Black spot, Boyg, Brainteaser, Business, Can of worms, Catch, Challenge, Conundrum, Crux, Difficulty, Dilemma, Egma, Enigma, Facer, Fault, Glitch, Hang-up, Hassle, Headache, Hiccup, Hitch, How d'ye do, Hurdle, Indaba, Issue, Knot(ty), Koan, Mind-body, Miniature, Musive, Mystery, Net, Nuisance, Obstacle, Pons asinorum, Poser, Predicament, Quandary, Question, Re, Rebus, Retractor, Riddle, Rider, Snag, Snarl-up, Sorites, Stimy, Sum, Teaser, Teething, Thing, Thorny, Tickler, Toughie, Trilemma, Tsuris, Weed, Yips

Proceed(s), Proceeding, Procedure Acta, Afoot, Algorithm, Assets, Case, Continue, Course, Derive, Drift, Drill, Emanate, Fand, Firedrill, Flow, Fond, Form, Goes, Haul, Heimlich, Issue, Machinery, March, Mechanics, Mine, MO,

Modal, Move, On (course), Paracentesis, Pass, Point of order, Practice, Praxis, Process, Profit, Punctilio, Pursue, Put, Rake, Receipts, Return, Rigmarole, Rite, Rope(s), Routine, Sap, Steps, Subroutine, System, Take, Tootle, Use, Yead(s), Yede, Yeed

Process(ing), Procession, Processor Acromion, Action, Ala, Ambarvalia, Anger, Axon, Ben Day, Bessemer, Calcination, Catalysis, Cibation, Coction, Concoction, Congelation, Conjunction, Corso, Cortège, DAP, Demo, Dissolution, Double, Exaltation, Exequy, Fermentation, Frack(ing), Haber(-Bosch), Handle, Markov, Method, Moharram, Mond, Motorcade, Muharram, Multiple pounding, Multiplication, Number-crunch, Olecranon, Open hearth, Operation, Pageant, Parade, Paseo, Photosynthesis, Pipeline, Pomp, Projection, Pterygoid, Puddling, Pultrusion, Purex, Putrefaction, Recycle, Ritual, Separation, Series, Single, Skimmington, Solvay, Speciation, Spinous, String, Sublimation, Tie and dye, Titration, Train, Transaction, Transverse, Treat, Trial, Vermiform, Xephisternum

Proclaim, Proclamation Announce, Annunciate, Ban, Blaze, Blazon, Boast, Broadsheet, Cry, Decree, Edict, Enounce, Enunciate, Herald, Indiction, Kerygma, Manifesto, Oyez, Preconise, Profess, Publish, Ring, Shout, Trumpet, Ukase

Prodigious, Prodigy Abnormal, Amazing, Huge, Immense, Little wonder, Monster, Monument, Mozart, Phenomenal, Portentous, Tremendous, Wonder, Wonderwork, Wunderkind

Produce(r), Producing Afford, Bear, Beget, Breed, Cause, Create, Crop, De Mille, Disney, D'Oyly Carte, Dramaturg, Ean, Edit, Effect, Engender, Entail, Evoke, Exhibit, Extend, Fabricate, Fruit, Generate, Get, Giulini, Goldwyn, Grow, Impresario, Ingenerate, Issue, Kind, Make, Offspring, Onstream, Originate, Output, Outturn, Propage, Propound, Puttnam, Raise, Realise, Roach, Selznick, Sloganeer, Son, Spielberg, Stage, Supply, Teem, Throw, Tree, Trot out, Upcome, Wares, Whelp, Yield, Zeffirelli, Ziegfeld

▷**Produces** *may indicate* an anagram

Product(ion), Productive(ness), Productivity Actualities, Apport, Artefact, Ashtareth, Ashtaroth, Astarte, Autogeny, Bore, Cartesian, Coefficient, Commodity, Creation, Cross, Depside, Dot, Drama, Effectual, End, Factorial, Fecund, Fertile, Fruit, Genesis, Global, Handiwork, Harvest, Inner, Line, Mass, Net domestic, Net national, Output, Outturn, Pair, Partial, Pastiche, Power(house), Primary, Prolific, Resinoid, Result, Rich, Scalar, Secondary, Set, Show, Speiss, Substitution, Uberous, Uberty, Vector, Waste, Work, Yield

▷**Production** *may indicate* an anagram

Profane, Profanation, Profanity Blaspheming, Coarse, Coprolalia, Desecrate, Impious, Irreverent, Sacrilege, Unholy, Violate

Profess(ed), Professor Absent-minded, Academic, Acknowledge, Adjoint, Admit, Artist, Aspro, Asset, Assistant, Associate, Challenger, Claim, Declare, Disney, Emeritus, Full, Higgins, Hodja, Kho(d)ja, Know-all, Ostensible, Own, Practise, Pundit, Regent, Regius, RP, STP

Profession(al) Accomplished, Admission, Assurance, Avowal, Buppy, Business, Calling, Career, Creed, Expert, Métier, Practice, Practitioner, Pretence, Pursuit, Regular, Salaried, Skilled, Trade, Vocation, Yuppie

Proficiency, Proficient Accomplished, Adept, Alert, Dan, Expert, Forte, Master, Past master, Practised, Skill, Technique

Profile Analysis, Contour, Half-cheek, Half-face, High, Loral, Market, Outline, Silhouette, Sketch, Statant, T(h)alweg, Vignette

Profit(able), Profiteer, Profits Advantage, Arbitrage, Asset stripper, Avail, Benefit, Bestead, Boon, Boot, Bunce, Cash cow, Cash in, Cere, Clear, Divi(dend), Earn, Economic, Edge, Emblements, Emoluments, Expedient, Exploit, Extortionist, Fat, Fruitful, Gain, Gelt, Graft, Gravy, Grist, Gross, Income, Increase, Increment, In pocket, Issue, Jobbery, Juicy, Landshark, Leech, Lucrative, Makings, Margin, Melon, Mesne, Milch cow, Mileage, Moneymaker, Money-spinner, Negative, Net, Overcharge, Pay(ing), Pay (off), Perk, Pickings, Plummy, Preacquisition, Productive, Quids in, Rake-off, Return, Reward, Royalty, Scalp, Spoils, Tout, Use, Usufruct, Utile, Utility, Vail, Windfall

Profuse, Profusion Abounding, Abundant, Copious, Excess, Free, Galore, Lavish, Liberal, Lush, Quantity, Rank, Rich, Two-a-penny

▶**Program(ming), Programming language, Programmer** *see* **COMPUTER PROGRAM(S)**

Programme(s) Agenda, Broadcast, Card, Chat show, Code, Community, Corrida, Countdown, Docudrama, Documentary, Docusoap, Docutainment, Double-header, Dramedy, Entitlement, Episode, Est, Event, Faction, Feature, Fly-on-the-wall, Format, Infotainment, Linear, Live show, Mastermind, Medicaid, Miniseries, Minisode, Mockumentary, Neighbours, Neurolinguistic, Newscast, Newsreel, PDL, Phone-in, Pilot, Plan, Playbill, Prank, Race card, Radiothon, RECHAR, Regimen, Report, Satellite, Schedule, Scheme, Sepmag, Serial, Shockumentary, Show, Simulcast, Sitcom, Sked, Soap, Software, Sportscast, Sustaining, Syllabus, System, Telecast, Teleplay, Telethon, Timetable, Twelve step, Webcast, YPO

Progress(ive), Progression →**ADVANCE**, Afoot, Arithmetic, Arpeggio, Avant garde, Course, Endosmometric, Fabian, Flow, Forge, Forward, Gain, Geometric, Get along, Go (ahead), Growth, Headway, Incede, Inroads, Knight's, Left, Leftist, Liberal, Move, Onwards, Paraphonia, Periegesis, Pilgrim's, Prosper, Rack, Radical, Rake's, Reformer, Roll, Run, Sequence, Series, Step, Stepping stone, Vaunce, Way, Yead, Yede, Yeed

Prohibit(ed), Prohibition(ist) Ban, Block, Debar, Dry, Embargo, Enjoin, Estop, Forbid, Hinder, Index, Injunct, Interdict, Noli-me-tangere, Off-limits, Preclude, Prevent, Pussyfoot, Rahui, Suppress, Taboo, Tabu, Verboten, Veto

Project(ile), Projecting, Projection, Projector Aim, Ammo, Antitragus, Assignment, Astral, Astrut, Axonometric, Azimuthal, Baby, Ball, Ballistic, Beetle, Bullet, Butt, Buttress, Cam, Canopy, Carina, Cast, Catapult, Channel, Cinerama®, Cog, Conceive, Conical, Console, Cremaster, Dendron, Discus, Ear, Eaves, Enterprise, Epidiascope, Episcope, Excrescence, Exsert, Extrapolate, Extrude, Fet(ter)lock, Flange, Gore, Grapeshot, Guess, Halter(e), Hangover, Helicity, Hoe, Homolosine, Housing, Human genome, Hurtle, Inion, Jut, Kern, Kinetoscope, Knob, Ledge, Lobe, Lug, Magic lantern, Map, Mohole, Mucro, Nab, Nose, Oblique, Opaque, Orthogonal, Orthographic, Outcrop, Outjet, Outjut, Outrigger, Outshot, Overhang, Overhead, Oversail, Palmation, Peak, Peters', Pitch, Planetarium, Planisphere, Prickle, Promontory, Prong, Propel, Proud(er), Prow, Pseudopod, Quillon, Roach, Rocket, Sail, Salient, Sally, Sanson-Flamsteed, Scheme, Scrag, Screen, Shelf, Shot, Shrapnel, Sinusoidal, Skeg, Slide, Sling, Snag, Snout, Spur, Stand out, Stick out, Stud, Tang, Tappet, Tenon, Thorn, Throw, Toe, Tongue, Tracer, Trimetric, Trippet, Turnkey, Turtleback, Tusk, Umbo, Underhung, Undertaking, Villiform, Whizzbang, Zenithal

Prolong(ed) Continue, Drag out, Extend, Lengthen, Persistent, Protract, Sostenuto, Spin, Sustain

Prom(enade) Alameda, Boulevard, Cakewalk, Catwalk, Concert, Crush-room, Esplanade, Front, Mall, Parade, Paseo, Pier, Sea-front, Stroll, →**WALK**

Prominence, Prominent Antitragus, Blatant, Bold, Colliculus, Condyle, Conspicuous, Egregious, Emphasis, Featured, Gonion, Headliner, High profile, Important, Insistent, Leading light, Luminary, Manifest, Marked, Mastoid, Noted, Obtrusive, Outstanding, Salient, Signal, Solar, Splash, Spotlight, Tall poppy, Teat, Toot, Tragus

Promise, Promising Accept, Agree, Assure, Augur, Auspicious, Avoure, Behest, Behight, Behote, Betrothal, Bode, Bright, Coming, Commit, Compact, Covenant, Earnest, Engagement, Foreshadow, Foretaste, Gratuitous, Guarantee, Hecht, Hest, Hete, Hight, IOU, Likely, Manifest, Oath, Parole, Pledge, Plight, Pollicitation, Potential, Pregnant, Recognisance, Recognizance, Resolution, Rosy, Sign, Sponsor, Swear, Tile, Troth, Undertake, Upbeat, Vow, Warranty, Word

Promote(r), Promotion Ad, Adman, Advance, Advancement, →**ADVERTISE**, Advocate, Aggrandise, Aid, Assist, Back, Banner ad, Blurb, Boost, Breed, Brevet, Buggins' turn, Campaign, Churn, Dog and pony show, Elevate, Encourage, Eulogy, Event, Exponent, Float, Foment, Foster, Further, Help, Hype, Incite, Increase, Kick upstairs, Leaflet, Lord of Misrule, Mailshot, Make, Market, Peddle, Plug, Pracharak, Prefer, Prelation, Promulgate, Provoke, Push, Queen, Raise, Rear, Remove, Roadshow, Run, Salutary, Sell, Sponsor, Spruik, Stage, Step (up), Subserve, Tendencious, Tendentious, Tout, Upgrade, Uplead, Uprate

Prompt(er), Promptly, Promptness Accelerate, Actuate, Alacrity, Autocue®, Believe, Cause, Celerity, Chop-chop, Cue, Early, Egg, Expeditious, Feed, Frack, Idiot-board, Immediate, Incite, Inspire, Instigate, Motivate, Move, Pernicious, Post-it note, Premove, Punctual, Quick, Ready, Sharp, Speed(y), Spur, Stage right, Stimulate, Stir, Sudden, Swift, Tight, Tit(e), Titely, Trigger, Tyte, Urgent

Prone Apt, Groof, Grouf, Grovel, Laid back, Liable, Lying, Prostrate, Recumbent, Subject, Susceptible

Pronounce(d), Pronouncement Adjudicate, Affirm, Agrapha, Articulate, Assert, Asseveration, Clear, Conspicuous, Declare, Definite, Dictum, Emphatic, Enunciate, Fatwa, Fiat, Indefinite, Marked, Opinion, Palatalise, Philosophise, Pontificate, Predication, Recite, Utter, Velarise, Vocal, Voice, Vote

Proof(s) Acid test, Apagoge, Argument, Artist's, Assay, Bona fides, Confirmation, Corroboration, Direct, Evidence, Firm, Foundry, Galley, Godel's, India, Indirect, Justification, Lemma, Positive, Preif(e), Probate, Pull, Quality, Receipt, Refutation, Remarque, Reproduction, Resistant, Revision, Secure, Slip, Smoking gun, Strength, Test, Tight, Token, Trial, Upmake, Validity, Watertight

Prop(s) Airscrew, Becket, Bolster, Buttress, Crutch, Dog-shore, Fulcrum, Leg, Loosehead, Misericord(e), Punch(eon), Rance, Rest, Scotch, Set, Shore, Sprag, Spur, Staff, Stay, Stempel, Stemple, Stilt, Stoop, Stoup, Strut, Stull, →**SUPPORT**, Tighthead, Underpin

Propaganda, Propagandist Agitprop, Ballyhoo, Brainwashing, Chevalier, Doctrine, Promotion, Psyop, Psywar, Publicity, Slogan

Propel(ler), Propellor Airscrew, Ca', Drive, Fin, Fling, Launch, Leg, Lox, →**MOVE**, Oar(sman), Paddle, Pedal, Pole, Project, Push, Rotor, Row, Screw, Send, Tail rotor, Throw, Thruster, Tilt-rotor, Tractor, Twin-screw, Vane

Proper(ly) Ain, Convenance, Correct, Courteous, Decent, Decorous, Due, Eigen, En règle, Ethical, →**FIT**, Genteel, Governessy, Kosher, Legitimate, Maidenish,

Nimity-pimity, Noun, Ought, Own, Pakka, Pathan, Prim, Pucka, Pukka, Puritanic, Real, Rightful, Seemly, Staid, Strait-laced, Suitable, Tao, Trew, True, Veritable, Well

Property, Properties Assets, Attribute, Aver, Belongings, Capacitance, Chattel, Chirality, Chose, Contenement, Dead-hand, Demesne, Des res, Dowry, Effects, Enclave, Enthalpy, Escheat, Escrow, Essence, Estate, Fee, Feu, Flavour, Fonds, Freehold, Goods, Haecceity, Hereditament, Heritable, Holding, Home, Hot, Hotchpot, Immoveable, Inertia, In rem, Intellectual, Jointure, Land, Leasehold, Living, Means, Mortmain, Mystique, Paraphernalia, Peculium, Personal, Personalty, Pertinent, Predicate, Premises, Private, Projective, Public, Quale, Quality, Realty, Second home, Settlement, Stock, Stolen, Theft, Thixotropy, Time-share, Timocracy, Trait, Usucapion, Usucaption

Prophesy, Prophecy, Prophesying, Prophet(s), Prophetess, Prophetic Amos, Augur, Bab, Balaam, Cassandra, Clairvoyant, Daniel, Deborah, Divine, Elias, Elijah, Elisha, Ezekiel, Ezra, Fatal, Forecast, Foretell, Haruspex, Hosea, Is, Isa, Is(a)iah, Jeremiah, Joel, Jonah, Mahdi, Major, Malachi, Mani, Mantic, Micah, Minor, Mohamet, Mohammed, Mormon, Moses, Mother Shipton, Nahum, Nathan, Necromancy, Nostradamus, Obadiah, Ominous, Oracle, Portend, Predictor, Prognosticate, Pythoness, Samuel, Second sight, Seer, Sibyl, Weather, Zephaniah, Zoroaster

Proportion(ate) Commensurable, Cotangent, Dimension, Fraction, Harmonic, Percentage, Portion, Pro rata, Quantity, Quota, Ratio, Reason, Regulate, Relation, Sine, Size, Soum, Sowm, Symmetry, Tenor

Propose(r), Proposal Advance, Advocate, Aim at, Approach, Ask, Bid, Bill, Eirenicon, Feeler, Fiancé, Idea, Irenicon, Mean, Motion, Move, Nominate, Offer, Overture, Plan, Pop, Premise, Proffer, Propound, Recommend, Resolution, Scheme, Slate, Submission, **→ SUGGEST**, Table, Tender, Toast, Volunteer, Woot, Would

Proposition Axiom, Corollary, Deal, Disjunction, Ergo, Hypothesis, Implicature, Lemma, Overture, Pons asinorum, Porism, Premise, Premiss, Rider, Sorites, Spec, Superaltern, Theorem, Thesis

Proprietor, Propriety Bienséance, Convenance, Correctitude, Decorum, Etiquette, Grundy, Keeper, Lord, Master, Owner, Patron, Rectitude

Prose, Prosy Haikai, Polyphonic, Purple patch, Saga, Stich, Verbose, Version, Writing

Prosecute, Prosecutor, Prosecution Allege, Arraign, Avvogadore, Charge, Crown, Do, Double jeopardy, Fiscal, Furtherance, Impeach, Indict, Lord Advocate, Practise, Public, Pursue, Sue, Wage

Prospect(or), Prospecting Costean, Dowser, Explore, Forty-niner, Fossick, Future, Look-out, Mine, **→ OUTLOOK**, Panorama, Perspective, Pleases, Reefer, Scenery, Search, Sourdough, Street, Sweep-washer, View, Vista, Visto, Wildcatter

Prosper(ity), Prospering, Prosperous Aisha, Ay(e)sha, Blessed, Blossom, Boom, Do well, Fair, Fat cat, Flourish, Get ahead, Heyday, Mérimée, Opulent, Palmy, Sleek, **→ SUCCEED**, Thee, Thrift, Thrive, Up, Warison, Wealth, Welfare, Well-heeled, Well-to-do, Well-to-live

Prostitute, Prostitution Brass, Broad, Catamite, Chippie, Cocotte, Comfort woman, Convertite, Debase, Dell, Dolly-mop, Doxy, Drab, Floozie, Floozy, Grande cocotte, Harlot, Hetaera, Hetaira, Hostess, Hustler, Jailbait, Laced mutton, Lady of the night, Loon, Loose woman, Lowne, Madam, Magdalen(e),

Moll, Mutton, Pict, Poule, Pro, Public woman, Pug, Rent-boy, Rough trade, Scrubber, Slap, Stale, Stew, Streetwalker, Strumpet, Tart, Tramp, Trull, Whore, Working girl

Protect(ed), Protection, Protective, Protector Adonise, Aegis, Aircover, Amulet, Antigropelo(e)s, Arm, Armour, Asylum, Auspice, Barbican, Bastion, Bodyguard, Boom, Brolly, Buckler, Bullbar, Bullet-proof, Cathodic, Chaffron, Chain mail, Chamfrain, Chamfron, Charm, Cherish, Cloche, Coat, Cocoon, Coddle, Conserve, Copyright, Cosset, Cover, Covert, Crash helmet, Cromwell, Curb, Cushion, Danegeld, Data, Defend, Defilade, Diaper, Egis, Enamel, Entrenchment, Escort, Featherbed, Fence, Fender, Firewall, Flank, Goggle, Grill(e), Groundsheet, Guard(ian), Gumshield, Hedge, House, Hurter, Immune, Indemnify, Indemnity, Indusium, Insulate, Insure, Integument, Keep, Kickback, Klendusic, Kneepad, Lag, Lee, Listed, Mac(k)intosh, Mail, Male, Mentor, Mollycoddle, Mother, Mothproof, Mouthpiece, Mudguard, Nannyish, Napkin, Nappy, Noddy suit, Noll, Nosey, Oliver, Ombrella, Overall, Pad, Palladium, Parados, Parapet, Patent, Patron, Pelta, Penthouse, Police, Polytunnel, Pomander, Preserve, Procrypsis, Rampart, Raymond, Reserve, Revetment, Ride shotgun, Sacrosanct, Safeguard, Sandbag, Save, Screen, Scug, Security, Serviette, Shadow, Sheathing, Sheeting, Shelter, →**SHIELD**, Skug, Souteneur, Splashback, Splashboard, Splasher, Starling, Stockade, Sunscreen, Sunshade, Supermax, Talisman, Telomere, Testa, Testudo, Thimble, Thumbstall, Tower, Tribune, Tribute, Tutelar, Twilled, Umbrella, Underlay, Underseal, Vaccine, Waist-cloth, Ward(ship), Weatherboard, Weatherproof, Weatherstrip, Windbreaker, Windshield, Winterweight, Write

Protein Complement, Conjugated, Repressor, Simple

Protest(er) Abhor, Anti, Aver, Avouch, Boycott, Clamour, Come, Complaint, Démarche, Demo, Demonstrate, Demur, Deprecate, Dhurna, Dissent, Expostulate, Fulminate, Gripe, Hartal, Inveigh, I say, Lady Godiva, Lock-out, Luddite, March, Object, Outcry, Peenge, Picket, Plea, Rail, Refus(e)nik, Remonstrate, Representation, Riot, Sit-in, Squawk, Squeak, Squeal, Stand, Work-to-rule

Protestant Amish, Anabaptist, Anglo, Arminian, Calvin, Congregationalism, Covenanter, Cranmer, Dissenter, Evangelic, Gospeller, Huguenot, Independent, Lady, Lutheran, Mennonite, Methodist, Moravian, Nonconformist, Oak-boy, Orangeman, Pentecostal, Pietism, Prod(die), Puritan, Reformed, Right-footer, Seventh Day Adventist, Stundist, Swaddler, Waldensian, Wesleyan

Protract(ed) Delay, →**EXTEND**, Lengthen, Livelong, Long, Prolong

Proud Arrogant, Boaster, Cocky, Conceited, Dic(k)ty, Egotistic, Elated, Flush, Haughty, Haut, Jutting, Level, Lordly, Orgulous, Outstanding, Superb, Vain

Prove(d), Proving Apod(e)ictic, Argue, Ascertain, Assay, Attest, Attribution, Authenticate, Aver, Confirm, Convince, Establish, Evince, Justify, Probative, →**PROOF**, →**SHOW**, Substantiate, Test, Trie, Try, Turn out

Proverb Adage, Axiom, Byword, Gnome, Maxim, Paroemia, Saw

▷**Proverbial** *may refer to* the biblical Proverbs

Provide(d), Provident(ial) Afford, Allow, Arrange, Besee, Bring, Cater, Compare, Conditional, Endow, Endue, Equip, Far-seeing, Feed, Fend, Find, Furnish, Generate, Give, Grubstake, If, Lay on, Lend, Maintain, Offer, Plenish, Proviso, Purvey, Quote, Render, Serve, So, Sobeit, →**SUPPLY**, Suttle

Province, Provincial(ism) Area, Circar, Countrified, County, District, Exclave, Land, Nomarchy, Nomos, Regional, Sirkar, Small-town, Suburban, Territory

Provision(s), Provisional Acates, Ap(p)anage, Board, Budget, Contingency, Cover(age), Endowment, Entrenched, Fodder, Foresight, Groceries, Insolvency, Jointure, Larder, Lend-lease, Mart, Proggins, Scran, Skran, Stock, Stuff, Supply, Suttle, Viands, Viaticum, Victuals

Proviso, Provisional Caution, Caveat, Clause, Condition, Interim, Interlocutory, IRA, Makeshift, Nisi, On trial, Reservation, Salvo, Stipulation, Temporary, Tentative

Provocation, Provocative, Provoke Agacant, Aggro, Alluring, Anger, Bait, Challenge, Egg, Elicit, Erotic, Exacerbate, Excite, Flirty, Gar, Goad, Harass, Impassion, Incense, Incite, Incur, Induce, Inflame, Instigate, In yer face, Irk, Irritate, Kindle, Needle, Nettle, Occasion, Pique, Prompt, Raise, Red rag, Sedition, Sound, Spark, Stimulate, Stir, Sultry, Tantalise, Tar, Tarty, Tease, Urge, Vex, Wind up

Prowl(er) Hunt, Lurch, Lurk, Mooch, Prog, Prole, Ramble, Roam, Rove, Snoke, Snook, Snowk, Tenebrio, Tom

Proxy Agent, Attorn, Deputy, PP, Regent, Sub, Surrogate, Vicar, Vice

Prude(nce), Prudent, Prudery, Prudish Bluenose, Canny, Caution, Circumspect, Comstocker, Conservative, Discreet, Discretion, Economy, Far-sighted, Foresight, Frugal, Grundyism, Metis, Mimsy, Mrs Grundy, Politic, Prig, Prissy, Provident, Restrained, Sage, Sensible, Sparing, Strait-laced, Strait-lacer, Thrifty, Vice-nelly, Victorian, Ware, Wary, Well-advised, Wise

Prune(r) Bill-hook, Clip, Dehorn, Lop, Plum, Proign, Proin(e), Reduce, Reform, Secateur, Slash, Sned, Snip, Thin, Trim

Pry Ferret, Force, Lever, Meddle, Nose, Paul, Peep, Question, Search, Snoop

Psalm Anthem, Cantate, Chant, Chorale, Hallel, Hymn, Introit, Jubilate, Metrical, Miserere, Neck-verse, Paean, Proper, Ps, Song, Tone, Tract, Tractus, Venite

Pseudonym Aka, Alias, Allonym, Anonym, Pen-name, Stage-name

Psychiatrist, Psychologist Adler, Alienist, Asperger, Clare, Coué, Ellis, Freud, Headshrinker, Jung, Kraft-Ebing, Laing, Müller-Lyer, Reich, Shrink, Skinner, Trick-cyclist

Psychic, Psychosis Clairvoyant, ESP, Fey, Lodge, Medium, Mind-reader, Seer, Telekinesis

Psychological, Psychology, Psychologist Analytical, Behaviourism, Binet, Clinical, Comparative, Constitutional, De Bono, Depth, Development, Dynamic, Educational, Experimental, Eysenck, Gestalt, Hedonics, Humanistic, Industrial, James, Latah, Occupational, Organisational, Piaget, Skinner, Social, Structural, Windt

Psychotherapist, Psychotherapy Coué, Laing, Rebirthing, Shen

Pub(lic) house Bar, Boozer, Brew, Free-house, Gin-palace, Groggery, Hostelry, Houf(f), House, Howf(f), Inn, Joint, Local, Lush-house, PH, Pothouse, Potshop, Roadhouse, Shanty, Tavern, Tiddlywink, Tied house, Watering-hole

Public Apert, Audience, Civil(ian), Common, Demos, Estate, General, Great unwashed, Janata, Lay, Limelight, National, Open, Out, Overt, Populace, State, Vulgar, World

Publican Ale-keeper, Bung, Host, Landlord, Licensee, Tapster, Taverner

Publication Announcement, Book, Booklet, Broadsheet, Edition, Exposé, E-zine, Issue, →**JOURNAL**, Lady, Mag, Magazine, Organ, Pamphlet, Pictorial, Red-top, Samizdat, Tabloid, Tatler, Tract, Tribune, Weekly, Yearbook

Publicise, Publicist, Publicity Ad(vert), Airing, Announce, Ballyhoo, Billing, Build up, Coverage, Declassify, Exposure, Flack, Glare, Headline, Hype, Leakage,

Limelight, Notoriety, Photocall, Plug, PR(O), Promo(te), Promotion, Promulgate, Propaganda, Réclame, Spin-doctor, Splash

Publish(er), Published, Publishing, Publicise Air, Blaze, Cape, Copyleft, Delator, Desktop, Disclose, Edit, Evulgate, Issue, Larousse, Noise, OUP, Out, Pirate, Plug, Post, Print(er), Proclaim, Propagate, Release, Ren, Run, Stationer, Vanity, Vent, Ventilate

Pudding Afters, Black, Blancmange, Bread (and butter), Brown Betty, Cabinet, Charlotte, Christmas, Clootie dumpling, College, Crumble, Custard, →**DESSERT**, Dog's body, Duff, Dumpling, Eve's, Flummery, Fool, Fritter, Fromenty, Frumenty, Furme(n)ty, Furmity, Haggis, Hasty, Ice-cream, Lokshen, Milk, Nesselrode, Panada, Pandowdy, Panna cotta, Parfait, Pease, Plum, Plum-duff, Pockmanky, Pockmantic, Pock-pudding, Popover, Portmanteau, Queen's, Rice, Roly-poly, Savarin, Sowens, Sponge, Spotted dick, Spotted dog, Stickjaw, Stodge, Suet, Summer, Sundae, Sweet, Tansy, Tapioca, Umbles, White, White hass, White hause, White hawse, Yorkshire, Zabaglione

Puff(ed), Puffer, Puffy Advertise, Bellows, Bloat, Blouse, Blow, Blowfish, Blurb, Bouffant, Breath, Chuff, Chug, Cream, Drag, Encomist, Eulogy, Exsufflicate, Fag, Flaff, Flatus, Fluffy, Fuff, Globe-fish, Grampus, Gust, Hype, Lunt, Pech, Pegh, Pluffy, Plug, Powder, Quilt, Recommend, Skiff, Slogan, Smoke, Steam, Swell, Toke, Twilt, Waff, Waft, Waif, Whiff, Whiffle

Pull (up), Pull out Adduce, Attraction, Charm, Crane, Cry off, Demand, Drag, Draw, Force, Gravity, Haul, Heave, Heeze, Hoist, Hook, →**INFLUENCE**, Lug, Mousle, Pluck, Pop-top, Rein, Ring, Rove, Row, Rug, Saccade, Sally, Seduce, Snatch, Sole, Sool(e), Sowl(e), Stop, Tit, Touse, Touze, Tow, Towse, Towze, Traction, Trice, Tug, Undertow, Withdraw, Wrench, Wrest, Yank

Pulp Cellulose, Chyme, Chymify, Crush, Flong, Kenaf, Marrow, Mash, Mush, Pap, Paste, Pomace, Pound, Puree, Rot, Rubbish, Squeeze, Squidge

Pulpit Ambo(nes), Bully, Lectern, Mimbar, Pew, Rostrum, Tent, Tub, Wood

Pulse Adsuki, Adzuki, Alfalfa, Beat, Calavance, Caravance, Chickpea, Daal, D(h)al, Dholl, Dicrotic, Fava (bean), Garbanzo, Gram, Groundnut, Heartbeat, Ictus, Lentil, Lucerne, Pea, Rhythm, Sain(t)foin, Snow pea, Soy beans, Sphygmic, Sync, Systaltic, Systole, Throb

▷**Pummelled** *may indicate* an anagram

Pump(ing) Aerator, Air, Bellows, Bicycle, Bilge, Bowser, Breast, Centrifugal, Chain, Compressor, Cross-examine, Cross-question, Diaphragm, Donkey, Drive, Electromagnetic, Elicit, Feed, Filter, Foot, Force, Fork, Geissler, Grease-gun, Grill, Heart, Heat, Hydropult, Inflate, Interrogate, Knee-swell, Lift, Monkey, Mud, Nodding-donkey, Optical, Parish, Petrol, Piston, Pulsometer, Question, Quiz, Rotary, Scavenge, Shoe, Sodium, Stirrup, Stomach, Suction, Turbine, Vacuum, Water, Wind

Pun Calembour, Clinch, Equivoque, Jeu de mots, Paragram, Paronomasia, Quibble, Quip, Ram

Punch(ed) Bell, Biff, Blow, Box, Bradawl, Card, Centre, Chad, Check, Chin, Chop, Clip, Cobbler's, Conk, Cross, Dong, Fist(ic), Fourpenny one, Gang, Haymaker, Hit, Hook, Horse, Jab, Key, Kidney, Knevell, Knobble, Knubble, KO, Lam, Lander, Milk, Nevel, One-er, One-two, Overhand, Perforate, Planter's, Plug, Poke, Polt, Pommel, Pounce, Prod, Pummel, Puppet, Rabbit, Roundhouse, Rum, Sangria, Slosh, Sock, Steed, Sting(o), Stoush, Stunner, Suffolk, Tape, Upper-cut, Wap, Wind, Zest

Punctuate, Punctuation (mark) Bracket, Colon, Comma, Em-dash, Emphasize, Em-rule, Hyphen, Interabang, Interrobang, Interrupt, Mark, Semicolon, Tittle

Puncture(d) Bore, Centesis, Criblé, Cribrate, Deflate, Drill, Flat, Hole, Lance, Lumbar, Pearse, Perforate, Pierce, Pounce, Prick, Thoracocentesis

Pungency, Pungent Acid, Acrid, Acrolein, Alum, Ammonia, Bite, Bitter, Caustic, Hot, Mordant, Nidorous, Piquant, Poignant, Point, Racy, Salt, Spice, Sting, Tangy, Witty

Punish(ment), Punished, Punishing Algates, Amerce, Baculine, Baffle, Bastinado, Beat, Birch, Bum rap, Cane, Cang, Capital, Cart, Castigate, Chasten, Chastise, Come-uppance, Corporal, Correct, Dam(nation), Defrock, Desert(s), Detention, →**DISCIPLINE**, Execution, Fatigue, Fine, Flog, Gate, Gauntlet, Gruel, Hellfire, Hiding, High jump, Hot seat, Imposition, Impot, Interdict, Jankers, Kang, Keelhaul, Knee-capping, Knout, Lambast(e), Leathering, Lines, Necklace, Nemesis, Pack-drill, Padre Pio, Pay out, Peine forte et dure, Penalise, Penance, Pensum, Perdition, Picket, Pillory, Pine, Rap, Red card, Reprisal, Retribution, Sanction, Scaffold, Scourge, Sentence, Serve out, Six of the best, Smack, Smite, Spank, Stick, Stocks, Stoning, Strafe, Strap, Strappado, Tar and feather, Thick-ear, Timber-mare, Toco, Toko, Torture, Treadmill, Trim, Trounce, Vice anglais, What for, Whip, Whirligig, Wild mare

▷**Punish** *may indicate* an anagram

Punt(er), Punting Antepost, Back, Bet, Gamble, Gondolier, Kent, Kick, Pound, Quant, Turfite

Pupil Abiturient, Academical, Adie's, Apple, Apprentice, Bluecoat, Boarder, Cadet, Catechumen, Daygirl, Disciple, Etonian, Eyeball, Fag, Follower, Greycoat, Gyte, Intake, Junior, L, Monitor, Prefect, Protégé(e), Scholar, Senior, Student, Tiro, Trainee, Tutee, Ward, Wykehamist

▷**Pupil** *may refer to* an eye

Puppet(s), Puppeteer Creature, Doll, Dummy, Fantoccini, Finger, Galanty show, Glove, Guignol, Judy, Marionette, Mawmet, Mommet, Motion generative, Pawn, Pinocchio, Punch(inello), Rod, Thunderbird, Tool

Purchase(r), Purchasing Acquisition, Bargain, Buy, Coff, Compulsory, Earn, Emption, End-user, Gadsden, Get, Grip, Halliard, Halyard, Hold, Layaway, →**LEVERAGE**, Louisiana, Money, Offshore, Oligopsony, Parbuckle, Perquisitor, Repeat, Secure, Shop, Toehold, Traction

Pure, Purist, Purity Absolute, Angelic, Cando(u)r, Cathy, Chaste, Chiarezza, Clean(ly), Cleanness, Cosher, Fine, Glenys, Good, Holy, Immaculate, Incorrupt, Innocent, Intemerate, Inviolate, Kathy, Kosher, Lily, Lilywhite, Maidenhood, Meer, Me(a)re, Net(t), Precisionist, Pristine, Quintessence, Refined, Sanctity, Sheer, Simon, Simple, Sincere, Snow-white, Snowy, Stainless, Sterile, Thoroughbred, True, Unalloyed, Unapplied, Undrossy, Virgin, Virtue, White

Purgative, Purge Aloes, Aryanise, Cascara, Castor-oil, Catharise, Catharsis, Comstockery, Delete, Detox, Drastic, Elaterium, Eliminate, Emetic, Erase, Evacuant, Expiate, Flux, Hydragogue, Ipecacuanha, Jalop, Laxative, Number nine, Physic, Pride's, Relaxant, Scur, Senna

Purification, Purifier, Purify(ing) Absolve, Bowdlerise, Catharsis, Clay, Clean(se), Depurate, Dialysis, Distil, Edulcorate, Eluent, Elution, Exalt, Expurgate, Filter, Fine, Gas-lime, Lustre, Lustrum, Osmosis, Refine, Retort, Reverse osmosis, Samskara, Sanctify, Sanitise, Scorify, Scrub, Smudging, Sublime, Try, Whiten

Puritan(ical) Ascetic, Bible belt, Bluenose, Browne, Cromwell, Digger(s), Ireton, Ironsides, Killjoy, Pi, Pilgrim, Precisian, Prig, Prude, Prynne, Roundhead, Seeker, Traskite, Waldenses, Wowser, Zealot

Purloin Abstract, Annex, Appropriate, Lift, Nab, Pilfer, Snaffle, Sneak, Steal

Purple Amaranthine, Amarantin(e), Amethyst, Aubergine, Burgundy, Cassius, Claret, Eminence, Fuchsia, Heather, Heliotrope, Hyacinthine, Indigo, Lavender, Lilac, Magenta, Mulberry, Pansy, Plum, Prune, Puce, Purpure, Royal, Violet

Purpose(ful) Advertent, Aim, Avail, Calculated, Cause, Cautel, Cross, Design, Errand, Ettle, Function, Goal, Here-to, Idea, → **INTENT**, Marrow, Mean(ing), Meant, Mint, Mission, Motive, Object, Plan, Point, Raison d'être, → **REASON**, Resolution, Resolve, Sake, Telic, Telos, Tenor, Use, View

Purse Ad crumenam, Bag, Bung, Caba, Clutch, Contract, Crease, Crumenal, Egg, Embouchure, Exchequer, Fisc, Fisk, Long Melford, Pocket, Prim, Privy, Prize, Pucker, Spleuchan, Sporran, Wallet, Whistle

▷**Pursed** *may indicate* one word within another

Pursue(r), Pursuing, Pursuit After, Alecto, Business, Chase, Chivvy, Course, Dog, Follow, Follow up, Harry, Hobby, Hot-trod, Hound, Hue and cry, Hunt, Line, Pastime, Practise, Proceed, Prosecute, Quest, Scouring, Stalk, Trivial

Push(er), Push in, Push out, Pushy Astrut, Barge, Birr, Boost, Brash, Buffet, Bunt, Ca', Detrude, Drive, Dunch, Edge, Effort, Elbow, Fire, Horn, Hustle, Hyper, Impulse, Invaginate, Jostle, Nose, Nudge, Nurdle, Obtrude, Offensive, Onrush, Pitchfork, Plod, Ply, Press, Promote, Propel, Railroad, Ram, Rush, Sell, Shog, Shoulder, Snoozle, Subtrude, Thrust, Urge

Put (off, on, out, up) Accommodate, Add, Alienate, Bet, Board, Cup, Daff, Defer, Dish, Do, Don, Douse, Implant, Impose, Include, Incommode, Inn, Lade, Launch, Lay, Locate, Lodge, Lump, Miff, Oust, Pit, Pitch, Place(d), Plonk, Set, Sheathe, Simulate, Sited, Smoor, Smore, Station, Stow, Temporise

Put down Abase, Degrade, Demean, Disparage, Floor, Humiliate, Land, Relegate, Repress, Reprime, Snuff, Write

▷**Put off** *may indicate* an anagram

Putty Glaziers', Jewellers', Mastic, Painters', Plasterers', Polishers'

Puzzle(r), Puzzled Acrostic, At a loss, Baffle, Bemuse, Bewilder, Brainteaser, Chinese, Confound, Confuse, Conundrum, Crossword, Crux, Crux medicorum, Egma, Elude, Enigma, Feague, Floor, Fox, Get, Glaik, Gravel, Intrigue, Jigsaw, Jumbo, Kakuro, Kittle, Logogriph, Magic pyramid, Maze, Mind-bender, Monkey, Mystery, Mystify, Nonplus, Perplex, Ponder, Pose(r), Rebus, Riddle, Rubik's Cube®, Sorites, Sphinx, Stick(l)er, Stump, Sudoku, Tangram, Teaser, Thematic, Tickler, Wordsearch, Wordsquare

Pyramid(s) Cheops, Chephren, Egyptology, Frustum, Magic, Stack, Teocalli

Qq

Quack Charlatan, Crocus, Dulcamara, Empiric, Fake, →**IMPOSTOR**, Katerfelto, Mountebank, Pretender, Saltimbanco

Quadrilateral Lambeth, Tetragon, Trapezium, Trapezoid

Quagmire Bog, Fen, Imbroglio, Marsh, Morass, Swamp, Wagmoire

Quail Asteria, Bevy, Bird, Blench, Bob-white, Button, Caille, Colin, Flinch, Harlot, Hen, Quake, Shrink, Tremble, Wince

Quaint Cute, Far(r)and, Farrant, Fie, Naive, Odd, Old-world, Picturesque, Strange, Twee, Wham, Whim(sy)

Quake(r), Quaking Aminadab, Broad-brim, Didder, Dither, Dodder, Fox, Friend, Fry, Hicksite, Obadiah, Palpitate, Penn, Quail, Seism, Shake(r), Shiver, →**TREMBLE**, Tremor, Trepid, Wamble

Qualification, Qualified, Qualify Able, Adapt, Adverb, Agrege, Alloy, But, Capacitate, Caveat, Competent, Condition, Credential, Degree, Diplomatic, Doctorate, Eligible, Entitle, Fit, Graduate, Habilitate, Higher Still, Meet, Moderate, Modifier, Nisi, Parenthetical, Pass, Past-master, Proviso, Quantify, Restrict, Temper, Versed

Quality Aroma, Attribute, Aura, Body, Calibre, Cast, Charisma, De luxe, Esse, Essence, Extra virgin, Fabric, Fame, First water, Five-star, Flavour, Grade, Inscape, Insight, It, Kite-mark, Letter, Long suit, Mystique, Nature, Phat, Pitch, Plus, Premium, Primary, Property, Q, Quale, Reception, Sanctitude, Savour, Sort, Standard, Stature, Style, Substance, Suchness, Terroir, Texture, Thew, Thisness, Timbre, Tone, Tophole, Top-notch, Total, Up-market, Vein, Vinosity, Virgin, Virtu(e), Water, Worth

Quantity →**AMOUNT**, Analog(ue), Batch, Bundle, Capacity, Deal, Dose, Feck, Fother, Hank, Heaps, Hundredweight, Idempotent, Intake, Jag, Lion's share, Loads, Lock, Lot, Mass, Measure, Melder, Multitude, Myriad, Niblet, Nip, Nonillion, Number, Ocean(s), Omnium, Operand, Output, Parameter, Parcel, Peck, Plenty, Posology, Pottle, Qs, Qt, Quire, Quota, Quotient, Radicand, Ream, Scalar, Slather, Slew, Slue, Sum, Surd, Tret, Unknown, Vector, Wad, Warp, Whips

Quarrel(some), Quarreler Altercate, Argue, Barney, Bate, Bicker, Brawl, Bust-up, Cantankerous, Cat and dog, Catfight, Clash, Contentious, Contretemps, Difference, Disagree, Dispute, Domestic, Dust-up, Fall out, Feisty, Feud, Fire-eater, Fracas, Fray, Hassle, Loggerheads, Miff, Pugnacious, Ruction, Squabble, Tangle, Tiff, Tile, Tink, Tweedledee, Tweedledum, Vendetta, Vitilitigation, Wrangle

Quarry, Quarry face Chalkpit, Currie, Curry, Game, Mark, Mine, Pit, Prey, Scabble, Scent, Stone pit, Victim

Quarter(ing), Quarters Airt, Barracks, Barrio, Billet, Camp, Canton(ment), Casbah, Casern(e), Chinatown, Chum, Clemency, Close, Coshery, District,

Dorm, E, Empty, Enclave, Fardel, Farl, First, Fo'c'sle, Forecastle, Forpet, Forpit, Fourth, Ghetto, Ham(s), Harbour, Haunch, Last, Latin, Medina, →MERCY, N, Note, Oda, Pity, Point, Principium, Quadrant, Region, S, Season, Sector, Tail, Trimester, Two bits, W, Wardroom, Warp, Winter

▷**Quarterdeck** *may indicate* a suit of cards

Quarto Crown, Demy, Foolscap, Imperial, Medium, Royal, Small

Quartz Adventurine, Agate, Amethyst, Bristol diamond, Buhrstone, Cacholong, Cairngorm, Chalcedony, Chert, Citrine, Crystal, Flint, Granophyre, Granulite, Itacolumite, Jasp(er), Love-arrow, Morion, Onyx, Plasma, Prase, Rainbow, Rose, Rubasse, Sapphire, Silex, Silica, Smoky, Spanish topaz, Stishovite, Tiger-eye, Tonalite, Whin Sill

Quash Abrogate, Annul, Nullify, Oppress, Quell, Rebut, Recant, Repress, Scotch, Subdue, Suppress, Terminate, Void

Quasimodo Bellringer, Gibbose, Hunchback

Quaver(ing) Shake, Trill, Vibrate, Warble

Quay Bund, Jetty, Landing, Levee, Staithe, Wharf

Queasy Delicate, Nauseous, Squeamish

Queen(ly) Adelaide, Alcestis, Alexandra, Anna, Anne, Artemesia, Atossa, Balkis, Beatrix, Beauty, Bee, Begum, Bess, Boadicea, Boudicca, Brun(n)hild(e), Camilla, Candace, Card, Caroline, Cat, Chesspiece, Christina, Cleopatra, Dido, Drag, Eleanor(a), Ellery, Esther, Gertrude, Guinevere, Harvest, Hatshepset, Hatshepsüt, Hecuba, Helen, Henrietta Maria, Hermione, Hippolyta, Isabel, Ishtar, Isolde, Jocasta, Juliana, Juno, Leda, Maam, Mab, Maeve, Margaret, Marie Antoinette, Mary (Tudor), Matilda, May, Monarch, Nefertiti, Omphale, Oriana, Pearly, Penelope, Persephone, Phaedra, Prom, Proserpina, Qu, R, Ranee, Regal, Regina(l), Semiramis, Sheba, Titania, Vashti, Victoria, Virgin

Queer(ness) Abnormal, Berdash, Bizarre, Crazy, Cure, Curious, Fey, Fie, Fifish, Fishy, Gay, →ODD, Outlandish, Peculiar, Pervert, Poorly, Quaint, Rum, Spoil, Uranism, Vert

Quench Assuage, Cool, Extinguish, Satisfy, Slake, Slo(c)ken, Sta(u)nch, Yslake

▶**Query** *see* QUESTION(ING)

Quest Goal, Graal, Grail, Hunt, Pursuit, Search, Venture, Vision

Question(ing), Questioner, Questionnaire Appose, Arraign, Ask, Bi-lateral, Burning, Catechise, Challenge, Chin, Consult, Contest, Conundrum, Cross-examine, Curious, Debrief, Dichotomous, Direct, Dispute, Dorothy Dixer, Doubt, Erotema, Eroteme, Erotesis, Examine, Fiscal, Good, Grill, Heckle, Homeric, Impeach, Impugn, Indirect, Information, Innit, Inquisitor, Interpellation, Interrogate, Interview, Investigate, Issue, Koan, Leading, Loaded, Maieutic, Matter, Open, Oppugn, Peradventure, Point of order, Pop, Pose, Previous, Probe, Problem, Pump, Q, Qu, Quaere, Quiz, Rapid-fire, Refute, Rhetorical, Riddle, Socratic method, Sound, Speer, Speir, Survey, Suspect, Tag, Teaser, Tickler, Vexed, West Lothian, WH, What, Worksheet

Queue Braid, Breadline, Cercus, Crocodile, Cue, Dog, File, →LINE, Line up, Pigtail, Plait, Plat, Tail(back), Track

Quibble(r), Quibbling Balk, Carp, Carriwitchet, Casuist, Cavil, Chicaner, Dodge, Elenchus, Equivocate, Haggle, Hairsplitting, Nitpick, Pedantry, Pettifoggery, Prevaricate, Pun, Quiddity, Quillet, Quirk, Sophist

Quick(en), Quickening, Quicker, Quickie, Quickly, Quickness, Quickwitted Accelerate, Acumen, Adroit, Agile, Alive, Animate, Breakneck, Bright, Brisk, Celerity, Chop-chop, Cito, Deft, Enliven, Existent, Expeditious,

Express, Fastness, Fleet, Hasten, Hie, Hotfoot, Hypersonic, Impetuous, Impulsive, Intelligent, Jiffy, Keen, Living, Mercurial, Meteoric, Mistress, Mosso, Nailbed, Nifty, Nimble, Nippy, Nooner, Pdq, Piercing, Post-haste, Prestissimo, Presto, Prompt, Pronto, Rapid, Ready, Sharp, Short cut, Slippy, Smart, Snappy, Soon, Spry, Streamline, Stretta, Stretto, Sudden, Swift, Tout de suite, Trice, Up tempo, Veloce, Vital, Vite, Volable

Quid Chaw, Chew, L, Nicker, Plug, Pound, Quo, Sov, Tertium, Tobacco

Quiet(en), Quieter, Quietly Accoy, Allay, Appease, Barnacle, Calm, Clam, Compose, Decrescendo, Diminuendo, Doggo, Ease, Easeful, Easy, Encalm, Entame, Gag, Grave, Hush, Kail, Laconic, Loun(d), Low, Lown(d), Low-profile, Lull, Meek, Mezzo voce, Millpond, Muffle, Mute, Orderly, P, Pacify, Pastel, Pause, Peace, Piano, Pipe down, Plateau, QT, Reserved, Reticent, Sedate, Settle, Sh, Shtoom, Shtum, Silence, Sober, Soothe, Sotto voce, Still(ness), Subact, Subdued, Tace, Taciturn, Tranquil, Whisht, Whist

Quilt(ed), Quilting Comfort(er), Counterpane, Cover, Doona®, Duvet, Echo, Eiderdown, Futon, Kantha, Matel(l)asse, Patch(work), Puff, Trapunto

Quip Carriwitchet, Crack, Epigram, Gibe, Jest, Jibe, Joke, Repartee, Taunt, Zinger

Quirk(y) Concert, Foible, Idiosyncrasy, Irony, Kink, Mannerism, Strange, Twist

Quit(s) Abandon, Absolve, Ap(p)ay, Cease, Desert, Desist, Even(s), Go, Leave, Meet, Part, Resign, Rid, Stash, → **STOP**, Stow, Vacate, Yield

Quite Actually, All, Altogether, Ap(p)ay, Clean, Dead, Enough, Enow, Fairly, Fully, Mezzo, Precisely, Rather, Real(ly), Right, Sheer, Very, Yes

Quiver(ing) Ashake, Aspen, Pulsate, Quake, Shake, Sheaf, Sheath, The yips, Tremble, Tremolo, Tremor, Tremulate, Trepid, Vibrant, Vibrate, Wobble

Quiz Bandalore, Banter, Catechism, Examine, Hoax, Interrogate, I-spy, Mastermind, Mockery, Oddity, Probe, Pub, Question, Smoke, Third degree, Trail, Yo-yo

Quota Proportion, Ration, Share

Quotation, Quote(d) Adduce, Citation, Cite, Co(a)te, Duckfoot, Epigraph, Estimate, Evens, Excerpt, Extract, Forward, Instance, List, Locus classicus, Name, Price, Recite, Reference, Say, Scare, Soundbite, Stock, Tag, Verbatim, Wordbite

Quotient Intelligence, Kerma, Quaternion, Ratio, Respiratory

Rr

Rabbit Angora, Astrex, Blather, Brer, Buck, Bun(ny), Bury, Chat, Chitchat, Chunter, Con(e)y, Cottontail, Daman, Dassie, Doe, Duffer, Gas, Goon, Harp, Hyrax, Jack, Jaw, Klipdas, Marmot, Muff, Natter, Nest, Novice, Oarlap, Patzer, Prate, Prattle, Rack, Rattle, Rex, Sage, Snowshoe, Tail-ender, Tapeti, Terricole, Waffle, Warrener, Yak, Yap, Yatter

Rabble, Rabble-rousing Canaille, Clamjamphrie, Clanjamfray, Colluvies, Crowd, Demagoguery, Doggery, Herd, Hoi-polloi, Horde, Legge, Meinie, Mein(e)y, Menyie, Mob, Raffle, Rag-tag, Rascaille, Rascal, Riff-raff, Rout, Scaff-raff, Shower, Tag, Tagrag

Race, Racing Alpine, Ancestry, Arms, Autocross, Autopoint, Aztec, Bathtub, Belt, Boat, Breed, Bumping, Career, Car rally, Caucus, Chantilly, Chase, Claiming, Classic, Comrades, Consolation, Contest, Country, Course, Criterium, Current, Cursus, Cyclo-cross, Dash, Dogs, Double sculls, Drag, Egg and spoon, Event, F1, Fastnet, Flat, Flow, Formula One, Fun-run, Generation, Ginger, Half-marathon, Handicap, Harness, Hialeah, High hurdles, Human(kind), Hurdles, Hurry, Inca, Keiren, Keirin, Kentucky Derby, Kind, Leat, Leet, Lick, Lignage, Line(age), Mankind, Marathon, Master, Mediterranean, Meets, Mile, Monza, Motocross, Nascar, Nation, → **NATIONAL**, National Hunt, Nursery, Nursery stakes, Obstacle, One-horse, Picnic, Plate, Point-to-point, Potato, Pre-Dravidian, Prep, Pursuit, Rallycross, Rallying, Rapids, Regatta, Relay, Rill, Road, Rod, Run-off, Sack, Scramble, Scratch, Scud, Scurry, Seed, Selling(-plate), Sheep, Slalom, Slipstream, Slot-car, Smock, Speedway, Sprint, Stakes, Steeplechase, Stem, Stock, Strain, Streak, Supermoto, Sweepstake, Tail, Tear, Three-legged, Tide, Torch, Torpids, Tribe, Trotting, TT, Turf, Two-horse, Walking, Walk-over, Waterway, Welter, Wetherby, White

Racehorse, Racer Arkle, Dragster, Eclipse, Filly, Hare, Kart, Maiden, Mudder, Neddy, Plater, Red Rum, Shergar, Snake, Steeplechaser, Trotter

Race meeting, Racecourse, Racetrack Aintree, Ascot, Ayr, Brands Hatch, Cambridgeshire, Catterick, Cesarewitch, Derby, Doggett's Coat and Badge, Doncaster, Dromical, Epsom, Goodwood, Grand National, Grand Prix, Guineas, Imola, Indy, Kentucky Derby, Leger, Le Mans, Longchamps, Madison, National Hunt, Newmarket, Oaks, Racino, Redcar, Regatta, St Leger, Silverstone, Super G, Thousand Guineas, Towcester, Two Thousand Guineas, Wetherby, Wincanton, York

Rack Anguish, Bin, Cloud, Cratch, Drier, Flake, Frame, Hack, Hake, Heck, Pipe, Pulley, Roof, Stretcher, Toast, Torment, Torture, Touse, Towse

Racket(eer) Bassoon, → **BAT**, Battledore, Bloop, Blue murder, Brattle, Caterwaul, Charivari, Chirm, Clamour, Con, Crime, Crosse, Deen, Din, Discord, Earner, → **FIDDLE**, Fuss, Gyp, Hubbub, Hullaballoo, Hustle, → **NOISE**,

Noisiness, Numbers, Protection, Ramp, Rattle, Rort, Ruction, Scam, Sokaiya, Stridor, Swindle, Tirrivee, Tumult, Uproar, Utis

▷**Racketeer** *may indicate* a tennis or squash player

Radar Acronym, Angel, AWACS, Beacon, DEW line, Doppler, Gadget, Gee, Gull, Lidar, Loran, Monopulse, Navar, Rebecca-eureka, Scanner, Shoran, Surveillance, Teleran®, Tracking

Radiance, Radiant Actinic, Aglow, Aureola, Beamish, Brilliant, Glisten(ing), Glittery, Glory, Glow, Happy, Luminous, Lustre, Refulgent, Sheen

Radiate, Radiating, Radiation, Radiator Actinal, Air-colour, Annihilation, Beam, Black body, Bremsstrahlung, Cavity, C(h)erenkov, Characteristic, Effulgence, Effuse, Emanate, Fluorescence, Glow, Heater, Infrared, Insolation, Isohel, Laser, Microwave, Millirem, Non-ionizing, Pentact, Photon, Picowave, Pulsar, Quasar, Rem(s), Rep, Roentgen, → **SHINE**, Sievert, Soft, Solar, Spherics, Spoke, Stellate, SU, Sun, Ultra violet, Van Allen

Radical Acetyl, Alkyl, Ammonium, Amyl, Aryl, Bolshevist, Bolshie, Butyl, Chartist, Dibutyl, Drastic, Egalitarian, Elemental, Ester, Ethynyl, Extreme, Free, Fundamental, Hexyl, Innate, Jacobin, Leftist, Methyl, Phenyl, Pink, Propyl, Red, Revolutionary, Root, Rudiment, Taliban, Taproot, Trot(sky), Vinyl, Vinylidene, Whig, Yippie, Yippy, Young Turk

Radio Beatbox, Blooper, Bluetooth, Boom-box, Broadcasting, Cat's whisker, CB, Cellular, Citizen's band, Clock, Cognitive, Community, Crystal set, Digital, Ether, Gee, Ghetto-blaster, Ham, Local, Long wave, Loudspeaker, Marconigraph, Pirate, Receiver, Receiving-set, Rediffusion®, Reflex, Rig, Set, Short wave, Simplex, Sound, Steam, Talk, Talkback, Tranny, Transceiver, Transistor, Transmitter, Transponder, Tuner, Walkie-talkie, Walkman®, Walky-talky, Wireless

Radioactive, Radioactivity Actinide, Americium, Astatine, Autinite, Bohrium, Cheralite, Cobalt 60, Curie, Darmstadtium, Emanation, Hot, Megacurie, Niton, Nucleonics, Steam, Thorianite, Thorite, Thorium, Torbernite, Unstable, Uranite, Uranium

Raft(ing) Balsa, Carley float, Catamaran, Float, Kon-Tiki, Life, Log, Mohiki, Pontoon, Slew

Rafter Barge-couple, Beam, Chevron, Jack, Joist, Principal, Ridge, Spar, Timber

Rag(ged), Ragged(ness), Rags Bait, Bate, Clout, Coral, Deckle, Dud(s), Duddery, Duddie, Duster, Fent, Figleaf, Glad, Gutter press, Guyed, Haze, Horror, Kid, Lap(pie), Lapje, Mop, Moth-eaten, → **NEWSPAPER**, Paper, Red(top), Remnant, Revel, Rivlins, Roast, Rot, Scabrous, Scold, Scrap, S(c)hmatte, → **SHRED**, Slate, Slut, Splore, Tat(t), Tatter(demalion), Tatty, Taunt, → **TEASE**, Tiger, Tongue, Uneven

▷**Rag(ged)** *may indicate* an anagram

Rage, Raging Amok, → **ANGER**, Ardour, Bait, Bate, Bayt, Boil, Chafe, Conniption, Explode, Fad, Fashion, Fierce, Fit, Fiz(z), Fume, Furibund, Furore, Fury, Gibber, Go, Irate, Ire, Madness, Mania, Mode, Paddy(-whack), Passion, Pelt, Pet, Rabid, Ramp, Rant, Road, 'roid, See red, Snit, Storm, Tear, Temper, Ton, Utis, Wax, Wrath

Raid(er) Assail, Assault, Attack, Bear, Bodrag, Bust, Camisado, Chappow, Commando, Do, Forage, For(r)ay, Imburst, Incursion, Inroad, Inrush, Invade, Jameson, Maraud, March-treason, Mosstrooper, Pict, Pillage, Plunder, Ransel, Razzia, Reive, Rob, Sack, Scrump, Skrimp, Skrump, Smash-and-grab, Sortie, Spreagh, Storm, Swoop, Viking

Rail(er), Railing Abuse, Arm(rest), Arris, Balustrade, Ban, Banister, →**BAR**, Barre, Barrier, Bird, Communion, Conductor, Coot, Corncrake, Crake, Criticise, Dado, Fender, Fiddle, Flanged, Flat-bottomed, Flite, Flow, Fulminate, Grab, Grinding, Guide, Gush, Insult, Inveigh, Light, Limpkin, Live, Metal, Monkey, Picture, Pin, Plate, Post, Pulpit, Pushpit, Rack, Rag, Rate, Rave, Rung, Scold, Slate, Slip, Sora, Soree, Spar, T, Taffrail, Takahe, Taunt, Third, Towel, Train

Railroad, Railway Aerial, Amtrak, BR, Branch line, Bulldoze, Cable, Cash, Coerce, Cog, Crémaillère, Dragoon, El, Elevated, Funicular, Gantlet, GWR, Inclined, L, Light, Lines, LMS, LNER, Loop-line, Maglev, Marine, Metro, Monorail, Mountain, Narrow-gauge, Press, Rack, Rack and pinion, Rly, Road, Rollercoaster, Ropeway, ROSCO, Ry, Scenic, Ship, Siding, SR, Stockton-Darlington, Switchback, Telpher-line, Track, Train, Tramline, Tramway, Trans-Siberian, Tube, Underground

Rain(y), Rainstorm Acid, Blash, Deluge, Downpour, Drizzle, Flood, Hyad(e)s, Hyetal, Mistle, Mizzle, Oncome, Onding, Onfall, Pelt, Pelter, Piss, Plump, Pluviose, Pluvious, Pour, Precipitation, Right, Roke, Scat, Scotch mist, Seil, Serein, Serene, Shell, Shower, Sile, Skiffle, Skit, Smir(r), Smur, Soft, Spat, Spet, Spit, Storm, Teem, Thunder-plump, Virga, Water, Weep, Wet

Raise(d), Raising Advance, Aggrade, Attollent, Aweigh, Boost, Bouse, Bowse, Broach, Build, Buoy up, Cat, Coaming, Cock, Collect, Elate, →**ELEVATE**, Emboss, Enhance, Ennoble, Erect, Escalate, Exalt, Fledge, Grow, Heave, Heezie, Heft, High(er), Hike, Hoick, Hoist, Increase, Inflate, Jack, Key, Leaven, Levy, Lift, Mention, Overcall, Perk, Prise, Rear, Regrate, Relievo, Repoussé, Revie, Rouse, Saleratus, Siege, Sky, Snarl, Sublimate, Take up, Up, Upgrade, Uprear, Weigh

Rake, Raker, Rakish Bag of bones, Bed-hopper, Buckrake, Casanova, Comb, Corinthian, Dapper, Dissolute, Don Giovanni, Don Juan, Enfilade, Gay dog, Jaunty, Lecher, Libertine, Lothario, Raff, Reprobate, Rip, Roam, Roué, Scan, Scour, Scowerer, Scrape, Scratch, Sporty, Strafe, Straff, Swash-buckler, Swinge-buckler, Wagons, Wolf, Womaniser

Rally, Rallying-point Assemble, Autocross, Autopoint, Badinage, Banter, Demo, Gather, Jamboree, Meeting, Mobilise, Monte Carlo, Morcha, Muster, Oriflamme, Persiflage, Raise, Recover, Regroup, Rely, Rest, Reunion, Revive, Risorgimento, Roast, Rouse, Scramble, Spirit, Treasure hunt

Ram Aries, Battering, Buck, Bunt, Butt, Butter, Corvus, Crash, Drive, Hidder, Hydraulic, Mendes, Pound, Pun, Sheep, Stem, Tamp, Thrust, Tup, Wether

Ramble(r), Rambling Aberrant, Aimless, Digress, Excursive, Hike, Incoherent, Liana, Liane, Maunder, Meander, Phrasy, Rabbit, Rigmarole, Roam, Rose, Rove, Skimble-skamble, Sprawl, Stray, Vagabond, Wander

Ramp Bank, Gradient, Helicline, Incline, Linkspan, Runway, Slipway, Slope, Speed, Vert

▷**Rampant** *may indicate* an anagram or a reversed word

Rampart Abat(t)is, Brisure, Butt, Defence, Fortification, Parapet, Terreplein, Vallum, Wall

Ranch Bowery, Corral, Estancia, Farm, Fazenda, Hacienda, Spread, Stump

Rancid Frowy, Rafty, Reast(y), Reest(y), Reist(y), Sour, Turned

Rancour Acrimony, Bad blood, Gall, Hate, Malgré, Malice, Resentment, Spite

Random Accidental, Ad hoc, Aleatoric, Arbitrary, →**AT RANDOM**, Blind, Casual, Desultory, Fitful, →**HAPHAZARD**, Harvest, Hit-or-miss, Indiscriminate, Lucky dip, Scattershot, Sporadic, Stochastic, Stray

▷**Random(ly)** *may indicate* an anagram

Range(r), Rangy Admiralty, Aga, Align, Ambit, Andes, Atlas, AZ, Band, Bushwhack, Capsule, Carry, Cascade, Chain, Cheviot, Compass, Cotswolds, Course, Dandenong, Darling, Diapason, Dolomites, Dynamic, Earshot, Err, →EXTENT, Eye-shot, Forest, Game warden, Gamme, Gamut, Grade, Great Dividing, Gunshot, Harmonic, Himalayas, Home, Interquartile, Kaikoura, Karakoram, Ken(ning), Kolyma, Limit, Line, Locus, Long, MacDonnell, Massif, →MOUNT, Musgrave, New England, Orbit, Otway, Oven, Owen Stanley, Palette, Pennine Hills, Point-blank, Prairie, Prism, Purview, Pyrenees, Radius, Rake, Reach, Register, Repertoire, Roam, Rocket, Rove, Ruivenzori, Run, Saga, Scale, Scope, Sc(o)ur, Selection, Serra, Shooting, Short, Sierra, Sloane, Spectrum, Sphere, Stanovoi, Stanovoy, Sweep, The Wolds, Urals, Wasatch, Waveband, Woomera

Rank(s), Ranking Arrant, Assort, Begum, Brevet, Caste, Category, Cense, Classify, Condition, Cornet, Degree, Dignity, Downright, Earldom, Echelon, Estate, État(s), Flag, General(issimo), Grade, Gree, Gross, High, Malodorous, Olid, Petty Officer, Place, Profuse, Queue, Rammish, Range, Rate, Reist, Rooty, Row, Sergeant, Serried, Sheer, Sort, Stance, →STATION, Status, Table, Taxi, Tier, →TITLE, Top drawer, Utter, Viscount

Ransack Fish, Loot, Pillage, Plunder, Rifle, Ripe, Rob, Rummage, Tot(ter)

Rant(er), Ranting Bluster, Bombast, Declaim, Fustian, Ham, Harangue, Rail, Rodomontade, Scold, Slang-whang, Sound off, Spout, Spruik, Stump, Thunder, Tirade, Tub-thump

Rap(ped) Blame, Censure, Clour, Gangsta, Halfpenny, Knock, Ratatat, Shand, Strike, Swapt, Tack, Tap

Rape Abuse, Assault, Belinda, Cole-seed, Colza, Creach, Creagh, Date, Deflower, Despoil, Gangbang, Grass(line), Hundred, Linseed, Lock, Lucretia, Navew, Oilseed, Plunder, Ravish, Stuprate, Thack, Violate, Vitiate

Rapid(ity), Rapidly Chute, Dalle, Express, Fast, Fleet, Meteoric, Mosso, Presto, Pronto, Quick-fire, Quicksilver, Riffle, Sault, Shoot, Speedy, Stickle, Swift, Veloce, Vibrato, Whiz(zing), Wildfire

Rapport Accord, Affinity, Agreement, Harmony

Rapture, Rapturous Bliss, →DELIGHT, Ecstasy, Elation, Euphoria, Joy, Trance

Rare, Rarity Blue moon, Curio, Earth, Geason, Gold dust, Infrequent, Intemerate, Oddity, One-off, Rear, Recherché, Scarce, Seeld, Seld(om), Singular, Surpassing, Thin, →UNCOMMON, Uncooked, Underdone, Unusual

Rascal(ly) Arrant, Bad hat, Cad, Cullion, Cur, Devil, Gamin, Hallian, Hallion, Hallyon, Limner, Loon, Lorel, Low, Lozel(l), Rip, Rogue, Scallywag, Scamp, Scapegrace, Schelm, Skeesicks, Skellum, Skelm, Smaik, Spalpeen, Tinker, Toe-rag, Varlet, Varmint, Villain

Rash(ness), Rasher Acne, Ate, Bacon, Brash, Collop, Daredevil, Eczema, Eruption, Erysipelas, Fast, Foolhardy, Gum, Harum-scarum, →HASTY, Headlong, Heat, Hives, Hotbrain, Hotspur, Ill-considered, Impetigo, Impetuous, Imprudent, Impulsive, Indiscreet, Lichen, Madbrain, Madcap, Nettle, Outbreak, Overhasty, Pox, Precipitate, Reckless, Road, Roseola, Rubella, St Anthony's fire, Sapego, Serpigo, Spots, Temerity, Thoughtless, Unheeding, Unthinking, Unwise, Urticaria

Rat(s), Ratty Agouta, Apostate, Bandicoot, Betray, Blackleg, Blackneb, Boodie, Brown, Bug-out, Cad, Camass, Cane, Cur, Cutting grass, Defect, Desert, Fink, Footra, Foutra, Geomyoid, Gym, Heck, Heel, Hood, Hydromys, Informer, Kangaroo, Malabar, Mall, Maori, Mole, Moon, Norway, Pack, Pig, Poppycock,

Potoroo, Pouched, Pshaw, Pup(py), Renegade, Renegate, Rice, Rink, Rodent, Roland, Rot(ten), Scab, Sewer, Shirty, Squeal, Stinker, Tell, Turncoat, Vole, Water, Wharf, Whiskers, White, Wood

Rate(s), Rating A, Able, Able-bodied, Apgar, Appraise, Appreciate, Assess, Base, Basic, Birth, Bit, Carpet, Castigate, Cess, Cetane, Chide, Classify, Click, Conception, Conversion, Cost, Count, Credit, Death, Deserve, Effective, ELO, Erk, Estimate, Evaluate, Exchange, Grade, Headline, Hearty, Horsepower, Hurdle, Incidence, Interest, ISO, Knot, Lapse, Leading, Lick, Mate's, Merit, Mortality, Mortgage, MPH, Mutation, Octane, Ordinary, OS, Pace, Penalty, Percentage, PG, Piece, Poor, Prime (lending), Rag, Rank, Rebuke, Red, Refresh, Reproof, Rocket, Row, Sailor, Scold, Sea-dog, Slew, →**SPEED**, Standing, Starting, Steerageway, Surtax, Take-up, TAM, Tariff, Tax, Tempo, Tick off, Tog, U, Upbraid, Value, Water, Wig, World-scale, X, Zero

Rather Affirmative, Agreed, Assez, Degree, Gay, Gey, Instead, Kinda, Lief, Liever, Loor, More, Not half, Prefer, Pretty, Some(what), Somedele, Sooner

Ratio Advance, Albedo, Aspect, Bypass, Cash, Compound, Compression, Cosine, Distinctiveness, Duplicate, Focal, Fraction, Gear, Golden, Gyromagnetic, Inverse, Liquidity, Loss, Mark space, Mass, Neper, PE, Pi, Picture, Pogson's, Poisson's, Position, Price-dividend, Price-earnings, Proportion, Protection, Quotient, Reserve, Savings, Signal-to-noise, Sin(e), Slip, Space, Tensor, Trigonometric

Ration(s) Allocate, Allot, Apportion, Compo, Dole, Étape, Iron, K, Quota, Restrict, Scran, Share, Short commons, Size, Stint, Whack

Rational(ism), Rationalisation, Rationalist, Rationalize Descartes, Dianoetic, Dispassionate, Free-thinker, Humanistic, Level-headed, Logical, Lucid, Matter-of-fact, Pragmatic, Reasonable, Sane, Sapient, Sensible, Sine, Sober, Tenable, Wice

Rattle (box), Rattling, Rattle on Alarm, Blather, Chatter, Clack, Clank, Clap, Clatter, Conductor, Death, Demoralise, Discombobulate, Discomfort, Discompose, Disconcert, Gas-bag, Hurtle, Jabber, Jangle, Jar, Natter, Nonplus, Rale, Rap, Reel, Rhonchus, Ruckle, Shake, Sistrum, Tirl, Upset, Vuvuzela

Ravage Depredation, Desecrate, Despoil, Havoc, Pillage, Prey, Ruin, Sack, Waste

Raven(ous) Black, Corbel, Corbie, Corvine, Croaker, Daw, Grip, Hugin, Munin, Prey, Unkindness, Wolfish

Ravine Arroyo, Barranca, Barranco, Canada, Canyon, Chasm, Chine, Clough, Coulée, Couloir, Dip, Flume, Ghyll, Gorge, Goyle, Grike, Gulch, Gully, Kedron, Khor, Khud, Kidron, Kloof, Lin(n), Nal(l)a, Nallah, Nulla(h), Pit, Purgatory

Ravish(ing) Abduct, A ravir, Constuperate, Constuprate, Debauch, Defile, Devour, Outrage, Rape, Stuprate, Transport, Violate

Raw Brut, Chill, Coarse, Crude, Crudy, Damp, Fresh, Green(horn), Natural, New, Recruit, Rude, Sashimi, Uncooked, Wersh

Ray(s), Rayed Actinic, Alpha, Beam, Beta, Bivium, Canal, Cathode, Cosmic, Cramp-fish, Delta, Devil, Devilfish, Diactine, Dun-cow, Eagle, Electric, Fish, Gamma, Grenz, Guitarfish, Homelyn, Laser, Manta, Medullary, Monactine, Polyact, R, Radioactive, Radius, Re, Roentgen, Roker, Röntgen, Sawfish, Sea-devil, Sea-vampire, Sephen, Shaft, Skate, Stick, Sting, Stingaree, T, Tetract, Thornback, Torpedo, UV

Reach(ed) Achieve, Ar(rive), Attain, Boak, Boke, Carry, Come, Extend, Gain, Get at, Get out, Grasp, Hent, Hit, Key-bugle, Lode, Octave, Peak, Raught, Rax, Retch, Ryke, Sease, Seize, Stretch, Touch, Win

React(or), Reaction(ary) Addition, Allergy, Answer, Backlash, Backwash, Behave, Blimp, Blowback, Boiling water, Breeder, Bristle, Calendria, Cannizzaro, Catalysis, Chain, Convertor, Core, Counterblast, Dibasic, Dounreay, Dyed-in-the-wool, Emotion, Endergonic, Exoergic, Falange, Fast(-breeder), Feedback, Flehmen, Flinch, Friedel-Crafts, Furnace, Gut, Heavy-water, Incomplete, Interplay, Inulase, Kickback, Knee-jerk, Lightwater, Molten salt, Nuclear, Old Guard, Outcry, Pebble-bed, Pile, Polymerization, Pressure-tube, Pressurized water, Reciprocate, Recoil, Reflex, Repercussion, Respond, Reversible, Rigid, Sensitive, Sprocket, Stereotaxis, Thermal, Topochemistry, Ultraconservative

▷**Reactionary** *may indicate* reversed or an anagram

Read(ing) Abomasum, Bearing, Browse, Decipher, Decode, Devour, Exegesis, First, Gauge, Grind, Grounden, Haftarah, Haphtarah, Haphtorah, Interpret, Learn, Lection, Lesson, Lu, Maftir, Maw, Paired, Pericope, Peruse, Pore, Rad, Rennet-bag, Say, Scan, Second, See, Sight, Skim, Solve, Speed, Stomach, →**STUDY**, Third, Uni(versity), Vell, Version, Ycond

Reader(s) ABC, Academic, Alidad(e), Bookworm, Editor, Epistoler, Gauge, Gentle, Lay, Lector, Microfilm, Phrenologist, Primer, Silas Wegg, Softa, Taster

Readiest, Readily, Readiness, Ready Alacrity, Alamain, Alert, Amber, Amenability, Apt, Atrip, Available, Boun, Bound, Braced, Brass, Cash, Conditional, Dosh, Dough, Eager, Early, Eftest, En garde, Fettle, Fit, Fiver, Forward, Game, Geared-up, Gelt, Go, In the wings, Keyed, Latent, Lolly, Masterman, Money, On (call), Petty cash, Predy, Prepared, Present, Prest, Primed, Procinct, Prompt, Promptitude, Ransom, Reckoner, Ripe, Running costs, Set, Soon, Spot, Tenner, To hand, Turnkey, Unhesitant, Usable, Wherewithal, Willing, Yare, Yark

Readymade Bought, Precast, Prepared, Prêt-à-porter, Slops, Stock, Store

Real, Reality, Realities, Really Actual, Ah, Augmented, Bona-fide, Brass tacks, Coin, Deed, De facto, Dinkum, Dinky-di(e), Earnest, Echt, Ens, Entia, Entity, Essence, Ever so, Fact(ion), →**GENUINE**, Hard, Honest (to God), Indeed, Mackay, McCoy, McKoy, Naive, Ontic, Positive, Quite, Royal, Simon Pure, Sooth, Sterling, Straight up, Substantial, Tangible, Tennis, The case, Thing(li)ness, True, Verismo, Verity, Very, Virtual

Realise, Realisation, Realism, Realistic Achieve, Attain, Attuite, Cash (in), Dirty, Down-to-earth, Embody, Encash, Entelechy, Fetch, Fruition, Fulfil, Hard-edged, Learn, Lifelike, Magic, Naive, Naturalism, Practical, Pragmatism, See, Sell, Sense, Social, Socialist, Suss, Understand, Verisimilitude, Verismo, Verité

▶**Realities, Reality** *see* **REAL**

Realm Dominion, Duchy, Field, Kingdom, Land, Notogaea, Region, Special(i)ty, UK

Ream Bore, Foam, Froth, Paper, Rime, Screed

Reap(er) Binder, Crop, Death, Earn, Gather, Glean, Harvest, Scythe, Shear, Sickleman, Solitary, Stibbler

Rear(ing) Aft, Back(side), Baft, Behind, Bottom, Bring-up, Bunt, Butt, Cabré, Derrière, Empennage, Foster, Haunch, Hind, Loo, Nousell, Nurture, Podex, Poop, Prat(t), →**RAISE**, Rampant, Retral, Rump, Serafile, Serrefile, Stern, Sternward, Tonneau, Train

Reason(able), Reasoning A fortiori, Agenda, Analytical, Apagoge, A priori, Argue, Argument, Basis, Call, Casuistry, Casus belli, Cause, Colour,

Consideration, Deduce, Economical, Expostulate, Fair, Ground(s), Ijtihad, Inductive, Inference, Intellect, Intelligent, Ipso facto, Logic, Logical, Logistics, Metamathematics, Mind, Moderate, Motive, Noesis, Petitio principii, Plausible, Point, Pretext, Pro, Proof, Purpose, Rational(e), Sane, Sanity, Sense, Sensible, Settler, Somewhy, Sophism, Syllogism, Synthesis, Think, Viable, What for, Why, Wit

Rebate Diminish, Lessen, Refund, Repayment, Return

Rebel(s), Rebellion, Rebellious Anarchist, Apostate, Beatnik, Blouson noir, Bolshy, Bounty, Boxer, Cade, Contra, Danton, Defiance, Diehard, Dissident, Drop out, Easter, Fifteen, Forty-five, Green Mountain Boys, Hippy, Iconoclast, Insubordinate, Insurgent, Insurrection, IRA, Jacobite, Kick, Luddite, Maccabee, Malignant, Mutine(er), Mutiny, Oates, Pilgrimage of Grace, Putsch, Recalcitrant, Recusant, Resist, → **REVOLT**, Rise, Sedition, Straw, Tyler, UDI, Unruly, Warbeck, Wat Tyler, Young Turk, Zealot

▷**Rebellious** *may indicate* a word reversed

Rebuff Censure, Check, Cold-shoulder, Earwig, Noser, Quelch, Repulse, Retort, Rubber, Setdown, Sneb, Snib, Snub

Rebuke Admonish, Berate, Check, Chide, Earful, Lecture, Neb, Objurgate, Rap, Rate, Razz, Reprimand, Reproof, Reprove, Rollick, Scold, Slap, Slate, Snub, Strop, Threap, Threep, Tick off, Trim, Tut, Upbraid, Wig

Recall(ing) Annul, Echo, Eidetic, Encore, Evocative, Flashback, Go over, Memory, Reclaim, Recollect, Redolent, Remember, Remind, Reminisce, Repeal, Retrace, Revoke, Total, Withdraw

▷**Recast** *may indicate* an anagram

Recede, Receding Decline, Ebb, Hairline, Lessen, Regress, Retrograde, Shrink, Withdraw

Receipt(s) Acknowledge, Chit, Docket, Gate, Quittance, Recipe, Revenue, Take, Voucher

Receive(d), Receiver Accept, Accoil, Acquire, Admit, Antenna, Assignee, Bailee, Bleeper, Cop, Dipole, Dish, Donee, Ear, Earphone, Earpiece, Fence, Get, Grantee, Greet, Hydrophone, Inherit, Pernancy, Phone, Pocket, Radio, Radiopager, Remit, Reset, Roger, Set, Sounder, Take, Tap, Transistor, Transponder, Tuner, Wireless

Recent(ly) Alate, Current, Fresh, Hot, Just, Late, Low, Modern, New, New-found, Of late, Yesterday, Yestereve, Yesterweek

Receptacle Ash-tray, Basket, Bin, Bowl, Box, Chrismatory, Ciborium, Container, Cyst, Hell-box, Hypanthium, Monstrance, Muffle, Outtray, Portfolio, Reliquary, Relique, Sacculus, Skip, Spermatheca, Spittoon, Tank, Thalamus, Tidy, Tore, Torus

Reception, Receptive Acceptance, Accoil, Antechamber, At home, Bel-accoyle, Couchée, Court, Durbar, First-class, Ghost, Greeting, Infare, Kursaal, Levée, Open, Ovation, Ruelle, Saloon, Sensory, Soirée, Superheterodyne, Teleasthetic, Ticker-tape, Warm, Welcome

Recess(ion) Alcove, Apse, Bay, Break, Breaktime, Bunk, Corner, Cove, Dinette, Ebb, Embrasure, Fireplace, Grotto, Indent, Inglenook, Interval, → **NICHE**, Nook, Pigeonhole, Respite, Rest, Toehold, Withdrawal

▷**Recess** *may indicate* 'reversed'

▷**Recidivist** *may indicate* 'reversed'

Recipient Assignee, Beneficiary, Disponee, Donee, End user, Grantee, Heir, Legatee, Receiver, Suscipient

Reciprocal, Reciprocate Corresponding, Elastance, Even the score, Exchange, Inter(act), Mutual, Repay, Return, Two-way

Recite(r), Recital, Recitation(ist) Ave, Declaim, Diseuse, Enumerate, Litany, Monologue, Mystic, Parlando, Quote, Reading, Reel, Relate, Rendition, Rhapsode, Say, Sing, Tell

Reckless(ness) Bayard, Blindfold, Careless, Catiline, Chicken, Desperado, Desperate, Devil-may-care, Gadarene, Harum-scarum, Hasty, Headfirst, Headlong, Hell-bent, Irresponsible, Jaywalker, Madcap, Perdu(e), Ramstam, Rantipole, → **RASH**, Slapdash, Tearaway, Temerity, Ton-up, Wanton, Wildcat
▷ **Reckless** *may indicate* an anagram

Reckon(ed), Reckoner, Reckoning Abacus, Assess, Bet, Calculate, Cast, Census, Computer, Consider, Count, Date, Doomsday, Estimate, Fancy, Figure, Guess, Impute, Number, Rate, Reputed, Settlement, Shot, Tab

Reclaim(ed), Reclamation Assart, Empolder, Impolder, Innings, Novalia, Polder, Recover, Redeem, Restore, Salvage, Swidden, Tame, Thwaite

Recognise(d), Recognition Accept, Accredit, Acknow(ledge), Admit, Anagnorisis, Appreciate, Apprehend, Ascetic, Character, Cit(ation), Count, Discern, Exequatur, Gaydar, Identify, Isolated, Ken, → **KNOW**, Kudos, Nod, Notice, Oust, Own, Perception, Resipiscence, Reward, Salute, Scent, Sense, Standard, Sung, Voice, Wate, Weet, Wit, Wot

Recoil Backlash, Bounce, Kick(back), Quail, Rebound, Redound, Repercussion, Resile, Reverberate, Shrink, Shy, Spring, Start, Whiplash

Recollect(ion) Anamnesis, Memory, Pelmanism, Recall, → **REMEMBER**, Reminisce
▷ **Recollection** *may indicate* an anagram

Recommend(ation) Advise, Advocate, Counsel, Direct, Encourage, Endorse, Move, Nap, Praise, Precatory, Promote, Rider, Suggest, Testimonial, Tip, Tout, Urge

Recompense Cognisance, Deodand, Deserts, Eric, Expiate, Guerdon, Pay, Remunerate, Repayment, Requite, Restitution, Reward

Reconcile(d), Reconciler, Reconciliation Accord, Adapt, Adjust, Affrended, Atone, Bridge builder, Harmonise, Henotic, Make up, Mend, Square

Record(er), Recorded, Recording (company) All-time, Blu-ray®, Book, Camera, Chart, Chronicle, Clock, Coat(e), Descant, Enrol, Enter, Entry, Ever, Fact, File, Hi-fi, Itemise, Log, Mark, Memorise, Notate, Note, Previous, Quote, Release, Remember, Seismograph, Set down, Somerset House, Sunshine, Take, Tally, Tallyman, Trace, Trip, Vote, VTR, Weigh, Write

Recover(y) Amend, Clawback, Comeback, Convalescence, Cure, Dead cat bounce, Heal, Lysis, Over, Perk (up), Pull round, Rally, Rebound, Reclaim, Recoup, Recuperation, Redeem, Regain, Rehab, Repaint, Replevin, Replevy, Repo(ssess), Rescript, Rescue, Resile, → **RETRIEVE**, Revanche, Salvage, Salve, Upswing, Upturn

Recruit(s) Attestor, Bezonian, Choco, Conscript, Crimp, Draft, Employ, Engage, Enlist, Enrol, Headhunt, Hire, Intake, Muster, New blood, Nignog, Nozzer, Rookie, Sprog, Volunteer, Wart, Yardbird, Yobbo

Rectifier, Rectify Adjust, Amend, Dephlegmate, Redress, Regulate, → **REMEDY**, Repair, Right

Recur(rent), Recurring Chronic, Ergodic, Quartan, Quintan, Recrudesce, Repeated, Repetend, Return
▷ **Recurrent** *may indicate* 'reversed'

Recycle(r), Recycling Freegan, Nephron, Pulp

Red(den), Redness Admiral, Anarch(ist), Angry, Arun, Ashamed, Auburn, Bashful, Beet, Bloodshot, Blush, Bolshevik, Brick, Burgundy, C, Cain-coloured, Carmine, Carrot-top, Carroty, Cent, Cerise, Cherry, Chianti, Chinese, Claret, Commie, Commo, Communist, Copper, Coral, Corallin(e), Crimson, Crocoite, Debit, Dubonnet, Duster, Embarrassed, Eosin, Eric, Erik, Erythema, Ffion, Flame, Flaming, Florid, Flush, Foxy, Garnet, Geranium, Ginger, Gory, Gule(s), Guly, Hat, Henna, Herring, Indian, Indigo, Inflamed, Infra, Inner, Iron, Judas-coloured, Lake, Left(y), Lenin, Letter, Magenta, Maoist, Maroon, Marxist, McIntosh, Medoc, Mulberry, Murrey, Neaten, Overdraft, Oxblood, Pillar-box, Pinko, Plum, Pompeian, Poppy, Raddle, Radical, Raspberry, Raw, Realgar, Rhodamine, Rhodopsin, Ridinghood, Roan, Rosaker, Rose, Rot, Rouge, Rubefaction, Rubefy, Rubella, Ruby, Ruddy, Rufus, Russ(e), Russet, Russian, Russky, Rust(y), Safranin(e), Sanguine, Santalin, Sard, Scarlet, Sea, Setter, Shame-faced, Tape, Tidy, Tile, Titian, Trot, Trotsky, Turkey, Venetian, Vermilion, Vinaceous, Wax, Wine

▷**Red** *may indicate* an anagram

Redeem(er), Redemption(ist) Cross, Liberate, Liguorian, Lowse, Mathurin, Ransom, Retrieve, Salvation, Save

▶**Red Indian** *see* **NORTH AMERICAN (INDIAN)**

▷**Rediscovered** *may indicate* an anagram

Reduce(d), Reducer, Reduction Abatement, Allay, Alleviate, Asyndeton, Attenuate, Bate, Beggar, Calcine, Clip, Commutation, Commute, Concession, Condense, Contract, Cull, Curtail, Cut, Cutback, Damping, Debase, Decimate, Decrease, Decrement, De-escalate, Demote, Deplete, Detract, Devalue, Dil(ute), Diminish, Diminuendo, Discount, Downgrade, Downscale, Downsize, Draw-down, Drop, Emasculate, Epitomise, Grate, Grind, Hatchet job, →**LESSEN**, Lite, Markdown, Miniature, Mitigate, Model, Moderate, Palliate, Pot, Proclitic, Pulp, Put, Rarefaction, Regression, Relegate, Remission, Retrench, Rundown, Scant, Shade, Shorten, Shrinkage, Slash, Strain, Streamline, Supersaver, Taper, Telescope, Thin, Weaken, Whittle, Write-off

Redundancy, Redundant FIFO, Frill, Futile, Lay-off, Needless, Otiose, Pink slip, Pleonasm, Retrenchment, Superfluous, Surplus

Reef Atoll, Barrier, Bombora, Bommie, Cay, Coral, Fringing, Great Barrier, Key, Knot, Lido, Motu, Sca(u)r, Skerry, Witwatersrand

Reel Bobbin, Dance, Drum, Eightsome, Hoolachan, Hoolican, Inertia, Lurch, Multiplier, Pirn, Spin, Spool, Stagger, Strathspey, Sway, Swift, Swim, Tirl, Totter, Wheel, Whirl, Wince, Wintle

Refer Advert, Allude, Assign, Cite, Direct, Mention, Pertain, Relate, Remit, Renvoi, Renvoy, See, Submit, Touch, Trade

Referee Arbiter, Commissaire, Linesman, Mediate, Oddsman, Ref, Umpire, Voucher, Whistler, Zebra

Reference(s), Reference room Allusion, Almanac, Apropos, Autocue, Biaxal, Chapter and verse, Character, Coat, Credentials, Cross, Grid, Guidebook, Index, Innuendo, Lexicon, Mention, Morgue, Passion, Promptuary, Quote, Regard, Renvoi, Respect, Retrospect, Testimonial, Thesaurus, Thumb index, Vide

Refine(d), Refinement, Refiner(y) Alembicated, Attic, Catcracker, Couth, Cultivate, Culture, Cupellation, Cut-glass, Dainty, Distil, Distinction, Elaborate, Elegance, Ethereal, Exility, Exquisite, Genteel, Grace, Horsy, Ladify, Nice, Nicety,

Polish(ed), Polite, Précieuse, Preciosity, Pure, Rare(fy), Recherché, Saltern, Sift, Smelt, Spiritualize, Spirituel, Subtilise, Subtlety, Try, U, Urbane, Veneer

Reflect(ing), Reflection, Reflective, Reflector Albedo, Apotheosis, Aspersion, Blame, Cat's eye®, Chew, Cogitate, → **CONSIDER**, Echo, Glass, Glint, Glisten, Image, Meditate, Mirror, Muse, Narcissus, Ponder, Redound, Repercuss, Ruminate, Thought

Reform(er), Reforming, Reformist AA, Agrarian, Amend, Apostle, Besant, Bloomer, Calvin, Chastise, Convert, Correct, Counter-Reformation, Enrage, Fourier, Fry, Gandhi, Glassite, Howard, Improve, Knox, Lafayette, Lollard, Luther, Mend, Modify, Penn, Pietism, PR, Progressionist, Protestant, Puritan, Rad(ical), Recast, Reclaim, Reconstruction, Rectify, Regenerate, Restyle, Ruskin, Simons, Stanton, Taskmaster, Transmute, Whig, Wilberforce, Wilkes, Worms, Zinzendorf

▷**Reform(ed)** *may indicate an anagram*

Refrain Abstain, Alay, Avoid, Bob, Burden, Chorus, Desist, Epistrophe, Faburden, Fa-la, Forbear, Haunting, Hemistich, Leave, Owreword, Repetend, Resist, Ritornello, Roundel, Rumbelow, Rum(p)ti-iddity, Rum-ti-tum, Spare, Tag, Tirra-lirra, Tirra-lyra, Tra-la, Undersong, Waive, Wheel

Refresh(ment), Refresher Air, Bait, Be(a)vers, Buffet, Cheer, Coffee, Elevenses, Enliven, Exhilarate, Food, Four-hours, Milk shake, Nap, New, Nourishment, Purvey, Refection, Reflect, Refocillate, Reinvigorate, Renew, Repast, Restore, Revive, Seltzer, Shire, Slake, Sorbet, Tea, Water

Refrigerator Chill, Chiller, Cold store, Cooler, Deep freeze, Esky®, Freezer, Freon, Fridge, Ice-box, Minibar, Reefer

Refuge Abri, Adytum, Asylum, Bolthole, Bothie, Bothy, Caravanserai, Dive, Fastness, Foxhole, Funkhole, Girth, Grith, Harbour, Haven, Hideaway, Hole, Holt, Home, Hospice, Oasis, Port, Reefer, Resort, Retreat, Sanctuary, Sheet-anchor, → **SHELTER**, Soil, Stronghold

Refurbish New, Refit, Renew

▷**Refurbished** *may indicate an anagram*

Refusal, Refuse Bagasse, Ba(u)lk, Bilge, Bin, Black, Blackball, Boycott, Bran, Brash, Breeze, Brock, Bull, Bunkum, Cane-trash, Chaff, Cinder, Clap-trap, Contumacy, Crane, Crap, Debris, Decline, Deny, Discountenance, Disown, Draff, Drivel, Dross, Dunder, Dung, Fag-end, Fenks, Finks, First, Frass, Garbage, Guff, Hogwash, Hold-out, Husk, Interdict, Jews' houses, Jews' leavings, Jib, Junk, Knub, Lay-stall, Leavings, Litter, Lumber, Mahmal, Marc, Megass(e), Midden, Mother, Mush, Nay(-say), Nill, No (dice), Noser, Nould(e), Nub, Offal, Off-scum, Orts, Passup, Pigswill, Pigwash, Potale, Punk, Raffle, Rags, Rape(cake), Rat(s), Rebuff, Red(d), Redline, Reest, Regret, Reject, Reneg(u)e, Renig, Repudiate, Resist, Rot, → **RUBBISH**, Ruderal, Scaff, Scrap, Scree, Screenings, Scum, Sewage, Sewerage, Shant, Shell heap, Slag, Spurn, Sullage, Sweepings, Swill, Tailings, Tinpot, Tip, Tosh, Trade, Trash, Tripe, Trumpery, Turndown, Twaddle, Unsay, Utter, Wash, Waste, Waste paper

▷**Re-fused** *may indicate an anagram*

Regal Maeve, Majestic, Organ

▶**Regal** *see* **ROYAL(TY)**

Regard(ing) Anent, Apropos, As to, Attention, Care, Consider, → **ESTEEM**, Eye, Gaum, Look, Observe, Odour, Pace, Rate, Re, Repute, Respect, Revere, Sake, See, Steem, Value, Vis-à-vis

Regardless Anyway, Despite, Heedless, In any event, Irrespective, No matter, Notwithstanding, Rash, Though, Uncaring, Willy-nilly

Regiment Black Watch, Buffs, Colour(s), Discipline, Foot, Greys, Ironsides, Life Guards, Marching, Monstrous, Nutcrackers, Organise, RA, RE, REME, Rifle, Royals, Scots Greys, Tercio, Tertia

▷**Regiment** *may indicate* an anagram

Region(s), Regional →AREA, Belt, Canton, Central, Climate, Climature, Clime, District, Domain, Enclave, End, Endemic, Locality, Offing, Part, Province, Quart(er), Realm, Sector, Side, Territory, Tract, Zone

Register(ing), Registration, Registry Actuarial, Almanac, Annal, Cadastral, Cadastre, Calendar, Cartulary, Cash, Census, Check-in, Child abuse, Dawn, Diptych, Docket, Enlist, Enrol, Enter, Flag out, Gross, Handicap, Index, Indicate, Inscribe, Inventory, Land, Ledger, List, Lloyd's, Log, Matricula, Menology, NAI, Net, Note, Notitia, Obituary, Parish, Park, Patent, Patent Rolls, Poll, Quotation, Read, Reception, Record, Reg(g)o, Rent-roll, Roll, Roule, Score, Shift(ing), Ship's, Sink in, Soprano, Terrier, Till, Voice

Regret(ful), Regrettable Alack, Alas, Apologise, Bemoan, Deplore, Deprecate, Ewhow, Forthink, Ichabod, If only, Lackaday, Lament, Mourn, Otis, Penitent, Pity, Remorse, Repentance, Repine, Resent, Rew, Ruth, Sorrow, Tragic

Regular(ity), Regularly, Regulars By turn, Clientele, Clockwork, Constant, Custom(er), Daily, Episodic, Equilateral, Even, Giusto, Goer, Habitual, Habitude, Habitué, Hourly, Insider, Level, Methodic, Nightly, Nine-to-five, Normal, Often, Orderly, Orthodox, Patron, Peloria, Periodic, Punter, Rhythmic, Routine, Set, Smooth, Soldier, →STANDARD, Stated, Statutory, Steady, Strict, Symmetric, Uniform, Usual, Yearly

Regulate, Regulation, Regulator Adjust, Appestat, Ballcock, Ballonet, Bye-law, Code, Control, Correction, Curfew, Customary, Direct, Dispensation, Gibberellin, Governor, Guide, Hormone, Logistics, Metrostyle, Modulate, Order, Ordinance, Police, Prescriptive, Protocol, Red tape, Rule, Snail, Square, Standard, Statute, Stickle, Sumptuary, Thermostat, Valve

Rehearsal, Rehearse Band-call, Dress, Drill, Dry-block, Dry-run, Dummy-run, Practice, Practise, Preview, Recite, Repeat, Run through, Technical, Trial, Walk through

Reign(ed) Era, Govern, Meiji, Prevail, Raine, Rang, Realm, Restoration, Ring, →RULE, Sway

Rein(s) Bearing, Caribou, Check, Control, Curb, Deer, Free, Long, Lumbar, Restrain, Ribbons, Safety, Stop, Tame, Tight, Walking

Reinforce(ment) Aid, Augment, Beef up, Bolster, Boost, Brace, Buttress, Cleat, Counterfort, Line, Plash, Pleach, Positive, Re-bar, Recruit, Reserve, Ripieno, →STRENGTHEN, Support, Tenaille, Tenaillon, Tetrapod, Underline, Welt

Reject(ion) Abhor, Abjure, Athetise, Bin, Blackball, Cast, Debar, Deny, Dice, Disallow, Discard, Disclaim, Disdain, Disown, Diss, Eliminate, Flout, Frass, Heave-ho, Jettison, Jilt, Kest, Kill, Knock-back, No(t)chel, Ostracise, Oust, Outcast, Outtake, Pip, Plough, Quash, Rebuff, Recuse, Refuse, Reny, Reprobate, Repudiate, Repulse, Retree, Scout, Scrub, Spet, Spike, Spin, Spit, Sputum, Thumbs-down, Trash, Turndown, Veto

Rejoice, Rejoicing Celebrate, Exult, Festivity, Gaude, Glory, Joy, Maffick, Sing

Rejoin(der), Rejoined Answer, Comeback, Counter, Relide, Reply, Response, Retort, Reunite

Relate(d), Relation(ship), Relations, Relative, Relativity About, Account, Affair, Agnate, Akin, Allied, Amour, Appertain, Apposition, Associate, Blood, Blude, Bluid, Causality, Cognate, Commune, Concern, Connection,

Connexion, Consanguinity, Cousin(-german), Coz, Dalliance, Dependent, Dispersion, Einstein, Eme, Enate, Equation, Equivalence, External, False, Formula, German(e), Goodfather, Granny, Guanxi, How's your father, Impart, Inbreeding, In-law, Internal, International, Item, Kin, Kinsman, Labour, Liaison, Link, Love-hate, Mater, Material, Matrix, Nan(n)a, Narrative, Naunt, Nooky, Object, One-to-one, Pertain, Phratry, Pi, Platonic, Poor, Predation, → **PROPORTION**, Pro rata, Proxemics, Public, Race, Rapport, Ratio, Recite, Recount, Refer(ence), Relevant, Respect(s), Saga, Sib(b), Sibling, Sine, Symbiosis, Syntax, Tale, Tell, Truck, Who

Relax(ation), Relaxant, Relaxed Abate, Atony, Calm, Casual, Chill (out), Com(m)odo, Dégagé, Délassement, Détente, Diversion, Downbeat, Ease, Easy-going, Flaccid, Informal, Laid-back, Laze, Leisured, Let-up, → **LOOSEN**, Mellow (out), Mitigate, Outspan, Peace, Recline, Relent, Relief, Remit, Rest, Settle, Sit down, Slacken, Sleep, Slump, Soma, Soothe, Toneless, Tranquil, Unbend, Unbrace, Unclench, Unknit, Unstiffen, Untie, Unwind, Yoga

▷ **Relaxed** *may indicate* an anagram

▷ **Relay(ing)** *may indicate* an anagram

Release Abreact, Abrogation, Announcement, Bail, Block, Cable, Catharsis, Clear, Day, Death, Deliver(y), Desorb, Disburden, Discharge, Disclose, Disengage, Disenthral, Disimprison, Dismiss, Disorb, Emancipate, Enfree, Exclaustration, Excuse, Exeem, Exeme, Exemption, Exonerate, Extricate, Exude, Free, Handout, Happy, → **LIBERATE**, Manumit, Merciful, Moksa, Nirvana, Outrush, Parole, Press, Quietus, Quitclaim, Quittance, Relinquish, Remission, Ripcord, Soft, Spring, Tre corde, Trip, Unchain, Unconfine, Uncouple, Undo, Unhand, Unharness, Unleash, Unlock, Unloose, Unpen, Unshackle, Unsnap, Unteam, Untether, Untie

Relevance, Relevant Ad rem, Appliable, Applicable, Apposite, Apropos, Apt, Germane, Material, Pertinent, Point, Real world, Valid

▶ **Reliable, Reliance** *see* **RELY**

Relic Antique, Ark, Artefact, Fossil, Leftover, Memento, Neolith, Remains, Sangraal, Sangrail, Sangreal, Souvenir, Survival, Vestige

Relief, Relieve(d) Aid, Air-lift, Allay, Alleviate, Alms, Anodyne, Assistance, Assuage, Bas, Cameo, Catharsis, Cavo-relievo, Comfort, Contrast, Cure, Détente, Ease(ment), Emboss, Emollient, Exempt, Free, Help, High, Indoor, Let-up, Lighten, Linocut, Low, Mafeking, MIRAS, Mitigation, On the parish, Outdoor, Palliate, Phew, Photo, Pog(e)y, Reassure, Redress, Refection, Remedy, Remission, Replacement, Repoussé, Reprieve, → **RESCUE**, Respite, Retirement, Rid, Scratch, Sigh, Spare, Spell, Stand-in, Succour, Taper, Tax, TENS, Thankful, Thermoform, Whew, Woodcut

Religion, Religious (sect) Congregant, Creed, Cult, Denomination, Devout, Doctrine, Eremite, Faith, Godfearing, God-slot, God-squad, Hieratic, Hospital(l)er, Messeigneurs, Missionary, Missioner, Monastic, Monseigneur, Nun, Oblate, Opium, Opus Dei, Orthodox, Pi, Russellite, Serious, Spiritual, State, Theology, Whore, Zealous

Relish(ing) Appetite, Aspic, Botargo, Caponata, Catsup, Chow-chow, Chutney, Condiment, Embellishment, Enjoy, Flavour, Gentleman's, Gout, Gust(o), Horseradish, Ketchup, Lap(-up), Lust, Opsonium, Palate, Pesto, Piccalilli, Sapid, Sar, Sauce, Savour, Seasoning, Tang, Tooth, Worcester sauce, Zest

Reluctant, Reluctance Averse, Backward, Chary, Circumspect, Cockshy, Cold feet, Grudging, Hesitant, Laith, Lethargy, Loath, Loth, Nolition, Prudish, Renitent, Shy, Under protest, Unwilling

Rely, Reliance, Reliant, Reliable Addiction, Authentic, Bank, Bread and butter, Brick, Confidence, Constant, Copper-bottomed, →COUNT, Dependent, Found, Honest, Hope, Inerrant, Jeeves, Leal, Lean, Loyal, Mensch, Predictable, Presume, Pukka, Rest, Robin, Safe, Secure, Solid, Sound, Sponge, Stalwart, Stand-by, Staunch, Steady, Straight, Sure, Trade on, Trump, Trustworthy, Trusty, Unfailing

Remain(s), Remainder, Remaining Abide, Ash(es), Balance, Bide, Carcass, Continue, Corse, Dreg(s), Dwell, Embers, Estate, Extant, Exuviae, Fag-end, Fossils, Heeltap, Kreng, Last, Late, Lave, Left, Lie, Locorestive, Manet, Nose, Oddment, Orts, Other, Outstand, Persist, Relic(ts), Reliquae, Residue, Rest, Ruins, Rump, Scourings, Scraps, Stand, Stay, Stick, Stub, Stump, Surplus, Survive, Tag-end, Talon, Tarry, Wait

Remark Aside, Aspersion, Barb, Bromide, Comment(ary), Compliment, Descry, Dig, Generalise, Mention, Noise, →NOTE, Notice, Obiter dictum, Observe, Personal, Platitude, Quip, Reason, Sally, Say, Shot, State

Remarkable, Remarkably A1, Amazing, A one, Arresting, Beauty, Bodacious, Come-on, Conspicuous, Dilly, Egregious, Eminent, Extraordinary, Heliozoan, Lamentable, Legendary, Lulu, Mirable, Notable, Notandum, Noteworthy, Personal, Phenomenal, Rattling, →SIGNAL, Singular, Some, Striking, Tall, Unco, Uncommon, Visible

Remedial, Remedy Adaptogen, Aid, Antacid, Antibiotic, Antidote, Antihistamine, Arnica, Bicarb, Boneset, Calomel, Corrective, Cortisone, →CURE, Cure-all, Decongestant, Drug, Elixir, Emetic, Febrifuge, Feverfew, Fumitory, Ginseng, Heal, Ipecac, Medicate, Medicine, Nostrum, Palliative, Panacea, Paregoric, Poultice, Rectify, Redress, Repair, Salve, Simple, Solve, Sovereign, Specific, Sucralfate, Therapeutic, Treatment

Remember(ed), Remembering, Remembrance Bethink, Catchy, Commemorate, Con, Mem, Memorial, Memorise, Mention, Mneme, Poppy, Recall, Recollect, Remind, Reminisce, Retain, Rosemary, Souvenir

▷**Remember** *may indicate* RE-member, *viz.* Sapper

Remind(er) Aftertaste, Aide-memoire, Bell ringer, Bethought, Bookmark, Evocatory, Evoke, Jog, Keepsake, Mark, Memento (mori), Memo, Mnemonic, Mnemotechnic, Monition, Nudge, Phylactery, Prod, Prompt, Shades of, Souvenir, Spur, Throwback, Token

Remission Abatement, Absolution, Acceptilation, Indulgence, Pardon, Pause

Remnant Butt, End, Fent, Heeltap, Leavings, Left-over, Odd-come-short, Offcut, Relic, Relict, →REMAINDER, Rump, Stub, Sweepings, Trace, Vestige, Witness

Remorse(ful) Angst, Apologetic, Ayenbite, Breast-beating, Compunction, Contrition, Had-i-wist, Pity, →REGRET, Repentance, Rue, Ruing, Ruth, Sorrow, Worm

Remote(ness) Afield, Aloof, Aphelion, Backveld, Backwater, Backwood, Boondocks, Bullamakanka, Bundu, Bush, →DISTANT, Forane, Foreign, Inapproachable, Insular, Irrelevant, Jericho, Lonely, Long(inquity), Mystique, Nowhere, Off-the-map, Out(part), Outback, Out of the way, Reassert, Scrub, Secluded, Shut-out, Slightest, Surrealistic, Unlikely, Withdrawn, Wop-wops

Removal, Remove(d) Abduct, Abstract, Airbrush, Assuage, Banish, Blot, Circumcision, Clear, Couch, Deaccession, Debridement, Declassify, Deduct, Dele(te), Depilate, Depose, Detach, Dethrone, Detract, Dislodge, Dismiss, Dispel, Displace, Doff, Efface, Eject, Eliminate, Eloi(g)n, Emend, Eradicate,

Erase, Esloin, Estrange, Evacuate, Evict, Exalt, Excise, Expunge, Expurgate, Extirpate, Far, Fillet, Flit, Gut, Huff, Nick, Obviation, Ouster, Raise, Raze, Recuse, Rid(dance), Scratch, Shift, Sideline, Spirit, Strip, Subtract, Supplant, Swipe, Transfer, Transport, Unbelt, Unload, Unseat, Unstep, Uproot, Wrest

Render(ing) Construe, Deliver, Do, Gie, Give, Interpretation, Make, Melt, Pebble-dash, Plaster, Provide, Recite, Represent, Restore, Setting, Submit, Tallow, Try, Yeve, Yield

Rendezvous Date, Meeting, Philippi, Tryst, Venue

Rendition Account, Delivery, Interpretation, Translation, Version

Renegade, Reneg(u)e Apostate, Default, Defector, Deserter, Pike, Rat(ton), Recreant, Traitor, Turncoat, Weasel out

▷**Renegade** *may indicate* a word reversal

Renew(al) Instauration, Neogenesis, Palingenesis, Refresh, Replace, Resumption, Retrace, Revival, Urban

Renounce, Renunciation Abandon, Abdicate, Abjure, Abnegate, Disclaim, Disown, Forfeit, For(e)go, Forisfamiliate, Forsake, For(e)say, Forswear, Kenosis, Pass up, Recede, Recuse, Refuse, Relinquish, Renay, Retract, Sacrifice

Renovate(d), Renovation Duff, Face-lift, Instauration, Makeover, Refurbish, Renew, Repair, Restore, Revamp, Touch up, Translate

Rent(er), Rented, Renting Asunder, Attorn, Broken, Charge, Cornage, Cost, Crack, Cranny, Cuddeehih, Cuddy, Division, Economic, Fair, Farm, Fee, Fissure, Gale, Gavel, Ground, →**HIRE**, Lease, Let, List, Mail, Market, Occupy, Opening, Pendicle, Penny(-mail), Peppercorn, Quit-rent, Rack, Rip, Rived, Riven, Screed, Seat, Slit, Split, Stallage, Subtenant, Tare, Tenant, Tithe, Tore, Torn, Tythe, White

▷**Reorganised** *may indicate* an anagram

Repair(s), Repairer, Reparation Amend(s), Anaplasty, Botch, Cobble, Damages, Darn, DIY, Doctor, Expiation, Fettle, Fitter, Fix, Garage, Go, Haro, Harrow, Heel, Make good, →**MEND**, Neoplasty, Overhaul, Patch, Point, Recompense, Recover, Redress, Refit, Reheel, Remedy, Renew, Repoint, Resort, Restore, Retouch, Roadworks, Satisfaction, Save, Service, Stitch, Stopgap, Tenorrhaphy, Ulling, Vamp, Volery, Wright

Repartee Backchat, Badinage, Banter, Cross talk, Persiflage, Rejoinder, Retort, Riposte, Wit, Wordplay

Repast Bever, Collection, Food, Meal, Tea, Treat

Repay(ment) Avenge, Compensate, Perseverate, Quit, Reassert, Refund, Reimburse, Requite, Retaliate, Revenge, Reward, Satisfaction

Repeat(ed), Repeatedly, Repetition, Repetitive Again, Alliteration, Belch, Bis, Burden, Burp, Copy, Cycle, Ditto(graphy), Do, Duplicate, →**ECHO**, Echolalia, Encore, Eruct, Facsimile, Habitual, Harp, Image, Imitate, Iterate, Leit-motiv, Parrot, Parrot-fashion, Passion, Perpetuate, Perseverate, Playback, Reassert, Recapitulate, Recite(r), Redo, Refrain, Regurgitate, Reiterate, Renew, Rep, Repetend, Rerun, Retail, Ritual, Rote, Same(y), Screed, Tautology, Thrum, Trite

Repel(lent) Aversive, Camphor, Deet, Estrange, Harsh, Offensive, Rebarbative, Reject, Repulse, Resist, Revolt, Scare, Shoo, Squalid, Turn-off, Ug(h), Ward

▶**Repetition** *see* **REPEAT(ED)**

Replace(ment), Replaceable, Replacing Change, Deputise, Diadochy, Euphorism, For, Instead, Novation, Overwrite, Pinch-hit, Pre-empt, Raincheck, Refill, Reinstate, Relief, Renew, Replenish, Restore, Spare part, Stand-in, Substitute, Supersede, Supplant, Surrogate, Taxis, Transform, Transliterate, Understudy, Upgrade, Usurp

Replete, Repletion Awash, Full, Gorged, Plenitude, Plethora, Sated, Satiation

Replica Clone, Copy, Duplicate, Facsimile, Image, Repetition, Spit

Reply Accept, Answer, Churlish, Counter-attack, Duply, Echo, Rejoinder, Replication, Repost, Rescript, Response, Retort, Surrebut, Surrejoinder

Report(s), Reporter Account, Announce, Annual, Auricular, Bang, Beveridge, Blacksmith, Bruit, Bulletin, Cahier, Clap, Columnist, Comment, Commentator, Compte rendu, Correspondent, Court, Court circular, Cover, Crack, Crump, Cub, Debrief, Describe, Despatch, Disclose, Dispatch, Dissertation, Document, Explosion, Fame, Fireman, Grapevine, Gunshot, Hansard, Hearsay, Informant, Item, Jenkins, Journalist, Legman, Libel, Narrative, News, Newsflash, Newshawk, Newshound, Newsman, Noise, Notify, On dit, Paper, Pop, Powwow, Pressman, Protocol, Rapporteur, Read-out, Recount, Relate, Relay, Representation, Repute, Return, Roorback, Rumour, Shot, Sitrep, Sound(bite), Staffer, State(ment), Stringer, Survey, Tale, → **TELL**, Thesis, Thunder (clap), Transactions, Transcribe, Tripehound, Troop, Update, Weather, Whang, White paper, Wolfenden, Write up

▷**Reported** *may indicate* the sound of a letter or word

Represent(ation), Representative, Represented Agent, Ambassador, Archetypal, Assembly-man, Caricature, Client, Commercial, Commissary, Commissioner, Cross-section, Delegate, Depict, Deputation, Describe, Display, Drawing, Drummer, Effigy, Elchee, Eltchi, Emblem, Embody, Emissary, Epitomise, Example, Histogram, Ikon, Image, Instantiate, John Bull, Legate, Limn, Lobby, Mandala, Map, Model, Mouthpiece, MP, Nuncio, Personate, Personify, Piechart, Portray, Proportional, Quintessence, Rep, Resemble, Salesman, Senator, Shop steward, Simulacrum, Spokesman, Stand-in, Statua, Status, Steward, Symbolic, Tableau, Tableau vivant, Token, Transcription, Traveller, Typical, Vice-consul, Visitor-general

▷**Represented** *may indicate* an anagram

Reprimand Blast, Bounce, Carpet, Castigate, → **CENSURE**, Chastise, Chide, Dressing-down, Earful, Jobe, Lace into, Lecture, Rating, Rebuke, Reproof, Rocket, Rollicking, Scold, Slate, Strafe, Targe, Tick off, Tongue-lashing, Wig

Reproach Besom, Bisom, Blame, Braid, Byword, Cataian, Catayan, Chide, Discredit, Dispraise, Exprobrate, Gib, Mispraise, Odium, Opprobrium, Rebuke, Ronyon, Runnion, Scold, Shend, Sloan, Stigma, Taunt, Truant, Twat, Twit, Upbraid, Upcast, Yshend

Reproduce(r), Reproduction, Reproductive (organ) Ambisonics®, Arrhenotoky, Bearing, Clone, Copy, Counterfeit, Depict, Duplicate, Edition, Egg(s), Etch, Eugenics, Generation, Genitalia, Loins, Megaspore, Mono, Monogenesis, Monogony, Multiply, Oogamy, Parthenogenesis, Phon(e)y, Pirate, Propagate, Refer, Replica, Roneo®, Seminal, Simulate, Stereo, Vegetative, Viviparism

▷**Reproduce** *may indicate* an anagram

Reproof, Reprove Admonish, Berate, Brickbat, Censure, Chide, Correction, Correption, Lecture, Rap, Rate, Rebuff, Rebuke, Reprehension, Scold, Sloan, Take to task, Tut, Upbraid

Reptile, Reptilian Agamid, Alligarta, Alligator, Base, Basilisk, Caiman, Cayman, Chameleon, Chelonian, Creeper, Crocodile, Cynodont, Diapsid, Dicynodont, Dinosaur, Gecko, Goanna, Herpetology, Lacertine, Lizard, Mamba, Pelycosaur, Pit viper, Pteranodon, Pterodactyl, Pterosaur, Rhynchocephalian, Sauroid, → **SNAKE**, Sphenodon, Squamata, Synapsid, Tegu(exin), Thecodont, Therapsid, Tortoise, Tuatara, Tuatera, Turtle, Worm

Republic(s) Antimonarchist, Banana, Second, State

Republican Antimonarchist, Belarussian, Democrat, Fenian, Fianna Fáil, Girondist, GOP, International Brigade, IRA, Iraqi, Leveller, Montagnard, Mugwump, Plato, Provisional, Provo, R, Red, Sansculotte, Sansculottic, Sinn Fein, Whig, Young Italy

Repudiate Abjure, Deny, Disaffirm, Disavow, Discard, Disclaim, Disown, Ignore, Recant, Reject, Renounce, Repel

Repugnance, Repugnant Abhorrent, Alien, Disgust, Distaste, Fulsome, Horror, Loathing, Nastiness, Noisome, Obscene, Odious, Revulsion

Reputable, Reputation, Repute(d) Bubble, Credit, Dit, Estimate, Fame, Good, Izzat, Loos, Los, Name, Note, Notoriety, Odour, Opinion, Prestige, Putative, Regard, Renown, Said, Sar, → **STANDING**, Stature, Status, Stink, Stock, Trustworthy

Request Adjure, Appeal, Application, Apply, Ask, Beg, Desire, D-notice, Entreaty, Implore, Invite, Petition, Plea, Prayer, Precatory, Solicit, Supplication, Touch

Require(d), Requirement Charge, Crave, De rigueur, Desideratum, Desire, Enjoin, Essential, Exact, Expect, Incumbent, Lack, Mandatory, Necessity, Need, Prerequisite, Priority, Proviso, Seek, Sine qua non, Stipulate, Then

Requisite, Requisition Commandeer, Due, Embargo, Essential, Indent, Necessary, Needful, Order, Press

Rescue(r) Aid, Air-sea, Bring off, Deliver, Free, Liberate, Lifeboat, Lifeline, Lifesave, Mountain, Noah, Ransom, Reclaim, Recover, Recower, Redeem, Regain, Relieve, Repatriate, Reprieve, Retrieve, Salvage, Salvation, → **SAVE**, White knight

Research(er) Audience, Boffin, Delve, Dig, Enquiry, Explore, Fieldwork, Indagator, Investigate, Legwork, Market, MORI, Near-market, Operational, Opposition, Pioneer, Post-doctoral, Psychical, Quest, Res, Scientist, Sus(s), Test, Thesis

Resemblance, Resemble, Resembling Affinity, Apatetic, Ape, Approach, Assimilate, Assonant, Homophyly, Likeness, Match, -oid, -opsis, Quasi, Replica, Similitude, Simulacrum, Simulate

Resent(ful), Resentment Acrimony, Anger, Bitter(ness), Bridle, Choler, Cross, Dudgeon, Embittered, Envy, Grudge, Indignation, Ire, Malic, Malign, Miff, Mind, Offence, Pique, Rancour, Rankle, Smart, Snarling, Spite, Umbrage

Reservation, Reserve(d), Reservist(s) Aloof, Arrière-pensée, Aside, Backlog, Bag, Bank, Bashful, Book, But, By, Capital, Caveat, Central, Cold, Condition, Coy, Demiss, Detachment, Distant, Earmark, Engage, Ersatz, Except, Fall-back, Federal, Fort Knox, Fund, General, Gold, Hold, Husband, Ice, Indian, Introvert, Landwehr, Layby, Locum, Median strip, Mental, Militiaman, Modesty, Nature, Nest-egg, Nineteenth man, Pool, Pound, Proviso, Qualification, Reddendum, Res, Rest, Restraint, Retain, Reticence, Retiring, Rez, Safari park, Salvo, Sanctuary, Save, Scenic, Scruple, Serengeti, Set aside, Shyness, Special, Spoken for, Stand-by, Stand-offishness, Starch, Stash, Stock(pile), Sub(stitute), TA (men), Taciturn, Twelfth man, Uncommunicate, Undemonstrative, Understudy, Warren, Waves, Withhold

Reservoir Basin, Cistern, Font, G(h)ilgai, Gilgie, Inkholder, Lake, Oilcup, Repository, Stock, Sump, Tank, Well

Reside(nce), Resident(s), Residential Abode, Address, Amban, Chequers, Commorant, Consulate, Denizen, Domicile, Dwell, Embassy, Establishment,

Expatriate, Exurb(anite), Gaff, Gremial, Guest, Home, Hostel, Housemate, Indweller, Inholder, Inmate, Intern, Ledger, Lei(d)ger, Lieger, Lodgement, Lodger, Masonry, Metic, Native, Pad, Parietal, Populace, Resiant, Roost, Settle, Settlement, Sojourn, Squat, Stay, Tenant, Tenement, Uptown, Villager, Yamen

Residual, Residue Ash, Astatki, Calx, Caput, Chaff, Cinders, Clinker, Crud, Draff, Dregs, Expellers, Greaves, Heeltap, Leavings, Mazout, Mortuum, Pitch, Prefecture, Raffinate, Remainder, Remanent, Remnant, Scourings, Sediment, Slag, Slurry, Snuff, Soot, Vinasse

Resign(ed), Resignation Abandon, Abdicate, Demit, Fatalism, Heigh-ho, Leave, Meek, Patience, Philosophical, →QUIT, Reconcile, Step down, Stoic, Submit

Resin Acaroid, Amber, Amine, Amino, Arar, Asaf(o)etida, Bakelite®, Balsam, Benjamin, Benzoin, Burgundy pitch, Cachou, Cannabin, Caranna, Carauna, Catechu, Charas, Churrus, Colophony, Conima, Copai(ba), Copaiva, Copal(m), Courbaril, Cutch, Dam(m)ar, Dammer, Dragon's blood, Elemi, Epoxy, Frankincense, Galbanum, Galipot, Gambi(e)r, Gamboge, Glyptal, Guaiacum, Gum, Hasheesh, Hashish, Hing, Jalapic, Jalapin, Kino, Lac, Ladanum, Limonene, Lupulin, Mastic, Melamine, Myrrh, Natural, Olibanum, Opopanax, Phenolic, Podophyl(l)in, Polyester, Polymer, Polypropylene, Propolis, Retinite, Roset, Rosin, Rosit, Rozet, Rozit, Sagapenum, Sandarac(h), Saran®, Scammony, Shellac, Silicone, Storax, Styrene, Synthetic, Tacamahac, Tacmahack, Takamaka, Thus, Urea, Xylenol

Resist, Resistance, Resistant, Resistor All-weather, Anti, Antibiotic, Barretter, Bleeder, Bristle, Buck, Ceramal, Cermet, Chetnik, Coccidiostat, Combat, Consumer, Contest, Defiance, Defy, Diehard, Drag, Element, Face, Fend, Friction, Gainstrive, Grapo, Hostile, Immunity, Impede, Impediment, Internal, Intifada, Invar, Klendusic, Klepht, Maquis, Maraging, Market, Megohm, Microhm, Negative, Obstacle, Ohm(age), Omega, Oppose, Partisan, Passive, Pull, R, Radiation, Redound, Reluct, Reluctance, Renitent, Resilient, Rheostat, Sales, Satyagraha, Shockproof, Soul-force, Specific, Stability, Stand (pat), Stonde, Stubborn, Tamil Tiger, Tough, Voltage divider

Resolute, Resolution Adamant, Analysis, Bold, Cast-iron, Closure, Courage, Decided, Decision, Denouement, Determined, Dogged, →FIRM, Fortitude, Granite, Grim, Grit, Hardiness, Insist, Iron, Manful, Motion, New Year, Pertinacity, Promotion, Rede, Reed(e), Resolve, Stable, Stalwart, Staunch, Stout(-hearted), Strength, Strong-willed, Sturdy, Tenacity, Tough, Unbending, Unmoved, Valiant, Willpower

Resolve(d), Resolver Aim, Analyse, Calculate, Conation, Conciliate, Decide, Declare, →DETERMINE, Deus ex machina, Factorise, Fix, Grit, Hellbent, Intent, Nerve, Pecker, →PURPOSE, Right, Settle, Sort out, Steadfast, Tenacity, Vow

▷**Resolved** *may indicate* an anagram

Resort Acapulco, Antibes, Arbroath, Aspen, Benidorm, Biarritz, Blackpool, Bognor, Bournemouth, Brighton, Cancun, Cannes, Centre, Chamonix, Clacton, Copacabana, Davos, Dive, Estoril, Étaples, Expedient, Frame, Frequent, Frinton, Gstaad, Haunt, Health, Herne Bay, Hove, Hydro, Invoke, Klosters, Lair, Last, Las Vegas, Llandudno, Locarno, Malaga, Malibu, Margate, Menton, Miami, Minehead, Morecambe, Nassau, Nice, Orlando, Ostend, Palm Beach, Pau, Penzance, Pis aller, Poole, Portrush, Ramsgate, Rapallo, Recourse, Redcar, Repair, Rhyl, Rimini, Riviera, St Ives, St Tropez, Seaside, Skegness, Southend, Spa(w), Swanage, Tampa, Thredbo, Torquay, Torremolinos, Troon, Use, Utilise,

Waikiki, Weston-super-Mare, Weymouth, Whitby, Worthing, Yalta
▷**Resort(ing)** *may indicate* an anagram

Resource(s), Resourceful Assets, Beans, Bottom, Chevisance, Clever, Faculty, Funds, Gumption, Ingenious, Input, Inventive, Manpower, Means, Renewable, Shared, Sharp, Smeddum, Stock-in-trade, →**VERSATILE**, Ways and means, Wealth, Webliography

Respect(ed), Respectability, Respectable, Respectful Admire, Ahimsa, Aspect, Behalf, Bien-séance, Clean cut, Consecrate, Consider, Cred(it), Curtsey, Decent, Deference, Devoir, Douleia, Doyen(ne), Duty, Eminent, Esteem, Fear, Genteel, Gigman, Homage, →**HONOUR**, Kempt, Kowtowing, Latria, Obeisant, Officious, Pace, Particular, Polite, Preppy, Presentable, Prestige, Proper, Reference, Regard, Relation, Reputable, Revere, Sir, S(t)irrah, U, Venerate, Way, Wellborn, Well-thought-of, Wise, Worthy

Respirator, Respire, Respiration Artificial, Blow, Breathe, Exhale, External, Gasmask, Inhale, Iron lung, Mouth-to-mouth, Pant, Snorkel

Respond, Response, Responsive Amenable, Answer, Antiphon, Autoreply, Backchat, Backlash, Bi, Comeback, Conditioned, Counteroffer, Duh, Echo, Feedback, Flechman, Grunt, Immune, Kneejerk, Kyrie, Litany, Meow, Nastic, Pavlovian, Photonasty, Plea, Prebuttal, Psychogalvanic, Racket, React(ion), Reagency, Rebutter, Reflex, Reply, Repost, Retort, Rheotaxis, Rheotropism, Rise, Sensitive, Stayman, Synapte, Syntonic, Tender, Thigmotropic, Tic, Tropism, Unconditioned, Voice, Warm, Wilco

Responsibility, Responsible Accountable, Anchor, Answerable, Baby, Behind, Blame, Buck, Charge, Collective, Culpable, Dependable, Diminished, Duty, Frankpledge, Guilty, Hot seat, Incumbent, Instrumental, Liable, Mantle, Mea culpa, Millstone, Noblesse oblige, Onus, Parental, Perpetrate, Pigeon, Sane, Solid, Stayman, Trust

Rest(ing), Rest day Abutment, Anchor, Balance, Bed, Break, Breather, Calm, Catnap, Depend, Dormant, Dwell, Ease, Easel, Etc(etera), Feutre, Gallows, Gite, Halt, Inaction, Jigger, Lance, Lave, Lay to, Lean, Leasure, Leisure, Lie, Lie-in, Light, Lodge, Loll, Lound, Lull, Minim, Nap, Noah, Oasis, Others, Outspan, Pause, Quiescence, Quiet, Relâche, Relax, Rely, Remainder, Repose, Requiem, Reserve, Respite, Sabbath, Shut-eye, Sick leave, Siesta, Silence, →**SLEEP**, Slumber, Spell, Spider, Static, Stopover, Support, Surplus, Teabreak, Waypoint

Restaurant, Restaurateur Automat, Beanery, Bistro, Brasserie, British, Cabaret, Café, Canteen, Carvery, Chew'n'spew, Chippy, Chip-shop, Chophouse, Coffee shop, Commissary, Cook shop, Creperie, Diner, Eatery, Eating-house, Estaminet, Gastropub, Greasy spoon, Grill, Grillroom, Grub shop, Luncheonette, Maxim's, Naafi, Noshery, Padrone, Pizzeria, Porter-house, Rathskeller, Ratskeller, Raw bar, Roadhouse, Rotisserie, Slap-bang, Steakhouse, Takeaway, Taqueria, Taverna, Tea garden, Teahouse, Tearoom, Teashop, Trat(toria)

Restive, Restless(ness) Agitato, Chafing, Chorea, Fantods, Feverish, Fidgety, Fikish, Fitful, Free-arm, Impatient, Itchy, Jactitation, Spring fever, Toey, Unsettled
▷**Restless** *may indicate* an anagram

Restoration, Restorative, Restore(d) Bring to, Cure, Descramble, Graft, Heal, Mend, New, Pentimento, Pick-me-up, Postliminy, Rally, Reclaim, Recondition, Recuperate, Redeem, Redintegrate, Redress, Redux, Refresh, Refurbish, Regenerate, Rehabilitate, Reinstate, Reintegrate, Rejuvenate, Remedial, Renew, Renovate, Replenish, Replevy, Repone, Restitute, Resuscitate, Retouch, Revamp, Revive, Righten, Salvage, Stet, Tonic, Undelete, Whole

Restrain(ed), Restraint Abstinence, Ban, Bar, Bate, Bit, Bottle, Branks, Bridle, Cage, Censor, Chain, Chasten, →**CHECK**, Checks and balances, Chokehold, Coerce, Cohibit, Compesce, Confinement, Contain, Control, Cramp, Curb, Dam, Decorum, Detent, Dry, Duress, Embargo, Enfetter, Fetter, Freeze, Gag-rein, Gyve, Halt, Hamshackle, Handcuffs, Harness, Heft, Hinder, Hopple, Immanacle, Impound, Inhibit, Jess, Leash, Leg-iron, Lid, Low-key, Manacle, Measure, Mince, Moderation, Muzzle, Patient, Pen, Pinion, Quiet, Rein, Repress, Restrict, Ritenuto, Seat belt, Shackle, Sober, Sobriety, Spancel, Squeeze, Stay, Stent, Stint, Straitjacket, Strait-waistcoat, Tabu, Temper(ate), Tether, Tie, Tieback, Trash, Underplay

Restrict(ed), Restriction Band, Bar, Bind, Bit, Block, Burden, Cage, Catch, Censorship, Chain, Circumscribe, Closet, Condition, Constrain, Cord, Corset, Cramp, Curb, Curfew, DORA, Entail, Fence, Fetter, Fold, Gate, Ground, Guard, Hamper, Hamstring, Handcuff, Hedge, Hidebound, Hobble, Inhibit, Intern, Irons, Kennel, Let, →**LIMIT**, Localise, Lock, Mere, Narrow, Net, Nick, No-go, Oche, Pale, Parochial, Pen, Pent, Pier, Pin, Poky, Pot-bound, Private, Proscribed, Qualify, Ration, Regulate, Rein, Rent, Repression, Rope, Safety belt, Scant, Seal, Section, Selected, Shackle, Snare, Squeeze, Stenopaic, Stent, Stint, Stop, Straiten, Stunt, Swaddle, Tether, Tie

Result(s) After-effect, Aftermath, Ans(wer), Arise, Bring, Causal, Consequence, Effect, Emanate, End, End-product, Ensue, Entail, Event, Eventuate, Finding, Fruict, Fruition, Fruits, Issue, Karmic, Lattermath, →**OUTCOME**, Outturn, Pan, Pay off, Proceeds, Product, Quotient, Score-line, Sequel, Side-effect, Sum, Therefore, Upshot, Verdict, Wale

Retain(er), Retains, Retention, Retentive Brief, Contain, Deposit, Fee, Hold, Keep, Long, Memory, Panter, Pantler, Reserve, Retinue, Servant, Ur(a)emia, Vassal

Retaliate, Retaliation Avenge, Carousel, Counter(measure), Lex talionis, Pay back, Pay home, Quit(e), Redress, Repay, Reprisal, Requite, Retort, Revenge, Talion, Tit for tat

Reticence, Reticent Boutonne, Clam, Close, Cowardly, Coy, Dark, Guarded, Introvert, Reserve, Restraint, Secretive, Shy, Taciturn

Retinue Comitatus, Company, Cortège, Equipage, Following, Meiney, Meinie, Meiny, Menyie, Sowarry, Suite

Retire(d), Retiree, Retirement, Retiring Abed, Aloof, Asocial, Baccare, Backare, Backpedal, Blate, Bowler-hat, Bow out, Cede, Coy, Demob, Demure, Depart, Ebb, Emeritus, Essene, Former, Leave, Lonely, Modest, Mothball, Nun, Outgoing, Pension, Private, Put out, Quit, Recede, Recluse, Reserved, Resign, Retract, Retreat, Retrocedent, Roost, Rusticate, Scratch, Sequester, Shy, Superannuate, Timid, Unassertive, Withdraw

▷**Retirement** *may indicate* 'bed' *around another word, or word reversed*

Retort Alembic, Comeback, Courteous, Floorer, Quip, Repartee, →**REPLY**, Retaliate, Riposte, Still

Retract(ion) Disavow, Epanorthosis, Palinode, Recall, Recant, Renounce, Revoke

Retreat Abbey, About turn, Arbour, Ashram(a), Asylum, Backwater, Berchtesgaden, Bower, Bug, Cell, Climb down, Cloister, Convent, Dacha, Departure, Donjon, Draw back, Funkhole, Girth, Grith, Growlery, Hermitage, Hibernaculum, Hideaway, Hide-out, Hole, Ivory-tower, Lair, Lama(sery), Mew, Monastery, Nest, Nook, Nunnery, Pullback, Recede, Recoil, Redoubt, Reduit,

Refuge, Retire, Retraite, Right-about, Rout, Shangri-La, Shelter, Skedaddle, Stronghold, Withdraw

Retribution Come-uppance, Deserts, Nemesis, Revenge, Reward, Utu, Vengeance

Retrieve(r), Retrieval Access, Bird-dog, Chesapeake Bay, Fetch, Field, Gundog, Labrador, Read-out, Recall, Reclaim, Recoup, Recover, Redeem, Rescue, Salvage

Return(s) Agen, Answer, Bricole, Census, Comeback, Counter, Day, Diminishing, Dividend, Earnings, Echo, Elect, Er, Exchange, Extradite, Gain, Homecoming, Nil, Pay, Payback, Proceeds, Profit, Rebate, Rebound, Recur, Redound, Regress, Reject, Rejoin, Render, Rent, Repair, Repay, Replace, Reply, Requital, Respond, Rest, Restitution, Restoration, Restore, Retort, Retour, Revenue, Reverse, Revert, Riposte, Takings, Tax, Tit for tat, Traffic, →**YIELD**

Reveal(ing), Revelation Acute, Admit, Advertise, Air, Apocalyptic, Bar, Bare, Betray, Bewray, Confess, Declare, Descry, Disclose, Discover, Discure, →**DIVULGE**, Epiphany, Evince, Exhibit, Explain, Expose, Eye-opener, Giveaway, Hierophantic, Impart, Indicate, Indiscreet, Ingo, Kythe, Leak, Low-cut, Manifest, Open, Out, Parade, Pentimento, Rake up, Satori, Scanty, Scry, →**SHOW**, Skimpy, Spill, Tell-tale, Unclose, Uncover, Unfold, Unheal, Unmask, Unveil

Revel(ling), Revelry Ariot, Bacchanalia, Bend, Carnival, Carouse, Comus, Dionysian, Disport, Feast, Gloat, Glory, Joy, Maffick, Merriment, On the tiles, Orgy, Rant, Rejoice, Riot, Roister, Rollicks, Rout, Royst, Saturnalia, Splore, Swig, Upsee, Ups(e)y, Wallow, Wassail, Whoopee

Revenge(r), Revengeful Aftergame, Avenge, Commination, Goel, Grenville, Montezuma's, Nightrider, Payback, Reprise, Requite, Retaliation, Revanche, Settlement, Tit for tat, Ultion, Utu, Vigilante, Vindictive

Revere(nce), Revered Admire, Adoration, Awe, Bostonian, Dread, Dulia, Esteem, Fear, Hallow, Hero, Hery, Homage, →**HONOUR**, Hyperdulia, Idolise, Latria, Obeisance, Paul, Prostration, Respect, Venerate

Reversal, Reverse, Reversing, Reversion, Reversible Anatropy, Antithesis, Antonym, Arsy-versy, Atavism, Back(slide), B-side, Change-over, Chiasmus, Counter(mand), Escheat, Evaginate, Exergue, Flip, Flip side, Inversion, Mirror image, Misfortune, →**OPPOSITE**, Overturn, Palindrome, Pile, Regress, Repeal, Retrograde, Revoke, Rheotropic, Setback, Switchback, Tails, Throwback, Transit, Turn, Turnabout, Two-faced, Un-, Undo, Upend, U-turn, Verso, Vice versa, Volte-face, Woman

Review(er) Appeal, Audit, Censor, Credit, Critic, Criticaster, Critique, Editor, Feuilleton, Footlights, Glimpse, Inspect, Iso-, Judicial, Magazine, March-past, Notice, Pan, Panorama, Peer, Pick over, Pundit, Quarterly, Recapitulate, Repeat, Retrospect, Revise, Rundown, Run over, Slate, Spithead, Summary, Summing-up, Survey, Write-up

▷**Review** *may indicate* an anagram or a reversed word

Revise(r), Revision(ist) Alter, Amend, Change, Correct, Diaskeuast, Diorthosis, Edit, Emend, Heretic, Peruse, Reappraise, Reassess, Recense, Reform, Rev, Rework, Update

▷**Revise(d)** *may indicate* an anagram

Revive(r), Revival(ist), Revivify, Reviving Araise, Classical, Enliven, Gothic, Kiss of life, Neo-classical, Rally, Reanimate, Reawake(n), Rebirth, Redintegrate, Redux, Refresh, Rekindle, Relive, Renaissance, Renascent, Renew, Renovate, Restore, Resurrect, Resuscitate, Risorgimento, Romantic, Romo, Rouse, Sal volatile, Smelling salts, Wake

Revolt(ing), Revolution(ary) Agitator, American, Anarchist, Apostasy, Barrel roll, Bloodless, Bolshevik, Boxer, Bukharin, Cade, Castro, Chartist, Che, Chinese, Circle, Coup d'état, Cultural, Cycle, Defection, Dervish, Desmoulins, De Valera, Disgust, Enragé, February, French, Girondin, Glorious, Green, Grody, Gyration, Ho Chi Minh, Icky, Industrial, → **IN REVOLT**, Insurgent, Insurrection, IRA, Lafayette, Lenin, Leninist, Mao, Marat, Marti, Marx, Marxist, Maximalist, Montagnard, Mutiny, Nauseating, October, Orbit, Paine, Palace, Paris Commune, Peasants, Pilgrimage of grace, Putsch, → **REBEL**, Red Guard, Red Shirt, Reformation, Reign of terror, Repellent, Riot, Robespierre, Roll, Rotation, Russian, Savimbi, Sedition, Septembrist, Sicilian Vespers, Spartacist, Spiral, Syndicalism, Titanomachy, Trot(sky), Ugly, Ultra, Unsavoury, → **UPRISING**, Upryst, Velvet, Weatherman, Whirl
▷**Revolutionary** *may indicate* 'reversed'
Revolve(r), Revolving Carrier, Catherine wheel, Centrifuge, Colt®, Gat, Girandole, Grindstone, → **GUN**, Gyrant, Gyrate, Iron, Klinostat, Lathe, Maelstrom, Merry-go-round, Peristrephic, Pistol, Pivot, Planet, Roll, Roller, Rotate, Rotifer, Rotor, Roul, Roundabout, Run, Spin, Swivel, Tone, Turn(stile), Turntable, Turret, Twiddle, Waterwheel, Wheel, Whirl(igig), Whirlpool
Revulsion Abhorrence, Distaste, Goose skin, Loathing, Repugnance, The creeps, Ugh
Reward(ing) Albricias, Bonus, Bounty, Compensate, Consideration, Desert, Emolument, Fee, Guerdon, Head money, Jackpot, Meed, Payment, Premium, Price, Prize, Profit, Purse, Push money, Reap, Recognise, Recompense, Reguerdon, Remuneration, Repay, Requital, Requite, S, Shilling, Stipend, Tanti, Wage, War(r)ison
Rhetoric(al) Alliteration, Anaphora, Anastrophe, Antimetabole, Antithesis, Antistrophe, Apophasis, Aposiopesis, Assonance, Asteism, Asyndeton, Aureate, Bombast, Brachylogia, Cacophony, Catachresis, Chiasmus, Eloquence, Enantiosis, Epanadiplosis, Epanados, Epanalepsis, Epanorthosis, Epexegesis, Epistrophe, Epizeuxis, Erotema, Eroteme, Erotesis, Euphemism, Hendiadys, Litotes, Metonymy, Oratory, Oxymoron, Paradox, Paral(e)ipsis, Periphrasis, Peroration, Pleonasm, Polysyndeton, Scesisonomaton, Speechcraft, Syllepsis, Trivial, Trivium, Zeugma
Rhyme(s), Rhymer, Rhyming Assonance, Clerihew, Closed couplet, Counting out, Couplet, Crambo, Cynghanedd, Doggerel, Double, Eye, Feminine, Head, Internal, Jingle, Macaronic, Masculine, Measure, Mother Goose, Nursery, Ode, Perfect, Poetry, Poulter's measure, Rondel, Runic, Sight, Slang, Slant, Tercet, Terza-rima, Thomas, Triple, → **VERSE**, Virelay
Rhythm(ic) Agoge, Alpha, Asynartete, Backbeat, Beat, Beta, Bo Diddley beat, Breakbeat, Cadence, Circadian, Clave, Dolichurus, Dotted, Drumbeat, Duple, Euouae, Evovae, Four-four, Ictic, In-step, Lilt, Meter, Movement, Oompah, Ostinato, Prosody, Pyrrhic, Rising, Rubato, Sdrucciola, Sesquialtera, Singsong, Sprung, Stride piano, Swing, Syncopation, Tala, Talea, Theta, Three-four, Time, Two-four, Voltinism
Rib(bed), Ribbing, Rib-joint Bar, Better half, Chaff, Cod, Cord, Costa, Cross-springer, Dutch, Eve, False, Floating, Futtock, Groin, Intercostal, Lierne, Nervate, Nervular, Nervure, Ogive, Persiflage, Rally, Spare, Springer, Subcosta, Tease, Tierceron, Tracery, True, Wife
Ribbon Band, Bandeau, Blue, Bow, Braid, Caddis, Caddyss, Cordon, Fattrels, Ferret, Fillet, Grosgrain, Hatband, Infula, Pad, Petersham, Radina, Red, Rein,

Riband, Rosette, Rouleau, Soutache, Taenia, Tape, Teniate, Tie, Topknot, Torsade

Rice (cake) Arborio, Basmati, Brown, Elmer, Entertainer, Golden, Idli, Indian, Kedgeree, Patna, Pilaf, Pilau, Pilaw, Reis, Risotto, Sushi, Twigs, Vialone nano, Wild, Zizania

Rich(es), Richness Abounding, Abundant, Affluent, Ample, Amusing, Bonanza, Buttery, Comfortable, Comic, Copious, Croesus, Dives, Edmund, Edwin, Fat, Feast, Fertile, Filthy, Flamboyant, Flush, Fruity, Full, Generous, Golconda, Haves, Heeled, High, Idle, Loaded, Luscious, Lush, Luxe, Luxurious, Mammon, Moneybags, Moneyed, Nabob, New, Oberous, Oofy, Plenteous, Plush, Plutocrat, Prolific, Rolling, Silvertail, Sumptuous, Tallent, Toff, Top hat, Treasure, Upper ten, Vulgarian, →**WEALTHY**, Well-heeled, Well off, Well-to-do
▷**Rickety** *may indicate* an anagram

Riddle(r) Boulter, Charade, Colander, Conundrum, Dilemma, Enigma, Koan, Logogriph, Pepper, Perforate, Permeate, Puzzle, Screen, Searce, Search, Seil, Sieve, Sift, Sile, Siler, Sorites, Sphinx, Strain, Tems(e), Trommel, Winnow

Ride, Riding Annoy, Bareback, Bestride, Bruise, Burn, Canter, Car(r)ousel, Coast, Cycle, District, Division, Draisene, Draisine, Drive, Equitation, Ferris wheel, Field, Free, Galloper, Hack, Harass, Haute école, Helter-skelter, Hitchhike, Lift, Merry-go-round, Mount, Pick(-a-)back, Piggyback, Postil(l)ion, Rape, Revere's, Roadstead, Rollercoaster, Rural, Sit, Spin, Stang, Surf, Switchback, Third, Transport, Trot, Waltzer, Weather, Welter, Wheelie, White-knuckle

Rider(s) Addendum, Addition, Adjunct, Afterthought, Appendage, Attachment, Boundary, Bucket, Cavalier, Charioteer, Circuit, Clause, Coachman, Codicil, Condition, Corollary, Dispatch, Equestrian, Eventer, Freedom, Gaucho, Godiva, Guidon, Haggard, Horseman, Jockey, Lochinvar, Messenger, Peloton, Postil(l)ion, Proviso, PS, Revere, Scrub, Spurrer, Transport, Walkyrie

Ridge(pole) Annapurna, Arête, As(ar), Aseismic, Bank, Bar, Baulk, Brow, Chine, Coteau, Crease, Crest, Culmen, Dune, Eskar, Esker, Hoe, Hog's back, Kaim, Kame, Ledge, List(er), Middleback, Moraine, Oche, Offset, Promontory, Riblet, Roof-tree, Wale, Weal, Welt, Whorl, Witwatersrand

Ridicule, Ridiculous Absurd, Badinage, Bathos, Chaff, Charade, Cockamamie, Debunk, Deride, Derisory, Egregious, Foolish, Gibe, Gird, Goad, Guy, Haze, Jeer, Jibe, Josh, Lampoon, Laughable, Ludicrous, Mimic, Mock, Paradox, Pasquin, Pillory, Pish, Pooh-pooh, Rag, Raillery, Rally, Rib, Rich, Risible, Roast, Satire, Scoff, Scout, Screwy, Send up, Sight, Silly, Skimmington, Sneer, Taunt, Travesty

Rifle(man) Air, Armalite®, Assault, Bone, Browning, Bundook, Burgle, Carbine, Chassepot, Enfield, Enfield musket, Escopette, Express, Ferret, Garand, →**GUN**, Jaeger, Kalashnikov, Loot, Magazine, Martini®, Mauser®, Minié, Pick, Pilfer, Pillage, Raid, Ransack, Reave, Reive, Repeater, Rieve, Rob, Saloon, Springfield, Winchester®

Rig(ging), Rigger Accoutre, Apparel, Attire, Bermuda, Deadeye, Drilling, Equip, Feer, Frolic, Gaff, Get-up, Gunter, Hoax, Jack-up, Jury, Manipulate, Marconi, Martingale, Oilwell, Outfit, Panoply, Platform, Ratline, Rattlin, Ropes, Roughneck, Schooner, Sport, Stack, Stuns'l, Swindle, Tackle, Togs, Top hamper, Trull, Yardarm
▷**Rigged** *may indicate* an anagram

Right(s), Righten, Rightful, Rightness Affirmative, Ancient lights, Animal, Appropriate, Ay, Bang, Befit, Blue-pencil, Cabotage, Civil, Claim, Competence,

Conjugal, Conservative, →**CORRECT**, Cuddy, Cure, Dead on, Direct, Divine, Droit, Due, Emend, Entitlement, Equity, Ethical, Exactly, Fascist, Fiar, Fitting, Forestage, Franchise, Freedom, Gay, Germane, Hedge-bote, Human, Inalienable, Interest, Jure, Jus (mariti), Legal, Liberty, Lien, Maternity, Meet, Merit, Miner's, Miranda, Moral, Neo-con, New, Ninepins, Offside, OK, Okay, Option, Pannage, Pasturage, Patent, Paternity, Performing, Pit and gallows, Pre-emption, Prerogative, Priority, Privilege, Proper, Property, Pukka, R, Rain, Reason, Rectify, Redress, Remedy, Repair, Ripe, Rt, Serial, Slap, So, Spot-on, Stage, Substantive, Suo jure, Suo loco, Tenants', Tickety-boo, Tory, Trover, True, Water, Women's

Rigid(ity) Acierated, Catalepsy, Catatonic, Craton, Extreme, Fixed, Formal, Hidebound, Inflexible, Lignin, Ossified, Renitent, Set, Slavish, Starch(y), Stern, Stiff, Stretchless, Strict, Stringent, Tense, Turgor

Rigorous, Rigo(u)r Accurate, Austere, Cruel, Exact, Firm, Hard, Harshness, Inclement, Iron-bound, Severe, Stern, Strait, Strict, Stringent, Thorough

▷**Rile(y)** *may indicate* an anagram

Rim Atlantic, Border, Chimb, Chime, Edge, Felloe, Felly, Flange, Girdle, →**LIP**, Margin, Strake, Verge

Ring(ed), Ringer, Ringing, Rings Anchor, Angelus, Annual, Annulus, Arena, Band, Bangle, Bayreuth, Bell, Benzine, Betrothal, Boom-iron, Call, Cambridge, Carabiner, Cartel, Change, Chime, Circle, Circlet, Circlip, Circus, Clang, Clink, Coil, Cordon, Cornice, Corona, Corral, Cramp, Cycle, Dead, Death's head, Dial, Diffraction, Ding, Disc, Dong, Donut, Doorbell, Dress, D(o)uar, Echo, Encircle, Enclosure, Encompass, Engagement, Enhalo, Enlace, Envelop, Environ, Enzone, Eternity, Extension, Eyelet, Fairy, Ferrule, Gas, Gimmer, Gird(le), Girr, Gloriole, Grom(m)et, Growth, Halo, Hank, Hob, →**HOOP**, Hoop-la, Hound, Hula-hoop, Ideal, Image, Inner, Inorb, Keeper, Key, Knell, Knock-out, Kraal, Lactam, Laer, Lifebelt, Link, Loop, Lute, Magpie, Manacle, Mourning, Napkin, Nimbus, Nose, O, Oil-control, Orb, Outer, Parral, Parrel, Peal, Pen, Phone, Ping, Piston, Potato, Price, Prize, Quoit, Re-echo, Resonant, Resound, Retaining, Reverberate, Round, Rove, Rowel, Runner, Rush, Sale, Scarf, Scraper, Screw eye, Seal, Signet, Slinger, Slip, Snap-link, Solomon, Sound, Spell, Split, Stonehenge, Surround, Swivel, Syndicate, Tang, Tattersall, Teething, Thimble, Thumb, Timbre, Ting, Tingle, Tink(le), Tintinnabulate, Toe, Token, Toll, Tore, Torquate, Torques, Torret, Torus, Trochus, Troth, Vice, Vortex, Wagnerian, Washer, Wedding, Whorl, Woggle, Zero

Rink Ice, Roller, Skating

Riot(er), Riotous(ly), Riots Anarchy, Brawl, Clamour, Demo, Deray, Gordon, Hilarious, Hubbub, Luddite, Medley, Mêlée, Orgy, Pandemonium, Peterloo, Porteous, Profusion, Quorum, Rag, Ragmatical, Rebecca, Rebel, Roister, Rout, Rowdy, Ruffianly, Sedition, Swing, Tumult

▷**Rioters, Riotous** *may indicate* an anagram

Rip(per), Ripping, Rip off Avulse, Basket, Buller, Cur, Dilacerate, Fleece, Grand, Handful, Horse, Jack, Lacerate, Rent, Rep, Roué, Scallywag, Splendid, Tear, Tide, Topnotch, To-rend, Unseam

Ripe, Ripen(ing) Auspicious, Full, Geocarpy, Mature, Mellow, Rathe, Ready

▷**Rippling** *may indicate* an anagram

Rise(r), Rising Advance, Appreciate, Ascend, Aspire, Assurgent, Bull, Butte, Cause, Dry, Easter, Eger, Elevation, Emanate, Emerge, Emerse, Émeute, Eminence, Erect, Escalate, Get up, Gradient, Hance, Hauriant, Haurient, Heave,

Hike, Hill, Hummock, Hunt's up, Improve, Increase, Incremental, Insurgent, Intifada, Intumesce, Jibe, Knap, Knoll, Lark, Leap, Levee, Levitate, Lift, Molehill, Motte, Mount, Mutiny, Orient, Origin, Peripety, Point, Putsch, Rear, Rebel, Resurgent, Resurrection, → **REVOLT**, Riot, Rocket, Saleratus, Scarp, Sky-rocket, Soar, Spiral, Stand, Stay, Stie, Sty, Stye, Surface, Surge, Tor, Tower, Transcend, Up, Upbrast, Upburst, Upcurl, Upgo, Uprest, Upshoot, Upspear, Upsurge, Upswarm, Upturn, Well

Risk(y) Actuarial, Adventure, Apperil, Back, Calculated, Chance, Compromise, Counterparty, → **DANGER**, Daring, Dice, Dicy, Emprise, Endanger, Fear, Gamble, Game, Hairy, Hazard, High-wire, Iffy, Imperil, Impetuous, Jeopardy, Liability, Morass, Nap, Parlous, Peril(ous), Precarious, Security, Spec(ulate), Stake, Throw, Unsafe, Venture

Rite(s) Asperges, Bora, Ceremony, Eastern, Exequies, Initiation, Last offices, Liturgy, Mystery, Nagmaal, Obsequies, Powwow, Ritual, Sacral, Sacrament, Sarum use, Solemnity, Superstition, York

Ritual Agadah, Arti, Ceremony, Chanoyu, Cultus, Customary, Formality, Haggada, Lavabo, Liturgy, Rite, Sacrament, Sacring, Seder, Social, Tantric, Telestic, Use

Rival(ry), Rivals Absolute, Acres, Aemule, Challenge, Compete, Contender, Emulate, Emule, Envy, Fo(n)e, → **MATCH**, Needle, Opponent, Touch, Vie

River(s) Bayou, Creek, Dalles, Ea, Eau, Estuary, Flood, Flower, Fluvial, Potamic, Potamology, R, Riverain, Runner, Stream, Tide(-way), Tributary, Waterway

Road(s), Roadside, Road surface A, A1, Access, Anchorage, Arterial, Asphalt, Autobahn, Autopista, Autostrada, Ave(nue), B, Beltway, Blacktop, Boulevard, Burma, Bypass, Carriageway, Causeway, Clay, Clearway, Close, Cloverleaf, Coach, Concession, Corduroy, Corniche, Course, Crossover, Crown, Cul-de-sac, Dirt, Drift-way, Driveway, Drove, Dunstable, Escape, Exit, Expressway, Fairway, Feeder, Fly-over, Fly-under, Foss(e) Way, Freeway, Frontage, Grid, Hampton, Hard, Highway, Horseway, Interstate, Kerb, Lane, Loan, Loke, M1, Macadam, Mall, Metal, Motorway, Off-ramp, Orbital, Overpass, Parkway, Path, Pike, Post, Private, Rat-run, Rd, Relief, Ride, Ridgeway, Ring, Royal, Service, Shoulder, Shunpike, Side, Silk, Skid, Slip, Speedway, Spur(way), St(reet), Superhighway, Switchback, Tarmac, Tar-seal, Terrace, Thoroughfare, Throughway, Tobacco, Toby, Tollway, Track(way), Trunk, Turning, Turnpike, Unadopted, Underpass, Unmade, Verge, Via, Viaduct, Way

Roam Enrange, Extravagate, Peregrinate, Rake, Ramble, Rove, Stray, Wander, Wheel

Roar(ing) Bawl, Bell(ow), Blare, Bluster, Boom, Boys, Cry, Forties, Guffaw, Laugh, Leonine, Roin, Rote, Rout, Royne, Thunder, Tumult, Vroom, Wuther, Zoom

Roast Bake, Barbecue, Baste, Birsle, Brent, Cabob, Cook, Crab, Crown, Decrepitate, Excoriate, Grill, Kabob, Pan, Parch, Pot, Ridicule, Scald, Scathe, Sear, Slate, Spit, Tan, Torrefy

Rob(bed), Robber(y) Abactor, Abduct, Bandit, Bereave, Bonnie, Brigand, Burgle, Bust, Cateran, Clyde, Dacoit, Daylight, Depredation, Dispossess, Do, Fake, Filch, Fleece, Footpad, Heist, Highjack, High toby, Highwayman, Hijack, Hold-up, Hustle, Job, Knock off, Kondo, Ladrone, Land-pirate, Larceny, Latron, Loot, Moskonfyt, Mug, Pad, Pillage, Pinch, Piracy, Pluck, Plunder, Ramraid, Rapine, Reave, Reft, Reive, Rieve, Rifle, Road agent, Robertsman, Roll, Roy, Rustler, Sack, Score, Screw, Sheppard, Short change, Sirup, Skinner,

Smash and grab, Snatch, Spoiler, Spring-heeled Jack, →**STEAL**, Steaming, Stick-up, Sting, Swindle, Syrup, Thief, Thug(gee), Toby, Turn-over, Turpin

Robe(s) Alb, Amice, Amis, Attrap, Buffalo, Camis, Camus, Canonicals, Cassock, Chimer, Chrisom(-cloth), Christom, Dalmatic, Djellabi, Dolman, →**DRESS**, Gown, Habit, Ihram, Kanga, Kanzu, Khalat, Khilat, Kill(a)ut, Kimono, Mantle, Night, Parament, Parliament, Pedro, Peplos, Pontificals, Purple, Regalia, Rochet, Saccos, Sanbenito, Soutane, Sticharion, Stola, Stole, Talar, Tire, Vestment, Yukata

Robot Android, Animatronic, Automaton, Cyborg, Dalek, Golem, Nanobot, Puppet, RUR, Telechir

Rock(s), Rocker, Rocking, Rocky Acid, Ages, Agitate, Astound, Ayers, Birthstone, Cairn, Cap, Cock, Country, Cradle, Destabilise, Edinburgh, Elvis, Erratic, Extrusive, Garage, Gem, Gib(raltar), Goth, Heavy metal, Jounce, Jow, Lithology, Mantle, Marciano, Marlstone, Matrix, Native, Nunatak(kr), Oscillate, Pelitic, Permafrost, Petrology, Petrous, Platform, Plymouth, Progressive, Punk, Quake, Reggae, Reservoir, Rimrock, Rip-rap, Sally, Scar, Scare, Scaur, Sclate, →**SHAKE**, Shoogle, Showd, Soft, Stonehenge, Stun, Sway, Swee, Swing, Ted, Teeter, Terra, Totter, Traverse, Tremble, Ultrabasic, Ultramafic, Uluru, Unstable, Unsteady, Wall, Weeping, Whin, Wind, Windsor, Wobble

Rocket Arugula, Blue, Booster, Capsule, Carpet, Carrier, Congreve, Delta, Drake, Dressing down, Earful, Engine, Flare, Iron horse, Jato, Life, Missile, Onion, Payload, Posigrade, Reprimand, Reproof, Retro, Rucola, SAM, Skylark, Soar, Sounding, Space probe, Stephenson, Thruster, Tourbillion, Upshoot, V1, Vernier, Warhead, Weld

▷**Rocky** *may indicate* an anagram

Rod(-shaped), Rodlike, Rods Aaron's, Angler, Axle, Bar, Barbel(l), Barre, Birch, Caduceus, Caim, Camshaft, Can, Cane, Cue, Cuisenaire®, Dipstick, Divining, Dopper, Dowser, Drain, Emu, Firearm, Fisher, Fly, Fuel, Gauging, Gold stick, Gun, Handspike, Laver, Lease, Linchpin, Lug, Mapstick, Measure, Measuring, Mopstick, Moses, Newel, Perch, Pin, Pistol, Piston, Pitman, Pointer, Poker, Poking-stick, Pole, Pontie, Pontil, Ponty, Puntee, Punty, Push, Raddle, Range, Riding, Rood, Shaft, Spindle, Spit, Stair, Staple, Stave, Stay-bolt, Stick, Sticker, Switch, Swizzle stick, Tie, Twig, Verge, Virgate, Virgulate, Wand, Withe

Rodent Acouchi, Acouchy, Agouty, Ag(o)uti, Bandicoot, Bangsring, Banxring, Beaver, Biscacha, Bizcacha, Bobac, Bobak, Boomer, Capybara, Cavy, Chickaree, Chincha, Chinchilla, Chipmunk, Civet, Coypu, Cricetus, Dassie, Deer-mouse, Degu, Delundung, Dormouse, Fieldmouse, Gerbil(le), Glires, Glutton, Gnawer, Gopher, Groundhog, Guinea pig, Ham(p)ster, Hedgehog, Hog-rat, Hutia, Hyrax, Hystricomorph, Jerboa, Jird, Lemming, Loir, Mara, Marmot, Mole rat, Mouse, Murid, Mus, Musk-rat, Musquash, Nutria, Ochotona, Ondatra, Paca, Porcupine, Potoroo, Prairie dog, Rat, Ratel, Ratton, Renegade, Runagate, Sciurine, Sewellel, Shrew, Simplicidentate, Spermophile, Springhaas, Springhase, Squirrel, S(o)uslik, Taguan, Taira, Tuco-tuco, Tucu-tuco, Vermin, Viscacha, Vole, Woodchuck, Woodmouse

Rogue, Roguish(ness) Aberrant, Arch, Bandit, Bounder, Charlatan, Chiseller, Crook, Drole, Dummerer, Elephant, Espiègle(rie), Ganef, Ganev, Ganof, Gonif, Gonof, Greek, Gypsy, Hedge-creeper, Heel, Hempy, Herries, Imp, Knave, Latin, Limmer, Miscreant, Monkey, Palliard, Panurge, Picaresque, Picaroon, Pollard, Poniard, Rapparee, Ra(p)scal(l)ion, Reprobate, Riderhood, Rotter, Savage, Scallywag, Scamp, Schellum, Schelm, Scoundrel, Skellum, Sleeveen, Slip-string, Sly, Swindler, Terror, Varlet, Villain, Wrong 'un

Roll(ed), Roller, Roll-call, Rolling, Rolls Absence, Bagel, Bap, Birmingham, Bolt, Bridge, Brioche, Bun, Calender, Cambridge, Comber, Cop, Couch, Court, Croissant, Cylinder, Dandy, Drum, Dutch, Electoral, Enwallow, Eskimo, Even, Finger, Forward, Furl, Go, Goggle, Holy, Hotdog, Labour, List, Loaded, Mangle, Marver, Morning, Moving, Music, Muster, Opulent, Pain au chocolat, Patent, Pay, Petit-pain, Piano, Pigeon, Pipe, Platen, Porteous, Ragman, Record, Reef, Reel, Register, Ren, Rent, Revolute, Revolve, Rich, Ring, Road, Rob, Rolag, Roster, Rota, Rotate, Roul(e), Roulade, Row, RR, Rumble, Run, Sausage, Skin up, Snap, Somersault, Souter's clod, Spool, Spring, Summar, Sway, Swell, Swiss, Table, Tandem, Taxi, Temple, Tent, Terrier, Thread, Toilet, Tommy, Toss, Trill, Trindle, Trundle, Tsunami, Tube, Upfurl, Valuation, Victory, Volume, Wad, Wallow, Wave, Weather, Well-heeled, Western, Yaw, Zorbing
▷**Rollicking** *may indicate an anagram*

Roman Agricola, Agrippa, Aurelius, Caesar, Calpurnia, Candle, Catholic, Cato, Centurion, Consul, CR, Crassus, Decemviri, Decurion, Empire, Flavian, Galba, Holiday, Italian, Jebusite, Latin, Maecenas, Nero, Papist, Patrician, PR, Quirites, Raetic, RC, Retarius, Rhaetia, Road, Scipio, Seneca, Sulla, Tarquin, Tiberius, Trebonius, Type(cast), Uriconian, Veneti

Romance, Romantic (talk) Affair, Amoroso, Amorous, Byronic, Casanova, Catalan, Chocolate box, Dreamy, Fancy, Fantasise, Fib, Fiction, Gest(e), Gothic, Invention, Ladin(o), Ladinity, Langue d'oc(ian), Langue d'oil, Langue d'oui, Liaison, Lie, Neo-Latin, New, Novelette, Poetic, Quixotic, Rhapsodic, R(o)uman, Ruritania, Sentimental, Stardust, Sweet nothings, Tale, Tear-jerker

▶**Romany** *see* GYPSY

Roof (edge), Roofing Asphalt, Belfast, Bell, Broach, Ceil, Cl(e)ithral, Cover, Curb, Divot, Dome, Drip, Eaves, French, Gable, Gambrel, Hardtop, Hip(ped), Home, Housetop, Hypostyle, Imperial, Jerkin-head, Leads, M, Mansard, Monopitch, Onion dome, Palate, Pavilion, Pop-top, Porte-cochère, Rag top, Rigging, Saddle, Shingle, Skirt, Targa top, Tectiform, Tectum, Tegula, Thatch, Thetch, Tiling, Top, Uraniscus, Vaulting, Yealm

Room(y) Capacity, Cavernous, Ceiling, Clearance, Commodious, Elbow, Latitude, Leeway, Margin, Place, Scope, Smoke-filled, →**SPACE**, Spacious, Standing, Tolerance, Wiggle, Zenana

Root(s), Rooted, Rooting, Rootstock Aruhe, Aryl, Asarum, Calamus, Cassava, Celeriac, Cheer, Cocco, Couscous, Cube, Cuscus, Delve, Derivation, Dig, Eddo, Eradicate, Etymon, Fern, Foundation, Ginseng, Grass, Grub, Heritage, Horseradish, Hurrah, Immobile, Incorrigible, Insane, Ipecac(huana), Khuskhus, Knee, Liquorice, Mandrake, Navew, Nuzzle, Pleurisy, Poke, Pry, Radicate, Radicle, Radish, Rhizome, Skirret, Snuzzle, Source, Spur, Square, Stilt, Stirpes, Strike, Tap, Taro, Tuber, Tulip, Turnip, Turpeth, Ventral, Zedoary

Rope(s) Backstay, Ba(u)lk, Bind, Bobstay, Boltrope, Bracer, Brail, Breeching, Bunt-line, Cable, Cablet, Cat's paw, Cord, Cordage, Cordon, Cringle, Downhaul, Drag, Earing, Fall, Flake, Flemish coil, Fly, Foot, Fore-brace, Foresheet, Forestay, Futtock-shroud, Gantline, Garland, Grass line, Guest, Guide, Guy, Halliard, Halser, Halter, Halyard, Hawser, Hawser-laid, Headfast, Inhaul, Jack-stay, Jeff, Jib-sheet, Jump, Kernmantel, Kickling, Ladder, Lanyard, Lasher, Lasso, Lazo, Leg, Lifeline, Line, Longe, Lunge, Mainbrace, Mainsheet, Manil(l)a, Marlin(e), Match-cord, Monkey, Mooring, Nip, Noose, Outhaul, Painter, Pastern, Prolonge, Prusik, Pudding, Rawhide, Reef point, Riata, Ridge, Ringstopper, Roband, Robbin, Rode, Runner, St Johnston's ribbon, St Johnston's tippet,

Sally, Salt-eel, Seal, Selvagee, Sennit, Sheet, Shroud, Sinnet, Span, Spun-yarn, Stay, Sternfast, Stirrup, String, Strop, Sugan, Swifter, Tackle, Tail, Tether, Tie, Timenoguy, Tow(line), Trace, Trail, Triatic, Triatic stay, Vang, Wanty, Widdy, Wire, Yarn

Rose(-red), Rosie, Rosy Albertine, Alexandra, Avens, Blooming, Bourbon, Briar, Brier, Burnet, Cabbage, Canker, China, Christmas, Compass, Crampbark, Damask, Dog, Eglantine, England, English, Floribunda, G(u)elder, Geum, Hybrid, Lancaster, Lee, Monthling, Moss, Multiflora, Musk, Noisette, Peace, Pink, Promising, Rambler, Red(dish), Rhoda, Rugosa, Scotch, Snowball, Sprinkler, Standard, Tea, Tokyo, Tudor, York

Rot(ten), Rotting Addle, Baloney, Biodegrade, Boo, Bosh, Botrytis, Brown, Bull, Caries, Carious, Corrode, Corrupt, Daddock, Decadent, → DECAY, Decompose, Degradable, Dotage, Dricksie, Druxy, Dry, Eat, Erode, Fester, Foul, Gangrene, Halt, Kibosh, Manky, Mildew, Noble, Nonsense, Off, Poppycock, Poxy, Punk, Putid, Putrefy, Putrescent, Putrid, Rail, Rancid, Rank, Rat, Red, Ret, Rhubarb, Rust, Sapropel, Septic, Sour, Squish, Twaddle, Vrot, Wet

Rotate, Rotating, Rotation, Rotator Axial, Backspin, Crankshaft, Crop, Gyrate, Laevorotation, Pivot, Pronate, Rabat(te), Reamer, Rebato, Revolve, Roll, Selsyn, Succession, Sway, Teres, Topspin, Trochilic, Trundle, Turn, Vortex, Wheel, Windmill

▶**Rotten** see ROT(TEN)

▷**Rotten** may indicate an anagram

Rough(en), Roughly, Roughness About, Abrasive, Approximate, Asper(ate), Blunt, Broad, Broad brush, Burr, C, Ca, Choppy, Circa, Coarse, Craggy, Craig, Crude, Draft, Frampler, Grained, Gross, Gruff, Guestimate, Gurly, Gusty, Hard, Harsh, Hirsute, Hispid, Hoarse, Hoodlum, Hooligan, Ill, Impolite, Imprecise, Incondite, Indecorous, Inexact, Irregular, Jagged, Karst, Keelie, Kokobeh, Muricate, Obstreperous, Of sorts, Or so, Push, Ragged, Ramgunshoch, Raspy, Raucle, Rip, Risp, Robust, Row, Rude, Rugged, Rusticate, Rusty, Scabrid, Scabrous, Scratchy, Sea, Shaggy, Sketchy, Some, Spray, Spreathe, Squarrose, Stab, Strong-arm, Stubbly, Swab, Tartar, Tearaway, Ted, Textured, Tiger country, Tousy, Touzy, Towsy, Towzy, Uncut, Violent, Yahoo

▷**Roughly** may indicate an anagram

Round(ed), Roundness About, Ammo, Ball, Beat, Bout, Cartridge, Catch, Circle, Circular, Complete, Cycle, Dance, Dome, Doorstep, Fat, Figure, Full, Geoidal, Global, Globose, Hand, Heat, Inorb, Jump-off, Lap, Leg, Milk, O, Oblate, Obtuse, Orb, Orbit, Orby, Paper, Patrol, Peri-, Pirouette, Plump, Pudsy, Qualifying, Quarter, Rev, Ring, Robin, Roly-poly, Rota, Rotund, Route, Routine, Rung, Salvo, Sandwich, Sarnie, Semi-final, Shot, Skirt, Slice, Sphere, Step, Table, Tour, Trick, Tubby, Tune, U-turn, Walk

▷**Round** may indicate a word reversed

Roundabout Ambages, Approximately, Bypass, Carousel, Circuit, Circumambient, Circumbendibus, Circus, Devious, Eddy, → INDIRECT, Peripheral, Rotary, Tortuous, Traffic circle, Turntable, Waltzer, Whirligig, Windlass

▷**Roundabout** may indicate an anagram

Routine Automatic, Day-to-day, Drill, Everyday, Grind, Groove, Habitual, Heigh-ho, Helch-how, Ho-hum, Jogtrot, Journeywork, Monotony, Pattern, Perfunctory, Pipe-clay, Prosaic, Red tape, Regular, Rota, Rote, Round, Run-of-the-mill, Rut, Schtik, S(c)htick, SOP, Stand-up, Treadmill, Workaday

Rove(r), Roving Car, Errant, Freebooter, Tramp

Row(er) Align, Altercation, Arew, Argue, Argument, Artillery, Bank, Barney, Bedlam, Bow, Brawl, Brulyie, Bru(i)lzie, Cacophony, Cannery, Cat fight, Clatter, Colonnade, Crescent, Death, Debate, Din, Dispute, Dust-up, Feud, File, Fireworks, Food, Hoo-ha, Hullabaloo, Leander, Line(-up), Noise, Oar, Octastich, Orthostichy, Paddle, Parade, Pluriserial, Ply, Pull, Quarrel, Queue, Range, Rank, Reproach, Rew, Rotten, Ruction, Rumpus, Savile, Scene, Scrap, Scull, Series, Set (to), Shindig, Shindy, Shine, Skid, Spat, Stern, Stound, Street, Stroke, Sweep, Terrace, Tier, Tiff, Torpid, Twelve-tone, Vendetta, Wetbob, Wherryman

Rowdy, Rowdiness Boisterous, Bovver, Hoo, Hooligan, Ladette, Loud, Noisy, Obstreperous, Rorty, Rough, Roughhouse, Ruffian, Scourer, Skinhead, Stroppy, Unruly, Uproarious

Royal(ty), Royalist Academy, Angevin, Basilical, Battle, Bourbon, Crowned, Emigré, Exchange, Fee, Hanoverian, HR(H), Imperial, Imposing, Inca, Kingly, Majestic, Malignant, Palatine, Payment, Pharaoh, Plantagenet, Prince, Purple, Queenly, Real, Regal, Regis, Regius, Regnal, Sail, Sceptred, Society, Tsarista

Rub(bing), Rubber(y), Rub out Abrade, Buff, Bungie, Bungy, Calk, Caoutchouc, Chafe, Chloroprene, Cold, Condom, Corrode, Cow gum®, Crepe, Delete, Destroy, Ebonite, Efface, Elastic, Elaterite, Embrocate, Emery, Eradicator, Erase, Factis, Fawn, Foam, Foursome, Fray, Fret, Friction, Frottage, Frotteur, Grate, Graze, Grind, Gum elastic, Gutta-percha, Hard, High-hysteresis, Hule, India, Irritate, Jelutong, Johnnie, Latex, Masseur, Obstacle, Polish, Root, Safe, Sandpaper, Scour, Scrape, Scrub, Scuff, Seringa, Smoked, Sorbo®, Sponge, Synthetic, Towel, Trace, Ule, Wipe

▷**Rubbed** *may indicate* an anagram

Rubbish Bad mouth, Balls, Bilge, Brash, Brock, Bull, Bunkum, Cack, Chaff, Clap-trap, Cobblers, Codswallop, Culch, Debris, Detritus, Dirt, Discredit, Dre(c)k, Drivel, Dross, Eyewash, Fiddlesticks, Garbage, Grot, Grunge, Gubbins, Guff, Hogwash, Hokum, Kack, Kak, Landfill, Leavings, Litter, Mullock, Mush, Nonsense, Pan, Pants, Phooey, Piffle, Pish, Raff, Raffle, Red(d), → **REFUSE**, Riff-raff, Scrap, Sewage, Slate, Spam, Stuff, Thrash, Tinpot, Tinware, Tip, Tom(fool), Tosh, Totting, Trade, Tripe, Trouch, Truck, Trumpery, Twaddle, Urethra

Rude(ness) Abusive, Barbaric, Bear, Bestial, Bumpkin, Callow, Carlish, Churlish, Coarse, Discourteous, Disrespect, Elemental, Goustrous, Green, Ignorant, Ill-bred, Impolite, Indecorous, Indelicate, Inficete, Ingram, Ingrum, Insolent, Ocker, Offensive, Peasant, Profane, Raw, Ribald, Risqué, Rough, Simple, Surly, Unbred, Uncivil, Uncomplimentary, Uncourtly, Unlettered, Unmannered, Vulgar, Yobbish

▷**Ruffle** *may indicate* an anagram

Rug Afghan, Bearskin, Bergama, Buffalo-robe, Carpet, Drugget, Ensi, Flokati, Gabbeh, Hearth, Herez, Heriz, Kelim, K(h)ilim, Kirman, Lap robe, Mat, Maud, Numdah, Oriental, Pilch, Prayer, Rag, Runner, Rya, Scatter, Steamer, Tatami, Throw, Travelling, Wig

Ruin(ed), Ruination, Ruins, Ruinous Annihilate, Banjax, Bankrupt, Blast, Blight, Blue, Butcher, Carcase, Collapse, Corrupt, Crash, Crock, Damn, Decay, Defeat, Demolish, Despoil, Destroy, Devastate, Dilapidation, Disaster, Disfigure, Dish, Disrepair, Dogs, Do in, Doom, Downcome, Downfall, Dry rot, End, Fine, Fordo, Hamstring, Heap, Hell, Insolvent, Inure, Kaput(t), Kibosh, Loss, Mar, Mockers, Mother's, Overthrow, Perdition, Perish, Petra, Pigs and whistles, Pot,

Puckerood, Ravage, Reck, Relic, Rust, Scotch, Screw, Scupper, Scuttle, Shatter, Sink, Smash, Spill, → **SPOIL**, Stramash, Subvert, Undo, Unmade, Unmake, Ur, Violate, Vitiate, Whelm, Woe, Wrack, Write off

▷**Ruined** *may indicate* an anagram

Rule(r), Rules, Ruling Advantage, Align, Bosman, Bylaw, Calliper, Canon, Chain, Club-law, Code, Commonly, Condominium, Constitution, Control, Criterion, Decree, Divine right, Dominate, Domineer, Dominion, Em, Empire, En, Establishment, Etiquette, Fatwa, Feint, Fetwa, Formation, Formula, Gag, Global, Golden, Govern, Ground, Gynocracy, Home, In, Institutes, Jackboot, Law, Leibniz's, Lex, Lindley, Liner, Majority, Markownikoff's, Mastery, Maxim, Measure, Mede, Method, Mobocracy, Motto, Norm(a), Ordinal, Organon, Organum, Pantocrator, Parallel, Parallelogram, Phase, Phrase-structure, Placitum, Plumb, Precedent, Precept, Predominant, Prevail, Principle, Proscribe, Protocol, Ptochocracy, Rafferty's, Realm, Reciprocity, Rector, Regal, Regnant, Reign, Rewrite, Ring, Routine, Rubric, Selection, Setting, Slide, Squirearchy, Standard, Statute, Straight edge, Stylebook, Sway, Syntax, System, Ten-minute, Ten-yard, Theorem, Three, Thumb, Transformation(al), Trapezoid, T-square, Tycoon, Tyrant, Uti possidetis, Wield, Yardstick

Rumble, Rumbling Borborygmus, Brool, Curmurring, Drum-roll, Groan, Growl, Guess, Lumber, Mutter, Roll, Rumour, Thunder, Tonneau, Twig

Rumour Breeze, Bruit, Buzz, Canard, Cry, Fame, Furphy, → **GOSSIP**, Grapevine, Hearsay, Kite, Noise, On-dit, Pig's-whisper, Report, Repute, Roar, Say-so, Smear, Talk, Underbreath, Unfounded, Vine, Voice, Whisper, Word

Run(ning), Run away, Run into, Run off, Runny, Runs Admin(ister), Arpeggio, Black, Bleed, Blue, Bolt, Break, Bunk, Bye, Canter, Career, Chase, Chicken, Clip, Consider, Control, Coop, Corso, Course, Cresta, Cross-country, Current, Cursive, Cursorial, Cut, Dart, Dash, Decamp, Diarrhoea, Dinger, Direct, Dog-trot, Double, Dribble, Drive, Dry, Dummy, Enter, Escape, Execute, Extra, Fartlek, Flee, Flit, Flow, Fly, Follow, Fun, Fuse, Gad, Gallop, Gauntlet, Glissando, Go, Green, Ground, Hare, Haste(n), Hennery, Hie, Hightail, Home, Hoof, Idle, Jog, Jump bail, Ladder, Lam, Lauf, Leg(work), Leg bye, Lienteric, Liquid, Lope, Manage, Marathon, Melt, Milk, Mizzle, Mole, Molt, Monkey, Neume, Now, Offset, On, On-line, Operate, Orchestration, Pace, Pacific, Paper chase, Parkour, Pelt, Pilot, Ply, Pour, Print, Purulent, R, Race, Range, Rear end, Red, Renne, Rin, Roadwork, Romp, Root, Roulade, Rounder, Ruck, Scamper, Scapa, Scarpa, Scarper, School, Schuss, Score, Scud, Scuddle, Scutter, Scuttle, See, Sequence, Shoot, Single, Skate, Skedaddle, Ski, Skid, Skirr, Skitter, Slalom, Slide, Smuggle, Spew, Split, Spread, Sprint, Sprue, Squitters, Stampede, Straight, Streak, Stream, Superintend, Taxi, Tear, Tenor, Test drive, Tick over, Tie-breaker, Tirade, Trial, Trickle, Trill, Trot, Well, Wide

Runner(s) Atalanta, Athlete, Bean, Blade, Bow Street, Candidate, Carpet, Chataway, Coe, Contrabandist, Courser, Dak, Deserter, Drug, Emu, Errand boy, Field, Foot, Geat, Gentleman, Harrier, Internuncio, Leg bye, Legman, Messenger, Miler, Milk, Oribi, Ovett, Owler, Pacemaker, Pacesetter, Policeman, Racehorse, Rhea, → **RIVER**, Rum, → **RUN(NING)**, Scarlet, Scud, Series, Slipe, Smuggler, Stolon, Stream, Tailskid, Trial

▷**Running, Runny** *may indicate* an anagram

Rural Agrarian, Agrestic, Backwoodsman, Boo(h)ai, Booay, Boondocks, Bucolic, Country(side), Forane, Georgic, Mofussil, Pastoral, Platteland, Praedial, Predial, Redneck, Rustic, Sticks, The Shires, Ulu, Upland, Wop-wops

Rush(ed) Accelerate, Barge, Bolt, Bustle, Career, Charge, Dart, Dash, Debacle, Dutch, Expedite, Fall, Feese, Flaw, Fly, Forty-nine, Gold, Hare, Hasten, Hectic, High-tail, Horsetail, → **HURRY**, Hurry and Scurry, Hurtle, Jet, Lance, Leap, Odd-man, Onset, Pellmell, Phase, Plunge, Pochard, Precipitate, Railroad, Rampa(u)ge, Rash, Reed, Rip, Sally, Scamp(er), Scour(ing), Scramble, Scud, Scurry, Scuttle, Sedge, Shave-grass, Spate, Speed, Stampede, Star(r), Streak, Streek, Surge, Swoop, Swoosh, Tantivy, Tear, Thrash, Thresh, Tilt, Torrent, Tule, Whoosh, Zap, Zoom

Russia(n), Russian headman, Russian villagers Alexei, Apparatchik, Ataman, Bashkir, Belorussian, Beria, Bolshevik, Boris, Boyar, Buryat, Byelorussian, Cesarevitch, Chechen, Circassian, Cossack, Dressing, D(o)ukhobor, Esth, Evenki, Ewenki, Igor, Ivan, Kabardian, Kalmuk, Kalmyck, Leather, Leonid, Lett, Mari, Menshevik, Minimalist, Mir, Misha, Muscovy, Octobrist, Old Believer, Osset(e), Putin, Red, Romanov, Rus, Russ(niak), Russki, Ruthene, Salad, Serge, Sergei, Slav, Stakhanovite, SU, Tatar, The Bear, Thistle, Udmurt, Ukrainian, Uzbeg, Uzbek, Vladimir, Vogul, Yuri, Zyrian

Rust(y) Aeci(di)um, Brown, Corrode, Cor(ro)sive, Eat, Erode, Etch, Ferrugo, Goethite, Iron-stick, Laterite, Maderise, Oxidise, Reddish, Rubiginous, Soare, Stem, Teleutospore, Telium, Uredine, Uredo, Verdigris, Wheat

Rustic Arcady, Bacon, Bor(r)el(l), Bucolic, Bumpkin, Carl, Carlot, Chawbacon, Churl, Clodhopper, Clown, Corydon, Countryman, Crackle, Damon, Doric, Forest, Georgic, Hayseed, Hick, Hillbilly, Hind, Hob, Hobbinoll, Hodge, Homespun, Idyl(l), Pastorale, Peasant, Pr(a)edial, Put(t), Rube, Rural, Silk, Strephon, Swain, Uplandish, Villager, Villatic, Yokel

▷**Rustic** *may indicate* an anagram

Rustle(r), Rustling Abactor, Crackle, Crinkle, Duff, Fissle, Frou-frou, Gully-raker, Poach, Silk, Speagh(ery), Sprechery, Steal, Stir, Stocktaking, Susurration, Swish, Thief, Whig

Rut Channel, Furrow, Groove, Heat, Routine, Track

Ruthless Brutal, Cruel, Dog eat dog, Fell, Fierce, Hard, Hardball, Hard-bitten, Indomitable, Inhuman

Ss

S Ogee, Saint, Second, Sierra, Society, South, Square

Sabotage, Saboteur Cripple, Destroy, Frame-breaker, Hacktivism, Ratten, Sab, Spoil, Worm, Wrecker

Sack(cloth), Sacking Axe, Bag, Bed, Boot, Bounce, Budget, Bulse(r), Burlap, Can, Cashier, Chasse, Coal, Compression, Congé, Congee, Dash, Depose, Depredate, Despoil, Discharge, Dismissal, Doss, Fire, Growbag, Gunny, Havoc, Heave-ho, Hessian, Jute, Knap, Loot, Mailbag, Maraud, Marching orders, Mat, Mitten, Pillage, Plunder, Poke, Postbag, Push, Raid, Rapine, Ravage, Reave, Rieve, Rifle, Road, Rob, Sad, Sanbenito, Self-abasement, Sherris, Sherry, Spoliate, Vandalise, Walking papers

▷**Sacks** *may indicate* an anagram

Sacrifice Corban, Cost, Forego, Gambit, Gehenna, Immolate, Lay down, Molochize, Oblation, →**OFFERING**, Paschal lamb, Relinquish, Suttee

Sad(den), Sadly, Sadness Alas, Attrist, Bittersweet, Blue, Con dolore, Dejected, Depressed, Desolate, Disconsolate, Dismal, Doleful, Dolent, Dolour, Downcast, Drear, Dull, Dumpy, Elegiac, Fadeur, Forlorn, Heartache, Heart-rending, Lamentable, Lovelorn, Low, Lugubrious, Mesto, Mournful, Niobe, Oh, Plaintive, Plangent, Poignancy, Proplastid, Sorrowful, Sorry, Tabanca, Tearful, Tear-jerker, Threnody, Tragic, Triste, Tristesse, Unhappy, Wan, Weltschmerz, Wo(e)begone

Saddle (bag, cloth, flap, girth, pad), Saddled Alforja, Aparejo, Arson, Bicycle, Burden, Cantle, Cinch, Col, Crupper, Demipique, Kajawah, Lumber, Numnah, Oppress, Pack, Panel, Pigskin, Pilch, Pillion, Seat, Sell(e), Shabrack, Side, Skirt, Stock, Tree, Unicycle, Western

▷**Sadly** *may indicate* an anagram

Safe(ty) Active, Awmrie, Blue-chip, Cert, Copper-bottomed, Deliverance, Deposit, Fireproof, Harmless, Hunk, Immunity, Impunity, Inviolate, Meat, Night, Passive, Peter, Proof, Reliable, Roadworthy, Sanctuary, Secure, Sheltered, Sound, Strong-box, Strongroom, Sure, Unadventurous, Whole-skinned, Worthy

Safebreaker Peterman, Yegg, Yeggman

Safeguard Air bag, Bulwark, Caution, Ensure, Fail-safe, Frithborh, Fuse, Hedge, Inoculate, Palladium, Preserve, Protection, Register, Shield, Ward

Saga Aga, Chronicle, Edda, Epic, Forsyte, Icelandic, Legend

Sahelian Chad, Mali, Mauritania, Niger

▷**Said** *may indicate* 'sounding like'

Sail(s), Sailing Balloon, Bunt, Canvas, Cloth, Coast, Course, Cruise, Fan, Gaff(-topsail), Gennaker, Genoa, Head, Jib, Jut, Land, Lateen, Leech, Luff, Lug, Moonraker, Muslin, Navigate, Orthodromy, Peak, Ply, Rag, Raven(s)-duck, Reef, Rig, Ring-tail, Royal, Sheet, Shoulder-of-mutton, Smoke, Solar, Spanker,

Spencer, Spinnaker, Spritsail, Square, Staysail, Steer, Storm-jib, Studding, Stuns'l, Top(-gallant), Up anchor, Windsurf, Yard

Sailor(s) AB, Admiral, Argonaut, Blue-jacket, Boater, Boatman, Boatswain, Bos'n, Bos(u)n, Budd, Canvas-climber, Commodore, Crew, Deckhand, Drake, Evans, First mate, Foremastman, Freshwater, Gob, Greenhand, Hand, Hat, Hearties, Helmsman, Hornblower, Hydronaut, Jack, Jaunty, Lascar, Leadsman, Liberty man, Limey, Lt, Lubber, Mariner, Matelot, Matlo(w), Middy, MN, Nelson, Noah, NUS, Oceaner, Oldster, OS, Petty Officer, Pirate, Polliwog, Pollywog, Popeye, Privateer, Rating, Reefer, RN, Salt, Seabee, Seacunny, Sea-dog, Seafarer, Sea-lord, → SEAMAN, Serang, Sin(d)bad, Steward, Submariner, Swabber, Swabby, Tar, Topman, Wandering, Wave, Wren, Yachtie, Yachtsman

Saint(ly) Canonise, Canonize, Hagiology, Hallowed, Holy, Latterday, Leger, Patron, Pillar, Plaster, St, Templar, Thaumaturgus

Sake Account, Behalf, Cause, Drink, Mirin

Salad Beetroot, Caesar, Chef's, Coleslaw, Cos, Cress, Cucumber, Days, Endive, Fennel, Finoc(c)hio, Frisée, Fruit, Greek, Guacamole, Horiatiki, Lettuce, Lollo rosso, Lovage, Mache, Mixture, Mizuna, Niçoise, Purslane, Radicchio, Radish, Rampion, Rocket, Russian, Slaw, Tabbouli, Tomato, Waldorf, Watercress
▷**Salad** *may indicate* an anagram

Salary Emolument, Fee, Hire, Pay, Prebend, Screw, Stipend, → WAGE

Sale(s) Attic, Auction, Boot, Breeze up, Cant, Car-boot, Clearance, Farm-gate, Fire, Garage, Jumble, Market, Outroop, Outrope, Pitch, Raffle, Retail, Roup, Rummage, Subhastation, Trade, Turnover, Upmarket, Venal, Vend, Vendue, Vent, Voetstoets, Voetstoots, Warrant, Wash, White, Wholesale, Yard

Salmon Atlantic, Char(r), Chinook, Chum, Cock, Coho(e), Grav(ad)lax, Grayling, Grilse, Kelt, Keta, Par(r), Pink, Redfish, Rock, Silver, Smelt, Smolt, Smowt, Sockeye, Springer, Umber

Salt(s), Salty AB, Acid, Alginate, Aluminate, Andalusite, Antimonite, Arseniate, Arsenite, Ascorbate, Aspartite, Attic, Aurate, Azide, Base, Bath, Benzoate, Bicarbonate, Bichromate, Boiler, Borate, Borax, Brackish, Brine, Bromate, Bromide, Capr(o)ate, Caprylate, Carbamate, Carbonate, Carboxylate, Celery, Cerusite, Chlorate, Chlorite, Chromate, Citrate, Columbate, Complex, Condiment, Corn, Cure(d), Cyanate, Cyclamate, Datolite, Deer lick, Diazonium, Dichromate, Dioptase, Dithionate, Double, Efflorescence, Enos, Eosin, Epsom, Ferricyanide, Formate, Glauber, Glutamate, Halite, Halo-, Health, Hydrochloride, Hygroscopic, Iodide, Ioduret, Isocyanide, Kosher, Lactate, Lake-basin, Linoleate, Lithate, Liver, Magnesium, Malate, Malonate, Manganate, Mariner, Matelot, Mersalyl, Microcosmic, Monohydrate, Mucate, Muriate, NaCl, Niobate, Nitrate, Nitrite, Oleate, Orthoborate, Orthosilicate, Osm(i)ate, Oxalate, Palmitate, Pandermite, Perborate, Perchlorate, Periodate, Permanganate, Phenolate, Phosphate, Phosphite, Phthalate, Picrate, Piquancy, Plumbate, Plumbite, Potassium, Powder, Propionate, Pyruvate, Rating, Reh, Resinate, Rochelle, Rock, Rosinate, Sailor, Sal ammoniac, Salicylate, Salify, Sal volatile, Saut, Sea-dog, Seafarer, Seasoned, Sebate, Selenate, Smelling, Soap, Sodium, Solar, Sorbate, Sorrel, Stannate, Stearate, Suberate, Succinate, Sulfite, Sulphate, Sulphite, Sulphonate, Table, Tannate, Tantalate, Tartrate, Tellurate, Tellurite, Thiocyanate, Thiosulphate, Titanate, Trithionate, Tungstate, Uranin, Uranylic, Urao, Urate, Vanadate, Volatile, Water-dog, Whewellite, White, Wit(ty), Xanthate

Salutation, Salute Acclaim, Address, Asalam-wa-leikum, Australian, Ave, Banzai, Barcoo, Bid, Cap, Cheer, Command, Coupé(e), Curtsey, Embrace,

Feu de joie, Fly-past, Genuflect, Greet, Hail, Hallo, Halse, Homage, Honour, Jambo, Kiss, Middle finger, Namas kar, Namaste, Present, Salaam, Salvo, Sieg Heil, Toast, Tribute, Wassail, Wave

Salvage Cannibalise, Dredge, Lagan, Ligan, Reclaim, Recover, Recycle, Rescue, Retrieve, Tot

Salve Anele, Anoint, Assuage, Ave, Lanolin(e), Lotion, Ointment, Remedy, Saw, Tolu, Unguent

Same(ness) Ae, Agnatic, Congruent, Contemporaneous, Do, Egal, Equal, Equiparate, Equivalent, Ib(id), Ibidem, Id, Idem, Identical, Identity, Ilk, Iq, Like, One, Rut, Thick(y), Thilk, Uniform, Ylke

Sample, Sampling Amniocentesis, Biopsy, Blad, Browse, Example, Extract, Foretaste, Handout, Muster, Pattern, Pree, Prospect, Quadrat, Random, Scantling, Smear, Snip, Specimen, Swatch, Switch, →**TASTE**, Taster, Toile, Transect, Try
▷**Sam Weller** *may indicate* the use of 'v' for 'w' or vice versa

Sanction(s), Sanctioned Allow, Appro, Approbate, Approof, Approve, Assent, Authorise, Bar, Confirm, Countenance, Economic, Enable, Endorse, Fatwa(h), Fetwa, Fiat, Green light, Homologate, Imprimatur, Legal, Legitimate, Mandate, OK, Pass, Pragmatic, Ratify, Smart, Sustain, Upstay, Warrant

Sanctuary, Sanctum Adytum, Ark, Asylum, By-room, Cella, Ch, Chancel, Church, Delubrum, Frithsoken, Frithstool, Girth, Grith, Haven, Holy, JCR, Lair, Naos, Oracle, Penetralia, Preserve, Refuge, Sacellum, Sacrarium, Salvation, SCR, →**SHELTER**, Shrine, Temple

Sandwich(es), Sandwiched Between, Bruschetta, Butty, Club, Clubhouse, Croque-monsieur, Cuban, Doorstep, Earl, Hamburger, Hoagie, Island, Knuckle, Open, Panini, Roti, Round, Sanger, Sango, Sarmie, Sarney, Sarnie, Smørbrød, Smörgåsbord, Smørrebrød, Squeeze, Sub, Submarine, Tartine, Thumber, Toastie, Toebie, Triple-decker, Twitcher, Victoria, Western, Zak(o)uski
▷**Sandwich(es)** *may indicate* a hidden word

Sane, Sanity Compos mentis, Formal, Healthy, Judgement, Rational, Reason, Right-minded, Sensible, Wice

Sanguine Confident, Haemic, Hopeful, Optimistic, Roseate, Ruddy

Sap Attenuate, Benzoin, Bleed, Cosh, Cremor, Depress, Drain, Enervate, Entrench, Ichor, Juice, Laser, Latex, Latice, Lymph, Mine, Mug, Nuclear, Pulque, Ratten, Resin, Roset, Rosin, Rozet, Rozit, Secretion, Soma, Sucker, Sura, Swot, Undermine, Unnerve, Weaken

Sarcasm, Sarcastic Acidity, Biting, Caustic, Cutting, Cynical, Derision, Irony, Mordacious, Mordant, Pungent, Quip, Sarky, Satire, Sharp, Sharp-tongued, Snide, Sting, Wisecrack, Wry

Sardonic Cutting, Cynical, Ironical, Scornful

Sash Baldric(k), Band, Belt, Burdash, Cummerbund, Fillister, French, Lungi, Obi, Scarf, Turban, Window

Satan Adversary, Apollyon, Arch-enemy, Arch-foe, Cram, →**DEVIL**, Eblis, Lucifer, Prince of darkness, Shaitan, The old serpent

Satellite Adrastea, Ananke, Ariel, Artificial, Astra, Atlas, Attendant, Aussat, Belinda, Bianca, Bird, Callisto, Calypso, Camenae, Carme, Charon, Communications, Comsat®, Cordelia, Cosmos, Cressida, Deimos, Desdemona, Despina, Dione, Disciple, Early bird, Earth, Echo, Elara, Enceladus, Europa, Explorer, Fixed, Follower, Galatea, Galilean, Ganymede, Geostationary, Helene, Henchman, Himalia, Hipparchus, Hyperion, Iapetus, Intelsat, Io, Janus, Lackey, Larissa, Leda, Lysithea, Meteorological, Metis, Mimas, Miranda, Moon, Mouse,

Naiad, Navigation, Nereid, Oberon, Ophelia, Orbiter, Pan, Pandora, Pasiphae, Phobos, Phoebe, Planet, Portia, Prometheus, Puck, Rhea, Rosalind, Sinope, Smallset, Space probe, SPOT, Sputnik, Syncom, Telesto, Telstar, Tethys, Thalassa, Thebe, Tiros, Titan, Titania, Triton, Umbriel, Weather

▶**Satin** *see* **SILK(Y)**

Satisfaction, Satisfactory, Satisfy(ing), Satisfied, Satisfactorily
Adequate, Agree, Ah, Answer, Ap(p)ay, Appease, Assuage, Atone, Change, Compensation, Complacent, → **CONTENT**, Defrayment, Enough, Feed, Fill, Fulfil, Glut, Gratify, Happy camper, Indulge, Jake, Job, Liking, Meet, Nice, OK, Okey-dokey, Pacation, Palatable, Pay, Please, Pride, Propitiate, Qualify, Redress, Relish, Repay, Replete, Reprisal, Revenge, Sate, Satiate, Sensual, Serve, Settlement, Slake, Smug, Square, Suffice, Supply, Tickety-boo, Well

Saturate(d) Drench, Glut, Imbue, Impregnate, Infuse, Permeate, → **SOAK**, Sodden, Steep, Surcharge, Waterlog

Sauce, Saucier, Saucy Agrodolce, Aioli, Alfredo, Allemanse, Apple, Arch, Avgolemono, Baggage, Barbecue, Béarnaise, Béchamel, Bigarade, Bold(-faced), Bolognese, Bordelaise, Bourguignonne, Bread, Brown, Caper, Carbonara, Catchup, Catsup, Chasseur, Chaudfroid, Cheek, Chef, Chilli, Chutney, Condiment, Coulis, Cranberry, Cream, Creme anglaise, Cumberland, Custard, Dapper, Dip, Dressing, Enchilada, Espagnole, Fenberry, Fondue, Fricassee, Fudge, Fu yong, Fu yung, Gall, Garum, Gravy, Hard, Hoisin, Hollandaise, Horseradish, HP®, Impudence, Jus, Ketchup, Lip, Malapert, Marinade, Marinara, Matelote, Mayo(nnaise), Melba, Meunière, Mint, Mirepoix, Mole, Monkeygland, Mornay, Mousseline, Mouth, Nam pla, Neck, Nerve, Newburg, Nuoc mam, Oxymal, Oyster, Panada, Parsley, Passata, Peart, Peking, Perky, Pert, Pesto, Piert, Piri-piri, Pistou, Pizzaiola, Ponzu, Portugaise, Puttanesca, Ragu, Ravigote, Relish, Remoulade, Rouille, Roux, Sabayon, Sal, Salad cream, Salpicon, Salsa, Salsa verde, Sambal, Sass, Satay, Shoyu, Soja, Soubise, Soy(a), Stroganoff, Sue, Sugo, Supreme, Sweet and sour, Tabasco®, Tamari, Tartar(e), Tomato, Topping, Tossy, Trimmings, Velouté, Vinaigrette, Vindaloo, White, Wine, Worcester, Worcestershire, Yakitori

Sausage(s) Andouille, Andouillette, Banger, Black pudding, Boerewors, Bologna, Bratwurst, Cervelat, Cheerio, Chipolata, Chorizo, Corn dog, Cumberland, Devon, Drisheen, Frankfurter, Garlic, Kielbasa, Knackwurst, Knockwurst, Liver(wurst), Lorne, Luncheon, Mortadella, Pep(p)eroni, Polony, Pudding, Salami, Sav(eloy), Snag(s), Snarler, Square, String, Vienna, Weenie, Weeny, White pudding, Wiener(wurst), Wienie, Wourst, Wurst, Zampone

Savage Barbarian, Bitter, Boor, Brute, Cruel, Fierce, Frightful, Grim, Hun, Immane, Inhuman, Maul, Remorseless, Sadistic, Truculent, Vitriolic, Wild

Save(r), Saving(s) Bank, Bar, Besides, But, Capital, Collect, Conserve, Cut-rate, Deposit, Economy, Except, Goalie, Hain, Hoard, Husband, Investment, ISA, Keep, Layby, Nest egg, Nirlie, Nirly, Not, PEPS, Post office, Preserve, Put by, Reclaim, Recycle, Redeem, Relieve, Reprieve, → **RESCUE**, Reskew, Sa', Salt (away), Salvage, SAYE, Scrape, Scrimp, Shortcut, Slate club, Soak away, Sock away, Sou-sou, Spare, Stint, Stokvel, Succour, Susu, TESSA, Unless

Saw Adage, Aphorism, Apothegm, Azebiki, Back, Band, Beheld, Bucksaw, Buzz, Chain, Circular, Cliché, Commonplace, Compass, Coping, Cross-cut, Crown, Cut, Dictum, Double-ender, Dovetail, Dozuki, Ensured, Flooring, Frame, Fret, Gang, Glimpsed, Gnome, Grooving, Hack, Hand, Jig, Keyhole, Legend, Log, Maxim, Met, Motto, Pad, Panel, Paroemia, Pitsaw, Proverb, Pruning, Quarter, Rabbeting, Rack, Ribbon, Rip, Ryoba, Sash, Saying, Scroll, Serra, Skil®,

Skip-tooth, Slasher, Slogan, Span, Spied, Stadda, Stone, Sweep, Tenon, Trepan, Trephine, Whip, Witnessed

Say, Saying(s) Adage, Agrapha, Allege, Aphorism, Apophthegm, Apostrophise, Articulate, Axiom, Beatitude, Bon mot, Bromide, Byword, Cant, Catchphrase, Centos, Cliché, Declare, Dict(um), Eg, Enunciate, Epigram, Expatiate, Express, Fadaise, For example, For instance, Gnome, Impute, Input, Logia, Logion, Mean, Mot, Mouth, Observe, Phrase, Platitude, Predicate, Pronounce, Proverb, Put, Quip, Recite, Rede, Relate, Remark, Report, Repute, Saine, Saw, Sc, Sententia, →SPEAK, Suppose, Sutra, Talk, Utter, Voice, Word

▷**Say, Saying(s)** *may indicate* a word sounding like another

Scale(s), Scaly API gravity, Ascend, Balance, Beaufort, Brix, Bud, Burnham, Celsius, Centigrade, Chromatic, →CLIMB, Cottony-cushion, Dander, Dandruff, Diagonal, Diatonic, Enharmonic(al), Escalade, Fahrenheit, Flake, Fujita, Full, Gamme, Gamut, Gapped, Gauge, Gravity, Gray, Heptatonic, Hexachord, Humidex, Indusium, Interval, Kelvin, Krab, Ladder, Lamina, Layer, Leaf, Lepid, Libra, Ligule, Magnitude, Major, Mercalli, Mesel, Metric, Minor, Mohs, Natural, Nominal, Ordinal, Oyster shell, Palet, Peel, Pentatonic, Plate, Platform, Proportion, →RANGE, Rankine, Ratio, Réau(mur), Regulo, Richter, San Jose, Scalade, Scan, Scent, Scurf, Shin, Sliding, Spring, Submediant, Tegula, Tonal, Tron(e), Unified, Vernier, Wage, Weighbridge, Wentworth, Whole-tome, Wind

▷**Scale(d)** *may indicate* a fish

Scan(ning), Scanner Barcode, CAT, CT, EEG, Examine, Flat-bed, Helical, Inspect, Iris, OCR, Oversee, Peruse, PET, Rake, Raster, Scrutinise, SEM, SPET, Study, Survey, Tomography, Ultrasound, Vet

Scandal(ous), Scandalise Belie, Canard, Commesse, Disgrace, Gamy, -gate, Hearsay, Muck-raking, Mud, Opprobrium, Outrage, Shame, Slander, Stigma, Tattle, Watergate

Scant(y), Scantness Bare, Brief, Exiguous, Jejune, Jimp, Low, Meagre, Oligotrophy, Parsimonious, Poor, Scrimpy, Short, Shy, Slender, Spare, Sparse, Stingy

Scapegoat, Scapegrace Butt, Fall-guy, Hazazel, Joe Soap, Martyr, Patsy, Skainesmate, Stooge, Target, Victim, Whipping-boy

Scarce(ly), Scarcity Barely, Dear, Dearth, Famine, Few, Hardly, Ill, Lack, Paucity, Rare, Scanty, Seldom, Short, Strap, Uncommon, Want

Scarecrow Bogle, Bugaboo, Dudder, Dudsman, Gallibagger, Gallibeggar, Gallicrow, Gallybagger, Gallybeggar, Gallycrow, Malkin, Mawkin, Potato-bogle, Ragman, S(h)ewel, Tattie-bogle

Scarf Babushka, Belcher, Cataract, Comforter, Cravat, Curch, Doek, Dupatta, Fascinator, Fichu, Hai(c)k, Haique, Hyke, Lambrequin, Madras, Mantilla, Muffettee, Muffler, Neckatee, Neckcloth, Neckerchief, Neckgear, Neckpiece, Necktie, Neckwear, Nightingale, Orarium, Pagri, Palatine, Patka, Rail, Rebozo, Sash, Screen, Shash, Stock, Stole, Tallith, Tippet, Trot-cosy, Trot-cozy, Vexillum

Scatter(ed), Scattering Bestrew, Broadcast, Diaspora, Disgregation, Disject, Dispel, Dissipate, Dot, Flurr, Inelastic, Litter, Rayleigh, Rout, Scail, Skail, Sow, Sparge, Sparse, Splutter, Sporadic, Sprad, Spread, Sprinkle, Squander, Straw, Strew, Strinkle

Scavenge(r) Ant, Dieb, Forage, Gully-hunter, Hunt, Hy(a)ena, Jackal, Rake, Ratton, Rotten, Scaffie, Sweeper, Totter, Vulture

Scene(ry) Arena, Backcloth, Boscage, Cameo, Coulisse, Decor, Diorama, Episode, Flat(s), Landscape, Locale, Outtake, Periaktos, Phantasmagoria, Prop, Prospect, Riverscape, Set, Sight, Site, Sketch, Stage, Tableau, Take, Tormenter, Tormentor, Venue, View, Wing

Scent Aroma, Attar, Chypre, Civet, Cologne, Essence, Fragrance, Frangipani, Fumet(te), Gale, Moschatel, Musk, Nose, Odour, Orris, Ottar, Otto, Perfume, Pomander, Sachet, Smell, Spoor, Vent, Waft, Wind

Sceptic, Sceptical(ly), Scepticism Askant, Cynic, Disbeliever, Doubter, Europhobe, Incredulous, Infidel, Jaundiced, Nihilistic, Nullifidian, Pyrrho(nic), Sadducee, Thomas

Schedule Agenda, Calendar, Classification, Itinerary, List, Prioritise, Programme, Register, Slot, Table, Time-sheet, Timetable

Scheme, Schemer, Scheming Angle, Calculate, CATS, Colour, Concoct, Connive, Conspire, Crafty, Cunning, Dare, Darien, Dart, Decoct, Décor, Design, Devisal, Diagram, Dodge, Draft, Evince, Gin, Honeytrap, Housing, Intrigue, Jezebel, Machiavellian, Machinate, Manoeuvre, Master plan, Nostrum, Pension, Pilot, → **PLAN**, Plat, Plot, Ponzi, Project, Proposition, Purpose, Put-up job, Pyramid, Racket, Rhyme, Ruse, Scam, Set-aside, Stratagem, System, Table, Top-hat, Wangle, Wheeler-dealer, Wheeze

Scholar, Scholiast Abelard, Academic, Alcuin, Alumni, BA, Bookman, Classicist, Clergy, Clerk, Commoner, Demy, Disciple, Don, Erasmus, Erudite, Etonian, Exhibitioner, Extern(e), Faculty, Graduate, Hebraist, Literate, MA, Maulana, Ollamh, Ollav, Pauline, Plutarch, Polymath, Pupil, Rhodes, Sap, Savant, Saxonist, Schoolboy, Soph, → **STUDENT**, Tom Brown, Varro

School Brainwash, Discipline, Drill, Educate, Exercise, Feeder, Peripatetic, Teach, → **TRAIN**, Tutor

Science Aerodynamics, Anatomy, Anthropology, Applied, Art, Astrodynamics, Astrophysics, Atmology, Avionics, Axiology, Behavioural, Biology, Biotech, Botany, Chemistry, Christian, Cognitive, Computer, Crystallography, Cybernetics, Dismal, Domestic, Earth, Ekistics, Electrodynamics, Entomology, Eth(n)ology, Eugenics, Euphenics, Exact, Forensic, Gay, Geodesy, Geology, Hard, Information, Knowledge, Life, Lithology, Macrobiotics, Materia medica, Mechanics, Metallurgy, Meteorology, Metrology, Military, Mineralogy, Mnemonics, Natural, Noble, Nomology, Noology, Nosology, Occult, Ology, Ontology, Optics, Optometry, Pedagogy, Penology, Phrenology, Physical, Physics, Policy, Political, Psychics, Pure, Rocket, Rural, Semantics, Semiology, Serology, Skill, Social, Soft, Soil, Sonics, Stinks, Stylistics, Tactics, Technics, Technology, Tectonics, Telematics, Thermodynamics, Thremmatology, Toxicology, Tribology, Trigonometry, Typhlology, Zootechnics

Scoff Belittle, Boo, Chaff, Deride, Devour, Dor, Eat, Feast, Flout, Food, Gall, Geck, Gibe, Gird, Gobble, → **JEER**, Jest, Mock, Rail, Rib, Ridicule, Roast, Scaff, Scorn, Send up, Sneer, Swallow, Taunt

Scold(ing) Admonish, Berate, Callet, Catamaran, Chastise, Chide, Clapperclaw, Do, Earful, Earwig, Flite, Flyte, Fuss, Jaw(bation), Jobation, Lecture, Nag, Objurgate, Philippic, Rag, Rant, Rate, → **REBUKE**, Reprimand, Reprove, Revile, Rollick, Rollock, Rouse on, Row, Sas(s)arara, Sis(s)erary, Slang, Slate, Termagant, Tick-off, Tongue-lash, Trimmer, Upbraid, Virago, What for, Wig, Xant(h)ippe, Yaff, Yankie, Yap

Scope Ambit, Bargaining, Breadth, Compass, Diapason, Domain, Elbow-room, Extent, Freedom, Gamut, Indulgence, Ken, Latitude, Leeway, Purview, Range, Remit, Room, Rope, Scouth, Scowth, Size, Sphere

Scorch(er) Adust, Birsle, Blister, Brasero, → **BURN**, Char, Destroy, Frizzle, Fry, Parch, Scouther, Scowder, Scowther, Sear, Singe, Soar, Speed, Swale, Swayl, Sweal, Sweel, Torrefy, Torrid, Wither

Score(s), Scoring Aggregate, Apgar, Arrange, Behind, Bill, Birdie, Bradford, Bye, Capot, Chalk up, Chase, Clock up, Conversion, Count, Crena, Debt, Dunk, Eagle, Etch, Full, Gash, Goal, Groove, Hail, Honours, Incise, Ingroove, Ippon, Koka, Law, Leaderboard, Lots, Magpie, Make, Mark, Music, Net, Nick, Notation, Notch, Nurdle, Open, Orchestrate, Partitur(a), Peg(board), Pique, Point, Record, Repique, Rit(t), Rouge, Run, Rut, Scotch, Scrat, Scratch, Scribe, Scrive, Set, Sheet music, Single, Spare, Stableford, Stria, String, Sum, Tablature, → **TALLY**, TE, Touchdown, Try, Twenty, Vocal, Waza-ari, Win, Yuko

▷**Scorer** *may indicate* a composer

▷**Scoring** *may indicate* an anagram

Scorn(ful) Arrogant, Bah, Contemn, Contempt, Contumely, Deride, Despise, Dis(s), Disdain, Dislike, Disparagement, Flout, Geck, Haughty, Insult, Meprise, Mock, Opprobrium, Phooey, Putdown, Raillery, Rebuff, Ridicule, Sarcastic, Sardonic, Sarky, Scathing, Scoff, Scout, Sdaine, Sdeigne, Sneer, Sniffy, Spurn, Wither

Scot(sman), Scots(woman), Scottish Alistair, Blue-bonnet, Fingal, Kelvinside, Morningside, Pecht, Shetlander, Tartan, Tax

Scotland Alban(y), Albion, Caledonia, Lallans, Lothian, NB, Norland, Scotia

Scoundrel Cad, Cur, Dog, Heel, Hound, Knave, Miscreant, Rat(bag), Reprobate, Scab, Smaik, Varlet, → **VILLAIN**, Wretch

▷**Scour** *may indicate* an anagram

Scout Akela, Baden-Powell, Beaver, Bedmaker, Bird dog, Colony, Deride, Disdain, Emissary, Explorer, Flout, Guide, Mock, Outrider, Pathfinder, Patrol(ler), Pickeer, Pioneer, Ranger, Reconnoitre, Rover, Runner, Scoff, Scorn, Scourer, Scurrier, Sixer, Talent, Tenderfoot, Tonto, Venture

Scrap(s), Scrappy Abandon, Abolish, Abrogate, Bin, → **BIT**, Brock, Cancel, Conflict, Discard, Ditch, Dump, End, Erase, → **FIGHT**, Fisticuffs, Fragment, Fray, Iota, Jot, Junk, Leftover, Mêlée, Mellay, Morceau, Morsel, Odd, Off-cut, Ort, Ounce, Patch, Piece, Pig's-wash, Rag, Rase, Raze, Remnant, Rescind, Rew, Row, Ruck, Scarmoge, Scintilla, Scissel, Scissil, Scroddled, Scrub, Set-to, Shard, Sherd, Shred, Skerrick, Skirmish, Snap, Snippet, Spall, Stoush, Tait, Tate, Tatter, Titbit, Trash, Truculent, Tussle, Whit, Wisp

Scrape(r) Abrade, Agar, Bark, Clat, Claw, Comb, Curette, D and C, Escapade, Grate, Graze, Gride, Harl, Hoe, Hole, Jar, Kowtow, Lesion, Lute, Pick, Predicament, Racloir, Rake, Rasorial, Rasp, Rasure, Raze, Razure, Saw, Scalp, Scart, Scrat(ch), Scroop, Scuff, Shave, Skimp, Skin, Skive, Squeegee, Strake, Strigil, Xyster

Scratch(es), Scratched, Scratching Cracked heels, Etch, Grabble, Key, Mar, Pork, Ritt, Score, Scrawp, Scrooch, Scrorp, Scuff, Streak, Striation, Withdraw

▷**Scratch(ed)** *may indicate* an anagram

Scream(er) Aargh, Amusing, Bellow, Cariama, Caterwaul, Comedian, Comic, Cry, Eek, Headline, Hern, Hoot, Kamichi, Laugh, Priceless, Primal, Riot, Scare-line, Screech, Seriema, Shriek, Skirl, Squall, Sutch, Yell

Screen(s), Screening Air, Arras, Back projection, Backstop, Blind(age), Block, Blue, Boss, Camouflage, Cervical, Chancel, Check, Chick, Cinerama®, Cloak, Comb, Cornea, Cover, Curtain, Divider, Dodger, Eclipse, Eyelid, Fight, Fire, Flat, Fluorescent, Glib, Grid, Grille, Hallan, Help, Hide, Hoard, Hoarding, Intensifying, Lattice, Long-persistence, Mantelet, Mask, Meat, Monitor, Net, Nintendo®, Nonny, Obscure, Organ, Overhead, Parclose, Partition, Pella, Plasma, Pulpitum, Purdah, Radar, Radarscope, Reardos, Reredorse, Reredos(se), Retable, Riddle, Rood, Scog, Sconce, Scope, Seclude, → **SHADE**, Shelter, Shield, Show, Sift, Sight, Silver, Skug, Small, Smoke, Split, Strain,

Sunblock, Televise, Tems, Test, Testudo, TFT, Touch, Traverse, Umbrella, VDU, Vet, Visor, Wide, Windbreak, Window, Windshield

Screw Adam, Allen, Archimedes, Blot, Butterfly, Cap, Cheat, Coach, Coitus, Countersunk, Double-threaded, Dungeoner, Endless, Extort, Female, Fleece, Grub, Guard, Gyp, Ice, Interrupted, Jack, Jailer, Jailor, Lag, Lead, Levelling, Lug, Machine, Male, Mar, Micrometer, Miser, Monkey-wrench, Niggard, Pay, Perpetual, Phillips®, Prop(ellor), Pucker, Raised head, Robertson, Rotate, Ruin, Salary, Screweye, Scrunch, Skinflint, Spiral, Squinch, Swiz(zle), Thumb(i)kins, Twin, Twine, Twist, Vice, Wages, Whitworth, Worm, Wreck

Script (reader) Book, Demotist, Devanagari, Gurmukhi, Hand, Hieratic, Hiragana, Italic, Jawi, Kana, Kufic, Libretto, Linear A, Linear B, Lines, Lombardic, Longhand, Miniscule, Nagari, Nashki, Nastalik, Nastaliq, Nes(h)ki, Og(h)am, Prompt book, Ronde, Scenario, Screenplay, Shorthand, Writing

Scripture(s), Scriptural version Adi Granth, Agadah, Alcoran, Antilegomena, Avesta, Bible, Gemara, Gematria, Gospel, Granth (Sahib), Guru Granth, Haggada(h), Hermeneutics, Hexapla, Holy book, Holy writ, Koran, K'thibh, Lectionary, Lesson, Lotus Sutra, Mishna(h), OT, Rig-veda, Smriti, Tantra, Targum, Testament, Upanishad, Veda, Vedic, Verse, Vulgate

Scrounge(r) Beg, Blag, Bludge(r), Borrow, Bot, Cadge, Forage, Freegan, Freeload, Layabout, Ligger, Scunge, Sponge

Scrub(ber), Scrubland, Scrubs Abandon, Cancel, Chaparral, Cleanse, Dele(te), Exfoliate, Expunge, Facial, Fynbos, Gar(r)igue, Heath, Horizontal, Loofa(h), Luffa, Masseur, Nailbrush, Negate, Pro, Rescind, Rub, Scour, Sticks, Strim, Tart, Wormwood

▷**Scrub** *may indicate* 'delete'

Scrutinize, Scrutiny Check, Docimasy, Examine, Inspect, Observe, Peruse, Pore, Pry, → **SCAN**, Size up, Study

▷**Scuffle** *may indicate* an anagram

Sculpt(ure) Bas-relief, Bronze, Bust, Carve, Chisel, Della-robbia, Figure, Glyptics, High-relief, Kouros, Marble, Mezzo-relievo, Mezzo-rilievo, Mobile, Nude, Pietà, Relievo, Shape, → **STATUARY**, Topiary

Scum, Scumbag Dregs, Dross, Epistasis, Film, Louse, Pellicle, Pond, Rat, Scorious, Scruff, Slag, Slime, Spume, Sullage, Vermin

Scurf, Scurvy Dander, Dandriff, Dandruff, Furfur, Horson, Lepidote, Lepra, Leprose, Scabrous, Scall, Scorbutic, Whoreson, Yaws, Yaw(e)y

Sea(s), Seawards Billow, Brine, Briny, Ditch, Drink, Electron, Epicontinental, Euxine, Foam, Herring-pond, Main, Mare, Mare clausum, Mare liberum, Maritime, Molten, → **OCEAN**, Offing, Offshore, Open, Out, Quantity, Strand, Tide, Water

Seaman, Seamen AB, Argonaut, Circumnavigator, Crew, Jack, Lascar, Lubber, Mariner, OD, Ordinary, PO, Rating, RN, → **SAILOR**, Salt, Swabby, Tar

Sear Brand, Burn, Catch, Cauterise, Char, Frizzle, Parch, Scath(e), Scorch, Singe, Wither

Search(ing) Beat, Body, Comb, Delve, Dowse, Dragnet, Examine, Ferret, Fish, → **FORAGE**, Fossick, Frisk, Google(-whack), Grope, Home, Hunt, Indagate, Inquire, Jerk, Jerque, Kemb, Manhunt, Perscrutation, Probe, Proll, Prospect, Proul, Prowl, Pursue, Quest, Rake, Rancel, Ransack, Ransel, Ranzel, Ravel, Ripe, Root, Rootle, Rummage, Scan, Scavenge, Scour, Scout, Scur, Sker, Skirr, Snoop, Strip, Surf, Sweep, Talent spotting, Thumb, Trace, Trawl, Zotetic

Season(able), Seasonal, Seasoned, Seasoning Accustom, Age, Aggrace, Autumn, Betimes, Christmas, Close, Condiment, Devil, Dress, Duxelles, Easter,

Enure, Etesian, Fall, Fennel, Festive, Fines herbes, Flavour, Garlic, G(h)omasco, Growing, Heat, Hiems, High, In, Inure, Lent, Marjoram, Master, Mature, Noel, Nutmeg, Off, Open, Paprika, Peak, Pepper, Powellise, Practised, Ripen, Salt, Sar, Seal, Seel, Sele, Silly, Solstice, Spice, Spring, Summer(y), Tahini, Ticket, Tide, Time, Timeous, Weather-beaten, Whit, Winter

Seat(ing) Barstool, Beanbag, Behind, Booty, Bosun's chair, Bunker, Catbird, Choirstall, Country, Duff, Inglenook, Judgement, Lap, Miserere, Rocker, Royal box, Sagbag, Sedile, Selle, Shooting stick, Siege Perilous, Stall, Stand, Thwart, Tip up, Window

Seaweed Agar, Alga(e), Arame, Badderlock, Bladderwort, Bladderwrack, Carrag(h)een, Ceylon moss, Chondrus, Conferva, Coralline, Cystocarp, Desmid, Diatom, Dulse, Enteromorpha, Florideae, Fucus, Gulfweed, Heterocontae, Kale, Karengo, Kelp, Kilp, Kombu, Laminaria, Laver, Maerl, Nori, Nulliphore, Oarweed, Ore, Peacock's tail, Porphyra, Redware, Rockweed, Sargasso, Seabottle, Sea-furbelow, Sea-girdle, Sea-lace, Sea-lettuce, Sea-mat, Sea-moss, Sea-tangle, Seaware, Sea-whistle, Sea-wrack, Tang(le), Ulva, Varec(h), Vraic, Wakame, Ware, Wrack

Seclude(d), Seclusion Cloister, Incommunicado, Isolate, Ivory tower, Maroon, Nook, Pleasance, Poke(y), Privacy, Purdah, Quarantine, Remote, Retiracy, Retreat, Secret, Sequester, Shyness, Solitude

Second(ary), Seconds Abet, Alternative, Another (guess), Appurtenance, Assist, Atomic, Back(er), Beta, Byplay, Chaser, Collateral, Coming, Comprimario, Congener, Cornerman, Deuteragonist, Fiddle, Flash, Flip, Friend, Handler, Imperfect, Indirect, Inferior, Instant, Jiffy, Latter, Lesser, Minor, Mo(ment), Nature, Other, Pig's-whisper, Red ribbon, Runner-up, Saybolt-Universal, Sec, Shake, Share, Side(r), Sideline, Sight, Silver, Split, Subsidiary, Subtype, Support, Tick, Tone, Trice, Twinkling, Universal, Wind

Second-hand Flea market, Hearsay, Reach-me-down, Trade in, Unoriginal, Used

Secrecy, Secret(s), Secretive Apocrypha, Arcana, Arcane, Backstairs, Cabbalistic, Cagey, Clam, Clandestine, Classified, Closet, Code, Conference, Confidence, Corner, Couvert, Covert, Cranny, Cryptic, Dark, Deep, Deep-laid, Devious, Esoteric, Furtive, Hidden, Hole and corner, Hush-hush, In camera, Inly, Inmost, Inner, In pectore, In petto, Know-nothing, Latent, Mysterious, Mystical, Mystique, Open, Oyster, Password, Penetralia, → **PRIVATE**, Privy, QT, Rune, Seal, Sensitive, Shelta, Silent, Slee, Sly, Sneaky, State, Stealth, Sub rosa, Surreptitious, Tight-lipped, Top, Trade, Unbeknown, Underboard, Undercover, Underhand, Unknown, Unre(a)d, Unrevealed, Untold

Secretary Aide, Amanuensis, Chancellor, Chronicler, CIS, Desk, Desse, Famulus, Minuteman, Moonshee, Munshi, Notary, Permanent, Prot(h)onotary, Scrive, Social, Stenotyper, Temp

Sect(arian), Secret society Ahmadiy(y)ah, Albigenses, Bigot, Campbellite, Christadelphian, Covenantes, Cynic, Disciples of Christ, Encratite, Familist, Fifth monarchy, Gabar, Glassite, Hassid, Hemerobaptist, Hesychast, Holy Roller, Hutterite, Ismaili, Jehovah's Witness, Jodo, Mendaites, Nasorean, Noetian, Ophites, Patripassian, Paulician, Perfectation, Pietist, Plymouth Brethren, Pure Land, Ranter, Rasta, Russellite, Saktas, Sandeman, Schwenkfelder, Seventh Day Adventist, Shafiite, Shembe, Shiite, Soka Gakkai, Sons of Freedom, Taliban, Utraquist, Vaishnava, Zealot

Section, Sector Appendix, Area, Balkanize, Caesarian, Chapter, Classify, Compartment, Conic, Cross, Cut, Department, Directorate, Division, Edge, Ellipse, Empennage, Episode, Eyalet, Gan, Golden, Gore, Hyperbola, Length,

Lith, Lune, Meridian, Metamere, Mortice, Movement, Octant, Outlier, Panel, Passus, Peraeon, → **PIECE**, Platoon, Private, Public, Pull-out, Quarter, Rhythm, Rib, S, Segment, Septum, Severy, Sextant, Shard, Sherd, Slice, Stage, Track, Ungula, Unit, Wing, Zone

Secure(d), Security Affix, Anchor, Assurance, Bag, Bail, Band, Bar, → **BASIC**, Batten, Belay, Bellwether, Belt and braces, Bolt, Bond, Buckle, Buck Rogers, Button, Calm, Cash ratio, Catch, Cement, Chain, Cinch, Clamp, Clasp, Clench, Clinch, Close, Cocoon, Collateral, Collective, Come by, Confine, Consolidate, Consols, Cosy, Counterseal, Cushy, Debenture, Deposit, Disreputable, Doorman, Earn, Earthwork, Engage, Enlock, Ensure, Equity, Establishment, Fasten, Fastness, Firm, Fortify, Fungibles, Gain, Gilt, Gilt-edged, Gird, Guarantee, Guy, Heritable, Hostage, Immune, Impregnable, Indemnity, Inlock, In the bag, Invest(ment), Knot, Lace, Land, Lash, Latch, Lien, Listed, Lock (up), Lockaway, Lockdown, Lockfast, Longs, Mortgage, Nail, National, Obtain, Padlock, Patte, Pin, Pledge, Pot, Pre-empt, Preference, Procure, Protect, Quad, Rope, Rug, → **SAFE**, Safety, Screw, Seal, Settle, Shutter, Snell, Snug, Social, Sound, Stable, Staple, Stock, Strap, Sure(ty), Tack, Take, Tie, Tight, Trap, Tyde, Vest, Warrant, Watertight, Wedge, Win

Sedative Amytal®, Anodyne, Aspirin, Barbitone, Bromal, Bromide, Chloral, Depressant, Deserpidine, Hypnic, Lenitive, Lupulin(e), Meprobamate, Metopryl, Miltown, Morphia, Narcotic, Nembutal®, Opiate, Painkiller, Paraldehyde, Pethidine, Phenobarbitone, Premed(ication), Rohypnol®, Roofie, Scopolamine, Seconal®, Snuff, Soothing, Temazepam, Thridace, Veronal®

Sediment Alluvium, Chalk, Deposit, Dregs, F(a)eces, Fecula, Flysch, Foots, Graded, Grounds, Incrustation, Lees, Molasse, Placer, Residue, Salt, Sapropel, Silt, Sludge, Terrigenous, Till, Varve, Warp

Seduce(r), Seduction, Seductive Bed, Beguilement, Bewitch, Come-hither, Debauch, Dishonour, Honeyed, Honied, Ixion, Jape, Lothario, Luring, Mislead, Sexpot, Sexy, Siren, Tempt, Vamp

▷**Seduce** *may indicate* one word inside another

See(ing) Bath and Wells, Behold, Believing, Bishopric, Carlisle, Consider, Date, Descry, Diocesan, Discern, Ebor, Episcopal, Exeter, Eye, Get, Glimpse, Holy, In as much as, Lo, Notice, Observe, Papal, Perceive, Realise, Rochester, Rubberneck, St David's, Salisbury, Sight, Spot, Spy, Twig, Understand, Vatican, Vid(e), View, Vision, Voilà, Witness

Seed(s), Seedy Achene, Apiol, Argan, Arilli, Arillode, Ash-key, Bean, Ben, Benne, Best, Blue, Bonduc, Cacoon, Caraway, Cardamom, Carvy, Cebadilla, Cedar-nut, Cevadilla, Chickpea, Coriander, Corn, Cum(m)in, Dragon's teeth, Embryo, Endosperm, Ergot, Favourite, Germ, Grain, Gritty, Inseminate, Issue, Ivory-nut, Kernel, Lentil, Lomentum, Mangy, Mawseed, Miliary, Mote, Nickar, Nicker, Nucellous, Nut, Oat, Offspring, Origin, Ovule, Pea, Peaky, Pinon, Pip, Pomegranate, Poorly, Poppy, Pyxis, Sabadilla, Samariform, Scuzz, Semen, Seminal, Senvy, Sesame, Shabby, Silique, Sordid, Sorus, Sow, Sperm, Spore, Stane, Stone, Thistledown, Urd, Zoosperm

Seek(er), Seeking Ask, Beg, Busk, Cap-in-hand, Chase, Court, Endeavour, Fish, Forage, Gun for, Pursue, Quest, Scavenge, Scur, Search, Skirr, Solicit, Suitor, Try

Seem(ing), Seemingly Apparent, Appear, As if, Look, Ostensible, Purport, Quasi, Think

Seemly Apt, Comely, Decent, Decorous, Fit, Proper, Suitable

Seer Balaam, Eye, Nahum, Nostradamus, Observer, Onlooker, Oracle, Prescience, Prophet, Sage, Sibyl, Soothsayer, Witness, Zoroaster

Segment(ation) Antimere, Arthromere, Cut, Division, Gironny, Gyronny, Intron, Joint, Lacinate, Lith, Lobe, Merogenesis, Merome, Merosome, Metamere, Metathorax, Piece, Pig, Proglottis, Prothorax, Quadrant, Scliff, Section, Share, Shie, Skliff, Somite, Split, Sternite, Syllable, Tagma, Telson, Urite, Uromere

Segregate, Segregation Apartheid, Exile, Insulate, Intern, →**ISOLATE**, Jim Crow, Seclude, Separate

Seize, Seizing, Seizure Angary, Apprehend, Appropriate, Areach, Arrest, Attach(ment), Bag, Bone, Capture, Catch, Claw, Cleek, Clutch, Cly, Collar, Commandeer, Confiscate, Cop, Coup, Distrain, Distress, For(e)hent, →**GRAB**, Grip, Hend, Hi-jack, Ictus, Impound, Impress, Maverick, Nab, Na(a)m, Nap, Nim, Poind, Possess, Pot, Raid, Ravin, Replevy, Rifle, Sease, Sequestrate, Smug, Snag, Snatch, Stroke, Tackle, Wingding, Wrest

Select(ion), Selecting, Selector Adopt, Artificial, Assortment, Bla(u)d, Cap, Casting, Catalogue, Choice, Choose, Classy, Clonal, Cream, Cull, Darwinism, Discriminate, Draft, Draw, Eclectic, Edit, Elite, Excerpt, Exclusive, Extract, Favour, Garble, Handpick, Inside, K, Nap, Natural, Pericope, →**PICK**, Pot-pourri, Prefer, Recherché, Redline, Sample, Seed, Single, Sort, Stream, Tipster, Triage, UCCA, Vote

Self Atman, Auto, Character, Ego, Person, Psyche, Seity, Sel, Soul

▶**Self-defence** *see* **MARTIAL (ARTS)**

Self-esteem Amour-propre, Conceit, Confidence, Egoism, Pride, Vainglory

Self-important, Self-indulgent, Self-interested, Self-regarding Aristippus, Arrogant, Bumptious, Conceited, Coxy, Egocentric, Hedonist, Immoderate, Jack-in-office, Licentious, Mugwump, Narcissistic, Pompous, Pooterish, Pragmatic, Primadonna, Profligate, Solipsist, Sybarite, Vainglorious

Selfish(ness) Avaricious, Dog eat dog, Dog-in-the-manger, Egocentric, Egoist, Egomaniac, Greedy, Hedonist, Hog, Mean, Solipsism

Self-possession Aplomb, Assurance, Composure, Cool, Nonchalant, Phlegm

Self-satisfied, Self-satisfaction Complacent, Narcissism, Smug, Tranquil

Sell(er), Selling Apprize, Auction, Barter, Bear, Betray, Blackmail, Blockbuster, Cant, Catch, Chant, Chaunt, Cold-call, Cope, Costermonger, Direct, Dispose, Divest, Do, Eggler, Fancier, Fellmonger, Flog, Go, Hard, Have, Hawk, Huckster, Hustle, Inertia, Knock down, Market, Marketeer, Ménage, Merchant, Missionary, Oligopoly, Pardoner, Party, Peddle, Peddler, Pick-your-own, Purvey, Push, Pyramid, Rabbito(h), Realise, Rep, Retail, Ruse, Scalp, Shift, Short, Simony, Soft, Stall-man, Sugging, Switch, Tout, →**TRADE**, Trick, Vend, Vent, Wholesaler

Semblance Appearance, Aspect, Guise, Likeness, Sign, Verisimilitude

Senator Antiani, Cicero, Concept father, Elder, Legislator, Patrician, Shadow, Solon

Send, Sent Consign, →**DESPATCH**, Disperse, Emanate, Emit, Entrance, Extradite, Issue, Launch, Order, Post, Rapt, Refer, Remit, Ship, Transmit, Transport

Send up Chal(l)an, Lampoon, Promote

Senile, Senility Caducity, Dementia, Disoriented, Doddery, Doited, Doitit, Dotage, E(i)ld, Gaga, Nostology, Twichild

Senior(ity) Aîné, Doyen, Elder, Father, Grecian, Major, Majorat, Old(er), Oldie, Oldster, Oubaas, Père, Primus, Superior, Upper

Sensation(al) Acolouthite, Aftershock, Anoesis, Aura, Blood, Blood and thunder, Commotion, Drop-dead, Emotion, Empfindung, Feeling, Furore, Gas, Lurid, Melodrama, Organic, Phosphene, Photism, Pyrotechnic, Rush, Sensory,

Shocker, Shock-horror, Splash, Stir, Styre, Synaesthesia, Thrill, Tingle, Vibes, Wow, Yellow

Sense, Sensual(ist), Sensing Acumen, Animalist, Attuite, Aura, Carnal, Coherence, Common, Conscience, Dress, Ear, ESP, Faculty, Feel, Gaydar, Gross, Gumption, Gustation, Hearing, Horse, Idea, Import, Instinct, Intelligence, Intuition, Lewd, Loaf, Logic, Marbles, Meaning, Moral, Nous, Olfactory, Palate, Perceptual, Proprioceptive, Rational, Receptor, Remote, Rumble-gumption, Rum(m)el-gumption, Rumgumption, Rum(m)le-gumption, Sanity, Satyr, Sight, Sixth, Slinky, Smell, Spirituality, Sybarite, Synesis, Taste, Taste bud, Touch, Voluptuary, Voluptuous, Wisdom, Wit

Senseless Absurd, Anosmia, Asinine, Illogical, Lean-witted, Mad, Numb, Silly, Stupid, Stupor, Unconscious, Unwise, Vegetal

Sensible Aware, Clear-headed, Dianoetic, Lucid, No-nonsense, Politic, Prudent, Raisonné, Rational, Realistic, Sane, Sapient, Solid, Together, Well-balanced

Sensitive, Sensitivity Aesthete, Alive, Allergic, Dainty, Delicate, Discreet, Emotive, Keen, Mimosa, Mystique, Niceness, Panchromatic, Passible, Quick, Radiesthesia, Sore, Sympathetic, Tactful, Tender, Thin-skinned, Ticklish, Touchy(-feely), Vulnerable

Sentence(s) Antiphon, Assize, Bird, Carpet, Clause, Commit, Condemn, Custodial, Death, Decree(t), Deferred, Doom, Fatwah, Indeterminate, Judgement, Life, Matrix, Paragraph, Period(ic), Porridge, Predicate, Punish, Rap, Rheme, Rune, Send up, Stretch, Suspended, Swy, Tagmene, Verdict, Versicle

Sentiment(al), Sentimentality Byronism, Chocolate box, Corn, Cornball, Drip, Emotive, Feeling, Goo, Govey, Gucky, Gush, Lovey-dovey, Maudlin, Mawkish, Mind, Mush, Nationalism, Opinion, Posy, Romantic, Rose-pink, Rosewater, Saccharin, Schmaltzy, Sloppy, Slushy, Smoochy, Sob-stuff, Softy, Soppy, Spoony, Swoony, Syrupy, Tear-jerker, Too-too, Traveller, Treacly, Twee, View, Weepy, Wertherian, Yucky

Sentry, Sentinel Caveman, Cordon sanitaire, Look-out, Picket, Sentinel, Vedette, Vidette, Watch

Separate(d), Separation, Separately, Separatist Abscise, Abstract, Analyse, Apart, Asunder, Bulkhead, Bust up, Comma, Compartmentalise, Cull, Curdle, Cut, Decollate, Decompose, Decouple, Deduct, Demarcate, Demerge, Detach, Dialyse, Disaggregate, Disally, Disconnect, Disintegrate, Disjunction, Dissect, Dissociate, Distance, Distinct, Disunite, Divide, Division, Divorce, Eloi(g)n, Elute, Elutriate, Esloin, Estrange, ETA, Extricate, Filter, Flaky, Grade, Gulf, Heckle, Hive, Hyphenate, Insulate, Intervene, Isolate, Judicial, Laminate, Lease, Legal, Liquate, Part, Particle, Partition, Partitive, Parturition, Peel off, Piece, Prescind, Prism, Red(d), Rift, Sashing, Scatter, Screen, Segregate, Sequester, Sever, Several, Shear, Shed, Shore, Shorn, Sift, Sleave, Sle(i)ded, Solitary, Sort, →**SPLIT**, Spread, Staccato, Stream, Sunder, Sundry, Tease, Tems(e), Tmesis, Try, Twin(e), Unclasp, Unhitch, Unravel, Winnow, Wrench

Sepulchral, Sepulchre Bier, Cenotaph, Charnel, Crypt, Easter, Funeral, Monument, Pyramid, Tomb, Vault, Whited

Sequence, Sequential Agoge, Algorithm, Byte, Cadence, Chronological, Consecution, Consensus, Continuity, Continuum, Cycle, Fibonacci, Gene, Intron, Line, Linear, Montage, Order, Plot, Program(me), Rotation, Run, Seriatim, Series, Shot, Sonnet, Storyboard, String, Succession, Suit, Suite, Train, Vector

Serene, Serenity Calm, Composed, Placid, Quietude, Repose, Sangfroid, Sedate, Seraphic, Smooth, →**TRANQUIL**

Serf(dom) Adscript, Bondman, Ceorl, Churl, Helot, Manred, →**SLAVE**, Thete, Thrall, Vassal, Velle(i)nage, Villein

Sergeant Buzfuz, Chippy, Chips, Cuff, Drill, Flight, Halberdier, Havildar, Kite, Master, Pepper, Platoon, RSM, Sarge, SL, SM, Staff, Technical, Troy

Series Actinide, Actinium, Arithmetical, Battery, Chain, Concatenation, Consecution, Continuum, Course, Cycle, Cyclus, Docusoap, Electromotive, Enfilade, En suite, Episode, Epos, Ethylene, Exponential, Geometric, Gradation, Harmonic, Homologous, Lanthanide, Line, Loop, Methane, Molasse, Neptunium, Partwork, Pedigree, Power, Process, →**PROGRESSION**, Radioactive, Rally, Random walk, Ranks, Rest, Rosalia, Rosary, Rounds, Routine, Rubber, Run, Sequence, Ser, Set, Sitcom, String, Succession, Suit, Test, Thorium, Time, Tone, Tournament, Train, Uranium, World

Serious(ly) Critical, Earnest, Extreme, For real, Grave, Gravitas, Harsh, Important, In earnest, Intense, Major, Momentous, Pensive, Radical, Real, Sad, Serpentine, Sober, Solemn, Sombre, Staid, Straight(-faced), Unamused, Very

Sermon Address, Discourse, Gatha, Homily, Khutbah, Lecture, Preachment, Prone, Ser, Spital

Serpent(ine) Adder, Anguine, Asp, Aspic(k), Basilisk, Bass horn, Boa, Cockatrice, Dipsas, Firedrake, Nagas, Pharaoh's, Reptile, Sea-snake, →**SNAKE**, Traitor, Verd-antique, Verde-antico, Viper

Serum Albumin, Antiglobulin, Antilymphocyte, Antitoxin, ATS, Fluid, Globulin, Humoral, Opsonin, Senega, Truth

Servant, Server Aid(e), Attendant, Ayah, Bartender, Batman, Bearer, Bedder, Bedmaker, Between-maid, Bond, Boot-catcher, Boots, Boy, Busboy, Butler, Caddie, Chambermaid, Chokra, Civil, Columbine, Cook, Cook-general, Daily, Dogsbody, Domestic, Dromio, Drudge, Employee, Esne, Factotum, File, Flunkey, Footboy, Footman, Friday, General, G(h)illie, Gip, Gorsoon, Gully, Gyp, Handmaid, Helot, Henchman, Hind, Hireling, Jack, Jack-slave, Kitchen-knave, Kitchen-maid, Knave, Lackey, Ladle, Lady's maid, Leroy, Maid, Major-domo, Man, Man Friday, Menial, Minion, Mixologist, Muchacha, Muchacho, Myrmidon, Obedient, Orderly, Page, Pantler, Parlourmaid, Pistol, Public, Pug, Redemption, Retainer, Retinue, Scout, Scullion, Servitor, Skivvy, Slavey, Soldier, Soubrette, Steward, Tablespoon, Tiger, Trotter, Turnspit, Tweeny, Underling, Valet, Valkyrie, Varlet, Vassal, Waiter

Serve(r), Service(s) Acas, Ace, Act, Active, Agency, All-up, Amenity, Answer, Army, Assist, Attendance, Avail, Baptism, Barista, Barman, Barperson, Benediction, Breakfast, Campaign, Candlemas, Cannonball, Canteen, China, Christingle, Civil, Communion, Community, Complin(e), Conscription, Credo, Devotional, Dien, Dinnerset, Diplomatic, Divine, Dollop, Drumhead, Dry, Duty, Ecosystem, Emergency, Employ, Evensong, Facility, Fault, Fee, Feudal, Fish, Foreign, Forensic, Forward, →**FUNCTION**, Funeral, Help, Helpline, Ibadat, Jury, Kol Nidre, Ladle, Lauds, Lip, Litany, Liturgy, Ma'ariv, Marriage, Mass, Mat(t)ins, Memorial, Memory, Mincha, Minister, Ministration, Ministry, Missa, National, Navy, Nocturn, Nones, Oblige, Offertory, Office, Oracle, Overarm, Overhaul, Pass, Pay, Personal, Pit stop, Placebo, Possum, Pottery, Pour, Prayer meeting, Prime, Proper, Public, Radio, RAF, Regular, Requiem, Rite, Sacrament, SAS, Satisfy, SBS, Secret, Selective, Senior, Sext, Shacharis, Shaharith, Shuttle, Silent, Silver, Skeleton, Social, Sue, Tableware, Tea, Tierce, Vespers, Wait, Waitron, Waitstaff, Watch-night, Wild, Worship, Yeoman('s)

▷**Serviceman** *may indicate* a churchman

Servile, Servility Abasement, Base, Crawling, Creep, Knee, Kowtowing, Lickspittle, Menial, Minion, Obsequious, Slavish, Slimy, Submissive, Suck-hole, Sycophantic, Tintookie, Truckle

Session(s) All-nighter, Bout, Executive, Galah, Hearing, Jam, Kirk, Meeting, Nightshift, Petty, Poster, Quarter, Rap, Round, Séance, Sederunt, Settle, Sitting, Special, Term

Set(ting) (about, aside, down, in, off, out, up) Activate, Apply, Array, Assail, Assiege, Backdrop, Brooch, Cabal, Coagulate, Codomain, Congelation, Cyclorama, Data, Dead, Detonate, Direct, Duchesse, Earmark, Enchase, Ensky, Explode, Film, Firm, Flash, Framed, F-stop, Gang, Gelatinise, Habitat, Hairdo, Heliacal, Inchase, Incrowd, Infinite, Inlay, Jet, Julia, Knit, Layette, Mental, Miserere, Nail, Open, Ordain, Ordered, Ossify, Ouch, Pair, Pavé, Permanent, Point, Power, Rate, Resolute, Rig, Rouse, Saw, Service, Settle(d), Slate, Smart, Solution, Stud, Subscriber, Televisor, The four hundred, Theme, Tiffany, Toilet, Trannie, Transistor, Trey, Trip, Truth, TV, Union, Universal

Setback Checkmate, Downturn, Glitch, Hiccough, Hiccup, Jolt, Knock, Relapse, Retard, Retreat, Reversal, Scarcement, Sickener, Tes, Vicissitude, Whammy

Settle(d), Settlement, Settler Adjust, Agree, Alight, Ante, Appoint, Arrange, Ascertain, Avenge, Balance, Bed, Bench, Boer, Borghetto, Borough, Botany Bay, Camp, Clear, Clench, Clinch, Colonial, Colonise, Colony, Compose, Compound, Compromise, Cough up, Cut and dry, Decide, Defray, Determine, Discharge, Dispose, Dowry, Encamp, Endow, Ensconce, Entail, Establish, Expat, Faze, Finalise, Fix, Foot, Foreclose, Gravitate, Guilder, Habitant, Hama, Hyannis, Illegitimate, Informal, Jamestown, Jointure, Kibbutz, Land, Ledge, Light, Lull, Manyat(t)a, Meet, Merino, Mise, Mission, Moreton Bay, Nest, Nestle, New Amsterdam, Opt, Ostman, Outpost, Outstation, Over, Pa(h), Paleface, Patroon, Pay, Payment, Penal, People, Perch, Pilgrim, Pioneer, Placate, Planter, Populate, Port Arthur, Port Nicholson, Pueblo, Readjust, Reckoning, Reconcile, Redditch, Reduction, Reimburse, Remit, Repay, Reside, Resolve, Rest, Roofie, Roost, Sate, Satisfaction, Saxon, Scare, Seal, Seat, Secure, Sedimentary, Set fair, Shtetl, Silt, Snuggle, Sofa, Soldier, Solve, Soweto, Square, Square up, State, Still, Straits, Subside, Sudden death, Township, Undertaker, Vest(ed), Viatical, Visigoth, Voortrekker, Wrap up

▷**Settlement** *may indicate* an anagram

▷**Settler** *may indicate* a coin

Seven(th), Seven-sided Ages, Days, Dials, Great Bear, Hebdomad, Hepta-, Hills, Nones, Pleiad(es), S, Sages, Seas, Septenary, Septilateral, Septimal, Sins, Sisters, Sleepers, Stars, Wonders, Zeta

Several Divers, Many, Multiple, Plural, Some, Sundry, Various

Severe(ly), Severity Acute, Astringent, Austere, Bad, Chronic, Cruel, Dour, Draconian, Drastic, Eager, Extreme, Grave, Grievous, Gruel(ling), Hard, →**HARSH**, Ill, Inclement, Morose, Penal, Rhadamanthine, Rigo(u)r, Roundly, Ruthless, Serious, Sharp, Snell(y), Sore, Spartan, Stark, Stern, Strict

Sew(ing), Sew up Baste, Cope, Darn, Embroider, Fell, Fine-draw, Hemstitch, Machine, Mitre, Overlock, Run up, Seam, Seel, Stitch, Tack, Whip

Sewage, Sewer Bacteria, Cesspool, Cloaca, Culvert, Dorcas, →**DRAIN**, Effluence, Jaw-box, Jaw-hole, Mimi, Needle, Privy, Seamster, Shore, Soil, Sough, Soughing-tile, Sure, Waste

Sex(ist), Sexual, Sexy Bed-hopping, Carnal, Congress, Cottaging, Coupling, Cybersex, Erotic, Favours, Female, Gam(ic), Gender, Greek love, Hump, Incest, Intercourse, Intimacy, Jailbait, Kind, Knee-trembler, Libidinous, Libido, Lingam,

Lumber, Male, Mate, Naughty, Non-penetrative, Nookie, Oomph, Oral, Outercourse, Paedophilia, Paraphilia, Pederasty, Phallocratic, Phat, Phone, Priapean, Prurient, Race, Randy, Raunchy, Rough trade, Rut(ish), Salacious, Screw, Sect, Six, Slinky, SM, Steamy, Stud, Sultry, Tantric, Teledildonics, Unsafe, Venereal, Venery, VI, Voluptuous

Shabby Base, Buckeen, Dingy, Dog-eared, Down-at-heel, Fusc(ous), Grotty, Grungy, Low-lived, Mean, Moth-eaten, Old hat, Oobit, Oorie, Oubit, Ourie, Outworn, Owrie, Raunch, Scaly, Scarecrow, Scruffy, Seedy, Shoddy, Squalid, Tatty, Tawdry, Threadbare, Unkempt, Worn, Woubit

Shackle(s) Bind, Bracelet, Chain, Constrain, Darbies, Entrammel, Fetter(lock), Hamper, Irons, Manacle, Restrict, Tie, Trammel, Yoke

Shade(d), Shades, Shading, Shadow, Shady Adumbrate, Arbour, Awning, Blear, Blend, Blind, Bongrace, Bowery, Brocken spectre, Buff, Cast, Cerise, Chiaroscuro, Chroma, Cloche, Cloud, Colo(u)r, Corrupt, Cross-hatch, Degree, Demirep, Dis, Dog, Dubious, Eclipse, Enigma, Eye, Fawn, Five o'clock, Galanty, Gamp, Ghost, Gnomon, Gradate, Gray, Hachure, Hatch, Hell, Herbar, Hint, Hue, Inumbrate, Larva, Lee, Magnolia, Mezzotint, Modena, Nuance, Opaque, Overtone, Parasol, Pastel, Phantom, Presence, Ray-Bans®, Satellite, Screen, Shroud, Sienna, Silhouette, Silvan, Skia-, Soften, Sound, Spectre, Spirit, Stag, Sunglasses, Swale, Swaly, Tail, Tenebrious, Tinge, Tint, Titian, Tone, Track, Trail, Ugly, Ultramarine, Umbra(tile), Umbrage(ous), Umbrella, Umbrose, Underhand, Underworld, Velamen, Velar(ium), Velum, Visitant, Visor, Wraith

Shaft(ed), Shafting Arbor, Arrow, Barb, Barrow-train, Beam, Befool, Capstan, Cardan, Chimney, Collet, Column, Crank, Cue, Disselboom, Dolly, Downcast, Drive, Escape, Fil(l), Flue, Fust, Gleam, Incline, Journal, Lay, Limber, Loom, Mandrel, Mandril, Moulin, Parthian, Passage, Pile, Pit, Pitbrow, Pitch, Pithead, Pole, Propeller, Ray, Rib, Rise, Scape, Scapus, Shank, Snead, Spindle, Staff, Stale, Steal(e), Steel, Steen, Stele, Stulm, Sunbeam, Telescopic, Thill, Tige, Tomo, Trave, Truncheon, Upcast, Winning, Winze

Shaggy Ainu, Beetle-browed, Bushy, Comate, Hairy, Hearie, Hirsute, Horrid, Horror, Maned, Rough, Rugged, Shock, Shough, Tatty, Tousy, Touzy, Towsy, Towzy, Untidy

Shake(n), Shake off, Shakes, Shakiest, Shaky Agitate, Ague(-fit), Astonish, Bebung, Brandish, Coggle, Concuss, Dabble, Dick(e)y, Didder, Diddle, Disconcert, Dither, Dodder, Epicentre, Feeble, Groggy, Hod, Hotch, Ictal, Jar, Jiggle, Joggle, Jolt, Jounce, Judder, Jumble, Lose, Milk, Mo, Nid-nod, Press flesh, Quake, Quiver, Quooke, Rattle, Rickety, Rickle, →ROCK, Rouse, Shimmer, Shimmy, Shiver, Shock, Shog, Shoogle, Shudder, Steel, Succuss(ation), Sweat, Swish, Thunderstruck, Tremble, Tremolo, Tremor, Tremulous, Trill(o), Tumbledown, Undulate, Unsteady, Vibrate, Vibrato, Wag, Waggle, Wind, Wobble, Wonky

▷**Shake** *may indicate an anagram*

Shallow(s) Ebb, Flat, Fleet, Flew, Flippant, Flue, Justice, Neritic, Rattlebrain, Riffle, Sandbank, Sandbar, Shoal, Slight, Superficial

Sham Apocryphal, Bluff, Bogus, Braide, Charade, Counterfeit, Deceit, Fake, →FALSE, Hoax, Idol, Impostor, Mimic, Mock, Phony, Pinchbeck, Pretence, Pseudo, Repro, Snide, Spurious, Straw man

Shame(ful), Shame-faced Abash, Aidos, Atimy, Aw, Confusion, Contempt, Crying, Degrade, Discredit, Disgrace, Dishonour, Disrepute, Embarrass, Fie, Gross, Guilt, Hangdog, Honi, Humiliate, Ignominy, Infamy, Inglorious, Modesty, Mortify, Ohone, Pity, Pudor, Pugh, Sad, Scandal, Shend, Sin, Slander, Stain, Stigma, Tsk, Vile, Yshend

Shape(d), Shapely, Shaping Blancmange, Boast, Cast, Contour, Cuneiform, Die-cast, Face, Fashion, Figure, Form, Format, Fractal, Geoid, Geometrical, Gnomon, Headquarters, Hew, Jello, Model, Morphology, →**MOULD**, Navette, Octagon(al), Polyomine, Quadrant, Ream, Rhomb(us), Roughcast, Scabble, Scalene, Scallop, Sculpt, Spheroid, Step-cut, Voluptuous, Wrought

Share(d), Shares, Sharing Allocation, Allotment, Allottery, Angels' cost, Apportion, Blue-chip, Chop, Co, Cohabit, Coho(e), Common, Communal, Contango, Co-portion, Co-tenant, Culter, Cut, Deferred, Divi(dend), Divide, Divvy (up), Dole, Dutch, Equity, Finger, Flatmate, Founders, Golden, Grubstake, Impart, Interest, Job, Kangaroo, Law, Lay, Lion's, Market, Moiety, Mutual, Odd lot, OFEX, Ordinary, →**PART**, Partake, Participate, Penny, PIBS, Plough, Plough-iron, Portfolio, Portion, Prebend, Pref(erred), Preference, Pro rata, Prorate, Quarter, Quota, Rake off, Ration, Rug, Scrip, Security, Shr, Slice, Snack, Snap, Sock, Split, Stock, Taurus, Time, Tranche, Two-way, Whack

Shark Angel, Basking, Beagle, Blue, Bonnethead, Bull, Carpet, Cestracion, Cow, Demoiselle, Dog(fish), Great white, Hammerhead, Houndfish, Huss, Lemonfish, Leopard catshark, Loan, Mackerel, Mako, Noah, Nurse, Penny-dog, Plagiostomi, Porbeagle, Requiem, Reremai, Rhin(e)odon, Rigg, Rook, Sail-fish, Sand, Sea-ape, Sea-fox, Sevengill, Sharp, Shortfin mako, Shovelhead, Smoothhound, Spotted ragged-tooth, Squaloid, Swindler, Thrasher, Thresher, Tiger, Tope, Usurer, Whale, Whaler, Wobbegong, Zygaena

Sharp(er), Sharpen(er), Sharply, Sharpness Abrupt, Accidental, Acerose, Acetic, Acidulous, Acrid, Aculeus, Acumen, Acuminate, Acutance, Acute, Alert, Angular, Arris, Astringent, Bateless, Becky, Bitter, Brisk, Cacuminous, Cheat, Clear, Coticular, Cutting, Dital, Edge(r), Fine, Gleg, Grind, Hone, Hot, Keen, Kurtosis, Massé, Mordant, Oilstone, Peracute, Piquant, Poignant, Precision, Prompt, Pronto, Pungent, Quick-witted, Razor, Rogue, Rook, Saw doctor, Set, Shrewd, Smart, Snap, Snell, Sour, Spicate, Stoccato, Strop, Swindler, Tart, Tomium, Varment, Vivid, Volable, Vorpal, Whet

Shawl Afghan, Buibui, Cashmere, Chuddah, Chuddar, Dopatta, Dupatta, Fichu, India, Kaffiyeh, Kashmir, Manta, Mantilla, Maud, Paisley, Partlet, Pashmina, Prayer, Serape, Sha(h)toosh, Stole, Tallis, Tallit(ot), Tallith, Tippet, Tonnag, Tozie, Tribon, Whittle, Wrap(per), Zephyr

Shed(ding), Shedder Autotomy, Barn, Byre, Cast, Cho(u)ltry, Coducity, Cootch, Cwtch, Depot, Discard, Doff, Downsize, Drop, Effuse, Exuviate, Hangar, Hovel, Hut, Infuse, Lair, Lean-to, Linhay, Linn(e)y, Mew, Moult, Outbuilding, Pent, Potting, Salmon, Shippen, Shippon, Shuck, Skeo, Skillion, Skio, Slough, Sow, Spend, Spent, Spill, Spit, Tilt, Tool

Sheep(ish) Ammon, Ancon(es), Aoudad, Argali, Ashamed, Barbary, Bell(wether), Bharal, Bident, Bighorn, Black, Blackface, Blate, Border Leicester, Broadtail, Burhel, Burrel(l), Caracul, Charollais, Cheviots, Coopworth, Corriedale, Cotswold, Cotswold lion, Coy, Crone, Dall('s), Dinmont, Domestic, Dorset Down, Dorset Horn, Down, Drysdale, Embarrassed, Ewe, Exmoor, Fank, Fat-tailed, Flock, Fold, Gimmer, Hair, Hampshire, Hampshire Down, Hangdog, Herdwick, Hidder, Hirsel, Hog(g), Hogget, Jacob, Jemmy, Jumbuck, Karakul, Kent, Kerry Hill, Lamb, Lanigerous, Leicester, Lincoln, Lo(a)ghtan, Loghtyn, Long, Lonk, Marco Polo, Masham, Merino, Mor(t)ling, Mouf(f)lon, Mountain, Muflon, Mug, Mus(i)mon, Mutton, Oorial, Ovine, Oxford Down, Perendale, Portland, Ram, Rambouillet, Romeldale, Romney Marsh, Rosella, Ryeland, Scottish Blackface, Shearling, Shetland, Shidder, Short, Shorthorn, →**SHY**, Soay,

Southdown, Spanish, Stone('s), Suffolk, Sumph, Swaledale, Teeswater, Teg(g), Texel, Theave, Trip, Tup, Twinter, Two-tooth, Udad, Urial, Vegetable, Welsh Mountain, Wensleydale, Wether, Wiltshire Horn, Woollyback, Yow(e), Yowie

Sheet(ing), Sheets Balance, Cel, Cere-cloth, Cerement, Charge, Chart, Crime, Cutch, Diet, Dope, Expanse, Film, Folio, Foolscap, Heft, Intrusive, Leaf, Membrane, Nappe, Out-hauler, Page, Pane, Pot(t), Pour, Proof, Prospectus, Rap, Ream, Rope, Sail, Scandal, Shroud, Stern, Stratus, Taggers, Tarpaulin(g), Tear, Tentorium, Terne, Thunder, Time, Web, Winding

Shell(ed), Shellfish, Shellwork Abalone, Acorn-shell, Admiral, Ambulacrum, Ammo, Ammonite, Argonaut, Balamnite, Balanus, Balmain bug, Barnacle, Belemnite, Bergmehl, Bivalve, Blitz, Boat, Bodywork, Bombard, Buckie, Camaron, Camera, Capiz, Capsid, Carapace, Cartridge, Casing, Chank, Chelonia, Chitin, Clam, Cleidoic, Clio, Coat-of-mail, Cochlea, Cockle, Cohog, Conch, Cone, Copepoda, Cover, Cowrie, Cowry, Crab, Cracked, Crustacea, Cuttlebone, Dariole, Deerhorn, Dentalium, Dop, Drill, Electron, Escallop, Eugarie, Foraminifer, Framework, Frustule, Gas, Geoduck, Globigerina, Haliotis, Hull, Husk, Hyoplastron, Isopoda, Kernel, Lamp, Langouste, Limacel, Limpet, Live, Lobster, Lorica, Lyre, Malacostraca, Midas's ear, Mitre, Mollusc, Money, Monocoque, Moon, Moreton Bay bug, Mother-of-pearl, Murex, Music, Mussel, Nacre, Nautilus, Olive, Ormer, Ostracod, Ostrea, Otter, Oyster, Paua, Pawa, Pea('s)cod, Peag, Peak, Pecten, Peel, Pereia, Periostracum, Periwinkle, Pilgrim's, Pipi, Pipsqueak, Plastron, Pod, Prawn, Projectile, Purple fish, Putamen, Quahaug, Quahog, Razor, Rocaille, Sal, Scalarium, Scallop, Scollop, Sea-ear, Sea-pen, Shale, Shard, Sheal, Sheel, Shiel, Shill, Shock, Shot, Shrapnel, Shrimp, Shuck, Sial, Smoke-ball, Snail, Spat, Spend, Spindle, Star, Stomatopod, Stonk, Straddle, Strafe, Stromb(us), Swan-mussel, Tear, Tellen, Tellin, Test(a), Thermidor, Toheroa, Tooth, Top, Torpedo, Tracer, Trivalve, Trough, Trumpet, Turbo, Turritella, Tusk, Univalve, Valency, Venus, Wakiki, Wampum, Whelk, Whiz(z)bang, Winkle, Xenophya, Yabbie, Yabby, Zimbi

▷**Shelled** *may indicate* an anagram

Shelter(ed) Abri, A l'abri, Anderson, Arbour, Asylum, Awn, Awning, Barn, Bay, Belee, Bender, Bield, Billet, Bivouac, Blind, Blockhouse, Booth, Bunker, Burladero, Butt, Byre, Cab, Carport, Casemate, Coop, Cot(e), Cove, Covert, Coverture, Defence, Dodger, Donga, Dovecote, Dripstone, Dug-out, Earth, Embower, Fall-out, Garage, Gunhouse, Gunyah, Harbour, Haven, Hithe, Hospice, Hostel, House, Hovel, Humpy, Hut, Hutchie, Hwl, Igloo, Imbosom, Kipsie, Lee, Lee-gage, Loun, Lound, Lown, Lownd, Mai mai, Mission, Morrison, Nissen, Nodehouse, Palapa, Pilothouse, →**REFUGE**, Retreat, Roadstead, Roof, Sanctuary, Scog, Sconce, Scoog, Scoug, Screen, Scug, Secluded, Shed, Shiel(ing), Shroud, Skug, Snowhole, Snowshed, Stell, Storm-cellar, Succah, Sukkah, Summerhouse, Suntrap, Tax, Tent, Te(e)pee, Testudo, Tortoise, Tupik, Twigloo, Umbrage, Weather, Wheelhouse, Wickyup, Wi(c)kiup, Wil(t)ja, Windbreak, Windscreen, Windshield

Shepherd(ess) Abel, Acis, Amaryllis, Amos, Bergère, Bo-peep, Bucolic, Chloe, Clorin, Conduct, Corin, Corydon, Cuddy, Daphnis, Dorcas, Drover, Endymion, Escort, Ettrick, Feeder, Flock-master, German, Grubbinol, Gyges, Herdsman, Hobbinol, Lindor, Marshal, Menalcas, Padre, Pastor(al), Pastorella, Phebe, Pilot, Sheepo, Strephon, Tar-box, Thenot, Thyrsis, Tityrus

Sherry Amoroso, Cobbler, Cream, Cyprus, Doctor, Dry, Fino, Gladstone, Jerez, Manzanilla, Oloroso, Sack, Solera, Sweet, Whitewash, Xeres

Shield(s), Shield-shaped Ablator, Achievement, Aegis, Ancile, Armour, Arms, Baltic, Biological, Bodyguard, Box, Brolly, Buckler, Canadian, Carapace, Cartouche,

Clypeus, Defend, Dress, Escutcheon, Fence, Gobo, Guard, Gumshield, Gyron, Hatchment, Heat, Hielaman, Human, Inescutcheon, Insulate, Laurentian, Lozenge, Mant(e)let, Mask, Pavis(e), Pelta, Plastron, Protect, Randolph, Ranfurly, Riot, Rondache, Scandinavian, Screen, Scutcheon, Scute, Scutum, Sheffield, Splashboard, Sternite, Targe(t), Thyroid, Toecap, Vair, Visor, Water

Shift(er), Shifty Amove, Astatic, Blue, Budge, Change, Chemise, Core, Cymar, Devious, Displace, Doppler, Dress, Dying, Evasive, Expedient, Fend, Graveyard, Hedging, Jiggle(r), Landslide, Lateral, Linen, Meve, Move, Night, Nightie, Nighty, Oil, Realign, Red, Relay, Remove, Ruse, Scorch, Shirt, Shovel, Shuffle, Shunt, Simar(re), Slicker, Slip(pery), Spell, Stagehand, Steal, Stint, Switch, Tergiversate, Tour, Transfer, Tunic, Turn, Turnabout, Vary, Veer, Warp

▷**Shift(ing)** *may indicate* an anagram

▷**Shimmering** *may indicate* an anagram

Shin Clamber, Climb, Cnemial, Leg, Shank, Skink, Swarm

Shine(r), Shining, Shiny Aglitter, Aglow, Beam, Buff, Burnish, Deneb, Effulge, Excel, Flash, Glaze, Gleam, Glisten, Gloss, → **GLOW**, Irradiant, Japan, → **LAMP**, Leam, Leme, Lucent, Luminous, Lustre, Micate, Mouse, Nitid, Nugget, Phoebe, Phosphoresce, Polish, Radiant, Radiator, Relucent, Resplend, Rutilant, Shellac, Shimmer, Skyre, Sleek, Twinkle, Varnish

▷**Shiny** *may indicate* a star

Ship(ping), Shipping area, Ships Boat, Convoy, → **DISPATCH**, Embark, Export, Fastnet, Flota, Her, Keel, Man, Nautical, Post, Prize, Prow, Raft, Ram, Sail, She, SS, Tub, Vessel

Shipshape Apple-pie, Neat, Orderly, Tidy, Trim

Shirt Aloha, Boiled, Brown, Caftan, Calypso, Camese, Camise, Chemise, Choli, Cilice, Dasheki, Dashiki, Dick(e)y, Dress, Fiesta, Garibaldi, Grandad, Hair, Hawaiian, Jacky Howe, Kaftan, Kaross, K(h)urta, Muscle, Nessus, Non-iron, Parka, Partlet, Polo, Rash, Red, Rugby, Safari, Sark, Serk, Set, Shift, Smock, Stuffed, Subucula, T, Uncle (Bert)

Shiver(ing), Shivers, Shivery Aguish, Aquiver, Atingle, Break, Brrr, Chitter, Crumble, Dash, Dither, Fragile, Frisson, Gooseflesh, Grew, Grue, Malaria, Matchwood, Oorie, Ourie, Owrie, Quake, Quiver, → **SHAKE**, Shatter, Shrug, Shudder, Smash, Smither, Smithereens, Splinter, Timbers, Tremble

▷**Shiver(ed)** *may indicate* an anagram

Shock(ed), Shocker, Shocking Acoustic, Aghast, Agitate, Amaze, Anaphylactic, Appal, Astone, Astony, Astound, Awful, Bombshell, Bunch, Criminal, Culture, Daze, Defibrillate, Devastate, Disconcert, Disgust, Dreadful, Drop, Dumbfound, Earthquake, ECT, Egregious, Electric, Electrocute, EST, Eye-opener, Fleg, Floccus, Galvanism, Gobsmack, Hair, Haycock, Haystack, Horrify, Horror, Impact, Infamous, Insulin, Isoseismic, Jar, Jolt, Knock cold, Live, Mane, Mop, Numb, Obscene, Outrage, Poleaxe, Putrid, Recoil, Return, Revolt, Rick(er), Rigor, Scandal(ise), Seismic, Septic, Shake, Sheaf, Shell, Shog, Stagger, Start(le), Stun, Stupor, Surgical, Tangle, Thermal, Thunderstruck, Torpedinidae, Trauma, Tremor, Turn

▷**Shocked** *may indicate* an anagram

Shoe(s) Accessory, Arctic, Athletic, Ballet, Balmoral, Bauchle, Birkenstock, Blocked, Boat, Boot, Bootee, Brake, Brogan, Brogue, Brothel creepers, Buskin, Calceate, Calk(er), Calkin, Carpet slipper, Casuals, Caulker, Cawker, Charlier, Chaussures, Chopin(e), Clodhopper, Clog, Co-respondent, Court, Creeper, Dap, Deck, Espadrille, Flattie, Flip-flops, → **FOOTWEAR**, Galage, Galoche, Galosh, Gatty, Geta, Ghillie, Golosh, Gumboot, Gumshoe, Gym, High-low, High tops,

Hot, Hush-puppies®, Jandal®, Jellies, Kamik, Kletterschue, Kurdaitcha, Lace up, Launch(ing), Loafer, Mary-Janes®, Mocassin, Moccasin, Muil, Mule, Open-toe, Oxford, Oxonian, Panton, Patten, Peeptoe, Pennyloafer, Pile, Plate, Plimsole, Plimsoll, Poulaine, Pump, Rivlin, Rope-soled, Rubbers, Rullion, Runner, Sabaton, Sabot, Saddle, Safety, Sandal, Sandshoe, Sannie, Scarpetto, Shauchle, Skid, Skimmer, Slingback, Slip-on, Slipper, Slip-slop, Sneaker, Snow, Sock, Soft, Solleret, Spike, Stoga, Stogy, Suede, Tabi, Tackies, Takkies, Tennis, Tie, Topboot, Track, Trainer, T-strap, Upper, Vamp(er), Veld-schoen, Veldskoen, Velskoen, Vibram®, Vibs, Wagon lock, Wedgie, Welt, Winkle-picker, Zori

Shoemaker Blacksmith, Choo, Clogger, Cobbler, Cordiner, Cordwainer, Cosier, Cozier, Crispi(a)n, Farrier, Leprechaun, Sachs, Smith, Snob, Soutar, Souter, Sowter, Sutor

Shoot(er), Shooting, Shoot out Ack-ack, Airgun, Arrow, Bine, Bostryx, Braird, Breer, Bud, Bulbil, Burgeon, Camera, Catapult, Chit, Cion, Cyme, Dart(le), Delope, Discharge, Drib, Elance, Enate, Eradiate, Film, Fire, Germ, Germain(e), Germen, Germin(ate), Glorious twelfth, →**GUN**, Gunsel, Head-reach, Hurl, Imp, In bud, Jet, Lateral, Layer, Lens, Limb, Loose, Marksmanship, Offset, Osier, Outgun, Pepper, Photograph, Pip, Plink, Pluff, Plug, Poot, Pop, Pot, Pout, Ramulus, Rapids, Ratoon, Riddle, Rod, Rough, Rove, Runner, Scion, Septembriser, Shell, Showdown, Sien(t), Skeet, Snipe, Spire, Spirt, Spout, Spray, Sprout, Spurt, Spyre, Start, Stole, Stolon, Strafe, Sucker, Syen, Tellar, Teller, Tendril, Tendron, Tiller, Turion, Twelfth, Twig, Udo, Vimen, Wand, Weapon, Whiz(z), Wildfowler

Shop(per), Shopping, Shops Agency, Arcade, Assembly, Atelier, Automat, Bag, Betray, Betting, Body, Boutique, Bucket, Buy, Cantina, Chain, Charcuterie, Charity, Chippy, Chop, Closed, Coffee, Commissary, Cook, Co-op, Cop, Corner, Cut-price, Dairy, Delicatessen, Denounce, Dobbin, Dolly, Duddery, Duka, Duty-free, Emporium, Factory, Five and dime, Food court, Galleria, Gift, Grass, In bond, Inform, Junk, Kiosk, Luckenbooth, Machine, Mail (order), Mall, Mall crawl, Mall-rat, Market, Megastore, Mercat, Messages, Minimart, Muffler, Mystery, Naafi, Never-never, Office, Officinal, Off-licence, Off-sales, Op(portunity), Open, Outlet, Parlour, Patisserie, Personal, Pharmacy, Precinct, Print, PX, Rat on, Report, Retail, RMA, Salon, Sex, Shambles, Share, Shebang, Spaza, Squat, →**STORE**, Strip mall, Studio, Sundry, Superette, Supermarket, Superstore, Swap, Talking, Tally, Tea (room), Thrift, Tick, Tommy, Trade, Truck, Tuck, Union, Vintry, Warehouse, Whistle-blow, Works

Shopkeeper British, Butcher, Chemist, Gombeen-man, Greengrocer, Grocer, Haberdasher, Hosier, Ironmonger, Merchant, Newsagent, Provisioner, Retailer, Stationer, Vendor

Shore Bank, Beach, Buttress, Coast, Coste, Landfall, Lee, Littoral, Machair, Offing, Prop, Rivage, Seaboard, Strand, Strandline

Short(en), Shortly Abbreviate, Abridge, Abrupt, Anon, Brief, Brusque, Close-in, Commons, Concise, Contract, Crisp, Cross, Curt, Curtail, Curtal, Cutty, Digest, Diminish, Drink, Epitomise, Ere-long, Flying, Hard up, Impolite, Inadequate, In a while, In brief, Lacking, Laconical, Light, Limited, Low, Mini, Near, Nip, Nirlie, Nutshell, Offing, Pithy, Punch, Reduce, Reef, Scantle, Scanty, Scarce, Shrift, Shy, Skimpy, Snatch, Soon, Sparse, Spirit, Squab, Staccato, Stint, Stocky, Strapped, Stubby, Succinct, Taciturn, Teen(s)y, Telescope, Temporal, Terse, Tight, Tot, Under, Wee

Shortage Brevity, Dearth, Deficiency, Deficit, Drought, Famine, Lack, Need, Paucity, Scarcity, Sparsity, Ullage, Wantage

Shorts Bermuda, Board, Boxer, Briefs, Culottes, Hot pants, Kaccha, Lederhosen, Plus-fours, Skort, Stubbies®, Trunks

Shot(s) Air, Ammo, Approach, Attempt, Backhand, Ball, Bank, Barrage, Blank, Blast, Bull, Bullet, Burl, Canna, Cannon(ball), Cartridge, Case, Catapulted, Chain, Chip, Close up, Corner, Cover, Crab, Crack, Daisy cutter, Dink, Dolly, Dram, Draw, Drop, Duckhook, Dum dum, Dunk, Elt, Essay, Exhausted, Explosion, Flew, Forehand, Fusillade, Gesse, Get, Glance, Go, Grape, Guess, Hazard, Hook, In-off, Iridescent, Jab, Jump, Kill, Lay-up, Marksman, Maroon, Massé, Matte, Mitraille, Money, Moon-ball, Mulligan, Musket, Nip, Noddy, Opalescent, Pack, Parthian, Parting, Passing, Pellet, Penalty, Photo, Pitch, Plant, Pop, Pot, Puff, Push, Rake, Rid, Round, Safety, Salvo, Scratch, Shell, Shy, Silk, Six, Slam-dunk, Slap, Slice, Slug, Slung, Smash, Snap, Snifter, Sped, Spell, Spent, Square cut, Stab, Still, Streaked, Tap in, Tee, Throw, Toepoke, Tonic, Tot, Tracking, Trial, Try, Turn, Volley, Warning, Wrist, Yahoo

Shout(er), Shouting Alley-oop, Barrack, Bawl, Bellow, Boanerges, Boo, Call, Claim, Clamour, Conclamation, Cry, Din, Exclaim, Heckle, Hey, Hoi(cks), Holla, Holla-ho(a), Holler, Hollo, Holloa, Hooch, Hosanna, Howzat, Hue, Och, Oi, Oy, Rah, Rant, Rave, Roar, Root, Round, Sa sa, Storm, Treat, Trumpet, Vociferate, Whoop, Yammer, Yell(och), Yicker, Yippee, Yodel, Yoohoo

Shovel Backhoe, Dustpan, Hat, Loy, Main, Peel, Power, Scoop, Shool, Spade, Steam, Trowel, Van

Show(ing), Shown, Showy Appearance, Aquacade, Bad, Bench, Betray, Branky, Broadcast, Burlesque, Cabaret, Cattle, Chat, Circus, Come, Con, Cruft's, Dashing, Define, Demo(nstrate), Depict, Describe, Dime museum, Diorama, Display, Do, Drama, Dramedy, Dressy, Dumb, Effere, Entertainment, Establish, Evince, →**EXHIBIT**, Expo, Express, Extravaganza, Exude, Facade, Fair, Fangled, Farce, Fine, Flamboyant, Flash (Harry), Flaunt, Floor, Fly, Folies Bergere, Game, Garish, Gaudy, Gay, Gig, Give, Glitter, Glitz(y), Gloss, Good, Horse, Indicate, Jazzy, Koni, Lay bare, Light, Loud, Manifest, Matinée, Minstrel, Moon, Musical, One-man, Ostentatious, Pageant, Panel game, Panto(mime), Parade, Patience, Peacock, Peep, Performance, Phen(o), Phone-in, Point, Pomp, Portray, Presentation, Pretence, Preview, Pride, Procession, Prog(ramme), Project, Prominence, Prove, Pseudery, Puff, Puppet, Quiz, Raree, Razzmatazz, Reality, Register, Represent, Reveal, Revue, Road, Rodeo, Ruddigore, Rushes, Screen, Shaw, Sight, Singspiel, Sitcom, Slang, Soap, Son et lumière, Specious, Spectacle, Splash, Splay, Stage, Stunt, Swankpot, Talk, Tattoo, Tawdry, Telecast, Telethon, Theatrical, Three-man, Tinhorn, Tinsel(ly), Tulip, Unbare, Uncover, Unveil, Usher, Vain, Variety, Vaudeville, Veneer, Viewy, Wear, Wild west

Shower Douche, Downfall, Exhibitor, Flurry, Hail, Indicant, Indicator, Lavish, Lot, Meteor, Panoply, Party, Pelt, Pepper, Precipitation, Rain, Regale, Scat, Scouther, Scowther, Scud, Skit, Snow, Spat, Spet, Spit, Splatter, Spray, Sprinkle, Ticker tape, Volley

▷**Showing, Shown in** *may indicate* a hidden word

Shred Clout, Filament, Grate, Mammock, Mince, Rag, Screed, Swarf, Tag, Tatter, Tear up, Thread, Wisp

Shrewd(ness) Acumen, Acute, Arch, Argute, Artful, Astucious, Astute, Callid, Canny, Clued-up, Cute, Far-sighted, File, Gnostic, Gumptious, Judicious, Knowing, Pawky, Politic, Prudent(ial), Sagacious, Sapient(al), Savvy, Sharp-sighted, Tactical, Wide boy, Wily, Wise

Shriek Cry, Scream, Shright, Shrike, Shrill, Shritch, Skirl, Yell

Shrine Adytum, Alamo, Altar, Dagaba, Dagoba, Dargah, Delphi, Fatima, Feretory, Harem, Holy, Joss house, Kaaba, Lourdes, Marabout, Memorial, Naos, Pagoda, Pilgrimage, Reliquary, Scrine, Scryne, Stupa, Tabernacle, Temple, Tope, Vimana, Walsingham

Shrink(age), Shrink from, Shrinking, Shrunk Abhor, Alienist, Blanch, Blench, Cling, Compress, Contract, Cour, Cower, Creep, Crine, Cringe, Dare, Decrew, Depreciate, Dread, Dwindle, Flinch, Funk, Less, Minimise, Nirl, → **PSYCHIATRIST**, Quail, Recoil, Reduce, Retract, Sanforised, Shrivel, Shy, Violet, Waste, Wince, Wither, Wizened

Shrove Tuesday Fastens, J'ouvert, Pancake

Shrub(bery) → **BUSH**, Petty whin, Plant, Undergrowth

▷**Shuffle(d)** *may indicate* an anagram

Shuttle Alternate, Challenger, Commute, Drawer, Flute, Go-between, Navette, Shoot, Shunt, Space, Tat(t), Weave

Shy Bashful, Blate, Blench, Cast, Catapult, Chary, Clam, Coconut, Coy, Deficient, Demure, Farouche, Flinch, Funk, Go, Heave, Introvert, Jerk, Jib, Laithfu', Lob, Mim, Modest, Mousy, Rear, Recoil, Reserved, Sally, Sheepish, Shrinking violet, Skeigh, Sling, Start, Throw, Timid, Tongue-tied, Toss, Try, Wallflower, Withdrawn

Sick(en), Sickener, Sickening, Sickliness, Sickly, Sickness Affection, Ague, Ail, Altitude, Anaemic, Bad, Bends, Bilious, Cat, Chunder, Cloying, Colic, Crapulence, Cringeworthy, Crook, Decompression, Delicate, Diseased, Disorder, Emetic, Emetin(e), Gag, Green, Hacked off, Hangover, Icky, Ill, Infection, Infirm, Lazar, Leisure, Loathsome, Mal, Mawkish, Milk, Morbid, Morning, Motion, Mountain, Nauseous, Off-colour, Pale, Peaky, Peelie-wallie, Peely-wally, Pestilent, Pindling, Plague, Poorly, Queasy, Radiation, Regorge, Repulsive, Retch, Serum, Sleeping, Sleepy, Space, Spue, Squeamish, Sweating, Travel, Twee, Valetudinarian, Virus, Vomit, Wan

Side, Sidepiece Abeam, Airs, B, Beam, Border, Camp, Distaff, Division, Edge, Effect, Elevation, Eleven, English, Epistle, Facet, Flank, Flip, Gunnel, Hand, Heavy, Hypotenuse, Iliac, Lateral, Lee(ward), Left, Long, Lore, Obverse, Off, On, OP, Pane, Part, Partisan, Party, Pleura, Port, Pretension, Profile, Prompt, Rave, Reveal, Reverse, Right, Rink, Scratch, Short, Silver, Slip, Spear, Spindle, Starboard, Swank, → **TEAM**, Tight, West, Windward, Wing, XI

Sight(ed) Aim, Barleycorn, Bead, Conspectuity, Eye(ful), Eyesore, Glimpse, Ken, Long, Oculated, Prospect, Range, Riflescope, Scene, Scotopia, Second, See, Short, Spectacle, Taish, Telescopic, Twenty-twenty, Vane, → **VIEW**, Visie, Vision, Vista, Vizy, Vizzie

Sign(ing), Signpost, Signs Accidental, Addition, Air, Ale-pole, Ampersand, Ankh, Apostrophe, Aquarius, Archer, Aries, Arrow, Auspice, Autograph, Badge, Balance, Beck, Beckon, Birth, Board, Brand, Bull, Bush, Call, Cancer, Capricorn, Caract, Caret, Character, Chevron, Clue, Cross, Cue, Dele, Denote, Di(a)eresis, Division, Dollar, DS, Earmark, Earth, Emblem, Endorse, Endoss, Enlist, Enrol(l), Equals, Evidence, Exit, Fascia, Fire, Fish, Gemini, Gesture, Goat, Hallmark, Harbinger, Harvey Smith, Hash, Hex, Hieroglyphic, Hint, Ideogram, Indian, Indicate, Indication, Initial, INRI, Inscribe, Ivy-bush, Leo, Libra, Local, Logogram, Milepost, Milestone, Minus, Motion, Mudra, Multiplication, Negative, Nod, Notice, Obelisk, Obelus, Omen, Peace, Pisces, Plus, Positive, Pound, Presage, Prodrome, Radical, Ram, Ratify, Red lattice, Rest, Rune, Sacrament, Sagittarius, Sain, Scorpio, Segno, Semeion, Semiotics, Shingle, Shorthand, Show, Sigil, Sigla, Signal, Star, Subscribe, Subtraction, Superscribe, Symbol, Symptom,

Syndrome, Tag, Taurus, Tic(k)tac(k), Tilde, Titulus, Token, Trace, Twins, Umlaut, V, Vestige, Virgo, Vital, Warison, Warning, Water, Waymark, Word, Zodiac

Signal(ler) Alarm, Alert, All clear, Amber, Assemble, Beacon, Beckon, Bell, Bleep, Bugle, Busy, Buzz, Call, Code, Cone, Cue, Detonator, Distant, Distress, Duplex, Earcon, Emit, Flag, Flagman, Flare, Flash, Fog, Gantry, Gesticulate, Gesture, Gong, Griffin, Gun, Hail, Harmonic, Heliograph, Heliostat, Herald, Heterodyne, High sign, Hooter, Icon, Important, Indicator, Input, Interrupt, Interval, Knell, Luminance, Mark, Mayday, Message, Modem, Morse, NICAM, Notation, Noted, Output, Password, Peter, Pheromone, Pinger, Pip, Pollice verso, Prod, Radio, Renowned, Reveille, Robot, Salient, Semaphore, Simplex, Singular, Smoke, Snook, Sonogram, SOS, Spoiler, Squawk, Storm, Taps, Target, Tattoo, Telegraph, Thumb, Tic(k)-tac(k), Time, Token, Traffic, Transmit, Troop, Vehicle-actuated, Very, Video, V-sign, Waff, Waft, Wave, Wink, Word, Yeoman

Signature Alla breve, Allograph, Autograph, By-line, Digital, Hand, John Hancock, John Henry, Key, Mark, Onomastic, Per pro, Sculpsit, Sheet, Specimen, Subscription, Tag, Time

Significance, Significant Cardinal, Consequence, Cosmic, Emblem, Epochal, Ethos, Impact, Important, Indicative, Key, Landmark, Magnitude, Major, Matter, M(a)cGuffin, Meaningful, Moment(ous), Notable, Noted, Noteworthy, Operative, Paramount, Pith, Pregnant, Red-letter day, Salient, Special, Telling, Totemic, Weight

Silence(r), Silent Choke-pear, Clam, Clamour, Creepmouse, Dead air, Dolby, Dumbfound, Dumbstruck, Earplug, Gag, Hist, Hush, Hushkit, Mim(budget), Muffler, Mum(p), Mute, Omertà, Quench, Quiesce, →QUIET, Reticence, Shtoom, Shtum, Shush, Speechless, Squelch, Still, Sulky, Tace(t), Tacit(urn), Throttle, Tight-lipped, Tongue-tied, Unvoiced, Wheesh(t)

Silk(y), Silk screen Alamode, Artificial, Atlas, Barathea, Blonde-lace, Brocade, Bur(r), Charmeuse®, Chenille, Chiffon, Cocoon, Corn, Crape, Crepe, Duchesse, Dupion, Faille, Filoselle, Florence, Florentine, Flosh, Floss, Flox, Foulard, Gazar, Georgette, Glossy, Grosgrain, Honan, Kente, Kincob, Lustrine, Lustring, Lutestring, Madras, Makimono, Marabou(t), Matelasse, Milanese, Near, Ninon, Organza, Ottoman, Paduasoy, Parachute, Peau de soie, Pongee, Prunella, Prunelle, Prunello, Pulu, QC, Raw, Samite, Sars(e)net, Satin, Schappe, Sendal, Seric, Sericeous, Serigraph, Shalli, Shantung, Sien-tsan, Sleave, Sleek, Smooth, Soft, Spun, Surah, Tabaret, Tabby, Taffeta, Tasar, Thistledown, Thrown, Tiffany, Tram, Tulle, Tussah, Tusseh, Tusser, Tussore, Velvet

Silly, Silliness Absurd, Apish, Brainless, Childish, Crass, Cuckoo, Daffy, Daft, Ditsy, Divvy, Dotish, Drippy, Dumb(o), Dunce, Dweeb, Fatuous, Feather-brained, Fluffy, Folly, Fool, Foolery, Footling, Frivolous, Goopy, Goosey, Gormless, Idiotic, Imbecile, Inane, Inept, Infield(er), Mid-off, Mid-on, Mopoke, Prune, Puerile, Scatterbrain, Season, Simple, Soft(y), Sot, Spoony, →STUPID, Tomfoolery, Tripe, Wacky, Wally

▷**Silver** *may indicate* a coin

Similar(ity) Affinity, Akin, Analog(ue), Analogical, Corresponding, Equivalent, Etc, Homoeoneric, Homogeneous, Homoiousian, Homologous, Homonym, Isomorphism, Kindred, →LIKE, Likeness, Likewise, Parallel, Resemblance, Samey

Simple(r), Simplicity, Simplify, Simply Arcadian, Artless, Austere, Bald, Bare, Basic, Bog-standard, Breeze, Chaste, Crude, Daw, Doddle, Doric, →EASY, Eath(e), Elegant, Elemental, ESN, Ethe, Eyebright, Facile, Fee, Folksy, Gotham, Green, Gullish, Herb(alist), Homespun, Idyllic, Incomposite, Inornate, Mere, Naive(té), Naked, Niaiserie, No brainer, One-fold, Open and shut,

Ordinary, Paraphrase, Pastoral, Peter, Plain, Pleon, Provincial, Pure, Reduce, Renormalise, Rustic, Sapid, Semplice, Sheer, Silly, Simon, Spartan, Straightforward, Streamline, Stupid, Suave, Uncluttered, Understated, Unicellular, Unsophisticated, Woollen

Sin(ful), Sinfulness Aberrant, Anger, Avarice, Besetting, Bigamy, Capital, Cardinal, Covetousness, Crime, Deadly, Debt, Envy, Err, Evil, Folly, Gluttony, Guile, Hamartiology, Harm, Hate, Impious, Impure, Lapse, Lust, Misdeed, Misdoing, Mortal, →**OFFENCE**, Original, Peccadillo, Piacular, Pride, Sacrilegious, Scape, Scarlet, Sine, Sloth, Transgress, Trespass, Unrighteous, Venial, Vice, Wicked, Wrath, Wrong

Sincere(ly), Sincerity Bona-fide, Candour, Earnest, Entire, Frank, Genuine, Heartfelt, Heartwhole, Honest, Open, Real(ly), Realtie, Simple-hearted, True, Verity, Whole-hearted

▶**Sinful** *see* **SIN(FUL)**

Sing(ing) Antiphony, Barbershop, Bel canto, Belt out, Carol, Chant, Cheep, Chorus, Coloratura, Community, Cough, Croon, Crow, Descant, Diaphony, Diddle, Glee club, Gregorian, Hum, Incant, Inform, Intone, Karaoke, La-la, Lilt, Lyricism, Melic, Parlando, Peach, Pen(n)illion, Pipe, Plainchant, Rand, Rant, Rap, Record, Render, Scat, Second(o), Serenade, Spinto, Squeal, Tell, Thrum, Trill, Troll, Unitary, Vocalese, Warble, Woodshedding, Yodel

Singer(s) A cappella, Alto, Baillie, Baker, Bard, Baritone, Bass, Beatle, Bing, →**BIRD**, Bono, Brel, Buffo, Canary, Cantatrice, Cantor, Car, Cash, Castrato, Chanteur, Chanteuse, Chantor, Chauntress, Chazan, Cher, Chorister, Coloratura, Countertenor, Crooner, Diva, Elvis, Falsetto, Gigli, Glee club, Gleeman, Gobbi, Griot, Hammond, Kettle, Lark, Lauder, Lay clerk, Lorelei, Meister, Melba, Melodist, Mezzo(-soprano), Minstrel, Opera, Orbison, Pavarotti, Piaf, Rapper, Semi-chorus, Shrike, Siren, Songman, Songstress, Soprano, Soubrette, Spinto, Succentor, Syren, Tenor, Tenure, Torch, Treble, Troubador, Vocalist, Voice, Warbler

Single, Singly Ace, Aefa(u)ld, Aefawld, Alone, Azygous, Bachelor, Celibate, Discriminate, EP, Exclusive, Feme sole, Haplo-, Individual, Lone, Matchless, Monact, Mono, Odd, One-off, One-shot, Only, Pick, Run, Seriatim, Sole, Solitary, Solo, Spinster, Unary, Unattached, Uncoupled, Uniparous, Unique, Unwed, Versal, Yin

Singular(ity) Curious, Especial, Exceptional, Extraordinary, Ferly, Odd, Once, One, Peculiar, Queer(er), Rare, S, Strange, →**UNIQUE**, Unusual

Sink(ing), Sinker, Sunk(en) Abandon, Basin, Bidet, Bog, Cadence, Carbon, Cower, Deep-set, Delapse, Depress, Descend, Devall, Dip, Down, Drain, Draught-house, Drink, Drop, Drown, Ebb, Embog, Flag, Founder, Gravitate, Heat, Hole, Immerse, Invest, Jawbox, Kitchen, Lagan, Laigh, Lapse, Ligan, Merger, Pad, Poach, Pot, Prolapse, Put(t), Relapse, Sag, Scupper, Scuttle, Set, Settle, Shaft, Shipwreck, Slump, Steep-to, Stoop, Sty, Submerge, Subside, Swag, Swamp, Titanic

Siren Alarm, Alert, Charmer, Delilah, Hooter, Houri, Ligea, Lorelei, Mermaid, Oceanides, Parthenope, Salamander, Shark, Teaser, Temptress, Vamp

Sister(s) Anne, Beguine, Carmelite, Fatal, Minim, →**NUN**, Nurse, Pleiades, Religeuse, Sib, Sibling, Sis, Sob, Soul, Swallow, Titty, Ugly, Ursuline, Verse, Ward, Weak, Weird

Sit(ter), Sitting All-night, Bestride, Clutch, Dharna, Duck, Gaper, Gimme, Incubate, Lime, Model, Perch, Pose, Reign, Roost, Séance, Sederunt, Sesh, Session, Squat

Site, Siting Area, Arpa, Brochure, Camp, Caravan, Chat room, Cobweb, Feng shui, Gap, Greenfield, Home-page, Locality, Location, Lot, Mirror, Orphan, Pad, Place, Plot, Ramsar, Rogue, Silo, Spot, Stance, Visie, Vizy, Vizzie, World Heritage

Situation Affair, Ballpark, Berth, Can of worms, Cart, Case, Catch, Catch-22, Chicken and egg, Cliff-hanger, Contretemps, Cow, Dilemma, Drama, Galère, Hole, Hornet's nest, Hot seat, Job, Knife-edge, Lie, Location, Lurch, Matrix, Mire, Nail-biter, Niche, Novel, No-win, Office, Outcome, Place, Plight, Position, Post, Scenario, Scene, Schmear, Schmeer, Seat, Set-up, Shebang, Showdown, State of play, Status quo, Sticky wicket, Strait, Stringalong, Where, Worst case

Size(able) Amplitude, Area, Bulk, Calibre, Clearcole, Countess, Demy, →**EXTENT**, Format, Girth, Glair, Glue, Guar, Gum, Imperial, Measure, Particle, Party, Physique, Pot(t), Princess, Proportion, Tempera, Tidy

Skate(r), Skateboard(er), Skateboarding, Skating Blade, Fakie, Figure, Fish, Half-pipe, Hot dog, In-line, Maid, Mohawk, Ollie, Overacid, Rink, Rock(er), Roller, Rollerblade®, Runner, Short-track, Sit spin, Torvill

Skeleton, Skeletal Anatomy, Atomy, Axial, Bones, Cadaverous, Cadre, Cage, Coenosteum, Coral, Corallum, Framework, Hydrostatic, Key, Ossify, Outline, Scenario, Sclere

Sketch(y) Bozzetto, Cameo, Character, Charade, Charcoal, Croquis, Delineate, Diagram, Draft, →**DRAW**, Ébauche, Esquisse, Illustration, Limn, Line, Map out, Maquette, Modello, Outline, Pencilling, Pen portrait, Playlet, Pochade, Précis, Profile, Representation, Rough, Skit, Study, Summary, Thumbnail, Trick, Vague, Vignette, Visual

Ski(er), Skiing Aquaplane, Carving, Free ride, Glide, Glissade, Hot-dog, Langlauf, Nordic, Schuss, Schussboomer, Super G, Telemark, Vorlage, Wedeln

Skilful, Skill(ed) Ability, Able, Accomplished, Ace, Address, Adept, Adroit, Art, Artistic, Bravura, Canny, Chic, Competence, Craft, Deacon, Deft, Demon, Dextrous, Endowment, Enoch, Expertise, Facility, Feat, Finesse, Flair, Gleg, Habile, Hand, Handicraft, Handy, Hend, Hot, Ingenious, Keepy-uppy, Knack, Know-how, Knowing, Lear(e), Leir, Lere, Masterly, Masterpiece, Mastery, Mean, Métier, Mistery, Mystery, Mystique, Practised, Proficient, Prowess, Quant, Resource, Savvy, Science, Skeely, Sleight, Soft, Speciality, Tactics, Talent, Technic, Technique, Touch, Trade, Transferable, Trick, Versed, Virtuoso, Wise, Workmanship

Skin(s) Ablate, Agnail, Armour, Bark, Basan, Basil, Bingo wing, Box-calf, Bronzed, Calf, Callus, Case, Cere, Chevrette, Coat, Cortex, Crackling, Cutaneous, Cuticle, Cutis, Deacon, Deer, Derm(a), Dermis, Dewlap, Disbark, Ectoderm, Enderon, Envelope, Epicarp, Eschar, Excoriate, Exterior, Fell, Film, Flaught, Flay, Flench, Flense, Flinch, Fourchette, Goldbeater's, Hangnail, Hide, Integra®, Jacket, Kip, Leather, Membrane, Muktuk, Nympha, Pachyderm, Patagium, Peau, Peel, Pell, Pellicle, Pelt, Plew, Prepuce, Rack, Rape, Rind, Scalp, Scarfskin, Serosa, Shagreen, Shell, Spetch, Strip, Swindle, Tegument, Veneer, Wattle, Woolfell

Skin disease, Skin problem, Skin trouble Boba, Boil, Buba, Chloasma, Chloracne, Cowpox, Cyanosis, Dartre, Dermatitis, Dermatosis, Dyschroa, Ecthyma, Eczema, Erysipelas, Exanthem(a), Favus, Framboesia, Herpes, Hives, Ichthyosis, Impetigo, Leishmaniasis, Leucodermia, Livedo, Lupus vulgaris, Maidism, Mal del pinto, Mange, Miliaria, Morula, Pellagra, Pemphigus, Pinta, Pityriasis, Prurigo, Pseudofolliculitis, Psoriasis, Pyoderma, Rash, Ringworm,

Rosacea, Rose-rash, Sapego, Scabies, Sclerodermia, Scurvy, Seborrhoea, Serpigo, Strophulus, Tetter, Tinea, Vaccinia, Verruca, Verruga, Vitiligo, Xanthoma, Xerosis, Yaws

Skip(ped), Skipper Boss, Bound, Caper, Captain, Cavort, Drakestone, Elater, Frisk, Hesperian, Jump, Jumping-mouse, Lamb, Luppen, Miss, Omit, Patroon, Ricochet, Roo, Sand, Saury, Scombresox, Spring, Tittup, Trip, Trounce(r)

Skirt(ing) Bypass, Fil(l)ibeg, Grass, Petticoat, Philibeg, Pinafore, Stringboard, Tube, Valance, Washboard, Wrapover

Skull Brainpan, Bregma(ta), Calvaria, Cranium, Death's head, Harnpan, Head, Head case, Malar, Obelion, Occiput, Pannikell, Phrenology, Scalp, Sinciput, Vault, Yorick

Sky(-high), Sky-tinctured, Skywards Air, Azure, Blue, Canopy, Carry, Cloud-kissing, El Al, E-layer, Element, Empyrean, Ether, Firmament, Heaven, Lift, Lob, Loft, Mackerel, Occident, Octa, Okta, Raise, Rangi, Welkin

Slab(s) Briquette, Cake, Cap(e)stone, Chunk, Dalle, Hawk, Ledger, Metope, Mihrab, Mud, Paver, Plank, Slice, Stela, Tab, Tablet, Tile, Wood-wool

Slack(en), Slacker, Slackness Abate, Careless, Clock-watch, Crank, Dilatory, Dross, Ease (off), Easy-going, Flaccid, Idle, Inanition, Languor, Lax(ity), Lazybones, Loose, Malinger, Nerveless, Off-peak, Off-season, Relax, Release, Remiss, Shirk, Skive, Slatch, Slow, Surge, Unscrew, Unwind, Veer

Slander(ous) Asperse, Backbite, Badmouth, Calumny, Defame, Derogatory, Disparage, Infame, Insult, Libel, Malediction, Malign, Mendacity, Missay, Mud, Mudslinging, Obloquy, Sclaunder, Smear, Traduce, Vilify, Vilipend, Vitriol

Slang Abuse, Argot, Back, Berate, Blinglish, Cant, Colloquial, Ebonics, Flash, Jargon, Lingo, Nadsat, Rhyming, Slate, Vernacular, Zowie

Slant(ed), Slanting Angle, Asklent, Atilt, Bevel, Bias, Brae, Cant, Careen, Catty-cornered, Chamfer, Clinamen, Diagonal, Escarp, Oblique, Prejudice, Rake, Slew, →**SLOPE**, Splay, Talus, Tilt, Virgule

Slash(ed) Chive, Cut, Diagonal, Gash, Jag, Laciniate, Leak, Oblique, Rash, Rast, Reduce, Scorch, Scotch, Separatrix, Slice, Slit, Solidus, Stroke, Virgule, Wee

Slaughter(house), Slaughterer Abattoir, Bleed, Bloodshed, Butcher, Carnage, Decimate, Hal(l)al, Holocaust, Immolation, Jhatka, Kill, Mactation, →**MASSACRE**, Off, Scupper, Shambles, S(c)hechita(h), Shochet, Smite, Trounce

Slave(ry), Slaves, Slavish Addict, Aesop, Aida, Androcles, Barracoon, Blackbird, Bond, Bond(s)man, Bondwoman, Boy, Caliban, Contraband, Dogsbody, Drudge, Drug, Dulosis, Enthralment, Esne, Galley, Helot, Jack, Mameluke, Mamluk, Marmaluke, Maroon, Minion, Nativity, Odali(s)que, Odalisk, Peasant, Pr(a)edial, Rhodope, Serf, Servitude, Spartacus, Terence, Theow, Thersites, Thete, Thrall, Toil, Topsy, Vassal, Villein, Wage, Wendic, White, Yoke

Slay(er), Slaying Destroy, Execute, Ghazi, →**KILL**, Mactation, Murder, Quell, Saul, Slaughter, Transport

Sled(ge), Sleigh(-ride) Bob, Dog train, Dray, Hurdle, Hurley-hacket, Kibitka, Komatic, Komatik, Lauf, Luge, Mush, Polack, Pulk(h)(a), Pung, Rocket, Skeleton bob(sleigh), Skidoo®, Slipe, Stoneboat, Tarboggin, Toboggan, Travois

Sleep, Sleeper(s), Sleepiness, Sleeping, Sleepy Beauty, Bed, Bivouac, Blet, Bundle, Bye-byes, Car, Catnap, Coma, Couchette, Crash, Cross-sill, Cross-tie, Dormant, Dormient, Dormouse, Doss, Doze, Drop off, Drowse, Flop, Forty winks, Gowl, Gum, Hibernate, Hypnology, Hypnos, Kip, Land of Nod, Lassitude, Lethargic, Lie, Morpheus, Nap, Narcolepsy, Narcosis, Nod, Oscitation, Over, Paradoxical, Petal, Policeman, Pop off, REM, Repast, Repose,

Rest, Rip Van Winkle, Roomette, Sandman, Shuteye, Siesta, Skipper, Sleepover, Sloom, Slumber, Snooz(l)e, Somnolent, Sopor(ose), Sownd, Spine bashing, Tie, Torpid, Twilight, Wagon-lit, Wink, Zeds, Zizz

Sleeve (opening) Arm(hole), Balloon, Batwing, Bishop's, Bush, Cap, Collet, Cover, Dolman, Gatefold, Gigot, Gland, Kimono, Lawn, Leg-o'-mutton, Liner, Magyar, Manche, Pagoda, Pudding, Querpo, Raglan, Record, Sabot, Scye, Slashed, Trunk, Turnbuckle, Wind

▶**Sleigh** *see* SLED(GE)

Slender(ness) Asthenic, Ectomorph, Elongate, Exiguity, Exility, Fine, Flagelliform, Flimsy, Gracile, Jimp, Leptosome, Loris, Narrow, Rangy, Skinny, Slight, Slim, Small, Spindly, Stalky, Styloid, Svelte, Swank, Sylph, Tenuous, Thready, Trim, Waif

Slice Cantle, Chip, Collop, Cut, Doorstep, Fade, Frustrum, Lop, Piece, Rasure, Round, Sector, Segment, Share, Sheave, Shive, Slab, Sliver, Spoon, Tranche, Wafer, Whang

Slide Barrette, Chute, Cursor, Diapositive, Drift, Fader, Glissando, Helter-skelter, Hirsle, Hollow-ground, Ice-run, Illapse, Lantern, Mount, Portamento, Pulka, Schuss, Scoop, Ski, Skid, Skite, Slip, Slither, Snowboard, Tailskid, Telescope, Transparency, Volplane

Slight(ly) Affront, Belittle, Cold shoulder, Cut, Detract, Disparage, Disregard, Disrespect, Elfin, Facer, Flimsy, Fragile, Halfway, Insult, Minor, Misprise, Neglect, Nominal, Partial, Pet, Petty, Puny, Rebuff, Remote, Scorn, →SLENDER, Slim, Slimsy, Slur, Small, Smattering, Sneaking, Snub, Sparse, Stent, Subtle, Superficial, Sylphine, Tenuous, Thin, Tiny, Trifling, Trivial, Wee, Wispy

Slime, Slimy Glair, Glareous, Glit, Gorydew, Guck, Gunk, Mother, Muc(o)us, Oily, Ooze, Sapropel, Slabbery, Slake, Sludge, Uliginous

Sling Balista, Catapult, Drink, Fling, Hang, Parbuckle, Prusik, Shy, Singapore, Support, Toss, Trebuchet

Slip(ped), Slipping, Slips Avalanche, Blunder, Boner, Boob, Come home, Coupon, Cutting, Deteriorate, Disc, Docket, Drift, EE, Elapse, Elt, Error, Escape, Faux pas, Fielder, Form, Freudian, Glide, Glissade, Infielder, Label, Landslide, Lapse, Lath, Leash, Lingerie, Lingual, Mistake, Muff, Nod, Overbalance, Oversight, Peccadillo, Petticoat, Plant, Prolapse, Quickset, Rejection, Relapse, Run, Scape, Sc(h)edule, Scoot, Set, Shim, Sin, Ski, Skid, Skin, Skite, Slade, Slidder, Slide, Slither, Slive, Spellican, Spillican, Stumble, Surge, Ticket, Trip, Tunicle, Underskirt, Unleash

Slipper(s) Baboosh, Babouche, Babuche, Banana skin, Calceolate, Carpet, Chappal, Eel, Errorist, Mocassin, Moccasin, Moyl, Muil, Mule, Pabouche, Pampootie, Pantable, Pantof(f)le, Panton, Pantoufle, Pump, Rullion, Runner, Ski, Sledge, Sneaker, Sock

Slippery Eely, Elusive, Errorist, Foxy, Glid, Icy, Lubric, Shady, Shifty, Skidpan, Slick, Slimy

▷**Slipshod** *may indicate* an anagram

Slit Cranny, Cut, Fent, Fissure, Fitchet, Gash, Loop, Pertus(at)e, Placket, Race, Rit, Scissure, Spare, Speld(er), Unseam, Vent

Slogan Amandla, Byword, Catchphrase, Catchword, Chant, Cry, Jai Hind, Jingle, Masakhane, Mot(to), Murdabad, Nayword, Phrase, Rallying-cry, Slughorn(e), Splash, Street cry, Warcry, Watchword

Slop(pily), Slops, Sloppy Careless, Lagrimoso, Lowse, Madid, Mushy, Remiss, Schmaltzy, Shower, Slapdash, Slipshod, Sloven, Slushy, Sozzly, Untidy, Weepie

Slope(s), Sloping Acclivity, Angle, Anticline, Bahada, Bajada, Bank, Batter, Bevel, Borrow, Borstal(l), Brae, Breast, Camber, Chamfer, Cle(e)ve, Cuesta, Declivity, Delve, Diagonal, Dip, Dry, Escarp, Escarpment, Fastigiate, Fla(u)nch, Foothill, Geanticline, Glacis, Grade, Gradient, Heel, Hill, Hipped, Incline, Isoclinical, Kant, Lean, Natural, Nursery, Oblique, Pediment, Pent, Periclinal, Piste, Pitch, Rake, Ramp, Rollway, Scarp, Schuss, Scrae, Scree, Shelve, Sideling, Skewback, Slade, Slant, Slippery, Slipway, Splay, Steep, Stoss, Talus, Tilt, Verge, Versant, Weather

▷**Sloppy** *may indicate* an anagram

Sloth(ful) Accidie, Acedia, Ai, Bradypus, Edentate, Ground, Idle, Inaction, Indolent, Inertia, Lazy, Lie-abed, Megatherium, Sweer(t), Sweir(t), Three-toed, Torpor

Slough(ing) Cast, Despond, Ecdysis, Eschar, Exfoliate, Exuviae, Lerna, Marsh, Mire, Morass, Paludine, Shed, Shorten, Shuck, Swamp

Sloven(ly) Careless, Dag(gy), D(r)aggle-tail, Dishevelled, Down-at-heel, Frowsy, Grobian, Jack-hasty, Mawkin, Slattern, Sleazy, Slipshod, Slummock, Slut, Untidy

Slow(er), Slowing, Slowly, Slow-witted Adagio, Allargando, Andante, Andantino, Behindhand, Brady, Brake, Broad, Calando, Calf, Crawl, Dawdle, Decelerate, Deliberate, Dilatory, Dim, Draggy, Dull, Dumka, ESN, Flag, Gradual, Halting, Hesitant, Inchmeal, Insulse, Lag, Langsam, Larghetto, Largo, Lash, Lassu, Late, Leisurely, Lentamente, Lentando, Lento, Lifeless, Loiter, Losing, Meno mosso, Obtuse, Pedetentous, Rall(entando), Rein, Reluctant, Retard, Ribattuta, Rit, Ritardando, Ritenuto, Roll-out, Slack, Slug, Sluggish, Snail's pace, Snaily, Solid, Stem, Tardigrade, Tardive, Tardy, Tardy-gaited, Thick

Slug(s) Ammo, Bêche-de-mer, Blow, Brain, Bullet, Cosh, Draught, Drink, Gast(e)ropod, Grapeshot, Knuckle sandwich, Lead, Limaces, Limax, Mollusc, Nerita, Pellet, Shot, Snail, Tot, Trepang

Sluggish Dilatory, Drumble, Idler, Inert, Jacent, Lacklustre, Laesie, Languid, Lazy, Lentor, Lethargic, Lug, Phlegmatic, Saturnine, Sleepy, → **SLOW**, Stagnant, Tardy, Torpid, Unalive

Slumber Doze, Drowse, Nap, Nod, Sleep, Sloom, Snooze

Slump Decrease, Depression, Deteriorate, Dip, Flop, Recession, Sag, Sink, Slouch, Sprawl, Stoop

Slur(ring) Defame, Drawl, Innuendo, Ligature, Opprobrium, Slight, Smear, Synaeresis, Tie

Sly, Slyness Canny, Christopher, Clandestine, Coon, Covert, Cunning, Foxy, Guile, Leery, Peery, Reynard, Secretive, Shifty, Slee, Sleeveen, Sneaky, Stallone, Stealthy, Subtle, Surreptitious, Tinker, Tod, Tricky, Weasel, Wily

▷**Slyly** *may indicate* an anagram

Smack(er) Aftertaste, Buss, Cuff, Flavour, Foretaste, Fragrance, Hooker, Kiss, Klap, Lander, Lips, Pra(h)u, Relish, Salt, Saut, Skelp, Slap, Slat, Smatch, Smell, Smouch, Soupçon, Spank, Spice, Splat, Tack, Taste, Thwack, Tincture, Trace, Twang, X, Yawl

Small (thing), Smaller, Smallest amount A minori, Atom, Bantam, Beer, Bijou, Bittie, Bitty, Chickenfeed, Chotta, Collops, Crumb, Denier, Diddy, Diminutive, Dinky, Dreg, Drib, Driblet, Elfin, Elfish, Endomorphic, Few, Fleabite, Fry, Grain, Haet, Ha'it, Half-pint, Handful, Hint, Hobbit, Holding, Hole-in-the-wall, Hyperosmia, Insect, Ion, Itsy-bitsy, Knurl, Leet, Leetle, Lepton, Lilliputian, Limited, Lite, → **LITTLE**, Lock, Low, Meagre, Mean, Measly, Microscopic, Midget, Mignon, Miniature, Minikin, Minority, Minute, Mite, Modest, Modicum, Neap, Nominal, Nurl, Peerie, Peewee, Petit(e), Petty, Pickle,

Pigmy, Pink(ie), Pinky, Pint-size, Pittance, Pocket, Poky, Puckle, Rap, Reduction, Runt, S, Scantling, Scattering, Scrump, Scrunt, Scruple, Scut, Shoebox, Shortarse, Shrimp, Single, Slight, Slim, Smattering, Smidge(o)n, Smidgin, Smithereen, Smout, Snippet, Soupçon, Sprinkling, Spud, Squirt, Stim, Stunted, Subminiature, Suspicion, Tad, Teenty, Thin, Tidd(l)y, Tiny, Titch(y), Tittle, Tot(tie), Totty, Trace, Trivial, Wee, Weedy, Whit

Smart(en), Smartest, Smartness Ache, Acute, Alec, Astute, Best, Bite, Burn, Chic, Classy, Clever, Cute, Dandy, Dapper, Dressy, Elegant, Flash, Flip, Fly, Groom, Jemmy, Kookie, Kooky, Larnery, Natty, Neat, New pin, Nifty, Nip, Nobby, Outwit, Pac(e)y, Pacy, Pert, Posh, Preen, Primp, Prink, Pusser, Raffish, Rattling, Ritzy, Saucy, Slick, Sly, Smoke, Smug, Snappy, Snazzy, Soigné(e), Spiff, Sprauncy, Sprightly, Spruce, Sprush, Spry, Sting, Street cred, Stylish, Swagger, Sweat, Swish, Tiddley, Tippy, Titivate, Toff, Trendy, U, Zippy

Smash(ed), Smasher, Smashing Atom, Brain, Break, Cannon, Corker, Crush, Demolish, Devastate, Dish, Drunk, High, Kaput, Kill, Lulu, Plastered, Ram, Shatter, Shiver, Slam, Squiffy, Stave, Super, Terrific, Tight, **→ WRECK**

▷**Smash(ed)** *may indicate* an anagram

Smear Anoint, Assoil, Besmirch, Blur, Calumniate, Cervical, Clam, Daub, Defile, Denigrate, Discredit, Drabble, Enarm, Gaum, Gorm, Lick, Mud, Oil, Oint, Pay, Plaster, Slairg, Slaister, Slander, Slather, Slime, Slubber, Slur, Smalm, Smarm, Smudge, Splodge, Spredd, Sully, Swipe, Teer, Traduce, Wax

Smell(ing), Smelly Aroma, BO, Cacodyl, Effluvium, Exhale, F(o)etid, Fetor, Fug, Funky, Gale, Gamy, Graveolent, Guff, Hing, Honk, Hum, Ionone, Mephitis, Miasm(a), Ming, Musk, Niff, Nose, Odour, Olent, Olfact(ory), Osmatic, Osmeterium, Osmic, Perfume, Pong, Ponk, Pooh, Rank, Redolent, Reech, Reek, Ripe, Sar, Savour, **→ SCENT**, Sensory, Smack, Sniff, Snifty, Snoke, Snook, Snuff, Steam, Stench, Stifle, Stink, Tang, Whiff

Smile(s), Smiling, Smily Agrin, Beam, Cheese, Emoticon, Favour, Gioconda, Grin, Rictus, Self-help, Simper, Smirk, Watch the birdie

Smoke(r), Smoking, Smoky Arbroath, Blast, Bloat, Censer, Chain, Chillum, Chimera, Chimney, **→ CIGAR(ETTE)**, Cure, Drag, Exhaust, Fog, Fuliginous, Fume, Fumigate, Funk, Gasper, Hemp, Incense, Indian hemp, Inhale, Kipper, Latakia, London ivy, Lum, Lunt, Manil(l)a, Nicotian, Opium, Panatella, Peaty, Pother, Pudder, Puff, Reech, Reefer, Reek, Reest, Roke, Secondary, Sidestream, Smeech, Smeek, Smirting, Smoor, Smother, Smoulder, Smudge, Snout, Tear, Tobacconalian, Toke, Vapour, Viper, Whiff, Wreath

Smooth(er), Smoothly Alabaster, Bald, Bland, Brent, Buff, Cantabile, Chamfer, Clean, Clockwork, Debonair, Dress, Dub, Easy, Even, Fettle, File, Flat, Fluent, Fretless, Glabrous, Glare, Glass paper, Glassy, Glib, Goose, Iron, Legato, Level, Levigate, Linish, Mellifluous, Mellow, Millpond, Oil, Plane, Planish, Plaster, Pumice, Rake, Roll, Rub, Sad-iron, Sand(er), Satiny, Scrape, Shiny, Sleek, Slick, Slickenslide, Slithery, Slur, Smug, Snod, Sostenuto, Straighten, Streamlined, Suave, Swimmingly, Terete, Terse, Trim, Unwrinkled, Urbane

Smother Burke, Choke, Dampen, Muffle, Oppress, Overlie, Smoor, Smore, Stifle, Suppress

Smug Complacent, Conceited, Gloating, Goody-goody, Goody-two-shoes, Neat, Oily, Pi, Self-satisfied, Trim

Smuggle(d), Smuggler, Smuggling Bootleg, Contraband, Coyote, Donkey, Fair trade, Free trader, Gunrunning, Moonshine, Mule, Owler, Rum-runner, Run, Secrete, Sneak, Steal, Traffic

Smut(ty) Bawdy, Black, Blight, Blue, Brand, Burnt-ear, Coom, Crock, Filth, Grime, Racy, Soot, Speck

Snack Bever, Bhaji, Bhelpuri, Bite, Blintz, Bombay mix, Breadstick, Breakfast bar, Brunch, Burger, Butty, Canapé, Chack, Choc bar, Churro, Crisps, Croque monsieur, Crudités, Doner kebab, Elevenses, Enchilada, Entremets, Finger buffet, Four-by-two, Gorp, Goujons, Hoagie, Hors (d'oeuvres), Hot dog, Knish, Meze, Munchies, Nacho, Nacket, Nibble, Nigiri, Nocket, Nooning, Nuncheon, Padkos, Pasty, Pie, Piece, Ploughman's lunch, Popcorn, Pork scratchings, Rarebit, Refreshment, Samo(o)sa, Sandwich, Sarney, Sarnie, Savoury, Scroggin, Sloppy joe, Small chop, Smorgasbord, Spring roll, Sushi, Tapa, Taste, Toast(y), Trail mix, Vada, Voidee, Wada, Wrap, Zakuska

Snag Aggro, Anoint, Catch, Contretemps, Drawback, Hindrance, Hitch, Impediment, Knob, Nog, Obstacle, Remora, Rub, Stumbling block, Tear

Snail(s) Brian, Cowrie, Cowry, Dodman, Escargot, Gast(e)ropod, Heliculture, Helix, Hodmandod, Limnaea, Lymnaea, Nautilus, Nerite, Roman, Slow, Slug, Strombus, Unicorn-shell, Univalve, Wallfish, Whelk

Snake, Snaking Drag, Meander, →**SERPENT**, Slither, Wind

Snap(per), Snappy, Snap up Abrupt, Alligator, Autolycus, Bite, Break, Brittle, Camera, Click, Cold, Cold wave, Crack, Crocodile, Cross, Curt, Edgy, Fillip, Gator, Girnie, Glitch, Glom, Gnash, Grab, Hanch, Impatient, Knacker, Knap, Livery, Mugshot, Photo, Photogene, Retort, Scotch, Snack, Snatch, Spell, Still, Swift, Tetchy, Vigour

Snare Bait, Benet, Engine, Entrap, Gin, Grin, Honeytrap, Hook, Illaqueate, Inveigle, Mantrap, Net, Noose, Rat-trap, Springe, Toil, →**TRAP**, Trapen, Trepan, Web, Weel, Wire

Snarl(ing) Chide, Complicate, Cynic, Enmesh, Gnar(l), Gnarr, Growl, Grumble, Knar, Knot, Snap, Tangle, Yirr

Sneak(y) Area, Carry-tale, Clipe, Clype, Creep, Furtive, Infiltrate, Inform, Lurk, Mumblenews, Nim, Peak, Scratch, Scunge, Skulk, Slip, Slither, Slyboots, Snitch, Snoop, Split, Steal, Stoolie, Tell(-tale)

Sneeze (at), Sneezing Atishoo, Errhine, Sternutation

Sniff, Sniffle E-nose, Inhale, Nose, Nursle, Nuzzle, Scent, Smell, Snivel, Snort, Snuffle, Vent, Whiff

Snob(bery), Snobbish Cobbler, Crachach, Crispin, Dic(k)ty, Genteel, High-hat, La-di-da, Prudish, Pseud, Scab, Side, Sloane, Snooty, Snow, Soutar, Souter, Sowter, Toffee-nose, Vain, Vamp

Snore, Snoring Rhonchus, Rout, Snort, Snuffle, Stertorous, Zz

Snort(er) Dram, Drink, Grunt, Nare, Nasal, Roncador, Snore, Toot

Snout Bill, Boko, Cigar, Informer, Muzzle, Nose, Nozzle, Proboscis, Schnozzle, Tinker, Tobacco, Wall

Snow(y), Snowdrift, Snowstorm Horse, Marine, Nivose, Noise, Powder, Red, Sleet, Spotless, Virga, Yellow

Snub Brush off, Cut, Diss, Go-by, Lop, Pug, Quelch, Rebuff, Reproof, Retroussé, Short, Slap, Slight, Sloan, Sneap, Snool, Wither

Snuff(le) Asarabacca, Douse, Dout, Errhine, Extinguish, Maccaboy, Ptarmic, Pulvil, Rappee, Smother, Snaste, Sneesh(an), Sniff, Snift, Snotter, Snush, Stop, Tobacco, Vent

Snuffbox Mill, Mull, Ram's horn

Snug(gery), Snuggle Burrow, Comfy, Cose, →**COSY**, Couthie, Couthy, Croodle, Cubby(hole), Cuddle, Embrace, Intime, Lion, Neat, Nestle, Nuzzle, Rug, Snod, Tight, Trim

So Ergo, Hence, Sic(h), Sol, Such, Therefore, Thus, True, Very, Yes

Soak(ed) Bate, Bath(e), Beath, Bewet, Bloat, Blot, Buck, Cree, Deluge, Drench, Drent, Drink, Drook, Drouk, Drown, Drunk, Duck, Dunk, Embay, Embrue, Fleece, Grog, Imbrue, Impregnate, Infuse, Inundate, Lush, Macerate, Marinate, Mop, Oncome, Permeate, Plastered, Rait, Rate, Ret(t), Rob, Saturate, Seep, Sipe, Sog, Sop, Sorb, Souce, Souse, Sows(s)e, Steep, Sype, Thwaite, Toper, Waterlog, Wet, Wino

Soap(y), Soap opera Brookside, Cake, Carbolic, Cleanser, Coronation St, Dallas, Eluate, ER, Flake, Flannel, Flattery, Glass, Green, Hard, Joe, Lather, Lux®, Marine, Metallic, Moody, Mountain, Pinguid, Saddle, Safrole, Saponaceous, Saponin, Sawder, Serial, Shaving, Slime, Soft, Spanish, Suds, Sudser, Sugar, Tablet, Tallow, The Bill, Toilet(ry), Washball, Yellow

Soar(ing) Ascend, Essorant, Fly, Glide, Plane, Rise, Tower, Zoom

Sociable, Sociability Affable, Cameraderie, Chummy, Clubby, Cosy, Couthie, Extravert, Folksy, Friendly, Genial, Gregarious, Mixer, Phatic

Socialism, Socialist Champagne, Chartist, Dergue, Fabian, Fourierism, Hardie, ILP, International, Karmathian, Lansbury, Left(y), Marxism, Nihilism, Owen(ist), Owenite, Parlour pink, Pasok, Pinko, Red, Revisionist, Sandinista, Second international, Spartacist, Utopian, Webb

Society Affluent, Alternative, Association, Band of Hope, Benefit, Black Hand, Body, Boxer, Brahma, Brahmo, Building, Camorra, Casino, Choral, Class, Club, College, Company, Consumer, Co-op, Cooperative, Culture, Debating, Dorcas, Duddieweans, Elite, Elks, Fabian, Fashion, Fellowship, Foresters, Freemans, Freemasons, Friendly, Friends, Glee club, Grand monde, Group, Guarantee, Guilds, Haut monde, High, High life, Humane, Institute, Invincibles, John Birch, Ku-Klux-Klan, Law, Linnean, Lodge, Mafia, Masonic, Mass, Mau-Mau, Ménage, Molly Maguire, National, Oddfellows, Open, Oral, Orangemen, Oratory, Order, Oxford Union, Permissive, Plural, Pop, Provident, Repertory, Risk, Rotary, Royal, S, Samaj, School, Secret, Soc, Sodality, Somaj, Soroptomist, Sorority, Stakeholder, Surveillance, Tammany, Theosophical, Toc H, Ton, Tong, Triad, U, Whiteboy

Socket Acetabulum, Alveole, Bayonet, Budget, Eyepit, Gudgeon, Hollow, Hosel, Hot shoe, Jack, Keeper, Lampholder, Nave, Nozzle, Orbit, Ouch, Outlet, Plug, Pod, Port, Power-point, Screw, Serial port, Strike

Sod Clump, Delf, Delph, Divot, Fail, Gazo(o)n, Mool, Mould, Mouls, Scraw, Sward, Turf

Sofa Canapé, Chaise longue, Chesterfield, Couch, Daybed, Divan, Dos-à-dos, Dosi-do, Lounge, Ottoman, Settee, Squab, Tête-à-tête

Soft(en), Softener, Softening, Softly Amalgam, Anneal, Assuage, B, BB, Blet, Boodle, Cedilla, Cottony, Cree, Cushion, Dim, Doughy, Emolliate, Emollient, Flabby, Furry, Gentle, Hooly, Humanise, Lash, Lax, Lenient, Limp, Low, Mease, Mellow, Melt, Mild, Milksop, Mitigate, Modify, Modulate, Mollify, Morendo, Mulch, Mush(y), Mute, Neale, Nesh, Option, P, Pad(ded), Palliate, Pastel, Piano, Plushy, Porous, Propitiate, Rait, Rate, Relent, Sentimental, Silly, Slack, Soda, Spongy, Squashy, Squidgy, Squishy, Temper, → **TENDER**, Tone, Velvet, Weak, Yielding

Soil(ed), Soily Acid, Adscript, Agrology, Agronomy, Alkali(ne), Alluvium, Azonal, Backfill, Bedraggle, Begrime, Bemire, Beray, Besmirch, Blacken, Chernozem, Clay, Cohesive, Contaminate, Defile, Desecrate, Desert, Dinge, Dirt(y), Discolour, Duricrust, Eard, Earth, Edaphic, Edaphology, Frictional,

Gault, Glebe, Grey, Grimy, Ground, Gumbo, Hotbed, Humus, Illuvium, Intrazonal, Lair, Land, Latosol, Lithosol, Loam, Loess, Lome, Loss, Marl, Mire, Mo(u)ld, Mool, Mud, Mulch, Mull, Night, Ordure, Peat, Ped, Pedogenic, Pedology, Phreatic, Planosol, Podsol, Podzol, Pollute, Prairie, Pure, Regar, Regolith, Regosol, Regur, Rendzina, Rhizosphere, Root-ball, Sal, Sedentary, Smudge, Smut, Solonchak, Solonetz, Solum, Soot, Stain, Stonebrash, Sub, Sully, Tarnish, Tash, Terrain, Terricolous, Tilth, Top, Udal, Umber, Virgin, Zonal

Soldier(s) Ant, Chocolate, Detachment, Fighter, Gyrene, Insect, Old Bill, Unknown

▷**Soldiers** *may indicate* bread for boiled eggs

Sole, Solitaire, Solitary Alone, Anchoret, Anchorite, Antisocial, Ascetic, Asocial, Clump, Corporation, Crepe, Eremite, Fish, Friendless, Incommunicado, Independent, Inner, Lemon, Lonesome, Meered, Megrim, Merl, Meunière, Monkish, One, On ice, Only, Pad, Palm, Patience, Pegboard, Pelma, Planta(r), Plantigrade, Platform, Recluse, Sand, Scaldfish, Single(ton), Skate, Slip, Smear-dab, Tap, Thenar, Unique, Vibram®, Vola

Solemn Austere, Devout, Earnest, Grave, Gravitas, Owlish, Po-faced, Sacred, Sedate, Serious, Sober, Sobersides, Sombre

Solicit Accost, Approach, Ask, Attract, Bash, → **BEG**, Canvass, Cottage, Drum up, Importun(at)e, Plead, Ply, Speer, Speir, Touch, Tout, Woo

Solid(arity), Solidify, Solidity Burly, Cake, Chunky, Clot, Clunky, Compact, Comradeship, Concrete, Cone, Congeal, Conoid, Consolidate, Cube, Cylinder, Dense, Dilitancy, Enneahedron, Esprit de corps, Ethal, Firm, Foursquare, Freeze, Frustrum, Fuchsin(e), Gel, Hard, Holosteric, Impervious, Kotahitanga, Merbromin, Octahedron, Pakka, Parallelepiped, Petrarchan, Platonic, Polyhedron, Prism, Pucka, Pukka, Purin(e), Robust, Rockhewn, Set, Square, Squatly, Stable, Staunch, Stereoscopic, Stilbene, Sturdy, Sublimate, Substantial, Tetrahedron, Thick (set), Trusty, Unanimous

▶**Solitary** *see* **SOLE**

Solo Aria, Cadenza, Cavatine, Concertante, Lone, Monodrama, Monody, Ombre, One-man, Recit, Scena, Single-handed, Unaided, Variation

Solution Amrit, Brine, Colloidal, Electrolyte, Final, Fix, Formalin, Hairspray, Liquid, Normal, Oleum, Reducer, Remedy, Rubber, Soup, Standard, Tone, Viscose

▷**Solution** *may indicate* an anagram

Solve(d), Solver Absolve, Assoil, Calculate, Casuist, Clear, Crack, Decode, Loast, Loose, Panacea, Read(er), Troubleshoot, Unclew, Unriddle, Work

Solvent Above water, Acetaldehyde, Acetone, Alcahest, Aldol, Alkahest, Anisole, Aqua-regia, Banana oil, Benzene, Chloroform, Cleanser, Cymene, Decalin, Denaturant, Diluent, Dioxan(e), Eleunt, Eluant, Ether, Funded, Furan, Heptane, Hexane, Ligroin, Megilp, Menstruum, Methanol, Methylal, Naphtha, Nitromethane, Paraldehyde, Picoline, Protomic, Pyridine, Sound, Stripper, Terebene, Terpineol, Terts, Tetrachloromethane, Thiophen, Toluene, Toluol, Trike, Trilene, Turpentine, White spirit

Sombre Dark, Drab, Drear, Dull, Funereal, Gloomy, Grave, Morne, Morose, Subfusc, Subfusk, Sullen, Triste

Some Any, Arrow, Ary, Certain, Divers, Few, One, Part, Portion, Quota, Sundry, These, They, Wheen

▷**Some** *may indicate* a hidden word

▷**Somehow** *may indicate* an anagram

Sometime(s) Erstwhile, Ex, Former, Intermittent, Occasional, Off and on, Otherwhiles, Quondam

Son Boy, Disciple, Epigon(e), Fils, Fitz, Lad, Lewis, M(a)c, Native, Offspring, Prodigal, Progeny, Scion

Sonata Minuet, Moonlight, Trio, Waldstein

Song Air, Amoret, Anthem, Aria, Ariette, Art, Aubade, Ballad, Barcarol(l)e, Berceuse, Blues, Burden, Cabaletta, Calypso, Cantata, Cante hondo, Cante jondo, Canticle, Canticum, Cantion, Carol, Catch, Chanson(ette), Cha(u)nt, Chantey, Conductus, Corroboree, Cycle, Descant, Dirge, Ditty, Drinking, Duettino, Dynasty, Elegy, Fitt, Flamenco, Folk, Gaudeamus, Gita, Glee, Hillbilly, Hymn, Internationale, Lament, Lay, Lied(er), Lilt, Lullaby, Lyric, Madrigal, Marseillaise, Melody, Minnesang, Negro spiritual, Number, Nunc dimittis, Octastichon, Paean, Part, Plain, Plantation, Pop, Psalm, Rap, Red Flag, Rhapsody, Roulade, Roundelay, Rune, Scat, Scolion, Sea-shanty, Serenade, Shanty, Shosholoza, Siren, Solo, Sososholoza, Spiritual, Stave, Stomper, Strain, Strophe, Swan, Taps, Theme, Torch, Trill, Tune, Tyrolienne, Vaudeville, Villanella, Waiata, War, Warble, Yodel

Sonnet Amoret, Italian, Petrarch(i)an, Shakespearean, Shakespearian, Spenserian

Soon(er) Anon, Betimes, Directly, Enow, Erelong, Imminent, Nearly, OK, Oklahoma, Presently, Shortly, Tight, Timely, Tit(ely), Tite, Tyte

Soothe(r), Soothing Accoy, Allay, Anetic, Appease, Assuage, Bucku, Calm, Compose, Demulcent, Ease, Emollient, Irenic, Lenitive, Lull, Mellifluous, Mollify, Obtundent, Pacific, Paregoric, Placate, Poultice, Quell, Rock, Stroke

Sophisticate(d) Blasé, Boulevardier, City slicker, Civilised, Classy, Cogniscento, Cosmopolitan, Couth, Cultured, Doctor, High-end, Hi-tech, Patrician, Polished, Sative, Slicker, Smooth, Suave, Svelte, Urbane, Worldly

▷**Sophoclean** *may indicate* Greek alphabet, etc.

Sorcerer, Sorceress, Sorcery Angek(k)ok, Ashipu, Black art, Circe, Conjury, Diablerie, Diabolist, Genie, Hoodoo, Kadaitcha, Kurdaitcha, Lamia, Mage, Magic(ian), Magus, Medea, Merlin, Morgan le Fay, Mother Shipton, Necromancer, Obi, Pishogue, Shaman, Sortilege, Voodoo, Warlock, Witch, Witch knot, Wizard

Sore(ly), Sores Abrasion, Bitter, Blain, Boil, Canker, Chancre, Chap, Chilblain, Cold, Dearnly, Felon, Gall, Impost(h)ume, Ireful, Kibe, Nasty, Noma, Pressure, Quitter, Quittor, Raw, Rupia(s), Saddle, Sair, Sensitive, Shiver, Sitfast, Soft, Surbate, Tassell, Tercel, Ulcer(s), Whitlow, Wound

Sorrow(ful) Affliction, Attrition, Deplore, Distress, Dole, Doloroso, Dolour, →**GRIEF**, Lament, Misery, Nepenthe, Ochone, Penance, Pietà, Plaintive, Remorse, Rue, Triste, Wae, Waugh, Wirra, Woe, Yoop

Sorry Apologetic, Ashamed, Contrite, Eh, Miserable, Oops, Paltry, Penitent, Pitiful, Poor, Regretful, Relent, Rueful, Simple, Wan, Wretched

▷**Sorry** *may indicate* an anagram

▶**Sorts** *see* OUT OF SORTS

▷**So to speak** *may indicate* 'sound of'

Soul(ful) Alma, Ame, Anima, Animist, Atman, Ba, Bod(y), Brevity, Deep, Eschatology, Essence, Expressive, Heart, Inscape, Ka, Larvae, Manes, Motown, Person, Psyche, Saul, Shade, Spirit, Traducian

Sound(ed), Sounding, Soundness, Sound system Accurate, Ach-laut, Acoustic, Albemarle, Allophone, All there, Alveolar, Aspirate, Audio, Blare,

Bleep, Blip, Bloop, Blow, Bong, Bray, Breathed, Cacophony, Chime, Chirl, Chirr(e), Chord, Chug, Clam, Clang, Clank, Clink, Cloop, Clop, Clunk, Compos, Consistent, Copper-bottomed, Dah, Dental, Diphthong, Dit, Dive, Dream, Dusky, Echo, Eek, Epenthesis, Fast, Fathom, Fettle, Fit, Flap, Flawless, Flow, Foley, Glide, Good, Hale, Harmonics, Hayle, Healthy, Hearty, Hiccup, Hi-fi, Hiss, Inlet, Intact, Islay, Jura, Kalmar, Knell, Lene, Lo-fi, Long Island, Low, Lucid, Mach, Madrilene, Mersey, Milford, Monophthong, Murmur, Musak, Music, Muzak®, Narrow, Nasal, Nicam, → **NOISE**, Off-glide, Onomatopoeia, Oompah, Optical, Orate, Orinasal, Orthodox, Palatal, Paragog(u)e, Peal, Pest, Phone(me), Phonetic, Phonic, Phonology, Phut, Pitter(-patter), Plap, Plink, Plonk, Plop, Plosion, Plosive, Plumb, Plummet, Plunk, Plymouth, Probe, Pronounce, Put-put, Quadraphonic(s), Rale, Rational, Rat-tat, Real, Reasonable, Reliable, Ring, Robust, Rumble, Rustle, Safe, Sandhi, Sane, Sensurround®, S(c)hwa, Skirl, Solid, Sondage, Sone, Souffle, Sough, Speech, Splat, Stereo, Stereophony, Strait, Stroke, Surround, Swish, Tannoy®, Tchick, Tenable, Thorough, Timbre, Ting, Tone, Toneme, Trig, Trill, Triphthong, Trumpet, Twang, Ultrasonic(s), Unharmed, Uvular, Valid, Viable, Voice, Vowel, Watertight, Well, Whine, Whinny, Whistle, Whole(some), Whoosh, Wolf

Soup Alphabet, Bird's nest, Bisque, Borsch, Bouillabaisse, Bouillon, Broth, Cal(l)aloo, Chowder, Cioppino, Clam chowder, Cock-a-leekie, Cockieleekie, Cockyleeky, Consommé, Crab chowder, Cullen skink, Gazpacho, Gumbo, Lokshen, Minestrone, Miso, Mock turtle, Mulligatawny, Oxtail, Pho, Pot(t)age, Pot-au-feu, Primordial, Puree, Ramen, Rice, Rubaboo, Sancoche, Scoosh, Scotch broth, Skink, Stock, Turtle, Vichyssoise

▷**Soup** *may indicate* an anagram

Sour(puss) Acerb, Acescent, Acid, Acidulate, Aigre-deux, Alegar, Bitter, Citric, Crab, Eager, Esile, Ferment, Moody, Stingy, Turn, Unamiable, Verjuice, Vinegarish

Source Authority, Basis, Bottom, Centre, Closed, Database, Derivation, Egg, Fons, Font, Fount, Fountain-head, Germ, Head-stream, Leak, Literary, Mine, Mother, Neutron, Origin, Parent, Pi, Pion, Point, Principle, Prot(h)yle, Provenance, Quarry, Reference, Rise, Root, Seat, Seed, Spa, Spring, Springhead, Stock, Supply, Upriver, Urn, Well, Wellhead, Wellspring, Ylem

South(ern), Southerner Austral, Confederacy, Decanal, Decani, Dixieland, Meridian, S, Scal(l)awag, Scallywag

South Africa(n) Caper, Grikwa, Griqua, Lebowa, SA, Soutie, Soutpiel, Springbok, Swahili, Xhosa, ZA, Zulu

South-east Home Counties, Roseland, SE

Souvenir Goss, Keepsake, Memento, Relic, Remembrance, Scalp, Token, Trophy

Sovereign(ty), Sovereign remedy Anne, Autocrat, Bar, Condominium, Couter, Dominant, Emperor, ER, Goblin, Haemony, Harlequin, Imperial, Imperium, James, King, L, Liege, Monarch, Napoleon, Nizam, Pound, Quid, Rangatiratanga, Reign, Royalty, Ruler, Shiner, Supreme, Swaraj, Synarchy

Sow(ing) Catchcrop, Elt, Foment, Gilt, Inseminate, Plant, Scatter, Seed, Sprue, Strew, Yelt

Spa Aachen, Baden, Baden-Baden, Bath, Ems, Evian, Fat farm, Harrogate, Hydro, Kurhaus, Kursaal, Leamington, Malvern, Pump-room, Vichy

Space, Spaced (out), Spaceman, Spacing, Spacious, Spatial Abyss, Acre, Airy, Alley, Area, Areola, Bay, Bedsit, Bolthole, Bracket, Breathing, Bronchus, Catatonic, Cellule, Cislunar, Clearing, Cofferdam, Concourse, Crawl, Cubbyhole, Daylight, Deducted, Deep, Distal, Distance, Elbow-room,

Elliptic, Em, En, Esplanade, Ether, Exergue, Expanse, Extent, Flies, Footprint,
Freeband, Gagarin, Gap, Glade, Glenn, Goaf, Gob, Groggy, Gutter, Hair,
Hash(mark), Headroom, Hell, Indention, Inner, Intergalactic, Interim,
Interlinear, Interplanetary, Interstellar, Interstice, Invader, Kneehole, Lacuna,
Lair, Leading, Legroom, Life, Lobby, Logie, Lumen, Lunar, Lung, Maidan,
Manifold, Manorial, Metope, Minkowski, Mosh pit, MUD, Muset, Musit, Orbit,
Outer, Palatial, Parking, Parvis(e), Personal, Polemics, Proportional, Proxemics,
Quad, Retrochoir, Riemannian, →**ROOM**, Ruelle, Sample, Sheets, Shelf room,
Sinus, Slot, Spandrel, Spandril, Sparse, Step, Steric, Storage, Third, Topological,
Tympanum, Ullage, Uncluttered, Vacua, Vacuole, Vacuum, Vast, Vector,
Virtual, Void, Volume, Well

Spacecraft, Space agency, Space object, Spaceship, Space station
Apollo, Capsule, Challenger, Columbia, Columbus, Deep Space, Explorer,
Galileo, Gemini, Genesis, Giotto, Lander, LEM, Luna, Lunik, Mariner, Mercury,
MIR, Module, NASA, Orbiter, Pioneer, Probe, Quasar, Ranger, Rocket ship,
Salyut, Shuttle, Skylab, Soyuz, Space lab, Sputnik, Starship, Tardis, Viking,
Voskhod, Vostok, Voyager, Zond

Spade Breastplough, Caschrom, Cas crom, Castrato, Detective, Graft, Loy,
Mole, Paddle, Paddle staff, Pattle, Peat, Pettle, Pick, S, Shovel, Slane, Spit,
Suit, Tus(h)kar, Tus(h)ker, Twiscar

Span Age, Arch, Attention, Bestride, Bridge, Chip, Ctesiphon, Extent, Life,
Octave, Range, Timescale

Spaniard, Spanish Alguacil, Alguazil, Asturian, Balearic, Barrio, Basque,
Cab, Caballero, Carlist, Castilian, Catalan, Chicano, Diego, Don, Fly, Grandee,
Hidalgo, Hispanic, José, Madrileno, Main, Mestizo, Mozarab, Pablo, Señor

Spaniel Cavalier, Field, Irish water, King Charles, Toady, Toy, Water, Welsh
springer

Spar Barite, Barytes, Blue John, Boom, Bowsprit, Box, Cauk, Cawk, Derbyshire,
Fight, Gaff, Heavy, Iceland, Icestone, Jib-boom, Mainyard, Martingale, Mast,
Mizzenmast, Nail-head, Outrigger, Rafter, Rail, Ricker, Satin, Shearleg,
Sheerleg, Snotter, Spathic, Sprit, Steeve, Stile, Triatic, Yardarm

Spare, Sparing(ly) Angular, Cast-off, Dup(licate), Economical, Fifth wheel,
Free, Frugal, Galore, Gash, Gaunt, Hain, Lean, Lenten, Narrow, Other, Pardon,
Relieve, Reprieve, Reserve, Rib, Save, Scant, Skinny, Slender, Stint, Subsecive,
Tape, Thin

Spark Animate, Arc, Beau, Blade, Bluette, Dandy, Flash, Flicker, Flint, Funk,
Ignescent, Ignite, Kindle, Life, Quenched, Scintilla, Smoulder, Spunk, Trigger,
Zest

Sparkle(r), Sparkling Aerated, Bling, Burnish, Coruscate, Crémant, Diamanté,
Effervesce, Élan, Emicate, Fire, Fizz, Flicker, Frizzante, Gem, Glint, Glisten,
Glister, Glitter, Patina, Pétillant, Scintillate, Seltzer, Seltzogene, Spangle,
Spirited, Spritzig, Spumante, Twinkle, Verve, Witty, Zap

Spartan(s) Ascetic, Austere, Basic, Enomoty, Hardy, Helot, Laconian, Lysander,
Menelaus, Severe, Valiant

Spasm(s), Spasmodic Ataxic, Blepharism, Chorea, Clonus, Convulsive,
Cramp, Crick, Fit(ful), Hiccup, Hippus, Intermittent, Irregular, →**JERK**, Kink,
Laryngismus, Nystagmus, Paroxysm, Periodical, Start, Strangury, Tetany, Throe,
Tonic, Tonus, Trismus, Twinge, Twitch, Vaginismus

▷**Spasmodic** *may indicate* an anagram
▶**Spatial** *see* **SPACE**

Speak(er), Speaking Address, Ad lib, Articulate, Bang on, Broach, Chat, Cicero, Collocuter, Communicate, Converse, Coo, Declaim, Diction, Dilate, Discourse, Diseur, Dwell, Earphone, Effable, Elocution, Eloquent, Expatiate, Express, Extemporise, Filibuster, Intercom, Intone, Inveigh, Jabber, Jaw, Lip, Loq, Loquitur, Management, Mang, Mention, Mike, Mina, Mouth, Mouthpiece, Nark, Native, Open, Orate, Orator, Palaver, Parley, Perorate, Pontificate, Prate, Preach, Prelector, Public, Recite, Rhetor, → **SAY**, Sayne, Soliloquize, Spout, Spruik, Stump, Talk, Tannoy®, Tongue, Trap, Tweeter, Utter, Voice, Waffle, Wibble, Windbag, Witter, Woofer, Word

Spear Ash, Asparagus, Assagai, Assegai, Barry, Dart, Demi-lance, Engore, Fishgig, Fizgig, Gad, Gavelock, Gig, Glaive, Gleave, Gum digger's, Gungnir, Harpoon, Hastate, Impale, Javelin, Lance(gay), Launcegaye, Leister, Morris-pike, Partisan, Pierce, Pike, Pilum, Prong, Skewer, Spike, Trident, Trisul(a), Waster

Special(ly) Ad hoc, Constable, Designer, Disparate, Distinctive, Extra, Important, Notable, Notanda, Particular, Peculiar, Red-letter, Specific, Strong suit, Vestigial

Specialise, Specialist(s), Speciality Allergist, Authority, Concentrate, Connoisseur, Consultant, ENT, Esoteric, Expert, Field, Forte, Illuminati, Internist, Logistician, Maestro, Major, Optometrist, Pomologist, Quant, Recondite, Technician

Specific(ally), Specification, Specified, Specify Adduce, Ad hoc, As, Ascribe, Assign, Cure, Define, Designate, Detail, Explicit, Formula, Given, Itemise, Medicine, Namely, Of, Precise, Quantify, Remedy, Sp, Special, Spell out, Stipulate, Stylesheet, The, To wit, Trivial, Vide licit

Speck, Speckle(d) Atom, Bit, Dot, Fleck, Floater, Freckle, Mealy, Mote, Muscae volitantes, Particle, Peep(e), Pip, Smut, Spreckle, Stud

Spectacle(s), Spectacled, Spectacular Bifocals, Blinks, Colourful, Epic, Escolar, → **GLASSES**, Goggles, Horn-rims, Lorgnette, Lorgnon, Meteoric, Optical, Pageant, Pebble glasses, Phenomenon, Pince-nez, Pomp, Preserves, Rose-coloured, Scene, Show, Sight, Son et lumière, Staggering, Stunt, Sunglasses, Tattoo, Trifocal, Varifocals

Spectate, Spectator(s) Audience, Bystander, Dedans, Etagère, Eyer, Gallery, Gate, Groundling, Kibitzer, Observer, Onlooker, Passer-by, Ringsider, Standerby, Terrace, Wallflower, Witness

Spectral, Spectre Apparition, Bogle, Bogy, Eidolon, Empusa, Ghost, Idola, Iridal, Larva, Malmag, Phantasm, Phantom, Phasma, Spirit, Spook, Tarsier, Walking-straw, Wraith

Speculate, Speculative, Speculator, Speculation Academic, Arb(itrage), Assume, Bear, Better, Boursier, Bull, Conjecture, Flier, Flyer, Gamble, Guess, Ideology, If, Imagine, Meditate, Notional, Operate, Pinhooker, Presume, Raider, Shark, Stag, Theoretical, Theorise, Theory, Thought, Trade, Transcendent, Wonder

Speech, Speech element Accents, Address, Argot, Articulation, Bat, Blah, Bunkum, Burr, Curtain, Declamation, Delivery, Dialect, Diatribe, Diction, Direct, Discourse, Dithyramb, Drawl, Éloge, Eloquence, English, Epilogue, Eulogy, Farewell, Filibuster, Free, Gab, Glossolalia, Grandiloquence, Guttural, Harangue, Helium, Idiolect, Idiom, Inaugural, Indirect, Intonation, Jargon, Keynote, King's, Lallation, → **LANGUAGE**, Lingua franca, Litany, Logopaedics, Maiden, Monologue, Morph(eme), Musar, Oblique, Occlusive, Oral, Oration, Parabasis, Parle, Peroration, Phasis, Philippic, Phonetics, Prolog(ue), Queen's,

Rant, Reported, Rhetoric, RP, Sandhi, Say, Scanning, Screed, Sermon, Set, Side, Slang, Soliloquy, Stemwinder, Stump, Tagmeme, Talk, Taxeme, Tirade, Toneme, Tongue, Uptalk, Vach, Verbal, Visible, Voice, Wawa, Whaikorero, Whistle-stop, Xenoglossia

Speed(ily), Speedy Accelerate, Alacrity, Amain, Amphetamine, ANSI, Apace, ASA, Average, Barrel, Bat, Baud, Belive, Belt, Benzedrine, Breakneck, Burn, C, Career, Cast, Celerity, Clip, Cruising, Dart, Despatch, Dictation, DIN, Dispatch, Expedite, Fang, Fast, Film, Fleet, Further, Gait, Gallop, Goer, Group, Gun, Hare, Haste, Hie, Hotfoot, Hypersonic, Induce, Instantaneous, Knot, Landing, Lick, Mach, Merchant, MPH, → **PACE**, Pelt, Phase, Pike, Post-haste, Prompt, Pronto, Race, Rapidity, Rate, Rev, RPS, Rush, Scorch, Scud, Scurr, Skirr, Soon, Spank, Split, Stringendo, Supersonic, Swift, Tach, Tear, Tempo, Teraflop, Ton up, V, Velocity, Ventre à terre, Vroom, Wave, Whid, Wing, Zoom

Spell(ing) Abracadabra, Bewitch, Bout, Cantrip, Charm, Conjuration, Do, Elf-shoot, Enchantment, Entrance, Fit, Go, Gri(s)-gri(s), Hex, Incantation, Innings, Jettatura, Juju, Knock, Knur, → **MAGIC**, Mojo, Need-fire, Nomic, Orthography, Period, Phase, Philter, Philtre, Pinyin, Relieve, Ride, Romaji, Run, Rune, Scat, Shift, Shot, Signify, Sitting, Snap, Snatch, Sorcery, Sp, Spasm, Splinter, Stint, Stretch, Tack, Term, Time, Tour, Trick, Turn, Weird, Whammy, Wicca, Witchcraft

Spend(er), Spending Anticipate, Birl, Blow, Blue, Boondoggling, Consume, Deficit, Deplete, Disburse, Exhaust, Extravagant, Fritter, Lay out, Live, Outlay, Pass, Pay, Splash, Splurge, Squander, Squandermania, Ware

Spendthrift Prodigal, Profligate, Profuser, Wastrel

Sphere, Spherical Armillary, Attraction, Ball, Benthoscope, Celestial, Discipline, Earth, Element, Field, Firmament, Globe, Magic, Mound, Orb(it), Planet, Primum mobile, Prolate, Province, Realm, Theatre, Wheel

Spice, Spicy Anise, Aniseed, Baby, Baltic, Caraway, Cardamom, Cayenne, Chili powder, Cinnamon, Clove, Clow, Coriander, Cough drop, Cum(m)in, Dash, Devil, Galingale, Garam masala, Ginger, Green ginger, Jerk, Mace, Marjoram, Masala, Myrrh, Nutmeg, Oregano, Paprika, Peppercorn, Picante, Pimento, Piquant, Posh, Risque, Root ginger, Saffron, Season, Sexed up, Tansy, Tarragon, Taste, Turmeric, Vanilla, Variety, Za'atar

Spider(s) Arachnid, Aranea, Araneida, Attercop, Bird, Black widow, Bobbejaan, Bolas, Cardinal, Cheesemite, Citigrade, Diadem, Epeira, Ethercap, Ettercap, Funnel-web, Harvest(er), Harvestman, House, Hunting, Huntsman, Jumping, Katipo, Lycosa, Mite, Money, Monkey, Mygale, Orb-weaver, Pan, Phalangid, Podogona, Program, Pycnogonid, Red, Redback, Rest, Ricinulei, Saltigrade, Scorpion, Solpuga, Spinner, Strap, Tarantula, Telary, Trapdoor, Violin, Water, Wolf, Zebra

Spike(d) Barb, Brod, Calk, Calt(h)rop, Chape, Cloy, Crampon, Doctor, Ear, Fid, Filopodium, Foil, Gad, Gadling, Goad, Grama, Herissé, Impale, Kebab, Lace, Locusta, Marlin(e), Nail, Needle, → **PIERCE**, Pin, Piton, Point, Pricket, Prong, Puseyite, Raceme, Rod, Sharp, Shod, Skewer, Spadix, Spear, Spicate, Spicule, Strobiloid, Surge, Tang, Thorn, Tine

Spill(age) Divulge, Drop, Fidibus, Jackstraw, Lamplighter, Leakage, Let, Lighter, Overflow, Overset, Scail, Scale, Shed, Skail, Slart, Slop, Stillicide, Swatter, Taper, Tumble, Ullage

Spin(ner), Spinning (wheel) Aeroplane, Arabian, Arachne, Aswirl, Bielmann, Birl, Camel, Centrifuge, Chark(h)a, Cribellum, Cut, Dance, Day trip, Dextrorse,

DJ, Eddy, Eke, Flat, Flax-wrench, Flip, Gimp, Googly, Gymp, Gyrate, Gyre,
Gyroscope, Hurl, Isobaric, Isotopic, Jenny, Lachesis, Mole, Nun, Peg-top,
Piecener, Piecer, Pirouette, Pivot, PR, Precess, Prolong, Purl, Reel, Rev(olve),
Ride, Rotate, Royal, Screw, Side, Sinistrorse, Slant, Slide, Somersault, Spider,
Stator, Strobic, Swirl, Swivel, Throstle, Tirl, Toss, Trill, Trundle, Turntable,
Twirl, Twist, Wheel, Whirl, Whirligig, Work

Spinal (cord), Spine(d), Spiny Acanthoid, Acerose, Acicular, Acromion,
Aculeus, Areole, Arête, Backbone, Barb, Chine, Coccyx, Column, Doorn,
Epidural, Muricate, Myelon, Notochord, Ocotillo, Prickle, Quill, Rachial,
R(h)achis, Ray, Ridge bone, Thorn, Torso, Tragacanth

▶**Spine** *see* **SPINAL (CORD)**

Spirit(s), Spirited Afreet, Afrit, Animal, Animation, Animus, Ardent, Blithe,
Bogeyman, Dash, → **DRINK**, Dutch courage, Élan, Element(al), Emit, Entrain,
Essence, Ethereal, Etheric, Ethos, Fettle, Fiend, Fight, Free, Game, Gasoline,
Geist, Ginger, Gism, Go, Grit, Gumption, Heart, Holy, Hugh, Kindred,
→ **LIQUOR**, Lively, Mettle, Morale, Mystique, Nobody, Oversoul, Panache,
Pecker, Pep, Presence, Pride, Racy, Rotgut, Scientology, Sloe gin, Soul, Spunk,
Steam, Stomach, Team, Ton, Verve, Vigour, Vim, Vital, Zing

Spiritual(ism), Spiritualist, Spirituality Aerie, Aery, Channelling,
Ecclesiastic, Ethereous, Eyrie, Eyry, Incorporeal, Inwardness, Mystic, Negro,
Planchette, Slate-writing, Swedenborg, Yogi

Spit(ting), Spittle Bar, Barbecue, Broach, Brochette, Chersonese, Dead ringer,
Dribble, Drool, Emptysis, Eructate, Expectorate, Fuff, Gob, Golly, Gooby, Grill,
Hawk, Impale, Jack, Lookalike, Peninsula, Phlegm, Ras, Ringer, Rotisserie,
Saliva, Shish kebab, Skewer, Slag, Spade(ful), Spawl, Sputter, Sputum, Tombolo,
→ **TONGUE**, Yesk, Yex

Spite(ful) Backbite, Bitchy, Catty, Grimalkin, Harridan, Irrespective, Malevolent,
Malgré, Malice, Mean, Mischievous, Nasty, Petty, Pique, Rancour, Spleen,
Venom, Viperish, Waspish

Splash Befoam, Blash, Blue, Dabble, Dash, Dog, Drip, Feature, Flouse, Fl(o)ush,
Gardyloo, Jabble, Ja(u)p, Jirble, Paddle, Plap, Plop, Plowter, Sket, Slosh, Soda,
Soss, Sozzle, Spairge, Spat(ter), Spectacle, Splat(ch), Splatter, Splodge, Splosh,
Splotch, Spot, Spray, Spree, Squatter, Swash, Swatter, Water, Wet

▷**Splash** *may indicate* an anagram

Splendid, Splendour Braw, Brilliant, Bully, Capital, Champion, Clinker,
Dandy, Divine, Éclat, Effulgent, Excellent, Fine, Finery, Fulgor, Gallant,
Garish, Glittering, Glorious, Glory, Gorgeous, Grand(eur), Grandiose, Heroic,
Hunky-dory, Lavish, Lustrous, Majestic, Noble, Palatial, Panache, Pomp, Proud,
Radiant, Rich, Ripping, Royal, Stunning, Super(b), Superduper, Tophole, Wally,
Zia

▷**Spliced** *may indicate* an anagram

Splinter(s) Flinder, Fragment, Matchwood, Shatter, Shiver, Skelf, Sliver, Spale,
Spicula, Spill

Split(ting) Areolate, Axe, Banana, Bifid, Bifurcate, Bisect, Breach, Break, Broach,
Burst, Chasm, Chine, Chop, Chorism, Cleave, Cleft, Clint, Clove(n), Crack, Crevasse,
Cut, Decamp, Disjoin, Distrix, Disunite, → **DIVIDE**, Division, Divorce, End,
Estrange, Fissile, Fissure, Flake, Fork(ed), Fragment, Grass, Headache, Lacerate,
Left, Maul, Partition, Red(d), Rift(e), Rip, Rive, Rupture, Russian, Ryve, Schism,
Scissor, Segment, Segregate, Separate, Sever, Share, Skive, Slit, Sliver, Spall, Spalt,
Speld, Spring, Tattle, Tmesis, Told, Trifurcate, Vamoose, Wedge, Xerochasy

▷**Split** *may indicate* a word to become two; one word inside another; or a connection with Croatia (or the former Yugoslavia)

Spoil(s), Spoiler, Spoilt Addle, Air dam, Blight, Booty, Botch, Bribe, Coddle, Corrupt, →**DAMAGE**, Dampen, Deface, Defect, Defile, Deform, Disfigure, Dish, Fairing, Feather-bed, Foul, Gum, Hames, Harm, Impair(ed), Impoverish, Indulge, Loot, Maltreat, Mar, Mollycoddle, Muck, Mutilate, Mux, Pamper, Party pooper, Pet, Pickings, Pie, Pillage, Plunder, Prejudicate, Prize, Queer, Rait, Rate, Ravage, Ret, Rot, Ruin, Screw up, Scupper, Spoon-fed, Swag, Taint, Tarnish, Turn, Vitiate, Winnings, Wreck

▷**Spoil(ed), Spoilt** *may indicate* an anagram

▷**Spoken** *may indicate* the sound of a word or letter

Sponge(r), Spongy Battenburg, Bum, Cadge, →**CAKE**, Diact, Free-loader, Lig, Loofa(h), Madeira, Madeleine, Mooch, Mop, Parasite, Rum baba, Scrounge, Shule, Sop, Sucker, Swab, Sweetbriar, Sycophant, Tectratine, Tetract, Tetraxon, Tiramisu, Wangle, Wipe, Zoophyte

Sponsor(ship) Aegis, Angel, Backer, Bankroll, Egis, Finance, Godfather, Godparent, Gossip, Guarantor, Lyceum, Patron, Surety, Undertaker

Spontaneous Autonomic, Exergonic, Free, Gratuitous, Immediate, Impromptu, Improvised, Impulsive, Instant, Intuitive, Lightning, Natural, Off-the-cuff, Unrehearsed, Untaught

Spoof Chouse, Cozenage, Deception, Delusion, Fallacy, →**HOAX**, Imposture, Ramp, Swindle, Trick

Spoon(ful), Spoon-shaped Apostle, Canoodle, Cochlear, Dollop, Dose, Eucharistic, Gibby, Horn, Labis, Ladle, Mote, Neck, Rat-tail, Runcible, Salt, Scoop, Scud, Server, Spatula, Stir, Sucket, Trout, Woo, Wooden

Sport(ing), Sportive, Sports, Sporty Amusement, Bet, Blood, Breakaway, Brick, By-form, Contact, Daff, Dalliance, Dally, Demonstration, Deviant, Extreme, Field, Freak, Frisky, Frolic, Fun, →**GAME**, Gent, In, Joke, Laik, Lake, Lark, Merimake, Merry, Morph, Mutagen, Nautics, Pal, Pastime, Recreate, Rogue, Rules, Shikar, Spectator, Tournament, Tourney, Toy, Wear, Winter

▷**Sport(s)** *may indicate* an anagram

Spot(s), Spotted, Spotter, Spotting, Spotty Ace, Acne, Area, Areola, Areole, Bead, Beauty, Befoul, Bespatter, Blackhead, Blain, Blemish, Blind, Blip, Blister, Blob, Blot, Blotch(ed), Blur, Brind(l)ed, Café-au-lait, Carbuncle, Caruncle, Cash, Check, Cloud, Colon, Comedo, Corner, Cyst, Dalmatian, Dance, Dapple(-bay), Defect, Descry, Detect, Dick, Dilemma, Discern, Discover, Dot, Drop, Eruption, Espy, Eye, Flat, Flaw, Fleck, Floater, Flyspeck, Foxed, Freak, Freckle, Furuncle, G, Gay, Glimpse, Gout, High, Hot, Identify, Jam, Leaf, Lentigo, Leopard, Light, Little, Liver, Locale, Location, Loran, Mackle, Macle, Macul(at)e, Mail, Meal, Measly, Microdot, Moil, Mole, Mote, Motty, Naevoid, Naevus, Nightclub, Note, Notice, Ocellar, Ocellus, Paca, Papule, Parhelion, Patch, Peep(e), Penalty, Perceive, Performance, Pied, Pimple, Pin, Pip, Place, Plague, Plight, Plot, Pock, Point, Poxy, Predicament, Punctuate, Pupil, Pustule, Quat, Radar, Rash, Recognise, Red, Rubella, Scene, Scout, Sight, Situation, Skewbald, Smut, Soft, Soil, Speck(le), Speculum, Splodge, Spoil, Spy, Stigma, Sully, Sun, Sweet, Taint, Tar, Tight, Touch, Trace, Trouble, Venue, Weak, Whelk, Whitehead, Witness, Woodpecker, X, Yellow, Zit

Spouse Better half, Companion, Consort, Dutch, Feare, Feer, F(i)ere, Hubby, Husband, Mate, Oppo, Other half, Partner, Pheer, Pirrauru, Wife, Xant(h)ippe

Spout(er) Adjutage, Erupt, Gargoyle, Geyser, Grampus, Gush, Impawn, Jet, Mouth, Nozzle, Orate, Parrot, Pawn, Pourer, Raile, Rote, Spurt, Stream, Stroup, Talk, Tap, Vent

Sprain(ed) Crick, Reckan, Rick, Stave, Strain, Wrench, Wrick

Spray Aerosol, Aigrette, Airbrush, Antiperspirant, Atomiser, Bespatter, Blanket, Bouquet, Buttonhole, Chap, Corsage, Egret, Hair, Nebuliser, Perse, Pesticide, Posy, Rose, Rosula, Scatter, Shower, Sparge, Spindrift, Splash, Sprent, Sprig, Sprinkle, Spritz, Strinkle, Syringe, Twig, Wet

▷**Spray** *may indicate* an anagram

Spread(ing), Spreader Air, Apply, Banquet, Bestrew, Beurre, Bid offer, Blow-out, Branch, Bush, Butter, Carpet, Centre, Circumfuse, Contagious, Couch, Coverlet, Coverlid, Deploy, Diffract, Diffuse, Dilate, Disperse, Dissemination, Distribute, Divulge, Double, Double-page, Drape, Dripping, Elongate, Emanate, Engarland, Expand, Extend, Fan, Feast, Flare, Guac(h)amole, Honeycomb, Infect, Jam, Lay, Mantle, Margarine, Marge, Marmite®, Meal, Metastasis, Middle-age(d), Multiply, Mushroom, Nutter, Oleo, Open, Overgrow, Palliate, Paste, Pâté, Patent, Patté, Patulous, Perfuse, Pervade, Picnic, Pour, Proliferate, Propagate, Radiant, Radiate, Rampant, Ran, Ranch, Run, Scale, Scatter, Sea-floor, Set, Sheet, Slather, Smear, Smörgåsbord, Sow, Span, Speld, Spelder, Spillover, Splay, Sprawl, Spray, Straddle, Straw, Stretch, Strew, Strow, Suffuse, Swell, Systemic, Tath, Teer, Unfold, Unfurl, Unguent, Unroll, Vegemite®, Widen, Wildfire

▷**Spread** *may indicate* an anagram

Spring(s), Springtime, Springy Air, Arise, Axel, Black smoker, Bolt, Bounce, Bound, Box, Bunt, Cabriole, Caper, Capriole, Cavort, Cee, Coil, Dance, Elastic, Emanate, Eye, Fount(ain), Free, Gambado, Germinate, Geyser, Grass, Hair, Helix, Hop, Hot, Jeté, Jump, Leaf, Leap, Lent, Lollop, May, Mineral, Originate, Persephone, Pierian, Pounce, Prance, Primavera, Prime, Resilient, Ribbon, Rise, Saddle, Season, Skip, Snap, Source, Spa, Spang, Spaw, Start, Stem, Stot, Submarine, Sulphur, Summer, Suspension, Teal, Thermae, Thermal, Valve, Vault, Vernal, Ware, Watch, Waterhole, Weeping, Well(-head), Well up, Whip

▷**Spring(y)** *may indicate* an anagram

Sprinkle(r), Sprinkling Asperge, Aspergill(um), Bedash, Bedew, Bedrop, Bescatter, Caster, Disponge, Dispunge, Dredge, Dust, Hyssop, Lard, Papper, Pouncet, Rose, Scatter, Shower, Sift, Sow, Spa(i)rge, Spatter, Splash, Spray, Spritz, Strinkle

Sprout Braird, Breer, Bud, Burgeon, Chit, Crop, Eye, Germ(inate), Grow, Pullulate, Shoot, Spire, Tendron, Vegetate

Spruce Balsam, Dapper, Engelmann, Hemlock, Natty, Neat, Norway, Picea, Pitch-tree, Prink, Shipshape, Sitka, Smart, Snazzy, Spiff, Tidy, Tree, Trim, Tsuga

Spur(s) Accourage, Activate, Aphrodisiac, Calcar(ate), Encourage, Fame, Fire, Fuel, Gee, Gilded, Goad, Groyne, Heel, Incite, Limb, Lye, Needle, Prick, Prong, Rippon, Rowel, Shoot, Spica, Stimulus, Strut, Stud, Tar, Urge

▷**Spurious** *may indicate* an anagram

Spy(ing), Spies Agent, Beagle, Blunt, Burgess, Caleb, CIA, Descry, Dicker, Double agent, Eavesdrop, Emissary, Fink, Infiltrate, Informer, Keeker, Maclean, Mata Hari, MI, Mole, Mossad, Mouchard, Nark, Ninja, Nose, Operative, Pickeer, Pimp, Plant, Pry, Recce, Scout, See, Setter, Shadow, Sinon, Sleeper, Snoop, Spetsnaz, Spook, Tachometer, Tarpeia, Tout, Voyeur, Wait

Squalid, Squalor Abject, Colluvies, Dinge, Dingy, Filth, Frowsy, Grungy, Mean, Poverty, Scuzzy, Seedy, Skid Row, Sleazy, Slum(my), Slurb, Sordid

Squall Blast, Blow, Commotion, Cry, Drow, Flaw, Flurry, Gust, Rainstorm, Sumatra, Wail, Williwaw, Yell, Yowl

Squander Blow, Blue, Dissipate, Fritter, Frivol, Misspend, Mucker, Scamble, Slather, Splash, Splurge, Ware, → **WASTE**

Square(d), Squares Agree, Anta, Arrière, Ashlar, Ashler, Bandanna, Bang, Barrack, Belgrave, Berkeley, Bevel, Block, Bribe, Chequer, Compone, Compony, Corny, Cube, Deal, Dinkum, Dodo, Even(s), Fair, Fog(e)y, Forty-nine, Fossil, Four, Gobony, Grey, Grosvenor, Latin, Least, Leicester, Level, Madison, Magic, Market, Meal, Mean, Mitre, Nasik, Neandert(h)aler, Nine, Norma, Old-fashioned, Old school, Old-time, Out, Palm, Passé, Pay, Perfect, Piazza, Place, Platz, Plaza, Quad(rangle), Quadrate, Quarry, Quits, Red, Rhomboid, Rood, S, Set(t), Sloane, Solid, Squier, Squire, Stick-in-the-mud, Straight, T, Tee, Tiananmen, Times, Traditionalist, Trafalgar, Try, Uncool, Unhip

Squash(y) Adpress, Butternut, Conglomerate, Crush, Flatten, Gourd, Kia-ora®, Knead, Marrow, Mash, Obcompress, Oblate, Pattypan, Press, Pulp, Pumpkin, Rebut, Shoehorn, Silence, Slay, Slew, Slue, Soft, Squeeze, Squidge, Squidgy, Summer, Suppress, Torpedo, Winter

Squeeze(r) Bleed, Chirt, Clench, Coll, Compress, Concertina, Constrict, Cram, Cramp, Crowd, Crush, Dispunge, Embrace, Exact, Express, Extort, Extrude, Hug, Jam, Mangle, Milk, Pack, Preace, Press, Reamer, Sandwich, Sap, Scrooge, Scrouge, Scrowdge, Scruze, Shoehorn, Squash, Squish, Strangle, Sweat, Thrutch, Vice, Wring

Squid Calamari, Calamary, Cephalopod, Cuttlefish, Ink-fish, Loligo, Mortar, Nautilus, Octopus

▷**Squiggle** *may indicate* an anagram

Squint(ing) Boss-eyed, Cast, Cock-eye, Cross-eye, Glance, Gledge, Glee, Gley, Heterophoria, Louche, Opening, Proptosis, Skellie, Skelly, Sken, Squin(n)y, Strabism, Swivel-eye, Vergence, Wall-eye

Squire Armiger(o), Beau, Donzel, Escort, Hardcastle, Headlong, Land-owner, Sancho Panza, Scutiger, Swain, Western

Squirm(ing) Fidget, Reptation, Twist, Worm, Wriggle, Writhe

Squirt(er) Chirt, Cockalorum, Douche, Jet, Scoosh, Scoot, Skoosh, Spirt, Spout, Spritz, Urochorda, Wet, Whiffet, Whippersnapper

Stab Bayonet, Chib, Chiv, Crease, Creese, Dag, Effort, Go, Gore, Guess, Jab, Knife, Kreese, Kris, Lancinate, Pang, Pierce, Pink, Poniard, Prick, Prong, Punch, Stick, Stiletto, Turk, Wound

Stabilise(r), Stability Aileron, Anchor, Balance, Ballast, Balloonet, Emulsifier, Even, Fin, Fixure, Gyroscope, Maintain, Peg, Permanence, Plateau, Poise, Steadfastness, Steady

Stable(s) Adjusted, Augean, Balanced, Barn, Byre, Certain, Consistent, Constant, Durable, Equerry, Equilibrium, Firm, Livery, Loose box, Manger, Mews, Permanent, Poise, Sane, Secure, Settled, Solid, Sound, Stall, Static(al), Steadfast, Steady, Stud, Sure, Together, Well-adjusted

Stack(s) Accumulate, Chimney, Clamp, Cock, End, Funnel, Heap, Lum, Nest, → **PILE**, Reckan, Rick, Ruck, Shock, Sight, Smoke, Staddle

Stadium Anfield, Arena, Astrodome, Ballpark, Bowl, Circus, Circus Maximus, Coliseum, Headingley, Hippodrome, Murrayfield, Trent Bridge, Velodrome, Wembley

Staff Aesculapius, Alpenstock, Ash-plant, Bato(o)n, Bouche, Bourdon, Bread, Burden, Caduceus, Cane, Crew, Crook, Crosier, Cross(e), Crozier, Crutch,

Cudgel, Entourage, Equerry, Establishment, État-major, Faculty, Ferula, Ferule, Flagpole, General, Ground, Jacob's, Jeddart, Linstock, Lituus, Mace, Man, Office, Omlah, Pastoral, Personnel, Pike, Pole, Ragged, Rod, Rung, Runic, Sceptre, Seniority, Skeleton, Stave, Stick, Supernumerary, Taiaha, Tapsmen, Tau, Thyrsus, Token, Truncheon, Verge, Wand, Workers, Workforce, Wring

Stage Act, Anaphase, Apron, Arena, Ashrama, Bandstand, Bema, Boards, Catasta, Chrysalis, Committee, Diligence, Dog-leg, Estrade, Fargo, Fit-up, Gastrula, Grade, Hop, Imago, Instar, Juncture, Key, Landing, Leg, Levee, Level, Metaphase, Milestone, Moment, Mount, Napron, Oidium, Orbital, Perform, Phase, Phasis, Pier, Pin, Platform, Podium, Point, Postscenium, Present, Prophase, PS, Puberty, Report, Resting, Rostrum, Scene, Sensorimotor, Sound, Stadium, Step, Stepping stone, Stor(e)y, Subimago, Theatre, Theatrical, Thrust, Transition, Trek, Wells Fargo, Yuga, Zoea

Stagger(ed), Staggering Alternate, Amaze, Astichous, Astonish, Astound, Dodder, Falter, Floor, Lurch, Recoil, Reel, Rock, Sensational, Shock, Startle, Stoiter, Stot(ter), Stumble, Sway, Teeter, Thunderstruck, Titubate, Tolter, Totter, Waddle
▷**Staggered** *may indicate* an anagram

Stain(er) Aniline, Bedye, Begrime, Besmirch, Blemish, Blob, Blot, Blotch, Chica, Discolour, Dishonour, Dye, Embrue, Ensanguine, Eosin, Fox, Gram-negative, Gram-positive, Gram's, Grime, Imbrue, Inkspot, Iodophile, Keel, Maculate, Mail, Meal, Mote, Portwine, Slur, Smirch, Smit, Soil, Splodge, Splotch, Stigma, Sully, Taint, Tarnish, Tinge, Tint, Vital, Woad

Stair(case), Stairs Apples, Apples and pears, Caracol(e), Cochlea, Companionway, Escalator, Flight, Moving, Perron, Rung, Scale (and platt), Spiral, Step, Tread, Turnpike, Vice, Wapping

Stake(s) Ante, Bet, Claim, Deposit, Eclipse, Extracade, Gage, Go, Holding, Impale, Impone, Interest, Lay, Loggat, Mark, Mise, Nursery, Paal, Pale, Paling, Palisade, Peel, Peg, Pele, Picket, Pile, Play, Post, Pot, Punt, Rest, Revie, Risk, Set, Spike, Spile, Stang, Stob, Sweep, Tether, Vie, Wager, Weir

Stale Aged, Banal, Chestnut, Flat, Fozy, Frowsty, Hackneyed, Handle, Hoary, Mouldy, Musty, Old, Pretext, Rancid, Stagnant, Urine, Worn
▷**Stale** *may indicate* an obsolete word

Stalemate Deadlock, Dilemma, Draw, Hindrance, Impasse, Mexican standoff, Saw-off, Standoff, Tie, Zugzwang

Stalk(er), Stalks Bennet, Bun, Cane, Follow, Funicle, Ha(u)lm, Pedicel, Pedicle, Peduncle, Petiole, Petiolule, Phyllode, Prowler, Pursue, Reed, Scape, Seta, Shaw, Spear, Spire, Stem, Still-hunter, Stipe(s), Strae, Straw, Stride, Strig, Strut, Stubble, Stump, Trail, Yolk

Stall(s) Arrest, Bay, Booth, Box, Bulk, Crib, →**DELAY**, Floor, Flypitch, Hedge, Horse-box, Kiosk, Loose-box, Orchestra, Pen, Pew, Prebendal, Procrastinate, Seat, Shamble, Sideshow, Stable, Stand, Stasidion, Sty, Sutlery, Temporise, Trap, Traverse, Travis, Trevis(s), Whipstall

Stamina Endurance, Fibre, Fortitude, Guts, Last, Stay, Steel, Vigour

Stammer(ing) Hesitate, Hum, Stumble, Waffle

Stamp(s), Stamped Albino, Appel, Cachet, Cast, Character, Coin, Date(r), Die, Dry print, Enface, Enseal, Fiscal, Frank, Gutter-pair, Health, Imperforate, Impress, Imprint, Incuse, Kind, Label, Matchmark, Mint, Mintage, Obsign, Pane, Penny black, Perfin, Philately, Pintadera, Postage, Press(ion), Print, Rubber, Seal, Seebeck, Se-tenant, Signet, Spif, Strike, Swage, Tête-bêche, Touch, Touchmark, Trading, Trample, Tread, Tromp, Type, Visa

Stand(ing), Stand for, Stand up Apron, Arraign, Attitude, Base, Bay, Be, Bear, Bide, Bier, Binnacle, Bipod, Bristle, Brook, Caste, Cock, Cradle, Crease, Dais, Degree, Desk, Dock, Dree, Dumb-waiter, Easel, Endure, Epergne, Étagère, Extant, Face, Firedog, Foothold, Freeze, Gantry, Gueridon, Hard, Hob, Importance, Insulator, Last, Lazy Susan, Lectern, Leg, Lime, Music, Nef, Odour, One-night, Ovation, Pedestal, Place, Plant, Podium, Pose, Position, Predella, Prestige, Promenade, Protest, Qua, Rack, Rank, Regent, Remain, Represent, Repute, Rise, Rouse, Shout, Stall, Statant, Station, Stay, Stillage, Stock, Stomach, Stool, Straddle, Striddle, Stroddle, Strut, Table, Tantalus, Taxi, Teapoy, Terrace, Toe, → **TREAT**, Tree, Tripod, Trivet, Umbrella, Upright, Whatnot, Witness

Standard(s) Banner, Base, Baseline, Basic, Benchmark, Bog, Bogey, Bread and butter, British, Canon, CAT, Classic(al), Cocker, Code, Colour(s), Conventional, Copybook, Criterion, Double, Eagle, English, Ethics, Etiquette, Examplar, Example, Exemplar, Fiducial, Flag, Ga(u)ge, Gold, Gonfalon, Grade, Guidon, Horsetail, Ideal, Jolly Roger, Kite-marker, Labarum, Level, Living, Measure, Model, Morals, Netiquette, Norm(a), Normal, Numeraire, Old Glory, Oriflamme, Par, Parker Morris, Pennon, Principle, Rate, Regular, Rod, Rose, Routine, Royal, → **RULE**, Scruples, Silver, Spec(ification), Staple, Stereotype, Sterling, Stock, Time, Touchstone, Tricolour, Troy, Two-power, Uniform, Usual, Valuta, Vexillum, Yardstick

Stanza Antistrophe, Ballad, Elegiac, Envoi, Envoy, Matoke, Ottava rima, Quatrain, Spasm, Tantum ergo, Troparion

Star(s) Adept, Aster(isk), Binary, Body, Celebrity, Champ, Class act, Coma Berenices, Companion, Constant, Constellation, Cushion, Cynosure, Dark, Death, Double, Esther, Exploding, Falling, Fate, Feather, Feature, Film, Fixed, Flare, Giant, Headline, Hero, Hester, Hexagram, Idol, Late type, Lead, Leading light, Lion, Main sequence, Mogen David, Movie, Mullet, Multiple, Pentacle, Personality, Phad, Pip, Plerion, Pointer, Principal, Pulsating, Red-top, Seven, Shell, Shine, Shooting, Sidereal, Solomon's seal, Spangle, Starn(ie), Stellar, Stern, Swart, (The) Pointers, Top banana, Top-liner, Ultraviolet, Valentine, Variable, Vedette

Stare Eyeball, Fisheye, Gape, Gapeseed, Gawp, Gaze, Glare, Goggle, Gorp, Look, Ogle, Outface, Peer, Rubberneck, Scowl

Stark Apparent, Austere, Bald, Bare, Bleak, Gaunt, Harsh, Naked, Nude, Sheer, Stiff, Utterly

Start(ed), Starter, Starting, Starting-point Abrade, Abraid, Abray, Activate, Actuate, Baseline, Begin, Bhajee, Boggle, Boot-up, Bot, Broach, Bug, Bully off, Bump, Chance, Commence, Consommé, Course, Crank, Create, Crudités, Curtain up, Dart, Debut, Ean, Embryo, Entrée, Face-off, False, Fire, Flinch, Float, Flotation, Flush, Flying, Found, Gambit, Gan, Generate, Genesis, Getaway, Gun, Handicap, Head, Hors-d'oeuvres, Hot-wire, Impetus, Imprimis, Incept(ion), Initiate, Instigate, Institute, Intro(duce), Jar, Jerk, Judder, Jump, Jump lead, Jump-off, Kick-off, L, Lag, Launch, Lead, Melon, Nidus, Novice, Off, Offset, Onset, Ope(n), Ord, Origin, Outset, Poppadom, Potage, Preliminary, Prelude, Push, Put-up, Reboot, Resume, Roll, Roul, Rouse, Scare, Set off, Shy, Slip, Snail, Soup, Source, Spark, Spring, Springboard, Spud, String, Syndicate, Tee-off, Terminus a quo, Toehold, Wince

▷**Start** *may indicate* an anagram or first letters

Starvation, Starve(d), Starving Anorexia, Anoxic, Cold, Diet, Famish, Foodless, Innutrition, Perish, Pine, Undernourished

▷**Starving** *may indicate* an 'o' in the middle of a word

Stash Hide, Hoard, Secrete

State(s), Stated, Stateside Affirm, Alle(d)ge, Aread, Arrede, Assert, Assever, Attest, Aver, Avow, Buffer, Case, Circar, Cite, Client, Commonwealth, Condition, Confederate, Construct, Country, Critical, Cutch, Declare, Dependency, Dirigisme, Emirate, Empire, État, Explicit, Express, Federal, Fettle, Flap, Formulate, Free, Going, Habitus, Humour, Kingdom, Land, Lesh, Limbo, Maintain, Mess, Metastable, Mode, Morocco, Name, Nanny, Nation, Native, Palatinate, Para, Plateau, Plenarty, Plight, Police, Posit, Power, Predicament, Predicate, Premise, Profess, Pronounce, Protectorate, Puppet, Quantum, Realm, Republic, Rogue, Samadhi, Sanctitude, Satellite, Satori, Say, Sircar, Sirkar, Slave, Sorry, Standard, Standing, Steady, Succession, Sunbelt, Threeness, Thusness, Uncle Sam, Union, Welfare, Yap

▷**Stated** *may indicate* a similar sounding word

Stately, Stately home August, Dome, Grand, Imposing, Junoesque, Majestic, Mansion, Noble, Pile, Regal, Solemn

Statement Accompt, Account, Affidavit, Aphorism, Assertion, Asseveration, Attestation, Avowal, Axiom, Bill, Bulletin, Case, Communiqué, Credo, Declaration, Deposition, Description, Dictum, Diktat, Encyclical, Enigma, Evidence, Expose, Factoid, Grand Remonstrance, Impact, Invoice, Jurat, Manifesto, Mission, Motto, Non sequitur, Note, Outline, Plaint, Pleading, Press release, Profession, Pronouncement, Pronunciamento, Proposition, Quotation, Release, Report, Return, Sentence, Shema, Shout out, Soundbite, Sweeping, Testament, Testimony, Theologoumenon, Truism, Utterance, Verbal

Station(s) Action, Aid, Air, Base, Berth, Birth, Camp, Caste, CCS, Channel, Charing Cross, Coaling, Comfort, Crewe, Deploy, Depot, Docking, Dressing, Earth, Euston, Filling, Fire, Garrison, Gas, Generation, Halt, Head, Hill, Hilversum, Ice, King's Cross, Lay, Location, London Bridge, Marylebone, Meridian, Mir, New Street, Nick, Outpost, Paddington, Panic, Pay, Petrol, Pitch, Place, Plant, Point, Police, Polling, Post, Power, Powerhouse, Quarter, Radio, Rank, Relay, Rowme, Seat, Service, Sheep, Sit, Situate, Space, Stance, Stand, Star, Status, Stond, Subscriber, Tana, Tanna(h), Terminus, Testing, Thana(h), Thanna(h), Tracking, Transfer, Triangulation, Vauxhall, Victoria, Waterloo, Waverley, Way, Weather, Whistlestop, Wind farm, Wireless, Work

Statuary, Statue(tte) Acrolith, Bronze, Bust, Discobolus, Effigy, Eros, Figure, Figurine, Galatea, Idol, Image, Kore, Kouros, Liberty, Marmoreal, Memnon, Monolith, Monument, Oscar, Palladium, Pietà, Sculpture, Sphinx, Stonework, Stookie, Tanagra, Torso, Xoanon

Staunch Amadou, Leal, Resolute, Steady, Stem, Stout, Styptic, Watertight

Stay(ing), Stayer, Stays Abide, Alt, Avast, Bide, Blay, Bolster, Cohab(it), Continue, Corselet, Corset, Embar, Endure, Forbear, Fulcrum, Gest, Guest, Guy, Hawser, Hold, Indwell, Jump, Lie, Lig, Linger, Moratorium, Pause, Pernoctate, Postpone, Prop, → REMAIN, Reprieve, Respite, Restrain, Rope, Settle, Sist, Sleepover, Sojourn, Stamina, Strut, Sustain, Tarry, Visit

Steadfast Abiding, Constance, Constant, Dilwyn, Firm, Immutable, Implacable, Perseverant, Resolute, Sad, Stable, Unswerving

Steadier, Steady Andantino, Ballast, Beau, Boyfriend, Composer, Consistent, Constant, Even, Faithful, Fast, Firm, Girlfriend, Level-headed, Malstick, Measured, Regular, Rock-solid, Stabilise, Stable, Sustained, Unswerving

Steak, Steakhouse Chateaubriand, Chuck, Diane, Entrecote, Fillet, Flitch, Garni, Grill room, Mignon, Minute, Pepper, Pope's eye, Porterhouse, Ribeye, Rump, Slice, Tartare, T-bone, Tenderloin, Tournedos, Vienna

Steal(ing), Steal away Abstract, Bag, Bandicoot, Bone, Boost, Cabbage, Cly, Convey, Creep, Crib, Duff, Edge, Elope, Embezzle, Filch, Glom, Grab, Half-inch, Heist, Joyride, Kidnap, Knap, Knock down, Knock off, Lag, Liberate, Lift, Loot, Mag(g), Mahu, Mill, Misappropriate, Naam, Nam, Nap, Nick, Nim, Nip, Nobble, Nym, Peculate, Phone-jack, Pilfer, Pillage, Pinch, Piracy, Plagiarise, Plunder, Poach, Pocket, Prig, Proll, Purloin, Purse, Ram-raid, Remove, Rifle, Rip-off, Rob, Rustle, Scrump, Sculk, Shoplift, Skrimp, Skulk, Smug, Snaffle, Snatch, Sneak, Snitch, Souvenir, Swipe, Take, Theft, Thieve, Tiptoe, TWOC, Whip

Steam(ed), Steaming, Steamy Boil, Condensation, Cushion, Dry, Fume, Gaseous, Het, Humid, Live, Livid, Mist, Porn, Radio, Roke, Sauna, Snift, Spout, Vapor, Vapour, Wet

Steel(y) Bainite, Cast, Chrome, Chromium, Cold, Concrete, Damascus, Damask, High-carbon, High-speed, Low-carbon, Magnet, Manganese, Mild, Nerve, Pedal, Shear, Silver, Spray, Taggers, Terne plate

Steep(ening) Abrupt, Arduous, Bold, Brent, Buck, Cliff-face, Embay, Expensive, Hilly, Immerse, Krans, Krantz, Kranz, Macerate, Marinade, Marinate, Mask, Monocline, Plo(a)t, Precipice, Precipitous, Rait, Rapid, Rate, Ret, Saturate, Scarp, Soak, Sog, Sop, Souse, Stey, Stickle, Towery

Steer(er), Steering Ackerman, Airt, Buffalo, Bullock, Bum, Cann, Castor, Con(n), Cox, Coxswain, Direct, →GUIDE, Handlebar, Helm, Navaid, Navigate, Ox, Pilot, Ply, Rudder, Stot, Whipstaff, Zebu

Stem Alexanders, Arrow, Axial, Bind, Bine, Bole, Caudex, Caulicle, Caulome, Check, Cladode, Cladophyll, Confront, Corm, Culm, Dam, Eddo, Epicotyl, Floricane, Ha(u)lm, Kex, Originate, Pedicle, Peduncle, Pin, Rachis, Ram, Rhizome, Rise, Sarment, Scapus, Seta, Shaft, Shank, Spring, Stalk, Staunch, Stipe, Stolon, Sympodium, Tail, Tamp, Terete

Step(s) Act, Apples and pears, Balancé, Chassé, Choctaw, Companionway, Corbel, Corbie, Curtail, Dance, Degree, Démarche, Echelon, Escalate, False, Flight, Fouetté, Gain, Gait, Glissade, Goose, Grade, Grapevine, Grecian, Greece, Grees(e), Greesing, Grese, Gressing, Grice, Griece, Grise, Grize, Halfpace, Increment, Lavolt, Lock, Measure, Move, Notch, Pace, Pas, Pas de souris, Perron, Phase, Pigeon('s) wing, Quantal, Raiser, Ratlin(e), Rattlin(e), Rattling, Roundel, Roundle, Rung, Sashay, Shuffle, Slip, Stage, Stair, Stalk, Stile, Stope, Stride, Sugarfoot, Toddle, Trap, Tread, Trip, Unison, Waddle, Walk, Whole, Winder

Stereotype(d) Hackney, Ritual, Spammy

Sterile, Sterilise(r), Sterilisation, Sterility Barren, Clean, Dead, Fruitless, Impotent, Infertile, Neuter, Pasteurise, Spay, Tubal ligation, Unproductive, Vasectomy

Stern Aft, Austere, Back, Counter, Dour, Flinty, Grim, Hard, Implacable, Iron, Isaac, Nates, Poop, Rear, Relentless, Rugged, Stark, Strict, Tailpiece

Stew(ed), Stews Bath, Blanquette, Boil, Bouillabaisse, Bouilli, Bourguignon, Braise, Bredie, Broth, Brothel, Burgoo, Carbonade, Casserole, Cassoulet, Chowder, Coddle, Colcannon, Compot(e), Daube, Flap, Fricassee, Fume, Fuss, Goulash, Haricot, Hash, Hell, Hot(ch)pot(ch), Irish, Jug, Lobscouse, Matelote, Mulligan, Navarin, Olla podrida, Osso bucco, Oyster, Paddy, Paella, Pepperpot, Pot-au-feu, Pot-pourri, Ragout, Ratatouille, Salmi, Sass, Scouse, Seethe, Simmer, Squiffy, Stie, Stove, Stovies, Sty, Succotash, Sweat, Swelter

Steward(ess) Bailiff, Cabin crew, Chiltern Hundreds, Flight attendant, Keeper, Major domo, Redcoat, Sewer, Smallboy

▷**Stewed** *may indicate* an anagram

Stick(ing) (out), Stickiness, Sticks, Stuck, Sticky Adhere, Affix,
Agglutinogen, Aground, Ash, Ashplant, Attach, Backwater, Baguette, Bamboo,
Bastinado, Bat, Baton, Bauble, Bayonet, Beanpole, Blackthorn, Bludgeon, Bond,
Boondocks, Broadside, Cambrel, Cane, Celery, Cement, Chalk, Chapman, Clag,
Clam(my), Clarty, Clave, Cleave, Cleft, Cling, Clog, Club, Cocktail, Cohere,
Coinhere, Composing, Control, Crab, Crayon, Crosier, Cross(e), Crotch, Crozier,
Cue, Distaff, Divining-rod, Dog, Dure, Endure, Execration, Exsert, Fag(g)ot,
Firewood, Fix, Flak, Flypaper, Founder, Fuse, Gad(e), Gambrel, Gelatine, Glair,
Glit, Gloopy, Glue, Goad, Gold, Goo, Gore, Ground-ash, Gum, Gunge, Gunk,
Harpoon, Hob, Hold on, Hurley, Immobile, Impale, Inhere, Isinglass, Jab,
Jam, Joss, Jut, Kebbie, Kid, Kindling, Kip, Kiri, Knife, Knitch, Knobkerrie,
Lance, Lath(i), Lug, Mallet, Message, Minder, Needle, Orange, Parasitic, Paste,
Penang-lawyer, Persist, Pierce, Pin, Plaster, Pogo, Poise, Pole, Posser, Pot,
Protrude, Protuberant, Q-tip, Quarterstaff, Rapier, Rash, Ratten, Resinous,
Rhubarb, Rhythm, Rod, Ropy, Rural, Scouring, Seat, Shillela(g)h, Shooting, Size,
Ski, Smeary, Smudge, Spanish windlass, Spear, Spillikin, Spurtle, Stab, Staff,
Stand, Stang, Stob, Stodgy, Stubborn, Swagger, Switch, Swizzle, Swordstick,
Tack(y), Tally, Tar, Thick, Throwing, Toddy, Tokotoko, Truncheon, Twig, Viscid,
Viscose, Viscous, Waddy, Wait, Walking, Wand, Wattle, Waxy, Wedge, White,
Woomera(ng), Yardwand

Sticker Barnacle, Bumper, Bur, Burr, Flash, Gaum, Glue, Label, Limpet, Pin,
Poster, Post-it®, Viscose

Stiff, Stiffen(er), Stiffening, Stiffness Anchylosis, Angular, Ankylosis,
Baleen, Bandoline, Body, Brace, Buckram, Budge, Cadaver, Corpse,
Corpus, Crick, Dead, Defunct, Dilate, Expensive, Fibrositis, Firm, Formal,
Frore(n), Goner, Gromet, Grummet, Gut, Hard, Inelastic, Interfacing, Mort,
Muscle-bound, Petrify, Pokerish, Prim, Ramrod, Rheumatic(ky), Rigid, Rigor,
Rigor mortis, Sad, Set, Size, Solid, Starch, Stark, Stay, Steep, Steeve, Stieve,
Stilted, Stoor, Stour, Stowre, Sture, Tarlatan, Tensive, Unbending, Unyielding,
Upper lip, Whalebone, Wigan, Wooden

Still Accoy, Airless, Alembic, Anymore, Assuage, At rest, Becalm, Breathless,
Calm, Check, Current, Doggo, Ene, Even(ness), Howbe, However, Hush, Idle,
Illicit, Inactive, Inert, Kill, Languid, Limbec(k), Lull, Motionless, Nevertheless,
Nonetheless, Notwithstanding, Patent, Peaceful, Photograph, Placate, Placid,
Polaroid, Posé, Practitioner, Quiescent, Quiet, Resting, Retort, Serene, Silent,
Snapshot, Soothe, Stagnant, Static, Stationary, Stock, Stone, Though, Tranquil,
Windless, Yet

Stimulate, Stimulus, Stimulant, Stimulation Activate, Adrenaline,
Anilingus, Ankus, Antigen, Aperitif, Aphrodisiac, Arak, Arouse, Benny, Brace,
Caffeine, Cardiac, Cinder, Coca, Conditioned, Cue, Dart, Dex(edrine)®, Digitalin,
Digoxin, Doxapram, Egg, Energise, Erotogenic, Evoke, Excitant, Fillip, Foreplay,
Fuel, Galvanize, Ginger, Goad, Grains of Paradise, G-spot, Guinea grains, Hop
up, Hormone, Incentive, Incitant, Incite, Innerve, Inspire, Irritate, Jog, K(h)at,
Key, Kick, Mneme, Motivate, Oestrus, Pa(a)n, Paratonic, Pep, Pep pill, Peyote,
Philtre, Pick-me-up, Piquant, Potentiate, Prod, Promote, Provoke, Psych, Qat,
Rim, Ritalin®, Roborant, Rowel, Rub, Sassafras, Sensuous, Somatosensory,
Spark, Spur, Sting, Stir, String, Suggestive, Tannin, Tar, Theine, Tickle, Tik-tik,
Titillate, Tone, Tonic, Tropism, Unconditioned, Upper, Urge, Whet(stone),
Winter's bark

Sting(er), Stinging Aculeate, Barb, Bite, Cheat, Cnida, Con, Goad, Nematocyst, Nettle(tree), Overcharge, Perceant, Piercer, Poignant, Prick, Provoke, Pungent, Rile, Scorcher, Scorpion, Sea anemone, Sephen, Smart, Spice, Stang, Stimulus, Surcharge, Tang, Tingle, Trichocyst, Urent, Urtica, Venom, Wasp

Stingy Cheeseparing, Chintzy, Close, Costive, Hard, Illiberal, Mean, Miserly, Narrow, Near, Nippy, Parsimonious, Save-all, Snippy, Snudge, Tight(wad), Tight-arse

▷**Stingy** *may indicate* something that stings

Stipulate, Stipulation Clause, Condition, Covenant, Insist, Provision, Proviso, Rider, Specify, String

Stir(red), Stirrer, Stirring Accite, Admix, Ado, Afoot, Agitate, Amo(o)ve, Animate, Annoy, Araise, Arouse, Awaken, Bother, Bustle, Buzz, Can, Churn, Cooler, Emotional, Emotive, Evocative, Excite, Foment, Furore, Fuss, Gaol, Hectic, Impassion, Incense, Incite, Inflame, Inspire, Insurrection, Intermix, Jee, Jog, Jug, Kitty, Limbo, Live, Makebate, →**MIX**, Molinet, Move, Newgate, Nick, Noy, Poach, Poss, Pother, →**PRISON**, Prod, Provoke, Quad, Quatch, Quetch, Qui(t)ch, Quinche, Quod, Rabble(-rouse), Rear, Roil, Rouse, Roust, Rummage, Rustle, Sod, Steer, Styre, Swizzle, To-do, Touch, Upset, Upstart, Wake

▷**Stir(red), Stirring** *may indicate* an anagram

Stitch(ing), Stitch up Bargello, Bar tack, Basket, Baste, Blanket, Blind, Box, Buttonhole, Cable, Chain, Couching, Crewel, Crochet, Cross, Daisy, Embroider, Fancy, Feather, Fell, Flemish, Florentine, Garter, Gathering, Grospoint, Hem, Herringbone, Honeycomb, Insertion, Kettle, Knit, Lazy daisy, Lock, Machine, Middle, Monk's seam, Moss, Needle, Open, Overlock, Pearl, Petit point, Pinwork, Plain, Purl, Queen, Rag, Railway, Rib, Rope, Running, Saddle, Satin, Screw, Sew, Slip, Smocking, Spider, Split, Stab, Stay, Steek, Stem, Stockinette, Stocking, Straight, Sutile, Suture, Tack, Tailor's tack, Tent, Topstitch, Wheat-ear, Whip, Whole, Zigzag

Stock(ed), Stockpile, Stocks, Stocky Aerie, Aery, Alpha, Ambulance, Arsenal, Barometer, Blue-chip, Bouillon, Bree, Breech, Buffer, But(t), Capital, Cards, Carry, Cattle, Choker, Cippus, Common, Congee, Court-bouillon, Cravat, Crop, Dashi, Debenture, Delta, Die, Endomorph, Equip, Evening, Fumet, Fund, Gamma, Gear(e), Government, Graft, Gravy, Growth, Gun, Hackneyed, Handpiece, He(a)rd, Hilt, Hoard, Hoosh, Industrial, Intervention, Inventory, Joint, Just-in-time, Kin, Larder, Laughing, Line, Little-ease, Log, Night-scented, Omnium, Pigeonhole, Preferred, Pycnic, Race, Ranch, Recovery, Rep(ertory), Replenish, Reserve, Resource, Rolling, Root, Scrip, Seed, Shorts, Soup, Squat, Staple, Stash, Steale, Steelbow, Stereotype, Stirp(e)s, →**STORE**, Strain, Stubby, Supply, Surplus, Talon, Tap, Taurus, Team, Thickset, Tie, Trite, Trust(ee), Usual, Utility, Virginian, Water

Stocking(s) Body, Fishnet, Hogger, Hold ups, Hose, Hosiery, Leather, Legwear, Moggan, Netherlings, Netherstocking, Nylons, Popsock, Seamless, Sheer, Silk, Sock, Spattee, Surgical, Tights

Stole(n) Bent, Boa, Epitrachelion, Fichu, Hot, Maino(u)r, Manner, Manor, Nam, Orarion, Orarium, Reft, Scarf, Screen, Soup, Staw, Tippet, Waif, Wrap

Stomach(ic) Abdomen, Abomasum, Accept, Alvine, Appetite, Belly, Bible, Bingy, Bonnet, Bread-basket, Brook, C(o)eliac, Corporation, Craw, Epiploon, Face, Gaster, Gastric, Gizzard, Gut, Heart, Inner man, Jejunum, King's-hood, Kite, Kyte, Little Mary, Manyplies, Mary, Maw, Mesaraic, Midriff, Omasum, Opisthosoma, Paunch, Potbelly, Psalterium, Puku, Pylorus, Rennet, Reticulum,

Rumen, Stand, Stick, Swagbelly, **→ SWALLOW**, Tripe, Tum, Tun-belly, Urite, Uromere, Vell, Venter, Wame, Washboard, Wem

Stool Bar, Buffet, Commode, Coppy, Cracket, Creepie, Cricket, Cucking, Curule, Cutty, Faeces, Foot, Hassock, Litany, Milking, Piano, Pouf(fe), Ruckseat, Seat, Sir-reverence, Step, Stercoral, Sunkie, Taboret, Tripod, Turd

Stop(page), Stopcock, Stopper, Stopping Abate, Abort, Adeem, Anchor, Aperture, Arrest, Aspirate, Avast, Avert, Bait, Ba(u)lk, Belay, Bide, Block, Brake, Buffer, Bung, Can, Carillon, **→ CEASE**, Cessation, Chapter, Check, Checkpoint, Cheese, Clarabella, Clarino, Clarion, Clog, Close, Cog, Colon, Comfort, Comma, Conclude, Conversation, Cork, Coupler, Cremo(r)na, Cut, Cut out, Deactivate, Debar, Demurral, Desist, Deter, Devall, Diapason, Diaphone, Discontinue, Discourage, Dit, Dock, Dolce, Dot, Drop, Echo, Embargo, Emergency, End, Enough, Expression, Extinguish, F, Fagotto, Fare stage, Field, Fifteenth, Flag (down), Flue, Flute, Forbid, Foreclose, Forestall, Foundation, Freeze, Frustrate, Full, Full point, Gag, Gamba, Gemshorn, Glottal, Gong, Halt, Hang, Hartal, Heave to, Hinder, Hitch, Ho, Hoa, Hoh, Hold, Hoy, Inhibit, Intermit, Jam, Kibosh, Kill, Lay to, Let-up, Lill, Lin, Lute, Media, Moratoria, Mutation, Nasard, Oboe, Obstruent, Obturate, Occlude, Oppilate, Organ, Outage, Outspan, Pack in, Pause, Period, Piccolo, Pit, Plug, Point, Poop, Preclude, Prevent, Principal, Prop, Prorogue, Pull-in, Pull over, Pull-up, Punctuate, Pyramidon, Quash, Quint, Quit, Racket, Red, Reed, Refrain, Register, Rein, Remain, Request, Rest, Roadblock, Salicional, Scotch, Screw-top, Semi-colon, Sext, Silence, Sist, Sneb, Snub, Snuff out, Sojourn, Solo, Spigot, Stall, Stanch, Standstill, Stap, Stash, Stasis, Station, Staunch, Stay, Stent, Stive, Strike, Subbase, Suction, Supersede, Suppress, Surcease, Suspend, T, Tab, Tackle, Tamp(ion), Tap, Tea break, Tenuis, Terminate, Thwart, Toby, Truck, Trumpet, Tuba, Twelfth, Voix celeste, Waypoint, When, Whistle, Whoa

Storage, Store(house) Accumulate, Archive, Armoury, Arsenal, Associative, Backing, Barn, Big box, Bin, Bookshop, Bottle, Bottom drawer, Boxroom, Buffer, Bunker, Buttery, Byte, Cache, Capacitance, Catacomb, Cell, Cellar(et), Chain, Cheek pouch, Clamp, Clipboard, Coffer, Convenience, Co-op(erative), Core, Corn-crib, Cupboard, Cutch, Database, Deep freeze, Deli, Dene-hole, Dépanneur, Department(al), Depository, Depot, Dime, Discount, Dolly-shop, Drive, EAROM, Elevator, Emporium, Ensile, Entrepot, Étape, External, Freezer, Fridge, Fund, Galleria, Garner, Gasholder, Girnal, Glory hole, Go-down, Granary, Hayloft, Hive, **→ HOARD**, Hog, Hold, Honeycomb, Hope chest, House, Houseroom, Humidor, Husband, Hypermarket, IKEA, Keep, Larder, Lastage, Liquor, Locker, Lumber room, Magazine, Main, Mart, Meat safe, Memory, Mine, Minimart, Morgue, Mothball, Mow, Multiple, Nest-egg, Off-licence, One-step, Ottoman, Package, Pantechnicon, Pantry, Pithos, Preserve, Provision, Pumped, Rack(ing), RAM, Reel, Repertory, Reposit, ROM, Root house, Save, Sector, Shed, **→ SHOP**, Silage, Silo, Sim card, Speakeasy, Spence, Springhouse, Squirrel, Stack, Stash, Stillroom, Stock, Stockpile, Stockroom, Stow, Superbaza(a)r, Superette, Supermarket, Supply, Tack-room, Tank, Thesaurus, Tithe-barn, Tommy-shop, Trading post, Uplay, Vestiary, Vestry, Virtual, Warehouse, Woodshed, Woodyard, Wool (shed), WORM

▶**Storey** *see* **STORY**

Storm(y) Ablow, Adad, Assail, Assault, Attack, Baguio, Blizzard, Bluster, Brouhaha, Buran, Charge, Cloudburst, Cockeye(d) bob, Cyclone, Devil, Dirty, Dust, Electric, Enlil, Expugn, Furore, Gale, Gusty, Haboob, Hurricane, Ice, Line,

Magnetic, Monsoon, Onset, Pelter, Rage(ful), Raid, Rain, Rampage, Rant, Rate, Rave, Red spot, Rugged, Rush, Shaitan, Snorter, Squall, Tea-cup, Tempest, Tornade, Tornado, Tropical, Turmoil, Unruly, Violent, Weather, White squall, Willy-willy, Zu

▷**Stormy** *may indicate* an anagram

Story, Storyline, Stories Account, Actioner, Allegory, Anecdote, Apocrypha, Apologise, Attic, Bar, Basement, Baur, Bedtime, Biog, Blood and thunder, Chapbook, Chestnut, Clearstory, Clerestory, Cock and bull, Conte, Cover, Decameron, Detective, Edda, Epic, Episode, Etage, Exclusive, Fable, Fabliau, Fabrication, Falsehood, Feature, Fib, Fiction, Flat, Floor, Folk-lore, Folk-tale, Gag, Geste, Ghost, Glurge, Hair-raiser, Hard-luck, Heptameron, Horror, Idyll, Iliad, Jataka, Lee, Legend, Lie, Lore, Märchen, Mezzanine, Myth(os), Mythus, Narrative, Nouvelle, Novel(la), Oratorio, Parable, Passus, Pentameron, Photo, Plot, Rede, Report, Roman a clef, Romance, Rumour, Saga, Scoop, Script, Serial, SF, Shaggy dog, Shocker, Short, Smoke-room, Sob, Spiel, Spine-chiller, Splash, Spoiler, Stage, Storey, Success, Tale, Tall, Thread, Thriller, Tier, Tragedy, Triforium, Upper, Version, Whodun(n)it, Yarn

Storyteller Aesop, Fibber, Grimm, Griot, Liar, Miller, Munchausen, Narrator, Raconteur, Sagaman, Shannachie, Tusitala, Uncle Remus

Stout(ness) Ale, Burly, Chopping, Chubby, Cobby, Corpulent, Doughty, Embonpoint, Endomorph, Entire, Fat, Fubsy, Guinness, Hardy, Heavyset, Humpty-dumpty, Lusty, Manful, Milk, Obese, Overweight, Plump, Porter, Portly, Potbelly, Robust, Rotund, Stalwart, Stalworth, Sta(u)nch, Strong, Stuggy, Sturdy, Substantial, Tall, Tufty

Stove Aga, Baseburner, Break, Calefactor, Chauf(f)er, Chiminea, Cockle, Cooker, Cooktop, Furnace, Gasfire, Hob, Oven, Potbelly, Primus®, Range, Salamander

Straggle(r), Straggly Estray, Gad, Meander, Ramble, Rat-tail, Spidery, Sprawl, Stray, Wander

Straight(en), Straightness Align, Bald, Beeline, Blunt, Boning, Correct, Die, Direct, Downright, Dress, Frank, Gain, Het(ero), Honest, Lank, Legit, Level, Line, Narrow, Normal, Ortho-, Rectilineal, Rectitude, Righten, Sheer, Slap, Tidy, True, Unbend, Unbowed, Uncoil, Unlay, Upright, Veracious, Virgate

Straightforward Candid, Direct, Downright, Easy, Even, Forthright, Honest, Jannock, Level, Plain sailing, Pointblank, Simple, Uncomplicated

Strain(ed), Strainer, Straining Agonistic, Air, Ancestry, Aria, Breed, Bulk, Carol, Charleyhorse, Clarify, Colander, Distend, Drawn, Effort, Exert, Filter, Filtrate, Fit, Fitt(e), Force, Fray, Fytt(e), Intense, Kind, Lineage, Lullaby, Melody, Milsey, Minus, Molimen, Music, Nervy, Note, Overstretch, Overtask, Passus, Percolate, Pressure, Pull, Rack, Raring, Reck(an), Repetitive, Retch, Rick, Seep, Seil(e), Set, Shear, Sieve, Sift, Sile, Stape, Start, Stirps, Stock, Streak, Stress, Stretch, Stripe, Sye, Tamis, Tammy, Taut, Tax, Tems(e), Tenesmus, Tense, Tension, Threnody, Try, Vein, Vice, Work, Wrick

Strait(s) Bab el Mandeb, Basilan, Desperate, Dire, Dover, Drake Passage, East River, Florida, Golden Gate, Great Belt, Hainan, Kerch, Mackinac, Mona Passage, North Channel, Oresund, Soenda, Sumba, Tatar, Tiran, Tsugaru, Windward Passage

Strange(ness), Stranger Abnormal, Alien, Aloof, Amphitryon, Bizarre, Curious, Dougal, Eccentric, Eerie, Exotic, Ferly, Foreign, Fraim, Freaky, Frem(d), Fremit, Frenne, Funny, Guest, Jimmy, Malihini, New, Novel, Odd(ball), Outlandish, Outsider, Quare, Quark, Queer, Rum, S, Screwy, Selcouth, Singular,

Surreal, Tea-leaf, Uncanny, Unco, Uncommon, Unfamiliar, Unked, Unket, Unkid, Unused, Unusual, Wacky, Weird, Weyard, Wondrous

▷**Strange** *may indicate* an anagram

Strap(ping) Able-bodied, Band, Barber, Beat, Bowyangs, Braces, Brail, Braw, Breeching, Browband, Cheekpiece, Crownpiece, Crupper, Cuir-bouilli, Curb, Deckle, Garter, Girth, G-string, Halter, Harness, Holdback, Jess, Jock(ey), Kicking, Larrup, Lash, Leather, Ligule, Lorate, Lore, Manly, Martingale, Nicky-tam, Octopus, Overcheck, Palmie, Pandy, Rand, Rein, Robust, Shoulder, Sling, Spaghetti, Spider, Strop, Surcingle, Suspender, T, Tab, Taws(e), T-bar, Thong, Thoroughbrace, Throatlash, Throatlatch, Trace, Tump-line, Wallop, Watch, Watchband

Stratagem, Strategist, Strategy Artifice, Clausewitz, Contrivance, Coup, Deceit, Device, Dodge, Exit, Fetch, Finesse, Fraud, Game plan, Generalship, Guile, Heresthetic, Kaupapa, Lady Macbeth, Malengine, Manoeuvre, Maskirovka, Masterstroke, Maximum, Minimax, Plan, Realpolitik, Rope-a-dope, Salami, Scheme, Scorched earth, Sleight, Subterfuge, Tack, Tactic(s), Tactician, Trick, Wheeze, Wile

Straw(s), Strawy Balibuntal, Boater, Buntal, Chaff, Cheese, Crosswort, Halm, Hat, Haulm, Hay, Insubstantial, Kemple, Last, Leghorn, Nugae, Oaten, Panama, Parabuntal, Pedal, Rush, Stalk, Strae, Stramineous, Strammel, Strummel, Stubble, Sucker, Trifles, Truss, Wisp, Ye(a)lm

Stray(ing) Abandoned, Aberrant, Alleycat, Chance, Depart, Deviate, Digress, Err, Excursion, Forwander, Foundling, Maverick, Meander, Misgo, Pye-dog, Ramble, Roam, Sin, Straggle, Streel, Street arab, Traik, Unowned, Waff, Waif, Wander, Wilder

Streak(ed), Streaker, Streaky Bended, Blue, Brindle, Comet, Flambé, Flaser, Flash, Fleck, Freak, Hawked, Hawkit, Highlights, Lace, Layer, Leonid, Lowlight, Marble, Mark, Merle, Mottle, Primitive, Race, Ra(t)ch, Run, Schlieren, Seam, Shot, Splodge, Striate, Striga, Strip(e), Vein, Venose, Vibex, Waif, Wake, Wale, Yellow

Stream Acheron, Beam, Beck, Blast, Bourne, Brook, Burn, Consequent, Course, Current, Driblet, Fast, Flow, Flower, Freshet, Ghyll, Gill, Gulf, Gush, Headwater, Influent, Influx, Jet, Kill, Lade, Lane, Leet, Logan, Meteor, Nala, Nalla(h), Nulla(h), Obsequent, Onflow, Pokelogan, Pour, Pow, Riffle, Rill, River, Rivulet, Rubicon, Run, Runnel, Sike, Slough, Spill, Spruit, Squirt, Star, Strand, Streel, Subsequent, Syke, The Fleet, Third, Thrutch, Tide-race, Torrent, Tributary, Trickle, Trout, Watercourse, Water-splash, Winterbourne

Streamer Banner(all), Ribbon, Tape, Tippet

Street Alley, Ave(nue), Bay, Boulevard, Bowery, Broad, Broadway, Carey, Carnaby, Cato, Causey, Cheapside, Civvy, Close, Corso, Court, Crescent, Downing, Drive, Easy, Ermine, Fleet, Gate, Grub, Harley, High(way), Lane, Main drag, Meuse, Mews, One-way, Parade, Paseo, Poultry, Queer, Road(way), Side, Sinister, St, Strand, Terrace, Thoroughfare, Threadneedle, Throgmorton, Wall, Wardour, Watling, Way, Whitehall

Strength(en), Strengthened, Strengthener, Strengthening Afforce, Anneal, Arm, Asset, Augment, Bant, Beef, Brace, Brawn, Build, Confirm, Consolidate, Edify, Embattle, Enable, Energy, Fish, Foison, Force, Force majeure, Forte, Fortify, Fortitude, Freshen, Fur, Fus(h)ion, Grit, Herculean, Horn, Integrity, Intensity, Invigorate, Iron, Lace, Line, Main, Man, Might, Munite, Muscle, Neal, Nerve, → **POWER**, Prepotence, Pre-stress, Proof, Reinforce,

Roborant, Shear, Sinew, Spike, Spine, Stamina, Steel, Sthenia, Stoutness,
→**STRONG**, Sustain, Tensile, Thews, Titration, Unity, Vigour, Vim, Willpower

Stress(ed), Stressful Actuate, Angst, Careworn, Creep, Drive home, Highlight,
Nerves, Oxidative, Paroxytone, Post-traumatic, Press, Primary, Proclitic,
Rhythm, Secondary, Sentence, Shear, Testing, Thetic, Tonic, Umlaut, Wind
shear, Word, Yield (point)

Stretch(able), Stretched, Stretcher, Stretching Acreage, Alength,
Amplitude, Belt, Brick, Crane, Distend, Doolie, Draw, Ectasis, Eke, Elastic,
Elongate, Exaggerate, Expanse, Extend, Extensile, Farthingale, Fib, Frame, Give,
Gurney, Home, Lengthen, Lie, Life, Limo, Litter, Narrows, Outreach, Pallet,
Porrect, Procrustes, Prolong, Protend, Pull, Rack, Rax, →**REACH**, Sentence,
Shiner, Spell, Spread, Strain, Streak, Taut, Tend, Tense, Tensile, Tenter, Term,
Time, Tract, Tractile, Traction, Tree, Trolley

Strict(ly) Authoritarian, De rigueur, Dour, Exacting, Fundamentalist, Hard and
fast, Harsh, Literal, Orthodox, Penal, Puritanical, Religious, Rigid, Rigorous,
Severe, Spartan, Stern, Strait(-laced)

Stride(s) Gal(l)umph, Jeans, Leg, Lope, March, Pace, Piano, Stalk, Sten, Stend,
Straddle, Stroam, Strut, Stump

Strident Brassy, Discordant, Grinding, Harsh, Raucous, Screech, Shrill

Strife Bargain, Barrat, Bate(-breeding), Brigue, Conflict, Contest, Discord,
Disharmony, Dissension, Feud, Food, Friction, Ignoble, Scrap(ping)

Strike(r), Striker, Striking, Strike out Affect, Air, Alight, Annul, Arresting,
Astonishing, Attitude, Backhander, Baff, Band, Bang, Bash, Bat, Baton, Batsman,
Batter, Beat, Belabour, Better, Biff, Black, Bla(u)d, Bludgeon, Bonanza, Bop, British
disease, Buff, Buffet, Butt, Cane, Catch, Chime, Chip, Clap, Clash, Clatch, Clip,
Clock, Clout, Club, Cob, Collide, Conk, Constitutional, Coup, Cue, Cuff, Dad, Dele,
Dent, Dev(v)el, Ding, Dint, Dismantle, Douse, Dowse, Dramatic, Drive, Dush,
Éclat, Effective, Emphatic, Especial, Fat, Fet(ch), Fillip, Firk, Fist, Flail, Flog, Frap,
General, Get, Gnash, Go-slow, Gowf, Hail, Handsome, Hartal, Head-butt, →**HIT**,
Horn, Hour, Hunger, Ictus, Illision, Impact, Impinge, Impress, Jarp, Jaup, Jole,
Joll, Joule, Jowl, Knock, Lam, Lambast, Laser, Lash, Lay(-off), Lightning, Match,
Memorable, Middle, Mint, Notable, Noticeable, Official, Out, Pash, Pat(ter), Pat,
Peen, Percuss, Picket, Plectrum, Pounce, Pound, Pronounced, Pummel, Punch,
Quarter-jack, Rag-out, Raid, Ram, Rap, Remarkable, Rolling, Salient, Scrub,
Scutch, Shank, Sick out, Sideswipe, Signal, Sitdown, Sit-in, Sizzling, Slam, Slap,
Slat, Slog, Slosh, Smack, Smash, Smite, Sock, Souse, Spank, Stayaway, Stop(page),
Stub, Swap, Swat, Swinge, Swipe, Switch, Swop, Sympathy, Tan, Tangent, Tat,
Thump, Thwack, Tip, Token, Tripper, Twat, Unconstitutional, Unofficial, Vivid,
Walk-out, Wallop, Wap, Whack, Whale, Whang, Whap, Wherret, Who does
what, Wildcat, Wipe, Wondrous, Zap

String(s), Stringy Anchor, Band, Bant, Beads, Bootlace, Bow, Cello, Chalaza,
Chanterelle, Cord, Cosmic, Drill, Enfilade, Fiddle, First, Floss, G, Glass, Gut,
Henequin, Hypate, Idiot, Injection, Keyed, Kill, Lace, Lag, Laisse, Leading,
Lichanos, Macramé, Mese, Necklace, Nete, Nicky-tam, Oil, Paranete,
Production, Proviso, Purse, Quint, Ripcord, Rope, Rosary, Rough, Second,
Series, Shoe(-tie), Silly®, Sinewy, Snare, Spit, Stable, Straggle, Strand, Sultana,
Sympathetic, Team, Tendon, Thairm, Tie, Tough, Train, Trite, Twiddling-line,
Viola, Violin, Worry-beads, Wreathed

Strip(ped), Stripper, Stripping, Striptease Agent orange, Airfield,
Armband, Asset, Band(eau), Bare, Bark, Batten, Belt, Bereave, Bimetallic,

Blowtorch, Caprivi, Chippendale, Comic, Cote, Defoliate, Denude, Deplume, Deprive, Derobe, Despoil, Devest, Disbark, Dismantle, Dismask, Disrobe, Divest, Doab, Dosing, Drag, Écorché, Excorticate, Fannel(l), Feeler gauge, Fiche, Film, Flashing, Flaught, Flay, Fleece, Flench, Flense, Flight, Flinch, Flounce, Flype, Furring, Gaza, Goujon, Hatband, Infula, Jib, Label, Landing, Lap-dancer, Lardon, Lath, Ledge, Linter, List, Littoral, Loading, Locust, Magnetic, Mail-rod, Maniple, Median, Möbius, Nature, Nude, Paint, Panhandle, Parting, Peel, Pillage, Pluck, Pull, Puttee, Puttie, Rand, Raunch, Raw, Reglet, Reservation, Riband, Ribbon, Rifle, Roon, Royne, Rumble, Rund, Runway, Scent, Screed, Scrow, Shear, Shed, Shim, Shorn, Shred, Shuck, Skin, Slat, Slit, Sliver, Spellican, Spilikin, Spill(ikin), Splat, Splent, Spline, Splint, Splinter, Spoil, Sportswear, Straik, Strake, Strap, Streak, Strop, Sugar soap, Swath(e), Sweatband, Tack, Tear, Tear-off, Tee, Thong, Tirl, Tirr, Tombolo, Tongue, Trash, Unbark, Uncase, Unclothe, Undeck, Undress, Unfrock, Unrig, Unrip, Unrobe, Valance, Weather, Zona, Zone

Strive, Striving Aim, Aspire, →**ATTEMPT**, Contend, Emulous, Endeavour, Enter, Kemp, Labour, Nisus, Persevere, Pingle, Press, Strain, Struggle, Toil, Try, Vie

Stroke Apoplex(y), Backhander, Bat, Bisque, Blow, Boast, Breast, Butterfly, Caress, Carom, Chip, Chop, Counterbuff, Coup, Coy, Crawl, Dab, Dash, Dint, Dog(gy)-paddle, Down-bow, Drear(e), Dropshot, Effleurage, Exhaust, Feat, Flick, Fondle, Forehand, Glance, Ground, Hairline, Hand(er), Hyphen, Ictus, In-off, Jenny, Jole, Joll, Joule, Jowl, Knell, Knock, Lash, Lightning, Like, Line, Loft, Long jenny, Loser, Master, Oarsman, Oblique, Odd, Off-drive, Outlash, Palp, Paw, Pile-driver, Pot-hook, Pull, Punto reverso, Put(t), Reverso, Ridding straik, Roquet, Rub, Scart, Scavenge, Sclaff, Scoop, Seizure, Serif, Seriph, Sheffer's, Short Jenny, Sider, Sixte, Slash, Slice, Smooth, Solidus, Spot, Strike, Stripe, Sweep, Swipe, Tact, Tittle, Touch, Touk, Trait, Trudgen, Trudgeon, Tuck, Upbow, Virgule, Wale, Whang, Wrist shot

Strong(est) Able, Boofy, Brawny, Buff, Cast-iron, Doughty, Durable, F, Fat, Fierce, Fit, Forceful, Forcible, Forte, Hale, Hercules, High-powered, Humming, Husky, Intense, Ironside, Keen, Marrowy, Mature, Mighty, Muscular, Nappy, Ox, Pithy, Pollent, Potent, Powerful, Predominant, Pronounced, Pungent, Racy, Rank, Robust, Samson, Solid, Sour, Stale, Stalwart, Stark, Steely, Sthenic, Stiff, Stout, Str, Strapping, →**STRENGTH**, Sturdy, Substantial, Suit, Tarzan, Theory, Thesis, Thewy, Thickset, Tough, Trusty, Valid, Vegete, Vehement, Vigorous, Violent, Well-set, Wight, Ya(u)ld

Stronghold Acropolis, Aerie, Bastion, Castle, Citadel, Eyrie, Fastness, Fortalice, Fortress, Holt, Keep, Kremlin, Redoubt, Tower

Structural, Structure Acrosome, Analysis, Anatomy, Arch, Armature, Atomic, Building, Centriole, Chromosome, Conus, Darga(h), Database, Edifice, Erection, Fabric, Fairing, Flaser, Format(ion), Frame, Gantry, Headframe, Helictite, Hut, Ice-apron, Idant, Lantern, Lattice, Malpighian, Manubrium, Mole, Organic, Ossature, Pagoda, Parawalker, Pea-trainer, Pediment, Pergola, Physique, Prophyll, Shape, Shell, Shoring, Skeleton, Squinch, Staging, Stand, Starling, Syntax, System, Texas, Texture, Thylakoid, Trabecula, Trilithon, Trochlea, Undercarriage

Struggle, Struggling Agon(ise), Agonistes, Amelia, Battle, Buckle, Camp, Chore, Class, Combat, Conflict, Contend, Contest, Cope, Debatement, Duel, Effort, Encounter, Endeavour, Exertion, Fag, Fight, Flounder, Grabble, Grapple,

Hassle, Jockey, Kampf, Labour, Luctation, Maul, Mill, Pingle, Rat-race, Reluct, Resist, Scrabble, Scramble, Scrape, Scrimmage, Scrum, Scrummage, Scuffle, Slugfest, Sprangle, Strain, Strift, → **STRIVE**, Toil, Tug, Tuilyie, Tussle, Up a tree, Uphill, Vie, War(sle), Warfare, Work, Wraxle, Wrest(le)

▷**Struggle** *may indicate* an anagram

Stubborn(ness) Adamant, Bigoted, Bulldog, Bull-headed, Contumacious, Cross-grained, Cussed, Diehard, Entêté, Hard(-nosed), Hidebound, Intransigent, Inveterate, Moyl(e), Mulish, Mumpsimus, Obdurate, Obstinate, Opinionated, Ornery, Ortus, Pertinacious, Perverse, Recalcitrant, Reesty, Refractory, Rigwiddie, Rigwoodie, Self-willed, Stiff, Stoor, Tenacious, Thrawn, Tough, Wrong-headed

Stud(ded) Doornail, Entire, Farm, Frost, Press, Shear, Shirt, Stop

Student(s) Abiturient, Alumnus, Apprentice, Bajan, Bejant, Bursar, Cadet, Candle-waster, Classmate, Coed, Collegian, Commoner, Dan, Dig, Disciple, Dresser, Dux, Exchange, Exhibitioner, External, Form, Fresher, Freshman, Goliard, Gownsman, Graduand, Green welly, Grind, Gyte, Hafiz, Ikey, Internal, Junior, → **LEARNER**, Lucubrator, Magistrand, Matie, Mature, Medical, Mootman, NUS, Opsimath, Ordinand, Oxonian, Plebe, Poll, Postgraduate, Preppy, Pupil, Reader, Rushee, Sap, → **SCHOLAR**, Self-taught, Semi, Seminar, Senior, Shark, Sixth former, Sizar, Sizer, Smug, Softa, Soph(omore), Sophister, Spod, Subsizar, Swat, Swot, Talibe, Templar, Tiro, Tosher, Trainee, Tuft, Tukkie, Tutee, Underclassman, Undergraduate, Welly, Witsie, Wooden spoon, Wooden wedge, Wrangler, Year

Study, Studies, Studied, Studious, Studying Analyse, Bionics, Bone, Brown, Carol, Carrell, Case, Classics, Comparability, Con(ne), Conscious, Consider, Course(work), Cram, Den, Dig, Étude, Examine, Eye, Feasibility, Field, Gen up, Intramural, Isagogics, Lair, Learn, Liberal, Media, Motion, Mug up, Mull, Muse, Nature, Ology, Perusal, Peruse, Pilot, Pore, Portrayal, Post-doctoral, Prep(aration), Probe, Read, Recce, Reconnoitre, Research, Revise, Sanctum, Sap, Scan, Science, Scrutinise, Shiur, Sketch, Swat, Swot, Take, Time and motion, Trade-off, Train, Tutorial, Typto, Voulu, Work

Stuff(iness), Stuffing, Stuffy Airless, Bloat, Canvas, Close, Cloth, Cloy, Codswallop, Cram, Crap, Dimity, Equipment, Farce, Feast, Fiddlesticks, Fill, Force, Forcemeat, Formal, Frows(t)y, Frowzy, Fug, Gear, Glut, Gobble, Gorge, Gubbins, Guff, Hair, Havers, Hooey, Horsehair, Inlay, Kapok, Lard, Line, Linen, → **MATERIAL**, Matter, No-meaning, Nonsense, Overeat, Pad, Pang, Panne, Pompous, Ram, Replete, Rot, Sate, Scrap, Sob, Stap, Steeve, Stew, Substance, Surfeit, Taxidermy, Trig, Upholster, Wad, Youth

Stumble Blunder, Daddle, Err, Falter, Flounder, Founder, Lurch, Peck, Snapper, Stoit, Titubate, Trip

Stun(ned), Stunning Astonish, Astound, Awhape, Bewilder, Bludgeon, Concuss, Cosh, Daze, Dazzle, Deafen, Dove(r), Drop-dead, Eclectic, Fantastic, Faze, Flabbergast, Glam, Gobsmack, KO, Numb, Poleaxe, Shell-shocked, Shock, Stoun, Stupefy

Stunt(ed) Aerobatics, Confine, Droichy, Dwarf, Exploit, Feat, Gimmick, Hot-dog, Hype, Jehad, Jihad, Loop, Nirl, Puny, Ront(e), Runt, Ruse, Scroggy, Scrub(by), Scrunt(y), Stub, Trick, Wanthriven

Stupid, Stupid person Anserine, Asinine, Besotted, Blithering, Blockish, Braindead, Clay-brained, Crass, Daft, Datal, Dense, Desipient, Dim(wit), Dip, Donner(e)d, Dozy, Dull(ard), Fatuous, Flat, Gaumless, Gross, Half-arsed,

Half-baked, Hammerheaded, Hare-brained, Hatter, Hen-witted, Inane, Insensate, Insipient, Lamming, Mindless, Natural, Obtuse, Senseless, Silly, Sodden-witted, Thick, Thick-witted, Torpid, Witless, Wooden(head)

Sturdy Burly, Dunt, Gid, Hardy, Hefty, Lusty, Robust, Rugged, Solid, Stalwart, Staunch, Steeve, Stocky, Strapping, Strong, Thickset, Turnsick, Vigorous

Style(s), Stylish, Stylist Adam, À la, A-line, Anime, Art nouveau, Band, Barocco, Barock, Baroque, Bel canto, Blocked, Blow-dry, Brachylogy, Burin, Call, Chic, Chi-chi, Chippendale, Class, Cultism, Cursive, Cut, Dapper, Dash, Decor, Decorated, Demotic, Diction, Dress sense, Dub, Dude, Élan, Elegance, Empire, Entitle, Execution, Face, Fancy Dan, Farand, →**FASHION**, Fetching, Finesse, Flamboyant, Flava, Flossy, Fly, Font, Form(at), Free, Friseur, Galant, Genre, Ghetto fabulous, Glamour, Gnomon, Gothic, Grace, Grand, Gr(a)ecism, Greek, Groovy, Hair-do, Hand, Hepplewhite, Heroic, Heuristic, Hip, Homeric, House, International (Gothic), Italianate, Katharev(o)usa, Locution, Louis quatorze, Louis quinze, Manner, Metrosexual, Mock heroic, Mod(e), Modernism, Modish, Natty, New, New Look, Nib, Nifty, Novelese, Old, Panache, Pattern, Pen, Perm, Perpendicular, Personal, Phrase, Picturesque, Pistil, Plateresque, Pointel, Port, Posh, Post-modernism, Preponderant, Probe, Prose, Queen Anne, Rakish, Rank, Regency, Retro, Ritzy, Rococo, Romanesque, Rudie, Sheraton, Signature, Silk, Slap-up, Smart, Snappy, Snazzy, Soigné, Spiffy, Sporty, Street, Surname, Swish, Taste, Term, Title, Ton, Tone, Tony, Touch, Traditional, Trendsetter, Tuscan, Uncial, Unisex, Vain, Va-va-voom, Verismo, Vogue, Way

Subconscious Inner, Instinctive, Not-I, Subliminal, Suppressed

Subdue(d) Abate, Allay, Chasten, Conquer, Cow, Dampen, Dim, Dominate, Lick, Low-key, Master, Mate, Mute, Overbear, Quail, Quieten, Reduce, Refrain, Repress, Restrain, Slow, Sober, Soft pedal, Suppress, Tame, Under

Subject(ed), Subjection, Subjectivity, Subjects, Subject to Amenable, Art, Bethrall, Caitive, Case, Citizen, Core, Cow, Dedicatee, Dhimmi, Enthrall, Gist, Guinea pig, Hobby, Hobby-horse, Inflict, Issue, Liable, Liege(man), Matter, Metic, Motif, National, On, Oppress, Overpower, PE, People, Personalism, Poser, PPE, RE, RI, Serf, Servient, Servitude, Sitter, Slavery, Snool, Submit, Suit, Syllabus, →**THEME**, Thirl, Thrall, Topic, Under, Undergo, Vassal, Villein

Sublime Ali, Alice, August, Empyreal, Grand, Great, Holy, Lofty, Majestic, Outstanding, Perfect, Porte, Splendid

Submarine(r) Boomer, Diver, Hydronaut, Nautilus, Polaris, Sub, U-boat, Undersea

▷**Submarine** *may indicate* a fish

Submerge(d) Dip, Dive, Drown, Embathe, Engulf, Imbathe, Impinge, Lemuria, Overwhelm, Ria, Sink, Take, Whelm

Submissive, Submission, Submit Acquiesce, Bow, Capitulate, Comply, Cringe, Defer, Docile, Folio, Gimp, Knuckle, Lapdog, Meek, Obedient, Passive, Pathetic, Pliant, Propound, Refer, Render, Resign, Snool, Stepford, Stoop, Succumb, Truckle, →**YIELD**

Subordinate Adjunct, Below, Dependent, Flunky, Inferior, Junior, Minion, Myrmidon, Nether, Offsider, Postpone, Secondary, Servient, Stooge, Subject, Subservient, Surrender, Under(ling), Underman, Under-strapper, Vassal

Subscribe(r), Subscription Approve, Assent, Cedilla, Conform, Due, Endorsement, Pay, Pay TV, Sign(atory), Signature, Undersign, Underwrite

Subsequent(ly) Anon, Consequential, Future, Later, Next, Postliminary, Since, Then

Subside, Subsidence, Subsidy Abate, Adaw, Aid, Assuage, Bonus, Cauldron, Diminish, Ebb, Grant, Headage, Lysis, Sink, Sit, Slake, Swag

Substance, Substantial Allergen, Ambergris, Antigen, Antitoxin, Apiol, Axerophthol, Blanco, Body, Castoreum, Cermet, Chalone, Chitin, Cofactor, Colloid, Considerable, Content, Creatine, Cytochalasin, Dense, Ectoplasm, Elemi, Endorphin, Enorm(ous), Enzyme, Essential, Ester, Ethambutol, Exudate, Fabric, Feck, Fixative, Flavanone, Getter, Gist, Gluten, Gossypol, Gravamen, Gutta-percha, Hearty, Hefty, Hirudin, Hylic, Imine, Indol, Inhibitor, Isatin(e), Isomer, Kryptonite, Lase, Lectin, Linin, Material, Matter, Meaning, Meat(y), Metabolite, Mineral, Misoprostol, Mitogen, Molal, Mole, Morphactin, Myelin, Neotoxin, Noselite, Nutrient, Orgone, P, Particulate, Pepsinogen, Perforine, Phosphor, Pith, Polymer, Proinsulin, Promoter, Prostaglandin, Protyl(e), Quid, Reagent, Reality, Resin, Salacin(e), Secretagogue, Sense, Sequestrant, Smeclic, Solid, Sorbitol, Stramonium, Stuff, Sturdy, Suint, Sum, Sunblock, Synergist, Syntonin, Taeniafuge, Tangible, Terra alba, Thermoplastic, Thiouracil, Thiourea, Tocopherol, Weighty, Ylem

▶**Substantial** *see* **SUBSTANCE**

Substitute, Substitution Acting, Alternative, Change, Changeling, Commute, Creamer, Deputy, Emergency, Ersatz, -ette, Euphemism, Exchange, Fill-in, Imitation, Improvise, Instead, Lieu(tenant), Locum, Makeshift, Mock, Nominee, Novation, Pinch-hit, Proxy, Regent, Relieve, Replace, Represent, Reserve, Resolution, Ringer, Sentence, Soya, Spare, Stalking-horse, Stand-in, Stead, Step in, Stopgap, Supernumerary, Supply, Surrogate, Switch, Swop, Twelfth man, Twentieth man, Understudy, Vicarious

Subterfuge Artifice, Chicane, Evasion, Hole, Manoeuvre, Off-come, Ruse, Strategy, Trick

Subtle(ty) Abstruse, Alchemist, Crafty, Delicate, Fine(spun), Finesse, Hair-splitting, Ingenious, Innuendo, Nice(ty), Nuance, Overtone, Refinement, Sly, Subdued, Suttle, Thin, Wily

Subtract(ion) Deduct, Discount, Remove, Take, Tithe, Withdraw

Suburb(s) Dormitory, Environs, Exurbia, Metroland, Outskirts, Purlieu, Uptown

Subverse, Subversion, Subversive, Subvert Agitprop, Fifth column, Overthrow, Reverse, Sabotage, Sedition, Treasonous, Undermine, Upset

Succeed, Success(ful), Successfully Accomplish, Achieve, Answer, Arrive, Big-hitter, Bingo, Blockbuster, Boffo, Breakthrough, Chartbuster, Coast, Come off, Contrive, Coup, Do well, Éclat, Effective, Efficacious, Ensue, Fadge, Fare, Felicity, Flourish, Follow, Fortune, Gangbuster, Get, Go, Heyday, Highflyer, Hit, Hotshot, Inherit, Killing, Landslide, Luck, Made, Make good, Make it, Make out, Manage, Masterstroke, Mega, Midas touch, Offcome, Parlay, Pass, Prevail, Procure, Profitable, Promising, Prosper, Pull off, Purple patch, Pyrrhic, Rags to riches, Reach, Replace, Result, Riot, Roll, Score, Seal, Seel, Sele, Sell out, Soaraway, Socko, Speed, Stardom, Superstar, Sure thing, Take, Tanistry, The bitch goddess, Thrive, Thumbs up, Triumph, Up, Up and coming, Upstart, Vault, Victory, Weather, Well, Win, Winnitude, W(h)iz(z)kid, Wow, Wunderkind

Successor Co(m)arb, Deluge, Descendant, Ensuite, Epigon(e), Heir, Incomer, Inheritor, Khalifa, Next, Syen

Succulent Aloe, Cactus, Echeveria, Hoodia, Ice-plant, Juicy, Lush, Rich, Saguaro, Sappy, Spekboom, Tender, Toothy

Suck(er), Sucking Absorb, Aphid, Aspirator, Ass, Dracula, Drink, Dupe, Fawn, Felch, Gnat, Gobstopper, Graff, Graft, Greenfly, Gull, Hoove, Lamia, Lamprey,

Leech, Liquorice, Lollipop, Mammal, Mouth, Mug, Patsy, Plunger, Scolex, Shoot, Siphon, Slurp, Smarm, Sweetmeat, Swig, Sycophant, Toad-eater, Vampire

Sudden(ly) Abrupt, Astart, Astert, Extempore, Ferly, Flash, Fleeting, Foudroyant, Hasty, Headlong, Impulsive, Overnight, Precipitate, Rapid, Slap (bang), Sodain, Subitaneous, Swap, Swop, Unexpected

Sue Apply, Ask, Beseech, Dun, Entreat, Implead, Implore, Petition, Pray, Process, Prosecute, Woo

Suffer(er), Suffering Abide, Aby(e), Ache, Affliction, Agonise, Auto, Bale, →BEAR, Brook, Calvary, Cop, Die, Distress, Dree, Endurance, Endure, Feel, Gethsemane, Golgotha, Grief, Hardship, Have, Hell, Incur, Indolent, Languish, Let, Luit, Mafted, Martyr, Ordeal, Pain, Passible, Passion, Passive, Patible, Patience, Pay, Pellagrin, Permit, Pine, Plague, Purgatory, Smart, Stand, Stomach, Stress, Sustain, Thole, Tolerate, Toll, Torment, Torture, Trial, Tribulation, Undergo, Use, Victim

Suffice, Sufficiency, Sufficient Abundance, Adequate, Ample, Basta, Do, Due, Enough, Enow, Nuff, Satisfy, Serve

Suffocate Asphyxiate, Choke, Smother, Stifle, Stive, Strangle, Throttle

Sugar(y), Sugar cane Aldohexose, Aldose, Amygdalin, Arabinose, Barley, Beet, Blood, Brown, Candy, Cane, Caramel, Cassonade, Caster, Cellobiose, Cellose, Confectioner's, Cube, Daddy, Demerara, Deoxyribose, Dextrose, Disaccharide, Flattery, Fructose, Fucose, Furanose, Galactose, Gallise, Glucose, Glucosoric, Glycosuria, Goo(r), Granulated, Granulose, Grape, Gur, Heptose, Hexose, Hexose, Honeydew, Hundreds and thousands, Iced, Icing, Inulin, Invert, Jaggary, Jaggery, Jagghery, Ketose, Lactose, Laevulose, Loaf, Lump, Maltose, Manna, Mannose, Maple, Milk, Money, Monosaccharide, Muscovado, Nectar, Nucleoside, Palm, Panocha, Pentose, Penuche, Pyranose, Raffinose, Rhamnose, Ribose, Saccharine, Saccharoid, Simple, Sis, Sorbose, Sorghum, Sorg(h)o, Sparrow, Spun, Sweet(ener), Syrup, Tetrose, Trehalose, Triose, White, Wood, Xylose

Suggest(ion), Suggestive Advance, Advice, Advise, Blue, Breath, Connote, Cue, Float, Guess, Hint, Hypnotic, Idea, Imply, Innuendo, Insinuate, Intimate, Kite, Mention, Modicum, Moot, Nominate, Posit, Posthypnotic, Postulate, Prompt, Proposal, Propound, Provocative, Racy, Raise, Recommend, Redolent, Reminiscent, Ring, Risqué, Savour, Scenario, Smacks, Soft core, Suspicion, Threat, Touch, Trace, Twang, Vestige, Vote

Suicide Felo-de-se, Hara-kiri, Hari-kari, Kamikaze, Lemming, Lethal, Sati, Seppuku, Suttee

Suit Action, Adapt, Adjust, Agree, Answer, Anti-G, Apply, Appropriate, Become, Befit, Beho(o)ve, Bequest, Besit, Birthday, Cards, Case, Cat, Clubs, Conform, Courtship, Demob, Diamonds, Dinner, Dittos, Diving, Do, Dress, Dry, Etons, Exec(utive), Fashion, Fit, G, Garb, Gee, Get on, Gree, Hearts, Hit, Jump, Lis pendens, Litigation, Long, Lounge, Major, Mao, Match, Menswear, Minor, Monkey, NBC, Noddy, Orison, Outcome, Paternity, Penguin, Petition, Pinstripe, Plaint, Play, Plea, Please, Point, Prayer, Pressure, Process, Pyjama, Quarterdeck, Queme, Res judicata, Romper(s), Safari, Sailor, Salopettes, Satisfy, Serve, Shell, Siren, Skeleton, Slack, Space, Spades, Strong, Sun, Sunday, Supplicat, Sweat, Swim, Swords, Tailleur, Three-piece, Track, Trial, Trouser, Trumps, Tsotsi, Tweeds, Twin, Two-piece, Uniform, Union, Wet, Wingsuit, Zoot

Suitable Apposite, Appropriate, Apt, Becoming, Capable, Competent, Congenial, Consonant, Convenance, Convenient, Decorous, Due, Eligible, Expedient, →FIT, Habile, Keeping, Meet, Opportune, Pertinent, Relevant, Seemly, Sittlichkeit, Worthy

Suite Allemande, Apartment, Chambers, Court, Dolly, Edit, Ensemble, Entourage, Hospitality, Lounge, Nutcracker, Partita, Retinue, Rooms, Serenade, Set, Tail, Three-piece, Train, Two-piece

Suitor Beau, Gallant, Lover, Petitioner, Pretendant, Pretender, Swain

Sulk(y), Sulkiness B(r)oody, Carriage, Disgruntled, Dod, Dort, Gee, Glout(s), Glower, Glum, Grouchy, Grouty, Grumps, Gumple-foisted, Huff, Hump, Jinker, Moody, Mope, Mump, Pet, Petulant, Pique, Pout, Snit, Spider, Strunt, Sullen

Sullen Black, Brooding, Dorty, Dour, Farouche, Glum(pish), Grim, Grumpy, Moody, Mumpish, Peevish, Po, Stunkard, Sulky, Sumph, Surly

Sully Assoil, Bedye, Besmirch, Blot, Deface, Defile, Glaur(y), Smear, Smirch, Soil(ure), Tarnish, Tar-wash

Sultry Houri, Humid, Sexy, Smouldering, Steamy, Tropical

Sum(s), Sum up Add(end), Aggregate, All (told), Amount, Bomb, Encapsulate, Foot, Logical, Lump, Number, Perorate, → **QUANTITY**, Re-cap, Refund, Remittance, Reversion, Slump, Solidum, Tidy, Total, Vector

Summarize, Summary Abridge, Abstract, Aperçu, Bird's eye, Breviate, Brief, Coda, Compendium, Condense, Conspectus, Digest, Docket, Epanodos, Epitome, Footnote, Gist, Headnote, Instant, Minute, Offhand, Outline, Overview, Pirlicue, Précis, Purlicue, Recap(itulate), Resume, Résumé, Round-up, Rundown, Short (shrift), Sitrep, Syllabus, Synopsis, Tabloid, Tabulate, Tabulation, Wrap-up

Summer(time) Abacus, Adder, Aestival, August, BST, Computer, Estival, Heyday, Indian, Lintel, Luke, Prime, St Luke's, St Martin's, Season, Sigma, Solstice, Totter

Summit Acme, Acro-, Apex, Brow, Climax, Conference, → **CREST**, Crown, Eminence, Height, Hillcrest, Jole, Jungfrau, Mont Blanc, Peak, Pike, Pinnacle, Ridge, Spire, Vertex, Vertical, Yalta

Summon(s) Accite, Arraign, Arrière-ban, Azan, Beck(on), Bleep, Call, Call in, Cist, Cital, Citation, Command, Convene, Drum, Evoke, Garnishment, Gong, Hail, Invocation, Muster, Order, Originating, Page, Post, Preconise, Rechate, Recheat, Reveille, Signal, Sist, Subpoena, Ticket, Warn, Warrant, What-ho, Whoop, Writ

Sun(-god), Sunlight, Sunny, Sunshine Amen-Ra, Amon-Ra, Apollo, Aten, Bright, Cheer, Day(star), Dry, Earthshine, Eye of the day, Glory, Heater, Heliacal, Helio(s), Helius, Horus, Mean, Midnight, Mock, New Mexico, Nova, Orb, Paper, Parhelion, Phoebean, Photosphere, Ra, Radiant, Rays, Re, Rising, Shamash, Sol(ar), Soleil, Sonne, Surya, Svastika, Swastika, Tabloid, Tan, Titan, UV

Sunder Divide, Divorce, Part, Separate, Sever, Split

▶**Sun-god** *see* SUN(-GOD)

▶**Sunken** *see* SINK(ING)

Sunshade Awning, Bongrace, Canopy, Parasol, Umbrella

Sup Dine, Eat, Feast, Sample, Sip, Swallow

Super A1, Actor, Arch, Extra, Fab(ulous), Great, Grouse, Ideal, Lulu, Paramount, Superb, Terrific, Tip-top, Top-notch, Tops, Walker-on, Wizard

Superb A1, Fine, Gorgeous, Grand, Majestic, Splendid, Top-notch

Supercilious Aloof, Arrogant, Bashaw, Cavalier, Haughty, Lordly, Snide, Sniffy, Snooty, Snotty, Snouty, Superior, Withering

Superficial Cosmetic, Cursenary, Cursory, Exterior, Facile, Glib, One-dimensional, Outside, Outward, Overlying, Perfunctory, Shallow, Sketchy, Skindeep, Smattering, Veneer, Window-dressing

▷**Superficial(ly)** *may indicate* a word outside another

Superfluous, Superfluity Appendix, De trop, Extra, Lake, Mountain, Needless, Otiose, Redundant, Spare, Unnecessary

Superhuman Bionic, Herculean, Heroic, Supernatural

Superintend(ent) Boss, Curator, Director, Foreman, Guide, Janitor, Oversee(r), Preside, Provost, Sewer, Surveillant, Warden, Zanjero

Superior(ity) Abbess, Abbot, Abeigh, Above, Advantage, Ahead, Aloof, Ascendant, Atop, Better, Brahmin, Choice, Classy, Condescending, Custos, De luxe, Dinger, Elite, Eminent, Excellent, Exceptional, Feuar, Finer, Forinsec, Gree, Herrenvolk, High-class, High-grade, Jethro, Lake, Liege, Master race, Mastery, Morgue, Mother, Nob, Noble, Outgrown, Outstanding, Over, Overlord, Oversee, Paramount, Plum, Pooh-Bah, Posh, Predominance, Premium, Prestige, Pretentious, Prevalent, Prior, Smug, Snooty, Speciesism, Stuck up, Superordinate, Supremacy, Swell, Top(-loftical), Transcendent(al), U, Udal, Upmarket, Upper(most), Upper crust, Uppish, Upstage

Superlative Best, Exaggerated, Peerless, Supreme, Utmost

Supernatural Divine, Eerie, Endemon, Fay, Fey, Fie, Fly, Gothic, Mana, Manito(u), Occult, Paranormal, Selky, Sharp, Siddhi, Tokoloshe, Unearthly, Wargod

Supernumerary Additional, Corollary, Extra, Mute, Orra

Supersede Replace, Stellenbosch, Supplant

Supervise(d), Supervision, Supervisor Administer, Chaperone, Check, Direct, Engineer, Foreman, Gaffer, Grieve, Handle, Honcho, Invigilate, Key grip, Manager, Marshal, Monitor, Officiate, Organise, Overman, Oversee(r), Probation, Proctor, Regulate, Seneschal, Shopwalker, Steward, Symposiarch, Targe, Taskmaster, Tool pusher, Under, Walla(h)

Supper Bar, Burns, Dinner, → **DRINK(ER)**, Fork, Hawkey, Hockey, Horkey, Last, Meal, Nagmaal, Repast, Soirée

Supplant Displace, Exchange, Overthrow, Pre-empt, Replace, Substitute, Supersede

Supple, Suppleness Agile, Compliant, Leish, Limber, Lissom(e), Loose, Loose-limbed, Lythe, Malleable, Plasticity, Pliable, Sinuous, Souple, Wan(d)le, Wannel, Whippy

Supplement(ary), Supplementing Addend(um), Addition, Adjunct, And, Annex(e), Appendage, Appendix, As well as, Auxiliary, Bolt-on, Colour, Eche, Eik, Eke, Extra, Footnote, Glucosamine, Inset, Mend, Paralipomena, Postscript, Practicum, PS, Relay, Ripienist, Ripieno, Rutin, Sports, TES, Weighting

Supply, Supplies, Supplier Accommodate, Advance, Afford, Amount, Cache, Cater, Commissariat, Contribute, Crop, Deal, Endue, Equip, Excess, Exempt, Feed, Fill, Find, Fit, Foison, Fund, Furnish, Give, Grant, Grist, Grubstake, Heel, Holp(en), Hydrant, Indew, Indue, Issue, Lay on, Lend, Lithely, Mains, Matériel, Ordnance, Pipeline, Plenish, Ply, Pool, → **PROVIDE**, Provision, Purvey, Push, RASC, Replenishment, Reservoir, Resource, Retailer, Serve, Source, Stake, Stock, → **STORE**, Viands, Vintner, Water, Widow's cruse, Yield

Support(er), Supporting Abet, Acco(u)rage, Adherent, Advocate, Aegis, Affirm, Aficionado, Aftercare, Aid, Aide, Ally, Anciliary, Andiron, Anta, Arch, Arm, Assistant, Athletic, Axle, Back(bone), Back-up, Baluster, Banister, Bankroll, Barrack, Barre, Base, Basis, Batten, Beam, Bear, Befriend, Behind, Belt, Benefactor, Bier, Bolster, Book end, Boom, Bra, Brace, Bracket, Brassiere, Breadwinner, Bridge, Buttress, Carlist, Caryatid, Cavalier, Chair, Champion, Cheerleader, Chenet, Cherish, Circumstantiate, Clientele, Clipboard, Colonnade, Column, Comfort, Confirm, Console, Cornerstone, Corroborate, Countenance,

Cradle, Cripple, Cross-beam, Cruck, Crutch, C(ee)-spring, Dado, Disciple, Doula, Easel, Encourage, Endorse, Endoss, Endow, Engager, Enlist, Enthusiast, Espouse, Evidence, Family, Fan, Favour, Fid, Finance, Flying buttress, Fly-rail, Footrest, Footstool, For, Foster, Friend, Fulcrum, Gamb, Gantry, Garter, Girder, Grapevine, Groundswell, Guy, Handrail, Hanger, Hat-peg, Headrest, Help, Henchman, Hold with, Home help, I-beam, Impost, Income, Indorse, Jack, Jackstay, Jockstrap, Joist, Keep, Keystone, Kingpost, Knee, Knife rest, Lath, Learning, Lectern, Leg, Lifebelt, Lifebuoy, Lobby, Loyalist, Mailstick, Mainbrace, Mainstay, Maintain, Makefast, Mill-rind, Miserere, Misericord(e), Moral, Mount, Neck, -nik, Nourish, Pack, Pack-frame, Packstaff, Partisan, Partners, Patronage, Pedestal, Peronist, Phalanx, Pier, Pile(-cap), Pillar, Pin, Plinth, Poppet, Post, Potent, Price, Promote, Prop, Proponent, PTA, Pull-for, Puncheon, Pylon, Queenite, Raft, Rally round, Rebato, Regular, Reinforce, Relieve, Respond, Rest, Rind, Rod, Root, Royalist, Samaritan, Sanction, Sarking, Sawhorse, Scaffolding, Sconce, Second, Shoetree, Shore, Skeg, Skeleton, Skid, Sleeper, Sling, Socle, Solidarity, Spectator, Splat, Splint, Sponson, Sponsor, Sprag, Spud, Squinch, Staddle, Staddlestone, Staff, Staging, Stake, Stalwart, Stanchion, Stand(-by), Stay, Steady, Step, Stick, Stirrup, Stool, Stringer, Strut, Stull, Subscribe, Subsidy, Succour, Summer, Suspender, Sustain, Sustentacular, Sustentaculum, Sustentation, Tartan army, Technical, Tee, Tendril, Third, Tie, Tige, Torsel, Trellis, Trestle, Tripod, Trivet, Trotter, Truss, Tumpline, Underlay, Underpin, Understand, Uphold, Upkeep, Verify, Vindicate, Viva, Walker, Waterwings, Welfare, Well-wisher, Yorkist, Zealot

Suppose(d), Supposedly, Supposition An, Assume, Believe, Conjecture, Daresay, Expect, Guess, Hypothetical, Idea, If, Imagine, Imply, Infer, Opine, Presume, Putative, Reputedly, Say, Sepad, Theory, What if

Suppress(ion), Suppressed Abate, Abolish, Adaw, Burke, Cancel, Censor, Check, Clampdown, Conditioned, Crackdown, Crush, Ecthlipsis, Elide, Elision, Epistasis, Gag, Gleichschaltung, Hide, Inhibit, Mob(b)le, Muffle, Quash, Quell, Quench, Restrain, Silence, Sit on, Smother, Squash, Squelch, Stand on, Stifle, Strangle, Subdue, Submerge, Subreption, Under

Supreme, Supremacy, Supremo Baaskap, Best, Caudillo, Consummate, Dominant, Kronos, Leader, Napoleon, Overlord, Paramount, Peerless, Pre-eminent, Regnant, Sovereign, Sublime, Sudder, Top, Utmost

Sure(ly) Assured, Ay, Bound, Cert(ain), Certes, Confident, Definite, Doubtless, Firm, Indeed, Inevitable, Know, Pardi(e), Pardy, Perdie, Positive, Poz, Safe, Secure, Self-confident, Shoo-in, Sicker, Syker, Uh-huh, Unerring, Yeah, Yes

Surety Bail, Guarantee, Mainprise, Security, Sponsional

Surface Aerofoil, Appear, Area, Arise, Astroturf®, Bitumen, Brane, Camber, Carpet, Caustic, Ceiling, Control, Crust, Cutis, Day, Dermal, Dermis, Emerge, Epigene, Exterior, External, Face, Facet, Finish, Flock, Interface, Linish, Macadam, Meniscus, Nanograss, Notaeum, Out, Outcrop, Outward, Overglaze, Paintwork, Patina, Pave, Plane, Reveal, Rise, Salband, Scarfskin, Side, Skim, Skin, Soffit, Spandrel, Superficial, Superficies, Supracrustal, Tarmac®, Tar-seal, Texture, Top, Topping, Toroid, Veneer, Wearing course, Worktop

Surfeit(ed) Blasé, Cloy, Excess, Glut, Overcloy, Plethora, Satiate, Stall, Staw

Surge Billow, Boom, Drive, Gush, Leap, Onrush, Seethe, Sway, Swell, Upgush, Wind

Surgeon Abernethy, Barber, BCh, Brain, BS, CHB, CM, Doctor, DS, Dupuytren, Hunter, Leech, Lister, Medic, Operator, Orthopod, Plastic, Sawbones, Tang, Tree, Vet(erinary)

Surgery Anaplasty, Bypass, Cordotomy, Cosmetic, Dentistry, Facelift, Hobday, Keyhole, Knife, Laparotomy, Laser, LASIK, Mammoplasty, Medicine, Nip and tuck, Nose job, Op, Open-heart, Orthop(a)edics, Osteoplasty, Plastic, Prosthetics, Section, Spare-part, Stereotaxis, Thoracoplasty, Tuboplasty, Zolatrics

Surly Bluff, Cantankerous, Chough, Chuffy, Churl(ish), Crusty, Cynic, Glum, Gruff, Grum, Grumpy, Huffy, Rough, Snarling, Sullen, Truculent

Surpass(ing) Bang, Beat, Best, Cap, Ding, Eclipse, Efface, Exceed, Excel, Frabjous, Outdo, Outfoot, Outgo, Outgun, Out-Herod, Outman, Outshine, Outstrip, Overshadow, Overtop, Transcend, Trump

Surplus De trop, Excess, Extra, Gash, Glut, Lake, Mountain, Offcut, Out-over, Over, Overabundance, Overcome, Remainder, Residue, Rest, Spare, Superplus, Surfeit

Surprise(d), Surprising Ag, Alert, Amaze, Ambush, Astonish, Aykhona wena, Bewilder, Blimey, Bombshell, By Jove, Caramba, Catch, Confound, Coo, Cor, Crikey, Criminé, Cripes, Crumbs, Dear, Eye-opener, Gadso, Gee, Geewhiz, Gemini, Gobsmacked, Godsend, Golly, Good-lack, Gorblimey, Gordon Bennett, Gosh, Gotcha, Great Scott, Ha, Hah, Hallo, Heavens, Hech, Heck, Heh, Hello, Hell's teeth, Hey, Hit for six, Ho, Holy cow, Hullo, Jeepers, Jeepers creepers, Jeez(e), Jinne, Jirre, Law, Lawks, Lor, Lordy, Lumme, Lummy, Man alive, Marry, Musha, My, Nooit, Och, Odso, Omigod, Oops, Open-mouthed, Overtake, Phew, Pop-eyed, Really, Sheesh, Shock, Singular, Sjoe, So, Spot, Stagger, Startle, Strewth, Stun, Sudden, Treat, Turn-up, Uh, Upset, Whew, Whoops, Whoops-a-daisy, Wide-eyed, Wonderment, Wow, Wrongfoot, Yikes, Yipes, Yow, Zart, Zowie

Surrender Abandon, Capitulate, Cave-in, Cede, Cessio honorum, Cession, Enfeoff, Extradite, Fall, Forego, Forfeit, Handover, Hulled, Recreant, Release, Relinquish, Renounce, Resign, Roll over, Strike, Submit, Succumb, Waive, → YIELD, Yorktown

Surround(ed), Surrounding(s) Ambient, Amid, Architrave, Background, Bathe, Begirt, Bego, Beset, Besiege, Bundwall, Cinct, Circumvallate, Circumvent, Compass, Doughnutting, Ecology, Embail, Encase, → ENCIRCLE, Enclave, Enclose, Encompass, Enfold, Entomb, Environ, Enwheel, Enwrap, Fence, Gherao, Gird, Girt, Hedge, Impale, Inorb, Invest, Mid, Orb, Orle, Outflank, Outside, Perimeter, Periphery, Setting, Wall

Surveillance, Survey(ing), Surveyor Behold, Browse, Cadastre, Case, Census, Chartered, Conspectus, Domesday, Doomwatch, Espial, Examination, Eye, Geodesy, Geological, Groma, Look-see, Map, Once-over, Ordnance, Overeye, Overview, Poll, Prospect, Recce, Reccy, Reconnaissance, Regard, Review, Rodman, Scan, Scrutiny, Staffman, Stakeout, Straw poll, Supervision, Terrier, Theodolite, Triangulate, Vigil, Watch, Y-level

Survival, Survive, Surviving, Survivor Bushcraft, Castaway, Cope, Die hard, Endure, Exist(ence), Extant, Finalist, Hibakusha, Last (out), Leftover, Live, Outlast, Outlive, Overlive, Persist, Pull through, Relic(t), Ride (out), Sole, Subsist, Weather, Withstand

Suspect, Suspicion, Suspicious Askance, Assume, Breath, Cagey, Distrust, Dodgy, Doubt, Dubious, Equivocal, Fishy, Grain, Grey list, Guess, Hinky, Hint, Hunch, Hunky, Iffy, Imagine, Inkling, Jalouse, Jealous, Leery, Misdeem, Misdoubt, Misgiving, Mistrust, Modicum, Notion, Paranoia, Queer, Scent, Sense, Smatch, Soupçon, Stealthy, Think, Thought, Tinge, Whiff

▷**Suspect, Suspicious** *may indicate* an anagram

Suspend(ed), Suspender, Suspense, Suspension Abate, Abeyance, Adjourn, Anti-shock, Cliffhanger, Colloid, Dangle, Defer, Delay, Dormant, Freeze, Garter, Ground, →**HANG**, Hang-gliding, Hovering, Hydraulic, Independent, Intermit, Lay off, Mist, Moratorium, Mystery, Nailbiter, Pensile, Poise, Prorogue, Put on ice, Reprieve, Respite, Rub out, Rusticate, Sideline, Sol, Stand off, Stay, String, Swing, Table, Tension, Tenterhooks, Truce, Undercurrent, Underslung, Withhold

▷**Suspended** *may indicate* 'ice' on ice at the end of a down light

Sustain(ed), Sustaining, Sustenance Abide, Aliment, Bear, Constant, Depend, Endure, Food, Keep, Last, Maintain, Nourish, Nutriment, Nutrition, Pedal, Prolong, Sostenuto, Succour, Support, Upstay

Suture Coronal, Lambda, Pterion, Sagittal, Stitch

Swab Dossil, Dry, Mop, Pledget, Scour, Sponge, Squeegee, Stupe, Tampon, Tompon, Wipe

Swagger(er), Swaggering Birkie, Bluster, Boast, Bobadil, Brag, Bragadisme, Bravado, Bucko, Cock, Cockiness, Crow, Jaunty, Matamore, Nounce, Panache, Pra(u)nce, Roist, Roll, Rollick, Roul, Royster, Ruffle, Sashay, Side, Strive, Strut, Swagman, Swank, Swash(-buckler)

Swallow(able), Swallowing Absorb, Accept, Barn, Bird, Bolt, Bredit, Buy, Consume, Credit, Devour, Down(flow), Drink, Eat, Endue, Engulf, Esculent, Glug, Gobble, Gulch, Gulp, Incept, Ingest, Ingulf, Ingurgitate, Itys, Lap, Martin, Martlet, Neck, Progne, Quaff, Shift, Sister, Slug, Stomach, Swift, Swig, Take

Swamp(y) Bog, Bunyip, Cowal, Deluge, Dismal, Drown, Engulf, Everglade, Flood, Inundate, Lentic, Lerna, Lerne, Loblolly, Mar(i)sh, Morass, Muskeg, Overrun, Overwhelm, Pakihi, Paludal, Poles'ye, Pripet Marshes, Purgatory, Quagmire, Slash, Slough, Sudd, Vlei, Vly

▷**Swap(ped)** *may indicate* an anagram

Swarm(ing) Abound, Alive, Bike, Bink, Byke, Cast, Clamber, Cloud, Crowd, Flood, Geminid, Host, Hotch, Hotter, Infest, Pullulate, Rife, Shin, Shoal, Teem, Throng

Sway(ing) Careen, Carry, Command, Diadrom, Domain, Dominion, Flap, Fluctuate, Govern, Hegemony, Influence, Lilt, Oscillate, Prevail, Reel, Reign, Rock, Roll, Rule, Sally, Shog, Shoogie, Shoogle, Swag, Swale, Swee, Swing(e), Teeter, Titter, Totter, Vacillate, Wobble

Swear(ing), Swearer, Swear word Asseverate, Attest, Avow, Billingsgate, Coprolalia, Curse, Cuss, Darn, Depose, Eff (and blind), Execrate, Jurant, Juratory, Oath, Objure, Pledge, Plight, Rail, Sessa, State, Tarnal, Tarnation, Trooper, Verify, Vow

Sweat(ing), Sweaty Agonise, Apocrine, Clammy, Dank, Diaphoresis, Eccrine, Egest, English, Excrete, Exude, Forswatt, Glow, Hidrosis, Lather, Muck, Ooze, Osmidrosis, Secretion, Slave, Stew, Sudament, Sudamina, Sudate, Suint, Swelter, Toil

Sweater Aran, Argyle, Circassian, Circassienne, Cowichan, Fair Isle, Gansey, Guernsey, Indian, Jersey, Polo, Pullover, Roll-neck, Siwash, Skinny-rib, Skivvy, Slip-on, Slop-pouch, Sloppy Joe, Turtleneck, V-neck, Woolly

Sweep(er), Sweeping(s) Besom, Broad, Broom, Brush, Chimney, Chummy, Clean, Curve, Debris, Detritus, Expanse, Extensive, Generalisation, Lash, Lottery, Net, Oars, Pan, Phasing, Range, Scavenger, Scud, Sling, Snowball, Soop, Spoom, Street, Stroke, Surge, Swathe, Sway, Vac(k), Vacuum, Waft, Well, Wholesale, Wide, Widespread

Sweet, Sweeten(er), Sweetmeat, Sweetness Acesulfame-K, Afters, Aspartame, Baclava, Baklava, Bonus, Bribe, Bung, Cassata, Charity, Charming, Cherubic, Cloying, Confect(ion), Confiserie, Conserve, Crème, Cute, Douce(t), Drop, Dulcet, Dulcie, Dulcitude, Edulcorate, FA, Flan, Flapjack, Flummery, Fool, Fragrant, Fresh, Glycerin, Goody, Honey(ed), Kiss, Lavender, Liqueur, Luscious, Melodious, Molasses, Money, Nectared, Nonpareil, Nothing, Pea, Pet, Pie, Pud(ding), Redolent, Saccharin(e), Seventeen, Sillabub, Sixteen, Soot(e), Sop, Sorbet, Spice, Split, Sucrose, Sugar, Sugary, Syllabub, Syrupy, Tart(let), Torte, Trifle, Twee, Uses, William, Winsome, Zabaglione

Sweetheart Amoret, Amour, Beau, Boyfriend, Darling, Dona(h), Dowsabel(l), Doxy, Dulcinea, Flame, Follower, Girlfriend, Honey(bunch), Honeybun, Jarta, Jo(e), Lass, Leman, Lover, Masher, Neaera, Peat, Romeo, Steady, Toots(y), True-love, Valentine, Yarta, Yarto

Swell(ing) Adenomata, Ague-cake, Anasarca, Aneurysm, Apophysis, Bag, Balloon, Bellying, Berry, Billow, Blab, Blister, Bloat, Blow, Boil, Boll, Bolster, Botch, Braw, Bubo, Bulb, Bulge, Bump, Bunion, Burgeon, Capellet, Carbuncle, Cat, Chancre, Chilblain, Cratches, Cyst, Dandy, Diapason, Dilate, Dom, Don, Edema, Eger, Elephantiasis, Encanthis, Enhance, Enlarge, Entasis, Epulis, Excellent, Farcy-bud, Frog, Gall, Gathering, Gent, Gnarl, Goiter, Goitre, Gout, Grandee, Ground, Head sea, Heave, Heighten, H(a)ematoma, Hove, Hydrocele, Increase, Inflate, Intumesce, Kibe, L, Lampas(se), Lampers, Lump, Macaroni, Milk leg, Mouse, Nodule, Odontoma, Oedema, OK, Onco-, Ox-warble, Parotitis, Plim, Plump, Protrude, Proud, Pulvinus, Rise, Roil, Roller, Scirrhus, Scleriasis, Sea, Strout, Struma, Stye, Stylopodium, Sudamina, Surge, Teratoma, Toff, Tuber(cle), Tumefaction, Tumour, Tympanites, Tympany, Upsurge, Varicose, Venter, Vesicle, Vulvitis, Vulvovaginitis, Warble, Wen, Whelk, Windgall, Xanthoma

▷**Swelling** *may indicate* a word reversed

Swerve, Swerving Bias, Broach, Careen, Deflect, Deviate, Dodge, Lean, Sheer, Shy, Snoke, Stray, Sway, Swing, Veer, Warp, Wheel

Swift(ly) Apace, Bird, Dean, Dromond, Fleet, Flock, Hasty, Martlet, Newt, Nimble, Presto, Prompt, Quick, → **RAPID**, Slick, Sodaine, Spanking, Speedy, Sudden, Velocipede, Wight

▷**Swilling** *may indicate* an anagram

Swim(ming) Bathe, Bogey, Bogie, Crawl, Dip, Float, Freestyle, Naiant, Natant, Natatorial, Paddle, Reel, Run, Skinny-dip, Soom, Synchro(nized), Trudgen, Whim, Whirl

▷**Swim** *may indicate* an anagram

▷**Swimmer** *may indicate* a fish

Swindle(r) Beat, Bunco, Cajole, Champerty, → **CHEAT**, Chiz(z), Con, Concoct, Defraud, Diddle, Do, Escroc, Fake, Fiddle, Finagle, Fleece, Fraud, Gazump, Gip, Gold brick, Graft, Grifter, Gull, Gyp, Hocus, Hustler, Leg, Leger, Mulct, Nobble, Peter Funk, Plant, Ponzi scheme, Racket, Ramp, Rig, Rogue, Scam, Sell, Shaft, Shakedown, Shark, Sharper, Shicer, Shyster, Skin, Slicker, Sting, Stitch-up, Suck, Swiz(z), Take, Trick, Tweedle, Twist, Two-time

Swing(er), Swinging Colt, Dangle, Flail, Gate, Hang, Hep, Hip, Kip(p), Lilt, Metronome, Mod, Music, Oscillate, Pendulate, Pendulum, Reverse, Rock, Rope, Shog, Shoogie, Shuggy, Slew, Slue, Swale, Sway, Swee, Sweep, Swerve, Swey, Swipe, Swivel, Trapeze, Veer, Vibratile, Voop, Wave, Western, Wheel, Whirl, Yaw

▷**Swirling** *may indicate* an anagram

Switch(ed), Switches, Switching Birch, Button, Change, Churn, Convert, Crossbar, Cryotron, Dead man's handle, Dimmer, Dip, Dolly, Exchange, Gang, Hairpiece, Isolator, Knife, Legerdemain, Master, Mercury, Mercury tilt, Message, Pear, Point, Relay, Replace, Retama, Rocker, Rod, Scutch, Shift, Swits, Thyristor, Time, Toggle, Transpose, Tress, Trip, Tumbler, Twig, Wave, Zap
▷**Switched** *may indicate an anagram*
Swivel Caster, Pivot, Root, Rotate, Spin, Terret, Territ, Torret, Turret, Wedein
Swollen Blown, Bollen, Bulbous, Full, Gourdy, Gouty, Incrassate, Nodose, Puffy, Tumid, Turgescent, Turgid, Varicose, Ventricose, Vesiculate
Swoon Blackout, Collapse, Dwa(l)m, Dwaum, Faint, Swarf, Swerf
Sword(-like), Swordplay Andrew Ferrara, Anelace, Angurvadel, Anlace, Arondight, Assegai, Balisarda, Balmunc, Balmung, Bilbo, Blade, Brand, Brandiron, Broad(sword), Brondyron, Cemitare, Claymore, Cold steel, Court, Curtal-ax, Curtana, Curtax, Cutlass, Damascene, Damocles, Dance, Dirk, Ensate, Ensiform, Epée, Espada, Estoc, Excalibur, Falchion, Faulchi(o)n, Foil, Gladius, Glaive, Glamring, Gleave, Glorious, Hanger, Iai-do, Jacob's staff, Joyeuse, Katana, Kendo, Khanda, Kirpan, Kreese, Kris, Kukri, Machete, Morglay, Parang, Rapier, Reverso, Sabre, Samurai, Schiavone, Schläger, Scimitar, Semita(u)r, Shabble, Shamshir, Sharp, Sigh, Simi, Skene-dhu, Slangwhanger, Smallsword, Spadroon, Spirtle, Spit, Spurtle(blade), Steel, Tachi, Toledo, Tulwar, Two-edged, Whinger, Whiniard, Whinyard, White-arm, Yatag(h)an
Sycophant(ic) Brown-nose, Claqueur, Crawler, Creeper, Fawner, Groveller, Hanger-on, Lickspittle, Parasite, Servile, Toad-eater, Toady, Yesman
Syllable(s) Acatalectic, Anacrusis, Aretinian, Om, Outride, Thesis, Tonic, Ultima
Syllabus Program(me), Prospectus, Résumé, Summary, Table, Timetable
Symbol(ic), Symbolism, Symbolist, Symbols Allegory, Ampussy-and, Character, Charactery, Decadent, Del, Diesis, Iconography, K, Klimt, Logotype, Metaphor, Minus, Moral, Mystical, Nominal, Notation, Operator, Placeholder, Plus, Quantifier, Regalia, Semicolon, Sex, Shadowy, Shamrock, Slur, Status, Syllabary, Synthetism, T-cross, Trisul, Type, Weather
Symmetric(al), Symmetry Balance, Bilateral, Digonal, Diphycercal, Even, Harmony, Isobilateral, Radial, Regular
Sympathetic, Sympathise(r), Sympathy Affinity, Agreeable, Approval, Commiserate, Compassion, Condole(nce), Condone, Congenial, Crypto, Dear-dear, Empathy, Fellow-traveller, Genial, Humane, Kind, Mediagenic, Par, Pathos, Pity, Rapport, Ruth, Side, Supportive, Understanding, Vicarious, Well-disposed
Symphony Alpine, Antar, Babi Yar, Bear, Clock, Concert, Drum-roll, Echo, Eroica, Farewell, Feuer, Fifth, Finlandia, Haffner, Horn-signal, Hunt, Ilya Murometz, Jupiter, Laudon, Leningrad, Linz, London, L'Ours, Manfred, Matin, Midi, Miracle, Music, New World, Ninth, Opus, Oxford, Pastoral, Prague, Queen, Resurrection, Rhenish, Sinfonia, Surprise, Tragic, Unfinished
Symptom(s) Epiphenomenon, Feature, Indicia, Merycism, Mimesis, Prodrome, Semiotic, Sign, Syndrome, Token, Trait, Withdrawal
Syncopated, Syncopation, Syncope Abridged, Breakbeat, Offbeat, Revamp, Zoppa, Zoppo
Syndrome Adams-Stokes, Alport's, Asperger's, Carpal tunnel, Cerebellar, Characteristic, China, Chinese restaurant, Chronic fatigue, Compartment, Couvade, Cri du chat, Crush, Cushing's, De Clerambault's, Down's,

Economy-class, Empty nest, Erotomania, False memory, Fetal alcohol, Fragile X, Goldenhar's, Gorlin, Guillain-Barré, Gulf War, Hughes, Hutchinson-Gilford, Irritable-bowel, Jerusalem, Klinefelter's, Korsakoff's, Locked-in, Long QT, Marfan, ME, Meniéres, Metabolic, Munch(h)ausen's, Nonne's, Overuse, Parkinson's, Pattern, POS, Postviral, Prader-Willi, Premenstrual, Proteus, Reiter's, Rett's, Revolving door, Reye's, SADS, SARS, Savant, Sezary, Shaken baby, Sick building, SIDS, Sjogren's, Stevens-Johnson, Stockholm, Stokes-Adams, Sturge-Weber, Tall-poppy, Temperomandibular, TMJ, Total allergy, Tourette's, Toxic shock, Turner's, Wag the dog, Wernicke-Korsakoff, Williams, Wobbler, XYY

Synopsis Abrege, Abstract, Blurb, Conspectus, Digest, Outline, Résumé, Schema, → **SUMMARY**

Synthetic Android, Dralon, Ersatz, Fake, False, Guanazolo, Mock, Neoprene, Polyamide, Resin, Spencerian, Tow, Urea

Syringe(s) Douche, Flutes, Harpoon, Hypo, Needle, Reeds, Spray, Squirt, Wash

Syrup(y) Cassareep, Cassis, Coquito, Corn, Flattery, Glycerol, Goo, Grenadine, Linctus, Maple, Molasses, Orgeat, Rob, Rosehip, Starch, Sugar, Treacle, Viscous, Wig

System(s), Systematic ABO, Alpha, An mo, Apartheid, Auditory, BACS, Beam, Binary, Black, Bordereau, Braille, Brunonian, Carboniferous, Ceefax, Centauri, Circulatory, Closed loop, Code, Colloidal, Colonial, Compander, Complexus, Continental, Cosmos, Course, Crystal, Cybernetics, Decimal, Dewey (Decimal), Dianetics, Distributed, Dolby®, DOS, Early warning, Economy, Eocene, Establishment, Ethic, Expert, Feng Shui, Feudal, Fixed, Folksonomy, Formal, Fourierism, Froebel, Front-end, Grading, Harvard, Haversian, Hexagonal, HLA, Holist, Honour, Hub and spoke, I Ching, Immune, Imperial, Imprest, Imputation, Induction loop, Inertial, ISA, Ism, Kalamazoo, Kanban, Life-support, Limbic, Lobby, Long wall, Loop, Lymphatic, Madras, Mercantile, Mereology, Merit, → **METHOD**, Metric, Midi, Minitel, MKSA, Movable, Muschelkalk, Natural, Navigational, Neat, Nervous, Network, Nicam, Notation, Number, Octal, Operating, Order, Organon, Orphism, Orrery, Panel, Periodic, Plenum, Points, Portal, Process, Public address, Purchase, Quota, Quote-driven, Raisonné, Regime, Regular, Reproductive, Respiratory, Root, Run-time, Scheme, Schmitt, Scientific, Selsyn, Servo, Sexual, SI, Sofar, Solar, Solmisation, Sonar, Sound, Spoils, Sprinkler, Squish lip, Stack(ing), Staff, Stakhanovism, Stand-alone, Star, STOL, Structure, Studio, Support, Sweating, Tactic, Talk-down, Tally, Ternary, Theory, Third-rail, Tommy, Totalitarianism, Touch, Truck, Turnkey, Tutorial, Two-party, Universe, Unix, Urogenital, Vestibular, VOIP, Warehousing, Water, Water vascular, Weapon, Windows

Tt

Table(-like), Tables Altar, Board, Bradshaw, Breakfast, Calendar, Capstan, →**CHART**, Coffee, Communion, Console, Corbel, Counter, Cricket, Decision, Desk, Diagram, Dinner, Dissecting, Draw-leaf, Draw-top, Dressing, Drop-leaf, Drum, Experience, Food, Gateleg, Gate-legged, Glacier, Graph, Green-cloth, Grub, High, Imposing, Index, Key, Ladder, League, Life, Light, →**LIST**, Log, Lord's, Lowboy, Mahogany, Matrix, Mensa(l), Mesa, Mortality, Multiplication, Nest, Occasional, Operating, Orientation, Pembroke, Periodic, Piecrust, Pier, Plane, Plateau, Platen, Pool, Pythagoras, Ready-reckoner, Reckoner, Refectory, Roll, Round, Sand, Schedule, Scheme, Slab, Sofa, Spoon, Stall, Statistical, Stone, Suggest, Tariff, Tea, Te(a)poy, Throwing, Tide, Times, Toilet, Toning, Top, Tray(mobile), Trestle, Trolley, Truth, Twelve, Washstand, Water, Whirling, Wool, Workbench, Writing

Tablet Abacus, Album, Aspirin, Caplet, Cartouche, E, Eugebine, Hatchment, Medallion, Opisthograph, Osculatory, Ostracon, Ostrakon, →**PAD**, →**PILL**, Plaque, Rune, Slate, Stele, Stone, Tabula, Tombstone, Torah, Triglyph, Triptych, Troche, Trochisk, Ugarit, Wax

Taboo, Tabu Ban(ned), Bar, Blackball, Forbidden, No-no, Tapu

Tack(y) Adhesive, Bar, Baste, Beat, Boxhaul, Brass, Cinch, Clubhaul, Cobble, Gybe, Harness, Kitsch, Leg, Martingale, Nail, Noseband, Saddlery, Salt-horse, →**SEW**, Sprig, Stirrup, Tasteless, Veer, White-seam, Yaw, Zigzag

Tackle Accost, Address, Approach, Attempt, Beard, Bobstay, Burton, Cat, Chin, Claucht, Claught, Clevis, Collar, Dead-eye, Garnet, Gear, Haliard, Halyard, Harness, Jury-rig, Kit, Ledger, Nose, Rig, Rigging, Sack, Scrag, Spear, Stick, Undertake

Tact, Tactful Delicacy, Diplomacy, Diplomatic, Discreet, Discretion, Kidglove, Politic, Savoir-faire

Tactic(s) Audible, Carrot and stick, Crossruff, Hardball, Manoeuvre, Masterstroke, Plan, Ploy, Salami, Scare, Shock, Smear, →**STRATEGY**, Strong-arm

Tactless(ness) Blundering, Brash, Crass, Gaffe, Gauche, Indelicate, Indiscreet, Loud mouth

Tail, Tailpiece, Tailboard All-flying, Amentum, →**APPENDAGE**, Bob, Brush, Bun, Caudal, Coda, Colophon, Cue, Dock, Endgate, Fan, Fee, →**FOLLOW**, Fud, Liripoop, Parson's nose, Point, Pole, Pope's nose, PS, Queue, Scut, Seat, Shirt, Stag, Stern, Telson, →**TIP**, Train, Uropod, Women

Tailor(ed) Bespoke, Bushel, Cabbager, Clothier, Couturier, Customise, Cutter, Darzi, Draper, Durzi, Epicene, Feeble, Form, Nine, Outfitter, Pick-the-louse, Pricklouse, Sartor, Seamster, Snip, Starveling, Style, Whipcat, Whipstitch

▷**Tailor** *may indicate* an anagram

Taint(ed) Besmirch, Blemish, Fly-blown, Foughty, High, Impure, Infect, Leper, Off, Poison, →**SPOIL**, Stain, Stale, Stigma, Trace, Unwholesome

Take(n), Take in, Taking(s), Take over, Takeover Absorb, →**ACCEPT**, Adopt, Annex, Appropriate, Assume, Attract, Bag, Beg, Besotted, Bewitch, Bite, Bone, Borrow, Bottle, →**CAPTURE**, Catch, Charming, Claim, Cop, Coup (d'etat), Detract, Dig, Dishy, Eat, Entr(y)ism, Epris, Exact, Expropriate, Film, Get, Grab, Greenmail, Handle, Haul, Hent, House, Howe, Huff, Impound, Incept, Ingest, Leveraged buy out, Loot, Mess, Misappropriate, Nationalise, Nick, Occupy, On, Pocket, Poison pill, Quote, R, Rec, Receipt, Receive, Recipe, Reserved, Reverse, Rob, Seise, Sequester, Ship, Smitten, Snaffle, Snatch, Sneak, Spoken for, →**STEAL**, Stomach, Subsume, Swallow, Sweet, Swipe, Toll, Trump, Turnover, Usher, Usurp, Wan, Winsome, Wrest

Take down, Take up Appropriate, Cap, Choose, Osmose, Shot, Snaffle, Unhook
▷**Taken up** *may indicate* reversed

Tale(s) Aga-saga, Allegory, Anecdote, Blood, Cautionary, Conte, Decameron, Edda, Fable, Fabliau, Fairy, Fiction, Gag, Geste, Hadith, Hair-raiser, Iliad, Jataka, Jeremiad, Legend, Lie, Mabinogion, Maise, Märchen, Ma(i)ze, Narrative, Odyssey, Rede, Saga, Score, Sinbad, Spiel, →**STORY**, Teratology, Toy, Tradition, Traveller's, Weird, Yarn

Talent(ed) Able, Accomplishment, Aptitude, Beefcake, Bent, Brilliance, Budding, Dower, Endowment, Faculty, Flair, Genius, Gift, Idiot savant, Knack, Nous, Obol, Prodigy, Schtick, Strong point, Tottie, Versatile, Virtuoso, Whiz-kid, W(h)iz(z)

Talk(ing), Talking point, Talker, Talks Address, Ana, Articulate, Babble, Blab, Blat, Blather, Blether-skate, Cant, Causerie, Chalk, Chat, Chew the fat, Chinwag, Chirp, Chitchat, Commune, Confer, Contact, Converse, Coo, Cross, Descant, Dialog(ue), Diatribe, Dilate, Discourse, Diseur, Dissert, Double, Earbash, Earful, Expatiate, Express, Fast, Froth, Gab, Gabble, Gabnash, Gas, Gibber, Gossip, Guff, Harp, High-level, Hobnob, Hot air, Imparl, Jabber, Jargon, Jaw-jaw, Jazz, Lalage, Lalla, Lip, Mang, Maunder, Mince, Monologue, Nashgab, Natter, Noise, Palaver, Parlance, Parley, Patter, Pawaw, Pep, Pidgin, Pillow, Pitch, Potter, Powwow, Prate, Prattle, Presentation, Prose, Proximity, Ramble, Rap, Rattle on, Regale, Rigmarole, Rote, Sales, SALT, Sermon, Shop, Slang(-whang), Small, Soliloquy, →**SPEAK**, Speech, Spiel, Spout, Straight, Summit, Sweet, Table, Tachylogia, Topic, Turkey, Twaddle, Twitter, Up(s), Utter, Vocal, Waffle, Wibble, Witter, Wrangle, Yabber, Yack, Yad(d)a-yad(d)a-yad(d)a, Yak, Yalta, Yammer, Yap, Yatter

Talkative Chatty, Expansive, Fluent, Gabby, Garrulous, Gash, Glib, Loquacious, Vocular, Voluble, Windbag

Tall Beanpole, Etiolated, Exaggerated, Far-fetched, Hie, High, Hye, Lanky, Lathy, Leggy, Lofty, Long, Order, Procerity, Randle-tree, Rangy, Spindly, Tangle, Taunt, Tower, Towery

Tally Accord, →**AGREE**, Census, Correspond, Count, Match, Nickstick, Notch, Record, →**SCORE**, Stick, Stock, Tab, Tag

Tame Amenage, Break, Docile, Domesticate, Gentle, Mail, Mansuete, Meek, Mild, Safe, Snool, Subdue

Tamper(ing) Bishop, Cook, Doctor, Fake, Fiddle, Meddle, Medicate, Monkey, Nobble, Phreaking

Tan(ned), Tanned skin, Tanning Adust, Bablah, Babul, Bark, Basil, Beige, Bisque, Bronze, →**BROWN**, Catechu, Insolate, Lambast, Leather, Neb-neb,

Paste, Pipi, Puer, Pure, Spank, Sun, Tenné, Umber, Valonea, Val(l)onia, Weather-beaten, Ybet

Tangle Alga, Badderlock, Burble, Driftweed, Dulse, Embroil, Enmesh, Entwine, Fank, Fankle, Heap, Hole, Implication, Ket, →**KNOT**, Labyrinth, Laminaria, Lutin, Mat, Mess, Mix, Nest, Oarweed, Ore, Perplex, Pleach, Raffle, Sea-girdle, Seaweed, Skean, Skein, Snarl, Taigle, Taut(it), Tawt, Thicket, Tousle, Varec
▷**Tangled** *may indicate* an anagram

Tank(ed) Abrams, Alligator, Amphibian, Aquarium, Back boiler, Belly, Bosh, Casspir, Centurion, Cesspool, Challenger, Chieftain, Cistern, Crusader, Dracone, Drop, Drunk, Fail, Feedhead, Float, Flotation, Fuel, Gasholder, Gasometer, Header, Keir, Kier, Panzer, Pod, Quiescent, →**RESERVOIR**, Ripple, Sedimentation, Septic, Sherman, Shield pond, Sponson, Sump, Surge, Think, Tiger, Vat, Venter, Ventral, Vivarium, Weasel

Tantalise Entice, Tease, Tempt, Torture

Tantrum Conniption, Paddy, Pet, Rage, Scene, Snit, Tirrivee, Tirrivie, Wobbly

Tap(ping), Taps Accolade, Ague, Blip, Bob, Broach, Bug, Cock, Dip into, Drum, Eavesdrop, Faucet, Fever, Fillip, Flick, Hack, H and C, Listen, Mixer, Paracentesis, Pat, Patter, Percuss, Petcock, →**RAP**, Screw, Spigot, Spile, Standpipe, Stopcock, Tack, Tat, Tit

Tape Adhesive, Chrome, DAT, Demo, →**DRINK**, Duct, Ferret, Finish, Friction, Gaffer, Grip, Idiot, Incle, Inkle, Insulating, Magnetic, Masking, Measure, Metal, Narrowcast, Paper, Passe-partout, Perforated, Punched, Record, Red, Reel to reel, Scotch, Sellotape®, Shape, Stay, Sticky, Ticker, Tit, Video, Welding

Taper(ed), Tapering Candle, Diminish, Fastigiate, Featheredge, Flagelliform, Fusiform, Lanceolate, Narrow, Nose, Spill, Subulate, Tail

Tapestry Alentous, Arras(ene), Bayeux, Bergamot, Crewel-work, Dosser, Gobelin, Hanging, Mural, Oudenarde, Sewing, Tapet, Weaving

Target Admass, →**AIM**, Ambition, Attainment, Blank, Butt, Clay, Clout, Cockshy, Dartboard, Drogue, End, Ettle, Hit, Home, Hub, Inner, Magpie, Mark, Mark-white, Motty, Nick, →**OBJECT**, Object ball, Outer, Peg, Pelta, Pin, Popinjay, Prey, Prick, Quintain, Sitter, Sitting (duck), Tee, Victim, Wand, Zero in, Zero on

Tarry Bide, Bituminous, Dally, Leng, →**LINGER**, Stay, Sticky

Tartar Argal, Argol, Beeswing, Crust, Hell, Plaque, Rough, Scale, Tam(b)erlane, Zenocrate

Task Assignment, Aufgabe, Clat, Commission, Drudgery, Duty, Emprise, Errand, Exercise, Fag, Imposition, Legwork, Marathon, Mission, Onus, Ordeal, Remit, Stint, Thankless, Uphill, Vulgus

Taste(ful), Taster, Tasty Acquired, Aesthetic, Appetite, Assay, Dash, Degust, Delibate, Delicious, Discrimination, →**EAT**, Elegant, Excerpt, Fad, Fancy, Fashion, Flavour, Form, Gout, Gust, Gustatory, Hint, Lekker, Lick, Liking, Palate, Penchant, Pica, Pree, Refinement, Relish, →**SAMPLE**, Sapor, Sar, Savour, Scrummy, Seemly, Sensation, S(c)hme(c)k, Sip, Smack, Smatch, Smattering, Snack, Soupçon, Specimen, Stomach, Succulent, Tang, Titbit, Toothsome, →**TRY**, Umami, Vertu, Virtu, Waft, Wine

Tasteless Appal, Coarse, Fade, Flat, Gaudy, Indelicate, Insipid, Insulse, Kitsch, Stale, Tawdry, Vapid, Vulgar, Watery, Wearish, Wersh

Tattle(r) Blab, Chatter, →**GOSSIP**, Prate, Rumour, Sneak, Snitch, Totanus, Willet

Taunt Bait, Catcall, Dig, Fling, Gibe, Gird, →**JEER**, Jest, Jibe, Rag, Razz, Ridicule, Twight, Twit

Tavern Bar, Bodega, Bousing-ken, Bush, Fonda, →**INN**, Kiddleywink, Kneipe, Mermaid, Mitre, Mughouse, Night-house, Pothouse, Shebeen, Taphouse

Tawdry Brash, Catchpenny, →**CHEAP**, Flashy, Gaudy, Gingerbread, Sleazy, Tatty

Tax(ation), Taxing ACT, Agist, Aid, Alms-fee, Arduous, Assess, Capital gains, Capitation, Carbon, Cense, Cess, →**CHARGE**, Corporation, Council, CRT, Custom, Danegeld, Death duty, Deferred, Direct, Duty, Energy, EPT, Escot, Escuage, Eurotax, Exact, Excise, Exercise, EZT, Fat, Geld, Gelt, Gift, Green, Head, Head money, Hearth money, Hidden, Impose, Imposition, Impost, Impute, Indirect, Inheritance, IR, Keelage, Land, Levy, Lot, Negative, Octroi, Operose, Overtask, Overwork, PAYE, Poll, Poundage, Precept, Primage, Property, Proportional, PT, Punish, Purchase, Rate, Regressive, Road, Sales, Scat(t), Scot (and lot), Scutage, Sess, SET, Ship money, Sin, Single, Skat, Stealth, Stent, Strain, Stretch, Stumpage, Super, Tall order, Tariff, Tartan, Task, Teind, Tithe, Tobin, Toilsome, Toll, Tonnage, Tribute, Try, Turnover, Tyre, Unitary, Value-added, VAT, Wattle, Wealth, Weary, White rent, Windfall, Window, Withholding

Tax-collector, Taxman Amildar, Cheater, Exciseman, Farmer, Gabeller, Ghostbuster, Inspector, IR(S), Publican, Stento(u)r, Tidesman, Tithe-proctor, Tollman, Undertaker, Vatman, Zemindar

Tea Afternoon, Assam, Beef, Black, Bohea, Brew, Brew-up, Brick, Bubble, Bush, Cambric, Camomile, Caper, Ceylon, Cha, Chai, Chamomile, Chanoyu, Char, China, Chirping-cup, Congo(u), Cream, Cuppa, Darjeeling, Earl Grey, Grass, Green, Gunfire, Gunpowder, Herb(al), High, Hybrid, Hyson, Ice(d), Indian, Jasmine, K(h)at, Kitchen, Labrador, Lapsang, Lapsang Souchong, Leaves, Ledum, Lemon, Malt, Manuka, Marijuana, Maté, Mexican, Mint, Morning, Mountain, New Jersey, Oolong, Orange pekoe, Oulong, Paraguay, Pekoe, Post and rail, Pot, Qat, Red-root, Rooibos, Rosie Lee, Russian, Sage, Senna, Souchong, Stroupach, Stroupan, Switchel, Tay, Thea, Theophylline, Tousy, Twankay, White, Yapon, Yerba (de Maté)

Teach(er), Teaching (material), Teachings Academe, Academician, Adjoint, Advisory, Agrege, Anthroposophy, Apostle, Aristotle, AUT, Beale, BEd, Buddha, Buss, Chalk and talk, →**COACH**, Communicate, Con(ne), Didactic, Doctrine, Dogma, Dominie, Dressage, Edify, →**EDUCATE**, Educationalist, Edutainment, Explain, Faculty, Froebel, Gospel, Governess, Guru, Head, Inculcate, Indoctrinate, Inform, Instil, Instruct, Ism, Kindergart(e)ner, Kumon (Method), Lair, Lear(e), Lecturer, Leir, Lere, Maam, Magister, Marker, Marm, Master, Mentor, Message, Miss, Mistress, Molla(h), Monitor, Mufti, Mullah, Munshi, Mwalimu, Nuffield, NUT, PAT, Pedagogue, Pedant, Peripatetic, Phonic method, Posture-master, Preceptor, Pr(a)efect, Proctor, Prof, Prog, PT, Pupil, Rabbetzin, Rabbi, Rav, Rebbe, Remedial, Rhetor, Scholastic, Schoolie, Schoolman, Scribe, Show, Sir, Socrates, Sophist, Specialist, Staff, Stinks, Substitute, Sufism, Sunna, Supply, Swami, Tantra, Team, Tonic sol-fa, Train(er), Tuition, Tutelage, Tutor, Tutress, Tutrix, Usher

Team All Blacks, Argyll, Colts, Crew, Dream, Écurie, Eleven, Équipe, Fifteen, Hearts, Man U, Nine, Outfit, Oxen, Panel, Possibles, Proto, Relay, Scrub, Set, →**SIDE**, Span, Spurs, Squad, Squadron, Staff, Syndicate, Troupe, Turnout, Unicorn, Unit, United, XI

Tear(s), Tearable, Tearful, Tearing Beano, Claw, Crocodile, Dismember, Drop(let), Eye-drop, Eye-water, Greeting, Hurry, Lacerate, Lachrymose, Laniary, Mammock, Maudlin, Pelt, Ranch, Rash, Reave, Rheum, Rip, Rive, Rume, Screed, Shred, Snag, Split, Spree, Sprint, Tire, Vale, Wet, Worry, Wrench, Wrest

Tease, Teaser, Teasing Arch, Backcomb, Badinage, Bait, Ballyrag, Banter, Chap, Chiack, Chip, Cod, Comb, Coquet, Discredit, Drag, Enigma, Grig, Guy, Hank, Imp, Ironic, Itch, Josh, Kemb, Kid, Mag, Nark, Persiflage, →**RAG**, Raillery, Rally, Razz, Rib, Rip on, Rot, Strip, →**TANTALISE**, Torment(or), Touse, Touze, Towse, Towze, Twit

Teat Dug, Dummy, Mamilla, Mastoid, Nipple, Pap, Soother, Tit

Technical, Technician, Technique Adept, Alexander, Art, Artisan, Brushwork, Campimetry, College, Craftsmanship, Cusum, Delphi, Execution, Foley artist, Footsteps editor, Harmolodics, Honey-trap, Junior, Kiwi, Know-how, Layback, Manner, Metamorphic, →**METHOD**, Operative, Phasing, Phlebotomist, Pixil(l)ation, Reflectography, Salami, Sandwich, Science, Scientist, Senior, Serial, Slam-dunk, Slo-mo, Split-screen, Stop-motion, System, Toe and heel, Touch, Western blotting, Work around

Tedium, Tedious Boring, Chore, Deadly, Drab, Drag, Dreariness, Dreich, Dull, Ennui, Foozle, Heaviness, Ho-hum, Laborious, Langueur, Long, Longspun, Mind-numbing, Monotony, Operose, Prosy, Rigmarole, Snore, Soul-destroying, Tiresome, →**TIRING**, Wearisome, Yawn

Teem(ing) Abound, Bustling, Empty, Great, Heaving, Pullulate, Swarm

Teenage(r) Adolescent, Bobbysoxer, Junior, Juvenile, Minor, Mod, Pubertal, Rocker, Sharpie

▶**Teeth** see **TOOTH(ED)**

Teetotal(ler) Abdar, Abstainer, Blue Ribbon, Nephalist, Rechabite, Sober, Temperate, TT, Water-drinker, Wowser

Telegram, Telegraph Bush, Cable, Ems, Facsimile, Fax, Grapevine, Greetings, Marconi, Message, Moccasin, Overseas, Quadruplex, Radiogram, Telautograph®, Telex, Wire

Telephone, Telephonist Ameche, ATLAS, Bell, Blackberry, Blower, BT, Call, Cellphone, Centrex, Cordless, Detectophone, Dial, Exchange, Freephone®, GRACE, Handset, Horn, Hotline, Intercom, Line, Mercury, Mob(e)y, Noki, Operator, Patchboard, Payphone, Pdq, Ring, Snitch line, Speakerphone, STD, Telebridge, Tie line, Touch-tone, Utility, Vodafone®, Wire

Telescope Altazimuth, Astronomical, Binocle, Cassegrain(ian), Collimator, Comet finder, Coronagraph, Coronograph, Coudé, Electron, Equatorial, Finder, Galilean, Gemini, Glass, Gregorian, Heliometer, Hubble, Interferometer, Intussuscept, Meniscus, Newtonian, Night-glass, Optical, Palomar, Perspective, Prospect(ive)-glass, Radio, Reading, Reflecting, Reflector, Refractor, Schmidt, Sector, Shorten, Sniperscope, Snooperscope, Speculum, Spyglass, Stadia, Terrestrial, Tube, X-ray, Zenith

Television, Telly Appointment, Box, Breakfast, Closed-circuit, Confessional, Digibox®, Digital, Diorama, Docu-soap, Flatscreen, Goggle box, Iconoscope, Interactive, ITV, MAC, Narrowcast, PAL, Reality, RTE, Set, Small screen, Terrestrial, Tube, →**TV**, Video

Tell(ing), Teller, Telltale Acquaint, Announce, Apprise, Beads, Blab, Cashier, Clipe, Clype, Confess, Direct, →**DISCLOSE**, Divulge, Effective, Fess, Give, Grass, Impart, Influential, Inform(er), →**NARRATE**, Noise, Nose, Notify, Number, Rat, Recite, Recount, Relate, Report, Retail, Rumour, Scunge, Sing, Sneak, Snitch, Spin, Teach, Unbosom, William

Temper, Temperate Abstinent, Adjust, Allay, Alloy, Anneal, Assuage, Attune, Balmy, Bate, Bile, Blood, Calm, Cantankerous, Choler, Continent, Dander, Delay, Ease, Fireworks, Flaky, Inure, Irish, Leaven, →**MILD**, Mitigate, Moderate,

Modify, →**MOOD**, Neal, Outburst, Paddy, Pet, Rage, Season, Sober, Soften, Spitfire, Spleen, Strop, Tantrum, Techy, Teen, Teetotal, Tetchy, Tiff, Tone, Trim, Tune, Wax

Temperament(al) Bent, Blood, Choleric, Crasis, Cyclothymia, Disposition, Equal, Just, Kidney, Mean-tone, Melancholy, Mettle, Moody, →**NATURE**, Neal, Over-sensitive, Phlegmatic, Prima donna, Sanguine, Unstable, Up and down, Viscerotonia

Temperature Absolute, Black body, Celsius, Centigrade, Chambré, Core, Curie, Eutectic, Fahrenheit, Fever, Flashpoint, Heat, Heterothermal, Hyperthermia, Ignition, Kelvin, Melting, Néel, Permissive, Regulo, Room, Supercritical, T, Transition, Weed, Weid

Temple, Temple gate Abu Simbel, Abydos, Amritsar, Capitol, Chapel, Church, Delphi, Delubrum, Ephesus, Erechtheum, Erechthion, Fane, Gurdwara, Heroon, Inner, Josshouse, Karnak, Masjid, Middle, Mosque, Museum, Naos, Pagod(a), Pantheon, Parthenon, Sacellum, Serapeum, →**SHRINE**, Shul(n), Teocalli, Teopan, Torii, Vihara, Wat

Temporary Acting, Caretaker, Casual, Cutcha, Ephemeral, Fleeting, Freelance(r), Hobjob, Impermanent, Interim, Jury-rigged, Kutcha, Lash-up, Locum, Makeshift, Pro tem, Provisional, Quick-fix, Scratch, Short-term, Stopgap, Temp, Transient, Transitional

Tempt(ation), Tempting, Tempter, Temptress Allure, Apple, Bait, Beguile, Beset, Dalilah, Dangle, Decoy, Delilah, Draw, →**ENTICE**, Eve, Femme fatale, Groundbait, Impulse, Induce, Irresistible, Lure, Mephistopheles, Peccable, Providence, Satan, Seduce, Serpent, Sexy, Siren, Snare, Tantalise, Test, Tice, Trial, Woo

Ten Commandments, Decad, Iota, Long, Tera-, Tribes, X

Tenacious, Tenacity Adhesive, Clayey, Determined, Dogged, Drive, Fast, Grim death, Guts, Hold, Intransigent, Persevering, Persistent, Resolute, Retentive, Sticky

Tenancy, Tenant(s) Boarder, Censuarius, Cosherer, Cottager, Cottar, Cotter, Cottier, Dreng, Feuar, Feudatory, Homage, Ingo, Inhabit, Kindly, Leaseholder, Lessee, Liege, →**LODGER**, Mailer, Metayer, Occupant, Occupier, Pendicler, Regulated, Rentaller, Renter, Shorthold, Sitting, Socager, Socman, Sokeman, Suckener, Tacksman, Valvassor, Vassal, Vavasour, Villein, Visit

Tend(ing) Apt, Care, Dress, Herd, Incline, Keep, Lean, Liable, Mind, Minister, Nurse, Prone, Run, Shepherd, Stoke, Verge, Volunteer

Tendency Apt, Bent, Bias, Conatus, Disposition, Drift, Import, Inclination, Leaning, Militant, Orientation, Penchant, Proclivity, Propensity, Trend

Tender(iser), Tenderly, Tenderness Affettuoso, Amoroso, Bid, Bill, Charitable, Coin, Con amore, Crank, Dingey, Ding(h)y, Fond, Frail, Gentle, Green, Humane, Jolly-boat, Legal, Nesh, Nurse(maid), →**OFFER**, Papain, Pinnace, Pra(a)m, Prefer, Present, Proffer, Proposal, Quotation, Red Cross, Sair, Shepherd, →**SOFT**, Sore, SRN, Submit, Sweet, Swineherd, Sympathy, Tendre

Tendon Achilles, Aponeurosis, Hamstring, Leader, Paxwax, Sinew, String, Vinculum, Whitleather

Tennis player Ashe, Edberg, Laver, Nastase

Tenor Caruso, Course, Direction, →**DRIFT**, Effect, Even, Feck, Gigli, Gist, Heldentenor, Purport, Sense, Singer, T, Timbre, Trial, Vein

Tense Agitato, Aor, Aorist, Case, Clench, Cliffhanger, Conditional, Drawn, Edgy, Electric, Essive, Flex, Fraught, Imperfect, Keyed up, Knife-edge, Laconic,

Mood(y), Nail-biting, Nervy, On edge, Overstrung, Past, Perfect, Pluperfect, Present perfect, Preterite, Rigid, Stiff, Stressed(-out), Strict, T, Tighten, Uptight

Tension Creative, Dialectic, High, Isometrics, Isotonic, Meniscus, Nail-biting, Nerviness, Premenstrual, →**strain**, Stress, Stretch, Surface, Tone, Tonicity, Tonus, Yips

Tent Bell, Bivouac, Bivvy, Cabana, Douar, Duar, Ger, Gur, Kedar, Kibitka, Marquee, Oxygen, Pavilion, Probe, Ridge, Shamiana(h), Shamiyanah, Shelter, Tabernacle, Teepee, Tepee, Tipi, Top, Topek, Trailer, Tupek, Tupik, Wigwam, Y(o)urt

Term(s), Terminal, Termly Air, Anode, Boundary, Buffer, Buzzword, Cathode, Coast, Container, Coste, Designate, Desinent(ial), Distal, Distributed, Dub, Dumb, Easy, Euphemism, Expression, Final, Gnomon, Goal, Half, Hilary, Inkhorn, Intelligent, Kathode, Law, Lent, Major, Michaelmas, Middle, Minor, Misnomer, Never-never, →**period**, Point-of-sale, Rail(head), Real, Remit, Removal, Sabbatical, School, Semester, Session, Smart, Spell, Stint, Stretch, Trimester, Trimestrial, Trinity, Verb, Waterloo, →**word**, Work station

Terminate, Termination, Terminus Abolish, Abort, Axe, Cease, Conclude, Depot, Desinent, Earth, →**end**, Euston, Expiry, →**finish**, Goal, King's Cross, Liquidate, Naricorn, Paddington, Railhead, Suffix, Waterloo

Terrace Barbette, Beach, Bench, Crescent, Kop, Linch, Lynchet, Patio, Perron, River, Row house, Shelf, Stoep, Tarras, Undercliff, Veranda(h)

Terrible, Terribly Atrocity, Awful, Deadly, Dire, Fearsome, Fell, Fiendish, Frightful, Ghastly, Heinous, Hellacious, Horrible, Humgruffi(a)n, Ivan, Much, Odious, Very

Terrier Australian silky, Bedlington, Cairn, Cesky, Dandie Dinmont, Fox, Glen of Imaal, Irish, Jack Russell, Schauzer, Scotch, Scottish, Soft-coated wheaten, Staffordshire bull, Sydney silky, West Highland white, Westie, Wheaten, Wire-haired, Yorkie

Terrific, Terrified, Terrify(ing) Affright, Aghast, Agrise, Agrize, Agryze, Appal, Awe, Enorm, Fear, Fine, Fley, Gast, Helluva, Huge, Mega, Nightmarish, Overawe, →**petrify**, Scare, Superb, Thumping, Unman, Yippee

Territory, Territorial(ist) Abthane, Ap(p)anage, Area, Colony, Coral Sea Islands, Doab, Domain, Dominion, Duchy, Emirate, Enclave, Exclave, Goa, Golan Heights, Irredentist, Kingdom, Lebensraum, Mandated, Manor, Margravate, No-man's-land, Northern, Nunavut, Panhandle, Patch, Princedom, Principality, Principate, Protectorate, Province, Realm, →**region**, Reserve, Rupert's Land, Sphere, Stamping ground, Sultanate, Swazi, Ter(r), Trieste, Trust, Tuath, Yukon

Test(er), Testing, Tests Achievement, Acid, Alpha, Ames, Analyse, Appro, Aptitude, Ashes, Assay, Audition, Barany, Bench, Bender, Benedict, Beta, Bioassay, Biopsy, Blood, Breath, Breathalyser®, Burn-in, Candle, Canopy, Check, Chi-square, Cis-trans, Cloze, Conn(er), Coomb's, Crash, Criterion, Crosscheck, Cross-match, Crucial, Crucible, Crunch, Dick, Driving, Drop, Dummy-run, Esda, Essay, Etudes, Exacting, Examine, Exercise, Experiment, Fehling's, Field, Finals, Flame, Frog, Hagberg, Ink-blot, Intelligence, International, Litmus, Lydian stone, Match, Mazzin, Means, Medical, Mom, MOT, Mug, Neckverse, Needs, Objective, Oral, →**ordeal**, Pale, Pap, Paraffin, Patch, Paternity, Performance, Personality, PH, Pilot, Ping, Pons asinorum, Pree, Preeve, Preve, Prieve, Probative, Probe, Projective, Proof, Prove, PSA, Pyx, Q-sort, Qualification, Quiz, Rally, Reagent, Reliability, Road, Rorschach, SAT, Scan, Schutz-Charlton,

Scientise, Scratch, Screen, Shadow, Shibboleth, Showdown, Shroff, Sign, Signed-ranks, Significance, Sixpence, Skidpan, Skin, Slump, Smear, Smoke, Snellen, Soap, Sound, Sounding, Spinal, Stress, Task, Tempt, Tensile, Thematic apperception, Tongue-twister, Touch, Touchstone, Trial, Trier, Trior, Try, Turing, Ultrasonic, Viva, Weigh, Zohar

Testament Bible, Heptateuch, Hexateuch, New, Old, Pentateuch, Scripture, Septuagint, Tanach, Targum, Will

Testicle(s) Ballocks, Balls, Bollix, Bollocks, Bush oyster, Cojones, Cruet, Doucets, Dowsets, Family jewels, Goolie, Gool(e)y, Knackers, Monorchid, Nuts, Orchis, Pills, Prairie oyster, Ridgel, Ridgil, Rig(gald), Rocks, Stone

Testify(ing), Testimonial, Testimony Attestation, Character, Chit, Declare, Depone, Deposition, →**EVIDENCE**, Hard, Rap, Reference, Scroll, Viva voce, Vouch, Witness

Tether Cord, Endurance, Knot, Lariat, Leash, Noose, Picket, Seal, Stringhalt, →**TIE**

Text(s), Textbook, Texting ABC, Alkoran, Apocrypha, Body, Brahmana, Church, Codex, Copy, Corpus, Donat, Ennage, Greeked, Harmony, Letterpress, Libretto, Lines, Mandaean, Mantra(m), Masoretic, Mezuzah, Minitel, Ms, Nynorsk, Octapla, Op-cit, Panegyricon, Philology, Plain, Proof, Purana, Pyramid, Quran, Responsa, Rubric, S(h)astra, Script, Sermon, Shema, SMS, →**SUBJECT**, Sura, Sutra, Tao Te Ching, Tefillin, Tephillin, Tetrapla, Thesis, Topic, Tripitaka, Tweet, Typography, Upanis(h)ad, Urtext, Variorum, Viewdata, Vulgate, Writing, Zohar

Thank(s), Thankful, Thanksgiving Appreciate, Collins, Deo gratias, Gloria, Grace, Gramercy, Grateful, Gratitude, Kaddish, Mercy, Roofer

Thatch(er), Thatching At(t)ap, Hair, Heard, Hear(i)e, Hele, Hell, Lath, Mane, PM, Reed, Straw, Sway, Thack, Theek, Wig, Ye(a)lm

▷**Thaw** *may indicate* 'ice' to be removed from a word

Theatre(s), Theatrical(ity) Abbey, Absurd, Adelphi, Aldwych, Arena, Auditorium, Balcony, Broadway, Camp, Cinema, Circle, Coliseum, Criterion, Crucible, Drama, Drury Lane, Epic, Event, Everyman, Field, Folies Bergere, Fourth-wall, Fringe, Gaff, Gaiety, Globe, Grand Guignol, Grandiose, Great White Way, Hall, Haymarket, Hippodrome, Histrionic, House, Kabuki, La Scala, Legitimate, Little, Living, Lyceum, Melodramatic, Mermaid, Moulin Rouge, Musical, Music-hall, National, News, Nickelodeon, Noh, Novello, Odeon, Odeum, Off-Broadway, Off-off-Broadway, Old Vic, Operating, OUDS, Palladium, Panache, Pennygaff, Pit, Playhouse, Political, Rep(ertory), Royal Court, Sadler's Wells, Shaftesbury, Sheldonian, Shop, Stage, Stalls, Stoll, Straw-hat, Street, Studio, Summer stock, Tivoli, Total, Touring, Vic, Windmill, Winter Garden(s), Wyndham's, Zarzuela

Theft, Thieving Appropriation, Bluesnarfing, Burglary, Haul, Heist, Identity, Kinchinlay, Larceny, Maino(u)r, Manner, Petty larceny, Pilfery, Pillage, Piracy, Plagiarism, Plunder, Pugging, Ram-raid, Rip off, Robbery, Shrinkage, Stealth, Stouth(rief), →**THIEF**, Touch, TWOC, Walk-in

Theme Crab canon, Donnée, Fugue, Idea, Leitmotiv, Lemma, Lemmata, →**MELODY**, Motif, Mythos, Mythus, Peg, Question, →**SUBJECT**, Subtext, Text, Topic, Topos

Theologian, Theologist, Theology Abelard, Ambrose, Aquinas, Arminius, Baur, Calvin, Christology, Colet, DD, Divine, Eckhart, Erastus, Eschatology, Eusebius, Exegetics, Faustus, Fideism, Harnack, Hase, Irenics, Isidore, Jansen,

Kierkegaard, Knox, Laelius, Luther, Mullah, Newman, Niebuhr, Origen, Paley, Pastoral, Patristics, Pelagius, Peritus, Pusey, Rabbi, Religious, Schoolman, Schwenkfeld, Socinus, Softa, STP, Swedenborg, Tertullian, Thomas à Kempis, Tirso de Molina, Ulema

Theory, Theorem, Theoretical, Theorist Abstract, Academic, Atomic, Attachment, Attribution, Auteur, Automata, Band, Big bang, Binomial, Boo-hurrah, Boolean, Calorific, Catastrophe, Chaos, Communications, Complexity, Connectionism, Conspiracy, Corpuscular, Cosmogony, Creationism, Decision, Deduction, Dependency, Dictum, Doctrinaire, Domino, Double aspect, Dow, Einstein, Emboîtement, Empiricism, Euhemerism, Exponential, Fermat's (last), Fortuitism, Gaia, Galois, Game, Gauge, Germ, Grand Unified, Grotian, Group, Guess, Holism, Hormic, Hypothesis, Ideal, Identity, Ideology, Information, Ism(y), Jordan curve, Kinetic, Kock's, Lemma, Lunar, MAD, Metaphysical, Milankovitch, Model, Mythical, Nebular, Neo-Lamarckism, Neovitalism, Nernst heat, Notion, Number, Object relations, On paper, Pancosmism, Pantologism, Perturbation, Petrinism, Pluralism, Positivism, Probability, Proof, Pure, Pythagoras, Quantity, Quantum, Quantum field, Queueing, Random walk, Rational choice, Reception, Relativism, Relativity, Satisfaction, Set, Solipsism, Steady state, String, Superdense, Superstring, Supersymmetry, Supposition, System, Traducianism, Trickle-down, Twistor, Tychism, Unified Field, Utilitarianism, Voluntarism, Vortex, Wages fund, Wave

Therapy, Therapeutic, Therapist Analyst, Family, Fever, Insight, Non directive, Past life, Remedial, →TREATMENT

Thermometer Aethrioscope, Centesimal, Cryometer, Glass, Katathermometer, Pyrometer, Wet and dry bulb

Thick(en), Thickening, Thickener, Thickness, Thickset Abundant, Agar-agar, Algin, Brainless, Burly, Bushy, Callosity, Callus, Clavate, Cloddy, Cruddle, Curdle, Dense, Dextrin(e), Dumb, Dumose, Engross, Fat, Grist, Grume, Guar, Gum, Hyperostosis, In cahoots, Incrassate, Inspissate, Kuzu, Liaison, Luxuriant, Nirlie, Pally, Panada, Ply, Reduce, Roux, Sclerosis, →SOLID, Soupy, Spissitude, Squat, Stocky, Stumpy, →STUPID, Thieves, This, Thixotropic, Turbid, Viscous, Waulk, Wooden, Xantham

Thicket Bosk, Brake, Brush, Cane-brake, Chamisal, Chap(paral), Coppice, Copse, Covert, Dead-finish, Fernshaw, Greve, Grove, Macchia, Maquis, Queach, Reedrand, Reedrond, Salicetum, Shola

Thief, Thieves, Thievish Area sneak, Autolycus, Blood, Bulker, Chummy, Coon, Corsair, Cracksman, Cutpurse, Dip, Filcher, Flood, Footpad, Forty, Freebooter, Gully-raker, Heist, Hotter, Ice-man, Jackdaw, Joyrider, Kiddy, Larcener, Lifter, Light-fingered, Looter, Mag, Magpie, Nip(per), Pad, Pickpocket, Pilferer, Pirate, Plagiarist, Poacher, Prig, Raffles, →ROBBER, Rustler, Safeblower, Safebreaker, Safecracker, Scrump, Shark, Shop-lifter, Sneak, Snowdropper, Taffy, Taker, Tarry-fingered, Tea-leaf, Thick, Twoccer

Thin(ner), Thinness Acetone, Atomy, Bald, Beanpole, Bony, Cadaverous, Cornstalk, Cull, Diluent, Dilute, Emaciated, Enseam, Filmy, Fine, Fine-drawn, Flimsy, Gaunt, Hair('s)-breadth, Inseam, Lanky, Lathy, Lean, Narrow, Puny, Rangy, Rare, Rarefied, Reedy, Scant, Scraggy, Scrawny, Sheer, Sieve, Skeletal, Skelf, Skimpy, Skinking, Slender, Slight, Slim, Slimline, Slink, →SPARE, Sparse, Spindly, Stilty, Stringy, Subtle, Svelte, Taper, Tenuous, Threadbare, Turpentine, Turps, Wafer, Washy, Waste, Watch, Water(y), →WEAK, Wear, Weedy, Wiry, Wispy, Wraith

Thing(s) Alia, Article, Chattel, Chose, Cratur, Craze, Doodah, Doofer, Entia, Fetish, First, Fixation, It, Item, Jingbang, Job, Last, Material, Matter, Near, Notanda, Noumenon, → **OBJECT**, Obsession, Paraphernalia, Phobia, Res, Tool, Vision, Whatnot

Thingumabob, Thingummy Dingbat, Dinges, Dingus, Doobrey, Doobrie, Doodad, Doodah, Doofer, Doohickey, Gubbins, Hootenanny, Hoot(a)nanny, Jigamaree, Oojah, Oojamaflip, Whatsit, Yoke

Think(er), Thinking Appraise, Associate, Audile, Believe, Brain, Brainstorm, Brood, Casuistry, Chew over, Cogitate, Cognition, Conjecture, Consider, Contemplant, Deem, Deliberate, Descartes, Devise, Dianoetic, Divergent, Esteem, Fancy, Fear, Feel, Fogramite, Forward, Ghesse, Gnostic, Guess, Hegel, Hold, → **IMAGINE**, Introspection, Judge, Lateral, Meditate, Mentation, Mindset, Mull, Muse, Opine, Pensive, Philosopher, Phrontistery, Ponder, Pore, Presume, Ratiocinate, Rational(e), Reckon, Reflect, Reminisce, Ruminate, Speculate, Synectics, Trow, Vertical, Ween, Wishful

Third, Third rate Bronze, C, Eroica, Gamma, Gooseberry, Interval, Major, Mediant, Minor, Picardy, Quartan, Tertius, Tierce, Trisect

Thirst(y) → **CRAVE**, Dives, Drought, Drouth, Dry, Hydropic, Nadors, Pant, Polydipsia, Thrist

Thirteen Baker's dozen, Long dozen, Riddle, Unlucky

Thistle Canada, Carduus, Carline, Cnicus, Creeping, Echinops, Musk, Rauriki, Safflower, Sow, Star, Thrissel, Thristle

Thomas Aquinas, Arnold, Christadelphian, De Quincey, Didymus, Doubting, Dylan, Erastus, Hardy, Loco, Parr, Rhymer, Tompion, True, Turbulent

Thorn(y) Acantha, Aculeus, Bael, Bel, Bhel, Bramble, Briar, Coyotillo, Doom, Edh, Eth, Irritation, Jerusalem, Jew's, Mahonia, Mayflower, Nabk, Nar(r)as, Nebbuk, Nebe(c)k, → **NEEDLE**, Paloverde, Prickle, Slae, Spine, Spinescent, Spinulate, Trial, Wagn'bietjie, Ye, Zare(e)ba, Zariba, Zeriba

Thorough(ly), Thoroughgoing À fond, Complete, Downright, Even-down, Firm, Fully, Good, In depth, Ingrained, Inly, Intensive, Not half, Out, Out and out, Painstaking, Pakka, Pucka, Pukka, Radical, Rigorous, Ripe, Sound, Strict, Total, Tout à fait, Up

Thought(s), Thoughtful(ness) Avisandum, Broody, Censed, Cerebration, Charitable, Cogitation, Concept, Conscience, Considerate, Contemplation, Dianoetic, Felt, Idea, Imagination, Indrawn, Innate, Kind, Maieutic, Mind, Musing, Notion, Opinion, Pansy, Pensée, Pensive, Philosophy, Reason, Reflection, Rumination, Second, Studious

Thoughtless Blindfold, Careless, Goop, Heedless, Inconsiderate, Pillock, → **RASH**, Reckless, Reflexive, Remiss, Scatter-brained, Stupid, Unintentional, Unkind, Vacant

Thousand(s) Chiliad, G, Gorilla, Grand, K, Lac, Lakh, M, Millenary, Millennium, Octillion, Plum, Sextillion, Toman

Thrash(ing) → **BEAT**, Belabour, Belt, Bepelt, Binge, Bless, Cane, Dress, Drub, Flail, Flog, Jole, Joll, Joule, Jowl, Lace, Laidie, Laidy, Lambast, Larrup, Lather, Leather, Lick, Marmelise, Onceover, Paste, Ploat, Quilt, Rout, Slog, Smoke, Strap-oil, Swaddle, Swat, Targe, Towel, Trim, Trounce, Whale, Whap, Work over

Thread(ed), Threadlike Acme screw, Addenda, Ariadne, Bar, Bottom, Bride, Buttress, Chalaza, Chromosome, Clew, Clue, Cord, Coventry blue, Eel-worm, End, Female, Fibre, Filament, File, Filiform, Filose, Float, Floss, Flourishing,

Gist, Gold, Gossamer, Hair, Heddle, Ixtle, Lace, Lap, Lingel, Lingle, Link, Lisle, Lurex®, Male, Meander, Microfibre, Needle, Organzine, Pack, Pearlin(g), Pick, Ravel, Reeve, Roon, Rope-yarn, Rove, Sacred, Screw, Sellers screw, Seton, Shoot, Silver, Single, Spider line, Spireme, Sporangiophore, Stamen, Stroma, Suture, Tassel, Tendril, Tenor, Theme, Thrid, Thrum, Trace, Tram, Trundle, Tussore, Twine, Twist, Two-start, Warp, Wax(ed) end, Weft, Wick, → **WIND**, Wisp, Worm, Zari

Threat(en), Threatened, Threatening Baleful, Black(en), Blackmail, Bluster, Brew, Brutum fulmen, Bully, Coerce, Comminate, Denounce, Discovered check, Duress, Extort, Face, Fatwa, Fraught, Greenmail, Greymail, Hazard, Impend, Imperil, Intimidate, Jeopardise, Loom, Lower, → **MENACE**, Minacious, Minatory, Mint, Nuclear, Omen, Ominous, Or else, Overcast, Overhang, Parlous, Peril, Portent, Ramp, Shore, Strongarm, Ugly, Veiled, Warning, Yellow peril

Three, Threefold, Three-wheeler, Thrice Cheers, Graces, Har, Harpies, Jafenhar, Leash, Muses, Musketeers, Pairial, Pair-royal, Parial, Prial, Ter, Tercet, Tern(ate), Terzetta, Thridi, Tid, T.i.d, Tierce, Tray, Trey, Triad, Trial, Tricar, Triennial, Trifid, Trigon, Trilogy, Trinal, Trine, Trinity, Trio, Triple, Triptote, Troika

Threshold Absolute, Brink, Cill, Difference, Doorstep, Limen, Liminal, Nuclear, Sill, Tax, Verge

▶**Thrice** *see* **THREE**

Thrift(y) Economy, Frugal, Husbandry, Oeconomy, Scrimping, Sea-grass, Sea-pink, Virtue, Wary

Thrill(er), Thrilling Atingle, Buzz, Charge, Delight, Dindle, Dinnle, Dirl, Dread, Dynamite, Electric, Emotive, → **ENCHANT**, Enliven, Excite, Film noir, Frisson, Gas, Jag, Kick, Page-turner, Perceant, Plangent, Pulsate, Pulse, Quiver, Sensation, Thirl, Tinglish, Titillate, Tremor, Vibrant, Whodunit, Wow(-factor), Zing

Thrive Batten, Blossom, Boom, Do, Fl, → **FLOURISH**, Flower, Grow, Mushroom, → **PROSPER**, Succeed, Thee

Throat(y) Craw, Crop, Deep, Dewlap, Fauces, Gorge, Gular, Gullet, Guttural, Jugular, Laryngeal, Maw, Oropharynx, Pereion, Pharynx, Prunella, Quailpipe, Roopit, Roopy, Strep, Swallet, Thrapple, Thropple, Throttle, Weasand, Wesand, Whistle, Windpipe

Throb(bing) Beat, Palpitate, Pant, Pit-a-pat, Pound, Pulsate, Quop, Stang, Tingle, Vibrato

▷**Throbbing** *may indicate* an anagram

Throne Bed-of-justice, Cathedra, Episcopal, Gadi, → **LAVATORY**, Rule, Seat, See, Siege, Stone of Scone, Stool, Tribune

Throttle → **CHOKE**, Gar(r)otte, Gun, Mug, Scrag, Silence, Stifle, Strangle, Strangulate, We(a)sand

Through, Throughout Along, Ana, By, Dia-, During, Everywhere, Over, Passim, Per, Pr, Sempre, Sic passim, To, Trans, Up and down, Via, Yont

Throw (up), Thrower, Throw-out Bin, Cast-off, Chunder, Egesta, Eject, Estrapade, Floor, Flummox, Flying mare, Go, Jettison, Mangonel, Pash, Puke, Reject, Slam-drunk, Spatter, Spew, Squirt, Squit, → **TOSS**, Ventriloquism

▶**Throw(n)** *see* **TOSS(ING)**

Thrust(er) Abdominal, Aventre, Bear, Boost, Botte, Burn, Burpee, Detrude, Dig, Drive, Elbow, Engine, Exert, Extrude, Foin, → **FORCE**, Gist, Hay, Hustle, Impulse, Jet, Job, Lift-off, Lunge, Muscle, Obtrude, Oust, Pass, Passado, Peg,

Penetrate, Perk, Pitchfork, Poach, Poke, Potch(e), Pote, Probe, Prog, Propel, Pun, Punto, →**PUSH**, Put, Ram, Remise, Repost, Run, Shoulder, Shove, Sock, Sorn, Squat, Stap, Stick, Stoccado, Stoccata, Stock, Stuck, Thrutch, Tilt, Tuck, Venue

Thug(s) Brute, Gangster, Goon(da), Gorilla, Gurrier, Heavy, Hood(lum), Keelie, Loord, Ninja, Ockers, Phansigar, Rough(neck), SS, Strangler, Ted, Tityre-tu, Tsotsi, Yahoo

Thump(ing) Blow, Bonk, Cob, Crump, Dawd, Ding, Dod, Drub, Dub, Enormous, Hammer, Knevell, Knock, Lamp, Nevel, Oner, Paik, Percuss, →**POUND**, Pummel, Ribroast, Slam, Slosh, Swat, Swingeing, Thud, Tund, Whump

Thunder(ing), Thunderstorm Astrophobia, Bolt, Boom, Clap, Donnerwetter, Foudroyant, Foulder, Fulminate, Intonate, Lei-king, Microburst, Pil(l)an, Raiden, →**ROAR**, Rumble, Summanus, Tempest, Thor, Tonant

Thwart Baffle, Balk, →**CROSS**, Dish, Foil, Forestall, Frustrate, Hamstring, Hogtie, Obstruct, Pip, Prevent, Scotch, Scupper, Snooker, Spike, Spite, Stonker, Stymie, Transverse

Tick, Ticking-off, Tick off Acarida, Acarus, Arachnid, Beat, Click, Cr, →**CREDIT**, Deer, HP, Idle, Instant, Jar, Ked, Mattress, Mile, Mo, Moment, Ricinulei, Second, Seed, Sheep, Soft, Strap, Wigging, Worm

Ticker Clock, Heart, Metronome, Watch

Ticket(s) Billet, Bone, Brief, Carnet, Commutation, Complimentary, Coupon, Day, Docket, Dream, E(lectronic), Excursion, Hot, Kangaroo, Label, Meal, One-day, One-way, Open-jaw, Parking, Pass, Pass-out, Pasteboard, Pawn, Platform, Raffle, Raincheck, Return, Round-trip, Rover, Saver, Scratchcard, Season, Single, Soup, Split, Straight, Stub, Supersaver, Tempest, Tessera(l), Through, Tix, Transfer, Tyburn, Unity, Voucher, Walking, Zone

Tickle, Ticklish Amuse, Delicate, Divert, Excite, Fondle, Gratify, Gump, →**ITCH**, Kittle, Queasy, Thrill, Titillate

Tide, Tidal Current, Drift, Eagre, Easter, Estuary, Flood, High, Low, Marigram, Neap, River, Roost, Sea, Seiche, Slack water, Spring, Trend, Wave

Tidy Big, Comb, Considerable, Curry, Fair, Fettle, Kempt, Large, Neat, Neaten, →**ORDER**, Pachyderm, Predy, Preen, Primp, Red(d), Slick, Snug, Sort, Spruce, Trim

Tie, Tied, Tying Ascot, Attach, Barcelona, Berth, Bind, Black, Bolo, →**BOND**, Bootlace, Bow, Bowyang, Cable, Chain, Clip-on, Cope, Cord, Cravat, Cup, Dead-heat, Drag, Draw, Fasten, Fetter, Four-in-hand, Frap, Halter, Halve, Handicap, Harness, Hitch, Holdfast, Kipper, →**KNOT**, Lace, Lash, Level, Ligament, Ligate, Ligature, Link, Marry, Match, Moor, Neck and neck, Oblige, Obstriction, Old School, Oop, Oup, Overlay, Raffia, Relation, Restrain, Rod, Rope, Scarf, School, Score draw, Scrunchie, Semifinal, Shackle, Sheave, Shoelace, Shoestring, Sleeper, Slur, Solitaire, Soubise, Splice, Stake, Standoff, Strap, String, Tawdry-lace, Tether, Together, Trice, Truss, Unite, White, Windsor

Tiff Bicker, Contretemps, Difference, Dispute, Exchange, Feed, Feud, Huff, Miff, Skirmish, Spat, Squabble

Tiger, Tigress Ambush, Bengal, →**CAT**, Clemenceau, Demoiselle, Lily, Machairodont, Machairodus, Man-eater, Margay, Paper, Sabre-tooth, She-cat, Shere Khan, Smilodon, Stripes, Tasmanian, Woods

Tight(en), Tightness, Tights Boozy, Bosky, Brace, Canny, Cinch, Close(-hauled), Constriction, Cote-hardie, Fishnet, Fleshings, High, Hose, Jam,

Leggings, Leotards, Lit, Loaded, Maillot, Mean(-spirited), Merry, Niggardly, Oiled, Pang, Pantihose, Phimosis, Pickled, Pinch(penny), Plastered, Prompt, Proof, Rigour, Snug, Squiffy, Stenosis, → **STINGY**, Stinko, Strict, Stringent, Swift, Swig, Taut, Tense, Tipsy, Trig, Woozy

Tile(s), Tiled Antefix, Arris, Azulejo, Dalle, Derby, Encaustic, → **HAT**, Hung, Imbrex, Imbricate, Lid, Mahjong(g), Ostracon, Ostrakon, Peever, Quarrel, Quarry, Rag(g), Ridge, Rooftop, Sclate, Shingle, Slat, Tegular, Tessella, Tessera, Titfer, Topper, Wall, Wally

Till Cashbox, Checkout, Coffer, Ear, Eulenspiegel, Farm, Hasta, Hoe, Husband, Lob, Peter, → **PLOUGH**, Rotavate, Set, Unto, Up to

Tilt(ed) Awning, Bank, Camber, Cant, Careen, Cock, Dip, Heel, Hut, Joust, Just, → **LIST**, Quintain, Rock, Tip, Trip, Unbalance, Version

Timber Apron, Ashlaring, Balk, Batten, Beam, Bolster, Bond, Bowsprit, Bridging, Cant-rail, Cedarwood, Chess, Clapboard, Compass, Cross-tree, Cruck, Dogshores, Driftwood, Druxy, Elmwood, Flitch, Float, Four-by-two, Greenheart, Groundsell, Hardwood, Harewood, Intertie, Iroko, Ironwood, Joist, Keel, Knee, Ligger, Lignum, Lintel, Log, Loggerhead, Lumber, Nogging, Purlin(e), Putlock, Putlog, Rib, Ridgepole, Roseweed, Roundwood, Rung, Sandalwood, Sapele, Sapodilla, Satinwood, Scantling, Shook, Shorts, Skeg, Sneezewood, Softwood, Souari, Stemson, Stere, Sternpost, Sternson, Straddle, Stud, Stull, Summer, Swing-stock, Tilting fillet, Towing-bitts, Transom, Two-by-four, Wale, Wall plate, Weatherboard, Whitewood, → **WOOD**, Yang

Time(s), Timer, Timing Access, African, Agoge, Apparent, Assymetric, Astronomical, Atlantic, Atomic, Autumn, Awhile, Bird, BST, By, Central, Chronaxy, Chronic, Chronometer, Chronon, Clock, Closing, Common, Compound, Connect, Core, Counter, Cryptozoic, Date, Day, Dead, Decade, Dimension, Double, Duple, Duration, Early, Eastern, Eastern Standard, Egg-glass, Enemy, Eon, Ephemeris, Epoch, Epocha, Epoque, Equinox, Era, EST, European, Eve(ning), Extra, Father, Flexitime, Fold, Forelock, Four-four, Fourth dimension, Free, Full, Geological, Gest, Glide, Half, Healer, High, Hour, Hourglass, Hr, Idle, Imprisonment, Injury, Innings, Instant, Interim, Interlude, Jiff, Juncture, Kalpa, Killing, Latent, Lead, Lean, Leisure, Length, Life, Lighting-up, Lilac, Local, Lowsing, Lustra, Man-day, Man-hour, Mean, Menopause, Metronome, Multiple, Needle, Nonce, Nones, Normal, Occasion, Oft, Opening, Pacific, Paralysis, Part, Peak, Period, Phanerozoic, Pinger, Porridge, Post, Precambrian, Prime, Proper, Quadruple, Quality, Question, Quick, Reaction, Real, Reaper, Recovery, Released, Response, Responsum, Reverberation, Rhythm, Run(ning), Sandglass, Sands, Schedule, Seal, → **SEASON**, Seel, Seil, Sentence, Serial, Session, Shelf-life, Sidereal, Sight, Simple, Sith(e), Slot, Slow, Solar, Solstice, Space, Spacious, Span, Spare, Spell, Spin, Split, Spring, Squeaky-bum, Standard, Stoppage, Stopwatch, Stound, Stownd, Stretch, Summer, Sundial, Sundown, Sync(h), Sythe, T, Tem, Tempo, Tempore, Tense, Thief, Three-four, Thunderer, Tick, Tid, Tide, Trice, Triple, True, Two-four, Universal, Usance, Whet, While, Winter, X, Yonks, Yukon, Zero(-hour)

Timekeeper, Timekeeping, Timepiece Ben, Clock, Clockwork, Hourglass, Ref, Sand-glass, Sundial, Ticker, Tompion, Watch

Timely Appropriate, Apropos, Happy, Heaven-sent, Opportune, Pat, Periodical, Prompt, Punctual

Timetable ABC(ee), Absee, Bradshaw, → **CHART**, Schedule

Timid, Timorous Afraid, Aspen, Bashful, Blate, Chicken, Cowardly, Eerie, Eery, Faint-hearted, Fearful, Fibreless, Hare, Hen-hearted, Meticulous, Milquetoast, Mouse, Mous(e)y, Pavid, Pigeon-hearted, Pusillanimous, Pussy, Quaking, Shrinking, →**SHY**, Skeary, Sook, Tremulous, Wuss, Yellow

Tin(ned), Tinfoil, Tinny Argentine, Britannia metal, Can, Cash, Debe, Dixie, Maconochie, →**MONEY**, Moola(h), Ochre, Plate, Rhino, Sn, Stannary, Stannic, Tain, Tole

Tincture Arnica, Brown, Bufo, Chroma, Elixir, Fur, Infusion, Laudanum, Metal, Or, Sericon, Sol, Spice, Taint, Tenné, Vert

Tinder Amadou, Faggot, Fuel, Funk, Punk, Spark, Spunk, Touchwood

Tingle, Tingling Dinnle, Dirl, Paraesthesia, Pins and needles, Prickle, Thrill, Throb, Tinkle

Tinker Bell, Caird, Coster, Didicoy, Didikoi, →**FIDDLE**, Gypsy, Meddle, Mender, Pedlar, Potter, Prig, Putter, Repair, Sly, Smouse, Snout, Tamper, Tramp, Traveller, Tweak

Tiny Atto-, Baby, Chickenfeed, Diddy, Dwarf, Fleabite, Ha'it, Infinitesimal, Itsy-bitsy, Leet(le), Lilliputian, Meagre, Midget, Minikin, Minim, Mite, Negligible, Petite, Pint-sized, Pitiful, Pittance, Small, Smidge(o)n, Smidgin, Stime, Teeny, Tim, Tine, Toy, Wee(ny)

Tip (off), Tipping Advice, Apex, Arrowhead, Asparagus, Backshish, Baksheesh, Batta, Beer-money, Cant, Capsize, Cert, Chape, Counsel, Coup, Cowp, Crown, Cue, Cumshaw, Doff, Douceur, Dump, Extremity, Fee, Felt, Ferrule, Filter, Forecast, Glans, Gratuity, Heel, →**HINT**, Hunch, Inkle, Iridise, Largess(e), Lean, List, Mag(g), Mess, Nap, Nib, Noop, Ord, Perk, Perquisite, Point, Pointer, Pour, Previse, Scrapheap, Slagheap, Suggestion, Summit, Tag, Tail, Tilt, Toom, Touch, Tronc, Upend, Upset, Vail, Vales, Warn, Whisper, Wrinkle

Tipsy Askew, Bleary, Boozy, Bosky, Elevated, Merry, Moony, Nappy, Oiled, On, Rocky, Screwed, Slewed, Slued, Squiffy, Stewed, Tight, Wet

▷**Tipsy** *may indicate* an anagram

Tirade Diatribe, Invective, Jobation, Laisse, Philippic, Rand, Rant, Rave, Screed, Slang

Tire(d), Tiredness, Tiring All-in, Aweary, Beat, Bejade, Bleary-eyed, Blown, Bore, Brain fag, Bushed, Caparison, Cooked, Dress, Drowsy, →**EXHAUST**, Fag, Fatigue, Flag, Footsore, Fordid, Fordod, Forjeskit, Frazzle, Gruel, Irk, Jack, Jade, Languor, Lassitude, Limp, ME, Poop, Puggled, →**ROBE**, Rubber, Sap, Shagged, Sicken, Sleepry, Sleepy, Sloomy, Snoozy, Swinkt, Tax, Tedious, Trying, Tucker, Wabbit, Wappend, Weary, World-weary, Wrecked

▶**Tiro** *see* **TYRO**

Tissue Adenoid, Adhesion, Adipose, Aerenchyma, Aponeurosis, Archesporium, Bast, Callus, Carbon, Cartilage, C(o)elom, Cementum, Chalaza, Cheloid, Chlorenchyma, Coenosarc, Collagen, Collenchyma, Commissure, Conducting, Connective, Corpus luteum, Corpus Striatum, Cortex, Dentine, Diploe, Elastic, Elastin, Endarch, Endosperm, Endosteum, Epigenesis, Epimysium, Epineurium, Epithelium, Eschar, Evocator, Fabric, Fascia, Fibroid, Filament, Flesh, Gamgee, Gauze, Gleba, Glia, Granulation, Granuloma, Gum, Handkerchief, Hankie, Heteroplasia, Histogen, Histoid, Hypoderm(is), Infarct, Interlay, Junk, Keloid, Kleenex®, Lamina, Liber, Lies, Ligament, Luteal, Lymphate, Lymphoid, Macroglia, Marrow, Matrix, Mechanical, Medulla, →**MEMBRANE**, Meristem, Mesenchyme, Mesophyll, Mestom(e), Mole, Muscle, Myelin(e), Myocardium, Neoplasia, Neoplasm, Neuroglia, Nucellus, Olivary, Pack, Palisade, Pannus,

Paper, Papilla, Parenchyma, Periblem, Perichylous, Pericycle, Peridesmium, Perimysium, Perinephrium, Perineurium, Perisperm, Phellogen, Phloem, Pith, Placenta, Plerome, Polyarch, Pons, Primordium, Procambium, Prosenchyma, Prothallis, Pterygium, Pulp, Radula, Retina, Sarcenet, Sars(e)net, Scar, Sclerenchyma, Scleroma, Sequestrum, Sinew, Siphonostele, Siphuncle, Soft, Somatopleure, Stereome, Stroma, Submucosa, Suet, Tarsus, Tela, Tendon, Toilet, Tonsil, Trace, Tunica, Vascular, Velum, Web, Wound, Xylem, Zoograft

Tit, Tit-bit(s) Analecta, Currie, Curry, Delicacy, Dug, Nag, Nipple, Pap, Quarry, Sample, Scrap, Snack, Snippet, Teat, Tug, Twitch, Zakuska

Titan(ic), Titaness Atlas, Colossus, Cronos, Enormous, Giant, Ginormous, Huge, Hyperion, Kronos, Large, Leviathan, Liner, Oceanus, Phoebe, Prometheus, Rhea, Superman, Themis, Vast

Title Abbé, →**ADDRESS**, Ag(h)a, Agname, Appellative, Bab, Baroness, Baronet, Bart, Bastard, Bhai, Burra sahib, Calif, Caliph, Caption, Charta, Chogyal, Claim, Conveyance, Count(ess), Courtesy, Credit, Dan, Datin, Dauphin, Dayan, Deeds, Denominative, Devi, Dom, Don, Don(n)a, Dowager, Dub, Duchess, Duke, Earl, Effendi, Eminence, Epithet, Esquire, Excellency, Fra, Frau(lein), Ghazi, Grand Master, Great Mogul, Handle, Header, Heading, Headline, Hereditary, Highness, Hojatoleslam, Hon, Honour, Il Duce, Imperator, Interest, Kabaka, Kalif, Kaliph, Khan, King, Kumari, Lady, Lala, Lemma, Lord, Mal(l)am, Marchesa, Marchese, Marquess, Marquis, Master, Masthead, Memsahib, Meneer, Miladi, Milady, Milord, Mr(s), Mynheer, Name, Native, Negus, Nemn, Nickname, Nizam, Nomen, Ownership, Pacha, Padishah, Pasha, Peerage, Pir, Polemarch, Prefix, Prince(ss), Queen, →**RANK**, Reb, Reverence, Reverend, →**RIGHT**, Rubric, Running, Sahib, Sama, San, Sardar, Sayid, Senhor(a), Señor(a), Shri, Singh, Sir, Sirdar, Son, Sowbhagyawati, Sri, Stratum, Tannie, Tenno, Titule, Torrens, Tuanku, Tycoon, U, Voivode, Worship

To(wards) At, Beside, Inby, Intil, Oncoming, Onto, Shet, Shut, Till, Until

Toad(y) Bootlicker, Bufo, Bumsucker, Cane, Clawback, Crawler, Fawn, Frog, Hanger-on, Horned, Jackal, Jenkins, Knot, Lackey, Lickspittle, Midwife, Minion, Natterjack, Nototrema, Paddock, Parasite, Pipa, Placebo, Platanna, Poodle, Pouch, Puddock, Sook, Spade-foot, Squit, Surinam, Sycophant, Tuft-hunter, Warty, Xenopus, Yesman

Toadstool Amanita, Death-cap, Death-cup, →**FUNGUS**, Grisette, Marasmus, Paddock-stool, Parrot, Saffron milk cap, Sickener, Sulphur tuft

Toast(er) Bacchus, Bell, Birsle, Brindisi, →**BROWN**, Bruschetta, Bumper, Cheers, Chin-chin, Crostini, Croute, Crouton, Drink-hail, French, Gesundheit, Grace-cup, Grill, Health, Heat, Iechyd da, Immortal memory, Kia-ora, L'chaim, Lechayim, Loyal, Melba, Pledge, Propose, Prosit, Round, Salute, Scouther, Scowder, Scowther, Sentiment, Sippet, Skoal, Slainte, Soldier, Sunbathe, Zwieback

Tobacco, Tobacco-field Alfalfa, Bacchi, Baccy, Bird's eye, Broadleaf, Burley, Burn, Canaster, Capa, Caporal, Cavendish, Chew, Dottle, Honeydew, Indian, Killikinnick, Kinnikinick, Latakia, Mundungus, Nailrod, Navy-cut, Negro-head, Nicotine, Perique, Pigtail, Pipe, Plug, Quid, Régie, Returns, Shag, Sneesh, Snout, Snuff, Stripleaf, Turkish, Twist, Vega, Virginia, Weed, Wrapper

Today Hodiernal, Now, Present

Toddle(r) Baim, Gangrel, Mite, Tot, Totter, Trot, Waddle

Toe(s), Toed Dactyl, Digit, Hallux, Hammer, Pigeon, Piggy, Pinky, Pointe, Poulaine, Prehallux, Tootsie

Toffee Butterscotch, Caramel, Cracknel, Gundy, Hard-bake, Hokey-pokey, Humbug, Tom-trot

Together Among, At-one, Atone, Attone, Col, Gathered, Hand-in-glove, Hand-in-hand, In concert, Infere, In mass, In step, Job lot, →**JOINT**, Juxtaposed, Pari-passu, Sam, Simultaneous, Tutti, Unison, Wed, Y, Yfere, Ysame

Toil(s) Drudge, Fag, Graft, Industry, →**LABOUR**, Mesh, Net, Seine, Sisyphus, Slog, Sweat, Swink, Tela, Tew, Trap, Travail, Tug, Web, →**WORK**, Wrest, Yacker, Yakka, Yakker

Toilet Can, Chemical, Coiffure, Garderobe, Gents, Head(s), John, Ladies, Lat(rine), Lavabo, →**LAVATORY**, Loo, Necessary house, Necessary place, Pan, Pot, Powder room, Restroom, Toot, WC

Token Abbey-counter, Abbey-piece, Buck, Chip, Counter, Coupon, Disc, Double-axe, Emblem, Favour, Gift, Indication, Mark, →**MEMENTO**, Monument, Nominal, Omen, Portend, Seal, Sign, Signal, Slug, Symbol, Symptom, Tessella, Tessera, Valentine, Voucher, White flag

Tolerable Acceptable, Bearable, Fair(ish), Mediocre, Passable, So-so

Tolerance, Tolerant, Tolerate(d) Abear, Abide, Accept, Admit, →**ALLOW**, Bear, Broadminded, Brook, Countenance, Endure, Enlightened, Good-natured, Hack, Had, Immunological, Latitude, →**LENIENT**, Liberal, Long-suffering, Lump, Mercy, Permit, Stand (for), Stick, Stomach, Studden, Suffer, Support, Thole, Wear, Zero

Toll Chime, Chok(e)y, Customs, Due, Duty, Excise, Jole, Joll, Joule, Jow, Octroi, Pierage, Pike, Pontage, Rates, →**RING**, Scat, Scavage, Streetage, Tariff, Tax, Turnpike

Tom(my) Atkins, Bell, Bowling, Bread, Brown, →**CAT**, Chimney sweep, Collins, Edgar, Gib, Grub, Gun, He-cat, Jerry, Jones, Mog(gy), Nosh, Peeping, Private, Pro(stitute), Pte, Puss, Ram-cat, Sawyer, Snout, Soldier, Stout, Thos, Thumb, Tiddler, Tucker

Tomato Beef(steak), Cherry, Husk, Love-apple, Plum, Strawberry, Tamarillo, Wolf's peach

Tomb(stone) Burial, Catacomb, Catafalque, Cenotaph, Cist, Coffin, Cromlech, Dargah, Durgah, Grave, Hypogeum, Inurn, Kistvaen, Marmoreal, Mastaba, Mausoleum, Megalithic, Monument, Pyramid, Repository, →**SEPULCHRE**, Sepulture, Serdab, Shrine, Speos, Tholos, Tholus, Through-stane, Through-stone, Treasury, Vault

Tomboy Gamine, Gilpey, Gilpy, Hoyden, Ladette, Ramp, Romp

Tomorrow Future, Manana, Morrow, The morn

Ton(nage) C, Century, Chic, Displacement, Freight, Gross, Hundred, Long, Measurement, Metric, Net register, Register, Shipping, Short, T

Tone, Tonality Aeolian, Brace, Colour, Combination, Compound, Difference, Differential, Fifth, Gregorian, Harmonic, Hypate, Inflection, Key, Klang, Mediant, Minor, Ninth, Partial, Passing, Pure, Qualify, Real, Ring, →**SOUND**, Strain, Summational, Temper, Tenor, Timbre, Trite, Whole

Tongue, Tonguing Brogue, Burr, Chape, Clack, Clapper, Doab, Final, Flutter, Forked, Glossa, Glossolalia, Glottal, Isthmus, Jinglet, →**LANGUAGE**, Languet(te), Lap, Ligula, Lill, Lingo, Lingual, Lingulate, Lytta, Mother, Organ, Radula, Ranine, Rasp, Red rag, Spit, Tab, Voice

Tonic Booster, Bracer, C(h)amomile, Cascara, Doh, Elixir, Key, Keynote, Mease, Medicinal, Mishmee, Mishmi, Oporice, Pick-me-up, Quassia, Refresher, Roborant, Sarsaparilla, Solfa

▷**Tonic** *may indicate* a musical note

Too Als(o), Besides, Eke, Excessive, Item, Likewise, Moreover, Oer, Over, Overly, Plus, Troppo

Tool(s), Tool-maker Countersink, Crampon, Flatter, →**IMPLEMENT**, →**INSTRUMENT**, Knapper, Maker, Penis, Percussion, Power, Property, Tongs, Utensil

Tooth(ed), Toothy, Teeth Baby, Bicuspid, Bit, Buck, Bunodont, Cadmean, Canine, Carnassial, Chactodon, Cheek tooth, Chisel, Choppers, Cog, Comb, Comer, Cott's, Crena(te), Ctenoid, Cusp, Deciduous, Denticle, Dentin(e), Dentures, Egg, Eye, False, Fang, Gam, Gap, Gat, Gnashers, Grinder, Heterodont, Impacted, Incisor, Ivory, Joggle, Laniary, Milk, Mill, Molar, Nipper, Odontoid, Orthodontics, Overbite, Pawl, Pearly gates, Pectinate, Periodontics, Peristome, Permanent, Phang, Plate, Poison-fang, Pre-molar, Prong, Radula, Ratch, Ratchet, Scissor, Secodont, Sectorial, Selenodont, Serration, Set, Snaggle, Sprocket, Stomach, Store, Sweet, Trophi, Tush, Tusk, Uncinus, Upper, Wallies, Wang, Wiper, Wisdom, Wolf, Zalambdodont, Zygodont

Top (drawer, hole, line, notcher), Topper, Topping, Topmost 1st, A1, Ace, Acme, Altissimo, Apex, Apical, Behead, Best, Better, Big, Blouse, Blouson, Boob tube, Brow, Bustier, Camisole, Cap, Capstone, Ceiling, Classic, Coma, Cop, Coping, Corking, Cream, →**CREST**, Crista, Crop, Crown, Culmen, Decapitate, De capo, Decollate, Diabolo, Dog, Dome, Dominant, Double, Drawer, Dux, Elite, Execute, Fighting, Finial, Flip, Foremost, Gentry, Gyroscope, Halterneck, Hard, Hat, →**HEAD**, Height, Hummer, Humming, Imperial, Impost, Jumper, Lead, Lid, Maillot, Marzipan, Nun, One-er, Optimate, Orb, Parish, →**PEAK**, Pediment, Peerie, Peery, Peg, Peplos, Peplus, Pinnacle, Pitch, Quark, Replenish, Ridge, Roof, Sawyer, Screw, Secret, Shaw, Shirt, Skim, Sky, Slay, Soft, Spinning, Star, Summit, Superb, Supreme, Supremo, Surface, Sweater, Table, Tambour, Targa, Teetotum, Texas, Tile, Trash, Trump, T-shirt, Unroof, Up(most), Uppermost, V, Vertex, Vest, Whipping, Whirligig, Winner

▷**Top** *may indicate* first letter

Topic(al) Agenda, Head, Issue, Item, Local, Motion, Place, Subject, Text, →**THEME**, Timely, Up to date

Topping Grand, Icing, Meringue, Pepperoni, Piecrust, Streusel

Topple Depose, Dethrone, Oust, Overbalance, Overturn, Tip, Upend, →**UPSET**

Topsy-turvy Careen, Cockeyed, Inverted, Summerset, Tapsalteerie, Tapsleteerie

Torch Blow, Brand, Cresset, Fire, Flambeau, Flashlight, Lamp, Lampad, Link, Penlight, Plasma, Tead(e), Weld, Wisp

Toreador Escamillo, Matador, Picador, Torero

Torment(ed), Tormentor Agony, Anguish, Bait, Ballyrag, Bedevil, Butt, Cruciate, Crucify, Curse, Distress, Excruciate, Frab, Gibe, Grill, Hag-ridden, Harass, Harry, Haunt, Hell, Martyrdom, Molest, Nag, Nettle, Oppress, Pang, Pine, Plague, →**RACK**, Sadist, Tantalise, Wrack

Torn Agnail, In two, Ripped

Torpedo Bangalore, Bomb, Missile, Ray, Weapon

Torpid, Torpor Comatose, Dormant, Gouch, Languid, Lethargic, Sluggish, Slumbering, Stupor

Torrid Amphiscian, Fiery, Hot, Sultry, Tropical

Torso Body, Midriff, Trunk

Tortoise Chelonia, Emydes, Emys, Galapagos, Hic(c)atee, Kurma, Pancake, Snapping-turtle, Terrapin, Testudo, Timothy, Turtle

Tortoiseshell Cat, Epiplastra, Hawksbill, Testudo

▷**Tortuous** *may indicate* an anagram

Torture, Torture chamber, Torture instrument Agonise, Auto-da-fé, Bastinade, Bastinado, Boot, Bootikin, Catasta, Chinese burn, Chinese water, Crucify, Devil-on-the-neck, Engine, Excruciate, Flageolet, Fry, Gadge, Gauntlet, Gyp, Hell, Iron maiden, Knee-cap, Naraka, Peine forte et dur, Persecute, Pilliwinks, Pine, Pinniewinkle, Pinnywinkle, →**RACK**, Sadism, Scaphism, Scarpines, Scavenger, Scavenger's daughter, Scourge, Skeffington's daughter, Skevington's daughter, Strappado, Tantalise, Third degree, Thumb(i)kins, Thumbscrew, Torment, Treadmill, Triphook, Tumbrel, Tumbril, Water, Wheel, Wrack

▷**Tortured** *may indicate* an anagram

Toss(ing), Throw(n) Abject, Bandy, Birl, Bounce, Buck, Bung, Buttock, Cant, Canvass, Cast, Catapult, Crabs, Crap, Cross-buttock, Dad, Daud, Dawd, Deal, Dink, Discomfit, Disconcert, Dod, Elance, Estrapade, Falcade, Faze, →**FLING**, Flip, Floor, Flump, Flutter, Flying (head)-mare, Gollum, Hanch, Haunch, Heave, Hipt, Hoy, →**HURL**, Jact(it)ation, Jaculation, Jeff, Jump, Lance, Launch, Lob, Loft, Nick, Pash, Pick, Pitch, Purl, Roll, Round-arm, Salad, Seamer, Shy, Slat, Sling, Squail, Unhorse, Unseat, Upcast, Wheech, Yuko

Tot Add, Babe, Bairn, →**CHILD**, Dop, Dram, Infant, Mite, Moppet, Nightcap, Nip(per), Nipperkin, Slug, Snifter, Snort, Tad

Total(ity), Totally, Toto Absolute, Aggregate, All(-out), All told, Amount, Balance, Be-all, →**COMPLETE**, Count, Entire, Gross, In all, Lot, Mass, Ouroborus, Outright, Overall, Sum(mate), Tale, Tally, Unqualified, Uroborus, Utter, Whole

Totter Abacus, Daddle, Daidle, Didakai, Didakei, Didicoi, Did(d)icoy, Halt, Lurch, Ragman, Reel, Rock, Shamble, →**STAGGER**, Swag, Sway, Topple, Waver, Wobble

Touch(ed), Touching, Touch up, Touchy Abut, Accolade, Adjoin, Affect, Against, Airbrush, Anent, Apropos, Badass, Barmy, Cadge, Captious, Carambole, Caress, Carom, Common, Concern, Connivent, Contact, Contiguous, Dash, Easy, Emove, →**FEEL**, Feisty, Final, Finger, Finishing, Flick, Fondle, Glance, Handle, Haptic, Heart-warming, Huffish, Huffy, Iracund, Irascible, Irritable, J'adoube, Kiss, Liaison, Libant, Loan, Loco, Meet, Midas, Miffy, Near, Nie, Nigh, Nudge, Palp, Pathetic, Paw, Potty, Re, Reach, Sense, Shade, Skiff, Soft, Sore, Spice, →**SPOT**, Tactile, Tactual, Tag, Tangible, Tap, Taste, Tat, Tetchy, Tickle, Tig, Tinderbox, Tinge, Titivate, Trace, Trait, Trifle, Tuck, Vestige

Touchstone Basanite, Criterion, Norm, Standard

Tough(en) Adamantine, Anneal, Apache, Arduous, Ballsy, Bruiser, Burly, Chewy, Dab, Exacting, →**HARD**, Hardball, Hard-boiled, Hard nut, Hardy, Heavy duty, He-man, Hood, Husky, Indurate, Keelie, Knotty, Leathern, Leathery, Nut, Pesky, Rambo, Resilient, Rigwiddie, Rigwoodie, Robust, Roughneck, Sinewy, Skinhead, Spartan, Steely, Stiff, Strict, String, Sturdy, Teuch, Thewed, Thug, Tityre-tu, Virile, Wiry, Withy, Yob

Tour(er), Tourism, Tourist Adventure, Barnstorm, Benefit, Circuit, Conducted, Cook's, Emmet, Excursion, Gig, Grand, Grockle, GT, Holiday-maker, Itinerate, →**JOURNEY**, Lionise, Mystery, Outing, Package, Posting, Pub crawl, Reality, Roadie, Road show, Rubberneck, Safari, Sightsee, Spin, Steerage, →**TRAVEL**, Trip(per), Viator, Weather, Whistle-stop

Tournament Basho, Bridge drive, Carousel, Drive, Event, Joust, Just, Open, Plate, Pro-am, Pro-celebrity, Round robin, Royal, Spear-running, Tilt-yard, Tourney, Whist drive, Wimbledon

Tow(ing), Towpath Button, Fibre, →**HAUL**, Hobbler, Pull, →**ROPE**, Skijoring, Stupe, Track road

▶**Towards** *see* **TO(WARDS)**

Towel Dry, Jack, Nappy, Pantyliner, Roller, Rub, Sanitary, Tea, Tea-cloth, Terry, Turkish

Tower, Tower over AA, Aspire, Atalaya, Babel, Barbican, Bastille, Bastion, Belfry, Bell, Blackpool, Bloody, Brattice, Brettice, Brogh, Campanile, Clock, Conning, Control, Cooling, Donjon, Dungeon, Dwarf, Edifice, Eiffel, Fly, Fortress, Gantry, Garret, Gate, Hawser, Horologium, Husky, Ivory, Keep, Leaning, Loom, Maiden, Martello, Minar(et), Monument, Mooring, Mouse, Nurhag, Overtop, Peel, Pinnacle, Pisa, Pound, Pylon, Rear, Rise, Rood, Round, Sail, Sears, Shot, Signal, Silo, Ski-lift, Skyscraper, Spire, Stealth, Steeple, Swiss Re, Tête-de-pont, Texas, Tractor, Tugboat, →**TURRET**, Victoria, Watch, Water, Ziggurat

Town, Township Boom, Borgo, Borough, Bourg, Burg(h), City, Company, Conurbation, County, Deme, Dormitory, Dorp, Favella, Five, Ghost, Ham(let), Market, Municipal, Nasik, One-horse, Open, Place, Podunk, Pueblo, Satellite, Shanty, Shire, Soweto, Tp, Twin, Urban, Whistle stop, Wick

Townee, Townsman Cad, Cit(izen), Dude, Freeman, Oppidan, Philister, Resident, Snob, Urbanist, Urbanite

Toxic(ity), Toxin Abrin, Aflatoxin, Antigen, Botox®, Botulin, Cadmium, Chlorin(e), Coumarin, Curare, Deadly, Dioxan, Dioxin, Eclampsia, Lethal, Melittin, Muscarine, Nicotine, Paraquat, Phenol, Phenothiazine, Pre-eclampsia, Psoralen, Sepsis, Serology, Venin, Venomous, Yellow rain

Toy Babyhouse, Bauble, Bottle-imp, Bull-roarer, Cartesian devil, Cockhorse, Coral, Cyberpet, Dally, Dandle, Dinky®, Doll, Doll's house, Dreid(e)l, Executive, Faddle, Fiddle, Finger, Flirt, Frisbee®, Gewgaw, Golly, Gonk, Jack-in-the-box, Jumping-jack, Kaleidoscope, Kickshaw, Knack, Lego®, Meccano®, Newton's cradle, Noah's ark, Novelty, Paddle, Pantine, Peashooter, Pinwheel, Plaything, Pogo stick, Popgun, Praxinoscope, Quiz, Rag doll, Rattle, Russian doll, Scooter, Shoofly, Skipjack, Stroboscope, Tamagotchi, Tantalus-cup, Taste, Teddy, Thaumatrope, Top, →**TRIFLE**, Trinket, Tu(r)ndun, Wheel of life, Whirligig, Windmill, Yoyo, Zoetrope

Trace Atom, Cast, Derive, Describe, Draft, Draw, Dreg, Echo, Footprint, Ghost, Gleam, →**HINT**, Mark, Outline, Relic, Relict, Remnant, Scan, Scintilla, Semblance, Sign, Smack, Soupçon, Spark, Streak, Suspicion, Tinge, →**TOUCH**, Track, Vestige, Whit

Track(s), Tracker, Tracking, Trackman Aintree, Aisle, Band, B-road, Caterpillar®, Cinder, Circuit, Course, Crawler, Cycleway, Dirt, Disrail, Dog, DOVAP, Drag strip, Drift, Ecliptic, El, Fast, Fettler, Flap(ping), Footing, Gandy dancer, Green road, Greenway, Groove, Hunt, Ichnite, Ichnolite, Icknield Way, Inside, Lane, Ley, Line, Loipe, Loopline, Mommy, Monitor, Monza, Orbit, Pad, →**PATH**, Persue, Piste, Pitlane, Pug, Pursue, Race, Raceway, Rail, Railway, Rake, Ridgeway, Riding, Route, Run, Runway, Rut, Scent, Siding, Sign, Skidway, Sleuth, Slot, Sonar, Speedway, Spoor, Stylus, Tan, Tan-ride, Taxiway, Tenure, Tideway, Title, Towpath, Trace, →**TRAIL**, Trajectory, Tram, Tramline, Tramroad, Tramway, Tread, Trode, Tug(boat), Twin, Wake, Wallaby, Way, Y

Tract(able), Tracts Area, Belt, Bench, Clime, Common, Dene, Digestive, Enclave, Enteral, Flysheet, Lande, Leaflet, Monte, Moor, →**PAMPHLET**, Park, Prairie, Province, Purlieu, Pusey, Pyramidal, Region, Scabland, Taluk, Tawie, Terrain, Wold

Trade(r), Tradesman, Trading Arb(itrageur), Art, Banian, Banyan, Bargain, Barrow boy, Barter, Bear, Bilateral, Bricks and clicks, Bull, Burgher, Business, Cabotage, Calling, Carriage, Chaffer, Chandler, Chapman, Cheapjack, Cheesemonger, Clicks and mortar, Coaster, →**COMMERCE**, Coper, Coster, Costermonger, Crare, Crayer, Custom, Deal(er), Decorator, Dicker, Eggler, Errand, Exchange, Exporter, Factor, Fair, Floor, Free, Galleon, Handle, Higgler, Horse, Hosier, Hot, Importer, Indiaman, Industry, Insider, Ironmonger, Jobber, Kidder, Line, Matrix, Mercantile, Mercer, Merchant, Mercosur, Métier, Middleman, Milkman, Mister, Monger, Mystery, Occupy, Outfitter, Paralleling, Pitchman, Plumber, Ply, Program(me), Rag, Retailer, Roaring, Rough, Roundtripping, Salesman, Scalp, Screen, Sell, Shrivijaya, Simony, Slave, Stallholder, Stationer, Sutler, Suttle, →**SWAP**, Tailor, Traffic, Transit, Trant, Truck, Union, Vaisya, Vend, Wheeler-dealer, Wholesaler, Wind, Worker

Trademark, Trade name Brand, Chop, Idiograph, Label, Logo, TN

Tradition(s), Traditional(ist) Ancestral, Classical, Convention, Custom(ary), Diehard, Eastern, Folksy, Folkway, Hadith, Heritage, Legend, Lore, Mahayana, Misoneist, Old guard, Old-line, Old-school, Orthodox, Pharisee, Pompier, Practice, Purist, Square, Suburban, Time-honoured, Trad, Tralaticious, Tralatitious, Unwritten

Traffic(ker), Traffic pattern Air, Barter, Broke, Cabotage, Clover-leaf, Commerce, Contraflow, Coyote, Deal, Export, Negotiate, Passage, Run, Sell, Slave trade, Smuggle, Tailback, Trade, Truck, Vehicular, Way

Tragedian, Tragedy, Tragic Aeschylus, Antigone, Buskin, Calamity, Cenci, Corneille, Dire, →**DRAMA**, Euripides, Lear, Macready, Melpomene, Oedipean, Oresteia, Otway, Pathetic, Seneca, Sophoclean, Thespian, Thespis

Trail(er), Trailing Abature, Advert, Appalachian, Bedraggle, Caravan, Creep, Dissipation, Drag, Draggle, Fire, Follow, Forerunner, Foretaste, Horsebox, Ipomaea, Ivy, Lag, Liana, Liane, Low-loader, Nature, Oregon, Paper, Path, Persue, Preview, Prevue, Promo(tion), Pursue, Repent, Runway, Scent, Shadow, Sickle-cell, Sign, Sleuth, Slot, Slowcoach, Snail, Spoor, Straggle, Stream, Streel, Tow, Trace, →**TRACK**, Trade, Traipse, Trape, Trauchle, Trayne, Troad, Vapour, Vine, Virga, Wake

Train(er), Training Accommodation, Advanced, Apprenticeship, APT, Autogenic, Baggage, Boot camp, BR, Break in, Breed, Brighton Belle, Bullet, Caravan, Cat, Cavalcade, Choo-choo, Circuit, Coach, Commuter, Condition, Cortège, Day release, Diesel, Direct, Discipline, Dog, Double-header, Dressage, Drill, Drive, Educate, Entourage, Enure, Eurostar®, Excursion, Exercise, Express, Fartlek, Field, Flier, Flight simulator, Freightliner®, Fuse, Gear, Ghan, Ghost, Gravy, Grounding, GWR, Handle(r), HST, →**INSET**, Instruct, Intercity®, Interval, Journey, Limber up, Liner, Link, LMS, LNER, Loco, Lunge, Maglev, Mailcar, Manège, Manrider, Mentor, Milk, Mixed, Multiple unit, Nopo, Nurture, Nuzzle, Omnibus, Orient Express, Outward Bound®, Owl, Pack, Paddy, Parliamentary, Passenger, Pavlov, PE, Pendolino, Personal, Potty, Power, Practise, →**PREPARE**, Procession, PT, Puffer, Puff-puff, Push-pull, Q, Qualified, Queue, Railcar, Rattler, Rehearse, Retinue, Road, Roadwork, Rocket, Roughrider, Royal Scot, Ry, Sack, Sacque, →**SCHOOL**, Series, Shoe,

Shuttle service, Siege, Simulator, Skill centre, Sleeper, Sloid, Sloyd, Sneaker, Sowarry, Special, Square-bashing, SR, Steer, String, Suite, Tail, Tame, **→ TEACH**, Through, Tire, Tone up, Track shoe, Trail, Trellis, Tube, Twin bill, Wage, Wagon, Wave, Way, Whale oil

▷**Train(ed)** *may indicate an anagram*

Traitor Betrayer, Casement, Dobber-in, Fifth column, Joyce, Judas, Nid(d)ering, Nid(d)erling, Nithing, Proditor, Quisling, Renegade, Reptile, Snake, Tarpeian, Traditor, Treachetour, Turncoat, Viper, Wallydraigle, Weasel

▷**Trammel** *may indicate an anagram*

Tramp, Trample Bum, Caird, Clochard, Clump, Deadbeat, Derelict, Derro, Dingbat, Dosser, Down and out, Drifter, Estragon, Footslog, Freighter, Gadling, Gangrel, Hike, Hobo, Knight of the road, Lumber, Override, Overrun, Pad, Piepowder, Piker, Plod, Poach, Potch(e), Prostitute, Rover, Scorn, Ship, Slog, Slut, Splodge, Sundowner, Swagman, **→ TINKER**, Toe-rag(ger), Tom, Track, Traipse, Tread, Trek, Trog, Tromp, Truant, Trudge, Tub, Vagabond, Vagrant, Weary Willie, Whore

Trance Aisling, Catalepsy, Cataplexy, Goa, Narcolepsy, Somnambulism

Tranquil(lity) Ataraxy, Calm, Compose, Composure, Halcyon, Lee, Peace(ful), Placid, Quietude, Restful, Sedate, **→ SERENE**, Still

Tranquillise(r) Appease, Ataractic, Ataraxic, **→ CALM**, Compose, Diazepam, Downer, Hypnone, Hypnotic, Largactil®, Librium®, Lullaby, Nervine, Nitrazepam, Oxazepam, Paregoric, Placate, Satisfy, Sedative, Soothe, Still, Valium®

Transcend(ent), Transcendental(ist), Transcendentalism Emerson, Excel, Mystic, Overtop, Surpass, Thoreau

Transfer(ence) Alien, Alienate, **→ ASSIGN**, Attorn, Bosman, Calk, Calque, Carryover, Cede, Chargeable, Communize, Consign, Convey(ance), Credit, Cross over, Crosstalk, Cutover, Dabbity, Decal(comania), Deed, Demise, Devolve, Download, Embryo, Exchange, Explant, Extradite, Ferry, Flit, Gene, Hive off, Incardinate, Iron-on, Letraset®, Make over, Mancipation, Metathesis, Mortmain, Nuclear, On-lend, Pass, Photomechanical, Print through, Provection, Reassign, Redeploy, Remit, Remove, Render, Repot, Second, Settlement, Slam, Spool, Thought, Transcribe, Transduction, Transfection, Transhume, Translocation, Uproot, Vire, Virement

▷**Transferred** *may indicate an anagram*

Transform(ation), Transformer Affine, Alchemist, Alter, Balun, Change, Linear, Lorentz, Makeover, Metamorphism, Metamorphose, Metamorphosis, Metaplasia, Metastasis, Morphallaxis, Morphing, Mutate, Permute, Rectifier, Sea change, Sepalody, Tesla coil, Tinct, Toroid, Toupee, Transfigure, Transmogrify, Variation, Wig

▷**Transform(ed)** *may indicate an anagram*

Transgress(ion) Encroach, Err, Infraction, Infringe, Offend, Overstep, Peccancy, **→ SIN**, Violate

Transient, Transit(ion), Transitory Brief, Caducity, Ecotone, Ephemeral, Evanescent, Fleeting, Fly-by-night, Fugacious, Hobo, Impermanent, Metabasis, Passage, Passing, Provisional, Rapid, Segue, Sfumato, T, Temporary

Translate, Translation, Translator Calque, Construe, Convert, Coverdale, Crib, Decipher, Decode, Decrypt, Encode, Explain, Free, Horse, Interpret, In vitro, Itala, Jerome, Key, Linguist, Loan, Machine, Metaphrase, Nick, Paraphrase, Pinyin, Polyglot, Pony, Reduce, Render, Rendition, Rhemist,

Septuagint, Simultaneous, Targum, Tr, Transcribe, Transform, Trot, Tyndale, Unseen, Version(al), Vulgate, Wycliffe

▷**Translate(d)** *may indicate* an anagram

Transmit(ter), Transmitted, Transmission Aerial, Air, Aldis lamp, Analogue, Band, Baseband, Beacon, →**BROADCAST**, Carry, CB, Communicate, Compander, Compandor, Consign, Contagion, Convection, Convey, Digital, Diplex, Forward, Gearbox, Gene, Heredity, Impart, Intelsat, Localizer, Manual, Mast, Mic(rophone), Modem, Nicol, Permittivity, Pipe, Propagate, Racon, Radiate, Radio (galaxy), Receiver, Responser, Send, Simulcast, Sonabuoy, Spark, Tappet, Telautograph®, Telecast, Telegony, Telematics, Telemetry, Telepathy, Teleprinter, Teletex, Televise, Telex, Telstar, Tiptronic®, Tiros, Traduce, Traject, Tralaticious, Tralatitious, UART, Ultrawideband, Uplink, Upload, Walkie-talkie, WAP, Webcam, Wi-Fi®

Transparent, Transparency Adularia, Clarity, Clear, Crystal(line), Diaphanous, Dioptric, Glassy, Glazed, Hyaloid, Iolite, Leno, Limpid, Lucid, Luminous, Patent, Pellucid, Porcelain, Sheer, Slide, Tiffany, Transpicuous

Transport(ed), Transporter, Transportation Aerotrain, Air-bus, Air-lift, Airline, Ar(a)ba, Argo, Barca, Bathorse, Beachbuggy, Bear, Bike, Black Maria, Boat, Boat-train, Broomstick, BRS, Buggy, Bus, Cable-car, Cargo, Carract, →**CARRY**, Cart, Casevac, Cat-train, Charabanc, Charm, Conductor, Convey, Cycle, Cyclo, Delight, Deliver, Dray, Ecstasy, Elation, Eloin, Enrapt, Enravish, Entrain, Esloin, Estro, Exalt, Ferriage, Ferry, Fishyback, Freight (train), Haul(age), Hearse, Helicopter, Hydrofoil, Jag, Jerrican, Jet ski, Joy, Kart, Kurvey, Landau, Lift, Maglev, Matatu, Medevac, Minicab, Minivan, Monorail, Motor cycle, Overjoy, Pack animal, Palanquin, Pantechnicon, Park and ride, Paytrain, Penny farthing, Pipeline, Plane, Portage, Public, Put, Q-train, Rape, Rapine, Rapture, Ravish, Rickshaw, Roadster, Ropeway, Ship, Shorthaul, Shuttle, Skateboard, Sledge, Sleigh, Sno-Cat, Snowmobile, Stagecoach, Supersonic, Tandem, Tape, Tardis, Taxi, Tote, Train, Tramway, Transit, Trap, Trolley, Troopship, Tuktuk, Tumbril, Ubiquinone, Waft, Waterbus, Wheelchair, Wheels, Wireway

Transpose, Transposition Anagram, Commute, Convert, Invert, Metathesis, Shift, Spoonerism, Switch, Tr

▷**Transposed** *may indicate* an anagram

Trap(s), Trapdoor, Trapped, Trappings Accoutrement, Ambush, →**BAGGAGE**, Bags, Belongings, Birdlime, Booby, Buckboard, Bunker, Carriage, Catch, Catch-pit, Clapnet, Cobweb, Corner, Creel, Crevasse, Cru(i)ve, Deadfall, Death, Decoy, Dip, Dogcart, Downfall, Drain, Eelset, Emergent, Enmesh, Ensnare, Entoil, Entrain, Fall, Fit-up, Fly, Flypaper, Frame-up, Fyke, Geel, Gig, Gin, Gob, Gravel, Grin, Haaf-net, Hatch, Honey, Housings, Ice-bound, Illaqueate, Jinri(c)ksha(w), Keddah, Kettle, Kheda, Kiddle, Kidel, Kipe, Kisser, Knur(r), Light, Lime, Live, Lobster pot, →**LUGGAGE**, Lure, Mesh, Mouth, Net, Nur(r), Oil, Paraphernalia, Pitfall, Plant, Polaron, Police, Pot, Poverty, Putcheon, Putcher, Quicksand, Radar, Regalia, Sand, Scruto, Scuttle, →**SNARE**, Speed, Spell, Spider, Springe, Stake-net, Star, Steam, Stench, Sting, Stink, Sun, Tangle, Tank, Teagle, Toil, Tonga, Tourist, Trapfall, Tripwire, Trojan horse, Trou-de-loup, Two-wheeler, U, U-bend, Vampire, Waterseal, Web, Weel, Weir, Wire

Trash(y) Bosh, Deface, Desecrate, Dre(c)k, Garbage, Junk, Kitsch, Off-scum, Pulp, →**RUBBISH**, Schlock, Scum, Tinpot, Trailer, Trumpery, Vandalise, Worthless, Write off

Travel(ler), Travelling Aeneas, Backpack, Bagman, Caird, Chapman, Columbus, Commercial, Commute, Crustie, Crusty, Drive, Drummer, Eurostar, Explorer, Fare, Fellow, Fly, Fogg, Geoffrey, Gipsen, Gipsy, Gitano, Globe-trotter, Go, Gulliver, Gypsy, Hike, Hitchhiker, Interrail, Itinerant, Jet-setter, Journey, Locomotion, Long-haul, Marco Polo, Meve, Migrant, Motor, Move, Mush, Nomad, Odysseus, Pardoner, Passepartout, Peregrination, Peripatetic, Pilgrim, Ply, Polo, Range, Rep, Ride, Road, Roam, Rom(any), Rove, Safari, Sail, Salesman, Samaritan, Sinbad, Sledger, Spaceman, Stowaway, Teleport, Tool, → **TOUR**, Tourist, Trek, Tripper, Tsigane, Viator, Voyage, Waft, Wayfarer, Wend, Wildfire, Zigan

Travesty Burlesque, Charade, Distortion, Parody, Show, Skit

Tray Antler, Carrier, Case, Charger, Coaster, Galley, In, Joe, Lazy Susan, Mould, Out, Plateau, Tea, Trencher, Typecase, Voider

Treacherous, Treachery Bad faith, Betrayal, Deceit, Delilah, Fickle, Ganelon, Guile, Insidious, Knife, Medism, Perfidious, Punic, Punic faith, Quicksands, Sedition, Serpentine, Sleeky, Snaky, Sneaky, Trahison, Traitor, Trappy, → **TREASON**, Two-faced, Unleal, Viper, Weasel

Tread Clamp, Clump, Dance, Pad, Step, Stomp, Stramp, Track, Trample

Treason Betrayal, Constructive, High, Insurrection, Lèse-majesté, Lese-majesty, Perduellion, Sedition, → **TREACHERY**

Treasure(r), Treasury Aladdin's cave, Banker, Bursar, Cache, Camera, Camerlengo, Camerlingo, Cherish, Chest, Cimelia, Coffer, Ewe-lamb, Exchequer, Fisc(al), Fisk, Godolphin, Golden, Heirloom, Heritage, Hoard, Hon(ey), Montana, Nugget, Palgrave, → **PRIZE**, Procurator, Purser, Quaestor, Relic, Riches, Steward, Sweetie, Thesaurus, Trove

Treat, Treatment Actinotherapy, Action, Acupressure, Acupuncture, Address, Allopathy, Antidote, Antiserum, Apitherapy, Aromatherapy, Arsphenamine, Beano, Beauty, Beneficiate, Besee, Body wrap, Botox®, Capitulate, Care, Chemotherapy, Condition, Course, Coverage, Crymotherapy, Cupping, Cure, Deal, Detox(ification), Dialysis, Do, → **DOCTOR**, Dose, Dress, Dutch, ECT, Electrotherapy, Entertain, EST, Facial, Faith-healing, Fango, Faradism, Figuration, Finish, Foment, Frawzey, Handle, Heliotherapy, Hellerwork, Holistic, Homeopathy, HRT, Hydrotherapy, Hypnotherapy, Insulin, Intermediate, Kenny, Laser, Manage, Massotherapy, Mechanotherapy, Medicament, Medicate, Mercerise, Mesotherapy, Narcotherapy, Naturopathy, Negotiate, Organotherapy, Orthoptics, Osteopathy, → **OUTING**, Pasteur, Pedicure, Pelotherapy, Camerlingo, Phototherapy, Physiatrics, Physic, Physiotherapy, Pie, Poultice, Process, Psychoanalysis, Psychodrama, Psychotherapy, Radiotherapy, Regale, Rehab(ilitation), Rest cure, Root, Secretage, Serotherapy, Setter, Shiatsu, Shout, Shrift, Sironise, Smile, Softener, Speleotherapy, → **STAND**, Statin, Tablet, TENS, → **THERAPY**, Thermotherapy, Titbit, Traction, Turkish bath, Twelve-step, UHT, Usance, Use, Vet

▷**Treated** *may indicate* an anagram

Treatise Almagest, Bestiary, Commentary, Cybele, Didache, Discourse, Monograph, Pandect, Profound, Summa, Tract(ate), Upanishad, Vedanta

Treaty Agreement, Alliance, Assiento, Concordat, Covenant, Entente, GATT, Lateran, Locarno, Lunéville, Maastricht, Nijmegen, → **PACT**, Paris, Protocol, Rapallo, Ryswick, San Stefano, Sovetsk, Test-ban, Utrecht, Westphalia

Treble Castrato, Choirboy, Chorist(er), Pairial, Soprano, → **TRIPLE**, Triune

Tree(s) Actor, → **ANCESTRY**, Axle, Beam, Bluff, Boom, Bosk, Chaparral, Conifer, Corner, Covin, Cross, Daddock, Deciduous, Decision, Dendrology, Descent,

Family, Fault, Fringe, Gallows, Greenery, Grove, Hang, Hardwood, Jesse, Nurse, Pedigree, Phanerophyte, Pole, Sawyer, Shoe, Silviculture, Softwood, Staddle, Stand, Stemma, Summer, Thicket, Timber, Tyburn, Ulmaceous, Wicopy, →**WOOD**

Tremble, Trembling, Tremor Aftershock, Aquiver, Butterfly, Dither, Dodder, Fremitus, Hotter, Judder, Marsquake, Milk sickness, Palpitate, Quail, Quake, Quaver, Quiver, Seismal, →**SHAKE**, Shiver, Shock, Shudder, Stound, Temblor, Titubation, Trepid, Twitchy, Vibrate; Vibration, Vibratiuncle, Vibrato, Wobble, Wuther, Yips

Tremendous Big, Enormous, Extreme, Gargantuan, Howling, Immense, Marvellous, Thundering

▶**Tremor** *see* **TREMBLE**

Trench(er), Trencherman Boyau, Cunette, Cuvette, Delf, Delph, Dike(r), →**DITCH**, Dyke(r), Encroach, Fleet, Foss(e), Foxhole, Fur(r), Furrow, Grip, Gullet, Gutter, Knife and fork, Leat, Line, Mariana, Moat, Oceanic, Outwork, Passage, Rill, Rille, Ring-dyke, Salient, Sap, Shott, Slidder, Slit, Sod, Sondage

Trend(y), Trendsetter Bellwether, Bent, Bias, Chic, Climate, Drift, Fashion, Groovy, Hep, Hip, Hipster, In, Latest, Mainstream, Mode, Modern, Newfangled, Pacemaker, Pop, Poserish, Posey, Rage, Smart, Style, Swim, Tendency, Tendenz, Tenor, Tide, Tonnish

Trespass(er), Trespassing Encroach, Errant, Hack, Impinge, Infringe, Offend, Peccancy, Sin, Trench, Wrong(doer)

Trial Acid test, Adversity, Affliction, Appro, Approbation, Approval, Assize, Attempt, Bane, Bernoulli, Bout, Burden, Case, Compurgation, Corsned, Court-martial, Cow, Cross, Dock, Drumhead, Dry run, Dummy run, Empirical, Essay, →**EXPERIMENT**, Field, Fitting, Go, Hearing, Jeddart justice, Jethart justice, Lydford law, Nuremberg, Ordeal, Pest, Pilot, Pree, Probation, Proof, Race, Rehearsal, Rigour, Salem, Scramble, State, Taste, Test, Test bed

Triangle(d), Triangular Acute, Bermuda, Cosec, Deltoid, Equilateral, Eternal, Frame, Gair, Golden, Gore, Gyronny, Isosceles, Obtuse, Pascal's, Pedimental, Pyramid, Rack, Right-angled, Scalene, Similar, Trigon, Triquetral, Tromino, Warning

Tribe(s), Tribal, Tribesman Angle, Cimmerii, Clan(nish), Cree, Crow, D(a)yak, Dynasty, Ephraim, Family, Gond, Guarani, Issachar, Iwi, Judah, Levite, Longobardi, Lost, Manasseh, Nair, Nation, Nayar, Ordovices, Picts, →**RACE**, Schedule, Strandloper, Ute, Zebulun

Tribune, Tribunal Aeropagus, Bema, Bench, →**COURT**, Divan, Forum, Hague, Industrial, Leader, Platform, Rienzi, Rota, Star-chamber

Tributary Affluent, Bogan, Branch, Confluent, Creek, Fork

Tribute Cain, Citation, Commemoration, Compliment, Crants, Danegeld, Deodate, →**DUE**, Encomium, Epitaph, Festschrift, Floral, Gavel, Heriot, Homage, Kain, Memento, Ode, Panegyric, Peter's pence, →**PRAISE**, Rome-penny, Rome-scot, Scat(t), Tax, Testimonial, Toast, Toll, Wreath, Wroth

Trick(ed), Trickery, Tricks(ter), Tricky Antic, Art, Artifice, Attrap, Awkward, Bamboozle, Begunk, Book, Bunco, Bunko, Cantrip, Capot, Catch, Charley pitcher, Cheat, Chicane(ry), Chouse, Claptrap, Cod(-act), Cog, Con(fidence), Coyote, Crook, Davenport, Deceit, Deception, Deck, Decoy, Deke, Delicate, Delude, Device, Dirty, →**DO**, →**DODGE**, Double, Dupe, Elf, Elfin, Elvan, Elven, Entrap, Fard, Feat, Fetch, Fiddle, Finesse, Finicky, Flam, Flim-flam, Fob, Fox, Fraud, Fun, Gambit, Game, Gammon, Gaud, Get, Gimmick, Gleek, Glike,

Gowk, Guile, Had, Hanky-panky, Hey presto, Hoax, Hocus(-pocus), Hoodwink, Hot potato, Hum, Illude, Illusion, Imposture, Jape, Jockey, John, Kittle, Knack, Lark, Legerdemain, Leg pull, Magsman, Mislead, Monkey, Monkey-shine, Murphy's game, Nap, Palter, Parlour, Pass, Pawk, Phish, Pleasantry, Prank, Prestige, Put-on, Quick, Ramp, Raven, Reak, Reik, Rex, Rig, Rope, Ropery, Ruse, Scam, Sell, Set-up, Shanghai, Shenanigan, Shifty, Shill, Skite, Skul(l)duggery, Skylark, Skyte, Slam, Sleight, Slight, Sophism, Spoof, Stall, Stealth, Stint, Stunt, Subterfuge, Take in, Three-card, Ticklish, Tip, Trait, Trap, Trump, Turn, Underplot, Vole, Wangle, Wheeze, Wile, Wrinkle

▷**Trick** *may indicate* an anagram

Trifle(s), Trifling Bagatelle, Banal, Bauble, Bibelot, Birdseed, Bit, Bric-a-brac, Bubkes, Cent, Chickenfeed, Coquette, Dabble, Dalliance, Denier, Dessert, Dilly-dally, Do, Doit, Faddle, Falderal, Falderol, Fallal, Feather, Fewtril, Fiddle, Fiddle-faddle, Fig, Fizgig, Flamfew, Fleabite, Flirt, Folderol, Fool, Footle, Fribble, Frippery, Fritter, Frivol, Gewgaw, Idle, Inconsequential, Insignificant, Iota, Kickshaw, Knick-knack, Mess, Mite, Nothing, Old song, Palter, Paltry, Peanuts, Peddle, Peppercorn, Petty, Philander, Piddle, Piffle, Pin, Pingle, Pittance, Play, Potty, Quelquechose, Quiddity, Quiddle, Sherry, Slight, Small beer, Small wares, Smatter, Song, Sport, Stiver, Strae, Straw, Sundry, Tiddle, Tom, Toy, Trinket, Trivia, Whit

Trigger Detent, Hair, Instigate, Pawl, Precipitate, Set off, Spark, Start, Switch on, Tripwire

Trill(ed), Triller, Trilling Burr, Churr, Hirrient, Quaver, Ribattuta, Roll, Staphyle, Trim, Twitter, Warble

Trim(med), Trimmer, Trimming Abridge, Adorn, Adornment, Ballast, Barb, Bleed, Braid, Bray, Chipper, Clip, Dapper, Defat, Dinky, Dress, Ermine, Face, Fettle, File, Froufrou, Garnish, Garniture, Gimp, Guimpe, Hog, Macramé, Macrami, Marabou, Neat, Net(t), Order, Ornament, Pare, Pipe, Plight, Posh, Preen, Pruin(e), Prune, Roach, Robin, Ruche, Sax, Sett, Shear, Shipshape, Smirk, Smug, Sned, Snod, Soutache, →**SPRUCE**, Straddle, Stroddle, Stylist, Svelte, →**TIDY**, Time-server, Top, Torsade, Trick, Wig

Trinket(s) Bauble, Bibelot, Bijou(terie), Charm, Falderal, Fallal, Folderol, Knickknack, Nicknack, Toy, Trankum

Trip(per) Awayday, Cook's tour, Cruise, Dance, Day, Druggie, Ecotour, Ego, Emmet, Errand, Expedition, →**FALL**, Field, Flight, Flip, Guilt, Head, High, Hop, Joint, Jolly, Journey, Junket, Kilt, Lap, Link, Outing, Passage, Pleasure, Ply, Power, Ride, Round, Run, Sail, Sashay, Spin, Spurn, →**STUMBLE**, Tootle, Tour, Trek, Trial, Voyage

▷**Trip** *may indicate* an anagram

Triple, Triplet Codon, Hemiol(i)a, Perfect, Sdrucciola, Ternal, Tiercet, Treble, Trifecta, Trilling, Trin(e), Tripling

Trite Banal, Boilerplate, Corny, Hackneyed, Hoary, Mickey Mouse, Novelettish, Pabulum, Rinky-dink, Stale, Stock, Time-worn, Truism, Worn

Triumph(ant) Cock-a-hoop, Codille, Cowabunga, Crow, Exult, Glory, Impostor, Jubilant, Killing, Oho, Olé, Ovation, Palm, Prevail, Victorious, →**WIN**

Trivia(l), Triviality Adiaphoron, Bagatelle, Balaam, Bald, →**BANAL**, Bathos, Footling, Frippery, Frothy, Futile, Idle, Inconsequential, Light, Minutiae, Nitpicking, No-brainer, Nonentity, Nothingism, Paltry, Pap, Peppercorn, Pettifoggery, Petty, Picayune, Piddling, Piffling, Puerile, Shallow, Small, Small beer, Small fry, Snippety, Squirt, Squit, Toy(s), Twaddle, Vegie

Trolley Brute, Cart, Crane, Dinner-wagon, Dolly, Gurney, Shopping, Tea, Teacart, Truck, Trundler

▶**Trollop** *see* **LOOSE(N)**

Troop(s), Trooper Alpini, Anzac, Band, BEF, Brigade, Cohort, Company, Depot, Detachment, Garrison, Guard, Horde, Household, Logistics, Midianite, Milice, Militia, Monkeys, Pultan, Pulton, Pultoon, Pultun, SAS, School, Scout, Shock, →**SOLDIER**, Sowar, State, Storm, Subsidiary, Tp, Turm(e), Velites

Trophy Adward, Ashes, →**AWARD**, Bag, Belt, Brush, Cup, Emmy, Jackpot, Memento, Palm, Plate, →**PRIZE**, Scalp, Schneider, Shield, Silverware, Spoils, Tourist, Triple crown, TT

Trot(ter), Trot out Air, Clip, Crib, Crubeen, Hag, Job, Jog, Passage, Pettitoes, Piaffe, Pony, Ranke, Red(-shirt), Rising, Tootsie, Trotskyist

Trouble(s), Troublemaker, Troublesome Ache, Ado, Affliction, Aggrieve, Aggro, Agitate, Ail, Alarm, Annoy, Assail, Bale, Barrat, Bedevil, Beset, →**BOTHER**, Bovver, Brickle, Burden, Care, Coil, Concern, Debate, Disaster, Dismay, Disquiet, Distress, Disturb, Dog, Dolour, Eat, Exercise, Fash, Finger, Firebrand, Fret, Frondeur, Fun and games, Fuss, Gram(e), Grief, Harass, Harry, Hassle, Hatter, Heat, Heist, Hellion, Hot potato, Hot water, Howdyedo, Incommode, Inconvenience, Infest, →**IN TROUBLE**, Irk, Jam, Kaugh, Malcontent, Mayhem, Mess, Mixer, Moil, Molest, Noy, Onerous, Perturb, Pester, Pestiferous, Picnic, Plague, Play up, Poke, Reck, Rioter, Rub, Ruffle, Scamp, Scrape, Shake, Shtook, Soup, Spiny, Stir, Stirrer, Storm, Sturt, Tartar, Teen, Teething, Thorny, Tine, Toil, Trial, Turn-up, Tyne, Typhoid Mary, Unpleasant, Unrest, Unsettle, Upsetter, Varmint, Vex, →**WORRY**

▷**Troublesome** *may indicate* an anagram

Trough Back, Backet, Bed, Buddle, Channel, Chute, Culvert, Graben, Gutter, Hod, Hutch, Manger, Stock, Straik, Strake, Syncline, Troffer, Tundish, Tye, Vale

Trouser(s) Bags, Bell-bottoms, Bloomers, Breeches, Bumsters, Capri pants, Cargo pants, Chinos, Churidars, Clam-diggers, Combat, Continuations, Cords, Corduroys, Cossacks, Culottes, Cut-offs, Daks, Denims, Drainpipe, Drawers, Ducks, Dungarees, Eel-skins, Flannels, Flares, Galligaskins, Gaskins, Gauchos, Hip-huggers, Hipsters, Indescribables, Inexpressibles, Innominables, Jazzpants, Jeans, Jeggings, Jodhpurs, Jog-pants, Kaccha, Ke(c)ks, Knee cords, Lederhosen, Levis, Longs, Loon-pants, Loons, Moleskins, Overalls, Oxford bags, Palazzo (pants), Palazzos, Pantalet(te)s, Pantaloons, Pants, Pedal pushers, Pegtops, Plus-fours, Plus-twos, Pyjamas, Rammies, Reach-me-downs, Salopettes, Shalwar, Ski pants, Slacks, Stirrup pants, Stovepipes, Strides, Strossers, Sweatpants, Thornproofs, Trews, Trouse, Trunk-breeches, Unmentionables, Unutterables, Utterless

Trout Aurora, Brook, Brown, Bull, Char(r), Coral, Cutthroat, Finnac(k), Finnock, Fish, Gillaroo, Herling, Hirling, Peal, Peel, Phinnock, Pogies, Quintet, Rainbow, Sewen, Sewin, Speckled, Splake, Steelhead, Togue, Whitling

Truant Absentee, AWOL, Bunk off, Dodge, Hooky, Idler, Kip, Mich(e), Mitch, Mooch, Mouch, Skive, Wag

Truce Armistice, Barley, Ceasefire, Fainites, Fains, Hudna, Interlude, Keys, Pax, Stillstand, Treague, Treaty

Truck Bakkie, Bogie, Breakdown, Business, Cabover, Cattle, Cocopan, Dealings, Dolly, Dray, Dumper, Flatbed, Forklift, Haul, Hopper, Journey(-weight), →**LORRY**, Low-loader, Monster, Pallet, Panel, Pick-up, Road-train, Semi, Sound, Stacking, Tipper, Tommy, Tow(ie), Traffic, Tram, Trolley, Trundle, Ute, Utility, Van, Wrecker

Trudge Footslog, Jog, Lumber, Pad, Plod, Stodge, Stramp, Taigle, Traipse, Trash, Trog, Vamp

True Accurate, Actual, Apodictic, Axiomatic, Constant, Correct, Exact, Factual, Faithful, Genuine, Honest, Indubitable, Leal, Literal, Loyal, Platitude, Plumb, Pure, Real, Realistic, Sooth, Vera, Very

Truly Certainly, Certes, Fegs, Forsooth, Honestly, Indeed, Insooth, Surely, Verily, Yea

Trump(s), Trumpet(er) Agami, Alchemy, Alchymy, Bach, Bass, Blare, Blast, Bray, Buccina, Bugle(r), Call, Card, Clang, Clarion, Conch, Cornet, Corona, Crossruff, Crow, Daffodil, Elephant, Extol, Fanfare, Hallali, Honours, → **HORN**, Invent, Jew's, Last, Lituus, Lur(e), Lurist, Manille, Marine, Megaphone, Overruff, Pedro, Proclaim, Ram's-horn, Resurrect, Rogue, Ruff, Salpingian, Salpinx, Sancho, Satchmo, Sennet, Shell, Shofar, Shophar, Slug-horn, Splash, Surpass, Swan, Tantara, Tantarara, Tar(at)antara, Theodomas, Tiddy, Triton, Triumph

Trunk(s) Aorta(l), A-road, Body, Bole, Box, Bulk, But(t), Caber, Carcase, Chest, Coffer, Hose, Imperial, Log, Nerve, Peduncle, Pollard, Portmanteau, Portmantle, Proboscis, Puncheon, Ricker, Road, Saratoga, Shorts, STD, Steamer, Stock, Stud, Suitcase, Synangium, Togs, Torso, Valise, Wardrobe

Trust(y), Trusting, Trustworthy Affy, Apex, Authentic, Belief, Bet on, Blind, Box, Camaraderie, Care, Carnegie, Cartel, Charge, Combine, Confide, Count on, Credit, Dependable, Dewy-eyed, Discretionary, Escrow, → **FAITH**, Fidelity, Fiduciary, Foundation, Gullible, Honest, Hope, Hospital, Investment, Leal, Lippen, Loyal, Naif, National, NT, Reliable, Reliance, Rely, Repose, Reputable, Responsible, Staunch, Tick, Trojan, Trow, True, Trump, Unit

Truth(ful), Truism Accuracy, Alethic, Axiom, Bromide, Cliché, Cold turkey, Dharma, Dialectic, → **FACT**, Facticity, Forsooth, Gospel, Griff, Home, Honesty, Idea(l), Logical, Maxim, Naked, Necessary, Pravda, Principle, Reality, Sooth, Soothfast, Strength, Troggs, Veracity, Veridical, Verisimilitude, Verity, Vraisemblance

Try(ing) After, Aim, Approof, Arraign, Assay, Attempt, Audition, Bash, Bate, Bid, Birl, Burden, Burl, Conative, Contend, Court martial, Crack, Effort, Empiric(utic), → **ENDEAVOUR**, Essay, Examine, Experiment, Fand, Fish, Fling, Foretaste, Go, Gun for, Harass, Hard, Hear, Importunate, Irk, Noy, Offer, Ordalium, Ordeal, Penalty, Pesky, Pop, Practise, Pree, Prieve, Prove, → **SAMPLE**, Seek, Shot, Sip, Stab, Strain, Strive, Struggle, Tackle, Taste, Tax, Tempt, Test, Touchdown, → **TRIAL**, Whirl

Tub(by), Tubbiness, Tubman, Tub-thumper Ash-leach, Back, Bath, Boanerges, Bran, Bucket, Cooper, Corf, Cowl, Dan, Demagogue, Diogenes, Endomorph, Firkin, Hip bath, Keeve, Kid, Kieve, Kit, Pin, Podge, Powdering, Pudge, Pulpit, Rolypoly, Seasoning, Tun, Vat, Wash, Whey

Tube, Tubing, Tubular Acorn, Arteriole, Artery, Barrel, Blowpipe, Bronchus, Buckyball, Buckytube, Burette, Calamus, Camera, Can(n)ula, Capillary, Casing, Catheter, Cathode-ray, Cave, Conduit, Crookes, Digitron, Diode, Discharge, Drain, Draw, Drift, Dropper, Duct, Electron, Endiometer, Eustachian, Extension, Fallopian, Fistula, Flash, Fluorescent, Germ, Glowstick, Grommet, Hawsepipe, Hose, Idiot box, Inner, Kinescope, Macaroni, Matrass, Metro, Morris, Nasogastric, Neural, Nixie, Optic, Orthicon, Oval, Oviduct, Pastille, Peashooter, Pentode, Picture, → **PIPE**, Pipette, Piping, Pneumatic, Pollen, Postal, Promethean, Salpinx, Saticon®, Saucisse, Saucisson, Schnorkel, Shock, Sieve, Siphon(al), Siphonet, Sleeve, Slide, Snorkel, Spaghetti, Speaking, Spout, Staple,

Static, Stem, Stent, Stone canal, Storage, Strae, Straw, Strip light, Subway, Sucker, Swallet, Syringe, Tele, Telescope, Teletron, Television, Telly, Terete, Test, Tetrode, Thermionic, Tile, Torpedo, Torricellian, Trachea, Travelling-wave, Trocar, Trochotron, Trunk, Tunnel, Tuppenny, TV, U, Underground, Ureter, Urethra, Vacuum, Vas, VDU, Vein, Vena, Venturi, Video, Vidicon®, Worm, X-ray

Tuber(s) Arnut, Arracacha, Bulb, Chufa, Coc(c)o, Dasheen, Earth-nut, Eddoes, Ginseng, Jicama, Mashua, Oca, Pignut, Potato, Root, Salep, Taproot, Taro, Tater, Tuckahoe, Yam, Yautia

Tuberculosis Consumption, Crewels, Cruel(l)s, Decline, Lupus, Lupus vulgaris, Phthisis, Scrofula

Tuck Dart, Friar, Gather, Grub, Hospital corner, Kilt, Pin, Pleat, Scran

Tuft(ed) Aigrette, Amentum, Beard, Candlewick, Catkin, C(a)espitose, Cluster, Coma, Comb, Cowlick, Crest, Dollop, Ear, Flaught, Floccus, Goatee, Hank, Hassock, Knot, Pappus, Penicillate, Pledget, Quiff, Scopate, Shola, Tait, Tassel, Toorie, Topknot, Toupee, Tourie, Tussock, Tuzz, Whisk

Tug Chain, Drag, Haul, Hoick, Jerk, Lug, Pug, →**PULL**, Rive, Rug, Ship, Sole, Soole, Sowl(e), Tit, Tow, Towboat, Yank

Tumble, Tumbler Acrobat, Cartwheel, Drier, Fall, →**GLASS**, Jack, Jill, Lock, Pitch, Popple, Purl, Realise, Roller-coaster, Spill, Stumble, Topple, Touser, Towser, Trip, Twig, Voltigeur, Welter

▷**Tumble** *may indicate* an anagram

Tumour Adenoma, Anbury, Angioma, Angiosarcoma, Astrocytoma, Burkitt('s) lymphoma, Cancer, Carcinoid, Carcinoma, Carcinosarcoma, Chondroma, Condyloma, Crab(-yaws), Craniopharyngioma, Dermoid, Encanthis, Encephaloma, Enchondroma, Endothelioma, Epulis, Exostosis, Fibroid, Fibroma, Ganglion, Glioblastoma, Glioma, Granuloma, Grape, →**GROWTH**, Gumma, Haemangioma, Haematoma, Hepatoma, Lipoma, Lymphoma, Medulloblastoma, Melanoma, Meningioma, Mesothelioma, Metastasis, Mole, Myeloma, Myoma, Myxoma, Neoplasm, Neuroblastoma, Neurofibroma, Neuroma, -oma, Oncogenesis, Oncology, Osteoclastoma, Osteoma, Osteosarcoma, Papilloma, Polypus, Retinoblastoma, Rous sarcoma, Sarcoma, Scirrhous, Seminoma, Steatoma, Struma, Talpa, Teratocarcinoma, Teratoma, Thymoma, Wart, Wen, Wilms', Windgall, Wolf, Xanthoma, Yaw

Tumult, Tumultuous Brattle, Brawl, Coil, Deray, Ferment, Fracas, Hirdy-girdy, Hubbub, Reird, Riot, →**ROAR**, Romage, Rore, Stoor, Stour, Stowre, Stramash, Tew, Tristan, Tristram, Turbulent, →**UPROAR**

Tuna Ahi, Eel, Pear, Skipjack, Yellowfin

Tune(s), Tuneful, Tuner, Tuning Adjust, Air, Aria, Ayre, Canorous, Carillon, Catch, Choral(e), Dial, Dump, Étude, Fork, Gingle, Harmony, Hornpipe, Hunt's up, Jingle, Key, Maggot, Measure, Melisma, →**MELODY**, Morrice, Morris, Old Hundred, Peg, Planxty, Port, Potpourri, Raga, Rant, Ranz-des-vaches, Reel, Scordatura, Signature, Snatch, Song, Spring, Strain, Sweet, Syntonise, Syntony, Temper, Theme, Tone, Toy, Tweak

Tungstate, Tungsten Scheelite, W, Wolfram

Tunic Ao dai, Caftan, Chiton, Choroid, Cote-hardie, Dalmatic, Dashiki, Gymslip, Hauberk, Kabaya, Kaftan, Kameez, K(h)urta, Tabard, Toga

Tunnel(ler) Bore, Channel, Condie, Countermine, Culvert, Cundy, Gallery, Head, Mine, Mole, Qanat, Sewer, Simplon, Stope, Subway, Sure, Syrinx, Transmanche, Tube, Underpass, Warren, Wind, Wormhole

Turban Bandanna, Hat, Mitral, Pagri, Puggaree, Puggery, Puggree, Sash, Scarf, Toque

Turbulence, Turbulent Atmospheric, Becket, Bellicose, Buller, Factious, Fierce, Overfall, Rapids, Roil, Stormy

▷**Turbulent, Turbulence** *may indicate* an anagram

Turf Caespitose, Clod, Divot, Earth, Fail, Feal, Flaught, Gazo(o)n, →**GRASS**, Greensward, Kerf, Peat, Racing, Scraw, →**SOD**, Sward, Territory

Turk(ish) Anatolian, Bashaw, Bashkir, Bey, Bimbashi, Bostangi, Byzantine, Caimac(am), Crescent, Effendi, Gregory, Horse(tail), Irade, Kaimakam, Kazak(h), Kurd, Mameluke, Mutessarif(at), Omar, Osman(li), Ottamite, Ottoman, Ottomite, Rayah, Scanderbeg, Selim, Seljuk(ian), Seraskier, Spahi, Tatar, Timariot, Usak, Uzbeg, Uzbek, Yakut

Turkey, Turkey-like Anatolia, Antioch, Brush, Bubbly(-jock), Curassow, Dud, Eyalet, Flop, Gobbler, Lame brain, Lemon, Norfolk, Sultanate, Talegalla, TR, Trabzon, Vulturn

Turmoil Ariot, Chaos, Confusion, Din, Disruption, Dust, Ferment, Maelstrom, Mess, Pother, Pudder, Stoor, Stour, Tornado, Tracasserie, Tumult, Unrest, →**UPROAR**, Welter

Turn(ing), Turn(ed) away, Turn(ed) up, Turns Act, Adapt, Addle, Advert, Antrorse, Avert, Bad, Bank, Become, Bend, Blow in, Bump, Careen, Cartwheel, Cast, Change, Char(e), Chore, Christiania, Christie, Christy, Churn, Coarsen, Cock, Coil, Convert, Corotate, Crank(le), Cuff, Curd(le), Curve, Defect, Deflect, Detour, Deviate, Dig, Digress, Divert, Ear, Earn, Elbow, Evert, Evict, Fadge, Ferment, Flip, Forfend, Go, Good, Gyrate, Hairpin, Handbrake, Head-off, Hie, High, Hinge, Hup, Influence, Innings, Invert, Jar, Jink, Jump, Keel, Kick, Lodging, Lot, Luff, Mohawk, Move, Nip, Number, Obvert, Parallel, Parry, Penchant, Pivot, Plough, Pronate, Prove, PTO, Quarter, Rebut, Refer, Refract, Retroflex, Retroussé, Retrovert, Rev, Revolt, Ride, Riffle, Rocker, Roll, Root, →**ROTATE**, Rote, Roulade, Rout, Routine, Screw, Sheer, →**SHOT**, Shout, Sicken, Skit, Slew, Slue, Solstice, Sour, →**SPELL**, Spin, Spot, Sprain, Star, Start, Stem, Step, Stunt, Swash, Swerve, Swing, Switch, Swivel, Telemark, Thigmotropism, Three-point, Throw, Tiptilt, Tirl, T-junction, Transpose, Trend, Trick, Trie, Turtle, Twiddle, Twist, Twizzle, U, Uey, U-ie, Up, Veer, Versed, Version, Vertigo, Volta, Volte-face, Volutation, Wap, Warp, Wend, Went, →**WHEEL**, Whelm, Whirl, Whorl, Wimple, Wind, Wrast, Wrest, Wriggle, Zigzag

▷**Turn(ing)** *may indicate* an anagram

Turn-coat Apostate, Cato, Defector, Quisling, Rat, Renegade, Rottan, Tergiversate, Traitor

Turner Axle, Capstan, Crank, Lana, Lathe, Page, Painter, Pivot, Remueur, Rose-engine, Spanner, Tina, Worm, Wrench

Turning point Crisis, Crossroads, Landmark, Solstice, Watershed

Turnip(-shaped) Baggy, Bagie, Hunter, Indian, Napiform, Navew, Neep, Rutabaga, Shaw, →**STUPID PERSON**, Swede, Tumshie

▷**Turnip** *may indicate* a watch

Turn over, Turnover Bridie, Capsize, Careen, Flip, Inversion, Mull, Production, PTO, Samosa, Somersault, TO, Up-end

Turret(ed) Barmkin, Bartisan, Belvedere, Garret, Gazebo, Louver, Louvre, Mirador, Pepperbox, Sponson, Tank top, →**TOWER**, Turriculate

Turtle, Turtle head Bale, Box, Calipash, Calipee, Chelone, Cooter, Diamondback, Emys, Floor, Green, Hawk(s)bill, Inverted, Leatherback,

Loggerhead, Matamata, Mossback, Mud, Musk, Painted, Ridley, Screen, Snapper, Snapping, Soft-shelled, Stinkpot, Terrapin, Thalassian

Tusk Gam, Horn, Ivory, Tooth, Tush

Tussle Giust, Joust, Mêlée, Scrimmage, Scrum, Scuffle, Skirmish, Touse, Touze, Towse, Towze, Tuilyie, Wrestle

Tutor Abbé, Aristotle, Ascham, Bear, → **COACH**, Crammer, Don, Edify, Instruct, Leader, Preceptor, Répétiteur, Starets, Staretz, Supervisor, Teacher, Train

TV Baird, Box, Breakfast, Cable, Closed circuit, Digibox®, Digital, Docudrama, Docusoap, Flat screen, Idiot-box, Lime Grove, Mini-series, Monitor, NICAM, PAL, SECAM, Sitcom, Sky, Tele, Telly, Tie-in, Triniscope, Tube, Video

Twaddle Blether, Drivel, Fadaise, Rot, Slipslop, Tripe

Tweak Pinch, Pluck, Primp, Twiddle, Twist, Twitch

Twelfth, Twelve Apostles, Dozen, Epiphany, Glorious, Grouse, Midday, Midnight, N, Night, Noon(tide), Ternion, Twal

▶**Twice** *see* **TWO(SOME)**

Twig(s) Besom, Birch, Brushwood, Cotton, Cow, Dig, Fathom, Grasp, Kow, Osier, Realise, Reis, Rice, Rod, Rumble, Sarment, See, Sprig, Stick, Sticklac, Switch, Understand, Wand, Wattle, Whip, Wicker, Withe

Twilight Astronomical, Civil, Cockshut, Crepuscular, Demi-jour, Dimpsy, Dusk, Gloam(ing), Götterdämmerung, Nautical, Ragnarok, Summerdim

Twin(s) Asvins, Castor, Coetaneous, Couplet, Didymous, Dioscuri, Ditokous, Dizygotic, Double, Dual, Fraternal, Gemel, Geminate, Gemini, Identical, Isogeny, Juxtaposition, Kindred, Kray, Look-alike, Macle, Monozygotic, Parabiotic, Pigeon-pair, Pollux, Remus, Romulus, Siamese, Thomas, Tweedledee, Tweedledum

Twine Binder, Braid, Coil, Cord, Inosculate, Packthread, Sisal, Snake, String, Twist, Wreathe

Twinkle, Twinkling Glimmer, Glint, Mo(ment), → **SPARKLE**, Starnie, Trice

▷**Twirling** *may indicate* an anagram

Twist(ed), Twister, Twisting, Twisty Aglee, Agley, Askant, Askew, Baccy, Becurl, Bought, Braid, Buckle, Card-sharper, Chisel, Coil, Contort, Convolution, Corkscrew, Crinkle, Crisp, Cue, Curl(icue), Curliewurlie, Cyclone, Deform, Detort, Diddle, Dishonest, Distort, → **DODGE**, Eddy, Embraid, Entrail, Entwine, Garrot, Helix, Kink, Lemon peel, Loop, Mangulate, Mat, Meander, Misshapen, Oliver, Plait, Quirk, Raddle, Ravel, Rick, Rogue, Rotate, Rove, Serpent, Skew, Slew, Slub(b), Slue, Snake, Snarl, Spin, Spiral, Sprain, Squiggle, Squirm, Strand, Swivel, Tendril, Thraw(n), Torc, Tornado, Torque, Torsade, Torsion, Tortile, Turn, Tweak, Twiddle, Twine, Twirl, Twizzle, Typhoon, Wamble, Warp, Wind, Wreathe, Wrench, Wrest, Wriggle, Wring, Writhe, Wry, Zigzag

▷**Twisted, Twisting** *may indicate* an anagram

Twit, Twitter Airhead, Birdbrain, Chaff, Cheep, Cherup, Chirrup, Dotterel, Gear(e), Giber, → **JEER**, Rag, Stupid, Taunt, Warble

Twitch(ing), Twitchy Athetosis, Birdwatch, Clonic, Fibrillation, Grass, Jerk, Life-blood, Saccadic, Sneer, Spasm, Start, Subsultive, Tic, Tig, Tippet, Tit, Toss, Tweak, Twinge, Vellicate, Yips

Two(some), Twofold, Twice Bice, Bis, Bisp, Both, Brace, Company, Couple(t), Deuce, Double, Duad, Dual, Duet, Duo, Duple, Dyad, Item, → **PAIR**, Snake-eyes, Swy, Tête-à-tête, Twain, Twins, Twister

Tycoon Baron, Entrepreneur, Fat cat, Gates, Magnate, Murdoch, Nabob, Onassis, Plutocrat, Shogun

Tympany Castanets, Cymbal, Drum, Kitchen, Triangle, Xylophone

Type(s), Typify, Typing A, Agate, Aldine, Antimony, Antique, B, Balaam, Baskerville, Bastard, Batter, Beard, Black-letter, Block, Blood, Body, Bold face, Bold Roman, Bourgeois, Braille, Brand, Brevier, Brilliant, Canon, Caslon, Category, Character, Chase, Cicero, Clarendon, Class, Columbian, Condensed, Cut, Egyptian, Elite, Elzevir, Em, Emblem, Emerald, En(nage), English, Epitomise, Exemplar, Face, Font, Footer, Form(e), Founder's, Fount, Fraktur, Fudge, Garamond, Gem, Genre, Gent, Gothic, Great primer, Hair, Hot metal, Ilk, Image, Key, Keyboard, Kidney, Kind, Late-star, Ligature, Light-faced, Logotype, Longprimer, Ludlow, Make, Mating, Melanochroi, Minion, Modern, Monospaced, Moon, Mould, Mullioned, Non-pareil, Norm, Old English, Old-face, Old Style, Paragon, Pattern, Pearl, Peculiar, Personality, Pi, Pica, Pie, Plantin, Point, Primer, Print, Quad(rat), Roman, Ronde, Ruby, Sanserif, Secretary, Semibold, Serif, Serological, Slug, Sp, Species, Spectral, Stanhope, Style, Times, Times Roman, Tissue, Touch, Variety, Version

▷**Type of** *may indicate* an anagram

Typical Average, Characteristic, Classic, Everyman, Natural, Normal, Representative, Standard, Symbolic, True-bred, Usual

Tyrant, Tyranny, Tyrannical Absolutism, Autocrat, Caligula, Czar, Despot, Dictator, Dominion, Drawcansir, Gelon, Herod, Ivan the Terrible, Lordly, Nero, Oppressor, Pharaoh, Pisistratus, Sardanapalus, Satrap, Stalin, Totalitarian, Tsar, Yoke

Tyre(s) Balloon, Cross-ply, Cushion, Earthing, Flat, Michelin®, Pericles, Pneumatic, Radial(-ply), Recap, Remould, Retread, Shoe, Sidewall, Slick, Snow, Spare, Stepney, Toe in, Tread, Tubeless, Whitewall

Tyro Beginner, Ham, → **NOVICE**, Rabbit, Rookie, Rooky, Starter

Uu

Ugly Abhorrent, Butters, Cow, Crow, Customer, Disfigured, Eyesore, Faceache, Foul, Gorgon, Grotesque, Gruesome, Hideous, Homely, Huckery, Jolie laide, Loath, Loth, Mean, Monstrosity, Ominous, Plain, Sight, Unsightly

Ulcer(ous) Abscess, Aphtha, Canker, Chancre, Chancroid, Decubitus, Duodenal, Enanthema, Gastric, Helcoid, Imposthume, Mouth, Noma, Peptic, Phagedaena, Plague-sore, Rodent, Rupia, Sore, Wolf

Ulster NI, Overcoat, Raincoat, Red hand, Ulad

Ultimate(ly) Absolute, Basic, Deterrent, Eventual, Final, Furthest, Last, Maximum, Mostest, Omega, So, Supreme, Thule, Ult

Umbrage Offence, Pique, Resentment, Shade

Umbrella(-shaped) Bumbershoot, Chatta, En tout cas, Gamp, Gingham, Gloria, Mush(room), Parasol, Sunshade, Tee

Umpire Arb(iter), Byrlawman, Daysman, Decider, Judge, Mediate, Oddjobman, Odd(s)man, Overseer, Referee, Rule, Stickler, Thirdsman

Unable Can't, Downa-do, Incapable

Unacceptable Beyond the pale, Ineligible, Non-U, Not on, Out, Repugnant, Stigmatic, Taboo

Unaccompanied A cappella, Alone, High-lone, Secco, Single, Solo, Solus

Unaffected Artless, Genuine, Homely, Insusceptible, Naif, Naive, Natural, Plain, Sincere, Unattached

Unanswerable Erotema, Irrefragable, Irrefutable

Unappealing Distasteful, Grim, Offensive, Off-putting, Rank

Unattached Disengaged, Fancy free, Freelance, Loose

Unattractive Demagnetised, Dowdy, Drac(k), Frump(y), Hideous, Lemon, Munter, Plain, Plug-ugly, Rebarbative, Scungy, Seamy, Skanky, Ugly

▷**Unauthentic** *may indicate an anagram*

Unavail(able), Unavailing Bootless, Futile, Ineluctable, Lost, NA, No use, Off, Vain

Unaware(ness) Blind-side, Cloistered, Coma, Heedless, Ignorant, Incognisant, Innocent, Oblivious, Stupor

Unbalanced Asymmetric, Deranged, Doolalli, Doolally, Loco, Lopsided, Nutty, Out to lunch, Skewwhiff, Twisted, Uneven

Unbecoming, Unbefitting Improper, Indecent, Infra dig, Shabby, Unfitting, Unseemly, Unsuitable, Unworthy

Unbelievable, Unbeliever Agnostic, Atheist, Cassandra, Doubter, Giaour, Heathen, Heretic, Incredible, Infidel, Pagan, Painim, Paynim, Sceptic, Tall, Zendik

Unbend(ing) Relax, Relent, Strict

Unbiased Fair, Impartial, Independent, Just, Neutral, Non-partisan, Objective, Open-minded, Unattainted

Unblock(ing) Clear, Free, Recanalization

Unbridled Fancy free, Footloose, Lawless, Uncurbed, Unrestricted, Unshackled, Untramelled

Uncanny Eerie, Eldritch, Extraordinary, Geason, Rum, Spooky, Wanchancie, Wanchancy, Weird

Uncertain(ty) Acatalepsy, Agnostic, Blate, Broken, Chancy, Chary, Confusion, Contingent, Delicate, Dicey, Dither, Dodgy, Doubtful, Dubiety, Equivocal, Hesitant, Iffy, Indeterminate, Indistinct, Irresolute, Limbo, Obscure, Parlous, Peradventure, Precarious, Queasy, Risky, Slippery, Suspense, Tentative, Vagary, Vor, Wide open

▷**Uncertain** *may indicate* an anagram

Unchangeable, Unchanged, Unchanging As is, Enduring, Eternal, Idempotent, Immutable, Intact, Monotonous, Perennial, Read only, Semper idem, Stable, Timeless

Unchaste Corrupt, Immodest, Immoral, Impure, Lewd, Light-heeled, Wanton

Uncivil(ised) Barbaric, Benighted, Boondocks, Brutish, Discourteous, Disrespectful, Giant-rude, Heathen, Impolite, Liberty, Military, Rude, Rudesby, Short, Unmannerly

Uncle Abbas, Afrikaner, Arly, Bob, Dutch, Eme, Nunky, Oom, Pawnbroker, Pawnee, Pawnshop, Pledgee, Pop-shop, Remus, Sam, Silas, Tio, Tom, U, Usurer, Vanya

Unclean Defiled, Dirty, Impure, Obscene, Ordure, Squalid, Tabu, T(e)refa(h)

Unclear Ambitty, Blurred, Cloudy, Grey area, Hazy, Inexplicit, Nebulous, Obscure, Opaque, Overcast, Sketchy, Slurred

Uncomfortable Awkward, Mean, Spartan, Uneasy

Uncommon Rara avis, Rare, Sparse, Strange, Unusual

▷**Uncommon(ly)** *may indicate* an anagram

Uncompromising Cutthroat, Hardline, Hardshell, Intransigent, Relentless, Rigid, Strict, Ultra, Zero tolerance

Unconcerned Bland, Careless, Casual, Cold, Impassive, Indifferent, Insouciant, Nonchalant, Strange

Unconditional Absolute, Free, No strings, Pure

Unconnected Asyndetic, Detached, Disjointed, Enodal, Off-line

Unconscious(ness) Asleep, Automatic, Catalepsy, Cold, Comatose, Instinctive, Non-ego, Subliminal, Syncope, Trance, Unaware, Under, Zonked out

Uncontrolled Adrift, Anarchic, Atactic, Free, Hysterical, Incontinent, Intemperate, Loose, Rampant, Skid, Wild

Unconventional Anti-hero, Avant garde, Beatnik, Bohemian, Divergent, Drop-out, Eccentric, Far-out, Freakish, Freeform, Gonzo, Heretic, Heterodox, Hippy, Informal, Irregular, Offbeat, Off-the-wall, Original, Outlandish, Outré, Out there, Raffish, Rebel, Screwball, Spac(e)y, Swinger, Unorthodox, Way-out, Wild

▷**Unconventional** *may indicate* an anagram

Uncooperative Bolshie, Recalcitrant, Stroppy

Uncouth(ness) Baboon, Backwoodsman, Bear, Boorish, Churlish, Crude, Gothic, Inelegant, Rube, Rude, Rugged, Slob, Sloven, Uncivil

Uncover(ed) Bare, Denude, Disclose, Expose, Inoperculate, Naked, Open, Peel, Reveal, Shave, Shill, Shuck, Uncap, Unhood

Unction, Unctuous(ness) Anele, Balm, Chrism, Extreme, Greasy, Last rites, Ointment, Oleaginous, Ooze, Smarm, Soapy

Uncultivated, Uncultured Artless, Bundu, Fallow, Feral, Ignorant, Incult, Lowbrow, Philistine, Rude, Tramontane, Waste, Wild, Wildland, Wildwood

Undecided Aboulia, Dithering, Double-minded, Doubtful, Havering, Hung, Moot, Non-committal, Open-ended, Pending, Pendulous, Torn, Uncertain, Wavering

Under(neath) Aneath, Below, Beneath, Hypnotized, Hypo-, Infra, Sotto, Sub-, Unconscious, Unneath

Undercover Cloak and dagger, Espionage, Secret, Veiled

▶**Undergarment** *see* **UNDERWEAR**

Undergo Bear, Dree, Endure, Sustain

Undergraduate Commoner, Fresher, L, Pup, Questionist, Sizar, Sophomore, Student, Subsizar

Underground (group) Basement, Catacomb, Cellar, Clandestine, Erebus, Fogou, Hell, Hypogaeous, Infernal, Irgun, Kiva, Macchie, Maquis, Mattamore, Metro, Phreatic, Pict, Plutonia, Pothole, Secret, Souterrain, Subsoil, Subterranean, Subway, Tube, Tunnel, Warren, Weem

Undergrowth Brush, Chaparral, Firth, Frith, Scrub

Underhand Arch, Backstair, Dirty, Haunch, Insidious, Lob, Oblique, Scullduggery, Secret, Shady, Sinister, Sly, Sneaky, Surreptitious

Underline Emphasise, Insist, Reinforce, Sublineation

Underling Bottle-washer, Cog, Inferior, Jack, Menial, Minion, Munchkin, Subordinate

Undermine Destabilise, Erode, Fossick, Handbag, Sap, Subvert, Tunnel, Weaken

Understand(able), Understanding, Understood Accept, Acumen, Agreement, Alliance, Apprehend, Capeesh, Catch on, Clear, Cognisable, Comprehend, Conceive, Concept, Connivance, Consideration, Cotton-on, Deal, Dig, Digest, Empathy, Enlighten, Entente, Exoteric, Fathom, Follow, Gather, Gauge, Gaum, Geddit, Get it, Gorm, Grasp, Grok, Have, Head, Heels, Hindsight, Implicit, Insight, Intelligible, Intuit, Ken, Kind, Knowhow, Latch on, Learn, Light(s), Lucid, OK, Omniscient, Pact, Perspicuous, Plumb, Prajna, Rapport, Rapprochement, Realise, Roger, Savey, Savvy, See, Sense, Sole, Subintelligitur, Substance, Tacit, Take, Tenderness, Tolerance, Treaty, Tumble, Twig, Unspoken, Unstated, Uptak(e), Wisdom, Wit

Understate(d), Understatement Litotes, Low-key, Minify, M(e)iosis

▶**Understood** *see* **UNDERSTAND(ABLE)**

Understudy Deputy, Double, Stand-in, Sub

Undertake, Undertaking Adventure, Attempt, Commitment, Contract, Covenant, Emprise, Endeavour, Enterprise, Essay, Guarantee, Misere, Pledge, Promise, Scheme, Shoulder, Tackle, Task, Warranty

Undertaker Editor, Entrepreneur, Mortician, Obligor, Sponsor, Upholder

Underwear Alb, Balbriggan, Balconette, Bloomers, Bodice, Body, Bodyshaper, Body stocking, Body suit, Boxers, Bra(ssiere), Briefs, Broekies, Butt bra, Camiknickers, Camisole, Chemise, Chemisette, Chuddies, Combinations, Combs, Corselet, Corset, Dainties, Drawers, (French) knickers, Frillies, Girdle, Grundies, G-string, Hosiery, Innerwear, Jump, Knick(er)s, Linen, Lingerie, Linings, Long johns, Pantalets, Pantaloons, Panties, Pantihose, Panty girdle, Petticoat, Scanties, Semmit, Shift, Shimmy, Shorts, Singlet, Skivvy, Slip, Smalls, Spencer, Stammel, Stays, Step-ins, Subucula, Suspender-belt, Suspenders, Tanga, Teddy, Thermal, Trunks, Underdaks, Undergarments, Underlinen,

Underpants, Underset, Undershirt, Underthings, Undies, Unmentionables, Vest, Wyliecoat, Y-fronts®

Underworld All-fired, Avernus, Chthonic, Criminal, Gangland, Hell, Lowlife, Mafia, Pluto, Shades, Tartar(e), Tartarus, Tartary

Underwrite, Underwritten Assure, Endorse, Guarantee, Insure, Lloyds, PS

Undeveloped Ament, Backward, Depauperate, Green, Inchoate, Latent, Ridgel, Ridgil, Ridgling, Rig, Riggald, Riglin(g), Rudimentary, Seminal

Undiluted Absolute, Neat, Pure, Sheer, Straight

Undivided Aseptate, Complete, Entire, Indiscrete, One

Undo(ing) Annul, Defeat, Destroy, Downfall, Dup, Poop, Poupe, Release, Rescind, Ruin, Unravel

Undone Arrears, Left, Postponed, Ran, Ruined, Unlast

Undoubted(ly) Ay, Certes, Clearly, Positively, Sure, To be sure

Undress(ed) Bare, Disarray, Disrobe, En cuerpo, Expose, Négligé, Nude, Nue, Peel, Querpo, Raw, Rough, Self-faced, Spar, Strip, Unapparelled

Undulate, Undulating Billow, Nebule, Ripple, Roll, Swell, Wave

▷**Unduly** *may indicate* an anagram

Unearth(ly) Astral, Dig, Discover, Disentomb, Exhumate, Indagate

Unease, Uneasiness, Uneasy Angst, Angular, Anxious, Creeps, Discomfort, Inquietude, Itchy, Malaise, Qualm, Queasy, Restive, Shy, Tense, The willies, Trepidation, Uptight, Windy, Womble-cropped

Unemployed, Unemployment Drone, Idle, Jobless, Laik, Lake, Latent, Lay-off, Neet, Redundant

Unending Chronic, Eternal, Lasting, Sempiternal

Unequal(led) Aniso-, Disparate, Non(e)such, Scalene, Unjust

Unerring Dead, Exact, Precise

Uneven(ness) Accident, Blotchy, Bumpy, Erratic, Irregular, Jaggy, Lopsided, Patchy, Ragged, Rough, Scratchy, Streaky

▷**Unevenly** *may indicate* an anagram

Unexceptional Ordinary, Run of the mill, Workaday

Unexciting Flat, Mundane, Staid, Tame

Unexpected(ly) Abrupt, Accidental, Adventitious, Bonus, Emergency, Fortuitous, Infra dig, Inopinate, Ironic, Snap, Sodain(e), Startling, Sudden, Turn-up, Unawares, Unforeseen, Untoward, Unware, Unwary, Windfall

Unfair Bias(s)ed, Crook, Dirty, Discriminatory, Inclement, Iniquitous, Invidious, Mean, One-sided, Partial, Raw deal, Thick, Unsportsmanlike

Unfaithful Adulterer, Cuckold, Disloyal, Godless, Infidel, Traitor

Unfashionable Cube, Daggy, Demode, Dowdy, Lame, Mumsy, Obsolescent, Passé, Square, Vieux jeu

▷**Unfashionable** *may indicate* 'in' to be removed

Unfasten Undo, Untie, Untruss

Unfathomable Abysmal, Bottomless, Deep

Unfavourable Adverse, Ill, Outsider, Poor, Untoward

Unfeeling Adamant, Brutish, Callous, Cold, Cruel, Dead, Empty, Hard, Inhuman(e), Insensate, Iron-witted, Numb, Robotic, Scared, Stony-hearted

Unfinished, Unfinishable Crude, Inchoate, Incondite, Raw, Scabble, Scapple, Sisyphean, Stickit

Unfit(ting) Disabled, Faulty, Ill, Impair, Inept, Outré, Seedy, Stiffie, Unable

▷**Unfit** *may indicate* an anagram

Unfocused Glazed, Grasshopper-mind, Vague

Unfold Deploy, Develop, Disenvelop, Display, Divulge, Evolve, Interpret, Open, Relate, Spread

Unfortunate(ly) Accursed, Alack, Alas, Catastrophic, Devil, Down and out, Hapless, Ill-omened, Ill-starred, Indecorous, Luckless, Shameless, Sorry, Star-crossed, Unlucky, Worse luck

Unfriendly Aloof, Antagonistic, Asocial, Chill(y), Cold, Cold fish, Crusty, Fraim, Fremd, Fremit, Frosty, Hostile, Icy, Inhospitable, Remote, Standoffish, Surly, Wintry

Unfruitful Abortive, Barren, Sterile

Ungainly Awkward, Gawkish, Uncouth, Weedy

Ungracious Cold, Mesquin(e), Offhand, Rough, Rude

Unguent Nard, Pomade, Salve

Ungulate Anta, Antelope, Dinoceras, Eland, Equidae, Hoofed, Moose, Pachydermata, Rhino, Ruminantia, Takin, Tapir, Tylopoda

Unhappily, Unhappy, Unhappiness Blue, Dejected, Depressed, Disconsolate, Disgruntled, Dismal, Doleful, Downcast, Down-hearted, Dysphoria, Glumpish, Ill-fated, Love-lorn, Lovesick, Miserable, Sad, Sore, Tearful, Unlief, Upset

▷**Unhappily** *may indicate* an anagram

Unhealthy Bad, Clinic, Diseased, Epinosic, Insalubrious, Morbid, Noxious, Peaky, Poxy, Prurient, Scrag, Sickly, Twisted

Uniform Abolla, Alike, Apparel, Battledress, Consistent, Constant, Doublet, Dress, Equable, Equal, Even, Flat, Forage-cap, Homogeneous, Identical, Khaki, Kit, Level, Livery, Monkey suit, Regimentals, Regular, Rig, Robe, Same, Sole, Standard, Steady, Strip, Suit, U, Unitary, Unvaried

Unimaginative Banausic, Cabbage, Earthbound, Literalistic, Meagre, Pedestrian, Pooter, Short-sighted, Slavish

Unimportant Academic, Cog, Down-the-line, Fiddling, Folderol, Footling, Frivolous, Hot air, Idle, Immaterial, Inconsequent, Inconsiderable, Insignificant, Junior, Light, MacGuffin, Makeweight, Miniscule, Minnow, Minutiae, Negligible, Nonentity, Nugatory, Peddling, Peripheral, Petty, Piddling, Slight, Small beer, Small-time, Trifling, Trivia(l)

Uninhabited Bundu, Deserted, Desolate, Lonely

Uninspired, Uninspiring Barren, Bored, Flat, Humdrum, Nondescript, Pedestrian, Pompier, Stereotyped, Sterile, Tame

Uninterested, Uninteresting Apathetic, Bland, Drab, Dreary, Dry, Dull, Grey, Incurious, Nondescript, Non-event

Uninterrupted Constant, Continuous, Incessant, Running, Steady

Union(ist) Affiance, African, Agreement, Allegiance, Alliance, Amicus, Art, ASLEF, Association, Bed, Benelux, Bond, Brotherhood, Brussels, Civil, Close, Coalition, Combination, Company, Concert, Confederacy, Craft, Credit, Customs, Diphthong, Economic, Enosis, Ensemble, Equity, EU, European, Federal, Federation, French, Frithgild, Fusion, Group, Guild, Heterogamy, Horizontal, Industrial, Integration, Isogamy, Junction, Latin, League, Liaison, Liberal, Link-up, Management, Marriage, Match, Merger, NUM, Nuptials, NUR, NUS, NUT, OILC, Pan-American, Pearl, Postal, Print, RU, Rugby, Samiti, Sex, Sherman, Shop-steward, Solidarity, Soviet, Splice, Sponsal, Student, Synthesis, Syssarcosis, Teamsters, Tenorrhaphy, TU, U, UNISON, USDAW, Uxorial, Vertical, Vienna, Wedding, Wedlock, Western European, Wield, Yoke, ZANU

Unique(ness) Alone, A-per-se, Farid, Hacceity, Inimitable, Lone, Matchless, Nonesuch, Nonpareil, Nonsuch, One-off, One(-to)-one, Onliest, Only, Peerless, Rare, Singular, Sole, Specific, Sui generis

Unit(s) Ampere-hour, Bargaining, Battery, Bel, Board of Trade, Brigade, Cadre, Cell, Cohort, Commando, Commune, Control, Corps, Derived, Detachment, Division, Dyad, Ecosystem, Element, Ensuite, Feedlot, Flight, Fundamental, Home, Horsepower, Hub, Income, Item, Kiloton, Last, Measure, Megabit, Message, Module, Monetary, Panzer, Peninsular, Period, Peripheral, Practical, Sealed, Secure, Shed, Squad(ron), Stock, Syllable, Team, Terminal, Theme, Timocracy, Tower

Unite(d), Uniting Accrete, Band, Bind, Cement, Close-knit, Coalesce, Combine, Concordant, Connate, Connect, Consolidate, Consubstantiate, Covalent, Ecumenical, Fay, Federal, Federate, Fuse, Gene, Graft, Harmonise, Injoint, Join, Joinder, Jugum, Kingdom, Knit, Lap, Link, Marry, Meint, Meng, Ment, Merge, Meynt, Ming, Nations, Oneness, Oop, Oup, Piece, Siamese, Solid, States, Tie, Tightknit, Unify, Utd, → **WED**, Weld, Yoke

Unity Cohesion, Harmony, One, Solidarity, Sympathy, Togetherness

Universal, Universe All, All-embracing, Catholic, Cosmogony, Cosmos, Creation, Ecumenic(al), Emma, General, Global, Infinite, Macrocosm, Mandala, Microcosm, Omnify, Oscillating, Sphere, U, World(wide)

University Academe, Academy, Alma mater, Aston, Bangor, Bath, Berkeley, Bonn, Brown, Campus, Civic, College, Columbia, Cornell, Dartmouth, Exeter, Gown, Harvard, Heidelberg, Ivy League, Keele, MIT, Open, OU, Oxbridge, Pennsylvania, Princeton, Reading, Redbrick, St Andrews, Sorbonne, Stamford, Syracuse, Varsity, Wittenberg, Witwatersrand, Yale

Unjust(ified) Groundless, Inequitable, Inequity, Iniquitous, Invalid, Tyrannical

Unknown, Unknowable Acamprosate, Agnostic, Anon, A.N. Other, Dark horse, Hidden, Ign, Incog(nito), Inconnu, Indeterminate, N, Nobody, Noumenon, Occult, Quantity, Recondite, Secret, Soldier, Strange, Symbolic, Tertium quid, Unchartered, Untold, Warrior, X, Y

Unless Nisi, Save, Without

Unlike(ly) As if, Difform, Disparate, Dubious, Far-fetched, Implausible, Improbable, Inauspicious, Last, Long shot, Outsider, Remote, Tall, Unlich

Unlimited Almighty, Borderless, Boundless, Indefinite, Measureless, Nth, Open-ended, Pure, Universal, Vast

Unload Disburden, Discharge, Drop, Dump, Jettison, Land, Unship

Unlucky Donsie, Hapless, Ill(-starred), Ill-fated, Ill-omened, Inauspicious, Infaust, Jonah, Misfallen, S(c)hlimazel, Sinister, Stiff, Thirteen, Untoward, Wanchancie, Wanchancy, Wanion

Unmanageable Handful, Riotous, Tartarian

Unmarried Bachelor, Celibate, Common-law, Lane, Lone, Single, Spinster, Tallywoman

Unmentionable(s) Bra, Foul, No-no, → **UNDERWEAR**, Undies

Unmindful Heedless, Oblivious, Regardless

Unmistakable Clear, Manifest, Plain

Unnatural Abnormal, Absonant, Affected, Artificial, Cataphysical, Contrived, Eerie, Far-fetched, Flat, Geep, Irregular, Man-made, Strange, Studied, Transuranian

▷**Unnaturally** *may indicate* an anagram

Unnecessary De trop, Extra, Gash, Gratuitous, Needless, Otiose, Redundant, Superfluous

Unobserved Backstage, Sly, Unseen
Unoccupied Désouvré, Empty, Idle, Inactive, Otiose, Vacant, Void
Unoriginal Banal, Copy, Déjà vu, Derivative, Imitation, Plagiarised, Slavish,
Trite
Unorthodox En passant, Heretic, Heterodox, Irregular, Maverick, Off-beat,
Off-the-wall, Outré, Stagyrite, Unconventional
▷**Unorthodox** *may indicate* an anagram
Unpaid Amateur, Brevet, Hon(orary), Voluntary
Unperturbed Bland, Calm, Collected, Serene
Unplanned Disorganised, Happenstance, Impromptu, Improvised,
Spontaneous
Unpleasant, Unpleasant person Creep, Drastic, Foul, God-awful, Grim,
Grotty, Gruesome, Gunk, Hoor, Horrible, Icky, Insalubrious, Invidious,
Mucky, Nasty, Obnoxious, Odious, Offensive, Painful, Pejorative, Poxy, Putrid,
Rebarbative, Reptile, Scrote, Shady, Shitty, Shocker, Skanky, Snot, Sour, Sticky,
Thorny, Toerag, Wart
Unpolished Coarse, Inelegant, Rough
Unpredictable Act of God, Aleatory, Capricious, Dicy, Erratic, Loose cannon,
Maverick, Scatty, Vagary, Wayward, Wild card
Unprepared Ad lib, Cold, Extempore, Green, Impromptu, Improvised, On the
hop, Raw, Unready
Unprincipled Amoral, Dishonest, Irregular, Opportunist, Reprobate
Unproductive Arid, Atokal, Atokous, Barren, Dead-head, Desert, Eild, Fallow,
Futile, Infertile, Lean, Poor, Shy, Sterile, Yeld, Yell
Unprofessional Amateur, Laic, Malpractice
Unprofitable Bootless, Fruitless, Lean, Thankless, Wasted
Unprotected Exposed, Nude, Vulnerable
Unqualified Absolute, Arrant, Categoric, Downright, Entire, Outright,
Profound, Pure, Quack, Sheer, Straight, Thorough, Total, Tout court, Utter
Unquestionably, Unquestioning, Unquestioned Absolute, Axiomatic,
Certain, Doubtless, Implicit
Unravel(ling) Construe, Denouement, Disentangle, Feaze, Fray, Solve, Undo
Unreal(istic) Academic, Alice-in-Wonderland, Cockamamie, Eidetic, En
l'air, Escapist, Fake, Fancied, Illusory, La-la-land, Mirage, Mythical, Oneiric,
Phantom, Phon(e)y, Pipe dream, Pseudo, Romantic, Sham, Spurious, Storybook,
Virtual
Unreasonable, Unreasoning Absurd, Bigot, Exorbitant, Extreme, Illogical,
Irrational, Misguided, Perverse, Rabid, Tall order
Unrecognised Incognito, Inconnu, Invalid, Obscure, Thankless, Unnoticed,
Unsung
Unrefined Bestial, Coarse, Common, Crude, Earthy, Gur, Impudent, Inelegant,
Natural, Rude, Slob, Vul(g), Vulgar
Unrelenting Implacable, Remorseless, Severe, Stern
Unreliable Broken reed, Chequered, Dishonest, Dodgy, Erratic, Fickle,
Flibbertigibbet, Flighty, Fly-by-night, Insincere, Kludge, Misleading, Shonky,
Skitter, Unstable, Wankle, Weak sister, Wonky
Unresponsive Aloof, Blank, Catatonic, Cold, Frigid, Nastic, Rigor
Unrest Discontent, Ferment, The Troubles
Unrestrained Ariot, Free, Freewheeling, Hearty, Homeric, Immoderate,
Incontinent, Lax, Loose, Lowsit, Orgic, Rampant, Wanton, Wild

Unruly Anarchic, Bodgie, Buckie, Camstairy, Camsteary, Camsteerie, Coltish, Disruptive, Exception, Fractious, Insubordinate, Lawless, Obstreperous, Obstropalous, Ragd(e), Raged, Ragged, Rambunctious, Rampageous, Rattlebag, Refractory, Riotous, Rowdy, Tartar, Torn-down, Turbulent, Turk, Wanton, Wayward, Zoo

▷**Unruly** *may indicate* an anagram

Unsafe Deathtrap, Fishy, Insecure, Perilous, Precarious, Unsound, Vulnerable

Unsatisfactory, Unsatisfying Bad, Disappointing, Lame, Lemon, Lousy, Meagre, Rocky, Thin, Wanting

Unseasonable, Unseasoned Green, Hors de saison, Murken, Raw, Untimely

Unseemly Coarse, Improper, Indecent, Indecorous, Indign, Risque, Tasteless, Untoward

Unsentimental Cynical, Gradgrindery, Hard-nosed

Unsettle(d) Disconcert, Grey area, Homeless, Hunky, Inconclusive, Indecisive, Nervous, Open, Outstanding, Overdue, Owed, Queasy, Restive, Restless

▷**Unsettled** *may indicate* an anagram

Unsight(ed), Unsightly Hideous, Repulsive, Ugly

Unskilled, Unskilful Awkward, Dilutee, Gauche, Green, Hunky, Inexpert, Menial, Raw, Rude, Stumblebum, Talentless, Whitechapel

Unsophisticated Alf, Basic, Boondocks, Boonies, Bushie, Cornball, Corny, Cracker-barrel, Direct, Down-home, Faux-naïf, Green, Hick, Hillbilly, Homebred, Homespun, Ingenu(e), Inurbane, Jaap, Jay, Naive, Natural, Primitive, Provincial, Rough, Rube, Rustic, Verdant, Yokel

Unsound Barmy, Infirm, Invalid, Shaky, Specious, Wildcat, Wonky

▷**Unsound** *may indicate* an anagram

Unspeakable Dreadful, Ineffable, Nefandous

Unspoiled, Unspoilt Innocent, Natural, Perfect, Pristine, Pure, Virgin

Unstable, Unsteady Anomic, Astatic, Bockedy, Casual, Crank(y), Dicky, Doddery, Erratic, Fitful, Flexuose, Flexuous, Flit(ting), Fluidal, Giddy, Groggy, Infirm, Insecure, Labile, Minute-jack, Quicksand, Rickety, Shifty, Skittish, Slippy, Tickle, Top-heavy, Tottery, Totty, Vacillating, Variable, Walty, Wambling, Wankle, Warby, Wobbly, Wonky

▶**Unsteady** *see* **UNSTABLE**

▷**Unstuck** *may indicate* an anagram

Unsubstantial Aeriform, Airy, Flimsy, Paltry, Shadowy, Slight, Thin, Yeasty

Unsuccessful Abortive, Also ran, Disastrous, Duff, Futile, Joyless, Loss-maker, Manqué, Vain

Unsuitable Amiss, Ill-timed, Impair, Improper, Inapt, Incongruous, Inexpedient, Malapropos, Misbecoming, Unfit

Untidy Daggy, Dishevelled, Dog's breakfast, Dog's dinner, Dowd(y), Frowzy, Frump, Guddle, Litterbug, Ragged, Ragtag, Scruff(y), Slipshod, Slob, Slovenly, Slut, Straggly, Tatty

▷**Untidy** *may indicate* an anagram

Untie Free, Undo, Unlace

Untold Secret, Umpteen, Unread, Unred, Vast

Untouchable Burakumin, Dalit, Harijan, Immune, Sealed

▷**Untrained** *may indicate* 'BR' to be removed

Untrue, Untruth Apocryphal, Eccentric, Fable, Faithless, False(hood), Lie, Lopsided, Prefabrication, Unleal

Untrustworthy Dishonest, Disloyal, Eel, Fickle, Shifty, Sleeky, Slippery, Tricky

Unused, Unusable Impracticable, New, Over, Spare, Wasted

Unusual(ly) Aberration, Abnormal, Anomalous, Atypical, Departure, Different, Especial, Exceptional, Exotic, Extra(ordinary), Eye-popping, Freak, Gonzo, Kinky, New, Non-standard, Novel, Odd, Offbeat, Other, Out-of-the-way, Outré, Particular, Peculiar, Phenomenal, Quaint, Queer, Rara avis, Rare (bird), Remarkable, Singular, Special, → **STRANGE**, Unco, Unique, Untypical, Unwonted, Variant, Wacko

▷**Unusual** *may indicate* an anagram

Unvarying Constant, Eternal, Monotonous, Repetitive, Stable, Static, Uniform

Unwanted Black list, De trop, Exile, Gooseberry, Nimby, Outcast, Pidog, Sorn

Unwelcome, Unwelcoming Frosty, Hostile, Icy, Intruder, Lulu, Obtrusive, (Persona) Non grata, Repugnant

Unwell Ailing, Bedridden, Crook, Dicky, Ill, Impure, Indisposed, Poorly, Rop(e)y, Rough, Seedy, Toxic

Unwholesome Insalutary, Miasmous, Morbid, Noxious, Stagnant, Stinkpot

Unwilling(ness) Averse, Disinclined, Intestate, Laith, Loath, Loth, Nolition, Nolo, Perforce, Reluctant, Shy, Tarrow

Unwind Descramble, Relax, Straighten, Unclew, Uncoil, Undo, Unravel, Unreave, Unreeve

▷**Unwind** *may indicate* an anagram

Unwise(ly) Foolish, Ill-advised, Ill-judged, Impolitic, Imprudent, Inexpedient, Injudicious, Insipient, Rash

Unworthy Below, Beneath, Golden calf, Indign, Inferior, Infra dig, Substandard, Undeserving

Unyielding Adamant, Eild, Firm, Granite, Inexorable, Intransigent, Mulish, Obdurate, Relentless, Rigid, Steadfast, Steely, Stern, Stiff, Stolid, Stubborn, Tough

Up(on), Upturned, Upper, Uppermost, Uppish, Uppity A, Afoot, Ahead, Antidepressant, Apical, Arrogant, Astir, Astray, Astride, Cloud-kissing, Elevated, Erect, Euphoric, Excited, Heavenward, Hep, Horsed, Incitant, Off, On, Overhead, Primo, Quark, Range, Ride, Riding, Senior, Skyward, Speed, → **UPPER CLASS**, Vamp, Ventral, Wart

Upbraid Abuse, Berate, Rebuke, Reproach, Reprove, Scold, Twit

Update Brief, Refresh, Renew, Report, Sitrep

Upheaval Cataclysm, Eruption, Maelstrom, Seismic, Shake out, Stir, Turmoil, Upturn, Volcano

▷**Upheld** *may indicate* 'up' in another word

Uphill Arduous, Borstal, Sisyphean

Upholster(ed), Upholstery Fleshy, Lampas, Moquette, Tabaret, Trim

Uplift Boost, Edify, Elate, Elevation, Exalt, Hoist, Levitation, Sky

Upper class, Upper crust Aristocrat, County, Crachach, Hooray Henry, Nobility, Patrician, Posh, Privileged, Sial, Top-hat, Tweedy, U

Upright(s), Uprightness Aclinic, Anend, Apeak, Apeek, Aplomb, Arrect, Beanpole, Bedpost, Doorpost, Erect, Goalpost, Honest, Jamb, Joanna, Merlon, Mr Clean, Mullion, Orthograde, Perpendicular, Piano, Pilaster(s), Post, Prig, Probity, Rectitude, Roman, Splat, Stanchion, Standing, Stares, Stile, Stud, Vertical, Virtuous, White

Uprising Incline, Insurrection, Intifada, Meerut, Naxalbari, Rebellion, Revolt, Tumulus

Uproar(ious) Bagarre, Ballyhoo, Bedlam, Blatancy, Brouhaha, Charivari, Clamour, Collieshangie, Commotion, Cry, Din, Dirdam, Dirdum, Durdum, Emeute,

Ferment, Flaw, Fracas, Furore, Garboil, Hell, Hooha, Hoopla, Hubbub(oo), Hullabaloo, Hurly(-burly), Imbroglio, Katzenjammer, Noise, Noyes, Outcry, Pandemonium, Racket, Raird, Randan, Razzmatazz, Reird, Riotous, Roister, Romage, Rough music, Rowdedow, Rowdydow(dy), Ruckus, Ruction, Rumpus, Shemozzle, Stramash, Tempest, Tumult, Turmoil, Utis, Whoobub

Uproot Averruncate, Dislodge, Eradicate, Evict, Outweed, Supplant, Weed

Upset(ting) Aerate, Aggrieve, Alarm, Applecart, Ate, Bother, Capsize, Catastrophe, Choked, Coup, Cowp, Crank, Derail, Derange, Dip, Disarrange, Discomboberate, Discombobulate, Discomfit, Discomfort, Discommode, Disconcert, Dismay, Disorganise, Displease, Disquiet, Distraught, Disturb, Dod, Eat, Fuss, Grieve, Gutted, Heart-rending, Inversion, Keel, Miff, Nauseative, Niggling, Offend, Overbalance, Overthrow, Overtip, Overturn, Peeve, Perturb, Pip, Pother, Purl, Rattle, Renverse, Rile, Ruffle, Rumple, Sad(den), Seel, Shake, Shatter, Shook up, Sore, Spill, Tapsalteerie, Teary, Tip, Topple, Trauma, Undo

▷**Upset** *may indicate* an anagram; a word upside down; or 'tes'

Upshot Outcome, Result, Sequel

Upside down Inverted, Resupinate, Tapsie-teerie, Topsy-turvy

▷**Upstart** *may indicate* 'u'

Up-to-date Abreast, Advanced, Contemporary, Current, Gear, Hip, Mod, New-fashioned, Rad, Right-on, State-of-the-art, Swinging, Switched on, Topical, Trendy

Upwards Acclivious, Aloft, Antrorse, Cabré

Urban, Urbanite Civic, Megalopolis, Municipal, Street, Town, Townsman

Urbane, Urbanity Civil, Debonair, Eutrapelia, Smooth, Townly

Urchin Arab, Asterias, Brat, Crinoid, Crossfish, Cystoid, Echinoidea, Echinus, Gamin, Gutty, Heart, Hedgehog, Mudlark, Nipper, Pedicellaria, Ragamuffin, Sand-dollar, Sea-egg, Spatangoidea, Spatangus, Street-arab, Township

Urge, Urgency, Urgent Acute, Admonish, Ca, Coax, Coerce, Constrain, Craving, Crying, Desperate, Dire, Drive, Egg, Enjoin, Exhort, Exigent, Goad, Hard, Haste, Hie, Hoick, Hunger, Hurry, Id, Immediate, Impel, Imperative, Importune, Impulse, Incense, Incite, Insist(ent), Instance, Instigate, Itch, Kick, Libido, Nag, Orexis, Peremptory, Persuade, Press(ing), Prod, Push, Scrub, Set on, Sore, Spur, Stat, Strenuous, Strident, Strong, Vehement, Wanderlust, Whig, Whim, Yen

▷**Urgent** *may indicate* 'Ur-gent', viz. Iraqi

Urinal Bog, John, Jordan, → **LAVATORY**, Loo, Pissoir

Urinate(d), Urine Chamber-lye, Emiction, Enuresis, Lant, Leak, Micturition, Number one, Pee, Piddle, Piss, Slash, Stale, Strangury, Tiddle, Uresis, Whiz(z), Widdle

Urn(s), Urn-shaped Canopic, Cinerarium, Ewer, Grecian, Lachrymal, Olla, Ossuary, Samovar, Storied, Vase

Us Me, Ourselves, 's, UK, Uns, We

Usage, Use(r), Used, Utilise Accustomed, Application, Apply, Avail, Boot, Consume, Custom, Deploy, Dow, → **EMPLOY**, Enure, Ex, Exercise, Exert, Exploit, Flesh, Function, Habit(uate), Hand-me-down, Inured, Loanee, Manner, Milk, Mores, Ply, Practice, Pre-owned, Sarum, Snorter, Spent, Sport, Stock, Stoner, Tradition, Treat, Try, Ure, Utilisation, Wield, With, Wont

Useful Asset, Availing, Commodity, Convenient, Dow, Expedient, Invaluable, Practical

Useless Appendix, Base, Bung, Cumber, Cumber-ground, Dead duck, Dead loss, Dead-wood, Dud, Empty, Futile, Gewgaw, Ground, Idle, Inane, Incapable,

Ineffective, Inutile, Lame, Lemon, Nugatory, Otiose, Plug, Pointless, Reject, Sculpin, Sterile, Swap, US, Vain, Void, Wet, White elephant

Usher Black Rod, Blue Rod, Chobdar, Commissionaire, Conduct(or), Doorman, Escort, Gentleman, Guide, Herald, Huissier, Macer, Marshal, Rod, Show, Steward

Usual, Usually Average, Common, Customary, Habit(ual), In general, In the main, Most, Natural, Normal, Ordinary, Routine, Rule, Solito, Standard, Stock, Tipple, Typical, Vanilla, Wont

Usurer, Usury Gombeen, Gripe, Lender, Loanshark, Moneylender, Note-shaver, Shark, Uncle

Utensil(s) Batterie, Battery, Cafetiere, Ca(u)ldron, Canteen, Chopsticks, Colander, Cookware, Corer, Double boiler, Egg-slice, Fish-kettle, Fork, Funnel, Gadget, Grater, Gridiron, Holloware, Implement, Instrument, Jagger, Kettle, Knife, Mandolin(e), Ricer, Scoop, Sieve, Skillet, Spatula, Spoon, Things, Tool, Whisk, Zester

▶**Utilise** *see* USAGE

Utilitarian Benthamite, Mill, Practical, Useful

Utility Elec(tricity), Gas, Mains, Water

Utmost Best, Extreme, Farthest, Maximum

Utopia(n) Adland, Cloud-cuckoo-land, Ideal, More, Never-never-land, Pantisocracy, Paradise, Perfect, Shangri-la

Utter(ance), Uttered, Utterly Absolute, Accent, Agrapha, Agraphon, Arrant, Aside, Cry, Dead, Deliver, Dictum, Dog, Downright, Ejaculate, Enunciate, Express, Extreme, Glossolalia, Issue, Judgement, Lenes, Lenis, Locution, Most, Oracle, Pass, Phonate, Pronounce, Pure, Quo(th), Rank, Rattle, Remark, Saw, → SAY, Sheer, Speak, Spout, Stark, State, Syllable, Tell, Thorough, Tongue, Ug, Unmitigated, Vend, Vent, Very, Voice

Vv

V Anti, Bomb, Del, Five, Nabla, See, Sign, Verb, Verse, Versus, Victor(y), Volt, Volume

Vacancy, Vacant Blank, Empty, Glassy, Goaf, Hole, Hollow, Inane, Place, Space, To let, Vacuum, Wooden

Vacation Holiday, Leave, Long, Outing, Recess, Trip, Voidance, Volunteer

Vaccination, Vaccine Antigen, Antiserum, Attenuated, Booster, Cure, HIB, Jenner, Sabin, Salk, Serum, Subunit

Vacuum Blank, Cleaner, Dewar, Eiky, Emptiness, Magnetron, Nothing, Nothingness, Plenum, Thermos®, Void

Vagabond Bergie, Gadling, →**GYPSY**, Hobo, Landlo(u)per, Outcast, Picaresque, Rapparee, Romany, Rover, Runagate, Tramp

Vague(ness) Amorphous, Bleary, Blur, Confused, Dim, Dreamy, Equivocal, Evasive, Faint, General, Hazy, Ill-defined, Ill-headed, Imprecise, Indecisive, Indefinite, Indeterminate, Indistinct, Inexact, Loose, Loste, Mist, Nebulous, Obscure, Shadowy, Sketchy, Woolly-minded

▷**Vaguely** *may indicate* an anagram

Vain Bootless, Conceited, Coxcomb, Coxcomical, Dandyish, Egoistic, Empty, Fruitless, →**FUTILE**, Hollow, Idle, Narcissistic, Pompous, Pown, Proud, Strutting, Unuseful, Useless, Vogie

Valet Aid, Andrew, Jeames, Jeeves, Lacquey, Man, Passepartout, Servant, Skip-kennel

Valiant Brave, Doughty, Heroic, Redoubtable, Resolute, Stalwart, Stouthearted, Wight

Valid(ity), Validate Confirm, Establish, Holding, Just, Legal, Legitimate, Probate, Right, Sound

Valley Argolis, Beqaa, Cleavage, Cleugh, Clough, Comb(e), Coomb, Cwm, Dale, Dean, Death, Defile, Dell, Den, Dene, Dingle, Dip, Drowned, Dry, Emmental, Ghyll, Glen, Glencoe, Gleneagles, Glyn, Gorge, Griff(e), Grindelwald, Gulch, Hollow, Imperial, Indus, Monument, Napa, Po, Ravine, Ria, Rift, Ruhr, Seaton, Silicon, Sonoma, Strathmore, Tempe, U-shaped, Vale, Vallis Alpes, Water gap, Yosemite

Valour Bravery, Courage, Gallantry, Heroism, Merit, Prowess

Valuable, Valuation, Value(s) Absolute, Acid, Appraise, Appreciate, Apprize, Assess(ment), Asset, Attention, Bargain, Blue chip, Book, Break up, Calibrate, Calorific, Carbon, Checksum, Cherish, CIF, Cop, Cost, Crossover, Datum, Dear, Denomination, Entry, Equity, Esteem, Estimate, Exit, Expected, Face, Feck, Hagberg, Intrinsic, Jew's eye, Limit, Market, Merit, Modulus, Money's worth, Museum piece, Net present, Net realizable, Nominal, Nuisance, Number, Omnium, Par, PH, Place, Prairie, Precious, Premium, Present, Price, Prize, Prys, Q, Quartile, Rarity, Rate, Rateable, Rating, Regard, Residual,

Respect, Rogue, Salt, Scarcity, Sentimental, Set, Snob, Steem, Stent, Store, Street, Surplus, Surrender, Taonga, Time, Treasure, Tristimulus, Truth, Utility, Valuta, → **WORTH**

Valve Air, Ball(cock), Bicuspid, Bleed, Blow, Butterfly, Check, Choke, Clack, Cock, Diode, Dynatron, Eustachian, Flip-flop, Gate, Inlet, Magnetron, Mitral, Non-return, Outlet, Pentode, Petcock, Piston, Poppet, Puppet, Resnatron, Safety, Seacock, Semilunar, Shut-off, Side, Sleeve, Sluice, Stopcock, Tap, Tetrode, Thermionic, Throttle, Thyratron, Tricuspid, Triode, Ventil, Vibrotron

Vampire Bat, Dracula, False, Ghoul, Lamia, Lilith, Nosferatu, Pontianak

Van(guard) Advance, Box-car, Brake, Breakdown, Camper, Cart, Cube, Dormobile®, Forefront, Foremost, Freight-car, Front, Head, Kombi®, Lead, Leader(s), Lorry, Loudspeaker, Panel, Pantechnicon, Pick-up, Removal, Spearhead, Tartana, Truck, Ute, Wagon

Vandal(ise), Vandalism Deface, Desecrate, Freebooter, Hooligan, Hun, Loot, Pillage, Ravage, Rough, Sab(oteur), Sack, Saracen, Skinhead, Slash, Smash, Trash, Wrecker

Vanish(ed), Vanishing Cease, Depart, Disappear, Disperse, Dissolve, Evanesce(nt), Evaporate, Extinct, Faint(ed), Mizzle, Slope, Transitory, Unbe

Vanity Amour-propre, Arrogance, Ego, Ego-trip, Esteem, Fair, Futility, Narcissism, Peacockery, Pomp, Pretension, Pride, Self-esteem, Self-importance

Vaporise, Vapour Aerosol, Boil, Cloud, Contrail, Fog, Fume, Halitus, Inhalant, Iodine, Miasma, Mist, Moisture, Reek, Roke, Skywriting, → **STEAM**, Steme, Water

▶**Variable, Variance, Variant, Variation** *see* **VARY(ING)**

▶**Varied, Variety** *see* **VARY(ING)**

▷**Varied** *may indicate* an anagram

Variegate(d) Dappled, Flecked, Fretted, Harlequin, Motley, Mottle, Pied, Rainbow, Skewbald, Tissue

▷**Variety of** *may indicate* an anagram

Various Divers(e), Manifold, Multifarious, Several, Sundry

Varnish(ing) Arar, Bee-glue, Copal, Cowdie-gum, Dam(m)ar, Dammer, Desert, Dope, Dragon's-blood, French polish, Glair, Japan, Lacquer, Lentisk, Mastic, Nail, Nibs, Resin, Shellac, Spirit, Tung-oil, Tung-tree, Vernis martin, Vernissage

Vary(ing), Variable, Variance, Variant, Variation, Varied, Variety, Various Ablaut, Alter, Amphoteric, Assorted, Assortment, Breed, Brew, Cepheid, Change, Chequered, Colour, Contrapuntal, Counterpoint, Dependent, Differ, Discrepancy, Dispute, Diverse, Diversity, Dummy, Eclectic, Eclipsing, Enigma, Fickle, Fluctuating, Form, Grid, Heterodox, Iid, Inconsistent, Inconstant, Independent, Intervening, Isotopy, Line, Local, Medley, Mix, Morph, Multifarious, Multiplicity, Music hall, Mutable, Nimrod, Nuance, Nutation, Odds and ends, Olio, Omniform, Parametric, Protean, Random, Remedy, Response, Smörgåsbord, Sort, Species, Spice, Sport, Stirps, Stochastic, Strain, String, Timeserver, Tolerance, Twistor, Uneven, Unknown, Var, Varicellar-zoster, Vaudeville, Versatile, Versiform, Version, Vicissitude, Vl, Wane, Wax, X, Y, Z

Vase Bronteum, Canopus, Diota, Hydria, Jardinière, Kalpis, Lachrymal, Lecythus, Lekythos, Lustre, Murr(h)a, Portland, Pot, Potiche, Stamnos, Urn, Vessel

Vast(ness) Big, Cosmic, Enormous, Epic, Extensive, Googol, Huge(ous), Immeasurable, Immense, Mighty, Ocean, Prodigious

Vat Back, Barrel, Bath, Blunger, Chessel, Copper, Cowl, Cuvée, Fat, Girnel, Keir, Kier, Mash tub, Tank, Tub, Tun

Vault(ed), Vaulting Arch, Barrel, Cavern, Cellar, Chamber, Charnel house, Clear, Cross, Crypt, Cul-de-four, Cupola, Dome, Dungeon, Fan, Firmament, Fornicate, Groin, Hypogeum, Jump, Kiva, Leap(frog), Lierne, Mausoleum, Overarch, Palm, Pend, Pendentive, Pole, Rib, Safe, Sepulchre, Serdab, Severy, Shade, Souterrain, Tomb, Undercroft, Vaut, Wagon, Weem

▷**Vault** *may indicate* an anagram

Veer Bag, Boxhaul, Broach, Clubhaul, Deviate, Gybe, Sway, Swerve, Tack, Turn, Wear, Yaw

Veg(etate), Vegetator, Vegetation Alga, Biome, Flora, Fynbos, Greenery, Herb, Laze, Lemna, Maquis, Quadrat, Scrub, Stagnate

Vegetable(s) Flora, Hastings, Inert, Jardinière, Olitory, Plant, Root, Salad, Sauce, Truck

Vegetarian Giraffe, Herbivore, Lactarian, Meatless, Tofu, Vegan, Veggie

Vehemence, Vehement(ly) Amain, Ardent, Fervid, Frenzy, Heat, Hot, Intense, Violent

Vehicle(s) Agent, Artic, Articulated, Base, Commercial, Conveyance, Double-bottom, Fleet, Half-track, High occupancy, Hybrid, Machine, Means, Medium, Multipurpose, Offroad, Oil, Rattletrap, Recovery, Recreational, Re-entry, Space, Superload, Tempera, Tracked, Ute, Utility, Wheels, Wrecker

Veil Burk(h)a, Calyptra, Chad(d)ar, Chador, Chuddah, Chuddar, Cloud, Cover, Curtain, Envelop, Eucharistic, Hejab, Hide, Hijab, Humeral, Kalyptra, Khimar, Kiss-me, Lambrequin, Mantilla, Mist, Nikab, Niqab, Obscure, Purdah, Scene, Sudarium, Veale, Volet, Weeper, Wimple, Yashmak

Vein Artery, Basilic, Brachiocephalic, Coronary, Costa, Epithermal, Fahlband, Gate, H(a)emorrhoid, Innominate, Jugular, Ledge, Lode, Mainline, Media, Midrib, Mood, Naevus, Nervure, Outcrop, Percurrent, Pipe, Portal, Postcava, Precava, Pulmonary, Radius, Rake, Reef, Rib, Saphena, Sectorial, Stockwork, Stringer, Style, Tone, Varicose, Varix, Vena, Venule

Velocity Circular, Muzzle, Parabolic, Radial, Rate, Speed, Terminal, V

Veneer Facade, Finish, Gloss, Varnish

Venerable Aged, August, Augustus, Bede, Guru, Hoary, Iconic, Sacred, Sage, Vintage

Venerate, Veneration Adore, Awe, Douleia, Dulia, Filiopietistic, GOM, Hallow, Homage, Honour, Hyperdulia, Iconise, Idolise, Latria, Respect, Revere, Worship

Vengeance, Vengeful Erinyes, Reprisal, Ultion, Vindictive, Wan(n)ion, Wrack, Wreak

Venom(ous) Bitchy, Black widow, Platypus, Poison, Rancour, Spite, Toxic, Virus, Zootoxin

Vent Aperture, Belch, Chimney, Emit, Express, Fumarole, Hornito, Issue, Louver, Louvre, Ostiole, Outlet, Solfatara, Spiracle, Undercast, Wreak

Ventilate, Ventilator Air, Air-brick, Air-hole, Discuss, Draught, Express, Louvre, Plenum, Shaft, Voice, Winze

Venture(d) Ante, Assay, Bet, Callet, Chance, Dare, Daur, Durst, Enterprise, Flutter, Foray, Handsel, Hazard, Mint, Opine, Presume, Promotion, Prostitute, Risk, Spec, Strive, Throw

Venue Bout, Locale, Place, Showground, Stadium, Stateroom, Tryst, Visne

Venus Armless, Clam, Cohog, Cytherean, Hesper(us), Love, Lucifer, Morning-star, Primavera, Quahaug, Quahog, Rokeby, Vesper

Veracity, Veracious Accurate, Factual, Sincere, Truth(ful)

Veranda(h) Balcony, Gallery, Lanai, Patio, Porch, Sleep-out, Stoep, Stoop, Terrace

Verb(al), Verbs Active, Auxiliary, Conative, Copula, Factitive, Finite, Infinitive, Intransitive, Irregular, Passive, Perfective, Performative, Phrasal, Preterite, Stative, Transitive, Vb, Word-of-mouth

Verbose, Verbosity Gassy, Padding, Prolix, Talkative, Wordy

Verdict Decision, Epitaph, Fatwah, Judg(e)ment, Narrative, Open, Opinion, Pronouncement, Resolution, Ruling

Verge Border, Brink, → **EDGE**, Hard shoulder, Incline, Limit, Rim, Roadside, Threshold

Verify, Verification Accredit, Affirm, Ascertain, Check, Constatation, Control, Crosscheck, Prove, Validate

Vermin(ous) Lice, Mice, Pest, Ratty, → **RODENT**, Scum

Vernacular Common, Dearnly, Dialect, Idiom, Jargon, Lingo, Native, Patois, Slang, Vulgate

Versatile Adaptable, All-rounder, Flexible, Handy, Many-sided, Multipurpose, Octavalent, One man band, Protean, Resourceful

Verse(s), Versed Dactyl, Fluent, Free, Linked, Logaoedic, Passus, Poetry, Political, Reported, Rhophalic, → **RHYME**, System

▷**Versed** *may indicate* reversed

Version Account, Authorised, Cephalic, Cover, Edition, Form, Paraphrase, Rede, Remake, Rendering, Rendition, Revised, Revision, Rhemish, Standard, Summary, Translation, Urtext, Variorum

Vertical Apeak, Apeek, Apothegm, Atrip, Erect, Lapse, Muntin(g), Ordinate, Perpendicular, Plumb, Sheer, Standing, Stemmed, Stile, Upright

Vertigo Dinic, Dizziness, Fainting, Giddiness, Megrim, Nausea, Staggers, Whirling

Very (good, well) A1, Ae, Assai, Awfully, Bonzer, Boshta, Boshter, Dashed, Dead, Def, Ever (so), Extreme(ly), Fell, Frightfully, Full, Gey, Grouse, Heap, Hellova, Helluva, Highly, Hugely, Jolly, Keen, Light, Mighty, Molto, Much, OK, Opt, Precious, Precise, Purler, Real(ly), Self same, So, Sore, Stinking, Très, Unco, Utter, V, VG, Way

Vessel(s) → **BOAT**, Capillary, Container, Craft, Dish, Lacteal, Logistics, Motor, Pressure, Receptacle, Retia, Seed, → **SHIP**, Tomentum, Utensil, Vascular, Weaker

Vest Beset, Confer, Crop top, Gilet, Modesty, Rash, Semmit, Singlet, Skivvy, Spencer, Sticharion, String, Undercoat, Waistcoat

Vestibule Anteroom, Atrium, Entry, Exedra, Foyer, Hall, Lobby, Narthex, Porch, Portico, Pronaos, Tambour

Vestment Alb, Breastplate, Chasuble, Cotta, Dalmatic, Ephod, Fannel, Fanon, Garb, → **GARMENT**, Mantelletta, Omophorion, Pallium, Parament, Ph(a)elonian, Pontificals, Raiment, Rational, Rochet, Rocquet, Saccos, Sakkos, Sticharion, Stole, Superhumeral, Surplice, Tunic(le)

Vet(ting), Veterinary, Vets Censor, Check, Doc(tor), Examine, Farrier, Herriot, Horse-doctor, Inspect, OK, Positive, Screen, Veteran, Zoiatria, Zootherapy

Veteran BL, Expert, GAR, Master, Old-stager, Oldster, Old sweat, Old-timer, Old 'un, Retread, Seasoned, Soldier, Stager, Stalwart, Stalworth, Vet, War-horse, Warrior

▷**Veteran** *may indicate* 'obsolete'

Veto Ban, Bar, Blackball, Debar, Item, Line-item, Local, Negative, Pocket, Reject, Taboo, Tabu

Vex(ing), Vexatious, Vexed Ail, Anger, Annoy, Bepester, Bother, Chagrin, Debate, Fret, Gall, Grieve, Harass, Haze, Irritate, Mortify, Noy, Peeve, Pester, Rankle, Rile, Sore, Spite, Tease, Torment, Trouble(some)

Via By, Per, Through

Viable Economic, Going, Healthy, Possible

Vibrate, Vibration(s), Vibrant Active, Atmosphere, Diadrom, Dinnle, Dirl, Flutter, Free, Fremitus, Hotter, Jar, Judder, Oscillate, Pulsate, Pulse, Purr, Quake, Resonance, Seiche, Shimmy, Shudder, Thrill, Throb, Tingle, Tremble, Tremor, Trill, Trillo, Twinkle, Wag, Whir(r)

Vicar Bray, Cleric, Elton, Incumbent, Pastoral, Plenarty, Primrose, Rector, Rev(erend), Trimmer

Vice Acting, Clamp, Cramp, Crime, Deputy, Eale, Evil, Foible, Greed, Iniquity, Instead, Jaws, Regent, Second (in command), → SIN, Stair

Viceroy Khedive, Nawab, Provost, Satrap, Willingdon

Vicinity Area, Environs, Locality, Neighbourhood, Region, Round about

Victim(s), Victimisation Abel, Butt, Casualty, Currie, Curry, Dupe, Easy meat, Fall guy, Frame, Hitlist, Host, Judenhetze, Lay-down, Mark, Martyr, Nebbich, Neb(b)ish, Pathic, Patsy, Prey, Quarry, Sacrifice, Scapegoat, Sitting duck, Target

Victor(y) Bangster, Banzai, Beater, Cadmean, Cannae, Captor, Champ(ion), Conqueror, Conquest, Epinicion, Epinikion, Eunice, Flagship, Fool's mate, Gree, Gris, Hugo, Jai, Jai Hind, Kobe, Landslide, Lepanto, Ludorum, Mature, Nike, Palm, Philippi, Pyrrhic, Romper, Runaway, Scalp, Shut-out, Signal, Squeaker, Sweeping, Triumph, V, VE (day), Vee, Vic, Walkover, Win(ner)

Vie Compete, Contend, Emulate, Strive

View(er) Aim, Angle, Aspect, Attitude, Behold, Belief, Bird's eye, Cineaste, Consensus, Consider, Cosmorama, Cutaway, Dekko, Dogma, Doxy, Endoscope, Estimation, Eye (shot), Facet, Gander, Glimpse, Grandstand, Heresy, Idea, Introspect, Jaundiced, Kaleidoscope, Landscape, Look, Notion, Observe, Opinion, Optic, Outlook, Pan, Panorama, Parallax, Perception, Perspective, Point, Private, Profile, → PROSPECT, Scan, Scape, Scene(ry), Scope, See, Sight, Sightlined, Slant, Snapshot, Spectate, Spectre, Specular, Spyglass, Standpoint, Stereoscope, Survey, Synop(sis), Tenet, Thanatopsis, Theory, Veduta, Vista, Visto, Watch, Witness, Worm's eye

Viewpoint Angle, Attitude, Belvedere, Conspectus, Elevation, Eyeshot, Grandstand, Instance, Observatory, Perspective, Sight, Sightline, Tendentious, Voxpop, Watch tower

Vigil(ance), Vigilant(e) Awake, Aware, Baseej, Basij, Deathwatch, Eve, Lyke-wake, On guard, Prudence, Wake, Wake-rife, Wary, Watch, Waukrife

Vigorous(ly), Vigour Aggressive, Agitato, Alive, Animation, Athletic, Bant, Bellona, Billy-o, Billy-oh, Birr, Blooming, Bouncing, Brio, Brisk, Con brio, Cracking, Drastic, Dynamic, Élan, Emphatic, Energetic, Flame, Forceful, Full-blooded, Furioso, Go, Green, Gusto, Heart(y), Heterosis, Hybrid, Lush, Lustihood, Lustique, Lusty, Manful, Moxie, P, Pep, Pith, Potency, Punchy, Pzazz, Racy, Rank, Raucle, Red-blooded, Robust, Round, Rude, Sap, Smeddum, Spirit, Sprack, Sprag, Steam, Sthenic, Stingo, Strength, Strenuous, Strong, Thews, Tireless, Tone, Tooth and nail, Trenchant, Two-fisted, Up, Vegete, Verve, Vim, Vinegar, Vitality, Vivid, Vivo, Voema, Zip

▷**Vigorously** *may indicate* an anagram

Vile(ness) Base, Corrupt, Depraved, Dregs, Durance, Earthly, Infamy, Infernal, Mean, Offensive, Scurvy, Vicious

Villa Bastide, Chalet, Dacha, House

Village Aldea, Auburn, Borghetto, Burg, Clachan, Dorp, Endship, Global, Gotham, Gram, Greenwich, Hamlet, Kainga, Kampong, Kirkton, Kraal, Legoland, Mir, Outlet, Outport, Pit, Pueblo, Rancheria, Rancherie, Shtetl, Thorp(e), Vill, Wick

Villain(y) Anti-hero, Baddy, Bluebeard, Bravo, Crim(inal), Crime, Dastard, Dog, Fagin, Heavy, Iago, Knave, Lawbreaker, Macaire, Miscreant, Mohock, Nefarious, Ogre, Rogue, Scelerat, Scoundrel, Sikes, Steerforth, Tearaway, Traitor

Vim Energy, Go, Vigour, Vitality, Zing

Vindicate, Vindication Absolve, Acquit, Apologia, Avenge, Clear, Compurgation, Darraign(e), Darrain(e), Darrayn, Defend, Deraign, Exculpate, Exonerate, Justify

Vindictive Bunny-boiler, Hostile, Malevolent, Repay(ing), Spiteful

Vinegar Acetic, Alegar, Balsam, Balsamic, Eisel(l), Esile, Oxymel, Tarragon, Wine

Vintage Classic, Crack, Cru, Old, Quality

Viol(a), Violet African, Alto, Amethyst, Archil, Dame's, Dog, Dog's tooth, Gamba, Gentian, Gridelin, Heart's ease, Ianthine, Indole, Iodine, Ionone, Kiss-me, Lilac, Lyra, Mauve, Orchil, Pansy, Parma, Prater, Quint(e), Rock, Saintpaulia, Shrinking, Tenor

Violate, Violating, Violation Abuse, Breach, Contravene, Defile, Desecrate, Fract, Infraction, March-treason, Outrage, Peccant, Rape, Ravish, Sacrilege, Solecism, Stuprate, Transgress, Trespass

Violence, Violent(ly) Acquaintance, Amain, Attentat, Bangster, Battery, Berserk, Bloody, Brutal, Brute force, Cataclysmic, Crude, Drastic, Droog, Extreme, Fierce, Flagrant, Force, Frenzied, Furious, Heady, Het, High, Hooliganism, Hot, Inbreak, Mighty, Onset, Rabid, Rage, Rampage, Rampant, Riot, Rogue, Rough, Rude, Rumbustious, Savage, Severe, Shoot 'em up, Slap, Stormy, Strongarm, Ta(r)tar, Tearaway, Thuggery, Tinderbox, Tub-thumping, Vehement, Vie, Wild

Violet Anil, Gentian, Neapolitan, Purple, →**VIOLA**

Violin(ist), Violin-maker, Violin-shaped Alto, Amati, Cremona, Fiddle, Griddle, Guarneri(us), Guarnieri, Heifetz, Kit, Leader, Luthier, Nero, Paganini, Rebec(k), Rote, Stradivarius

VIP Bashaw, Bigshot, Bigwig, Brass, Cheese, Cob, Effendi, Envoy, Imago, Kingpin, Magnate, Magnifico, Mugwump, Nabob, Nib, Nob, Pot, Snob, Someone, Swell, Tuft, Tycoon, Worthy

Virago Amazon, Battle-axe, Beldam(e), Harpy, Randy, Shrew, Termagant

Virgin(al), Virginity, Virgin Mary Celibate, Chaste, Cherry, Intact, Ladykin, Madonna, Maiden, Maidenhead, Maidenhood, Marian, May, New, Our lady, Pan(h)agia, Pietà, Pucel(l)age, Pucelle, Pure, Queen, Snood, Tarpeia, Theotokos, Vestal, Zodiacal

Virile, Virility Energetic, Lusty, Machismo, Macho, Male, Manly, Red-blooded

Virtue(s), Virtuous, Virtual Angelic, Aret(h)a, Assay-piece, Attribute, Cardinal, Caritas, Charity, Chastity, Continent, Cyber, Dharma, Efficacy, Ethical, Excellent, Faith, Foison, Fortitude, Fus(h)ion, Good, Grace, Honesty, Hope, Justice, Moral(ity), Natural, Patience, Plaster-saint, Practical, Principal, Prudence, Pure, Qua, Say-piece, Squeaky-clean, Straight and narrow, Temperance, Theological, Upright, Worth

Virulent Acrimonious, Deadly, Hostile, Malign, Noxious, Toxic, Vitriolic, Waspish

Viscera Bowels, Entrails, Giblets, Guts, Harigal(d)s, Haslet, Innards, Omentum, Umbles, Vitals

Viscous (liquid), Viscosity Absolute, Glaireous, Gleety, Gluey, Gummite, Gummy, Kinematic, Slab, Specific, Sticky, Stoke, Tacky, Tar, Thick

Visible, Visibility Clear, Conspicuous, Evident, Explicit, Export, In sight, Obvious, Zero-zero

Vision(ary) Abstraction, Aery, Aisling, Apparition, Awareness, Binocular, Bourignian, Day-dreamer, Double, Dream(er), Emmetropia, Fancy, Fantast, Fey, Foresight, Idealist, Ideologist, Illusionist, Image, Kef, Moonshine, Mouse-sight, Mystic, Ocular, Phantasm(a), Phantom, Pholism, Photism, Photopia, Revelation, Romantic, Seeing, Seer, Sight, Sightline, Stereo, Stereopsis, Tunnel, Twenty-twenty, Viewy

Visit(or) Affliction, Alien, Away, Caller, Day-tripper, Domiciliary, ET, Event, First-foot, Guest, Habitué, Haunt, Hit, Inflict, Kursaal, Look in, Look up, Pop in, See, Sightseer, Sojourn, State, Stay, Stranger, Take, Theatregoer, Tourist, Wait upon, Weekender

Visor, Vizor Eyeshade, Face-saver, Mesail, Mezail, Umbrel, Umbr(i)ere, Umbril, Vent(ayle)

Vital(ity) Alive, Bounce, Central, Critical, Crucial, Energy, Esprit, Essential, Existent, Foison, Gusto, Indispensable, Juice, Key, Kick, Life-blood, Lifeline, Linchpin, Lung, Mites, Momentous, Necessary, Oomph, Organ, Pizzazz, Pulse, Salvation, Sap, Verve, Viable, Vigour, Zing, Zoetic

Vitriol(ic) Acid, Acrimonious, Biting, Caustic, Mordant

Vituperate Abuse, Berate, Castigate, Censure, Defame, Inveigh, Lash, Rail, Scold

Vivid Bright, Brilliant, Colourful, Dramatic, Eidetic, Fresh, Graphic, Keen, Live, Lurid, Pictorial, Picturesque, Sharp, Shocking, Violent

▶**Vizor** *see* **VISOR**

Vocabulary Idiolect, Idioticon, Jargon, (Kata)kana, Lexicon, Lexis, Meta-language, Nomenclator, Wordbook

Vocation Call, Career, Métier, Mission, Priesthood, Profession, Pursuit, Shop

Vogue Chic, Day, →**FASHION**, Groovy, Mode, Rage, Style, Ton, Trend

Voice(d) Active, Air, Alto, Ancestral, Bass, Chest, Contralto, Countertenor, Descant, Edh, Emit, Eth, Express, Falsetto, Glottis, Harp, Head, Inner, Intonate, Lyric, Mastersinger, Meistersinger, Mezzo-soprano, Middle, Mouth, Opinion, Passive, Phonic, Pipe, Presa, Quill, Say, Sonant, Soprano, Speak, Spinto, Sprechstimme, Steven, Syrinx, Tais(c)h, Tenor, Throat, Tone, →**TONGUE**, Treble, Utter, White

Voiceless Aphonia, Aphony, Dumb, Edh, Eth, Mute, Silent, Tacit

Void Abyss, Annul, Belch, Blank, Chasm, Counter, Defeasance, Defecate, Diriment, Empty, Erase, Evacuate, Gap, Hollow, Inane, Inoperative, Invalid, Irritate, Lapse, Negate, Nullify, Quash, Space, Vacuum

Volatile Excitable, Explosive, Inconsistent, Latin, Live(ly), Mercurial, Skittish, Tear gas, Temperamental, Terpene, Tinderbox, Unstable

Volcano(es), Volcanic Agglomerate, Basalt, Black smoker, Burning mountain, Composite, Cone, Conic, Fumarole, Greystone, Hornito, Ice, Idocrase, Igneous, Ignimbrite, Monticule, Mud, Obsidian, Pele, Pelée, Plinian, Pozz(u)olana, Pumice, Puzzolana, Sandblow, Shield, Soffioni, Solfatara, Stratovolcano, Tephra, Trass, Tuff

Volley Barrage, Boom, Broadside, Platoon, Round, Salvo, Tirade, Tire

Volume Atomic, Band, Bande, Barrel, Book, Bushel, Capacity, CC, Code(x), Content, Cubage, Gallon, Hin, Loudness, Mass, Ml, Omnibus, Peck, Pint, Quart(o), Roll, Roul(e), Size, Space, Stere, Tom, Tome, Ullage, Vol

Voluntary, Volunteer Docent, Enlist, Fencible, Free, Honorary, Offer, Postlude, Reformado, Spontaneous, Tender, Tennessee, Terrier, TN, Ultroneous, Yeoman

Voluptuary, Voluptuous Carnal, Hedonist, Luscious, Sensuist, Sensuous, Sybarite

Vomit(ing) Barf, Black, Boak, Boke, Cascade, Cat, Chuck up, Chunder, Disgorge, Egest, Egurgitate, Emesis, Honk, Keck, Kotch, Posset, Puke, Ralph, Regorge, Retch, Rolf, Spew, Technicolour yawn, Upchuck

Voracious, Voracity Bulimia, Edacity, Gluttony, Greed, Man-eater, Ravenous, Serrasalmo

Vote(r), Votes, Voting Alternative, Assentor, Aye, Ballot, Ballotee, Block, Card, Casting, Choose, Colonist, Constituent, Coopt, Cross, Crossover, Cumulative, Division, Donkey, Fag(g)ot, Floating, Franchise, Free, Grey, Informal, Mandate, Nay, Negative, No, Opt, People, Placet, Plebiscite, Plump, Plural, Poll, Postal, PR, Preferential, Proportional representation, Protest, Qualified majority, Referendum, Return, Scrutin de liste, Scrutiny, Show of hands, Side, Single transferable, Straw(-poll), Suffrage, Swinging, Sympathy, Tactical, The stump, Theta, Ticket, Token, Transferable, Voice, X, Yea, Yes

Vouch(er), Vouchsafe Accredit, Assure, Attest, Beteem(e), Chit, Coupon, Credit note, Endorse, Gift, Guarantee, Luncheon, Meal-ticket, Promise, Receipt, Slip, Ticket, Token, Warrant

Vow Affirm, Baptismal, Behight, Behot(e), Earnest, Ex voto, Hecht, Hest, I do, Nuncupate, →**OATH**, Obedience, Pledge, Plight, Promise, Simple, Solemn, Swear, Troth

Vowel(s) Ablaut, Anaptyxis, Aphesis, Breve, Cardinal, Diphthong, Indeterminate, Monophthong, Murmur, Seg(h)ol, S(c)hwa, Svarabhakti, Triphthong

Voyage(r) Anson, Columbus, Course, Cruise, Launch, Passage, Peregrinate, Salt, Sinbad, Travel

Vulgar(ian) Base, Earthy, Filthy, Gorblim(e)y, Gross, Kitsch, Lavatorial, Parvenu, Plebby, Ribald, Rude, Scurrilous, Slag, Snob, Tarty, Twopenny

Vulnerable, Vulnerability Achilles heel, Defenceless, Endangered, Exposed, Frangible, Open, Pregnable, Susceptible, Unguarded, Weak, Wide-open

Vulture Aasvogel, Bearded, Bird, Buzzard, California (condor), Condor, Culture, Falcon, Gallinazo, Gier, Griffon, Gripe, Grype, King, Lammergeier, Lammergeyer, Ossifrage, Predator, Turkey, Urubu, Zopilote

Wad(ding) Batt(ing), Lump, Pad, Pledget, Roll, Swab, Wodge

Wade(r), Wading Antigropelo(e)s, Ardea, Crane, Curlew, Dikkop, Egret, Flamingo, Ford, Grallae, Grallatorial, Greenshank, Gumboot, Heron, Ibis, Jacksnipe, Lapwing, Limpkin, Paddle, Phalarope, Plodge, Plover, Pukeko, Ree, Sandpiper, Sarus, Seriema, Shoebill, Snipe, Splodge, Stilt(bird), Terek, Virginia, Wellington

Wafer Biscuit, Cracker, Crisp, Gaufer, Gaufre, Gofer, Gopher, Host, Papad, Seal

Waffle Adlib, Blather, Cake, Equivocate, Fudge, Gas, Gaufer, Gaufre, Gofer, Gopher, Hedge, Padding, Poppycock, Prate, Rabbit, Wibble

Wag(gish), Waggle Arch, Card, Comedian, Joker, Lick, Nod, Rogue, Shake, Sway, Swee, Wit(snapper), Wobble

Wage(s) Ante, Award, Fee, Greengage, Hire, Income, Living, Meed, Minimum, Nominal, Pay, Portage, Practise, Prosecute, Rate, Salary, Screw, Subsistence

Wage-earner Breadwinner, Employee, Proletariat(e)

Wager Ante, Back, → BET, Gamble, Lay, Pascal's, Stake, Wed

Wagon(er) Ar(a)ba, Aroba, Boötes, Boxcar, Brake, Break, Buck, Buckboard, Buggy, Caisson, Carriage, Cart, Cattle truck, Chuck, Coachman, Cocopan, Conestoga, Corf, Covered, Democrat, Drag, Dray, Flatcar, Fourgon, Freight-car, Gambo, Go-cart, Hopper, Hutch, Low-loader, Mammy, Paddy, Palabra, Patrol, Plaustral, Police, Prairie schooner, Rave, Reefer, Rubberneck, Shandry, Stage, Station, Tank, Tartana, Telega, Tender, Trap, Trekker, Truck, Van, Victoria, Wain, Water

Wail(er) Banshee, Bawl, Blubber, Howl, Keen, Lament, Moan, Skirl, Threnody, Threnos, Ululate, Vagitus, Wah-wah, Yammer

Waist(band) Belt, Cummerbund, Girdlestead, Hour-glass, Middle, Midship, Obi, Sash, Shash, Wasp, Zoster

Waistcoat Gilet, Jerkin, Lorica, MB, Sayon, Sleeve(d), Stabvest, Tuxedo, Vest, Weskit

Wait(er), Waiting Abid(e), Ambush, Attend, Barista, Bide, Busboy, Butler, Buttle, Carhop, Commis, Cupbearer, Dally, Delay, Estragon, Expect, Flunkey, Frist, Garçon, Hang on, Hesitate, Hover, Interval, Khidmutgar, Lead time, Lime, Linger, Loiter, Lurch, Maître d', Maître d'hôtel, Minority, Omnibus, Pannier, Pause, Penelope, Pozzo, Queue, Remain, Serve(r), Sommelier, Stacking, Stay, Steward, Suspense, Taihoa, Tarry, Tend(ance), Tray, Vladimir, Wine, Won

Waitress Bunny girl, Hebe, Miss, Mousme(e), Nippy, Server

Waive Abandon, Defer, Forgo, Overlook, Postpone, Relinquish, Renounce, Suspend

Wake(n) Abrade, Abraid, Abray, Aftermath, Alert, Animate, Arouse, Astern, Backwash, Deathwatch, Excite, Finnegan's, Hereward, Keen, Prod, Rear, Revive, Surface, Trail, Train, Wash

Walk(er), Walking, Walkabout, Walkway Aisle, Alameda, Alley, Alure, Amble, Ambulate, Arcade, Birdcage, Charity, Cloister, Clump, Constitutional,

Daddle, Dander, Emu, Esplanade, EVA, Festination, Flânerie, Forefoot, Gait, Gallery, Gangplank, Ghost, Go, Gradient, Hike, Hookey, Hump, Lambeth, Leg, Lumber, Mall, March, Mince, Mooch, Mosey, Nordic, Pace, Pad, Paddle, Pasear, Paseo, Passage, Passerby, Path, Pavement, Ped(estrianism), Perambulate, Pergola, Perp, Piaffe, Piazza, Pole, Pound, Power, Prance, Prom(enade), Rack, Ramble, Rampart, Random, Ring, Routemarch, Sashay, Scamble, Schlep, Shamble, Sidle, Slommock, Space, Spanish, Sponsored, Stalk, Step, Stoa, Stride, Stroll, Strut, Stump, Taligrade, Terrace, Toddle, Tramp, Trash, Travolator, Tread, Trog, Truck, Trudge, Turn, Wade, Wander, Wayfare

Wall Bail, Bailey, Barrier, Berlin, Berm, Cavity, Cell, Chinese, Climbing, Crib, Curtain, Dado, Dam, Dike, Dry-stone, Fail-dike, Fourth, Frustule, Gable, Great, Groyne, Hadrian's, Hanging, Hangman, Head, Immure, Mutual, Non-bearing, Parapet, Parpane, Parpen(d), Parpent, Partition, Party, Peribolos, Perpend, Perpent, Podium, Puteal, Retaining, Reveal, Revet(ment), Ring, River, Roman, Roughcast, Screen, Sea, Septum, Side, Street, Studding, Tambour, Tariff, Vallation, Video, Wa', Wailing, Western, Withe

Wallaby Brusher, Dama, Kangaroo, Pademelon, Pad(d)ymelon, Quokka, Tammar

Wall-covering, Wallpaper Anaglypta®, Arras, Burlap, Lincrusta, Paper, Tapestry, Tapet

Wallet Billfold, Case, Flybook, Folder, Notecase, Pochette, Purse, Scrip

Wallop Axe, Bash, Baste, Batter, Beat, Biff, Clout, Cob, Gigantic, → **HIT**, Lam, Lounder, Oner, Polt, Pound, Slog, Strap, Swinge, Tan, Tat, Thud, Trounce

Wallow(ing) Bask, Flounder, Luxuriate, Revel, Roll, Slubber, Splash, Swelter, Tolter, Volutation, Welter

Walrus Morse, Moustache, Pinniped, Rosmarine, Sea-cow, Sea-horse, Tash, Ugly

Wan Lurid, Pale, Pallid, Pasty, Sanguine, Sorry

Wander(er), Wandering Adrift, Bedouin, Berber, Bum, Caird, Daiker, Daydream, Delirious, Deviate, Digress, Diverge, Drift, Errant, Estray, Excursive, Expatiate, Gad(about), Grope, Hobo, Itinerant, Jew, Landloper, Maunder, Meander, Mill, Mither, Moider, Moither, Moon, Noctivagant, Nomad(e), Odysseus, Peregrine, Peripatetic, Prodigal, Ramble, Range, Romany, Room, Rove, Stooge, Straggle, Stray, Stroam, Stroll, Swan, Ta(i)ver, Tramp, Troll, Truant, Vagabond, Vagile, Vagrant, Vague, Waif, Wend, Wheel, Wilder

▷**Wandering** *may indicate* an anagram

Want(ing), Wants Absence, Conative, Covet, Crave, Dearth, Defect, Deficient, Derth, Desiderata, → **DESIRE**, Destitution, Distress, Envy, For, Hardship, Indigent, Itch, Lack, Like, Long, Mental, Moldwarp, Mole, Need, Penury, Require, Scarceness, Scarcity, Shortfall, Shy, Void, Wish, Yen

Wanton(ness) Bona-roba, Cadgy, Chamber, Cocotte, Deliberate, Demirep, Filly, Flirt-gill, Gammerstang, Giglet, Giglot, Gillflirt, Hussy, Jay, Jezebel, Jillflirt, Lewd, Licentious, Light o' love, Loose, Nice, Protervity, Roué, Slut, Smicker, Sportive, Sybarite, Toyish, Twigger, Unchaste, Wayward

War(fare), Wars American Civil, American Independence, Ares, Armageddon, Arms, Asymmetrical, Attrition, Bacteriological, Bate, Battle, Biological, Blitz(krieg), Chemical, Civil, Clash, Class, Cod, Cold, Combat, Conflict, Crimean, Crusade, Culture, Electronic, Emergency, Feud, → **FIGHT**, Flagrante bello, Flame, Food, Franco-Prussian, Fray, Germ, Great, Guer(r)illa, Gulf, Holy, Hostilities, Hot, Hundred Years', Information, Internecine, Jenkins' ear, Jihad, Korean, Limited, Mars, Mexican, Nam, Napoleonic, Nuclear, Opium, Peasants', Peloponnesian, Peninsular, Phon(e)y, Price, Private, Propaganda, Psychological,

Punic, Push-button, Queen Anne's, Rebellion, Revolutionary, Roses, Russo-Japanese, Secession, Seven against Thebes, Seven Years', Shooting, Six Day, Social, Spanish-American, Spanish Civil, Star, Sword, Theomachy, Thirty Years', Total, Trench, Trojan, Turf, Vietnam, Winter, World, Yom Kippur

Warble(r) Carol, Cetti's, Chiff-chaff, Chirl, Fauvette, Peggy, Rel(l)ish, Singer, Sylvia, Trill, Vibrate, Yodel, Yodle

Ward (off) Artemus, Averruncate, Avert, Care, Casual, Casualty, Charge, Defend, District, Fend, Guard, Inner, Keyhole, Marginal, Maternity, Minor, Nightingale, Oppose, Orphan, Outer, Parry, Protégé, Pupil, Soc, Soken, Thunderbolt, Vintry, Wear, Weir

Warden Beefeater, Caretaker, Church, Concierge, Constable, Curator, Custodian, Game, Guardian, Keeper, Meter maid, Pear, Provost, Ranger, Septimus, Sidesman, Spooner, Steward, Traffic

Ware(s) Alga, Arretine, Basalt, Beware, Biscuit, Cameo, Canton, Chelsea, China, Etruria, Fabergé, Faience, Goods, Hollow(w)are, Jasper, Lapis lazuli, Lustre, Merchandise, Palissy, Plate(d), Queen's, Samian, Sanitary, Satsuma, Shippo, Truck, Wemyss

Warehouse Bonded, Data, Depository, Entrepôt, Freight-shed, Go-down, Hong, Store

▶**Warfare** *see* **WAR(FARE)**

Wariness, Wary Ca'canny, Cagey, Careful, Cautel, Caution, Chary, Discreet, Distrust, Gingerly, Guarded, Leerie, Leery, Mealy-mouthed, Prudent, Sceptical, Suspicious, Vigilant

Warlike Battailous, Bellicose, Gung-ho, Lachlan, Martial, Militant

Warm(er), Warming, Warmth Abask, Admonish, Air, Ardour, Atingle, Balmy, Bonhomie, British, Calefacient, Calid(ity), Cardigan, Chambré, Cordial, Cosy, Eager, El Nino, Empressement, Enchafe, Fervour, Flame, Foment, Genial, Gladden, Global, Glow, → **HEAT**, Hospitable, Hot, Incalescent, Kang, Kindly, Lew, Logic, Loving, Muff, Muggy, Mull, Nuke, Radiator, Tepid, Thermal, Toast, Toasty, Tog

Warn(ing) Admonish, Alar(u)m, Alert, Amber, Apprise, Beacon, Bell, Beware, Bleep, Buoy, Caution, Cave, Caveat, Caveat emptor, Cone, Counsel, Cowbell, Detector, DEW, Document, Early, En garde, Example, Foghorn, Fore, Foreshadow, Foretoken, Gardyloo, Garnishment, Griffin, Harbinger, Hazchem, Heads up, Hoot, Horn, Illocution, Klaxon, Knell, Larum, Lesson, Light, Maroon, Minatory, Nix, Noli-me-tangere, Nota bene, Notice, Notification, Omen, Pi-jaw, Portent, Premonish, Premonitory, Presage, Profit, Protevangelium, Red alert, Red flag, Red light, Remind, Riot Act, Rumble strip, Scaldings, Signal, Siren, Spindle, Stoplight, Storm, Tattler, Threat, Timber, Tip-off, Token, Toot, Yellow card

Warp(ed) Bent, Bias, Buckle, Cast, Contort, Distort, Hog, Kam, Kedge, Pandation, Spring, Time, Twist, Weft, Zag

▷**Warped** *may indicate* an anagram

Warrant(y), Warrant officer Able, Authorise, Behight, Behote, Bosun, Capias, Caption, Certificate, Charter, Deserve, Detainer, Distress, Dividend, Fiat, Fiaunt, Fugle, Guarantee, Justify, Merit, Mittimus, Mortgage, Peace, Permit, Precept, Reprieve, Royal, Search, Sepad, Swear, Transire, Vouch, Warn, Writ

Warrior Achilles, Agamemnon, Ajax, Amazon, Anzac, Arimasp, Attila, Brave, Cold, Crusader, Eorl, Fighter, Finlay, Finley, Geronimo, Gurkha, Haiduk, Heyduck, Impi, Jihadi, Lewis, Louis, Myrmidon, Nestor, Roger, Samurai, Soldier, Tatar, Unknown, Wardog, Warhorse, Warwolf, Zulu

Warship Battleship, Blockship, Castle, Cog, Corvette, Cruiser, Destroyer, Drake, Dromon(d), Galleass, Galliass, Invincible, Man-o-war, Mine-layer, Monitor, Privateer, Ram, Repulse

▶**Wary** *see* **WARINESS**

Wash(ed), Washer, Washing (up), Wash out Ablution, Affusion, Alluvion, Bath, Bay(e), Bidet, Bur(r), Calcimine, Circlip, Clean(se), Cradle, D, Dashwheel, Dele(te), Dip, Edulcorate, Elute, Enema, Erode, Fen, Flush, Freshen, Front-loader, Gargle, Grom(m)et, Grummet, Hose, Hush, Irrigate, Kalsomine, Lap, →**LAUNDER**, Lavabo, Lave, Leather, Lip, Lotion, Marsh, Maundy, Mop, Nipter, Pan, Pigswill, Poss, Purify, Rinse, Sapple, Scrub, Shampoo, Shim, Sind, Sloosh, Sluice, Soogee, Soojee, Soojey, Squeegie, Stand-up, Sujee, Swab, Synd, Syne, Tempera, Tie, Toiletry, Twin tub, Tye, Wake

Wasp(ish) Bembex, Bink, Bite, Chalcid, Cuckoo-fly, Cynipidae, Cynips, Digger, Fig, Fretful, Gall(-fly), Hornet, Horntail, Hoverfly, Irritable, Marabunta, Mason, Miffy, Muddauber, Paper, Peevish, Pompilid, Potter, Seed, Solitary, Spider, Syrphus, Vespa, Yellow jacket

▷**Wasp** *may indicate* a rugby player

Wastage, Waste(d), Wasting, Wasteful, Wasteland, Wastepipe, Waster, Wastrel Amyotrophy, Atrophy, Bilge, Blight, Blow, Blue, Bluer, Boondoggle(r), Cesspit, Cirrhosis, Colliquative, Consume, Coom(b), Cotton, Crud, Culm, Decay, Desert, Detritus, Devastate, Dilapidate, Dissipate, Dregs, Dross, Dung, Dwindle, Dwine, Dystrophy, Effluent, Egesta, Emaciate, Erode, Excrement, Exhaust, Expend, Faeces, Flue, Fribble, Fritter, Garbage, Gash, Gob, Grog, Guano, Gunge, Haggard, Half-cut, Havoc, Hazardous, High, High-level, Hi(r)stie, Husk, Ice-field, Inefficient, Kill, Knub, Landfill, Lavish, Lean, Loose, Lose, Loss, Low-level, Merino, Misspent, Moor, Muir, Mungo, Natural, Ne'er-do-well, Nub, Nuclear, Offal, Offcut, Off-scouring, Oller, Ordure, Pellagra, Perish, Pigswill, Pine, Prodigalise, Rack and manger, Radioactive, Rammel, Ravage, Red mud, Red tape, →**REFUSE**, Rubble, Ruderal, Ruin, Scant o' grace, Scissel, Scoria, Scrap, Scum, Sew(er)age, Skeletal, Slag, Slurry, Spend, Spill(age), Spoil(age), Squander, Sullage, Swarf, Tailing, Thin, Thwaite, Toxic, Trash, Tundra, Ureal, Urine, U-trap, Vast, Wear, Wilderness

▷**Wasted** *may indicate* an anagram

Watch(er), Watch out Accutron®, Analog(ue), Argus, Await, Bark, Behold, Big brother, Bird-dog, Black, Case, Cave, Chronograph, Clock, Coastguard, Digital, Dog, Eryl, Espy, Eyeball, Fob, Gregory, Guard, Half-hunter, Huer, Hunter, Lever, Lo, Look, Look-out, Lykewake, Middle, Monitor, Morning, Nark, Neighbourhood, Night, Nit, Note, Observe, Overeye, Patrol, Posse, Quartz, Regard, Repeater, Rolex®, Rubberneck, Scout, Sentinel, Sentry, Shadow, Snoop, Spectate, Spie, Spotter, Spy, Stake out, Stemwinder, Suicide, Surveillance, Tend, Ticker, Timekeeper, Timepiece, Timer, Tompion, Tout, Turnip, Vedette, View, →**VIGIL**, Voyeur, Wait, Wake, Ward, Weather eye, Wrist(let)

Watchman Argus, Bellman, Charley, Charlie, Cho(w)kidar, Chok(e)y, Guard, Huer, Sentinel, Sentry, Speculator, Tompion, Viewer

Watch-tower Atalaya, Barbican, Beacon, Garret, Mirador, Sentry-go, Turret

Water(ed), Waters, Watery Adam's ale, Adam's wine, Aerated, Apollinaris, Aq(ua), Aquatic, Aqueous, Ascites, Barley, Bayou, Bedabble, Bilge, Bound, Branch, Brine, Broads, Brook, Burn, Canal, Cancer, Chlorine, Chuck, Cold, Cologne, Compensation, Conductivity, Connate, Dead, Deg, Dew, Dill, Dilute, Dribble, Drinking, Eau, Ebb, Element, Evian®, First, Flood, Ford, Fossil, Functional, Grey, Gripe, Ground, Hard, Heavy, Hellespont, High, Holy, Hot,

Irrigate, Javel(le), Kyle, Lagoon, Lagune, Lake, Laurel, Lavender, Leachate, Light, Lime, Loch(an), Lode, Lough, Low, Lubricated, Lymph, Mains, Melt, Meteoric, Mineral, Miner's inch, Moiré, Mother, Nappe, North, Oasis®, Oedema, Orange-flower, Overfall, Pani, Pawnee, Pee, Perrier®, Pisces, Polly, Poppy, Potash, Potass, Pump, Purest, Quarry, Quick, Quinine, Rain, Rapids, Rate, Reach, Rheumy, Rice, Rip, Riverine, Rose, Running, Runny, Rydal, Saltchuck, Scorpio, Sea, Seltzer, Sera, Serous, Serum, Shoal, Shower, Skinkling, Slack, Slick, Sloshy, Sluice, Soda, Sodden, Soft, Sound, Souse, Southampton, Sprinkle, Standpipe, Steam, Stream, Surface, Tabby, Table, Tap, Tar, Tarn, Temper, Territorial, Thermocline, Thin, Tide, Toilet, Tonic, Urine, Utility, Vichy, Viscous, Wai, Wake, Wash(y), Weak, Wee, Whey, White, White coal, Wild, Wishy-washy

Water-carrier Aqueduct, Bheestie, Bheesty, Bhistee, Bhisti, Bucket, Carafe, Chatty, Drain, Furphy, Hose, Hydra, Hydria, Kirbeh, Pail, Pitcher, Rigol

Water-course Arroyo, Billabong, Canal, Ditch, Dyke, Falaj, Furrow, Gutter, Khor, Lead, Leat, Nala, Nalla(h), Nulla, Nullah, Rean, Rhine, Rill, River(et), Serpentine, Shott, Spruit, Wadi

Waterfall Angel (Falls), Cataract, Churchill, Chute, Cuquenan, Espelands, → **FALL(S)**, Force, Foss, Kahiwa, Kile, Lasher, Lin(n), Lower Mar Valley, Mardel, Montmorency, Mtarazi, Niagara, Overfall, Rapid, Salmon leap, Sault, Sutherland, Takakkaw, Tugela, Tyssestrengene, Utigord, Yosemite

Waterless Arid, Dry, Neat

Waterman Aquarius, Bargee, Ferryman, Oarsman

Water-plant Alga, Alisma, Aquatic, Cress, Crowfoot, Elodea, Gulfweed, Lace-leaf, Lattice-leaf, Nelumbo, Nenuphar, Nuphar, Ouvirandra, Pontederia, Quillwort, Reate, Sea-mat, Sedge, Seg, Stratiotes, Urtricularia, Vallisneria

Waterproof, Water-tight Cagoul(e), Caisson, Camlet, Caulk, Cerecloth, Cofferdam, Corfam®, Curry, Dampcourse, Dubbin(g), Groundsheet, Loden, Mac, Mino, Oilcloth, Oilers, Oilpaper, Oilskin, Pay, Sealant, Sealskin, Seaworthy, Sta(u)nch, Stank, Suberin, Tar-paper, Tarpaulin, Waders

Water-sprite Kelpie, Kelpy, Nix(ie), Nixy, Tangie, Undine, Water-nymph

Waterway Aqueduct, Canal, Channel, Creek, Culvert, Ditch, Dyke, Igarapé, Illinois, Intracoastal, Lode, River, St Lawrence Seaway, Sny(e), Sound, Straight, Suez

Water-wheel Noria, Pelton, Sakia, Saki(y)eh, Tympanum

Wave(s), Waved, Waveform, Wavelength, Waver, Wavy Alpha, Beachcomber, Beam, Beck, Beta, Billow, Bore, Bow, Brain, Brandish, Breaker, Carrier, Cold, Comber, Complex, Continuous, Crest, Crime, Crimp, Crispate, Delta, Dominant, Dumper, Electromagnetic, Feather, Finger, Flap, Flaunt, Float, Flote, Flourish, Fourier series, Gesticulate, Gravitational, Gravity, Graybeard, Ground, Groundswell, Harmonic, Haystack, Head sea, Heat, Impulse, Internal, Ionospheric, Lee, Long, Longitudinal, Marcel, Matter, Medium, Mexican, New, Perm(anent), Plunger, Primary, Pulse, Radar, Radiation, Radio, Rip, Ripple, Roller, Rooster, Sea, Secondary, Seiche, Seismic, Shake, Shock, Short, Sine, Sinuate, Sinuous, Skipper's daughter, Sky, Skyrmion, Snaky, Sound, Spiller, Square, Squiggle, Standing, Stationary, Stern, Stream, Supplementary, Surf, Surge, Sway, Tabby, Theta, Third, Thought, Tidal, Tidal bore, Tide, Train, Transverse, Travelling, Tsunami, Ultrasonic, Undate, Unde, Undertow, Undulate, Waffle, Waft, Wag, Waive, Wand, Wash, Waw, Wawe, Whelm, Whitecap, White-horse, Wigwag

▷ **Wave(s)** *may indicate an anagram*

Waver(ing), Waverer Dither, Double-minded, Falter, Flag, Gutter, Hesitate, Indecision, Oscillate, Reel, Stagger, Sway, Swither, Teeter, Vacillate, Waffle, Wet, Wow

Wax(ed), Waxing, Waxy Ambergris, Appal, Bate, Bees, Bone, Brazilian, Cere, Ceresin, Cerumen, Chinese, Cobbler's, Cutin, Earth, Effuse, Enseam, Ethal, Geraldton, Grave, Greaves, Grow, Heelball, Honeycomb, Increase, Increscent, Inseam, Ire, Japan, Kiss, Livid, Lost, Lyrical, Mineral, Mummy, Myrtle, Paraffin, Pela, Petroleum, Rage, Seal, Sealing, Spermaceti, Tallow, Tantrum, Temper, Toxaphene, Vegetable, White, Yielding

Way(s), Wayside Access, Agate, Appian, Autobahn, Avenue, Borstal(l), Budo, Bypass, Companion, Course, Crescent, Defile, Direction, Door, Draw, E, Each, Entrance, Family, Fashion, Flaminian, Foss(e), Four-foot, Gate, Greek, Habit, Hatch, Hedge, High, Hither, How, Icknield, Lane, Manner, Means, Method, Milky, MO, Mode, N, Pass, Passage, Path, Permanent, Pilgrim's, Procedure, Railroad, Regimen, Ridge, →ROAD, Route, S, Sallypost, St(reet), Style, System, Technique, Thoroughfare, Thus, Trace, Trail, Troade, Turning, Turnpike, Underpass, Untrodden, Via, W, Wise

Way-out Advanced, Bizarre, Egress, Esoteric, Exit, Exotic, Extreme, Offbeat, Trendy

Wayward Capricious, Disobedient, Errant, Erratic, Loup-the-dyke, Obstreperous, Perverse, Scapegrace, Stray, Unruly, Wilful

WC Fields, Gents, Ladies, Lav, Loo

Weak(er), Weaken(ing), Weakest, Weakness Achilles' heel, Adynamia, Appair, Appal, Arsis, Assuage, Attenuate, Blot, Brittle, Chink, Cissy, Cripple(d), Debile, Debilitate, Decrease, Delay, Delicate, Deplete, Dilling, Dilute, Disable, Effete, Emasculate, Embrittle, Enervate, Enfeeble, Entender, Fade, Faible, Failing, Faint, Fallible, Fatigue, Feeble, Fissile, Flag, Flaw, Flimsy, Foible, Fragile, Frailty, Give, Glass chin, Gone, Groggy, Ham, Helpless, Honeycomb, Impair, Impotence, Infirm, Knock-kneed, Lame, Lassitude, Loophole, Low, Low ebb, Malaise, Meagre, Mild, Milk and water, Namby-pamby, Pale, Pall, Paresis, Penchant, Puny, Push-over, Pusillanimous, Reduce, Runt, Simp, Slack, Soft spot, Spineless, Starveling, Tenuous, Thesis, Thin, Thready, Tottery, Unable, Underdog, Undermine, Unman, Unnerve, Unstable, Vapid, Vessel, Vulnerability, W, Washy, Water(y), Wish(y)-wash(y)

Wealth(y) Abundance, Affluence, Bonanza, Bullion, Capital, Croesus, Digerati, Ease, Fat-cat, Fortune, Golconda, Jet-set, Klondike, Klondyke, Loaded, Loadsamoney, Lolly, Magnate, Mammon, Means, Mine, Mint, Moneyed, Nabob, Opulence, Ore, Pelf, Plutocrat, Privileged, Prosperous, Reich, Rich, Ritzy, Solid, Substance, Treasure, Trustafarian, Untold, Well-heeled, Well-off, Well-to-do

Weapon(s) Ammo, Antitank, Arm, Arsenal, Assault, Binary, Cultural, Deterrent, Greek fire, →GUN, Hoplology, Long-range, Missile, Munition, Nuclear, Nuke, Ordnance, Piece, →PISTOL, →SWORD, Theatre, Thermonuclear, Tool, Traditional

Weapon-carrier Frog, Holster, Quiver, Rocket-launcher, Sheath

Wear(ing), Wear Out Abate, Ablative, Abrade, Attrition, Chafe, Clothing, Corrade, Corrode, Deteriorate, Detrition, Efface, Enfeeble, Erode, Erosion, Fashion, Fatigue, For(e)spend, Fray, Frazzle, Fret, Garb, Garni, Impair, In, Mush, Pack, Sap, Scuff, Sport, Stand, Tedy, Tolerate

▷**Wear** *may indicate* the NE, e.g. Sunderland

Weariness, Wearisome, Weary(ing) Beat, Bejade, Blethered, Bore, Cloy, Dog-tired, Effete, Ennui, Ennuyé, Exhaust, Fag, Fatigate, Fatigue, Flag(ging), Harass, Hech, Heigh-ho, Irk, Jade, Lacklustre, Lassitude, Pall, Puny, Ramfeezle, Sick, Sleepy, Spent, Tire, Tiresome, Trash, Try, Tucker, Wabbit, Worn

Weasel Beech-marten, Cane, Delundung, Ermine, Ferret, Foumart, Glutton, Grison, Kolinsky, Marten, Mink, Mustela, Otter, Pekan, Pine-marten, Polecat,

Skunk, Stoat, Taira, Tayra, Vermin, Whit(t)ret, Whitterick, Whittrick, Wolverine, Woodshock, Zorilla

Weather, Weather forecast Atmosphere, Cyclone, Discolour, Dreich, Ecoclimate, Elements, Endure, Hail, La Nina, Met, Monkey's wedding, Outlive, Rain, Ride, Sky, Snow, Sprat, Stand, Survive, Synoptic, Tiros, Undergo, Withstand

Weave(r), Weaves, Weaving Arachne, Basket, Broché, Cane, Complect, Contexture, Entwine, Finch, Heald, Heddle, Interlace, Jacquard, Lace, Lease, Leno, Lion, Loom, Marner, Osiery, Penelope, Plain, Plait, Raddle, Ripstop, Rya, Shuttle, Sparrow, Spider, Splice, Stevengraph, Taha, Textorial, Texture, Throstle, Throwster, Tissue, Tweel, Twill, Twine, Wabster, Waggle, Webster, Zigzag

Web(bed), Webbing, Web-footed, Web-site Aranea, Food, Forum, Fourchette, Hit, Infomediary, Internet, Mat, Maze, Mesh(work), Network, Offset, Palama, Palmate, Palmiped, Patagium, Pinnatiped, Portal, Skein, Snare, Tela, Tissue, Toil, Totipalmate, Vane, World Wide

Wed(ding), Wedlock Alliance, Bet, Destination, Diamond, Espousal, Golden, Hymen, Join, Knobstick, Liaison, Link, Marriage, Marry, Mate, Meng(e), Me(i)nt, Meynt, Ming, Nuptials, Pair, Penny, Ruby, Sacrament, Shotgun, Silver, Spousage, Spousal, → **UNION**, Unite, Wad, White, Y

Wedge(d) Chock, Chunk, Cleat, Cotter, Cuneal, Doorstop, Feather, Forelock, Gad, Gagger, Gib, Jack, Jam, Key, Lofter, Niblick, Prop, Quoin, Scotch, Shim, Spaceband, Sphenic, Stick, Texas, Trig, Vomerine, Whipstock

Wee Leak, Little, Pee, Slash, Sma(ll), Tinkle, Tiny, → **URINATE**, Widdle

Weed(y) Adderwort, Agrestal, Alga, Allseed, Anacharis, Arenaria, Bedstraw, Bell-bind, Blinks, Burdock, Buttercup, Carpetweed, Catch, Charlock, Chickweed, Chlorella, Cigar(ette), Cissy, Clotbur, Clover, Cobbler's pegs, Cockle, Cocklebur, Colonist, Coltsfoot, Corncockle, Couch, Daisy, Dallop, Dandelion, Darnel, Dock, Dollop, Dulse, Elder, Elodea, Ers, Fag, Fat hen, Femitar, Fenitar, Fluellen, Fluellin, Fork, Fucoid, Fumitory, Gangly, Goutweed, Goutwort, Ground elder, Groundsel, Helodea, Hoe, Indian, Joe-pye, Knapweed, Knawel, Knot-grass, Lanky, Lemna, Mare's-tail, Marijuana, Matfelon, Mayweed, Nard, Nettle, Nipplewort, Nostoc, Onion, Oxygen, Paterson's curse, Pearlwort, Peed, Perique, Pilewort, Pineapple, Piri-piri, Plantain, Potamogeton, Purslane, Ragi, Ragwort, Reate, Rest-harrow, Ribbon, Rib-grass, Ribwort, Ruderal, Runch, Sagittaria, Sargasso, Scal(l)awag, Scallywag, Senecio, Shrimp, Softy, Sorrel, Speedwell, Spurge, Spurrey, Stink, Sudd, Sun-spurge, Swine's-cress, Tab, Tansy, Tare, Thistle, Tine, Tobacco, Tormentil, Twitch, Ulotrichale, Ulva, Vetch, Viper's bugloss, Wartcress, Widow's, Winnow, Yarr

▷ **Weed** *may indicate* 'urinated'

Weedkiller Arsenic, Atrazine, Dalapon, Diquat, Diuron, Herbicide, Hoe, Paraquat®, Simazine

Week(s), Weekly Ember, Expectation, Great, Hebdomadary, Holy, Omer, Orientation, Ouk, Oulk, Passion, Periodical, Prophetic, Rag, Rogation, Schoolies, Sennight, Working

Weep(er), Weeping, Weepy, Wept Bawl, Blubber, Cry, Grat, Greet, Lachrymose, Lament, Leak, Loser, Maudlin, Niobe, Ooze, Pipe, Sob, Tearful, Wail, Waterworks

Weigh(ing), Weigh down, Weight(y) All-up, Atomic, Avoirdupois, Balance, Ballast, Bantam, Barbell, Bob, Bow, Bulk, Burden, Clout, Consider, Count, Counterpoise, Cruiser, Dead, Deliberate, Denier, Drail, Dumbbell, Emphasis, Equivalent, Feather, Formula, Great, Handicap, Heaviness, Heft, Import, Importance, Impost, Incumbent, Journey, Kerb, Live, Load, Mark,

Massive, Matter, Metage, Metrology, Minimum, Molecular, Moment, Mouse, Onerous, One-sided, Oppress, Overpoise, Payload, Perpend, Plumb-bob, Plummet, Poise, Preponderance, Prey, Rate, Sinker, Slang, Stress, Tare, Throw, Ton(nage), Tophamper, Tron(e), Troy, Unmoor, Welter, Wey

Weir Cauld, Dam, Garth, Kiddle, Kidel, Lasher, Pen, Watergate

Weird Bizarre, Curious, Dree, Eerie, Eery, Eldritch, Far out, Kookie, Odd, Offbeat, Spectral, Spooky, Strange, Supernatural, Taisch, Uncanny, Unearthly, Zany

Welch, Welsh Abscond, Cheat, Default, Embezzle, Levant, Rat, Reneg(u)e, Renig, Skedaddle, Weasel

Welcome, Welcoming Acclaim, Aloha, Ave, Bel-accoyle, Ciao, Embrace, Entertain, Glad-hand, Godsend, Greet, Haeremai, Hail, Hallo, Halse, Handshake, Heil, Hello, Hospitable, How, Hullo, Open-armed, Open house, Ovation, Receive, Reception, Salute, Snug, Ticker-tape, Wotcha, Wotcher

Welfare Advantage, Alms, Benison, Common weal, Ha(y)le, Heal, Health, Sarvodaya, Weal

Well (done) Artesian, Atweel, Ave, Aweel, Bien, Bore(hole), Bravo, Carbon, Casinghead, Cenote, Chipper, Development, Discovery, Downhole, Dry hole, Easily, Euge, Famously, Fine, Fit, Foot, Gasser, Geyser, Good, Gosh, Gusher, Hale, →**HEALTHY**, Hot, Inkpot, Ka pai, Law, Mickery, My, Namma hole, Odso, Oh, Oil(er), Phreatic, Potential, Pour, So, Source, Spa, Spouter, Spring, Sump, Surge, Teek, Tube, Um, Upflow, Wildcat, Wishing, Worthily, Zemzem

Wellbeing Atweel, Bien-être, Comfort, Eudemonic, Euphoria, Euphory, Good, Health, Welfare

Well-known Famous, Iconic, Illustrious, Infamous, Notorious, Notour, Prominent

Well-off Affluent, Bien, Far, Rich, Wealthy

Welsh(man), Welshwoman Aled, Briton, Brittonic, Brython, Cake, Cambrian, Celtic, Cog, Crachach, Cym(ric), Cymry, Dafydd, Dai, Emlyn, Emrys, Enid, Evan, Fluellen, Gareth, Harp, Idris, Ifor, Ivor, Keltic, Megan, P-Celtic, P-Keltic, Rabbit, Rarebit, Rees, Rhys, Sion, Taff(y), Tudor, W, Walian

▶**Welsh** see **WELCH**

West(ern), Westerly Ang mo, Favonian, Film, Hesperian, Mae, Movie, Oater, Occidental, Ponent, Spaghetti, Sunset, W, Westlin, Wild

▷**West end** may indicate 't' or 'W1'

Wet(ting), Wetland Bedabble, Bedraggled, Clammy, Daggle, Damp, Dank, Dew, Dip, Douse, Dowse, Drench, Drip(ping), Drook, Drouk, Dunk, Embrue, Enuresis, Feeble, Foppish, Humect, Humid, Hyetal, Imbrue, Imbue, Irrigate, Irriguous, Macerate, Madefy, Madid, Marshy, Moil, Moist(en), Molly, Namby-pamby, Pee, Piddle, Pouring, Rainy, Ramsar site, Ret(t), Rheumy, Roral, Roric, Runny, Saturate, Seepy, Shower, Simp(leton), Sipe, Sissy, Sluice, →**SOAK**, Sodden, Sopping, Sour, Steep, Tiddle, Tipsy, Urinate, Wat, Wee, Widdle, Wimpy, Wringing

Whale(meat), Whaling Baleen, Beaked, Beluga, Blower, Blubber, Blue, Bottlehead, Bottlenose, Bowhead, Cachalot, Calf, Cetacea(n), Cete, Cetology, Dolphin, Fall, Fin(back), Finner, Gam, Glutton, Grampus, Greenland (right), Grey, Humpback, Ishmael, Killer, Kreng, Leviathan, Manatee, Minke, Monodon, Mysticeti, Orc(a), Paste, Pilot, Pod, Porpoise, Right, River dolphin, Rorqual, School, Scrag, Sei, Sperm, Thrasher, Toothed, Toothless, White, Ziphius

▷**Whale** may indicate an anagram

What, Whatever Anan, Any, Come again, Eh, How, Owt, Pardon, Que, Regardless, Siccan, Sorry, Such, That, Which

Whatnot, What's-its-name Dinges, Dingus, Doings, Doobrey, Doobrie, Étagère, Gismo, Jigamaree, Jiggumbob, Thingamy, Thingumajig, Thingumbob, Thingummy, Timenoguy

Wheat Allergen, Amber, Amelcorn, Bald, Beard(ed), Beardless, Blé, Bulg(h)ur, Cracked, Durum, Einkorn, Emmer, Federation, Fromenty, Frumenty, Furme(n)ty, Furmity, Grain, Hard, Mummy, Red, Rivet, Sarrasin, Sarrazin, Seiten, Semolina, Sharps, Spelt, Summer, Triticum, White

Wheedle Banter, Barney, Blandish, Cajole, Coax, Cog, Cuiter, Cuittle, Flatter, Inveigle, Tweedle, Whilly(whaw)

Wheel(er) Balance, Bedel, Bevel, Bicycle, Big, Bogy, Breast, Bucket, Buff(ing), Cart's tail, Caster, Castor, Catherine, Chain, Chark(h)a, Circle, Cistern, Count, Crown, Cycle, Daisy, Diamond, Disc, Driving, Emery, Epicycloidal, Escape, Fan, Felloe, Felly, Ferris, Fifth, Fortune, Gear, Grinding, Gyrate, Helm, Hurl, Idle(r), Jagger, Jigger, Jolley, Joy, Kick, Lantern, Magnate, Master, Medicine, Mitre, Monkey, Nabob, Nave, Nose, Paddle, Pattern, Pedal, Pelton, Perambulator, Persian, Pin, Pinion, Pitch, Pivot, Planet, Potter's, Prayer, Pulley, Rag, Ratchet, Roll, Roller, Rotate, Roulette, Rowel, Sheave, Snail, Spare, Spider, Spinning, Sprocket, Spur, Star, Steering, Stitch, Swing, Tail, Throwing-table, Training, Tread, Treadmill, Trindle, Trolley, Truckle, Trundle, →**TURN**, Water, Web, Whirling-table, Wire, Worm

Wheeze Asthma, Breathe, Jape, Joke, Pant, Pech, Ploy, Rale, Reak, Reik, Rhonchus, Ruse, Stridor, Trick, Whaisle, Whaizle

Where(abouts) Location, Neighbourhood, Place, Site, Vicinity, Whaur, Whither

Wherewithal Finance, Means, Money, Needful, Resources

Whet(stone) Coticular, Excite, Hone, Oilstone, Rubstone, Sharpen, Stimulate, Stroke

Which(ever), Which is Anyway, As, QE, Whatna, Whilk, Who

While Although, As, Interim, Since, Space, Span, Spell, Though, Throw, Time, When, Whenas, Whereas, Yet

Whim(s), Whimsical, Whimsy Bizarre, Caprice, Conceit, Crotchet, Droll, Fad, Fancy, Fay, Fey, Fie, Flisk, Kicksy-wicksy, Kink, Maggot, Notion, Quaint, Quirk, Tick, Toy, Vagary

Whine, Whinge(r) Cant, Carp, Complain, Cry baby, Grumble, Kvetch, Mewl, Miaow, Moan, Peenge, Pule, Snivel, Sword, Whimper, Yammer

Whip(ped), Whip out, Whipping Beat, Braid, Bullwhip, Cat, Cat o' nine tails, Chastise, Chief, Colt, Crop, Drive, Firk, Five-line, Flagellate, Flay, Gad, Hide, Jambok, Knout, Larrup, →**LASH**, Leather, Limber, Lunge, Quirt, Rawhide, Riem, Scourge, Sjambok, Slash, Steal, Stock, Swinge, Swish, Switch, Taw, Thong, Three-line, Thresh, Trounce, Welt, West Country, Whap

Whirl(er), Whirling Circumgyrate, Dervish, Eddy, Gyrate, →**IN A WHIRL**, Maelstrom, Pivot, Reel, Spin, Swing, Swirl, Vortex, Vortical, Whirry

Whirlpool Eddy, Gulf, Gurge, Maelstrom, Moulin, Swelchie, Vorago, Vortex, Weel, Wiel

Whirlwind Cyclone, Dust devil, Eddy, Tornado, Tourbillion, Typho(o)n, Vortex, Willy-willy

Whisker(s) Beard, Beater, Bristles, Burnsides, Cat's, Dundreary, Eggbeater, Excrement, Face fungus, Hackle, Hair, Moustache, Mutton-chop, Samuel, Side(-boards), Side-burns, Sidelevers, Stibble, Stubble, Vibrissa

Whisk(e)y Alcohol, Bond, Bourbon, Canadian, Cape smoke, Corn, Creature, Fife, Fire-water, Grain, Hard stuff, Hoo(t)ch, Irish, Islay, Malt, Moonshine, Morning, Mountain dew, Nip, Peat-reek, Pot(h)een, Red eye, Rye, Scotch, Southern Comfort®, Stirrup-dram, Tun, Usquebaugh, W

▷**Whisky** *may indicate* an anagram

Whisper Aside, Breath(e), Bur(r), Chinese, Hark, Hint, Innuendo, Murmur, Pig's, Round, Rumour, Rustle, Sigh, Stage, Susurrus, Tittle, Undertone, Whittie-whattie

Whistle(r) Blow, Calliope, Catcall, Feedback, Flute, Hewgh, Hiss, Marmot, Pedro, Penny, Phew, Ping, Pipe, Quail-pipe, Ref, Siffle(ur), Sowf(f), Sowth, Steam, Stop, Stridor, Swab(ber), Swanee, Tin, Toot, Tweedle, Tweet, Warbler, Wheeple, Wheugh, Whew, Wolf

Whistle-blower Informer, Nark, Ref

White(n), Whitener, Whiteness, White-faced Agene, Agenise, Alabaster, Albedo, Albescent, Albino, Albumen, Argent, Ashen, Au lit, Blameless, Blanch, Blanche, Blanco, Bleach, Buckra, Cabbage, Calm, Cam, Camstone, Candid, Candida, Candour, Canescent, Canities, Caucasian, Chalk(y), Chardonnay, Chaste, China, Chinese, Christmas, Cliffs, Collar, Company, Cream, Cue ball, Egg, Elephant, Ermine, European, Fang, Fard, Feather, Flag, Flake, French, Glair, Gwen(da), Gwendolen, Gwyn, Hawked, Hoar(y), Hock, Honorary, Hore, House, Innocent, Ivory, Large, Leucoma, Lie, Lily, Livid, Man, Marbled, Mealy, Muscadet, Opal, Oyster, Pale(face), Pallor, Paper, Paris, Pearl(y), Poor, Pure, Redleg, Russian, Sclerotic, Sheep, Silver, Small, Snow(y), Spanish, Taw, Wan, Wedding, Wine, Wyn, Zinc

White man Ba(c)kra, Buckra, Caucasian, Corn-cracker, Cracka, Gora, Gub(bah), Haole, Honkie, Honky, Larney, Mzungu, Norteno, Occidental, Ofay, Pakeha, Paleface, Redleg, Redneck, WASP, Wigga, Wigger

Whole, Wholehearted, Wholeness, Wholly All, Cosmos, Eager, Entire(ty), Entity, Every inch, Fully, Hale, Intact, Integer, Integral, Integrity, In toto, Largely, Lot, Shebang, Sound, Sum, Systemic, Thoroughly, Total, Tout à fait, Unbroken, Uncut

Wholesale(r) Cutprice, En bloc, Engrosser, Ingross, Jobber, Stockjobber, Sweeping, Trader

Whoop(er), Whooping cough Alew, Celebrate, Chincough, Crane, Cry, Excite, Kink(cough), Kink-host, Pertussis, Swan

Whopper, Whopping Barn, Crammer, Goliath, Huge, Immense, Jumbo, Lie, Lig, Oner, Out and outer, Plumper, Scrouger, Slapper, Slockdolager, Soc(k)dalager, Soc(k)dolager, Soc(k)doliger, Soc(k)dologer, Sogdolager, Sogdoliger, Sogdologer, Tale, Taradiddle

Whore Drab, Harlot, Loose woman, Pinnace, Pro, Prostitute, Quail, Road, Strumpet, Tart

Wicked(ness) Atrocity, →**BAD**, Candle, Criminal, Cru(i)sie, Crusy, Depravity, Devilish, Evil, Goaty, Godless, Heinous, Immoral, Impious, Improbity, Iniquity, Lantern, Miscreant, Naughty, Nefarious, Night-light, Pernicious, Perverse, Pravity, Rush, Satanic, Scelerate, Sin(ful), Splendid, Super, Taper, Turpitude, Unchaste, Unholy, Vile

▷**Wicked** *may indicate* containing a wick

Wicket Crease, Gate, Hatch, Maiden, Pitch, Square, Sticky, Stool, Stump, W, Yate

Wide, Widen(ing), Width Abroad, Ample, Bay, Braid, Broad, Comprehensive, Dilate, Drib, Eclectic, Expand, Extend, Far, Flanch, Flange, Flare, Flaunch, Ga(u)ge, General, Miss, Prevalent, Roomy, Scope, Set, Spacious, Span, Spread, Sundry, Sweeping, Vast

Widespread Diffuse, Epidemic, Extensive, General, Pandemic, Panoramic, Pervasive, Prevalent, Prolate, Routh(ie), Sweeping, Universal

Widow(ed) Black, Dame, Discovert, Dowager, Golf, Grass, Jointress, Relict, Sati, Sneerwell, Suttee, Twankey, Vidual, Viduous, Whydah-bird, Widdy

Wife, Wives Ball and chain, Better half, Bride, Common-law, Concubine, Consort, Devi, Dutch, Enid, Evadne, Feme, Feme covert, Frau, Goody, Haram, Harem, Harim, Helpmate, Helpmeet, Hen, Her indoors, Kali, Little woman, Mate, Memsahib, Missis, Missus, Mrs, Partner, Penelope, Potiphar's, Rib, Seraglio, Spouse, Squaw, Stepford, Trophy, Trouble and strife, Umfazi, Ux(or), Vrou, W, Wag

Wig Bagwig, Bob(wig), Brutus, Buzz-wig, Campaign, Carpet, Cauliflower, Caxon, Chevelure, Chide, Cockernony, Dalmahoy, Full-bottomed, Gizz, Gregorian, Hair(piece), Heare, Jas(e)y, Jazy, Jiz, Major, Periwig, Peruke, Postiche, Ramil(l)ie(s), Rate, Reprimand, Rug, Scold, Scratch, Sheitel, Spencer, Syrup, Targe, Tie, Toupee, Toupet, Tour

Wild(er), Wildness Abandoned, Aberrant, Agitato, Agrestal, Amok, Amuck, Angry, Barbarous, Baresark, Berserk, Bundu, Bush, Chimeric, Crazy, Demented, Earl, Enraged, Enthusiastic, Errant, Erratic, Extravagant, Farouche, Feral, Frantic, Frenetic, Frontier, Gene, Gohardery, Haggard, Hectic, Lawless, Mad(cap), Maenadic, Manic, Meshugge, Myall, Natural, Outlaw, Rampant, Raver, Riotous, Romantic, Rumbustious, → **SAVAGE**, Skimble-skamble, Tearaway, Unmanageable, Unruly, Untamed, Violent, Warrigal, West, Woolly
▷**Wild(ly)** *may indicate* an anagram

Wile, Wily Art, Artful, Artifice, Astute, Braide, → **CUNNING**, Deceit, Foxy, Peery, Ruse, Shifty, Shrewd, Slee, Slippery, → **SLY**, Spider, Stratagem, Streetwise, Subtle, Trick, Versute, Wide

Wilful(ly) Deliberate, Headstrong, Heady, Obstinate, Recalcitrant, Scienter, Wayward

Will, Willing(ly) Alsoon, Amenable, Bard, Bequeath, Bewildered, Biddable, Bill(y), Can do, Complaisant, Compliant, Conation, Content, Desire, Devise, Fain, Force, Free, Game, General, Hay, Holographic, Leave, Legator, Leve, Lief, Lieve, Living, Mind, Nerve, Noncupative, Obedient, On, Open, Pacable, Please, Prone, Purpose, Raring, Rather, Ready, Receptive, Resolution, Scarlet, Shakespeare, Soon, Spirit, Swan, Testament, Testate, Thelma, Tolerant, Up for, Velleity, Volens, Volition, Voluntary, Volunteer, Way, Wimble, Woot
▷**Will** *may indicate* an anagram

William(s) Bill(y), Conqueror, Occam, Orange, Pear, Rufus, Silent, Sweet, Tell, Tennessee

Willow(ing), Willowy Arctic, Crack, Lissom(e), Lithe, Osier, Poplar, Pussy, Sale, Salix, Sallow, Sauch, Saugh, Seal, Slender, Supple, Twilly, Weeping, Withy
▶**Wily** *see* **WILE**

Wimp(ish) Drip, Milksop, Mouse, Namby-pamby, Pantywaist, Saddo, Snool, Weed
▷**Wimple** *may indicate* an anagram

Win(ner), Winning Achieve, Acquire, Adorable, Ahead, Appealing, Attain, Backgammon, Bangster, Banker, → **BEAT**, Capot, Carry off, Cert, Champion, Charm, Conciliate, Conquer, Cup, Cute, Decider, Disarming, Dividend, Dormie, Dormy, Earn, Effect, Endearing, Engaging, Fetching, First, Fool's mate, Gain, Gammon, Grand slam, Hit, Jackpot, Land(fall), Landslide, Laureate, Lead, Luck out, Medallist, Motser, Motza, Nap hand, Nice, On a roll, Pile, Pot, Prepossessing, Prevail, Profit, Purler, Reap, Repique, Result, Rollover, Rubicon, Scoop, Shoo-in, Slam, Snip, Success, Sweet, Take, Top dog, → **TRIUMPH**, Up, Vellet, Velvet, Victor(y), Vole, Walk over, Wrest, Yellow jersey, Yokozuna

Wind(er), Winding(s), Windy Air, Airstream, Anfractuous, Backing, Ball, Bend, Blow, Bottom, Brass, Burp, Capstan, Chill, Coil, Colic, Crank, Creeky, Curl, Curve, Cutter, Draught, Draw, Entwine, Entwist, Evagation, Fart, Fearful,

Flatulence, Flatus, Flaw, Gas, Gust, Meander, Nervous, Periodic, Ponent, Poop, Prevailing, Purl, Quarter, Quill, Reeds, Reel, Roll, Screw, Sea, Second, Series, Serpentine, Serpentize, Sinuous, Slant, Snake, Spiral, Spool, Surface, Swirl, Tail, Tendril, Thread, Throw, Tortuous, Trade, Trend, Turn, Twaddle, Twine, Twisty, Veer, Veering, Ventose, Waffle, Weave, Wiggle, Winch, Windle, Winnle, Wrap, Wreathe, Wrest

Window(s) Atmosphere, Bay, Bow, Casement, Catherine-wheel, Companion, Compass, Day, Deadlight, Dormer, Double-hung, Dream-hole, Entry, Eye, Eyelids, Fanlight, Fenestella, Fenestra, French, Gable, Garret, Glaze, Guichet, Jalousie, Jesse, Judas, Jut, Lancet, Lattice, Launch, Light, Loop-light, Louver, Louvre, Lozen, Lucarne, Lunette, Luthern, Lychnoscope, Marigold, Mezzanine, Mirador, Monial, Mullion, Oculus, Oeil-de-boeuf, Ogive, Opportunity, Orb, Oriel, Ox-eye, Pane, Pede, Picture, Plate glass, Pop-under, Pop-up, Porthole, Program, Quarterlight, Radio, Re-entry, Rosace, Rose, Round, Sash, Sexfoil, Shed dormer, Shop, Shot, Skylight, Spyhole, Storm, Transom, Trellis, Ventana, Weather, Wheel, Wicket, Windock, Windore, Winnock

Windsor Barbara, Castle, Knot

Wine Bin, Blush, Cabinet, Case, Cup, Cuvée, Dessert, Doc, Espumoso, Essence, Fortified, Grand cru, Low, Mulled, Must, Piece, Pigment, Premier cru, Prisage, Rotgut, Rouge, Semi-dry, Sparkling, Steen, Tannin, Terroir, The grape, Tirage, Unoaked, Varietal, Vat, Vintage, Zymurgy

Wing(s), Winged, Winger, Wing-like Aerofoil, Ala(r), Aliform, Alula, Annexe, Appendage, Arm, Bastard, → **BIRD**, Branch, Buffalo, Canard, Cellar, Corium, Coulisse, Delta, Dipteral, El(l), Elevon, Elytral, Elytriform, Elytron, Elytrum, Fan, Fender, Flap, Flew, Flipper, Forward, Halteres, Hurt, Left, Limb, Offstage, Parascenia, Parascenium, Patagium, Pegasus, Pennate, Pennon, Pinero, Pinion, Pip, Pterygoid, Putto, Right, Rogallo, Sail, Satyrid, Scent-scale, Segreant, Seraphim, Sweepback, Sweptback, Sweptwing, Swift, Swingwing, Tailplane, Tectrix, Tegmen, Tormentor, Transept, Van, Vol(et), Water, Wound(ed)

▷**Winger** *may indicate* a bird

Wink (at) Bat, Condone, Connive, Eliad, Flicker, Ignore, Illiad, Instant, Nap, Nictitate, Oeillade, Pink, Twinkle

Winnow Fan, Riddle, Separate, Sift, Van, Wecht

Winter, Wintry Bleak, Brumal, Cold, Dec, Fimbul, Frigid, Frore, Hibernate, Hiemal, Hiems, Hodiernal, Jasmine, Nuclear, Shrovetide, Snowy, Subniveal

Wipe (out), Wiping Abolish, Abrogate, Absterge, Amortise, Annihilate, Cancel, Cleanse, Demolish, Destroy, Deterge, Dicht, Dight, Efface, Erase, Expunge, Forget, Hanky, Kleenex®, Mop, Nose-rag, Null, Purge, Raze, Rub, Sponge, Tersion, Tissue

Wire(s), Wirework, Wiry Aerial, Barb(ed), Cable, Cat's whiskers, Chicken, Coil, Earth, Element, Fencing, Filament, Filar, File, Filigree, Heald, Heddle, High, In on, Kirschner, Lead, Lean, Lecher, Live, Marconigram, Messenger, Mil, Nichrome®, Nipper, Number eight, Piano, Pickpocket, Razor, Sevice, Shroud, Sinewy, Snake, Solenoid, Spit, Staple, Stilet, Strand, String, Stylet, Telegram, Telegraph, Thoth, Thread, Tightrope, Trace, Trip

Wise(acre), Wisdom Advisedly, Athena, Athene, Canny, Conventional, Cracker barrel, Depth, Ernie, Gothamite, Gudrun, Hep, Hindsight, Horse sense, Judgement, Knowledge, Learned, Long-headed, Lore, Manner, Mimir, Minerva, Norman, Oracle, Owl, Pearl, Philosopher, Philosophy, Politic, Polymath, Prajna,

Profound, Prudence, Sagacity, Sage, Salomonic, Sapience, Savvy, Shrewd, Smartie, Solon, Sophia, Tooth, Wice

Wise man Balthazar, Caspar, Gaspar, Hakam, Heptad, Melchior, Nestor, Pandit, Sage, Sapient, Seer, Solomon, Swami, Thales, Worldly

Wish(es), Wishing Ache, Ake, Aspire, Covet, Crave, Death, Desiderate, →DESIRE, Envy, For, Hope, Itch, List, Long, Nill, Pleasure, Pray, Precatory, Regards, RIP, Velleity, Want, Yearn

Wit(s), Witticism, Witty Acumen, Attic, Badinage, Banter, Bon mot, Brevity, Card, Commonsense, Concetto, Cunning, Dry, Epigram, Esprit (de l'escalier), Estimation, Eutrapelia, Eutrapely, Facetious, Fantasy, Gnome, Hartford, Horse sense, Humour, Imagination, Intelligence, Irony, Jest, Jeu d'esprit, Joke, Marbles, Marinism, Memory, Mind, Mot, Mother, Native, Nous, One-liner, Oscar Wilde, Pawky, Pun, Quipster, Repartee, Rogue, Sally, Salt, Saut, Sconce, →SENSE, Shaft, Smart, Sparkle, Videlicet, Viz, Wag, Weet, Wisecrack, Word-play

Witch(craft) Beldam(e), Besom-rider, Broomstick, Cantrip, Carline, Circe, Coven, Craigfluke, Crone, Cutty Sark, Diabolism, Ensorcell, Galdragon, Glamour, Goety, Gramary(e), Gyre-carline, Hag, Hecat(e), Hex, Lamia, Magic, Medea, Myal(ism), Night-hag, Obeahism, Obia, Obiism, Pishogue, Pythoness, Salem, Selim, She-devil, Sibyl, Sieve, Sorceress, Speller, Sycorax, Termagant, Trout, Valkyrie, Vaudoo, Vilia, Voodoo, Water, Weird, Wicca, Wise woman

With And, By, Con, Cum, Hereby, In, Mit, Of, Using, W

Withdraw(al), Withdrawn Abdicate, Abstract, Alienate, Aloof, Back out, Backpedal, Breakaway, Climb down, Cloistered, Cold turkey, Cry off, Deduct, Desertion, Detach, Disengage, Distrait, Enshell, Estrange, Evacuate, Extract, Hive off, Inshell, Introvert, Leave, Offish, Palinode, Phantom, Precede, Preserve, Recant, Recede, Recoil, Renegue, Repair, Rescind, Resile, Reticent, Retire, Retract(ion), Retreat, Revoke, Revulsion, Scratch, Secede, Secesh, Sequester, Shrink, Shy, Stand down, Subduce, Subduct, Subtract, Tap, Unreeve, Unsay

Wither(ed), Withering, Withers Arefy, Atrophy, Blast, Burn, Corky, Decadent, Die, Droop, Dry, Evanish, Fade, Forpine, Gizzen, Googie, Languish, Marcescent, Miff, Nose, Sarcastic, Scram, Sere, Shrink, Shrivel, Welk, Welt

▷**With gaucherie** *may indicate* an anagram

Withhold(ing), Withheld Abstain, Conceal, Curt, Deny, Detain, Detinue, Hide, Keep, →RESERVE, Ritenuto, Trover

Within Enclosed, Endo-, Immanent, Indoors, Inside, Interior, Intra

Without Bar, Beyond, Ex, Lack(ing), Less, Minus, Orb, Outdoors, Outside, Sans, Save, Sen, Senza, Sine, X

▷**Without** *may indicate* one word surrounding another

▷**Without restraint** *may indicate* an anagram

Witness Attend, Attest, Behold, Bystander, Catch, Character, Confirm, Deponent, Depose, Endorse, Evidence, Experience, Expert, Eye, Glimpse, Hostile, Jehovah's, Mark, Martyr, Material, Muggletonian, Note, Notice, Observe, Obtest, Onlooker, Passer-by, Perceive, Proof, →SEE, Show, Sight, Sign, Spy, Stander-by, Survey, Testament, Teste, Testify, Testimony, View, Vouchee, Watch

▶**Witticism** *see* WIT(S)

Wizard (priest) Archimage, Awesome, Carpathian, Conjuror, Demon, Expert, Gandalf, Hex, Mage, Magician, Merlin, Obiman, Oz, Prospero, Shaman, Sorcerer, Super, Warlock

Wobble, Wobbling, Wobbly Chandler's, Coggle, Hissy fit, Precess, Quaver, Rock, Shimmy, Shoggle, Shoogle, Teeter, Totter, Tremble, Trillo, Unsteady, Wag, Waggle, Walty, Waver

Woe(ful), Woebegone, Woeful Agony, Alack, Alas, Bale, Bane, Distress, Dool(e), Dule, Ewhow, Execrable, Gram, Grief, Hurt, Jeremiad, Lack-a-day, Misery, Pain, Plague, →**SORROW**, Tribulation, Triste, Wailful, Wednesday's child

Wolf(ish), Wolf-like Akela, Assyrian, Bolt, Cancer, Carcajou, Casanova, Coyote, Cram, Dangler, Dasyure, Dire, Earth, Engorge, Fenrir, Fenris, Gorge, Grey, Ise(n)grim, Lobo, Lone, Lothario, Lupine, Luster, Lycanthrope, MI, Michigan, Pack, Philanderer, Prairie, Rake, Ravenous, Red, Rip, Roué, Rout, Rudolph, Rye, Scoff, Sea, Seducer, Strand, Tasmanian, Thylacine, Tiger, Timber, Wanderer, Were, Whistler

Woman(hood), Women Aguna(h), Anile, Beldam(e), Besom, Biddy, Bimbo, Bint, Bit, Boiler, Broad, Callet, Caryatid, Chai, Chap(p)ess, Chook, Cotquean, Crone, Crumpet, Cummer, Dame, Daughter, Distaff, Doe, Dona(h), Dorcas, Doris, Doyenne, Drab, Duenna, Eve, F, Fair, Fair sex, →**FEMALE**, Feme, Femme fatale, Flapper, Floozy, Frail, Frow, Gammer(stang), Gin, Girl, Gyno-, -gyny, Harpy, Harridan, Hausfrau, Hen, Her, Ho, Housewife, Inner, It, Jade, Jane, Kloo(t)chman, Lady, Liberated, Lilith, Lorette, Madam(e), Mademoiselle, Mary, Miladi, Milady, Millie, Minge, Mob, Modicum, Mort, Ms, Painted, Pandora, Peat, Petticoat, Pict, Piece, Piece of goods, Placket, Point, Popsy, Puna(a)ni, Puna(a)ny, Pussy, Quean, Queen, Ramp, Rib, Ribibe, Rudas, Runnion, Sabine, Scarlet, Shawlay, Shawlie, She, Skirt, Sloane Ranger, Sort, Squaw, Tail, Tib, Tiring, Tit, Tottie, Totty, Trot, Wahine, Weaker sex, Wifie, Zena

Wonder(s) Admire, Agape, Amazement, AR, Arkansas, Arrah, Awe, Chinless, Colossus, Ferly, Grape-seed, Hanging Gardens, Humdinger, Marle, →**MARVEL**, Mausoleum, Meteor, Mirabilia, Miracle, Muse, Nine-day, One-hit, Pharos, Phenomenon, Prodigy, Pyramids, Speculate, Statue of Zeus, Stupor, Suppose, Surprise, Temple of Artemis, Thaumatrope, Wheugh, Whew, Wow(ee)

Wonderful(ly) Amazing, Bees' knees, Bitchin(g), Chinless, Divine, Épatant, Fantastic, Far-out, Ferly, Geason, Gee-whiz, Glorious, Gramercy, Grand, Great, Heavenly, Lal(l)apalooza, Magic, Mirable, Must-see, Old, Priceless, Purely, Ripping, Smashing, Stellar, Sublime, Wicked

Wood(s), Wooden, Woodland, Woody Arboretum, Batten, Beam, Birken, Board, Boord(e), Bough, Brake, Cask, Channel, Chipboard, Chuck, Chump, Clapboard, Conductor, Dead, Deadpan, Expressionless, Fardage, Fathom, Fire, Fish, Funk, Furious, Gantry, Gauntree, Guthrie, Hanger, Hard, Hyle, Kindling, Knee, Krummholz, Late, Lath, Loggerhead, Lumber, Mad, Magnetic, Miombo, Nemoral, Nemorous, Offcut, Pallet, Pegboard, Pulp(wood), Punk, Silvan, Slat, Spilikin, Spill, Spinney, Splat, Spline, Splint, Stolid, Sylvan, Tenon, Three-ply, Tiger, Timber, Tinder, Touch, Treen, Trees, Twiggy, Two-by-four, Vert, Xylem, Xyloid

▷**Wood** *may indicate* an anagram in sense of mad

Woodpecker Bird, Descent, Flicker, Hairy, Hickwall, Picalet, Picarian, Pileated, Rainbird, Sapsucker, Saurognathae, Witwall, Woodspite, Woodwale, Woody, Yaffle

Woodwind Bassoon, Clarinet, Cornet, Flute, Oboe, Piccolo, Pipe, Recorder, Reed

Wool(len), Woolly (haired) Alpaca, Angora, Aran, Beige, Berlin, Botany, Bouclé, Cardi(gan), Cashmere, Clean, Clip, Combings, Cotton, Dog, Doily, Down, Doyley, Drugget, Duffel, Fadge, Fingering, Fleece, Flock, Fuzz, Glass, Guernsey,

Hank, Heather mixture, Jaeger, Jersey, Kashmir, Ket, Knitwear, Lanate, Llama, Lock, Merino, Mineral, Noil(s), Offsorts, Oo, Paco, Pashm, Pelage, Persian, Pine, Rock, Say, Shetland, Shoddy, Skein, Skin, Slag, Slipe, Slip-on, Slub, Smart, Spencer, Staple, Steel, Stuff, Swansdown, Tammy, Tank top, Telltale, Three-ply, Tod, Tricot, Tweed, Ulotrichous, Vague, Vicuña, Virgin, Wire, Yarn

Word(s), Wording, Wordy Al(l)-to, Argument, Aside, Buzz, Cataphor(a), Catch, Cheville, Claptrap, Clipped, Clitic, Code, Coinage, Comment, Content, Dick, Dicky bird, Dit(t), Echoic, Effable, Embolalia, Epitaph, Epithet, Epos, Etymon, Faith, Four-letter, Function, Functor, Ghost, Grace, Hapax legomenon, Hard, Heteronym, Hint, Holophrase, Homograph, Homonym, Horseman's, Household, → **IN A WORD**, → **IN TWO WORDS**, Janus, Jonah, Key, Last, Lexeme, Lexicon, Lexis, Loan, Logia, Logos, Long-winded, Lyrics, Mantra, Meronym, Message, Mot, Neologism, News, Nonce, Nonsense, Noun, Oath, Om, Operative, Oracle, Order, Palabra, Paragram, Paranym, Parenthesis, Parlance, Parole, Paronym, Particle, Peristomenon, Phrase, Piano, Pledge, Pleonasm, Polysemen, Portmanteau, Preposition, Prolix, Promise, Pronoun, Reserved, Rhyme, Rumbelow, Rumour, Saying, Semantics, Signal, Soundbite, Subtitle, Surtitle, Syntagma, Talkative, Tatpurusha, Term, Tetragram, Text, Tirade, Trigger, Trope, Typewriter, Verb, Verbiage, Verbose, Vocab(ulary), Vogue, Warcry, Weasel, Winged, Written

▷**Work** *may indicate* a book or play, etc.

Workaholic, Work(er), Working(-class), Workman, Workmen, Works, Workman(ship) Act(ivate), Aga saga, Ant, Application, Appliqué, Apronman, Artefact, Artel, Artifact, Artificer, Artisan, At it, At task, Barmaid, Beamer, Beaver, Bee, Blue-collar, Blue-singlet, Bohunk, Boon(er), Brief, Bull, Business, Busy, Careerist, Casual, Char, Chare, Chargehand, Chigga, Chippy, Chore, Claim, Clock, Colon, Community, Computer, Contingent, Corvée, Craftsman, Crew, Cultivate, Dig, Diss(ertation), Do, Dog, Dogsbody, Donkey, Draft-mule, Drudge, Drug, Earn, Effect, Effort, Elbow grease, Em, Ergon, Ergonomics, Eta, Everything, Evince, Exercise, Exergy, Exploit, Factotum, Facture, Fast, Fat, Ferment, Fettler, Field, Filter, Flat cap, Flex(i)time, Fret, Fuller, → **FUNCTION**, Gae, Gel, Girl Friday, Go, Graft, Grass, Grind, Grunt, Guest, Hand, Harness, Hat, Hobo, Horse, Hot-desking, Hunky, Indian, Industry, Innards, Intray, Jackal, Job, Journeyman, Key, Knead, Knowledge, Labour, Laid, Leave, Luddite, Lump, Machinist, Maid, Man, Manipulate, Manpower, McJob, Mechanic(ian), Menge, Menial, Midinette, Mine, Ming, MO, Moil, Moonlight, Movement, Navvy, Neuter, Number, Oeuvre, On, On (the) job, Op, Opera(tion), Operative, Operator, Opus, Orderly, Outreach, Outside, Ouvrier, Ox, Part, Partisan, Passage, Peasant, Peg, Pensum, Peon, Pink-collar, Plasterer, Ply, Poker, Portfolio, Postlude, Potboiler, Practicum, Practise, Production, Project, Prole(tariat), Public, Pursuit, Red-neck, Reduction, Rep, Ride, Robot, Rotovate, Roughneck, Round, Rouseabout, Roustabout, Run, Salaryman, Sandhog, Satisfactory, Scabble, Scullion, Secretariat, Sedentary, Servant, Serve, Service, Servile, Seven, Sewage, Shift, Shop (floor), Situation, Skanger, Slogger, Smithy, Social, Soldier, Spiderman, Staff, Stagehand, Stevedore, Stint, Strap, Straw, Strive, Support, Surface, Swaggie, Swagman, Sweat, Swink, Take, Tamper, Task, Team, Technician, Telecommuter, Temp, Tenail(le), Termite, Tew, Text, Tick, Till, Toccata, Toil, Travail, Treatise, Trojan, TU, TUC, Turk, Tut, Tutman, Uphill, Walla(h), Welfare, White-collar, Wright, Yarco

▷**Working** *may indicate* an anagram

Works, Workplace, Workshop Atelier, Engine, Factory, Forge, Foundry, Garage, Hacienda, Hangar, Innards, Lab, Mill, Passage, Plant, Public, Shed, Sheltered, Shipyard, Shop, Skylab, Smithy, Studio, Study, Sweatshop, Tannery, Telecottage, Time, Tin, Turnery, Upper

World(ly), Worldwide Adland, Carnal, Chthonic, Cosmopolitan, Cosmos, Cyberspace, Dream, Earth, First, Fleshly, Fourth, Free, Ge, Global village, Globe, Kingdom, Lay, Lower, Mappemond, Meatspace, Microcosm, Midgard, Mondaine, Mondial, Mould, Mundane, Natural, Nether, New, Old, Orb, Other, Oyster, Planet, Possible, Second, Secular, Sensual, Small, Society, Sphere, Spirit, Temporal, Terra, Terrene, Terrestrial, Third, Universe, Vale, Web, Welt, Whole

Worm(-like), Worms, Wormy Acorn, Angle, Anguillula, Annelid, Annulata, Apod(e), Apodous, Army, Arrow, Articulata, Ascarid, Bilharzia, Bladder, Blind, Blood, Bob, Bootlace, Brandling, Bristle, Caddis, Capeworm, Caseworm, Catworm, Cercaria, Cestode, Cestoid, Chaetopod, Clamworm, Clew, Copper, Dew, Diet, Diplozoon, Dracunculus, Edge, Enteropneust, Fan, Filander, Filaria, Flag, Flat, Flesh, Fluke, Galley, Gape, Gilt-tail, Gordius, Gourd, Gru-gru, Guinea, Hair, Hair-eel, Hairworm, Heartworm, Helminth, Hemichordata, Hookworm, Horsehair, Idle, Inchworm, Leech, Liver-fluke, Lob, Lumbricus, Lytta, Maw, Measuring, Merosome, Miner's, Mopani, Muck, Nemathelminthes, Nematoda, Nematode, Nematodirus, Nematomorpha, Nemertean, Nemertina, Nereid, Night-crawler, Oligochaete, Onychophoran, Paddle, Palmer, Palolo, Paste-eel, Peripatus, Phoronid, Pile, Pin, Piper, Planarian, Platyhelminth, Polychaete, Ragworm, Redia, Ribbon, Rootworm, Roundworm, Sabella, Sand mason, Schistosome, Scoleciform, Scolex, Screw, Seamouse, Serpula, Servile, Ship, Sipunculacea, Sipunculoidea, Spiny-headed, Stomach, Strawworm, Strongyl(e), Taenia, Tag-tail, Taint, Tapeworm, Tenioid, Teredo, Termite, Threadworm, Tiger, Tiger tail, Tongue, Toxocara, Trematode, Trichin(ell)a, Trichinosed, Triclad, Tube, Tubifex, Turbellaria, Vermiform, Vinegar, Vinegar eel, Wheat-eel, Wheatworm, Whipworm

Worn (out) Attrite, Bare, Decrepit, Detrition, Effete, Épuisé, Exhausted, Forfairn, Forfoughten, Forjaskit, Forjeskit, Frazzled, Gnawn, Old, On, Passé, Raddled, Rag, Seedy, Shabby, Shopsoiled, Shot, Spent, Stale, Tatty, Threadbare, Tired, Traikit, Trite, Used, Weathered, Whacked

Worried, Worrier, Worry Agonise, Ail, Annoy, Anxiety, Badger, Bait, Beset, Bother, Brood, Burden, Care(worn), Cark, Chafe, Concern, Consternate, Deave, Deeve, Distraught, Distress, Disturb, Dog, Eat, Exercise, Faze, Feeze, Frab, Frantic, Fret, Fuss, Gnaw, Harass, Harry, Hyp, Inquietude, Knag, Nag, Niggle, Perturb, Pester, Pheese, Pheeze, Phese, Pingle, Pium, Rattle, Rile, Sool, Stew, Tew, Touse, Towse, Trouble, Unsettle, Vex, Wherrit, Worn

▷**Worried** *may indicate* an anagram

Worse(n) Adversely, Aggravate, Compound, Degenerate, Deteriorate, Exacerbate, Impair, Inflame, Pejorate, Regress, Relapse, War(re), Waur, Well away

Worship(per) Adore, Adulation, Allostery, Ancestor, Angelolatry, Aniconism, Animist, Autolatry, Bardolatry, Bless, Churchgoer, Congregation, Cosmolatry, Cult, Deify, Devotion, Dote, Douleia, Doxology, Dulia, Elementalism, Epeolatry, Exalt, Exercise, Fetish, Glorify, Groupie, Gurdwara, Happy-clappy, Henotheism, Hero, Ibadah, Iconology, Idolatry, Idolise, Latria, Lauds, Lionise, Liturgics, Lordolatry, Mariolatry, Meeting-house, Monolatry, Odinism, Oncer, Orant, Praise, Puja, Revere, Sabaism, Sakta, Service, Shacharis, Shakta, Sun, Synaxis, Thiasus, Vaishnava, Venerate, Votary, Wodenism

Worst Beat, Best, Better, Conquer, Defeat, Get, Less, Nadir, Outdo, Overpower, Pessimum, Rock-bottom, Scum, Severest, Throw, Trounce

Worsted Caddis, Caddyss, Challis, Coburg, Crewel, Genappe, Lea, Ley, Serge, Shalli, Tamin(e), Whipcord

▷**Worsted** *may indicate* an anagram

Worth(while), Worthy, Worthies Admirable, Ad valorem, Asset, Be, Cop, Cost effective, Deserving, Eligible, Estimable, Face value, Feck, →**MERIT**, Notable, Significant, Substance, Tanti, Use, Value, Vertu, Virtu(e), Virtuous, Wealth

Worthless (person) Average, Bad egg, Base, Beggarly, Bilge, Blown, Bodger, Bootless, Bum, Candy floss, Catchpenny, Chaff, Cheapjack, Crumb, Cypher, Damn, Despicable, Doit, Dreck, Dross, Duff, Ephemeron, Fallal, Frippery, Gimcrack, Gingerbread, Gubbins, Hilding, Ignoble, Jimcrack, Knick-knack, Left, Light, Mauvais sujet, Mud, Naughty, Nugatory, Nyaff, Obol, Ornery, Orra, Otiose, Pabulum, Paltry, Pin, Poxy, Punk, Raca, Rag, Rap, Razoo, Riffraff, Rubbishy, Rump, Scabby, Scrote, Scum, Shotten, Siwash, Sorry, Straw, Tawdry, Tinhorn, Tinpot, Tinsel, Tittle, Toerag, Trangam, Trashy, Tripy, Trumpery, Tuppenny, Twat, Two-bit, Twopenny, Useless, Vain, Vile, Zero

Wound(ed) Battery, Bite, Bless, Blighty, Bruise, Chagrin, Coiled, Crepance, Cut, Dere, Dunt, Engore, Entry, Exit, Ganch, Gash, Gaunch, Gore, Harm, Hurt, Injury, Knee, Lacerate, Lesion, Maim, Maul, Molest, Mortify, Offend, Pip, Sabre-cut, Scab, Scar, Scath, Scotch, Scratch, Shoot, Snaked, Snub, Sore, Stab, Sting, Trauma, Twined, Umbrage, Vuln, Vulnerary, Walking, Wing, Wint

Wrangle(r), Wrangling Altercate, Argie-bargie, →**ARGUE**, Bandy, Bicker, Brangle, Broil, Cample, Controvert, Dispute, Haggle, Hassle, Herder, Horse, Mathematical, Rag, Rodeo, Vitilitigation

Wrap(per), Wrapped, Wrapping, Wraparound, Wrap up Amice, Amis, Bag, Bandage, Bathrobe, Bind, Boa, Bubble, Bundle, Carton(age), Cellophane®, Cere, Clingfilm, Cloak, Clothe, Cocoon, Conclude, Cover-up, Drape, Emboss, Encase, Enfold, Enrol(l), Ensheath(e), Envelop(e), Enwind, Foil, Folio, Furl, Gladwrap®, Hap, Hem, Infold, Kimono, Kraft, Lag, Lap, Mail, Muffle, Negligee, Outsert, Package, Parcel, Plastic, Roll, Rug, Sarong, Shawl, Sheath(e), Sheet, Shrink, Shroud, Stole, Swaddle, Swathe, Tinfoil, Tsutsumu, Velamen, Wap, Wimple

Wreath(e) Adorn, Anadem, Chaplet, Civic crown, Coronal, Crown, Entwine, Festoon, Garland, Laurel, Lei, Steven, Torse, Tortile, Twist

Wreck(age), Wrecked, Wrecker Banjax, Blight, Crab, Debris, Demolish, Devastate, Flotsam, Founder, Goner, Hesperus, Hulk, Lagan, Ligan, Luddite, Mutilate, Ruin(ate), Sabotage, Saboteur, Shambles, Shatter, Sink, Smash, Spif(f)licate, Stramash, Subvert, Torpedo, Trash, Vandalise, Wrack

▷**Wrecked** *may indicate* an anagram

Wrench Allen, Fit, Jerk, Lug, Mole, Monkey, Nut, Pin, Pull, Rick, Screw, Socket, Spanner, Sprain, Stillson®, Strain, Tear, Twist, Windlass, Wrest

Wrestle(r), Wrest, Wrestling All-in, Arm (lock), Backbreaker, Basho, Bearhug, Bodycheck, Boston crab, Catchweight, Clinch, Clothes line, Cross buttock, Cross press, Featherweight, Flying mare, Foil, Forearm smash, Freestyle, Full-nelson, Grapple, Gr(a)eco-Roman, Grovet, Half-nelson, Hammerlock, Haystacks, Headlock, Hip-lock, →**HOLD**, Indian, Judo, Knee-drop, Milo, Monkey climb, Mud, Nelson, Niramiai, Pinfall, Posting, Sambo, Stable, Straight arm lift, Stranglehold, Struggle, Sumo, Suplex, Tag (team), Toehold, Tussle, Whip, Wristlock, Writhe

Wretch(ed) Abject, Blackguard, Blue, Caitiff, Chap-fallen, Crumb, Cullion, Cur, Darned, Forlorn, Git, Goddamned, Hapless, Ignoble, Lorn, Measly, Miscreant, Miser, Miserable, Peelgarlic, Pilgarlick, Pipsqueak, Poltroon, Poor, Punk, Rakeshame, Rascal, Rat, Scoundrel, Scroyle, Seely, Snake, Sorry, Toerag, Unblest, Waeful, Wo(e)
▷**Wretched** *may indicate* an anagram

Wrinkle(d), Wrinkly Clue, Cockle, Corrugate, Crankle, Crease, Crepy, Crimple, Crimpy, Crinkle, Crow's-foot, Crumple, Fold, Frounce, Frown, Frumple, Furrow, Gen, Groove, Headline, Hint, Idea, Knit, Line, Lirk, Plissé, Plough, Pucker, Purse, Ridge, Rimple, Rivel, Rop(e)y, Ruck(le), Rugose, Rumple, Runkle, Seamy, Shrivel, Sulcus, Time-worn, Tip, Whelk, Wizened, Wrizled

Writ(s) Attachment, Capias, Certiorari, Cursitor, Dedimus, Devastatit, Distringas, Elegit, Fieri facias, Filacer, Habeas corpus, Holy, Injunction, Latitat, Law-burrows, Mandamus, Mittimus, Noverint, Praemunire, Process, Quare impedit, Replevin, Scirefacias, Significat, Subpoena, Summons, Supersedeas, Tolt, Venire, Warrant

Write(r), Writing Amphigory, Apocrypha, →**AUTHOR**, Automatic, Balladist, Ballpoint, Belles lettres, Bellet(t)rist, BIC®, Biographer, Biro®, Blog, Bloomsbury Group, Book-hand, Calligraphy, Causerie, Cento, Chalk, Charactery, Clerk, Clinquant, Columnist, Continuity, Copperplate, Creative, Cursive, Diarist, Dissertation, Dite, Draft, Endorse, Endoss, Engross, Enrol, Epigrammatise, Epistle, →**ESSAYIST**, Expatiate, Farceur, Feudist, Fist, Form, Formulary, Freelance, Ghost, Graffiti, Graphite, Hack, Hairline, Hand, Haplography, Hieratic, Hieroglyphics, Hierology, Hiragana, Homiletics, Indite, Ink, Inkhorn-mate, Ink-jerker, Inkslinger, Inscribe, Join-hand, Jot(tings), Journalese, Journalist, Journo, Kaleyard School, Kana, Leader, Leetspeak, Lexigraphy, Lexis, Linear A, Lipogram, Littérateur, Longhand, Lucubrate, Memoirist, Mimographer, Mirror, Miscellany, Monodist, Monograph, Ms(s), Nib, Notary, Notate, Novelese, →**NOVELIST**, Palaeography, Pamphleteer, Pen, Pencil, Penmanship, Penny-a-liner, Pentel®, Phrasemonger, Picture, Planchette, →**POET**, Polemic, Polygraphy, Pot-hook, Prosaist, Proser, Psychogram, Psychography, Purana, Purple patch, Quill, Rhymer, Roundhand, Runic, Sanskrit, Scenarist, Sci-fi, Score, Scratch, Scrawl, Screed, Screeve, Scribble, Scribe, Scrip(t), Scripture, Scrivener, Secretary, Sign, Sing, Sling-ink, Small-hand, Space, Spirit, Stichometry, Style, Stylist, Stylography, Subscript, Superscribe, Sutra, Syllabary, Syllabic, Syllabism, Synoptist, Tantra, Telegraphese, Text, Tractarian, Transcribe, Treatise, Type, Uncial, Varityper®, Wisdom, Wordsmith, Zend-Avesta
▷**Writhing** *may indicate* an anagram

Wrong(ful), Wrongdoer, Wrongdoing Aggrieve, Agley, Amiss, Astray, Awry, Bad, Chout, Defect, Delict, Disservice, Err, Fallacious, False, Harm, Ill, Immoral, Improper, Incorrect, Injury, Mischief, Misconduct, Misfaring, Misintelligence, Misled, Mistake(n), Misuse, Nocent, Offbase, Offend, Pear-shaped, Peccadillo, Perpetrator, Perverse, Sin(ful), Sinner, Tort, Tortious, Transgress, Unethical, Unright, Unsuitable, Withershins, Wryly, X
▷**Wrong** *may indicate* an anagram

Wry Askew, Contrary, Devious, Distort, Droll, Grimace, Ironic

X(-shaped) Buss, By, Chi, Christ, Cross, Decussate, Drawn, Generation, Kiss, Ten, Times, Unknown, X-ray

▶**Xmas** *see* **CHRISTMAS(TIME)**

X-ray Angiogram, Arthrogram, Characteristic, Cholangiography, Emi-Scanner, Encephalogram, Encephalograph, Fermi, Grenz, Mammogram, Plate, Pyelogram, Radiogram, Radioscopy, Rem, Roentgen, Sciagram, Screening, Sigmatron, Skiagram, Skiagraph, Tomography, Venogram, X

Xylophone Marimba, Semantra, Sticcado, Sticcato

Yy

Yacht Britannia, Dragon, Ice, Keelboat, Ketch, Land, Maxi, Sailboat, Sand, Yngling

Yachtsman, Yachtsmen Chichester, Heath, RYS

Yank(ee) Bet, Carpetbagger, Hitch, Jerk, Jonathan, Lug, Northerner, Pluck, Pull, Rug, Schlep(p), So(o)le, Sowl(e), →**TUG**, Tweak, Twitch, Wrench, Wrest, Y
▷**Yank** *may indicate* an anagram

Yard(s) Area, CID, Close, Court, Farm-toun, Garden, Hard, Haw, Hof, Junk, Kail, Knacker's, Lay, Main, Marshalling, Mast, Measure, Met, Navy, Patio, Poultry, Prison, Ree(d), Sail, Scotland, Show, Spar, Sprit, Steel, Stick, Stockyard, Stride, Switch, Tilt, Timber, Victualling, Y, Yd, Y-track

Yarn(s) Abb, Anecdote, Berlin, Bouclé, Caddice, Caddis, Chenille, Clew, Clue, Cop, Cord, Crewel, Fib, Fibroline, Fingering, Genappe, Gimp, Gingham, Guimp(e), Gymp, Homespun, Jaw, Knittle, Knot, Lay, Lea, Ley, Line, Lisle, Lurex®, Marl, Merino, Nylon, Organzine, Orlon®, Ply, Rigmarole, Ripping, Saxony, Sennit, Sinnet, Skein, Small stuff, Story, Strand, Tale, Taradiddle, Thread, Thrid, Thrum(my), Tram, Twice-laid, Warp, Water twist, Weft, Woof, Wool, Worsted, Zephyr

Yawn(ing) Boredom, Chasmy, Fissure, Gant, Gape, Gaunt, Greys, Hiant, Oscitation, Pandiculation, Rictus

Year(ly), Years A, Age, Anno, Annual, Anomalistic, Astronomical, AUC, Autumn, Calendar, Canicular, Civil, Common, Cosmic, Decennium, Donkey's, Dot, Ecclesiastical, Egyptian, Embolismic, Equinoctial, Financial, Fiscal, Gap, Grade, Great, Hebrew, Holy, Indiction, Julian, Leap, Legal, Light, Locust, Lunar, Lunisolar, Natural, PA, Perfect, Platonic, Prophetic week, Riper, Sabbatical, School, Sidereal, Solar, Sothic, Spring, Summer, Sun, Tax, Theban, Time, Towmon(d), Towmont, Tropical, Twelvemonth, Vintage, Wander(jahr), Winter, Zodiac

Yearn(ing) Ache, Ake, Aspire, Brame, Burn, Covet, Crave, Curdle, Desire, Erne, Greed, Green, Grein, Hanker, Hone, →**LONG**, Lust, Nostalgia, Pant, Pine, Sigh, Wistful
▷**Yearning** *may indicate* an anagram

Yeast Barm, Bees, Brewer's, Ferment, Flor, Leaven, Saccharomycete, Torula, Vegemite®

Yellow(ish) Amber, Auburn, Back, Beige, Bisque, Bistre, Buff, Butternut, Canary, Champagne, Chartreuse, Chicken, Chrome, Citrine, Clay-bank, Cowardly, Craven, Daffadowndilly, Daffodil, Eggshell, Etiolin, Fallow, Fever, Filemot, Flavin(e), Flaxen, Gamboge, Gaudy-green, Gold, Icteric, Isabel(le), Isabella, Jack, Jaundiced, King's, Lemon(y), Lurid, Luteous, Maize, Mustard, Nankeen, Naples, Oaker, Ochroid, Or(eide), Pages, Peach, Peril, Pink, Primrose,

Queen's, River, Saffron, Sallow, Sand, Sear, Sherry, Spineless, Strae, Straw, Sulfur, Sulphur, Tawny, Topaz, Tow, Unheroic, Weld, Yolk

Yes Agreed, Ay(e), Da, I, Indeed, Ja, Jokol, Nod, OK, Oke, Quite, Sure, Truly, Uh-huh, Whoopee, Wilco, Yah, Yea, Yokul, Yup

Yesterday Démodé, Eve, Hesternal, Pridian

Yield(ing), Yielded Abandon, Afford, Bear, Bend, Bow, Breed, Capitulate, Catch, Cede, Come, Comply, Concede, Crack, Crop, Defer, Dividend, Docile, Ductile, Easy, Elastic, Facile, Flaccid, Flexible, Give, Harvest, Interest, Knock under, Knuckle, Meek, Meltith, Mess, Obtemper, Output, Pan, Pay, Pliant, Produce, Quantum, Relent, Render, Return, Sag, Soft, Squashy, →**SUBMIT**, Succumb, Supple, Surrender, Susceptible, Sustained, Temporise, Tolerant, Truckle, Yold

Yob Lager lout, Lout, Oaf, Ted

Yoke Bow, Cang(ue), Collar, Couple, Harness, Inspan, Jugal, Pair, Span

Yokel Boor, Bumpkin, Chaw(-bacon), Clumperton, Culchie, Hayseed, Hick, Jake, Jock, Joskin, Peasant, Rube, Rustic

Yon(der) Distant, Further, O'erby, Thae, There, Thether, Thither

York(shire), Yorkshireman Batter, Bowl, Dales, Ebor, Pudding, Ridings, See, Tyke, White rose

You One, Second person, Sie, Thee, Thou, Usted, Wena, Ye

Young (person), Youngster, Youth(ful) Adolescent, Ageless, Bairn, Bev(an), Bit, Boy, Boyhood, Bub, Buckeen, Buppie, Calf-time, Ch, Charver, Chick, Chicken, Chiel, Child, Chile, Cion, Cock(erel), Cockle, Colt, Cub, Day-old, Dell, Dilling, DJ, Early, Ephebe, Ephebus, Esquire, Flapper, Fledgling, Foetus, Fox, Fresh, Fry, Gigolo, Gilded, Girl, Hebe, Hobbledehoy, Immature, Imp, Infant, Issue, Jeunesse d'orée, Junior, Juvenal, Juvenesce, Juvenile, Kid, Kiddo, Kiddy, Kipper, Lad, Lamb, Latter-day, Leaping-time, Less, Litter, Little, Middle, Minor, Misspent, Mod, Mormon, Mot, Muchacha, Narcissus, Ned(ette), Nestling, New, New Romantic, Nipper, Nurs(e)ling, Nymph, Plant, Popsy, Poult, Pre-teen, Progeny, Protégé(e), Punk, Pup, Rude boy, Salad days, Sapling, Scent, Scion, Screenager, Shaveling, Shaver, Sien(t), Skinhead, Slip, Small, Son, Spark, Spawn, Spide, Sprig, Stripling, Subteen, Swain, Ted, Teenager, Teens, Teenybopper, Tir na n'Og, Tit, Tot, Toyboy, Waif, Well-preserved, Whelp, Whippersnapper, Widge, Wigga, Wigger, Wimp, Yukon

Younger, Youngest Baby, Benjamin, Cadet, Last born, Less, Minimus, Seneca, Wallydrag, Wallydraigle, Yr

▶**Youth** see **YOUNG (PERSON)**

Zz

Z Izzard, Izzet, Zambia, Zebra

Zeal(ous) Ardour, Bigotry, Devotion, Eager, Earnest, Enthusiasm, Evangelic, Fanatical, Fanaticism, Fervour, Fire, Hamas, Happy-clappy, Perfervid, Rabid, Study, Zest

Zealot Bigot, Crusader, Devotee, Essene, Extremist, Fan(atic), St Simon, Votary

Zenith Acme, Apogee, Height, Pole, Summit, Vertex

Zeppelin Airship, Balloon, Dirigible

Zero Absolute, Blob, Cipher, Circle, Double, Ground, Nil, Nilpotent, None, Nothing, Nought, O, Year, Z

Zest Brio, Condiment, Crave, Élan, Enthusiasm, Gusto, Peel, Pep, Piquancy, Relish, Spark, Spice, Tang, Taste, Zap, Zing

Zigzag Crémaillère, Crinkle-crankle, Dancette, Feather-stitch, Indent, Pink, Ric-rac, Slalom, Stagger, Tack, Traverse, Vandyke, Yaw

Zinc Blende, Gahnite, Mossy, Sherardise, Spelter, Sphalerite, Tutenag, Tutty, Willemite, Wurtzite, Zn

Zip(per) Dart, Dash, Energy, Fastener, Fly, Go, Nada, O, Oomph, Pep, Presto, Slide fastener, Stingo, Verve, Vim, Vivacity, Whirry, Zero

Zodiac(al) Aquarius, Archer, Aries, Bull, Cancer, Capricorn, Counter-glow, Crab, Fish, Gegenschein, Gemini, Goat, Horoscope, Leo, Libra, Lion, Ophiuchus, Pisces, Ram, Sagittarius, Scales, Scorpio(n), Taurus, Trigon, Twins, Virgin, Virgo, Watercarrier

Zone(s) Abyssal, Aerospace, Anacoustic, Area, Arid, Auroral, Band, Bathyal, Belt, Benioff, Buffer, Canal, Climate, Collision, Comfort, Convergence, Crumple, Dead, Demilitarized, District, Drop, Economic, Ecotone, End, Enterprise, Erogenous, Eruv, Euro, Exclusion, Exclusive, F layer, Fracture, Free(-fire), Fresnel, Frigid, Hadal, Home, Hot, Impact, Ionopause, Krumhole, Low velocity, Mix, Neutral, No-fly, Nuclear-free, Precinct, → **REGION**, Rift, Ring, Russian, Sahel, Saturation, Schlieren, Sector, Shear, Skip, Smokeless, Soviet, Stratopause, Strike, Subduction, T, Taiga, Temperate, Time, Tolerance, Torrid, Tundra, Twilight, Vadose, Z